D0945603

Gleim Publications, Inc., offers six university-level study manuals:

| | |
|---|---|
| *Auditing & Systems Exam Questions and Explanations* | $19.95 |
| *Business Law/Legal Studies Exam Questions and Explanations* | 16.95 |
| *Federal Tax Exam Questions and Explanations* | 19.95 |
| *Financial Accounting Exam Questions and Explanations* | 19.95 |
| *Cost/Managerial Accounting Exam Questions and Explanations* | 19.95 |

The following is a list of Gleim examination review books:

| | |
|---|---|
| *CIA Review: Part I, Internal Audit Process* | $22.95 |
| *CIA Review: Part II, Internal Audit Skills* | 22.95 |
| *CIA Review: Part III, Management Control and Information Technology* | 22.95 |
| *CIA Review: Part IV, The Audit Environment* | 22.95 |

*CIA Test Prep* software ($35 per section) is also available to complement your study.

| | |
|---|---|
| *CMA/CFM Review: Part 1, Economics, Finance, and Management* | $22.95 |
| *CFM Review: Part 2CFM, Corporate Financial Management* | 22.95 |
| *CMA Review: Part 2CMA, Financial Accounting and Reporting* | 22.95 |
| *CMA/CFM Review: Part 3, Mgmt. Reporting, Analysis, and Behavioral Issues* | 22.95 |
| *CMA/CFM Review: Part 4, Decision Analysis and Information Systems* | 22.95 |

*CMA/CFM Test Prep* software ($35 per section) and *CMA/CFM Review* audiotapes ($60 per section) are also available to complement your study.

| | |
|---|---|
| *CPA Review: Financial* | $24.50 |
| *CPA Review: Auditing* | 24.50 |
| *CPA Review: Business Law* | 24.50 |
| *CPA Review: TAX-MAN-GOV* | 24.50 |

*CPA Test Prep* software ($35 per section) and *CPA Review* audiotapes ($75 per section) are also available to complement your study.

Order forms for these and all of our other publications are provided at the back of this book.

# REVIEWERS AND CONTRIBUTORS

Bettina Fernandez, M.Acc., CPA, University of Florida, provided extensive editorial assistance throughout the manuscript.

Karen Hom, B.A., University of Florida, is our book production coordinator. Ms. Hom coordinated the production staff and provided production assistance throughout the project.

Grady M. Irwin, J.D., University of Florida, has taught in the University of Florida College of Business. Mr. Irwin provided many answer explanations and extensive editorial assistance throughout.

Travis Moore, M.B.A., University of Florida, provided technical and editorial assistance, prepared the page layout, and reviewed the final manuscript.

Nancy Raughley, B.A., Tift College, is our editor. Ms. Raughley reviewed the entire manuscript and assisted in all phases of production.

Bradley Smerage, M.Acc., University of Florida, provided extensive editorial assistance throughout the manuscript.

# A PERSONAL THANKS

This manual would not have been possible without the extraordinary effort and dedication of Jim Collis and Terry Hall, who typed the entire manuscript and all revisions as well as prepared the camera-ready pages.

We appreciate the production and editorial assistance of Shannon Bunker, Ryan DePeiza, Rob Gallardo, and Jan Morris, as well as the critical reading assistance of Lana Cox, Tiffany Dunbar, Eric Hall, Jamie McGinn, Tricia Slaton, and Greg Zacharias.

Finally, I appreciate the encouragement and tolerance of my family throughout the project.

# ———— Sixth Edition ————

# COST/MANAGERIAL ACCOUNTING

## Exam Questions and Explanations

by

Irvin N. Gleim, Ph.D., CPA, CIA, CMA, CFM

with the assistance of
Grady M. Irwin, J.D.

## ABOUT THE AUTHOR

Irvin N. Gleim is Professor Emeritus in the Fisher School of Accounting at the University of Florida and is a member of the American Accounting Association, Academy of Legal Studies in Business, American Institute of Certified Public Accountants, Association of Government Accountants, Florida Institute of Certified Public Accountants, The Institute of Internal Auditors, and the Institute of Management Accountants. He has had articles published in the *Journal of Accountancy, The Accounting Review,* and *The American Business Law Journal* and is author/ coauthor of numerous accounting and aviation books and CPE courses.

Gleim Publications, Inc.
P.O. Box 12848
University Station
Gainesville, Florida 32604
(800) 87-GLEIM
(352) 375-0772
FAX (352) 375-6940
Internet: www.gleim.com

ISSN 1092-4205
ISBN 1-58194-031-9

This is the first printing of the sixth edition of *Cost/Managerial Accounting Exam Questions and Explanations*. Please send e-mail to update@gleim.com with MAN EQE 6-1 as the subject or text. You will receive our current update as a reply.

EXAMPLE:

To:         update@gleim.com
From:       your e-mail address
Subject:    MAN EQE 6-1

## ACKNOWLEDGMENTS

Material from Uniform Certified Public Accountant Examination questions and unofficial answers, Copyright © 1969 - 1994 by the American Institute of Certified Public Accountants, Inc. is reprinted and/or adapted with permission.

The authors also appreciate and thank the Institute of Internal Auditors, Inc. for permission to use the Institute's Certified Internal Auditor Examination questions, copyright © 1976 - 1995 by The Institute of Internal Auditors, Inc.

The authors also appreciate and thank the Institute of Certified Management Accountants of the Institute of Management Accountants (formerly the National Association of Accountants) for permission to use questions from past CMA examinations, copyright © 1973 - 1995 by the Institute of Management Accountants.

---

*This publication is designed to provide accurate and authoritative information with regard to the subject matter covered. It is sold with the understanding that the publisher is not engaged in rendering legal, accounting, or other professional service.*

*If legal advice or other expert assistance is required, the services of a competent professional person should be sought.*

(From a declaration of principles jointly adopted by a Committee of the American Bar Association and a Committee of Publishers.)

Visit our Internet site (www.gleim.com) for the latest updates and information on all of our products.

# PREFACE FOR ACCOUNTING STUDENTS

The purpose of this book is to help you understand cost/managerial accounting concepts and procedures, and their applications. In turn, these skills will enable you to perform better on your undergraduate examinations, as well as look ahead to (and prepare for) professional certification examinations (e.g., CIA, CMA, CFM, and CPA).

One of the major benefits of this book is comprehensive coverage of cost/managerial accounting topics. Accordingly, when you use this book to help prepare for cost/managerial accounting courses and examinations, you are assured of covering virtually all topics that can reasonably be expected to be studied in typical college or university courses. See Appendix A for a comprehensive list of cross-references.

The question-and-answer format is designed and presented to facilitate effective study. Students should be careful not to misuse this text by referring to the answers, which appear to the immediate right of each question, before independently answering each question. One way to overcome the temptation is to use our *Test Prep* software, which is packed with features and priced with the student's budget in mind. See page 18 for additional information.

The majority of the questions in this book are from past CIA, CMA, and CPA examinations. Although a citation for the source of each question is provided, some have been modified to accommodate changes in professional pronouncements, to clarify questions, and/or to emphasize an accounting concept or its application. In addition, hundreds of publisher-written questions test areas covered in current textbooks but not directly tested on accounting certification examinations.

Note that this book should not be relied upon to prepare for professional examinations. You should utilize review manuals specifically developed for each examination. Gleim's *CIA Review, CMA/CFM Review,* and *CPA Review* are up-to-date manuals that comprehensively cover all material necessary for successful completion of each examination. An order form for these other books, software, and audiotapes is provided on page 703.

Thank you for your interest in this book. We deeply appreciate the many letters and suggestions received from accounting students and educators during the past years, as well as from CIA, CMA, and CPA candidates. Please send us your suggestions, comments, and corrections concerning this manual. The last two pages have been designed to help you note corrections and suggestions throughout your study process.

Please read the Introduction carefully. It is very short but nevertheless very important.

Good Luck on Your Exams,

*Irvin N. Gleim*

December 1998

---

Gleim Publications' Customer Service Procedures

To continue providing our customers with first-rate service, we request that questions about our books and software be sent to us via mail, e-mail, or fax. The appropriate staff member will give it thorough consideration and a prompt response. Questions concerning orders, prices, shipments, or payments will be handled via telephone by our competent and courteous customer service staff.

Thank you.

# PREFACE FOR ACCOUNTING PRACTITIONERS

The first purpose of this book is to permit you to assess your technical proficiency concerning cost and managerial accounting and related special skills such as quantitative methods, planning, and control. The second purpose is to facilitate your review and update of cost accounting concepts with our compendium of over 1,400 objective questions. The third purpose is to provide CPE credit for your self-assessment and review/update study effort.

This approach to CPE is both interactive and intense. You should be continually challenged to answer each question correctly. When you answer a question incorrectly or have difficulty, you should pursue a complete understanding by reading the answer explanation and consulting reference sources as necessary.

Most of the questions in *Cost/Managerial Accounting Exam Questions and Explanations* were taken from various professional examinations, but many have been revised, adapted, etc., to provide broader and up-to-date coverage of the managerial accounting body of technical knowledge. While some are from the CPA exam, many are from the CIA and CMA exams. Thus, you have an opportunity to consider the appropriateness of pursuing these other accounting certifications. In addition, hundreds of publisher questions cover material not directly tested on the accounting certification examinations. Also, this book contains multiple-choice questions developed from essay questions/computational problems that appeared on the CIA, CMA, and CPA exams.

Finally, we ask for any supplemental comments, reactions, suggestions, etc., that you may have as you complete our CPE program. Please attach them to the Course Evaluation (handwritten notes are fine). The last two pages of this study book have been designed to help you note corrections and suggestions throughout your study process.

Practitioners interested in multiple certification will find the discussion of the CIA and CMA/CFM and other certification programs in the Introduction to be useful. If, as you work through this study book and take the open-book CPE final exams, you find you need to refer to a cost or quantitative methods textbook, Appendix A contains a list of current titles. You should be sure to read carefully the introductory pages of your *Cost/Managerial Accounting CPE* book.

Thank you for your interest, and I look forward to hearing from you.

Best Wishes in Your CPE Endeavors,

*Irvin N. Gleim*

December 1998

# TABLE OF CONTENTS

# CONTRIBUTING PROFESSORS

We are especially grateful to the following professors who submitted questions for the Third, Fourth, and Fifth Editions. Their participation has made *Cost/Managerial Accounting Exam Questions and Explanations* truly a community project. We welcome further submissions of questions for the Seventh Edition of *Cost/Managerial Accounting Exam Questions and Explanations* or for future editions of our other exam question and explanation books. Call, write, fax, or e-mail us for more information.

Boze, K. . . . . . . . . . . . . . . . . . . . . . . . . . . . . . . . . . . . . . . . . . . . . . . . . . University of Alaska at Fairbanks
Ferry, J.W. . . . . . . . . . . . . . . . . . . . . . . . . . . . . . . . . . . . . . . . . . . . . . . . . . Pittsburg State University
Gruber, R. . . . . . . . . . . . . . . . . . . . . . . . . . . . . . . . . . . . . . . . . University of Wisconsin at Whitewater
Mayne, F. . . . . . . . . . . . . . . . . . . . . . . . . . . . . . . . . . . . . . . . . . . . University of Texas at El Paso
McCarthy, L.J. . . . . . . . . . . . . . . . . . . . . . . . . . . . . . . . . . . . . . . . . . . . . . Slippery Rock University
Romal, J.B. . . . . . . . . . . . . . . . . . . . . . . . . . . . . . . . . . . . . . . . . . . . . . SUNY College at Fredonia
Skender, C.J. . . . . . . . . . . . . . . . . . . . . . . . . . . . . . . . . . . . . . . . . . North Carolina State University
Wagner, C. . . . . . . . . . . . . . . . . . . . . . . . . . . . . . . . . . . . . . . . . . . . . . . Mankato State University
Wilson, A. . . . . . . . . . . . . . . . . . . . . . . . . . . . . . . . . . . . . . . . . . . . . . . . . . . . . Auburn University

# INTRODUCTION

The format and content of this study manual are innovative in the accounting text market. The first purpose is to provide accounting students with a well-organized, comprehensive compendium of summary outlines and corresponding objective questions covering the topics taught in typical cost, managerial, and quantitative methods undergraduate courses. The second purpose is to provide accounting professionals with a comprehensive presentation of diagnostic objective questions for self-diagnostic use and/or review of basic level cost/managerial standards and procedures including quantitative methods.

The Gleim exam question and explanation books really work! You can pretest yourself before class to see if you are strong or weak in the assigned area. You can retest after class to see if you really understand the material. The questions in these books cover **all** topics in your related courses, so you will encounter few questions on your exams for which you will not be well prepared.

The chapter titles and organization of Chapters 1 through 18 are based on the current cost/managerial accounting and quantitative methods textbooks listed in Appendix A. Some textbooks may have been inadvertently omitted. If you are using a textbook that is not included in our list, please fax, mail, or e-mail us the table of contents so that we may provide you with a cross-reference. In your correspondence to us, please include your name, address, school, professor, and course name.

## OUR USE OF MODULES

Each chapter of this book is divided into subtopics to assist your study program. We call these subtopics "modules." Modules permit broad and perhaps overwhelming topics to be divided into more manageable study components.

Choosing modules and arranging questions within these subtopics was difficult. As a result, there is some overlapping of topics and questions. The number of questions is large enough for comprehensive coverage but does not present an insurmountable task. We have defined each module narrowly enough to cover a single topic but broadly enough to prevent questions from being repetitious.

Within each module, multiple-choice questions are presented in a sequence moving from the general to the specific, elementary to advanced, etc., to provide an effective learning sequence. Duplicate questions and redundant explanations have been kept to a minimum.

## SOURCES OF OBJECTIVE QUESTIONS

Past CIA, CMA, and CPA examinations and sample questions are the primary sources of questions included in this study manual.

Additionally, your authors have prepared questions (coded in this text as *Publisher*) based upon the content of the cost/managerial accounting and quantitative methods textbooks listed in Appendix A. These *Publisher* questions were developed to review topics not adequately covered by questions from the other sources. Also, professors from schools around the country have contributed questions. See page viii for a list of their names and school affiliations.

## IDENTIFICATION OF THE SOURCE OF EACH QUESTION

The source of each question appears in the first line of its answer explanation, in the column to the right of the question. Summary of source codes:

| | |
|---|---|
| *CIA* | Certified Internal Auditor Examination |
| *CMA* | Certified Management Accountant Examination |
| *CPA* | Uniform Certified Public Accountant Examination |
| *Publisher* | Your authors |
| *Individual name* | Name of professional or professor who contributed the question |

If you, your professor, or your classmates wish to submit questions, we will consider using them in future editions. Please send questions you develop, complete with answers and explanations, to the following address:

> Gleim Publications, Inc.
> EQE Question Bank
> P.O. Box 12848, University Station
> Gainesville, FL 32604

Writing and analyzing multiple-choice questions is an excellent way to prepare yourself for your exams. We will make every effort to consider, edit, and use questions you submit. However, we ask that you send us only serious, complete, carefully considered efforts.

## UNIQUENESS OF OBJECTIVE QUESTIONS

The major advantage of objective questions is their ability to cover (for study or test purposes) a large number of topics with little time and effort when compared to essay questions and/or computational problems.

A multiple-choice question is actually a series of statements of which all but one are incorrect given the facts of the question. The advantage of multiple-choice questions over true-false questions is that they require more analysis and result in a lower score for those with little or no knowledge. Random guessing on questions with four answer choices results in an expected grade of 25%. Random guessing on a true-false test results in an expected grade of 50%.

Students and practitioners both like multiple-choice questions. Because they present alternative answers from which only one needs to be selected, students find them relatively easy to answer. Professors also like objective questions because they are easy to grade and because much more material can be tested in the same period of time.

## ANSWER EXPLANATIONS ALONGSIDE THE QUESTIONS

Our format presents objective questions and their answer explanations side by side. The answer explanations are to the right of each question. The example below is from the CPA exam.

**8.** What is the normal effect on the numbers of cost pools and cost assignment bases when an activity-based cost (ABC) system replaces a traditional cost system?

| | Cost Pools | Cost Assignment Bases |
|---|---|---|
| A. | No effect | No effect |
| B. | Increase | No effect |
| C. | No effect | Increase |
| D. | Increase | Increase |

The correct answer is (D). *(CPA, adapted)*
**REQUIRED:** The normal effect of an ABC system on the numbers of cost pools and cost assignment bases.
**DISCUSSION:** In an ABC system, cost assignment is more precise than in traditional systems because activities rather than functions or departments are defined as cost objects. This structure permits assignment to more cost pools and the identification of a driver specifically related to each. A driver is a factor that causes a change in a cost. Thus, an ABC system uses more cost pools and cost assignment bases than a traditional system.
Answers (A), (B), and (C) are incorrect because the numbers of cost pools and cost assignment bases increase.

The format in this study manual is designed to facilitate your study of objective questions, their answers, and the answer explanations. The intent is to save you time and effort by eliminating the need to turn pages back and forth from questions to answers.

Be careful, however. Do not misuse this format by consulting the answers before you have answered the questions. Misuse of the readily available answers will give you a false sense of security and result in poor performance on examinations and decreased benefit from your studies. The best way to use this study manual is to cover the answer explanations with the bookmark provided for this purpose in the back of the book (or sheet of paper) as you read and answer each question. As a crucial part of the learning process, you must honestly commit yourself to an answer before looking at the answer explanation. Whether you are right or wrong, your memory of the correct answer will be reinforced by this process.

## OVERVIEW OF ACCOUNTING CERTIFICATION PROGRAMS

The CPA (Certified Public Accountant) exam is the grandparent of all the professional accounting examinations. Its origin was in the 1896 public accounting legislation of New York. In 1917 the American Institute of CPAs (AICPA) began to prepare and grade a uniform CPA exam. It is currently used to measure the technical competence of those applying to be licensed as CPAs in all 50 states, Guam, Puerto Rico, the Virgin Islands, and the District of Columbia. More than 60,000 candidates sit for each CPA exam which is given twice a year in May and November.

The CIA (Certified Internal Auditor), CMA (Certified Management Accountant), and CFM (Corporate Financial Management) examinations are relatively new certification programs compared to the CPA. The CMA exam was first administered in 1972, and the first CIA exam in 1974. The CFM exam was first administered in December 1996. Why were these certification programs begun? Generally, the requirements of the CPA designation instituted by the boards of accountancy, especially the necessity for public accounting experience, led to the development of the CIA, CMA, and CFM programs.

Certification is important to professional accountants because it provides

1.   Participation in a recognized professional group
2.   An improved professional training program arising out of the certification program
3.   Recognition among peers for attaining the professional designation
4.   An extra credential for the employment market/career ladder
5.   The personal satisfaction of attaining a recognized degree of competency

These reasons hold particularly true in the accounting field due to wide recognition of the CPA designation. Accountants and accounting students are often asked if they are CPAs when people learn they are accountants. Thus, there is considerable pressure for accountants to become *certified*.

A new development is multiple certifications, which is important for the same reasons as initial certification. Accounting students and recent graduates should look ahead and obtain multiple certifications. Obtaining multiple certifications will help to broaden your career opportunities. The table of selected CIA, CMA, CFM, and CPA examination data on the following page provides an overview of these accounting examinations.

## RATIONALE FOR ACCOUNTING CERTIFICATION PROGRAMS

The primary purpose of the CIA, CMA, CFM, and CPA examinations is to measure the technical competence of candidates. Competence includes technical knowledge, ability to apply such knowledge with good judgment, and comprehension of professional responsibility. Additionally, the nature of these examinations (low pass rate, broad and rigorous coverage, etc.) has several very important effects.

1.   Candidates are forced to learn all of the material that should have been presented and learned in a good accounting educational program.

2.   Relatedly, candidates must integrate the topics and concepts that are presented in individual courses in accounting education programs.

3.   The content of each examination provides direction to accounting education programs; i.e., what is tested on the examinations will be taught to accounting students.

## EXAMINATION CONTENT

The content of these examinations is specified by their governing boards with lists of topics to be tested. In the Gleim review manuals -- *CIA Review, CMA/CFM Review,* and *CPA Review* -- the material tested is divided into subtopics called study units. A study unit is a more manageable undertaking than an overall part of each exam. The listings of topics on pages 6 through 8 provide an overview of the content of these exams.

## CIA, CMA/CFM, CPA EXAMINATION SUMMARY

| | CIA | CMA/CFM | CPA |
|---|---|---|---|
| Sponsoring Organization | Institute of Internal Auditors 249 Maitland Avenue Altamonte Springs, FL 32701 (407) 830-7600 www.theiia.org | Institute of Certified Management Accountants 10 Paragon Drive Montvale, NJ 07645-1759 (201) 573-9000 (800) 638-4427 www.ima.org | American Institute of Certified Public Accountants Harborside Financial Center 201 Plaza III Jersey City, NJ 07311-3881 (201) 938-3419 www.aicpa.org |
| Passing Score | 75% | 70% | 75% |
| Average Pass Rate by Exam Part | 45% | 40% | 33% |
| Cost | $300 (50% student discount) | $240 (50% student discount; requires IMA membership) | $35-315 (Varies by state) |
| Year Examination Was First Administered | 1974 | 1972 | 1916 |
| Major Exam Sections and Length | I. Internal Audit Process (3½ hours) | 1. Economics, Finance, and Management (3 hours) | 1. Business Law & Professional Responsibilities (3 hours) |
| | II. Internal Audit Skills (3½ hours) | 2. Financial Accounting and Reporting (3 hours)  2CFM. Corporate Financial Management (3 hours) | 2. Auditing (4½ hours) |
| | III. Management Control and Information Tech. (3½ hours) | 3. Management Reporting, Analysis, and Behavioral Issues (3 hours) | 3. Accounting & Reporting -- Taxation, Managerial, & Governmental and Not-for-Profit Organizations (3½ hours) |
| | IV. The Audit Environment (3½ hours) | 4. Decision Analysis and Information Systems (3 hours) | 4. Financial Accounting & Reporting -- Business Enterprises (4½ hours) |
| Length of Exam | 14 hours | 12 hours (CMA or CFM) 15 hours (CMA *and* CFM) | 15½ hours |
| When Administered | 2 weeks after CPA Wed, Thur | On Demand | 1st week of May, Nov Wed, Thur |
| Candidates Sitting for Exam: | Total number of candidates sitting for two examinations; many are repeaters. | | |
| 1990 | 4,363 | 4,839 | 143,572 |
| 1991 | 4,597 | 6,404 | 140,042 |
| 1992 | 4,961 | 7,464 | 136,541 |
| 1993 | 5,103 | 7,879 | 140,100 |
| 1994 | 4,557 | 8,259 | 131,000 |
| 1995 | 4,649 | 8,675 | 126,000 |
| 1996 | 4,646 | 8,679 | 122,232 |
| 1997 | 5,169 | 7,481 | 121,437 |

Other professional accounting-related designations include: CBA (Certified Bank Auditor), CDP (Certificate in Data Processing), CFA (Chartered Financial Analyst), CFE (Certified Fraud Examiner), CISA (Certified Information Systems Auditor), Enrolled Agent (one enrolled to practice before the IRS).

---

**CIA REVIEW**

Gleim makes your study process straightforward with 10 study units per exam part. Pass the first time with Gleim.

**Part I:  Internal Audit Process**
Introduction to Internal Auditing
Independence, Status, and Objectivity
Standards and Proficiency
Internal Control
Planning and Administering the Audit Assignment
Audit Evidence and Procedures
Managing the Internal Auditing Department
Information Technology Auditing
Ethics
Fraud

**Part II:  Internal Audit Skills**
Problem Solving
Decision Making
Pronouncements on Audit Evidence
Types of Audit Evidence
Flowcharting and Data Gathering
Using Electronic Media
Working Papers
Communicating Results
Mathematics
Statistics and Sampling

**Part III:  Management Control and Information Technology**
Internal Control Concepts
The Controlling Process
Budgeting
Responsibility Accounting
Product Cost Control Systems
Decision Analysis I
Decision Analysis II
Information Technology I
Information Technology II
Information Technology - Control

**Part IV:  The Audit Environment***
Standards and Statements
Assets
Liabilities and Shareholders' Equity
Financial Accounting - Special Topics
Finance I
Finance II
Managerial Accounting - Cost Behavior and Allocation
Managerial Accounting - Additional Topics
Regulatory Environment I
Regulatory Environment I

*Persons who have passed the CPA or CMA exams (and many other professional exams) are not required to take Part IV of the CIA exam.

---

Each of the four parts consists of 80 multiple-choice questions and is 3½ hours in length (8:30 - 12:00 and 1:30 - 5:00).

The first two parts of the CIA exam focus on the theory and practice of internal auditing. The body of knowledge of internal auditing and the auditing skills to be tested consist of

1.   The typical undergraduate auditing class (as represented by auditing texts, e.g., Arens and Loebbecke, Taylor and Glezen, etc.)

2.   Internal auditing textbooks (e.g., Sawyer and Sumners, *The Practice of Modern Internal Auditing,* and Atkisson, Brink, and Witt, *Modern Internal Auditing*)

3.   Various IIA (Institute of Internal Auditors) pronouncements (e.g., The IIA *Code of Ethics*, Standards for the Professional Practice of Internal Auditing, and Statement of Responsibilities of Internal Auditing)

4.   Reasoning ability, communications, and problem-solving skills, and dealing with auditees within an audit context (i.e., the questions will cover audit topics, but test audit skills)

The remaining 50% of the exam, parts III and IV, assures that internal auditors are conversant with topics, methodologies, and techniques ranging from individual and organizational behavior to economics.

Management cannot personally observe the functioning of all officers, employees, and specialized functions (finance, marketing, operations, etc.). Each has a unique perspective. Only internal auditing is in a position to take a total company point of view.

## CMA and CFM REVIEW

Gleim makes your study process straightforward with 10 study units per exam part.  Pass the first time with Gleim.

**Part 1:  Economics, Finance, and Management**

Microeconomics
Macroeconomics
International Business Environment
Domestic Institutional Environment of Business
Working Capital Finance
Capital Structure Finance
Risk
Organizational Theory
Motivation and the Directing Process
Communication

**Part 2CMA:  Financial Accounting and Reporting***

Accounting Standards
Financial Statements
Conceptual Framework
Assets
Liabilities
Shareholders' Equity
Other Income Items
Other Reporting Issues
Financial Statement Analysis
External Auditing

**Part 2CFM:  Corporate Financial Management****

Financial Statements and Annual Reports
Financial Statements:  Special Topics
Long-Term Capital Financing
Financial Markets and Interest Rates
Investment Banking and Commercial Banking
Financial Statement Analysis
Business Combinations and Restructurings
Risk Management
External Financial Environment
Accounting Standard Setting

**Part 3:  Management Reporting, Analysis, and Behavioral Issues**

Cost and Managerial Accounting Definitions
Product Costing and Related Topics
Cost Behavior
Statements on Management Accounting
Planning
Budgeting
The Controlling Process
Standard Costs and Variance Analysis
Responsibility Accounting
Behavioral Issues

**Part 4:  Decision Analysis and Information Systems**

Decision Analysis
Cost-Volume-Profit Analysis
Capital Budgeting
Decision Making Under Uncertainty
Quantitative Methods I
Quantitative Methods II
Information Systems I
Information Systems II
Internal Control
Internal Auditing

*Persons who have passed the CPA exam are not required to take Part 2 of the CMA exam.

**CMAs in good standing need only pass this part to earn the CFM designation.

The CMA and CFM exams have broader coverage than the CPA exam in several areas.  For example,

1.  Management information systems is tested more extensively on the CMA exam.

2.  SEC Financial Reporting Releases and Cost Accounting Standards Board pronouncements are covered on the CMA exam but not on the CPA exam.

3.  Topics like economics, finance, and management on Part 1 and Part 2CFM are covered lightly, if at all, on the CPA exam.

4.  The CMA exam tests internal auditing to a far greater degree than does the CPA exam.

5.  The CMA exam tests business ethics, but not business law.

CMA questions are generally more analysis oriented than CPA questions.  On the CPA exam, the typical requirement is the solution of an accounting problem, e.g., consolidated worksheet, funds statement, etc.

Each part of the CMA/CFM consists of 110 multiple-choice, computer-administered questions, of which five will be unscored for pretesting.

---

## CPA REVIEW

Gleim makes your study process straightforward with 19 to 21 study units per exam part.  Pass the first time with Gleim.

### Business Law
AICPA Ethics
CPAs and the Law
Agency
Partnerships
Corporations
Estates and Trusts
Contract Formation
Contract Performance
Rights and Duties
Guarantors
Bankruptcy
Securities
Employment
Environmental Regulation
Commercial Paper
Sales
Secured Transactions
Documents of Title
Real Property and Insurance
Personal Property, Bailments, and Computers

### TAX-MAN-GOV
Gross Income
Deductions
Tax Computations
Tax Procedures
Property Transactions
Corporate Taxable Income
Corporate Tax Computations
Corporate Tax Special Topics
S Corporations
Partnerships
Estates and Trusts
Exempt Organizations/Preparer's Responsibilities
Governmental Concepts
Governmental Accounting and Reporting
Not-for-Profit Concepts
Not-for-Profit Accounting and Reporting
Cost Accounting
Budgeting
Analytical Methods

### Auditing
Engagement Responsibilities
Risk Assessment
Strategic Planning Issues
Internal Control Concepts
Internal Control -- Sales-Receivables-Cash Receipts Cycle
Internal Control -- Purchases-Payables-Cash Disbursements Cycle
Internal Control -- Payroll and Other Cycles
Tests of Controls
Internal Control Communications
Evidence -- Objectives and Nature
Evidence -- The Sales-Receivables-Cash Cycle
Evidence -- The Purchases-Payables-Inventory Cycle
Evidence -- Other Assets, Liabilities, and Equities
Evidence -- Key Considerations
Evidence -- Sampling
Reports --  Standard, Qualified, Adverse, and Disclaimer
Reports -- Other Modifications
Special Reports
Related Reporting Topics
Review and Compilation
Governmental Audits

### Financial
Concepts and Standards
Revenue Recognition
Financial Statements
Other Income Statement Items
Financial Statement Disclosure
Statement of Cash Flows
Cash and Investments
Receivables and Accruals
Inventories
Property, Plant, and Equipment
Intangibles and Other Assets
Payables and Accruals
Accounting for Income Taxes
Employee Benefits
Bonds and Notes Payable
Leases and Contingencies
Equity Accounts -- Corporations
Equity Accounts -- Other
Business Combinations
Foreign Currency Issues and Other Topics

---

1.  The table below presents the CPA exam schedule and exam composition by question type.

| Section | Day | Time | Objective | | Essay/Problem |
|---|---|---|---|---|---|
| | | | MC | Other | |
| Business Law | Wednesday | 9:00-12:00 | 50-60% | 20-30% | 20-30% |
| Auditing | Wednesday | 1:30-6:00 | 50-60% | 20-30% | 20-30% |
| TAX-MAN-GOV | Thursday | 8:30-12:00 | 50-60% | 40-50% | 0 |
| Financial | Thursday | 1:30-6:00 | 50-60% | 20-30% | 20-30% |

2.  The "other objective format" (OOF) question is any question that can be answered on an answer sheet that can be optically scanned, except four-answer multiple-choice.

3.  Essay questions will be graded for writing skills.

4.  Calculators will be provided for both Thursday sessions (Sharp Model EL-231L).

5.  Every aspect of the exam is explained and analyzed in *CPA Review:  A System for Success.* Faculty and student organizations should order this free booklet in bulk for distribution.

## EXAMINATION SCHEDULES AND FUTURE DATES

The CPA exam is given during the first week of May and November on Wednesday and Thursday. The CIA exam is given on a Wednesday and Thursday 1 or 2 weeks after the CPA examination. The CMA and CFM exams are offered in a computer-based, on-demand format.

Note that all four examinations can be taken within a 3-week period, which is ideal owing to the great amount of overlap of the material tested.

|  | 1999 | | 2000 | | 2001 | |
|---|---|---|---|---|---|---|
| **CPA EXAM** | May 5, 6 | Nov. 3, 4 | May 3, 4* | Nov. 1, 2* | May 2, 3* | Nov. 7, 8* |
| **CIA EXAM** | May 19, 20* | Nov. 17, 18* | May 17, 18* | Nov. 15, 16* | May 16, 17* | Nov. 21, 22* |
| **CMA EXAM** | Computer-Based/On-Demand | | Computer-Based/On-Demand | | Computer-Based/On-Demand | |
| **CFM EXAM** | Computer-Based/On-Demand | | Computer-Based/On-Demand | | Computer-Based/On-Demand | |

*Predicted dates. Check your registration card for actual dates.

### When to Sit for the Exams

Sit for all four examinations as soon as you can. The CIA, CMA, and CFM exams can be taken in your last undergraduate quarter or semester, and both offer a 50% reduction in fees to full-time students. In many states you may also take the CPA exam in your last quarter or semester. If you are graduating in May, consider taking the CPA exam the first week of May, the CIA exam 2 weeks thereafter, and the CMA or CFM exam in early June. Your preparation program for all of these exams is very synergistic and not appreciably more work than preparing for just the CPA exam.

## EXAMINATION PASS RATES

The pass rates on the CIA and CMA exams are about the same and are somewhat higher than the pass rate on the CPA exam. Nationally, the pass rate on the CPA exam is about 33% on each of the four parts. The pass rates on the CIA and CMA exams average 40%-45% per part (see the tables on page 10).

Unfortunately, a great deal of confusion surrounds CPA exam pass rates. There is considerable variation in the pass rate from state to state, even though the national rate is fairly constant. Nationally, about 20% pass all four parts on the first sitting, even though the pass rate on each part is about 33%. Approximately 20% of all candidates sitting for each CPA exam successfully complete the exam (this includes those passing the entire exam on one sitting and those passing their final parts for successful completion). Over 80% of *serious* CPA candidates eventually complete the CPA exam.

There is confusion between CPA pass rates and condition rates. While 75% is the passing grade for each part, *conditional* status is assigned to candidates who pass some, but not all, parts. The combined pass and condition rate is therefore higher than the pass rate. Relatedly, the qualifications and the requirements of conditional status vary from state to state.

Many schools and CPA review courses advertise the quality of their programs by reporting pass rates. Obviously, the best rates are emphasized. Thus, the reported percentage may be that for first-time candidates, all candidates, candidates passing a specific section of the examination, candidates completing the examination, or even candidates successfully completing the exam after a specified number of sittings.

| CPA Exam | Pass Rates -- First-Time Candidates | | | | Pass Rates -- Repeat Candidates | | | |
|---|---|---|---|---|---|---|---|---|
|  | 5/96 | 11/96 | 5/97 | 11/97 | 5/96 | 11/96 | 5/97 | 11/97 |
| Auditing | 29.5 | 31.0 | 27.2 | 26.5 | 30.7 | 33.4 | 33.8 | 35.8 |
| Business Law | 31.1 | 31.9 | 30.6 | 28.4 | 31.2 | 37.8 | 34.9 | 35.1 |
| TAX-MAN-GOV | 29.8 | 29.5 | 27.7 | 22.8 | 30.1 | 33.5 | 30.5 | 29.3 |
| Financial | 30.8 | 32.3 | 28.4 | 24.1 | 29.9 | 34.3 | 26.7 | 26.2 |
| All* | 15.5 | 16.3 | 15.1 | 12.5 | 28.1 | 30.6 | 28.8 | 26.5 |

*Percentage of first-time and repeat candidates who pass all remaining parts on a particular exam.

## Reasons for the Low Pass Rates

Although a very high percentage of serious candidates successfully complete each of the examinations, the 33% CPA pass rate and the 40% - 45% CIA and CMA pass rates warrant an explanation. First, the pass rates are low (relative to bar and medical exams) because these examinations reflect the high standards of the accounting profession, which contribute greatly to the profession's reputation and also attract persons with both competence and aspiration.

Second, the pass rates are low because many accounting educational programs are at the undergraduate rather than graduate level. Undergraduates may look on their program as a number of individual courses required for graduation rather than as an integrated program to prepare them for professional practice. We encourage accounting undergraduates to take accounting seriously by helping them look ahead to graduate school, professional practice, and the CIA, CMA, CFM, and CPA exams.

Third, the pass rates are low because accounting programs and curricula at most colleges and universities are not given the budgetary priority they deserve. Accounting faculties are often understaffed for the number of accounting majors, the number and nature of accounting courses (problem-oriented vs. descriptive), etc., relative to other faculties. However, you cannot use this as an excuse or reason for not achieving your personal goals. You must do your best to improve your control systems and study resources.

| CIA Exam Pass Rates | | | | |
|---|---|---|---|---|
|  | 5/96 | 11/96 | 5/97 | 11/97 |
| Part I | 45.0 | 50.3 | 58.2 | 47.7 |
| Part II | 41.9 | 43.2 | 45.1 | 49.7 |
| Part III | 45.1 | 43.9 | 43.3 | 46.9 |
| Part IV | 44.4 | 42.5 | 44.3 | 44.1 |

| CMA/CFM Exams The CMA/CFM exams are administered on-demand at Sylvan Testing Centers. | |
|---|---|
| Part 1 | 49% |
| Part 2CMA | 41% |
| Part 2CFM | 41% |
| Part 3 | 50% |
| Part 4 | 46% |

## COST TO OBTAIN AND MAINTAIN PROFESSIONAL CERTIFICATION

The cost to take the CIA exam is a $60 registration fee plus $70-per-part examination fee, which totals $340 (assuming you pass all parts the first time you take them). Full-time students save 50%. A $20-per-year record-keeping fee is charged to maintain CPE records for nonmembers of The Institute of Internal Auditors (The IIA). Membership in The IIA is not required.

The cost to take the CMA/CFM exam is $80 for each of the parts and a $50 application fee plus Institute of Management Accountants (IMA) membership dues, which varies from $27 for students to $135 for regular members. Membership in the IMA is required. Students may take the examination once at a reduced fee of $40 per part and do NOT pay an application fee.

The cost of the CPA exam varies by state. The table on page 13 lists the examination fee in each state. Additionally, most states require an annual fee to maintain the CPA certificate and/or license.

## WHERE TO TAKE THE CPA EXAM

If you are not going to practice public accounting, you may wish to become certified in a state that

I.    Issues a CPA certificate separate from a license to practice
II.   Does **not** require experience to receive a CPA certificate
III.  Does **not** require continuing professional education of CPA certificate holders
IV.  Does **not** require residency to sit for the CPA exam

You may also be concerned with the 150-hour requirement to sit for the CPA exam. Consult the table on page 13. This topic and more specific recommendations are presented in Chapter 1 of the free 112-page Gleim booklet, *CPA Review: A System for Success*. Visit the AICPA's web page at www.aicpa.org for more information.

## STEPS TO BECOME A CPA

1.   Decide when you are going to take the CPA exam (the sooner, the better!).

2.   Determine the state board to which you will apply to sit for the CPA exam. Read "Where to Take the CPA Exam" above.

3.   Obtain, complete, and submit your application form, including transcripts, etc.

4.   Commit to thorough, systematic preparation for the exam as described in our free booklet, *CPA Review: A System for Success*.

5.   Work systematically through each study unit in the four Gleim *CPA Review* books (*Business Law*, *Auditing*, *TAX-MAN-GOV*, and *Financial*).

6.   Use Gleim's **CPA Test Prep** software: over 5,000 CPA questions, all updated to current tax law, FASB Statements, etc., as testable on the CPA exam.

7.   Sit for and PASS the CPA exam while you are in control, as described in Chapter 8 of *CPA Review: A System for Success*. Gleim will make it easy. Call (800) 87-GLEIM for more information.

## STATE BOARDS OF ACCOUNTANCY

All 50 states (and the District of Columbia, Guam, Puerto Rico, and the Virgin Islands) have an administrative agency that administers the laws and rules which regulate the practice of public accounting in each state. Each of these 54 jurisdictions contracts with the AICPA to use the AICPA's Uniform CPA Examination.

While the 54 jurisdictions agree on using the same examination, the rules and procedures for applying to take the exam and becoming licensed to practice public accounting vary considerably. Accordingly, you should call or write to your state board for a CPA exam application form. With the form you will receive that board's rules, regulations, and directions to you as a CPA candidate.

The next page contains a list of the state boards, their addresses, phone numbers, and the following information relevant to most CPA candidates.

## CPA REQUIREMENTS BY STATE (next page)

**Residency:** Some states have in-state guidelines to meet in order to sit for the CPA exam: R = residency, E = employment, O = office (business), C = U.S. citizenship requirement.

**150-hour requirement:** As of August 1998, 44 states have legislated the requirement for 150 semester hours to take the CPA exam, which is generally a baccalaureate plus 30 hours. The effective dates of this requirement are listed on the table on the next page. Contact individual boards for exact information.

**Education beyond high school (in years) required to take exam/apply for certificate:** A number = years of education beyond high school; B = bachelor's; A = emphasis in accounting; + = hours in excess of bachelor's. The slashes are used to separate various levels of education, which affect the amount of experience required to practice (see Experience, below). Please check with your state board to inquire about specific hour requirements.

**Experience (in public accounting) required to practice:** Years of experience correspond to education which is listed in the column just to the left. Varying education requirements and varying experience requirements are separated by slashes. For example, Alaska permits persons to take the CPA exam if one of the following requirements is met:

1. A bachelor's degree not in accounting
2. A bachelor's degree with an accounting major

After passing the CPA exam, either 3 or 2 years' experience is required before a CPA certificate is issued.

1. Three years if the exam was taken with a bachelor's degree not in accounting
2. Two years if the exam was taken with a bachelor's degree in accounting

**Exam application deadline -- first time:** New candidates

**Exam application deadline -- re-exam:** For candidates with conditional status (see below)

**Exam conditioning requirements:** Number of parts to pass, followed by minimum grade on other parts, if any

**Exam fee:** For all four parts, usually less if conditioned

**Ethics test:** An E indicates a separate ethics test is given (not during the CPA exam). A dash indicates no ethics test. A pound sign (#) means the ethics test is required at the time of certification.

**CPA certificate issued separately from a license to practice:** Indicated by a "Y"

# CPA REQUIREMENTS BY STATE
## as of August 1998

**NOTE: Each State Board is currently updating requirements to accommodate the 1997 changes in the CPA exam. Contact your State Board for complete up-to-date information.**

| STATE BOARD • ADDRESS | Telephone # | Residency | 150-Hr. Requirement | Education | Experience | Application Deadline First Time | Application Deadline Re-Exam | Condition Requirements | Exam Fee | Ethics | Separate Certificate |
|---|---|---|---|---|---|---|---|---|---|---|---|
| AK P.O. Box 110806 • Juneau, AK 99811 | (907) 465-2580 | -- | 2001 | B/BA | 3/2 | 60 days | 60 days | 2, 50 | $100.00 | E | Y |
| AL 770 Washington Ave., Ste. 236 • Montgomery, AL 36130 | (334) 242-5700 | C | 1995 | B+ | 2/5 | 2/28; 8/31 | 3/31; 9/30 | 2, 50 | $190.00 | -- | Y |
| AR 101 East Capitol, Ste. 430 • Little Rock, AR 72201 | (501) 682-1520 | R/E | 1998 | BA/+ | 2/1 | 60 days | 30 days | 2, 50 | $160.00 | -- | Y |
| AZ 3877 N. 7th St., Ste. 106 • Phoenix, AZ 85014 | (602) 255-3648 | -- | | BA/+ | 2/1 | 2/28; 8/31 | 2/28; 8/31 | 2, 50 | $175.00 | # | -- |
| CA 2000 Evergreen St., Ste. 250 • Sacramento, CA 95815 | (916) 263-3680 | -- | | B/BA | 3/2 | 3/1; 9/1 | 3/1; 9/1 | 2 | $160.00 | E | Y |
| * CO 1560 Broadway, Ste. 1370 • Denver, CO 80202 | (303) 894-7800 | -- | 2002 | BA | 1 | 3/1; 9/1 | 3/1; 9/1 | 2, 50 | $200.00 | # | |
| * CT 30 Trinity Street • Hartford, CT 06106 | (860) 509-6179 | -- | 2000 | BA | 3 | 60 days | 60 days | 2, 50 | $220.00 | # | |
| DC P.O. Box 37200 • Washington, DC 20013-7200 | (202) 727-7468 | -- | 2000 | BA | 2 | 90 days | 60 days | 2, 50 | $120.00 | -- | Y |
| * DE Cannon Bldg., Ste. 203, P.O. Box 1401 • Dover, DE 19903 | (302) 739-4522 | -- | | 2/BA/+ | 4/2/1 | 3/1; 9/1 | 3/1; 9/1 | 2, 50 | $195.00 | # | Y |
| FL 2610 NW 43rd St., Ste. 1-A • Gainesville, FL 32606 | (352) 955-2165 | -- | 1983 | BA+ | 0 | 2/1; 8/1 | 3/1; 9/1 | 2, 50 | $235.00 | # | |
| * GA 166 Pryor Street, S.W. • Atlanta, GA 30303 | (404) 656-2281 | -- | 1998 | BA+ | 2 | 2/1; 8/1 | 3/1; 9/1 | 2, 50 | $200.00 | -- | |
| GU P.O. Box P • Agana, GU 96910 | (671) 475-2672 | C/R/E/O | 2000 | BA/+ | 2/1 | 60 days | 60 days | 2, 50 | $35.00 | -- | |
| * HI P.O. Box 3469 • Honolulu, HI 96801 | (808) 586-2694 | -- | 1978 | BA+ | 2 | 3/1; 9/1 | 3/1; 9/1 | 2, 50 | $270.00 | -- | Y |
| * IA 1918 SE Hulsizer Avenue • Ankeny, IA 50021 | (515) 281-4126 | R/E/O | 2001 | 0/BA/+ | 3/2/0 | 2/28; 8/31 | 2/28; 8/31 | 2, 50 | $210.00 | E | Y |
| ID 1109 Main St., Ste. 470 • Boise, ID 83720-0002 | (208) 334-2490 | R | 2000 | BA/+ | 2/2 | 3/1; 9/1 | 3/1; 9/1 | 2, 50 | $175.00 | E | Y |
| IL 320 W. Washington St., 3rd Fl. • Springfield, IL 62786 | (217) 785-0800 | -- | 2001 | BA | 1 | 3/1; 8/1 | 3/1; 9/1 | 2, 50 | $180.00 | E | Y |
| * IN 302 West Washington St, E034 • Indianapolis, IN 46204 | (317) 232-3935 | R | 2000 | BA/+ | 3/2 | 3/1; 9/1 | 3/1; 9/1 | 2, 50 | $220.00 | -- | |
| * KS 900 SW Jackson St., Ste. 556 • Topeka, KS 66612 | (913) 296-2162 | R/E/O | 1997 | BA/+ | 1-2 | 3/1; 9/1 | 3/1; 9/1 | 2, 50 | $200.00 | E | Y |
| KY 332 W. Broadway, Ste. 310 • Louisville, KY 40202 | (502) 595-3037 | R | 2000 | BA | 1-2 | 3/1; 9/1 | 3/1; 9/1 | 2, 50 | $140.00 | # | |
| * LA 601 Poydras St., Ste. 1770 • New Orleans, LA 70130 | (504) 566-1244 | R | 1996 | BA/+ | 2/1 | 3/1; 9/1 | 3/1; 9/1 | 2, 50 | $200.00 | -- | Y |
| * MA 100 Cambridge St, Rm. 1315 • Boston, MA 02202 | (617) 727-1806 | -- | 2002 | BA/+ | 3/2 | 3/15; 9/15 | 3/15; 9/15 | 2, 50 | $220.00 | -- | |
| ** MD 500 N. Calvert Street, Room 308 • Baltimore, MD 21202-3651 | (410) 333-6322 | -- | 1999 | BA | 0 | 60 days | 60 days | 2, 50 | $98.00 | E | |
| * ME 35 State House Station • Augusta, ME 04333 | (207) 624-8603 | R | 2002 | B/+ | 2/1 | 3/1; 9/1 | 3/1; 9/1 | 2 | $225.00 | -- | Y |
| ** MI P.O. Box 30018 • Lansing, MI 48909-7518 | (517) 241-9249 | R/E/O | | BA/+ | 2/1 | 3/1; 9/1 | 3/1; 9/1 | 2, 50 | $145.00 | -- | Y |
| MN 85 East 7th Place • St Paul, MN 55101 | (612) 296-7937 | R/E/O | | 0/2/B/BA/+ | 6/5/3/2/1 | 3/1; 9/1 | 3/1; 9/1 | 2, 50 | $150.00 | E | Y |
| * MO P.O. Box 613 • Jefferson City, MO 65102 | (573) 751-0012 | R/E/O | 1999 | BA | 2 | 3/1; 9/1 | 3/1; 9/1 | 2, 50 | $200.00 | # | Y |
| MS 653 North State Street • Jackson, MS 39202-3304 | (601) 354-7320 | R/O | 1995 | BA+ | 1 | 3/1; 9/1 | 3/1; 9/1 | 2, 50 | $200.00 | -- | Y |
| MT 111 N. Jackson, P.O. Box 200513 • Helena, MT 59620 | (406) 444-3739 | -- | 1997 | B/BA+ | 2/1 | 3/15; 9/15 | 3/15; 9/15 | 2, 50 | $225.00 | # | Y |
| NC P.O. Box 12827 • Raleigh, NC 27605 | (919) 733-4222 | C | 2001 | B | 2 | 1/31; 7/31 | 2/28; 8/31 | 2, 50 | $175.00 | E | Y |
| ND 2701 S. Columbia Rd • Grand Forks, ND 58201 | (800) 532-5904 | R | 2000 | 0/BA | 4/0 | 3/15; 9/15 | 3/15; 9/15 | 2, 40 | $140.00 | E | Y |
| NE P.O. Box 94725 • Lincoln, NE 68509 | (402) 471-3595 | R/E/C | 1998 | B+ | 2/1 | 3/31; 9/30 | 3/31; 9/30 | 2, 50 | $200.00 | E | Y |
| NH 57 Regional Drive • Concord, NH 03301 | (603) 271-3286 | -- | | B/B+ | 2/1 | 3/15; 9/15 | 3/15; 9/15 | 2, 50 | $225.00 | -- | |
| * NJ P.O. Box 45000 • Newark, NJ 07101 | (973) 504-6380 | -- | 2000 | BA | 2 | 3/1; 9/1 | 2/1; 8/1 | 2, 50 | $290.00 | -- | |
| NM 1650 University NE, Ste. 400A • Albuquerque, NM 87102 | (505) 841-9108 | -- | | B/BA | 3/1 | 3/1; 9/1 | 3/1; 9/1 | 2 | $125.00 | E | Y |
| NV 200 South Virginia St., #670 • Reno, NV 89501 | (702) 786-0231 | -- | 2001 | B | 2 | 3/1; 11/1 | 3/1; 11/1 | 2, 50 | $150.00 | # | |
| * NY Cultural Ed Center, Rm. 3013 • Albany, NY 12230 | (518) 474-3836 | -- | 2002 | BA/+ | 2/1 | 2/1; 8/1 | 3/1; 9/1 | 2 | $345.00 | -- | |
| OH 77 S. High St., 18th FL., Ste. 222 • Columbus, OH 43266 | (614) 466-4135 | R/E/O | 2000 | BA/+ | 2/1 | 3/2; 9/1 | 3/2; 9/1 | 2, 50 | $245.00 | E | |
| OK 4545 Lincoln Blvd., Ste. 165 • Ok. City, OK 73105 | (405) 521-2397 | R | 2003 | BA | 0 | 60 days | 60 days | 2, 50 | $120.00 | -- | |
| OR 3218 Pringle Road SE, Ste. 110 • Salem, OR 97302-6307 | (503) 378-4181 | -- | 2000 | 0/BA/+ | 4/2/1 | 3/1; 9/1 | 3/1; 9/1 | 2, 50 | $150.00 | E | |
| ** PA P.O. Box 2649 • Harrisburg, PA 17105 | (717) 783-1404 | R/E/O | 2000 | BA/+ | 2/2 | 2/15; 8/15 | 3/1; 9/1 | 2 | $103.75 | -- | Y |
| * PR P.O. Box 3271 • San Juan, PR 00902-3271 | (787) 722-2122 | C/R/E/O | 2000 | 0/B/BA | 6/4/0 | 3/1; 9/1 | 60 days | 2 | $275.00 | -- | |
| * RI 233 Richmond St., Ste. 236 • Providence, RI 02903 | (401) 277-3185 | R/E | 1999 | BA/+ | 2/1 | 3/15; 9/15 | 3/15; 9/15 | 2 | $260.00 | # | |
| SC P.O. Box 11329 • Columbia, SC 29211-1329 | (800) 272-3926 | -- | 1997 | BA+ | 2 | 3/15; 9/15 | 3/15; 9/15 | 2, 40 | $200.00 | -- | |
| SD 301 E. 14th St., Ste. 200 • Sioux Falls, SD 57104 | (605) 367-5770 | -- | 1998 | BA/+ | 2/1 | 3/1; 9/1 | 3/1; 9/1 | 2, 50 | $200.00 | # | Y |
| * TN 500 J. Robertson Pkwy., 2nd FL. • Nashville, TN 37243-1141 | (615) 741-2550 | R | 1993 | B/BA+ | 1 | 3/1; 9/1 | 3/1; 9/1 | 2, 50 | $200.00 | E | |
| TX 333 Guadalupe Tower III, Ste. 900 • Austin, TX 78701 | (512) 305-7800 | -- | 1997 | BA/+ | 2/1 | 2/28; 8/31 | 2/28; 8/31 | 2, 50 | $170.00 | # | |
| UT 160 E 300 S., Box 45805 • Salt Lake City, UT 84145 | (801) 530-6628 | -- | 1994 | BA+ | 1 | 2/1; 8/1 | 3/1; 9/1 | 2, 50 | $251.00 | E | Y |
| * VA 3600 West Broad Street • Richmond, VA 23230 | (804) 367-8505 | -- | | BA/+ | 2/1 | 3/1; 9/1 | 60 days | 2, 50 | $162.00 | E | Y |
| VI 1-B King Street • Christiansted, St. Croix, VI 00820 | (809) 773-0096 | R/E/O | | 0/B/BA | 6/3/2 | 3/15; 9/15 | 3/15; 9/15 | 2 | $150.00 | -- | |
| * VT 109 State Street • Montpelier, VT 05609-1106 | (800) 272-3926 | -- | | 0/2A | 2/2 | 3/15; 9/15 | 3/15; 9/15 | 2, 50 | $315.00 | # | |
| WA P.O. Box 9131 • Olympia, WA 98507-9131 | (360) 664-9191 | -- | 2000 | BA | 1 | 3/1; 9/1 | 3/1; 9/1 | 2, 50 | $200.00 | E | Y |
| WI P.O. Box 8935 • Madison, WI 53708 | (608) 266-5511 | -- | 2001 | BA | 3 | 3/1; 9/1 | 3/1; 9/1 | 2, 50 | $132.00 | E | -- |
| WV 201 L&S Bldg., 812 Quarrier St. • Charleston, WV 25301 | (304) 558-3557 | R/E/O | 2000 | BA | 2 | 2/15; 8/15 | 2/15; 8/15 | 2, 50 | $170.00 | E | Y |
| WY First Bank Bldg., 2020 Carey Ave. • Cheyenne, WY 82002 | (307) 777-7551 | R/E/O | 2000 | BA | 2 | 3/1; 9/1 | 3/1; 9/1 | 2, 50 | $200.00 | E | Y |

*CPA Examination Services, a division of the National Association of State Boards of Accountancy, administers the CPA exam including exam application in these 22 states. Call (800) CPA-EXAM

**LGR Examinations administers the CPA exam including exam application in these 3 states. Call (800) 877-EXAM

# USING EXAM QUESTION AND EXPLANATION BOOKS TO IMPROVE GRADES

Use the other Gleim exam question books to ensure your understanding of each topic you study in your accounting and business law courses. Access the largest bank of exam questions (including thousands from past certification exams) that is widely used by professors. Get immediate feedback on your study effort, while you take your "practice" tests.

## AUDITING & SYSTEMS EXAM QUESTIONS AND EXPLANATIONS
(Eighth Edition)

Introduction
1 External Auditing Standards and Professional Responsibilities
2 Audit Planning and Risk Assessment
3 Internal Control
4 Audit Evidence and Procedures
5 Information Systems
6 Statistical Sampling
7 Audit Reports
8 Special Reports and Other Reporting Issues
9 Internal Auditing

## FINANCIAL ACCOUNTING EXAM QUESTIONS AND EXPLANATIONS
(Eighth Edition)

Introduction
1 Conceptual Framework
2 The Accounting Process
3 Comprehensive Income and the Statement of Income
4 Present Value and Future Value
5 Current Assets, Cash, Accounts Receivable, and Short-Term Notes Receivable
6 Inventory
7 Property, Plant, and Equipment
8 Depreciation and Depletion
9 Intangible Assets and Research and Development Costs
10 Investments in Debt Securities, Equity Securities, and Derivatives
11 Current Liabilities, Compensated Absences, and Contingencies
12 Long-Term Liabilities
13 Pensions, Other Postretirement Benefits, and Postemployment Benefits
14 Leases
15 Shareholders' Equity
16 Earnings Per Share
17 Accounting for Income Taxes
18 Accounting Changes and Error Corrections
19 Statement of Cash Flows
20 Accounting for Changing Prices
21 Financial Statement Disclosures
22 Long-Term Construction-Type Contracts, Installment Sales, and Consignments
23 Financial Statement Analysis Based on Percentage Relationships
24 GAAP Accounting for Partnerships
25 Business Combinations, Consolidations, and Branch Accounting
26 Interim Financial Reporting
27 Foreign Currency Translation and Transactions
28 Accounting for State and Local Government Entities
29 Not-for-Profit Organizations
30 Specialized Accounting Issues

## COST/MANAGERIAL ACCOUNTING EXAM QUESTIONS AND EXPLANATIONS
(Sixth Edition)

Introduction
**Part I: Cost Accounting**
1 Overview and Terminology
2 Activity-Based Costing
3 Job-Order Costing
4 Process Costing
5 Quality
6 Cost Allocations: Support Costs and Joint Costs
7 Absorption and Variable Costing

**Part II: Planning and Control**
8 Cost-Volume-Profit Analysis
9 Budgeting
10 Standard Costs and Variances
11 Responsibility Accounting, Performance Measurement, and Transfer Pricing

**Part III: Nonroutine Decisions and Quantitative Methods**
12 Nonroutine Decisions
13 Capital Budgeting
14 Inventory Management: Traditional and Modern Approaches
15 Probability and Statistics
16 Regression Analysis
17 Linear Programming
18 Other Quantitative Approaches

## FEDERAL TAX EXAM QUESTIONS AND EXPLANATIONS                     (Eighth Edition)

## BUSINESS LAW/LEGAL STUDIES EXAM QUESTIONS AND EXPLANATIONS         (Fourth Edition)

**FREE UPDATES, SOFTWARE, AND SUPPORT:  THE GLEIM HOME PAGE (www.gleim.com)!**

Our extensive web page is updated regularly to provide convenient, up-to-date information. Some of the features include

- Free Demonstration Versions of Our Software
- Updates and Corrections for Gleim Books and Software
- Listings of Bookstores that Carry Gleim's *CPA Review*

- Technical Support Request Form
- Links to Other Helpful Sites
- Information about Other Gleim Products
- Order Forms

# NEW!

## update@gleim.com

**GLEIM E-MAIL UPDATE SERVICE**

Your message (in the subject or body of your e-mail) to Gleim must include the acronym of your book or software (see below), followed by the edition-printing for books, or version for software.  The edition-printing is indicated on the book's spine.  The software version is indicated on the diskette label.

| | Book* | Software* |
|---|---|---|
| **Exam Questions and Explanations** | | |
| *Auditing & Systems* | AUD EQE | |
| *Business Law/Legal Studies* | LAW EQE | |
| *Federal Tax* | TAX EQE | |
| *Financial Accounting* | FIN EQE | |
| *Cost/Managerial Accounting* | MAN EQE | |
| **CIA Review:** | | |
| *Part I, Internal Audit Process* | CIA I | CIATP I |
| *Part II, Internal Audit Skills* | CIA II | CIATP II |
| *Part III, Management Control and Information Technology* | CIA III | CIATP III |
| *Part IV, The Audit Environment* | CIA IV | CIATP IV |
| **CMA/CFM Review:** | | |
| *Part 1, Economics, Finance, and Management* | CMA/CFM Part 1 | CMA/CFMTP 1 |
| *Part 2CFM, Corporate Financial Management* | CMA/CFM Part 2CFM | CMA/CFMTP 2CFM |
| *Part 2CMA, Financial Accounting and Reporting* | CMA/CFM Part 2CMA | CMA/CFMTP 2CMA |
| *Part 3, Management Reporting, Analysis, and Behavioral Issues* | CMA/CFM Part 3 | CMA/CFMTP 3 |
| *Part 4, Decision Analysis and Information Systems* | CMA/CFM Part 4 | CMA/CFMTP 4 |
| **CPA Review:** | | |
| *Auditing* | CPA AUD | CPATP AUD |
| *Business Law* | CPA LAW | CPATP LAW |
| *TAX-MAN-GOV* | CPA TMG | CPATP TMG |
| *Financial* | CPA FIN | CPATP FIN |
| *A System for Success* | CPA SFS | |

*Add the printing-edition of your book or version of your software to this acronym to get your update.

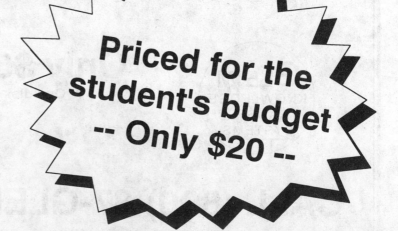

# CHAPTER ONE
# OVERVIEW AND TERMINOLOGY

**Traditional cost/managerial accounting systems** were developed to provide external financial reports by companies that mass produced a few standardized products. These systems have a full- (absorption-) cost perspective in accordance with GAAP. They also assume that costs may be treated as fixed or variable depending on their behavior when unit output changes. Hence, costs are assigned on the basis of **unit-level drivers**, for example, units produced, direct labor hours or dollars, and machine hours. Because many other drivers may cause the incurrence of costs, a traditional system tends to assign many costs on some basis other than cause and effect. Furthermore, a traditional system is oriented toward reporting inventories and cost of goods sold solely in terms of production costs, so it does not capture the other product costs in the **value chain**. Another aspect of a traditional system is that its planning and control (**responsibility accounting**) function is oriented to cost control and financial measures of performance. Individual organizational units are assigned responsibility for costs, and outcomes are compared with budgeted amounts.

However, a variety of factors have led to a rapid evolution of accounting methods in this field. For example, more intense competition has compelled firms to become more cost efficient and to provide better **customer value**. Thus, accountants must be able to gather information about all activities in the value chain and to understand all the functions that affect total product cost. An emphasis solely on the manufacturing function is no longer sufficient.

Another feature of the new environment is that **quality and time** are increasingly viewed as competitive weapons. Prompt delivery of reliable (defect-free) products and services necessitates development of methods that accumulate financial and nonfinancial information about quality and time. Given the speed of technological change and the shortening of the **product life cycle**, enterprises must expedite the development and delivery of new products and services, and they must also be able to react flexibly and quickly to changing market conditions. Accordingly, the relationship of quality, cost, and time must be a focus of modern accounting systems.

Advances in information technology, including substantial reductions in its cost, have made more elaborate and detailed accounting systems feasible. Furthermore, the increased amounts of information are almost instantly available for analysis with sophisticated software tools. Improved technology also permits automation of production processes. For example, the results of **computer-integrated manufacturing** include real-time monitoring, control, and reporting; better quality and scheduling; lower inventories and costs; and the feasibility of small-lot production of customized goods.

Advances in technology and a heightened emphasis on quality have coincided with the emergence of a **just-in-time (JIT)** production philosophy. In a JIT system, demand pulls units through production. Each operation's output consists only of what is demanded by the next operation. Thus, inventory is greatly reduced or eliminated, defect-free output is an imperative, and processes must be reorganized and improved.

Still another factor in the evolution of cost/managerial accounting is the rapid growth of the **service sector** of the economy. Service enterprises face the same competitive pressures as manufacturing firms. Moreover, deregulation of many services (banking, transportation, telecommunications, etc.) has further increased competition. Service organizations therefore have focused on the same issues of quality, time, customer value, cost minimization, and productivity as manufacturers. One outcome is that cost/ managerial accounting methods are increasingly applied or adapted to service organizations.

The foregoing factors have created a need for, and facilitated the development of, better methods of generating accounting information. One response to this need is the emergence of **activity-based management**, an approach built on **activity-based costing (ABC)** and **process value analysis**. ABC provides more detailed and precise cost assignments to products and services. It focuses on the multiple activities that cause the consumption of resources (costs). Process value analysis is a systematic understanding of the activities involved in making a product or rendering a service. It identifies those that add value and those that may be eliminated because they do not.

Despite these recent trends, however, traditional cost/managerial accounting concepts and techniques remain the core of the body of knowledge presented in textbooks and tested on professional examinations. Consequently, this book will continue to address this subject matter while providing comprehensive coverage of new developments.

In addition to the foregoing overview, this introductory chapter also presents a selection of key definitions. For important additional definitions, see the glossary related to activity-based costing in Chapter 2. Students should be aware that terminology varies somewhat among authoritative sources and from textbook to textbook. Compare, for example, the definition of cost allocation given below with the definitions of allocation and tracing in an ABC context provided in the glossary in Chapter 2.

References in this chapter to SMAs are to Statements of Management Accounting. A committee of the Institute of Management Accountants issues SMAs to communicate the organization's positions on management accounting practices.

This chapter concludes with a section on professional responsibilities.

# COST AND MANAGERIAL ACCOUNTING GLOSSARY

**Absorption (full) costing** is the accounting method that considers all manufacturing costs as product costs. These costs include variable and fixed manufacturing costs whether direct or indirect.

**Activity-based costing** is defined in SMA 2A, *Management Accounting Glossary*, as an accounting system that "identifies the causal relationship between the incurrence of cost and activities, determines the underlying driver of the activities, establishes cost pools related to individual drivers, develops costing rates, and applies cost to product on the basis of resources consumed (drivers)."

**Actual costing** assigns actual direct costs to cost objects. It also assigns overhead on the basis of actual rates and the actual quantity of the base used for cost assignment. Contrast with normal costing.

**Applied (absorbed) overhead** is factory (manufacturing) overhead that has been allocated to products, usually on the basis of a predetermined rate. Overhead is over- or underapplied (absorbed) when overhead charged is greater or less than overhead incurred, respectively.

**Appraisal costs** are the costs of quality that are incurred to detect nonconformance of products or services with specifications or customer needs. They include the costs of inspection and testing of materials, product acceptance (sampling of finished goods), process acceptance (sampling of goods in process), equipment used in measurement, packaging inspection, supervising appraisal, and outside endorsements.

**Avoidable costs** are those that may be eliminated by not engaging in an activity or by performing it more efficiently.

**Backflush costing** is often used with a just-in-time (JIT) production system. It delays costing until goods are finished. Standard costs are then flushed backward through the system to assign costs to products. The result is that detailed tracking of costs is eliminated. The system is best suited to companies that maintain low inventories because costs then flow directly to cost of goods sold.

**Balanced scorecard** approach uses multiple measures to evaluate managerial performance. These measures may be financial or nonfinancial, internal or external, and short-term or long-term. The scorecard allows a determination as to whether a manager is achieving certain objectives at the expense of others that may be equally or more important.

**Benchmarking** (also called competitive benchmarking or best practices) compares one's own product, service, or practice with the best known similar activity. The objective is to measure the key outputs of a business process or function against the best and to analyze the reasons for the performance difference. Benchmarking applies to services and practices as well as to products and is an ongoing systematic process. It entails both quantitative and qualitative measurements that allow both an internal and an external assessment.

**Budget variance** (also known as the flexible-budget variance or spending variance) is the difference between actual and budgeted fixed factory overhead in a four-way analysis of overhead variances. In three-way analysis, the spending variance combines the variable overhead spending variance and the fixed overhead budget variance. In two-way analysis, the budget (flexible-budget or controllable) variance is that part of the total factory overhead variance not attributed to the production volume variance.

**Budgeting** is the formal quantification of management's plans. Budgets are usually expressed in quantitative terms and are used to motivate management and evaluate its performance in achieving goals. In this sense, standards are established.

**By-products** are one or more products of relatively small total value that are produced simultaneously from a common manufacturing process with products of greater value and quantity (joint products).

**Committed costs** result when a going concern holds fixed assets (property, plant, and equipment). Examples are insurance, long-term lease payments, and depreciation.

**Common (joint) costs** are incurred in the production of two or more inseparable products up to the point at which the products become separable (the split-off point).

**Computer-integrated manufacturing (CIM)** systems automate the design, engineering, production, and accounting functions. A **computer-assisted design (CAD)** system is used to design products that are tested using a **computer-assisted engineering (CAE)** system. They are manufactured using a **computer-assisted manufacturing system (CAM)** that consists of machinery controlled by computers, possibly including some applications of robotics. These functions are linked by an information system. For a specific type of CAM, see flexible manufacturing systems.

**Contribution margin** is calculated by subtracting all variable costs of the product or service from sales revenue. Variable costs include both variable cost of goods sold and variable selling and administrative costs. Fixed costs are not subtracted. The contribution margin ratio equals unit contribution margin divided by unit sales price.

**Controllable costs** are directly regulated by management of a given responsibility center at a given level of activity within a given time span; e.g., fixed costs are not controllable.

**Controllable variance** in two-way analysis is the part of the total factory overhead variance not attributable to the volume variance.

**Controller (or comptroller)** is a financial officer having responsibility for the accounting functions (management and financial) as well as budgeting and the internal control structure.

**Conversion costs** are direct labor and factory overhead, the costs of converting raw materials into finished goods.

**Cost**. In SMA 2A, the IMA defines cost as follows: "(1) In management accounting, a measurement in monetary terms of the amount of resources used for some purpose. The term by itself is not operational. It becomes operational when modified by a term that defines the purpose, such as acquisition cost, incremental cost, or fixed cost. (2) In financial accounting, the sacrifice measured by the price paid or required to be paid to acquire goods or services. The term 'cost' is often used when referring to the valuation of a good or service acquired. When 'cost' is used in this sense, a cost is an asset. When the benefits of the acquisition (the goods or services) expire, the cost becomes an expense or loss."

**Cost accounting** includes (1) managerial accounting in the sense that its purpose can be to provide internal reports for use in planning and control and in making nonroutine decisions and (2) financial accounting because its product costing function satisfies requirements for reporting to shareholders, government, and various outside parties.

**Cost Accounting Standards Board (CASB)** is an agency established by Congress with "exclusive authority to make, promulgate, amend, and rescind cost accounting standards and interpretations thereof" pertaining to contracts negotiated with the U.S. government. It is an independent entity within the Office of Federal Procurement Policy. CASB standards are included in the Federal Acquisition Regulations.

**Cost allocation** is the process of assigning and reassigning costs to cost objects. It may also be defined as a distribution of costs that cannot be directly assigned (traced) to the cost objects that are assumed to have caused them. In this sense, allocation involves choosing a cost object, determining the direct and indirect costs assignable thereto, deciding how costs are to be accumulated in cost pools before allocation, and selecting the allocation base. Allocation is necessary for product costing, pricing, investment decisions, managerial performance evaluation, profitability analysis, make-or-buy decisions, etc.

**Cost center** is a responsibility center that is accountable for costs only.

**Cost driver** "is a measure of activity, such as direct labor hours, machine hours, beds occupied, computer time used, flight hours, miles driven, or contracts, that is a causal factor in the incurrence of cost to an entity" (SMA 2A).

**Cost objects** are the intermediate and final dispositions of cost pools. Intermediate cost objects receive temporary accumulations of costs as the cost pools move from their originating points to the final cost objects. Final cost objects, such as a job, product, or process, should be logically linked with the cost pool based on a cause-and-effect relationship.

**Cost of goods manufactured (CGM)** is equivalent to a retailer's purchases. It equals all manufacturing costs (direct materials, direct labor, and factory overhead) incurred during the period, plus beginning work-in-process (BWIP), minus ending work-in-process (EWIP). CGM is the amount transferred to finished goods.

**Cost of goods sold (CGS)** equals beginning finished goods (or merchandise) inventory, plus cost of goods manufactured (or purchases), minus ending finished goods (or merchandise) inventory.

**Cost pools** are accounts in which a variety of similar costs with a common cause are accumulated prior to assignment to cost objects on some common basis. The overhead account is a cost pool into which various types of overhead are accumulated prior to their allocation. Under ABC, a cost pool is established for each activity.

**Cost-volume-profit (breakeven) analysis** is a means of predicting the relationships among revenues, variable costs, and fixed costs at various production levels. It allows management to discern the probable effects of changes in sales volume, sales price, costs, product mix, etc.

**Customer profitability** analysis assigns revenues and costs to major customers or groups of customers rather than to organizational units products, or other objects. The results may direct organizational resources toward more profitable uses.

**Differential (incremental) cost** is the difference in total cost between two decisions.

**Direct cost** is one that can be specifically associated with a single cost object in an economically feasible way.

**Direct labor costs** are wages paid to labor that can feasibly be specifically identified with the production of finished goods or the rendering of services.

**Direct materials costs** are the costs of raw materials that can feasibly be specifically identified with the production of finished goods or the rendering of services.

**Direct method of service cost allocation** apportions service department costs directly to production departments. It makes no allocation of services rendered to other service departments.

**Direct (variable) costing** (See variable costing.)

**Discretionary costs** are characterized by uncertainty about the relationship between input (the costs) and the value of the related output. They tend to be subject to periodic (e.g., annual) outlay decisions. Advertising and research costs are examples.

**Economic value added (EVA)** is a variation of residual income that defines the variable in specific ways. One version of EVA® equals after-tax net operating profit minus the product of the weighted-average cost of capital (WACC) and operating capital. The WACC is an after-tax average of the costs of all sources of funds, equity as well as debt, used by the firm. Moreover, certain adjustments may be made in measuring net operating profit, e.g., amortizing R&D expense over a period of years. Operating capital equals total assets minus current liabilities.

**Efficiency variances** compare the actual use of inputs with the budgeted quantity of inputs allowed for the activity level achieved. When the difference is multiplied by the budgeted rate per unit of input, the resulting variance isolates the cost effect of using more or fewer units of input than budgeted.

**Electronic data interchange (EDI)** is the communication of electronic documents directly from a computer in one entity to a computer in another entity, for example, to order goods from a supplier or to transfer funds. EDI was developed to enhance just-in-time (JIT) production systems.

**Engineered costs** are costs having a clear relationship to output. Direct materials cost is an example.

**Equivalent unit of production** is a set of inputs required to manufacture one physical unit. Calculating equivalent units for each factor of production facilitates measurement of output and cost allocation when work-in-process exists.

**Extended normal costing** assigns direct costs to cost objects using budgeted rates and actual quantities of the inputs. It assigns overhead based on budgeted rates and the actual quantity of the base used for cost assignment.

**External failure costs** are the costs of quality that are incurred when products and services do not conform with specifications or customer needs after delivery. They include the costs of recalls, lost sales, returns and allowances, product liability, warranties, and reduced market share.

**Factory (manufacturing) overhead (indirect manufacturing costs)** consists of all costs other than direct materials and direct labor that are associated with the manufacturing process. It includes both fixed and variable costs.

**Fixed costs** remain unchanged in total within the relevant range for a given period despite fluctuations in activity. Fixed costs per unit change as the level of activity changes.

**Flexible manufacturing systems (FMSs)** use computerized methods to reduce setup or changeover times and facilitate the production of differentiated products in small numbers. The shift in emphasis is from mass production of a few products to a job-shop environment in which customized orders are manufactured. Automation allows for better quality and scheduling, rapid changes in product lines, and lower inventories and costs. See computer-integrated manufacturing.

**Gross margin (profit)** is the difference between sales and the full absorption cost of goods sold. It should be contrasted with contribution margin (sales – variable costs).

**Imputed costs** are properly attributable to a cost object even though no transaction has occurred that would be routinely recognized in the accounts. They may be outlay costs or opportunity costs, but in either case they should be considered in decision making. An example of an imputed cost is the profit lost as a result of being unable to fill orders because the inventory level is too low.

**Indirect costs** cannot be specifically associated with a given cost object in an economically feasible way. They are also defined as costs that are not directly identified with one final cost object but that are identified with two or more final cost objects or with at least one intermediate cost object.

**Internal failure costs** are the costs of quality that are incurred because of nonconformance of products and services with specifications or customer needs. These costs are identified before delivery to outside parties. They include the costs of scrap, rework, downtime, design modifications, and repeat testing.

**Investment center** is a responsibility center that is accountable for revenues (markets), costs (sources of supply), and invested capital.

**Job-order cost system** of accounting is appropriate when products or services have individual characteristics or when identifiable groupings are possible, e.g., batches of certain styles or types of furniture. The unique aspect of job-order costing is the identification of costs to specific units or a particular job.

**Joint products** are two or more separate products produced by a common manufacturing process from a common input. The common (joint) costs of two or more joint products with significant values are customarily allocated to the joint products.

**Just-in-time (JIT) production systems** are based on a demand pull philosophy. Purchases of materials and output depend on actual customer demand. Inventories are reduced greatly or eliminated, a few suppliers must reliably deliver small amounts on a frequent basis, plant layouts must become more efficient, a zero defects policy is established, and workers must be able to perform multiple tasks, including continuous monitoring of quality.

**Kaizen** is the Japanese term for continuous improvement. Kaizen budgeting incorporates expectations for continuous improvement into budgetary estimates. Kaizen costing determines target cost reductions for a period, such as a month. Thus, variances are the differences between actual and targeted cost reduction. The objective is to reduce actual costs below standard costs. The cost-reduction activities associated with the Kaizen approach minimize costs throughout the entire product life cycle. Thus, it has the advantage of being closely related to the entity's profit-planning procedures. See the definition of target costing in Chapter 2.

**Life-cycle costing** accounts for all product costs in the value chain from research and development and design of products and processes through production, marketing, distribution, and customer service. It focuses on minimizing locked-in costs, for example, by reducing the number of parts, promoting standardization of parts, and using equipment that can make more than one kind of product.

**Managerial accounting** primarily concerns the planning and control of organizational operations, considers nonquantitative information, and is usually less precise than cost accounting.

**Manufacturing cycle efficiency** is the quotient of the time required for value-added production divided by total manufacturing lead (cycle) time. Lead time is the time elapsed from when an order is ready for production until it becomes a finished good.

**Margin of safety** is the excess of budgeted revenues or unit sales over the breakeven point.

**Marginal cost** is the sum of the costs necessary to effect a one-unit increase in the activity level.

**Mix variances** measure the effects of changes in the proportions of various inputs, e.g., different mixes of direct materials or labor. See also sales mix variance.

**Mixed (semivariable) costs** combine fixed and variable elements.

**Normal capacity** is the long-term average level of activity that will approximate demand over a period that includes seasonal, cyclical, and trend variations. Deviations in a given year will be offset in subsequent years.

**Normal costing** assigns actual direct costs to cost objects. It assigns overhead using budgeted (normalized) rates and the actual quantity of the base used for cost assignment. Contrast with actual costing and extended normal costing.

**Operating leverage** is the change in operating income resulting from a change in sales. The assumption is that firms with greater fixed costs will have higher contribution margins and more operating leverage.

**Operation costing** is a hybrid of job-order and process costing systems. It is used by companies that manufacture goods that undergo some similar and some dissimilar processes. Operation costing accumulates total conversion costs and determines a unit conversion cost for each operation. However, direct materials costs are charged specifically to products as in job-order systems.

**Opportunity cost** is the maximum benefit forgone by using a scarce resource for a given purpose. It is the benefit, for example, the contribution to income, provided by the best alternative use of that resource.

**Out-of-pocket (outlay) costs** require negative cash outflows (expenditures) currently or in the near future.

**Outsourcing** is the acquisition of products and services from sources outside the organization instead of producing them internally.

**Partial productivity** is ordinarily calculated as output divided by a single input.

**Period costs** are charged to expense as incurred and not to a particular product. They are not identifiable with a product and are not inventoried. Period costs may be classified as either revenue expenditures or capital expenditures. Revenue expenditures, e.g., advertising and officers' salaries, are charged to the income statement in the period the costs are incurred because they usually do not benefit future periods. Capital expenditures, e.g., those for depreciable assets, are initially recorded as assets and then expensed as they are consumed, used, or disposed of.

**Periodic inventory systems** rely on physical counts to determine quantities.

**Perpetual inventory records** provide for continuous record keeping of the quantities of inventory (and possibly unit costs or total costs). This method requires a journal entry every time items are added to or taken from inventory.

**Practical capacity** is the maximum level at which output is produced efficiently. It usually results in underapplied overhead.

**Prevention costs** are the costs of quality that are incurred to avoid defects in products or services. They include the costs of quality engineering, design engineering, employee training, quality planning and reporting, new materials, preventive maintenance, quality audits, and quality circles.

**Price (rate) variance** equals the difference between the actual and standard price of an input, multiplied by the actual quantity.

**Prime costs** are the costs of direct materials and direct labor.

**Process costing** should be used to assign costs to similar products or service units that are mass produced on a continuous basis. Costs are accumulated by process or department rather than by jobs, and unit costs are established by measuring output for a specified period and dividing into the process costs. Process costing is an averaging process that calculates the average cost of all units.

**Process reengineering** involves analysis of business processes that results in radical change rather than incremental improvement. Redesign of processes is intended to result in elimination of unnecessary steps, reduction of circumstances in which mistakes can occur, cost minimization, quicker response times, and better quality.

**Product (inventoriable) costs** are incurred to produce units of output and are deferred to future periods to the extent output is not sold (kept on hand for sale in future periods). They are expensed in the period the product is sold. Hence, product costs are those that can be associated with specific revenues. Examples are direct materials, direct labor, and factory (not general and administrative) overhead.

**Productivity** is the relationship of input and output.

**Profit center** is a segment of a company responsible for both revenues and costs. A profit center has the authority to make decisions concerning markets (revenues) and sources of supply (costs).

**Quality.** (See total quality management, appraisal costs, internal failure costs, external failure costs, and prevention costs.)

**Quantity (usage) variance** is an efficiency variance for direct materials.

**Rate variance** is a price variance for direct labor.

**Reciprocal method** uses simultaneous equations to allocate each service department's costs among the departments providing mutual services before reallocation to other users.

**Relative sales value method** is used to allocate joint costs at split-off to joint products based upon their relative proportions of total sales value. If a product is not salable at the split-off point, its net realizable value (NRV) may be used to approximate its relative sales value. One variant of this method is the constant gross margin percentage method. Still another way to allocate joint costs is by physical quantities.

**Relevant costs** are those expected future costs that vary with the action taken. All other costs are assumed to be constant and thus have no effect on (are irrelevant to) the decision.

**Relevant range** is the range of activity within which assumed cost relationships are deemed to be true. For example, given a cost function assumed to be linear, variable unit costs are constant and fixed costs are constant in total. In this range, the incremental cost of one additional unit is also constant.

**Residual income** is the excess of the return on an investment over a targeted amount equal to an imputed interest charge on invested capital. The rate used is ordinarily the weighted-average cost of capital. Some enterprises prefer to measure managerial performance in terms of the amount of residual income rather than the percentage return on investment (ROI). The principle is that the enterprise is expected to benefit from expansion as long as residual income is earned. Using a percentage ROI approach, expansion might be rejected if it lowered ROI even though residual income would increase. See economic value added.

**Responsibility accounting** is a means of managerial control that entails assignment of responsibility, determination of performance benchmarks, evaluation of performance, and distribution of rewards. In a traditional system, responsibility defined in financial terms is assigned to the head of an organizational unit. In a modern system, the emphasis shifts to processes and teams, and multiple, dynamic performance measures are established that relate to process efficiency and output, e.g., cycle time, on-time delivery, quality, and unit cost.

**Return on investment (ROI)** equals income divided by investment. ROI is a measure of managerial performance that is sometimes called the accounting rate of return. "Income" and "investment" are defined in a variety of ways.

**Revenue center** in a responsibility accounting system is accountable for revenues only.

**Sales mix variance** measures the effect on the contribution margin of a change in the projected proportions of the different products or services composing an entity's total sales.

**Sales quantity variance** is the product of the difference between actual and budgeted units sold and the budgeted weighted-average unit contribution margin for the budgeted sales mix.

**Sales volume variance** is the sum of the sales mix and sales quantity variances. It is the difference in the contribution margin attributable to the difference between actual sales and budgeted sales.

**Scrap** consists of raw materials left over from the production cycle but still usable for purposes other than those for which it was originally intended. Scrap may be sold to outside customers, usually for a nominal amount, or may be used in a different production process.

**Separable costs** are those incurred beyond the split-off point and identifiable with specific products.

**Spending variance** is a factory overhead variance. For variable overhead, it is the difference between actual costs and the product of the actual activity and the budgeted application rate. For fixed overhead, the spending (also known as the budget) variance is the difference between actual and budgeted fixed costs. In three-way analysis, the two spending variances isolated in four-way analysis are combined. In two-way analysis, the two spending variances and the variable overhead efficiency variance are combined.

**Split-off point** is the stage of production at which joint products become separately identifiable.

**Standard cost** is a predetermined unit cost. Standard cost systems isolate deviations (variances) of actual from expected costs. Standard costs can be used with job-order and process costing systems.

**Step-cost functions** are nonlinear cost functions. These costs are constant over small ranges of output but increase by steps (discrete amounts) as levels of activity increase. They may be fixed or variable. If the steps are relatively narrow, these costs are usually treated as variable. If the steps are wide, they are more akin to fixed costs.

**Step-down method** of service department cost allocation is a sequential (but not a reciprocal) process. These costs are allocated to other service departments as well as to users. One common starting point is the service department that renders the greatest percentage of its services to other service departments.

**Sunk cost** is a past cost or a cost that the entity has irrevocably committed to incur. Because it is unavoidable and will therefore not vary with the option chosen, it is not relevant to future decisions.

**Theoretical (ideal) capacity** is the maximum capacity assuming continuous operations with no holidays, downtime, etc.

**Theory of constraints** is an approach to continuous improvement (reducing operating expenses and inventory and increasing throughput) based on a five-step procedure: (1) identifying constraints, (2) exploiting the binding constraints, (3) subordinating everything else to the decisions made in the second step, (4) increasing the capacity of the binding constraints, and (5) repeating the process when new binding constraints are identified.

**Total productivity** (also called total factor productivity) equals the quantity of output divided by the cost of all inputs.

**Total quality management (TQM)** is an approach to quality that emphasizes continuous improvement, a philosophy of "doing it right the first time," and striving for zero defects and elimination of all waste.

**Transfer price** is the price charged in an intracompany transaction.

**Transferred-in costs** are those incurred in a preceding department and received in a subsequent department in a multi-department production setting.

**Treasurer** has the responsibility for safeguarding financial assets (including the management of cash) and arranging financing.

**Variable cost** is an operating expense that varies directly and proportionately with activity.

**Variable (direct) costing** considers only variable manufacturing costs to be product (inventoriable) costs. Fixed manufacturing costs are considered period costs and are expensed as incurred.

**Variance analysis** concerns the study of deviations of actual costs from budgeted amounts.

**Volume (idle capacity or production volume) variance** is the amount of under- or overapplied fixed factory overhead. It is the difference between budgeted fixed factory overhead and the amount applied based on a predetermined rate and the standard input allowed for actual output. It measures the use of capacity rather than specific cost outlays.

**Waste** is the amount of raw materials left over from a production process or production cycle for which there is no further use. Waste is usually not salable at any price and must be discarded.

**Work-in-process (manufacturing)** account is used to accumulate the costs of goods that have been placed in production but have not yet been completed.

**Yield variances** determine the effect of varying the total input of a factor of production (e.g., direct materials or labor) while holding constant the input mix (the proportions of the types of materials or labor used) and the weighted-average unit price of the factor of production.

## PROFESSIONAL RESPONSIBILITY

Like CPAs and internal auditors, management accountants have recognized their professional responsibilities to their various constituencies. The Institute of Management Accountants (IMA), through its Management Accounting Practices Committee, issued a revised code of ethics for management accountants in April 1997. This code reflects the official position of the organization. The code is printed on the following pages in its entirety. (Source: Statement on Management Accounting 1C (Revised), Objectives: Standards of Ethical Conduct for Practitioners of Management Accounting and Financial Management, *Management Accounting*, April 1997, pp. 69-70). The final section, Resolution of Ethical Conflict, is especially significant.

## STANDARDS OF ETHICAL CONDUCT FOR PRACTITIONERS
## OF MANAGEMENT ACCOUNTING AND FINANCIAL MANAGEMENT

*Practitioners of management accounting and financial management have an obligation to the public, their profession, the organizations they serve, and themselves, to maintain the highest standards of ethical conduct. In recognition of this obligation, the Institute of Management Accountants has promulgated the following standards of ethical conduct for practitioners of management accounting and financial management. Adherence to these standards, both domestically and internationally, is integral to achieving the <u>Objectives of Management Accounting.</u> Practitioners of management accounting and financial management shall not commit acts contrary to these standards nor shall they condone the commission of such acts by others within their organizations.*

### Competence

*Practitioners of management accounting and financial management have a responsibility to:*

- *Maintain an appropriate level of professional competence by ongoing development of their knowledge and skills.*
- *Perform their professional duties in accordance with relevant laws, regulations, and technical standards.*
- *Prepare complete and clear reports and recommendations after appropriate analyses of relevant and reliable information.*

### Confidentiality

*Practitioners of management accounting and financial management have a responsibility to:*

- *Refrain from disclosing confidential information acquired in the course of their work except when authorized, unless legally obligated to do so.*
- *Inform subordinates as appropriate regarding the confidentiality of information acquired in the course of their work and monitor their activities to assure the maintenance of that confidentiality.*
- *Refrain from using or appearing to use confidential information acquired in the course of their work for unethical or illegal advantage either personally or through third parties.*

## Integrity

*Practitioners of management accounting and financial management have a responsibility to:*

- *Avoid actual or apparent conflicts of interest and advise all appropriate parties of any potential conflict.*
- *Refrain from engaging in any activity that would prejudice their ability to carry out their duties ethically.*
- *Refuse any gift, favor, or hospitality that would influence or would appear to influence their actions.*
- *Refrain from either actively or passively subverting the attainment of the organization's legitimate and ethical objectives.*
- *Recognize and communicate professional limitations or other constraints that would preclude responsible judgment or successful performance of an activity.*
- *Communicate unfavorable as well as favorable information and professional judgments or opinions.*
- *Refrain from engaging in or supporting any activity that would discredit the profession.*

## Objectivity

*Practitioners of management accounting and financial management have a responsibility to:*

- *Communicate information fairly and objectively.*
- *Disclose fully all relevant information that could reasonably be expected to influence an intended user's understanding of the reports, comments, and recommendations presented.*

## Resolution of Ethical Conflict

*In applying the standards of ethical conduct, practitioners of management accounting and financial management may encounter problems in identifying unethical behavior or in resolving an ethical conflict. When faced with significant ethical issues, practitioners of management accounting and financial management should follow the established policies of the organization bearing on the resolution of such conflict. If these policies do not resolve the ethical conflict, such practitioners should consider the following courses of action:*

- *Discuss such problems with the immediate superior except when it appears that the superior is involved, in which case the problem should be presented initially to the next higher managerial level. If satisfactory resolution cannot be achieved when the problem is initially presented, submit the issues to the next higher managerial level. If the immediate superior is the chief executive officer, or equivalent, the acceptable reviewing authority may be a group such as the audit committee, executive committee, board of directors, board of trustees, or owners. Contact with levels above the immediate superior should be initiated only with the superior's knowledge, assuming the superior is not involved. Except where legally prescribed, communication of such problems to authorities or individuals not employed or engaged by the organization is not considered appropriate.*
- *Clarify relevant ethical issues by confidential discussion with an objective advisor (e.g., IMA Ethics Counseling Service) to obtain a better understanding of possible courses of action.*
- *Consult your own attorney as to legal obligations and rights concerning the ethical conflict.*
- *If the ethical conflict still exists after exhausting all levels of internal review, there may be no other recourse on significant matters than to resign from the organization and to submit an informative memorandum to an appropriate representative of the organization. After resignation, depending on the nature of the ethical conflict, it may also be appropriate to notify other parties.*

## 1.1 Cost/Managerial Accounting

**1.** Managerial accounting differs from financial accounting in that financial accounting is

- A. More oriented toward the future.
- B. Primarily concerned with external financial reporting.
- C. Concerned with nonquantitative information.
- D. Heavily involved with decision analysis and implementation of decisions.

The correct answer is (B). *(Publisher)*
**REQUIRED:** The concept that applies more to financial than to managerial accounting.
**DISCUSSION:** Financial accounting is primarily concerned with historical accounting, i.e., traditional financial statements, and with external financial reporting to creditors and shareholders. Managerial accounting applies primarily to the planning and control of organizational operations, considers nonquantitative information, and is usually less precise.

Answer (A) is incorrect because managerial accounting is future oriented. Answer (C) is incorrect because financial accounting is primarily concerned with quantitative information. Answer (D) is incorrect because decision analysis and implementation are characteristics of managerial accounting.

**2.** Which one of the following is least likely to be an objective of a cost accounting system?

- A. Product costing and inventory valuation.
- B. Departmental efficiency.
- C. Sales commission determination.
- D. Income determination.

The correct answer is (C). *(CMA, adapted)*
**REQUIRED:** The item that is the least likely to be an objective of a cost accounting system.
**DISCUSSION:** A cost accounting system has internal and external reporting objectives. These include product costing; assessment of departmental efficiency; inventory valuation; income determination; and planning, evaluating, and controlling operations. Determining sales commissions is not an objective because they are not based on costs.

Answers (A), (B), and (D) are incorrect because product costing and inventory valuation, departmental efficiency, and income determination are objectives of a cost accounting system.

**3.** Which is the best description of traditional cost accounting?

- A. The entire general ledger and subsidiary ledgers and related journals, etc., of a manufacturer.
- B. The general ledger and subsidiary accounts and related records, etc., used to accumulate the costs of goods or services provided by an entity.
- C. The accounts used to determine the costs of goods sold by an entity.
- D. All of the journals, ledgers, records, and financial statements used by an enterprise to record, classify, summarize, and report economic activity of an enterprise.

The correct answer is (B). *(Publisher)*
**REQUIRED:** The best explanation of traditional cost accounting.
**DISCUSSION:** Cost accounting includes all of the accounts and records used to accumulate the cost of goods and services provided by an entity. In a retail enterprise, the inventory accounts, i.e., accounts for the costs of goods purchased from others for resale, serve this function. In manufacturing companies, service enterprises, etc., goods and services are created by the enterprise rather than purchased from others. The means of accounting for the costs of these enterprises is a cost accounting system.

Answer (A) is incorrect because the entire general ledger and subsidiary ledgers serve many other financial accounting functions besides the accumulation of cost data. Answer (C) is incorrect because a retailer uses only inventory and CGS accounts to determine CGS. In a manufacturing company, other accounts are used in the costing system, such as WIP and finished goods. Answer (D) is incorrect because the accounting system in general includes all of the journals, ledgers, records, and financial statements.

**4.** Management should implement a different and/or more expensive accounting system only when

- A. The cost of the system exceeds the benefits.
- B. Management thinks it appropriate.
- C. The board of directors dictates a change.
- (D.) The benefits of the system exceed the cost.

The correct answer is (D). *(Publisher)*

**REQUIRED:** The reason for using a different and/or more expensive accounting system.

**DISCUSSION:** Changing to a different and/or more expensive accounting system requires cost-benefit analysis. Changes should be undertaken only if the benefits of the proposed change exceed its cost.

Answer (A) is incorrect because it is economically irrational to implement a system in which the cost exceeds the benefits. Answer (B) is incorrect because cost-benefit analysis should not be ignored. An accounting system should be selected on an objective basis. Answer (C) is incorrect because dictation of a change by the board of directors implies a system selection on an other than objective basis.

**5.** Cost and managerial accounting systems are goods in the economic sense and, as such, their benefits must exceed their costs. When managerial accounting systems change, the cost that is frequently ignored is the cost of

- (A) Educating users.
- B. Gathering and analyzing data.
- C. Training accounting staff.
- D. Preparing reports.

The correct answer is (A). *(Publisher)*

**REQUIRED:** The cost typically ignored in cost-benefit analysis of proposed changes in accounting systems.

**DISCUSSION:** Users, i.e., managers, must be both willing and able to use new accounting systems. Accordingly, they should be encouraged to participate in the design and implementation of the new system. If they do not, they may not understand or want to use the new information.

Answer (B) is incorrect because the costs of gathering and analyzing data are direct costs of changing managerial accounting systems and are usually considered. Answer (C) is incorrect because training costs for staff are usually considered. Answer (D) is incorrect because report preparation is explicitly considered in systems development.

**6.** An accounting system that collects financial and operating data on the basis of the underlying nature and extent of the cost drivers is

- A. Activity-based costing.
- B. Target costing.
- C. Cycle-time costing.
- D. Variable costing.

The correct answer is (A). *(CMA, adapted)*

**REQUIRED:** The accounting system that collects data on the basis of cost drivers.

**DISCUSSION:** An activity-based costing (ABC) system identifies the causal relationship between the incurrence of costs and activities, determines the cost driver for each activity, and applies costs to products on the basis of resources (drivers) consumed.

Answer (B) is incorrect because target costing determines the maximum allowable cost of a product before the product is designed or produced; it deducts an acceptable profit margin from a forecasted selling price. Answer (C) is incorrect because cycle time is the period from the time a customer places an order to the time that product is delivered. Answer (D) is incorrect because variable costing expenses fixed factory overhead as incurred.

**7.** Companies characterized by the production of heterogeneous products will most likely use which of the following methods for the purpose of averaging costs and providing management with unit cost data?

- A. Process costing.
- B. Job-order costing.
- C. Direct costing.
- D. Absorption costing.

The correct answer is (B). *(CIA, adapted)*

**REQUIRED:** The method of averaging costs and providing management with unit cost data used by companies with heterogeneous products.

**DISCUSSION:** The job-order cost system of accounting is appropriate when products have varied characteristics and/or when identifiable groupings are possible, e.g., batches of certain styles or types of furniture. The unique aspect of job-order costing is the identification of costs to specific units or a particular job.

Answer (A) is incorrect because process costing accounts for continuous processing of homogeneous products. Answer (C) is incorrect because direct costing includes only variable manufacturing costs in unit cost. Answer (D) is incorrect because absorption costing includes all manufacturing costs in unit cost.

**8.** Companies characterized by the production of basically homogeneous products will most likely use which of the following methods for the purpose of averaging costs and providing management with unit-cost data?

 A. Process costing.

B. Job-order costing.

C. Variable costing.

D. Absorption costing.

The correct answer is (A). *(CIA, adapted)*

**REQUIRED:** The costing method used by companies with homogeneous products.

**DISCUSSION:** Like products that are mass produced should be accounted for using process costing to assign costs to products. Costs are accumulated by processes rather than by jobs, work-in-process is stated in terms of equivalent units, and unit costs are established. Process costing is an averaging process that calculates the average cost of all units.

Answer (B) is incorrect because job-order costing is employed when manufacturing involves different (heterogeneous) products. Answers (C) and (D) are incorrect because variable costing and absorption costing may be used whether products are homogeneous or heterogeneous and with either process or job-order costing.

**9.** The primary reason for adopting total quality management is to achieve

 A. Greater customer satisfaction.

B. Reduced delivery time.

C. Reduced delivery charges.

D. Greater employee participation.

The correct answer is (A). *(CIA, adapted)*

**REQUIRED:** The primary reason for adopting TQM.

**DISCUSSION:** TQM is an integrated system that identifies internal and external customers and establishes their requirements. The ultimate (external) customer is best served when internal customers are also well served.

Answers (B) and (C) are incorrect because reduced delivery time and reduced delivery charges are two of many potential activities that need improvement. Answer (D) is incorrect because increased employee participation is necessary to achieve TQM, but it is not the primary purpose for establishing the program.

**10.** Companies that adopt just-in-time purchasing systems often experience

 A. A reduction in the number of suppliers.

B. Fewer deliveries from suppliers.

C. A greater need for inspection of goods as the goods arrive.

D. Less need for linkage with a vendor's computerized order entry system.

The correct answer is (A). *(CMA, adapted)*

**REQUIRED:** The true statement about companies that adopt just-in-time (JIT) purchasing systems.

**DISCUSSION:** The objective of JIT is to reduce carrying costs by eliminating inventories and increasing the deliveries made by suppliers. Ideally, shipments of raw materials are received just in time to be incorporated into the manufacturing process. The focus of quality control under JIT is the prevention of quality problems. Quality control is shifted to the supplier. JIT companies typically do not inspect incoming goods; the assumption is that receipts are of perfect quality. Suppliers are limited to those who guarantee perfect quality and prompt delivery.

Answer (B) is incorrect because more deliveries are needed. Each shipment is smaller. Answer (C) is incorrect because, in a JIT system, materials are delivered directly to the production line ready for insertion in the finished product. Answer (D) is incorrect because the need for communication with the vendor is greater. Orders and deliveries must be made on short notice, sometimes several times a day.

**11.** The perpetual inventory method differs from the periodic in that the former

    A.  Includes only variable manufacturing costs in the product cost calculation.

    B.  Requires a physical inventory count to determine amounts of inventories used and/or remaining.

    C.  Maintains a continuous record of transactions affecting the inventory balances.

    D.  Includes manufacturing and nonmanufacturing costs in inventory.

The correct answer is (C). *(Publisher)*

    **REQUIRED:** The difference between the perpetual and periodic inventory methods.

    **DISCUSSION:** Perpetual inventory records provide for continuous record keeping of the quantities of inventory (and possibly unit costs and/or total costs). Perpetual inventory records can be maintained either in units or in units and dollars. This method requires a journal entry every time items are added to or taken from inventory.

    Answer (A) is incorrect because variable costing is a method that treats all fixed costs as period costs. It may be applied in either a perpetual or a periodic system. Answer (B) is incorrect because the periodic inventory system relies on physical counts to determine quantities. Answer (D) is incorrect because only manufacturing costs are included in inventory.

**12.** The budgeting tool or process in which estimates of revenues and expenses are prepared for each product beginning with the product's research and development phase and traced through to its customer support phase is a(n)

    A.  Master budget.

    B.  Activity-based budget.

    C.  Zero-base budget.

    D.  Life-cycle budget.

The correct answer is (D). *(CMA, adapted)*

    **REQUIRED:** The budget tool that involves estimating a product's revenues and expenses from R&D through customer support.

    **DISCUSSION:** A life-cycle budget estimates a product's revenues and expenses over its expected life cycle. This approach is especially useful when revenues and related costs do not occur in the same periods. It emphasizes the need to budget revenues to cover all costs, not just those for production. Hence, costs are determined for all value-chain categories: upstream (R&D, design), manufacturing, and downstream (marketing, distribution, and customer service). The result is to highlight upstream and downstream costs that often receive insufficient attention.

    Answer (A) is incorrect because a master budget summarizes all of a company's budgets and plans. Answer (B) is incorrect because an activity-based budget emphasizes the costs of activities, which are the basic cost objects in activity-based costing. Answer (C) is incorrect because a zero-base budget requires each manager to justify his/her subunit's entire budget each year.

**13.** Controllers are ordinarily not concerned with

    A.  Preparation of tax returns.

    B.  Reporting to government.

    C.  Protection of assets.

    D.  Investor relations.

The correct answer is (D). *(Publisher)*

    **REQUIRED:** The activity with which controllers are usually not concerned.

    **DISCUSSION:** Controllers are usually in charge of budgets, accounting, accounting reports, and related controls. Treasurers are most often involved with control over cash, receivables, short-term investments, financing, and insurance. Thus, treasurers rather than controllers are concerned with investor relations.

    Answer (A) is incorrect because the preparation of tax returns is a typical responsibility of the controller. Answer (B) is incorrect because external reporting is a function of the controller. Answer (C) is incorrect because the accounting system helps to safeguard assets.

**14.** The treasury function is usually not concerned with

- A. Financial reporting.
- B. Short-term financing.
- C. Cash custody and banking.
- D. Credit extension and collection of bad debts.

The correct answer is (A). *(Publisher)*
**REQUIRED:** The function usually not fulfilled by the treasurer.
**DISCUSSION:** Treasurers are usually concerned with investing cash and near-cash assets, the provision of capital, investor relations, insurance, etc. Controllers, on the other hand, are responsible for the reporting and accounting activities of an organization, including financial reporting.
Answer (B) is incorrect because short-term financing lies within the normal range of a treasurer's functions.
Answer (C) is incorrect because the treasurer has custody of assets. Answer (D) is incorrect because credit operations are often within the treasurer's purview.

**15.** Which professional organization represents management accountants in the United States?

- A. The American Institute of Certified Public Accountants (AICPA).
- B. The Institute of Internal Auditors (IIA).
- C. The Institute of Certified Management Accountants (ICMA).
- D. The Institute of Management Accountants (IMA).

The correct answer is (D). *(Publisher)*
**REQUIRED:** The professional organization representing management accountants in the U.S.
**DISCUSSION:** The primary purpose of the IMA (formerly the National Association of Accountants) is to enhance the professionalism of management accountants. Membership is open to all persons interested in management accounting. Unlike the AICPA, which restricts membership to CPAs, the IMA does not require a member to have a CMA certificate.
Answer (A) is incorrect because the AICPA primarily represents the public accounting profession. Answer (B) is incorrect because The IIA represents internal auditors. Answer (C) is incorrect because the ICMA is a division of the IMA that administers the Certified Management Accountant (CMA).

**16.** The professional certification program most suited for one interested in a career in management accounting leads to which of the following designations?

- A. CDP.
- B. CIA.
- C. CISA.
- D. CMA.

The correct answer is (D). *(Publisher)*
**REQUIRED:** The professional certification program most appropriate for a career in management accounting.
**DISCUSSION:** The Certified Management Accountant (CMA) program is administered by the IMA through the ICMA. The CMA certificate is awarded to those who pass four 4-hour examinations on economics, finance, and management; financial accounting and reporting; management reporting, analysis, and behavioral issues; and decision analysis and information systems.
Answer (A) is incorrect because a Certificate in Data Processing (CDP) is issued by the Institute for Certification of Computer Professionals. Answer (B) is incorrect because the Certified Internal Auditor (CIA) by The IIA. Answer (C) is incorrect because the Information Systems Audit and Control Association (ISACA) offers the Certified Information Systems Auditor (CISA) certificate.

## 1.2 Cost Definitions

**17.** One of the purposes of standard costs is to

- A. Simplify costing procedures and expedite cost reports.
- B. Replace budgets and budgeting.
- C. Serve as a basis for product costing for external reporting purposes.
- D. Eliminate accounting for under- or overapplied factory overhead at the end of the period.

The correct answer is (A). *(CPA, adapted)*
**REQUIRED:** The purpose of standard costs.
**DISCUSSION:** A standard cost system differentiates the expected cost from the actual cost, thus identifying deviations from expected (attainable) results on a routine basis. One of the purposes of standard costs is to simplify costing procedures and expedite cost reports.
Answer (B) is incorrect because standard costs are used to prepare budgets. Answer (C) is incorrect because standard costs cannot be used for external reporting if material variances exist. Answer (D) is incorrect because standard costs help measure over- and underapplied overhead.

**18.** Relevant costs are

   A. All fixed and variable costs.

   B. Costs that would be incurred within the relevant range of production.

   C. Past costs that are expected to be different in the future.

   D. Anticipated future costs that will differ among various alternatives.

The correct answer is (D). *(CMA, adapted)*
   **REQUIRED:** The definition of relevant costs.
   **DISCUSSION:** Relevant costs are anticipated costs that will vary among the choices available. In other words, if two courses of action share some costs, those costs are not relevant because they will be incurred regardless of the decision made.
   Answer (A) is incorrect because both fixed and variable costs can be either relevant or irrelevant depending upon the circumstances. Answer (B) is incorrect because relevant costs are those that differ among decision choices. Answer (C) is incorrect because past costs are sunk costs. Because they cannot be changed by management action, they are not relevant.

**19.** Incremental cost is

   A. The difference in total costs that results from selecting one choice instead of another.

   B. The profit forgone by selecting one choice instead of another.

   C. A cost that continues to be incurred in the absence of activity.

   D. A cost common to all choices in question and not clearly or feasibly allocable to any of them.

The correct answer is (A). *(CMA, adapted)*
   **REQUIRED:** The definition of incremental cost.
   **DISCUSSION:** Incremental cost is the difference in total cost between two courses of action. "Decremental cost" is the term used when the difference is noted as a decline although "incremental" is the more common term. Incremental cost is also referred to as differential cost.
   Answer (B) is incorrect because opportunity cost is the profit forgone by selecting one choice instead of another. Answer (C) is incorrect because a fixed cost is incurred even though no output is produced. Answer (D) is incorrect because common or joint costs are not allocable among the possible choices.

**20.** A company will produce 20,000 units of product A at a unit variable cost of $7 and a unit selling price of $13. Fixed costs are $40,000. However, the company will still have 40% idle capacity. The company can use this idle capacity to produce 6,000 units of a different product B, which it can sell for $7 per unit. The incremental variable cost of producing a unit of B is $6. Present fixed costs that will be allocated to B amount to $10,000. To decide whether to produce B, the company should use

   A. Differential cost analysis.

   B. Information economics.

   C. Regression analysis.

   D. Markov chain analysis.

The correct answer is (A). *(CIA, adapted)*
   **REQUIRED:** The method to determine if idle capacity should be used to produce another product.
   **DISCUSSION:** Nonroutine decisions involve such questions as whether to make or buy or accept a special order. These decisions should be made in part on the basis of relevant costs. Analysis of differential costs is therefore essential. The difference between the relevant costs of two decision choices is differential (incremental) cost.
   Answer (B) is incorrect because information economics concerns cost-benefit analysis of obtaining information for decision making. Answer (C) is incorrect because regression analysis attempts to find an equation describing the change in a dependent variable related to a change in an independent variable. Answer (D) is incorrect because Markov analysis is useful when a problem involves a variety of states of nature, and the probability of moving from one state to another is dependent only upon the current state.

**21.** Which one of the following costs would be relevant in short-term decision making?

   A. Incremental fixed costs.

   B. All costs of inventory.

   C. Total variable costs that are the same in the considered alternatives.

   D. Costs of fixed assets to be used in the alternatives.

The correct answer is (A). *(CMA, adapted)*
   **REQUIRED:** The cost relevant to short-term decision making.
   **DISCUSSION:** Relevant costs are those future costs that differ among the options. Incremental or differential cost is the difference in total cost between two decisions. Consequently, incremental fixed cost is a relevant cost.
   Answer (B) is incorrect because inventory costs may not always differ among options. Answer (C) is incorrect because costs that do not vary are not relevant to the decision process. Answer (D) is incorrect because the costs of fixed assets may be relevant or irrelevant depending upon whether they vary with the choice made.

**22.** When a decision is made in an organization, it is selected from a group of alternative courses of action. The loss associated with choosing the alternative that does not maximize the benefit is the

    A.   Net realizable value.

    B.   Expected value.

    C.   Opportunity cost.

    D.   Incremental cost.

The correct answer is (C). *(CMA, adapted)*

    **REQUIRED:** The loss associated with choosing the option that does not maximize the benefit.

    **DISCUSSION:** Opportunity cost is the maximum benefit obtainable from the next best alternative use of a resource. It is the benefit given up by not selecting that option.

    Answer (A) is incorrect because net realizable value is the value of an asset net of any disposal costs. Answer (B) is incorrect because expected value is a probabilistically weighted average of potential outcomes. Answer (D) is incorrect because an incremental cost is the additional cost of selecting one option rather than another.

**23.** Controllable costs

    A.   Arise from periodic appropriation decisions and have no well-specified function relating inputs to outputs.

    B.   Are primarily subject to the influence of a given manager of a given responsibility center for a given time span.

    C.   Arise from having property, plant, and equipment, and a functioning organization.

    D.   Result specifically from a clear-cut measured relationship between inputs and outputs.

The correct answer is (B). *(CIA, adapted)*

    **REQUIRED:** The definition of controllable costs.

    **DISCUSSION:** Controllable costs can be changed by action taken at the appropriate management (responsibility) level. All costs are controllable, but they are controlled at different management levels; e.g., the decision to build another plant is made at a higher level of management than the decision to buy office supplies.

    Answer (A) is incorrect because periodic appropriation decisions that have no well-specified function relating inputs to outputs apply to discretionary costs. Answer (C) is incorrect because property, plant, and equipment costs are committed costs. Answer (D) is incorrect because engineered costs result from a measured relationship between inputs and outputs.

**24.** A cost that bears an observable and known relationship to a quantifiable activity base is a(n)

    A.   Engineered cost.

    B.   Indirect cost.

    C.   Target cost.

    D.   Fixed cost.

The correct answer is (A). *(CMA, adapted)*

    **REQUIRED:** The cost that bears an observable and known relationship to a quantifiable activity base.

    **DISCUSSION:** An engineered cost is determined by formulas and measurements developed by experts, not by analysis of historical data. Engineered costs have a clear relationship to output. Direct materials cost is an example.

    Answer (B) is incorrect because an indirect cost does not have a clear relationship to output. Answer (C) is incorrect because a target cost is the maximum allowable cost of a product and is calculated before the product is designed or produced. Answer (D) is incorrect because a fixed cost remains unchanged within the relevant range for a given period despite fluctuations in activity; it usually has no direct relationship to activity.

**25.** In cost terminology, conversion costs consist of

A. Direct and indirect labor.

B. Direct labor and direct materials.

C. Direct labor and factory overhead.

D. Indirect labor and variable factory overhead.

The correct answer is (C). *(CMA, adapted)*

**REQUIRED:** The components of conversion costs.

**DISCUSSION:** Conversion costs consist of direct labor and factory overhead. These are the costs of converting raw materials into a finished product.

Answer (A) is incorrect because all factory overhead is included in conversion costs, not just indirect labor. Answer (B) is incorrect because direct materials are not an element of conversion costs; they are a component of prime costs. Answer (D) is incorrect because direct labor is also an element of conversion costs.

**26.** An imputed cost is

A. The difference in total costs that results from selecting one choice instead of another.

B. A cost that may be shifted to the future with little or no effect on current operations.

C. A cost that cannot be avoided because it has already been incurred.

D. A cost that does not entail any dollar outlay but is relevant to the decision-making process.

The correct answer is (D). *(CMA, adapted)*

**REQUIRED:** The definition of an imputed cost.

**DISCUSSION:** An imputed cost is properly attributed to a cost object even though no transaction is involved that would be routinely recognized in the accounting records. An imputed cost may be an outlay cost or an opportunity cost, but it should be considered in decision making in either case. An example involving an outlay is a loan to a supplier at a lower-than-market interest rate given in exchange for price concessions. Part of the outlay should be treated as a cost of the product. An example of an opportunity cost is the profit lost as a result of a stockout.

Answer (A) is incorrect because an incremental cost is the difference in total costs that results from selecting one choice instead of another. Answer (B) is incorrect because a postponable cost may be shifted to the future with little current effect. Answer (C) is incorrect because sunk costs have already been incurred.

**27.** Out-of-pocket costs

A. Are not recoverable.

B. Are under the influence of a supervisor.

C. Require expenditure of cash.

D. Are committed and unavoidable.

The correct answer is (C). *(Publisher)*

**REQUIRED:** The definition of out-of-pocket costs.

**DISCUSSION:** Out-of-pocket costs require negative cash flows (expenditures) currently or in the near future.

Answer (A) is incorrect because many out-of-pocket costs can be recovered over time; e.g., spending on a machine may produce a cash flow over its useful life. Answer (B) is incorrect because costs under the influence of a supervisor are controllable costs. From the perspective of a specific supervisor, out-of-pocket costs may not be controllable. Answer (D) is incorrect because committed and unavoidable costs are sunk costs.

**28.** Joint costs are those costs

    A.  Of products requiring the services of two or more processing departments.

    B.  Of a product from a common process that has relatively little sales value and only a small effect on profit.

    C.  Of production that are combined in the overhead account.

    D.  Of two or more products produced from a common process.

The correct answer is (D). *(Publisher)*

    **REQUIRED:** The definition of joint costs in cost accounting.

    **DISCUSSION:** Joint costs are the common costs of producing two or more inseparable products up to the point at which they become separable (the split-off point). The products are then sold as identifiably separate products or are processed further.

    Answer (A) is incorrect because the costs accumulated in prior processing steps are considered raw materials costs for purposes of subsequent processing. Answer (B) is incorrect because common products with relatively little sales value are by-products, e.g., woodchips from a sawmill. Joint cost is usually not allocated to them. Answer (C) is incorrect because indirect costs are combined in the overhead account.

**29.** Cost is the amount measured by the current monetary value of economic resources given up or to be given up in obtaining goods and services. Costs may be classified as unexpired or expired. Which of the following costs is not always considered to be expired immediately upon being recognized?

    A.  Cost of goods sold.

    B.  Sales salaries.

    C.  Depreciation expense for plant machinery.

    D.  Loss from bankruptcy of a major debtor not provided for in the annual adjustment.

The correct answer is (C). *(C. Wagner)*

    **REQUIRED:** The cost not always considered expired when recognized.

    **DISCUSSION:** Unexpired costs are assets and apply to the production of future revenues. Expired costs, which are those not applicable to production of future revenues, are deducted from current revenues or, in a very few cases, charged against retained earnings. Depreciation on plant machinery is a component of factory overhead that reflects the reclassification of a portion of the machinery cost to product (inventory) cost. This portion of inventory cost is an unexpired cost until the product is sold. At that time it becomes part of cost of goods sold (an expense).

    Answers (A) and (B) are incorrect because cost of goods sold and sales salaries are period costs. Answer (D) is incorrect because the loss from bankruptcy of a major debtor indicates that the expected future benefit from the receivable will not be obtained. Hence, the loss is the expiration of a future benefit.

Questions 30 through 35 are based on the following information.

Huron Industries has developed two new products but has only enough plant capacity to introduce one product during the current year. The following data will assist management in deciding which product should be selected.

Huron's fixed overhead includes rent and utilities, equipment depreciation, and supervisory salaries. Selling and administrative expenses are not allocated to products.

| | Product A | Product B |
|---|---|---|
| Raw materials | $   44.00 | $   36.00 |
| Machining @ $12/hr. | 18.00 | 15.00 |
| Assembly @ $10/hr. | 30.00 | 10.00 |
| Variable overhead @ $8/hr. | 36.00 | 18.00 |
| Fixed overhead @ $4/hr. | 18.00 | 9.00 |
| Total cost | $ 146.00 | $   88.00 |
| Suggested selling price | $ 169.95 | $   99.98 |
| Actual R&D costs | $240,000 | $175,000 |
| Proposed advertising and promotion costs | $500,000 | $350,000 |

**30.** For Huron's Product A, the unit costs for raw materials, machining, and assembly represent

A. Conversion costs.

B. Separable costs.

C. Prime costs.

D. Common costs.

The correct answer is (C). *(CMA, adapted)*

**REQUIRED:** The type of cost represented by raw materials, machining, and assembly.

**DISCUSSION:** Raw materials and direct labor (such as machining and assembly) are a manufacturer's prime costs.

Answer (A) is incorrect because conversion costs consist of direct labor and overhead. Answer (B) is incorrect because separable costs are incurred beyond the point at which jointly produced items become separately identifiable. Answer (D) is incorrect because common costs (joint costs) are incurred in the production of two or more inseparable products up to the point at which the products become separable.

**31.** The difference between the $99.98 suggested selling price for Huron's Product B and its total unit cost of $88.00 represents the unit's

A. Contribution margin ratio.

B. Gross profit.

C. Contribution.

D. Gross profit margin ratio.

The correct answer is (B). *(CMA, adapted)*

**REQUIRED:** The difference between selling price and unit cost.

**DISCUSSION:** Gross profit is the difference between sales price and the full absorption cost of goods sold.

Answer (A) is incorrect because contribution margin ratio is the ratio of contribution margin (sales – variable costs) to sales. Answer (C) is incorrect because contribution (margin) is the difference between unit selling price and unit variable costs. Fixed costs are not considered. Answer (D) is incorrect because the gross profit margin ratio equals gross profit divided by sales.

**32.** The total overhead cost of $27.00 for Huron's Product B is a

A. Carrying cost.

B. Sunk cost.

C. Mixed cost.

D. Committed cost.

The correct answer is (C). *(CMA, adapted)*

**REQUIRED:** The nature of total overhead.

**DISCUSSION:** A mixed cost is a combination of fixed and variable elements. The total overhead cost is mixed because it contains both fixed and variable overhead.

Answer (A) is incorrect because a carrying cost is the cost of carrying inventory; examples are insurance and rent. Answer (B) is incorrect because a sunk cost is a past cost or a cost that the entity has irrevocably committed to incur. Answer (D) is incorrect because a committed cost results when an entity holds fixed assets.

**33.** Research and development costs for Huron's two new products are

A.   Conversion costs.

B.   Sunk costs.

C.   Relevant costs.

D.   Avoidable costs.

The correct answer is (B). *(CMA, adapted)*

**REQUIRED:** The nature of R&D costs.

**DISCUSSION:** Before they are incurred, R&D costs are often considered to be discretionary. However, Huron's R&D costs have already been incurred. Thus, they are sunk costs. A sunk cost is a past cost or a cost that the entity has irrevocably committed to incur. Because it is unavoidable, it is not relevant to future decisions.

Answer (A) is incorrect because conversion costs (direct labor and factory overhead) are incurred to convert materials into a finished product. Answer (C) is incorrect because relevant costs are expected future costs that vary with the action taken. Answer (D) is incorrect because avoidable costs may be eliminated by not engaging in an activity or by performing the activity more efficiently.

**34.** The advertising and promotion costs for the product selected by Huron will be

A.   Discretionary costs.

B.   Opportunity costs.

C.   Prime costs.

D.   Incremental costs.

The correct answer is (A). *(CMA, adapted)*

**REQUIRED:** The nature of advertising and promotion costs.

**DISCUSSION:** A discretionary cost (a managed or program cost) results from a periodic decision about the total amount to be spent. It is also characterized by uncertainty about the relationship between input and the value of the related output. Examples are advertising and R&D costs.

Answer (B) is incorrect because an opportunity cost is the benefit provided by the best alternative use of a particular resource. Answer (C) is incorrect because prime costs are the costs incurred for raw materials and direct labor. Answer (D) is incorrect because incremental costs are the differences in costs between two decision choices.

**35.** The costs included in Huron's fixed overhead are

A.   Joint costs.

B.   Committed costs.

C.   Opportunity costs.

D.   Prime costs.

The correct answer is (B). *(CMA, adapted)*

**REQUIRED:** The nature of fixed overhead.

**DISCUSSION:** Committed costs are those for which management has made a long-term commitment. They typically result when a firm holds fixed assets. Examples include long-term lease payments and depreciation. Committed costs are typically fixed costs.

Answer (A) is incorrect because joint (common) costs are incurred in the production of two or more inseparable products up to the point at which they become separable. Answer (C) is incorrect because an opportunity cost is the benefit provided by the best alternative use of a particular resource. Answer (D) is incorrect because prime costs are composed of raw material and direct labor costs.

## 1.3 Cost of Goods Manufactured and Sold

**36.** In a retailing enterprise, the income statement includes cost of goods sold. Cost of goods sold is, in effect, purchases adjusted for changes in inventory. In a manufacturing company, the purchases account is replaced by which account?

    A. Inventory.

    B. Cost of goods manufactured.

    C. Finished goods.

    D. Cost of goods sold.

The correct answer is (B). *(Publisher)*
    **REQUIRED:** The account in a manufacturing company equivalent to purchases.
    **DISCUSSION:** Instead of purchasing goods and services for resale, a manufacturing company manufactures goods and services for sale. Accordingly, the CGM account is similar to the purchases account. CGS is equal to the BI of finished goods, plus CGM, minus the EI of finished goods. CGM includes the costs of labor, materials, and overhead for goods completed within the current period and transferred to finished goods inventory.
    Answers (A) is incorrect because both manufacturing and retailing companies have inventory accounts. Answer (C) is incorrect because the finished goods account of a manufacturer is akin to the merchandise inventory (goods held for resale) of a retailer. Answer (D) is incorrect because CGS is purchases or CGM adjusted for changes in inventory.

**37.** The information contained in a cost of goods manufactured budget most directly relates to the

    A. Materials used, direct labor, overhead applied, and ending work-in-process budgets.

    B. Materials used, direct labor, overhead applied, and work-in-process inventories budgets.

    C. Materials used, direct labor, overhead applied, work-in-process inventories, and finished goods inventories budgets.

    D. Materials used, direct labor, overhead applied, and finished goods inventories budgets.

The correct answer is (B). *(CMA, adapted)*
    **REQUIRED:** The items contained in a cost of goods manufactured budget.
    **DISCUSSION:** Cost of goods manufactured is equivalent to a retailer's purchases. It equals all manufacturing costs incurred during the period, plus beginning work-in-process, minus ending work-in-process. A cost of goods manufactured budget is therefore based on materials, direct labor, factory overhead, and work-in-process.
    Answer (A) is incorrect because a cost of goods manufactured budget includes both beginning and ending work-in-process budgets. Answers (C) and (D) are incorrect because a cost of goods manufactured budget excludes finished goods inventory budgets. They are the end product of the manufacturing process.

**38.** What is the nature of the work-in-process account?

    A. Inventory.

    B. Cost of goods sold.

    C. Productivity.

    D. Nominal.

The correct answer is (A). *(Publisher)*
    **REQUIRED:** The nature of the work-in-process account.
    **DISCUSSION:** Work-in-process is an inventory account. All the manufacturing costs charged to work-in-process this period and those remaining in the account from last period (BWIP) are allocated between goods that are completed and goods that are incomplete at year-end (EWIP). However, the costs of abnormal spoilage will be removed and charged to a loss account.
    Answer (B) is incorrect because CGS is CGM adjusted for the change in finished goods inventory. Hence, it is an expense (nominal) account. Answer (C) is incorrect because productivity is a nonsense term in this context. Answer (D) is incorrect because an inventory account is a real rather than a nominal account.

**39.** Theoretically, cash discounts permitted on purchased raw materials should be

A. Added to other income, whether taken or not.

B. Added to other income, only if taken.

C. Deducted from inventory, whether taken or not.

D. Deducted from inventory, only if taken.

The correct answer is (C). *(CPA, adapted)*

**REQUIRED:** The treatment of purchase discounts.

**DISCUSSION:** Cash discounts on purchases should be treated as reductions in the invoiced prices of specific purchases so that goods available for sale reflect net purchase prices. Any discounts not taken are recorded as losses in the income statement. The net method is preferable to recording inventories and payables at gross amounts because the net amounts are the most accurate exchange prices. Moreover, it measures management's stewardship by recording as financing charges any discounts not taken.

Answers (A) and (B) are incorrect because cash discounts are never added to other income. Answer (D) is incorrect because deducting only discounts taken (the gross method) is theoretically inferior.

**40.** The following information appeared in the accounting records of a retail store for the year ended December 31, 1998:

| | |
|---|---|
| Sales | $300,000 |
| Purchases | 140,000 |
| Inventories | |
| January 1 | 70,000 |
| December 31 | 100,000 |
| Sales commissions | 10,000 |

The gross margin was

A. $190,000

B. $180,000

C. $160,000

D. $150,000

The correct answer is (A). *(CPA, adapted)*

**REQUIRED:** The gross margin.

**DISCUSSION:** The gross margin (profit) equals sales minus cost of goods sold. The cost of goods sold equals purchases, plus beginning inventory, minus ending inventory. Consequently, the gross margin is $190,000 [$300,000 – ($140,000 + $70,000 – $100,000)].

Answer (B) is incorrect because sales commissions ($10,000) are deducted from the gross margin in arriving at net operating income. They are not included in cost of goods sold. Answer (C) is incorrect because $160,000 is the difference between sales and purchases, but an adjustment to purchases must also be made for the change in inventory (–$30,000). Answer (D) is incorrect because $150,000 is the result of improperly deducting sales commissions and not making an adjustment for the inventory change.

**41.** The following cost data were taken from the records of a manufacturing company:

| | |
|---|---|
| Depreciation on factory equipment | $ 1,000 |
| Depreciation on sales office | 500 |
| Advertising | 7,000 |
| Freight-out (shipping) | 3,000 |
| Wages of production workers | 28,000 |
| Raw materials used | 47,000 |
| Sales salaries and commissions | 10,000 |
| Factory rent | 2,000 |
| Factory insurance | 500 |
| Materials handling | 1,500 |
| Administrative salaries | 2,000 |

Based upon this information, the manufacturing cost incurred during the year was

A. $78,500

B. $80,000

C. $80,500

D. $83,000

The correct answer is (B). *(CIA, adapted)*

**REQUIRED:** The amount of manufacturing cost.

**DISCUSSION:** Manufacturing costs include direct labor, direct materials, and any other indirect costs (overhead) connected with production. Selling and administrative costs (e.g., depreciation on sales office, freight-out, sales salaries, and commissions, advertising, and administrative salaries) are not included. Thus, manufacturing cost is $80,000.

| | |
|---|---|
| Production wages | $28,000 |
| Raw materials | 47,000 |
| Factory rent | 2,000 |
| Factory insurance | 500 |
| Factory depreciation | 1,000 |
| Materials handling | 1,500 |
| | $80,000 |

Answer (A) is incorrect because the materials handling cost ($1,500) must also be added. Answer (C) is incorrect because sales office depreciation ($500) should be excluded. Answer (D) is incorrect because freight-out ($3,000) is a selling cost.

**42.** Glen Company has the following data pertaining to the year ended December 31:

| | |
|---|---|
| Purchases | $450,000 |
| Beginning inventory | 170,000 |
| Ending inventory | 210,000 |
| Freight-in | 50,000 |
| Freight-out | 75,000 |

How much is the cost of goods sold for the year?

A. $385,000

B. $460,000

C. $485,000

D. $535,000

The correct answer is (B). *(CPA, adapted)*
**REQUIRED:** The cost of goods sold for the year.
**DISCUSSION:** Freight-in is the cost of receiving inventory and is a product cost. Freight-out is the cost of shipping products to customers and should be treated as a selling expense (period cost). Thus, CGS is $460,000.

| | | |
|---|---|---|
| Beginning inventory | | $170,000 |
| Purchases | $450,000 | |
| Freight-in | 50,000 | 500,000 |
| Goods available | | $670,000 |
| Ending inventory | | (210,000) |
| Cost of goods sold | | $460,000 |

Answer (A) is incorrect because freight-out should be excluded from ending inventory. Answer (C) is incorrect because freight-in, not freight-out, should be included in the cost of goods available. Answer (D) is incorrect because freight-out should not be added to the cost of goods available.

---

Questions 43 through 46 are based on the following information. Madtack Company's beginning and ending inventories for the month of November 1998 are

| | November 1 | November 30 |
|---|---|---|
| Direct materials | $ 67,000 | $ 62,000 |
| Work-in-process | 145,000 | 171,000 |
| Finished goods | 85,000 | 78,000 |

Production data for November follows:

| | |
|---|---|
| Direct labor | $200,000 |
| Actual factory overhead | 132,000 |
| Direct materials purchased | 163,000 |
| Transportation in | 4,000 |
| Purchase returns and allowances | 2,000 |

Madtack uses one factory overhead control account and charges factory overhead to production at 70% of direct labor cost. The company does not formally recognize over- or underapplied overhead until year-end.

---

**43.** Madtack Company's prime cost for November is

A. $370,000

B. $363,000

C. $170,000

D. $368,000

The correct answer is (A). *(CMA, adapted)*
**REQUIRED:** The definition and calculation of prime cost.
**DISCUSSION:** Prime costs are direct materials and direct labor. They equal $370,000 ($170,000 DM as calculated below and $200,000 DL).

| | |
|---|---|
| Beginning materials inventory | $ 67,000 |
| Plus purchases | 163,000 |
| Plus transportation in | 4,000 |
| Minus purchase returns | (2,000) |
| Materials available for use | $232,000 |
| Minus ending materials inventory | (62,000) |
| Materials used | $170,000 |

Answer (B) is incorrect because $363,000 incorporates the change in finished goods inventories. Answer (C) is incorrect because the $170,000 is only the raw materials used. Answer (D) is incorrect because $368,000 fails to consider purchase returns and transportation in.

---

**44.** Madtack Company's total manufacturing cost for November is

A. $502,000

B. $503,000

C. $363,000

D. $510,000

The correct answer is (D). *(CMA, adapted)*
**REQUIRED:** The total manufacturing costs.
**DISCUSSION:** Total manufacturing costs consist of materials, labor, and overhead. Total prime costs were $370,000. Overhead applied was $140,000 (70% x $200,000 DL), so total manufacturing cost is $510,000 ($170,000 + $200,000 + $140,000).
Answer (A) is incorrect because $502,000 is based on actual overhead. Answer (B) is incorrect because $503,000 incorporates the change in finished goods inventories. Answer (C) is incorrect because $363,000 excludes overhead but includes the change in finished goods inventory.

**45.** Madtack Company's cost of goods transferred to finished goods inventory for November is

A. $469,000

B. $477,000

C. $495,000

D. $484,000

The correct answer is (D). *(CMA, adapted)*

**REQUIRED:** The cost of goods transferred to finished goods inventory during the month.

**DISCUSSION:** Total manufacturing costs are adjusted for the change in work-in-process to arrive at the cost of goods transferred. Total manufacturing cost was $510,000, so the cost of goods transferred (CGM) is $484,000 ($510,000 + $145,000 − $171,000).

Answer (A) is incorrect because $469,000 uses actual overhead and adjusts the figures for the change in finished goods inventory. Answer (B) is incorrect because $477,000 includes the change in finished goods inventory in the calculation. Answer (C) is incorrect because $495,000 uses materials purchased rather than materials used and also fails to adjust properly for transportation in.

**46.** Madtack Company's net charge to factory overhead control for the month of November is

A. $8,000 debit, overapplied.

B. $8,000 debit, underapplied.

C. $8,000 credit, overapplied.

D. $8,000 credit, underapplied.

The correct answer is (C). *(CMA, adapted)*

**REQUIRED:** The net charge to the factory overhead control account for the month.

**DISCUSSION:** The factory overhead control account was debited for $132,000 of actual overhead. Credits totaled $140,000 (70% x $200,000 DL). Thus, overhead was overapplied by $8,000.

Answer (A) is incorrect because an overapplication of overhead results in a credit balance. Answers (B) and (D) are incorrect because the overhead was overapplied for the month.

## 1.4 Variable vs. Fixed Costs

**47.** The difference between variable costs and fixed costs is

A. Unit variable costs fluctuate, and unit fixed costs remain constant.

B. Unit variable costs are fixed over the relevant range, and unit fixed costs are variable.

C. Total variable costs are variable over the relevant range and fixed in the long term, while fixed costs never change.

D. Unit variable costs change in varying increments, while unit fixed costs change in equal increments.

The correct answer is (B). *(CMA, adapted)*

**REQUIRED:** The difference between variable and fixed costs.

**DISCUSSION:** Fixed costs remain unchanged within the relevant range for a given period despite fluctuations in activity, but per-unit fixed costs do change as the level of activity changes. Thus, fixed costs are fixed in total but vary per unit as activity changes. Total variable costs vary directly with activity. They are fixed per unit within a given range, but vary in total.

Answer (A) is incorrect because variable costs are fixed per unit; they do not fluctuate. Fixed costs per unit change as production changes. Answer (C) is incorrect because all costs are variable in the long term. Answer (D) is incorrect because unit variable costs are fixed in the short term.

**48.** The difference between the sales price and total variable costs is

A. Gross operating profit.

B. Net profit.

C. The breakeven point.

D. The contribution margin.

The correct answer is (D). *(CMA, adapted)*

**REQUIRED:** The difference between sales price and total variable costs.

**DISCUSSION:** Contribution margin equals sales revenue minus all variable costs. It is the portion of sales available for covering fixed costs and profit.

Answer (A) is incorrect because gross operating profit results from deducting all manufacturing costs from sales. Answer (B) is incorrect because net profit is the remainder after deducting all costs from revenue. Answer (C) is incorrect because the breakeven point is the level of sales that equals the sum of fixed and variable costs.

**49.** Unit fixed costs

    A. Are constant per unit regardless of units produced or sold.

    B. Are determined by dividing total fixed costs by a denominator such as production or sales volume.

    C. Vary directly with the activity level when stated on a per-unit basis.

    D. Include both fixed and variable elements.

The correct answer is (B). *(Publisher)*
    **REQUIRED:** The correct statement about unit fixed costs.
    **DISCUSSION:** A unit fixed cost is equal to total fixed costs divided by an appropriate denominator or activity level. The resulting average or unit fixed cost must be used with extreme caution in decision making.
    Answer (A) is incorrect because variable costs are constant per unit. Answer (C) is incorrect because unit fixed costs vary inversely with activity. Answer (D) is incorrect because the question concerns only unit fixed costs.

**50.** A company has always used the full cost of its product as the starting point in the pricing of that product. The price set by competitors and the demand for the company's only product, the Widget, have never been predictable. Lately, the company's market share has been increasing as it continues to lower its price, but total revenues have not changed significantly relative to the gain in sales volume. The likely reason for the stability of total revenues is the

    A. Variable cost component of the full cost.

    B. Unstable contribution margin.

    C. Fixed cost component of the full cost.

    D. Drop in the incremental cost of the units in the increased sales volume.

The correct answer is (C). *(CIA, adapted)*
    **REQUIRED:** The likely reason for stability of total revenue given full costing, a lower price, and greater volume.
    **DISCUSSION:** Fixed costs remain fixed in total at different activity levels. Thus, unit fixed cost will vary inversely with the activity level. The use of full cost pricing results in a lowering of unit fixed cost used as a basis for unit price as sales increase. The consequence is a reduction of the unit sales price (assuming a constant unit profit margin is maintained). Total revenues may remain approximately the same as sales volume increases.
    Answer (A) is incorrect because variable cost per unit remains the same at all activity levels. Answer (B) is incorrect because an unstable contribution margin would affect total revenues. Answer (D) is incorrect because the drop in the incremental cost is the result of the decline in unit fixed cost.

**51.** Sales of a company's product have suffered because of intense price competition. As a result, the company must lower the price of the product. The lowest feasible short-run price would just exceed the product's

    A. Fixed cost per unit.

    B. Variable cost per unit.

    C. Fixed cost per unit plus variable cost per unit.

    D. Variable cost per unit minus fixed cost per unit.

The correct answer is (B). *(CIA, adapted)*
    **REQUIRED:** The lowest feasible short-run price.
    **DISCUSSION:** Theoretically, fixed costs are sunk costs in the short run: they will be incurred even if the firm closes down. The decision to continue in operation is therefore dependent on whether the firm can recover its incremental (variable) costs. Consequently, the firm should continue to operate in the short run if it can recover its variable costs and some portion of its fixed costs. In the short run, closing down results in the loss of the full amount of fixed costs (those incurred without regard to the level of production). Thus, a price just in excess of unit variable cost permits the firm to continue to operate. In the long run, all costs are variable, and the price must be set accordingly.
    Answer (A) is incorrect because fixed costs are sunk costs. In the short run, a loss-minimizing firm must cover its incremental (variable) costs. A price equal to unit fixed cost may or may not accomplish that goal. Answer (C) is incorrect because fixed cost per unit plus variable cost per unit is higher than the lowest feasible short-run price. Answer (D) is incorrect because variable cost per unit minus fixed cost per unit is a lower than feasible short-run price.

**52.** The relevant range in cost accounting is the range over which

    A. Costs may fluctuate.

    B. Cost relationships are valid.

    C. Production may vary.

    D. Relevant costs are incurred.

The correct answer is (B). *(CPA, adapted)*

    **REQUIRED:** The definition of the relevant range in cost accounting.

    **DISCUSSION:** The relevant range is the range of activity (production volume) within which variable unit costs are constant and fixed costs are constant in total. In this range, the incremental cost of one additional unit of production, i.e., the unit variable cost, does not vary.

    Answer (A) is incorrect because total cost fluctuates both within and outside the relevant range because variable costs vary. Answer (C) is incorrect because production levels may be above or below the relevant range; they are not confined to the relevant range. Answer (D) is incorrect because relevant costs are incurred at any level, not just within the relevant range.

**53.** Depreciation based on the number of units produced is classified as what type of cost?

    A. Out-of-pocket.

    B. Marginal.

    C. Variable.

    D. Fixed.

The correct answer is (C). *(CPA, adapted)*

    **REQUIRED:** The cost resulting from depreciation based on the number of units produced.

    **DISCUSSION:** A variable cost is uniform per unit but, in total, fluctuates in direct proportion to changes in the related activity or volume. Thus, a per-unit depreciation charge is a variable cost.

    Answer (A) is incorrect because the purchase of an asset, not the subsequent depreciation, is an out-of-pocket cost. Answer (B) is incorrect because a marginal cost is incurred by producing and/or selling an additional or partial unit. Marginal costs include materials, labor, etc. Answer (D) is incorrect because total fixed costs do not fluctuate with activity levels; they are not based on units produced.

**54.** Depreciation based on the straight-line method is classified as what type of cost?

    A. Out-of-pocket.

    B. Marginal.

    C. Variable.

    D. Fixed.

The correct answer is (D). *(J.W. Ferry)*

    **REQUIRED:** The classification of depreciation when it is based on the straight-line method.

    **DISCUSSION:** By definition, a fixed cost is a cost that remains unchanged over a given time period regardless of the related level of production activity. Straight-line depreciation is thus properly classified as fixed since it is correlated with the passage of time, not the level of activity.

    Answer (A) is incorrect because payment for an asset, not the subsequent depreciation, is an out-of-pocket cost. Answer (B) is incorrect because a marginal cost is incurred by producing and/or selling an additional or partial unit. Answer (C) is incorrect because variable costs fluctuate with activity levels. For example, depreciation based on the units-of-production method is a variable cost.

**55.** Which one of the following categories of cost is most likely not considered a component of fixed factory overhead?

    A. Rent.

    B. Property taxes.

    C. Supervisory salaries.

    D. Power.

The correct answer is (D). *(CMA, adapted)*

    **REQUIRED:** The item of cost most likely not considered a component of fixed factory overhead.

    **DISCUSSION:** A fixed cost is one that remains unchanged within the relevant range for a given period despite fluctuations in activity. Such items as rent, property taxes, depreciation, and supervisory salaries are normally fixed costs because they do not vary with changes in production. Power costs, however, are at least partially variable because they increase as usage increases.

    Answers (A), (B), and (C) are incorrect because rent, property taxes, and supervisory salaries are overhead items.

**56.** When the number of units manufactured increases, the most significant change in average unit cost will be reflected as

- A.   An increase in the nonvariable element.
- B.   A decrease in the variable element.
- C.   A decrease in the nonvariable element.
- D.   An increase in the semivariable element.

The correct answer is (C). *(CIA, adapted)*
**REQUIRED:** The most significant change in average unit cost when the number of units manufactured increases.
**DISCUSSION:** As production increases or decreases, the most significant change in the average unit cost will occur in the fixed (nonvariable) cost element. When production increases, the average cost of the nonvariable element per unit will decrease because total fixed cost is constant.
Answer (A) is incorrect because the nonvariable fixed element varies indirectly with production level; fixed cost per unit decreases with an increase in the production level. Answer (B) is incorrect because the variable element per unit is assumed to remain constant for changes in the production level within the relevant range. Answer (D) is incorrect because the semivariable element decreases to the extent it consists of fixed costs and remains constant to the extent it includes variable costs.

**57.** Costs that increase as the volume of activity decreases within the relevant range are

- A.   Average costs per unit.
- B.   Average variable costs per unit.
- C.   Total fixed costs.
- D.   Total variable costs.

The correct answer is (A). *(CIA, adapted)*
**REQUIRED:** The costs that increase as the volume of activity decreases within the relevant range.
**DISCUSSION:** As production levels decrease, total fixed costs must be allocated over fewer units. This increase in average fixed costs per unit increases total average cost per unit.
Answer (B) is incorrect because average variable costs per unit remain constant as the volume of activity decreases. Answer (C) is incorrect because total fixed costs are constant within the relevant range. Answer (D) is incorrect because total variable costs decrease as volume decreases.

**58.** Quo Co. rented a building to Hava Fast Food. Each month Quo receives a fixed rental amount plus a variable rental amount based on Hava's sales for that month. As sales increase, so does the variable rental amount but at a reduced rate. Which of the following curves reflects the monthly rentals under the agreement?

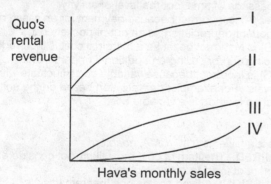

Hava's monthly sales

- A.   I
- B.   II
- C.   III
- D.   IV

The correct answer is (A). *(CPA, adapted)*
**REQUIRED:** The nature of fixed and variable costs.
**DISCUSSION:** Fixed cost remains unchanged within the relevant range for a given period despite fluctuations in activity, but variable costs vary directly with the activity. Because a portion of the rental revenue is a fixed cost, it will never be zero regardless of sales. Because the total variable cost increases at a reduced rate as sales increase, the per-unit variable cost is not fixed. Furthermore, as sales increase over time, the rental revenue increases at a diminishing amount as represented by Curve I.
Answer (B) is incorrect because, as sales increase, the variable rental amount increases at a reduced rate. Answers (C) and (D) are incorrect because the rental revenue is based on both a fixed and a variable component.

**59.** The following data were collected from the records of the shipping department of a company:

| Month | Units Shipped | Cost of Shipping Supplies |
|---|---|---|
| 1 | 7,000 | $35,000 |
| 2 | 5,000 | 25,000 |
| 3 | 3,000 | 14,900 |
| 4 | 13,000 | 65,000 |
| 5 | 11,000 | 55,200 |
| 6 | 10,000 | 50,200 |
| 7 | 15,000 | 74,900 |

The cost of shipping supplies is most likely to be a

A. Variable cost.

B. Fixed cost.

C. Step cost.

D. Semi-fixed cost.

The correct answer is (A). *(CIA, adapted)*

**REQUIRED:** The character of the cost of shipping supplies.

**DISCUSSION:** Variable costs are constant per unit but fluctuate in total with activity or volume (the rate of use of capacity). The cost per unit for shipping supplies is relatively constant at about $5, so this cost is variable.

Answer (B) is incorrect because total fixed costs do not change within the relevant range. Hence, the per-unit fixed cost declines as production increases. Answer (C) is incorrect because a step cost is fixed over a relatively small range of activity but increases by a discrete amount (a step) as activity increases. For example, the cost of one direct labor hour is the same regardless of the output generated during that hour, but the cost will increase by a discrete amount (the hourly rate) when the activity level is increased by one step (an hour). If the steps are small enough, the cost is essentially variable. As the steps increase, however, the cost may be classified as semi-fixed or fixed. Answer (D) is incorrect because the cost is variable. It changes over relatively small steps of activity.

**60.** Assuming all manufacturing costs for finished goods are known, which of the following statements explains why the accountant's unit cost used in inventory valuation for the annual financial statements would differ from the economist's marginal unit cost?

A. The company used LIFO or FIFO assumptions to compute inventory cost.

B. Accounting information that is based on historical manufacturing costs ignores current cost trends.

C. The economist's definition of marginal cost excludes a provision for profit per unit.

D. The manufacturing cost per unit reflected in financial statements includes fixed costs.

The correct answer is (D). *(CIA, adapted)*

**REQUIRED:** The difference between the economist's marginal cost and the accountant's unit cost.

**DISCUSSION:** The economist's marginal cost equals the cost to produce one additional unit; no fixed costs are included in the computation. It is the equivalent of the accountant's unit variable cost, which is an incremental unit cost. However, the accountant's unit cost for financial statement purposes includes an allocation of fixed costs.

Answer (A) is incorrect because the cost flow assumption is separate from the assumption of which costs are included. Answer (B) is incorrect because variable costs are stated at current-period prices. Answer (C) is incorrect because both accountants and economists usually exclude profit from inventory unit costs.

**61.** A manufacturing firm planned to manufacture and sell 100,000 units of product during the year at a variable cost per unit of $4.00 and a fixed cost per unit of $2.00. The firm fell short of its goal and only manufactured 80,000 units at a total incurred cost of $515,000. The firm's manufacturing cost variance was

A. $85,000 favorable.

B. $35,000 unfavorable.

C. $5,000 favorable.

D. $5,000 unfavorable.

The correct answer is (C). *(CMA, adapted)*

**REQUIRED:** The manufacturing cost variance.

**DISCUSSION:** The company planned to produce 100,000 units at $6 each ($4 variable + $2 fixed cost), or a total of $600,000, consisting of $400,000 of variable costs and $200,000 of fixed costs. Total production was only 80,000 units at a total cost of $515,000. The flexible budget for a production level of 80,000 units includes variable costs of $320,000 ($4 x 80,000 units). Fixed costs would remain at $200,000. Thus, the total flexible budget costs are $520,000. Given that actual costs were only $515,000, the variance is $5,000 favorable.

Answer (A) is incorrect because $85,000 favorable is based on a production level of 100,000 units. Answers (B) and (D) are incorrect because the variance is favorable.

## 1.5 Product vs. Period Costs

**62.** Inventoriable costs

    A.   Include only the prime costs of manufacturing a product.

    B.   Include only the conversion costs of manufacturing a product.

    C.   Are expensed when products become part of finished goods inventory.

    D.   Are regarded as assets before the products are sold.

The correct answer is (D). *(CMA, adapted)*

    **REQUIRED:** The nature of inventoriable costs.

    **DISCUSSION:** Under an absorption costing system, inventoriable (product) costs include direct materials and conversion costs (direct labor and fixed and variable factory overhead). Inventoriable costs are treated as assets until the products are sold because they represent future economic benefits.

    Answer (A) is incorrect because overhead costs are included in inventory. Answer (B) is incorrect because materials costs are also included. Answer (C) is incorrect because inventory costs are expensed when the goods are sold.

**63.** Internal auditors must often distinguish between product costs and period costs. Product costs are properly assigned to inventory when incurred. Period costs are always expensed in the same period in which they are incurred. Which of the following items is a product cost for a manufacturing company?

    A.   Insurance on the corporate headquarters building.

    B.   Property taxes on a factory.

    C.   Depreciation on salespersons' automobiles.

    D.   Salary of a sales manager.

The correct answer is (B). *(CIA, adapted)*

    **REQUIRED:** The item that is a product cost for a manufacturing company.

    **DISCUSSION:** For a manufacturer, product costs include direct materials, direct labor, and factory overhead. Property taxes on a factory are a product cost because they are included in factory overhead.

    Answer (A) is incorrect because insurance on the corporate headquarters building is not a cost of production and is therefore a period cost. Answer (C) is incorrect because depreciation on salespersons' automobiles is a selling cost, which is a period cost. Answer (D) is incorrect because the salary of a sales manager is a selling cost.

**64.** The cost of the direct labor associated with the manufacture of a product should be classified as an expense when the

    A.   Labor is performed.

    B.   Product is transferred to finished goods inventory.

    C.   Product is sold.

    D.   Employees are paid.

The correct answer is (C). *(CIA, adapted)*

    **REQUIRED:** The time when direct labor cost is expensed.

    **DISCUSSION:** Direct labor costs include the wages of all labor that can be identified in an economically feasible manner with the production of finished goods. Thus, it is a product cost and becomes an element of cost of goods sold that is expensed when the finished goods are sold.

    Answer (A) is incorrect because direct labor is part of the cost of the finished goods inventory (an asset) until sold. Answer (B) is incorrect because the cost of finished goods inventory is an asset. Answer (D) is incorrect because direct labor is an inventoriable cost. It is not expensed as incurred.

**65.** All costs related to the manufacturing function in a company are

    A.   Prime costs.

    B.   Direct costs.

    C.   Product costs.

    D.   Conversion costs.

The correct answer is (C). *(CIA, adapted)*

    **REQUIRED:** The classification of costs related to the manufacturing function.

    **DISCUSSION:** Product costs are the costs of producing the product and are usually directly identifiable with it. Thus, product costs include the costs of the factors of production identifiable with the product, which usually include direct materials, direct labor, and factory (not general) overhead. Factory overhead includes both fixed and variable elements. Product costs are inventoried until the product is sold, at which time they are expensed.

    Answer (A) is incorrect because prime costs are direct materials costs plus direct labor costs. Answer (B) is incorrect because direct costs are directly traceable to a single cost objective. Manufacturing costs can be indirect as well as direct. Answer (D) is incorrect because conversion costs are direct labor costs plus factory overhead costs.

**66.** Following are Mill Co.'s production costs for October:

| | |
|---|---|
| Direct materials | $100,000 |
| Direct labor | 90,000 |
| Factory overhead | 4,000 |

What amount of costs should be traced to specific products in the production process?

A. $194,000

B. $190,000

C. $100,000

D. $90,000

The correct answer is (B). *(CPA, adapted)*

**REQUIRED:** The amount of costs traceable to specific products.

**DISCUSSION:** Direct materials and direct labor can feasibly be identified with the production of specific goods. Factory overhead cannot be traced to a specific product but is allocated to all products produced. Thus, the amount of costs traceable to specific products in the production process equals $190,000 ($100,000 + $90,000).

Answer (A) is incorrect because $194,000 includes factory overhead. Answer (C) is incorrect because $100,000 excludes direct labor. Answer (D) is incorrect because $90,000 excludes direct materials.

**67.** West Co.'s 1998 manufacturing costs were as follows:

| | |
|---|---|
| Direct materials and direct labor | $700,000 |
| Other variable manufacturing costs | 100,000 |
| Depreciation of factory building and manufacturing equipment | 80,000 |
| Other fixed manufacturing overhead | 18,000 |

What amount should be considered product cost for external reporting purposes?

A. $700,000

B. $800,000

C. $880,000

D. $898,000

The correct answer is (D). *(CPA, adapted)*

**REQUIRED:** The product cost for external reporting purposes.

**DISCUSSION:** According to GAAP, absorption (full) costing is required for external reporting purposes. Absorption costing includes fixed and variable factory overhead in product cost. Direct materials and direct labor are other elements of product cost. Consequently, the total product cost is $898,000 ($700,000 + $100,000 + $80,000 + $18,000).

Answer (A) is incorrect because the other variable (presumably overhead) costs and the fixed factory overhead (including depreciation on plant assets) should be inventoried. Answer (B) is incorrect because the depreciation and the other fixed factory overhead are product costs. Answer (C) is incorrect because the other fixed factory overhead is also a product cost.

**68.** Period costs

A. Are always expensed in the same period in which they are incurred.

B. Vary from one period to the next.

C. Remain unchanged over a given period of time.

D. Are associated with the periodic inventory method.

The correct answer is (A). *(CIA, adapted)*

**REQUIRED:** The true statement about period costs.

**DISCUSSION:** Period costs are charged to expense as incurred and not to a particular product. They are not identifiable with a product and are not inventoried. Period costs may be classified as either revenue expenditures or capital expenditures. Revenue expenditures, e.g., advertising and officers' salaries, are charged to the income statement in the period the costs are incurred because they usually do not benefit future periods. Period costs classified as capital expenditures, e.g., depreciation, are initially recorded as assets and then charged to expense as they are consumed, used, or disposed of.

Answer (B) is incorrect because whether a cost varies from period to period does not determine whether it is a period cost or product cost. Answer (C) is incorrect because period costs can be either fixed or variable. Answer (D) is incorrect because the periodic inventory system is a method of maintaining inventory records.

**69.** Which one of the following costs is classified as a period cost?

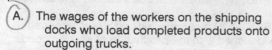

- A. The wages of the workers on the shipping docks who load completed products onto outgoing trucks.
- B. The wages of a worker paid for idle time resulting from a machine breakdown in the molding operation.
- C. The payments for employee (fringe) benefits paid on behalf of the workers in the manufacturing plant.
- D. The wages paid to workers for rework on defective products.

The correct answer is (A). *(CIA, adapted)*

**REQUIRED:** The cost classified as a period cost.

**DISCUSSION:** Period costs are expensed when incurred. They are not inventoriable because they are not sufficiently identifiable with specific production. The wages of the truck loaders are not associated with production and therefore should be classified as a selling expense and period cost.

Answer (B) is incorrect because the cost of idle time is a manufacturing overhead item and thus a product cost. Answer (C) is incorrect because fringe benefits for manufacturing workers are treated as direct labor or manufacturing overhead, both of which are product costs. Answer (D) is incorrect because the cost of rework is a manufacturing overhead item (product cost).

**70.** Which of the following are usually considered period costs?

|  | A | B | C | D |
|---|---|---|---|---|
| Direct labor |  |  | X | X |
| Direct materials |  | X |  | X |
| Sales materials | X | X | X |  |
| Advertising costs | X | X |  |  |
| Indirect factory materials |  |  |  | X |
| Indirect labor |  |  |  | X |
| Sales commissions | X | X | X |  |
| Factory utilities |  | X |  | X |
| Administrative supplies expense | X | X | X |  |
| Administrative labor | X | X | X | X |
| Depreciation on administration building | X | X | X | X |
| Cost of research on customer demographics | X | X | X |  |

- A. A.
- B. B.
- C. C.
- D. D.

The correct answer is (A). *(CIA, adapted)*

**REQUIRED:** The items usually considered period costs.

**DISCUSSION:** Period costs are charged to expense as incurred and not to a particular product. They are not identifiable with a product and are not inventoried. Period costs may be classified as either revenue expenditures or capital expenditures. Revenue expenditures, e.g., advertising and officers' salaries, are charged to the income statement in the period the costs are incurred because they usually do not benefit future periods. Period costs classified as capital expenditures, e.g., depreciation, are initially recorded as assets and then charged to expense as they are consumed, used, or disposed of. Accordingly, all the items listed are period costs except for the direct materials, direct labor, and the factory overhead items.

Answer (B) is incorrect because direct materials and factory utilities are product costs. Answer (C) is incorrect because direct labor is a product cost, and advertising costs are period costs. Answer (D) is incorrect because direct labor, direct materials, indirect factory materials, indirect labor, and factory utilities are product costs. Sales materials and advertising costs, sales commissions, supplies expense, and demographic research are period costs.

**71.** A fixed cost that would be considered a direct cost is

  A.  A cost accountant's salary when the cost object is a unit of product.

  B.  The rental cost of a warehouse to store inventory when the cost object is the Purchasing Department.

  C.  A production supervisor's salary when the cost object is the Production Department.

  D.  Board of directors' fees when the cost object is the Marketing Department.

The correct answer is (C). *(CMA, adapted)*
  **REQUIRED:** The fixed cost that is a direct cost.
  **DISCUSSION:** A direct cost can be specifically associated with a single cost object in an economically feasible way. Thus, a production supervisor's salary can be directly associated with the department (s)he supervises.
  Answer (A) is incorrect because a cost accountant's salary cannot be directly associated with a single product. Cost accountants work with many different products during a pay period. Answer (B) is incorrect because warehouse rent is not directly traceable to the Purchasing Department. Other departments have influence over the level of inventories stored. Answer (D) is incorrect because directors' fees cannot be directly associated with the Marketing Department. Directors provide benefits to all departments within a corporation.

**72.** In a traditional manufacturing operation, direct costs normally include

  A.  Machine repairs in an automobile factory.

  B.  Electricity in an electronics plant.

  C.  Wood in a furniture factory.

  D.  Commissions paid to sales personnel.

The correct answer is (C). *(CIA, adapted)*
  **REQUIRED:** The direct cost in a traditional manufacturing operation.
  **DISCUSSION:** Direct costs are readily identifiable with and attributable to specific units of production. Wood is a raw material (a direct cost) of furniture.
  Answer (A) is incorrect because machine repairs are usually treated as an overhead (indirect) cost. Answer (B) is incorrect because electricity is an overhead (indirect) cost. Answer (D) is incorrect because sales commissions are period costs. They are neither direct nor indirect costs of products.

**73.** For product costing purposes, the cost of production overtime caused by equipment failure that represents idle time plus the overtime premium should be classified as a(n)

  A.  Indirect cost.

  B.  Direct cost.

  C.  Controllable cost.

  D.  Discretionary cost.

The correct answer is (A). *(CIA, adapted)*
  **REQUIRED:** The classification of the cost of production overtime caused by equipment failure.
  **DISCUSSION:** Indirect cost is not directly traceable to specific units of production. It is a component of overhead. The overtime premium (the excess of the overtime pay rate over the regular rate, multiplied by total overtime hours) and idle time are considered indirect costs and overhead because their occurrence usually results from an abnormal volume of work and is thus borne by all units produced.
  Answer (B) is incorrect because the overtime premium (even for direct labor) and idle time are indirect costs. Answer (C) is incorrect because controllable cost is not relevant to product costing per se, but to responsibility accounting. Answer (D) is incorrect because discretionary costs, such as advertising, are period costs.

**74.** The salary of the line supervisor in the assembly division of an automobile company should be included in

  A.  Conversion costs.

  B.  Opportunity costs.

  C.  General and administrative costs.

  D.  Prime costs.

The correct answer is (A). *(CIA, adapted)*
  **REQUIRED:** The costs in which the salary of a line supervisor in the assembly division should be included.
  **DISCUSSION:** Conversion costs include direct labor and factory overhead. They are the costs of converting raw materials into finished products. Factory overhead normally includes indirect labor expense, supplies expense, and other production facility expenses, such as plant depreciation and plant supervisors' salaries. The line supervisor's salary is a factory overhead cost and should be included in conversion costs.
  Answer (B) is incorrect because opportunity cost is the profit forgone by making one decision rather than another. Answer (C) is incorrect because general and administrative costs are period costs and not inventoriable or identifiable with a particular product. Answer (D) is incorrect because prime costs, e.g., direct labor and material, are directly traceable to specific units of production.

**75.** Indirect materials are a

| | Conversion Cost | Manufacturing Cost | Prime Cost |
|---|---|---|---|
| A. | Yes | Yes | Yes |
| B. | Yes | Yes | No |
| C. | No | Yes | Yes |
| D. | No | No | No |

The correct answer is (B). *(J.W. Ferry)*

**REQUIRED:** The classification of indirect material cost.

**DISCUSSION:** Indirect materials are a manufacturing cost and a conversion cost. Indirect materials constitute a manufacturing cost that cannot be directly identified with a specific unit of production and is therefore a part of manufacturing overhead. Conversion cost consists of direct labor and factory overhead, but not direct materials (the direct materials are being converted). Prime cost consists of direct materials and direct labor.

Answer (A) is incorrect because indirect materials are not a prime cost. Answer (C) is incorrect because indirect materials are a conversion cost but not a prime cost. Answer (D) is incorrect because indirect materials are a conversion cost and a manufacturing cost.

**76.** The fixed portion of the semivariable cost of electricity for a manufacturing plant is a

| | Conversion Cost | Product Cost |
|---|---|---|
| A. | No | No |
| B. | No | Yes |
| C. | Yes | Yes |
| D. | Yes | No |

The correct answer is (C). *(CPA, adapted)*

**REQUIRED:** The classification(s) of fixed electricity cost for a manufacturer.

**DISCUSSION:** Electricity costs in a manufacturing plant are a part of manufacturing overhead. Manufacturing overhead is both a conversion cost and a product cost.

Answer (A) is incorrect because the fixed portion of a semivariable cost is a conversion cost and a product cost. Answer (B) is incorrect because the fixed portion of a semivariable cost is also a conversion cost. Answer (D) is incorrect because the fixed portion of a semivariable cost is also a product cost.

**77.** The wages of the factory janitorial staff should be classified as

A. Factory overhead cost.

B. Direct labor cost.

C. Period cost.

D. Prime cost.

The correct answer is (A). *(CIA, adapted)*

**REQUIRED:** The classification of the wages of the factory janitorial staff.

**DISCUSSION:** Factory overhead normally includes indirect labor expense, supplies expense, and other production facility expenses, such as plant depreciation, taxes, and plant supervisors' salaries. It includes all manufacturing costs except for direct materials and direct labor. Janitorial costs are not directly traceable to specific units of production; thus, they are indirect labor costs included in fixed factory overhead and are inventoried as a product cost.

Answer (B) is incorrect because direct labor costs are directly traceable to specific units of production. Answer (C) is incorrect because period costs are any costs that are not inventoriable. Answer (D) is incorrect because prime costs are direct labor and materials costs.

## 1.6 Professional Responsibility

**78.** Sheila is a management accountant who has discovered that her company is violating environmental regulations. If her immediate superior is involved, her appropriate action is to

A. Do nothing because she has a duty of loyalty to the organization.

B. Consult the audit committee.

C. Present the matter to the next higher managerial level.

D. Confront her immediate superior.

The correct answer is (C). *(Publisher)*

**REQUIRED:** The proper action when the accountant's immediate superior is involved in an ethical problem.

**DISCUSSION:** To resolve an ethical problem, the accountant's first step is usually to consult his/her immediate superior. If that individual is involved, the matter should be taken to the next higher level of management.

Answer (A) is incorrect because "management accountants have an obligation to the organizations they serve, their profession, the public, and themselves to maintain the highest standards of ethical conduct." Answer (B) is incorrect because the audit committee would be consulted first only if it were the next higher managerial level. Answer (D) is incorrect because, if the superior is involved, the next higher managerial level should be consulted first.

**79.** Integrity is an ethical requirement for all management accountants. One aspect of integrity requires

   A. Performance of professional duties in accordance with applicable laws.

   B. Avoidance of conflict of interest.

   C. Refraining from improper use of inside information.

   D. Maintenance of an appropriate level of professional competence.

The correct answer is (B). *(Publisher)*

   **REQUIRED:** The aspect of the integrity requirement.

   **DISCUSSION:** According to the IMA Code of Ethics, management accountants must "avoid actual or apparent conflicts of interest and advise all appropriate parties of any potential conflict."

   Answers (A) and (D) are incorrect because performance of professional duties in accordance with applicable laws and maintenance of an appropriate level of professional competence are aspects of the competence requirement. Answer (C) is incorrect because refraining from improper use of inside information is an aspect of the confidentiality requirement.

**80.** Under the express terms of the IMA Code of Ethics, a management accountant may not

   A. Advertise.

   B. Encroach on the practice of another management accountant.

   C. Disclose confidential information unless authorized or legally obligated.

   D. Accept other employment while serving as a management accountant.

The correct answer is (C). *(Publisher)*

   **REQUIRED:** The action explicitly proscribed by the IMA Code of Ethics.

   **DISCUSSION:** Management accountants may not disclose confidential information acquired in the course of their work unless authorized or legally obligated to do so. They must inform subordinates about the confidentiality of information and monitor their activities to maintain that confidentiality. Moreover, management accountants should avoid even the appearance of using confidential information to their unethical or illegal advantage.

   Answers (A) and (B) are incorrect because the ethics code does not address advertising and encroachment. Answer (D) is incorrect because other employment may be accepted unless it constitutes a conflict of interest.

**81.** Which ethical standard is most clearly violated if a management accountant knows of a problem that could mislead users but does nothing about it?

   A. Competence.

   B. Legality.

   C. Objectivity.

   D. Confidentiality.

The correct answer is (C). *(Publisher)*

   **REQUIRED:** The ethical standard most clearly violated when a management accountant does nothing about information that is misleading to users.

   **DISCUSSION:** Objectivity is the fourth part of the IMA Code of Ethics. It requires that information be communicated "fairly and objectively" and that all information that could reasonably influence users be fully disclosed.

   Answer (A) is incorrect because the competence standard pertains to the management accountant's responsibility to maintain his/her professional skills and knowledge. It also pertains to the performance of activities in a professional manner. Answer (B) is incorrect because legality is not addressed in the IMA Code of Ethics. Answer (D) is incorrect because the confidentiality standard concerns the management accountant's responsibility not to disclose or use the firm's confidential information.

**82.** The IMA Code of Ethics includes an integrity standard, which requires the management accountant to

A.   Identify and make known anything that may hinder his/her judgment or prevent satisfactory completion of any duties.

B.   Report any relevant information that could influence users of financial statements.

C.   Disclose confidential information when authorized by his/her firm or required under the law.

D.   Refuse gifts from anyone.

The correct answer is (A). *(Publisher)*
**REQUIRED:** The action required of the management accountant by the integrity standard.
**DISCUSSION:** One of the responsibilities of the management accountant under the integrity standard is to "recognize and communicate professional limitations or other constraints that would preclude responsible judgment or successful performance of an activity."
Answer (B) is incorrect because the objectivity standard requires the management accountant to "disclose fully all relevant information that could reasonably be expected to influence an intended user's understanding of the reports, comments, and recommendations presented." Answer (C) is incorrect because the confidentiality standard requires the accountant to "refrain from disclosing confidential information acquired in the course of his/her work except when authorized, unless legally obligated to do so." Answer (D) is incorrect because the integrity standard requires the accountant to "refuse any gift, favor, or hospitality that would influence or would appear to influence his/her actions."

**83.** The IMA Code of Ethics includes a competence standard, which requires the management accountant to

A.   Report information, whether favorable or unfavorable.

B.   Develop his/her accounting proficiency on a continual basis.

C.   Discuss ethical conflicts and possible courses of action with an unbiased counselor.

D.   Discuss, with subordinates, their responsibilities regarding the disclosure of information about the firm.

The correct answer is (B). *(Publisher)*
**REQUIRED:** The action required of the management accountant by the competence standard.
**DISCUSSION:** One of the responsibilities of the management accountant under the competence standard is to "maintain an appropriate level of professional competence by ongoing development of his/her knowledge and skills."
Answer (A) is incorrect because the integrity standard requires the management accountant to "communicate unfavorable as well as favorable information and professional judgments or opinions." Answer (C) is incorrect because one of the suggestions from the "Resolution of Ethical Conflict" paragraph is to "clarify relevant concepts by confidential discussion with an objective advisor to obtain an understanding of possible courses of action." Answer (D) is incorrect because the confidentiality standard requires the accountant to "inform subordinates as appropriate regarding the confidentiality of information acquired in the course of their work and monitor their activities to assure the maintenance of that confidentiality."

# CHAPTER TWO
# ACTIVITY-BASED COSTING

**Activity-based costing (ABC)** may be used by manufacturing, service, or retailing entities and in job-order or process costing systems.  It has been popularized because of the rapid advance of technology, which has led to a significant increase in the incurrence of indirect costs and a consequent need for more accurate cost assignment.  However, developments in computer and related technology (such as bar coding) also allow management to obtain better and more timely information at relatively low cost.  ABC is one means of improving a cost system to avoid what has been called **peanut-butter costing**.  Inaccurately averaging or spreading costs like peanut butter over products or service units that use different amounts of resources results in **product-cost cross-subsidization**.  This term describes the condition in which the miscosting of one product causes the miscosting of other products.  In a traditional system, direct labor and direct materials are traced to products or service units, a single pool of costs (overhead) is accumulated for a given organizational unit, and these costs are then assigned using an allocative rather than a tracing procedure.  The effect is an averaging of costs that may result in significant inaccuracy when products or service units do not use similar amounts of resources.

To improve its costing system, an organization can attempt to identify as many direct costs as economically feasible.  It can also increase the number of separate pools for costs not directly attributable to cost objects.  Each of these pools should be homogeneous; that is, each should consist of costs that have substantially similar relationships with the driver or other base used for assignment to cost objects.  Thus, choosing the appropriate base, preferably one with a driver or cause-and-effect relationship (a high correlation) between the demands of the cost object and the costs in the pool, is another way to improve a costing system.

ABC attempts to improve costing by assigning costs to activities rather than to an organizational unit.  Accordingly, ABC requires identification of the activities that consume resources and that are subject to demands by ultimate cost objects.  Design of an ABC system starts with **process value analysis**, a comprehensive understanding of how an organization generates its output.  It involves a determination of which activities that use resources are **value-adding** or **nonvalue-adding** and how the latter may be reduced or eliminated.  This linkage of product costing and continuous improvement of processes is **activity-based management (ABM)**.  It encompasses driver analysis, activity analysis, and performance measurement.

Once an ABC system has been designed, costs may be assigned to the identified activities, costs of related activities that can be reassigned using the same driver or other base are combined in **homogeneous cost pools**, and an overhead rate is calculated for each pool. The next step, as in traditional methods, is to assign costs to ultimate cost objects. In other words, cost assignment is a two-stage process: First, costs are accumulated for an activity based on the resources it can be directly observed to use and on the resources it can be assumed to use based on its consumption of **resource drivers** (factors that cause changes in the costs of an activity); second, costs are reassigned to ultimate cost objects on the basis of **activity drivers** (factors measuring the demands made on activities). In ABC, these objects may include not only products and services but also customers, distribution channels, or other objects for which activity and resource costs may be accumulated.

An essential element of ABC is **driver analysis** that emphasizes the search for (1) the cause-and-effect relationship between an activity and its consumption of resources and (2) an activity and the demands made on it by a cost object. For this purpose, activities and their drivers have been classified in accounting literature as follows: (1) unit-level, (2) batch-level, (3) product-level, and (4) facility-level. **Unit-level** (volume-related) activities occur when a unit is produced, e.g., direct labor and direct materials activities. **Batch-level** activities occur when a batch of units is produced, e.g., ordering, setup, or materials handling. **Product- or service-level** (product- or service-sustaining) activities provide support of different kinds to different types of output, e.g., engineering changes, inventory management, or testing. **Facility-level** (facility-sustaining) activities concern overall operations, e.g., management of the physical plant, personnel administration, or security arrangements.

Using this model, activities are grouped by level, and drivers are determined for the activities. At the unit level, examples of drivers are direct labor hours or dollars, machine hours, and units of output. At the batch level, drivers may include number or duration of setups, orders processed, number of receipts, weight of materials handled, or number of inspections. At the product level, drivers may include design time, testing time, number of engineering change orders, or number of categories of parts. At the facility level, drivers may include any of those used at the first three levels. Within each grouping of activities, the cost pools for activities that can use the same driver are combined into homogeneous cost pools. In contrast, traditional systems assign costs largely on the basis of unit-level drivers.

A difficulty in applying ABC is that, whereas the first three levels of activities pertain to specific products or services, facility-level activities do not. Thus, facility-level costs are not accurately assignable to products. The theoretically sound solution may be to treat these costs as **period costs**. Nevertheless, organizations that apply ABC ordinarily assign them to products to obtain a full absorption cost suitable for external financial reporting in accordance with GAAP.

As the foregoing discussion indicates, an advantage of ABC is that overhead costs are accumulated in multiple cost pools related to activities instead of in a single pool for a department, process, plant, or company. ABC also is more likely than a traditional system to assign costs to activities and reassign them to ultimate cost objects using a base that is highly correlated with the resources consumed by activities or with the demands placed on activities by cost objects. Furthermore, process value analysis provides information for eliminating or reducing nonvalue-adding activities (e.g., scheduling production, moving components, waiting for the next operating step, inspecting output, or storing inventories). The result is therefore not only more accurate cost assignments, especially of overhead, but also better cost control and more efficient operations. A disadvantage of ABC is that it is costly to implement because of the more detailed information required. Another disadvantage is that ABC-based costs of products or services may not conform with GAAP; for example, ABC may assign research costs to products but not such traditional product costs as plant depreciation, insurance, or taxes.

Organizations most likely to benefit from using ABC are those with (1) products or services that vary significantly in volume, diversity of activities, and complexity of operations; (2) relatively high overhead costs; or (3) operations that have undergone major technological or design changes. However, service organizations may have some difficulty in implementing ABC because they tend to have relatively high levels of facility-level costs that are difficult to assign to specific service units. They also engage in many nonuniform human activities for which information is not readily accumulated. Furthermore, output measurement is more problematic in service than in manufacturing entities. Nevertheless, ABC has been adopted by various insurers, banks, railroads, and health care providers.

This chapter summary concludes with a glossary of activity accounting terms that we have developed with the assistance of Mr. Gary Cokins, CPIM, Director of Industry Relations for ABC Technologies, Inc. It provides a coherent and comprehensive set of terms for ABC. However, readers should understand that textbook usage in this field is nonstandard. Accordingly, this book attempts to provide a sense of the range of terminology used in practice. For more information, please feel free to contact Mr. Cokins:

Gary Cokins, CPIM
garyc@abctech.com
www.abctech.com
ABC Technologies Inc.
503-617-7100 ext. 328

# GLOSSARY

**ABC** See *activity-based costing*.

**ABC model** A one-time translation of resource costs consumed through work activities and traced to products, services, customers, or internal needs.

**ABC visualization** A visual and usually manual diagraming technique that maps the ABC cost flow data and assignment paths. Aids modeler by giving a high level view.

**Action verb** A description of an activity worded such that employees can clearly relate to the work described. The verb is usually followed by an adjective and noun.

**Activity** Work actions performed by people or equipment, using supplies, technology, and environment, within an organization. Activities are usually described by the "action verb-adjective-noun" grammar convention.

**Activity analysis** The identification and cataloging of activities in an organization for detailed analysis of the activities' efficiency and effectiveness. Activity analysis involves determining what activities are done within a department, how many people perform the activities, how much time they spend performing the activities, what resources are required to perform the activities, what operational data best reflect the performance of the activities, and what value the activity has for the organization. Activity analysis is accomplished by means of interviews, questionnaires, observation, and review of physical records of work.

**Activity attributes** Characteristics of activities. Attributes can be organized, sorted, or summarized according to the attribute categories. For example, a measure of the elapsed time required to complete an activity is an attribute. (See *cost driver* and *performance measures*.)

**Activity capacity** The demonstrated or expected capacity of an activity under normal operating conditions, assuming a specified set of resources and a long time period. An example of this would be a rate of output for an activity expressed as 500 cycles per hour.

**Activity center** A pool of the costs of two or more activities.

**Activity cost assignment** The process in which the cost of activities are attached to cost objects using activity drivers. (See *cost object* and *activity cost driver*.)

**Activity cost driver** (second-stage cost driver) The best single measure of the frequency and intensity of the demands placed on activities by intermediate and final cost objects. It is used to reassign activity costs to cost objects. It represents a line item on the bill of activities for a product or customer. An example is the number of part numbers, which is used to measure the consumption of material-related activities by each product, material type, or component. The number of customer orders measures the consumption of order-entry activities by each customer. Sometimes an activity driver is used as an indicator of the output of an activity, such as the number of purchase orders prepared by the purchasing activity. (See *intensity*, *cost object*, and *bill of activities*.)

**Activity cost pool** A grouping of all cost elements associated with an activity. (See *cost element*.)

**Activity dictionary** A listing and description of generic activities. It can include activity, activity description, business process, function source, whether value-added, inputs, outputs, supplier, customer, output measures, and cost drivers.

**Activity driver analysis** The identification and evaluation of the activity drivers used to trace the cost of activities to cost objects. Activity driver analysis may also involve selecting activity drivers with a potential for cost reduction. (See *Pareto analysis*.)

**Activity level** A description of how an activity is used by a cost object or other activity. Some activity levels describe the cost object that uses the activity and the nature of this use. These levels include activities that are traceable to the product (i.e., unit-level, batch-level, and product-level costs), to the customer (customer-level costs), to a market (market-level costs), to a distribution channel (channel-level costs), and to a project, such as a research and development project (project-level costs).

**Activity sequence-sensitive** The calculation of time-based process costs taking into consideration the sequential relationships among activities.

**Activity-based budgeting (ABB)** An approach to budgeting that involves quantitative expression of the activities/business processes of the organization reflecting forecasts of workload (quantity of drivers) and other financial requirements to achieve strategic goals or planned changes to improve performance.

**Activity-based cost system** In contrast with an ABC model, which is a single snapshot or time-slice (period) of cost, a system maintains currency of data and processes financial and operating data on an organization's resources, activities, drivers, objects, and measures.

**Activity-based costing (ABC)** A method that measures the cost consumption rates and performance of process-related activities and their outputs (cost objects). It assigns the costs to activities based on the activities' use of resources, and reassigns activity cost to cost objects. ABC assigns activity costs to cost objects (outputs) based on the cost objects' proportional use of activities. ABC recognizes the causal relationship of cost drivers with activities.

**Activity-based management (ABM)** A discipline focusing on the management of activities within business processes as the route to continuously improve both the value received by customers and the profit earned by providing this value. Causes of activities are identified, measured, and used along with other activity information for performance evaluation. ABC draws on ABC data as a major source for information. A formal management system that compels employees to understand how they contribute to achieving strategic objectives; influences changes to emulate best practices; and supports continuous improvement.

**Actual cost** Costs measured by historical resource consumption.

**Allocation** (1) The calculation of the cost of a cost object without using physical observation or a cause-and-effect basis, or (2) A process of assigning cost to an activity or cost object when a direct measure does not exist. For example, assigning the cost of power to a machine activity by means of machine hours is an allocation because machine hours are an indirect measure of power consumption. In some cases, allocations can be converted to tracings by incurring additional measurement costs. Instead of using machine hours to allocate power consumption, for example, a company can place a power meter on machines to measure actual power consumption. (See *tracing*.)

**Assignment path, cost** The link between a cost and one of its two or more cost objects.

**Attributes** Characteristics of activities, such as cost drivers and performance measures. (See *cost driver* and *performance measure*.)

**Attribution** See *tracing*.

**Backflush costing** A costing method that first focuses on the throughput or output quantities of an organization, and then works backward using historical rates or balances to determine input and output quantities, cost of goods sold, and inventories. (Backflushing can occur at intermediate stages as well as for finished goods.) These quantities are usually costed using standard costs. The process assumes that the bill of material (or bill of activities) and the standard costs at the time of backflushing represent the actual quantities and resources used in the manufacture of the product. This is important, because no shop orders are usually maintained to collect costs. (2) A costing method usually associated with repetitive manufacturing. (See *repetitive manufacturing* in this glossary and *standard costs* in Chapter 1.)

**Benchmarking** (competitive benchmarking, best practices) A methodology that identifies an activity as the benchmark by which a similar activity will be judged. This methodology is used to assist in identifying a process or technique that can increase the effectiveness or efficiency of an activity. The source may be internal (e.g., taken from another part of the company) or external (e.g., taken from a competitor). Another term used is *competitive benchmarking*.

**Bill of activities** A listing of the activities and activity volumes and associated costs required by a product, service, process output, or other cost object.

**Bottleneck** An activity for which the work required equals or exceeds the capacity of the activity.

**Budget** A financial plan of an organization's commitment to planned activities, resource consumption, and resource use.

**Business intelligence** Using cost and related data to better understand activity behavior, define problems, draw conclusions, make recommendations, and take actions.

**Business process** See *process*.

**Capacity** The total resource cost available for consumption by activities. The ability of an activity/business process to produce output.

**Capacity cost** The fixed cost of providing the ability to operate at a particular level of output. The cost is unaffected by the actual output achieved.

**Capital decay** (1) A quantification of the lost revenues or reduction in net cash flows sustained by an entity due to obsolete technology. (2) A measure of noncompetitiveness.

**Carrying cost** See *holding cost*.

**Closed system** An enterprise-wide scope of organization resource costs that are all reassigned through activities to final cost objects.

**Constraint-based costing** A method that assigns resource costs to products and services based on the existence and location of a capacity constraint. Often governed by revenue maximization, implying that pricing is combined with costing.

**Continuous improvement program** A program to eliminate waste, reduce response time, simplify the design of both products and processes, and improve quality.

**Cost** A financial measure of resources sacrificed, consumed, or forgone to achieve an objective. A measure of the effect of a cost driver.

**Cost allocation** See *allocation*.

**Cost assignment** The tracing or allocation of resources to activities or cost objects. (See *allocation* and *tracing*.) The 1998 draft defines cost assignment more narrowly as the tracing of cost to cost objects (to other resources, activities, or final cost objects) using causal-based cost drivers. Thus, the 1998 draft treats assignment and tracing as synonyms. However, throughout this book, assignment is used as a broad term encompassing both allocation and tracing.

**Cost driver** Any factor or event that causes a change in the consumption of a resource o activity cost. Cost drivers are used to trace and reassign costs to cost objects in direct proportion to the object's cost consumption. Drivers themselves may have drivers. (See *operational cost driver*, *transaction volume cost driver*, *100% apportioned cost driver*, *surrogate cost driver*, and *weighted cost driver*.)

**Cost driver analysis** The examination, quantification, and explanation of the effects of cost drivers. The results are often used for continuous improvement programs to reduce throughput times, improve quality, and reduce cost.

**Cost element** The most disaggregated level of resource cost. For example, power cost, engineering cost, and depreciation may be cost elements in the activity cost pool for a machine activity. (See *activity cost pool*, *bill of activities*, and *resource costs*.)

**Cost management** The management and control of activities to help set enterprise strategies and to determine an accurate product and service cost, improve business processes, eliminate waste, identify cost drivers, and plan operations.

**Cost modules** A convention that is used to classify cost by its point of incurrence (resource module), its use (activity module), and its ultimate user (final cost object module). Activities also feed a Process Module.

**Cost object** (cost receiver, work object) Any activity, customer, product, service, contract, project, process output, or other work unit for which a separate cost measurement is desired. An intermediate cost object consists of the outputs of an activity that will have additional work done on them before they are delivered to an external customer or cost receiver. A final cost object consists of organizational outputs such as "end-of-the-line" external customers or finished salable parts, products, or services usually associated with a sales invoice. However, they can also be within the processes. A family cost object is a group of cost objects (e.g., products, customers) that have a defined relationship with each other. A base service cost object is, in a service industry, the standard service that does not differ between customers. Non-standard portions of the service are customer-specific.

**Cost pool** A group of costs.

**Cross-subsidy** The improper assignment of costs among cost objects such that certain cost objects are overcosted while other cost objects are undercosted relative to the activity costs assigned. For example, traditional cost accounting systems tend to overcost high-volume products and undercost low-volume products.

**Customer profitability analysis** Analyzing the profit generated for an organization by each of the customers of the organization.

**Customer value** The difference between customer realization and sacrifice. *Realization* is what the customer receives, which includes product features, quality, and service. This takes into account the customer's cost to use, maintain, and dispose of the product or service. *Sacrifice* is what the customer gives up, which includes the amount the customer pays for the product plus time and effort spent acquiring the product and learning how to use it. Maximizing customer value means maximizing the difference between realization and sacrifice.

**Cumulative activity cost** The cost of two or more activities added together. The build-up of activity costs so that each successive total includes activity costs that precede it.

**Cycle time** The time required to produce and deliver a product or service.

**Cycle time compression** Reducing the time required to produce and deliver a product or service, in order to increase throughput and become more flexible and responsive to customers.

**Differential cost** See *incremental cost*.

**Design for ____ilities** Designing a product or service for manufacturability (DFM), repairability, and serviceability. It assumes that problems with cost and quality stem from poor initial design.

**Direct cost** A cost (resource or activity) that is traced directly to an activity, an intermediate activity, or a cost object. The basis for assigning is cause-and-effect related. A cost that can be physically, easily, and accurately traced to a cost object. For example, the material issued to a particular work order and the engineering time devoted to a specific product are direct costs to the work orders or products. (See *tracing*.)

**Direct tracing** See *tracing*.

**Discounted cash flow** A technique used to evaluate the future cash flows generated by a capital investment. Discounted cash flow is computed by discounting cash flows to determine their present value.

**Diversity** Conditions in which cost objects place different demands on activities, activities place different demands on resources, or processes place different demands on resources. This situation arises, for example, when there is a difference in mix or volume of products that causes an uneven assignment of costs. Different types of diversity include: *batch size, customer, market, product mix, distribution channel,* and *volume.*

**Diversity segmentation** Recognizing varying levels of demand by using cost drivers.

**Employee empowerment** Placing the authority to make critical decisions with those closest to the problem, for example, those in the work area directly affected.

**Enterprise resource planning (ERP)** A method for the translation of an order planning, production, and logistics schedule into the necessary components, parts, material, machines, and people capacities.

**First-stage allocation** See *resource cost assignment.*

**Fixed cost** (1) A cost that in total does not fluctuate with the level of activity within the relevant range in a given period. (2) A resource cost or activity cost that does not vary with changes in the volume of cost drivers. The depreciation of a machine, for example, may be direct to a particular activity, but it is fixed with respect to changes in the number of units of the activity driver. The designation of a cost element as fixed or variable may vary depending on the time frame of the decision in question and the extent to which the volume of production, activity drivers, or cost drivers changes.

**Flexible factory** The objective of a flexible factory is to provide a wide range of services across many product lines in a timely manner. An example is a fabrication plant with several integrated manufacturing cells that can perform many functions for unrelated product lines with relatively short lead times.

**Focused factory** The objective of a focused factory is to organize around a specific set of resources to provide low cost and high throughput over a narrow range of products.

**Forcing** Allocating the costs of a sustaining activity to a cost object even though that cost object may not clearly consume or causally relate to that activity. Allocating a plant-level activity (such as heating) to product units using an activity driver such as direct labor hours, for example, forces the cost of this activity to the product. (See *sustaining activity cost.*)

**Functional decomposition** Identifies the activities performed in the organization. It yields a hierarchical representation of the organization and shows the relationship between the different levels of the organization and its activities. For example, a hierarchy may start with the division and move down through the plant, function, process, activity, and task levels.

**Granularity** Decomposition, e.g., of an activity or process.

**Heterogeneity** See *diversity segmentation.*

**Hierarchy of cost** An approach to group activity costs as they vary with external end-unit volume, internal volumes, batch-related volumes, and cost object diversity-sensitivity.

**Holding cost** The cost of retaining an asset, such as finished goods inventory or a building. May also include an imputed cost of capital expense. Generally, the calculation includes a cost of capital in addition to other costs such as insurance, taxes, and space.

**Homogeneity** Cost of an activity that has a similar cause-and-effect relationship with a cost object. Occurs when all the cost elements in an activity's cost pool are consumed in the same proportion by all cost objects. (See *cost element, activity cost pool,* and *activity cost driver.*)

**Implementation, bottom up approach** An approach to implementing ABC with emphasis on achieving operational improvements. Activities and cost objects are disaggregated for high resolution; accuracy requirements are high.

**Implementation, top down approach** An approach to implementing ABC with emphasis on achieving quick strategic results. Activities and cost objects are grouped with less resolution; accuracy requirements are not high.

**Incremental cost** (1) The cost associated with increasing the output of an activity or project above some base level. (2) The additional cost associated with selecting one economic or business alternative over another, such as the difference between working overtime or subcontracting the work. (3) The cost associated with increasing the quantity of a cost driver. (Also known as *differential cost.*)

**Indirect cost** A cost that cannot be easily traced to a cost object. For example, the costs of supervision or heat may be allocated to an activity on the basis of direct labor hours. (See *allocation.*)

**Insourcing** The opposite of outsourcing.

**Intensity** The cost consumed by each unit of the activity driver. It is assumed that the intensity of each unit of the activity driver for a single activity is equal. Unequal intensity means that the activity should be broken into smaller activities or that a different activity driver should be chosen. (See *diversity.*)

**Lead time** The amount of time between the request for material or parts and their receipt.

**Life cycle costing** Forecasting and measuring revenues with costs for a product or service over the life of that product or service (which will span multiple ABC time-slice periods).

**Multi-step cost reassignment** A reassignment of resource costs requiring one or more intermediate activity cost reassignments prior to cost assignment into the final cost objects.

**Nodal cost flow network** A network view of ABC in which the sources of the cost reassignments and downstream cost objects are thought of as "sending" and "receiving" nodes in a closed-system network.

**Non-value-added activity** An activity that is considered not to contribute to customer value or to the organization's needs. The designation "non-value-added" reflects a belief that the activity can be redesigned, reduced, or eliminated without reducing the quantity, responsiveness, or quality of the output required by the customer or the organization. (See *customer value* and *value analysis*.)

**Obsolescence** A product or service that has lost its value to the customer due to changes in need or technology.

**Operational cost driver** A higher order driver of an activity cost driver. Usually thought of as the driver of a business process.

**Outsourcing** Deciding to buy a product or service from a supplier rather than producing the product or providing the service within the organization.

**Pareto analysis** An analysis that measures the frequency of various types of defects. It shows how the majority of the impact is caused by a minority of the causal events. It is the identification and interpretation of significant factors using Pareto's rule that 20 percent of a set of independent variables is responsible for 80 percent of the result. Pareto analysis can be used to identify cost drivers or activity drivers that are responsible for the majority of cost incurred by ranking the cost drivers in order of value. (See *cost driver analysis* and *activity driver analysis*.)

**Performance measures** Indicators of the work performed and the results achieved in an activity, process, or organizational unit. Performance measures may be financial or nonfinancial. An example of a performance measure of an activity is the number of defective parts per million. An example of a performance measure of an organizational unit is return on sales.

**Process** (business process) A sequence or arterial network of logically related and time-based work activities structured to provide a specific output for an internal or external customer. For example, the assembly of a television set or the paying of a bill or claim entails several linked activities.

**Process cost** A cost assigned to a business process based on the cost of the activities that compose the process.

**Process mapping** A method of graphically displaying how processes are related to each other.

**Process-based management** Managing business processes to achieve a desired result.

**Product family** A group of products or services that have a defined relationship because of physical and production similarities. (The term *product line* is used interchangeably.)

**Product life cycle** The period that starts with the initial product specification and ends with the withdrawal of the product from the marketplace. A product life cycle is characterized by certain defined stages, including research, development, introduction, maturity, decline, and abandonment.

**Product line** See *product family*.

**Product/service cost** A cost that is assigned to the product or base service and expensed when the product or service is sold.

**Profitability object** The level cost accumulation at which revenues are matched to cost consumption to analyze profitability.

**Project** A planned undertaking, usually related to a specific activity, such as the research and development of a new product or the redesign of the layout of a plant.

**Project costing** A cost system that collects information on activities and costs associated with a specific activity, project, or program.

**Reengineering** The radical redesign of a process, product, or service (in contrast with incremental improvements) intended to simplify them in order to increase responsiveness to customers.

**Repetitive manufacturing** The manufacture of identical products (or a family of products) in a continuous flow.

**Resource costs** The costs of economic elements or inputs used to perform activities. They include people's salaries as well as the cost of materials, supplies, equipment, technologies, and facilities. (See *cost element*.)

**Resource cost assignment** The process by which cost is attached to activities. The process requires the assignment of cost from general ledger accounts to activities using resource drivers. For example, the chart of accounts may list information services at a plant level. It then becomes necessary to trace (assuming that tracing is practical) or to allocate (when tracing is not practical) the cost of information services to the activities that benefit from the information services by means of appropriate resource drivers. It may be necessary to set up intermediate activity cost pools to accumulate related costs from various resources before the assignment can be made. (See *activity cost pool* and *resource cost driver*.)

**Resource cost driver** (first-stage, initial, or zero-stage cost driver) The best single measure of the quantity of resources consumed by an activity. An example of a resource driver is the percentage of total square feet occupied by an activity. This factor is used to allocate a portion of the cost of operating the facilities to the activity.

**Responsibility accounting** An accounting method that focuses on identifying persons or organizational units that are accountable for the performance of revenue or expense plans.

**Risk** The subjective assessment of the possible positive or negative consequences of a current or future action. In a business sense, risk is the premium asked or paid for engaging in an investment or venture. Often, risk is incorporated into business decisions through such factors as cost of capital, hurdle rates, or the interest premium paid over a prevailing base interest rate.

**Root cause analysis** Identification of the underlying cause(s) of specific areas of deficiency in business processes.

**Second-stage allocation** See *activity cost assignment*.

**Sequentiality** Recognition that activity costs are governed by a logical order that mirrors how work is performed.

**Step fixed costs** A resource cost or activity cost that varies in discrete steps with changes in the volume of cost drivers.

**Subsequent activity** An activity that receives service from another activity.

**Sunk costs** Costs that have been invested in assets for which there is little (if any) alternative or continued value except salvage. Using sunk costs as a basis for evaluating alternatives may lead to incorrect decisions. Examples are the invested cost in a scrapped part or the cost of an obsolete machine.

**Supply chain management** Managing the "virtual" enterprise composed of suppliers and customers. Collaborative behavior will lead to streamlined business processes and mutual benefits.

**Support costs** Costs of activities not directly associated with production. Examples are the costs of process engineering and purchasing.

**Surrogate activity driver** An activity driver that is not descriptive of an activity, but that is closely correlated to the performance of the activity. The use of a surrogate activity driver should reduce measurement costs without significantly increasing the costing bias. The number of production runs, for example, is not descriptive of the material-disbursing activity, but the number of production runs may be used as an activity driver if material disbursements coincide with production runs.

**Surrogate cost driver** An acceptable substitute for a cost driver. It is used because the driver cannot be easily measured.

**Sustaining activity cost** Cost of an activity that benefits the organization but is not caused by any specific supplier, product, service, or customer cost object. Examples of such activities are preparation of financial statements, plant management, and support of community programs.

**Target costing** A method used in the analysis of product design that involves estimating a target cost, via a desired profit and sales price, and then designing the product/service to meet that cost. This method precedes Kaizen costing.

**Tasks** Disaggregated activities.

**Technology costs** A category of cost associated with the development, acquisition, implementation, and maintenance of technology assets. It can include costs such as the depreciation of research equipment, tooling amortization, maintenance, and software development.

**Technology valuation** A nontraditional approach to valuing technology acquisitions that may incorporate such elements as purchase price, startup costs, current market value adjustments, and the risk premium of an acquisition.

**Throughput** The rate of production of a defined process over a stated period of time. Rates may be expressed in terms of units of products, batches produced, dollar turnover, or other meaningful measurements.

**Time-based management** Using time as a strategic weapon by identifying market opportunities, responding to customers' needs, and eliminating waste.

**Total cost of ownership (TCO)** Tracing costs to a person or organization responsible for costs related to their designated products, services, and/or customers.

**Traceability** The ability to assign a cost directly to an activity or a cost object in an economically feasible way by means of a causal relationship. (See *tracing*.)

**Tracing** The assignment of cost to an activity or a cost object using an observable measure of the consumption of resources by an activity. Tracing is generally preferred to allocation if the data exist or can be obtained at a reasonable cost. For example, if a company's cost accounting system captures the cost of supplies according to which activities use the supplies, the costs may be traced -- as opposed to allocated -- to the appropriate activities. Tracing is also called *direct tracing*. The 1998 draft also defines cost tracing broadly as the ability to assign a cost to a cost object. Thus, it treats assignment and tracing as synonymous.

**Traditional cost allocations** Allocating indirect costs without using cost drivers. A cause-and-effect relationship may not exist between the cost and the base used for the allocation.

**Transaction-volume cost driver** A type of cost driver that draws on a measurement from a feeder sub-system which not only varies with cost magnitude but proportionately assigns the costs to its cost objects. It yields a per-unit cost.

**Unit cost** The cost associated with a single unit of a product, including direct costs, indirect costs, traced costs, and allocated costs.

**Value-added activity** An activity that is judged to contribute to customer value or satisfy an organizational need. The attribute "value-added" reflects a belief that the activity cannot be eliminated without reducing the quantity, responsiveness, or quality of output required by a customer or organization. (See *customer value*.)

**Value analysis** A method to determine how features of a product or service relate to cost, functionality, appeal, and utility to a customer.

**Value chain** The sequence of activities that convert input into output.

**Value-chain costing** An activity-based cost model (the ABM view) that contains all of the activities in the value-chain (design, procure, produce, market, distribute/render, and post-service a product or service) of one organization.

**Variable cost** (1) A cost that in total fluctuates with the level of activity within the relevant range in a given period. Usually assumed to be constant per unit of activity. (2) A resource cost or activity cost that linearly varies with changes in the volume of cost drivers. The cost of material handling to an activity, for example, varies according to the number of material deliveries and pickups to and from that activity. (See *cost element*, *fixed cost*, and *activity cost driver*.)

**Weighted cost driver** A technique of increasing or decreasing the cost consumption intensity of an individual cost object by weighting the measured quantity of the cost driver.

**Willie Sutton rule** A reminder to focus on the high-cost activities. The rule is named after bank robber Willie Sutton, who -- when asked "why do you rob banks?" -- is reputed to have replied "because that's where the money is."

**Work cell** A physical or logical grouping of resources that performs a defined job or task. The work cell may contain more than one.

**Workflow** A sequence of actions accomplishing a business goal. A toolset to proactively analyze, compress, and automate information-based activities.

**100% apportioned cost driver** A type of cost driver that relies entirely on an informed estimator's judgment of how much cost should be traced to each cost object and to which cost objects. Does not provide rates per unit of the cost driver (for predictive planning).

## 2.1 Activity-Based Costing (ABC)

**1.** Multiple or departmental manufacturing overhead rates are considered preferable to a single or plantwide overhead rate when

    A. Manufacturing is limited to a single product flowing through identical departments in a fixed sequence.

    B. Various products are manufactured that do not pass through the same departments or use the same manufacturing techniques.

    C. Individual cost drivers cannot accurately be determined with respect to cause-and-effect relationships.

    D. The single or plantwide rate is related to several identified cost drivers.

The correct answer is (B). *(CMA, adapted)*
    **REQUIRED:** The situation in which multiple or departmental overhead rates are considered preferable.
    **DISCUSSION:** Multiple rates are appropriate when a process differs substantially among departments or when products do not go through all departments or all processes. The trend in cost accounting is toward activity-based costing (ABC), which divides production into numerous activities and attempts to identify the driver(s) most relevant to each. A driver is a factor that causes changes in a cost. Thus, ABC emphasizes cost assignment based on tracing rather than allocation. The result is a more accurate assignment of costs.
    Answer (A) is incorrect because one rate may be cost beneficial when a single product proceeds through homogeneous processes. Answer (C) is incorrect because multiple rates will not be preferable if they do not result in more accurate costing. Identifying causal relationships between the incurrence of cost and the demands made by cost objects is necessary to improve costing accuracy. Answer (D) is incorrect because, if one rate is related to several cost drivers, it can be used as a surrogate for multiple rates.

**2.** An accounting system that collects financial and operating data on the basis of the underlying nature and extent of the cost drivers is

    A. Activity-based costing.

    B. Target costing.

    C. Delivery cycle time costing.

    D. Variable costing.

The correct answer is (A). *(CMA, adapted)*
    **REQUIRED:** The accounting system that collects data on the basis of cost drivers.
    **DISCUSSION:** An activity-based costing (ABC) system identifies the causal relationship between the incurrence of costs and activities, determines the driver for each activity, and applies costs to products or services on the basis of resources (drivers) consumed.
    Answer (B) is incorrect because target costing determines the maximum allowable cost of a product or service before it is designed or produced; it deducts an acceptable profit margin from a forecasted selling price. Answer (C) is incorrect because delivery cycle time is the period from the time a customer places an order to the time that product or service is delivered. Answer (D) is incorrect because variable costing expenses fixed overhead as incurred.

**3.** Activity-based costing (ABC) has become increasingly more feasible because of technological advances that allow managers to obtain better and more timely information at a relatively low cost. For this reason, a manufacturer is considering using bar-code identification for recording information on parts used by the manufacturer. A reason to use bar codes rather than other means of identification is to ensure that

    A. The movement of all parts is recorded.

    B. The movement of parts is easily and quickly recorded.

    C. Vendors use the same part numbers.

    D. Vendors use the same identification methods.

The correct answer is (B). *(CIA, adapted)*
    **REQUIRED:** The reason to use bar codes.
    **DISCUSSION:** Bar-code scanning is a form of optical character recognition. Bar codes are a series of bars of different widths that represent critical information about the item. They can be read and the information can be instantly recorded using a scanner. Thus, bar coding records the movement of parts with minimal labor costs.
    Answer (A) is incorrect because any identification method may fail to record the movement of some parts. Answer (C) is incorrect because each vendor has its own part-numbering scheme. Answer (D) is incorrect because each vendor has its own identification method, although vendors in the same industry often cooperate to minimize the number of bar-code systems they use.

**4.** Cost drivers are

   A. Activities that cause costs to increase as the activity increases.

   B. Accounting techniques used to control costs.

   C. Accounting measurements used to evaluate whether performance is proceeding according to plan.

   D. A mechanical basis, such as machine hours, computer time, size of equipment, or square footage of factory, used to assign costs to activities.

The correct answer is (A). *(CMA, adapted)*
   **REQUIRED:** The definition of a cost driver.
   **DISCUSSION:** According to SMA 2A, a cost driver is "a measure of activity, such as direct labor hours, machine hours, beds occupied, computer time used, flight hours, miles driven, or contracts, that is a causal factor in the incurrence of cost to an entity." It is a basis used to assign costs to cost objects.
   Answer (B) is incorrect because cost drivers are not controls. Answer (C) is incorrect because cost drivers are measures of activities that cause costs. Answer (D) is incorrect because, although cost drivers may be used to assign costs, they are not necessarily mechanical. For example, a cost driver for pension benefits is employee salaries.

**5.** Process value analysis is a key component of activity-based management that links product costing and

   A. Reduction of the number of cost pools.

   B. Continuous improvement.

   C. Accumulation of heterogeneous cost pools.

   D. Overhead rates based on broad averages.

The correct answer is (B). *(Publisher)*
   **REQUIRED:** The element of process value analysis.
   **DISCUSSION:** Design of an ABC system starts with process value analysis, a comprehensive understanding of how an organization generates its output. It involves a determination of which activities that use resources are value-adding or nonvalue-adding and how the latter may be reduced or eliminated. This linkage of product costing and continuous improvement of processes is activity-based management (ABM). It encompasses driver analysis, activity analysis, and performance measurement.
   Answer (A) is incorrect because ABC tends to increase the number of cost pools and drivers used. Answers (C) and (D) are incorrect because ABC's philosophy is to accumulate homogeneous cost pools. Thus, the cost elements in a pool should be consumed by cost objects in proportion to the same driver. Homogenizing cost pools minimizes broad averaging of costs that have different drivers.

**6.** Which of the following statements about activity-based costing is not true?

   A. Activity-based costing is useful for assigning marketing and distribution costs.

   B. Activity-based costing is more likely to result in major differences from traditional costing systems if the firm manufactures only one product rather than multiple products.

   C. In activity-based costing, cost drivers are what cause costs to be incurred.

   D. Activity-based costing differs from traditional costing systems in that products are not cross-subsidized.

The correct answer is (B). *(CIA, adapted)*
   **REQUIRED:** The false statement about ABC.
   **DISCUSSION:** ABC determines the activities associated with the incurrence of costs and then accumulates a cost pool for each activity. Costs are then reassigned to cost objects using cost drivers if possible. However, given one product, all costs are assigned to the one product; the particular method used to assign the costs does not matter.
   Answer (A) is incorrect because marketing and distribution costs should be assigned to specific cost objects. Answer (C) is incorrect because, by definition, a cost driver is a factor that affects (drives) the incurrence of a cost. Thus, it is highly correlated with the cost. Answer (D) is incorrect because product-cost cross-subsidization occurs when products are miscosted through a broad averaging process. The more accurate cost assignment provided by ABC minimizes the subsidy received by undercosted products at the expense of overcosted products.

**7.** Because of changes that are occurring in the basic operations of many firms, all of the following represent trends in the way indirect costs are assigned except

- A. Treating direct labor as an indirect manufacturing cost in an automated factory.

- B. Using throughput time as an application base to increase awareness of the costs associated with lengthened throughput time.

- C. Preferring plantwide application rates that are based on machine hours rather than incurring the cost of detailed cost assignments.

- D. Using several machine cost pools to measure product costs on the basis of time in a machine center.

The correct answer is (C). *(CMA, adapted)*
**REQUIRED:** The item not a trend in the way indirect costs are being assigned.
**DISCUSSION:** Given the automation of factories and the corresponding emphasis on ABC, plantwide application rates are being used less often because better information can be provided at a reasonable cost. ABC results in a more accurate application of indirect costs because it provides more refined data. Instead of a single cost pool for a process, a department, or an entire plant, an indirect cost pool is established for each identified activity. Costs are then reassigned to cost objects using cost drivers if possible.
Answer (A) is incorrect because one effect of automation is a decrease in direct labor usage. Thus, some companies no longer track direct labor costs closely. They treat direct labor as overhead. Answer (B) is incorrect because throughput time (manufacturing cycle time) is the rate of production over a stated time. It clearly drives (influences) the costs of such items as waiting time, inspection time, and transit time. Answer (D) is incorrect because multiple cost pools permit a better assignment of indirect costs to cost objects.

**8.** What is the normal effect on the numbers of cost pools and cost assignment bases when an activity-based cost (ABC) system replaces a traditional cost system?

|   | Cost Pools | Cost Assignment Bases |
|---|---|---|
| A. | No effect | No effect |
| B. | Increase | No effect |
| C. | No effect | Increase |
| D. | Increase | Increase |

The correct answer is (D). *(CPA, adapted)*
**REQUIRED:** The normal effect of an ABC system on the numbers of cost pools and cost assignment bases.
**DISCUSSION:** In an ABC system, cost assignment is more precise than in traditional systems because activities rather than functions or departments are defined as cost objects. This structure permits assignment to more cost pools and the identification of a driver specifically related to each. A driver is a factor that causes a change in a cost. Thus, an ABC system uses more cost pools and cost assignment bases than a traditional system.
Answers (A), (B), and (C) are incorrect because the numbers of cost pools and cost assignment bases increase.

**9.** Activities, their drivers, and their costs may be classified as unit-level, batch-level, product-level, and facility-level. If activity-based costing information is prepared for internal purposes, which costs are most likely to be treated as period costs?

- A. Unit-level.

- B. Batch-level.

- C. Product-level.

- D. Facility-level.

The correct answer is (D). *(Publisher)*
**REQUIRED:** The level of costs in an ABC analysis most likely to be treated as period costs.
**DISCUSSION:** A difficulty in applying ABC is that, whereas the first three levels of activities pertain to specific products or services, facility-level activities do not. Thus, facility-level costs are not accurately assignable to products. The theoretically sound solution may be to treat these costs as period costs. Nevertheless, organizations that apply ABC ordinarily assign them to products to obtain a full absorption cost suitable for external financial reporting in accordance with GAAP. However, for internal purposes, facility-level costs should be treated as period costs to avoid distorting decisions about cost efficiency, pricing, and profitability.
Answers (A), (B), and (C) are incorrect because unit-level, batch-level, and product-level costs relate to particular products (or services).

**10.** In an activity-based costing (ABC) system, cost reduction is accomplished by identifying and eliminating

| | All Cost Drivers | Nonvalue-Adding Activities |
|---|---|---|
| A. | No | No |
| B. | Yes | Yes |
| C. | No | Yes |
| D. | Yes | No |

The correct answer is (C). *(CPA, adapted)*
**REQUIRED:** The item(s), if any, identified and eliminated when reducing costs in an ABC system.
**DISCUSSION:** An ABC system determines activities associated with the incurrence of costs and then accumulates a cost pool for each activity. It then identifies the driver(s) used to trace those costs to such cost objects as products or services. A driver is a factor that causes a change in a cost. Activities that do not add customer value are identified and eliminated to the extent possible. A clear understanding of what causes a cost (the driver) helps eliminate the nonvalue-adding activities. However, all drivers cannot be eliminated.
Answers (A), (B), and (D) are incorrect because nonvalue-adding activities are unnecessary and therefore are eliminated, but not all drivers are eliminated.

**11.** Nile Co.'s cost assignment and product costing procedures follow activity-based costing principles. Activities have been identified and classified as being either value-adding or nonvalue-adding as to each product. Which of the following activities, used in Nile's production process, is nonvalue-adding?

A. Design engineering activity.

B. Heat treatment activity.

C. Drill press activity.

D. Raw materials storage activity.

The correct answer is (D). *(CPA, adapted)*
**REQUIRED:** The nonvalue-adding activity under ABC.
**DISCUSSION:** ABC assigns costs more precisely than traditional systems because cost pools are accumulated for activities rather than functions or departments. This structure permits assignment to more cost pools and the identification of the driver(s) to be used to reassign costs to cost objects. Analysis by activity also provides for better cost control because of identification of nonvalue-adding activities. For example, raw materials storage may be greatly reduced or eliminated in a JIT system without affecting customer value.
Answers (A), (B), and (C) are incorrect because design engineering activity, heat treatment activity, and drill press activity add value to products in the production process.

**12.** Which of the following would be a reasonable basis for assigning the materials handling costs to the units produced in an activity-based costing (ABC) system?

A. Number of production runs per year.

B. Number of components per completed unit.

C. Amount of time required to produce one unit.

D. Amount of overhead applied to each completed unit.

The correct answer is (B). *(CIA, adapted)*
**REQUIRED:** The basis for assigning materials handling costs in an activity-based costing system.
**DISCUSSION:** ABC identifies the causal relationship between costs and activities, determines the drivers of the activities, establishes cost pools, develops costing rates, and applies cost to products on the basis of resources consumed (drivers), that is, on the basis of the demands made by ultimate cost objects on the activities. The relationship between the number of components in a finished product (the unit-level driver of the activity) and materials handling (the activity the costs of which are to be reassigned to products) is direct and causal.
Answer (A) is incorrect because the number of production runs per year is a batch-level driver. It is not well correlated with materials handling. Answer (C) is incorrect because the time to produce one unit is traditionally used to assign overhead to units produced in a labor-intensive process. Answer (D) is incorrect because overhead applied to each completed unit is the result of, not a basis for, cost assignment.

**13.** Factory Company makes two products, X and Z. X is being introduced this period, whereas Z has been in production for 2 years. For the period about to begin, 1,000 units of each product are to be manufactured. Assume that the only relevant overhead item is the cost of engineering change orders; that X and Z are expected to require eight and two change orders, respectively; that X and Z are expected to require 2 and 3 machine hours, respectively; and that the cost of a change order is $600. If Factory applies engineering change order costs on the basis of machine hours, the cross-subsidy per unit arising from this peanut-butter costing approach is

A. $1.20

B. $2.40

C. $3.60

D. $4.80

The correct answer is (B). *(Publisher)*

**REQUIRED:** The cross-subsidy per unit.

**DISCUSSION:** ABC is one means of improving a cost system to avoid what has been called peanut-butter costing. Inaccurately averaging or spreading costs like peanut butter over products or service units that use different amounts of resources results in product-cost cross-subsidization. This term describes the condition in which the miscosting of one product causes the miscosting of other products. In a traditional system, direct labor and direct materials are traced to products or service units, a single pool of costs (overhead) is accumulated for a given organizational unit, and these costs are then assigned using an allocative rather than a tracing procedure. The effect is an averaging of costs that may result in significant inaccuracy when products or service units do not use similar amounts of resources. The total change order cost is $6,000 [$600 x (8 + 2)], the cost per machine hour is $1.20 {$6,000 ÷ [(2 x 1,000) + (3 x 1,000)] hours}, and the unit costs assigned on a machine-hour basis to X and Z are $2.40 ($1.20 x 2 hours) and $3.60 ($1.20 x 3 hours), respectively. However, if the change order costs are traced directly to X and Z, the unit costs assigned will be $4.80 [(8 orders x $600) ÷ 1,000 units] and $1.20 [(2 orders x $600) ÷ 1,000 units], respectively. Hence, the unit amount by which machine-hour-based assignment overcosts Z and undercosts X (the cross-subsidy) is $2.40 ($3.60 – $1.20 or $4.80 – $2.40).

Answer (A) is incorrect because $1.20 is the unit cost per machine hour or the unit cost directly attributable to Z. Answer (C) is incorrect because $3.60 is the unit cost assigned to Z on the machine-hour basis. Answer (D) is incorrect because $4.80 is the unit cost assigned to X on a direct-tracing basis.

Questions 14 and 15 are based on the following information. Zeta Company is preparing its annual profit plan. As part of its analysis of the profitability of individual products, the controller estimates the amount of overhead that should be assigned to the individual product lines from the information given as follows:

|  | Wall Mirrors | Specialty Windows |
|---|---|---|
| Units produced | 25 | 25 |
| Material moves per product line | 5 | 15 |
| Direct labor hours per unit | 200 | 200 |
| Budgeted materials handling | | |

**14.** Under a costing system that assigns overhead on the basis of direct labor hours, the materials handling costs allocated to one unit of wall mirrors would be

A. $1,000

B. $500

C. $2,000

D. $5,000

The correct answer is (A). *(CMA, adapted)*

**REQUIRED:** The unit materials handling cost of wall mirrors if direct labor hours is the base used to assign overhead.

**DISCUSSION:** The $50,000 of costs is assigned over 10,000 hours [(25 x 200 hrs.) + (25 x 200 hrs.)]. Thus, the overhead cost per hour is $5 ($50,000 ÷ 10,000 hrs.), and the per-unit overhead cost of wall mirrors is $1,000 ($5 x 200 direct labor hours).

Answer (B) is incorrect because $500 is based on the number of material moves. Answer (C) is incorrect because $2,000 assumes that all the overhead is assigned to the wall mirrors. Answer (D) is incorrect because $5,000 assumes overhead of $250,000.

**15.** Under activity-based costing (ABC), the materials handling costs assigned to one unit of wall mirrors would be

A. $1,000

B. $500

C. $1,500

D. $2,500

The correct answer is (B). *(CMA, adapted)*

**REQUIRED:** The amount of materials handling costs assigned to one unit of wall mirrors under ABC.

**DISCUSSION:** ABC assigns overhead costs on the basis of some causal relationship between the incurrence of cost and activities. Because the moves for wall mirrors constitute 25% (5 ÷ 20) of total moves, the mirrors should absorb 25% of the total materials handling costs, or $12,500 (25% x $50,000). The remaining $37,500 is assigned to specialty windows. The cost per unit of wall mirrors is $500 ($12,500 ÷ 25).

Answer (A) is incorrect because $1,000 uses direct labor as the basis used to assign overhead. Answer (C) is incorrect because $1,500 is the assigned overhead per unit of specialty windows. Answer (D) is incorrect because $2,500 is not based on the number of material moves.

Questions 16 and 17 are based on the following information. Believing that its traditional cost system may be providing misleading information, an organization is considering an activity-based costing (ABC) approach. It now employs a full-cost system and has been applying its manufacturing overhead on the basis of machine hours.

The organization plans on using 50,000 direct labor hours and 30,000 machine hours in the coming year. The following data show the manufacturing overhead that is budgeted.

| Activity | Cost Driver | Budgeted Activity | Budgeted Cost |
|---|---|---|---|
| Materials handling | No. of parts handled | 6,000,000 | $ 720,000 |
| Setup costs | No. of setups | 750 | 315,000 |
| Machining costs | Machine hours | 30,000 | 540,000 |
| Quality control | No. of batches | 500 | 225,000 |
| | Total manufacturing overhead cost: | | $1,800,000 |

Cost, sales, and production data for one of the organization's products for the coming year are as follows:

Prime costs:

| | |
|---|---|
| Direct material cost per unit | $4.40 |
| Direct labor cost per unit | |
| .05 DLH @ $15.00/DLH | .75 |
| Total prime cost | $5.15 |

Sales and production data:

| | |
|---|---|
| Expected sales | 20,000 units |
| Batch size | 5,000 units |
| Setups | 2 per batch |
| Total parts per finished unit | 5 parts |
| Machine hours required | 80 MH per batch |

**16.** If the organization uses the traditional full-cost system, the cost per unit for this product for the coming year will be

A. $5.39

B. $5.44

C. $6.11

D. $6.95

The correct answer is (C). *(CIA, adapted)*
   **REQUIRED:** The unit cost under traditional full costing.
   **DISCUSSION:** Given that manufacturing overhead is applied on the basis of machine hours, the overhead rate is $60 per hour ($1,800,000 ÷ 30,000), or $.96 per unit [($60 x 80 machine hours per batch) ÷ 5,000 units per batch]. Accordingly, the unit full cost is $6.11 ($5.15 unit prime cost + $.96).
   Answer (A) is incorrect because $5.39 assumes that 80 machine hours are required for the total production of 20,000 units. Answer (B) is incorrect because $5.44 is based on the machining overhead rate ($18). Answer (D) is incorrect because $6.95 is based on the direct labor hour manufacturing overhead rate.

**17.** If the organization employs an activity-based costing system, the cost per unit for the product described for the coming year will be

A. $6.00

B. $6.08

C. $6.21

D. $6.30

The correct answer is (D). *(CIA, adapted)*
   **REQUIRED:** The unit cost under the ABC system.
   **DISCUSSION:** Materials handling cost per part is $.12 ($720,000 ÷ 6,000,000), cost per setup is $420 ($315,000 ÷ 750), machining cost per hour is $18 ($540,000 ÷ 30,000), and quality cost per batch is $450 ($225,000 ÷ 500). Hence, total manufacturing overhead applied is $22,920 [(5 parts per unit x 20,000 units x $.12) + (4 batches x 2 setups per batch x $420) + (4 batches x 80 machine hours per batch x $18) + (4 batches x $450)]. The total unit cost is $6.296 [$5.15 prime cost + ($22,920 ÷ 20,000 units) overhead].
   Answer (A) is incorrect because $6.00 assumes one setup per batch and 80 total machine hours. Answer (B) is incorrect because $6.08 assumes that only 80 machine hours were used. Answer (C) is incorrect because $6.21 assumes one setup per batch.

Questions 18 through 20 are based on the following information. A company has identified the following overhead costs and cost drivers for the coming year:

| Overhead Item | Cost Driver | Budgeted Cost | Budgeted Activity Level |
|---|---|---|---|
| Machine setup | Number of setups | $ 20,000 | 200 |
| Inspection | Number of inspections | $130,000 | 6,500 |
| Material handling | Number of material moves | $ 80,000 | 8,000 |
| Engineering | Engineering hours | $ 50,000 | 1,000 |
| | | $280,000 | |

The following information was collected on three jobs that were completed during the year:

| | Job 101 | Job 102 | Job 103 |
|---|---|---|---|
| Direct materials | $5,000 | $12,000 | $8,000 |
| Direct labor | $2,000 | $ 2,000 | $4,000 |
| Units completed | 100 | 50 | 200 |
| Number of setups | 1 | 2 | 4 |
| Number of inspections | 20 | 10 | 30 |
| Number of material moves | 30 | 10 | 50 |
| Engineering hours | 10 | 50 | 10 |

Budgeted direct labor cost was $100,000, and budgeted direct material cost was $280,000.

**18.** If the company uses activity-based costing, how much overhead cost should be assigned to Job 101?

A. $1,300

B. $2,000

C. $5,000

D. $5,600

The correct answer is (A). *(CIA, adapted)*

**REQUIRED:** The overhead assigned to Job 101 under activity-based costing (ABC).

**DISCUSSION:** ABC assigns overhead costs more precisely than traditional methods. It identifies the activities associated with the incurrence of costs, determines the cost driver for each activity, and assigns cost accordingly. Thus, the cost per setup is $100 ($20,000 ÷ 200); per inspection, $20 ($130,000 ÷ 6,500); per material move, $10 ($80,000 ÷ 8,000); and per engineering hour, $50 ($50,000 ÷ 1,000). The overhead assigned to Job 101 is therefore $1,300 [(1 setup x $100) + (20 inspections x $20) + (30 material moves x $10) + (10 engineering hours x $50)].

Answer (B) is incorrect because $2,000 equals the overhead assigned to Job 103. Answer (C) is incorrect because $5,000 equals the assigned overhead using direct materials cost as a base. Answer (D) is incorrect because $5,600 equals 2% ($2,000 DL cost ÷ $100,000 budgeted annual DL cost) of budgeted overhead.

**19.** If the company uses activity-based costing, compute the cost of each unit of Job 102.

  A.  $340

  B.  $392

  C.  $440

  D.  $520

The correct answer is (A). *(CIA, adapted)*

**REQUIRED:** The cost per unit of Job 102 under ABC.

**DISCUSSION:** The overhead costs for the activities are $100 per setup, $20 per inspection, $10 per material move, and $50 per engineering hour. Thus, overhead assigned to Job 102 is $3,000 [(2 setups x $100) + (10 inspections x $20) + (10 material moves x $10) + (50 engineering hours x $50)]. The production cost of Job 102 is $17,000 ($12,000 DM + $2,000 DL + $3,000 OH), and the cost per unit is $340 ($17,000 ÷ 50).

Answer (B) is incorrect because $392 assumes overhead is assigned based on direct labor cost. Answer (C) is incorrect because $440 assumes overhead assigned is $8,000. Answer (D) is incorrect because $520 assumes overhead is assigned based on direct materials cost.

**20.** The company prices its products at 140% of cost. If the company uses activity-based costing, the price of each unit of Job 103 would be

  A.  $98

  B.  $100

  C.  $116

  D.  $140

The correct answer is (A). *(CIA, adapted)*

**REQUIRED:** The price to charge per unit of Job 103.

**DISCUSSION:** The costs per job for the activities are $100 per setup, $20 per inspection, $10 per material move, and $50 per engineering hour. Overhead assigned to Job 103 is $2,000 [(4 setups x $100) + (30 inspections x $20) + (50 material moves x $10) + (10 engineering hours x $50)]. Hence, the production cost of Job 103 is $14,000 ($8,000 DM + $4,000 DL + $2,000 OH), the cost per unit is $70 ($14,000 ÷ 200), and the price is $98 (140% x $70).

Answer (B) is incorrect because $100 is the unit cost if overhead is assigned based on direct materials cost. Answer (C) is incorrect because $116 is the unit cost if overhead is assigned based on direct labor cost. Answer (D) is incorrect because $140 assumes cost is $100.

Questions 21 through 24 are based on the following information. This information was presented as part of Question 3 on Part 3 of the June 1992 CMA examination, which covered activity-based costing.

Alaire Corporation manufactures several different types of printed circuit boards; however, two of the boards account for the majority of the company's sales. The first of these boards, a television (TV) circuit board, has been a standard in the industry for several years. The market for this type of board is competitive and therefore price-sensitive. Alaire plans to sell 65,000 of the TV boards next year at a price of $150 per unit. The second high-volume product, a personal computer (PC) circuit board, is a recent addition to Alaire's product line. Because the PC board incorporates the latest technology, it can be sold at a premium price; plans include the sale of 40,000 PC boards at $300 per unit.

Alaire's management group is meeting to discuss strategies, and the current topic of conversation is how to spend the sales and promotion dollars for next year. The sales manager believes that the market share for the TV board could be expanded by concentrating Alaire's promotional efforts in this area. In response to this suggestion, the production manager said, "Why don't you go after a bigger market for the PC board? The cost sheets that I get show that the contribution from the PC board is more than double the contribution from the TV board. I know we get a premium price for the PC board; selling it should help overall profitability."

Alaire uses a standard cost system, and the following data apply to the TV and PC boards:

|  | TV Board | PC Board |
|---|---|---|
| Direct materials | $80 | $140 |
| Direct labor | 1.5 hours | 4 hours |
| Machine time | .5 hours | 1.5 hours |

Variable factory overhead is applied on the basis of direct labor hours. For next year, variable factory overhead is budgeted at $1,120,000, and direct labor hours are estimated at 280,000. The hourly rates for machine time and direct labor are $10 and $14, respectively. Alaire applies a materials handling charge at 10% of materials cost; this materials handling charge is not included in variable factory overhead. Total 1999 expenditures for materials are budgeted at $10,600,000.

Ed Welch, Alaire's controller, believes that, before the management group proceeds with the discussion about allocating sales and promotional dollars to individual products, they should consider the activities involved in their production. As Welch explained to the group, "Activity-based costing integrates the cost of all activities, known as cost drivers, into individual product costs rather than including these costs in overhead pools." Welch has prepared the schedule shown below to help the management group understand this concept.

"Using this information," Welch explained, "we can calculate an activity-based cost for each TV board and each PC board and then compare it with the standard cost we have been using. The only cost that remains the same for both cost methods is the cost of direct materials. The cost drivers will replace the direct labor, machine time, and overhead costs in the standard cost."

| Budgeted Cost | | Cost Driver | Annual Activity for Cost Driver |
|---|---|---|---|
| **Materials overhead:** | | | |
| Procurement | $ 400,000 | Number of parts | 4,000,000 parts |
| Production scheduling | 220,000 | Number of boards | 110,000 boards |
| Packaging and shipping | 440,000 | Number of boards | 110,000 boards |
| | $1,060,000 | | |
| **Variable overhead:** | | | |
| Machine setup | $ 446,000 | Number of setups | 278,750 setups |
| Hazardous waste disposal | 48,000 | Pounds of waste | 16,000 pounds |
| Quality control | 560,000 | Number of inspections | 160,000 inspections |
| General supplies | 66,000 | Number of boards | 110,000 boards |
| | $1,120,000 | | |
| **Manufacturing:** | | | |
| Machine insertion | $1,200,000 | Number of parts | 3,000,000 parts |
| Manual insertion | 4,000,000 | Number of parts | 1,000,000 parts |
| Wave soldering | 132,000 | Number of boards | 110,000 boards |
| | $5,332,000 | | |

| Required per unit | TV Board | PC Board |
|---|---|---|
| Parts | 25 | 55 |
| Machine insertions | 24 | 35 |
| Manual insertions | 1 | 20 |
| Machine setups | 2 | 3 |
| Hazardous waste | .02 lb. | .35 lb. |
| Inspections | 1 | 2 |

**21.** On the basis of standard costs, the total contribution budgeted for the TV board is

A. $1,950,000

B. $2,275,000

C. $2,340,000

D. $2,470,000

The correct answer is (A). *(Publisher)*

**REQUIRED:** The total contribution budgeted for the TV board on a standard cost basis.

**DISCUSSION:** As calculated below, the budgeted standard unit cost of a TV board is $120. This amount includes $6 of variable overhead [1.5 DLH x ($1,120,000 total VOH ÷ 280,000 DLH)]. Given a unit price of $150, the unit contribution margin is therefore $30. Total budgeted contribution is $1,950,000 ($30 UCM x 65,000 budgeted units).

| | |
|---|---:|
| Direct materials | $ 80 |
| DM handling (10% × $80) | 8 |
| Direct labor (1.5 hr. × $14) | 21 |
| Machine time (.5 hr. × $10) | 5 |
| Variable overhead (1.5 hr. × $4) | 6 |
| Budgeted unit cost | $120 |

Answer (B) is incorrect because $2,275,000 excludes the cost of machine time ($5 x 65,000 units = $325,000). Answer (C) is incorrect because $2,340,000 excludes the variable overhead ($6 x 65,000 units = $390,000). Answer (D) is incorrect because $2,470,000 excludes the direct materials handling cost ($8 x 65,000 units = $520,000).

**22.** On the basis of activity-based costs (ABC), the total contribution budgeted for the TV board is

A. $1,594,000

B. $1,950,000

C. $2,037,100

D. $2,557,100

The correct answer is (D). *(Publisher)*

**REQUIRED:** The total contribution budgeted for the TV board on an ABC basis.

**DISCUSSION:** As calculated below, the budgeted activity-based unit cost of a TV board is $110.66. Given a unit price of $150, the unit contribution margin is $39.34. Total budgeted contribution is $2,557,100 ($39.34 UCM x 65,000 budgeted units).

| | |
|---|---:|
| Direct materials | $ 80.00 |
| Procurement [($400,000 ÷ 4,000,000 parts) × 25 parts] | 2.50 |
| Scheduling ($220,000 ÷ 110,000 boards) | 2.00 |
| Packaging and shipping ($440,000 ÷ 110,000 boards) | 4.00 |
| Setups [($446,000 ÷ 278,750 setups) × 2 setups] | 3.20 |
| Waste disposal [($48,000 ÷ 16,000 lb.) × .02] | .06 |
| Quality control ($560,000 ÷ 160,000 inspections) | 3.50 |
| General supplies ($66,000 ÷ 110,000 boards) | .60 |
| Machine insertion [(1,200,000 ÷ 3,000,000 parts) × 24 parts] | 9.60 |
| Manual insertion ($4,000,000 ÷ 1,000,000 parts) | 4.00 |
| Soldering ($132,000 ÷ 110,000 boards) | 1.20 |
| Budgeted ABC unit cost | $110.66 |

Answer (A) is incorrect because $1,594,000 is the CM for the PC board based on an ABC calculation. Answer (B) is incorrect because $1,950,000 is the CM for the TV board based on a standard-cost calculation. Answer (C) is incorrect because $2,037,100 erroneously includes $8 per board for materials handling ($8 x 65,000 units = $520,000).

Questions 23 and 24 are based on the information presented on page 74.

**23.** On the basis of standard costs, the total contribution budgeted for the PC board is

- A. $3,000,000
- B. $2,960,000
- C. $2,920,000
- D. $2,360,000

The correct answer is (D). *(Publisher)*

**REQUIRED:** The total contribution budgeted for the PC board on a standard cost basis.

**DISCUSSION:** As calculated below, the budgeted standard unit cost of a PC board is $241. This amount includes $16 of variable overhead [4 DLH x ($1,120,000 total VOH ÷ 280,000 DLH)]. Given a unit price of $300, the unit contribution margin is $59. Consequently, total budgeted contribution is $2,360,000 ($59 x 40,000 units).

| | |
|---|---|
| Direct materials | $140 |
| DM handling (10% × $140) | 14 |
| Direct labor (4 hr. × $14) | 56 |
| Machine time (1.5 hr. × $10) | 15 |
| Variable overhead (4 hr. × $4) | 16 |
| Budgeted unit cost | $241 |

Answer (A) is incorrect because $3,000,000 excludes the variable overhead ($16 x 40,000 units = $640,000). Answer (B) is incorrect because $2,960,000 excludes the cost of machine time ($15 x 40,000 units = $600,000). Answer (C) is incorrect because $2,920,000 excludes the direct materials handling cost ($14 x 40,000 units = $560,000).

**24.** On the basis of activity-based costs, the total contribution budgeted for the PC board is

- A. $1,594,000
- B. $1,950,000
- C. $2,360,000
- D. $2,557,100

The correct answer is (A). *(Publisher)*

**REQUIRED:** The total contribution budgeted for the PC board on an ABC basis.

**DISCUSSION:** As calculated below, the budgeted activity-based unit cost of a PC board is $260.15. Given a unit price of $300, the unit contribution margin is $39.85. Total budgeted contribution is $1,594,000 ($39.85 UCM x 40,000 units).

| | |
|---|---|
| Direct materials | $140.00 |
| Procurement [($400,000 ÷ 4,000,000 parts) × 55 parts] | 5.50 |
| Scheduling ($220,000 ÷ 110,000 boards) | 2.00 |
| Packaging and shipping ($440,000 ÷110,000 boards) | 4.00 |
| Setups [($446,000 ÷ 278,750 setups) × 3 setups] | 4.80 |
| Waste disposal [$48,000 ÷ 16,000 lb.) × .35] | 1.05 |
| Quality control [($560,000 ÷ 160,000 inspections) × 2] | 7.00 |
| General supplies ($66,000 ÷ 110,000 boards) | .60 |
| Machine insertions [($1,200,000 ÷ 3,000,000 parts) × 35] | 14.00 |
| Manual insertions [($4,000,000 ÷ 1,000,000 parts) × 20] | 80.00 |
| Soldering ($132,000 ÷ 110,000 boards) | 1.20 |
| Budgeted ABC unit cost | $260.15 |

Answer (B) is incorrect because $1,950,000 is the CM for the TV board based on a standard-cost calculation. Answer (C) is incorrect because $2,360,000 is the CM for the PC board based on a standard-cost calculation. Answer (D) is incorrect because $2,557,100 is the CM for the TV board based on an ABC calculation.

**25.** ALF Co. is an assisted-living facility that provides services in the form of residential space, meals, and other occupant assistance (OOA) to its occupants. ALF currently uses a traditional cost accounting system that defines the service provided as assisted living, with service output measured in terms of occupant days. Each occupant is charged a daily rate equal to ALF's annual cost of providing residential space, meals, and OOA divided by total occupant days. However, an activity-based costing (ABC) analysis has revealed that occupants' use of OOA varies substantially. This analysis determined that occupants could be grouped into three categories (low, moderate, and high usage of OOA) and that the activity driver of OOA is nursing hours. The driver of the other activities is occupant days. The following quantitative information was also provided:

| Occupant Category | Annual Occupant Days | Annual Nursing Hours |
|---|---|---|
| Low usage | 36,000 | 90,000 |
| Medium usage | 18,000 | 90,000 |
| High usage | 6,000 | 120,000 |
| | 60,000 | 300,000 |

The total annual cost of OOA was $7.5 million, and the total annual cost of providing residential space and meals was $7.2 million. Accordingly, the ABC analysis indicates that the daily costing rate should be

A. $182.50 for occupants in the low-usage category.

B. $145.00 for occupants in the medium-usage category.

C. $245.00 for occupants in the high-usage category.

D. $620.00 for all occupants.

The correct answer is (A). *(Publisher)*

**REQUIRED:** The true statement about daily costing rates based on an ABC analysis.

**DISCUSSION:** This service organization produces three "products" (the three occupant categories), and the "units produced" equal occupant days. According to the ABC analysis, production involves two activities: (1) provision of residential space and meals and (2) OOA. The drivers of these activities are occupant days and nursing hours, respectively. Thus, the cost pool rate for the first activity (residential space and meals) is $120 per occupant day ($7,200,000 ÷ 60,000 days), and the cost pool rate for the second activity (OOA) is $25 ($7,500,000 ÷ 300,000 hours). The total cost for providing services to occupants in the low-usage category is $6,570,000 [($120 x 36,000 days) + ($25 x 90,000 hours)]. The daily cost rate for these occupants is therefore $182.50 ($6,570,000 ÷ 36,000 occupant days).

Answer (B) is incorrect because $145.00 equals the sum of the cost pool rates ($120 + $25). Answer (C) is incorrect because $245 equals the rate per day for medium-usage occupants. Answer (D) is incorrect because $620 is the rate per day for high-usage occupants.

# CHAPTER THREE
# JOB-ORDER COSTING

Job-order costing and process costing are the two fundamental methods for assigning costs to products or services based on the nature of the output. Either may be used with activity-based costing (ABC). **Job-order costing** identifies costs to specific units, lots, or batches. It is appropriate when products or services have unique characteristics, such as custom-made furniture or audit services that vary with the client. **Process costing** assigns costs to large numbers of homogeneous products or services, with costs accumulated by processes, departments, or cost centers. Unit cost equals the costs of the process for the period divided by the number of units. The major distinction between the two methods is that job-order costing requires a subsidiary ledger to be maintained for the work-in-process and finished goods inventory accounts. The purpose is to accumulate information about specifically identifiable projects, services, or batches of goods. In process costing, subsidiary ledgers are unnecessary because units are homogeneous and processing is continuous. Use of **just-in-time (JIT)** manufacturing methods does not mitigate the need for such cost accumulation and cost assignment procedures.

Job-order costing records costs by classification (direct materials, direct labor, and overhead) on a **job-cost sheet** specifically prepared for each job. Job-cost sheets serve as a subsidiary ledger; thus, the total of all job-cost sheets for in-process jobs should equal the balance in the general ledger work-in-process account. The sources of documents for costs incurred include stores' requisitions for direct materials and work (or time) tickets for direct labor.

The most common means of measuring the costs to be assigned to products and services are **actual costing** and normal costing. Both methods assign direct materials and direct labor costs based on actual costs. However, **normal costing** applies overhead based on predetermined rates and the actual usage of the base used to assign such costs. This method smooths fluctuations in overhead costs that occur during the year. It also provides timely costing information that would not be available if the firm waited until year-end to determine the actual rates. A variation of normal costing is budgeted or **extended normal costing**, a method that multiplies the actual direct-cost input by budgeted rates. This approach is prevalent in the service sector. Accordingly, overhead is assigned under normal costing to each job through a predetermined overhead rate equal to the budgeted overhead divided by the budgeted amount of the appropriate denominator measure. In a traditional system, a single overhead rate might be established for an entire department, e.g., $3 of overhead for every direct labor hour. If **ABC** is used, however, the multiple activities that use resources classified as overhead will be identified, a cost pool will be established for each activity, and the costs in each pool will be assigned based on the driver specific to the activity. I. a driver cannot feasibly be identified, overhead is assigned to products or services using an allocative procedure; that is, it is determined using some indirect measure.

The following diagram illustrates the **cost flow** among accounts for a typical manufacturer.  This cost flow is substantially the same under job-order and process costing:

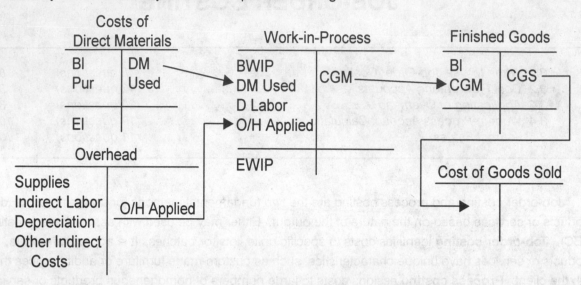

**Work-in-process** is an inventory account to which direct materials, direct labor, and applied overhead are charged.  The sum of these costs plus the cost of BWIP is the total production cost to be accounted for in any one period.  This total is allocated to goods completed during the period (cost of goods manufactured) and to EWIP.  Work-in-process may also be credited when a loss is recognized for abnormal loss of units.  In traditional systems, some spoilage is expected to occur under normal, efficient working conditions.  **Normal spoilage** is a product cost.  **Abnormal spoilage** is a period cost.  However, firms that have adopted a zero-defects (perfection) standard have quality programs that emphasize "doing it right the first time," workers' inspection of their own output, and on-the-spot correction.  Such firms essentially treat all spoilage as abnormal.

**Materials** are usually accounted for separately by a debit to materials (stores control) and a credit to accounts payable or cash.  When materials are transferred to work-in-process, inventory is credited.  **Direct labor** is usually debited directly to work-in-process when the payroll is recorded.  Any wages not attributable directly to production, e.g., those for janitorial services, are considered indirect labor and debited to overhead.  Shift differentials and overtime premium may also be treated as overhead unless a specific job is the cause of their incurrence.  Employer taxes on payroll and fringe benefits (e.g., pensions and insurance) paid to employees are treated as direct labor costs.  The justification is that payroll taxes and fringe benefits are necessary to obtain such labor.  **Overhead** is a separate account to which costs of production other than direct materials and labor are debited.  Examples are insurance, supplies, and depreciation.  Overhead is credited and work-in-process is debited based on predetermined overhead rates.  The objective is to charge all overhead incurred over a period of time, such as a year, to work-in-process.  A single overhead account may be used, but many firms prefer to debit actual costs to an overhead control account and to credit the amounts charged to work-in-process to a separate overhead applied account.  The latter has a credit balance.  As products are completed, their cost is credited to work-in-process and debited to **finished goods inventory**.  As the finished goods are sold, their cost is debited to **cost of sales**.  The procedures just described are readily adapted to jobs undertaken by service organizations.  For example, a firm of attorneys may treat a particular case as a job; legal forms and other inputs as direct materials; billable hours by attorneys as direct labor; and office rental, depreciation, clerical costs, law library maintenance, etc., as overhead.

Overhead consists of production costs other than direct labor and direct materials. It may be assigned using predetermined overhead application rates. The denominator of the overhead rate may be defined in terms of various capacity concepts. **Practical capacity** is the maximum level at which output is produced efficiently. It includes consideration of idle time resulting from holidays, downtime, changeover time, etc., but not from inadequate sales demand. Practical capacity exceeds the other commonly used denominator levels included in the calculation of the fixed overhead rate. Because practical capacity will almost always exceed the actual use of capacity, it will result in an unfavorable production volume variance. The unfavorable production volume variance is charged to income summary, so the effect of using a larger denominator volume is the more rapid write-off of fixed overhead. **Maximum (theoretical or ideal) capacity** is the level at which output is maximized assuming perfectly efficient operations at all times. Firms dedicated to the active pursuit of continuous improvement expect their operations to approach this level. It ordinarily results in underapplied overhead. **Normal capacity** is the level that will approximate demand over a period of years that includes seasonal, cyclical, and trend variations. Deviations in one year will be offset in other years. **Expected actual capacity** is a short-run level based on demand. It minimizes under- or overapplied overhead but does not provide a consistent basis for assigning overhead cost. Per-unit overhead will fluctuate because of short-term changes in the expected level of output.

**Capacity management** largely concerns how an organization manages its costs of unused (excess) capacity. The unused capacity in production facilities, distribution channels, marketing organizations, etc., are ordinarily not assignable to products or services on a cause-and-effect basis, so their inclusion in overhead rates may distort pricing decisions. Including the fixed costs of unused capacity in a cost-based price results in higher prices and in what is known as the **downward (black hole) demand spiral**.

As higher prices depress demand, unused capacity costs increase, the fixed costs included in prices increase, and demand will continue to spiral downward. One way to avoid this problem is not to assign unused capacity costs to products or services. The result should be better operating decisions and better evaluation of managerial performance. Unused capacity arises because currently used capacity includes not only the "just right" amount but also nonvalue-adding activities. Moreover, it may also include capacity maintained because of expected difficulties in coordination with such external parties as customers and suppliers. Still another component of unused capacity is that obtained to provide for growth. However, the costs of unused capacity must be set against the possibility of operational bottlenecks. Furthermore, managers must consider whether capacity may be increased and costs reduced through redesign of products, processes, etc.

Rarely will the amount of overhead incurred equal the amount applied at the end of the period. **Overapplied** overhead (a credit balance in overhead) results when product or service costs are overstated because the actual quantity of the base used to assign overhead was higher than expected, or actual overhead costs were lower than expected. **Underapplied** overhead (a debit balance in overhead) results when product costs are understated because the actual quantity of the base used to assign overhead was lower than expected, or actual overhead costs were higher than expected. The improvements in information technology and decreases in its cost have made **restatement of overhead rates** more appealing. This approach is implemented at the end of the period to calculate the actual overhead rates and then restate every entry involving overhead. The effect is that job cost records, the inventory accounts, and cost of sales are accurately stated with respect to actual overhead. This means of disposing of overhead variances is costly but has the advantage of improving the analysis of profitability. If a restatement approach is not taken, the treatment of the balance in the overhead account (over- or underapplied overhead) depends on the materiality of the amount.  For example, a manufacturer may write off the amount to cost of goods sold if it is not material.  If the amount is material, it should be prorated to work-in-process, finished goods, and cost of goods sold on the basis of the currently applied overhead in each of the accounts.  An alternative is to prorate the variance based on the total balances in the accounts.

### 3.1 When to Use Job-Order Costing

**1.** Two basic costing systems for assigning costs to products or services are job costing and process costing. These two costing systems are usually viewed as being on opposite ends of a spectrum. The fundamental criterion employed to determine whether job costing or process costing should be employed is

A. Proportion of direct (traceable) costs expended to produce the product or service.

B. Number of cost pools employed to allocate the indirect costs to the product or service.

C. Type of bases used in allocating the indirect cost pools to the product or service.

D. The nature and amount of the product or service brought to the marketplace for customer consumption.

The correct answer is (D). *(CIA, adapted)*
**REQUIRED:** The criterion for determining whether process or job costing is used.
**DISCUSSION:** Job costing is used if resources are expended to bring a distinct, identifiable product or service to the market; a company would be providing heterogeneous products or services that are often customized for the consumer. Process costing is used when masses of identical or similar units of product or services are provided for general consumer use.
Answers (A), (B), and (C) are incorrect because the proportion of direct costs, the number of cost pools, and the types of allocation bases do not affect the selection of a costing system.

**2.** A nonmanufacturing organization may use

A. Job-order costing but not process costing.

B. Process costing but not job-order costing.

C. Either job-order or process costing.

D. Neither job-order costing nor process costing.

The correct answer is (C). *(CPA, adapted)*
**REQUIRED:** The appropriate method(s) of cost accumulation in a nonmanufacturing organization.
**DISCUSSION:** A nonmanufacturing organization may use either cost accumulation procedure. For example, banks frequently use process costing for certain departments and job-order costing for others. Public accounting firms ordinarily use job-order costing.
Answers (A), (B), and (D) are incorrect because a nonmanufacturer may use either job-order or process costing.

**3.** In a manufacturing environment, job-order cost accounting systems and process cost accounting systems differ in the way

A. Costs are assigned to production runs and the number of units for which costs are averaged.

B. Orders are taken and the number of units in the orders.

C. Product profitability is determined and compared with planned costs.

D. Processes can be accomplished and the number of production runs that may be performed in a year.

The correct answer is (A). *(CIA, adapted)*
**REQUIRED:** The way job-order and process cost accounting systems differ.
**DISCUSSION:** A cost system determines the manufacturing cost to be expensed (because output was sold) and the portion to be deferred (because output was still on hand). Process costing is used for continuous process output of units that are relatively homogeneous (e.g., oil refining and automobile production). Job-order costing is used to account for the cost of specific jobs or projects when output is heterogeneous. The difference is often overemphasized. Job-order costing simply requires subsidiary ledgers (to keep track of the specific jobs) for the same work-in-process and finished goods accounts that are basic to process costing.
Answer (B) is incorrect because how orders are taken is irrelevant to whether job-order or process costing is used. Answer (C) is incorrect because profit is determined in the same way in both job-order and process costing. Answer (D) is incorrect because the cost system is not necessarily related to the manufacturing processes.

**4.** How does a job-order cost accounting system differ from a process cost accounting system?

- A. Subsidiary ledgers for the work-in-process and finished goods inventories are necessary in job-order costing.
- B. The procedures to apply overhead to product cost are different.
- C. Both the timing and nature of entries to transfer cost from the work-in-process account to the finished goods inventory account are different.
- D. Most of the journal entries that require debits and/or credits to the work-in-process account are different.

The correct answer is (A). *(Publisher)*

**REQUIRED:** The difference between a job-order system and process costing.

**DISCUSSION:** Job-order systems account for processes that produce distinctly different products or groups of products. By contrast, process costing is suitable to production of a homogeneous product. Given identifiably different products, costs need to be collected separately for each product or group of products. Accordingly, although the same general ledger accounts are used for both cost systems, subsidiary ledgers are maintained in job-order costing for the inventory accounts.

Answer (B) is incorrect because the overhead application procedures are similar. Answer (C) is incorrect because cost flow among general ledger accounts is not affected by using subsidiary ledgers for specific jobs. Answer (D) is incorrect because the two systems make similar entries to the general ledger.

**5.** In job-order costing, the basic document to accumulate the cost of each order is the

- A. Invoice.
- B. Purchase order.
- C. Requisition sheet.
- D. Job-cost sheet.

The correct answer is (D). *(CPA, adapted)*

**REQUIRED:** The basic document to accumulate the cost of each order in job-order costing.

**DISCUSSION:** The job-cost sheet, or job-order sheet, is used to accumulate product costs in a job-order costing system. Direct materials, direct labor, and overhead are the costs accumulated.

Answer (A) is incorrect because an invoice shows the price and quantity of the product purchased or sold. Answer (B) is incorrect because the purchase order states the specifications, quantities, and prices of items to be purchased. Answer (C) is incorrect because a requisition sheet is an internal document used by production to request materials or other resources from another department.

**6.** A company services office equipment. Some customers bring their equipment to the company's service shop; other customers prefer to have the company's service personnel come to their offices to repair their equipment. The most appropriate costing method for the company is

- A. A job-order costing system.
- B. An activity-based costing system.
- C. A process costing system.
- D. An operation costing system.

The correct answer is (A). *(CIA, adapted)*

**REQUIRED:** The appropriate costing method for a service company.

**DISCUSSION:** Job-order costing systems accumulate costs for tasks or projects that are unique and nonrepetitive. A company that services office equipment is interested in identifying the costs applicable to each customer each service call.

Answer (B) is incorrect because ABC identifies the activities that affect costs and uses a separate driver for each activity to assign costs to cost objects. It may be used with job-order or process costing. Answer (C) is incorrect because process costing applies to homogeneous products mass produced in continuous production runs. Answer (D) is incorrect because operation costing is a hybrid of job-order and process costing.

**7.** A new advertising agency serves a wide range of clients including manufacturers, restaurants, service businesses, department stores, and other retail establishments. The accounting system the advertising agency has most likely adopted for its record keeping in accumulating costs is

A. Job-order costing.

B. Operation costing.

C. Relevant costing.

D. Process costing.

The correct answer is (A). *(CIA, adapted)*
**REQUIRED:** The most likely accounting system adopted by a company with a wide range of clients.
**DISCUSSION:** Job-order costing is used by organizations whose products or services are readily identified by individual units or batches. The advertising agency accumulates its costs by client. Job-order costing is the most appropriate system for this type of nonmanufacturing firm.

Answer (B) is incorrect because operation costing would most likely be employed by a manufacturer producing goods that have common characteristics plus some individual characteristics. Answer (C) is incorrect because relevant costing refers to expected future costs that are considered in decision making. Answer (D) is incorrect because process costing is employed when a company mass produces a homogeneous product in a continuous fashion.

**8.** Which method of measuring the costs to be assigned to products or services uses budgeted rates for direct costs but applies those rates to the actual quantities of the inputs?

A. Actual costing.

B. Normal costing.

C. Extended costing.

D. Standard costing.

The correct answer is (C). *(Publisher)*
**REQUIRED:** The cost measurement method that uses budgeted rates for direct costs but applies those rates to the actual quantities of the inputs.
**DISCUSSION:** Extended costing assigns both direct costs (such as labor and materials) and overhead to cost objects by using budgeted rates. The direct cost assigned equals the budgeted rate times the actual amount of the direct-cost input. The overhead assigned equals the budgeted rate times the actual amount of whichever driver or other base is used for cost assignment purposes. The use of budgeted rates for overhead as well as direct costs may be helpful to avoid fluctuations during the year. It is also helpful when some direct costs, such as direct labor, may not be known until year-end.

Answer (A) is incorrect because actual costing uses only actual direct and overhead costs. Answer (B) is incorrect because normal costing uses budgeted rates only for overhead costs. Answer (D) is incorrect because standard costing applies budgeted rates to the standard (not actual) inputs allowed.

### 3.2 Cost Flow among Accounts

**9.** The work-in-process account is

A. Neither a real nor a nominal account.

B. An inventory account indicating the beginning and ending inventory of goods being processed.

C. A hybrid account (both a real and a nominal account).

D. A nominal account to which overhead costs are charged as incurred and credited as these costs are charged to production.

The correct answer is (B). *(Publisher)*
**REQUIRED:** The nature of work-in-process.
**DISCUSSION:** Work-in-process is an inventory account to which direct materials, direct labor, and factory overhead costs are charged as they are incurred in the production process. The sum of these costs plus the cost of BWIP is the total production cost to be accounted for in any one period. The total is assigned to goods completed during the period, i.e., to finished goods and to EWIP. Work-in-process may also be credited for abnormal spoilage.

Answers (A) and (C) are incorrect because work-in-process is an inventory or real account. Answer (D) is incorrect because factory overhead is a real account that pools overhead costs as incurred.

**10.** The debits in work-in-process are BWIP, direct labor, direct materials, and factory overhead. The account should be credited for production that is completed and sent to finished goods inventory. The balance is

- A. Zero.
- B. EWIP (credit).
- C. EWIP (debit).
- D. Total production costs to be accounted for.

The correct answer is (C). *(Publisher)*
**REQUIRED:** The composition of the balance of work-in-process after the account is credited for goods produced.
**DISCUSSION:** The sum of the debits to WIP equals total production costs. Ignoring possible spoilage, production consists either of completed goods or of those still in process. Accordingly, after the account is credited for the cost of goods completed and transferred to the FG inventory, the debit balance in the account is EWIP.
Answer (A) is incorrect because the balance is zero only if there is no EWIP. Answer (B) is incorrect because EWIP is credited when completed units are transferred but should never have a credit balance. Answer (D) is incorrect because total production costs to be accounted for include finished goods as well as EWIP.

**11.** What is the journal entry to record the purchase of materials on account?

| | | |
|---|---|---|
| A. Raw materials inventory | XXX | |
|   Accounts payable | | XXX |
| B. Accounts payable | XXX | |
|   Raw materials inventory | | XXX |
| C. Accounts receivable | XXX | |
|   Accounts payable | | XXX |
| D. Cash | XXX | |
|   Accounts receivable | | XXX |

The correct answer is (A). *(Publisher)*
**REQUIRED:** The journal entry to record the purchase of materials on account.
**DISCUSSION:** The correct entry to record a purchase of materials on account is to increase the appropriate asset and liability accounts. Materials are charged to an inventory account, e.g., stores control or supplies, and the corresponding liability is credited to accounts payable. Also, subsidiary ledgers may be used to account for various individual items (a perpetual inventory system). The term control implies that a subsidiary ledger is being used.
Answer (B) is incorrect because the entry to record the return of materials to suppliers debits accounts payable and credits raw materials inventory. Answer (C) is incorrect because this entry reclassifies credit balances in accounts receivable as liabilities or debit balances in accounts payable as assets. Answer (D) is incorrect because this entry records cash received on account.

**12.** In a traditional job-order cost system, the issuance of supplies to a production department increases

- A. Stores control.
- B. Work-in-process control.
- C. Factory overhead control.
- D. Factory overhead applied.

The correct answer is (C). *(CPA, adapted)*
**REQUIRED:** The account that increases when supplies are issued to a production department.
**DISCUSSION:** As overhead is incurred, factory overhead control is debited, and accounts payable, stores, etc., are credited. When overhead is applied, work-in-process is debited, and factory overhead applied is credited. The difference between the debited and credited amounts is over- or underapplied overhead.
Answer (A) is incorrect because stores control decreases (is credited). Answer (B) is incorrect because work-in-process increases (is debited) when overhead is applied. Answer (D) is incorrect because factory overhead applied increases (is credited) when overhead is applied.

**13.** In a job-order cost system, the use of direct materials previously purchased usually is recorded as an increase in

   A. Work-in-process control.

   B. Factory overhead control.

   C. Factory overhead applied.

   D. Stores control.

The correct answer is (A). *(CPA, adapted)*

   **REQUIRED:** The account increased by the use of direct materials already on hand.

   **DISCUSSION:** The purchase of direct materials requires a debit to (an increase in) direct materials inventory (stores control). This account is credited and work-in-process control is debited when direct materials are issued to a production department.

   Answer (B) is incorrect because factory overhead control is debited (increased) when materials not categorized as direct are issued. Answer (C) is incorrect because factory overhead applied is increased (credited) only when overhead is charged to work-in-process at a predetermined rate using an appropriate driver or other base. Answer (D) is incorrect because stores control is increased when direct materials are purchased.

**14.** In a job-order cost system, direct labor costs usually are recorded initially as an increase in

   A. Factory overhead applied.

   B. Factory overhead control.

   C. Finished goods control.

   D. Work-in-process control.

The correct answer is (D). *(CPA, adapted)*

   **REQUIRED:** The account to which direct labor is first charged in a job-order cost system.

   **DISCUSSION:** Direct labor costs are inventoriable costs. They are initially debited to the work-in-process control account.

   Answer (A) is incorrect because direct labor costs are not part of applied factory overhead. Answer (B) is incorrect because direct labor cost is not included in actual factory overhead. Answer (C) is incorrect because, in a job-order cost system, direct labor is initially charged to WIP control. When the goods are finished, direct labor cost will be transferred from WIP control to finished goods control.

**15.** In a job-order cost system, the application of factory overhead is usually reflected in the general ledger as an increase in

   A. Factory overhead control.

   B. Finished goods control.

   C. Work-in-process control.

   D. Cost of goods sold.

The correct answer is (C). *(CPA, adapted)*

   **REQUIRED:** The account that is increased when overhead is applied in a job-order cost system.

   **DISCUSSION:** The entry to record the application of factory overhead to specific jobs is to charge WIP control and credit factory overhead applied (or factory overhead control) using a predetermined overhead rate. The effect is to increase the WIP control account.

   Answer (A) is incorrect because factory overhead control increases when actual factory overhead costs are incurred. Answer (B) is incorrect because finished goods control increases only when goods are completed. Answer (D) is incorrect because cost of goods sold is increased only when products are sold.

**16.** A direct labor overtime premium should be charged to a specific job when the overtime is caused by the

   A. Increased overall level of activity.

   B. Customer's requirement for early completion of the job.

   C. Management's failure to include the job in the production schedule.

   D. Management's requirement that the job be completed before the annual factory vacation closure.

The correct answer is (B). *(CPA, adapted)*

   **REQUIRED:** The circumstances in which a direct labor overtime premium should be charged to a specific job.

   **DISCUSSION:** A direct labor overtime premium is ordinarily considered an indirect cost, charged to overhead, and allocated to all jobs. The association of overtime with a specific job may be attributable solely to random scheduling and an abnormally large production volume, a condition affecting all jobs. However, if overtime directly results from the demands of a specific job, it is a direct cost of that job.

   Answers (A) and (C) are incorrect because overtime arising from increased overall activity or management error is not caused by the demands of a specific job. Answer (D) is incorrect because, assuming all jobs are to be completed prior to the closing, no specific job is the cause of the overtime.

**17.** A company experienced a machinery breakdown on one of its production lines.  As a consequence of the breakdown, manufacturing fell behind schedule, and a decision was made to schedule overtime to return manufacturing to schedule.  Which one of the following methods is the proper way to account for the overtime paid to the direct laborers?

A.   The overtime hours times the sum of the straight-time wages and overtime premium would be charged entirely to manufacturing overhead.

B.   The overtime hours times the sum of the straight-time wages and overtime premium would be treated as direct labor.

C.   The overtime hours times the overtime premium would be charged to repair and maintenance expense, and the overtime hours times the straight-time wages would be treated as direct labor.

D.   The overtime hours times the overtime premium would be charged to manufacturing overhead, and the overtime hours times the straight-time wages would be treated as direct labor.

The correct answer is (D).  *(CIA, adapted)*
 **REQUIRED:**  The proper way to account for the overtime paid to the direct laborers.
 **DISCUSSION:**  Direct labor costs are wages paid to labor that can feasibly be specifically identified with the production of finished goods.  Factory overhead consists of all costs, other than direct materials and direct labor, that are associated with the manufacturing process.  Thus, straight-time wages would be treated as direct labor; however, because the overtime premium is a cost that customarily should be borne by all production, the overtime hours times the overtime premium should be charged to manufacturing overhead.
 Answer (A) is incorrect because the straight-time wages times the overtime hours should still be treated as direct labor.  Answer (B) is incorrect because only the overtime premium times the overtime hours is charged to overhead.  Answer (C) is incorrect because labor costs are not related to repairs and maintenance expense.

**18.** What is the entry to record completion of a particular product or group of products?

| | | |
|---|---|---|
| A.   Finished goods | XXX | |
|       Cost of goods sold | | XXX |
| B.   Work-in-process | XXX | |
|       Finished goods | | XXX |
| C.   Finished goods | XXX | |
|       Work-in-process | | XXX |
| D.   Cost of goods sold | XXX | |
|       Work-in-process | | XXX |

The correct answer is (C).  *(Publisher)*
 **REQUIRED:**  The entry to record completion of a job.
 **DISCUSSION:**  The entry to record completion of a job is to charge finished goods inventory and credit WIP for the amounts of actual direct materials and actual direct labor used and of factory overhead applied.
 Answer (A) is incorrect because a debit to FG and a credit to CGS is the reverse of the entry to expense inventory that is sold.  Answer (B) is incorrect because a debit to WIP and a credit to FG reverses the entry to transfer cost of goods finished from WIP to FG.  Answer (D) is incorrect because all items sold are charged to FG inventory before being transferred to CGS; no entries should transfer costs directly from WIP to CGS.

**19.** Under a job-order system of cost accounting, the dollar amount of the general ledger entry involved in the transfer of inventory from work-in-process to finished goods is the sum of the costs charged to all jobs

A.   Started in process during the period.

B.   In process during the period.

C.   Completed and sold during the period.

D.   Completed during the period.

The correct answer is (D).  *(CPA, adapted)*
 **REQUIRED:**  The costs included in the general ledger entry to transfer inventory to finished goods.
 **DISCUSSION:**  The entry to transfer inventory from WIP to FG is to debit finished goods and credit work-in-process.  The amount of the entry is the sum of the costs (irrespective of the period in which they were incurred) charged to all jobs completed during the period.
 Answer (A) is incorrect because the sum of the costs of jobs started in process during the period does not include the cost of goods started in a prior period and completed in this period.  Also, it includes EWIP.  Answer (B) is incorrect because the sum of the costs of jobs in process during the period includes the cost of EWIP.  Answer (C) is incorrect because the sum of the costs of jobs completed and sold excludes the cost of goods completed but not yet sold.

**20.** In job-order costing, payroll taxes paid by the employer for factory employees are usually accounted for as

A. Direct labor.

B. Factory overhead.

C. Indirect labor.

D. Administrative costs.

The correct answer is (A). *(CPA, adapted)*

**REQUIRED:** The accounting for employer payroll taxes.

**DISCUSSION:** Employer taxes on factory payroll and fringe benefits (e.g., pensions and insurance) paid to factory employees are treated as direct labor costs. The justification is that payroll taxes and fringe benefits are necessary to obtain such labor. The IMA in Statement of Management Accounting 4C, *Definition and Measurement of Direct Labor Cost*, supports this position.

Answer (B) is incorrect because accounting for employer payroll taxes as direct labor costs is preferable, although some companies treat these costs as overhead. Answer (C) is incorrect because indirect labor is a component of factory overhead. Answer (D) is incorrect because administrative costs are period costs.

## 3.3 Application of Overhead

**21.** In a job-cost system, factory (manufacturing) overhead is

|    | An Indirect Cost of Jobs | A Necessary Element of Production |
|----|----|----|
| A. | No  | Yes |
| B. | No  | No  |
| C. | Yes | Yes |
| D. | Yes | No  |

The correct answer is (C). *(CPA, adapted)*

**REQUIRED:** The nature of factory overhead.

**DISCUSSION:** Factory overhead consists of indirect manufacturing costs that cannot feasibly be traced to specific units but are necessarily incurred as part of the production process. Examples are depreciation, utilities expense, insurance, and supervisors' salaries. Factory overhead, in a traditional system, is usually allocated to products based upon some indirect measure, e.g., direct labor hours or machine hours.

Answers (A), (B), and (D) are incorrect because factory overhead is an indirect cost and necessary to production.

**22.** Which of the following items is not included in (charged to) factory overhead?

A. Factory depreciation and supplies.

B. Costs of service departments.

C. Costs of marketing departments.

D. Costs of maintenance departments.

The correct answer is (C). *(Publisher)*

**REQUIRED:** The item not charged to factory overhead.

**DISCUSSION:** Marketing costs, for example, salaries of sales personnel, sales commissions, and advertising, are period costs and are expensed as incurred. They cannot be assigned to the product because these marketing costs are not associated with the manufacturing process.

Answers (A), (B), and (D) are incorrect because factory depreciation, supplies, service department costs, and maintenance costs are indirectly associated with manufacturing and are assigned to products through the overhead account.

**23.** Many companies recognize three major categories of costs of manufacturing a product. These are direct materials, direct labor, and overhead. Which of the following is an overhead cost in the production of an automobile?

A. The cost of small tools used in mounting tires on each automobile.

B. The cost of the tires on each automobile.

C. The cost of the laborers who place tires on each automobile.

D. The delivery costs for the tires on each automobile.

The correct answer is (A). *(CIA, adapted)*

**REQUIRED:** The overhead cost in the production of an automobile.

**DISCUSSION:** The cost of small tools used in mounting tires cannot be identified solely with the manufacture of a specific automobile. This cost should be treated as factory overhead because it is identifiable with production.

Answer (B) is incorrect because tire costs are readily and directly identifiable with each automobile as direct materials costs. Answer (C) is incorrect because the cost of the laborers who place tires on each automobile is readily and directly identifiable with each automobile as a direct labor cost. Answer (D) is incorrect because delivery costs are readily and directly identifiable with the tires delivered. Thus, they are direct materials costs.

**24.** During the current accounting period, a manufacturing company purchased $70,000 of raw materials, of which $50,000 of direct materials and $5,000 of indirect materials were used in production. The company also incurred $45,000 of total labor costs and $20,000 of other factory overhead costs. An analysis of the work-in-process control account revealed $40,000 of direct labor costs. Based upon the above information, what is the total amount accumulated in the factory overhead control account?

A.  $25,000

B.  $30,000

C.  $45,000

D.  $50,000

The correct answer is (B). *(CIA, adapted)*

**REQUIRED:** The total amount accumulated in the factory overhead control account.

**DISCUSSION:** Factory overhead consists of all costs, other than direct materials and direct labor, that are associated with the manufacturing process. It includes both fixed and variable costs. The factory overhead control account should have the following costs:

| | |
|---|---:|
| Indirect materials | $ 5,000 |
| Indirect labor ($45,000–$40,000) | 5,000 |
| Other factory overhead | 20,000 |
| Total overhead | $30,000 |

Answer (A) is incorrect because $25,000 excludes the indirect materials. Answer (C) is incorrect because $45,000 is the total labor cost. Answer (D) is incorrect because $50,000 is the direct materials cost.

**25.** Why are annual overhead application rates used?

A.  To budget overhead.

B.  To smooth seasonal variability of overhead costs.

C.  To smooth seasonal variability of output levels.

D.  Both (B) and (C).

The correct answer is (D). *(Publisher)*

**REQUIRED:** The reason for annual overhead rates.

**DISCUSSION:** Annual overhead application rates smooth seasonal variability of overhead costs and output levels. If overhead were applied to products or service units as incurred, the overhead rate per unit in most cases would vary considerably from week to week or month to month. The purpose of an annual overhead application rate is to simulate constant overhead throughout the year.

Answer (A) is incorrect because overhead is budgeted by estimating the total costs to be incurred. Answers (B) and (C) are incorrect because overhead rates are used to smooth seasonal variability of both output levels and overhead costs.

**26.** There are several alternative denominator measures for applying overhead. Which is not commonly used?

A.  Direct labor hours.

B.  Direct labor cost.

C.  Machine hours.

D.  Sales value of product produced.

The correct answer is (D). *(Publisher)*

**REQUIRED:** The denominator measure not appropriate for applying overhead.

**DISCUSSION:** Overhead in traditional systems is normally applied to production according to an allocation base such as direct labor hours, direct labor cost, or machine hours. An allocation base is an indirect measure, but it should have a relatively close correlation with the incurrence of overhead. The sales value of the product produced is not a variable with a causal relationship to the incurrence of overhead.

Answer (A) is incorrect because direct labor hours is an appropriate base when overhead is incurred uniformly by all types of employees. Answer (B) is incorrect because direct labor cost is often used as a base in labor-intensive industries. Answer (C) is incorrect because machine hours is a frequently used base in capital-intensive industries.

**27.** Units of production is an appropriate method of assigning overhead when

    A.  Several well-differentiated products are manufactured.

    B.  Direct labor costs are low.

    C.  Only one product is manufactured.

    D.  The manufacturing process is complex.

The correct answer is (C). *(CMA, adapted)*

**REQUIRED:** The situation in which units of production is an appropriate method of assigning overhead.

**DISCUSSION:** Assigning overhead on the basis of the number of units produced is usually not appropriate. Costs should be assigned on the basis of some plausible relationship between the cost object and the incurrence of the cost, preferably cause and effect. Overhead costs, however, may be incurred regardless of the level of production. Nevertheless, if a firm manufactures only one product, this method may be acceptable because all costs are to be charged to the single product.

Answer (A) is incorrect because the number of units of production may have no logical relationship to overhead when several different products are made. Answer (B) is incorrect because a low level of direct labor costs means that fixed overhead is substantial, and appropriate cost drivers should be used to make the assignment. If drivers cannot be feasibly identified, an appropriate indirect measure should be chosen. Answer (D) is incorrect because a complex manufacturing process is likely to have many cost drivers, and overhead preferably should be allocated on the basis of what drives (causes) the costs.

**28.** In a capital-intensive industry, which is most likely to be an appropriate basis for applying overhead?

    A.  Direct labor hours.

    B.  Direct labor cost.

    C.  Machine hours.

    D.  Sales value of product produced.

The correct answer is (C). *(Publisher)*

**REQUIRED:** The most appropriate basis for applying overhead in a capital-intensive industry.

**DISCUSSION:** In capital-intensive industries, the amount of overhead will probably be related more to machine hours than to either direct labor hours or direct labor cost.

Answer (A) is incorrect because direct labor hours is a more appropriate basis for applying overhead in a labor-intensive industry. Answer (B) is incorrect because direct labor cost is often used as a base in labor-intensive industries. Answer (D) is incorrect because the sales value of product produced is virtually never an appropriate base on which to allocate overhead.

**29.** In a labor-intensive industry in which more overhead (service, support, more expensive equipment, etc.) is incurred by the more highly skilled and paid employees, what denominator measure is most likely to be appropriate for applying overhead?

    A.  Direct labor hours.

    B.  Direct labor cost.

    C.  Machine hours.

    D.  Sales value of product produced.

The correct answer is (B). *(Publisher)*

**REQUIRED:** The most appropriate basis for applying overhead in a labor-intensive industry.

**DISCUSSION:** In labor-intensive industries, overhead is traditionally assigned on the basis of labor time. However, if more overhead is incurred by the more highly skilled and paid employees, the overhead rate should be based upon direct labor cost rather than direct labor hours.

Answer (A) is incorrect because direct labor hours is appropriate when overhead is incurred uniformly by all types of employees. Answer (C) is incorrect because machine hours is an appropriate base when overhead varies with machine time used. Answer (D) is incorrect because sales value is virtually never an appropriate base for assigning overhead.

**30.** Practical capacity as a plant capacity concept

   A. Assumes all personnel and equipment will operate at peak efficiency and total plant capacity will be used.

   B. Does not consider idle time caused by inadequate sales demand.

   C. Includes consideration of idle time caused by both limited sales orders and human and equipment inefficiencies.

   D. Is the production volume that is necessary to meet sales demand for the next year.

The correct answer is (B). *(CMA, adapted)*
   **REQUIRED:** The true statement about practical capacity.
   **DISCUSSION:** Practical capacity is the maximum level at which output is produced efficiently. It includes consideration of idle time resulting from holidays, downtime, change-over time, etc., but not from inadequate sales demand.
   Answer (A) is incorrect because theoretical capacity assumes all personnel and equipment will operate at peak efficiency and total plant capacity will be used. Answer (C) is incorrect because practical capacity ignores demand. Answer (D) is incorrect because the production volume to meet sales demand may be more or less than practical capacity.

**31.** Application rates for factory overhead best reflect anticipated fluctuations in sales over a cycle of years when they are computed under the concept of

   A. Maximum capacity.

   B. Normal capacity.

   C. Practical capacity.

   D. Expected actual capacity.

The correct answer is (B). *(CPA, adapted)*
   **REQUIRED:** The concept of capacity for best applying overhead over a cycle of years.
   **DISCUSSION:** Normal capacity is the output level that will approximate demand over a period of years that includes seasonal, cyclical, and trend variations. Deviations in one year will be offset in other years.
   Answer (A) is incorrect because maximum (theoretical or ideal) capacity is the level at which output is maximized assuming perfectly efficient operations at all times. This level is impossible to maintain and results in underapplied overhead. Answer (C) is incorrect because practical capacity is the maximum level at which output is produced efficiently. It usually also results in underapplied overhead. Answer (D) is incorrect because expected actual capacity is a short-run output level. It minimizes under- or overapplied overhead but does not provide a consistent basis for assigning overhead cost. Per-unit overhead will fluctuate because of short-term changes in the expected production level.

**32.** The denominator of the overhead application rate can be based on one of several production capacities. Which would result in the lowest expected over- or underapplied overhead?

   A. Theoretical capacity.

   B. Expected capacity.

   C. Normal capacity.

   D. Practical capacity.

The correct answer is (B). *(Publisher)*
   **REQUIRED:** The production capacity resulting in the lowest expected over- or underapplied overhead.
   **DISCUSSION:** If actual output differs from the predetermined capacity level, a volume variance will occur. This variance equals the over- or underapplied overhead. The expected volume is that predicted for the period. Thus, the use of expected capacity as a denominator should result in the lowest expected over- or underapplied overhead.
   Answer (A) is incorrect because theoretical capacity is the maximum capacity. Answer (C) is incorrect because normal capacity is an average expected capacity over a series of years. It will vary from the expected capacity on a year-by-year basis. Answer (D) is incorrect because practical capacity is theoretical capacity adjusted downward for holidays, maintenance time, etc. It is very difficult to attain.

**33.** Which concept of capacity applies the least amount of overhead to units of production?

   A. Theoretical capacity.

   B. Expected capacity.

   C. Normal capacity.

   D. Practical capacity.

The correct answer is (A). *(Publisher)*
   **REQUIRED:** The concept of capacity that applies the least overhead to production.
   **DISCUSSION:** The larger the denominator in the overhead application rate, the smaller the rate and the lower the cost assigned to the product. Theoretical capacity, which is the absolute capacity during continuous operations, ignoring holidays, maintenance time, etc., provides the largest denominator in the ratio.
   Answers (B), (C), and (D) are incorrect because expected capacity, normal capacity, and practical capacity are less than theoretical capacity.

**34.** Effective cost capacity management

    A.  Minimizes the values delivered to customers.

    B.  Maximizes required future investments.

    C.  Matches the firm's resources with market opportunities.

    D.  Is limited to eliminating short-term worth.

The correct answer is (C). *(Publisher)*

**REQUIRED:** The true statement about effective cost capacity arrangement.

**DISCUSSION:** Maximizing the value created within an organization starts with understanding the nature and capabilities of all of the company's resources (capacity), which may be defined from several different perspectives. Managing capacity cost starts when a product or process is first envisioned. It continues through the subsequent disposal of resources downstream. Effective capacity cost management requires supporting effective matching of a firm's resources with current and future market opportunities.

    Answer (A) is incorrect because effective capacity management maximizes value delivered to customers. Answer (B) is incorrect because effective capacity management minimizes required future investment. Answer (D) is incorrect because effective capacity management minimizes waste in the short, intermediate, and long run.

**35.** Accounting for factory overhead costs involves averaging in

| | Job-Order Costing | Process Costing |
|---|---|---|
| A. | Yes | No |
| B. | Yes | Yes |
| C. | No | Yes |
| D. | No | No |

The correct answer is (B). *(CPA, adapted)*

**REQUIRED:** The accounting system(s) using average factory overhead costs.

**DISCUSSION:** Overhead consists of costs other than direct materials and labor that are averaged over the entire period, usually a year, based upon an estimated output level. The total of the estimated indirect costs is divided by the base used for cost assignment, e.g., direct labor hours, and assigned to the product based upon the actual output level. Consequently, factory overhead costs are averaged in both job-order and process costing systems.

    Answers (A), (C), and (D) are incorrect because averaging of overhead is done in process costing and in job-order costing.

**36.** Many firms use two overhead accounts: factory overhead control and factory overhead applied. During the period, which account receives numerous debits and credits?

    A.  Factory overhead applied.

    B.  Factory overhead control.

    C.  Both.

    D.  Neither.

The correct answer is (D). *(Publisher)*

**REQUIRED:** The overhead account(s) with numerous debits and credits during the period.

**DISCUSSION:** When both factory overhead control and factory overhead applied are used, all overhead incurred is debited to factory overhead control. All overhead applied is credited to factory overhead applied.

    Answer (A) is incorrect because the only debits to factory overhead applied are to close the account at the end of the period and to correct errors. Answer (B) is incorrect because the only credits to factory overhead control are to close the account at the end of the period and to correct errors. Answer (C) is incorrect because neither account is both debited and credited frequently.

**37.** Cox Company found that the differences in product costs resulting from the application of predetermined overhead rates rather than actual overhead rates were immaterial even though actual production was substantially less than planned production. The most likely explanation is that

- A. Overhead was composed chiefly of variable costs.

- B. Several products were produced simultaneously.

- C. Fixed factory overhead was a significant cost.

- D. Costs of overhead items were substantially higher than anticipated.

The correct answer is (A). *(CPA, adapted)*
**REQUIRED:** The likely explanation for a small difference between applied and actual overhead.
**DISCUSSION:** Total variable overhead costs change in proportion to changes in the activity level. Total fixed costs do not. For the difference between applied and actual overhead to be immaterial when actual production is substantially less than planned production, overhead costs must be composed chiefly of variable costs.
Answer (B) is incorrect because, for overhead application purposes, the simultaneous production of several products is similar to producing one product. Answer (C) is incorrect because, if fixed factory overhead had been significant, a material difference would have arisen. Answer (D) is incorrect because, if actual costs are substantially higher than anticipated, overhead will be underapplied by a substantial amount.

**38.** A job-order cost system uses a predetermined factory overhead rate based on expected volume and expected fixed cost. At the end of the year, underapplied overhead might be explained by which of the following situations?

|    | Actual Volume | Actual Fixed Costs |
|----|---------------|--------------------|
| A. | Greater than expected | Greater than expected |
| B. | Greater than expected | Less than expected |
| C. | Less than expected | Greater than expected |
| D. | Less than expected | Less than expected |

The correct answer is (C). *(CPA, adapted)*
**REQUIRED:** The reason(s) for underapplied overhead.
**DISCUSSION:** If too little fixed overhead is applied at the predetermined rate (expected fixed cost ÷ expected volume), the result is underapplied overhead (actual factory overhead exceeds overhead applied). If the actual and expected fixed costs are the same, but the actual volume is less than the expected (denominator) volume, overhead will be underapplied. If the actual volume equals expected volume, but actual fixed costs exceed the expected (numerator) fixed costs, overhead is likewise underapplied.
Answers (A), (B), and (D) are incorrect because, if actual volume is greater than expected or actual fixed costs are less than expected, overhead may be overapplied.

**39.** When the amount of overapplied factory overhead is significant, the entry to close overapplied factory overhead will most likely require

- A. A debit to cost of goods sold.

- B. Debits to cost of goods sold, finished goods inventory, and work-in-process inventory.

- C. A credit to cost of goods sold.

- D. Credits to cost of goods sold, finished goods inventory, and work-in-process inventory.

The correct answer is (D). *(CIA, adapted)*
**REQUIRED:** The most likely entry to close overapplied factory overhead.
**DISCUSSION:** Under a normal costing system, overhead is applied to all jobs worked on during the period at a predetermined rate. Because cost of goods sold, finished goods inventory, and work-in-process inventory all relate to these jobs, each should be adjusted by its proportionate share of over- or underapplied overhead. This apportionment may be based on either the percentage of total overhead (theoretically preferable) or the percentage of total cost. The entry to close overapplied overhead requires credits to these three accounts.
Answers (A), (B), and (C) are incorrect because cost of goods sold, finished goods inventory, and work-in-process inventory should be credited (not debited).

**40.** Assuming two overhead accounts are used, what is the entry to close them and to charge underapplied overhead to cost of goods sold?

A. Cost of goods sold     XXX
      Finished goods          XXX

B. Factory O/H applied     XXX
      Factory O/H control       XXX
      Cost of goods sold        XXX

C. Cost of goods sold     XXX
      Factory O/H applied       XXX

D. Cost of goods sold     XXX
    Factory O/H applied     XXX
      Factory O/H control       XXX

The correct answer is (D). *(Publisher)*
**REQUIRED:** The journal entry to close the overhead accounts and to charge underapplied overhead to CGS.
**DISCUSSION:** Total under- or overapplied overhead is often debited (credited) to CGS rather than allocated among CGS, EWIP, and finished goods. The correct entry to close the overhead accounts and to charge underapplied overhead to CGS is to debit the factory overhead applied account for the amount of overhead applied for the period and to credit factory overhead control for the amount of overhead actually incurred for the period. The amount actually incurred exceeds the amount of overhead applied because overhead is underapplied. The difference is the amount charged to CGS.
Answer (A) is incorrect because an entry debiting CGS and crediting finished goods expenses inventoried costs related to items sold. Answer (B) is incorrect because the closing entry credits CGS when overhead has been overapplied. Answer (C) is incorrect because crediting overhead applied does not close the account.

**41.** Mason Co. uses a job-order cost system and applies manufacturing overhead to jobs using a predetermined overhead rate based on direct-labor dollars. The rate for the current year is 200% of direct-labor dollars. This rate was calculated last December and will be used throughout the current year. Mason had one job, No. 150, in process on August 1 with raw materials costs of $2,000 and direct-labor costs of $3,000. During August, raw materials and direct labor added to jobs were as follows:

| | No. 150 | No. 151 | No. 152 |
|---|---|---|---|
| Raw materials | $ -- | $4,000 | $1,000 |
| Direct labor | 1,500 | 5,000 | 2,500 |

Actual manufacturing overhead for the month of August was $20,000. During the month, Mason completed Job Nos. 150 and 151. For August, manufacturing overhead was

A. Overapplied by $4,000.

B. Underapplied by $7,000.

C. Underapplied by $2,000.

D. Underapplied by $1,000.

The correct answer is (C). *(CPA, adapted)*
**REQUIRED:** The under- or overapplied manufacturing overhead.
**DISCUSSION:** Mason incurred direct-labor costs in August of $9,000 ($1,500 Job 150 + $5,000 Job 151 + $2,500 Job 152). Hence, overhead applied was $18,000 (200% x $9,000). The amount underapplied was $2,000 ($20,000 actual OH – $18,000).
Answer (A) is incorrect because overhead would have been overapplied by $4,000 if the direct-labor costs in beginning work-in-process had been treated as incurred during August. Answer (B) is incorrect because overhead would have been underapplied by $7,000 if Job 152 had been ignored. Answer (D) is incorrect because overhead would have been underapplied by $1,000 if the direct-labor costs in beginning work-in-process had been treated as incurred during August and if Job 152 had been ignored.

**42.** The following information is available from the records of a manufacturing company that applies factory overhead based on direct labor hours:

| | |
|---|---|
| Estimated overhead cost | $500,000 |
| Estimated labor hours | 200,000 |
| Actual overhead cost | $515,000 |
| Actual labor hours | 210,000 |

Based on this information, factory overhead is

A. Underapplied by $9,524.

B. Overapplied by $10,000.

C. Overapplied by $15,000.

D. Overapplied by $40,750.

The correct answer is (B). *(CIA, adapted)*
**REQUIRED:** The amount of factory overhead based on direct labor hours.
**DISCUSSION:** Applied overhead equals the actual labor hours (210,000) times the estimated application rate ($500,000 ÷ 200,000 DLH = $2.50 per direct labor hour), or $525,000. This amount is $10,000 ($525,000 – $515,000 actual cost) higher than the actual overhead cost incurred. Hence, overhead was overapplied by $10,000.
Answer (A) is incorrect because this amount results from treating the actual overhead and labor hours as the estimated values and vice versa. Answer (C) is incorrect because $15,000 is the excess of actual over estimated overhead. Answer (D) is incorrect because this amount results from treating actual overhead as the estimated value and vice versa.

**43.** Worley Company has underapplied overhead of $45,000 for the year. Before disposition of the underapplied overhead, selected year-end balances from Worley's accounting records were

| | |
|---|---|
| Sales | $1,200,000 |
| Cost of goods sold | 720,000 |
| Direct materials inventory | 36,000 |
| Work-in-process inventory | 54,000 |
| Finished goods inventory | 90,000 |

Under Worley's cost accounting system, over- or underapplied overhead is assigned to appropriate inventories and CGS based on year-end balances. In its year-end income statement, Worley should report CGS of

   A. $682,500

   B. $684,000

   C. $757,500

   D. $765,000

The correct answer is (C). *(CPA, adapted)*
   **REQUIRED:** The amount of cost of goods sold after allocation of underapplied overhead.
   **DISCUSSION:** The assignment of underapplied overhead increases CGS. The underapplied overhead of $45,000 for the year should be assigned on a pro rata basis to work-in-process ($54,000), finished goods ($90,000), and CGS ($720,000). The sum of these three items is $864,000. Thus, $37,500 should be assigned to CGS [($720,000 ÷ $864,000) x $45,000]. CGS after assignment is $757,500 ($37,500 + $720,000). The remaining $7,500 should be assigned proportionately to work-in-process and finished goods.
   Answer (A) is incorrect because $682,500 is the appropriate CGS balance if overhead was overapplied by $45,000 and $37,500 was assigned to CGS. Answer (B) is incorrect because $684,000 is the CGS balance if overhead was overapplied by $45,000 and direct materials inventory was incorrectly included in the denominator of the ratio used to assign overhead. Answer (D) is incorrect because $765,000 is the result of debiting the full amount of underapplied overhead ($45,000) to CGS.

**44.** At the beginning of the year, Smith Inc. budgeted the following:

| | |
|---|---|
| Units | 10,000 |
| Sales | $100,000 |
| Minus: | |
|   Total variable expenses | 60,000 |
|   Total fixed expenses | 20,000 |
| Net income | $ 20,000 |
| | |
| Factory overhead: | |
|   Variable | $ 30,000 |
|   Fixed | 10,000 |

There were no beginning inventories. At the end of the year, no work was in process, total factory overhead incurred was $39,500, and underapplied factory overhead was $1,500. Factory overhead was applied on the basis of budgeted unit production. How many units were produced this year?

   A. 10,250

   B. 10,000

   C. 9,875

   D. 9,500

The correct answer is (D). *(Publisher)*
   **REQUIRED:** The number of units produced given various overhead data.
   **DISCUSSION:** Given actual overhead of $39,500 and underapplied overhead of $1,500, overhead applied was $38,000 ($39,500 – $1,500). Overhead is applied at the rate of $4 per unit ($40,000 budgeted overhead ÷ 10,000 budgeted units). Accordingly, 9,500 units were produced ($38,000 applied overhead ÷ $4 per unit application rate).
   Answer (A) is incorrect because 10,250 would have been produced if overhead had been overapplied by $1,500 [($39,500 + $1,500) ÷ $4]. Answer (B) is incorrect because 10,000 is the result of dividing budgeted, not applied, overhead by the application rate. Answer (C) is incorrect because 9,875 units would have been produced if $39,500 had been the amount of applied overhead.

**45.** A company manufactures plastic products for the home and restaurant market. The company also does contract work for other customers and uses a job-order costing system. The flexible budget covering next year's expected range of output is

| Direct labor hours | 50,000 | 80,000 | 110,000 |
|---|---|---|---|
| Machine hours | 40,000 | 64,000 | 88,000 |
| Variable O/H costs | $100,000 | $160,000 | $220,000 |
| Fixed O/H costs | 150,000 | 150,000 | 150,000 |
| Total O/H costs | $250,000 | $310,000 | $370,000 |

A predetermined overhead rate based on direct labor hours is used to apply total overhead. Management has estimated that 100,000 direct labor hours will be used next year. The predetermined overhead rate per direct labor hour to be used to apply total overhead to the individual jobs next year is

A. $3.36

B. $3.50

C. $3.70

D. $3.88

The correct answer is (B). *(CIA, adapted)*
**REQUIRED:** The predetermined overhead rate per direct labor hour.
**DISCUSSION:** The predetermined overhead rate is calculated by dividing the total fixed overhead by the activity level to arrive at a unit fixed overhead cost that is added to the unit variable overhead cost. The unit variable overhead rate is the same at each activity level. Thus, the predetermined overhead rate is $3.50 [($150,000 FOH ÷ 100,000 hrs.) + ($220,000 VOH ÷ 110,000 hrs.)].
Answer (A) is incorrect because $3.36 per direct labor hour is based on use of an activity level of 110,000 direct labor hours to determine the fixed overhead rate. Answer (C) is incorrect because $3.70 is the result of assuming that $220,000 of variable overhead will be incurred for 100,000 (not 110,000) direct labor hours. Answer (D) is incorrect because $3.88 (rounded) results from using an activity level of 80,000 direct labor hours to determine the fixed overhead rate.

**46.** Schneider, Inc. had the following information relating to year 1:

| | |
|---|---|
| Budgeted factory overhead | $74,800 |
| Actual factory overhead | $78,300 |
| Applied factory overhead | $76,500 |
| Estimated direct labor hours | 44,000 |

If Schneider decides to use the actual results from year 1 to determine the year 2 overhead rate, what is the year 2 overhead rate?

A. $1.700

B. $1.738

C. $1.740

D. $1.780

The correct answer is (C). *(R. Gruber)*
**REQUIRED:** The overhead rate for year 2 using year 1 data.
**DISCUSSION:** The year 1 overhead rate was $1.70 ($74,800 budgeted overhead ÷ 44,000 estimated DLH). Because applied factory overhead equals actual DLH times the overhead rate, the actual direct labor hours for year 1 were 45,000 ($76,500 ÷ $1.70). Hence, the overhead rate for year 2 is $1.74 ($78,300 actual year 1 overhead ÷ 45,000 actual year 1 DLH).
Answer (A) is incorrect because $1.700 was the year 1 rate. Answer (B) is incorrect because $1.738 equals year 1 applied overhead divided by estimated (not actual) year 1 hours. Answer (D) is incorrect because $1.780 (rounded) equals actual year 1 overhead divided by estimated year 1 hours.

**47.** Carley Products has no work-in-process or finished goods inventories at year-end. The balances of Carley's accounts include the following:

| | |
|---|---|
| Cost of goods sold | $2,040,000 |
| General selling and administrative expenses | 900,000 |
| Sales | 3,600,000 |
| Factory overhead control | 700,000 |
| Factory overhead applied | 648,000 |

Carley's pretax income for the year is

A. $608,000

B. $660,000

C. $712,000

D. $1,508,000

The correct answer is (A). *(CMA, adapted)*
**REQUIRED:** The pretax income assuming an overhead application difference.
**DISCUSSION:** The pretax income is equal to sales minus cost of goods sold, general selling and administrative expenses, and underapplied factory overhead (the excess of actual overhead over the amount applied).

| | |
|---|---|
| Sales | $3,600,000 |
| CGS | (2,040,000) |
| Underapplied overhead | (52,000) |
| Gross margin | $1,508,000 |
| GS&A expenses | (900,000) |
| Income before income taxes | $ 608,000 |

Answer (B) is incorrect because $660,000 is the result of failing to deduct the underapplied overhead. Answer (C) is incorrect because $712,000 is the pretax income assuming $52,000 of overhead was overapplied and therefore added in the calculation of the gross margin. Answer (D) is incorrect because $1,508,000 is the gross margin.

**48.** Regan Company operates its factory on a two-shift basis and pays a late-shift differential of 15%. Regan also pays a premium of 50% for overtime work. Because Regan manufactures only for stock, the cost system provides for uniform direct-labor hourly charges for production done without regard to shift worked or work done on an overtime basis. Overtime and late-shift differentials are included in Regan's factory overhead application rate. The May payroll for production workers is as follows:

| | |
|---|---|
| Wages at base direct-labor rates | $325,000 |
| Shift differentials | 25,000 |
| Overtime premiums | 10,000 |

For the month of May, what amount of direct labor should Regan charge to work-in-process?

- A. $325,000
- B. $335,000
- C. $350,000
- D. $360,000

The correct answer is (A). *(CPA, adapted)*

**REQUIRED:** The amount of direct labor given shift pay differentials and overtime premiums.

**DISCUSSION:** Regan's cost system provides for uniform direct hourly charges for production done without regard to shift work or work done on an overtime basis. The shift pay differentials and overtime premiums are included in factory overhead. Accordingly, both the $25,000 and $10,000 amounts should be charged to overhead, and $325,000 should be charged to the WIP account as direct labor.

Answer (B) is incorrect because $335,000 includes overtime premiums. Answer (C) is incorrect because $350,000 includes shift differentials. Answer (D) is incorrect because $360,000 includes both the shift differentials and overtime premiums.

---

Questions 49 through 53 are based on the following information. Baehr Company is a manufacturing company with a fiscal year that runs from July 1 to June 30. The company uses a job-order accounting system for its production costs. A predetermined overhead rate based upon direct labor hours is used to apply overhead to individual jobs. A flexible budget of overhead costs was prepared for the fiscal year as shown below.

| Direct labor hours | 100,000 | 120,000 | 140,000 |
|---|---|---|---|
| Variable overhead costs | $325,000 | $390,000 | $455,000 |
| Fixed overhead costs | 216,000 | 216,000 | 216,000 |
| Total overhead | $541,000 | $606,000 | $671,000 |

Although the annual ideal capacity is 150,000 direct labor hours, company officials have determined 120,000 direct labor hours to be normal capacity for the year.

The information presented below and in the opposite column is for November. Jobs 83-50 and 83-51 were completed during November.

Inventories November 1

| | |
|---|---|
| Raw materials and supplies | $ 10,500 |
| Work-in-process (Job 83-50) | 54,000 |
| Finished goods | 112,500 |

Purchases of raw materials and supplies

| | |
|---|---|
| Raw materials | $135,000 |
| Supplies | 15,000 |
| | $150,000 |

Materials and supplies requisitioned for production

| | |
|---|---|
| Job 83-50 | $ 45,000 |
| Job 83-51 | 37,500 |
| Job 83-52 | 25,500 |
| Supplies | 12,000 |
| | $120,000 |

Factory direct labor hours

| | |
|---|---|
| Job 83-50 | 3,500 |
| Job 83-51 | 3,000 |
| Job 83-52 | 2,000 |
| | 8,500 |

Labor costs

| | |
|---|---|
| Direct labor wages | $51,000 |
| Indirect labor wages (4,000 hours) | 15,000 |
| Supervisory salaries | 6,000 |
| | $72,000 |

Building occupancy costs (heat, light, depreciation, etc.)

| | |
|---|---|
| Factory facilities | $6,500 |
| Sales offices | 1,500 |
| Administrative offices | 1,000 |
| | $9,000 |

Factory equipment costs

| | |
|---|---|
| Power | $4,000 |
| Repairs and maintenance | 1,500 |
| Depreciation | 1,500 |
| Other | 1,000 |
| | $8,000 |

**49.** The predetermined overhead rate to be used to apply overhead to individual jobs during the fiscal year is

A. $3.25 per DLH.

B. $4.79 per DLH.

C. $5.05 per DLH.

D. $5.41 per DLH.

Note: Without prejudice to your answer to question 49, assume the predetermined overhead rate is $4.50 per direct labor hour. Use this amount in answering questions 50 through 53.

**50.** The total cost of Job 83-50 is

A. $81,750

B. $135,750

C. $142,750

D. $146,750

**51.** The factory overhead costs applied to Job 83-52 during November were

A. $9,000

B. $21,000

C. $46,500

D. $8,000

The correct answer is (C). *(CMA, adapted)*

**REQUIRED:** The predetermined rate to apply overhead to individual jobs.

**DISCUSSION:** The predetermined overhead rate is the estimated total overhead divided by the direct labor hours at normal capacity. The normal capacity for the year is 120,000 hours and related overhead costs are $606,000. The overhead rate is therefore $5.05 ($606,000 ÷ 120,000 hours).

Answer (A) is incorrect because $3.25 per DLH only takes the variable overhead costs into account for the normal capacity of 120,000 hours. Answer (B) is incorrect because $4.79 is the overhead rate for a capacity of 140,000 direct labor hours. Answer (D) is incorrect because $5.41 is the overhead rate for a capacity of 100,000 direct labor hours.

The correct answer is (B). *(CMA, adapted)*

**REQUIRED:** The total cost for a job begun in a prior period and completed currently.

**DISCUSSION:** Job 83-50 was completed during November after having been started in a previous period (BWIP was $54,000). During the period, $45,000 in materials costs was added. Additionally, direct labor was incurred at the rate of $6.00 per hour ($51,000 ÷ 8,500 total DLH). Direct labor cost for November for Job 83-50 was thus $21,000 ($6.00 x 3,500 DLH). Overhead applied was $15,750 (given overhead rate of $4.50 x 3,500 DLH). Total cost was $135,750 ($54,000 + $45,000 + $21,000 + $15,750).

Answer (A) is incorrect because $81,750 omits beginning work-in process. Answer (C) is incorrect because $142,750 applies one-third, or $7,000 [($15,000 + $6,000) ÷ 3], of the indirect labor wages and supervisory salaries to the total cost of Job 83-50. Answer (D) is incorrect because $146,750 applies one-third, or $7,000, of the indirect labor wages and supervisory salaries, and one-third, or $4,000 ($12,000 ÷ 3), of the supplies requisitioned for production to the total cost of Job 83-50.

The correct answer is (A). *(CMA, adapted)*

**REQUIRED:** The factory overhead costs applied to an incomplete job at the end of the period.

**DISCUSSION:** The overhead rate is given as $4.50 per hour. Job 83-52 incurred 2,000 direct labor hours resulting in $9,000 ($4.50 x 2,000 DLH) of overhead applied to that job in November.

Answer (B) is incorrect because $21,000 includes the direct labor cost for November for Job 83-52 of $12,000. Answer (C) is incorrect because $46,500 is the total cost for November for Job 83-52. Answer (D) is incorrect because $8,000 applies an overhead rate of $4.00 per DLH instead of the given rate of $4.50.

**52.** Refer to the information preceding questions 49 and 50. The total amount of overhead applied to jobs during November was

A. $29,250

B. $38,250

C. $47,250

D. $56,250

The correct answer is (B). *(CMA, adapted)*

**REQUIRED:** The total overhead applied to jobs during the current period.

**DISCUSSION:** During November, 8,500 direct labor hours were incurred. The overhead application rate is given as $4.50 per hour. Thus, the total overhead applied was $38,250 ($4.50 x 8,500 DLH).

Answer (A) is incorrect because $29,250 subtracts the $9,000 of building occupancy costs from the total overhead applied of $38,250. Answer (C) is incorrect because $47,250 adds the $9,000 of building occupancy costs to the total overhead applied of $38,250. Answer (D) is incorrect because $56,250 reallocates November's portion of $18,000 ($216,000 ÷ 12) of fixed overhead costs to the total overhead applied of $38,250. The overhead rate, however, takes fixed and variable overhead costs into account.

**53.** Refer to the information preceding questions 49 and 50. Actual factory overhead incurred during November was

A. $38,000

B. $41,500

C. $47,500

D. $50,500

The correct answer is (C). *(CMA, adapted)*

**REQUIRED:** The actual factory overhead incurred during the period.

**DISCUSSION:** Actual factory overhead incurred during November consisted of factory equipment costs, factory occupancy costs (heat, light, depreciation, etc.), indirect labor wages and supervisory salaries ($15,000 + $6,000), and supplies requisitioned for production.

| | |
|---|---:|
| Factory equipment costs | $ 8,000 |
| Factory occupancy costs | 6,500 |
| Indirect labor wages and supervisory salaries | 21,000 |
| Supplies | 12,000 |
| Actual overhead | $47,500 |

Answer (A) is incorrect because $38,000 includes the building occupancy costs of the sales and administrative offices, but it does not include the cost of the supplies requisitioned for production. Answer (B) is incorrect because $41,500 does not include the supervisory salaries. Answer (D) is incorrect because $50,500 includes the actual purchase cost of supplies of $15,000 instead of the cost of the supplies requisitioned for production of $12,000.

## 3.4 Work-in-Process Account Calculations

**54.** Under Pick Co.'s job-order costing system, manufacturing overhead is applied to work-in-process using a predetermined annual overhead rate. During January 1998, Pick's transactions included the following:

| | |
|---|---:|
| Direct materials issued to production | $90,000 |
| Indirect materials issued to production | 8,000 |
| Manufacturing overhead incurred | 125,000 |
| Manufacturing overhead applied | 113,000 |
| Direct labor costs | 107,000 |

Pick had neither beginning nor ending work-in-process inventory. What was the cost of jobs completed in January 1998?

A. $302,000

B. $310,000

C. $322,000

D. $330,000

The correct answer is (B). *(CPA, adapted)*

**REQUIRED:** The cost of jobs completed.

**DISCUSSION:** Given no beginning or ending work-in-process, the cost of jobs completed equals the sum of direct materials, direct labor, and manufacturing overhead applied. Indirect materials costs are charged to overhead control and are not included in the amount transferred from work-in-process to finished goods except to the extent they are reflected in applied overhead. The difference between overhead incurred and overhead applied, if material, is assigned to finished goods, cost of goods sold, and ending work-in-process ($0 in this case). Hence, the cost of jobs completed was $310,000 ($90,000 + $113,000 + $107,000).

Answer (A) is incorrect because $302,000 results from subtracting indirect materials from the cost of jobs completed. Answer (C) is incorrect because $322,000 is based on overhead incurred. Answer (D) is incorrect because $330,000 includes indirect materials and overhead incurred.

**55.** A manufacturer employs a job-order cost system. All jobs ordinarily pass through all three production departments, and Job 101 and Job 102 were completed during the current month.

| Production Departments | Direct Labor Rate | Manufacturing Overhead Application Rates |
|---|---|---|
| Department 1 | $12.00 | 150% of direct materials cost |
| Department 2 | 18.00 | $8.00 per machine hour |
| Department 3 | 15.00 | 200% of direct labor cost |

| | Job 101 | Job 102 | Job 103 |
|---|---|---|---|
| BWIP | $25,500 | $32,400 | $ -0- |
| **DM:** | | | |
| Department 1 | $40,000 | $26,000 | $58,000 |
| Department 2 | 3,000 | 5,000 | 14,000 |
| Department 3 | -0- | -0- | -0- |
| **DL:** | | | |
| Department 1 | 500 | 400 | 300 |
| Department 2 | 200 | 250 | 350 |
| Department 3 | 1,500 | 1,800 | 2,500 |
| **MH:** | | | |
| Department 1 | -0- | -0- | -0- |
| Department 2 | 1,200 | 1,500 | 2,700 |
| Department 3 | 150 | 300 | 200 |

The cost of completed Job 101 is

A. $131,500

B. $189,700

C. $202,600

D. $215,200

The correct answer is (D). *(CIA, adapted)*
**REQUIRED:** The cost of completed Job 101.
**DISCUSSION:** The cost of completed Job 101 includes all direct costs, applied overhead from each department, and the beginning WIP inventory. Consequently, total cost is $215,200 {($40,000 + $3,000) DM + [($12 x 500) + ($18 x 200) + ($15 x 1,500)] DL + [(150% x $40,000 DM cost in Dept. 1) + ($8 x 1,200 MH in Dept. 2) + (200% x $15 x 1,500 DLH in Dept. 3)] OH}.

Answer (A) is incorrect because $131,500 excludes the costs from Departments 2 and 3. Answer (B) is incorrect because $189,700 excludes the beginning WIP inventory balance. Answer (C) is incorrect because $202,600 excludes direct materials from Department 2 and direct labor from Departments 1 and 2.

**56.** The Childers Company manufactures widgets. During the fiscal year just ended, the company incurred prime costs of $1.5 million and conversion costs of $1.8 million. Overhead is applied at the rate of 200% of direct labor cost. How much of the above costs represent direct materials cost?

A. $1,500,000

B. $300,000

C. $900,000

D. $600,000

The correct answer is (C). *(A. Wilson)*
**REQUIRED:** The calculation of direct materials costs for the fiscal year just ended.
**DISCUSSION:** Prime cost is the sum of direct materials and direct labor costs. Conversion cost is the sum of direct labor and factory overhead costs.

$$O/H = 200\% \times DL$$
$$DL + O/H = \$1,800,000$$

$$DL + 2DL = \$1,800,000$$
$$DL = \$600,000$$

$$DM + DL = \$1,500,000$$
$$DM + \$600,000 = \$1,500,000$$
$$DM = \$900,000$$

Answer (A) is incorrect because $1,500,000 is the prime costs, which include direct labor costs. Answer (B) is incorrect because $300,000 is the difference between conversion costs and prime costs. Answer (D) is incorrect because DL is equal to $600,000.

**57.** Birk Co. uses a job-order cost system. The following debits (credit) appeared in Birk's work-in-process account for the month of April 1998:

| April | Description | Amount |
|---|---|---|
| 1 | Balance | $ 4,000 |
| 30 | Direct materials | 24,000 |
| 30 | Direct labor | 16,000 |
| 30 | Factory overhead | 12,800 |
| 30 | To finished goods | (48,000) |

Birk applies overhead to production at a predetermined rate of 80% of direct labor cost. Job No. 5, the only job still in process on April 30, 1998, has been charged with direct labor of $2,000. What was the amount of direct materials charged to Job No. 5?

A. $3,000

B. $5,200

C. $8,800

D. $24,000

The correct answer is (B). *(CPA, adapted)*
**REQUIRED:** The dollar value of direct materials in ending work-in-process.
**DISCUSSION:** Total debits to WIP are $56,800 ($4,000 + $24,000 + $16,000 + $12,800). Given a credit of $48,000 for finished goods, EWIP is $8,800 ($56,800 – $48,000). Of this amount, $2,000 is direct labor and $1,600 (80% x $2,000) is overhead. Hence, the amount of direct materials charged to Job No. 5 was $5,200 ($8,800 – $2,000 – $1,600).
Answer (A) is incorrect because $3,000 is a random figure. Answer (C) is incorrect because $8,800 is the total EWIP credit. Answer (D) is incorrect because $24,000 is the debit for direct materials during the month.

**58.** Ajax Corporation transferred $72,000 of raw materials to its production department in February and incurred $37,000 of conversion costs ($22,000 of direct labor and $15,000 of overhead). At the beginning of the period, $14,000 of inventory (direct materials and conversion costs) was in process. At the end of the period, $18,000 of inventory was in process. What was the cost of goods manufactured?

A. $105,000

B. $109,000

C. $123,000

D. $141,000

The correct answer is (A). *(Publisher)*
**REQUIRED:** The cost of goods manufactured for the period.
**DISCUSSION:** The total cost incurred in the production process, the sum of BWIP, direct materials, direct labor, and overhead, minus the cost of goods not completed during the period (EWIP), is the cost of goods manufactured.

| | |
|---|---|
| BWIP | $ 14,000 |
| Materials | 72,000 |
| Conversion costs | 37,000 |
| Total | $123,000 |
| Minus EWIP | (18,000) |
| CGM | $105,000 |

Answer (B) is incorrect because $109,000 is the actual cost for the current period. BWIP should be added and EWIP subtracted to arrive at CGM. Answer (C) is incorrect because the $18,000 in EWIP was not deducted from the total cost of $123,000. Answer (D) is incorrect because the $18,000 of EWIP was added to (not subtracted from) the total costs incurred.

**59.** Lucy Sportswear manufactures a specialty line of T-shirts using a job-order cost system. During March, the following costs were incurred in completing Job ICU2: direct materials, $13,700; direct labor, $4,800; administrative, $1,400; and selling, $5,600. Factory overhead was applied at the rate of $25 per machine hour, and Job ICU2 required 800 machine hours. If Job ICU2 resulted in 7,000 good shirts, the cost of goods sold per unit would be

A. $6.50

B. $6.30

C. $5.70

D. $5.50

The correct answer is (D). *(CMA, adapted)*
**REQUIRED:** The cost of goods sold per unit.
**DISCUSSION:** Cost of goods sold is based on the manufacturing costs incurred in production but does not include selling or general and administrative expenses. Manufacturing costs equal $38,500 [$13,700 DM + $4,800 DL + (800 hours x $25) FOH]. Thus, per-unit cost is $5.50 ($38,500 ÷ 7,000 units).
Answer (A) is incorrect because $6.50 includes selling and administrative expenses. Answer (B) is incorrect because $6.30 includes selling costs. Answer (C) is incorrect because $5.70 includes administrative expenses.

Questions 60 and 61 are based on the following information. Kaden Corp. has two divisions -- Ace and Bow. Ace has a job-order cost system and manufactures machinery on special order for unrelated customers. Bow has a process cost system and manufactures Product Zee, which is sold to Ace as well as to unrelated companies. Ace's work-in-process account at April 30 included the following:

Ace applies factory overhead at 90% of direct labor cost. Job No. 125, which was the only job in process at April 30, has been charged with factory overhead of $4,500. Bow's cost to manufacture Product Zee is $3.00 per unit, which is sold to Ace for $5.00 per unit and to unrelated customers for $6.00 per unit.

| | |
|---|---:|
| Balance, April 1 | $ 24,000 |
| Direct materials (including transferred-in cost) | 80,000 |
| Direct labor | 60,000 |
| Factory overhead | 54,000 |
| Transferred to finished goods | (200,000) |

**60.** Direct materials (including transferred-in cost) charged to Job No. 125 amounted to

A. $5,000

B. $8,500

C. $13,500

D. $18,000

The correct answer is (B). *(CPA, adapted)*

**REQUIRED:** The amount of direct materials in EWIP.

**DISCUSSION:** The EWIP consists of direct materials, direct labor, and overhead. EWIP is

| | |
|---|---:|
| BWIP | $ 24,000 |
| DM | 80,000 |
| DL | 60,000 |
| FOH | 54,000 |
| CGM | (200,000) |
| EWIP | $ 18,000 |

FOH is applied at 90% of DL, and FOH was $4,500 on Job 125. Thus, direct labor is $5,000 ($4,500 ÷ .9). Direct materials charged therefore amounted to $8,500 ($18,000 EWIP – $4,500 FOH – $5,000 DL).

Answer (A) is incorrect because DL is equal to $5,000 ($4,500 ÷ .9). Answer (C) is incorrect because $13,500 is the total of DL and DM (prime costs). Answer (D) is incorrect because $18,000 is the total cost charged to Job No. 125.

**61.** How much is the transfer price for Product Zee?

A. $2.00

B. $3.00

C. $5.00

D. $6.00

The correct answer is (C). *(CPA, adapted)*

**REQUIRED:** The transfer price of Product Zee.

**DISCUSSION:** The transfer price is the price at which an item is sold in intracompany transactions. This price is usually less than the market price, but it may, at times, be set at a price equal to or greater than market to achieve overall corporate objectives. Here, the transfer price is given as $5.00.

Answer (A) is incorrect because $2.00 is the difference between the transfer price of $5.00 to Ace and Bow's cost of $3.00 to manufacture Product Zee. Answer (B) is incorrect because $3.00 is Bow's cost to manufacture Product Zee. Answer (D) is incorrect because $6.00 is the sale price to unrelated customers.

**62.** The work-in-process of Parrott Corporation increased $11,500 from the beginning to the end of November. Costs incurred during November included $12,000 for direct materials, $63,000 for direct labor, and $21,000 for overhead. What was the cost of goods manufactured during November?

A. $75,000

B. $84,500

C. $96,000

D. $107,500

The correct answer is (B). *(Publisher)*
**REQUIRED:** The cost of goods manufactured.
**DISCUSSION:** Because the work-in-process inventory increased by $11,500 from the beginning to the end of November, not all of the $96,000 in costs incurred during the period was transferred out. Consequently, the cost of goods manufactured must have been $84,500 ($12,000 DM + $63,000 DL + $21,000 O/H − $11,500).

Answer (A) is incorrect because $75,000 equals the sum of direct materials and direct labor. Answer (C) is incorrect because $96,000 equals the costs incurred during the period. Answer (D) is incorrect because $107,500 equals the costs incurred during the period plus $11,500.

**63.** If the CGS for the Cole Manufacturing Co. is $105,000 and FG inventory decreased by $9,000 during the year, what was the year-end CGM?

A. $9,000

B. $96,000

C. $105,000

D. $114,000

The correct answer is (B). *(Publisher)*
**REQUIRED:** The cost of goods manufactured given a decline in the finished goods inventory.
**DISCUSSION:** The cost of goods manufactured is the cost of goods sold minus the inventory decrease during the year. Inventory decreased by $9,000. Hence, $96,000 ($105,000 − $9,000) of the cost related to goods manufactured during the period.

Answer (A) is incorrect because $9,000 is the inventory change. Answer (C) is incorrect because $105,000 is the CGS. Answer (D) is incorrect because $114,000 is the sum of CGS ($105,000) and the FG inventory decrease ($9,000).

**64.** Luna Co.'s year-end manufacturing costs were as follows:

| | |
|---|---:|
| Direct materials and direct labor | $500,000 |
| Depreciation of manufacturing equipment | 70,000 |
| Depreciation of factory building | 40,000 |
| Janitor's wages for cleaning factory premises | 15,000 |

How much of these costs should be inventoried for external reporting purposes?

A. $625,000

B. $610,000

C. $585,000

D. $500,000

The correct answer is (A). *(CPA, adapted)*
**REQUIRED:** The computation of inventory costs for external reporting purposes.
**DISCUSSION:** Inventoriable costs are those costs directly related to the product including direct materials, direct labor, factory overhead and any other expenses necessary to produce the product. All the costs listed are inventoriable:

| | |
|---|---:|
| DM and DL | $500,000 |
| Depreciation of equipment | 70,000 |
| Depreciation of building | 40,000 |
| Janitor's wages | 15,000 |
| Total inventoriable costs | $625,000 |

Answer (B) is incorrect because $15,000 of the janitor's wages should be included. Answer (C) is incorrect because depreciation of the factory building ($40,000) should be included. Answer (D) is incorrect because depreciation of the manufacturing equipment, depreciation of the factory building, and the janitor's wages should be included.

Questions 65 and 66 are based on the following information. Blum Corp. manufactures plastic-coated metal clips. The information in the next column was among Blum's year-end manufacturing costs.

| Wages | |
|---|---|
| Machine operators | $200,000 |
| Maintenance workers | 30,000 |
| Factory supervisors | 90,000 |
| **Materials Used** | |
| Metal wire | $500,000 |
| Lubricant for oiling machinery | 10,000 |
| Plastic coating | 380,000 |

65. Blum's year-end direct labor amounted to

A. $200,000

B. $230,000

C. $290,000

D. $320,000

The correct answer is (A). *(CPA, adapted)*

**REQUIRED:** The amount of direct labor costs for the accounting period.

**DISCUSSION:** Direct labor consists of the labor costs incurred for those employees who work on the actual production of the product. In this problem, only the machine operators' wages ($200,000) are considered direct labor. The wages of the factory supervisors and maintenance workers are indirect labor and therefore part of factory overhead.

Answer (B) is incorrect because maintenance workers' wages should not be included. Answer (C) is incorrect because factory supervisors' wages should not be included. Answer (D) is incorrect because the wages of the factory supervisors and maintenance workers should not be included.

66. Blum's year-end direct materials amounted to

A. $890,000

B. $880,000

C. $510,000

D. $500,000

The correct answer is (B). *(CPA, adapted)*

**REQUIRED:** The amount of direct materials costs for the accounting period.

**DISCUSSION:** Direct materials are part of the product. Given that plastic-coated metal clips are being made, only the plastic coating and metal wire ($880,000) used to make the clips are considered direct materials. All other supplies, including lubricant for oiling the machinery, are part of manufacturing overhead.

Answer (A) is incorrect because the lubricant for oiling machinery is not a direct material. Answer (C) is incorrect because the plastic coating but not the lubricant should be included as a direct material. Answer (D) is incorrect because the plastic coating should also be included as a direct material.

Questions 67 and 68 are based on the following information. Hamilton Company uses job-order costing. Factory overhead is applied to production at a predetermined rate of 150% of direct labor cost. Any over- or underapplied factory overhead is closed to the cost of goods sold account at the end of each month. Additional information is available as follows:

Job 101 was the only job in process at January 31, with accumulated costs as follows:

| | |
|---|---:|
| Direct materials | $4,000 |
| Direct labor | 2,000 |
| Applied factory overhead | 3,000 |
| | $9,000 |

Jobs 102, 103, and 104 were started during February.

Direct materials requisitions for February totaled $26,000.

Direct labor cost of $20,000 was incurred for February.

Actual factory overhead was $32,000 for February.

The only job still in process on February 28 was Job 104, with costs of $2,800 for direct materials and $1,800 for direct labor.

**67.** The cost of goods manufactured for February was

A. $77,700

B. $78,000

C. $79,700

D. $85,000

The correct answer is (A). *(CPA, adapted)*
    **REQUIRED:** The cost of goods manufactured (CGM).
    **DISCUSSION:** CGM is the sum of the costs in BWIP and all the costs incurred during the period, minus the costs in EWIP. In computing CGM, applied overhead is used ($30,000 = 150% x $20,000 DL cost). The $7,300 in EWIP includes $2,800 for direct materials, $1,800 for direct labor, and $2,700 for applied overhead (at 150% of DL cost).

| | |
|---|---:|
| BWIP | $ 9,000 |
| Direct labor | 20,000 |
| Applied O/H (150% of DL cost) | 30,000 |
| Direct materials | 26,000 |
| EWIP | (7,300) |
| CGM | $77,700 |

Answer (B) is incorrect because $78,000 ignores BWIP and EWIP and uses actual factory O/H. Answer (C) is incorrect because actual factory O/H of $32,000 was used. Answer (D) is incorrect because EWIP was not subtracted.

**68.** Over- or underapplied factory overhead should be closed to the cost of goods sold account at February 28 in the amount of

A. $700 overapplied.

B. $1,000 overapplied.

C. $1,700 underapplied.

D. $2,000 underapplied.

The correct answer is (D). *(CPA, adapted)*
    **REQUIRED:** The amount of over- or underapplied factory overhead closed to CGS.
    **DISCUSSION:** The amount of over- or underapplied overhead is the difference between the actual overhead incurred and the overhead applied. The amount of overhead applied was $30,000 (150% x $20,000 DL cost). The amount of overhead incurred was $32,000. Consequently, underapplied overhead of $2,000 ($32,000 actual – $30,000 applied) should be closed to CGS.
    Answer (A) is incorrect because $700 overapplied equals applied overhead in EWIP minus the difference between actual February overhead and overhead applied in February. Answer (B) is incorrect because the $3,000 of applied factory overhead in BWIP should not be used in determining the current month's over- or underapplied overhead. Answer (C) is incorrect because the amounts of applied overhead in BWIP and EWIP should not be used in calculating the current month's over- or underapplied overhead.

Questions 69 and 70 are based on the following information. Paradise Company budgets on an annual basis for its fiscal year. The following beginning and ending inventory levels (in units) are planned for the fiscal year of July 1 through June 30:

|  | July 1 | June 30 |
|---|---|---|
| Raw materials* | 40,000 | 50,000 |
| Work-in-process | 10,000 | 10,000 |
| Finished goods | 80,000 | 50,000 |

*Two (2) units of raw materials are needed to produce each unit of finished product.

**69.** If Paradise Company plans to sell 480,000 units during the fiscal year, the number of units it would have to manufacture during the year would be

A. 440,000 units.

B. 480,000 units.

C. 510,000 units.

D. 450,000 units.

The correct answer is (D). *(CMA, adapted)*
**REQUIRED:** The number of units that would be manufactured for a given sales level.
**DISCUSSION:** The company needs 480,000 units of finished goods to sell plus 50,000 for the ending inventory, or a total of 530,000 units. Beginning inventory is 80,000 units. Thus, only 450,000 units (530,000 – 80,000) need to be manufactured this year.
Answer (A) is incorrect because the 10,000 units of EWIP were incorrectly subtracted. Answer (B) is incorrect because it is the number of units Paradise Co. plans to sell during the fiscal year. Answer (C) is incorrect because $FG_{BI}$ should be subtracted from (not added to) the 480,000-unit sales estimate, and $FG_{EI}$ should be added (not deducted).

**70.** If 500,000 finished units were to be manufactured during the fiscal year by Paradise Company, the units of raw materials needed to be purchased would be

A. 1,000,000 units.

B. 1,020,000 units.

C. 1,010,000 units.

D. 990,000 units.

The correct answer is (C). *(CMA, adapted)*
**REQUIRED:** The number of units of raw materials needed to be purchased during the year for a given production volume.
**DISCUSSION:** Each unit of finished goods requires two units of raw materials, and 1,000,000 units (500,000 x 2) of raw materials are needed for production. Because 50,000 units of raw materials are required for the ending inventory, the total needed is 1,050,000 units. Given that 40,000 are in beginning inventory, only 1,010,000 will have to be purchased.
Answer (A) is incorrect because 1,000,000 units are required for production. Answer (B) is incorrect because the 10,000-unit increase in raw materials inventory was incorrectly doubled. Answer (D) is incorrect because the 10,000-unit increase in raw materials inventory should be added to (not subtracted from) the materials requirements.

**71.** Tillman Corporation uses a job-order cost system and has two production departments, M and A. Budgeted manufacturing costs for the year are

|  | Dept. M | Dept. A |
|---|---|---|
| Direct materials | $700,000 | $100,000 |
| Direct labor | 200,000 | 800,000 |
| Manufacturing overhead | 600,000 | 400,000 |

The actual materials and labor costs charged to Job No. 432 during the year were as follows:

| Direct materials |  | $25,000 |
|---|---|---|
| Direct labor: |  |  |
| Dept. M | $ 8,000 |  |
| Dept. A | 12,000 | 20,000 |

Tillman applies manufacturing overhead to production orders on the basis of direct labor cost using separate departmental rates predetermined at the beginning of the year based on the annual budget. The total annual manufacturing costs associated with Job No. 432 should be

A. $50,000

B. $55,000

C. $65,000

D. $75,000

The correct answer is (D). *(CPA, adapted)*
**REQUIRED:** The total manufacturing costs associated with a job if overhead is based on direct labor cost applied using departmental rates.
**DISCUSSION:** Total manufacturing costs consist of materials, labor, and overhead. Materials and labor are given; overhead rates are to be determined for each department. Departmental rates are calculated by dividing departmental manufacturing overhead by direct labor costs.

$$Dept.\ M = \frac{\$600,000}{\$200,000} = \$3\ per\ \$1\ of\ DLC$$

$$Dept.\ A = \frac{\$400,000}{\$800,000} = \$.50\ per\ \$1\ of\ DLC$$

For Job No. 432:
Dept. M overhead = $3 × $8,000 = $24,000
Dept. A overhead = $.50 × $12,000 = $6,000

Thus, total manufacturing costs for Job No. 432 equal $75,000 ($25,000 materials + $20,000 labor + $24,000 M overhead + $6,000 A overhead).
Answer (A) is incorrect because $50,000 omits materials costs. Answer (B) is incorrect because $55,000 results from applying a single departmental overhead rate of $.50 per direct labor dollar. Answer (C) is incorrect because $65,000 results from applying a single departmental overhead rate of $1.00 per direct labor dollar [($600,000 + $400,000) total annual overhead ÷ ($200,000 + $800,000) total annual direct labor cost].

**72.** Lucas Co. has a job-order cost system. For the month of April, the following debits (credits) appeared in the general ledger account, work-in-process:

| April |  |  |
|---|---|---|
| 1 | Balance | $ 24,000 |
| 30 | Direct materials | 80,000 |
| 30 | Direct labor | 60,000 |
| 30 | Factory overhead | 54,000 |
| 30 | To finished goods | (200,000) |

Lucas applies overhead to production at a predetermined rate of 90% based on direct labor cost. Job No. 100, the only job still in process at the end of April, has been charged with factory overhead of $4,500. The amount of direct materials charged to Job No. 100 was

A. $18,000

B. $8,500

C. $5,000

D. $4,500

The correct answer is (B). *(CPA, adapted)*
**REQUIRED:** The amount of direct materials charged to the only job in process at the end of the period.
**DISCUSSION:** The ending balance in the WIP account is $18,000 ($24,000 + $80,000 + $60,000 + $54,000 – $200,000), the sum of all debits, $218,000, to the account less the $200,000 credit. The $18,000 balance consists of materials, labor, and overhead for Job No. 100. Overhead is given as $4,500 (90% of direct labor cost). Direct labor is thus $5,000 ($4,500 ÷ .90) and the amount of direct materials is $8,500.

$$DM + DL + OH = \$18,000$$
$$DM + DL + .9\ DL = \$18,000$$
$$DM + \$5,000 + \$4,500 = \$18,000$$
$$DM = \$8,500$$

Answer (A) is incorrect because $18,000 is the ending balance in the WIP account. Answer (C) is incorrect because $5,000 is the direct labor cost of Job No. 100. Answer (D) is incorrect because $4,500 is the amount of factory overhead charged to Job No. 100.

## 3.5 Journal Entries

**73.** ABC Company estimates its total vacation costs for the year to be $360,000. Direct labor costs are $180,000 monthly, and indirect labor costs are $45,000. ABC has chosen to accrue vacation costs monthly instead of recognizing them as incurred. Select the journal entry to record payroll and accrue the estimated vacation costs for the month of January.

| | | | |
|---|---|---|---|
| A. | Work-in-process | $180,000 | |
| | Factory O/H control | 75,000 | |
| | Est. liability for | | |
| | vacation pay | | $ 30,000 |
| | Accrued payroll | | 225,000 |
| | | | |
| B. | Wage expense | $225,000 | |
| | Accrued payroll | | $225,000 |
| | | | |
| C. | Vacation expense | $300,000 | |
| | Accrued payroll | | $300,000 |
| | | | |
| D. | Work-in-process | $225,000 | |
| | Accrued payroll | | $225,000 |

The correct answer is (A). *(Publisher)*
**REQUIRED:** The journal entry to accrue estimated vacation costs for the month of January.
**DISCUSSION:** Work-in-process should be debited for direct labor incurred, factory overhead control should be debited for indirect labor and estimated vacation costs [$45,000 + ($360,000 ÷ 12)], estimated liability for vacation pay should be credited for 1/12 of the annual expected cost of $360,000, and accrued payroll should be credited for the gross payroll (total due to employees including their deductions). The liability for vacation pay should be debited for any vacation pay taken.

Total vacation costs for the year are estimated to be $360,000. The explanation assumes that the annual cost is divided by 12 to arrive at a monthly cost of $30,000. More sophisticated approaches are available, e.g., accruing vacation costs in proportion to total labor expense.

Answer (B) is incorrect because direct labor should be charged to WIP, factory O/H control should be debited for indirect labor and estimated vacation costs, and estimated liability for vacation pay should be credited for 1/12 of its annual expected cost. Answer (C) is incorrect because direct labor and indirect labor should be charged to WIP and factory O/H control, respectively. A credit should also be made for the estimated liability for vacation pay, and accrued payroll should be credited for $225,000. Answer (D) is incorrect because WIP should be debited for direct labor, and factory O/H control should be debited for indirect labor and estimated vacation costs. Estimated liability for vacation pay and accrued payroll should be credited.

**74.** The Herron Company has a gross payroll of $2,000 per day based on a normal 40-hour work-week. Withholdings for income taxes amount to $200 per day. Gross payroll consists of $1,200 direct labor, $400 indirect labor, $280 selling expenses, and $120 administrative expenses each day. Assuming the weekly payroll and employer payroll taxes payable (but not employees' withholdings) have already been accrued, what is the journal entry to record the payment of the weekly payroll?

| | | | |
|---|---|---|---|
| A. | Accrued payroll | $5,000 | |
| | Cash | | $5,000 |
| | | | |
| B. | Accrued payroll | $10,000 | |
| | Cash | | $8,330 |
| | Employees' income | | |
| | taxes payable | | 1,000 |
| | Employees' FICA | | |
| | taxes payable | | 670 |
| | | | |
| C. | Accrued payroll | $10,000 | |
| | Cash | | $8,330 |
| | Work-in-process | | 1,670 |
| | | | |
| D. | Work-in-process | $6,000 | |
| | Factory overhead | 2,900 | |
| | Selling and administra- | | |
| | tive expense | 2,000 | |
| | Accrued payroll | | $10,000 |
| | Employer payroll | | |
| | taxes payable | | 900 |

The correct answer is (B). *(Publisher)*
**REQUIRED:** The journal entry to record the payment of the weekly payroll.
**DISCUSSION:** Accrued payroll should be debited for the balance in the account, cash should be debited for the actual amount of cash disbursed, employees' income taxes payable should be credited for the amount of taxes withheld from the employees' paychecks, and employees' FICA taxes payable and other liabilities should be credited for the amount of FICA taxes and other items withheld from the employees' paychecks.

Income taxes of $200 per day ($1,000 per week) should be withheld from the employees for income taxes payable. An amount should also be withheld for the employees' portion of FICA taxes. In this instance, the assumption must be made that the amount is $670, although no basis for the calculation is given. Employees' FICA taxes payable should be recognized, and no other entry given will satisfy the requirement.

Alternatively, if the employee withholdings had been recognized as liabilities when the payroll was accrued, the entry would be to debit the payroll liability and credit cash for $8,330.

Answer (A) is incorrect because $8,330 (not $5,000) is the amount of cash disbursed. Furthermore, employee taxes payable are not recorded. Answer (C) is incorrect because employee tax withholding liabilities, not WIP, are credited. Answer (D) is incorrect because debits to WIP, O/H control, and expense accounts, with credits to various payables, record the payroll liability rather than its payment.

**75.** What is the journal entry to record Legal Corporation's payment of state unemployment taxes for $600 if the tax has been accrued?

A.  State unemployment
      taxes payable            $600
        Cash                              $600

B.  State unemployment
      taxes payable            $600
        Accrued payroll                   $600

C.  Factory overhead          $600
        State unemployment
          taxes payable                   $600

D.  Accrued payroll           $600
        Cash                              $600

The correct answer is (A). *(Publisher)*
  **REQUIRED:** The journal entry to record payment of state unemployment taxes.
  **DISCUSSION:** The correct journal entry to record the payment of accrued state unemployment taxes is to debit state unemployment taxes payable and credit cash for the amount of state unemployment taxes paid.
  Answer (B) is incorrect because cash is credited when a liability is paid. Answer (C) is incorrect because debiting overhead and crediting a payable is the entry to accrue an expense, not record payment. Answer (D) is incorrect because the question indicates that a tax liability, not accrued payroll, had been credited.

**76.** Ajax Candy Company has a gross payroll of $75,000 per month consisting of $65,000 of direct labor and $10,000 of indirect factory labor. Assume that the tax rate on employers is .8% for federal unemployment, 1.55% for state unemployment, and 7.65% for Social Security benefits, a total payroll tax rate of 10%. What is the journal entry to accrue the monthly payroll and payroll taxes?

A.  Salary expense        $75,000
        Accrued wages                $75,000

B.  Salary expense        $82,500
        Accrued wages                $75,000
        Accrued payroll tax            7,500

C.  Work-in-process       $65,000
      Factory O/H control   17,500
        Accrued payroll              $75,000
        Employer payroll
          taxes payable                 7,500

D.  Work-in-process        $7,500
        Accrued payroll
          taxes payable              $7,500

The correct answer is (C). *(Publisher)*
  **REQUIRED:** The journal entry to accrue company payroll taxes.
  **DISCUSSION:** Work-in-process should be debited for the amount of direct labor costs, factory overhead should be debited for the amount of indirect labor costs plus the employer payroll tax ($10,000 + $7,500), accrued payroll should be credited for the amount of total direct and indirect labor costs, and employer's payroll taxes payable should be credited for the amount of the payroll tax (.10 x $75,000 = $7,500).
  Answer (A) is incorrect because payroll taxes are not taken into consideration, and payroll is not being charged to WIP (for direct labor costs) and factory O/H (for indirect labor costs). Answer (B) is incorrect because payroll must be charged to WIP for direct labor costs and factory O/H for indirect labor costs. Answer (D) is incorrect because WIP should be debited for the amount of direct labor costs, factory O/H should be debited for the amount of indirect labor costs plus the employer payroll taxes, accrued payroll should be credited for the amount of total direct and indirect labor costs, and taxes payable should be credited for 10% of the total wages.

**77.** What is the journal entry for the purchase of $500 of direct materials and $250 of supplies for cash?

A.  Supplies and materials   $750
        Accounts payable             $750

B.  Work-in-process          $500
      Factory overhead         250
        Accounts payable             $750

C.  Stores control          $750
        Cash                         $750

D.  Work-in-process         $750
        Cash                         $750

The correct answer is (C). *(Publisher)*
  **REQUIRED:** The journal entry for the cash purchase of materials and supplies.
  **DISCUSSION:** The correct entry to record the purchase of materials and supplies is to debit the stores control account for the combined cost of the materials and supplies ($750) and to credit cash.
  Answer (A) is incorrect because cash, not a payable, is credited. Answer (B) is incorrect because the supplies and materials were purchased with cash. Also, the materials and supplies are not debited to WIP and factory overhead, respectively, until they are used or transferred out of storage. Answer (D) is incorrect because raw material is charged to WIP only when put into production. Supplies are charged to overhead when used.

**78.** If $200 of direct materials and $125 of supplies were issued to work-in-process, which of the following entries is correct?

| A. | Work-in-process | $325 | |
| | Materials | | $200 |
| | Supplies | | 125 |

| B. | Work-in-process | $125 | |
| | Overhead control | 200 | |
| | Materials | | $200 |
| | Supplies | | 125 |

| C. | Work-in-process | $200 | |
| | Overhead control | 125 | |
| | Stores control | | $325 |

| D. | Materials and supplies | $325 | |
| | Stores control | | $325 |

The correct answer is (C). *(Publisher)*
**REQUIRED:** The entry to record the issuance of direct materials and supplies.
**DISCUSSION:** The cost of direct materials should be debited to the WIP account as the materials are used in the production of goods. The cost of supplies should be debited to factory overhead control as the supplies are used because their use cannot be identified with particular products. The credit should be to stores control or, if used, separate direct materials and supplies accounts.
Answer (A) is incorrect because supplies are charged to overhead as they are used. Answer (B) is incorrect because the overhead and WIP figures are reversed. Answer (D) is incorrect because direct materials and supplies transferred out of stores control are debited to WIP and overhead control, respectively.

**79.** What is the correct journal entry if $5,000 of direct labor and $1,250 of indirect labor were incurred?

| A. | Work-in-process | $6,250 | |
| | Accrued payroll | | $6,250 |

| B. | Work-in-process | $5,000 | |
| | Overhead control | 1,250 | |
| | Accrued payroll | | $6,250 |

| C. | Work-in-process | $6,250 | |
| | Overhead control | 1,250 | |
| | Accrued payroll | | $6,250 |
| | Applied overhead | | 1,250 |

| D. | Payroll expense | $6,250 | |
| | Accrued payable | | $6,250 |

The correct answer is (B). *(Publisher)*
**REQUIRED:** The journal entry to record the incurrence of direct and indirect labor.
**DISCUSSION:** The WIP account is charged with the $5,000 direct labor cost. The $1,250 of indirect labor is debited to factory overhead control because the labor cannot be identified with a particular product; e.g., general maintenance is a cost of production that cannot be allocated to specific products. The liability of $6,250 must also be recognized. Accounting for payroll taxes is assumed to be done when the payroll is paid by debiting accrued payroll and crediting cash and the employee withholding liabilities.
Answer (A) is incorrect because the indirect labor should be charged to overhead. Answer (C) is incorrect because only $5,000 goes to WIP. The remaining $1,250 is charged to overhead. Answer (D) is incorrect because factory labor costs must be inventoried rather than expensed.

**80.** The completion of Job #21, with total costs of $4,900, results in which of the following entries?

| A. | Finished goods | $4,900 | |
| | Work-in-process | | $4,900 |

| B. | Finished goods | $4,900 | |
| | Job #21 | | $4,900 |

| C. | Cost of goods available | $4,900 | |
| | Work-in-process | | $4,900 |

| D. | Work-in-process | $4,900 | |
| | Finished goods | | $4,900 |

The correct answer is (A). *(Publisher)*
**REQUIRED:** The entry to record the completion of a job.
**DISCUSSION:** During production, all the labor, material, and overhead are charged to WIP. Upon completion, the account must be credited for the total cost of the job. Thus, WIP will be credited and finished goods will be debited for $4,900. Upon sale, the cost will be transferred from finished goods to CGS.
Answer (B) is incorrect because, in the general ledger, the credit is to WIP rather than a specific subsidiary account, although there are subsidiary ledgers or job-cost cards for both the WIP and the FG accounts. Answer (C) is incorrect because the cost of goods available account does not exist. Cost of goods available for sale is the sum of beginning inventories plus purchases or CGM. Answer (D) is incorrect because finished goods should be debited and WIP credited.

**81.** If the year's overhead costs incurred are $29,000, and $25,000 in costs have been applied to the product, what is the appropriate closing entry (assuming separate accounts and no proration)?

| | | |
|---|---|---|
| A. | Cost of goods sold | $ 4,000 | |
| | Overhead applied | 25,000 | |
| |    Overhead control | | $29,000 |
| | | | |
| B. | Overhead control | $25,000 | |
| | Cost of goods sold | 4,000 | |
| |    Overhead applied | | $29,000 |
| | | | |
| C. | Cost of goods sold | $29,000 | |
| |    Overhead applied | | $29,000 |
| | | | |
| D. | Work-in-process | $29,000 | |
| |    Overhead control | | $29,000 |

The correct answer is (A). *(Publisher)*

**REQUIRED:** The journal entry to close actual overhead and applied overhead without proration.

**DISCUSSION:** When separate overhead control and overhead applied accounts are used, all overhead incurred is charged to the overhead control account. As overhead is applied, it is credited to overhead applied. Accordingly, the entry to close these accounts is to debit the applied account and credit the control account. Given no proration, the difference is taken directly to CGS. Material differences should be prorated among the WIP, FG, and CGS accounts. The proration should be in proportion to the amount of the current period's overhead already applied to the accounts.

Answer (B) is incorrect because overhead control should be credited. Answer (C) is incorrect because overhead applied should not be closed in entirety to CGS. Answer (D) is incorrect because it would be the correct entry to apply overhead for the entire period if overhead applied had been credited.

**82.** If $29,000 of factory overhead costs have been incurred and $25,000 of factory overhead has been applied, which of the following entries will close the overhead accounts and prorate the underapplied overhead among the relevant accounts? (Of the $25,000 applied, $2,500 is still in EWIP, and $5,000 is still in finished goods as part of unsold inventory.)

| | | |
|---|---|---|
| A. | Cost of goods sold | $ 1,333 | |
| | Finished goods | 1,333 | |
| | Work-in-process | 1,334 | |
| | Overhead control | 25,000 | |
| |    Overhead applied | | $29,000 |
| | | | |
| B. | Cost of goods sold | $ 2,800 | |
| | Finished goods | 800 | |
| | Work-in-process | 400 | |
| | Overhead applied | 25,000 | |
| |    Overhead control | | $29,000 |
| | | | |
| C. | Cost of goods sold | $ 2,000 | |
| | Finished goods | 1,500 | |
| | Work-in-process | 500 | |
| | Factory overhead applied | 25,000 | |
| |    Overhead summary | | $29,000 |
| | | | |
| D. | Overhead applied | $29,000 | |
| |    Overhead control | | $25,000 |
| |    Cost of goods sold | | 2,000 |
| |    Finished goods | | 1,500 |
| |    Work-in-process | | 500 |

The correct answer is (B). *(Publisher)*

**REQUIRED:** The entry that will close the overhead accounts and prorate the underapplied overhead.

**DISCUSSION:** Overhead applied has a credit balance. Hence, the closing entry must include a debit to the account. The reverse is true of the control account. In this case, only 10% of the $25,000 overhead applied remains in the WIP account ($2,500 ÷ $25,000). Accordingly, 10% of the $4,000 of underapplied overhead should be charged to work-in-process (10% x $4,000). Finished goods contains 20% ($5,000 ÷ $25,000) of the already applied overhead. Accordingly, $800 (20% x $4,000) should be charged to finished goods. The remaining 70% of applied overhead has been charged to cost of goods sold. Thus, 70% of the underapplied overhead ($2,800) should be charged to cost of goods sold. Proration based on the amounts of applied overhead in the inventory accounts is preferable, but the assignment is sometimes made on a total cost basis.

Answer (A) is incorrect because the proration should be 70%, 20%, and 10%, respectively, not 33%, 33%, and 34%. Also, the credit should be to overhead control. Answer (C) is incorrect because the proration should be 70%, 20%, and 10%, respectively, not 50%, 37.5%, and 12.5%. Also, the credit should be to overhead control. Answer (D) is incorrect because the amounts are wrong, and the entry is reversed.

**83.** A company manufactures pipes and uses a job-order costing system. During May, the following jobs were started (no other jobs were in process) and the following costs were incurred:

|                          | Job X    | Job Y    | Job Z    | Total    |
|--------------------------|----------|----------|----------|----------|
| Direct materials         |          |          |          |          |
| requisitioned            | $10,000  | $20,000  | $15,000  | $45,000  |
| Direct labor             | 5,000    | 4,000    | 2,500    | 11,500   |
|                          | $15,000  | $24,000  | $17,500  | $56,500  |

In addition, factory overhead of $300,000 and direct labor costs of $150,000 were estimated to be incurred during the year. Actual overhead of $24,000 was incurred in May; overhead is applied on the basis of direct labor dollars. If only Job X and Job Z were completed during the month, the appropriate entry to record the initiation of all jobs would be

A. Work-in-process     $79,500
    Direct materials           $45,000
    Direct labor               11,500
    Applied factory overhead      23,000

B. Work-in-process     $80,500
    Direct materials           $45,000
    Direct labor                11,500
    Factory overhead           24,000

C. Work-in-process     $80,500
    Direct materials           $45,000
    Direct labor                11,500
    Applied factory overhead      24,000

D. Direct labor          $11,500
    Direct materials       45,000
    Work-in-process           $56,500

The correct answer is (A). *(CIA, adapted)*

**REQUIRED:** The entry to record work-in-process for the month.

**DISCUSSION:** Work-in-process is debited for the direct materials, direct labor, and factory overhead charged to jobs initiated during the month. Materials and labor are given as $45,000 and $11,500, respectively. Overhead applied is calculated by multiplying the predetermined rate by the activity base. The $2 rate ($300,000 ÷ $150,000) times the $11,500 activity base equals overhead applied (charged to WIP), or $23,000.

Answer (B) is incorrect because the incurrence of overhead is reflected by a debit to factory overhead and credits to various accounts. Answer (C) is incorrect because it reflects the amount of overhead incurred ($24,000), not applied ($23,000). Answer (D) is incorrect because direct materials, direct labor, and applied factory overhead should be credited and WIP debited.

# CHAPTER FOUR
# PROCESS COSTING

**Process costing** is appropriate when many homogeneous products or service units pass through the same processes and are assigned similar amounts of costs. It is at the opposite end of the costing continuum from **job-order costing**, a method that accounts for differentiated products and services that are not subjected to the same processes. However, many firms apply a combination of these methods because units may undergo both similar and dissimilar processes (see the discussion of operation costing on the following page). Thus, process costing may be applied in some departments and job-order costing in others. Nevertheless, the cost flows through the accounts and the journal entries are substantially the same in the two methods. The primary difference is that job-order costing uses **job cost sheets** to account for specific jobs. By contrast, process costing averages costs for all units. Furthermore, process costing systems establish a **work-in-process** account to record accumulated costs in each department. When units are moved to the next department, those costs (transferred-in costs with respect to the transferee department) are attached.

**Transferred-in costs** are similar to materials added at a point in the process because both attach to (become part of) the product at that point, usually the beginning of the process. However, transferred-in costs are dissimilar because they attach to the units of production that move from one process to another. Thus, they are the basic units being produced. By contrast, materials are added to the basic units during processing. Computations for transferred-in costs are usually separate from those for other materials costs and conversion costs.

The objective of process costing is to determine the portion of production cost to be expensed (because the units were sold) and the portion to be deferred (because the units are still on hand). Like products that are mass produced should be accounted for using process costing techniques to assign costs. Costs are accumulated for a department (process) rather than a job, work-in-process is stated in terms of equivalent completed units so that average costs may be calculated, and unit costs are established. Thus, process costing is an averaging process that calculates the average cost of all units. Moreover, instead of a job cost sheet, the key document is the **production report** prepared in each department. In includes information about the physical flow of units, transferred-in costs, equivalent units, unit costs, valuation of EWIP, and transferred-out costs.

Process costing is employed in such manufacturing settings as chemical production, oil refining, bakery goods, paint processing, plastics, canned and boxed foods, semiconductors, and bottled liquids. In the service sector, process costing may be applied in accounting for such homogeneous, mass-produced services as check and deposit processing by financial institutions, routine delivery of mail, air travel, and laundering of clothing. Retailers may also use process costing. Examples are grain dealing and processing of newspaper subscriptions.

Process costing for service organizations and retailers is considerably simpler than for manufacturers because work-in-process ordinarily does not exist. For example, x-ray services are unlikely to result in work-in-process. Furthermore, manufacturers that have adopted the **just-in-time (JIT)** production philosophy also attempt to achieve equivalent simplification by reducing all inventories to immaterial levels. They also try to reorganize and simplify their procedures so that process costing is feasible. For example, **work cells** may be established that produce a product or major component from start to finish. By accumulating a cell's costs and measuring its output for a period, a simple unit-cost calculation is possible.

**Operation costing** is appropriate when similar products are produced in different models or styles or otherwise have distinctive traits. It is a hybrid of job-order and process costing systems. Operation costing is used by firms that produce batches of similar units that are subject to selected processing steps (operations). Different batches may pass through different sets of operations, but all units are processed identically within a given operation. Operation costing may also be appropriate when different materials are processed through the same basic operations, such as the woodworking, finishing, and polishing of different product lines of furniture. Operation costing accumulates total conversion costs and determines a unit conversion cost for each operation. This procedure is similar to overhead assignment. However, direct materials costs are charged specifically to products as in job-order systems. More work-in-process accounts are needed because one is required for each operation. Operation costing is often used for such items as clothes, shoes, electronics, and jewelry.

**Equivalent units of production (EUP)** measure the amount of work performed in each production phase in terms of fully processed units during a given period. An equivalent unit of production is a set of inputs required to manufacture one physical unit. Calculating equivalent units for each factor of production facilitates measurement of output and cost assignment when work-in-process exists. Incomplete units are restated as the equivalent amount of completed units. The calculation is made separately for **materials** (transferred-in costs are treated as materials for this purpose) and **conversion cost** (direct labor and overhead). One EUP is the amount of conversion cost (direct labor and overhead) or direct materials cost required to produce one unit of finished goods. For example, if 10,000 units are 25% complete, they equal 2,500 (10,000 x 25%) equivalent units. Some units may be more advanced in the production process with respect to one factor than another. Thus, a unit may be 75% complete as to direct materials but only 15% complete as to conversion cost.

Cost assignment in accordance with relative EUP may be based on either a FIFO assumption or a weighted-average assumption.  Under the **FIFO assumption**, only the costs incurred this period are allocated between finished goods and EWIP.  Beginning inventory costs are maintained separately from current-period costs.  Products finished this period are costed separately as either started last period and completed this period or started this period and completed this period.  The FIFO method determines EUP by subtracting the work done on the BWIP in the prior period from the weighted-average total.  The **weighted-average assumption** averages all materials and all processing (conversion) costs (both those incurred this period and those in BWIP).  Thus, no differentiation is made between products started in the preceding and the current periods.  The result is that weighted-average EUP differ from FIFO EUP by the amount of EUP in beginning work-in-process.  EUP under the weighted-average assumption are equal to the EUP transferred to finished goods plus the EUP in ending work-in-process.  Total EUP completed in beginning work-in-process are not subtracted.  Whichever assumption is used, computations may be burdensome when many batches of differing products must be accounted for.  Furthermore, when the output of a process consists of multiple products, using averages of historical costs for materials and conversion to be applied to all products results in miscosting.  A simpler alternative to the FIFO and weighted-average methods is **standard costing**.  This approach requires development of standard (equivalent-unit) materials and conversion costs for each product.  It also necessitates recognition of variances related to the work performed in the current period.

## 4.1 Basic Process Costing

**1.** A true process costing system could make use of each of the following except

    A. Standard costs.

    B. Individual lots.

    C. Variable costing.

    D. Responsibility accounting.

The correct answer is (B). *(CPA, adapted)*

    **REQUIRED:** The element not found in a process costing system.

    **DISCUSSION:** A process costing system is used for mass and continuous production processes. It assigns unit costs on the basis of the average costs of all units. A job-order costing system is appropriate when producing individual, differentiable jobs, batches, or units (lots).

    Answers (A), (C), and (D) are incorrect because standard costs, variable costing, and responsibility accounting can be used in both process and job-order costing.

**2.** A corporation manufactures two brands of barbed wire fencing for sale to wholesalers and large ranchers. Which of the following would be the best type of costing system for such a company to use?

    A. EOQ system.

    B. Job-order system.

    C. Process system.

    D. Retail inventory system.

The correct answer is (C). *(CIA, adapted)*

    **REQUIRED:** The costing system to be used by a company that manufactures two brands of one product.

    **DISCUSSION:** A process costing system is used when a company mass produces a standardized product on a continuous basis. Costs are assigned to large groups of similar items, and average unit costs are calculated.

    Answer (A) is incorrect because an EOQ system is an inventory control tool. Answer (B) is incorrect because a job-order system is used when products are heterogeneous. Each job (customer) is a separate cost center. Answer (D) is incorrect because this company is a manufacturer. The retail method converts ending inventory stated at retail to cost.

**3.** In a process cost system, the application of factory overhead usually is recorded as an increase in

    A. Cost of goods sold.

    B. Work-in-process inventory control.

    C. Factory overhead control.

    D. Finished goods inventory control.

The correct answer is (B). *(CPA, adapted)*

    **REQUIRED:** The account in which the application of factory overhead is recorded in a process costing system.

    **DISCUSSION:** The principal distinction between process costing and job-order costing systems is that the latter use subsidiary WIP and finished goods ledgers to account for separate jobs. However, the same general ledger accounts are used in both systems, and cost flow among accounts is also the same. Both systems increase work-in-process control to record applied overhead.

    Answer (A) is incorrect because CGS is debited when finished goods are sold. Answer (C) is incorrect because factory overhead control is debited when actual factory overhead is incurred. Answer (D) is incorrect because finished goods control is debited when goods are completed.

**4.** Which of the following characteristics applies to process costing but not to job-order costing?

    A. Identifiable batches of production.

    B. Equivalent units of production (EUP).

    C. Averaging process.

    D. Use of standard costs.

The correct answer is (B). *(CPA, adapted)*

    **REQUIRED:** The item that applies to process costing but not to job-order costing.

    **DISCUSSION:** EUP are calculated in a process costing system. EUP allow WIP to be stated in terms of completed units, a step not necessary in a job-order system, which assigns costs individually to each job. Stating WIP in terms of EUP permits calculation of average unit costs for mass-produced homogeneous goods.

    Answer (A) is incorrect because job-order costing is used for identifiable batches of production. Answer (C) is incorrect because both process costing and job-order costing use an averaging process. Answer (D) is incorrect because standard costs can be used with either costing method.

**5.** An equivalent unit of direct materials or conversion cost is equal to

A. The amount of direct materials or conversion cost necessary to complete one unit of production.

B. A unit of work-in-process inventory.

C. The amount of direct materials or conversion cost necessary to start a unit of production in work-in-process.

D. Fifty percent of the direct materials or conversion cost of a unit of finished goods inventory (assuming a linear production pattern).

The correct answer is (A). *(CPA, adapted)*
   **REQUIRED:** The definition of equivalent units.
   **DISCUSSION:** Equivalent units of production (EUP) measure the amount of work performed in each production phase in terms of fully processed units during a given period. Incomplete units are restated as the equivalent amount of completed units. The calculation is made separately for direct materials and conversion cost (direct labor and overhead).
   Answer (B) is incorrect because a unit of WIP inventory is not completed; an EUP is equal to one completed unit. Answer (C) is incorrect because an EUP is the amount of direct materials and conversion cost to complete, not start, a unit. Answer (D) is incorrect because an EUP is the amount of direct materials and conversion cost to complete 100%, not 50%, of a unit.

**6.** In the computation of manufacturing cost per equivalent unit, the weighted-average method of process costing considers

A. Current costs only.

B. Current costs plus cost of beginning work-in-process inventory.

C. Current costs plus cost of ending work-in-process inventory.

D. Current costs minus cost of beginning work-in-process inventory.

The correct answer is (B). *(CPA, adapted)*
   **REQUIRED:** The costs used in the weighted-average method.
   **DISCUSSION:** The weighted-average method of process costing combines the costs of work done in the previous period and the current period. Thus, the cost of the equivalent units is equal to the current cost (current period) plus the cost of BWIP (previous period).
   Answer (A) is incorrect because the FIFO method considers only current costs. Answer (C) is incorrect because the costs are being counted twice. The costs in EWIP are already included in current costs. Answer (D) is incorrect because BWIP costs are added to, not subtracted from, the current costs in the weighted-average method.

**7.** An error was made in the computation of the percentage of completion of the current year's ending work-in-process (EWIP) inventory. The error resulted in assigning a lower percentage of completion to each component of the inventory than actually was the case. Consequently, the following were misstated:

1. The computation of total equivalent units
2. The computation of costs per equivalent unit
3. Costs assigned to cost of goods completed for the period

What were the effects of the error?

| | 1 | 2 | 3 |
|---|---|---|---|
| A. | Understate | Overstate | Overstate |
| B. | Understate | Understate | Overstate |
| C. | Overstate | Understate | Understate |
| D. | Overstate | Overstate | Understate |

The correct answer is (A). *(CPA, adapted)*
   **REQUIRED:** The effects of understating the percentage of completion of EWIP.
   **DISCUSSION:** If the percentage of completion assigned is lower than actually attained, total equivalent units (EUP) will be understated. For example, if the actual percentage is 75%, but 50% is assigned and 100 units are in process, EUP will be 50 instead of 75. This error results in higher (overstated) costs per equivalent unit and higher (overstated) costs assigned to finished goods for the period (assuming costs are constant).
   Answers (B), (C), and (D) are incorrect because total equivalent units will be understated if an error resulted in assigning a lower-than-actual percentage of completion. Moreover, costs per equivalent unit and cost of goods completed (assuming constant costs) will be overstated.

**8.** A valid reason for using predetermined overhead rates for process costing is

A. The unrepresentative unit cost that will otherwise result when total factory overhead fluctuates significantly from period to period.

B. The noncomparability of the degree of completion of units in work-in-process from 1 month to the next when predetermined rates are not used.

C. The noncomparability of FIFO and weighted-average equivalent units of production for overhead when predetermined rates are not used.

D. The difference in transfer prices that will occur between two different plants of a company when predetermined rates are not used.

The correct answer is (A). *(CIA, adapted)*
**REQUIRED:** The reason for using predetermined overhead rates.
**DISCUSSION:** Predetermined overhead rates are used for costing purposes to minimize the effect of fluctuating overhead from period to period. These fluctuations may be caused by seasonal factors or other causes of variability. If not annualized or normalized, these fluctuations will result in significantly different unit costs for the same products in different periods.
Answers (B) and (C) are incorrect because predetermined overhead rates are not used in calculating the degree of completion of work-in-process or the equivalent units of production. Answer (D) is incorrect because predetermined overhead rates may result in transfer prices that less accurately measure the actual costs of products internally produced in comparison with those externally purchased.

**9.** In developing a predetermined factory overhead application rate for use in a traditional process costing system, which of the following could be used in the numerator and denominator?

| | Numerator | Denominator |
|---|---|---|
| A. | Actual factory overhead | Actual machine hours |
| B. | Actual factory overhead | Estimated machine hours |
| C. | Estimated factory overhead | Actual machine hours |
| D. | Estimated factory overhead | Estimated machine hours |

The correct answer is (D). *(CPA, adapted)*
**REQUIRED:** The possible numerator and denominator of a predetermined factory overhead rate.
**DISCUSSION:** The predetermined factory overhead rate is calculated by dividing the estimated factory overhead (the numerator) by the estimated measure of capacity (the denominator). The latter may be direct labor hours, direct labor dollars, machine hours, or some other reasonable base.
Answers (A), (B), and (C) are incorrect because actual amounts of factory overhead and machine hours are not known.

**10.** In a process costing system, the application of factory overhead usually is recorded as an increase in

A. Cost of goods sold.

B. Work-in-process inventory control.

C. Factory overhead control.

D. Finished goods control.

The correct answer is (B). *(CPA, adapted)*
**REQUIRED:** The account in which the application of factory overhead is recorded in a process costing system.
**DISCUSSION:** The principal distinction between a process costing system and a job-order system is that the latter uses subsidiary WIP and finished goods ledgers to account for separate jobs. However, the same general ledger accounts are used in both systems, and cost flow among accounts is also the same. Accordingly, both systems increase (debit) work-in-process control (a general ledger account) to record applied factory overhead and other production costs.
Answer (A) is incorrect because CGS is debited (increased) when finished goods are sold. Answer (C) is incorrect because factory overhead control is debited (increased) when actual factory overhead is incurred. Answer (D) is incorrect because finished goods control is debited (increased) when goods are completed.

**11.** The completion of goods is recorded as a decrease in work-in-process control when using

| | Job-Order Costing | Process Costing |
|---|---|---|
| A. | Yes | No |
| B. | Yes | Yes |
| C. | No | Yes |
| D. | No | No |

The correct answer is (B). *(CPA, adapted)*
**REQUIRED:** The costing system(s) in which work-in-process control is decreased when goods are completed.
**DISCUSSION:** The cost flow among accounts in process costing is similar to that for job-order costing. Both use the basic general ledger accounts, for example, materials control, work-in-process control, factory overhead control, finished goods control, and cost of goods sold. Consequently, each system credits (decreases) work-in-process control and debits (increases) finished goods control when goods are completed.
Answers (A), (C), and (D) are incorrect because both methods credit work-in-process when goods are completed.

## 4.2 Operation Costing

**12.** Operation costing is appropriate for products that are

A. Unique.

B. Produced in batches or production runs.

C. Homogeneous.

D. Related to food and beverage industries.

The correct answer is (B). *(Publisher)*
**REQUIRED:** The kind of product appropriate for operation costing.
**DISCUSSION:** Operation costing is used when different groups of products are subject to some but not all of the same processing steps (operations). Every unit passing through a given operation is processed in the same way, and conversion costs are accumulated by operation. Direct materials costs are accumulated by batch.
Answer (A) is incorrect because job-order costing is used for unique products. Answer (C) is incorrect because process costing is used for homogeneous products. Answer (D) is incorrect because food and beverage products may be unique or homogeneous and may be produced in jobs, lots, or batches.

**13.** An operation costing system is

A. Identical to a process costing system except that actual cost is used for manufacturing overhead.

B. The same as a process costing system except that materials costs are assigned on the basis of batches of production.

C. The same as a job-order costing system except that materials are accounted for in the same way as they are in a process costing system.

D. A system in which manufacturing activities are finely divided into individual, discrete steps or operations.

The correct answer is (B). *(CMA, adapted)*
**REQUIRED:** The definition of operation costing.
**DISCUSSION:** Operation costing is a hybrid of job-order and process costing systems that assigns materials costs on the basis of batches of production. It is used by companies that manufacture goods that undergo some similar and some dissimilar processes. Operation costing accumulates total conversion costs and determines a unit conversion cost for each operation. However, direct materials costs are charged specifically to products or batches as in job-order systems.
Answers (A) and (C) are incorrect because operation costing differs from process costing in the treatment of materials. Answer (D) is incorrect because conversion costs are accumulated by operations, not by discrete steps. Thus, operation may be synonymous with department or process.

**14.** Operation costing is a product costing system best described as

A. Job-order costing.

B. The cost accounting system designed for hospitals.

C. Process costing.

D. A blend of job-order and process costing.

The correct answer is (D). *(Publisher)*
**REQUIRED:** The best description of operation costing.
**DISCUSSION:** Operation costing is a hybrid of job-order costing and process costing. As in process costing, a single average unit conversion cost is applied to units passing through an operation. Direct materials costs are applied to the individual batches in the same manner as in job-order costing. It is used to account for the costs of batch processing of relatively large numbers of similar units in individual production runs.
Answers (A) and (C) are incorrect because operation costing is a hybrid form of job-order and process costing. Answer (B) is incorrect because operation costing was developed for batch processing operations.

**15.** Three commonly employed systems for product costing are job-order costing, operation costing, and process costing. Match the type of production environment with the costing method used.

|   | Job-Order Costing | Operation Costing | Process Costing |
|---|---|---|---|
| A. | Auto repair | Clothing manufacturing | Oil refining |
| B. | Loan processing | Drug manufacturing | Custom printing |
| C. | Custom printing | Paint manufacturing | Paper manufacturing |
| D. | Engineering design | Auto assembly | Motion picture production |

The correct answer is (A). *(CIA, adapted)*
**REQUIRED:** The match of the types of production environments with the costing methods.
**DISCUSSION:** Job-order costing is appropriate when producing products with unique characteristics. Process costing should be used to assign costs to similar products that are mass produced on a continuous basis. Operation costing is a hybrid of job-order and process costing systems. It is used by companies that manufacture goods that undergo some similar and some dissimilar processes. Thus, job-order costing is appropriate for auto repair, operation costing for clothing manufacturing, and process costing for oil refining.
Answer (B) is incorrect because job-order costing would be used for custom printing. Answer (C) is incorrect because process costing would be used for paint manufacturing. Answer (D) is incorrect because motion picture production would require job-order costing.

## 4.3 Transferred-in Costs

**16.** In a production cost report using process costing, transferred-in costs are similar to

A. Direct materials added at a point during the process.

B. Conversion costs added during the process.

C. Costs transferred to the next process.

D. Costs included in beginning inventory.

The correct answer is (A). *(CPA, adapted)*
**REQUIRED:** The type of cost most similar to transferred-in costs.
**DISCUSSION:** Transferred-in costs are similar to materials added at a point during the process because both attach to (become part of) the product at that point, which is usually the beginning of the process. Computations for transferred-in costs are usually separate from those for other direct materials costs and conversion costs.
Answer (B) is incorrect because conversion costs (direct labor and overhead) are usually continuously added throughout the process. Answer (C) is incorrect because transferred-out costs are those attached to completed units. Answer (D) is incorrect because the beginning inventory of a period (the ending inventory of the prior period) usually includes direct materials costs and conversion costs.

**17.** What are transferred-in costs in a process costing system?

A. Labor costs incurred for transferring employees from another department within the same plant instead of hiring temporary workers from the outside.

B. Costs of the product of a previous internal process that is subsequently used in a succeeding internal process.

C. Supervisory salaries that are transferred from an overhead cost center to a production cost center.

D. Ending work-in-process inventory of a previous process that will be used in a succeeding process.

The correct answer is (B). *(CPA, adapted)*
**REQUIRED:** The definition of transferred-in costs.
**DISCUSSION:** Transferred-in costs are the costs of the product of a previous internal process that is subsequently used in a succeeding internal process. Transferred-in costs are similar to direct materials costs added at the beginning of the process.
Answers (A) and (C) are incorrect because the costs of employees transferred from another department and supervisory salaries transferred from an overhead cost center to a production cost center are not product costs attached to units when they were transferred in from a preceding internal process. Answer (D) is incorrect because another department's EWIP has not yet been transferred.

**18.** In a process costing system, how is the unit cost affected in a production cost report when direct materials are added in a department subsequent to the first department and the added materials result in additional units?

- A. The first department's unit cost is increased, which necessitates an adjustment of the transferred-in unit cost.

- B. The first department's unit cost is decreased, which necessitates an adjustment of the transferred-in unit cost.

- C. The first department's unit cost is increased, which does not necessitate an adjustment of the transferred-in unit cost.

- D. The first department's unit cost is decreased, which does not necessitate an adjustment of the transferred-in unit cost.

The correct answer is (B). *(CPA, adapted)*
**REQUIRED:** The effect of adding direct materials in a subsequent department, thereby creating additional units.
**DISCUSSION:** If additional units are created in a process (e.g., by adding direct materials in a subsequent department), the number of equivalent units increases and the unit cost decreases because the total transferred-in cost remains constant. Thus, an adjustment to the transferred-in unit cost is necessary.

Answer (A) is incorrect because, as additional units are created, the number of equivalent units increases and the unit cost decreases. Answer (C) is incorrect because, as additional units are created, the number of equivalent units increases and the unit cost decreases. Additionally, a retroactive adjustment to the transferred-in unit cost is necessary. Answer (D) is incorrect because a retroactive adjustment to the transferred-in unit cost is necessary when more units are subsequently created.

**19.** Purchased direct materials are added in the second department of a three-department process. This addition increases the number of units produced in the second department and will

- A. Always change the direct labor cost percentage in the ending work-in-process inventory.

- B. Never cause an adjustment to the unit cost transferred in from the first department.

- C. Always increase total unit costs.

- D. Always decrease total ending work-in-process inventory.

The correct answer is (A). *(CPA, adapted)*
**REQUIRED:** The effect of adding materials in a subsequent department, thereby creating more units.
**DISCUSSION:** When direct materials are added to the production process in the second department, thereby increasing the number of units produced, more units are available to absorb the direct labor and overhead costs. Accordingly, the labor and overhead cost percentages are reduced (relative to direct materials cost).

Answer (B) is incorrect because, if work done in a subsequent department increases the units produced in a previous department, an adjustment to the transferred-in unit cost is necessary. Answer (C) is incorrect because, as the number of units produced increases, the unit cost of production usually decreases. Answer (D) is incorrect because, although the number of units has increased and unit cost has decreased, total inventory value is not affected.

**20.** Purchased direct materials are added in the second department of a three-department process. This addition does not increase the number of units produced in the second department and will

- A. Not change the dollar amount transferred to the next department.

- B. Decrease total ending work-in-process inventory.

- C. Increase the factory overhead portion of the ending work-in-process inventory.

- D. Increase total unit cost.

The correct answer is (D). *(CPA, adapted)*
**REQUIRED:** The effect of adding direct materials in a subsequent department given constant production.
**DISCUSSION:** Adding materials to a production process without changing the number of units produced increases the unit cost. The numerator (total cost) increases while the denominator (total units) remains the same.

Answer (A) is incorrect because, if purchased materials are added to the process, the cost will be added to the total cost transferred to the next department. Answer (B) is incorrect because the unit cost, and therefore the cost of EWIP, increases when materials are added. Answer (C) is incorrect because materials cost is separate from overhead.

**21.** Why are transferred-in costs differentiated from direct materials?

A. They usually consist of the basic units being produced.

B. They are of greater value than most other materials added.

C. They are greater in value than the value of all other materials added.

D. They are added at the beginning of the process, unlike other direct materials.

The correct answer is (A). *(Publisher)*

**REQUIRED:** The reason transferred-in costs are distinguished from other types of direct materials.

**DISCUSSION:** Usually, transferred-in costs pertain to the units of production that move from one process to another. Thus, they are the basic units being produced. Direct materials are added to the basic units during processing.

Answers (B) and (C) are incorrect because value is not an issue in differentiating transferred-in costs from direct materials. Answer (D) is incorrect because direct materials may be added at the beginning of a process and, conceivably, the transferred-in materials (i.e., basic units) could be added to the process after the direct materials are processed.

## 4.4 Equivalent Units of Production (EUP)

**22.** Equivalent units of production are used in process accounting to

A. Measure the efficiency of the production process.

B. Establish standard costs.

C. Provide a means of assigning cost to partially completed units.

D. Allocate overhead to production.

The correct answer is (C). *(Publisher)*

**REQUIRED:** The purpose of calculating equivalent units of production (EUP).

**DISCUSSION:** EUP are used to allocate cost to incomplete goods. Thus, if 50% of the direct materials have been added to 100 units in process, there are 50 EUP of materials. Similarly, if 30% of the conversion costs has been incurred for 1,000 units, 300 EUP have been produced.

Answers (A) and (B) are incorrect because EUP are calculated to allocate production costs, not to measure production efficiency. Answer (D) is incorrect because overhead is usually assigned based on a measure of activity, e.g., labor cost or machine hours.

**23.** EUP analysis is usually applied to

A. Direct materials and conversion costs.

B. Direct materials costs only.

C. Conversion costs only.

D. Overhead costs.

The correct answer is (A). *(Publisher)*

**REQUIRED:** The costs relevant to EUP analysis.

**DISCUSSION:** EUP analysis is usually done separately for direct materials and conversion costs. A production process may use several types of materials, e.g., transferred-in cost plus additional raw materials. Several conversion activities may be required as well. Hence, the percentage of completion is rarely the same for both costs.

Answers (B) and (C) are incorrect because EUP analysis is usually applied to both direct materials and conversion costs. Answer (D) is incorrect because overhead is part of conversion costs.

**24.** In process 2, material G is added when a batch is 60% complete. Ending work-in-process units, which are 50% complete, would be included in the computation of equivalent units for

|     | Conversion Costs | Material G |
| --- | --- | --- |
| A.  | Yes | No |
| B.  | No | Yes |
| C.  | No | No |
| D.  | Yes | Yes |

The correct answer is (A). *(CPA, adapted)*

**REQUIRED:** The computation(s) of equivalent units that will include ending work-in-process.

**DISCUSSION:** Conversion costs (direct labor and factory overhead) are the costs of transforming direct materials into finished products. If EWIP is 50% complete, it is presumably 50% complete as to conversion costs (all costs other than direct materials). But if material G is added only at the 60% point, no equivalent units of G have been produced. Thus, EWIP is included in the computation of equivalent units of conversion costs but not material G.

Answers (B), (C), and (D) are incorrect because EWIP is included in the EUP computation for conversion costs but not material G.

**25.** The following information pertains to a company's Finishing Department operations in May.

| | Units | % Completion |
|---|---|---|
| Work-in-process, May 1 | 2,000 | 40% |
| Units started during May | 10,000 | |
| Units completed and transferred to FG | 8,000 | |
| Work-in-process, May 31 | ? | 25% |

Materials are added at the end of the process, and conversion costs are incurred evenly throughout the process. The equivalent units of materials added during May were

A. 8,000

B. 8,200

C. 9,100

D. 10,000

The correct answer is (A). *(CIA, adapted)*
**REQUIRED:** The equivalent units of materials added in May.
**DISCUSSION:** Given that the materials are added at the end of the process, no equivalent units of materials are included in beginning or ending work-in-process. Thus, the equivalent units of materials equal the 8,000 units [(100% x 2,000) + (8,000 – 2,000) + (0% x 4,000)] transferred out during May.
Answer (B) is incorrect because 8,200 equals the equivalent units of conversion costs for May. Answer (C) is incorrect because 9,100 equals the equivalent units of conversion costs that result from reversing the degrees of completion for beginning and ending work-in-process. Answer (D) is incorrect because 10,000 equals the equivalent units of production if the materials were added at the beginning of the process.

**26.** Separate equivalent units calculations are often not made for

A. Conversion costs.

B. Transferred-in costs.

C. Direct materials costs.

D. Direct labor costs.

The correct answer is (D). *(Publisher)*
**REQUIRED:** The cost for which a separate EUP calculation is often not made.
**DISCUSSION:** Overhead in traditional costing systems is often applied on the basis of a direct labor activity base such as hours or cost. Thus, a single EUP calculation is made for conversion costs (direct labor and overhead). There is no basis for separating these costs if they are incurred uniformly.
Answer (A) is incorrect because EUP must be calculated for conversion costs. Answer (B) is incorrect because transferred-in costs are usually included at the beginning of the process. They consist of costs incurred in preceding departments and are therefore conceptually similar to direct materials. Hence, they are separate from other costs. Answer (C) is incorrect because direct materials may be added at various points in the operation. Each kind of material should be the basis for a separate EUP calculation.

**27.** Kew Co. had 3,000 units in work-in-process at April 1 that were 60% complete as to conversion cost. During April, 10,000 units were completed. At April 30, the 4,000 units in work-in-process were 40% complete as to conversion cost. Direct materials are added at the beginning of the process. How many units were started during April?

A. 9,000

B. 9,800

C. 10,000

D. 11,000

The correct answer is (D). *(CPA, adapted)*
**REQUIRED:** The number of units started in April.
**DISCUSSION:** The following physical flow formula may be used to calculate the unknown:

$$BWIP + Units\ started = Units\ completed + EWIP$$
$$3,000 + Units\ started = 10,000 + 4,000$$
$$Units\ started = 11,000$$

Answer (A) is incorrect because units started in April equal units completed during April + EWIP – BWIP. Answer (B) is incorrect because beginning work-in-process at April 1 is 3,000 (not 1,800) units, and the ending work-in-process at April 30 is 4,000 (not 1,600) units. Answer (C) is incorrect because 10,000 units were completed (not started) during April.

## 4.5  FIFO vs. Weighted-Average Assumption for EUP

**28.** In comparing the FIFO and weighted-average methods for calculating equivalent units

   A.   The FIFO method tends to smooth costs out more over time than the weighted-average method.

   B.   The weighted-average method is more precise than the FIFO method because the weighted-average method is based only on the work completed in the current period.

   C.   The two methods will give similar results even if physical inventory levels and production costs (material and conversion costs) fluctuate greatly from period to period.

   D.   The FIFO method is better than the weighted-average method for judging the performance in a period independently from performance in preceding periods.

The correct answer is (D). *(CIA, adapted)*

**REQUIRED:** The true statement about the FIFO and weighted-average methods of calculating equivalent units.

**DISCUSSION:** The calculation of the cost per equivalent unit using the FIFO method keeps the costs in one period separate from the costs of prior periods. Under the weighted-average method, the costs in the beginning work-in-process inventory are combined with current-period costs.

Answer (A) is incorrect because the weighted-average method tends to smooth costs over time. Answer (B) is incorrect because the FIFO method is more precise. It is based only on the work completed in the current period. Answer (C) is incorrect because the two methods will provide dissimilar results when physical inventory levels and the production costs (materials and conversion costs) fluctuate greatly from period to period.

**29.** A process costing system was used for a department that began operations in January 1998. Approximately the same number of physical units, at the same degree of completion, were in work-in-process at the end of both January and February. Monthly conversion costs are assigned to ending work-in-process and units completed. Compared with the FIFO method, would the weighted-average method use the same or a greater number of equivalent units to calculate the monthly cost assignments?

|  | Equivalent Units for Weighted-Average Compared with FIFO | |
| --- | --- | --- |
|  | January | February |
| A. | Same | Same |
| B. | Greater number | Greater number |
| C. | Greater number | Same |
| D. | Same | Greater number |

The correct answer is (D). *(CPA, adapted)*

**REQUIRED:** The comparison of equivalent units calculated under the FIFO and weighted-average methods.

**DISCUSSION:** The weighted-average method calculates equivalent units by adding the equivalent units in EWIP to the total of all units completed during the period, regardless of when they were started. The FIFO method determines equivalent units by subtracting the work done on the BWIP in the prior period from the weighted-average total. If the number of equivalent units in BWIP is zero, as it was for the month of January, the two methods produce the same result. Otherwise, the weighted-average computation is greater.

Answer (A) is incorrect because the weighted-average method calculates the greater number of equivalent units except when the number of equivalent units in BWIP is zero. Answer (B) is incorrect because both the FIFO and the weighted-average methods produce the same result for the first month of operations. Answer (C) is incorrect because the weighted-average total is greater for February and the same for January.

**30.** The units transferred in from the first department to the second department should be included in the computation of the equivalent units for the second department under which of the following methods of process costing?

|  | FIFO | Weighted-Average |
| --- | --- | --- |
| A. | Yes | Yes |
| B. | Yes | No |
| C. | No | Yes |
| D. | No | No |

The correct answer is (A). *(CPA, adapted)*

**REQUIRED:** The cost flow method(s) that include(s) transferred-in costs in EUP calculations.

**DISCUSSION:** The units transferred from the first to the second department should be included in the computation of equivalent units for the second department regardless of the cost flow assumption used. The transferred-in units are considered raw materials added at the beginning of the period.

Answers (B), (C), and (D) are incorrect because the units transferred in from the first to the second department should be included in the EUP computation for the second department under both FIFO and weighted-average.

**31.** In a given process costing system, the EUP are computed using the weighted-average method. With respect to conversion costs, the percentage of completion for the current period only is included in the calculation of the

|     | Beginning Work-in-Process Inventory | Ending Work-In-Process Inventory |
|-----|-----------------|-----------------|
| A.  | No              | No              |
| B.  | No              | Yes             |
| C.  | Yes             | No              |
| D.  | Yes             | Yes             |

**32.** Assuming no beginning work-in-process (BWIP) inventory, and that the ending work-in-process (EWIP) inventory is 50% complete as to conversion costs, the number of equivalent units as to conversion costs would be

A. The same as the units completed.

B. The same as the units placed in process.

C. Less than the units completed.

D. Less than the units placed in process.

**33.** Assuming no beginning work-in-process inventory, and that the ending work-in-process inventory is 100% complete as to materials costs, the number of equivalent units as to materials costs is

A. The same as the units placed in process.

B. The same as the units completed.

C. Less than the units placed in process.

D. Less than the units completed.

**34.** One approach to calculating EUP is to begin with the total work that could be done, i.e., the units in BWIP and those transferred in. Is there another approach?

A. Yes, begin with the total work that could not be done, e.g., work already completed in BWIP.

B. Yes, begin with the total work that has been done (units transferred out and the completed EUP in EWIP).

C. Yes, begin with the total work that has been done (units transferred out and the EUP required to complete EWIP).

D. No, EUP may be calculated in only one way.

The correct answer is (B). *(CPA, adapted)*
**REQUIRED:** The in-process inventory(ies) in which conversion costs are calculated.
**DISCUSSION:** The weighted-average process costing method considers only the degree of completion of EWIP in the calculation of EUP. Because this method includes the costs incurred in the prior period for units in BWIP, EUP are equal to units completed and transferred out plus the EUP completed in EWIP.
Answers (A), (C), and (D) are incorrect because the total units in beginning work-in-process inventory are used in the calculation of conversion costs; the percentage of completion of the ending work-in-process inventory is included in the calculation of conversion costs.

The correct answer is (D). *(CPA, adapted)*
**REQUIRED:** The number of EUP as to conversion costs.
**DISCUSSION:** Given no BWIP, it is immaterial whether FIFO or weighted average is used. Thus, conversion cost EUP equal the units that were started and completed this period, plus the EUP in EWIP. Because the units in EWIP are 50% complete as to conversion costs, they will not be fully counted for purposes of determining EUP.
Answer (A) is incorrect because, given no BWIP, the only units completed were those started in the current period. Total EUP include these units plus the EUP in EWIP. Answer (B) is incorrect because, given no BWIP, conversion cost EUP would equal units started if there were no EWIP. Answer (C) is incorrect because conversion cost EUP include units completed plus work in EWIP.

The correct answer is (A). *(CPA, adapted)*
**REQUIRED:** The number of EUP as to materials costs.
**DISCUSSION:** Given no BWIP, whether FIFO or weighted average is used is immaterial. Because EWIP is 100% complete as to materials costs, the EUP for materials costs are equal to the number of units placed in process (units in EWIP + units transferred to finished goods).
Answer (B) is incorrect because the number of equivalent units is equal to the units completed only if there is no EWIP. Answer (C) is incorrect because the number of equivalent units is less than the units placed in process when EWIP is less than 100% complete as to materials costs. Answer (D) is incorrect because the EUP must at least equal the number of units completed.

The correct answer is (B). *(Publisher)*
**REQUIRED:** The alternate approach to computing EUP.
**DISCUSSION:** Total work that can be done is one starting point for computing EUP. Total work that can be done is the sum of the units in BWIP and those transferred in. In FIFO, only EUP to complete BWIP are added. Under the weighted-average method, the work done to date is included in addition to work in the current period. The EUP required to complete EWIP are deducted from the total work that can be done. The other approach is to consider all the work done, i.e., to add the units transferred out to the units already completed in EWIP.
Answer (A) is incorrect because EUP calculations concern work that was done. Answer (C) is incorrect because, to compute the work that was done, one must add the completed EUP in EWIP. Answer (D) is incorrect because there are at least two methods to calculate EUP. Two of the methods are to begin with the total work that could be done and to begin with the total work that has been done.

Questions 35 through 38 are based on the following information.  Nine concepts are listed below:

Questions 35 through 38 are based on the following information.  Nine concepts are listed below:

1. EUP to complete BWIP
2. EUP from last period in BWIP
3. Units transferred in
4. Total units transferred out
5. Units transferred out that were started and completed this period

6. Units transferred out that were started last period and completed this period
7. EUP to complete EWIP
8. EUP completed in EWIP
9. Total units in BWIP

**35.** What is a correct formula for weighted-average EUP?

A.  $1 + 2 + 3 + 7$

B.  $2 + 4 - 8$

C.  $1 + 2 + 3 - 7$

D.  $4 + 5 + 6 + 8$

The correct answer is (C). *(Publisher)*
**REQUIRED:** The formula for weighted-average EUP.
**DISCUSSION:** Weighted-average EUP are computed as all the work that could have been done (the total units transferred in), minus work that was not done (the EUP required to complete EWIP).  The formula is $1 + 2 + 3 - 7$.

Answer (A) is incorrect because the EUP required to complete EWIP should be subtracted (not added). Answer (B) is incorrect because this formula results in double counting:  the work done last period in BWIP is also included in the total units transferred out.  Answer (D) is incorrect because units started and completed this period plus the units started last period and completed this period equal the total units transferred out.

**36.** What is another correct formula for weighted-average EUP?

A.  $8 + 6 + 5$

B.  $8 + 4 + 2 + 1$

C.  $8 + 7 + 4 + 2$

D.  $8 + 6 + 5 - 2$

The correct answer is (A). *(Publisher)*
**REQUIRED:** The alternative formula for weighted-average EUP.
**DISCUSSION:** Another approach is to consider the total work that has been done.  The sum of the units started and completed this period and those started last period and completed this period (total units transferred out) plus the EUP completed in EWIP is the total work done ($8 + 6 + 5$).

Answer (B) is incorrect because the units in BWIP are included in the units transferred out.  Answer (C) is incorrect because the EUP to complete WIP have not been done and should not be part of this period's EUP.  Answer (D) is incorrect because it is the formula for FIFO EUP.

**37.** What is the correct formula for FIFO EUP?

A.  $1 + 3 - 7$

B.  $1 + 2 + 3 - 8$

C.  $1 + 4 - 7$

D.  $9 - 5 - 6$

The correct answer is (A). *(Publisher)*
**REQUIRED:** The formula for determining FIFO EUP.
**DISCUSSION:** One FIFO approach is to determine the EUP that could be produced in this period.  The total work that can be done is that needed to finish BWIP and complete all the goods transferred in.  The EUP needed to finish any EWIP should then be deducted ($1 + 3 - 7$).

Answer (B) is incorrect because the work done last period in BWIP is not part of FIFO EUP, nor is the work completed this period subtracted.  Answer (C) is incorrect because the EUP to complete BWIP are included in the total units transferred out.  Answer (D) is incorrect because this formula gives the number of physical units (not EUP) in EWIP.

**38.** What is another correct formula for FIFO EUP?

A.  8 + 4

B.  8 + 4 – 2

C.  8 + 7 + 6 + 5

D.  7 + 4 + 2 + 1

The correct answer is (B). *(Publisher)*

**REQUIRED:** The alternative formula for FIFO EUP.

**DISCUSSION:** Another approach to computing FIFO EUP is to begin with the work that was done, which is the EUP completed in EWIP plus the units transferred out. Subtracting the work that had been done in the prior period gives the FIFO EUP (8 + 4 – 2).

Answer (A) is incorrect because EUP from last period in BWIP should be subtracted. Answer (C) is incorrect because this formula includes the work needed to complete EWIP. Answer (D) is incorrect because BWIP is included in units transferred out.

**39.** Which is the true statement about the cost of completed goods transferred under FIFO to the next production department or to finished goods inventory?

A.  The two amounts are kept separate.

B.  The two amounts are kept separate but are combined by the next department.

C.  The two amounts are considered combined as the goods are transferred.

D.  The goods started and completed this period are transferred prior to those started last period and completed this period.

The correct answer is (C). *(Publisher)*

**REQUIRED:** The true statement about the cost of completed goods transferred under FIFO.

**DISCUSSION:** Under FIFO, goods started last period and completed this period are costed separately from goods started and completed this period. When the goods are transferred to the next department or to finished goods, however, they are considered transferred out at one average cost so that a multitude of layers of inventory is not created. This procedure is consistent with the basic concept of process costing.

Answer (A) is incorrect because, if the amounts are kept separate, inventory layers will continue to multiply as the units of product are passed through additional WIP accounts. Answer (B) is incorrect because the amounts are combined before transfer. Answer (D) is incorrect because, under FIFO, the goods that were started last period and completed this period are deemed to be completed first and transferred first.

**40.** On November 1, Yankee Company had 20,000 units of WIP in Department No. 1 which were 100% complete as to material costs and 20% complete as to conversion costs. During November, 160,000 units were started in Department No. 1 and 170,000 units were completed and transferred to Department No. 2. WIP on November 30 was 100% complete as to material costs and 40% complete as to conversion costs. By what amount would the equivalent units for conversion costs for the month of November differ if the FIFO method were used instead of the weighted-average method?

A.  20,000 decrease.

B.  16,000 decrease.

C.  8,000 decrease.

D.  4,000 decrease.

The correct answer is (D). *(CPA, adapted)*

**REQUIRED:** The difference in EUP between the FIFO and the weighted-average method.

**DISCUSSION:** The weighted-average method combines previous and current period work, while the FIFO method includes only the EUP for the work done in the current period. Thus, the difference will be the EUP for BWIP.

| Units in Department No. 1 | |
|---|---|
| BWIP (20%)   20,000 | 170,000 Transferred |
| Started         160,000 | |
| | 10,000 EWIP (40%) |

Conversion Costs

| Wtd.-Avg. EUP | |
|---|---|
| Transferred | 170,000 |
| EWIP (40% × 10,000) | 4,000 |
| Wtd.-Avg. EUP | 174,000 |

| FIFO EUP | |
|---|---|
| Transferred: | |
| BWIP (80% × 20,000) | 16,000 |
| Started and completed | 150,000 |
| EWIP (40% × 10,000) | 4,000 |
| FIFO EUP | 170,000 |

The difference is that weighted average includes the work done in the previous period (20% of BWIP was completed in the prior period). Accordingly, the difference is that weighted-average EUP is greater than FIFO EUP by 20% of 20,000, or 4,000.

| | |
|---|---:|
| Questions 41 and 42 are based on the following information. A manufacturing company employs a process cost system. The company's product passes through both Department 1 and Department 2 in order to be completed. Conversion costs are incurred uniformly throughout the process in Department 2. The direct material is added in Department 2 when conversion is 80% complete. This direct material is a preservative that does not change the volume. Spoiled units are discovered at the final inspection and are recognized then for costing purposes. The physical flow of units for the current month is presented in the next column. | Beginning work-in-process in Department 2 (90% complete with respect to conversion costs)　14,000<br><br>Transferred in from Department 1　76,000<br>Completed and transferred to finished goods　80,000<br>Spoiled units - all normal　1,500<br>Ending work-in-process in Department 2 (60% complete with respect to conversion costs)　8,500 |

**41.** If the manufacturing company uses the weighted-average method, the equivalent units for direct materials in Department 2 for the current month would be

A. 67,500

B. 80,000

C. 81,500

D. 90,000

The correct answer is (C). *(CIA, adapted)*
**REQUIRED:** The equivalent units for direct materials based on the weighted-average method.
**DISCUSSION:** The weighted-average method does not distinguish between work done currently and in the prior period. Given that materials are added when units are 80% complete, that ending work-in-process is 60% complete, and that goods are inspected when they are 100% complete, and assuming that equivalent units are calculated for normal spoilage, the total weighted-average equivalent units for direct materials equal 81,500 (80,000 units transferred + 1,500 normally spoiled units).
Answer (A) is incorrect because 67,500 equivalent units of direct materials were added in accordance with the FIFO method. Answer (B) is incorrect because 80,000 units were transferred. Answer (D) is incorrect because 90,000 units equal the actual physical flow for the month.

**42.** If the manufacturing company uses the FIFO (first-in, first-out) method, the equivalent units for conversion costs in Department 2 for the current month would be

A. 72,500

B. 74,000

C. 85,200

D. 86,600

The correct answer is (B). *(CIA, adapted)*
**REQUIRED:** The equivalent units for conversion costs based on the FIFO method.
**DISCUSSION:** The FIFO method distinguishes between work done in the prior period and work done currently. The total FIFO equivalent units equal the work done currently on beginning work-in-process, plus the work done on ending work-in-process, plus all units started and completed currently. Hence, total FIFO equivalent units equal 74,000 {(10% x 14,000 units in BWIP) + (60% x 8,500 units in EWIP) + [100% x (81,500 spoiled and transferred – 14,000 units in BWIP)]}.
Answer (A) is incorrect because 72,500 ignores spoilage. Answer (C) is incorrect because 85,200 includes 90% of the beginning work-in-process. Answer (D) is incorrect because 86,600 calculates the equivalent units for conversion costs according to the weighted-average method.

| | Units | CC |
|---|---|---|
| WIP at January 1 | 25,000 | $ 22,000 |
| Units started and costs incurred during January | 135,000 | 143,000 |
| Units completed and transferred to next department during January | 100,000 | |

Questions 43 through 45 are based on the following information. The Cutting Department is the first stage of Mark Company's production cycle. BWIP for this department was 80% complete as to conversion costs. EWIP was 50% complete. Information as to conversion costs in the Cutting Department for January is presented in the next column.

**43.** Using the FIFO method, what was the conversion cost of WIP in the Cutting Department at January 31?

A. $22,000

B. $33,000

C. $39,000

D. $78,000

The correct answer is (C). *(CPA, adapted)*
**REQUIRED:** The FIFO conversion cost of EWIP.
**DISCUSSION:** Under the FIFO method, EUP for a period include only the work done that period and exclude any work done in a prior period. The total of conversion cost EUP for the period is calculated below.

| | Units | Work Done in Current Period | CC (EUP) |
|---|---|---|---|
| BWIP | 25,000 | 20% | 5,000 |
| Started & completed | 75,000 | 100% | 75,000 |
| EWIP | 60,000 | 50% | 30,000 |
| Total EUP | | | 110,000 |

The total of the conversion costs for the period is given as $143,000. Dividing by total EUP of 110,000 gives a unit cost of $1.30. Thus, the conversion cost of the EWIP inventory is $39,000 ($1.30 x 30,000 EUP in EWIP).
Answer (A) is incorrect because $22,000 is the BWIP. Answer (B) is incorrect because $33,000 equals the unit conversion cost for the preceding period [$22,000 ÷ (80% x 25,000)] times 30,000 EUP. Answer (D) is incorrect because $78,000 equals $1.30 times 60,000 units.

**44.** What is the per-unit conversion cost of goods started last period and completed this period?

A. $22,000 ÷ 25,000

B. $1.10

C. $28,500 ÷ 25,000

D. $1.30

The correct answer is (C). *(Publisher)*
**REQUIRED:** The unit conversion cost of goods.
**DISCUSSION:** The total of the units started last period and completed this period is 25,000. These units were 80% completed at the start of the period, at a cost of $22,000. The cost to complete was $6,500 (5,000 EUP x $1.30). The total cost of $28,500 is divided by 25,000 to obtain the unit cost.
Answer (A) is incorrect because $22,000 ÷ 25,000 does not consider the conversion cost of $6,500 to complete BWIP. Answer (B) is incorrect because $1.10 is the conversion cost per EUP for last period. Answer (D) is incorrect because $1.30 is the conversion cost per EUP for this period.

**45.** What is the unit conversion cost of goods started this period and completed this period using the weighted-average method?

A. $1.10

B. $1.14

C. $1.27

D. $1.30

The correct answer is (C). *(Publisher)*
**REQUIRED:** The weighted-average unit conversion cost.
**DISCUSSION:** The weighted-average method combines the costs in BWIP and the current-period costs. Thus, it calculates total EUP as total units to account for minus the work yet to be done on EWIP. The total cost to account for is $165,000 ($22,000 BWIP + $143,000 current costs). Total units to account for are 160,000 (25,000 BWIP + 135,000 started in January), and units in EWIP 50% complete equal 60,000 (160,000 – 100,000 transferred). Hence, weighted-average EUP equal 130,000 [160,000 – (50% x 60,000)], and the unit cost is $1.27 ($165,000 ÷ 130,000).
Answer (A) is incorrect because $1.10 is the conversion cost per EUP for last period. Answer (B) is incorrect because $1.14 is the unit conversion cost of goods started last period and completed this period. Answer (D) is incorrect because $1.30 is the current FIFO unit conversion cost.

## 4.6 FIFO EUP Calculations

**46.** A company employs a process cost system using the first-in, first-out (FIFO) method. The product passes through both Department 1 and Department 2 in order to be completed. Units enter Department 2 upon completion in Department 1. Additional direct materials are added in Department 2 when the units have reached the 25% stage of completion with respect to conversion costs. Conversion costs are added proportionally in Department 2. The production activity in Department 2 for the current month was as follows:

| | |
|---|---|
| Beginning work-in-process inventory (40% complete with respect to conversion costs) | 15,000 |
| Units transferred in from Department 1 | 80,000 |
| Units to account for | 95,000 |
| Units completed and transferred to finished goods | 85,000 |
| Ending work-in-process inventory (20% complete with respect to conversion costs) | 10,000 |
| Units accounted for | 95,000 |

How many equivalent units for direct materials were added in Department 2 for the current month?

- A. 70,000 units.
- B. 80,000 units.
- C. 85,000 units.
- D. 95,000 units.

The correct answer is (A). *(CIA, adapted)*
**REQUIRED:** The equivalent units for direct materials added in Department 2 for the current month.
**DISCUSSION:** Beginning inventory is 40% complete. Hence, direct materials have already been added. Ending inventory has not reached the 25% stage of completion, so direct materials have not yet been added to these units. Thus, the equivalent units for direct materials calculated on a FIFO basis are equal to the units started and completed in the current period (85,000 units completed – 15,000 units in BWIP = 70,000 units started and completed).

Answer (B) is incorrect because 80,000 total units were transferred in from Department 1. Answer (C) is incorrect because 85,000 equals the equivalent units for direct materials calculated on a weighted-average basis. Answer (D) is incorrect because 95,000 equals the total units to be account for.

**47.** The following data pertain to a company's cracking-department operations in December:

| | Units | Completion |
|---|---|---|
| Work-in-process, December 1 | 20,000 | 50% |
| Units started | 170,000 | |
| Units completed & transferred to the distilling department | 180,000 | |
| Work-in-process, December 31 | 10,000 | 50% |

Materials are added at the beginning of the process and conversion costs are incurred uniformly throughout the process. Assuming use of the FIFO method of process costing, the equivalent units of conversion performed during December were

- A. 170,000 equivalent units.
- B. 175,000 equivalent units.
- C. 180,000 equivalent units.
- D. 185,000 equivalent units.

The correct answer is (B). *(CIA, adapted)*
**REQUIRED:** The equivalent units of conversion.
**DISCUSSION:** The number of equivalent units computed under this method excludes work done on BWIP in the prior period. Thus, the total of equivalent units of conversion cost for the period is calculated as follows:

$$
\begin{array}{rr}
\text{10,000 units in EWIP} \times 50\% = & 5,000 \\
\text{180,000 completed units} \times 100\% = & \underline{180,000} \\
& 185,000 \\
\text{20,000 units in BWIP} \times 50\% = & \underline{(10,000)} \\
& \underline{175,000}
\end{array}
$$

Answer (A) is incorrect because 170,000 is the number of equivalent units of materials for the period. Answer (C) is incorrect because 180,000 is the total amount of work done on the completed units. Answer (D) is incorrect because 185,000 is the amount determined using the weighted-average method.

**48.** The Cutting Department is the first stage of Mark Company's production cycle. BWIP for this department was 80% complete as to conversion costs. EWIP was 50% complete. Conversion costs in the Cutting Department for January were as follows:

| | Units | CC |
|---|---|---|
| WIP at January 1 | 25,000 | $ 22,000 |
| Units started and costs incurred during January | 135,000 | 143,000 |
| Units completed and transferred to next department during January | 100,000 | |

Using the FIFO method, what was the conversion cost of WIP in the Cutting Department at January 31?

- A. $22,000
- B. $33,000
- C. $39,000
- D. $78,000

The correct answer is (C). *(CPA, adapted)*
**REQUIRED:** The FIFO conversion cost of EWIP.
**DISCUSSION:** Under the FIFO method, EUP for a period include only the work done that period and exclude any work done in a prior period. The total of conversion cost EUP for the period is calculated below.

| | Units | Work Done in Current Period | CC (EUP) |
|---|---|---|---|
| BWIP | 25,000 | 20% | 5,000 |
| Started & completed | 75,000 | 100% | 75,000 |
| EWIP | 60,000 | 50% | 30,000 |
| Total EUP | | | 110,000 |

The total of the conversion costs for the period is given as $143,000. Dividing by total EUP of 110,000 gives a unit cost of $1.30. Thus, the conversion cost of the EWIP inventory is $39,000 ($1.30 x 30,000 EUP in EWIP).

Answer (A) is incorrect because $22,000 is the BWIP. Answer (B) is incorrect because $33,000 equals the unit conversion cost for the preceding period [$22,000 ÷ (80% x 25,000)] times 30,000 EUP. Answer (D) is incorrect because $78,000 equals $1.30 times 60,000 units.

**49.** The Wilson Company manufactures the famous Ticktock watch on an assembly-line basis. January 1 work-in-process consisted of 5,000 units partially completed. During the month, an additional 110,000 units were started, and 105,000 units were completed. The ending work-in-process was 60% complete as to conversion costs. Conversion costs are added evenly throughout the process. The following conversion costs were incurred:

| | |
|---|---|
| Beginning costs for work-in-process | $ 1,500 |
| Total current conversion costs | 273,920 |

The conversion costs assigned to ending work-in-process totaled $15,360 using the FIFO method of process costing. What was the percentage of completion as to conversion costs of the 5,000 units in BWIP?

- A. 20%
- B. 40%
- C. 60%
- D. 80%

The correct answer is (D). *(A. Wilson)*
**REQUIRED:** The percentage completion of BWIP as to conversion costs.
**DISCUSSION:** Ending work-in-process consists of 10,000 (5,000 + 110,000 − 105,000) units 60% complete, or 6,000 equivalent units of conversion (10,000 x 60%). Conversion cost is $2.56 per unit ($15,360 ÷ 6,000 units). Total equivalent conversion units for the month are 107,000 ($273,920 ÷ $2.56 per unit). Total equivalent units equal the sum of equivalent units to finish BWIP, units started and completed, and equivalent units in EWIP. Assuming that 100,000 units were started this period and completed, the amount of conversion cost-equivalent units added to BWIP this period is determined below:

107,000 *units* = BWIP + *Units started & completed* + *EWIP*
107,000 *units* = BWIP + 100,000 *units* + 6,000 *units*
BWIP = 1,000 *units this period*

Thus, BWIP consisted of 4,000 EUP with respect to conversion; that is, it was 80% complete (4,000 ÷ 5,000).

Answer (A) is incorrect because 20% takes into account only the 1,000 conversion cost-equivalent units added to BWIP this period and divides it by 5,000 units partially completed in beginning work-in-process. Answer (B) is incorrect because BWIP consisted of 4,000 EUP with respect to conversion that was 80% complete (4,000 ÷ 5,000). Answer (C) is incorrect because 60% is the percentage of units complete in ending work-in-process.

**50.** The following data were provided by Boze Co.:

|  | Units | % Complete (Conversion) |
|---|---|---|
| BWIP | 100 | 75% |
| Units started | 10,000 | |
| EWIP | 150 | 40% |

Assuming the FIFO method is used, what were the EUP for conversion costs?

A. 10,250

B. 10,040

C. 9,935

D. 9,910

The correct answer is (C). *(K. Boze)*

**REQUIRED:** The EUP for conversion costs based on the FIFO assumption.

**DISCUSSION:** The FIFO method for EUP assumes the units in beginning inventory are finished first, and then those units started this period are finished second. In this period, BWIP required only 25% conversion to be complete, 9,850 units (10,000 started – 150 EWIP) were started and completed, and EWIP is only 40% complete as to conversion costs.

| Finished BWIP | 100 × .25 = | 25 |
|---|---|---|
| Units started and completed | 9,850 × 1.00 = | 9,850 |
| Conversion applied to EWIP | 150 × .40 = | 60 |
| Equivalent units | | 9,935 |

Answer (A) is incorrect because 10,250 (100 + 10,000 + 150) does not take into account the percent complete as to conversion costs. Also, EWIP is double counted. Answer (B) is incorrect because BWIP required only 25% conversion to be complete, 9,850 units were started and completed, and EWIP is only 40% complete as to conversion costs. Answer (D) is incorrect because 9,910 (9,850 + 60) does not take into account the conversion costs required to complete BWIP.

**51.** With a beginning inventory of 20,000 units in work-in-process that were 30% complete, a hard goods manufacturer completed 190,000 units in 1998 and finished the year with 15,000 units in work-in-process that were only 20% complete. Using the FIFO method, what is the number of equivalent units of production?

A. 187,000

B. 193,000

C. 196,000

D. 205,000

The correct answer is (A). *(CIA, adapted)*

**REQUIRED:** The number of equivalent units using the FIFO method.

**DISCUSSION:** The number of equivalent units calculated using the FIFO method of process costing is determined by the work done in the current period. No work, materials, or costs accumulated in the previous period are included in the calculation. In this case, 14,000 [20,000 units x (100% – 30%)] equivalent units of production effort were necessary to complete the beginning work-in-process, 170,000 units (190,000 completed – 20,000 in BWIP) were started and completed during the year, and the ending work-in-process represented 3,000 (20% x 15,000 units) equivalent units, a total of 187,000 (14,000 + 170,000 + 3,000).

Answer (B) is incorrect because 193,000 [190,000 completed units + (20% x 15,000 units in EWIP)] is the number of EUP calculated using the weighted-average method. Answer (C) is incorrect because the percentage of EWIP completed, not the percentage required to complete EWIP, is used to determine EUP. Answer (D) is incorrect because 205,000 (190,000 units completed + 15,000 in EWIP) is the number of physical units to account for.

**52.** A company produces plastic drinking cups and uses a process cost system. Cups go through three departments: mixing, molding, and packaging. During the month of June, the following information is known about the mixing department:

| | |
|---|---|
| Work-in-process at June 1 | 10,000 units |
| | An average 75% complete |
| Units completed during June | 140,000 units |
| Work-in-process at June 30 | 20,000 units |
| | An average 25% complete |

Materials are added at two points in the process. Material A is added at the beginning of the process and Material B at the midpoint of the mixing process. Conversion costs are incurred uniformly throughout the mixing process. Assuming a FIFO costing flow, the equivalent units for Material A, Material B, and conversion costs, respectively, for the month of June (assuming no spoilage) are

A. 150,000, 130,000, and 137,500.

B. 150,000, 140,000, and 135,000.

C. 160,000, 130,000, and 135,000.

D. 160,000, 140,000, and 137,500.

The correct answer is (A). *(CIA, adapted)*

**REQUIRED:** The equivalent units for Material A, Material B, and conversion costs.

**DISCUSSION:** The FIFO calculation considers only the work done in the current period. Given that A is added at the beginning of the process, the BWIP was complete with regard to A. Thus, assuming no spoilage, the equivalent units of production (EUP) for A equaled 150,000 (140,000 units completed + 20,000 EWIP – 10,000 BWIP). B is added at the midpoint, so the units in BWIP, but not those in EWIP, had received B. The EUP for B were therefore 130,000 (140,000 units completed – 10,000 BWIP). The FIFO EUP for conversion costs were 137,500 [130,000 units started and completed + 2,500 EUP to complete BWIP (10,000 x 25%) + 5,000 EUP (20,000 x 25%) in EWIP].

Answer (B) is incorrect because 140,000 EUP for Material B includes the 10,000 units in BWIP in which Material B was added in a prior period. Furthermore, 135,000 (130,000 + 5,000) EUP for conversion costs does not take into account the 2,500 EUP to complete BWIP. Answer (C) is incorrect because 160,000 (140,000 + 20,000) EUP for Material A includes the 10,000 units in BWIP in which Material A was added in the previous period. Furthermore, 135,000 (130,000 + 5,000) EUP for conversion costs does not take into account the 2,500 EUP to complete BWIP. Answer (D) is incorrect because 160,000 (140,000 + 20,000) EUP for Material A includes the 10,000 units in BWIP in which Material A was added in the previous period. Furthermore, 140,000 EUP for Material B includes the 10,000 units in BWIP in which Material B was added in a prior period.

## 4.7 Weighted-Average EUP Calculations

**53.** A company uses weighted-average process costing for the product it manufactures. All direct materials are added at the beginning of production, and conversion costs are applied evenly during production. The following data apply to the past month:

| | |
|---|---|
| Total units in beginning inventory (30% complete as to conversion costs) | 1,500 |
| Total units transferred to finished goods inventory | 7,400 |
| Total units in ending inventory (60% complete as to conversion costs) | 2,300 |

Assuming no spoilage, equivalent units of conversion costs total

A. 7,400

B. 8,330

C. 8,780

D. 9,700

The correct answer is (C). *(CIA, adapted)*

**REQUIRED:** The equivalent units of production for conversion costs.

**DISCUSSION:** The weighted-average method of process costing commingles prior-period (BWIP) and current costs. It does not consider the degree of completion of BWIP when computing EUP.

| | Units | % Complete | CC EUP |
|---|---|---|---|
| Completed | 7,400 | 100 | 7,400 |
| EWIP | 2,300 | 60 | 1,380 |
| Equivalent units | | | 8,780 |

Answer (A) is incorrect because 7,400 equals the completed units. Answer (B) is incorrect because the EUP for conversion costs would be 8,330 [8,780 weighted-average EUP – (30% x 1,500 units in BWIP)] if the FIFO method were used. Answer (D) is incorrect because 9,700 is the sum of the physical, not equivalent, units completed and in EWIP.

**54.** Dex Co. had the following production for the month of June:

| | Units |
|---|---|
| Work-in-process at June 1 | 10,000 |
| Started during June | 40,000 |
| Completed and transferred to finished | |
| goods during June | 33,000 |
| Abnormal spoilage incurred | 2,000 |
| Work-in-process at June 30 | 15,000 |

Materials are added at the beginning of the process. As to conversion cost, the beginning work-in-process was 70% completed, and the ending work-in-process was 60% completed. Spoilage is detected at the end of the process. Using the weighted-average method, the equivalent units for June, with respect to conversion costs, were

A. 42,000

B. 44,000

C. 45,000

D. 50,000

The correct answer is (B). *(CPA, adapted)*
**REQUIRED:** The EUP for conversion costs using the weighted-average method.
**DISCUSSION:** The weighted-average method averages BWIP costs and current costs. Thus, all the work completed this period, including that started last period, is included in EUP. Although its cost will be recognized as a loss rather than inventoried, abnormal spoilage is included in the EUP calculation. The spoiled units are 100% complete as to conversion costs because inspection for spoilage is at the end of the process. The EUP calculation for conversion costs is 44,000 [(100% x 33,000 units completed) + (100% x 2,000 units spoiled) + (60% x 15,000 units in EWIP)].

Answer (A) is incorrect because 42,000 (33,000 + 9,000) omits abnormal spoilage. Answer (C) is incorrect because 45,000 equals the sum of units completed, spoiled units, and BWIP. Answer (D) is incorrect because 50,000 equals units started plus units in BWIP.

**55.** Forming Department is the first of a two-stage production process. Spoilage is identified when units complete the forming process. Costs of spoiled units are assigned to units completed and transferred to the second department in the period spoilage is identified. The following concerns Forming's conversion costs:

| | Units | Conversion Costs |
|---|---|---|
| Beginning work-in-process | | |
| (50% complete) | 2,000 | $10,000 |
| Units started during month | 8,000 | 75,500 |
| Spoilage-normal | 500 | |
| Units completed & | | |
| transferred | 7,000 | |
| Ending work-in-process | | |
| (80% complete) | 2,500 | |

What was Forming's weighted-average conversion cost transferred to the second department?

A. $59,850

B. $64,125

C. $67,500

D. $71,250

The correct answer is (C). *(CPA, adapted)*
**REQUIRED:** The conversion costs transferred to the second production department.
**DISCUSSION:** Under the weighted-average method, total equivalent units include the equivalent units transferred and the equivalent units in ending work-in-process. Because normal spoilage costs attach to the good output, the transferred costs equal the costs of both the good units and the spoiled units. Total conversion costs under the weighted-average method are $85,500 ($10,000 BWIP + $75,500 May costs). Total equivalent units are 9,500 [7,000 good units transferred + (80% x 2,500 uninspected units in EWIP) + 500 completed units spoiled]. Accordingly, the conversion cost per equivalent unit is $9 ($85,500 ÷ 9,500), and total costs transferred are $67,500 [$9 x (7,000 good units transferred + 500 completed units spoiled)].

Answer (A) is incorrect because $59,850 equals 7,000 units times $8.55 ($85,500 ÷ 10,000 units). Answer (B) is incorrect because $64,125 equals 7,500 units times $8.55 ($85,500 ÷ 10,000 units). Answer (D) is incorrect because $71,250 results from not calculating equivalent units for spoilage in determining unit conversion cost. It equals $9.50 times 7,500 units.

**56.** A company manufactures a product that passes through two production departments, molding and assembly. Direct materials are added in the assembly department when conversion is 50% complete. Conversion costs are incurred uniformly. The activity in units for the assembly department during April is as follows:

|  | Units |
|---|---|
| Work-in-process inventory, April 1 | |
| (60% complete as to conversion costs) | 5,000 |
| Transferred in from molding department | 32,000 |
| Defective at final inspection | |
| (within normal limits) | 2,500 |
| Transferred out to finished goods | |
| inventory | 28,500 |
| Work-in-process inventory, April 30 | |
| (40% complete as to conversion costs) | 6,000 |

The number of equivalent units for direct materials in the assembly department for April calculated on the weighted-average basis is

A. 26,000 units.

B. 31,000 units.

C. 34,000 units.

D. 37,000 units.

**57.** The Wiring Department is the second stage of Flem Company's production cycle. On May 1, the BWIP contained 25,000 units 60% complete as to conversion costs. During May, 100,000 units were transferred in from the first stage of Flem's production cycle. On May 31, EWIP contained 20,000 units 80% complete as to conversion costs. Materials are added at the end of the process. Using the weighted-average method, the EUP on May 31 were

| | Transferred-In Costs | Materials | Conversion Costs |
|---|---|---|---|
| A. | 100,000 | 125,000 | 100,000 |
| B. | 125,000 | 105,000 | 105,000 |
| C. | 125,000 | 105,000 | 121,000 |
| D. | 125,000 | 125,000 | 121,000 |

The correct answer is (B). *(CIA, adapted)*
**REQUIRED:** The equivalent units for direct materials on the weighted-average basis.
**DISCUSSION:** The weighted-average approach averages the costs in beginning work-in-process with those incurred during the period. Accordingly, the degree of completion of the BWIP is ignored in computing the equivalent units for direct materials. Direct materials equivalent units therefore consist of units transferred to finished goods (28,500) and units that failed inspection (2,500), or 31,000. Ending work-in-process inventory has not reached the point at which materials are added.

Answer (A) is incorrect because 26,000 (31,000 weighted-average EUP – 5,000 EUP in BWIP) is the number of direct materials equivalent units calculated using the FIFO method. Answer (C) is incorrect because 34,000 [5,000 units in BWIP + 32,000 units transferred in – (60% x 5,000 units in BWIP)] is the number of physical units minus the conversion work previously done on the BWIP. Answer (D) is incorrect because 37,000 is the sum of defective units, units transferred, and units in EWIP (2,500 + 28,500 + 6,000).

The correct answer is (C). *(CPA, adapted)*
**REQUIRED:** The EUP for materials, conversion costs, and transferred-in costs using the weighted-average method.
**DISCUSSION:** Materials are added at the end of the process, and conversion costs are assumed to be incurred uniformly. By definition, transferred-in costs are always 100% complete. The number of units completed equals 105,000 (25,000 BWIP + 100,000 transferred in – 20,000 EWIP).

| | | T-I | | Mat. | | CC |
|---|---|---|---|---|---|---|
| | Units | EUP | % | EUP | % | EUP |
| Completed | 105 | 105 | 100 | 105 | 100 | 105 |
| EWIP | 20 | 20 | 0 | -- | 80 | 16 |
| EUP | | 125 | | 105 | | 121 |

Answer (A) is incorrect because 100,000 EUP for transferred-in costs and conversion costs are the units transferred in from the first stage of Flem's production cycle. 125,000 EUP for materials are the EUP for transferred-in costs. Answer (B) is incorrect because the 16,000 (20,000 x 80%) equivalent units in ending inventory should be included in the EUP calculation for conversion costs. Answer (D) is incorrect because the 20,000 units in ending inventory should not be included in the EUP calculation for materials.

**58.** The following information pertains to Lap Co.'s Palo Division for the month of April:

|  | Number of Units | Cost of Materials |
|---|---|---|
| Beginning work-in-process | 15,000 | $ 5,500 |
| Started in April | 40,000 | 18,000 |
| Units completed | 42,500 |  |
| Ending work-in-process | 12,500 |  |

All materials are added at the beginning of the process. Using the weighted-average method, the cost per equivalent unit for materials is

A. $0.59

B. $0.55

C. $0.45

D. $0.43

**The correct answer is (D).** *(CPA, adapted)*
**REQUIRED:** The cost per equivalent unit for materials using the weighted-average method.
**DISCUSSION:** The weighted-average method does not distinguish between work done in the previous period and that done in the current period. Consequently, given that materials are added at the start of the process, the total equivalent units equal 55,000 (42,500 units completed + 12,500 units in EWIP), the total cost of materials is $23,500, and the cost per equivalent unit for materials is $0.43 (rounded).

Answer (A) is incorrect because $0.59 results from deducting the units in BWIP from the total equivalent units. Answer (B) is incorrect because $0.55 equals cost divided by units completed. Answer (C) is incorrect because $0.45 is based on the FIFO method.

**59.** Roy Company manufactures Product X in a two-stage production cycle in Departments A and B. Materials are added at the beginning of the process in Department B. Roy uses the weighted-average method. BWIP (6,000 units) for Department B was 50% complete as to conversion costs. EWIP (8,000 units) was 75% complete. During February, 12,000 units were completed and transferred out of Department B. An analysis of the costs relating to WIP and production activity in Department B for February follows:

|  | Transferred-In Costs | Materials Costs | Conversion Costs |
|---|---|---|---|
| WIP, February 1: |  |  |  |
| Costs attached | $12,000 | $2,500 | $1,000 |
| Feb. activity: |  |  |  |
| Costs added | 29,000 | 5,500 | 5,000 |

The total cost per equivalent unit transferred out for February of Product X, rounded to the nearest penny, was

A. $2.75

B. $2.78

C. $2.82

D. $3.01

**The correct answer is (B).** *(CPA, adapted)*
**REQUIRED:** The total cost per equivalent unit transferred out using the weighted-average method.
**DISCUSSION:** The total cost per equivalent unit transferred out is equal to the unit cost for transferred-in costs, materials costs, and conversion costs. Transferred-in costs are by definition 100% complete. Given that materials are added at the beginning of the process in Department B, all units are complete as to materials. Conversion costs are assumed to be uniformly incurred.

| | Units | T-I | % | Mat. | % | CC |
|---|---|---|---|---|---|---|
| Completed | 12 | 12 | 100 | 12 | 100 | 12 |
| EWIP | 8 | 8 | 100 | 8 | 75 | 6 |
| Equivalent units | | 20 | | 20 | | 18 |

Transferred-in: $\dfrac{(\$12{,}000 + \$29{,}000)}{20{,}000 \text{ EUP}} = \$2.05$

Materials cost: $\dfrac{(\$2{,}500 + \$5{,}500)}{20{,}000 \text{ EUP}} = .40$

Conversion cost: $\dfrac{(\$1{,}000 + \$5{,}000)}{18{,}000 \text{ EUP}} = .33$

Total unit cost $\underline{\$2.78}$

Answer (A) is incorrect because unit conversion cost should be calculated using 18,000 EUP. Answer (C) is incorrect because unit materials cost should be calculated using 20,000 EUP. Answer (D) is incorrect because unit transferred-in cost should be calculated based on 18,000 EUP.

**60.** During March, Bly Company's Department Y equivalent unit product costs, computed under the weighted-average method, were as follows:

| | |
|---|---|
| Materials | $1 |
| Conversion | 3 |
| Transferred-in | 5 |

Materials are introduced at the end of the process in Department Y. There were 4,000 units (40% complete as to conversion costs) in WIP at March 31. The total costs assigned to the March 31 WIP inventory should be

A. $36,000

B. $28,800

C. $27,200

D. $24,800

The correct answer is (D). *(CPA, adapted)*
    **REQUIRED:** The total costs of EWIP using the weighted-average method.
    **DISCUSSION:** The unit costs of EUP under weighted-average are given. EWIP consists of 4,000 units 40% complete as to conversion costs (1,600 EUP). Given also that materials are added at the end of the process, no materials cost is included in EWIP. Thus, the EWIP reflects only transferred-in costs and conversion costs.

| | |
|---|---|
| Transferred-in (4,000 × $5) | $20,000 |
| Conversion (1,600 × $3) | 4,800 |
| EWIP | $24,800 |

Answer (A) is incorrect because $36,000 ($20,000 + 12,000 + 4,000) is the total cost for 4,000 completed units. Answer (B) is incorrect because materials are not added until the end of the process. Answer (C) is incorrect because conversion costs for 1,600 EUP (4,000 x 40%) in EWIP (not conversion costs to complete EWIP) should be added to transferred-in cost.

**61.** Information for the month of January concerning Department A, the first stage of Ogden Corporation's production cycle, is as follows:

| | Materials | Conversion |
|---|---|---|
| BWIP | $ 8,000 | $ 6,000 |
| Current costs | 40,000 | 32,000 |
| Total costs | $48,000 | $38,000 |
| Equivalent units using weighted-average method | 100,000 | 95,000 |
| Average unit costs | $ 0.48 | $ 0.40 |
| Goods completed | | 90,000 units |
| EWIP | | 10,000 units |

Materials are added at the beginning of the process. The ending work-in-process is 50% complete as to conversion costs. How would the total costs accounted for be distributed, using the weighted-average method?

| | Goods Completed | Ending Work-In-Process |
|---|---|---|
| A. | $79,200 | $6,800 |
| B. | $79,200 | $8,800 |
| C. | $86,000 | $0 |
| D. | $88,000 | $6,800 |

The correct answer is (A). *(CPA, adapted)*
    **REQUIRED:** The weighted-average distribution of total costs between goods completed and EWIP.
    **DISCUSSION:** The weighted-average method combines the costs in BWIP with those for the current period. Materials are added at the beginning of the process and conversion costs are assumed to be incurred uniformly. Equivalent unit and average unit cost calculations were given.

Completed goods:
| | |
|---|---|
| Materials ($.48 × 90,000) | $43,200 |
| Conversion costs ($.40 × 90,000) | 36,000 |
| Cost of completed goods | $79,200 |

Given that conversion costs for EWIP are 50% complete, there are 5,000 (50% x 10,000) equivalent units of conversion cost in ending inventory.

EWIP:
| | |
|---|---|
| Materials ($.48 × 10,000) | $ 4,800 |
| Conversion costs ($.40 × 5,000) | 2,000 |
| Cost of EWIP | $ 6,800 |

Answers (B), (C), and (D) are incorrect because the total to be distributed is $86,000. Of this amount, some portion must be assigned to EWIP.

## 4.8 Comprehensive

Questions 62 through 66 are based on the processing operations of HDG Enterprises. Assume that process conversion costs are uniform but a number of materials are added at different points in the process. Material 1 is added at the beginning of the process. The transferred-in costs are added at the 20% point in the process. Material 2 is added uniformly from the 50% to the 70% points in the process. Material 3 is added at the 75% point in the process, and Material 4 is added uniformly at the 90% to the 100% points in the process. The January BWIP was 10,000 units 60% complete, 60,000 units were added, and EWIP was 20,000 units 95% complete.

**62.** What was the number of Material 3 EUP for the month?

|     | FIFO | Weighted Average |
| --- | --- | --- |
| A. | 50,000 | 60,000 |
| B. | 60,000 | 60,000 |
| C. | 60,000 | 70,000 |
| D. | 70,000 | 70,000 |

The correct answer is (D). *(Publisher)*
**REQUIRED:** The EUP for Material 3 for the month.
**DISCUSSION:** Material 3 is added at the 75% point in the process. None of Material 3 was in BWIP. Accordingly, it had to be added to the 10,000 units in BWIP and all the 60,000 units started this period since the EWIP was 95% complete. Accordingly, the month's Material 3 EUP are 70,000 units for both FIFO and weighted average.
Answer (A) is incorrect because 50,000 units for FIFO subtracts BWIP from the 60,000 units that were added, and 60,000 units for weighted average does not include BWIP. Answer (B) is incorrect because 60,000 units EUP for FIFO and weighted average does not include Material 3 added for BWIP units. Answer (C) is incorrect because 60,000 units for FIFO does not include Material 3 added for BWIP.

**63.** What was the number of Material 1 EUP for the month?

|     | FIFO | Weighted Average |
| --- | --- | --- |
| A. | 50,000 | 60,000 |
| B. | 60,000 | 60,000 |
| C. | 60,000 | 70,000 |
| D. | 70,000 | 70,000 |

The correct answer is (C). *(Publisher)*
**REQUIRED:** The EUP for Material 1 for the month.
**DISCUSSION:** Material 1 is added at the very beginning of the process. Accordingly, BWIP had 10,000 units of Material 1 in it. During the period, 60,000 units were added. Thus, for FIFO, the EWIP is 60,000 units (current work done); for weighted average, it is 70,000 units (60,000 units added this period plus the 10,000 units in BWIP).
Answer (A) is incorrect because 50,000 units for FIFO subtracts BWIP from the 60,000 units that were added, and 60,000 units for weighted average does not include the BWIP. Answer (B) is incorrect because 60,000 units for weighted average does not include BWIP. Answer (D) is incorrect because 70,000 units for FIFO includes BWIP.

**64.** What was the number of conversion EUP for the month?

|     | FIFO | Weighted Average |
| --- | --- | --- |
| A. | 50,000 | 60,000 |
| B. | 63,000 | 69,000 |
| C. | 60,000 | 70,000 |
| D. | 53,000 | 59,000 |

The correct answer is (B). *(Publisher)*
**REQUIRED:** The EUP for conversion for the month.
**DISCUSSION:** Under weighted average, the conversion EUP include the 50,000 units complete (10,000 BWIP plus 60,000 started less 20,000 EWIP) plus the 19,000 EUP in EWIP (20,000 x 95%), or 69,000 EUP. For FIFO, the 69,000 EUP for weighted average is reduced by the 6,000 (10,000 units x 60%) of work completed in BWIP.
Answer (A) is incorrect because 50,000 units for FIFO equals the units completed, and 60,000 units for weighted average equals the units that were added. Answer (C) is incorrect because 60,000 units for FIFO equals the units that were added, and 70,000 units for weighted average equals the units that were added, plus BWIP. Answer (D) is incorrect because 53,000 units for FIFO is the conversion EUP for FIFO minus BWIP, and 59,000 units for weighted average is the conversion EUP for weighted average minus BWIP.

**65.** What was the number of Material 2 EUP for the month?

| | FIFO | Weighted Average |
|---|---|---|
| A. | 50,000 | 60,000 |
| B. | 60,000 | 70,000 |
| C. | 65,000 | 70,000 |
| D. | 63,000 | 67,000 |

The correct answer is (C). *(Publisher)*
**REQUIRED:** The EUP for Material 2 for the month.
**DISCUSSION:** Material 2 is added uniformly from the 50% to the 70% portion of the process. Accordingly, of the 10,000 BWIP at the 60% completion point, only 5,000 EUP would be in BWIP. Thus, an additional 5,000 units would be added to BWIP. Also, Material 2 had been added to all 60,000 units started during the period because EWIP is at the 95% point. Accordingly, EWIP would be 65,000 for FIFO and 70,000 for weighted average.

Answer (A) is incorrect for FIFO because it subtracts all of BWIP from the 60,000 units added, and 60,000 units for weighted average does not include BWIP. Answer (B) is incorrect because 60,000 units for FIFO does not include the 50,000 units of BWIP to which Material 2 was added. Answer (D) is incorrect because 63,000 units for FIFO is the conversion EUP for the month, and 67,000 units for weighted average is the weighted-average conversion EUP less one-half of the FIFO conversion EUP in BWIP [69,000 − .5 (4,000)].

**66.** What was the number of Material 4 EUP for the month?

| | FIFO | Weighted Average |
|---|---|---|
| A. | 50,000 | 60,000 |
| B. | 60,000 | 60,000 |
| C. | 65,000 | 70,000 |
| D. | 70,000 | 70,000 |

The correct answer is (B). *(Publisher)*
**REQUIRED:** The EUP for Material 4 for the month.
**DISCUSSION:** Material 4 is added uniformly between the 90% and the 100% point in the process. Accordingly, BWIP which was 60% complete would have no Material 4. Thus, weighted-average and FIFO EUP are the same. All 50,000 units completed would contain Material 4, plus there would be 10,000 EUP in EWIP, half of the 20,000 EWIP because Material 4 is added uniformly between the 90% and 100% points.

Answer (A) is incorrect because 50,000 units for FIFO does not include the 10,000 units in EWIP that contain Material 4. Answer (C) is incorrect because 65,000 units for FIFO is the number of Material 2 EUP, and 70,000 units for weighted average includes the 10,000 units in EWIP that do not contain Material 4. Answer (D) is incorrect because 70,000 units for FIFO and weighted average includes the 10,000 units in EWIP that do not contain Material 4.

Questions 67 through 74 are based on the following information. Kimbeth Manufacturing uses a process cost system to manufacture Dust Density Sensors for the mining industry. The following information pertains to operations for the month of May 1998.

|  | Units |
|---|---|
| Beginning work-in-process inventory, May 1 | 16,000 |
| Started in production during May | 100,000 |
| Completed production during May | 92,000 |
| Ending work-in-process inventory, May 31 | 24,000 |

The beginning inventory was 60% complete for materials and 20% complete for conversion costs. The ending inventory was 90% complete for materials and 40% complete for conversion costs.

Costs pertaining to the month of May are as follows:

- Beginning inventory costs are materials, $54,560; direct labor, $20,320; and factory overhead, $15,240.

- Costs incurred during May are materials used, $468,000; direct labor, $182,880; and factory overhead, $391,160.

**67.** Using the first-in, first-out (FIFO) method, the equivalent units of production (EUP) for materials are

- A. 97,600 units.
- B. 104,000 units.
- C. 107,200 units.
- D. 113,600 units.

The correct answer is (B). *(CMA, adapted)*
**REQUIRED:** The equivalent units of production for materials under FIFO.
**DISCUSSION:** Under FIFO, EUP are based solely on work performed during the current period. The EUP equal the sum of the work done on the beginning work-in-process inventory, units started and completed in the current period, and the ending work-in-process inventory. Given that beginning work-in-process was 60% complete as to materials, the current period is charged for 6,400 EUP (40% × 16,000 units). Because 92,000 units were completed during the period, 76,000 (92,000 – 16,000 in BWIP) must have been started and completed during the period. They represent 76,000 EUP. Finally, the EUP for ending work-in-process equal 21,600 (90% × 24,000 units). Thus, total EUP for May are 104,000 (6,400 + 76,000 + 21,600).
Answer (A) is incorrect because 97,600 units omits the 6,400 EUP added to beginning work-in-process. Answer (C) is incorrect because 107,200 units assumes beginning work-in-process was 40% complete. Answer (D) is incorrect because 113,600 units equals the EUP under the weighted-average method.

**68.** Using the FIFO method, the equivalent units of production for conversion costs are

- A. 85,600 units.
- B. 95,200 units.
- C. 98,400 units.
- D. 101,600 units.

The correct answer is (C). *(CMA, adapted)*
**REQUIRED:** The equivalent units of production for conversion costs under FIFO.
**DISCUSSION:** The beginning inventory was 20% complete as to conversion costs. Hence, 12,800 EUP (80% × 16,000 units) were required for completion. EUP for units started and completed equaled 76,000 [100% × (92,000 completed units – 16,000 units in BWIP)]. The work done on ending work-in-process totaled 9,600 EUP (40% × 24,000 units). Thus, total EUP for May are 98,400 (12,800 + 76,000 + 9,600).
Answer (A) is incorrect because 85,600 units omits the work done on beginning work-in-process. Answer (B) is incorrect because 95,200 units assumes the beginning work-in-process was 40% complete as to conversion costs. Answer (D) is incorrect because 101,600 units equals EUP under the weighted-average method.

**69.** Using the FIFO method, the equivalent unit cost of materials for May is

   A. $4.12

   B. $4.50

   C. $4.60

   D. $4.80

The correct answer is (B). *(CMA, adapted)*

   **REQUIRED:** The equivalent unit cost of materials under FIFO.

   **DISCUSSION:** Under the FIFO method, EUP for materials equal 104,000 [(16,000 units in BWIP × 40%) + (76,000 units started and completed × 100%) + (24,000 units in EWIP × 90%)]. Consequently, the equivalent unit cost of materials is $4.50 ($468,000 total materials cost in May ÷ 104,000 EUP).

   Answer (A) is incorrect because $4.12 is based on EUP calculated under the weighted-average method. Answer (C) is incorrect because $4.60 is the weighted-average cost per equivalent unit. Answer (D) is incorrect because $4.80 omits the 6,400 EUP added to beginning work-in-process.

**70.** Using the FIFO method, the equivalent unit conversion cost for May is

   A. $5.65

   B. $5.83

   C. $6.00

   D. $6.20

The correct answer is (B). *(CMA, adapted)*

   **REQUIRED:** The conversion cost per equivalent unit under FIFO.

   **DISCUSSION:** Under the FIFO method, EUP for conversion costs equal 98,400 [(16,000 units in BWIP × 80%) + (76,000 units started and completed × 100%) + (24,000 units in EWIP × 40%)]. Conversion costs incurred during the current period equal $574,040 ($182,880 DL + $391,160 FOH). Hence, the equivalent unit cost for conversion costs is $5.83 ($574,040 ÷ 98,400).

   Answer (A) is incorrect because $5.65 is based on EUP calculated under the weighted-average method. Answer (C) is incorrect because $6.00 is the cost per equivalent unit calculated under the weighted-average method. Answer (D) is incorrect because $6.20 results from combining conversion costs for May with those in beginning work-in-process and dividing by 98,400 EUP.

**71.** Using the FIFO method, the total cost of units in the ending work-in-process inventory at May 31, 1998 is

   A. $153,168

   B. $154,800

   C. $155,328

   D. $156,960

The correct answer is (A). *(CMA, adapted)*

   **REQUIRED:** The total cost of units in ending work-in-process under FIFO.

   **DISCUSSION:** The FIFO costs per equivalent unit for materials and conversion costs are $4.50 and $5.83, respectively. EUP for materials in ending work-in-process equal 21,600 (90% × 24,000). Thus, total FIFO materials cost is $97,200 (21,600 EUP × $4.50). EUP for conversion costs in ending work-in-process equal 9,600 (40% × 24,000). Total conversion costs are therefore $55,968 (9,600 EUP × $5.83). Consequently, total work-in-process costs are $153,168 ($97,200 + $55,968).

   Answer (B) is incorrect because $154,800 is based on a FIFO calculation for materials and a weighted-average calculation for conversion costs. Answer (C) is incorrect because $155,328 is based on a weighted-average calculation for materials and a FIFO calculation for conversion costs. Answer (D) is incorrect because $156,960 is the weighted-average cost of ending work-in-process.

For questions 72 through 74, refer to the information preceding question 67 on page 140.

**72.** Using the weighted-average method, the equivalent unit cost of materials for May is

- A. $4.12
- B. $4.50
- C. $4.60
- D. $5.68

The correct answer is (C). *(CMA, adapted)*

**REQUIRED:** The weighted-average equivalent unit cost for materials.

**DISCUSSION:** The weighted-average method averages the work done in the prior period with the work done in the current period. There are two layers of units to analyze: those completed during the period and those still in ending inventory. The units completed totaled 92,000. The 24,000 ending units are 90% complete as to materials, so EUP equal 21,600. Hence, total EUP for materials are 113,600 (92,000 + 21,600). The total materials costs incurred during the period and accumulated in beginning work-in-process are $522,560 ($468,000 + $54,560). Thus, weighted-average unit cost is $4.60 ($522,560 ÷ 113,600 EUP).

Answer (A) is incorrect because $4.12 equals materials costs for May divided by weighted-average EUP. Answer (B) is incorrect because $4.50 is the equivalent unit cost based on the FIFO method. Answer (D) is incorrect because $5.68 equals weighted-average costs divided by 92,000 units completed.

**73.** Using the weighted-average method, the equivalent unit conversion cost for May is

- A. $5.65
- B. $5.83
- C. $6.00
- D. $6.20

The correct answer is (C). *(CMA, adapted)*

**REQUIRED:** The weighted-average conversion cost per equivalent unit.

**DISCUSSION:** The weighted-average method does not distinguish between the work done in the prior period and the work done in the current period. Accordingly, the 92,000 completed units represent 92,000 weighted-average EUP. The 24,000 units in ending work-in-process are 40% complete as to conversion costs, so they equal 9,600 EUP. Hence, total EUP for conversion costs are 101,600 (92,000 + 9,600). The sum of the conversion costs accumulated in beginning work-in-process and incurred during the period is $609,600 ($20,320 + $15,240 + $182,880 + $391,160). Thus, weighted-average unit cost is $6.00 ($609,600 ÷ 101,600 EUP).

Answer (A) is incorrect because $5.65 omits the conversion costs in beginning work-in-process. Answer (B) is incorrect because $5.83 is the equivalent unit conversion cost based on FIFO. Answer (D) is incorrect because $6.20 is based on a FIFO calculation of equivalent units and a weighted-average calculation of costs.

**74.** Using the weighted-average method, the total cost of the units in the ending work-in-process inventory at May 31, 1998 is

- A. $153,168
- B. $154,800
- C. $155,328
- D. $156,960

The correct answer is (D). *(CMA, adapted)*

**REQUIRED:** The ending work-in-process under the weighted-average method.

**DISCUSSION:** The weighted-average costs per equivalent unit for materials and conversion costs are $4.60 and $6.00, respectively. EUP for materials in ending work-in-process equal 21,600 (90% × 24,000). Thus total weighted-average materials cost is $99,360 ($4.60 × 21,600). EUP for conversion costs in ending work-in-process equal 9,600 (40% × 24,000 units). Total conversion costs are therefore $57,600 ($6.00 × 9,600 EUP). Consequently, total ending work-in-process costs are $156,960 ($99,360 + $57,600).

Answer (A) is incorrect because $153,168 is the FIFO cost of ending work-in-process. Answer (B) is incorrect because $154,800 is based on a FIFO calculation for materials and a weighted-average calculation for conversion costs. Answer (C) is incorrect because $155,328 is based on a weighted-average calculation for materials and a FIFO calculation for conversion costs.

# CHAPTER FIVE
# QUALITY

**Quality** is a vital issue in an ever more competitive world economy. Improving quality increases demand (and market share) through heightened customer satisfaction, significantly lowers costs, creates goodwill, and increases employee expertise. The importance of quality is reflected in the creation of prestigious national awards for quality. For example, the U.S. Congress has created the **Malcolm Baldridge National Quality Awards**, with categories for manufacturing, service, educational, health, and small business entities. Furthermore, numerous countries, especially those of the European Union (EU), have adopted the **ISO 9000** standards issued by the International Organization for Standardization. These standards, which may be adapted to the needs of service organizations, provide uniform rules for evaluating an entity's quality assurance efforts regarding the design, development, manufacturing, installation, and servicing of products. Certification under ISO 9000 is a competitive advantage because purchasers, especially in JIT environments, increasingly rely on timely delivery of defect-free products by suppliers.

Quality has been defined in numerous ways. For example, according to the American Society for Quality Control (ASQC), it is "the totality of features and characteristics of a product made or a service performed according to specifications, to satisfy customers at the time of purchase and during use." Another approach found in the professional literature is to focus on the dimensions of quality. **Performance** concerns a product's operating characteristics and how they compare with those of competing products. For a service, this dimension also includes the responsiveness and empathy of the service provider and the assurance conveyed. **Aesthetics** is the dimension of subjective judgments about the appearance of tangible products or of the facilities, personnel, etc., related to services. **Features** are the design traits of a product or service that distinguish it from others with the same basic functions. **Reliability** is the likelihood that a product or service will fail within a designated time. **Durability** is the operational life of a product. **Serviceability** is the ease, rapidity, competence, and courtesy associated with maintenance of a product. **Fitness of use** concerns whether a product can perform its intended functions. Thus, a product may conform to specifications and yet fail because of a basic flaw in its design. **Perceived quality** is the reputation of a product or service derived from customers' past experience with the provider. **Conformance** is how well a product and its components meet applicable standards. The traditional view is that conforming products are those with characteristics that lie within an acceptable specified range of values that includes a target value. This view also regarded a certain percentage of defective (nonconforming) units as acceptable. The traditional view was superseded by the **zero-defects** approach that sought to eliminate all nonconforming output. An extension of this approach is the **robust quality** concept. Its goal is to reach the target value in every case for the reason that hidden quality costs occur when output varies from the target even though the units are within specifications.

**Total quality management (TQM)** is a comprehensive approach to quality that has been widely adopted. It treats quality as a basic organizational function. TQM is the continuous pursuit of quality in every aspect of organizational activities through a philosophy of doing it right the first time, employee training and empowerment, promotion of teamwork, **continuous improvement** of **processes**, and attention to satisfaction of customers, both internal and external. TQM emphasizes the supplier's relationship with the customer, identifies customer needs, and recognizes that everyone in a process is at some time a customer or supplier of someone else, either within or without the organization. Thus, TQM begins with external customer requirements, identifies internal customer-supplier relationships and requirements, and establishes requirements for external suppliers.

TQM uses various management processes, tools, and measures. **Policy deployment** is systematic strategic planning that connects corporate objectives and plans with the detailed ways in which organizational subunits will approach the accomplishment of their related goals. The purpose is goal congruence. It is an umbrella concept most useful in an environment in which the **Plan-Do-Check-Act (PDCA) Cycle** (the Deming Wheel) is used at all levels. PDCA is a "management by fact" or scientific method approach to continuous improvement. PDCA creates a process-centered environment because it involves studying the current process, collecting and analyzing data to identify causes of problems, planning for improvement, and deciding how to measure improvement (Plan). The plan is then implemented on a small scale if possible (Do). The next step is to determine what happened (Check). If the experiment was successful, the plan is fully implemented (Act). The cycle is then repeated using what was learned from the preceding cycle. **Quality function deployment** ensures that customer requirements (the dimensions desired by customers) are translated into design requirements at each step in product development. **Kaizen** is the Japanese word for the continuous pursuit of improvement in every aspect of organizational operations. For example, a budget prepared on the kaizen principle projects costs (possibly based on learning curves or the stage in the product's life cycle) in anticipation of future improvements. The probability of such improvements must be determined, and the cost of implementation and the savings therefrom must be estimated. Unfavorable variances result if budgeted improvements are not realized. **Employee involvement** means training and empowering employees to harness their creativity for problem solving. It also emphasizes **quality at the source**, or the responsibility of every employee, work group, department, or supplier to inspect the work. **Suppliers' management** is the careful selection of suppliers and the cultivation of long-term relationships based on the consistent ability to meet mutual expectations. **Competitive benchmarking** is the ongoing evaluation of the practices of best-in-class organizations and the adaptation of company processes to incorporate the best practices. It analyzes and measures the key outputs of a process or function, compares them with the best, and identifies the underlying key actions and root causes of the performance difference. Benchmarking is a continuous process that entails quantitative and qualitative measurement of the difference between an organization's performance of an activity and the performance by the best organization in the world. The benchmark organization need not be a competitor. **Quality training** familiarizes all employees with the means for preventing, detecting, and eliminating nonquality. The educational processes are tailored to the appropriate groups. **Reward and recognition** for quality improvement should be group oriented and should be based on quality measures. **Customer retention** is a vitally important measure of service quality because loyal customers spend more, refer new customers, and are less costly to service. **Statistical and other quantitative methods** are used to identify quality problems. Probability and statistics techniques, flowcharting, network analysis (PERT and CPM), cause-and-effect diagrams, Pareto analysis, histograms, scattergrams, statistical control charts, trend analysis, and the Taguchi quality loss function are among these methods. See Chapters 12, 13, and 15.

The **costs of quality** must be assessed in terms of relative costs and benefits.  Thus, an organization should attempt to minimize its total cost of quality.  **Conformance** (control) costs include costs of prevention and costs of appraisal, which are financial measures of internal performance.  **Prevention** costs result in high returns because preventing a problem is cheaper than finding and correcting it.  These costs include systems development; design, process, and quality engineering; quality training, planning, and reporting; quality circles; field trials; quality audits; statistical process control programs (the cost of these programs may also be considered appraisal costs); preventive maintenance; review of equipment design; and evaluation and selection of suppliers.  **Appraisal** embraces such activities as inspection and testing of materials, in-process items, finished goods, and packaging.  **Nonconformance (failure) costs** include internal failure costs (a financial measure of internal performance) and external failure costs (a financial measure of customer satisfaction).  **Internal failure** costs occur when nonconforming products or services are detected before delivery.  Examples are spoilage, scrap, rework, tooling changes, design changes, reinspection and testing, and downtime.  **External failure** costs arise when problems occur after delivery. They occur because products or services are nonconforming or otherwise do not satisfy customers.  Thus, external failure costs may be catastrophic.  They include the costs of customer support (complaint adjustment), repair, transportation, product recalls, process reengineering, warranties, liability claims, returns and allowances, lost sales, lost market share, and lost goodwill.  Quality costing is similar in service and manufacturing organizations.  However, external failure costs in service enterprises are even more important than in manufacturing environments.  Faulty goods sometimes may be reworked or replaced to a customer's satisfaction, but poor service tends to result in loss of customers.  Indeed, customer retention tends to have a greater effect on profitability in service enterprises than the factors (unit cost, economies of scale) traditionally reported by cost accountants.  Furthermore, labor costs are usually a higher percentage of total costs in service enterprises.  One implication of this circumstance for quality management is that lost time is always lost, whereas raw materials may be reworked or reused and machines may be repaired. A second implication is that quality improvements resulting in more efficient use of labor time and lower failure costs may be viewed by employees as leading to workforce reduction.  Thus, their cooperation with quality improvement efforts may be unenthusiastic.

**Environmental costs** are also external failure costs, e.g., fines for nonadherence to environmental law and loss of customer goodwill. To minimize environmental damage and its resulting costs, the International Organization for Standardization has issued **ISO 14000** standards to promote the reduction of environmental damage by an organization's products, services, and operations and to develop environmental auditing and performance evaluation systems.

Most quality costs are observable, or available from accounting records. However, some external failure costs are hidden costs that must be estimated. The **multiplier method** multiplies the known external failure costs by a constant (k) determined by the organization's experience to calculate the total cost. **Market research** is another method of estimating hidden costs. Yet another method is the **Taguchi quality loss function** (see Chapter 15). Quality costs should be presented by category in a **cost of quality report**. One possibility is to present these reports comparatively for consecutive periods. Another is to include a column expressing each category's costs as a percentage of sales. The optimal level of quality costs traditionally has been deemed to occur where the conformance cost curve intersects the nonconformance cost curve, which corresponds to the minimum point on the total cost curve. Thus, beyond some point, incurrence of prevention and appraisal costs is not cost beneficial. However, the modern robust quality view is that this relationship does not always hold. Improving quality and reducing costs in each category may be possible if the most efficient prevention methods are applied. For example, selection of a supplier meeting high quality standards regarding defect rates and delivery times may drive down not only failure costs but also the prevention and appraisal costs incurred when supplier performance was less reliable. From an activity-based management perspective, failure activities and their costs are nonvalue-added and should be eliminated. Efficient prevention activities are value-added, but most appraisal activities are nonvalue-added. Moreover, identifying quality-related activities and their drivers helps to improve cost assignments, eliminate or restructure activities, and reduce quality costs. Some useful ratios for analysis of quality costs are total quality costs to net sales, conformance costs to total quality costs, nonconformance costs to total quality costs, nonconformance costs to net sales, and total quality costs to direct labor cost.

The foregoing discussion stresses financial measures of customer satisfaction (external failure costs), but organizations also use nonfinancial measures to identify problems and future customer wants, for example, on-time delivery ratios, customer response time (time from order placement to delivery), customer complaints, ratio of defective items shipped, and survey data. Nonfinancial measures of internal performance are also used. They supplement the financial measures (prevention, appraisal, and internal failure costs) because they pinpoint out-of-control processes, provide rapid feedback about quality efforts, and are easy to calculate and comprehend. Among the many nonfinancial measures of internal performance are manufacturing lead or cycle time (time from when an order is ready for production to when it is completed), ratio of good output to total output (process yield), defects per product line, employee turnover, and the half-life method (time required to reduce the defect ratio by 50%). The nonfinancial measures are most useful when included in a trend analysis. Moreover, managerial performance assessment increasingly is based on a **balanced scorecard** approach. Thus, multiple measures of quality performance permit a determination as to whether a manager is achieving certain objectives at the expense of others that may be equally or more important.

**Spoiled goods** are defective items that cannot be feasibly reworked. Traditional cost accounting systems distinguish between normal and abnormal spoilage because, in some operations, a degree of spoilage is viewed as inevitable. However, organizations that have adopted rigorous approaches to quality regard normal spoilage as minimal or even nonexistent. Thus, all spoilage may be identified as abnormal. **Normal spoilage** occurs under normal, efficient operating conditions. It is spoilage that is uncontrollable in the short run and therefore should be expressed as a function of good output (treated as a product cost). Accordingly, normal spoilage is assigned to all good units in process costing systems, that is, all units that have passed the inspection point at which the spoilage was detected. The normal spoilage rate is based on the actual good output or on the normal input for the actual good output. Moreover, some authorities advocate the calculation of equivalent units for spoilage in process costing systems. This calculation may be based on the FIFO, weighted-average, or standard costing methods. In job-order costing, normal spoilage may be applicable to all jobs. The accounting treatment is to apply the normal spoilage cost of a given job to all jobs by charging it to overhead control (debit inventory for the salvage value, debit overhead control, and credit WIP for the total normal spoilage costs). If normal spoilage is attributable to a specific job, only the disposal value of the normally spoiled goods is removed from work-in-process, thereby assigning the cost of normal spoilage to the good units remaining in the specific job. **Abnormal spoilage** is not expected to occur under normal, efficient operating conditions. The cost of abnormal spoilage should be separately identified and reported. Abnormal spoilage is typically treated as a period cost (a loss) because it is unusual.

**Scrap** consists of raw materials left over from the production cycle but still usable for purposes other than those for which they were originally intended. Scrap may be sold to outside customers, usually for a nominal amount, or it may be used for a different production process. Scrap is recorded either at the time of production or at the time of sale. If scrap is recorded at the time of production, inventory is debited and work-in-process (if the scrap pertains to a particular job) or overhead control (if the scrap pertains to all units) is credited. If scrap is recorded at the time of sale, the debit is to cash or accounts receivable and the credit is to work-in-process (if the scrap pertains to a particular job) or to either sales or overhead control (if the scrap pertains to all units). **Normal rework** costs are customarily debited to factory overhead control, with credits to materials, wages payable, and overhead control. If they pertain to a specific job, they are debited to work-in-process for that job. Abnormal rework is debited to a loss account.

## 5.1 Quality

**1.** The International Standards Organization (ISO) has developed standards for ring networks that include fault management, configuration management, accounting management, security management, and performance monitoring. Which of the following controls is included in the performance-monitoring standards?

A. Reporting the failure of network fiber-optic lines.

B. Recording unauthorized access violations.

C. Compiling statistics on the number of times that application software is used.

D. Allocating network costs to system users of the network.

The correct answer is (C). *(CIA, adapted)*

**REQUIRED:** The controls included in ISO performance-monitoring standards.

**DISCUSSION:** The ISO consists of standards organizations from more than 75 countries. The U.S. affiliate is the ANSI (American National Standards Institute). The ISO's performance-monitoring standards pertain to management's ongoing assessment of the quality of performance over time. Recording software usage is a performance-monitoring control concerned with the extent and efficiency of network software use.

Answer (A) is incorrect because the failure of network fiber-optic lines is a fault management control. Answer (B) is incorrect because recording unauthorized access violations is a security management control. Answer (D) is incorrect because allocating network costs to system users of the network is an accounting management control.

**2.** A traditional quality control process in manufacturing consists of mass inspection of goods only at the end of a production process. A major deficiency of the traditional control process is that

A. It is expensive to do the inspections at the end of the process.

B. It is not possible to rework defective items.

C. It is not 100% effective.

D. It does not focus on improving the entire production process.

The correct answer is (D). *(CIA, adapted)*

**REQUIRED:** The major deficiency of mass inspection of goods only at the end of production.

**DISCUSSION:** The process used to produce the goods is not thoroughly reviewed and evaluated for efficiency and effectiveness. A total quality management approach is superior because it focuses on continuous improvement in every aspect of organizational activities. Preventing defects and increasing efficiency by improving the production process raise quality standards and decrease costs.

Answer (A) is incorrect because other quality control processes can also be expensive. Answer (B) is incorrect because reworking defective items may be possible although costly. Answer (C) is incorrect because no quality control system will be 100% effective.

**3.** Focusing on customers, promoting innovation, learning new philosophies, driving out fear, and providing extensive training are all elements of a major change in organizations. These elements are aimed primarily at

A. Copying leading organizations to better compete with them.

B. Focusing on the total quality of products and services.

C. Being efficient and effective at the same time, in order to indirectly affect profits.

D. Managing costs of products and services better, in order to become the low-cost provider.

The correct answer is (B). *(CIA, adapted)*

**REQUIRED:** The purpose of focusing on customers, promoting innovation, learning new philosophies, driving out fear, and providing extensive training.

**DISCUSSION:** TQM is a comprehensive approach to quality. It treats the pursuit of quality as a basic organizational function that is as important as production or marketing. TQM is the continuous pursuit of quality in every aspect of organizational activities through a philosophy of doing it right the first time, employee training and empowerment, promotion of teamwork, improvement of processes, and attention to satisfaction of customers, both internal and external. TQM emphasizes the supplier's relationship with the customer, identifies customer needs, and recognizes that everyone in a process is at some time a customer or supplier of someone else, either within or without the organization.

Answer (A) is incorrect because competitive benchmarking is just one tool for implementing TQM. Answers (C) and (D) are incorrect because TQM is aimed primarily at quality improvement rather than profitability or cost reduction.

**4.** Total quality management in a manufacturing environment is best exemplified by

   A.  Identifying and reworking production defects before sale.

   B.  Designing the product to minimize defects.

   C.  Performing inspections to isolate defects as early as possible.

   D.  Making machine adjustments periodically to reduce defects.

The correct answer is (B). *(CIA, adapted)*
   **REQUIRED:** The activity characteristic of TQM.
   **DISCUSSION:** Total quality management emphasizes quality as a basic organizational function. TQM is the continuous pursuit of quality in every aspect of organizational activities. One of the basic tenets of TQM is doing it right the first time. Thus, errors should be caught and corrected at the source, and quality should be built in (designed in) from the start.
   Answers (A), (C), and (D) are incorrect because TQM emphasizes prevention, not inspection, rework, or adjustment. The approach of TQM is to build in and design in quality, not to "fix it in" or "inspect it in."

**5.** One of the main reasons that implementation of a total quality management program works better through the use of teams is

   A.  Teams are more efficient and help an organization reduce its staffing.

   B.  Employee motivation is always higher for team members than for individual contributors.

   C.  Teams are a natural vehicle for sharing ideas, which leads to process improvement.

   D.  The use of teams eliminates the need for supervision, thereby allowing a company to reduce staffing.

The correct answer is (C). *(CIA, adapted)*
   **REQUIRED:** The reason that implementation of a TQM program works better through the use of teams.
   **DISCUSSION:** TQM promotes teamwork by modifying or eliminating traditional (and rigid) vertical hierarchies and instead forming flexible groups of specialists. Quality circles, cross-functional teams, and self-managed teams are typical formats. Teams are an excellent vehicle for encouraging the sharing of ideas and removing process improvement obstacles.
   Answer (A) is incorrect because teams are often inefficient and costly. Answer (B) is incorrect because high motivation does not directly affect the process improvement that is the key to quality improvement. Answer (D) is incorrect because the use of teams with less supervision and reduced staffing may be by-products of TQM, but they are not ultimate objectives.

**6.** One of the main reasons total quality management (TQM) can be used as a strategic weapon is that

   A.  The cumulative improvement from a company's TQM efforts cannot readily be copied by competitors.

   B.  Introducing new products can lure customers away from competitors.

   C.  Reduced costs associated with better quality can support higher shareholder dividends.

   D.  TQM provides a comprehensive planning process for a business.

The correct answer is (A). *(CIA, adapted)*
   **REQUIRED:** The reason TQM can be used as a strategic weapon.
   **DISCUSSION:** TQM is a comprehensive approach to quality. It treats the pursuit of quality as a basic organizational function that is as important as production or marketing. Because TQM affects every aspect of the organization's activities, it permeates the organizational culture. Thus, the cumulative effect of TQM's continuous improvement process can attract and hold customers and cannot be duplicated by competitors.
   Answer (B) is incorrect because new products can be quickly copied by competitors and therefore do not provide a sustained competitive advantage. Answer (C) is incorrect because TQM does not focus solely on cost reduction. Answer (D) is incorrect because TQM is only one tool of strategic management.

**7.** Under a total quality management (TQM) approach

- A. Measurement occurs throughout the process, and errors are caught and corrected at the source.
- B. Quality control is performed by highly trained inspectors at the end of the production process.
- C. Upper management assumes the primary responsibility for the quality of the products and services.
- D. A large number of suppliers are used in order to obtain the lowest possible prices.

The correct answer is (A). *(CIA, adapted)*
**REQUIRED:** The true statement about total quality management.
**DISCUSSION:** Total quality management emphasizes quality as a basic organizational function. TQM is the continuous pursuit of quality in every aspect of organizational activities. One of the basic tenets of TQM is doing it right the first time. Thus, errors should be caught and corrected at the source.
Answer (B) is incorrect because total quality management emphasizes discovering errors throughout the process, not inspection of finished goods. Answer (C) is incorrect because all members of the organization assume responsibility for quality of the products and services. Answer (D) is incorrect because the total quality management philosophy recommends limiting the number of suppliers to create a strong relationship.

**8.** Which of the following is a characteristic of total quality management (TQM)?

- A. Management by objectives.
- B. On-the-job training by other workers.
- C. Quality by final inspection.
- D. Education and self-improvement.

The correct answer is (D). *(CIA, adapted)*
**REQUIRED:** The characteristic of TQM.
**DISCUSSION:** According to management theorist W. Edwards Deming's well-known 14 points, education and self-improvement are essential. Knowledge is opportunity. Hence, continuous improvement should be everyone's primary career objective.
Answer (A) is incorrect because one of the 14 points recommends elimination of numerical quotas. MBO causes aggressive pursuit of numerical quotas. Answer (B) is incorrect because informal learning from coworkers serves to entrench bad work habits. One of the 14 points stresses proper training of everyone. Answer (C) is incorrect because another of the 14 points states that quality by final inspection is unnecessary if quality is built in from the start.

**9.** In which of the following organizational structures does total quality management (TQM) work best?

- A. Hierarchal.
- B. Teams of people from the same specialty.
- C. Teams of people from different specialties.
- D. Specialists working individually.

The correct answer is (C). *(CIA, adapted)*
**REQUIRED:** The structure in which TQM works best.
**DISCUSSION:** TQM advocates replacement of the traditional hierarchal structure with teams of people from different specialities. This change follows from TQM's emphasis on empowering employees and teamwork. Employees should have proper training, necessary information, and the best tools; be fully engaged in the decision process; and receive fair compensation. If such empowered employees are assembled in teams of individuals with the required skills, TQM theorists believe they will be more effective than people performing their tasks separately in a rigid structure.
Answer (A) is incorrect because hierarchal organization stifles TQM. Answer (B) is incorrect because TQM works best with teams of people from different specialties. Answer (D) is incorrect because teamwork is essential for TQM.

**10.** Which one of the following is not a characteristic of an innovative manufacturing company?

    A. Emphasis on continuous improvement.

    B. Responsiveness to the changing manufacturing environment.

    C. Emphasis on existing products.

    D. Improved customer satisfaction through product quality.

The correct answer is (C). *(CIA, adapted)*

    **REQUIRED:** The item not a characteristic of an innovative manufacturing company.

    **DISCUSSION:** Innovative companies are customer driven. Because customers demand ever better quality and competitors are attempting to provide that quality, continuous improvement (called kaizen by the Japanese) is essential for such companies. Thus, the flow of innovative products and services must be continuous. Simply emphasizing existing products is not an effective strategy for most organizations.

    Answer (A) is incorrect because continuous improvement is important for achieving and maintaining high levels of performance. Answer (B) is incorrect because more and more manufacturers are automating to achieve high quality, deliver customized products on time, minimize inventory, and increase flexibility. Answer (D) is incorrect because customer satisfaction is the highest priority according to modern management practice.

**11.** The most important component of quality control is

    A. Ensuring goods and services conform to the design specifications.

    B. Satisfying upper management.

    C. Conforming with ISO-9000 specifications.

    D. Determining the appropriate timing of inspections.

The correct answer is (A). *(CIA, adapted)*

    **REQUIRED:** The most important component of quality control.

    **DISCUSSION:** The intent of quality control is to ensure that goods and services conform to the design specifications. Whether the focus is on feedforward, feedback, or concurrent control, the emphasis is on ensuring product or service conformity.

    Answer (B) is incorrect because quality control is geared towards satisfying the customer, not upper management. Answer (C) is incorrect because ensuring the conformance with ISO-9000 specifications is a component of a compliance audit, not quality control. Answer (D) is incorrect because determining the appropriate timing of inspections is only one step towards approaching quality control. Consequently, it is not the primary component of the quality control function.

**12.** The primary reason for adopting total quality management is to achieve

    A. Greater customer satisfaction.

    B. Reduced delivery time.

    C. Reduced delivery charges.

    D. Greater employee participation.

The correct answer is (A). *(CIA, adapted)*

    **REQUIRED:** The primary reason for adopting TQM.

    **DISCUSSION:** TQM is an integrated system that identifies internal and external customers and establishes their requirements. The ultimate (external) customer is best served when internal customers are also well served.

    Answers (B) and (C) are incorrect because reduced delivery time and reduced delivery charges are two of many potential activities that need improvement. Answer (D) is incorrect because increased employee participation is necessary to achieve TQM, but it is not the primary purpose for establishing the program.

**13.** If a company is customer-centered, its customers are defined as

- A. Only people external to the company who have purchased something from the company.
- B. Only people internal to the company who directly use its product.
- C. Anyone external to the company and those internal who rely on its product to get their job done.
- D. Everybody external to the company who is currently doing, or may in the future do, business with the company.

The correct answer is (C). *(CIA, adapted)*
**REQUIRED:** The definition of customers if a company is customer-centered.
**DISCUSSION:** One of the tenets of TQM is customer orientation, whether the customer is internal or external. An internal customer is a member of the organization who relies on another member's work to accomplish his/her task.
Answers (A), (B), and (D) are incorrect because customers are internal as well as external.

**14.** An example of an internal nonfinancial benchmark is

- A. The labor rate of comparably skilled employees at a major competitor's plant.
- B. The average actual cost per pound of a specific product at the company's most efficient plant becoming the benchmark for the company's other plants.
- C. The company setting a benchmark of $50,000 for employee training programs at each of the company's plants.
- D. The percentage of customer orders delivered on time at the company's most efficient plant becoming the benchmark for the company's other plants.

The correct answer is (D). *(CIA, adapted)*
**REQUIRED:** The internal nonfinancial benchmark.
**DISCUSSION:** Competitive benchmarking is the ongoing evaluation of the practices of best-in-class organizations and the adaptation of company processes to incorporate the best practices. It analyzes and measures the key outputs of a process or function, compares them with the best, and identifies the underlying key actions and root causes of the performance difference. The percentage of orders delivered on time at the company's most efficient plant is an example of an internal nonfinancial benchmark.
Answers (A), (B), and (C) are incorrect because the labor rate of a competitor, the cost per pound of a product at the company's most efficient plant, and the cost of a training program are financial benchmarks.

**15.** The four categories of costs associated with product quality costs are

- A. External failure, internal failure, prevention, and carrying.
- B. External failure, internal failure, prevention, and appraisal.
- C. External failure, internal failure, training, and appraisal.
- D. Warranty, product liability, training, and appraisal.

The correct answer is (B). *(CMA, adapted)*
**REQUIRED:** The categories of product quality costs.
**DISCUSSION:** The four categories of quality costs are prevention, appraisal, internal failure, and external failure (lost opportunity). Prevention attempts to avoid defective output, e.g., by employee training, review of equipment design, preventive maintenance, and evaluation of suppliers. Appraisal includes inspection and testing. Internal failure costs are incurred when detection of defective products occurs before shipment, including scrap, rework, tooling changes, and downtime. External failure costs are incurred after the product has been shipped, including the costs associated with warranties, product liability, and loss of customer goodwill.
Answers (A), (C), and (D) are incorrect because carrying costs, training costs, warranty costs, and product liability costs are not quality cost categories.

**16.** Management of a company is attempting to build a reputation as a world-class manufacturer of quality products. On which of the four costs should it spend the majority of its funds?

A. Prevention costs.

B. Appraisal costs.

C. Internal failure costs.

D. External failure costs.

The correct answer is (A). *(CIA, adapted)*

**REQUIRED:** The type of cost on which the company should spend the majority of its funds.

**DISCUSSION:** The firm should spend the majority of its funds on prevention. The emphasis should be on "doing it right the first time" if the company follows TQM precepts. Except at relatively high levels of quality assurance, expenditures for prevention reduce total quality cost.

Answer (B) is incorrect because appraisal does not prevent errors. Answers (C) and (D) are incorrect because internal failure costs and external failure costs (nonconformance costs) must be reduced if total quality cost is to be minimized. Except at relatively high levels of quality assurance, $1 of conformance costs saves more than $1 of nonconformance costs.

**17.** Product-quality-related costs are part of a total quality control program. A product-quality-related cost incurred in detecting individual products that do not conform to specifications is an example of a(an)

A. Prevention cost.

B. Appraisal cost.

C. Internal failure cost.

D. External failure cost.

The correct answer is (B). *(CMA, adapted)*

**REQUIRED:** The term for quality-related costs incurred in detecting nonconforming products.

**DISCUSSION:** Appraisal costs embrace such activities as inspection and testing. Thus, the cost of detecting nonconforming products is an appraisal cost.

Answer (A) is incorrect because prevention costs are incurred in an attempt to avoid defective output. Answer (C) is incorrect because internal failure costs are incurred when detection of defective products occurs before shipment. Answer (D) is incorrect because external failure costs arise when quality problems occur after shipment.

**18.** The cost of statistical quality control in a product quality cost system is categorized as a(n)

A. External failure cost.

B. Internal failure cost.

C. Prevention cost.

D. Appraisal cost.

The correct answers are (C and D). *(CMA, adapted)*

**REQUIRED:** The nature of statistical quality control.

**DISCUSSION:** The categories of quality costs are prevention, appraisal, internal failure, and external failure. Appraisal costs include inspection and testing. However, some writers treat statistical quality control and statistical process control as prevention activities because they not only detect faulty work but also allow for adjustment of processes to avoid future defects.

Answer (A) is incorrect because statistical quality control is designed to detect quality problems before external failure can occur. Answer (B) is incorrect because internal failure costs include scrap, rework, etc.

**19.** In a quality control program, which of the following is(are) categorized as internal failure costs?

  I. Rework
 II. Responding to customer complaints
III. Statistical quality control procedures

A. I only.

B. II only.

C. III only.

D. I, II, and III.

The correct answer is (A). *(CPA, adapted)*

**REQUIRED:** The item(s) categorized as internal failure costs.

**DISCUSSION:** Cost accounting systems can contribute to improved product quality programs by accumulating and reporting their costs. Internal failure costs are incurred when detection of defective products occurs before shipment. Examples are scrap, rework, tooling changes, and downtime.

Answers (B), (C), and (D) are incorrect because responding to customer complaints and statistical quality control procedures result in external failure costs and appraisal (or prevention) costs, respectively

**20.** Management of a company is attempting to build a reputation as a world-class manufacturer of quality products. Which of the four costs would be the most damaging to its ability to build a reputation as a world-class manufacturer?

A. Prevention costs.

B. Appraisal costs.

C. Internal failure costs.

D. External failure costs.

The correct answer is (D). *(CIA, adapted)*

**REQUIRED:** The cost most damaging to a manufacturer's reputation.

**DISCUSSION:** The company must avoid external failures. If customers perceive its products to be of low quality, the company will not be able to build a reputation as a world-class manufacturer. It should therefore emphasize conformance (prevention and appraisal).

Answers (A), (B), and (C) are incorrect because the company must avoid shipment of poor quality products. Thus, incurrence of the costs of prevention, appraisal, and internal failure is preferable to external failure costs.

**21.** In 1998, a manufacturing company instituted a total quality management (TQM) program producing the following report:

Summary Cost of Quality Report
(in thousands)

|  | 1997 | 1998 | % Change |
|---|---|---|---|
| Prevention costs | $  200 | $  300 | +50 |
| Appraisal costs | 210 | 315 | +50 |
| Internal failure costs | 190 | 114 | −40 |
| External failure costs | 1,200 | 621 | −48 |
| Total quality costs | $1,800 | $1,350 | −25 |

On the basis of this report, which one of the following statements is most likely correct?

A. An increase in conformance costs resulted in a higher-quality product and a decrease in nonconformance costs.

B. An increase in inspection costs was solely responsible for the decrease in quality costs.

C. Quality costs such as scrap and rework decreased by 48%.

D. Quality costs such as returns and repairs under warranty decreased by 40%.

The correct answer is (A). *(CMA, adapted)*

**REQUIRED:** The true statement about a report prepared by a company instituting a TQM program.

**DISCUSSION:** TQM emphasizes the supplier's relationship with the customer and recognizes that everyone in a process is at some time a customer or supplier of someone else, either within or outside the organization. The costs of quality include costs of conformance and costs of nonconformance. Costs of conformance include prevention costs and appraisal costs. Nonconformance costs are composed of internal failure costs and external failure costs. Conformance costs (prevention and appraisal) increased substantially, whereas the nonconformance costs (internal and external failure) decreased. Hence, the increase in conformance costs resulted in a higher-quality product.

Answer (B) is incorrect because prevention costs also increased substantially, which could also have led to higher-quality products. Answer (C) is incorrect because scrap and rework are internal failure costs, which decreased by 40%. Answer (D) is incorrect because returns and repairs are external failure costs, which decreased by 48%.

**22.** All of the following would generally be included in a cost-of-quality report except

A. Warranty claims.

B. Design engineering.

C. Supplier evaluations.

D. Lost contribution margin.

The correct answer is (D). *(CMA, adapted)*

**REQUIRED:** The item that does not normally appear in a cost-of-quality report.

**DISCUSSION:** A cost-of-quality report includes most costs related to quality, including the costs of external failure, internal failure, prevention, and appraisal. Lost contribution margins from poor product quality are external failure costs that normally do not appear on a cost-of-quality report because they are opportunity costs. Opportunity costs are not usually recorded by the accounting system, thereby understating the costs of poor quality.

Answer (A) is incorrect because the costs of warranty claims are readily measurable external failure costs captured by the accounting system. Answers (B) and (C) are incorrect because the costs of design engineering and supplier evaluations are prevention costs that are usually included in cost-of-quality reports.

**23.** Nonfinancial performance measures are important to engineering and operations managers in assessing the quality levels of their products. Which of the following indicators can be used to measure product quality?

  I. Returns and allowances
  II. Number and types of customer complaints
  III. Production cycle time

  A. I and II only.

  B. I and III only.

  C. II and III only.

  D. I, II, and III.

The correct answer is (A). *(CPA, adapted)*
  **REQUIRED:** The indicators of product quality.
  **DISCUSSION:** Nonfinancial performance measures, such as product quality, are useful for day-to-day control purposes. Examples (indicators) of nonfinancial performance measures pertaining to individual product quality include percentage of defects, returned merchandise, allowances, and customer satisfaction.
  Answers (B), (C), and (D) are incorrect because the production or manufacturing cycle time is a nonfinancial measure of performance, but it does not measure the quality of individual products.

**24.** Management of a company is attempting to build a reputation as a world-class manufacturer of quality products. Which of the following measures would not be used by the firm to measure quality?

  A. The percentage of shipments returned by customers because of poor quality.

  B. The number of parts shipped per day.

  C. The number of defective parts per million.

  D. The percentage of products passing quality tests the first time.

The correct answer is (B). *(CIA, adapted)*
  **REQUIRED:** The measure not used for quality measurement.
  **DISCUSSION:** The number of parts shipped per day would most likely be used as a measure of the effectiveness and efficiency of shipping procedures, not the quality of the product. This measure does not consider how many of the parts are defective.
  Answers (A), (C), and (D) are incorrect because the percentage of shipments returned and the number of defective parts per million measure quality by the number of defective units. The percentage of products passing quality tests the first time measures quality by the number of nondefective products.

**25.** Quality cost indices are often used to measure and analyze the cost of maintaining a given level of quality. One example of a quality cost index, which uses a direct labor base, is computed as

$$\text{Quality cost index} = \frac{\text{Total quality costs}}{\text{Direct labor costs}} \times 100$$

The following quality cost data were collected for May and June:

|  | May | June |
| --- | --- | --- |
| Prevention costs | $ 4,000 | $ 5,000 |
| Appraisal costs | $ 6,000 | $ 5,000 |
| Internal failure costs | $12,000 | $ 15,000 |
| External failure costs | $14,000 | $ 11,000 |
| Direct labor costs | $90,000 | $100,000 |

Based upon these cost data, the quality cost index

  A. Decreased 4 points from May to June.

  B. Was unchanged from May to June.

  C. Increased 10 points from May to June.

  D. Decreased 10 points from May to June.

The correct answer is (A). *(CIA, adapted)*
  **REQUIRED:** The charge, if any, in the quality cost index.
  **DISCUSSION:** The index for May was 40% [($4,000 + $6,000 + $12,000 + $14,000) ÷ $90,000], and the index for June was 36% [($5,000 + $5,000 + $15,000 + $11,000) ÷ $100,000]. Thus, the index decreased 4 points (40% – 36%) from May to June.
  Answer (B) is incorrect because the index decreased. Answer (C) is incorrect because the increase in prevention costs was 10% of the increase in labor costs. Answer (D) is incorrect because the decrease in appraisal costs was 10% of the increase in labor costs.

**26.** Conformance is how well a product and its components meet applicable standards. According to the robust quality concept,

    A. A certain percentage of defective units is acceptable.

    B. Units are acceptable if their characteristics lie within an acceptable range of values.

    C. The goal is for all units to be within specifications.

    D. Every unit should reach a target value.

The correct answer is (D). *(Publisher)*

    **REQUIRED:** The true statement about robust quality.

    **DISCUSSION:** Conformance is how well a product and its components meet applicable standards. The traditional view is that conforming products are those with characteristics that lie within an acceptable specified range of values that includes a target value. This view also regarded a certain percentage of defective (nonconforming) units as acceptable. The traditional view was superseded by the zero-defects approach that sought to eliminate all nonconforming output. An extension of this approach is the robust quality concept. Its goal is to reach the target value in every case. The reason is that hidden quality costs occur when output varies from the target even though the units are within specifications.

    Answers (A) and (B) are incorrect because the traditional view of quality treats a certain number of defective units as acceptable. Moreover, a unit is deemed to be acceptable if it is within a range of specified values. Answer (C) is incorrect because the robust quality concept is an extension of the zero-defects approach. The goal of robust quality is in every case to reach a target value, not merely a range of acceptable values.

**27.** According to current accounting literature, the dimensions of quality most likely include

| | Perceived Quality | Aesthetics | Cost |
|---|---|---|---|
| A. | Yes | Yes | Yes |
| B. | Yes | Yes | No |
| C. | No | No | Yes |
| D. | No | No | No |

The correct answer is (B). *(Publisher)*

    **REQUIRED:** The listed dimension(s), if any, of quality.

    **DISCUSSION:** The dimensions of quality include perceived quality, aesthetics, performance, features, reliability, durability, serviceability, fitness of use, and conformance. Perceived quality is the reputation of a product or service derived from customers' past experience with the provider. Aesthetics is the dimension of subjective judgments about the appearance of tangible products or of the facilities, personnel, etc., related to services. However, cost is not normally regarded as a separate dimension of quality. It may be one of the factors that influence the perception of quality, but it is not the sole factor. Moreover, cost does not bear on fitness for use. Thus, a cheaper product is not necessarily a lower-quality product.

    Answers (A), (C), and (D) are incorrect because perceived quality and aesthetics but not cost are normally considered to be dimensions of quality.

**28.** The Plan-Do-Check-Act (PDCA) Cycle is a quality tool devised by W.E. Deming. It is best described as

    A. A "management by fact" approach to continuous improvement.

    B. An ongoing evaluation of the practices of best-in-class organizations.

    C. The translation of customer requirements into design requirements.

    D. The responsibility of every employee, work group, department, or supplier to inspect the work.

The correct answer is (A). *(Publisher)*

    **REQUIRED:** The best description of PDCA.

    **DISCUSSION:** PDCA is a "management by fact" or scientific method approach to continuous improvement. PDCA creates a process-centered environment because it involves studying the current process, collecting and analyzing data to identify causes of problems, planning for improvement, and deciding how to measure improvement (Plan). The plan is then implemented on a small scale if possible (Do). The next step is to determine what happened (Check). If the experiment was successful, the plan is fully implemented (Act). The cycle is then repeated using what was learned from the preceding cycle.

    Answer (B) is incorrect because competitive benchmarking is an ongoing evaluation of the practices of best-in-class organizations. Answer (C) is incorrect because quality deployment is the translation of customer requirements into design requirements. Answer (D) is incorrect because the "quality at the source" concept emphasizes the responsibility of every employee, work group, department, or supplier to inspect the work.

**29.** Which of the following quality costs are nonconformance costs?

   A. Systems development costs.

   B. Costs of inspecting in-process items.

   C. Environmental costs.

   D. Costs of quality circles.

The correct answer is (C). *(Publisher)*
**REQUIRED:** The nonconformance costs.
**DISCUSSION:** Nonconformance costs include internal and external failure costs. External failure costs include environmental costs, e.g., fines for violations of environmental laws and loss of customer goodwill.
Answer (A) is incorrect because systems development costs are prevention (conformance) costs. Answer (B) is incorrect because costs of inspecting in-process items are appraisal (conformance) costs. Answer (D) is incorrect because costs of quality circles are prevention (conformance) costs.

**30.** Quality costing is similar in service and manufacturing organizations. Nevertheless, the differences between these organizations have certain implications for quality management. Thus,

   A. Direct labor costs are usually a higher percentage of total costs in manufacturing organizations.

   B. External failure costs are relatively greater in service organizations.

   C. Quality improvements resulting in more efficient use of labor time are more likely to be accepted by employees in service organizations.

   D. Poor service is less likely to result in loss of customers than a faulty product.

The correct answer is (B). *(Publisher)*
**REQUIRED:** The true statement distinguishing quality considerations in service and manufacturing organizations.
**DISCUSSION:** External failure costs arise when problems occur after delivery. They occur because products or services are nonconforming or otherwise do not satisfy customers. External failure costs in service enterprises are even more important than in manufacturing environments. Faulty goods sometimes may be reworked or replaced to a customer's satisfaction, but poor service tends to result in a loss of customers.
Answer (A) is incorrect because direct labor costs are usually a higher percentage of total costs in service organizations. Answer (C) is incorrect because service activities are usually more labor intensive than in modern manufacturing environments. Thus, more efficient labor usage is more likely to be viewed as a threat to employee job security in service organizations. Answer (D) is incorrect because the badwill resulting from poor service may be even more likely than a defective product to result in loss of customers.

**31.** According to the robust quality concept,

   A. The minimum point on the total quality cost curve occurs when conformance cost per unit equals nonconformance cost per unit.

   B. Improving quality requires tradeoffs among categories of quality costs.

   C. Beyond some point, incurrence of prevention and appraisal costs is not cost beneficial.

   D. Costs in all categories of quality costs may be reduced while improving quality.

The correct answer is (D). *(Publisher)*
**REQUIRED:** The robust quality view about quality costs.
**DISCUSSION:** The optimal level of quality costs traditionally has been deemed to occur where the conformance cost curve intercepts the nonconformance cost curve, which corresponds to the minimum point on the total cost curve. Thus, beyond some point, incurrence of prevention and appraisal costs is not cost beneficial. However, the modern robust quality view is that this relationship does not always hold. Improving quality and reducing costs in each category may be possible if the most efficient prevention methods are applied. For example, selection of a supplier meeting high quality standards regarding defect rates and delivery times may drive down not only failure costs but also the prevention and appraisal costs incurred when supplier performance was less reliable.
Answers (A), (B), and (C) are incorrect because, according to the robust quality concept, conformance costs do not necessarily have to continue to increase to obtain additional reductions in nonconformance costs.

**32.** The following information is available for Portia Co. for its past 2 fiscal years:

|  | Year 1 | Year 2 |
| --- | --- | --- |
| Statistical process control | $ 70,000 | $ 100,000 |
| Quality audits | 35,000 | 50,000 |
| Training | 40,000 | 80,000 |
| Inspection and testing | 100,000 | 150,000 |
| Rework | 90,000 | 50,000 |
| Spoilage | 80,000 | 55,000 |
| Warranties | 180,000 | 80,000 |
| Estimated customer losses | 800,000 | 450,000 |
| Net sales | 3,000,000 | 3,200,000 |

In its cost of quality report for year 2, Portia will disclose that the ratio of

A. Conformance costs to total quality costs increased from 17.56% in year 1 to 37.44% in year 2.

B. Nonconformance costs to total quality costs increased from 62.56% in year 1 to 82.44% in year 2.

C. Nonconformance costs to net sales equaled 19.84% in year 1.

D. Conformance costs to net sales equaled 8.17% in year 2.

The correct answer is (A). *(Publisher)*
  **REQUIRED:** The true statement about quality cost ratios.
  **DISCUSSION:** Conformance costs are the costs of prevention and appraisal, e.g., statistical process control, quality audits, training, inspection, and testing. These costs equal $245,000 ($70,000 + $35,000 + $40,000 + $100,000) in year 1 and $380,000 ($100,000 + $50,000 + $80,000 + $150,000) in year 2. Total quality costs for years 1 and 2 are $1,395,000 ($245,000 + $90,000 + $80,000 + $180,000 + $800,000) and $1,015,000 ($380,000 + $50,000 + $55,000 + $80,000 + $450,000), respectively. Accordingly, the ratio of conformance costs to total quality costs increased from 17.56% ($245,000 ÷ $1,395,000) in year 1 to 37.44% ($380,000 ÷ $1,015,000) in year 2.
  Answer (B) is incorrect because the ratio of nonconformance costs to total quality costs decreased from 82.44% in year 1 to 62.56% in year 2. Answer (C) is incorrect because the ratio of nonconformance costs to net sales equaled 38.33% in year 1 and 19.84% in year 2. Answer (D) is incorrect because the ratio of conformance costs to net sales equaled 8.17% in year 1 and 11.88% in year 2.

## 5.2 Spoilage

**33.** A company produces stereo speakers for automobile manufacturers. The automobile manufacturers emphasize total quality control (TQC) in their production processes and reject approximately 3% of the stereo speakers received as being of unacceptable quality. The company inspects the rejected speakers to determine which ones should be reworked and which ones should be discarded. The discarded speakers are classified as

A. Waste.

B. Scrap.

C. Spoilage.

D. Rework costs.

The correct answer is (C). *(CIA, adapted)*
  **REQUIRED:** The classification of discarded units.
  **DISCUSSION:** Spoilage has been defined variously. Horngren, Foster, and Datar (*Cost Accounting: A Managerial Emphasis*, 9th ed., Englewood Cliffs, New Jersey: Prentice Hall, Inc., 1997, p. 652) define spoilage as "unacceptable units of production that are discarded or sold for net disposal proceeds. Partially completed or fully completed units may be spoiled."
  Answer (A) is incorrect because waste is material that is lost, evaporates, or shrinks in a manufacturing process, or is residue that has no measurable recovery value. Answer (B) is incorrect because scrap is material residue from a manufacturing process that has measurable but relatively minor recovery value. Answer (D) is incorrect because rework costs are incurred to make unacceptable units appropriate for sale or use.

**34.** Spoilage from a manufacturing process was discovered during an inspection of work-in-process. In a process costing system, the cost of the spoilage is added to the cost of the good units produced if the spoilage is

|  | Abnormal | Normal |
| --- | --- | --- |
| A. | No | Yes |
| B. | No | No |
| C. | Yes | Yes |
| D. | Yes | No |

The correct answer is (A). *(CPA, adapted)*
  **REQUIRED:** The kind(s) of spoilage added to the cost of good units in a process costing system.
  **DISCUSSION:** Normal spoilage is the spoilage that occurs under normal operating conditions. It is essentially uncontrollable in the short run. Normal spoilage arises under efficient operations and is treated as a product cost. Abnormal spoilage is spoilage that is not expected to occur under normal, efficient operating conditions. Because it is unusual, abnormal spoilage is typically treated as a loss when incurred, that is, as a period cost.
  Answers (B), (C), and (D) are incorrect because normal spoilage is a product cost, and abnormal spoilage is a period cost.

**35.** Normal spoilage is defined as

A. Spoilage that results from normal operations.

B. Uncontrollable waste as a result of a special production run.

C. Spoilage that arises under inefficient operations.

D. Controllable spoilage.

The correct answer is (A). *(Publisher)*
**REQUIRED:** The definition of normal spoilage in the production process.
**DISCUSSION:** Normal spoilage is the spoilage that occurs under normal operating conditions. It is essentially uncontrollable in the short run. Normal spoilage arises under efficient operations and is treated as a product cost.

Answer (B) is incorrect because, if spoilage occurs from a special production run, it is abnormal. Answer (C) is incorrect because spoilage is abnormal if it arises under inefficient operations. Answer (D) is incorrect because, if spoilage is controllable, it should be controlled under normal circumstances.

**36.** A manufacturing firm has a normal spoilage rate of 4% of the units inspected; anything over this rate is considered abnormal spoilage. Final inspection occurs at the end of the process. The firm uses the FIFO inventory flow assumption. The processing for the current month was as follows:

| | |
|---|---|
| Beginning work-in-process inventory | 24,600 units |
| Units entered into production | 470,400 units |
| Good units completed | (460,800) units |
| Units failing final inspection | (22,600) units |
| Ending work-in-process inventory | 11,600 units |

The equivalent units assigned to normal and abnormal spoilage for the current month would be

| | Normal Spoilage | Abnormal Spoilage |
|---|---|---|
| A. | 18,432 units | 4,168 units |
| B. | 18,816 units | 3,784 units |
| C. | 19,336 units | 3,264 units |
| D. | 19,800 units | 2,800 units |

The correct answer is (C). *(CIA, adapted)*
**REQUIRED:** The equivalent units assigned to normal and abnormal spoilage.
**DISCUSSION:** Normal spoilage equals 4% of the units inspected. The equivalent units of normal spoilage equal 19,336 [.04 x (460,800 units passing inspection + 22,600 units failing inspection)]. The equivalent units of abnormal spoilage are simply the residual of the spoiled units, or 3,264 (22,600 total spoiled units – 19,336 normal spoilage).

Answer (A) is incorrect because normal spoilage is 4% of the total goods inspected, not 4% of the completed units passing inspection. Answer (B) is incorrect because normal spoilage is 4% of the units inspected, not of the units entering production. Answer (D) is incorrect because 19,800 equals 4% of total units to account for.

**37.** Costs of normal spoilage are usually charged to goods manufactured during the period. They should also be assigned to EWIP when

A. The inspection point is at the end of the process.

B. No BWIP exists.

C. No EWIP exists.

D. The inspection point is prior to the end of the process, and goods in EWIP have passed the inspection point.

The correct answer is (D). *(Publisher)*
**REQUIRED:** The circumstances in which normal spoilage costs should be assigned to EWIP.
**DISCUSSION:** Normal spoilage costs should be assigned to all good units, i.e., all units that have passed the inspection point. In typical accounting problems, the inspection point is at the end of the process. Thus, goods in EWIP have not been inspected. If inspection is prior to the end of the process, however, and goods in EWIP have passed the inspection point, a portion of the normal spoilage costs should be assigned to EWIP.

Answer (A) is incorrect because, when the inspection point is at the end of the process, goods in EWIP have not yet passed the inspection point. Answer (B) is incorrect because the cost assignment question arises only at the inspection point, which is not related to the existence of BWIP. Answer (C) is incorrect because costs cannot be assigned to EWIP if there is no EWIP.

**38.** If a process has several inspection points, how should the costs of normal spoilage be accounted for?

    A. Charged to the cost of goods completed during the period.

    B. Assigned to EWIP and goods completed during the period based on their relative values.

    C. Assigned to the good units passing through each inspection point.

    D. Assigned to EWIP and goods completed during the period based on units.

The correct answer is (C). *(Publisher)*
    **REQUIRED:** The way to assign normal spoilage costs given several inspection points.
    **DISCUSSION:** At each inspection point, the costs of normal spoilage should be assigned to the good units passing through the inspection point. Consequently, the cost of moving the good units to the inspection point includes the direct materials and conversion costs of the normally spoiled units as well as those of the good units.
    Answer (A) is incorrect because normal spoilage is assigned to good units as they pass through each inspection point, not just to goods completed during the period. Answer (B) is incorrect because normal spoilage must be assigned to all good units as they pass through each inspection point. Answer (D) is incorrect because normal spoilage is assigned to good units as they pass through each inspection point based on their relative values (not based on units).

**39.** In a process costing system in which normal spoilage is assumed to occur at the end of a process, the cost attributable to normal spoilage should be assigned to

    A. Ending work-in-process inventory.

    B. Cost of goods manufactured and ending work-in-process inventory in the ratio of units worked on during the period to units remaining in work-in-process inventory.

    C. Cost of goods manufactured (transferred out).

    D. A separate loss account in order to highlight production inefficiencies.

The correct answer is (C). *(CPA, adapted)*
    **REQUIRED:** The inventory to which normal spoilage is assigned when it occurs at the end of the process.
    **DISCUSSION:** Normal spoilage is a product cost because it attaches to a product and is expensed when sold. When normal spoilage occurs at the end of the process, the product must be complete before the spoilage can be detected. Thus, all normal spoilage costs should be assigned to finished goods inventory.
    Answers (A) and (B) are incorrect because the EWIP contains no spoiled units because spoilage does not occur until processing is complete. Answer (D) is incorrect because normal spoilage costs attach to the product because they are expected. Abnormal spoilage costs are charged to a separate loss account.

**40.** In a job-order accounting application, $45,000 has been charged to a job ($25,000 of direct materials, $10,000 direct labor, and $10,000 applied overhead). The job yields 500 units of a product, of which 100 are rejected as spoiled with no salvage value. The cost of the spoilage is determined to be $9,000. If the firm wishes to use this job as the basis for setting a spoilage standard for comparison with future work, the conceptually superior way to express the spoilage rate is

    A. 20% of total inputs.

    B. 25% of good outputs.

    C. 90% of labor inputs.

    D. 36% of material inputs.

The correct answer is (B). *(F. Mayne)*
    **REQUIRED:** The calculation of a normal spoilage rate to be used for future comparison.
    **DISCUSSION:** Normal spoilage occurs under efficient operating conditions. It is uncontrollable in the short run and therefore should be expressed as a function of good output (treated as a product cost). The rate can be determined using the ratio of the cost of spoiled units to the cost of good units minus the cost of spoiled units. The ratio may also be stated in terms of units. Thus, the rate is 25% [$9,000 ÷ ($45,000 − $9,000)] or [100 units ÷ (500 − 100) units].
    Answer (A) is incorrect because normal spoilage is expressed as a function of good output. Answer (C) is incorrect because normal spoilage is not directly related to labor. Answer (D) is incorrect because normal spoilage is not directly related to materials.

**41.** Shrinkage should be accounted for as

 A. Miscellaneous revenue.

 B. An offset to overhead.

 C. Reworked units.

 D. Spoilage.

The correct answer is (D). *(Publisher)*
 **REQUIRED:** The accounting treatment of shrinkage.
 **DISCUSSION:** Shrinkage consists of materials lost through the manufacturing process (e.g., heat, compression, etc.). It is accounted for in the same manner as spoilage. If shrinkage is normal, it is charged to the product. If it is abnormal, it is charged as a loss.
 Answers (A) and (B) are incorrect because shrinkage usually does not result in scrap or waste products that can be sold and accounted for as a revenue or a contra cost. Answer (C) is incorrect because reworked units are those reprocessed to produce good units.

**42.** Abnormal spoilage is

 A. Not expected to occur when perfection standards are used.

 B. Not usually controllable by the production supervisor.

 C. The result of unrealistic production standards.

 D. Not expected to occur under efficient operating conditions.

The correct answer is (D). *(CIA, adapted)*
 **REQUIRED:** The definition of abnormal spoilage.
 **DISCUSSION:** Abnormal spoilage is spoilage that is not expected to occur under normal, efficient operating conditions. The cost of abnormal spoilage should be separately identified and reported to management. Abnormal spoilage is typically treated as a period cost (a loss) because of its unusual nature.
 Answer (A) is incorrect because perfection standards are based on perfect operating conditions, and negative deviation from such standards is expected. Answer (B) is incorrect because abnormal spoilage may result from any of a variety of conditions or circumstances that are usually controllable by first-line supervisors. Answer (C) is incorrect because abnormal spoilage may result from any of a variety of conditions or circumstances that are not necessarily related to standards.

**43.** A manufacturing firm may experience both normal and abnormal spoilage in its operations. The costs of both normal and abnormal spoilage are accounted for in the accounting records. The costs associated with any abnormal spoilage are

 A. Assigned to the good units transferred to finished goods.

 B. Assigned to the units transferred to finished goods and those remaining in work-in-process.

 C. Charged to the manufacturing overhead control account.

 D. Charged to a special abnormal spoilage loss account.

The correct answer is (D). *(CIA, adapted)*
 **REQUIRED:** The treatment of costs associated with abnormal spoilage.
 **DISCUSSION:** Abnormal spoilage should be written-off to a special account that is separately reported in the income statement. Costs associated with abnormal spoilage are not inventoried and are therefore treated as a loss in the period of detection.
 Answer (A) is incorrect because assigning spoilage costs to finished goods is an appropriate method of accounting for normal spoilage traceable to a job or process. Answer (B) is incorrect because assigning spoilage costs to finished goods and work-in-process is an appropriate method of accounting for normal spoilage traceable to a job or process, provided the units in process have passed the inspection point. Answer (C) is incorrect because charging spoilage costs to manufacturing overhead is an appropriate method of accounting for normal spoilage, assuming the allowance for normal spoilage is incorporated into the predetermined overhead rate.

**44.** What is a quantity of production report?

A.  A report of the units completed this period in comparison with the immediately preceding period, and a moving average of the number completed during the twelve preceding periods.

B.  A report that details the units transferred into one or more manufacturing accounts during a period and the disposition of these units, i.e., the units completed, spoiled, and in EWIP.

C.  A cost of goods manufactured statement.

D.  A report that lists and accounts for all debits to the manufacturing account during the period and the disposition of these costs, i.e., the costs of units completed, spoiled, and in EWIP.

The correct answer is (B). *(Publisher)*
**REQUIRED:** The description of a quantity of production report.
**DISCUSSION:** A quantity of production report adds the units in BWIP and those entering the process during the period, and indicates the disposition of those units, i.e., the units completed, spoiled, and in EWIP, respectively.
Answer (A) is incorrect because the quantity of production report is concerned only with the units put into and transferred out of the process in the current period. Answer (C) is incorrect because the cost of goods manufactured statement gives the cost of goods completed rather than an accounting for all of the units that went into the process. Answer (D) is incorrect because a cost of production report details the costs debited to and credited from the manufacturing account.

**45.** What is a cost of production report?

A.  A report that lists and accounts for all debits to the manufacturing account during the period and the disposition of these costs, i.e., the costs of units completed, spoiled, and in EWIP.

B.  A report that details the units transferred into one or more manufacturing accounts during a period and the disposition of these units, i.e., the units completed, spoiled, and in EWIP.

C.  A cost of goods manufactured statement.

D.  A report that analyzes all of the variances from standard costs and the disposition of these variances by allocation among inventory accounts and CGS or by a charge only to CGS.

The correct answer is (A). *(Publisher)*
**REQUIRED:** The description of a cost of production report.
**DISCUSSION:** A cost of production report is a formalized statement of the data in a manufacturing or work-in-process account or accounts. All the debits in the account are added to determine the total cost for which the process is accountable. A listing gives the disposition of those costs to cost of goods completed, spoilage, EWIP, etc.
Answer (B) is incorrect because a quantity of production report details the units transferred into and out of manufacturing accounts. Answer (C) is incorrect because the cost of goods manufactured account states the cost of goods completed, not the disposition of the costs incurred during the period. Answer (D) is incorrect because an analysis of standard cost variances report analyzes the variances from standard costs and the disposition of those variances.

**46.** In its July production, Gage Corp., which does not use a standard cost system, incurred total production costs of $800,000, of which Gage attributed $30,000 to normal spoilage and $20,000 to abnormal spoilage. Gage should account for this spoilage as

A.  Inventoriable cost of $30,000 and period cost of $20,000.

B.  Period cost of $30,000 and inventoriable cost of $20,000.

C.  Inventoriable cost of $50,000.

D.  Period cost of $50,000.

The correct answer is (A). *(CPA, adapted)*
**REQUIRED:** The treatment of normal and abnormal spoilage.
**DISCUSSION:** Abnormal spoilage is not expected to occur under efficient operating conditions and is a loss, i.e., a period cost. Normal spoilage arises under efficient operating conditions and is an inventoriable (product) cost. Thus, the $30,000 associated with normal spoilage is an inventoriable cost, and the $20,000 related to abnormal spoilage is a period cost.
Answer (B) is incorrect because the normal spoilage ($30,000) is an inventoriable cost, and the abnormal spoilage ($20,000) is a period cost. Answer (C) is incorrect because the abnormal spoilage ($20,000) is a period cost. Answer (D) is incorrect because the normal spoilage ($30,000) is an inventoriable cost.

| | |
|---|---|
| Questions 47 and 48 are based on the following information. Harper Co.'s Job 501 for the manufacture of 2,200 coats was completed during August at the unit costs presented as follows. Final inspection of Job 501 disclosed 200 spoiled coats, which were sold to a jobber for $6,000. | Direct materials $20<br>Direct labor 18<br>Factory overhead (includes an allowance<br>  of $1 for spoiled work) 18<br>$56 |

**47.** Assume that spoilage loss is charged to all production during August. What would be the unit cost of the good coats produced on Job 501?

A. $57.50

B. $55.00

C. $56.00

D. $58.60

The correct answer is (C). *(CPA, adapted)*

**REQUIRED:** The unit cost of goods produced when spoilage is charged to all production.

**DISCUSSION:** The unit cost of goods produced includes direct materials, direct labor, and factory overhead. Given that the spoilage is included in the calculation of overhead, it must be considered normal and a product cost. Thus, the unit cost remains $56.

Answer (A) is incorrect because $57.50 is the unit cost for 2,000 units, assuming that $6,000 is subtracted from a total cost of $121,000 ($55 x 2,200 units). Answer (B) is incorrect because $55 excludes the $1 of factory overhead for spoiled work. Answer (D) is incorrect because $58.60 is the unit cost for 2,000 units that results from subtracting $6,000 from the total cost of the 2,200 units produced.

**48.** Assume instead that the spoilage loss is attributable to the exacting specifications of Job 501 and is charged to this specific job. What would be the unit cost of the good coats produced on Job 501?

A. $55.00

B. $57.50

C. $58.60

D. $61.60

The correct answer is (B). *(CPA, adapted)*

**REQUIRED:** The unit cost of goods produced if the actual spoilage loss is charged to this job.

**DISCUSSION:** If the spoilage is charged to this specific job (rather than to factory overhead), the spoilage allowance should be removed from the factory overhead rate. The overhead application rate thus drops to $17 because this job's spoilage is not typical and will not be averaged with other jobs. The costs of producing the 2,000 good coats include the costs incurred in the production of the 2,200 coats, minus the $6,000 received for the spoiled coats. The unit cost is the net cost of production divided by the number of good coats produced (2,000).

$$\frac{2,200(\$20 + \$18 + \$17) - \$6,000}{2,000} = \$57.50$$

Answer (A) is incorrect because the total production should be multiplied by $55 ($56 – $1 spoilage allowance). Furthermore, the $6,000 received for spoiled goods should be allocated over the 2,000 good units. Answer (C) is incorrect because the $1-per-unit spoilage allowance in overhead should be deducted. Answer (D) is incorrect because the $1-per-unit spoilage allowance in overhead should be deducted. Furthermore, the $6,000 received for spoiled goods should be allocated over the good units.

**49.** A department adds materials at the beginning of a process and identifies defective units when the process is 40% complete. At the beginning of the period, there was no work-in-process. At the end of the period, the number of work-in-process units equaled the number of units transferred to finished goods. If all units in ending work-in-process were 66⅔% complete, ending work-in-process should be assigned

A.  50% of all normal defective unit costs.

B.  40% of all normal defective unit costs.

C.  50% of the materials costs and 40% of the conversion costs of all normal defective unit costs.

D.  None of the normal defective unit costs.

The correct answer is (A). *(CPA, adapted)*
**REQUIRED:** The normal spoilage costs assigned to EWIP.
**DISCUSSION:** Inspection occurs when the units are 40% complete. Hence, EWIP, which is 66⅔% complete, contains good units only. Because normal spoilage attaches to good units, and the units transferred to finished goods equal those in EWIP, the normal defective unit costs should be assigned 50% to EWIP and 50% to finished goods.

Answer (B) is incorrect because EWIP contains 50% of the good units produced. Answer (C) is incorrect because EWIP should be assigned 50% of all normal spoilage costs. Answer (D) is incorrect because normal spoilage costs should be assigned to EWIP if it contains inspected units.

**50.** In manufacturing its products for the month of March, Elk Co. incurred normal spoilage of $10,000 and abnormal spoilage of $12,000. How much spoilage cost should Elk charge as a period cost for the month of March?

A.  $22,000

B.  $12,000

C.  $10,000

D.  $0

The correct answer is (B). *(CPA, adapted)*
**REQUIRED:** The amount of spoilage charged as a period cost.
**DISCUSSION:** Normal spoilage arises under efficient operating conditions and is therefore a product cost. Abnormal spoilage is not expected to occur under efficient operating conditions. It is accounted for as a period cost. Thus, the amount of spoilage charged as a period cost is the $12,000 related to abnormal spoilage.

Answer (A) is incorrect because $22,000 includes the normal spoilage ($10,000), which is a product cost. Answer (C) is incorrect because the $10,000 normal spoilage is a product cost. Answer (D) is incorrect because the abnormal spoilage ($12,000) is a period cost.

**51.** A company that manufactures baseballs begins operations on January 1. Each baseball requires three elements: a hard plastic core, several yards of twine that are wrapped around the plastic core, and a piece of leather to cover the baseball. The plastic core is started down a conveyor belt and is automatically wrapped with twine to the approximate size of a baseball, at which time the leather cover is sewn to the wrapped twine. Finished baseballs are inspected, and defective ones are pulled out. Defective baseballs cannot be economically salvaged and are destroyed. Normal spoilage is 3% of the number of baseballs that pass inspection. Cost and production reports for the first week of operations are

| | |
|---|---:|
| Raw materials cost | $ 840 |
| Conversion cost | 315 |
| | $1,155 |

During the week, 2,100 baseballs were completed, and 2,000 passed inspection. There was no ending work-in-process. Calculate abnormal spoilage.

A.  $33

B.  $22

C.  $1,100

D.  $55

The correct answer is (B). *(CIA, adapted)*
**REQUIRED:** The abnormal spoilage for the week.
**DISCUSSION:** Abnormal spoilage is calculated as the total unit cost times the amount of spoilage in excess of expected normal spoilage. Total unit cost is

| | |
|---|---:|
| Materials cost ($840 ÷ 2,100 EUP) | $0.40 |
| Conversion cost ($315 ÷ 2,100 EUP) | 0.15 |
| | $0.55 |

Spoilage in excess of normal spoilage is 40 units [100 spoiled units − (.03 x 2,000 good units)]. Abnormal spoilage is thus $22 ($.55 x 40).

Answer (A) is incorrect because $33 is the normal spoilage cost [(.03 x 2,000) x $.55]. Answer (C) is incorrect because $1,100 is the cost of good baseballs produced ($.55 x 2,000). Answer (D) is incorrect because $55 is the cost of normal and abnormal spoilage (100 x $.55).

**52.** During May 1990, Mercer Company completed 50,000 units costing $600,000, exclusive of spoilage allocation. Of these completed units, 25,000 were sold during the month. An additional 10,000 units, costing $80,000, were 50% complete at May 31. All units are inspected between the completion of manufacturing and the transfer to finished goods inventory. Normal spoilage for the month was $20,000, and abnormal spoilage of $50,000 was also incurred during the month. The portion of total spoilage that should be charged against revenue in May is

A. $20,000

B. $50,000

C. $60,000

D. $70,000

**53.** Assume 550 units were worked on during a period in which a total of 500 good units were completed. Normal spoilage consisted of 30 units; abnormal spoilage, 20 units. Total production costs were $2,200. The company accounts for abnormal spoilage separately on the income statement as loss due to abnormal spoilage. Normal spoilage is not accounted for separately. What is the cost of the good units produced?

A. $2,000

B. $2,080

C. $2,120

D. $2,200

**54.** The normal spoilage rate for a company is 5% of normal input. A current job consisted of 31,000 total units, of which 28,500 good units were produced and 2,500 units were defective. The amount of abnormal spoilage on this job is

A. 950 units.

B. 1,000 units.

C. 1,075 units.

D. 1,550 units.

The correct answer is (C). *(CMA, adapted)*
**REQUIRED:** The portion of total spoilage that should be charged against revenue.
**DISCUSSION:** Normal spoilage is an inventoriable cost of production that is charged to cost of goods sold when the units are sold. Abnormal spoilage is a period cost recognized when incurred. The $50,000 of abnormal spoilage is therefore expensed during May. In addition, 50% of the normal spoilage is debited to cost of goods sold because 50% (25,000 ÷ 50,000) of the units completed were sold during the period. No spoilage is assigned to work-in-process because inspection occurs after completion. Thus, the normal spoilage expensed during the month is $10,000 (50% x $20,000). Total spoilage charged against revenue is $60,000 ($50,000 + $10,000).
Answer (A) is incorrect because $50,000 of abnormal spoilage and $10,000 ($20,000 x 50%) of normal spoilage should be charged against May revenue. Answer (B) is incorrect because $10,000 ($20,000 x 50%) of the normal spoilage should also be charged against May revenue. Answer (D) is incorrect because only 50% (not 100%) of the normal spoilage should be charged against May revenue.

The correct answer is (C). *(CIA, adapted)*
**REQUIRED:** The cost of the good units produced given normal and abnormal spoilage.
**DISCUSSION:** Abnormal spoilage is not expected to occur under efficient operating conditions. Thus, abnormal spoilage is excluded from the cost of the good units. Hence, the total production cost of $2,200 is reduced by $80 [20 units x ($2,200 ÷ 550 total units)] to arrive at the $2,120 cost of good units.
Answer (A) is incorrect because $2,000 does not include the normal spoilage ($120). Answer (B) is incorrect because normal spoilage ($120), not abnormal spoilage ($80), should be included in the cost of good units produced. Answer (D) is incorrect because the total production costs should be reduced by the abnormal spoilage ($80) to find the cost of good units produced.

The correct answer is (B). *(CIA, adapted)*
**REQUIRED:** The amount of abnormal spoilage.
**DISCUSSION:** Normal input (input for the good units and normal spoilage) is calculated by dividing the good units produced by the proportion left after the spoiled units are removed, or 95% (100% – 5%). Thus, normal input is the input for 30,000 units (28,500 ÷ .95), normal spoilage is 1,500 units (30,000 – 28,500), and abnormal spoilage is the difference between total and normal spoilage [(31,000 – 28,500) – 1,500].
Answer (A) is incorrect because 950 units equals total spoiled units minus 5% of 31,000 units. Answer (C) is incorrect because 1,075 units equals total spoiled units minus 5% of 28,500 units. Answer (D) is incorrect because 1,550 units equals 5% of 31,000 units.

## 5.3 Scrap and Rework

**55.** Scrap material consists of

A. Defective units that may be used or sold.

B. Raw materials remaining from the production cycle but usable for purposes other than the original purpose.

C. Raw materials remaining from the production cycle but not usable for any purpose.

D. Finished goods that do not meet quality control standards and cannot be reworked.

The correct answer is (B). *(Publisher)*
**REQUIRED:** The definition of scrap material.
**DISCUSSION:** Scrap material consists of raw materials left over from the production cycle but still usable for purposes other than those for which it was originally intended. Scrap material may be sold to outside customers, usually for a nominal amount, or may be used for a different production process.

Answer (A) is incorrect because scrap is raw material that may not necessarily be defective. Answer (C) is incorrect because it defines waste material. Answer (D) is incorrect because scrap is raw material, not finished goods.

**56.** During June, Delta Co. experienced scrap, normal spoilage, and abnormal spoilage in its manufacturing process. The cost of units produced includes

A. Scrap, but not spoilage.

B. Normal spoilage, but neither scrap nor abnormal spoilage.

C. Scrap and normal spoilage, but not abnormal spoilage.

D. Scrap, normal spoilage, and abnormal spoilage.

The correct answer is (C). *(CPA, adapted)*
**REQUIRED:** The accounting for scrap and spoilage.
**DISCUSSION:** One method of accounting for scrap is to credit a revenue account. A common alternative is to credit factory overhead control (or work-in-process for a specific job if the scrap relates only to that job). In the first case, the full costs associated with the scrap remain in work-in-process. In the second case, the amounts realized indirectly reduce the costs of all units or directly reduce the cost of specific units. Regardless of the method used, good units continue to bear at least those costs associated with scrap that cannot be recovered by its sale. The net cost of normal spoilage is likewise included in the cost of good units. But the cost of abnormal spoilage is credited to work-in-process, with the balancing debits to a loss account and to an account that records the disposal value.

Answer (A) is incorrect because good units bear normal spoilage costs. Answer (B) is incorrect because good units bear the costs of scrap. Answer (D) is incorrect because work-in-process is credited for abnormal spoilage.

**57.** The sale of scrap from a manufacturing process usually is recorded as a(n)

A. Decrease in factory overhead control.

B. Increase in factory overhead control.

C. Decrease in finished goods control.

D. Increase in finished goods control.

The correct answer is (A). *(CPA, adapted)*
**REQUIRED:** The usual accounting for a sale of scrap.
**DISCUSSION:** The sale of the normal amount of scrap arising from a manufacturing process is usually recorded by debiting cash or a receivable and crediting factory overhead control. The effect is to assign the net cost of the scrap (total cost-disposal value) to the good units produced; that is, the total cost remains in work-in-process control, but the factory overhead allocated is decreased.

Answer (B) is incorrect because factory overhead control is credited for the amounts realized upon sale. Answer (C) is incorrect because crediting finished goods would not allocate the disposal value to all good units. Answer (D) is incorrect because amounts received from the sale of scrap reduce the costs inventoried.

**58.** Assuming the value of scrap sales is material, when is it not necessary to record the value of scrap in inventory as it is produced?

    A.  When it is sold regularly, e.g., daily, weekly, etc.

    B.  When the unit value fluctuates.

    C.  If it is recognized as miscellaneous revenue.

    D.  If it is recognized as an offset to overhead.

The correct answer is (A). *(Publisher)*
    **REQUIRED:** The circumstances in which a company need not record a significant inventory value of scrap.
    **DISCUSSION:** If scrap material is sold on a regular basis, e.g., daily, its value should be recorded either as a contra cost or as a revenue on a regular basis, and income will be accounted for properly. If it is not sold regularly and not recorded in inventory, income may be misstated.
    Answer (B) is incorrect because failure to record significant scrap value can misstate income. Answers (C) and (D) are incorrect because the issue is timing the recognition of scrap value, not the account used.

**59.** A product that does not meet quality control standards and needs to be reworked to be salable as either an irregular or a good product is classified as

    A.  Spoiled goods.

    B.  Defective goods.

    C.  Scrap material.

    D.  Waste material.

The correct answer is (B). *(Publisher)*
    **REQUIRED:** The classification of a product requiring rework to be salable.
    **DISCUSSION:** Defective goods are products that have not met the quality control standards at the completion of the production process. Defective goods require rework to be salable as either an irregular item or a good product.
    Answer (A) is incorrect because spoiled goods are sold for salvage value or destroyed. Answer (C) is incorrect because scrap is raw material that may be put back into a different production process or sold to outsiders. Answer (D) is incorrect because waste material has no further use.

**60.** A manufacturing process normally produces defective units equal to 1% of production. Defective units are subsequently reworked and sold. The cost of reworking these defective units should be charged to

    A.  Factory overhead control.

    B.  Work-in-process control.

    C.  Finished goods control.

    D.  Cost of goods sold.

The correct answer is (A). *(CIA, adapted)*
    **REQUIRED:** The account charged for rework.
    **DISCUSSION:** Normal rework costs incurred because of factors common to all units produced ordinarily are charged to factory overhead control to spread the costs over all good units.
    Answer (B) is incorrect because, in a process costing application, normal rework is customarily charged to overhead. In a job-order costing application, normal rework costs related to specific jobs are usually charged to the work-in-process account for the given job, not the control account. Answer (C) is incorrect because rework costs are not charged to finished goods. Answer (D) is incorrect because rework costs are applied to good units or, in the case of abnormal rework, charged to a loss account.

**61.** Some units of output failed to pass final inspection at the end of the manufacturing process. The production and inspection supervisors determined that the estimated incremental revenue from reworking the units exceeded the cost of rework. The rework of the defective units was authorized, and the following costs were incurred in reworking the units:

Materials requisitioned from stores:

| | |
|---|---|
| Direct materials | $ 5,000 |
| Miscellaneous supplies | $   300 |
| Direct labor | $14,000 |

The manufacturing overhead budget includes an allowance for rework. The predetermined manufacturing overhead rate is 150% of direct labor cost. The account(s) to be charged and the appropriate charges for the rework cost would be

A.  Work-in-process inventory control for $19,000.

B.  Work-in-process inventory control for $5,000 and factory overhead control for $35,300.

C.  Factory overhead control for $19,300.

D.  Factory overhead control for $40,300.

The correct answer is (D). *(CIA, adapted)*
**REQUIRED:** The account(s) to be charged and the appropriate charges for the rework cost.
**DISCUSSION:** The rework charge for direct materials, indirect materials (supplies), direct labor, and overhead applied on the basis of direct labor cost is $40,300 [$5,000 + $300 + $14,000 + (1.5 x $14,000)]. If an allowance for rework is included in a company's manufacturing overhead budget, rework of defective units is spread over all jobs or batches as part of the predetermined overhead application rate. Hence, the debit is to overhead control.
Answers (A) and (B) are incorrect because factory overhead should be charged for direct materials, supplies, direct labor, and applied overhead Incurred for rework. Answer (C) is incorrect because $19,300 excludes the predetermined manufacturing overhead.

**62.** Hart Company incurred the following costs on Job 109 for the manufacture of 200 motors:

Original cost accumulation:

| | |
|---|---|
| Direct materials | $ 660 |
| Direct labor | 800 |
| Factory overhead (150% of DL) | 1,200 |
| | $2,660 |

Direct costs of reworking 10 units:

| | |
|---|---|
| Direct materials | $ 100 |
| Direct labor | 160 |
| | $ 260 |

The rework costs were attributable to the exacting specifications of Job 109, and the full rework costs were charged to this specific job. What is the cost per finished unit of Job 109?

A.  $15.80

B.  $14.60

C.  $13.80

D.  $13.30

The correct answer is (A). *(CPA, adapted)*
**REQUIRED:** The cost per finished unit of a job, given rework costs.
**DISCUSSION:** The rework costs are attributable to the exacting specifications of Job 109, so the full rework costs should be charged to this specific job. Accordingly, the cost of reworking the 10 units must include $260 of direct costs and an additional charge for overhead.

| | |
|---|---|
| Original cost | $2,660.00 |
| Rework direct costs | 260.00 |
| Rework O/H (150% × $160 DL) | 240.00 |
| Job 109 total costs | $3,160.00 |
| Divided by 200 motors | ÷   200 |
| Job 109 unit cost | $   15.80 |

Answer (B) is incorrect because $14.60 does not include the overhead for the rework. Answer (C) is incorrect because $13.80 excludes the overhead and direct labor costs of rework. Answer (D) is incorrect because $13.30 does not include the direct and overhead costs for the rework.

## 5.4 Comprehensive

Questions 63 through 67 are based on the following information. JC Company employs a process cost system. A unit of product passes through three departments -- molding, assembly, and finishing -- before it is complete. Finishing Department information for May follows:

|  | Units |
|---|---|
| Work-in-process inventory--May 1 | 1,400 |
| Units transferred in from the Assembly Department | 14,000 |
| Units spoiled | 700 |
| Units transferred out to finished goods inventory | 11,200 |

Raw materials are added at the beginning of the processing in the Finishing Department without changing the number of units being processed.

WIP was 70% complete as to conversion on May 1 and 40% complete as to conversion on May 31. All spoilage was discovered at final inspection before the units were transferred to finished goods; 560 of the units spoiled were within the limit considered normal.

The JC Company employs the weighted-average costing method. The equivalent units and the current costs per equivalent unit of production for each cost factor are as follows:

|  | EUP | Current Costs per EUP |
|---|---|---|
| Transferred-in | 15,400 | $5.00 |
| Raw materials | 15,400 | 1.00 |
| Conversion cost | 13,300 | 3.00 |
| Total cost per EUP |  | $9.00 |

**63.** The cost of production transferred to the finished goods inventory is

A. $100,800

B. $105,840

C. $107,100

D. $102,060

The correct answer is (B). *(CMA, adapted)*

**REQUIRED:** The weighted-average cost of production transferred to finished goods.

**DISCUSSION:** The costs assigned to finished goods inventory consist of the costs attached to the units transferred out plus the costs of normal spoilage (so the good units absorb the cost of normal spoilage). Because spoilage is detected at the end of the process, its unit cost ($9) is the same as the unit cost for good units. The cost of production transferred to finished goods is $105,840 [(11,200 good units + 560 spoiled units) × $9]. The remaining 140 units are abnormal spoilage and are written off as a period cost.

Answer (A) is incorrect because $100,800 does not include the cost of normal spoilage. Answer (C) is incorrect because $107,100 includes the cost of abnormal spoilage. Answer (D) is incorrect because $102,060 includes the cost of abnormal spoilage instead of normal spoilage.

**64.** The cost assigned to WIP on May 31 is

A. $28,000

B. $21,000

C. $25,200

D. $30,240

The correct answer is (C). *(CMA, adapted)*

**REQUIRED:** The cost of EWIP using the weighted-average method.

**DISCUSSION:** To determine the cost assigned to EWIP, one must first determine the EUP in EI. BI plus units transferred in, minus the units completed and transferred, minus the spoilage, equals EWIP of 3,500 units (1,400 + 14,000 – 11,200 – 700). Material is added at the beginning of the process, and transferred-in costs are treated as if they were materials added at the beginning of the process. Because conversion is 40% complete, the EUP for conversion costs are 1,400 (3,500 x 40%).

| | |
|---|---|
| Transferred-in (3,500 × $5) | $17,500 |
| Materials (3,500 × $1) | 3,500 |
| Conversion cost (1,400 × $3) | 4,200 |
| EWIP costs | $25,200 |

Answer (A) is incorrect because $28,000 includes no materials cost and includes all of the conversion cost for the 3,500 units in WIP. Answer (B) is incorrect because $21,000 omits conversion costs. Answer (D) is incorrect because $30,240 includes the cost of 560 spoiled units.

Refer to the information preceding question 63 on page 172.

**65.** If the total costs of prior departments included in the WIP of the Finishing Department on May 1 amounted to $6,300, the total cost transferred in from the Assembly Department to the Finishing Department during May is

- A. $70,000
- B. $62,300
- C. $70,700
- D. $63,700

The correct answer is (C). *(CMA, adapted)*
**REQUIRED:** The total costs transferred in during the period using the weighted-average method.
**DISCUSSION:** The total transferred-in cost is calculated by multiplying the transferred-in equivalent units by the cost per equivalent unit (15,400 x $5 = $77,000). Given that $6,300 was included in the BWIP, the remainder ($77,000 – $6,300 = $70,700) must have been transferred in during the month.

Answer (A) is incorrect because $70,000 is the cost of units transferred in during May. Answer (B) is incorrect because the total transferred-in costs equal $70,700 {[(1,400 + 14,000) x $5] – $6,300}. Answer (D) is incorrect because the transferred-in cost of BWIP (1,400 x $5) should be included.

**66.** The cost associated with the abnormal spoilage is

- A. $6,300
- B. $1,260
- C. $560
- D. $840

The correct answer is (B). *(CMA, adapted)*
**REQUIRED:** The cost associated with abnormal spoilage.
**DISCUSSION:** The cost of abnormal spoilage is calculated by multiplying the total unit cost (spoilage is detected at final inspection after all costs have been incurred) by the amount of abnormal spoilage. There are 140 units of abnormal spoilage (700 spoiled – 560 considered normal spoilage). The cost of abnormal spoilage is $1,260 (140 units x $9).

Answer (A) is incorrect because $6,300 is the cost associated with all spoilage. Answer (C) is incorrect because $560 is the raw materials cost of normal spoilage. Answer (D) is incorrect because $840 does not include the conversion costs for the abnormal spoilage.

**67.** The costs associated with abnormal spoilage ordinarily are charged to

- A. Inventory.
- B. A materials variance account.
- C. Manufacturing overhead.
- D. A special loss account.

The correct answer is (D). *(CMA, adapted)*
**REQUIRED:** The accounting for abnormal spoilage.
**DISCUSSION:** Abnormal spoilage costs are usually charged to a loss account (treated as a period cost), whereas normal spoilage costs are usually attached to the good units produced (treated as a product cost).

Answer (A) is incorrect because normal spoilage is absorbed by the good units produced. Answer (B) is incorrect because variances of materials prices or usage are charged to the material variance account. Answer (C) is incorrect because charging abnormal spoilage to manufacturing overhead is possible, but it is not the ordinary method. If charged to overhead, it is subsequently treated as a product rather than period cost.

Questions 68 through 75 are based on the following information. This information was presented as part of Question 8 on Part 4 of the December 1977 CMA examination.

Ranka Company manufactures high-quality leather products. The company's profits have declined during the past 9 months. Ranka has used unit cost data (which were developed 18 months ago) in planning and controlling its operations. In an attempt to isolate the causes of poor profit performance, management is investigating the manufacturing operations of each of its products.

One of Ranka's main products is fine leather belts. The belts are produced in a single, continuous process in the Bluett Plant. During the process, leather strips are sewn, punched, and dyed. Buckles are attached by rivets when the belts are 70% complete as to direct labor and overhead (conversion costs). The belts then enter a final finishing stage to conclude the process. Labor and overhead are applied continuously during the process.

The leather belts are inspected twice during the process: (1) right before the buckles are attached (70% point in the process) and (2) at the conclusion of the finishing stage (100% point in the process). Ranka uses the weighted-average method to calculate its unit costs.

The leather belts produced at the Bluett Plant sell wholesale for $9.95 each. Management wants to compare the current manufacturing costs per unit with the prices on the market for leather belts. Top management has asked the Bluett Plant to submit data on the cost of manufacturing the leather belts for the month of October. These data will be used to evaluate whether modifications in the production process should be initiated or whether an increase in the selling price of the belts is justified. The cost per equivalent unit being used for planning and control purposes is $5.35 per unit.

The work-in-process inventory consisted of 400 partially completed units on October 1. The belts were 25% complete as to conversion costs. The costs included in the inventory on October 1 were

| Leather strips | $1,000 |
| Conversion costs | 300 |
| | $1,300 |

During October, 7,600 leather strips were placed in production. A total of 6,800 good leather belts were completed. A total of 300 belts were identified as defective at the two inspection points -- 100 at the first inspection point (before buckle is attached) and 200 at the final inspection point (after finishing). This quantity of defective belts was considered normal. In addition, 200 belts were removed from the production line when the process was 40% complete as to conversion costs because they had been damaged as a result of a malfunction during the sewing operation. This malfunction was considered an unusual occurrence, so the spoilage was classified as abnormal. Defective (spoiled) units are not reprocessed and have zero salvage value. The work-in-process inventory on October 31 consisted of 700 belts 50% complete as to conversion costs.

The costs charged to production for October were

| Leather strips | $20,600 |
| Buckles | 4,550 |
| Conversion costs | 20,700 |
| Total | $45,850 |

**68.** What are the total equivalent units for the leather strips for the month?

A. 7,000

B. 8,000

C. 7,500

D. 7,800

The correct answer is (B). *(Publisher)*
**REQUIRED:** The total equivalent units for leather strips.
**DISCUSSION:** Leather strip equivalent units are the total completed during the month, plus normal spoilage, plus abnormal spoilage, plus any work-in-process at month-end.

| Completed during the month | 6,800 |
| Normal spoilage: | |
| 1st inspection | 100 |
| 2nd inspection | 200 |
| Abnormal spoilage | 200 |
| Work-in-process at 10/31 | 700 |
| Total equivalent units | 8,000 |

Answer (A) is incorrect because 7,000 excludes normal spoilage and EWIP. Answer (C) is incorrect because normal and abnormal spoilage should be included. Answer (D) is incorrect because 7,800 excludes abnormal spoilage.

Refer to the information preceding question 68 on page 173.

**69.** What is the cost per equivalent unit for the buckles?

A.  $.65

B.  $.67

C.  $.64

D.  $.59

The correct answer is (A). *(Publisher)*

**REQUIRED:** The cost per equivalent unit for buckles.

**DISCUSSION:** The buckles are attached when the belts are 70% complete, which is immediately after the first inspection. Hence, the 100 units of normal spoilage detected at the first inspection point did not have buckles and are not included in this EUP calculation. The cost per EUP for the buckles is the cost assigned to the buckles divided by the EUP. The 6,800 buckles added to belts completed during the month plus 200 units of normal spoilage identified at the second inspection point equal 7,000 EUP (the units in EWIP do not have buckles because they are only 50% complete). Given that $4,550 in costs is attributable to the 7,000 buckles, the cost per EUP is $.65 ($4,550 ÷ 7,000).

Answer (B) is incorrect because $.67 equals $4,550 divided by 6,800. Answer (C) is incorrect because $.64 equals $4,550 divided by 7,100. Answer (D) is incorrect because $.59 equals $4,550 divided by 7,700.

**70.** What is the total production cost to account for in October?

A.  $45,850

B.  $47,150

C.  $52,150

D.  $43,516

The correct answer is (B). *(Publisher)*

**REQUIRED:** The total cost of production to account for.

**DISCUSSION:** Total BWIP cost is $1,300, and costs charged to production during the month are $45,850. Thus, the total cost to account for is $47,150. Alternatively, the cost can be calculated by adding each component.

| | |
|---|---:|
| Material ($1,000 + $20,600) | $21,600 |
| Buckles | 4,550 |
| Conversion ($300 + $20,700) | 21,000 |
| Total costs | $47,150 |

Answer (A) is incorrect because $45,850 does not include the cost of BWIP ($1,300). Answer (C) is incorrect because $52,150 does not reflect the total of BWIP ($1,300) and the costs charged to production during the month ($45,850). Answer (D) is incorrect because $43,516 does not reflect the total cost of BWIP ($1,300) and the costs charged to production during the month ($45,850).

Refer to the information preceding question 68 on page 173.

**71.** What is the total cost per equivalent unit?

A. $5.50

B. $6.33

C. $6.49

D. $6.15

The correct answer is (D). *(Publisher)*

**REQUIRED:** The total cost per equivalent unit.

**DISCUSSION:** The total cost per EUP is the sum of EUP costs for strips, buckles, and conversion. The 100 units of normal spoilage detected by the first inspection were 70% complete (70 EUP), and the 200 units of normal spoilage identified at the second inspection point were 100% complete. The 200 units of abnormal spoilage were 40% complete (80 EUP). EWIP was 50% complete.

| | Leather Strips | Buckles | Conversion Cost |
|---|---|---|---|
| Completed during the month | 6,800 | 6,800 | 6,800 |
| Normal spoilage | | | |
|   1st inspection | 100 | -- | 70 |
|   2nd inspection | 200 | 200 | 200 |
| Abnormal spoilage | 200 | -- | 80 |
| WIP at 10/31 | 700 | -- | 350 |
| Equivalent units | 8,000 | 7,000 | 7,500 |

Cost per EUP:

| | |
|---|---|
| Strips [($1,000 + $20,600) ÷ 8,000] | $2.70 |
| Buckles ($4,550 ÷ 7,000) | .65 |
| Conversion [($300 + $20,700) ÷ 7,500] | 2.80 |
| Total cost per EUP | $6.15 |

Answer (A) is incorrect because $5.50 does not include the unit cost for buckles ($.65). Answer (B) is incorrect because $6.33 excludes the EUP for leather strips related to spoilage. Answer (C) is incorrect because $6.49 excludes all EUP for spoilage.

**72.** What is the total cost of normal spoilage?

A. $1,845

B. $1,566

C. $1,696

D. $2,460

The correct answer is (C). *(Publisher)*

**REQUIRED:** The total cost of normal spoilage.

**DISCUSSION:** The cost of normal spoilage is equal to the sum of the products of the EUP attributable to normal spoilage and the EUP cost for each component.

| | |
|---|---|
| Leather {300 EUP × [($1,000 + $20,600) ÷ 8,000 EUP]} | $ 810 |
| Buckles [200 EUP × ($4,550 ÷ 7,000 EUP)] | 130 |
| Conversion {270 EUP* × [($300 + $20,700) ÷ 7,500 EUP]} | 756 |
| Total | $1,696 |

* Consists of 200 units 100% complete and 100 units 70% complete.

Answer (A) is incorrect because $1,845 equals 300 spoiled units times $6.15 (total cost per EUP). Answer (B) is incorrect because $1,566 omits the cost of spoiled buckles. Answer (D) is incorrect because $2,460 includes abnormal spoilage.

Refer to the information preceding question 68 on page 173.

**73.** What is the total work-in-process as of October 31?

A. $1,890

B. $1,696

C. $4,305

D. $2,870

The correct answer is (D). *(Publisher)*
REQUIRED: The total ending work-in-process inventory.
DISCUSSION: The cost of EWIP is equal to the EUP in each category times the appropriate unit cost. Leather strips, the only item in EI as of October 31, are 100% complete as to leather and 50% complete as to conversion.

| | |
|---|---|
| Leather strips (700 × $2.70) | $1,890 |
| Conversion (700 × .5 × $2.80) | 980 |
| Total | $2,870 |

Answer (A) is incorrect because the cost of conversion ($980) should be included. Answer (B) is incorrect because $1,696 equals the cost of normal spoilage. Answer (C) is incorrect because $4,305 equals 700 units times $6.15 (total cost per EUP).

**74.** What is the average cost per unit for finished goods?

A. $5.89

B. $6.40

C. $6.15

D. $6.51

The correct answer is (B). *(Publisher)*
REQUIRED: The average cost per unit for finished goods.
DISCUSSION: The average cost for finished goods is the total cost of the good units completed plus the cost of normal spoilage, divided by the number of good units completed. The cost of good units completed is $41,820 (6,800 × $6.15 total cost per EUP). The cost of normal spoilage is $1,696. Thus, $43,516 ($41,820 + $1,696) is the total cost transferred, and the unit cost is $6.40 ($43,516 ÷ 6,800).

Answer (A) is incorrect because $5.89 equals the total cost of production to be accounted for divided by total physical units. Answer (C) is incorrect because $6.15 is the total cost per EUP. Answer (D) is incorrect because $6.51 includes abnormal spoilage in the numerator.

**75.** If the 300 defective belts (normal spoilage) were repaired and management wanted to be sure the incremental costs did not exceed the cost of producing new units, how would the rework costs be accounted for?

A. As normal materials, labor, and overhead.

B. Charged only to those belts repaired.

C. Expensed as extraordinary.

D. Charged to overhead and spread over the cost of all products.

The correct answer is (B). *(Publisher)*
REQUIRED: The appropriate accounting treatment to maximize control over rework costs.
DISCUSSION: To maximize control, the costs relating to the repair of the 300 defective belts should be separated from other costs. The costs might flow through the WIP accounts but should be kept separate (like a specific job in job-order costing). Alternatively, another WIP-type account for rework might be established on a job lot basis, which would prevent spending more for the rework than manufacturing a new product. Generally, manufacturers prefer to rework items rather than throw them away.

Answer (A) is incorrect because, if the rework costs are accounted for as normal materials, labor, and overhead, the costs of reworking are averaged in with the costs of production, which would bury rework costs exceeding the costs of normal production. Answer (C) is incorrect because extraordinary items must be both unusual and infrequent; normal spoilage is neither. Answer (D) is incorrect because charging the costs to overhead would give no effective control over the cost to rework.

# CHAPTER SIX
# COST ALLOCATION:
# SUPPORT COSTS AND JOINT COSTS

**Cost allocation** is a procedure of assigning costs that cannot feasibly be directly associated with or traced to particular cost objects. When resources are expended to produce two or more products or services, **common costs** are incurred that must be allocated. The reasons for potentially arbitrary allocations of common costs include the need to make pricing decisions, to determine profitability, to value inventory for external reporting purposes (not a relevant purpose for service organizations), to reach planning and control objectives (e.g., to select the optimal mix of services), and to motivate employees. Four guidelines are typically cited as being helpful in allocating common costs. **Cause and effect** should be used if possible because of its objectivity and acceptance by operating management. **Benefits received** is the most frequently used criterion when cause and effect cannot be determined. However, it requires an assumption about the benefits of costs, for example, that advertising promoting the company but not specific products or services increased sales by the various divisions. **Fairness** is sometimes mentioned in government contracts but appears to be more of a goal than an objective allocation base. **Ability to bear** (based on profits) is usually unacceptable because of its dysfunctional effect on managerial motivation.

**Support (service) department costs** are among the costs that normally require allocation. They are considered to be part of overhead and cannot feasibly be directly traced to cost objects. Thus, they must be allocated to the operating departments that use the resources. When support departments also provide services to each other, their costs may be allocated to each other before allocation to operating departments. Furthermore, support department costs should preferably be allocated using dual rates so that variable costs and fixed costs may be assigned using different bases.

The **direct method** is the simplest and most common method of support cost allocation.  It allocates costs directly to the producing departments without recognition of services provided among the support departments.  No attempt is made to allocate the costs of support departments to other support departments under the direct method.  Allocations of support department costs are made only to production departments based on their relative use of services.  The **step** or **step-down method** includes an allocation of support costs to other support departments in addition to the producing departments.  The allocation may begin with the costs of the support department that provides the highest percentage of its total support to other support departments, provides support to the greatest number of other support departments, or has the greatest dollar cost of support provided to other support departments.  The costs of the remaining support departments are then allocated in the same manner, but no cost is assigned to support departments whose costs have already been allocated.  The process continues until all support costs are allocated.  The **reciprocal method** is the most theoretically sound.  It allows reflection of all reciprocal support among support departments.  It is also known as the simultaneous-solution method, cross-allocation method, matrix-allocation method, or double-distribution method.  The step method considers only support provided among support departments in one direction, but the reciprocal method considers support in both directions.  If all reciprocal support is recognized, linear algebra may be used to reach a solution.  The typical problem on a professional examination can be solved using two or three simultaneous equations.

The common costs of a cost object shared by multiple users must also be allocated in many other circumstances.  One alternative cost allocation technique is the **stand-alone method**.  It allocates a portion of common costs to each user by applying a ratio equal to the stand-alone cost of providing benefits to that user divided by the sum of the stand-alone costs for all users.  A variation of the stand-alone technique is the **incremental cost-allocation method**.  It establishes a priority among users and allocates common costs to the primary party up to the amount of that user's stand-alone costs.  The remaining common costs are then allocated to the incremental party or parties.

Cost allocation is also necessary when two or more separate products are produced by a common manufacturing process from a common input.  The outputs from the process are **joint products**.  The joint costs of two or more joint products with significant values are usually allocated to the joint products at the point at which they became separate.  **Joint costs** (sometimes called common costs) are incurred prior to the split-off point to produce two or more goods manufactured simultaneously by a single process or series of processes.  Joint costs, which include direct materials, direct labor, and overhead, are not separately identifiable and must be allocated to the individual joint products.  At the **split-off point**, the joint products acquire separate identities.  Costs incurred after split-off are separable costs.  **Separable costs** can be identified with a particular joint product and assigned to a specific unit of output.  They are the costs incurred for a specific product after the split-off point.

Several methods are used to allocate joint costs. Each assigns a proportionate amount of the total cost to each product on a quantitative basis. The **physical-unit method** is based on some physical measure such as volume, weight, or a linear measure. The **relative sales-value (sales-value) method** is based on the relative sales values of the separate products at split-off. The **estimated net-realizable-value (NRV) method** is a variant of the sales-value method that is based on final sales value minus separable costs. The **constant gross margin percentage NRV** method is based on allocating joint costs so that the percentage is the same for every product. This method determines the overall percentage, deducts the appropriate gross margin from the final sales value of each product to calculate total costs for that product, and then subtracts the separable costs to arrive at the joint cost amount.

Joint costs are normally allocated to joint products but not by-products. **By-products** are one or more products of relatively small total value that are produced simultaneously from a common manufacturing process with products of greater value and quantity (joint products). The most cost-effective method for the initial recognition of by-products is to account for their value at the time of sale as a reduction in the cost of goods sold or as a revenue. Thus, cost of sales is not recognized for by-products. The alternative is to recognize their value at the time of production, a method that results in the recording of by-product inventory. Under this method, the value of the by-product may also be treated as a reduction in cost of goods sold or as a separate revenue item, and, again, cost of sales is not recognized for the by-product. The value to be reported for by-products may be sales revenue, sales revenue minus a normal profit, or estimated net realizable value. Regardless of the timing of their recognition in the accounts, by-products usually do not receive an allocation of joint costs because the cost of this accounting treatment ordinarily exceeds the benefit. However, allocating joint costs to by-products is acceptable. In that case, they are treated as joint products despite their small relative values. Although **scrap** is similar to a by-product, joint costs are almost never allocated to scrap.

The **relative sales-value method** is the most frequently used way to allocate joint costs to joint products. It allocates joint costs based upon each product's proportion of total sales revenue. For joint products salable at the split-off point, the relative sales value is the selling price at split-off. If further processing is needed, the relative sales value may be approximated by subtracting the additional anticipated processing and marketing costs from the final sales value to arrive at the estimated net realizable value. Thus, the allocation of joint costs to Product X is determined as follows:

$$\frac{\textit{Sales value or NRV of X}}{\textit{Total sales value or NRV of joint products}} \times \textit{Joint costs}$$

In determining whether to sell a product at the split-off point or process the item further at additional cost, the joint cost of the product is irrelevant because it is a sunk (already expended) cost. The cost of additional processing (incremental costs) should be weighed against the benefits received (incremental revenues). The sell-or-process decision should be based on that relationship.

## 6.1 Cost Allocation

**1.** Which of the following statements best describes cost allocation?

    A.  A company can maximize or minimize total company income by selecting different bases on which to allocate indirect costs.

    B.  A company should select an allocation base to raise or lower reported income on given products.

    C.  A company's total income will remain unchanged no matter how indirect costs are allocated.

    D.  A company should ordinarily allocate indirect costs randomly or based on an ability-to-bear criterion.

The correct answer is (C). *(CPA, adapted)*
    **REQUIRED:** The best statement about cost allocation.
    **DISCUSSION:** Allocation is a distribution of costs that cannot be directly traced to the cost objects that are assumed to have caused them. The process entails choosing a cost object, determining the indirect (nontraceable) costs that should be assigned to the cost object, deciding how costs are to be aggregated (accumulated in cost pools) prior to allocation, and selecting the allocation base, not a driver. Indirect costs cannot feasibly be directly associated with a given cost object. Hence, they must be allocated. However, how they are allocated has no effect on net income of the overall entity.
    Answer (A) is incorrect because the method of allocation of indirect costs affects net income figures of individual segments of the enterprise but not net income of the overall entity. Answer (B) and (D) are incorrect because the allocation base should be the most representative of the usage of resources by cost objects.

**2.** The allocation of costs to particular cost objects allows a firm to analyze all of the following except

    A.  Whether a particular department should be expanded.

    B.  Why the sales of a particular product have increased.

    C.  Whether a product line should be discontinued.

    D.  Why a particular product should be purchased rather than manufactured in-house.

The correct answer is (B). *(CMA, adapted)*
    **REQUIRED:** The item that cannot be analyzed as the result of allocating costs to particular cost objects.
    **DISCUSSION:** Cost allocation is necessary for, among other things, product costing (including determination of overhead rates), pricing, investment and disinvestment decisions, managerial performance measurement, make-or-buy decisions, determination of profitability, and employee motivation. However, an allocation of costs does not enable a company to determine why the sales of a particular product have increased. Many factors affect consumer demand, such as advertising, consumer confidence, availability of substitutes, and changes in tastes. Cost allocation is an internal matter that does not affect demand except to the extent it results in a change in price.
    Answers (A), (C), and (D) are incorrect because cost allocation permits analysis of profitability to facilitate investment, disinvestment, and make-or-buy decisions.

**3.** Costs are allocated to cost objects in many ways and for many reasons. Which one of the following is a purpose of cost allocation?

    A.  Evaluating revenue center performance.

    B.  Measuring income and assets for external reporting.

    C.  Budgeting cash and controlling expenditures.

    D.  Implementing activity-based costing.

The correct answer is (B). *(CMA, adapted)*
    **REQUIRED:** The purpose of cost allocation.
    **DISCUSSION:** Cost allocation is the process of assigning and reassigning costs that cannot feasibly be directly associated with specific cost objects. Cost allocation is often used for purposes of measuring income and assets for external reporting purposes. Cost allocation is less meaningful for internal purposes because decision making may be more accurate if more or less arbitrary allocations are avoided. Allocation (as opposed to tracing) may result in product (service)-cost cross-subsidization.
    Answer (A) is incorrect because a revenue center is evaluated on the basis of revenue generated, without regard to costs. Answer (C) is incorrect because cost allocation is not necessary for cash budgeting and controlling expenditures. Answer (D) is incorrect because activity-based costing is a means of assigning costs, not a purpose.

**4.** The allocation of general overhead costs to operating departments can be least justified in determining

   A. Income of a product or functional unit.

   B. Costs for short-term decisions.

   C. Costs of products sold and remaining in inventory.

   D. Costs for the federal government's cost-plus contracts.

The correct answer is (B). *(CIA, adapted)*
   **REQUIRED:** The inappropriate use of allocating cost data to operating departments.
   **DISCUSSION:** In the short term, management decisions are based on incremental costs without regard to fixed overhead because it cannot be changed in the short term. Thus, the emphasis in the short term should be on controllable costs. For example, support department costs allocated as a part of overhead may not be controllable in the short term.
   Answers (A), (C), and (D) are incorrect because determining the income of a product or functional unit, the costs of products sold and remaining in inventory, or the costs for the federal government's cost-plus contracts requires absorption (full-cost) data.

**5.** To identify costs that relate to a specific product, an allocation base should be chosen that

   A. Does not have a cause-and-effect relationship.

   B. Has a cause-and-effect relationship.

   C. Considers variable costs but not fixed costs.

   D. Considers direct materials and direct labor but not factory overhead.

The correct answer is (B). *(CPA, adapted)*
   **REQUIRED:** The allocation base that best identifies costs related to a specific product.
   **DISCUSSION:** A cost allocation base is the means by which costs are allocated. The cost allocation base is some variable (activity) that has a strong correlation with the incurrence of cost by the cost object. For example, direct labor hours is a cost allocation base in traditional accounting systems because indirect costs in labor-intensive manufacturing environments are often correlated with such activity.
   Answer (A) is incorrect because random allocation will not lead to useful or relevant total cost analysis. Answer (C) is incorrect because fixed costs are product costs. Answer (D) is incorrect because factory overhead is a product cost.

**6.** Allocation of support department costs to the production departments is necessary to

   A. Control costs.

   B. Determine overhead rates.

   C. Maximize efficiency.

   D. Measure use of plant capacity.

The correct answer is (B). *(CMA, adapted)*
   **REQUIRED:** The reason support department costs are allocated to production departments.
   **DISCUSSION:** Support department costs are indirect costs allocated to production departments to better determine overhead rates when the measurement of full (absorption) costs is desired. Overhead should be charged to production on some equitable basis to provide information useful for such purposes as allocation of resources, pricing, measurement of profits, and cost reimbursement.
   Answer (A) is incorrect because costs can be controlled by the support departments without allocation. However, allocation encourages cost control by the production departments. If the costs are allocated, managers have an incentive not to use support services indiscriminately. Answer (C) is incorrect because allocation of costs has no effect on the efficiency of support services when the department that receives the allocation has no control over the costs being controlled. Answer (D) is incorrect because activity in the support departments is not a measure of the use of production plant capacity.

**7.** Cost objects

   A.  May be intermediate if the costs charged are later reallocated to another cost object.

   B.  May be final if the cost object is the job, product, or process itself.

   C.  Should be logically linked with the cost pool.

   D.  All of the answers are correct.

The correct answer is (D). *(Publisher)*
   **REQUIRED:** The true statement(s) about cost objects.
   **DISCUSSION:** Cost objects are the intermediate and final dispositions of cost pools. Cost objects may be intermediate as cost pools move from their originating points to the final cost objects. They may be final, e.g., a job, activity, product, or process itself, and should be logically related to the cost pool, preferably on a cause-and-effect basis.
   Answers (A), (B), and (C) are incorrect because cost objects may be intermediate or final, and should be logically related to the cost pool.

**8.** A computer company charges indirect manufacturing costs to a project at a fixed percentage of a cost pool. This project is covered by a cost-plus government contract. Which of the following is an appropriate guideline for determining how costs are assigned to the pool?

   A.  Establish separate pools for variable and fixed costs.

   B.  Assign prime costs and variable administrative costs to the same pool.

   C.  Establish a separate pool for each assembly line worker to account for wages.

   D.  Assign all manufacturing costs related to the project to the same pool.

The correct answer is (A). *(CIA, adapted)*
   **REQUIRED:** The best way to assign indirect manufacturing costs to cost pools.
   **DISCUSSION:** Cost pools are accounts in which a variety of similar costs are accumulated prior to allocation to cost objects. The overhead account is a cost pool for indirect manufacturing costs. Because different allocation methods are applied to variable and fixed costs, separate pools should be established to permit the determination of dual overhead rates rather than a single rate. As a result, the assessment of capacity costs, the charging of appropriate rates to user departments, and the isolation of variances are facilitated.
   Answer (B) is incorrect because prime costs are direct costs, and variable administrative costs are period, not manufacturing, costs. Answer (C) is incorrect because establishing a separate pool for each assembly line worker to account for wages is not necessary under most cost allocation schemes. Answer (D) is incorrect because different allocation methods are usually applied to variable costs and fixed costs.

## 6.2 Support Department Costs

**9.** When allocating support department costs to production departments, the method that does not consider different cost behavior patterns is the

   A.  Step method.

   B.  Reciprocal method.

   C.  Single-rate method.

   D.  Dual-rate method.

The correct answer is (C). *(CMA, adapted)*
   **REQUIRED:** The method of support department cost allocation that does not consider cost behavior patterns.
   **DISCUSSION:** The single-rate method combines fixed and variable costs. However, dual rates are preferable because they allow variable costs to be allocated on a different basis from fixed costs.
   Answers (A) and (B) are incorrect because the step and reciprocal methods can be used on a single- or dual-rate basis. Answer (D) is incorrect because a dual-rate method considers different cost behavior patterns.

**10.** Several methods are used to allocate support department costs to the production departments. The method that recognizes support provided by one department to another but does not allow for two-way allocation of costs among support departments is the

A. Direct method.

B. Linear method.

C. Reciprocal method.

D. Step-down method.

The correct answer is (D). *(CMA, adapted)*
**REQUIRED:** The allocation method that recognizes one-way but not two-way support department cost allocation.
**DISCUSSION:** The direct method allocates all support department costs to production departments without recognizing any sevice provided by one support department to another. The step-down method is a sequential process that allocates support costs among support as well as production departments. However, once a department's costs have been allocated, no additional allocations are made back to that department. The reciprocal method uses simultaneous equations to recognize mutual services.

Answer (A) is incorrect because the direct method does not make allocations to other support departments. Answer (B) is incorrect because the term linear method is nonsensical. Answer (C) is incorrect because the reciprocal method recognizes reciprocal interdepartmental support activities.

**11.** The step-down method of support department cost allocation often begins with allocation of the costs of the support department that

A. Provides the greatest percentage of its support to the production departments.

B. Provides the greatest percentage of its support to other support departments.

C. Provides the greatest total output of support.

D. Has the highest total costs among the support departments.

The correct answer is (B). *(CIA, adapted)*
**REQUIRED:** The basis for determining the order of step-down allocation.
**DISCUSSION:** The step-down method may start with the department that renders the highest percentage of its total support to other support departments. It then progresses in descending order to the support department rendering the least percentage of its support to the other support departments. An alternative is to begin with the department that renders the highest dollar value of support to other support departments. A third possibility is to begin with the department that provides support to the greatest number of other support departments.

Answer (A) is incorrect because the step-down method may start with the department that provides the highest percentage of its total support to other support (not production) departments. Answers (C) and (D) are incorrect because beginning with the support department with the greatest output or the highest costs is not customary.

**12.** Which of the following overhead allocation methods does not charge support department costs to a support department after its costs have been allocated?

A. The reciprocal and direct methods.

B. The step-down and reciprocal methods.

C. The direct and step-down methods.

D. The simultaneous solution method.

The correct answer is (C). *(Publisher)*
**REQUIRED:** The cost allocation methods in which no costs can be charged back to a support department after its own costs have been allocated.
**DISCUSSION:** Under the direct method, support department costs are not allocated to other support departments. Under the step-down method, support department costs are acknowledged and allocated to other support departments but no reallocation occurs.

Answers (A) and (B) are incorrect because the reciprocal method allocates support department costs among support departments providing reciprocal services. This method requires reallocation and the use of simultaneous equations. Answer (D) is incorrect because the simultaneous solution method is a synonym for the reciprocal method.

**13.** The variable costs of support departments should be allocated to production departments by using

    A.   Actual short-run output based on predetermined rates.

    B.   Actual short-run output based on actual rates.

    C.   The support department's expected costs of long-run capacity.

    D.   The support department's actual costs based on actual use of services.

The correct answer is (A). *(Publisher)*

**REQUIRED:** The allocation basis of support departments' variable costs to production departments.

**DISCUSSION:** The most appropriate method of overhead allocation of variable support department costs to production departments is to multiply the actual usage of the production department by the predetermined rate. This basis establishes the user department's responsibility for the actual usage at the predetermined rate.

Answer (B) is incorrect because the actual rate may differ substantially from the estimated rate, and the production department usually has no control over the actual rate. Answer (C) is incorrect because the capacity costs of the support department should be allocated by a fixed overhead rate or lump-sum charge based upon the capacity needs of the production department. Answer (D) is incorrect because user departments do not control support department costs.

**14.** The fixed costs of support departments should be allocated to production departments based on

    A.   Actual short-run use based on predetermined rates.

    B.   Actual short-run units based on actual rates.

    C.   The support department's expected costs of long-run capacity.

    D.   The support department's actual costs based on actual use of services.

The correct answer is (C). *(Publisher)*

**REQUIRED:** The appropriate basis for allocating fixed costs of support departments to production departments.

**DISCUSSION:** The fixed costs of support departments should be allocated to production departments in lump-sum amounts on the basis of the support department's budgeted costs of long-term capacity to serve. This basis allows the production department to develop (budget) a certain capacity needed from the support departments and to agree on the assessment of costs. Analysis of actual results permits evaluation of the support departments' ability to provide the estimated volume of service.

Answers (A), (B), and (D) are incorrect because fixed cost allocation based on actual short-run use, actual short-run units, or actual costs transfers any efficiencies or inefficiencies of the support department to the production department.

**15.** In allocating factory support department costs to producing departments, which one of the following items would most likely be used as an activity base?

    A.   Units of product sold.

    B.   Salary of support department employees.

    C.   Units of electric power consumed.

    D.   Direct materials usage.

The correct answer is (C). *(CMA, adapted)*

**REQUIRED:** The item most likely used as an activity base when allocating factory support department costs.

**DISCUSSION:** Support department costs are considered part of factory overhead and should be allocated to the production departments that use the services. A basis reflecting cause and effect should be used to allocate support department costs. For example, the number of kilowatt hours used by each producing department is probably the best allocation base for electricity costs.

Answers (A) and (D) are incorrect because making allocations on the basis of units sold or direct materials usage may not meet the cause-and-effect criterion. Answer (B) is incorrect because the salary of support department employees is the cost allocated, not a basis of allocation.

Questions 16 through 18 are based on the following information. A company has two support departments, Power and Maintenance, and two production departments, Machining and Assembly. All costs are regarded as strictly variable. For September, the following information is available:

| | Support Departments | | Production Departments | |
| | Power | Maintenance | Machining | Assembly |
| --- | --- | --- | --- | --- |
| Direct costs | $62,500 | $40,000 | $25,000 | $15,000 |
| Actual activity: | | | | |
| Kilowatt hrs. | | 50,000 | 150,000 | 50,000 |
| Maintenance hours | 250 | | 1,125 | 1,125 |

**16.** If the company uses the direct method for allocating support department costs to production departments, what dollar amount of Power Department cost will be allocated to the Machining Department for September?

A. $37,500

B. $15,625

C. $39,062.50

D. $46,875

The correct answer is (D). *(CIA, adapted)*
REQUIRED: The cost allocated under the direct method.
DISCUSSION: Under the direct method, support department costs are allocated directly to the producing departments without recognition of support provided to other service departments. Allocation of support department costs is made only to production departments based on their relative use of support, in this case, kilowatt hours. Thus, the cost allocated to the Machining Department is $46,875 [$62,500 x (150,000 ÷ 200,000)].
Answer (A) is incorrect because $37,500 results from allocating the cost based on total kilowatt hours used by support and production departments. Answer (B) is incorrect because $15,625 is the amount allocated to the Assembly Department. Answer (C) is incorrect because $39,062.50 results from allocating the cost based on direct costs for each production department.

**17.** If the company uses the direct method for allocating support department costs to production departments, what dollar amount of Power Department cost will be allocated to the Maintenance Department for September?

A. $12,500

B. $15,625

C. $8,000

D. $0

The correct answer is (D). *(CIA, adapted)*
REQUIRED: The cost allocated under the direct method.
DISCUSSION: Under the direct method, support department costs are allocated directly to the producing departments without recognition of support provided to other support departments. Allocation of support department costs is made only to production departments based on their relative use of services. Thus, none of the cost will be allocated to the Maintenance Department.
Answers (A), (B), and (C) are incorrect because no cost should be allocated to other support departments under the direct method.

**18.** Assume the company uses the sequential or step method for allocating support department costs to production departments. The company begins with the support department that receives the least support from other support departments. What dollar amount of Power Department costs will be allocated to the Maintenance Department for September?

A. $0

B. $12,500

C. $6,250

D. $8,000

The correct answer is (B). *(CIA, adapted)*
REQUIRED: The cost allocated using the step method.
DISCUSSION: Under the step method, support costs are allocated to producing departments and to other support departments. This method does not allocate any cost back to the departments whose costs have already been allocated. This company will allocate Power Department costs first because the Maintenance Department receives relatively more support from the Power Department. The amount of Power Department cost allocated to the Maintenance Department is $12,500 [$62,500 x (50,000 ÷ 250,000)]. This allocation is based on the total kilowatt hours used by all departments (support and production).
Answer (A) is incorrect because, under the step method, support costs are allocated to both production and support departments. Answer (C) is incorrect because $6,250 results from allocating Power Department costs based on maintenance hours used. Answer (D) is incorrect because $8,000 results from allocating the Maintenance Department's direct costs to itself based on kilowatt hours used.

**19.** A company has two production and two support departments that are housed in the same building. The most reasonable basis for allocating building costs (rent, insurance, maintenance, security) to the production and support departments is

A. Direct labor hours.

B. Number of employees.

C. Square feet of floor space occupied.

D. Direct materials cost.

The correct answer is (C). *(CIA, adapted)*

**REQUIRED:** The most reasonable basis for allocating building costs to the production and support departments.

**DISCUSSION:** Allocation of indirect costs should be systematic and rational, that is, based on some variable that has a strong correlation with the incurrence of cost by the cost object. Thus, building costs (rent, insurance, maintenance, security) are closely related to the amount of floor space occupied by each department.

Answer (A) is incorrect because direct labor hours is clearly less related to the incurrence of building costs than square footage. Answer (B) is incorrect because the number of employees is more appropriate for allocating personnel department costs. Answer (D) is incorrect because direct materials cost is clearly less related to the incurrence of building costs than square footage.

---

Questions 20 and 21 are based on the following information. The Power and Maintenance Departments of a manufacturing company are support departments that provide support to each other as well as to the organization's two production departments, Plating and Assembly. The manufacturing company employs separate departmental manufacturing overhead rates for the two production departments requiring the allocation of the support department costs to the two manufacturing departments. Square footage of area served is used to allocate the Maintenance Department costs, and percentage of power usage is used to allocate the Power Department costs. Department costs and operating data are as follows:

| | Support Depts. | | Production Depts. | |
| --- | --- | --- | --- | --- |
| Costs: | Power | Maintenance | Plating | Assembly |
| Labor | $ 60,000 | $180,000 | | |
| Overhead | 1,440,000 | 540,000 | | |
| Total costs | $1,500,000 | $720,000 | | |
| Operating Data: | | | | |
| Square feet | 6,000 | 1,500 | 6,000 | 24,000 |
| Percent of usage: | | | | |
| Long-run capacity | | 5% | 60% | 35% |
| Expected actual use | | 4% | 70% | 26% |

---

**20.** The allocation method that would provide this manufacturer with the theoretically best allocation of support department costs would be

A. A dual-rate allocation method allocating variable cost on expected actual usage and fixed costs on long-run capacity usage.

B. The step-down allocation method.

C. The direct allocation method.

D. The reciprocal (or linear algebra) allocation method.

The correct answer is (D). *(CIA, adapted)*

**REQUIRED:** The best support cost allocation method.

**DISCUSSION:** The reciprocal method is the theoretically most defensible allocation method. By recognizing the mutual support provided among all support departments, it acknowledges all sources of cost.

Answer (A) is incorrect because dual rates may be used with any allocation method. Answer (B) is incorrect because the step-down method provides only for partial recognition of support provided by other support departments. Answer (C) is incorrect because the direct method does not give any recognition to the services rendered by other support departments.

---

**21.** Without prejudice to your answer in question 20, assume that the manufacturing company employs the step-down allocation method to allocate support department costs. If it allocates the cost of the Maintenance Department first, then the amount of the Maintenance Department's costs that are directly allocated to the Plating Department would be

A. $144,000

B. $120,000

C. $115,200

D. $90,000

The correct answer is (B). *(CIA, adapted)*

**REQUIRED:** The amount of maintenance costs directly allocated to the Plating Department under the step-down method.

**DISCUSSION:** The allocation base is 36,000 square feet (6,000 + 6,000 + 24,000). Plating's share is one-sixth (6,000 ÷ 36,000) of the total cost of maintenance services, or $120,000 ($720,000 ÷ 6).

Answer (A) is incorrect because $144,000 is the allocation based on the direct method. Answer (C) is incorrect because $115,200 is based on the total square footage of the entire plant. Answer (D) is incorrect because $90,000 results from allocating overhead costs only.

Questions 22 and 23 are based on the following information. Fabricating and Finishing are the two production departments of a manufacturing company. Building Operations and Information Services are support departments that provide support to the two production departments as well as to each other. The company employs departmental overhead rates in the two production departments to allocate the support department costs to the production departments. Square footage is used to allocate building operations, and computer time is used to allocate information services. The costs of the support departments and relevant operating data for the departments are as follows:

| | Building Operations | Information Services | Fabricating | Finishing |
|---|---|---|---|---|
| Costs: | | | | |
| Labor and benefit costs | $200,000 | $ 300,000 | | |
| Other traceable costs | 350,000 | 900,000 | | |
| Total | $550,000 | $1,200,000 | | |
| Operating Data: | | | | |
| Square feet occupied | 5,000 | 10,000 | 16,000 | 24,000 |
| Computer time (in hours) | 200 | | 1,200 | 600 |

**22.** If the company employs the direct method to allocate the costs of the support departments, then the amount of building operations costs allocated to Fabricating would be

A. $140,000

B. $160,000

C. $176,000

D. $220,000

The correct answer is (D). *(CIA, adapted)*
**REQUIRED:** The amount of building operations costs allocated to Fabricating under the direct method.
**DISCUSSION:** The direct method does not allocate support costs to other support departments. Hence, the allocation base is the square footage in the two production departments. Fabricating's share is 40% (16,000 ÷ 40,000) of the total cost incurred by Building Operations, or $220,000 (40% x $550,000).
Answer (A) is incorrect because $140,000 is 40% of other traceable costs. Answer (B) is incorrect because $160,000 assumes an allocation base of 55,000 square feet. Answer (C) is incorrect because $176,000 assumes an allocation base of 50,000 square feet, the base that would be used under the step method if the costs of building operations are allocated first.

**23.** If the company employs the step method to allocate the costs of the support departments and if information services costs are allocated first, then the total amount of support department costs (Information Services and Building Operations) allocated to Finishing would be

A. $657,000

B. $681,600

C. $730,000

D. $762,000

The correct answer is (D). *(CIA, adapted)*
**REQUIRED:** The total support department costs allocated to Finishing under the step method.
**DISCUSSION:** The step method of support department cost allocation is a sequential (but not a reciprocal) process. These costs are allocated to other support departments as well as to users. The process usually starts with the support department that renders the greatest percentage of its services to other support departments, the department that provides support to the greatest number of other departments, or the department with the greatest costs of support provided to other support departments. If the $1,200,000 of information services costs is allocated first, the allocation base is 2,000 computer hours (200 + 1,200 + 600). Thus, $120,000 [(200 ÷ 2,000) x $1,200,000] will be allocated to Building Operations and $360,000 [(600 ÷ 2,000) x $1,200,000] to Finishing. The total of the building operations costs to be allocated to production equals $670,000 ($550,000 + $120,000). The allocation base will be 40,000 square feet because no costs are allocated back to Information Services. Accordingly, the total of support costs allocated to Finishing equals $762,000 {$360,000 + [$670,000 x (24,000 ÷ 40,000)]}.
Answer (A) is incorrect because $657,000 results from allocating building operations costs first. Also, the information services costs are allocated using total computer hours. Answer (B) is incorrect because $681,600 results from allocating building operations costs to Information Services. Answer (C) is incorrect because $730,000 allocates the costs of both support departments according to the direct method rather than the step method.

Questions 24 through 28 are based on the following information. The managers of Rochester Manufacturing are discussing ways to allocate the cost of support departments such as Quality Control and Maintenance to the production departments. To aid them in this discussion, the controller has provided the following information:

|  | Quality Control | Maintenance | Machining | Assembly | Total |
|---|---|---|---|---|---|
| Budgeted overhead costs before allocation | $350,000 | $200,000 | $400,000 | $300,000 | $1,250,000 |
| Budgeted machine hours | -- | -- | 50,000 | -- | 50,000 |
| Budgeted direct labor hours | -- | -- | -- | 25,000 | 25,000 |
| Budgeted hours of service: | | | | | |
| Quality control | -- | 7,000 | 21,000 | 7,000 | 35,000 |
| Maintenance | 10,000 | -- | 18,000 | 12,000 | 40,000 |

**24.** If Rochester Manufacturing uses the direct method of allocating support department costs, the total support costs allocated to the assembly department would be

A. $80,000

B. $87,500

C. $120,000

D. $167,500

The correct answer is (D). *(CMA, adapted)*
**REQUIRED:** The total support costs allocated to the Assembly Department using the direct method.
**DISCUSSION:** Under the direct method, support department costs are allocated directly to the production departments, with no allocation to other support departments. The total budgeted hours of service by the Quality Control Department to the two production departments is 28,000 (21,000 + 7,000). Given that the Assembly Department is expected to use 25% (7,000 ÷ 28,000) of the total hours budgeted for the production departments, it will absorb 25% of total quality control costs (25% x $350,000 = $87,500). The total budgeted hours of service by the Maintenance Department to the production departments is 30,000 (18,000 + 12,000). The Assembly Department is expected to use 40% (12,000 ÷ 30,000) of the total maintenance hours budgeted for the production departments. Thus, the Assembly Department will be allocated 40% of the $200,000 of maintenance costs, or $80,000. The total support department costs allocated to the Assembly Department is $167,500 ($87,500 + $80,000).
Answers (A), (B), and (C) are incorrect because the total of the support department costs allocated to the Assembly Department is $167,500.

**25.** Using the direct method, the total amount of overhead allocated to each machine hour at Rochester Manufacturing would be

A. $2.40

B. $5.25

C. $8.00

D. $15.65

The correct answer is (D). *(CMA, adapted)*
**REQUIRED:** The total overhead allocated to each machine hour.
**DISCUSSION:** Machining uses 75% (21,000 ÷ 28,000) of the total quality control hours and 60% (18,000 ÷ 30,000) of the total maintenance hours budgeted for the production departments. Under the direct method, it will therefore be allocated $262,500 (75% x $350,000) of quality control costs and $120,000 (60% x $200,000) of maintenance costs. In addition, Machining is expected to incur another $400,000 of overhead costs. Thus, the total estimated Machining overhead is $782,500 ($262,500 + $120,000 + $400,000), and the overhead cost per machine hour is $15.65 ($782,500 ÷ 50,000 hours).
Answers (A), (B), and (C) are incorrect because the overhead cost per machine hour is $15.65.

**26.** If Rochester Manufacturing uses the step-down method of allocating support costs beginning with quality control, the maintenance costs allocated to the Assembly Department would be

A. $70,000

B. $108,000

C. $162,000

D. $200,000

The correct answer is (B). *(CMA, adapted)*

**REQUIRED:** The maintenance costs allocated to the Assembly Department if the step-down method is applied beginning with quality control costs.

**DISCUSSION:** The step-down method allocates support costs to both support and production departments but does not permit mutual allocations. Accordingly, Quality Control will receive no allocation of maintenance costs. The first step is to allocate quality control costs to the Machining Department. Maintenance is expected to use 20% (7,000 ÷ 35,000) of the available quality control hours and will be allocated $70,000 (20% x $350,000) of quality control costs. Thus, total allocable maintenance costs equal $270,000 ($70,000 + $200,000). The Assembly Department is estimated to use 40% (12,000 ÷ 30,000) of the available maintenance hours. Consequently, it will be allocated maintenance costs of $108,000 (40% x $270,000).

Answers (A), (C), and (D) are incorrect because the Assembly Department will be allocated maintenance costs of $108,000.

**27.** If Rochester Manufacturing uses the reciprocal method of allocating support costs, the total amount of quality control costs (rounded to the nearest dollar) to be allocated to the other departments would be

A. $284,211

B. $336,842

C. $350,000

D. $421,053

The correct answer is (D). *(CMA, adapted)*

**REQUIRED:** The quality control costs to be allocated to the other departments using the reciprocal method.

**DISCUSSION:** The reciprocal method permits mutual allocations of support costs among support departments. For this purpose, a system of simultaneous equations is necessary. The total costs for the Quality Control Department consist of $350,000 plus 25% (10,000 hours ÷ 40,000 hours) of maintenance costs. The total costs for the Maintenance Department equal $200,000 plus 20% (7,000 hours ÷ 35,000 hours) of quality control costs. These relationships can be expressed by the following equations:

$$Q = \$350,000 + .25M$$

$$M = \$200,000 + .2Q$$

To solve for Q, the second equation can be substituted into the first as follows:

$$Q = \$350,000 + .25(\$200,000 + .2Q)$$

$$Q = \$350,000 + \$50,000 + .05Q$$

$$.95Q = \$400,000$$

$$Q = \$421,053$$

Answers (A), (B), and (C) are incorrect because the total quality control costs to be allocated equal $421,053.

**28.** If Rochester Manufacturing decides not to allocate support costs to the production departments, the overhead allocated to each direct labor hour in the Assembly Department would be

A. $3.20

B. $3.50

C. $12.00

D. $16.00

The correct answer is (C). *(CMA, adapted)*

**REQUIRED:** The overhead cost per direct labor hour in the Assembly Department if no support costs are allocated to production departments.

**DISCUSSION:** With no allocation of support department costs, the only overhead applicable to the Assembly Department is the $300,000 budgeted for that department. Hence, the overhead cost applied per direct labor hour will be $12 ($300,000 budgeted overhead ÷ 25,000 hours).

Answers (A), (B), and (D) are incorrect because the overhead cost applied per direct labor hour will be $12.

**29.** A company has two support departments (S1 and S2) and two production departments (P1 and P2). Departmental data for January were as follows:

|  | S1 | S2 |
|---|---|---|
| Costs incurred: | $27,000 | $18,000 |
| Service provided to: |  |  |
| S1 . . . . . | ---- | 20% |
| S2 . . . . . | 10% | ---- |
| P1 . . . . . | 50% | 30% |
| P2 . . . . . | 40% | 50% |

What are the total allocated support department costs to P2 if the company uses the reciprocal method of allocating its support department costs? (Round calculations to the nearest whole number.)

A. $19,800

B. $21,949

C. $22,500

D. $23,051

The correct answer is (D). *(CIA, adapted)*

**REQUIRED:** The total allocated support department costs to P2.

**DISCUSSION:** The reciprocal method allocates support department costs to other support departments as well as to production departments by means of simultaneous equations, as shown below. Thus, total support cost allocated to P2 is $23,051 [(40% x $31,224) + (50% x $21,122)].

S1 = $27,000 + .2S2  
    $27,000 + [.2($18,000 + .1S1)]  
    $27,000 + $3,600 + .02S1  
.98S1 = $30,600  
  S1 = $31,224

S2 = $18,000 + .1($31,224)  
    $18,000 + $3,122  
S2 = $21,122

Answer (A) is incorrect because $19,800 equals the sum of 40% of S1's pre-allocation costs and 50% of S2's pre-allocation costs. Answer (B) is incorrect because $21,949 is the total service cost allocated to P1. Answer (C) is incorrect because $22,500 equals the average of the pre-allocation costs of S1 and S2.

---

Questions 30 through 37 are based on the following information. Barnes Company has two support departments and three production departments, each producing a separate product. For a number of years, Barnes has allocated the costs of the support departments to the production departments on the basis of the annual sales revenue dollars. In a recent audit report, the internal auditor stated that the distribution of support department costs on the basis of annual sales dollars would lead to support inequities. The auditor recommended that maintenance and engineering hours be used as a better support cost allocation basis. For illustrative purposes, the following information was appended to the audit report:

|  | Support Departments | | Production Departments | | |
|---|---|---|---|---|---|
|  | Maintenance | Engineering | Product A | Product B | Product C |
| Maintenance hours used |  | 400 | 800 | 200 | 200 |
| Engineering hours used | 400 |  | 800 | 400 | 400 |
| Department direct costs | $12,000 | $54,000 | $80,000 | $90,000 | $50,000 |

**30.** After applying the simultaneous equations (reciprocal) method, what is the total Engineering Department cost to be allocated?

A. $12,000

B. $54,000

C. $57,000

D. $60,000

The correct answer is (D). *(CIA, adapted)*

**REQUIRED:** The total cost to be allocated.

**DISCUSSION:** The reciprocal method uses simultaneous equations. Solving the following simultaneous equations indicates that Engineering's total cost to be allocated is $60,000. Total maintenance hours equal 1,600, of which 400, or 25%, are used by Engineering. Total engineering hours equal 2,000, of which 400, or 20%, are used by Maintenance.

$M$ = Maintenance Department's total cost  
$E$ = Engineering Department's total cost  
$M$ = $12,000 + .2E$  
$E$ = $54,000 + .25M$  
$E$ = $54,000 + .25($12,000 + .2E)$  
$E$ = $60,000$

Answer (A) is incorrect because $12,000 equals the original maintenance costs. Answer (B) is incorrect because none of the maintenance costs have been allocated to Engineering. Answer (C) is incorrect because $57,000 results from using the step-down method and beginning with the Maintenance Department.

**31.** After applying the simultaneous equations (reciprocal) method, assume that the Engineering Department's total cost to be allocated is $60,000. How much of this cost is allocated to Departments A, B, and C?

   A. $48,000

   B. $54,000

   C. $60,000

   D. $66,000

The correct answer is (A). *(Publisher)*

**REQUIRED:** The total engineering costs allocated to the production departments.

**DISCUSSION:** The Engineering Department's $60,000 in costs is allocated based on the denominator of 2,000 total hours (400 + 800 + 400 + 400).

$$\begin{aligned}
A\ (800 \div 2{,}000) &\times \$60{,}000 = \$24{,}000 \\
B\ (400 \div 2{,}000) &\times \$60{,}000 = \phantom{\$}12{,}000 \\
C\ (400 \div 2{,}000) &\times \$60{,}000 = \underline{\phantom{\$}12{,}000} \\
&\phantom{\times \$60{,}000 = } \$48{,}000
\end{aligned}$$

Answer (B) is incorrect because $54,000 is the amount allocated to Departments A, B, and C under the direct method. Answer (C) is incorrect because $60,000 is the total to be allocated. Answer (D) is incorrect because $66,000 is the total support cost incurred.

**32.** Assume that the Engineering Department's total cost to be allocated is $60,000 after applying the simultaneous equations (reciprocal) method. What is the total Maintenance Department cost to be allocated?

   A. $24,000

   B. $18,000

   C. $22,500

   D. $12,000

The correct answer is (A). *(Publisher)*

**REQUIRED:** The Maintenance Department's total cost to be allocated.

**DISCUSSION:** Substituting the Engineering Department's $60,000 of total cost into the equation for maintenance costs,

$$\begin{aligned}
E &= \$60{,}000 \\
M &= \$12{,}000 + .2E \\
M &= \$12{,}000 + \$12{,}000 = \$24{,}000
\end{aligned}$$

Answer (B) is incorrect because $18,000 is the amount allocated to the production departments. Answer (C) is incorrect because $22,500 equals $12,000 (costs incurred) plus 20% (400 ÷ 2,000) of engineering costs incurred. Answer (D) is incorrect because $12,000 equals the maintenance costs actually incurred.

**33.** Assume that the Maintenance Department's total cost to be allocated is $24,000. Under the reciprocal method, what portion of Maintenance Department cost is allocated to Department A?

   A. 800 ÷ 1,600

   B. 800 ÷ 1,200

   C. 200 ÷ 1,200

   D. 200 ÷ 1,600

The correct answer is (A). *(Publisher)*

**REQUIRED:** The portion of maintenance expense allocated to Department A under the reciprocal method.

**DISCUSSION:** The Maintenance Department's total cost to be allocated in accordance with the reciprocal method is $24,000. Of this amount, 50% (800 ÷ 1,600) is allocated to A, 12.5% (200 ÷ 1,600) to B, and 12.5% (200 ÷ 1,600) to C. Thus, $18,000 of maintenance cost is allocated to Departments A, B, and C, but only $12,000 was actually incurred. Also, the Engineering Department's actual expense was $54,000, but only $48,000 was allocated to the production departments. However, the total allocated to the production departments ($48,000 + $18,000 = $66,000) equals the total incurred ($12,000 + $54,000 = $66,000).

Answer (B) is incorrect because the denominator should be the total maintenance hours (1,600). Answer (C) is incorrect because 200 ÷ 1,200 is the proportion of maintenance hours devoted to production departments that was provided to Department A. Answer (D) is incorrect because the numerator should be the hours provided to Department A (800).

For Questions 34 through 37, refer to the information on page 190 and assume that maintenance costs are allocated first because the Maintenance Department provides a greater percentage of its total support to the other support department.

**34.** Using the step-down method of cost allocation, how much maintenance cost is allocated to the Engineering Department?

    A. $6,000

    B. $3,000

    C. $1,500

    D. $0

The correct answer is (B). *(Publisher)*
    **REQUIRED:** The maintenance cost allocated to Engineering using the step-down method.
    **DISCUSSION:** Under the step-down or sequential method, no reciprocal allocation occurs. Hence, maintenance costs are allocated to the Engineering Department, but engineering costs are not allocated to the Maintenance Department. Accordingly, $3,000 [$12,000 of costs incurred x (400 ÷ 1,600)] is allocated to the Engineering Department.
    Answer (A) is incorrect because the maintenance cost allocated to the Engineering Department using the reciprocal method is $6,000. Answer (C) is incorrect because $1,500 equals the maintenance cost allocated to Department B. Answer (D) is incorrect because $0 equals the costs allocated under the direct method.

**35.** Using the step-down method of cost allocation, what amount of maintenance cost is allocated to Department B?

    A. $1,500

    B. $6,000

    C. $3,000

    D. $15,750

The correct answer is (A). *(Publisher)*
    **REQUIRED:** The maintenance cost allocated to Department B using the step-down method.
    **DISCUSSION:** Under the step-down method of cost allocation, the proportion of hours of maintenance provided to Department B (200 ÷ 1,600) determines B's share of the maintenance cost. Thus, the allocation is $1,500 [$12,000 x (200 ÷ 1,600)].
    Answer (B) is incorrect because $6,000 is the maintenance cost allocated to Department A using the step-down method. Answer (C) is incorrect because $3,000 is the total maintenance cost allocated to B and C. Answer (D) is incorrect because $15,750 is the total of maintenance and engineering costs allocated to B under the step-down method.

**36.** Using the step-down method of cost allocation, what amount of engineering costs is allocated to the Maintenance Department?

    A. $12,000

    B. $10,800

    C. $3,000

    D. $0

The correct answer is (D). *(Publisher)*
    **REQUIRED:** The engineering costs allocated to Maintenance under the step-down method.
    **DISCUSSION:** Under the step-down method, once a department's costs have been allocated to subsequent departments, no reallocation back to that department takes place. Thus, no engineering costs are reallocated to the Maintenance Department.
    Answer (A) is incorrect because $12,000 is allocated to the Maintenance Department under the reciprocal method. Answer (B) is incorrect because $10,800 assumes that engineering costs are allocated first. Answer (C) is incorrect because $3,000 is the maintenance cost allocated to the Engineering Department under the step-down method.

**37.** Using the step-down method of cost allocation, what amount of engineering cost is allocated to Department C?

    A. $6,000

    B. $28,500

    C. $14,250

    D. $0

The correct answer is (C). *(Publisher)*
    **REQUIRED:** The engineering costs allocated to Department C using the step-down method.
    **DISCUSSION:** Using the step-down method, the total engineering costs allocated to Department C equal the actual engineering costs ($54,000) plus $3,000 of maintenance costs, times the proportion of engineering hours used by Department C. Hence, the allocation is $14,250 [($54,000 + $3,000) x (400 ÷ 1,600)].
    Answer (A) is incorrect because $6,000 is the maintenance cost allocated to Department A using the step-down method. Answer (B) is incorrect because $28,500 is the allocation to Department A. Answer (D) is incorrect because $0 is the allocation to the Maintenance Department.

Questions 38 and 39 are based on the following information. The Photocopying Department provides photocopy support for both Departments A and B and has prepared its total budget using the following information for next year:

| | |
|---|---|
| Fixed costs | $100,000 |
| Available capacity | 4,000,000 pages |
| Budgeted usage | |
| Department A | 1,200,000 pages |
| Department B | 2,400,000 pages |
| Variable cost | $0.03 per page |

**38.** Assume that the single-rate method of cost allocation is used and the allocation base is budgeted usage. How much photocopying cost will be allocated to Department B in the budget year?

A. $72,000

B. $122,000

C. $132,000

D. $138,667

The correct answer is (D). *(CMA, adapted)*

**REQUIRED:** The support cost allocated to Department B using a single rate based on budgeted usage.

**DISCUSSION:** Department B is budgeted to use 66⅔% of total production (2,400,000 ÷ 3,600,000), so it should be allocated fixed costs of $66,667 (66⅔% x $100,000). The variable cost allocation is $72,000 (2,400,000 pages x $.03 per page), and the total allocated is therefore $138,667 ($66,667 + $72,000).

Answer (A) is incorrect because $72,000 is the variable cost allocation. Answer (B) is incorrect because $122,000 assumes that fixed costs are allocated equally between A and B. Answer (C) is incorrect because $132,000 assumes fixed costs are allocated at a per-page rate based on available capacity ($100,000 ÷ 4,000,000 pages = $.025 per page), not on budgeted usage ($100,000 ÷ 3,600,000 pages = $.0278 per page).

**39.** Assume that the dual-rate cost allocation method is used and the allocation basis is budgeted usage for fixed costs and actual usage for variable costs. How much cost would be allocated to Department A during the year if actual usage for Department A is 1,400,000 pages and actual usage for Department B is 2,100,000 pages?

A. $42,000

B. $72,000

C. $75,333

D. $82,000

The correct answer is (C). *(CMA, adapted)*

**REQUIRED:** The support cost allocated to Department A if a dual-rate allocation method is used.

**DISCUSSION:** Based on budgeted usage, Department A should be allocated 33⅓% [1,200,000 pages ÷ (1,200,000 pages + 2,400,000 pages)] of fixed costs, or $33,333 (33⅓% x $100,000). The variable costs are allocated at $.03 per unit for 1,400,000 pages, or $42,000. The sum of the fixed and variable elements is $75,333.

Answer (A) is incorrect because $42,000 equals the variable costs allocated to Department A. Answer (B) is incorrect because $72,000 is the allocation to Department B using a single rate. Answer (D) is incorrect because $82,000 assumes fixed costs are allocated at a per-page rate based on actual usage ($100,000 ÷ 3,500,000 pages = $.0286 per page).

## 6.3 Introduction to Joint Costs

**40.** If a company obtains two salable products from the refining of one ore, the refining process should be accounted for as a(n)

- A. Mixed cost process.
- B. Joint process.
- C. Extractive process.
- D. Reduction process.

The correct answer is (B). *(CPA, adapted)*
**REQUIRED:** The type of costing process in which two products are refined from one raw material.
**DISCUSSION:** When two or more separate products are produced by a common manufacturing process from a common input, the outputs from the process are called joint products. The common costs of two or more joint products with significant values are generally allocated to the joint products based upon the products' net realizable values at the point they became separate products.
Answer (A) is incorrect because mixed costs are costs that have both fixed and variable components. Answer (C) is incorrect because extractive process is a technical manufacturing term and has no special meaning in cost accounting. Answer (D) is incorrect because reduction process is a technical manufacturing term and has no special meaning in cost accounting.

**41.** Joint costs are useful for

- A. Setting the selling price of a product.
- B. Determining whether to continue producing an item.
- C. Evaluating management by means of a responsibility reporting system.
- D. Determining inventory cost for accounting purposes.

The correct answer is (D). *(CIA, adapted)*
**REQUIRED:** The usefulness of joint costs in cost accounting.
**DISCUSSION:** Joint costs are useful for inventory costing when two or more identifiable products emerge from a common production process. The joint costs of production must be allocated on some basis, such as relative sales value.
Answer (A) is incorrect because items such as additional processing costs, competitive conditions in sales markets, and the relative contribution margins of all products derived from the common process must be considered in setting selling prices. Joint costs are useful only for inventory costing of unsold units. Answer (B) is incorrect because items such as additional processing costs, competitive conditions in sales markets, and the relative contribution margins of all products derived from the common process must be considered in determining whether to continue producing an item. Answer (C) is incorrect because management of one department may have no control over joint costs.

**42.** Which of the following components of production are allocable as joint costs when a single manufacturing process produces several salable products?

- A. Direct materials, direct labor, and overhead.
- B. Direct materials and direct labor only.
- C. Direct labor and overhead only.
- D. Overhead and direct materials only.

The correct answer is (A). *(CPA, adapted)*
**REQUIRED:** The components allocable as joint costs.
**DISCUSSION:** Joint costs are those costs incurred prior to the split-off point to produce two or more goods manufactured simultaneously by a single process or series of processes. Joint costs, which include direct materials, direct labor, and overhead, are not separately identifiable and must be allocated to the individual joint products.
Answer (B) is incorrect because joint costs also include overhead. Answer (C) is incorrect because joint costs also include direct materials. Answer (D) is incorrect because joint costs also include direct labor.

**43.** A joint process is a manufacturing operation yielding two or more identifiable products from the resources employed in the process. The two characteristics that identify a product generated from this type of process as a joint product are that it

    A.  Is identifiable as an individual product only upon reaching the split-off point, and it has relatively minor sales value when compared with the other products.

    B.  Is identifiable as an individual product before the production process, and it has relatively significant physical volume when compared with the other products.

    C.  Is identifiable as an individual product only upon reaching the split-off point, and it has relatively significant sales value when compared with the other products.

    D.  Has relatively significant physical volume when compared with the other products, and it can be sold immediately without any additional processing.

The correct answer is (C). *(CIA, adapted)*
    **REQUIRED:** The two characteristics of a joint product.
    **DISCUSSION:** Joint products are two or more separate products generated by a common process from a common input that are not separable prior to the split-off point. Moreover, in contrast with by-products, they have significant sales values in relation to each other either before or after additional processing.
    Answer (A) is incorrect because a by-product is identifiable as an individual product only upon reaching the split-off point, and it has relatively minor sales value compared with the other products. Answer (B) is incorrect because products that are separately identifiable before the production process are not joint products. Furthermore, physical volume has nothing to do with determining a joint product. Some joint products with significant physical volume may not have significant sales value. Answer (D) is incorrect because products do not have to be salable at the split-off point to be considered joint products; in fact, many joint products have to be processed after the split-off point before they can be sold.

**44.** A chemical company processes a single raw material. Three products are obtained at the end of the process. Each batch of 100 gallons of raw material is processed into 45 gallons of product X, 30 gallons of product Y, and 25 gallons of product Z. Product X can be sold at split-off for $10 per gallon, product Y for $20 per gallon, and product Z for $1 per gallon. Based upon this information, which of the following statements is true?

    A.  Products X and Y should be treated as joint products.

    B.  Products X and Z should be treated as joint products.

    C.  Products Y and Z should be treated as joint products.

    D.  Products X, Y, and Z should be treated as joint products.

The correct answer is (A). *(CIA, adapted)*
    **REQUIRED:** The true statement about the treatment of products generated from one process.
    **DISCUSSION:** The difference between joint products and by-products lies in their relative sales values. Joint products (X, Y) have relative sales values that are significant in relation to each other. A by-product (Z) has minor sales value compared with the major product(s).
    Answer (B) is incorrect because product Z has a comparatively minor sales value and should be regarded as a by-product. Answer (C) is incorrect because X is a joint product and Z is a by-product. Answer (D) is incorrect because Z is a by-product.

**45.** Which of the following is not a method to allocate joint costs?

    A.  Estimated net realizable value.

    B.  Physical units.

    C.  Relative profitability.

    D.  Sales value at split-off.

The correct answer is (C). *(Publisher)*
    **REQUIRED:** The method not used to allocate joint costs.
    **DISCUSSION:** There are several methods of allocating joint production costs, including the quantitative (physical-unit) method, based on some physical measure such as volume, weight, or a linear measure; the relative sales-value method, based on the sales values at split-off or estimated NRV; the weighted-average method, based on a predetermined standard or index of production; and the constant gross margin NRV method. Relative profitability cannot be used to allocate joint costs because the method of joint cost allocation determines profitability.
    Answers (A) and (D) are incorrect because relative sales value is used to allocate joint costs. Answer (B) is incorrect because relative weight, volume, or linear measure is used to allocate joint costs.

**46.** The principal disadvantage of using the physical quantity method of allocating joint costs is that

    A.  Costs assigned to inventories may have no relationship to value.

    B.  Physical quantities may be difficult to measure.

    C.  Additional processing costs affect the allocation base.

    D.  Joint costs, by definition, should not be separated on a unit basis.

The correct answer is (A). *(CMA, adapted)*

**REQUIRED:** The principal disadvantage of using the physical quantity method of allocating joint costs.

**DISCUSSION:** Joint costs are most often assigned on the basis of relative sales values. Basing allocations on physical quantities, such as pounds, gallons, etc., is usually not desirable because the costs assigned may have no relationship to value. When large items have low selling prices and small items have high selling prices, the large items might always sell at a loss when physical quantities are used to allocate joint costs.

Answer (B) is incorrect because physical quantities are usually easy to measure. Answer (C) is incorrect because additional processing costs have no more effect on the allocation of joint costs based on physical quantities than any other base. Answer (D) is incorrect because the purpose of allocating joint costs, under any method, is to separate such costs on a unit basis.

**47.** Which of the following is(are) often subject to further processing in order to be salable?

| | By-Products | Scrap |
| --- | --- | --- |
| A. | No | No |
| B. | No | Yes |
| C. | Yes | Yes |
| D. | Yes | No |

The correct answer is (D). *(CPA, adapted)*

**REQUIRED:** The item(s) often requiring further processing to be salable.

**DISCUSSION:** Scrap and by-products are often similar, both physically and from an accounting point of view. Scrap might even be considered a by-product of a manufacturing process. However, by-products usually have a greater sales value than scrap. Also, scrap rarely receives any additional processing.

Answers (A), (B), and (C) are incorrect because by-products usually have a greater sales value than scrap and may be further processed; scrap rarely receives any additional processing.

**48.** Lankip Company produces two main products and a by-product out of a joint process. The ratio of output quantities to input quantities of direct material used in the joint process remains consistent from month to month. Lankip has employed the physical-volume method to allocate joint production costs to the two main products. The net realizable value of the by-product is used to reduce the joint production costs before the joint costs are allocated to the main products. Data regarding Lankip's operations for the current month are presented in the chart below. During the month, Lankip incurred joint production costs of $2,520,000. The main products are not marketable at the split-off point and, thus, have to be processed further.

| | First Main Product | Second Main Product | By-Product |
|---|---|---|---|
| Monthly output in pounds | 90,000 | 150,000 | 60,000 |
| Selling price per pound | $30 | $14 | $2 |
| Separable process costs | $540,000 | $660,000 | |

The amount of joint production cost that Lankip would allocate to the second main product by using the physical-volume method to allocate joint production costs would be

A. $1,200,000

B. $1,260,000

C. $1,500,000

D. $1,575,000

The correct answer is (C). *(CMA, adapted)*

**REQUIRED:** The joint cost allocated to the second main product based on physical volume.

**DISCUSSION:** The joint cost to be allocated is $2,400,000 [$2,520,000 total joint cost – ($2 x 60,000 pounds of the by-product)]. Accordingly, the joint cost to be allocated to the second main product on a physical-volume basis is $1,500,000 {$2,400,000 x [150,000 pounds ÷ (90,000 pounds + 150,000 pounds)]}.

Answer (A) is incorrect because $1,200,000 assumes that the by-product is charged with a portion of the net joint cost. Answer (B) is incorrect because $1,260,000 assumes that the by-product is charged with a portion of the gross joint cost. Answer (D) is incorrect because $1,575,000 does not deduct by-product NRV from the joint cost.

## 6.4 Relative Sales Value

**49.** For purposes of allocating joint costs to joint products, the sales price at point of sale, reduced by cost to complete after split-off, is assumed to be equal to the

A. Total costs.

B. Joint costs.

C. Sales price minus a normal profit margin at point of sale.

D. Relative sales value at split-off.

The correct answer is (D). *(CPA, adapted)*

**REQUIRED:** The assumption about the sales price at point of sale, reduced by cost to complete after split-off.

**DISCUSSION:** The relative sales-value method is the most frequently used method to allocate joint costs to joint products. It allocates joint costs based upon the products' proportion of total sales revenue. For joint products salable at the split-off point, the relative sales value is the selling price at split-off. However, if further processing is needed, the relative sales value is approximated by subtracting the additional anticipated processing costs from the final sales value to arrive at the estimated net realizable value.

Answer (A) is incorrect because total costs include the cost to complete after split-off. Answer (B) is incorrect because joint costs are computed up to the split-off point. Answer (C) is incorrect because the normal profit margin does not necessarily equal the cost to complete after split-off.

**50.** For purposes of allocating joint costs to joint products, the relative sales-value method could be used in which of the following situations?

|   | No Costs Beyond Split-off | Costs Beyond Split-off |
|---|---|---|
| A. | Yes | Yes |
| B. | Yes | No |
| C. | No | Yes |
| D. | No | No |

The correct answer is (A). *(CPA, adapted)*
   **REQUIRED:** The situation(s) in which the relative sales-value method could be used to allocate joint costs.
   **DISCUSSION:** The relative sales-value method is used to allocate joint costs to the separate products at the split-off point. Joint costs are allocated based upon each product's proportion of total sales revenue. For joint products salable at the split-off point, the relative sales value is the selling price at split-off. If further processing is needed, the relative sales value is approximated by subtracting additional processing costs from the final sales value.
   Answers (B), (C), and (D) are incorrect because the relative sales-value method can be used for both joint products salable at the split-off point and those requiring further processing.

**51.** The method of accounting for joint product costs that will produce the same gross profit rate for all products is the

A. Relative sales-value method.

B. Physical-measure method.

C. Actual costing method.

D. Services-received method.

The correct answer is (A). *(CPA, adapted)*
   **REQUIRED:** The method resulting in the same gross profit rate for all joint products.
   **DISCUSSION:** The relative sales-value method produces the same gross profit as a percentage of sales value at split-off (or estimated NRV at split-off) for each product. The reason is that it allocates joint costs in proportion to sales values.
   Answer (B) is incorrect because physical measure may not be related to the fair value of separate products. Answer (C) is incorrect because the actual cost of each product cannot be determined. Answer (D) is incorrect because services received has no meaning in joint product costing.

**52.** Actual sales values at the split-off point for joint products Y and Z are not known. For purposes of allocating joint costs to products Y and Z, the relative sales-value method is used. Costs beyond split-off increase for product Z, while those of product Y remain constant. If the selling prices of finished products Y and Z remain constant, the percentage of the total joint costs allocated to product Y and product Z will

A. Decrease for product Y and product Z.

B. Decrease for product Y and increase for product Z.

C. Increase for product Y and product Z.

D. Increase for product Y and decrease for product Z.

The correct answer is (D). *(CPA, adapted)*
   **REQUIRED:** The effect on the allocation of joint costs, given an increase in separable costs for one product.
   **DISCUSSION:** The actual sales values of Y and Z at split-off may be approximated by calculating their estimated NRVs (final sales values – separable costs). Assuming constant selling prices and increased costs for Z, the NRV at split-off for Z must necessarily decrease. The relative sales-value method allocates joint costs in accordance with the ratio of each joint product's estimated NRV at split-off to the total for all joint products. Thus, the costs allocated to Z decrease, and the costs allocated to Y increase.
   Answers (A), (B), and (C) are incorrect because the costs allocated to Z will decrease and the costs allocated to Y will increase.

**53.** The diagram below represents the production and sales relationships of joint products P and Q. Joint costs are incurred until split-off; then separable costs are incurred in refining each product. Fair values of P and Q at split-off are used to allocate joint costs.

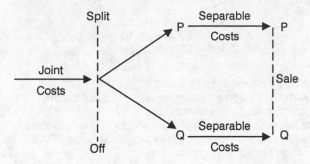

If the fair value of P at split-off increases and all other costs and selling prices remain unchanged, the gross margin of

| | P | Q |
|---|---|---|
| A. | Increases | Decreases |
| B. | Increases | Increases |
| C. | Decreases | Decreases |
| D. | Decreases | Increases |

The correct answer is (D). *(CPA, adapted)*
   **REQUIRED:** The effects on the gross margins of joint products if the fair value of one product at split-off increases while other costs and prices are constant.
   **DISCUSSION:** The allocation of joint costs to P and Q is in accordance with their relative sales values at split-off. If P's fair value at split-off increases, its allocation of joint costs will increase and Q's will decrease. Given that other costs and final selling prices are constant, P's gross margin (final sales revenue – cost of goods sold, which includes the allocation of joint costs) decreases and Q's increases.
   Answers (A), (B), and (C) are incorrect because P's gross margin decreases and Q's increases.

**54.** Lowe Co. manufactures products A and B from a joint process. Sales value at split-off was $700,000 for 10,000 units of A and $300,000 for 15,000 units of B. Using the sales value at split-off approach, joint costs properly allocated to A were $140,000. Total joint costs were

A. $98,000

B. $200,000

C. $233,333

D. $350,000

The correct answer is (B). *(CPA, adapted)*
   **REQUIRED:** The total joint costs given the joint costs properly allocated to one product.
   **DISCUSSION:** The relative sales value is a cost allocation method that allocates joint costs in proportion to the relative sales value of the individual products. Total sales value is $1,000,000 ($700,000 for A + $300,000 for B). The $140,000 of joint costs allocated to product A was 70% ($700,000 ÷ $1,000,000) of total joint costs. The calculation for total joint costs (Y) is

$$.7Y = \$140,000$$
$$Y = \$140,000 \div .7$$
$$Y = \$200,000$$

   Answer (A) is incorrect because $98,000 is 70% of the $140,000 joint cost allocated to A. To arrive at total joint costs, $140,000 needs to be divided by 70%. Answer (C) is incorrect because total joint costs are determined by dividing the joint costs allocated to A by A's percentage of sales value at split-off. Answer (D) is incorrect because total joint costs are based on sales value, not units produced.

**55.** A company processes a raw material into products F1, F2, and F3. Each ton of raw material produces five units of F1, two units of F2, and three units of F3. Joint processing costs to the split-off point are $15 per ton. Further processing results in the following per-unit figures:

|                                    | F1   | F2   | F3   |
| ---------------------------------- | ---- | ---- | ---- |
| Additional processing costs per unit | $28 | $30 | $25 |
| Selling price per unit             | 30   | 35   | 35   |

If joint costs are allocated based on the net realizable value of finished product, what proportion of joint costs should be allocated to F1?

A.  20%

B.  30%

C.  33⅓%

D.  50%

The correct answer is (A). *(CIA, adapted)*
**REQUIRED:** The proportion of joint costs that should be allocated to product F1.
**DISCUSSION:** To determine the proportion of joint costs to be allocated to F1, the NRVs of the three products must be calculated. NRV per unit is selling price minus additional processing costs.

$$
\begin{aligned}
\text{F1: } 5(\$30 - \$28) &= \ \ \$10 \\
\text{F2: } 2(\$35 - \$30) &= \ \ \ \ 10 \\
\text{F3: } 3(\$35 - \$25) &= \ \ \underline{\ \ 30} \\
&\ \ \ \ \ \$50
\end{aligned}
$$

The joint costs allocated to F1 equal 20% ($10 ÷ $50).

Answer (B) is incorrect because 30% is based on the proportion of selling price attributable to F1. Answer (C) is incorrect because joint costs are not divided equally among the three products. Answer (D) is incorrect because 50% is the allocation based on physical units.

**56.** A company manufactures products X and Y using a joint process. The joint processing costs are $10,000. Products X and Y can be sold at split-off for $12,000 and $8,000, respectively. After split-off, product X is processed further at a cost of $5,000 and sold for $21,000, whereas product Y is sold without further processing. If the company uses the net-realizable-value method for allocating joint costs, the joint cost allocated to X is

A.  $4,000

B.  $5,000

C.  $6,000

D.  $6,667

The correct answer is (C). *(CIA, adapted)*
**REQUIRED:** The joint costs allocated to product X.
**DISCUSSION:** Under the NRV method, joint costs are allocated based on relative NRVs unless sales prices are known at split-off. Such prices are available, so the amount of joint costs allocated to X is calculated as $6,000 {$10,000 joint costs x [$12,000 ÷ ($12,000 + $8,000)]}.

Answer (A) is incorrect because $4,000 is the joint cost allocated to Y. Answer (B) is incorrect because $5,000 is the cost to further process X. Answer (D) is incorrect because $6,667 is based on the NRV of X.

**57.** A cheese company produces natural cheese from cow's milk. As a result of the process, a secondary product, whey, is produced in the proportion of one pound for each pound of cheese. The following are the standards for 1,000 pounds of milk:

Input: 1,000 pounds of milk at $.20/pound
40 hours of labor at $10/hour
Overhead applied equaling 100% of direct labor cost

Output: 450 pounds of cheese
450 pounds of whey

The following prices and demand are expected:

| | Price per Pound | Demand in Pounds |
|---|---|---|
| Cheese | $2.00 | 450 |
| Whey | .80 | 375 |

Given that the company allocates common costs on the basis of NRVs, the allocated common costs per 1,000 pounds of milk (rounded) are

| | Cheese | Whey |
|---|---|---|
| A. | $450 | $150 |
| B. | $500 | $500 |
| C. | $714 | $286 |
| D. | $750 | $250 |

The correct answer is (D). *(CIA, adapted)*
**REQUIRED:** The common cost allocation.
**DISCUSSION:** The relative sales-value method allocates costs in proportion to the relative sales value of the individual products. The total common costs are

| | |
|---|---|
| Milk (1,000 lb. × $.20) | $ 200 |
| Labor (40 hr. × $10) | 400 |
| O/H (1.0 × $400 DL cost) | 400 |
| Common costs | $1,000 |

| Sales Value: | | |
|---|---|---|
| Cheese ($2 × 450) | $ 900 | 75% |
| Whey ($.80 × 375) | 300 | 25% |
| Total | $1,200 | |

| | |
|---|---|
| Cost to cheese (75% × 1,000) | $ 750 |
| Cost to whey (25% × 1,000) | 250 |
| | $1,000 |

If only 375 pounds of whey can be sold, the other 75 pounds is worthless and is not allocated any common cost.

Answer (A) is incorrect because allocations of $450 to cheese and $150 to whey result from omitting overhead from total common costs. Answer (B) is incorrect because an allocation of $500 to both cheese and whey is based on output in pounds. Answer (C) is incorrect because allocations of $714 to cheese and $286 to whey are based on relative unit sales prices.

**58.** Andy Company manufactures products N, P, and R from a joint process. The following information is available:

| | N | P | R | Total |
|---|---|---|---|---|
| Units produced | 12,000 | ? | ? | 24,000 |
| Joint costs | $ 48,000 | ? | ? | $120,000 |
| Sales value at split-off | ? | ? | $50,000 | $200,000 |
| Additional costs if processed further | $ 18,000 | $14,000 | $10,000 | $ 42,000 |
| Sales value if processed further | $110,000 | $90,000 | $60,000 | $260,000 |

Assuming that joint product costs are allocated using the relative sales value at split-off approach, what was the sales value at split-off for products N and P?

| | Product N | Product P |
|---|---|---|
| A. | $66,000 | $56,000 |
| B. | $80,000 | $70,000 |
| C. | $98,000 | $84,000 |
| D. | $150,000 | $50,000 |

The correct answer is (B). *(CPA, adapted)*
**REQUIRED:** The relative sales value at split-off of two joint products.
**DISCUSSION:** The relative sales-value method allocates joint costs in proportion to the relative sales value of the individual products.

| | Sales Value | Weighting Factor | Joint Cost Allocated |
|---|---|---|---|
| N | X | (X ÷ 200) × $120,000 | $ 48,000 |
| P | Y | | ? |
| R | $ 50,000 | (50 ÷ 200) × $120,000 | ? |
| | $200,000 | | $120,000 |

X is calculated below from the information given. If 40% of the cost is allocated to product N, the sales value of N must be 40% of the total sales value. Y is equal to the difference between total sales value at split-off ($200,000) and the sales value for products N and P ($80,000 + $50,000), or $70,000.

$$(X \div \$200,000) \times \$120,000 = \$48,000$$
$$X \div \$200,000 = .4$$
$$X = \$80,000$$

Answer (A) is incorrect because $66,000 and $56,000 are the total costs of N and P, respectively. Answer (C) is incorrect because the total sales value at split-off of N and P must be $150,000. Answer (D) is incorrect because $150,000 is the total sales value at split-off of N and P, and $50,000 is the sales value of R at split-off.

**59.** Ashwood Company manufactures three main products, F, G, and W, from a joint process. Joint costs are allocated on the basis of relative sales value at split-off. Additional information for June production activity follows:

|  | F | G | W | Total |
|---|---|---|---|---|
| Units produced | 50,000 | 40,000 | 10,000 | 100,000 |
| Joint costs | ? | ? | ? | $450,000 |
| Sales value at split-off | $420,000 | $270,000 | $60,000 | $750,000 |
| Additional costs if processed further | $ 88,000 | $ 30,000 | $12,000 | $130,000 |
| Sales value if processed further | $538,000 | $320,000 | $78,000 | $936,000 |

Assuming that the 10,000 units of W were processed further and sold for $78,000, what was Ashwood's gross profit on this sale?

A. $21,000

B. $28,500

C. $30,000

D. $36,000

The correct answer is (C). *(CPA, adapted)*

**REQUIRED:** The gross profit on the sale of a joint product that is processed beyond split-off.

**DISCUSSION:** The relative sales-value method allocates joint costs in proportion to the relative sales value of the individual products. Because the split-off sales value of $60,000 is known, this value should be used to determine the joint cost allocation to the products. The total sales value at split-off is $750,000.

|  | Sales Value | Weighting Factor | Joint Cost Allocated |
|---|---|---|---|
| W | $60,000 | (60 ÷ 750) × $450,000 | $36,000 |

The joint cost allocated at split-off is thus $36,000. The units are processed further at a cost of $12,000 and sold for $78,000. The gross profit is thus $30,000 ($78,000 – $36,000 – $12,000).

Answer (A) is incorrect because $21,000 uses units produced (10,000 units of W ÷ 100,000 total units) as a weighting factor. Answer (B) is incorrect because $28,500 uses sales value if processed further ($78,000 W ÷ $936,000 total) as a weighting factor. Answer (D) is incorrect because $36,000 is the joint cost allocated to W.

**60.** Warfield Corporation manufactures products C, D, and E from a joint process. Joint costs are allocated on the basis of relative sales value at split-off. Additional information is presented below.

|  | C | D | E | Total |
|---|---|---|---|---|
| Units produced | 6,000 | 4,000 | 2,000 | 12,000 |
| Joint costs | $ 72,000 | ? | ? | $120,000 |
| Sales value at split-off | ? | ? | $30,000 | $200,000 |
| Additional costs if processed further | $ 14,000 | $10,000 | $ 6,000 | $ 30,000 |
| Sales value if processed further | $140,000 | $60,000 | $40,000 | $240,000 |

How much of the joint costs should Warfield allocate to product D?

A. $24,000

B. $28,800

C. $30,000

D. $32,000

The correct answer is (C). *(CPA, adapted)*

**REQUIRED:** The joint costs allocated to product D.

**DISCUSSION:** Given that total joint costs are $120,000 and total sales value at split-off is $200,000, the ratio of joint costs to sales value is 60% ($120,000 ÷ $200,000). The joint costs of product C are $72,000. Thus, C's sales value at split-off is $120,000 ($72,000 ÷ 60%). If product C's sales value is $120,000, D's sales value is $50,000 ($200,000 – $30,000 E – $120,000 C). Accordingly, the joint costs of product D are $30,000, which is 60% of D's $50,000 sales value at split-off.

Answer (A) is incorrect because the $48,000 of joint costs to be allocated to products D and E should be allocated based on relative sales values at split-off, not allocated equally between products D and E. Answer (B) is incorrect because the joint cost allocation is based on sales value at split-off, not on sales value if processed further. Furthermore, the allocation is based on total sales values of products C, D, and E, not just products D and E. Answer (D) is incorrect because the $48,000 of joint costs to be allocated to products D and E should be allocated based on relative sales values at split-off, not on units produced. Furthermore, the allocation is based on total sales values of products C, D, and E, not just products D and E.

Questions 61 and 62 are based on the following information. Petro-Chem Inc. is a small company that acquires high-grade crude oil from low-volume production wells owned by individuals and small partnerships. The crude oil is processed in a single refinery into Two Oil, Six Oil, and impure distillates. Petro-Chem does not have the technology or capacity to process these products further and sells most of its output each month to major refineries. There were no beginning inventories of finished goods or work-in-process on November 1. The production costs and output of Petro-Chem for November are in the right column.

| | |
|---|---:|
| Crude oil acquired and placed in production | $5,000,000 |
| Direct labor and related costs | 2,000,000 |
| Factory overhead | 3,000,000 |

Production and sales

• Two Oil, 300,000 barrels produced; 80,000 barrels sold at $20 each.

• Six Oil, 240,000 barrels produced; 120,000 barrels sold at $30 each.

• Distillates, 120,000 barrels produced and sold at $15 per barrel.

**61.** The portion of the joint production costs assigned to Six Oil based upon physical output would be

A. $3,636,000

B. $3,750,000

C. $1,818,000

D. $4,800,000

The correct answer is (A). *(CMA, adapted)*

**REQUIRED:** The joint production costs assigned to Six Oil based on physical output.

**DISCUSSION:** The total production costs incurred are $10 million, consisting of crude oil of $5 million, direct labor of $2 million, and factory overhead of $3 million. The total physical output was 660,000 barrels, consisting of 300,000 barrels of Two Oil, 240,000 barrels of Six Oil, and 120,000 barrels of distillates. Thus, the allocation (rounded) is $3,636,000 [(240,000 ÷ 660,000) x $10,000,000].

Answer (B) is incorrect because $3,750,000 is based on the physical quantity of units sold, not units produced. Answer (C) is incorrect because $1,818,000 is the amount that would be assigned to distillates. Answer (D) is incorrect because $4,800,000 is the amount assigned if the relative sales-value method is used.

**62.** The portion of the joint production costs assigned to Two Oil based upon the relative sales value of output would be

A. $4,800,000

B. $4,000,000

C. $2,286,000

D. $2,500,000

The correct answer is (B). *(CMA, adapted)*

**REQUIRED:** The joint production costs assigned to Two Oil based on relative sales value.

**DISCUSSION:** The total production costs incurred are $10 million, consisting of crude oil of $5 million, direct labor of $2 million, and factory overhead of $3 million. The total value of the output is as follows:

| | |
|---|---:|
| Two Oil (300,000 × $20) | $ 6,000,000 |
| Six Oil (240,000 × $30) | 7,200,000 |
| Distillates (120,000 × $15) | 1,800,000 |
| Total sales value | $15,000,000 |

Because Two Oil composes 40% of the total sales value ($6,000,000 ÷ $15,000,000), it will be assigned 40% of the $10,000,000 of joint costs, or $4,000,000.

Answer (A) is incorrect because $4,800,000 is the amount that would be assigned to Six Oil. Answer (C) is incorrect because $2,286,000 is based on the relative sales value of units sold. Answer (D) is incorrect because $2,500,000 is based on the physical quantity of barrels sold.

## 6.5 By-Products

**63.** In accounting for by-products, their value may be recognized at the time of

| | Production | Sale |
|---|---|---|
| A. | Yes | Yes |
| B. | Yes | No |
| C. | No | No |
| D. | No | Yes |

The correct answer is (A). *(CPA, adapted)*
**REQUIRED:** The timing of recognition of by-products.
**DISCUSSION:** Practice with regard to recognizing by-products in the accounts is not uniform. The most cost-effective method for the initial recognition of by-products is to account for their value at the time of sale as a reduction in the joint cost or as a revenue. The alternative is to recognize the net realizable value at the time of production, a method that results in the recording of by-product inventory.
Answers (B), (C), and (D) are incorrect because by-products may be initially recognized at the time of sale or at the time of production.

**64.** In contrast with joint products, by-products

A. Have relatively significant sales value.
B. Are separately identifiable prior to the split-off point.
C. Have relatively minor sales value.
D. Require processing beyond the split-off point.

The correct answer is (C). *(CIA, adapted)*
**REQUIRED:** The definition of by-products.
**DISCUSSION:** When two or more separate products are produced by a common manufacturing process from a common input, the outputs are joint products. The common costs of joint products with significant values are usually allocated to the joint products based upon their relative sales values at split-off. By-products are joint products that have minor sales values compared with the sales values of the major product(s).
Answer (A) is incorrect because a relatively significant sales value is characteristic of a joint product. Answer (B) is incorrect because by-products are not separately identifiable prior to the split-off point. Answer (D) is incorrect because by-products do not necessarily require further processing.

**65.** By-products may have which of the following characteristics?

| | Zero Costs Beyond Split-off | Additional Costs Beyond Split-off |
|---|---|---|
| A. | No | No |
| B. | No | Yes |
| C. | Yes | Yes |
| D. | Yes | No |

The correct answer is (C). *(CPA, adapted)*
**REQUIRED:** The characteristic(s) of by-products.
**DISCUSSION:** By-products are joint products that have minor sales values compared with the sales values of the main product(s). To be salable, by-products may or may not require additional processing beyond the split-off point. Thus, the incurrence of separable costs beyond the split-off point may or may not be required.
Answers (A), (B), and (D) are incorrect because by-products may or may not require additional processing beyond the split-off point.

**66.** For the purposes of cost accumulation, which of the following are identifiable as different individual products before the split-off point?

| | By-Products | Joint Products |
|---|---|---|
| A. | Yes | Yes |
| B. | Yes | No |
| C. | No | No |
| D. | No | Yes |

The correct answer is (C). *(CPA, adapted)*
**REQUIRED:** The product(s), if any, identifiable before the split-off point for purposes of cost allocation.
**DISCUSSION:** In a joint production process, neither by-products nor joint products are separately identifiable as individual products until the split-off point. This is the definition of the split-off point. Joint costs up to the split-off point are usually related to both joint products and by-products. After split-off, additional (separable) costs can be traced, and charged to, the individual products.
Answers (A), (B), and (D) are incorrect because neither by-products nor joint products are separately identifiable until split-off.

**67.** Under an acceptable method of costing by-products, inventory costs of the by-product are based on the portion of the joint production cost allocated to the by-product

    A. But any subsequent processing cost is debited to the cost of the main product.

    B. But any subsequent processing cost is debited to revenue of the main product.

    C. Plus any subsequent processing cost.

    D. Minus any subsequent processing cost.

The correct answer is (C). *(CPA, adapted)*
    **REQUIRED:** The true statement about inventory costs of by-products.
    **DISCUSSION:** By-product is a term used to denote one or more products of relatively small total value that are produced simultaneously with a product of greater value and quantity, normally called the main product. One method of accounting for by-products is to recognize their value in inventory as they are produced. These inventory costs of the by-products may be based on an allocation of some portion of joint costs plus any subsequent processing costs.
    Answers (A) and (B) are incorrect because subsequent processing costs must be assigned to by-products. Answer (D) is incorrect because subsequent processing costs are added to the inventory costs of the by-product.

**68.** In the preceding question, why was joint cost allocated to by-products?

    A. They were treated as joint products even though they presumably met the definition of by-products because of their small relative sales values.

    B. All by-products must be allocated some portion of joint costs.

    C. Such allocation is required by the Cost Accounting Standards Board (CASB).

    D. The by-products produced a loss.

The correct answer is (A). *(Publisher)*
    **REQUIRED:** The explanation of the allocation of joint cost to by-products.
    **DISCUSSION:** The usual treatment of by-products is to account for their revenues or net realizable values as a reduction in cost or as a revenue item without allocation of joint costs. However, joint cost may be allocated to by-products as well as to joint products. In that case, they are treated as joint products even though their relative values are small.
    Answer (B) is incorrect because allocation of joint cost to by-products is not required by GAAP. Answer (C) is incorrect because allocation of joint cost to by-products is not required by the CASB. Answer (D) is incorrect because no information is given indicating that the by-products' subsequent processing resulted in a loss.

**69.** The main issues concerning recognition of by-products in the accounts are similar to those for

    A. Joint products.

    B. Scrap.

    C. Product costs.

    D. Main products.

The correct answer is (B). *(Publisher)*
    **REQUIRED:** The item that involves issues similar to those dealing with by-products.
    **DISCUSSION:** Scrap and by-products are usually similar, both physically and for accounting purposes. Scrap might even be considered a by-product of a manufacturing process. Whereas joint cost is almost never allocated to scrap, joint cost may be allocated to by-products. The main issue, however, is whether to recognize scrap or by-products in the accounts at the time of production or at the time of sale. Another issue is whether to treat the recognized values as contra costs or as revenues.
    Answers (A) and (D) are incorrect because the timing of recognition is usually not an issue concerning joint (main) products. Answer (C) is incorrect because product costs are by definition inventoriable. The value of by-products may or may not be inventoried.

**70.** Mig Co., which began operations in 1998, produces gasoline and a gasoline by-product. The following information is available pertaining to 1998 sales and production:

| | |
|---|---|
| Total production costs to split-off point | $120,000 |
| Gasoline sales | 270,000 |
| By-product sales | 30,000 |
| Gasoline inventory, 12/31/98 | 15,000 |
| Additional by-product costs: | |
| Marketing | $10,000 |
| Production | 15,000 |

Mig accounts for the by-product at the time of production. What is Mig's 1998 cost of sales for gasoline and the by-product?

| | Gasoline | By-Product |
|---|---|---|
| A. | $105,000 | $25,000 |
| B. | $115,000 | $0 |
| C. | $108,000 | $37,000 |
| D. | $100,000 | $0 |

The correct answer is (D). *(CPA, adapted)*
**REQUIRED:** The cost of sales for both the gasoline and the by-product.
**DISCUSSION:** If the by-product is accounted for at the time of production, by-product inventory is recorded at its selling price (or NRV in this case, given separable by-product costs) because by-products usually do not receive an allocation of joint costs. Thus, the by-product's cost of sales is zero. Assuming sales of the by-product reduced joint costs included in the main product's cost of sales, the cost of sales of the gasoline was $100,000 ($120,000 cost to split-off – $30,000 sales of the by-product + $25,000 additional by-product costs – $15,000 EI).
Answer (A) is incorrect because the cost of sales of the by-product is $0. The cost of sales of the gasoline equals $105,000 if the NRV of the by-product is treated as other revenue. Answer (B) is incorrect because $115,000 ignores the $15,000 ending inventory. Answer (C) is incorrect because allocating joint costs to by-products based on relative sales value is not cost effective, and by-product cost of sales should be $0.

---

Questions 71 through 76 are based on the following information. Earl Corporation manufactures a product that gives rise to a by-product called Zafa. The only costs associated with Zafa are selling costs of $1 for each unit sold. Earl accounts for Zafa sales first by deducting its separable costs from such sales and then by deducting this net amount from cost of sales of the major product. This year, 1,000 units of Zafa were sold at $4 each.

---

**71.** If Earl changes its method of accounting for Zafa sales by recording the net amount as additional sales revenue, Earl's gross margin will

A. Be unaffected.

B. Increase by $3,000.

C. Decrease by $3,000.

D. Increase by $4,000.

The correct answer is (A). *(CPA, adapted)*
**REQUIRED:** The effect on gross margin of changing the treatment of by-product sales.
**DISCUSSION:** The gross margin equals sales minus cost of sales. Before the change, the net amount was deducted from cost of sales (i.e., it increased the gross margin). After the change, the net amount is added to regular sales with no additional increase in cost of goods sold. Hence, the gross margin will be the same.
Answers (B), (C), and (D) are incorrect because the change in accounting method has no effect on gross margin.

**72.** If Earl changes its method of accounting for Zafa sales by recording the net amount as other income, Earl's gross margin will

A. Be unaffected.

B. Increase by $3,000.

C. Decrease by $3,000.

D. Decrease by $4,000.

The correct answer is (C). *(CPA, adapted)*
**REQUIRED:** The effect on gross margin of accounting for by-product sales as other income.
**DISCUSSION:** Sales revenue minus cost of goods sold is gross margin. If the net revenue from the by-product is recorded as other income rather than being deducted from cost of goods sold, the gross margin will decrease by $3,000 [1,000 x ($4 sales – $1 CGS)].
Answer (A) is incorrect because gross margin will be affected. Answer (B) is incorrect because the gross margin will decrease by $3,000. Answer (D) is incorrect because $4,000 is the gross amount of Zafa sales.

**73.** If Earl records the net realizable value of Zafa as inventory as it is produced, what will the per-unit value be?

A. $1

B. $2

C. $3

D. $4

The correct answer is (C). *(Publisher)*
    **REQUIRED:** The unit net realizable value.
    **DISCUSSION:** The NRV is selling price minus cost to complete and cost to dispose. The selling price of Zafa is $4, and the selling costs are $1. Given no completion or additional processing costs, unit net realizable value is $3.
    Answer (A) is incorrect because $1 is the selling cost. Answer (B) is incorrect because the unit net realizable value is $3. Answer (D) is incorrect because $4 is the selling price of Zafa.

**74.** Earl sold 1,000 units of Zafa. Assuming that 1,500 units were produced for the year and that net realizable value is recorded as inventory, Earl's net income will increase by

A. $6,000

B. $4,500

C. $3,000

D. $1,500

The correct answer is (B). *(Publisher)*
    **REQUIRED:** The change in net income if 1,500 units are produced and inventory is valued at net realizable value.
    **DISCUSSION:** If the 1,500 units of the by-product are recognized at the time of production, net income must increase by $4,500 ($3 unit NRV x 1,500). Ending inventory of Zafa reduces cost of sales, and by-product revenue either decreases costs or increases other income.
    Answer (A) is incorrect because $6,000 is the potential gross revenue from Zafa. Answer (C) is incorrect because $3,000 is the net revenue from sales of 1,000 units. Answer (D) is incorrect because $1,500 equals 1,500 units times the $1 unit selling cost.

**75.** If Earl records Zafa inventory at net realizable value as it is produced this year, what will be the profit recognized next year on a sale of 500 units?

A. $0

B. $500

C. $1,000

D. $1,500

The correct answer is (A). *(Publisher)*
    **REQUIRED:** The profit from the sale of inventory valued at net realizable value.
    **DISCUSSION:** Because net realizable value is selling price minus completion and disposal cost, there is no profit upon sale. The sale of 500 units of Zafa with an inventory value of $3 per unit will produce no profit ($4 unit selling price – $3 inventory cost – $1 selling cost = $0).
    Answer (B) is incorrect because $500 equals 500 units times the $1 selling cost. Answer (C) is incorrect because $1,000 is the selling cost of 1,000 units. Answer (D) is incorrect because $1,500 is the $3 inventory cost multiplied by the 500 units sold.

**76.** If the values of by-products are recorded as produced, why should they be recorded at net realizable value minus normal profit?

A. To permit a sales profit to be recognized upon sale.

B. To be valued at the lower of cost or market.

C. To control the loss upon sale.

D. To recognize a profit when the inventory value is recorded.

The correct answer is (A). *(Publisher)*
    **REQUIRED:** The reason by-products should be valued at net realizable value minus normal profit.
    **DISCUSSION:** If inventory is valued at NRV minus normal profit, recognition of normal profit is deferred until sale of the product. This treatment also results in a more conservative valuation of inventory.
    Answer (B) is incorrect because NRV minus normal profit may be greater than cost. Answer (C) is incorrect because valuation at NRV minus normal profit implies that some profit is to be recognized upon sale. Answer (D) is incorrect because, if a cost is credited for the value of the inventory, no profit is recognized when inventory is recorded at NRV minus normal profit.

Questions 77 through 81 are based on the following information. Atlas Foods produces three supplemental food products simultaneously through a refining process costing $93,000.

The joint products, Alfa and Betters, have a final selling price of $4 per pound and $10 per pound, respectively, after additional processing costs of $2 per pound of each product are incurred after the split-off point. Morefeed, a by-product, is sold at the split-off point for $3 per pound.

| | |
|---|---|
| Alfa | 10,000 pounds of Alfa, a popular but relatively rare grain supplement having a caloric value of 4,400 calories per pound. |
| Betters | 5,000 pounds of Betters, a flavoring material high in carbohydrates with a caloric value of 11,200 calories per pound. |
| Morefeed | 1,000 pounds of Morefeed, used as a cattle feed supplement with a caloric value of 1,000 calories per pound. |

**77.** Assuming Atlas Foods inventories Morefeed, the by-product, the joint cost to be allocated to Alfa, using the net-realizable-value method is

A. $3,000

B. $30,000

C. $31,000

D. $60,000

The correct answer is (B). *(CMA, adapted)*

**REQUIRED:** The joint cost allocated to Alfa based on net realizable values if the by-product is inventoried.

**DISCUSSION:** The NRV at split-off for each of the joint products must be determined. Given that Alfa has a $4 selling price and an additional $2 of processing costs, the value at split-off is $2 per pound. The total value at split-off for 10,000 pounds is $20,000. Betters has a $10 selling price and an additional $2 of processing costs. Thus, the value at split-off is $8 per pound. The total value of 5,000 pounds of Betters is therefore $40,000. The 1,000 pounds of Morefeed has a split-off value of $3 per pound, or $3,000. Assuming that Morefeed (a by-product) is inventoried (recognized in the accounts when produced) and treated as a reduction of joint costs, the allocable joint cost is $90,000 ($93,000 – $3,000). (NOTE: Other methods of accounting for by-products are possible.) The total net realizable value of the main products is $60,000 ($20,000 Alfa + $40,000 Betters). The allocation to Alfa is $30,000 [($20,000 ÷ $60,000) x $90,000].

Answer (A) is incorrect because $3,000 is the value of the by-product. Answer (C) is incorrect because $31,000 fails to adjust the joint processing cost for the value of the by-product. Answer (D) is incorrect because $60,000 is the amount allocated to Betters.

**78.** Assuming Atlas Foods inventories Morefeed, the by-product, the joint cost to be allocated to Alfa, using the physical quantity method is

A. $3,000

B. $30,000

C. $31,000

D. $60,000

The correct answer is (D). *(CMA, adapted)*

**REQUIRED:** The joint cost allocated to Alfa based on the physical quantity method if the by-product is inventoried.

**DISCUSSION:** Joint cost is $93,000, and Morefeed has a split-off value of $3,000 (see preceding question). Assuming the latter amount is treated as a reduction in joint cost, the allocable joint cost is $90,000. The total physical quantity (volume) of the two joint products is 15,000 pounds (10,000 Alfa + 5,000 Betters). Hence, $60,000 [(10,000 ÷ 15,000) x $90,000] of the net joint costs should be allocated to Alfa.

Answer (A) is incorrect because $3,000 is the value of the by-product. Answer (B) is incorrect because $30,000 is based on the net-realizable-value method. Answer (C) is incorrect because $31,000 is based on the net-realizable-value method and fails to adjust the joint processing cost for the value of the by-product.

**79.** Assuming Atlas Foods inventories Morefeed, the by-product, the joint cost to be allocated to Betters using the weighted-quantity method based on caloric value per pound is

A. $39,208

B. $39,600

C. $50,400

D. $52,080

The correct answer is (C). *(CMA, adapted)*
   **REQUIRED:** The joint cost allocated to Betters based on the weighted-quantity method.
   **DISCUSSION:** As determined in the preceding two questions, the net allocable joint cost is $90,000. The caloric value of Alfa is 44,000,000 (4,400 x 10,000 pounds), the caloric value of Betters is 56,000,000 (11,200 x 5,000 pounds), and the total is 100,000,000. Of this total volume, Alfa makes up 44% and Betters 56%. Thus, $50,400 (56% x $90,000) should be allocated to Betters.
   Answer (A) is incorrect because $39,208 is the amount allocated to Alfa if the 1,000,000 calories attributable to Morefeed is included in the computation. Answer (B) is incorrect because $39,600 is the allocation to Alfa. Answer (D) is incorrect because $52,080 is the allocation to Betters if the joint cost is not adjusted for the value of the by-product.

**80.** Assuming Atlas Foods inventories Morefeed, the by-product, the joint cost to be allocated to Alfa using the gross market-value method is

A. $36,000

B. $40,000

C. $41,333

D. $50,000

The correct answer is (B). *(CMA, adapted)*
   **REQUIRED:** The joint cost allocated to Alfa using the gross market-value method if the by-product is inventoried.
   **DISCUSSION:** Alfa has a gross sales value of $40,000 ($4 x 10,000 pounds), Betters has a gross sales value of $50,000 ($10 x 5,000 pounds), and Morefeed has a split-off value of $3,000. If the value of Morefeed is inventoried and treated as a reduction in joint cost, the allocable joint cost is $90,000 ($93,000 – $3,000). The total gross sales value of the two main products is $90,000 ($40,000 + $50,000). Of this total value, $40,000 should be allocated to Alfa [($40,000 ÷ $90,000) x $90,000].
   Answer (A) is incorrect because $36,000 is based on 40%, not 4/9. Answer (C) is incorrect because $41,333 fails to adjust the joint cost by the value of the by-product. Answer (D) is incorrect because $50,000 is the joint cost allocated to Betters.

**81.** Assuming Atlas Foods does not adjust the joint cost for the value of Morefeed, the by-product, the joint cost to be allocated to Betters using the net-realizable-value method is

A. $30,000

B. $31,000

C. $52,080

D. $62,000

The correct answer is (D). *(CMA, adapted)*
   **REQUIRED:** The joint cost allocated to Betters based on net realizable values if the by-product is not inventoried.
   **DISCUSSION:** As determined in question 77, the NRV of Alfa is $20,000, and the NRV of Betters is $40,000. If the joint cost is not adjusted for the value of the by-product, the amount allocated to Betters is $62,000 {[$40,000 ÷ ($20,000 + $40,000)] x $93,000}.
   Answer (A) is incorrect because $30,000 is the amount allocated to Alfa when the by-product is treated as a reduction of joint cost. Answer (B) is incorrect because $31,000 is the amount allocated to Alfa when the by-product is not treated as a reduction of joint cost. Answer (C) is incorrect because $52,080 assumes that a weighting method using caloric value is used.

## 6.6 Sell-or-Process Decisions

**82.** There is a market for both product X and product Y. Which of the following costs and revenues would be most relevant in deciding whether to sell product X or process it further to make product Y?

- A. Total cost of making X and the revenue from sale of X and Y.
- B. Total cost of making Y and the revenue from sale of Y.
- C. Additional cost of making Y, given the cost of making X, and additional revenue from Y.
- D. Additional cost of making X, given the cost of making Y, and additional revenue from Y.

The correct answer is (C). *(CIA, adapted)*
**REQUIRED:** The costs relevant to the decision to further process a product.
**DISCUSSION:** Incremental costs are the additional costs incurred for accepting one alternative rather than another. Questions involving incremental costing (sometimes called differential costing) decisions are based upon a variable costing analysis. The typical problem for which incremental cost analysis can be used involves two or more alternatives, for example, selling or processing further. Thus, the relevant costs and revenues are the marginal costs and marginal revenues.
Answer (A) is incorrect because the cost of making X is a sunk cost (irrelevant). In addition, only X or Y, not both, can be sold. Answer (B) is incorrect because only the relevant, incremental costs are considered. Answer (D) is incorrect because Y is made only after X is completed.

**83.** In joint-product costing and analysis, which one of the following costs is relevant when deciding the point at which a product should be sold to maximize profits?

- A. Separable costs after the split-off point.
- B. Joint costs to the split-off point.
- C. Sales salaries for the period when the units were produced.
- D. Purchase costs of the materials required for the joint products.

The correct answer is (A). *(CMA, adapted)*
**REQUIRED:** The cost relevant to deciding when a joint product should be sold.
**DISCUSSION:** Joint products are created from processing a common input. Common costs are incurred prior to the split-off point and cannot be identified with a particular joint product. As a result, common costs are irrelevant to the timing of sale. However, separable costs incurred after the split-off point are relevant because, if incremental revenues exceed the separable costs, products should be processed further, not sold at the split-off point.
Answer (B) is incorrect because joint costs (common costs) have no effect on the decision as to when to sell a product. Answer (C) is incorrect because sales salaries for the production period do not affect the decision. Answer (D) is incorrect because purchase costs are joint costs.

**84.** Copeland Inc. produces X-547 in a joint manufacturing process. The company is studying whether to sell X-547 at the split-off point or upgrade the product to become Xylene. The following information has been gathered:

I. Selling price per pound of X-547
II. Variable manufacturing costs of upgrade process
III. Avoidable fixed costs of upgrade process
IV. Selling price per pound of Xylene
V. Joint manufacturing costs to produce X-547

Which items should be reviewed when making the upgrade decision?

- A. I, II, and IV.
- B. I, II, III, and IV.
- C. I, II, IV, and V.
- D. II and III.

The correct answer is (B). *(CMA, adapted)*
**REQUIRED:** The items reviewed when making a sell-or-process decision.
**DISCUSSION:** Common, or joint, costs cannot be identified with a particular joint product. By definition, joint products have common costs until the split-off point. Costs incurred after the split-off point are separable costs. The decision to continue processing beyond split-off is made separately for each product. The costs relevant to the decision are the separable costs because they can be avoided by selling at the split-off point. They should be compared with the incremental revenues from processing further. Thus, items I (revenue from selling at split-off point), II (variable costs of upgrade), III (avoidable fixed costs of upgrade), and IV (revenue from selling after further processing) are considered in making the upgrade decision.
Answers (A), (C), and (D) are incorrect because the joint manufacturing costs are the only irrelevant item.

Questions 85 and 86 are based on the following information. N-Air Corporation uses a joint process to produce three products: A, B, and C, all derived from one input. The company can sell these products at the point of split-off (end of the joint process) or process them further. The joint production costs during October were $10,000. N-Air allocates joint costs to the products in proportion to the relative physical volume of output. Additional information is presented in the opposite column.

| Product | Units Produced | Unit Sales Price at Split-off | If Processed Further Unit Sales Price | If Processed Further Unit Additional Cost |
|---------|----------------|-------------------------------|---------------------------------------|-------------------------------------------|
| A | 1,000 | $4.00 | $5.00 | $ .75 |
| B | 2,000 | 2.25 | 4.00 | 1.20 |
| C | 1,500 | 3.00 | 3.75 | .90 |

**85.** Assuming that all products were sold at the split-off point during October, the gross profit from the production process would be

A. $13,000

B. $10,000

C. $8,625

D. $3,000

The correct answer is (D). *(CIA, adapted)*

**REQUIRED:** The gross profit from the production process if all products are sold at the split-off point.

**DISCUSSION:** If all products are sold at split-off, the gross profit is computed as follows:

| | |
|---|---|
| Product A ($4.00 × 1,000) | $ 4,000 |
| Product B ($2.25 × 2,000) | 4,500 |
| Product C ($3.00 × 1,500) | 4,500 |
| Total sales | $13,000 |
| Joint costs | (10,000) |
| Gross profit | $ 3,000 |

Answer (A) is incorrect because $13,000 is the total sales if all products are sold at split-off. Answer (B) is incorrect because $10,000 is the joint production cost during October. Answer (C) is incorrect because, if all products were sold at split-off, total sales are determined by multiplying units produced by the unit sales price at split-off, not the unit sales price if processed further.

**86.** Assuming sufficient demand exists, N-Air could sell all the products at the prices above at either the split-off point or after further processing. To maximize its profits, N-Air Corporation should

A. Sell product A at split-off and perform additional processing on products B and C.

B. Sell product B at split-off and perform additional processing on products C and A.

C. Sell product C at split-off and perform additional processing on products A and B.

D. Sell products A, B, and C at split-off.

The correct answer is (C). *(CIA, adapted)*

**REQUIRED:** The product(s) that should be processed further to maximize profits.

**DISCUSSION:** To maximize profits, it must be determined whether each product's incremental revenues will exceed its incremental costs. Joint costs are irrelevant because they are sunk costs.

| | A | B | C |
|---|---|---|---|
| Unit sales price if processed further | $5.00 | $4.00 | $3.75 |
| Minus unit sales price at split-off | (4.00) | (2.25) | (3.00) |
| Incremental revenue per unit | $1.00 | $1.75 | $ .75 |
| Minus incremental unit cost | (.75) | (1.20) | (.90) |
| Excess unit revenue over unit cost | $ .25 | $ .55 | $(.15) |

It is most profitable for N-Air to process products A and B further and to sell product C at the split-off point.

Answers (A), (B), and (D) are incorrect because N-Air should further process products A and B and sell product C at split-off.

**87.** A firm produces two joint products (A and B) from one unit of raw material, which costs $1,000. Product A can be sold for $700 and product B can be sold for $500 at the split-off point. Alternatively, both A and/or B can be processed further and sold for $900 and $1,200, respectively. The additional processing costs are $100 for A and $750 for B. Should the firm process products A and B beyond the split-off point?

    A. Both A and B should be processed further.

    B. Only B should be processed further.

    C. Only A should be processed further.

    D. Neither product should be processed further.

The correct answer is (C). *(CIA, adapted)*
    **REQUIRED:** The best decision regarding additional processing.
    **DISCUSSION:** The incremental costs ($100) for A are less than the incremental revenue ($200). However, the incremental costs of B ($750) exceed the incremental revenue ($700). Consequently, the firm should process A further and sell B at the split-off point.
    Answers (A), (B), and (D) are incorrect because only A should be processed further.

## 6.7 Journal Entries

| | |
|---|---|
| Questions 88 through 91 are based on the following information. The information was presented as part of Question 5 on the Practice II section of the May 1982 CPA examination. | Raw materials    $150,000<br>Direct labor    120,000<br>Factory overhead    30,000 |

Lares Confectioners, Inc. makes a candy bar called Rey that sells for $.50 per pound. The manufacturing process also yields a product known as Nagu. Without further processing, Nagu sells for $.10 per pound. With further processing, Nagu sells for $.30 per pound. During the month of April, total joint manufacturing costs up to the point of separation consisted of the charges to work-in-process presented in the opposite column.

Production for the month aggregated 394,000 pounds of Rey and 30,000 pounds of Nagu. To complete Nagu during the month of April and obtain a selling price of $.30 per pound, further processing of Nagu during April would entail the following additional costs:

| | |
|---|---|
| Raw materials | $2,000 |
| Direct labor | 1,500 |
| Factory overhead | 500 |

**88.** Select the proper journal entry for Nagu if it is recorded as inventory at sales value without further processing, with a corresponding reduction of Rey's manufacturing costs.

  A. By-product inventory   $3,000
       Finished goods            $3,000

  B. By-product inventory   $3,000
       Work-in-process           $3,000

  C. Work-in-process       $3,000
       By-product inventory      $3,000

  D. Cost of goods sold      $3,000
       By-product inventory      $3,000

The correct answer is (B). *(Publisher)*
    **REQUIRED:** The appropriate journal entry to record a by-product transfer.
    **DISCUSSION:** To transfer a by-product at sales value with a corresponding reduction of manufacturing costs requires estimation of the sales value of the transferred item. The selling price of Nagu is $3,000 (30,000 lb. produced x $.10/lb. incremental cost) without further processing. The sales value is to be accounted for as a reduction in manufacturing costs. Therefore, the debit and credit are to by-product inventory and work-in-process, respectively, if Rey is still in process.
    Answer (A) is incorrect because the credit should be to work-in-process for $3,000 to reduce the manufacturing costs. Answers (C) and (D) are incorrect because by-product inventory should be debited and work-in-process should be credited for $3,000 to reduce manufacturing costs.

**89.** What are the journal entries for Nagu if it is processed further and transferred to finished goods, with joint costs being allocated between Rey and Nagu based on relative sales value at the split-off point?

| A. | Work-in-process (Nagu) | $4,500 | |
| | Work-in-process (Rey) | | $4,500 |
| | Work-in-process (Nagu) | $4,000 | |
| | Raw materials | | $2,000 |
| | Direct labor | | 1,500 |
| | Factory overhead | | 500 |
| | Finished goods (Nagu) | $8,500 | |
| | Work-in-process (Nagu) | | $8,500 |
| | | | |
| B. | Work-in-process (Nagu) | $8,500 | |
| | Work-in-process (Rey) | | $8,500 |
| | Finished goods (Nagu) | $8,500 | |
| | Work-in-process (Nagu) | | $8,500 |
| | | | |
| C. | Finished goods (Nagu) | $8,500 | |
| | Work-in-process (Nagu) | | $8,500 |
| | | | |
| D. | Work-in-process (Rey) | $4,500 | |
| | Work-in-process (Nagu) | | $4,500 |
| | Work-in-process (Rey) | $4,000 | |
| | Raw materials | | $2,000 |
| | Direct labor | | 1,500 |
| | Factory overhead | | 500 |
| | Finished goods (Rey) | $8,500 | |
| | Work-in-process (Rey) | | $8,500 |

The correct answer is (A). *(Publisher)*

**REQUIRED:** The journal entries for joint products and further processing.

**DISCUSSION:** The initial journal entry requires the joint costs to be allocated between Rey and Nagu based on relative sales value at split-off. Total joint costs are $300,000 ($150,000 raw materials + $120,000 direct labor + $30,000 factory overhead). The ratio to calculate Nagu's joint costs is

$$\frac{\text{Sales value of Nagu}}{\text{Total sales value of Rey and Nagu}}$$

$$\frac{30,000 \; lb. \times \$.10}{(394,000 \; lb. \times \$.50) + (30,000 \; lb. \times \$.10)}$$

$$= \frac{\$3,000}{\$200,000} = .015 \; joint \; cost \; ratio$$

Nagu's share of the joint costs is $4,500 ($300,000 x .015), and the journal entry is a debit to WIP (Nagu) and a credit to WIP (Rey) for this amount. The next journal entry to reflect the cost of further processing of Nagu is to debit WIP (Nagu) and credit raw materials, direct labor, and factory overhead for the additional costs incurred. The final journal entry would be to transfer the WIP costs of $8,500 to finished goods.

Answers (B), (C), and (D) are incorrect because the first journal entry should be a debit to WIP (Nagu) and a credit to WIP (Rey). The second journal entry should be a debit to WIP (Nagu). The third journal entry should be a debit to finished goods (Nagu) and a credit to WIP (Nagu).

**90.** What is the journal entry for Nagu if it is further processed as a by-product and recorded as inventory at net realizable value, which reduces Rey's manufacturing costs?

| A. | By-product inventory (Nagu) | $3,000 | |
| | Work-in-process (Rey) | | $3,000 |
| | | | |
| B. | By-product inventory (Nagu) | $4,000 | |
| | Raw materials | | $2,000 |
| | Direct labor | | 1,500 |
| | Factory overhead | | 500 |
| | | | |
| C. | Work-in-process (Rey) | $5,000 | |
| | Raw materials | | 2,000 |
| | Direct labor | | 1,500 |
| | Factory overhead | | 500 |
| | By-product inventory (Nagu) | | $9,000 |
| | | | |
| D. | By-product inventory (Nagu) | $9,000 | |
| | Raw materials | | $2,000 |
| | Direct labor | | 1,500 |
| | Factory overhead | | 500 |
| | Work-in-process (Rey) | | 5,000 |

The correct answer is (D). *(Publisher)*

**REQUIRED:** The journal entry to transfer a by-product at net realizable value.

**DISCUSSION:** Net realizable value is the selling price minus the cost necessary to process further. After further processing, the net realizable value of Nagu is $5,000 [(30,000 lb. x $.30 per lb.) – $2,000 materials – $1,500 DL – $500 O/H]. Thus, the journal entry is a debit to by-product inventory of Nagu for the selling price and corresponding credits to raw materials, direct labor, and factory overhead. The final credit of $5,000 is to work-in-process (Rey), assuming that Rey is still in process.

Answers (A), (B), and (C) are incorrect because the journal entry is to debit by-product inventory (Nagu) for the selling price of $9,000 and to credit raw materials for $2,000, direct labor for $1,500, factory overhead for $500, and work-in-process (Rey) for $5,000.

Refer to the information preceding question 88 on page 212.

**91.** If the joint costs of $300,000 are allocated based on relative net realizable values and Nagu is considered a joint product rather than a by-product, what are the journal entries for Nagu and Rey to record the cost allocation and subsequent processing to the point at which both are in finished goods inventory?

A.
| | | |
|---|---|---|
| Finished goods (Rey) | $292,574 | |
| Work-in-process (Nagu) | 7,426 | |
|    Work-in-process (joint) | | $300,000 |
| Work-in-process (Nagu) | $4,000 | |
|    Raw materials | | $2,000 |
|    Direct labor | | 1,500 |
|    Factory overhead | | 500 |
| Finished goods (Nagu) | $11,426 | |
|    Work-in-process (Nagu) | | $11,426 |

B.
| | | |
|---|---|---|
| Work-in-process (Nagu) | $4,000 | |
|    Raw materials | | $2,000 |
|    Direct labor | | 1,500 |
|    Factory overhead | | 500 |

C.
| | | |
|---|---|---|
| Work-in-process (Nagu) | $4,967 | |
|    Work-in-process (joint) | | $4,967 |
| Work-in-process (Nagu) | $4,000 | |
|    Raw materials | | $2,000 |
|    Direct labor | | 1,500 |
|    Factory overhead | | 500 |

D.
| | | |
|---|---|---|
| Finished goods (Rey) | $295,033 | |
| Work-in-process (Nagu) | 4,967 | |
|    Work-in-process (joint) | | $300,000 |
| Work-in-process (Nagu) | $4,000 | |
|    Raw materials | | $2,000 |
|    Direct labor | | 1,500 |
|    Factory overhead | | 500 |
| Finished goods (Nagu) | $8,967 | |
|    Work-in-process (Nagu) | | $8,967 |

The correct answer is (A). *(Publisher)*

**REQUIRED:** The journal entries to reflect transfer of joint products to finished goods after joint cost allocation based on relative net realizable value.

**DISCUSSION:** The final sales value of Nagu is $9,000 (30,000 lb. x $.30). The cost of additional processing is $4,000 ($2,000 + $1,500 + $500). Its net realizable value is therefore $5,000. The sales value of Rey continues to be $197,000 (394,000 x $.50). Thus, the allocation of the $300,000 of common costs is $292,574 to Rey {[$197,000 ÷ ($197,000 + $5,000)] x $300,000} and $7,426 to Nagu {[$5,000 ÷ ($197,000 + $5,000)] x $300,000}. Consequently, the amount transferred to finished goods (Nagu) is the sum of the joint cost allocation and the additional processing costs ($7,426 + $4,000 = $11,426).

Answer (B) is incorrect because an entry that debits finished goods (Rey) for $292,574 and work-in-process (Nagu) for $7,426 with a corresponding credit to work-in-process (joint) for $300,000 should be included. Also, an entry that debits finished goods (Nagu) for $11,426 and credits work-in-process (Nagu) for $11,426 should be included as the sum of the joint cost allocation and the additional processing costs ($7,426 + $4,000 = $11,426). Answer (C) is incorrect because the entry to allocate joint costs should be debits to finished goods (Rey) for $292,574 and work-in-process (Nagu) for $7,426, with a corresponding credit to work-in-process (joint) for $300,000. The third entry is a debit to finished goods (Nagu) for $11,426 and a corresponding credit to work-in-process (Nagu) for $11,426. Answer (D) is incorrect because the entry to allocate joint costs should be debits to finished goods (Rey) for $292,574 and work-in-process (Nagu) for $7,426, with a corresponding credit to work-in-process (joint) for $300,000. The third entry should be a debit to finished goods (Nagu) for $11,426 with a corresponding credit to work-in-process (Nagu) for $11,426.

## 6.8 Comprehensive

Questions 92 and 93 are based on the following information. A manufacturing company uses a joint production process that produces three products at the split-off point. Joint production costs during April were $720,000. The company uses the sales-value method for allocating joint costs. Product information for April was as follows:

|  | Product | | |
|---|---|---|---|
|  | R | S | T |
| Units produced | 2,500 | 5,000 | 7,500 |
| Units sold | 2,000 | 6,000 | 7,000 |
| Sales prices: |  |  |  |
| At the split-off | $100 | $ 80 | $20 |
| After further processing | $150 | $115 | $30 |
| Costs to process after split-off | $150,000 | $150,000 | $100,000 |

**92.** Assume that all three products are main products and that they can be sold at the split-off point or processed further, whichever is economically beneficial to the company. What is the total cost of product S in April if joint cost allocation is based on sales value at split-off?

A. $375,000

B. $390,000

C. $510,000

D. $571,463

The correct answer is (C). *(CIA, adapted))*
**REQUIRED:** The total cost of product S in April.
**DISCUSSION:** Total sales value at split-off is $800,000 [(2,500 x $100) + (5,000 x $80) + (7,500 x $20)]. Product S accounts for 50% (5,000 x $80 = $400,000) of the sales value and therefore $360,000 (50% x $720,000) of the joint costs. Moreover, additional processing is beneficial because the incremental cost ($150,000) is less than the incremental benefit [($115 – $80) x 5,000 units = $175,000]. Thus, the total cost of product S is $510,000 ($360,000 allocated costs + $150,000 incremental cost).
Answer (A) is incorrect because $375,000 is the total cost of R. Answer (B) is incorrect because $390,000 is based on the physical-units method of allocating the joint costs. Answer (D) is incorrect because $571,463 uses the sales value at split-off based on actual sales.

**93.** Assume that product T is treated as a by-product and that the company accounts for the by-product at net realizable value as a reduction of joint cost. Assume also that products S and T must be processed further before they can be sold. What is the total cost of product R in April if joint cost allocation is based on net realizable values?

A. $220,370

B. $370,370

C. $374,630

D. $595,000

The correct answer is (A). *(CIA, adapted)*
**REQUIRED:** The total cost of product R for April.
**DISCUSSION:** The net-realizable-value (NRV) method is an appropriate method of allocation when products cannot be sold at split-off. Further processing of R, which is salable at split-off, is not economical because the cost ($150,000) exceeds the benefit [($150 – $100) x 2,500 units = $125,000]. Thus, R's NRV is $250,000 ($100 price at split-off x 2,500 units). However, S and T must be processed further. S's NRV is $425,000 [($115 x 5,000 units) – $150,000], and T's NRV is $125,000 [($30 x 7,500 units) – $100,000]. Given that the NRV of T is a reduction of joint cost, the total joint cost to be allocated is therefore $595,000 ($720,000 – $125,000 NRV of T). Accordingly, based on the NRV method, the joint cost allocated to R is $220,370 {[$250,000 R's NRV ÷ ($250,000 R's NRV + $425,000 S's NRV)] x $595,000 allocable joint cost}. Because further processing of R is uneconomical, the total cost of R is $220,370.
Answer (B) is incorrect because $370,370 includes additional processing costs. Answer (C) is incorrect because $374,630 is the joint cost allocated to S. Answer (D) is incorrect because $595,000 is the allocable joint cost.

Questions 94 through 99 are based on the following information. The information was presented as part of Question 7 on Part 4 of the June 1981 CMA examination.

Doe Corporation grows, processes, cans, and sells three main pineapple products – sliced pineapple, crushed pineapple, and pineapple juice. The outside skin is cut off in the Cutting Department and processed as animal feed. The skin is treated as a by-product. Doe's production process is as follows:

Pineapples first are processed in the Cutting Department. The pineapples are washed, and the outside skin is cut away. Then the pineapples are cored and trimmed for slicing. The three main products (sliced, crushed, juice) and the by-product (animal feed) are recognizable after processing in the Cutting Department. Each product is then transferred to a separate department for final processing.

The trimmed pineapples are forwarded to the Slicing Department where they are sliced and canned. Any juice generated during the slicing operation is packed in the cans with the slices.

The pieces of pineapple trimmed from the fruit are diced and canned in the Crushing Department. Again, the juice generated during this operation is packed in the can with the crushed pineapple.

The core and surplus pineapple generated from the Cutting Department are pulverized into a liquid in the Juicing Department. An evaporation loss equal to 8% of the weight of the good output produced in this department occurs as the juices are heated.

The outside skin is chopped into animal feed in the Feed Department.

The Doe Corporation uses the net-realizable-value (relative sales-value) method to assign costs of the joint process to its main products. The by-product is inventoried at its net realizable value. The NRV of the by-product reduces the joint costs of the main products.

A total of 270,000 pounds entered the Cutting Department during May. The schedule below shows the costs incurred in each department, the proportion by weight transferred to the four final processing departments, and the selling price of each product.

Doe uses the net-realizable-value method of determining inventory values for all products and by-products.

### May Processing Data and Costs

| Department | Costs Incurred | Proportion of Product by Weight Transferred to Departments | Selling Price per Pound of Final Product |
|---|---|---|---|
| Cutting | $60,000 | -- | None |
| Slicing | 4,700 | 35% | $.60 |
| Crushing | 10,580 | 28 | .55 |
| Juicing | 3,250 | 27 | .30 |
| Animal Feed | 700 | 10 | .10 |
| Total | $79,230 | 100% | |

**94.** How many net pounds of pineapple juice were produced in May?

   A.  72,900

   B.  79,200

   C.  64,525

   D.  67,500

The correct answer is (D). *(Publisher)*
   **REQUIRED:** The net pounds of pineapple juice produced during the period.
   **DISCUSSION:** The gross pounds of pineapple juice are 27% of the 270,000 total pounds entered into the various production units, or 72,900 pounds. Also, 8% of the good output is lost to evaporation. The net amount of pineapple juice is

$$X = 72,900 - .08X$$
$$1.08X = 72,900$$
$$X = 67,500 \text{ lb.}$$

   Answer (A) is incorrect because 72,900 is the gross pounds of pineapple juice. Answers (B) and (C) are incorrect because the net amount of pineapple juice is 67,500 lb. (72,900 gross pounds ÷ 1.08).

**95.** What is the net realizable value at the split-off point of pineapple slices?

  A. $52,000

  B. $56,700

  C. $49,800

  D. $39,200

The correct answer is (A). *(Publisher)*

  **REQUIRED:** The net realizable value at split-off of pineapple slices.

  **DISCUSSION:** The net realizable value at the split-off point can be estimated as the final sales revenue minus separable costs for further processing. Sales value equals the pounds of slices (270,000 x 35% = 94,500) times the selling price ($.60 per pound), or $56,700. The separable costs are given as $4,700. Accordingly, the net realizable value at split-off is $52,000 ($56,700 − $4,700).

  Answer (B) is incorrect because $56,700 is the sales revenue of the slices. Separable costs of $4,700 should be subtracted from $56,700 to arrive at the net realizable value at split-off of $52,000. Answers (C) and (D) are incorrect because $52,000 is the net realizable value of pineapple slices at the split-off point, which is equal to $56,700 sales revenue minus $4,700 separable costs.

**96.** What is the total amount of separable costs for the three main products?

  A. $15,280

  B. $18,530

  C. $16,750

  D. $12,280

The correct answer is (B). *(Publisher)*

  **REQUIRED:** The total amount of separable costs for the three main products.

  **DISCUSSION:** Separable costs for the three main products are the sum of the costs to further process the items to a salable state. The incremental costs incurred in slicing, crushing, and juicing are given. They total $18,530 ($4,700 + $10,580 + $3,250). The incremental costs incurred for animal feed are not included because they are the separable costs for the by-product.

  Answer (A) is incorrect because $15,280 includes only incremental costs incurred in slicing and crushing and should also include incremental costs of $3,250 incurred in juicing. Answers (C) and (D) are incorrect because the total amount of separable costs for the three main products is $18,530 ($4,700 slicing + $10,580 crushing + $3,250 juicing).

**97.** What is the total amount of joint costs for the Cutting Department to be assigned to each of the three main products in accordance with Doe's policy?

  A. $60,000

  B. $57,300

  C. $58,000

  D. $62,300

The correct answer is (C). *(Publisher)*

  **REQUIRED:** The total joint costs to be allocated to the main products.

  **DISCUSSION:** The joint costs to be allocated to main products are the Cutting Department costs minus any net revenue from the by-product. The animal feed's net revenue is $2,000 [sales value of $2,700 (270,000 lb. x 10% x $.10/lb.) − separable costs of $700]. The balance of joint costs of $58,000 ($60,000 total joint costs − $2,000 net by-product revenue) must be allocated to the main products in proportion to their net realizable values.

  Answer (A) is incorrect because $60,000 is the total joint costs. Answer (B) is incorrect because $57,300 results from subtracting animal feed sales value of $2,700 from $60,000 of total joint costs, instead of subtracting animal feed net by-product revenue of $2,000. Answer (D) is incorrect because the maximum joint costs to be allocated is $60,000.

Refer to the information preceding question 94 on page 216.

**98.** How much of the joint costs is allocated to crushed pineapple?

- A.  $30,160
- B.  $18,350
- C.  $9,860
- D.  $17,980

The correct answer is (D). *(Publisher)*

**REQUIRED:** The joint costs allocated to crushed pineapple.

**DISCUSSION:** The weights are found as percentages of total pounds. The pounds produced in Slicing equal 94,500 (270,000 x 35%), and the production of Crushing is 75,600 (270,000 x 28%).

| Product | Pounds Produced | Selling Price | Sales Revenue | Separable Costs |
|---|---|---|---|---|
| Slices | 94,500 | $.60 | $ 56,700 | $ 4,700 |
| Crushed | 75,600 | .55 | 41,580 | 10,580 |
| Juice | 67,500* | .30 | 20,250 | 3,250 |
| | | | $118,530 | $18,530 |

\* Amount computed in question 94

| | Net Realizable Value | |
|---|---|---|
| | Amount | Percent |
| Slices | $ 52,000 | 52% |
| Crushed | 31,000 | 31 |
| Juice | 17,000 | 17 |
| | $100,000 | 100% |

The joint costs to be allocated are $60,000 minus $2,000 net by-product revenue, or $58,000 (as computed in question 97). The joint costs allocated to crushed pineapple are $17,980 (31% x $58,000).

Answer (A) is incorrect because $30,160 is the amount allocated to sliced pineapple. Answer (B) is incorrect because $18,350 equals total separable costs. Answer (C) is incorrect because $9,860 is the joint cost allocated to pineapple juice.

**99.** What is the gross margin for the pineapple juice?

- A.  $9,860
- B.  $7,140
- C.  $3,250
- D.  $20,250

The correct answer is (B). *(Publisher)*

**REQUIRED:** The gross margin for pineapple juice.

**DISCUSSION:** Gross margin for pineapple juice equals the sales revenue minus the separable costs and the juice's allotted proportion of joint costs. The allotted amount of joint costs equals $9,860 (17% allocation percentage calculated in question 98 x $58,000 total joint cost calculated in question 97).

| | |
|---|---|
| Sales revenue (67,500 lb. × $.30) | $20,250 |
| Separable cost | (3,250) |
| Proportionate joint costs | (9,860) |
| Gross margin | $ 7,140 |

Answer (A) is incorrect because $9,860 is the joint cost allocated to the pineapple juice. Answer (C) is incorrect because $3,250 is the separable cost of the pineapple juice. Answer (D) is incorrect because $20,250 is the sales revenue for the pineapple juice. A gross margin of $7,140 is obtained by subtracting $3,250 separable cost and $9,860 joint cost from the sales revenue of $20,250.

Questions 100 through 103 are based on the following information. Sonimad Sawmill manufactures two lumber products from a joint milling process. The two products developed are mine support braces (MSB) and unseasoned commercial building lumber (CBL). A standard production run incurs joint costs of $300,000 and results in 60,000 units of MSB and 90,000 units of CBL. Each MSB sells for $2 per unit, and each CBL sells for $4 per unit.

**100.** Assuming no further processing work is done after the split-off point, the amount of joint cost allocated to commercial building lumber (CBL) on a physical quantity allocation basis would be

- A. $75,000
- B. $180,000
- C. $225,000
- D. $120,000

The correct answer is (B). *(CMA, adapted)*
**REQUIRED:** The joint cost allocated to CBL based on physical quantities.
**DISCUSSION:** Given 60,000 units of MSB and 90,000 units of CBL (a total of 150,000 units), CBL makes up 60% of the total quantity (90,000 ÷ 150,000). Hence, CBL should be charged with 60% of the joint costs (60% x $300,000 = $180,000).

Answer (A) is incorrect because $75,000 is the joint cost allocated to MSB based on the relative sales-value method. Answer (C) is incorrect because $225,000 is the joint cost allocated to CBL based on the relative sales-value method. Answer (D) is incorrect because $120,000 is the joint cost allocated to MSB based on physical quantities.

**101.** If there are no further processing costs incurred after the split-off point, the amount of joint cost allocated to the mine support braces (MSB) on a relative sales-value basis would be

- A. $75,000
- B. $180,000
- C. $225,000
- D. $120,000

The correct answer is (A). *(CMA, adapted)*
**REQUIRED:** The joint cost allocated to MSB based on the relative sales-value method.
**DISCUSSION:** At $2 each, the 60,000 units of MSB sell for $120,000. At $4 each, the 90,000 units of CBL sell for $360,000. Because 25% [$120,000 ÷ ($120,000 + $360,000)] of the total sales is produced by MSB, it should absorb 25% of the joint cost. Thus, $75,000 (25% x $300,000 joint cost) is allocated to MSB.

Answer (B) is incorrect because $180,000 is the joint cost allocated to CBL based on physical quantities. Answer (C) is incorrect because $225,000 is the joint cost allocated to CBL based on the relative sales-value method. Answer (D) is incorrect because $120,000 is the joint cost allocated to MSB based on physical quantities.

Questions 102 and 103 are based on the following additional information. Continuing with the data provided above questions 100 and 101 on page 219, assume the commercial building lumber is not marketable at split-off but must be further planed and sized at a cost of $200,000 per production run. During this process, 10,000 units are unavoidably lost; these spoiled units have no discernible value. The remaining units of commercial building lumber are salable at $10.00 per unit. The mine support braces, although salable immediately at the split-off point, are coated with a tar-like preservative that costs $100,000 per production run. The braces are then sold for $5 each.

**102.** Using the net-realizable-value (NRV) basis, the completed cost assigned to each unit of commercial building lumber would be

   A.  $2.92

   B.  $5.625

   C.  $2.50

   D.  $5.3125

The correct answer is (D). *(CMA, adapted)*

**REQUIRED:** The completed cost assigned to each unit of commercial building lumber using the NRV method.

**DISCUSSION:** The first step is to compute the sales for each product. The 60,000 units of MSB will sell for $5 each after further processing at a cost of $100,000. Their NRV is $200,000 [($5 × 60,000 units) – $100,000]. The 80,000 units of CBL sell for $10 each, or $800,000, after further processing. But to determine the NRV for CBL, the costs of this processing must be deducted from sales. Consequently, the NRV for CBL is $600,000 ($800,000 – $200,000). CBL therefore contributes 75% [$600,000 ÷ ($200,000 + $600,000)] of the realizable value and should bear an equal proportion of the $300,000 of joint costs, or $225,000. The total cost of CBL is $425,000 ($225,000 + $200,000), and the unit cost is $5.3125 ($425,000 ÷ 80,000).

Answer (A) is incorrect because $2.92 is the completed cost assigned to each MSB using the NRV method [($75,000 joint cost + $100,000 further processing costs) ÷ 60,000 units]. Answer (B) is incorrect because $5.625 is arrived at by using a sales price for MSB of $2.00 instead of $5.00, which is the sales price for MSB after further processing. Answer (C) is incorrect because the completed cost assigned to each unit of CBL using the NRV method is $5.3125 [($225,000 joint cost + $200,000 additional processing costs) ÷ 80,000 units of CBL].

**103.** If Sonimad Sawmill chose not to process the mine support braces beyond the split-off point, the contribution from the joint milling process would be

   A.  $120,000 higher.

   B.  $180,000 lower.

   C.  $100,000 higher.

   D.  $80,000 lower.

The correct answer is (D). *(CMA, adapted)*

**REQUIRED:** The difference in contribution from the joint milling process if MSB are not processed further.

**DISCUSSION:** MSB sell for $120,000 ($2 × 60,000 units) at the split-off point. By processing further, the company earns $200,000 ($300,000 in sales – $100,000 in preservative costs). Thus, the contribution from the joint milling process would be $80,000 lower ($200,000 – $120,000) if MSB are sold at the split-off point.

Answer (A) is incorrect because $120,000 is the sales value at split-off. Answer (B) is incorrect because $180,000 ignores the preservative costs. Answer (C) is incorrect because $100,000 is the cost of processing MSB further.

# CHAPTER SEVEN
# ABSORPTION AND VARIABLE COSTING

Absorption costing and variable costing reflect different views about whether fixed manufacturing cost should be assigned to products. The prevailing view for external reporting purposes is that product cost should include all manufacturing costs: direct labor, direct materials, and overhead. This method is commonly known as full costing or **absorption costing**. Absorption costing is currently required for federal income tax purposes and for external reporting under GAAP. However, **variable (direct) costing** has won increasing support. This method assigns only variable manufacturing costs to products. Thus, the term direct costing is misleading. Variable manufacturing costs include variable overhead, an indirect cost that is allocated, not traced. Many accountants believe that **variable costing** is a more suitable term, and some even call the method **contribution margin reporting**. Variable and absorption costing are just two of a continuum of possible inventory costing methods. At one extreme is **supervariable costing**, which treats direct materials as the only variable cost. At the other extreme is **superabsorption costing**, which treats costs from all links in the value chain as inventoriable.

Under variable costing, all direct labor, direct materials, and variable manufacturing overhead costs are handled in precisely the same manner as in absorption costing. Only fixed manufacturing overhead costs are treated differently. These fixed costs are accounted for as period costs under variable costing; that is, they are treated in the same way as fixed and variable selling and administrative costs. However, they are accounted for as product (inventoriable) costs under absorption costing. This difference results in changes in how the income statement is organized. Under variable costing, the variable cost of goods sold (beginning inventory + variable cost of manufacturing - - ending inventory) is subtracted from sales to determine the manufacturing contribution margin. The variable selling and administrative costs are then subtracted to determine the **contribution margin**. From this amount, all fixed costs are subtracted to calculate pretax variable-costing net income. Under absorption costing, sales minus cost of goods sold (beginning inventory + full cost of goods manufactured - - ending inventory) equals the **gross margin (profit)**. The gross margin minus fixed and variable selling and administrative costs equals pretax absorption-costing net income. The derivation of the contribution margin is an important element in the variable-costing income statement. It indicates how much sales contribute toward paying the fixed costs and providing a profit. Accordingly, variable costing provides a better measure than absorption costing of the relative profitability of individual products, product lines, territories, or customers because it provides information about cost-volume-profit (CVP) relationships (see Chapter 8). This CVP information is the primary objective of variable costing.

Absorption and variable costing result in different inventory values and incomes. Inventories computed under variable costing are lower than under absorption costing; income may be higher or lower depending upon whether inventories are increased or liquidated. Moreover, under absorption costing, if operations are above or below some capacity set as normal or standard, adjustments are made for fixed overhead volume variances (see Chapter 10 for discussion of variances). However, under variable costing, because fixed costs are not applied to products, no such variances arise.

Assuming other factors are constant, when production and sales are equal for a period, variable costing and absorption costing report the same net income. Total fixed costs expensed during the period are equal under the two methods. When production exceeds sales and ending inventories increase, the net income reported under absorption costing is higher than under variable costing. Under absorption costing, the fixed costs deferred in the ending inventories increase. Under variable costing, the total fixed costs are expensed. When sales exceed production and ending inventories decrease, variable costing reports the higher net income. Under absorption costing, the fixed costs expensed exceed the fixed costs incurred during the period. Accordingly, variable-costing net income always moves in the same direction as sales volume. Net income reported under absorption costing behaves erratically and sometimes moves in the opposite direction from sales. Moreover, net income differences tend to be larger when calculations are made for short periods. In the long run, the two methods will report the same total net income if sales are equal to production. The inequalities between production and sales are usually minor over an extended period. Production cannot continually exceed sales because an enterprise will not produce more than it can sell in the long run.

Although the use of variable costing for financial statements is controversial, most authorities agree about its superiority for internal reporting. It is far better suited than absorption costing to the needs of management. Management requires a knowledge of cost behavior under various operating conditions. For planning and control, management is more concerned with treating fixed and variable costs separately than with calculating full costs. Full costs are usually of dubious value because they contain arbitrary allocations of fixed costs. Under variable costing, the cost data for profit planning and decision making are readily available from accounting records and statements. Reference to auxiliary records and supplementary analyses is not necessary. For example, CVP relationships, such as the effects of changes in sales volume on net income, can easily be computed from the variable-costing income statement, but not from the conventional full-cost income statement based on the same data. Moreover, net income reported under variable costing has a relationship to sales revenue and is not affected by inventory or production variations. However, absorption-costing income statements may report decreases in income when sales are rising and increases when sales are decreasing, which may be confusing to management. Attempts at explanation by means of fixed manufacturing overhead volume variances may compound rather than clarify the confusion.

Another benefit of variable costing is that the favorable margin between selling prices and variable cost should provide a constant reminder of income forgone because of lack of sales volume. A favorable margin justifies a higher production level. In addition, the presentation of the total amounts of fixed costs on a variable-costing income statement emphasizes their full impact on net income, an effect partially hidden in inventory values under absorption costing. Adherents of variable costing also maintain that fixed manufacturing overhead should be treated as a period cost because it is more closely correlated with capacity to produce than with the production of individual units. Still another benefit of variable costing is that production managers cannot manipulate income by producing more or fewer products than needed during a period. Under absorption costing, however, a production manager could increase income simply by producing more units than are currently needed for sales.

**Segmented reporting** provides information about the contributions of organizational subunits. Segmented income statements differ from other income statements because they display amounts for direct (traceable) fixed costs (costs avoidable if the segment is eliminated) and for common or allocated fixed costs (costs that will continue to be incurred even if the segment is eliminated). Presenting segmented income statements on a variable-costing rather than an absorption-costing basis is preferable because it results in more accurate studies of relative profitability of divisions, plants, products, territories, activities, and other segments of an organization. It concentrates on the contribution (the segment margin) that each segment makes to the recovery of common fixed costs. Under variable-costing procedures, the marginal income concept leads to better pricing, investment, and other decisions. Marginal income data facilitate appraisal of segments without the bias (cross-subsidies) introduced by allocated common fixed costs. Furthermore, out-of-pocket expenditures required to manufacture products conform closely with the variable-costing valuation of inventory, and the relationship between income and the major factors of selling price, sales mix, sales volume, and variable manufacturing and nonmanufacturing costs is measured in terms of a single index of profitability (the contribution margin). For the foregoing reasons, variable costing facilitates comparison of the effects of two or more courses of action, profit planning, disinvestment decisions, and breakeven computations.

**Customer profitability analysis** is an application of segmented reporting in which a customer group is treated as a segment. This analysis may be done using variable costing to determine a customer contribution margin or absorption costing to determine a customer gross margin based on full-cost cost of sales. It is especially helpful when combined with an activity-based costing approach that determines which activities are performed for each group and assigns costs based on appropriate drivers. Activities include those required to gain new customers and to maintain relationships with current customers as well as ordering, packaging, handling, customer service, etc. Furthermore, assignment of costs for a customer profitability analysis is based on cost-hierarchy concepts similar to those used in product profitability analysis. For example, activities, their drivers, and their costs may be classified as order level, customer level, channel level, market level, or enterprise level. Assignment of revenues is also a critical concern in customer profitability analysis. Thus, sales returns and allowances, the effects of coupon offers, price discounts, etc., should be traced to specific customer groups.

## 7.1 Variable Costing

**1.** Which of the following is a term more descriptive of the type of cost accounting often called direct costing?

    A.  Out-of-pocket costing.

    B.  Variable costing.

    C.  Relevant costing.

    D.  Prime costing.

The correct answer is (B). *(CPA, adapted)*
    **REQUIRED:** The term that best describes direct costing.
    **DISCUSSION:** Variable costing is the more accurate term. Variable (direct) costing considers only variable manufacturing costs to be product costs, i.e., inventoriable. However, these costs include variable manufacturing overhead, an indirect cost.
    Answer (A) is incorrect because out-of-pocket costs refer to those requiring immediate expenditure. Answer (C) is incorrect because relevant costs are those that vary with alternative decisions. Answer (D) is incorrect because prime costing Includes only direct labor and direct materials costs (i.e., no variable factory overhead).

**2.** Which of the following must be known about a production process to institute a variable costing system?

    A.  The variable and fixed components of all costs related to production.

    B.  The controllable and noncontrollable components of all costs related to production.

    C.  Standard production rates and times for all elements of production.

    D.  Contribution margin and breakeven point for all goods in production.

The correct answer is (A). *(CPA, adapted)*
    **REQUIRED:** The elements needed to institute a variable costing system.
    **DISCUSSION:** Variable costing considers only variable manufacturing costs to be product costs, i.e., inventoriable. Fixed manufacturing costs are treated as period costs. Thus, one need only be able to determine the variable and fixed manufacturing costs to institute a variable costing system.
    Answer (B) is incorrect because even fixed costs are controllable in the long run. Answer (C) is incorrect because standard costing is not necessary to institute variable costing. Actual costs may be used. Answer (D) is incorrect because selling prices as well as variable and fixed costs must be known to calculate the contribution margin and breakeven point.

**3.** What costs are treated as product costs under variable costing?

    A.  Only direct costs.

    B.  Only variable production costs.

    C.  All variable costs.

    D.  All variable and fixed manufacturing costs.

The correct answer is (B). *(CPA, adapted)*
    **REQUIRED:** The costs allocated to product under variable costing.
    **DISCUSSION:** Product costs under variable costing include direct materials, direct labor, and variable factory overhead. Each is a variable production cost.
    Answer (A) is incorrect because variable factory overhead must also be included. Answer (C) is incorrect because only variable production costs, not variable selling and administrative costs, are product costs in variable costing. Answer (D) is incorrect because absorption costing, not variable costing, includes all variable and fixed production costs.

**4.** Inventory under the variable costing method includes

    A.  Direct materials cost, direct labor cost, but no factory overhead cost.

    B.  Direct materials cost, direct labor cost, and variable factory overhead cost.

    C.  Prime cost but not conversion cost.

    D.  Prime cost and all conversion cost.

The correct answer is (B). *(CPA, adapted)*
    **REQUIRED:** The elements included in variable-costing inventory.
    **DISCUSSION:** Variable-costing inventory includes only variable manufacturing costs: direct materials, direct labor, and variable factory overhead. Fixed factory overhead is treated as a period cost.
    Answer (A) is incorrect because variable factory overhead should be included. Answer (C) is incorrect because variable-costing inventory costs include direct labor and variable factory overhead, which are conversion costs. Answer (D) is incorrect because conversion cost includes fixed factory overhead, which is not a component of inventory under variable costing.

**5.** In the application of variable costing as a cost-allocation process in manufacturing,

A.  Variable direct costs are treated as period costs.

B.  Nonvariable indirect costs are treated as product costs.

C.  Variable indirect costs are treated as product costs.

D.  Nonvariable direct costs are treated as product costs.

The correct answer is (C). *(CIA, adapted)*
**REQUIRED:** The true statement about variable costing.
**DISCUSSION:** Variable costing considers only variable manufacturing costs to be product costs. Variable indirect costs included in variable factory overhead are therefore inventoriable. Fixed costs are considered period costs and are expensed as incurred.
Answer (A) is incorrect because variable manufacturing costs, whether direct (direct materials and direct labor) or indirect (variable factory overhead), are accounted for as product costs, not period costs. Answer (B) is incorrect because nonvariable indirect costs are treated as period costs in variable costing. Answer (D) is incorrect because, in variable costing, nonvariable direct costs are treated as period costs, not product costs.

**6.** Cay Co.'s 1998 fixed manufacturing overhead costs totaled $100,000, and variable selling costs totaled $80,000. Under variable costing, how should these costs be classified?

|    | Period Costs | Product Costs |
| --- | --- | --- |
| A. | $0 | $180,000 |
| B. | $80,000 | $100,000 |
| C. | $100,000 | $80,000 |
| D. | $180,000 | $0 |

The correct answer is (D). *(CPA, adapted)*
**REQUIRED:** The classification of fixed manufacturing overhead and variable selling costs.
**DISCUSSION:** Product costs are incurred to produce units of output, and they are expensed when the product is sold. Such costs include direct materials, direct labor, and factory (not general and administrative) overhead. Period costs are charged to expense as incurred because they are not identifiable with a product. Variable costing considers only variable manufacturing costs to be product costs. Fixed manufacturing costs and fixed and variable selling costs are considered period costs and are expensed as incurred. Thus, period costs equal $180,000 ($100,000 + $80,000).
Answers (A), (B), and (C) are incorrect because the fixed overhead and selling costs are not identifiable with a product.

**7.** Under the variable-costing concept, unit product cost would most likely be increased by

A.  A decrease in the remaining useful life of factory machinery depreciated on the units-of-production method.

B.  A decrease in the number of units produced.

C.  An increase in the remaining useful life of factory machinery depreciated on the sum-of-the-years'-digits method.

D.  An increase in the commission paid to salesmen for each unit sold.

The correct answer is (A). *(CPA, adapted)*
**REQUIRED:** The change most likely to increase unit product cost under variable costing.
**DISCUSSION:** Variable costing considers only variable manufacturing costs to be product costs. Fixed manufacturing costs are period costs. Units-of-production depreciation is included in variable factory overhead. Thus, a decrease in the remaining useful life of machinery will increase the unit product cost.
Answer (B) is incorrect because variable costs per unit remain constant. Answer (C) is incorrect because SYD depreciation affects fixed, not variable, factory overhead. Answer (D) is incorrect because commissions are a selling expense, i.e., a period cost, not a product cost.

**8.** Which costing method is properly classified as to its acceptability for both external and internal reporting?

|    |    | External Reporting | Internal Reporting |
| --- | --- | --- | --- |
| A. | Activity-based costing | Yes | Yes |
| B. | Job costing | No | Yes |
| C. | Variable costing | Yes | No |
| D. | Process costing | No | Yes |

The correct answer is (A). *(CMA, adapted)*
**REQUIRED:** The costing method properly classified as to its acceptability for internal and external reporting.
**DISCUSSION:** Activity-based costing, job-order costing, process costing, and standard costing can all be used for both internal and external purposes. Variable costing is not acceptable under GAAP for external reporting purposes because it treats fixed manufacturing costs as period costs.
Answer (B) is incorrect because job costing is acceptable for external reporting. Answer (C) is incorrect because variable costing is acceptable for internal purposes only. Answer (D) is incorrect because process costing is acceptable for external reporting.

**9.** A basic tenet of variable costing is that period costs should be currently expensed. What is the rationale behind this procedure?

    A. Period costs are uncontrollable and should not be charged to a specific product.

    B. Period costs are usually immaterial in amount, and the cost of assigning them to specific products will outweigh the benefits.

    C. Allocation of period costs is arbitrary at best and could lead to erroneous decisions by management.

    D. Because period costs will occur whether or not production occurs, it is improper to allocate these costs to production and defer a current cost of doing business.

The correct answer is (D). *(CPA, adapted)*

    **REQUIRED:** The rationale behind the variable costing method.

    **DISCUSSION:** Fixed costs are a basic expense of being in business; they are incurred to continue operating the business regardless of production levels. Accordingly, they are not controllable in the short run and should not be deferred.

    Answer (A) is incorrect because period costs are controllable at higher levels of management in the long run. Answer (B) is incorrect because period costs are usually material. Answer (C) is incorrect because, although the allocation of period costs may be arbitrary, the more basic rationale behind variable costing is the lack of controllability in the short run.

**10.** Which of the following is an argument against the use of variable costing?

    A. Absorption costing overstates the balance sheet value of inventories.

    B. Variable factory overhead is a period cost.

    C. Fixed factory overhead is difficult to allocate properly.

    D. Fixed factory overhead is necessary for the production of a product.

The correct answer is (D). *(CIA, adapted)*

    **REQUIRED:** The argument against the use of variable costing.

    **DISCUSSION:** Variable costing treats fixed manufacturing costs as period costs, whereas absorption costing accumulates them as product costs. If product costs are viewed as all manufacturing costs incurred to produce output, fixed factory overhead should be inventoried because it is necessary for production. The counter argument in favor of variable costing is that fixed factory overhead is more closely related to capacity to produce than to the production of individual units. Internal reporting for cost behavior analysis is more useful if it concentrates on the latter.

    Answer (A) is incorrect because variable costing arguably understates inventory. Answer (B) is incorrect because variable factory overhead is a product cost under any cost system. Answer (C) is incorrect because the difficulty of allocating fixed factory overhead is an argument against absorption costing.

**11.** In an income statement prepared as an internal report using the variable costing method, which of the following terms should appear?

| | Gross Profit (Margin) | Operating Income |
|---|---|---|
| A. | Yes | Yes |
| B. | Yes | No |
| C. | No | No |
| D. | No | Yes |

The correct answer is (D). *(CPA, adapted)*

    **REQUIRED:** The income classification for a variable-costing income statement.

    **DISCUSSION:** Gross profit (margin) is selling price minus CGS. The computation of CGS takes into account fixed manufacturing overhead in inventory. Absorption costing calculates gross profit. Variable costing treats fixed manufacturing overhead as an expense in the period of incurrence. In variable costing, the contribution margin (sales – variable costs) is calculated, not a gross profit (margin). Both methods, however, compute operating income on their income statements.

    Answers (A), (B), and (C) are incorrect because the variable-costing income statement does not show gross profit, but it does include operating income.

**12.** In an income statement prepared as an internal report using the variable costing method, variable selling and administrative expenses are

    A.  Not used.

    B.  Treated the same as fixed selling and administrative expenses.

    C.  Used in the computation of operating income but not in the computation of the contribution margin.

    D.  Used in the computation of the contribution margin.

The correct answer is (D). *(CPA, adapted)*
    **REQUIRED:** The treatment of variable selling and administrative expenses in an income statement based on variable costing.
    **DISCUSSION:** In a variable-costing income statement, the contribution margin equals sales minus all variable costs, which include the variable selling and administrative expenses as well as variable manufacturing costs (direct materials, direct labor, and variable factory overhead). Operating income equals the contribution margin minus all fixed costs.
    Answers (A) and (C) are incorrect because variable selling and administrative expenses are included in the determination of the contribution margin. Answer (B) is incorrect because fixed selling and administrative expenses are subtracted from the contribution margin to arrive at operating income.

**13.** When using a variable costing system, the contribution margin (CM) discloses the excess of

    A.  Revenues over fixed costs.

    B.  Projected revenues over the breakeven point.

    C.  Revenues over variable costs.

    D.  Variable costs over fixed costs.

The correct answer is (C). *(CPA, adapted)*
    **REQUIRED:** The definition of contribution margin (CM) in a variable costing system.
    **DISCUSSION:** Contribution margin is the difference between revenues and variable costs. No distinction is made between variable product costs and variable selling costs; both are deducted from revenue to arrive at CM.
    Answer (A) is incorrect because CM is the excess of total revenue over total variable costs, not over fixed costs. Answer (B) is incorrect because projected revenues over the breakeven point is the projected net income. Answer (D) is incorrect because CM is the excess of total revenue over total variable costs, not variable costs over fixed costs.

**14.** In an income statement prepared as an internal report using the variable costing method, fixed factory overhead would

    A.  Not be used.

    B.  Be used in the computation of operating income but not in the computation of the contribution margin.

    C.  Be used in the computation of the contribution margin.

    D.  Be treated the same as variable factory overhead.

The correct answer is (B). *(CPA, adapted)*
    **REQUIRED:** The treatment of fixed factory overhead in an income statement based on variable costing.
    **DISCUSSION:** Under the variable costing method, the contribution margin equals sales minus variable expenses. Fixed selling and administrative costs and fixed factory overhead are deducted from the contribution margin to arrive at operating income. Thus, fixed costs are included only in the computation of operating income.
    Answer (A) is incorrect because fixed factory overhead is deducted from the contribution margin to determine operating income. Answer (C) is incorrect because only variable expenses are used in the computation of the contribution margin. Answer (D) is incorrect because variable factory overhead is included in the computation of contribution margin and fixed factory overhead is not.

**15.** Which of the following statements is true for a firm that uses variable costing?

A.    The cost of a unit of product changes because of changes in number of units manufactured.

B.    Profits fluctuate with sales.

C.    An idle facility variation is calculated.

D.    Product costs include direct (variable) administrative costs.

The correct answer is (B). *(CMA, adapted)*
    **REQUIRED:** The true statement about variable costing.
    **DISCUSSION:** In a variable costing system, only the variable costs are recorded as product costs. All fixed costs are expensed in the period incurred. Because changes in the relationship between production and sales do not cause changes in the amount of fixed manufacturing cost that is expensed, profits more directly follow the trends in sales.
    Answer (A) is incorrect because, in variable costing, fixed costs are charged as period costs and cannot cause a change in unit cost as production increases. Answer (C) is incorrect because idle facility variation is calculated under an absorption costing system. Answer (D) is incorrect because neither variable nor absorption costing includes administrative costs in inventory.

## 7.2 Absorption Costing vs. Variable Costing

**16.** Which method of inventory costing treats direct manufacturing costs and manufacturing overhead costs, both variable and fixed, as inventoriable costs?

A.    Direct costing.

B.    Variable costing.

C.    Absorption costing.

D.    Conversion costing.

The correct answer is (C). *(CMA, adapted)*
    **REQUIRED:** The method of inventory costing that treats direct manufacturing costs and all factory overhead as inventoriable.
    **DISCUSSION:** Absorption (full) costing considers all manufacturing costs to be inventoriable as product costs. These costs include variable and fixed manufacturing costs, whether direct or indirect. The alternative to absorption is known as variable (direct) costing.
    Answers (A) and (B) are incorrect because variable (direct) costing does not inventory fixed factory overhead. Answer (D) is incorrect because conversion costs include direct labor and factory overhead but not direct materials.

**17.** Using absorption costing, fixed manufacturing overhead costs are best described as

A.    Direct period costs.

B.    Indirect period costs.

C.    Direct product costs.

D.    Indirect product costs.

The correct answer is (D). *(CIA, adapted)*
    **REQUIRED:** The manufacturing overhead costs under absorption costing.
    **DISCUSSION:** Using absorption costing, fixed manufacturing overhead is included in inventoriable (product) costs. Fixed manufacturing overhead costs are indirect costs because they cannot feasibly be directly traced to specific units produced.
    Answers (A), (B), and (C) are incorrect because fixed manufacturing overhead costs are neither direct nor period costs under absorption costing.

**18.** When a firm prepares financial reports by using absorption costing,

A.    Profits will always increase with increases in sales.

B.    Profits will always decrease with decreases in sales.

C.    Profits may decrease with increased sales even if there is no change in selling prices and costs.

D.    Decreased output and constant sales result in increased profits.

The correct answer is (C). *(CMA, adapted)*
    **REQUIRED:** The profit relationship between output and sales under absorption costing.
    **DISCUSSION:** In an absorption costing system, fixed overhead costs are included in inventory. When sales exceed production, more overhead is expensed under absorption costing due to fixed overhead carried over from the prior inventory. If sales increase over production, more than one period's factory overhead is recognized as expense. Accordingly, if the increase in factory overhead expensed is greater than the contribution margin of the increased units sold, there may be less profit with an increased level of sales.
    Answers (A) and (B) are incorrect because profit is a function of both sales and production, so it will not always move in the same direction as sales. Answer (D) is incorrect because decreased output will increase the unit cost of items sold. Fixed factory overhead per unit will increase.

**19.** Which one of the following statements is correct regarding absorption costing and variable costing?

A. Overhead costs are treated in the same manner under both costing methods.

B. If finished goods inventory increases, absorption costing results in higher income.

C. Variable manufacturing costs are lower under variable costing.

D. Gross margins are the same under both costing methods.

The correct answer is (B). *(CMA, adapted)*
**REQUIRED:** The true statement regarding absorption costing and variable costing.
**DISCUSSION:** Under variable costing, inventories are charged only with the variable costs of production. Fixed manufacturing costs are expensed as period costs. Absorption costing charges to inventory all costs of production. If finished goods inventory increases, absorption costing results in higher income because it capitalizes some fixed costs that would have been expensed under variable costing. When inventory declines, variable costing results in higher income because some fixed costs capitalized under the absorption method in prior periods are expensed in the current period.
Answer (A) is incorrect because fixed factory overhead is treated differently under the two methods. Answer (C) is incorrect because variable costs are the same under either method. Answer (D) is incorrect because gross margins will be different. Fixed factory overhead is expensed under variable costing and capitalized under the absorption method.

**20.** Absorption costing and variable costing are different methods of assigning costs to units produced. Which cost item listed below is not correctly accounted for as a product cost?

| | Part of Product Cost under | |
| --- | --- | --- |
| | Absorption Cost | Variable Cost |
| A. Manufacturing supplies | Yes | Yes |
| B. Insurance on factory | Yes | No |
| C. Direct labor cost | Yes | Yes |
| D. Packaging and shipping costs | Yes | Yes |

The correct answer is (D). *(CMA, adapted)*
**REQUIRED:** The cost not correctly accounted for.
**DISCUSSION:** Under absorption costing, all manufacturing costs, both fixed and variable, are treated as product costs. Under variable costing, only variable costs of manufacturing are inventoried as product costs. Fixed manufacturing costs are expensed as period costs. Packaging and shipping costs are not product costs under either method because they are incurred after the goods have been manufactured. Instead, they are included in selling and administrative expenses for the period.
Answers (A) and (C) are incorrect because manufacturing supplies and direct labor are variable costs inventoried under both methods. Answer (B) is incorrect because factory insurance is a fixed manufacturing cost inventoried under absorption costing but written off as a period cost under variable costing.

**21.** The Blue Company has failed to reach its planned activity level during its first 2 years of operation. The following table shows the relationship among units produced, sales, and normal activity for these years and the projected relationship for year 3. All prices and costs have remained the same for the last 2 years and are expected to do so in year 3. Income has been positive in both year 1 and year 2.

| | Units Produced | Sales | Planned Activity |
| --- | --- | --- | --- |
| Year 1 | 90,000 | 90,000 | 100,000 |
| Year 2 | 95,000 | 95,000 | 100,000 |
| Year 3 | 90,000 | 90,000 | 100,000 |

Because Blue Company uses an absorption costing system, gross margin for year 3 should be

A. Greater than year 1.

B. Greater than year 2.

C. Equal to year 1.

D. Equal to year 2.

The correct answer is (C). *(CIA, adapted)*
**REQUIRED:** The true interperiod gross margin relationship.
**DISCUSSION:** Gross margin equals sales minus CGS (BI + CGM – EI). An absorption costing system applies fixed as well as variable factory overhead to products. Because Blue's production has always been less than planned activity, fixed factory overhead was underapplied each year. Hence, Blue must have debited underapplied fixed factory overhead (an unfavorable production volume variance) each year to CGS, WIP, and FG. Because production always equaled sales, however, no inventories existed at any year-end, and each annual underapplication should have been debited entirely to CGS. Consequently, the gross margins for years 1 and 3 must be the same because the gross revenue and CGS were identical for the two periods.
Answer (A) is incorrect because the gross margins for years 1 and 3 are equal. Answers (B) and (D) are incorrect because the greater sales volume in year 2 should have produced a greater gross margin than in year 1 or 3.

**22.** A company manufactures a single product for its customers by contracting in advance of production. Thus, the company produces only units that will be sold by the end of each period. For the last period, the following data were available:

| | |
|---|---|
| Sales | $40,000 |
| Direct materials | 9,050 |
| Direct labor | 6,050 |
| Rent (9/10 factory, 1/10 office) | 3,000 |
| Depreciation on factory equipment | 2,000 |
| Supervision (2/3 factory, 1/3 office) | 1,500 |
| Salespeople's salaries | 1,300 |
| Insurance (2/3 factory, 1/3 office) | 1,200 |
| Office supplies | 750 |
| Advertising | 700 |
| Depreciation on office equipment | 500 |
| Interest on loan | 300 |

The gross margin percentage (rounded) was

A. 41%

B. 44%

C. 46%

D. 51%

The correct answer is (C). *(CIA, adapted)*

**REQUIRED:** The gross margin percentage given sales and cost data.

**DISCUSSION:** The gross margin percentage equals gross profit (sales – CGS) divided by sales. Sales are given as $40,000, and expenses included in cost of goods sold are listed below. The gross margin is $18,400, which is 46% of $40,000.

| | | |
|---|---|---|
| Sales | | $40,000 |
| Cost of goods sold | | |
| Direct materials | $9,050 | |
| Direct labor | 6,050 | |
| Rent (9/10 × $3,000) | 2,700 | |
| Depreciation | 2,000 | |
| Supervision (2/3 × $1,500) | 1,000 | |
| Insurance (2/3 × $1,200) | 800 | (21,600) |
| | | $18,400 |

Office expenses are usually general and administrative expenses, which are period rather than product costs.

Answer (A) is incorrect because 41% results from including sales salaries and advertising expenses in the calculation. Answer (B) is incorrect because 44% results from including 100% of the rent and supervision expenses. Answer (D) is incorrect because 51% omits depreciation on factory equipment from the calculation.

**23.** In an income statement prepared as an internal report, total fixed costs normally are shown separately under

| | Absorption Costing | Variable Costing |
|---|---|---|
| A. | No | No |
| B. | No | Yes |
| C. | Yes | Yes |
| D. | Yes | No |

The correct answer is (B). *(CPA, adapted)*

**REQUIRED:** The income statement(s) in which total fixed costs are normally shown separately.

**DISCUSSION:** In a variable-costing income statement, all variable costs are deducted from sales revenue to arrive at the contribution margin. Total fixed costs are then deducted from the contribution margin to determine operating income. In an absorption-costing income statement, fixed factory overhead included in the cost of goods sold is deducted from sales revenue in the calculation of the gross margin. Other fixed costs are subtracted from the gross margin to determine operating income.

Answers (A), (C), and (D) are incorrect because total fixed costs are normally shown separately under variable but not absorption costing.

**24.** A manufacturing company prepares income statements using both absorption and variable costing methods. At the end of a period, actual sales revenues, total gross margin, and total contribution margin approximated budgeted figures, whereas net income was substantially below the budgeted amount. There were no beginning or ending inventories. The most likely explanation of the net income shortfall is that, compared to budget, actual

A. Sales price and variable costs had declined proportionately.

B. Sales prices had declined proportionately more than variable costs.

C. Manufacturing fixed costs had increased.

D. Selling and administrative fixed expenses had increased.

The correct answer is (D). *(CPA, adapted)*
**REQUIRED:** The most likely explanation of the net income shortfall.
**DISCUSSION:** Gross margin equals sales minus cost of goods sold. The cost of goods sold equals the cost of goods manufactured (direct materials, direct labor, and variable and fixed factory overhead) adjusted for the change in inventory. Given that sales and gross margin approximated budgeted amounts, the net income shortfall must be attributable to an increase in selling and administrative expenses. The contribution margin (sales − all variable expenses) also approximated budget, so the shortfall could not be the result of an increase in variable expenses. Consequently, an increase in fixed selling and administrative expenses must be the cause of the net income decline.

Answer (A) is incorrect because, if sales prices and variable costs had declined proportionately, total contribution margin would have declined. Answer (B) is incorrect because both total and relative contribution margin would have declined. Answer (C) is incorrect because an increase in fixed factory overhead would have decreased the gross margin given constant sales revenues.

**25.** Jansen, Inc. pays bonuses to its managers based on operating income. The company uses absorption costing, and overhead is applied on the basis of direct labor hours. To increase bonuses, Jansen's managers may do all of the following except

A. Produce those products requiring the most direct labor.

B. Defer expenses such as maintenance to a future period.

C. Increase production schedules independent of customer demands.

D. Decrease production of those items requiring the most direct labor.

The correct answer is (D). *(CMA, adapted)*
**REQUIRED:** The action that will not increase bonuses based on operating income.
**DISCUSSION:** Under an absorption costing system, income can be manipulated by producing more products than are sold because more fixed manufacturing overhead will be allocated to the ending inventory. When inventory increases, some fixed costs are capitalized rather than expensed. Decreasing production, however, will result in lower income because more of the fixed manufacturing overhead will be expensed.

Answer (A) is incorrect because producing more of the products requiring the most direct labor will permit more fixed overhead to be capitalized. Answer (B) is incorrect because deferring expenses such as maintenance will increase current income (but may result in long-term losses caused by excessive downtime). Answer (C) is incorrect because increasing production without an increase in demand applies more fixed costs to inventory.

**26.** Net earnings determined using full absorption costing can be reconciled to net earnings determined using variable costing by computing the difference between

A. Inventoried fixed costs in the beginning and ending inventories and any deferred over- or underapplied fixed factory overhead.

B. Inventoried discretionary costs in the beginning and ending inventories.

C. Gross margin (absorption costing method) and contribution margin (variable costing method).

D. Sales as recorded under the variable costing method and sales as recorded under the absorption costing method.

The correct answer is (A). *(CPA, adapted)*
**REQUIRED:** The reconciliation of net earnings using absorption costing and variable costing.
**DISCUSSION:** Net earnings under variable costing and absorption costing differ because of the difference in treatment of fixed manufacturing costs. Variable costing treats all fixed manufacturing costs as period costs; absorption costing treats fixed manufacturing costs as product costs. When production and sales are equal, net income is the same under both methods. When production and sales differ, however, net income amounts differ and are reconciled by determining the changes in fixed costs inventoried.

Answer (B) is incorrect because inventoried discretionary costs, which is not a normal accounting term, may include both fixed and variable elements. Answer (C) is incorrect because the difference between gross margin and contribution margin does not determine the change in the fixed costs inventoried. Answer (D) is incorrect because sales are recorded the same way under both costing methods.

**27.** The management of a company computes net income using both the absorption and variable costing approaches to product costing. In the current year, the net income under the variable costing approach was greater than the net income under the absorption costing approach. This difference is most likely the result of

A. A decrease in the variable marketing expenses.

B. An increase in the finished goods inventory.

C. An excess of sales volume over production volume.

D. Inflationary effects on overhead costs.

The correct answer is (C). *(CIA, adapted)*

**REQUIRED:** The reason net income is greater under variable costing than under absorption costing.

**DISCUSSION:** Absorption costing (full costing) considers all manufacturing costs to be product costs, including variable and fixed manufacturing costs, whether direct or indirect. However, variable costing treats fixed factory overhead as a period cost. Thus, when sales exceed production, the absorption costing method recognizes fixed factory overhead inventoried in a prior period. Variable costing does not. Accordingly, net income under variable costing will be greater than net income under absorption costing.

Answer (A) is incorrect because a change in a variable period cost will affect absorption and variable costing in the same way. Answer (B) is incorrect because, if the finished goods inventory increases, absorption costing assigns more fixed overhead costs to the balance sheet and less to cost of goods sold on the income statement than does variable costing. Answer (D) is incorrect because inflationary effects will usually affect absorption and variable costing in the same way.

**28.** Net profit under absorption costing may differ from net profit determined under variable costing. This difference equals the change in the quantity of all units

A. In inventory times the relevant fixed costs per unit.

B. Produced times the relevant fixed costs per unit.

C. In inventory times the relevant variable cost per unit.

D. Produced times the relevant variable cost per unit.

The correct answer is (A). *(CPA, adapted)*

**REQUIRED:** The calculation for the difference in net profit between absorption costing and variable costing.

**DISCUSSION:** Variable costing treats all fixed costs as period costs; absorption costing treats fixed costs as product costs. The difference between net profit under the two methods can be determined by multiplying the fixed manufacturing cost per unit by the change in the number of units in inventory (assuming a constant per-unit fixed manufacturing cost).

Answers (B), (C), and (D) are incorrect because the effect of units sold must be considered. Also, the difference is caused by fixed costs.

**29.** A company's net income recently increased by 30% while its inventory increased to equal a full year's sales requirements. Which of the following accounting methods would be most likely to produce the favorable income results?

A. Absorption costing.

B. Direct costing.

C. Variable costing.

D. Standard direct costing.

The correct answer is (A). *(CIA, adapted)*

**REQUIRED:** The method likely to produce favorable income when inventory increases.

**DISCUSSION:** Inventory increases when production exceeds sales. In absorption costing, fixed costs that would be expensed under variable costing are deferred to future periods. If a company has very high fixed costs and a relatively low contribution margin, income may be increased by producing in excess of sales.

Answers (B), (C), and (D) are incorrect because variable-costing (direct-costing) net income is less than that under absorption costing when production exceeds sales.

**30.** When comparing absorption costing with variable costing, which of the following statements is not true?

A. Absorption costing enables managers to increase operating profits in the short run by increasing inventories.

B. When sales volume is more than production volume, variable costing will result in higher operating profit.

C. A manager who is evaluated based on variable costing operating profit would be tempted to increase production at the end of a period in order to get a more favorable review.

D. Under absorption costing, operating profit is a function of both sales volume and production volume.

The correct answer is (C). *(CIA, adapted)*
REQUIRED: The false statement comparing absorption costing and variable costing.
DISCUSSION: Absorption (full) costing is the accounting method that considers all manufacturing costs as product costs. These costs include variable and fixed manufacturing costs whether direct or indirect. Variable (direct) costing considers only variable manufacturing costs to be product costs, i.e., inventoriable. Fixed manufacturing costs are considered period costs and are expensed as incurred. If production is increased without increasing sales, inventories will rise. However, all fixed costs associated with production will be an expense of the period under variable costing. Thus, this action will not artificially increase profits and improve the manager's review.
Answer (A) is incorrect because increasing inventories increases absorption costing profit as a result of capitalizing fixed factory overhead. Answer (B) is incorrect because, when sales volume exceeds production, inventories decline. Thus, fixed factory overhead expensed will be greater under absorption costing. Answer (D) is incorrect because, under variable costing, operating profit is a function of sales. Under absorption costing, it is a function of sales and production.

**31.** Fleet, Inc. manufactured 700 units of Product A, a new product, during the year. Product A's variable and fixed manufacturing costs per unit were $6.00 and $2.00, respectively. The inventory of Product A on December 31 consisted of 100 units. There was no inventory of Product A on January 1. What would be the change in the dollar amount of inventory on December 31 if variable costing were used instead of absorption costing?

A. $800 decrease.

B. $200 decrease.

C. $0

D. $200 increase.

The correct answer is (B). *(CPA, adapted)*
REQUIRED: The difference in inventory using variable rather than absorption costing.
DISCUSSION: Given an inventory increase of 100 units during the year and the fixed manufacturing cost per unit of $2.00, $200 (100 units x $2.00) of overhead would be deferred using absorption costing but expensed immediately using variable costing. Thus, variable-costing inventory would be $200 less than absorption costing.
Answer (A) is incorrect because $800 is the total increase in inventories for the year. Answer (C) is incorrect because the cost per unit will differ. Fixed manufacturing costs are a product cost under absorption costing and a period cost under variable costing. Answer (D) is incorrect because inventory will decrease.

## 7.3 Calculations

**32.** During May, Roy Co. produced 10,000 units of Product X. Costs incurred by Roy during May:

| | |
|---|---:|
| Direct materials | $10,000 |
| Direct labor | 20,000 |
| Variable manufacturing overhead | 5,000 |
| Variable selling and general expenses | 3,000 |
| Fixed manufacturing overhead | 9,000 |
| Fixed selling and general expenses | 4,000 |
| Total | $51,000 |

Under absorption costing, Product X's unit cost was

A. $5.10

B. $4.40

C. $3.80

D. $3.50

The correct answer is (B). *(CPA, adapted)*
REQUIRED: The product's unit cost under absorption costing.
DISCUSSION: Unit cost under absorption costing is equal to the sum of manufacturing costs divided by the units produced. Selling and general expenses are not considered product costs.

$$\frac{\$10,000 + \$20,000 + \$5,000 + \$9,000}{10,000 \ units} = \$4.40$$

Answer (A) is incorrect because unit cost under absorption costing does not include variable or fixed selling and general expenses. Answer (C) is incorrect because $3.80 includes variable selling and general expenses but not fixed manufacturing overhead. Answer (D) is incorrect because $3.50 is the unit cost under variable costing.

**33.** During the month of April, Vane Co. produced and sold 10,000 units of a product. Manufacturing and selling costs incurred during April were as follows:

| | |
|---|---|
| Direct materials | $400,000 |
| Variable manufacturing overhead | 90,000 |
| Fixed manufacturing overhead | 20,000 |
| Variable selling costs | 10,000 |

The product's unit cost under variable costing was

  A. $49

  B. $50

  C. $51

  D. $52

The correct answer is (A). *(CPA, adapted)*
  **REQUIRED:** The product's unit cost under variable costing.
  **DISCUSSION:** Variable costing includes variable manufacturing costs only: direct materials, direct labor, and variable manufacturing overhead. Fixed manufacturing overhead and selling expenses are treated as period costs. Hence, the unit cost is $49 [($400,000 + $90,000) ÷ 10,000 units].
  Answer (B) is incorrect because variable selling costs ($1 per unit) should not be included. Answer (C) is incorrect because unit cost under absorption costing is $51. Answer (D) is incorrect because unit cost under variable costing does not include fixed manufacturing overhead or variable selling costs.

---

Questions 34 and 35 are based on the following information. Kirklin Co., a manufacturer operating at 95% of capacity, has been offered a new order at $7.25 per unit requiring 15% of capacity. No other use of the 5% current idle capacity can be found. However, if the order were accepted, the subcontracting for the required 10% additional capacity would cost $7.50 per unit.

The variable cost of production for Kirklin on a per-unit basis follows:

| | |
|---|---|
| Materials | $3.50 |
| Labor | 1.50 |
| Variable overhead | 1.50 |
| | $6.50 |

---

**34.** In applying the contribution margin approach to evaluating whether to accept the new order, assuming subcontracting, what is the average variable cost per unit?

  A. $6.83

  B. $7.17

  C. $7.25

  D. $7.50

The correct answer is (B). *(CIA, adapted)*
  **REQUIRED:** The average variable unit cost of the order.
  **DISCUSSION:** Variable cost is equal to the direct costs associated with a product, an order, or other decision. In this case, one-third of the order has a variable cost of $6.50, and two-thirds of the order has a variable cost of $7.50. Thus, the average variable cost is $7.17 [($6.50 x ⅓) + ($7.50 x ⅔)].
  Answer (A) is incorrect because $6.83 assumes two-thirds of the order is produced at $6.50 per unit and one-third at $7.50 per unit. Answer (C) is incorrect because the sales price per unit of the new order is $7.25. Answer (D) is incorrect because $7.50 is the unit cost above 100% capacity.

**35.** Assuming the average variable cost per unit of the new order is $7.17, the expected contribution margin per unit of the new order is

  A. $.08

  B. $.25

  C. $.33

  D. $.42

The correct answer is (A). *(CIA, adapted)*
  **REQUIRED:** The unit contribution margin of the new order.
  **DISCUSSION:** The unit contribution margin of the new order is the selling price of $7.25 minus the average variable cost. The average variable cost is $7.17. Accordingly, the unit contribution margin on the order is $.08.
  Answer (B) is incorrect because a $.25 contribution margin assumes a cost per unit of $7.00. Answers (C) and (D) are incorrect because the contribution margin is determined by subtracting the average variable cost ($7.17) from the unit sales price ($7.25).

Questions 36 and 37 are based on the following information. A company manufactures and sells a single product. Planned and actual production in 1998, its first year of operation, was 100,000 units. Planned and actual costs in 1998 were as follows:

|  | Manufacturing | Nonmanufacturing |
|---|---|---|
| Variable | $600,000 | $500,000 |
| Fixed | 400,000 | 300,000 |

The company sold 85,000 units of product in 1998 at a selling price of $30 per unit.

**36.** Using absorption costing, the company's operating income in 1998 would be

A. $750,000

B. $900,000

C. $975,000

D. $1,020,000

The correct answer is (B). *(CIA, adapted)*

**REQUIRED:** The absorption-costing operating income.

**DISCUSSION:** Under absorption costing, product costs include fixed and variable manufacturing costs. The unit product cost under absorption costing is $10 [($600,000 + $400,000) ÷ 100,000 units produced]. All nonmanufacturing costs are expensed in the period incurred. Thus, operating income is $900,000.

| | |
|---|---|
| Revenue (85,000 units × $30) | $2,550,000 |
| Cost of goods sold (85,000 units × $10) | (850,000) |
| Nonmanufacturing costs ($500,000 + $300,000) | (800,000) |
| Operating income | $ 900,000 |

Answer (A) is incorrect because $750,000 equals absorption-costing net income minus ending inventory ($15,000 units x $10). Answer (C) is incorrect because $975,000 treats the variable nonmanufacturing costs as manufacturing costs. Answer (D) is incorrect because $1,020,000 assumes that all costs are manufacturing costs.

**37.** Using variable costing, the company's operating income in 1998 would be

A. $750,000

B. $840,000

C. $915,000

D. $975,000

The correct answer is (B). *(CIA, adapted)*

**REQUIRED:** The variable-costing operating income.

**DISCUSSION:** Under variable costing, the product cost includes only variable manufacturing costs. All fixed costs are expensed in the period incurred. Unit product cost under variable costing is $6 ($600,000 ÷ 100,000 units produced).

| | |
|---|---|
| Revenue (85,000 units × $30) | $2,550,000 |
| Variable cost of goods sold (85,000 units × $6) | (510,000) |
| Variable nonmanufacturing costs | (500,000) |
| Contribution margin | $1,540,000 |
| Fixed costs | (700,000) |
| Operating income | $ 840,000 |

Answer (A) is incorrect because $750,000 equals variable costing net income minus ending inventory (15,000 units x $6). Answer (C) is incorrect because $915,000 treats all variable costs as manufacturing costs. Answer (D) is incorrect because $975,000 treats all variable costs and fixed manufacturing costs as product costs.

**38.** During its first year of operations, a company produced 275,000 units and sold 250,000 units. The following costs were incurred during the year:

Variable costs per unit:

| | |
|---|---|
| Direct materials | $15.00 |
| Direct labor | 10.00 |
| Manufacturing overhead | 12.50 |
| Selling and administrative | 2.50 |

Total fixed costs:

| | |
|---|---|
| Manufacturing overhead | $2,200,000 |
| Selling and administrative | 1,375,000 |

The difference between operating income calculated on the absorption costing basis and on the variable costing basis is that absorption-costing operating income is

A.  $200,000 greater.

B.  $220,000 greater.

C.  $325,000 greater.

D.  $62,500 less.

The correct answer is (A). *(CIA, adapted)*
**REQUIRED:** The difference between absorption-costing and variable-costing operating income.
**DISCUSSION:** Absorption-costing operating income will exceed variable-costing operating income because production exceeds sales, resulting in a deferral of fixed manufacturing overhead in the inventory calculated using the absorption method. The difference of $200,000 is equal to the fixed manufacturing overhead per unit ($2,200,000 ÷ 275,000 = $8.00) times the difference between production and sales (275,000 − 250,000 = 25,000, which is the inventory change in units).
Answer (B) is incorrect because units produced, not units sold, should be used as the denominator to calculate the fixed manufacturing cost per unit. Answer (C) is incorrect because fixed selling and administrative costs are not properly inventoriable under absorption costing. Answer (D) is incorrect because variable selling and administrative costs are period costs under both variable and absorption cost systems in the determination of operating income.

**39.** Keller Company, a manufacturer of rivets, uses absorption costing. Keller's manufacturing costs were as follows:

| | |
|---|---|
| Direct materials and direct labor | $800,000 |
| Depreciation of machines | 100,000 |
| Rent for factory building | 60,000 |
| Electricity to run machines | 35,000 |

How much of these costs should be inventoried?

A.  $800,000

B.  $835,000

C.  $935,000

D.  $995,000

The correct answer is (D). *(CPA, adapted)*
**REQUIRED:** The amount of costs inventoried.
**DISCUSSION:** Under absorption costing, the inventoried costs consist of all direct materials, direct labor, and manufacturing overhead. Manufacturing overhead includes depreciation, factory rent, and power for the machines. Thus, the total cost to be inventoried is $995,000 ($800,000 + $100,000 + $60,000 + $35,000).
Answer (A) is incorrect because inventoriable costs also include all manufacturing overhead. Answer (B) is incorrect because inventoriable costs under absorption costing include the depreciation of machines ($100,000) and the factory rent ($60,000). Answer (C) is incorrect because rent for the factory building ($60,000) is a cost that is charged to inventory.

Questions 40 through 43 are based on the following information. Peterson Company's records for the year ended December 31 show that no finished goods inventory existed at January 1 and no work was in process at the beginning or end of the year.

| | | |
|---|---|---|
| Net sales | | $1,400,000 |
| Cost of goods manufactured: | Variable | $  630,000 |
| | Fixed | $  315,000 |
| Operating expenses: | Variable | $    98,000 |
| | Fixed | $  140,000 |
| Units manufactured | | 70,000 |
| Units sold | | 60,000 |

**40.** What is Peterson's finished goods inventory cost at December 31 under the variable costing method?

A.  $90,000

B.  $104,000

C.  $105,000

D.  $135,000

The correct answer is (A). *(CPA, adapted)*
**REQUIRED:** The finished goods inventory cost.
**DISCUSSION:** Variable costing considers only variable manufacturing costs as product costs. Fixed manufacturing costs are considered period costs. The total variable manufacturing cost is given as $630,000. For the 70,000 units produced, unit cost was $9.00 ($630,000 ÷ 70,000 units). If EI is 10,000 units (70,000 produced − 60,000 sold), total cost of FG inventory is $90,000 ($9 x 10,000).
Answer (B) is incorrect because variable operating expenses should not be included in CGM. Answer (C) is incorrect because $105,000 equals 10,000 units times $630,000 divided by 60,000 units. Answer (D) is incorrect because $135,000 is the inventory balance under absorption costing.

**41.** What would be Peterson's finished goods inventory cost at December 31 under the absorption costing method?

   A. $90,000

   B. $104,000

   C. $105,000

   D. $135,000

The correct answer is (D). *(Publisher)*
   **REQUIRED:** The finished goods inventory cost under absorption costing.
   **DISCUSSION:** Absorption costing considers both variable and fixed manufacturing costs as product costs. Unit CGM is equal to the sum of the variable ($630,000) plus fixed ($315,000) costs divided by the number of units manufactured (70,000), or $13.50 per unit. Given that 10,000 units remain in inventory (70,000 produced – 60,000 sold), EI is $135,000.
   Answer (A) is incorrect because $90,000 is the finished goods inventory cost under variable costing. Answer (B) is incorrect because variable operating expenses should not be included in CGM. Furthermore, fixed costs of manufacturing need to be included in the calculation of EI. Answer (C) is incorrect because $105,000 equals 10,000 units times $630,000 divided by 60,000 units.

**42.** Under the absorption costing method, Peterson's operating income for the year is

   A. $217,000

   B. $307,000

   C. $352,000

   D. $374,500

The correct answer is (C). *(CPA, adapted)*
   **REQUIRED:** The operating income.
   **DISCUSSION:** In absorption costing, the unit costs include both fixed and variable manufacturing costs. Fixed manufacturing costs are given as $315,000.

| | |
|---|---:|
| Sales | $1,400,000 |
| CGS (60,000 × $13.50) | (810,000) |
| Gross margin | $ 590,000 |
| Operating expenses | |
|   Variable | (98,000) |
|   Fixed | (140,000) |
| Operating income | $ 352,000 |

   Answer (A) is incorrect because $217,000 is the operating income if all units manufactured are sold. Answer (B) is incorrect because $307,000 is the operating income under variable costing. Answer (D) is incorrect because units manufactured, not units sold, should be the denominator in determining the unit cost of inventory.

**43.** Under the variable costing method, Peterson's operating income for the year is

   A. $217,000

   B. $307,000

   C. $352,000

   D. $762,000

The correct answer is (B). *(Publisher)*
   **REQUIRED:** The operating income.
   **DISCUSSION:** In variable costing, the unit CGS includes only the variable manufacturing costs, which were $9.00 per unit ($630,000 ÷ 70,000). The income statement follows:

| | |
|---|---:|
| Sales | $1,400,000 |
| CGS (60,000 × $9) | (540,000) |
| Variable operating expenses | (98,000) |
| Contribution margin | $ 762,000 |
| Fixed costs: | |
|   CGM | (315,000) |
|   Operating | (140,000) |
| Operating income | $ 307,000 |

   Answer (A) is incorrect because $217,000 is the operating income if all units manufactured were sold. Answer (C) is incorrect because $352,000 is the operating income under absorption costing. Answer (D) is incorrect because $762,000 is the contribution margin.

Questions 44 through 47 are based on the following information. The annual flexible budget below was prepared for use in making decisions relating to Product X:

| | 100,000 Units | 150,000 Units | 200,000 Units |
|---|---|---|---|
| Sales volume | $800,000 | $1,200,000 | $1,600,000 |
| Manufacturing costs: | | | |
| Variable | $300,000 | $ 450,000 | $ 600,000 |
| Fixed | 200,000 | 200,000 | 200,000 |
| | $500,000 | $ 650,000 | $ 800,000 |
| Selling and other expenses: | | | |
| Variable | $200,000 | $ 300,000 | $ 400,000 |
| Fixed | 160,000 | 160,000 | 160,000 |
| | $360,000 | $ 460,000 | $ 560,000 |
| Income (or loss) | $ (60,000) | $ 90,000 | $ 240,000 |

The 200,000-unit budget has been adopted and will be used for allocating fixed manufacturing costs to units of Product X. At the end of the first 6 months, the following information is available:

| | Units |
|---|---|
| Production completed | 120,000 |
| Sales | 60,000 |

All fixed costs are budgeted and incurred uniformly throughout the year, and all costs incurred coincide with the budget. Over- and underapplied fixed manufacturing costs are deferred until year-end. Annual sales have the following seasonal pattern:

| | Portion of Annual Sales |
|---|---|
| First quarter | 10% |
| Second quarter | 20% |
| Third quarter | 30% |
| Fourth quarter | 40% |

**44.** The amount of fixed factory costs applied to product during the first 6 months under absorption costing is

A. Overapplied by $20,000.

B. Equal to the fixed costs incurred.

C. Underapplied by $40,000.

D. Underapplied by $80,000.

The correct answer is (A). *(CPA, adapted)*

**REQUIRED:** The true statement about the amount of applied factory overhead.

**DISCUSSION:** Under absorption costing, fixed factory overhead is applied based on the number of units produced. Fixed factory overhead equals $200,000. Given that production is budgeted at 200,000 units, the fixed factory overhead rate is $1 per unit. Production completed in the first 6 months equals 120,000 units, so $120,000 of overhead was applied. Because all costs incurred coincide with the budget, only $100,000 [$200,000 x (6/12)] of the budgeted fixed factory overhead was incurred. Therefore, factory overhead is overapplied by $20,000 ($120,000 – $100,000).

Answer (B) is incorrect because $100,000 was incurred and $120,000 was applied. Answer (C) is incorrect because fixed factory overhead is applied based on units produced, not units sold. Answer (D) is incorrect because $80,000 equals annual fixed factory overhead minus the amount applied to 120,000 units.

**45.** Reported net income (or loss) for the first 6 months under absorption costing is

A. $160,000

B. $0

C. $40,000

D. $(40,000)

The correct answer is (C). *(CPA, adapted)*

**REQUIRED:** The net income (loss) under the absorption costing method.

**DISCUSSION:** Variable manufacturing cost is $3 per unit and fixed manufacturing cost is $1 per unit. Selling price is $8 per unit ($1,600,000 ÷ 200,000 units). The variable selling expenses are $2 per unit ($400,000 ÷ 200,000 units). The fixed selling expenses equal $80,000 for the 6-month period (50% of the $160,000 annual selling expense).

| | |
|---|---|
| Revenue | $480,000 |
| CGS | (240,000) |
| Gross margin | $240,000 |
| Variable selling expense | (120,000) |
| Fixed selling expense | (80,000) |
| Net income | $ 40,000 |

Answer (A) is incorrect because the variable selling expense ($120,000) was not subtracted. Answer (B) is incorrect because $0 is the variable costing net income. Answer (D) is incorrect because a net income of $40,000, not a loss, should be reported.

**46.** Reported net income (or loss) for the first 6 months under variable costing is

A.  $180,000

B.  $40,000

C.  $0

D.  $(180,000)

The correct answer is (C).  *(CPA, adapted)*

**REQUIRED:**  The net income (loss) under the variable costing method.

**DISCUSSION:**  Sales were 60,000 units at $8, variable manufacturing cost was $3 per unit, variable selling cost was $2 per unit, and fixed costs were 50% of the annual amounts.

| | |
|---|---:|
| Revenue | $480,000 |
| CGS | (180,000) |
| Variable selling expense | (120,000) |
| Fixed manufacturing expense | (100,000) |
| Fixed selling expense | (80,000) |
| Net income | $   -0-   |

Answer (A) is incorrect because $180,000 is the contribution margin.  Answer (B) is incorrect because $40,000 is the absorption-costing net income.  Answer (D) is incorrect because $(180,000) results from subtracting the annual fixed costs.

**47.** Assuming that 90,000 units of Product X were sold during the first 6 months and that this is to be used as a basis, the revised budget estimate for the total number of units to be sold during this year is

A.  360,000

B.  240,000

C.  200,000

D.  300,000

The correct answer is (D).  *(CPA, adapted)*

**REQUIRED:**  The annual sales budget based on the first 6 months of the year.

**DISCUSSION:**  To calculate the revised annual sales budget based on the first 6 months of the year, the number of units sold during the first 6 months and the appropriate portion of the annual sales that the 90,000 units represent must be examined.  The 90,000 units of Product X sold during the first 6 months represent 30% of the annual sales (10% first quarter + 20% second quarter), so annual sales would be projected at 300,000 units (90,000 ÷ .30).

Answers (A) and (B) are incorrect because the revised estimate of sales for the year is 300,000 units.  Answer (C) is incorrect because 200,000 units is the original annual sales budget.  The sales estimate needs to be revised by using the actual sales information for the first 6 months of the year.

Questions 48 through 54 are based on the following information. Valyn Corporation employs an absorption costing system for internal reporting purposes; however, the company is considering using variable costing. Data regarding Valyn's planned and actual operations for the 1998 calendar year are presented below.

| | Planned Activity | Actual Activity |
|---|---|---|
| Beginning finished goods inventory in units | 35,000 | 35,000 |
| Sales in units | 140,000 | 125,000 |
| Production in units | 140,000 | 130,000 |

The planned per-unit cost figures shown in the schedule were based on production and sale of 140,000 units in 1998. Valyn uses a predetermined manufacturing overhead rate for applying manufacturing overhead to its product; thus, a combined manufacturing overhead rate of $9.00 per unit was employed for absorption-costing purposes in 1998. Any over- or underapplied manufacturing overhead is closed to cost of goods sold at the end of the reporting year.

| | Planned Costs Per Unit | Total | Incurred Costs |
|---|---|---|---|
| Direct materials | $12.00 | $1,680,000 | $1,560,000 |
| Direct labor | 9.00 | 1,260,000 | 1,170,000 |
| Variable manufacturing overhead | 4.00 | 560,000 | 520,000 |
| Fixed manufacturing overhead | 5.00 | 700,000 | 715,000 |
| Variable selling expenses | 8.00 | 1,120,000 | 1,000,000 |
| Fixed selling expenses | 7.00 | 980,000 | 980,000 |
| Variable administrative expenses | 2.00 | 280,000 | 250,000 |
| Fixed administrative expenses | 3.00 | 420,000 | 425,000 |
| Total | $50.00 | $7,000,000 | $6,620,000 |

The 1998 beginning finished goods inventory for absorption costing purposes was valued at the 1997 planned unit manufacturing cost, which was the same as the 1998 planned unit manufacturing cost. There are no work-in-process inventories at either the beginning or the end of the year. The planned and actual unit selling price for 1998 was $70.00 per unit.

**48.** The value of Valyn Corporation's 1998 actual ending finished goods inventory on the absorption costing basis was

A. $900,000

B. $1,200,000

C. $1,220,000

D. $2,000,000

The correct answer is (B). *(CMA, adapted)*
REQUIRED: The actual finished goods ending inventory.
DISCUSSION: Under the absorption method, unit cost is $30 ($12 direct materials + $9 direct labor + $4 variable overhead + $5 fixed overhead). Given beginning inventory of 35,000 units, the ending inventory equals 40,000 units (35,000 BI + 130,000 produced – 125,000 sold). Hence, ending inventory was $1,200,000 ($30 x 40,000 units).
Answer (A) is incorrect because $900,000 assumes an ending inventory of 30,000 units. Answer (C) is incorrect because planned unit cost, not actual unit cost, should be used. Answer (D) is incorrect because $2,000,000 equals $50 times 40,000 units.

**49.** The value of Valyn Corporation's 1998 actual ending finished goods inventory on the variable costing basis was

A. $1,400,000

B. $1,200,000

C. $1,000,000

D. $750,000

The correct answer is (C). *(CMA, adapted)*
REQUIRED: The actual finished goods ending inventory.
DISCUSSION: Using variable (direct) costing, the unit cost of ending inventory is $25 ($12 direct materials + $9 direct labor + $4 variable overhead). Given beginning inventory of 35,000 units, the ending inventory equals 40,000 units (35,000 BI + 130,000 produced – 125,000 sold). Thus, ending inventory was $1,000,000 ($25 x 40,000).
Answer (A) is incorrect because variable selling and administrative expenses were included. Answer (B) is incorrect because $1,200,000 equals absorption-costing ending inventory. Answer (D) is incorrect because ending inventory equals 40,000 units, not 30,000 units.

**50.** Valyn Corporation's actual manufacturing contribution margin for 1998 calculated on the variable costing basis was

A. $4,375,000

B. $5,500,000

C. $4,910,000

D. $5,625,000

The correct answer is (D). *(CMA, adapted)*

**REQUIRED:** The actual contribution margin on the variable costing basis.

**DISCUSSION:** At $70 per unit, sales revenue was $8,750,000 for 125,000 units. Variable costs of manufacturing were $25 per unit ($12 + $9 + $4). Thus, total variable manufacturing cost was $3,125,000 ($25 x 125,000 units). Consequently, manufacturing contribution margin was $5,625,000 ($8,750,000 – $3,125,000).

Answer (A) is incorrect because variable selling and administrative expenses should not be deducted. Answer (B) is incorrect because $5,500,000 results from deducting the variable manufacturing costs of 130,000 units. Answer (C) is incorrect because $4,910,000 results from deducting fixed manufacturing overhead.

**51.** Valyn Corporation's total fixed costs in 1998 on the absorption costing basis were

A. $2,095,000

B. $2,120,000

C. $2,055,000

D. $2,030,000

The correct answer is (A). *(CMA, adapted)*

**REQUIRED:** The total fixed costs under the absorption costing basis.

**DISCUSSION:** Under the absorption method, all selling and administrative fixed costs are charged to the current period. Accordingly, $980,000 of selling expenses and $425,000 of actual fixed administrative expenses were expensed during 1998. The fixed manufacturing costs must be calculated after giving consideration to the increase in inventory during the period (some fixed costs were capitalized) and to the underapplied O/H. The beginning finished goods inventory included 35,000 units, each of which had absorbed $5 of fixed manufacturing O/H. Each unit produced during the year also absorbed $5 of fixed manufacturing O/H. Given that 125,000 of those units were sold, CGS was debited for $625,000 of fixed O/H (125,000 units x $5). At year-end, the underapplied O/H was also added to CGS. Because production was expected to be 140,000 units, the O/H application rate for the $700,000 of planned fixed manufacturing O/H was $5 per unit. Only 130,000 units were manufactured. Hence, $650,000 ($5 x 130,000 units) of O/H was applied to units in process. Actual O/H was $715,000, so the underapplied O/H was $65,000 ($715,000 – $650,000). This amount was charged to CGS at year-end. The total of the fixed costs debited to CGS was therefore $2,095,000 ($980,000 selling expenses + $425,000 administrative expenses + $625,000 standard manufacturing costs + $65,000 underapplied O/H).

Answer (B) is incorrect because only $625,000 (125,000 units sold x $5) of the fixed manufacturing O/H should be expensed under absorption costing. Furthermore, underapplied O/H of $65,000 [$715,000 fixed manufacturing O/H incurred – ($5 x 130,000 units produced)] should also be included in Valyn's total fixed costs. Answer (C) is incorrect because only $625,000 (125,000 units sold x $5) of the fixed manufacturing O/H should be expensed under absorption costing. Additionally, underapplied O/H should be added to, not subtracted from, Valyn's total fixed costs. Answer (D) is incorrect because underapplied O/H of $65,000 [$715,000 fixed mfg. O/H incurred – ($5 x 130,000 units produced)] should be included in Valyn's total fixed costs.

Refer to the information preceding question 48 on page 240.

**52.** The total variable cost expensed in 1998 by Valyn Corporation on the variable costing basis was

  A.  $4,375,000

  B.  $4,500,000

  C.  $4,325,000

  D.  $4,550,000

The correct answer is (A). *(CMA, adapted)*

  **REQUIRED:** The total variable cost expensed under the variable costing method.

  **DISCUSSION:** The unit variable manufacturing cost was $25 ($12 direct materials + $9 direct labor + $4 variable overhead). Other variable costs included selling expenses ($8 per unit) and administrative expenses ($2 per unit). Thus, total unit variable cost was $35 ($25 + $8 + $2). The total expensed was therefore $4,375,000 ($35 x 125,000 units sold).

  Answers (B), (C), and (D) are incorrect because the total variable costs expensed under variable costing include the variable manufacturing ($25 per unit), selling ($8 per unit), and administrative ($2 per unit) costs for the units sold.

**53.** Valyn Corporation's absorption-costing operating income in 1998 was

  A.  Higher than variable-costing operating income because actual production exceeded actual sales.

  B.  Lower than variable-costing operating income because actual production exceeded actual sales.

  C.  Lower than variable-costing operating income because actual production was less than planned production.

  D.  Lower than variable-costing operating income because actual sales were less than planned sales.

The correct answer is (A). *(CMA, adapted)*

  **REQUIRED:** The true statement comparing absorption-costing and variable-costing income.

  **DISCUSSION:** Absorption costing results in a higher income figure than variable costing whenever production exceeds sales. The reason is that absorption costing capitalizes some fixed factory overhead as part of inventory. These costs are expensed during the period incurred under variable costing. Consequently, variable costing recognizes greater expenses and lower income. The reverse is true when sales exceed production. In that case, the absorption method results in a lower income because some fixed costs of previous periods absorbed by the beginning inventory are expensed in the current period as cost of goods sold. Variable costing income is never burdened with fixed costs of previous periods.

  Answer (B) is incorrect because an increase in inventory results in a higher income under absorption costing. Answer (C) is incorrect because the important relationship is between actual production and actual sales. Answer (D) is incorrect because planned sales do not determine actual income.

**54.** The difference between Valyn Corporation's 1998 operating income calculated on the absorption costing basis and calculated on the variable costing basis was

  A.  $25,000

  B.  $45,000

  C.  $75,000

  D.  $100,000

The correct answer is (A). *(CMA, adapted)*

  **REQUIRED:** The difference between absorption-costing and variable-costing income.

  **DISCUSSION:** The difference is caused by the capitalization of some of the fixed manufacturing overhead. When inventories increase, the absorption method capitalizes that overhead. The variable costing method deducts it in the current period. Inventories increased by 5,000 units during the period, and each unit would have included $5 of fixed manufacturing overhead under absorption costing. Accordingly, the $25,000 of fixed manufacturing overhead capitalized is the difference in income between the two costing methods.

  Answer (B) is incorrect because $45,000 equals unit manufacturing overhead cost ($9) times the inventory increase. Answer (C) is incorrect because $75,000 equals unit fixed cost ($15) times the inventory increase. Answer (D) is incorrect because $100,000 equals unit selling and administrative expenses times the inventory increase.

| | |
|---|---|
| Questions 55 and 56 are based on the following information. The excerpt presented in the next column was taken from Valenz Company's records for the fiscal year ended November 30. | |

| | |
|---|---|
| Direct materials used | $300,000 |
| Direct labor | 100,000 |
| Variable factory overhead | 50,000 |
| Fixed factory overhead | 80,000 |
| Sell. & admin. costs -- variable | 40,000 |
| Sell. & admin. costs -- fixed | 20,000 |

**55.** If Valenz Company uses variable costing, the inventoriable costs for the current fiscal year are

A. $400,000

B. $450,000

C. $490,000

D. $530,000

The correct answer is (B). *(CMA, adapted)*

**REQUIRED:** The inventoriable costs using the variable costing method.

**DISCUSSION:** Under variable costing, the only costs that are capitalized are the variable costs of manufacturing. These include

| | |
|---|---|
| Direct materials used | $300,000 |
| Direct labor | 100,000 |
| Variable factory overhead | 50,000 |
| Total inventoriable costs | $450,000 |

Answer (A) is incorrect because variable factory overhead ($50,000) must be included. Answer (C) is incorrect because variable selling and administrative costs ($40,000) should not be included. Answer (D) is incorrect because fixed factory overhead is not inventoried under variable costing.

**56.** Using absorption (full) costing, inventoriable costs are

A. $400,000

B. $450,000

C. $530,000

D. $590,000

The correct answer is (C). *(CMA, adapted)*

**REQUIRED:** The inventoriable costs using the absorption costing method.

**DISCUSSION:** The absorption method is required for financial statements prepared according to GAAP. It charges all costs of production to inventories. The variable cost of direct materials ($300,000), direct labor ($100,000), variable factory overhead ($50,000), and the fixed factory overhead ($80,000) are included. They total $530,000.

Answer (A) is incorrect because $400,000 equals direct materials and labor. Answer (B) is incorrect because $450,000 is the inventoriable costs using the variable costing method. Answer (D) is incorrect because selling and administrative costs are not included.

Questions 57 and 58 are based on the following information. Osawa, Inc. planned and actually manufactured 200,000 units of its single product in 1998, its first year of operations. Variable manufacturing costs were $30 per unit of product. Planned and actual fixed manufacturing costs were $600,000, and selling and administrative costs totaled $400,000 in 1998. Osawa sold 120,000 units of product in 1998 at a selling price of $40 per unit.

**57.** Osawa's 1998 operating income using absorption (full) costing is

   A. $200,000

   B. $440,000

   C. $600,000

   D. $840,000

The correct answer is (B). *(CMA, adapted)*
   **REQUIRED:** The operating income under absorption costing.
   **DISCUSSION:** Absorption costing net income is computed as follows:

| | |
|---|---:|
| Sales (120,000 × $40) | $4,800,000 |
| Variable production costs ($30 × 200,000 units) | $6,000,000 |
| Fixed production costs | 600,000 |
| Total production costs (200,000 units) | $6,600,000 |
| Ending inventory (80,000 × $33) | (2,640,000) |
| Cost of goods sold | $3,960,000 |
| Gross profit | $ 840,000 |
| Selling and administrative expenses | (400,000) |
| Operating income | $ 440,000 |

   Answer (A) is incorrect because $200,000 is the operating income under variable costing. Answer (C) is incorrect because $600,000 is the operating income that results from capitalizing $240,000 of fixed manufacturing costs and $160,000 of selling and administrative costs (the $160,000 is incorrect as all selling and administrative costs should be expensed). Answer (D) is incorrect because $840,000 is the gross profit under absorption costing, i.e., before selling and administrative expenses.

**58.** Osawa's 1998 operating income using variable costing is

   A. $200,000

   B. $440,000

   C. $800,000

   D. $600,000

The correct answer is (A). *(CMA, adapted)*
   **REQUIRED:** The operating income under variable costing.
   **DISCUSSION:** The contribution margin from manufacturing (sales – variable costs) is $10 ($40 – $30) per unit sold, or $1,200,000 (120,000 units x $10). The fixed costs of manufacturing ($600,000) and selling and administrative costs ($400,000) are deducted from the contribution margin to arrive at an operating income of $200,000. The difference between the absorption income of $440,000 (see preceding question) and the $200,000 of variable costing income is attributable to capitalization of the fixed manufacturing costs under the absorption method. Since 40% of the goods produced are still in inventory (80,000 ÷ 200,000), 40% of the $600,000 in fixed costs, or $240,000, was capitalized under the absorption method. That amount was expensed under the variable costing method.
   Answer (B) is incorrect because $440,000 is the operating income under absorption costing. Answer (C) is incorrect because $800,000 is the operating income if fixed costs of manufacturing are not deducted. Answer (D) is incorrect because $600,000 is the operating income that results from capitalizing 40% of both fixed manufacturing costs and selling and administrative costs.

Questions 59 and 60 are based on the following information. A and B are autonomous segments of a corporation. They have no beginning or ending inventories, and the number of units produced is equal to the number of units sold. Following is financial information relating to the two divisions.

|  | A | B |
|---|---|---|
| Sales | $150,000 | $400,000 |
| Other revenue | 10,000 | 15,000 |
| Direct materials | 30,000 | 65,000 |
| Direct labor | 20,000 | 40,000 |
| Variable factory overhead | 5,000 | 15,000 |
| Fixed factory overhead | 25,000 | 55,000 |
| Variable S&A expense | 15,000 | 30,000 |
| Fixed S&A expense | 35,000 | 60,000 |
| Central corporate expenses (allocated) | 12,000 | 20,000 |

**59.** What is the total contribution to corporate profits generated by Segment A before allocation of central corporate expenses?

A. $18,000

B. $20,000

C. $30,000

D. $90,000

The correct answer is (C). *(CIA, adapted)*
**REQUIRED:** The total contribution to profits by A.
**DISCUSSION:** Segment A's total contribution to corporate profits includes everything except the central corporate expense allocation. Thus, the total contribution is $30,000 ($150,000 sales + $10,000 other revenue – $30,000 direct materials – $20,000 direct labor – $5,000 variable overhead – $25,000 fixed overhead – $15,000 variable S&A expense – $35,000 fixed S&A expense).
Answer (A) is incorrect because $18,000 is the result of deducting the central corporate expenses. Answer (B) is incorrect because $20,000 is the result of excluding other revenue. Answer (D) is incorrect because $90,000 is the result of failing to deduct the fixed costs.

**60.** What is the contribution margin of Segment B?

A. $150,000

B. $205,000

C. $235,000

D. $265,000

The correct answer is (D). *(CIA, adapted)*
**REQUIRED:** The contribution margin of B.
**DISCUSSION:** The contribution margin equals revenue minus variable costs. Thus, Segment B's contribution margin is $265,000 ($400,000 sales + $15,000 other revenue – $65,000 direct materials – $40,000 direct labor – $15,000 variable overhead – $30,000 variable S&A expense).
Answer (A) is incorrect because $150,000 is the result of subtracting fixed costs. Answer (B) is incorrect because $205,000 is the result of subtracting fixed S&A costs. Answer (C) is incorrect because $235,000 is the result of subtracting fixed S and A costs but not variable S&A costs.

# CHAPTER EIGHT
# COST-VOLUME-PROFIT ANALYSIS

Cost-volume-profit (CVP) analysis (sometimes called breakeven analysis) is a means of predicting the relationships among revenues, variable costs, and fixed costs at various production levels. It allows management to discern the probable effects of changes in unit volume, sales price, revenue (sales) mix, etc. CVP variables include revenue as a function of price per unit and quantity produced, fixed costs, variable cost per unit or as a percentage of revenues, and profit per unit or as a percentage of revenues. Furthermore, certain simplifying CVP assumptions are inherent in this type of analysis. Costs and revenues are deemed to be predictable and linear over the relevant range of activity and specified time span. For example, reductions in prices are not necessary to increase revenues, and no learning curve effect operates to reduce unit variable labor costs at higher output levels. Thus, a relevant range exists in which the various relationships are true for a given time span. Within these limits, all costs are either fixed or variable relative to a given cost object, and the time value of money is ignored. Total variable costs change proportionally with activity level, but unit variable costs are constant over the relevant range. Moreover, total fixed costs remain constant over the relevant range, but per-unit fixed costs vary indirectly with the activity level. Unit sales prices and market conditions are also constant, and the revenue mix does not change (or the firm makes only one product). Other assumptions are that technology and productive efficiency are constant and that costs and revenues vary only with changes in physical unit volume. Thus, volume of output is the sole revenue driver and cost driver. Furthermore, any change in inventory is immaterial. Accordingly, the breakeven point is directly related to costs and indirectly related to the budgeted margin of safety and the contribution margin.

Certain additional definitions are fundamental to CVP analysis. The breakeven point is the level of output at which total revenues equal total costs. The margin of safety is a measure of risk. It is the excess of budgeted revenues over breakeven revenues, that is, operating income. The revenue (sales) mix is the composition of total revenues in terms of various products, i.e., the percentages of each product included in total revenues. It is deemed to be maintained for all volume changes. The unit contribution margin (UCM) is the unit selling price minus the unit variable cost. It is the contribution from the sale of one unit to cover fixed costs (and possibly a target operating income). It is expressed as either a percentage of the selling price (contribution margin ratio) or a dollar amount. The UCM is the slope of the total cost curve plotted so that quantity sold is on the x axis and cost is on the y axis.

The **breakeven formula** equates operating income with revenues (quantity sold × unit price) minus fixed costs and variable costs (quantity sold × unit variable cost).  One application is to determine the breakeven point in units by setting revenues equal to the sum of fixed costs and variable costs.  The same result can be obtained by dividing fixed costs by the UCM.  The breakeven point in dollars can be calculated by dividing fixed costs by the contribution margin ratio.  Another typical application calculates a target operating income, either in dollars or as a percentage of revenues.  If the target is stated as a per-unit amount or a percentage, it is treated as a variable cost.  If the desired amount is stated in total dollars, it is treated as a fixed cost.  A variation of this problem asks for net income (an after-tax amount) instead of operating income (a pretax amount).  In this case, the computation requires converting the target net income to target operating income by dividing the target net income by one minus the income tax rate.  Income tax liability does not change the breakeven point because, at that output level, operating income and therefore income tax expense are zero.  However, other taxes, such as sales tax, do change the breakeven point.

Multiple products also may be involved in calculating a breakeven point.  For example, if A and B account for 60% and 40% of total revenues, respectively, and variable costs are 60% and 85%, respectively, the breakeven point in dollars of revenue, given fixed costs of $150,000, is $500,000 [S = $150,000 + .6(.6S) + .85(.4S)].  In effect, the result is obtained by calculating a weighted-average contribution margin ratio (30%) and dividing it into the fixed costs to arrive at the breakeven point in dollars.  Another approach to multiproduct breakeven problems is to divide fixed costs by the UCM for a composite unit (when unit prices are known) to determine the number of composite units.  The number of individual units can then be calculated based on the stated mix.

Still another application of CVP analysis is determination of the profitability of special orders.  This application is essentially contribution margin analysis.

The foregoing discussion of breakeven applications assumes that **variable costing** (see Chapter 7) is used.  Under variable costing, the breakeven level of unit sales does not vary with production.  It is a function solely of total fixed costs and the UCM.  Under **absorption costing**, however, the breakeven level of unit sales also depends on units produced and the amount of the denominator value used to assign fixed manufacturing costs to inventory.  As the formula below indicates, the greater the units produced, the lower the breakeven point in units sold.  This inverse relationship arises because some fixed manufacturing costs are inventoried under absorption costing.  Accordingly, the breakeven point (BEP) in units sold under absorption costing equals total fixed costs (TFC) plus the product of the fixed manufacturing cost application rate (FMCAR) and the difference between the BEP in units sold and total units produced (UP), all divided by the UCM:

$$BEP = \frac{TFC + [FMCAR(BEP - UP)]}{UCM}$$

The **degree of operating leverage (DOL)** is the change in operating income (earnings before interest and taxes) resulting from a percentage change in revenues. It measures the extent to which a firm incurs fixed rather than variable costs in operations. Thus, the greater the DOL, the greater the risk of loss when sales decline and the greater the reward when sales increase.

$$Operating\ leverage\ =\ \frac{Percentage\ change\ in\ operating\ income}{Percentage\ change\ in\ revenues}$$

The assumption is that organizations with larger investments (and greater fixed costs) will have higher contribution margins and more operating leverage. Thus, as they invest in better and more expensive equipment, their variable production costs should decrease. For example, if revenues increase by 40% and operating income increases by 50%, the operating leverage is 1.25 (50% ÷ 40%). Given that Q equals the number of units sold, P is unit price, V is unit variable cost, and F is fixed cost, the DOL can also be calculated from the formula below, which equals total contribution margin divided by operating income (total contribution margin – fixed cost). This formula is derived from the previous formula, but the derivation is not given.

$$\frac{Q(P\ -\ V)}{Q(P\ -\ V)\ -\ F}\ =\ \frac{Total\ Contribution\ Margin\ (TCM)}{Operating\ income}$$

The DOL is calculated with respect to a given base level of revenues. The significance of the DOL is that a given percentage increase in revenues yields a percentage increase in operating income equal to the DOL for the base level times the percentage increase in revenues. Furthermore, the DOL is related to the **margin of safety percentage (MSP)**. The DOL equals 1 divided by the MSP, and the MSP equals 1 divided by the DOL. The reason for this relationship is that the margin of safety (operating income) is the excess of the CM over fixed costs (the amount by which the TCM may be reduced without incurring a loss). Thus, the MSP equals operating income divided by the TCM, which is the inverse of the DOL (TCM ÷ operating income).

**Sensitivity analysis** may be used to extend CVP procedures. CVP methods are based on deterministic estimates of costs and prices, but sensitivity analysis permits the decision maker to quantify the effects of risk and uncertainty by measuring the effects of errors in those deterministic estimates (certainty equivalents), which are developed by the best means available and assumed for purposes of a given decision model to be certain. The model then may be evaluated by changing certain data variables critical to the success of the entity and observing the outcomes. This process allows the decision maker to quantify the effects of forecasting (prediction) errors and to identify the most critical variables. For example, different estimates of unit variable cost, selling price, sales mix, total fixed costs, and target income may be tested in a CVP analysis. The outcomes will indicate how sensitive the results are to changes in these input values. Spreadsheet programs run on personal computers permit these calculations to be done quickly, cheaply, and accurately. Determination of the **margin of safety** is one type of sensitivity analysis performed in a CVP context.

An **activity-based costing (ABC)** approach provides for a more detailed CVP analysis. Traditional CVP analysis considers two cost classifications: (1) variable costs that vary with unit sales and (2) fixed costs. ABC explicitly considers that some costs treated as strictly fixed under traditional CVP methods actually vary with nonunit-based drivers. For example, such costs may vary with batch-level drivers (number of orders, pounds of materials handled, number of setups, etc.) and product-level drivers (product testing, product design, etc.). However, facility-level costs are treated as fixed in this approach because, in theory, they should not be added to products. Accordingly, the total cost in an ABC framework equals fixed cost, plus unit-based variable cost (units sold × unit variable cost), plus batch-level costs (amount of batch-level driver × cost per driver), plus product-level costs (amount of product-level driver × cost per driver). Furthermore, the breakeven point in units equals total cost minus unit-based variable cost, divided by the UCM. The result will be the same breakeven point in units as determined under traditional CVP analysis only if fixed cost under the traditional method equals the sum of fixed cost and nonunit-based variable cost in the ABC analysis. This equality of results will occur if the two methods calculate the nonunit-based variable cost using the same amounts of the batch-level and product-level drivers. However, if these activity amounts are changed after the more detailed consideration involved in the ABC analysis, the computed breakeven points will differ. Consequently, ABC in a CVP context is a type of sensitivity analysis because it can determine the effects of decisions about batch-level and product-level activities.

The **high-low method** is useful in CVP analysis because it is an easy method of estimating variable cost. It divides the difference in costs incurred at the highest and lowest observed levels of activity by the difference in activity. Once the variable cost is found, the fixed portion is determinable. The high-low method has the advantage of simplicity, and the costs of using more sophisticated methods sometimes outweigh the benefits of the incremental accuracy achieved.

CVP analysis is applicable not only in for-profit manufacturing settings but also in for-profit **service** organizations and **not-for-profit** entities. For example, a not-for-profit social services agency might be able to determine its maximum level of service by equating its revenues, such as an appropriation, with the sum of its fixed costs and variable costs (number of people served × cost per person).

## 8.1 Concepts

**1.** Cost-volume-profit (CVP) analysis allows management to determine the relative profitability of a product by

- A. Highlighting potential bottlenecks in the production process.

- B. Keeping fixed costs to an absolute minimum.

- C. Determining the contribution margin per unit and the projected profits at various levels of production.

- D. Assigning costs to a product in a manner that maximizes the contribution margin.

The correct answer is (C). *(CPA, adapted)*

**REQUIRED:** The purpose of cost-volume-profit analysis.

**DISCUSSION:** CVP analysis studies the relationships among sales volume, sales price, fixed costs, variable costs, and profit. It allows management to determine the unit contribution margin (UCM), that is, the difference between unit sales price and unit variable cost. The UCM is used to project the breakeven point (BEP) as well as profits at various levels of production.

Answer (A) is incorrect because CVP analysis does not control physical production. Answer (B) is incorrect because CVP analysis does not control production costs. Answer (D) is incorrect because CVP analysis is a means of estimating profitability at various sales levels rather than a technique of accounting for costs.

**2.** At the breakeven point, the contribution margin equals total

- A. Variable costs.

- B. Sales revenues.

- C. Selling and administrative costs.

- D. Fixed costs.

The correct answer is (D). *(CPA, adapted)*

**REQUIRED:** The amount of contribution margin at the breakeven point.

**DISCUSSION:** At the breakeven point, the point at which no profit or loss occurs, fixed cost must equal the contribution margin (total revenue – total variable cost).

Answers (A) and (B) are incorrect because variable costs and sales revenues are used to determine the contribution margin. Answer (C) is incorrect because selling and administrative costs may be fixed or variable.

**3.** Cost-volume-profit analysis is a key factor in many decisions, including choice of product lines, pricing of products, marketing strategy, and use of productive facilities. A calculation used in a CVP analysis is the breakeven point. Once the breakeven point has been reached, operating income will increase by the

- A. Gross margin per unit for each additional unit sold.

- B. Contribution margin per unit for each additional unit sold.

- C. Variable costs per unit for each additional unit sold.

- D. Sales price per unit for each additional unit sold.

The correct answer is (B). *(CMA, adapted)*

**REQUIRED:** The amount by which operating income will increase once the breakeven point has been reached.

**DISCUSSION:** At the breakeven point, total revenue equals fixed costs plus variable costs. Beyond the BEP, each unit sale will increase operating income by the unit contribution margin (unit sales price – unit variable cost) because fixed cost will already have been recovered.

Answer (A) is incorrect because the gross margin equals sales price minus cost of goods sold, including fixed cost. Answer (C) is incorrect because operating income will increase by the sales price minus the variable costs (contribution margin) for each additional unit sold. Answer (D) is incorrect because operating income will increase by the UCM.

**4.** Which of the following is a characteristic of a contribution income statement?

  A. Fixed and variable expenses are combined as one line.

  B. Fixed expenses are listed separately from variable expenses.

  C. Fixed and variable manufacturing costs are combined as one line item, but fixed operating expenses are shown separately from variable operating expenses.

  D. Fixed and variable operating expenses are combined as one line item, but fixed manufacturing expenses are shown separately from variable manufacturing expenses.

The correct answer is (B). *(CIA, adapted)*
**REQUIRED:** The characteristic of a contribution income statement.
**DISCUSSION:** The contribution income statement emphasizes the distinction between fixed and variable costs. Making this distinction facilitates determination of CVP relationships and the effects of changes in sales volume on income. Thus, fixed manufacturing costs and other fixed costs are separated from variable manufacturing costs and other variable costs. The basic categories in the contribution income statement are variable costs, contribution margin, fixed costs, and operating income.
  Answers (A), (C), and (D) are incorrect because the contribution income statement shows the contribution margin (sales – variable costs) before it subtracts the fixed costs. Fixed costs are not combined with variable costs.

**5.** The method of cost accounting that lends itself to breakeven analysis is

  A. Variable costing.

  B. Standard costing.

  C. Absolute costing.

  D. Absorption costing.

The correct answer is (A). *(CPA, adapted)*
**REQUIRED:** The method of cost accounting used in breakeven analysis.
**DISCUSSION:** Variable costs are emphasized in breakeven analysis. Total revenue minus the total variable costs equals the contribution margin, which is a major tool in breakeven analysis.
  Answer (B) is incorrect because standard costs may be fixed as well as variable. Breakeven analysis emphasizes variable costs. Answer (C) is incorrect because the term absolute cost accounting is nonsensical in this context. Answer (D) is incorrect because absorption costs also include fixed costs. Breakeven analysis emphasizes variable costs.

**6.** Cost-volume-profit relationships that are curvilinear may be analyzed linearly by considering only

  A. Fixed and semivariable costs.

  B. Relevant fixed costs.

  C. Relevant variable costs.

  D. A relevant range of volume.

The correct answer is (D). *(CPA, adapted)*
**REQUIRED:** The circumstances in which curvilinear cost-volume-profit relationships may be analyzed linearly.
**DISCUSSION:** CVP analysis is assumed to be linear over a relevant range of activity (volume). Over the relevant range, total fixed costs and unit variable costs are assumed to be constant.
  Answer (A) is incorrect because the range of volume (activity), not the costs, must be limited in order to analyze curvilinear cost-volume-profit relationships. Answer (B) is incorrect because the linear approximation of a curvilinear CVP relationship is achieved not by limiting the costs considered but by restricting analysis to a given range of activity. Answer (C) is incorrect because a CVP analysis of a curvilinear relationship is performed by restricting the level of activity to a relevant range.

**7.** When an organization is operating above the breakeven point, the degree or amount that revenues may decline before losses are incurred is the

  A. Residual income rate.

  B. Marginal rate of return.

  C. Margin of safety.

  D. Target (hurdle) rate of return.

The correct answer is (C). *(CMA, adapted)*
**REQUIRED:** The rate or amount that revenues may decline before losses are incurred.
**DISCUSSION:** The margin of safety is the excess of budgeted revenues over breakeven revenues. It is considered in sensitivity analysis.
  Answer (A) is incorrect because residual income is the excess of earnings over an imputed charge for the given investment base. Answer (B) is incorrect because a marginal rate of return is the return on the next investment. Answer (D) is incorrect because a target or hurdle rate of return is the required rate of return. It is also known as the discount rate or the opportunity cost of capital.

Questions 8 and 9 are based on the following information. See the cost-volume-profit chart below:

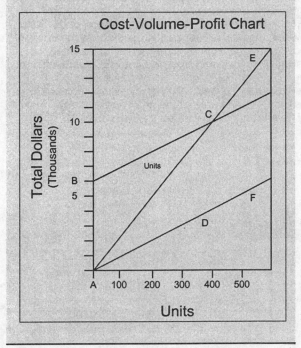

**Cost-Volume-Profit Chart**

**8.** Which of the following labeled points on this chart is the breakeven point?

A. Point A.

B. Point B.

C. Point C.

D. Point D.

The correct answer is (C). *(CIA, adapted)*

**REQUIRED:** The labeled point that is the breakeven point.

**DISCUSSION:** Point C is the intersection of the total cost line and the total revenue line, which is the breakeven point.

Answer (A) is incorrect because Point A is the origin, where total revenues are zero and there is a loss equal to the amount of fixed costs. Answer (B) is incorrect because Point B is the total cost line at zero activity, which is the amount of total fixed costs. Answer (D) is incorrect because Point D is on the total variable cost curve and represents the total variable costs at the breakeven point.

**9.** Which of the following items is graphically represented on the cost-volume-profit chart as the difference between labeled points E and F?

A. Total profit.

B. Total variable costs.

C. Total fixed costs.

D. Total contribution margin.

The correct answer is (D). *(CIA, adapted)*

**REQUIRED:** The item graphically represented on the CVP chart as the difference between labeled points E and F.

**DISCUSSION:** The difference between point E (on the total revenue line) and point F (on the total variable cost line) is total contribution margin.

Answer (A) is incorrect because profit is the difference between point E (which is on the total revenue line) and the total cost line. Answer (B) is incorrect because point F is on the total variable cost curve and represents the total variable costs at that point. Answer (C) is incorrect because total fixed costs is the difference between point F (which is on the total variable cost line) and the total cost line.

**10.** Presented below is a cost-volume-profit chart for a firm. Various reference points are marked on the chart with letters.

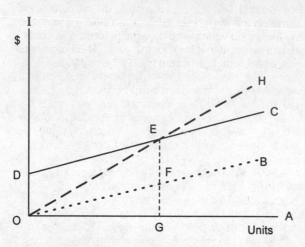

The letters CEH on the chart represent the

A.  Total sales.

B.  Total expenses.

C.  Area of the chart where total revenues exceed total expenses.

D.  Area of the chart where total expenses exceed total revenues.

The correct answer is (C). *(CIA, adapted)*
REQUIRED: The meaning of the letters CEH on the chart.
DISCUSSION: A cost-volume-profit chart contains elements (lines, points, axes) that identify variable cost, fixed cost, the breakeven point, total revenue, profit, and volume in units. When the total revenues line rises above the total cost line, a company will have positive operating income.

Answer (A) is incorrect because line HEO represents total revenues. Answer (B) is incorrect because line CED represents total expenses. Answer (D) is incorrect because the loss area, i.e., the area of the chart where total expenses exceed revenues, is represented by the area OED.

**11.** The diagram below is a cost-volume-profit chart.

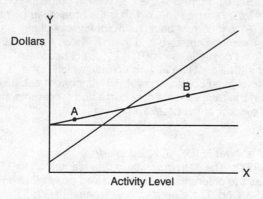

At point A compared with point B, as a percentage of revenues,

| | Variable Costs Are | Fixed Costs Are |
|---|---|---|
| A. | Greater | Greater |
| B. | Greater | The same |
| C. | The same | The same |
| D. | The same | Greater |

The correct answer is (D). *(CPA, adapted)*
REQUIRED: The true comparison of variable and fixed costs as percentages of revenues at points A and B.
DISCUSSION: In CVP analysis, unit sales price and unit variable cost are constant. Hence, total variable costs increase as the activity level rises from A to B, but they remain a constant percentage of revenues. Fixed costs do not vary within the relevant range. As the activity level increases, fixed costs therefore decrease as a percentage of revenues.

Answer (A) is incorrect because the variable costs as a percentage of revenues are constant from point A to point B because both variable costs and revenues increase at a constant rate as the activity level increases. Answer (B) is incorrect because the variable costs are the same as a percentage of revenues at both points. Also, the fixed costs as a percentage of revenues are greater at point A than at point B because fixed costs do not change over the relevant range. Answer (C) is incorrect because the fixed costs are greater as a percentage of revenues at point A. There is less revenue at point A with which to cover identical fixed costs.

**12.** In the profit-volume chart below, EF and GH represent the profit-volume graphs of a single-product company for 1997 and 1998, respectively.

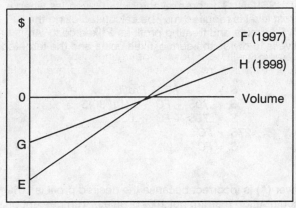

If 1997 and 1998 unit sales prices are identical, how did total fixed costs and unit variable costs of 1998 change compared with 1997?

|   | 1998 Total Fixed Costs | 1998 Unit Variable Costs |
|---|---|---|
| A. | Decreased | Increased |
| B. | Decreased | Decreased |
| C. | Increased | Increased |
| D. | Increased | Decreased |

The correct answer is (A). *(CPA, adapted)*

**REQUIRED:** The change in total fixed costs and unit variable costs.

**DISCUSSION:** Profit (loss) is plotted on the vertical axis and volume on the horizontal axis. Given zero volume, the company incurs no variable costs, and its total fixed costs will therefore equal its net loss for the year. Thus, points E and G represent total fixed costs for 1997 and 1998, respectively. Because point G is closer to the origin than E, total fixed costs must have decreased from 1997 to 1998.

In this profit-volume chart, the slope of a line equals the contribution margin per unit of volume (unit price – unit variable cost). The greater the unit contribution margin, that is, the lower the unit variable cost given a constant unit price, the steeper the slope. Consequently, unit variable cost must have increased and the unit contribution margin must have decreased from 1997 to 1998 because the slope of line GH (1998) is less than that of line EF (1998).

Answer (B) is incorrect because the variable costs increased from 1997 to 1998. The profit line is steeper for 1997, indicating a higher contribution margin for each unit sold. Answer (C) is incorrect because the fixed costs decreased. The 1998 profit line starts closer to the origin ($0 line). Answer (D) is incorrect because the fixed costs were lower in 1998, and the variable cost per unit was higher.

**13.** The dollar amount of revenues needed to attain a desired income is calculated by dividing the contribution margin ratio (CMR) into

A. Fixed cost.

B. Desired income.

C. Desired income plus fixed costs.

D. Desired income less fixed costs.

The correct answer is (C). *(CPA, adapted)*

**REQUIRED:** The formula to calculate the amount of revenues resulting in a desired income.

**DISCUSSION:** Breakeven analysis treats the desired income in the same way as fixed costs. The CMR {[(revenues – variable costs) ÷ revenues] or (UCM ÷ unit selling price)} is divided into the sum of fixed costs plus desired profit.

Answer (A) is incorrect because the result would be the BEP, not the revenues needed to earn a desired income. Answers (B) and (D) are incorrect because fixed costs must be added to desired income.

**14.** If a company's variable costs are 70% of revenues, which formula represents the computation of revenues that will yield a profit equal to 10% of the contribution margin when S equals revenues in dollars for the period and FC equals total fixed costs for the period?

A.  $S = .2 \div FC$

B.  $S = FC \div .2$

C.  $S = .27 \div FC$

D.  $S = FC \div .27$

The correct answer is (D). *(CPA, adapted)*
**REQUIRED:** The correct breakeven formula given a variable cost percentage and a desired profit.
**DISCUSSION:** The breakeven point in revenues when a given profit level is required may be calculated using the basic CVP formula and treating profit as a fixed cost. An alternative is to divide the sum of fixed costs and the targeted profit by the CMR.

$$S = VC + FC + Profit$$
$$S = .70S + FC + (.10)(.30)S$$
$$S = .70S + FC + .03S$$
$$.27S = FC$$
$$S = FC \div .27$$

Answer (A) is incorrect because the desired profit is 10% of the contribution margin, not 10% of sales. Ten percent of the contribution margin would equal 3% of revenues. Furthermore, FC would be the numerator, not the denominator. Answer (B) is incorrect because the desired profit is 10% of the contribution margin, not 10% of revenues. Ten percent of the contribution margin would equal 3% of revenues. Answer (C) is incorrect because .27 is divided into, not divided by, the FC.

**15.** The breakeven point in units increases when unit costs

A.  Increase and sales price remains unchanged.

B.  Decrease and sales price remains unchanged.

C.  Remain unchanged and sales price increases.

D.  Increase and sales price increases.

The correct answer is (A). *(CMA, adapted)*
**REQUIRED:** The event that causes the breakeven point in units to increase.
**DISCUSSION:** The breakeven point in units is calculated by dividing the fixed costs by the unit contribution margin (UCM). If selling price is constant and costs increase, the UCM will decline, resulting in an increase of the breakeven point.

Answer (B) is incorrect because a decrease in costs will lower the breakeven point. The UCM will increase. Answer (C) is incorrect because an increase in the selling price will also increase the UCM, resulting in a lower breakeven point. Answer (D) is incorrect because the magnitude of the increases in costs and in sales price must be known to determine their overall effect on the UCM.

**16.** A company's breakeven point (BEP) in dollars of revenue may be affected by equal percentage increases in both selling price and variable cost per unit (assume all other factors are constant within the relevant range). The equal percentage changes in selling price and variable cost per unit will cause the breakeven point in dollars of revenue to

A.  Decrease by less than the percentage increase in selling price.

B.  Decrease by more than the percentage increase in the selling price.

C.  Increase by the percentage change in variable cost per unit.

D.  Remain unchanged.

The correct answer is (D). *(CIA, adapted)*
**REQUIRED:** The effect of equal percentage changes in selling price and variable cost on the BEP in dollars of revenue.
**DISCUSSION:** The BEP in dollars of revenue is equal to the fixed cost divided by the CMR. Accordingly, equal percentage changes in selling price and variable cost per unit will not affect the BEP. For example, assume the unit price of a product is $1 and its unit variable cost is $.60. The CMR equals 40% [($1 – $.60)UCM ÷ $1 unit price]. If fixed cost is $100, the BEP is $250 ($100 ÷ 40%). Raising the selling price and variable cost by 20% to $1.20 and $.72, respectively, leaves the CMR at 40% ($.48 ÷ $1.20). Similarly, lowering the selling price and variable cost to $.80 and $.48, respectively, also leaves the CMR at 40% ($.32 ÷ $.80). Because fixed costs remain constant, the BEP in dollars will not change.

Answers (A), (B), and (C) are incorrect because the BEP in dollars will not change.

**17.** Given the following notations, what is the breakeven sales level in units?

SP = selling price per unit
FC = total fixed cost
VC = variable cost per unit

   A.  SP ÷ (FC ÷ VC)

   B.  FC ÷ [1 – (VC ÷ SP)]

   C.  VC ÷ (SP – FC)

   D.  FC ÷ (SP – VC)

The correct answer is (D). *(CPA, adapted)*
   **REQUIRED:** The correct formula to determine the breakeven level in units.
   **DISCUSSION:** The breakeven point in units is equal to fixed costs divided by the UCM. The UCM is equal to unit selling price minus unit variable costs.
   Answer (A) is incorrect because it provides nonsense results. Answer (B) is incorrect because it defines the BEP in dollars of revenue. Answer (C) is incorrect because it provides nonsense results. Fixed costs should be divided by the unit contribution margin.

**18.** The percentage change in earnings before interest and taxes associated with the percentage change in revenues is the degree of

   A.  Operating leverage.

   B.  Financial leverage.

   C.  Breakeven leverage.

   D.  Combined leverage.

The correct answer is (A). *(CIA, adapted)*
   **REQUIRED:** The term for the percentage change in earnings before interest and taxes associated with the percentage change in revenues.
   **DISCUSSION:** Operating leverage is based on the degree to which fixed costs are used in production. Firms may increase fixed costs, such as by automation, to reduce variable costs. The result is a greater degree of operating leverage (DOL), which is the percentage change in operating income (earnings before interest and taxes) divided by the percentage change in revenues. Thus, operating leverage is related to the price elasticity concept in economics. It can also be determined from dividing the total contribution margin by operating income as expressed in the following formula, given that Q is quantity of units sold, P is unit price, V is unit variable cost, and F is fixed cost:

$$\frac{Q(P - V)}{Q(P - V) - F}$$

   Answer (B) is incorrect because the degree of financial leverage equals the percentage change in net income divided by the percentage change in operating income. Answer (C) is incorrect because the breakeven point is the volume at which total revenue equals total costs. Answer (D) is incorrect because the degree of total (combined) leverage equals the percentage change in net income divided by the percentage change in revenues.

**19.** In preparing a cost-volume-profit analysis for his candle manufacturing business, Joe Stark is considering raising his prices $1.00 per candle. Stark is worried about the impact the increase will have on his revenues from craft fairs. Stark is concerned about the

   A.  Elasticity of demand.

   B.  Substitution effect.

   C.  Nature of supply.

   D.  Maximization of utility.

The correct answer is (A). *(CMA, adapted)*
   **REQUIRED:** The concept related to a concern about the effect of a price increase on sales.
   **DISCUSSION:** As prices are increased, total revenue may increase or decrease depending on the price elasticity of demand (percentage change in quantity demanded ÷ percentage change in price). If demand is elastic (elasticity > 1.0), a price increase will tend to reduce total revenues. If demand is inelastic, a price increase will tend to raise total revenues.
   Answer (B) is incorrect because the substitution effect is implicit in the concept of elasticity. The fewer substitutes, the less elastic will be the demand for a good. Answer (C) is incorrect because, in cost-volume-profit analysis, the nature of the supply curve is not considered. Answer (D) is incorrect because utility theory is implicit in the concept of elasticity. If demand is elastic, consumers derive less utility from paying a higher price.

**20.** A cost-volume-profit model developed in a dynamic environment determined that the estimated parameters used may vary between limits. Subsequent testing of the model with respect to all possible values of the estimated parameters is termed

    A. A sensitivity analysis.

    B. Statistical estimation.

    C. Statistical hypothesis testing.

    D. A time-series study.

The correct answer is (A). *(CIA, adapted)*

    **REQUIRED:** The term for subsequent testing of a model with respect to all possible values of the parameters.

    **DISCUSSION:** Sensitivity analysis permits measurement of the effects of errors in certainty equivalents, which are estimated amounts developed by the best means available and assumed for purposes of a given decision model to be certain. The model then may be evaluated by changing certain data variables (certainty equivalents) critical to the success of the entity and observing the outcomes. This analysis allows quantification of the effects of forecasting or prediction errors and identification of the most critical variables.

    Answer (B) is incorrect because statistical estimation involves the estimation of parameters. Answer (C) is incorrect because statistical hypothesis testing calculates the conditional probability that both the hypothesis is true and the sample results have occurred. Answer (D) is incorrect because a time-series study involves forecasting data over time.

## 8.2 Assumptions

**21.** Cost-volume-profit analysis assumes over the relevant range that

    A. Total costs are linear.

    B. Fixed costs are nonlinear.

    C. Variable costs are nonlinear.

    D. Selling prices are nonlinear.

The correct answer is (A). *(CPA, adapted)*

    **REQUIRED:** The assumption underlying cost-volume-profit analysis.

    **DISCUSSION:** Cost-volume-profit analysis assumes that the cost and revenue factors used in the formula are linear and do not fluctuate with volume. Hence, fixed costs are deemed to be fixed over the relevant range of volume, and variable cost per unit remains constant as volume changes within the relevant range.

    Answer (B) is incorrect because fixed costs are assumed to be constant in breakeven analysis. Answer (C) is incorrect because variable costs per unit are constant and therefore linear in breakeven analysis. Answer (D) is incorrect because the selling price is assumed to be linear in breakeven analysis.

**22.** In calculating the breakeven point for a multiproduct company, which of the following assumptions are commonly made when variable costing is used?

    I. Sales volume equals production volume.

    II. Variable costs are constant per unit.

    III. A given revenue (sales) mix is maintained for all volume changes.

    A. I and II.

    B. I and III.

    C. II and III.

    D. I, II, and III.

The correct answer is (D). *(CPA, adapted)*

    **REQUIRED:** The assumptions used in calculating the breakeven point.

    **DISCUSSION:** CVP analysis assumes that costs and revenues are linear over the relevant range. It further assumes that total fixed costs and unit variable costs are constant. Thus, total variable costs are directly proportional to volume. CVP analysis also assumes that no material change in inventory occurs (sales = production) and that the mix of products is constant (or that only one product is produced).

    Answer (A) is incorrect because the revenue (sales) mix is deemed to be constant. Answer (B) is incorrect because unit variable cost is assumed to be constant. Answer (C) is incorrect because the assumption is that inventories do not change.

**23.** An assembly plant accumulates its variable and fixed manufacturing overhead costs in a single cost pool, which is then applied to work-in-process using a single application base. The assembly plant management wants to estimate the magnitude of the total manufacturing overhead costs for different volume levels of the application activity base using a flexible budget formula. If there is an increase in the application activity base that is within the relevant range of activity for the assembly plant, which one of the following relationships regarding variable and fixed costs is correct?

A. The variable cost per unit is constant, and the total fixed costs decrease.

B. The variable cost per unit is constant, and the total fixed costs increase.

C. The variable cost per unit and the total fixed costs remain constant.

D. The variable cost per unit increases, and the total fixed costs remain constant.

The correct answer is (C). *(CIA, adapted)*
**REQUIRED:** The effect on variable and fixed costs of a change in activity within the relevant range.
**DISCUSSION:** Total variable cost changes when changes in the activity level occur within the relevant range. The cost per unit for a variable cost, however, is constant for all activity levels within the relevant range. Furthermore, if the volume of activity increases within the relevant range, total fixed costs will remain unchanged.
Answers (A), (B), and (D) are incorrect because the variable cost per unit and the total fixed costs will remain constant if the activity level increases within the relevant range.

**24.** Cost-volume-profit analysis assumes that over the relevant range

A. Variable costs are nonlinear.

B. Fixed costs are nonlinear.

C. Selling prices are unchanged.

D. Total costs are unchanged.

The correct answer is (C). *(CPA, adapted)*
**REQUIRED:** The assumption underlying cost-volume-profit analysis.
**DISCUSSION:** CVP analysis assumes that unit selling price and unit variable cost are constant within the relevant range. Accordingly, unit contribution margin, marginal revenue, and marginal cost are also constant.
Answer (A) is incorrect because all costs are deemed to be linear. Total variable cost changes by a constant amount with each change in volume. Answer (B) is incorrect because fixed costs are constant. Answer (D) is incorrect because total costs vary directly with volume.

**25.** Cost-volume-profit analysis assumes that over the relevant range total

A. Revenues are linear.

B. Costs are unchanged.

C. Variable costs are nonlinear.

D. Fixed costs are nonlinear.

The correct answer is (A). *(CPA, adapted)*
**REQUIRED:** The assumption underlying cost-volume-profit analysis.
**DISCUSSION:** CVP analysis assumes that all costs and revenues are linear and that unit price is constant within the relevant range. Consequently, total revenues are represented on a CVP chart by a line of constant positive slope (constant marginal revenue) originating at the origin, the point corresponding to zero volume and zero revenue.
Answer (B) is incorrect because total fixed costs but not total variable costs are constant. Thus, total costs increase in direct proportion to volume. Answer (C) is incorrect because all costs are linear. Answer (D) is incorrect because fixed costs are constant.

**26.** Cost-volume-profit analysis assumes that over the relevant range

A. Total fixed costs are nonlinear.

B. Total costs are unchanged.

C. Unit variable costs are unchanged.

D. Unit revenues are nonlinear.

The correct answer is (C). *(CPA, adapted)*
**REQUIRED:** The assumption underlying cost-volume-profit analysis.
**DISCUSSION:** CVP analysis assumes that unit selling price and unit variable costs are constant within the relevant range. It further assumes that costs and revenues are linear.
Answers (A) and (D) are incorrect because costs and revenues are linear. Answer (B) is incorrect because total costs vary with production level.

## 8.3 High-Low Calculations

**27.** The least exact method for separating fixed and variable costs is

A. The least squares method.

B. Computer simulation.

C. The high-low method.

D. Matrix algebra.

The correct answer is (C). *(Publisher)*
**REQUIRED:** The least exact method of estimating the proportions of fixed and variable costs.
**DISCUSSION:** The fixed and variable portions of mixed costs may be estimated by identifying the highest and the lowest costs within the relevant range. The difference in cost divided by the difference in activity is the variable rate. Once the variable rate is found, the fixed portion is determinable. The high-low method is a simple approximation of the mixed cost formula. The costs of using more sophisticated methods sometimes outweigh the incremental accuracy achieved. In these cases, the high-low method is sufficient.

Answer (A) is incorrect because the least squares method is a sophisticated method of identifying the fixed and variable costs. Answer (B) is incorrect because a computer simulation is a more exact method of separating fixed and variable costs. Answer (D) is incorrect because matrix algebra is a precise method of separating fixed and variable costs.

**28.** Mat Co. estimated its materials handling costs at two activity levels as follows:

| Kilos Handled | Cost |
|---|---|
| 80,000 | $160,000 |
| 60,000 | 132,000 |

What is Mat's estimated cost for handling 75,000 kilos?

A. $150,000

B. $153,000

C. $157,500

D. $165,000

The correct answer is (B). *(CPA, adapted)*
**REQUIRED:** The estimated cost for handling.
**DISCUSSION:** The high-low method estimates variable cost by dividing the difference in costs incurred at the highest and lowest observed levels of activity by the difference in activity. Once the variable cost is found, the fixed portion is determinable. Hence, unit variable handling cost is $1.40 [($160,000 – $132,000) ÷ (80,000 kilos – 60,000 kilos)], the fixed cost is $48,000 [$132,000 – ($1.40 x 60,000 kilos)], and the cost of handling 75,000 kilos is $153,000 [$48,000 + ($1.40 x 75,000 kilos)].

Answer (A) is incorrect because $150,000 assumes that all handling costs are variable and that the unit cost is $2 ($160,000 ÷ 80,000 kilos). Answer (C) is incorrect because $157,500 assumes that all handling costs are variable and that the unit cost is $2.10. Answer (D) is incorrect because the cost of handling 75,000 kilos must be less than the cost of handling 80,000 kilos.

**29.** Jackson, Inc. is preparing a flexible budget for next year and requires a breakdown of the cost of steam used in its factory into the fixed and variable elements. The following data on the cost of steam used and direct labor hours worked are available for the last 6 months of this year:

| Month | Cost of Steam | Direct Labor Hours |
|---|---|---|
| July | $ 15,850 | 3,000 |
| August | 13,400 | 2,050 |
| September | 16,370 | 2,900 |
| October | 19,800 | 3,650 |
| November | 17,600 | 2,670 |
| December | 18,500 | 2,650 |
| Total | $101,520 | 16,920 |

Assuming that Jackson uses the high-low method of analysis, the estimated variable cost of steam per direct labor hour is

A. $4.00

B. $5.42

C. $5.82

D. $6.00

The correct answer is (A). *(CPA, adapted)*
**REQUIRED:** The variable cost per direct labor hour.
**DISCUSSION:** The high-low method estimates variable cost by dividing the difference in costs incurred at the highest and lowest observed levels of activity by the difference in activity. The highest level of activity is 3,650 hours in October, and the lowest is 2,050 hours in August. The variable cost is found by dividing the change in cost by the change in activity (direct labor hours).

$$\frac{\$19,800 - \$13,400}{3,650 - 2,050} = \frac{\$6,400 \ cost}{1,600 \ DLH} = \$4.00/DLH$$

Answer (B) is incorrect because $5.42 is the cost per direct labor hour of the highest-cost month (October), which includes fixed costs as well as variable costs. Answer (C) is incorrect because the high-low method divides the difference in (not the sum of) costs by the difference in (not the sum of) hours between the months of highest and lowest activity in order to determine the variable cost per direct labor hour. Answer (D) is incorrect because $6 per direct labor hour is the total 6-month cost of steam divided by the 6-month total of direct labor hours.

Questions 30 and 31 are based on the following information. Total production costs of prior periods for a company are listed to the right of this paragraph. Assume that the same cost behavior patterns can be extended linearly over the range of 3,000 to 35,000 units and that the cost driver for each cost is the number of units produced.

| Production in units per month | 3,000 | 9,000 | 16,000 | 35,000 |
|---|---|---|---|---|
| Cost X | $23,700 | $ 52,680 | $ 86,490 | $178,260 |
| Cost Y | 47,280 | 141,840 | 252,160 | 551,600 |

**30.** What is the average cost per unit at a production level of 8,000 units for cost X?

A. $5.98

B. $5.85

C.. $7.90

D. $4.83

The correct answer is (A). *(CIA, adapted)*
**REQUIRED:** The average cost per unit for cost X.
**DISCUSSION:** Cost X is a mixed cost (part variable and part fixed). The high-low method can be used to determine the fixed and variable portions. Dividing the total cost of X at two different production volumes by the difference in units produced gives a unit variable cost of $4.83 [($178,260 – $23,700) ÷ (35,000 units – 3,000 units)]. Fixed cost must therefore be $9,210 [$178,260 cost of X for 35,000 units – ($4.83 x 35,000 units)]. Total cost of X for 8,000 units is $47,850 [$9,210 + ($4.83 x 8,000 units)], and the average cost is $5.98 ($47,850 ÷ 8,000 units).
Answer (B) is incorrect because $5.85 is the average cost of 9,000 units. Answer (C) is incorrect because $7.90 is the average cost of 3,000 units. Answer (D) is incorrect because $4.83 is the unit variable cost.

**31.** Identify the cost curve for the average cost per unit for cost Y.

A. Curve 1.

B. Curve 2.

C. Curve 3.

D. Curve 4.

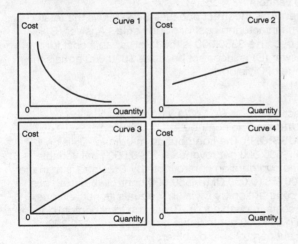

The correct answer is (D). *(CIA, adapted)*
**REQUIRED:** The curve describing the average cost per unit of cost Y.
**DISCUSSION:** Cost Y is a purely variable cost. The high-low method can be used to determine that no fixed portion exists. Dividing the amount of cost Y at each production volume within the relevant range by the units produced gives a constant average cost of $15.76 (e.g., $47,280 ÷ 3,000 units = $15.76, and $551,600 ÷ 35,000 units = $15.76). If cost Y included a fixed portion, average unit cost would decline as production increased. Consequently, Curve 4 describes the behavior of cost Y.
Answer (A) is incorrect because Curve 1 is an average cost curve for a fixed cost. Answer (B) is incorrect because Curve 2 is a total cost curve for a mixed cost. Answer (C) is incorrect because Curve 3 is a total cost curve for a variable cost.

## 8.4 Basic Breakeven Problems

**32.** A company is concerned about its operating performance, as summarized below:

| | |
|---|---:|
| Revenues ($12.50 per unit) | $300,000 |
| Variable costs | 180,000 |
| Operating loss | (40,000) |

How many additional units should have been sold in order for the company to break even in 1998?

  A.  32,000

  B.  24,000

  C.  16,000

  D.  8,000

The correct answer is (D). *(CIA, adapted)*

**REQUIRED:** The additional units that should have been sold to break even.

**DISCUSSION:** The contribution margin ratio is 40% [($300,000 – $180,000 VC) ÷ $300,000 revenues]. Hence, the UCM is $5 (40% x $12.50 unit SP), and the additional units that should have been sold equaled 8,000 ($40,000 NOL ÷ $5 UCM).

Answer (A) is incorrect because 32,000 is the breakeven sales volume. Answer (B) is incorrect because 24,000 is the actual unit sales volume. Answer (C) is incorrect because 16,000 treats the operating loss as operating income.

---

Questions 33 and 34 are based on the following information. Data available for the current year are presented below.

| | Whole Company | Division 1 | Division 2 |
|---|---:|---:|---:|
| Variable manufacturing cost of goods sold | $ 400,000 | $220,000 | $ 80,000 |
| Unallocated costs (e.g., president's salary) | 100,000 | | |
| Fixed costs controllable by division managers (e.g., advertising, engineering supervision costs) | 90,000 | 50,000 | 40,000 |
| Net revenue | 1,000,000 | 600,000 | 400,000 |
| Variable selling and administrative costs | 130,000 | 70,000 | 60,000 |
| Fixed costs controllable by others (e.g., depreciation, insurance) | 120,000 | 70,000 | 50,000 |

---

**33.** Based upon the information presented above, the contribution margin for the company was

  A.  $400,000

  B.  $470,000

  C.  $530,000

  D.  $600,000

The correct answer is (B). *(CIA, adapted)*

**REQUIRED:** The contribution margin for the company.

**DISCUSSION:** Contribution margin equals revenues minus variable costs. Accordingly, the CM is $470,000 ($1,000,000 net revenues – $400,000 variable CGS – $130,000 variable S&A costs).

Answer (A) is incorrect because $400,000 is the total variable manufacturing cost of goods sold. Answer (C) is incorrect because $530,000 is the total variable cost for the year. Answer (D) is incorrect because $600,000 equals the net revenue of Division 1.

---

**34.** Using the information presented above, the contribution by Division 1 was

  A.  $190,000

  B.  $260,000

  C.  $310,000

  D.  $380,000

The correct answer is (A). *(CIA, adapted)*

**REQUIRED:** The contribution by Division 1.

**DISCUSSION:** The contribution margin for Division 1 is $310,000 ($600,000 net revenue – $290,000 total variable costs). The contribution controllable by Division 1's manager is $260,000 ($310,000 CM – $50,000 controllable fixed cost). The total contribution by Division 1 equals its net revenue minus all costs traceable to it. Thus, the total contribution is $190,000 ($260,000 controllable contribution – $70,000 allocated but controllable by others).

Answer (B) is incorrect because $260,000 is the contribution controllable by the Division 1 manager. Answer (C) is incorrect because $310,000 is the contribution margin for Division 1. Answer (D) is incorrect because $380,000 equals net revenue minus variable manufacturing costs.

**35.** The following information pertains to Syl Co.:

| | |
|---|---|
| Revenues | $800,000 |
| Variable costs | 160,000 |
| Fixed costs | 40,000 |

What is Syl's breakeven point in revenues?

    A. $200,000

    B. $160,000

    C. $50,000

    D. $40,000

The correct answer is (C). *(CPA, adapted)*
**REQUIRED:** The breakeven point in revenues.
**DISCUSSION:** The breakeven point in revenues is the fixed costs divided by the contribution margin ratio. Variable costs equal 20% of sales ($160,000 ÷ $800,000). Hence, the contribution margin ratio is 80%, and the breakeven point in dollars is $50,000 ($40,000 FC ÷ 80%).

Answer (A) is incorrect because $200,000 is the sum of FC and VC at the $800,000 sales level. Answer (B) is incorrect because $160,000 is VC at the $800,000 revenue level. Answer (D) is incorrect because $40,000 is FC.

**36.** BEH Co. is considering dropping a product. Variable costs are $6.00 per unit. Fixed overhead costs, exclusive of depreciation, have been allocated at a rate of $3.50 per unit and will continue whether or not production ceases. Depreciation on the equipment is $20,000 a year. If production is stopped, the equipment can be sold for $18,000; if production continues, however, it will be useless at the end of 1 year and will have no salvage value. The selling price is $10 a unit. Ignoring taxes, the minimum units to be sold in the current year to break even on a cash flow basis is

    A. 4,500 units.

    B. 5,000 units.

    C. 1,800 units.

    D. 36,000 units.

The correct answer is (A). *(CMA, adapted)*
**REQUIRED:** The cash flow breakeven point in units.
**DISCUSSION:** The BEP in units is equal to fixed costs divided by the difference between unit selling price and unit variable cost (UCM). The $18,000 salvage value, the cash flow to be received if production is discontinued, is treated here as a fixed cost. Hence, continuation of the product line will permit the firm to break even or make a profit only if the total CM is $18,000 or more.

$$BEP = \frac{\$18,000}{\$10 - \$6} = 4,500 \ units$$

Fixed overhead allocated is not considered in this calculation because it is not a cash flow and will continue regardless of the decision.

Answer (B) is incorrect because 5,000 units is equal to the depreciation divided by the UCM of $4. Answer (C) is incorrect because 1,800 units equals $18,000 divided by $10. Answer (D) is incorrect because 36,000 units subtracts unit fixed costs in determining the unit contribution margin.

**37.** Kent Co.'s operating percentages were as follows:

| | | |
|---|---|---|
| Revenues | | 100% |
| Cost of goods sold | | |
|   Variable | 50% | |
|   Fixed | 10 | 60 |
| Gross profit | | 40% |
| Other operating expenses | | |
|   Variable | 20 | |
|   Fixed | 15 | 35 |
| Operating income | | 5% |

Kent's sales totaled $2 million. At what revenue level would Kent break even?

    A. $1,900,000

    B. $1,666,667

    C. $1,250,000

    D. $833,333

The correct answer is (B). *(CPA, adapted)*
**REQUIRED:** The breakeven point in revenues.
**DISCUSSION:** The BEP in revenues equals fixed costs divided by the CMR (CM ÷ sales). The CM equals the sales price minus variable costs. The CMR is

| | | |
|---|---|---|
| Revenues | | 100% |
| Minus variable expenses: | | |
|   Cost of goods sold | 50% | |
|   Other operating expenses | 20 | (70) |
| Contribution margin ratio | | 30% |

Total fixed costs are $500,000 [(10% + 15%) x $2,000,000]. The BEP in revenues is $1,666,667 ($500,000 ÷ 30%).

Answer (A) is incorrect because $1,900,000 is the total cost at a revenue level of $2,000,000. Answer (C) is incorrect because $1,250,000 equals fixed costs divided by the gross profit percentage. Answer (D) is incorrect because $833,333 equals fixed costs divided by the cost of goods sold percentage.

**38.** The following information relates to Clyde Corporation, which produced and sold 50,000 units during a recent accounting period.

| | |
|---|---|
| Revenues | $850,000 |
| Manufacturing costs | |
|   Fixed | 210,000 |
|   Variable | 140,000 |
| Selling and administrative costs | |
|   Fixed | 300,000 |
|   Variable | 45,000 |
| Income tax rate | 40% |

For the next accounting period, if production and sales are expected to be 40,000 units, the company should anticipate a contribution margin per unit of

A. $1.86

B. $3.10

C. $7.30

D. $13.30

The correct answer is (D). *(CMA, adapted)*

**REQUIRED:** The contribution margin per unit.

**DISCUSSION:** Unit contribution margin is the difference between unit selling price and unit variable cost. Unit selling price is $17 ($850,000 ÷ 50,000 units), and unit variable cost is $3.70 [($140,000 variable manufacturing cost + $45,000 variable S&A cost) ÷ 50,000 units sold]. Accordingly, unit contribution margin is $13.30 ($17 – $3.70).

Answer (A) is incorrect because $1.86 is an after-tax amount based on the inclusion of all fixed costs in the calculation. Answer (B) is incorrect because $3.10 is erroneously based on the inclusion of all fixed costs in the calculation of the UCM. Answer (C) is incorrect because $7.30 includes the $300,000 of fixed S&A costs in the calculation of the UCM.

**39.** Two companies are expected to have annual sales of 1 million decks of playing cards next year. Estimates for next year are presented below:

| | Company 1 | Company 2 |
|---|---|---|
| Selling price per deck | $3.00 | $3.00 |
| Cost of paper per deck | .62 | .65 |
| Printing ink per deck | .13 | .15 |
| Labor per deck | .75 | 1.25 |
| Variable overhead per deck | .30 | .35 |
| Fixed costs | $960,000 | $252,000 |

Given these data, which of the following responses is correct?

| | Breakeven Point in Units for Company 1 | Breakeven Point in Units for Company 2 | Volume in Units at Which Profits of Company 1 and Company 2 Are Equal |
|---|---|---|---|
| A. | 800,000 | 420,000 | 1,180,000 |
| B. | 800,000 | 420,000 | 1,000,000 |
| C. | 533,334 | 105,000 | 1,000,000 |
| D. | 533,334 | 105,000 | 1,180,000 |

The correct answer is (A). *(CIA, adapted)*

**REQUIRED:** The breakeven points and the indifference point for the companies.

**DISCUSSION:** The BEP in units is found by dividing the fixed costs by the UCM.

$$Company\ 1 = \frac{\$960,000}{\$3 - .62 - .13 - .75 - .30} = 800,000$$

$$Company\ 2 = \frac{\$252,000}{\$3 - .65 - .15 - 1.25 - .35} = 420,000$$

The volume at which profits are equal occurs when the difference between total revenue and total cost is also the same. Both charge $3 per deck, so total revenue for the two companies at the indifference volume (U) will be equal. Consequently, total costs should also be equal.

$$U(\$.62 + .13 + .75 + .30) + \$960,000 =$$
$$U(\$.65 + .15 + 1.25 + .35) + \$252,000$$
$$\$1.80U + \$960,000 = \$2.40U + \$252,000$$
$$\$.60U = \$708,000$$
$$U = 1,180,000$$

Answers (B), (C), and (D) are incorrect because the BEP for Company 1 is 800,000 units, the BEP for Company 2 is 420,000 units, and the indifference volume is 1,180,000 units.

**40.** A company with $280,000 of fixed costs has the following data:

| | Product A | Product B |
|---|---|---|
| Sales price per unit | $5 | $6 |
| Variable costs per unit | $3 | $5 |

Assume three units of A are sold for each unit of B sold. Revenues for product B at the breakeven point will equal

A. $200,000

B. $240,000

C. $600,000

D. $840,000

The correct answer is (B). *(CIA, adapted)*
REQUIRED: The breakeven point for B in dollars.
DISCUSSION: The breakeven point equals fixed costs divided by unit contribution margin. The composite unit contribution margin for A and B is $7 {[3 units of A x ($5 – $3)] + 1 unit of B x ($6 – $5)}. Thus, 40,000 composite units ($280,000 ÷ $7), including 40,000 units of B, are sold at the breakeven point. Revenues for B at the breakeven point equal $240,000 (40,000 units x $6).
Answer (A) is incorrect because $200,000 results from applying product A's price (40,000 x $5). Answer (C) is incorrect because $600,000 equals product A revenues at the breakeven point (120,000 x $5). Answer (D) is incorrect because $840,000 equals product A revenues and product B revenues at the breakeven point.

**41.** Lyman Company has the opportunity to increase annual revenues $100,000 by selling to a new, riskier group of customers. The bad debt expense is expected to be 15%, and collection costs will be 5%. The company's manufacturing and selling expenses are 70% of revenues, and its effective tax rate is 40%. If Lyman should accept this opportunity, the company's after-tax profits would increase by

A. $6,000

B. $10,000

C. $9,000

D. $18,000

The correct answer is (A). *(CMA, adapted)*
REQUIRED: The after-tax increase in profit.
DISCUSSION: Revenues increase by $100,000. Collection costs and bad debt expense are 20% of sales (15% + 5%). Total variable expenses for the new revenues will be 90% (20% + 70%) of each dollar. Thus, additional after-tax profit is $6,000 {[(100% – 90%) x $100,000] x [100% – 40% tax rate]}.
Answer (B) is incorrect because $10,000 is the pretax profit. Answer (C) is incorrect because $9,000 omits collection costs. Answer (D) is incorrect because $18,000 omits collection costs and bad debt expense.

**42.** Two companies produce and sell the same product in a competitive industry. Thus, the selling price of the product for each company is the same. Company 1 has a contribution margin ratio of 40% and fixed costs of $25 million. Company 2 is more automated, making its fixed costs 40% higher than those of Company 1. Company 2 also has a contribution margin ratio that is 30% greater than that of Company 1. By comparison, Company 1 will have the <List A> breakeven point in terms of dollar sales volume and will have the <List B> dollar profit potential once the indifference point in dollar sales volume is exceeded.

| | List A | List B |
|---|---|---|
| A. | Lower | Lesser |
| B. | Lower | Greater |
| C. | Higher | Lesser |
| D. | Higher | Greater |

The correct answer is (A). *(CIA, adapted))*
REQUIRED: The breakeven points and dollar profit potentials for two manufacturers.
DISCUSSION: Company 1's breakeven point is lower because its fixed costs are lower. Company 1's breakeven point is $62,500,000 ($25,000,000 ÷ 40%). Company 2's breakeven point is $67,307,692 [($25,000,000 x 1.4) ÷ (40% x 1.3)]. If X equals the unit sales price, the indifference point, at which dollar profits are equal, is $83,333,333 ($25,000,000 + .60X = $35,000,000 + .48X). Once the indifference point is passed, Company 1 will make lower profits than Company 2 because Company 2 has a higher contribution margin ratio.
Answers (B), (C), and (D) are incorrect because Company 1's breakeven point is lower, but its profits will be lower past the indifference point.

**43.** A company manufactures a single product. Estimated cost data regarding this product and other information for the product and the company are as follows:

| | |
|---|---:|
| Sales price per unit | $40 |
| Total variable production cost per unit | $22 |
| Sales commission (on sales) | 5% |
| Fixed costs and expenses: | |
|   Manufacturing overhead | $5,598,720 |
|   General and administrative | $3,732,480 |
| Effective income tax rate | 40% |

The number of units the company must sell in the coming year in order to reach its breakeven point is

  A.  388,800 units.

  B.  518,400 units.

  C.  583,200 units.

  D.  972,000 units.

The correct answer is (C). *(CIA, adapted))*
**REQUIRED:** The number of units to reach the breakeven point.
**DISCUSSION:** The breakeven point is determined by dividing total fixed costs by the unit contribution margin. The total fixed costs are $9,331,200 ($5,598,720 manufacturing overhead + $3,732,480 general and administrative). The contribution margin is $16.00 ($40 sales price – $22 variable production cost – $2.00 commission). Thus, the breakeven point is 583,200 units ($9,331,200 ÷ $16).

Answer (A) is incorrect because 388,800 units results from not subtracting the variable costs per unit from sales price. Answer (B) is incorrect because 518,400 units does not reflect the sales commissions in the total variable costs. Answer (D) is incorrect because 972,000 units includes taxes in the total variable costs, which understates the unit contribution margin.

**44.** A manufacturing concern sells its sole product for $10 per unit, with a unit contribution margin of $6. The fixed manufacturing cost rate per unit is $2 based on a denominator capacity of 1 million units, and fixed marketing costs are $1.5 million. If 900,000 units are produced, the absorption-costing breakeven point in units sold is

  A.  425,000 units.

  B.  583,333 units.

  C.  900,000 units.

  D.  1,000,000 units.

The correct answer is (A). *(Publisher)*
**REQUIRED:** The absorption-costing breakeven point in units sold.
**DISCUSSION:** The absorption-costing breakeven point in units sold equals the sum of (1) the total fixed costs and (2) the product of the fixed manufacturing cost application rate and the difference between the BEP in units sold (X) and units produced, with the sum divided by the UCM. Thus, the absorption-costing breakeven point in units sold is 425,000 units:

$$X = \frac{(\$2 \times 1,000,000 \text{ } denominator \text{ } capacity) + \$1,500,000 + \$2(X - 900,000)}{\$6}$$

$$X = \frac{(\$3,500,000 + \$2X - \$1,800,000)}{\$6}$$

$$\$6X = \$1,700,000 + \$2X$$

$$X = 425,000$$

Answer (B) is incorrect because 583,333 units is the variable-costing BEP. Answer (C) is incorrect because 900,000 units is the actual production level. Answer (D) is incorrect because 1,000,000 units is the capacity used to calculate the fixed overhead application rate.

**45.** A not-for-profit social agency provides home health care assistance to as many patients as possible. Its budgeted appropriation (X) for next year must cover fixed costs of $5 million, and the annual per-patient cost (Y) of its services. However, the agency is preparing for a possible 10% reduction in its appropriation that will lower the number of patients served from 5,000 to 4,000. The reduced appropriation and the annual per-patient cost equal

| | Reduced Appropriation | Per-Patient Annual Cost |
|---|---|---|
| A. | $5,000,000 | $4,000 |
| B. | $8,333,333 | $833 |
| C. | $9,000,000 | $1,000 |
| D. | $10,000,000 | $5,000 |

The correct answer is (C). *(Publisher)*
**REQUIRED:** The reduced appropriation and the annual per-patient cost.
**DISCUSSION:** This question applies CVP analysis in a not-for-profit context in which the agency wishes to assist as many people as possible. Thus, a breakeven point must be calculated. Total revenue (the appropriation) equals fixed cost plus the product of unit variable cost (per-patient annual cost) and the number of patients who can be assisted given the available resources. The following are simultaneous equations stated in the two unknowns:

$$X - 5,000Y = \$5,000,000$$
$$.9X - 4,000Y = \$5,000,000$$

Because X must equal 5,000Y + $5,000,000, the second equation may be solved as follows for the per-patient annual cost (Y):

$$.9(5,000Y + \$5,000,000) - 4,000Y = \$5,000,000$$
$$4,500Y + \$4,500,000 - 4,000Y = \$5,000,000$$
$$500Y = \$500,000$$
$$Y = \$1,000$$

Accordingly, the budgeted appropriation (X) must be $10,000,000 [(5,000 x $1,000) VC + $5,000,000 FC], and the reduced appropriation must be $9,000,000 (90% x $10,000,000).
Answer (A) is incorrect because $5,000,000 is the fixed cost and 4,000 is the number served given a reduced appropriation. Answer (B) is incorrect because $8,333,333 and $833 are the appropriation and per-patient annual cost, respectively, for the next year that result from a 10% increase in the appropriation of the current year instead of a 10% decrease in the next year's appropriation. Answer (D) is incorrect because $10,000,000 is the budgeted appropriation and 5,000 is the number of people it would serve.

## 8.5 Changes in CVP Variables

**46.** On January 1, 1998, Lake Co. increased its direct labor wage rates. All other budgeted costs and revenues were unchanged. How did this increase affect Lake's budgeted breakeven point and budgeted margin of safety?

| | Budgeted Breakeven Point | Budgeted Margin of Safety |
|---|---|---|
| A. | Increase | Increase |
| B. | Increase | Decrease |
| C. | Decrease | Decrease |
| D. | Decrease | Increase |

The correct answer is (B). *(CPA, adapted)*
**REQUIRED:** The effect on the breakeven point and margin of safety of an increase in direct labor cost.
**DISCUSSION:** The BEP is the level of revenues at which total revenue equals total cost. The margin of safety is the excess of budgeted revenues over the breakeven revenues. Given that all other costs and revenues are constant, an increase in direct labor cost will increase the BEP and decrease the margin of safety.
Answers (A), (C), and (D) are incorrect because the BEP will increase and the margin of safety will decrease.

**47.** A retail company determines its selling price by marking up variable costs 60%. In addition, the company uses frequent selling price markdowns to stimulate sales. If the markdowns average 10%, what is the company's contribution margin ratio?

A.   27.5%

B.   30.6%

C.   37.5%

D.   41.7%

The correct answer is (B). *(CIA, adapted)*
   **REQUIRED:** The contribution margin ratio.
   **DISCUSSION:** The contribution margin equals revenues minus variable costs. The CMR equals the UCM divided by the selling price. For example, if variable costs average $10 per unit, the average selling price is $16 (1.60 x $10). However, the 10% markdown implies that the actual average selling price is $14.40 (.90 x $16). The CMR is therefore 30.6% [($14.40 – $10.00) ÷ $14.40].
   Answer (A) is incorrect because 27.5% omits markdowns from the denominator. Answer (C) is incorrect because 37.5% ignores markdowns. Answer (D) is incorrect because 41.7% omits markdowns from the numerator.

**48.** Which of the following would decrease unit contribution margin the most?

A.   A 15% decrease in selling price.

B.   A 15% increase in variable costs.

C.   A 15% decrease in variable costs.

D.   A 15% decrease in fixed costs.

The correct answer is (A). *(CMA, adapted)*
   **REQUIRED:** The change in a CVP variable causing the greatest decrease in UCM.
   **DISCUSSION:** A decrease in selling price or an increase in variable costs decreases UCM (unit sales price – unit variable cost). However, a given percentage change in unit sales price must have a greater effect than an equal but opposite percentage change in unit variable cost because the former is greater than the latter. For example, if the price is $100 and unit variable cost is $50, the CM is $50. If the unit price decreases by 15%, the CM becomes $35. If the unit VC increases by 15%, the CM becomes $42.50.
   Answer (B) is incorrect because a 15% increase in variable costs will not decrease the CM as much as a 15% decrease in sales price. Answer (C) is incorrect because a decrease in variable costs increases the UCM. Answer (D) is incorrect because a decrease in fixed costs has no effect on the UCM.

**49.** The contribution margin increases when revenues remain the same and

A.   Variable cost per unit decreases.

B.   Variable cost per unit increases.

C.   Fixed costs decrease.

D.   Fixed costs increase.

The correct answer is (A). *(CPA, adapted)*
   **REQUIRED:** The cause of an increased CM when revenues remain constant.
   **DISCUSSION:** CM equals revenues minus variable costs. With constant revenues, an increase in the CM may occur only if either the unit sales price increases or the variable costs decrease.
   Answer (B) is incorrect because, when variable cost per unit increases, CM decreases if revenues and price remain the same. Answers (C) and (D) are incorrect because the CM does not vary with fixed costs.

**50.** If the fixed costs attendant to a product increase while variable costs and sales price remain constant, what will happen to contribution margin (CM) and breakeven point (BEP)?

|     | CM | BEP |
| --- | --- | --- |
| A. | Increase | Decrease |
| B. | Decrease | Increase |
| C. | Unchanged | Increase |
| D. | Unchanged | Unchanged |

The correct answer is (C). *(CPA, adapted)*
   **REQUIRED:** The effect of an increase in fixed costs on the CM and the BEP.
   **DISCUSSION:** The BEP in units is equal to fixed costs divided by the UCM (sales price – variable cost per unit). Consequently, an increase in fixed costs has no effect on the CM but causes the BEP to increase; that is, more units have to be sold to cover the increased fixed costs.
   Answer (A) is incorrect because the CM will not be affected by a change in fixed costs. Also, the BEP will increase. Answer (B) is incorrect because the CM will not be affected by a change in fixed costs. Answer (D) is incorrect because the BEP will increase. More units need to be sold to cover the increased fixed costs.

**51.** A company increased the selling price of its product from $1.00 to $1.10 a unit when total fixed costs increased from $400,000 to $480,000 and variable cost per unit remained unchanged. How will these changes affect the breakeven point?

   A. The breakeven point in units will be increased.

   B. The breakeven point in units will be decreased.

   C. The breakeven point in units will remain unchanged.

   D. The effect cannot be determined from the information given.

The correct answer is (D). *(CPA, adapted)*
   **REQUIRED:** The effect on the BEP of an increase in both selling price and fixed costs.
   **DISCUSSION:** The breakeven point in units equals fixed costs divided by the UCM (selling price – variable costs). To determine the new breakeven point, the variable cost per unit must be known as well as the total fixed costs and the new selling price per unit. Because the increase in selling price lowers the breakeven point and the increase in fixed costs raises it, the net effect of these changes cannot be determined when variable costs are not known.
   Answers (A), (B), and (C) are incorrect because the variable cost per unit needs to be provided in order to determine the effect of the changes.

**52.** The contribution margin per unit is the difference between the selling price and the variable cost per unit, and the contribution margin ratio is the ratio of the unit contribution margin to the selling price per unit. If the selling price and the variable cost per unit both increase 10% and fixed costs do not change, what is the effect on the contribution margin per unit and the contribution margin ratio?

   A. Both remain unchanged.

   B. Both increase.

   C. Contribution margin per unit increases, and the contribution margin ratio remains unchanged.

   D. Contribution margin per unit increases, and the contribution margin ratio decreases.

The correct answer is (C). *(CPA, adapted)*
   **REQUIRED:** The effect on the UCM and CMR of an equal percentage increase in the selling price and unit variable cost.
   **DISCUSSION:** UCM equals selling price minus variable costs. Thus, equal percentage increases in the selling price and the variable cost per unit will cause a proportionate increase in the UCM. The CMR equals the UCM divided by the selling price. If the selling price and variable cost per unit increase in the same proportion, the CMR will be unchanged. For example, if SP is $20 and the unit variable cost is $10, the CMR is 50%. If the selling price and unit variable cost are increased by 10% to $22 and $11, respectively, the CMR remains 50%.
   Answers (A), (B), and (D) are incorrect because the UCM will increase and the CMR will not change.

**53.** The most likely strategy to reduce the breakeven point would be to

   A. Increase both the fixed costs and the contribution margin.

   B. Decrease both the fixed costs and the contribution margin.

   C. Decrease the fixed costs and increase the contribution margin.

   D. Increase the fixed costs and decrease the contribution margin.

The correct answer is (C). *(CPA, adapted)*
   **REQUIRED:** The strategy to reduce the breakeven point.
   **DISCUSSION:** The breakeven point in units is equal to the fixed costs divided by the unit contribution margin. The breakeven point in revenues equals the fixed costs divided by the contribution margin ratio. Because fixed costs are in the numerator and the contribution margin is in the denominator, decreasing the fixed costs and increasing the contribution margin reduces the breakeven point.
   Answer (A) is incorrect because increasing the fixed costs increases the breakeven point. Answer (B) is incorrect because decreasing the contribution margin increases the breakeven point. Answer (D) is incorrect because increasing fixed costs and decreasing the contribution margin increases the breakeven point.

**54.** Marston Enterprises sells three chemicals: petrol, septine, and tridol. Petrol is the company's most profitable product; tridol is the least profitable. Which one of the following events will definitely decrease the firm's overall breakeven point for the upcoming accounting period?

   A.  The installation of new computer-controlled machinery and subsequent layoff of assembly-line workers.

   B.  A decrease in tridol's selling price.

   C.  An increase in anticipated sales of petrol relative to sales of septine and tridol.

   D.  An increase in petrol's raw material cost.

The correct answer is (C). *(CMA, adapted)*
   **REQUIRED:** The event that will decrease the firm's overall breakeven point.
   **DISCUSSION:** A company's breakeven point will be reduced if fixed costs are lowered or the average UCM is increased. Given that petrol is the company's most profitable product, and assuming that it has a higher UCM than septine and tridol, an increase in revenues from petrol relative to the other products will result in a higher average UCM and a lower breakeven point (fixed costs ÷ average UCM).
   Answer (A) is incorrect because the acquisition of new machinery will result in greater fixed costs and the possibility of a higher breakeven point. Answer (B) is incorrect because a decrease in selling price reduces the UCM, which in turn increases the breakeven point. Answer (D) is incorrect because an increase in raw materials cost (a variable cost) will result in a lower average UCM and a higher breakeven point.

Questions 55 through 59 are based on the following information. The SAB Company uses a profit-volume graph similar to the one shown below to represent the cost-volume-profit relationships of its operations. The vertical (y-axis) is the profit in dollars and the horizontal (x-axis) is the volume in units. The diagonal line is the contribution margin line.

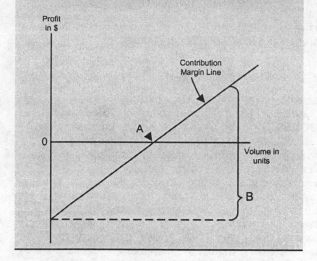

**55.** Point A on the profit-volume graph represents

   A.  The point at which fixed costs equal revenues.

   B.  A volume level of zero units.

   C.  The point at which total costs equal total revenues.

   D.  The point at which the rate of contribution margin increases.

The correct answer is (C). *(CMA, adapted)*
   **REQUIRED:** The nature of point A on the P-V graph.
   **DISCUSSION:** Point A is the intersection of the contribution margin line and the zero profit (zero loss) line; i.e., total costs equal total revenues at point A.
   Answer (A) is incorrect because the graph does not provide information about revenues. Answer (B) is incorrect because a volume level of zero units lies at point 0, the intersection of the x and y axes. Answer (D) is incorrect because the contribution rate does not increase in cost-volume-profit analysis, which assumes linearity.

**56.** The vertical distance (B) from the dotted line to the contribution margin line on the profit-volume graph represents

   A.   The total contribution margin.

   B.   The contribution margin per unit.

   C.   The contribution margin rate.

   D.   The sum of the variable and fixed costs.

The correct answer is (A). *(CMA, adapted)*
   **REQUIRED:** The nature of the vertical distance labeled B.
   **DISCUSSION:** The vertical distance denoted by B is the total contribution margin.
   Answer (B) is incorrect because the UCM is the slope of the CM line, i.e., the vertical increase per one unit increase in unit volume. Answer (C) is incorrect because the CMR is the same as the UCM. Answer (D) is incorrect because the graph provides information about fixed costs only, which are equal to the difference between the origin (0) and the intersection of the dotted line with the vertical axis.

**57.** If SAB Company's fixed costs increase,

   A.   The contribution margin line will shift upward parallel to the current line.

   B.   The contribution margin line will shift downward parallel to the current line.

   C.   The slope of the contribution margin line will be more pronounced (steeper).

   D.   The contribution margin line will coincide with the current contribution margin line.

The correct answer is (B). *(CMA, adapted)*
   **REQUIRED:** The effect of increased fixed costs on the contribution margin line.
   **DISCUSSION:** If fixed costs increase, the fixed cost line (the broken line) will shift downward. This shift will result in a higher BEP (currently point A, which will move to the right as the CM line moves down) and a CM line parallel to, but below and to the right of, the existing line. The new CM line will therefore begin at a lower point on the vertical axis.
   Answer (A) is incorrect because the CM line will shift upward if fixed costs decrease, not increase. Answer (C) is incorrect because the slope of the CM line cannot change if the CM itself (sales – variable costs) does not change. Changes in fixed costs do not affect the CM itself. Answer (D) is incorrect because, when fixed costs increase, the CM line will shift downward, not remain in the same place.

**58.** If SAB Company's variable costs per unit increase but its unit selling price stays constant,

   A.   The contribution margin line will shift upward parallel to the present line.

   B.   The contribution margin line will shift downward parallel to the present line.

   C.   The slope of the contribution margin line will be less pronounced (flatter).

   D.   The slope of the contribution margin line will change but not in a determinable manner.

The correct answer is (C). *(CMA, adapted)*
   **REQUIRED:** The effects of changes in variable costs per unit on the contribution margin line.
   **DISCUSSION:** If the variable costs per unit increase but selling price is constant, the UCM and the CM will decrease and the slope of the CM line will also decrease. The slope equals the UCM.
   Answer (A) is incorrect because a decrease in fixed costs shifts the CM line upward. Answer (B) is incorrect because an increase in fixed costs shifts the CM line downward. Answer (D) is incorrect because, if the CM increases, the slope will increase; if the CM decreases, the slope will decrease.

**59.** If SAB Company decided to increase its unit selling price to offset exactly the increase in the variable cost per unit, the

   A.   Contribution margin line would shift upward parallel to the existing line.

   B.   Slope of the contribution margin line would be pronounced (steeper).

   C.   Slope of the contribution margin line would be less pronounced (flatter).

   D.   Contribution margin line would coincide with the existing contribution margin line.

The correct answer is (D). *(CMA, adapted)*
   **REQUIRED:** The effect on the contribution margin line of an equal increase in both selling price and unit variable cost.
   **DISCUSSION:** If the selling price is increased by an amount exactly equal to the increase in variable costs per unit, the new CM (revenues – VC) would equal the old CM. Hence, the new CM line will coincide with the existing CM line. The only effect is that the sales price and variable costs per unit are greater. Neither is shown on the breakeven chart.
   Answer (A) is incorrect because the CM line will not shift. Fixed costs were not changed. Answers (B) and (C) are incorrect because the UCM remains constant, and no change in the slope will occur.

**60.** The Childers Company sells widgets. The company breaks even at an annual sales volume of 75,000 units. Actual annual sales volume was 100,000 units, and the company reported a profit of $200,000. The annual fixed costs for the Childers Company are

A. $800,000

B. $600,000

C. $200,000

D. Insufficient information to determine amount of fixed costs.

The correct answer is (B). *(A. Wilson)*

**REQUIRED:** The annual fixed costs.

**DISCUSSION:** The profit increased by $200,000, and the sales volume increased by 25,000 units over the BEP. This increase in profit is a result of an increase in the contribution margin (revenues – variable costs). UCM is $8 ($200,000 ÷ 25,000 units). The BEP in units is equal to fixed costs divided by the UCM. If the BEP is 75,000 units, fixed costs are $600,000 ($8 UCM x 75,000 units).

Answer (A) is incorrect because $800,000 is the contribution margin on sales volume of 100,000 units. Answer (C) is incorrect because $200,000 is the CM on the additional units. Answer (D) is incorrect because there is sufficient information to determine the fixed costs.

**61.** A company has revenues of $500,000, variable costs of $300,000, and pretax profit of $150,000. If the company increased the sales price per unit by 10%, reduced fixed costs by 20%, and left variable cost per unit unchanged, what would be the new breakeven point in dollars?

A. $88,000

B. $100,000

C. $110,000

D. $125,000

The correct answer is (A). *(CIA, adapted)*

**REQUIRED:** The new breakeven point in dollars.

**DISCUSSION:** The breakeven point in dollars is equal to the sum of fixed cost plus any desired pretax profit, divided by contribution margin ratio [(revenues – variable costs) ÷ revenues]. Fixed cost was $50,000 ($500,000 revenues – $300,000 VC – $150,000 pretax profit). Given the increase in revenues of 10% and decrease in fixed costs of 20%, the breakeven point in dollars is $88,000.

$$\frac{\text{Fixed costs } (\$50,000 \times .8) + \text{Desired pretax profit } 0}{[\text{Revenues } (\$500,000 \times 1.1) - \text{Variable costs } (\$300,000)] / \text{Revenues } (\$500,000 \times 1.1)} = \frac{\$40,000}{\$250,000 \div \$550,000}$$

Answer (B) is incorrect because $100,000 ignores the 10% price increase. Answer (C) is incorrect because $110,000 ignores the 20% decrease in fixed costs. Answer (D) is incorrect because $125,000 ignores the changes in price and fixed costs.

**62.** Tonykinn Company is contemplating marketing a new product. Fixed costs will be $800,000 for production of 75,000 units or less and $1.2 million if production exceeds 75,000 units. The variable cost ratio is 60% for the first 75,000 units. This ratio will increase to 50% for units in excess of 75,000. If the product is expected to sell for $25 per unit, how many units must Tonykinn sell to break even?

A. 120,000

B. 111,000

C. 96,000

D. 80,000

The correct answer is (B). *(C.J. Skender)*

**REQUIRED:** The breakeven point in units with changing fixed and variable cost behavior patterns.

**DISCUSSION:** At a production of 75,000 or fewer units, fixed costs are $800,000 and the UCM is $10 [$25 – (60% x $25)]. At this UCM, 80,000 units ($800,000 ÷ $10) must be sold, but this volume is not within the relevant range. At any production level greater than 75,000 units, total fixed costs are $1.2 million, but there are two UCM layers. The first 75,000 units sold will produce a contribution margin of $750,000 (75,000 x $10). Hence, another $450,000 ($1,200,000 – $750,000) must be contributed. The UCM is $12.50 [$25 – (50% x $25)] for units in excess of 75,000, and 36,000 ($450,000 ÷ $12.50) additional units must be sold. Total unit sales at the BEP are 111,000 (75,000 + 36,000).

Answer (A) is incorrect because 120,000 assumes all units have a UCM of $10. Answer (C) is incorrect because 96,000 assumes all units have a UCM of $12.50. Answer (D) is incorrect because 80,000 assumes a UCM of $10 and fixed costs of $800,000.

Questions 63 through 65 are based on the following information. MultiFrame Company has the following revenue and cost budgets for the two products it sells:

|  | Plastic Frames | Glass Frames |
|---|---|---|
| Sales price | $10.00 | $15.00 |
| Direct materials | (2.00) | (3.00) |
| Direct labor | (3.00) | (5.00) |
| Fixed overhead | (3.00) | (2.75) |
| Net income per unit | $ 2.00 | $ 4.25 |
| Budgeted unit sales | 100,000 | 300,000 |

The budgeted unit sales equal the current unit demand, and total fixed overhead for the year is budgeted at $975,000. Assume that the company plans to maintain the same proportional mix. In numerical calculations, MultiFrame rounds to the nearest cent and unit.

**63.** The total number of units MultiFrame needs to produce and sell to break even is

A. 150,000 units.

B. 153,947 units.

C. 100,000 units.

D. 300,000 units.

The correct answer is (A). *(CMA, adapted)*
REQUIRED: The total units sold at the breakeven point.
DISCUSSION: If the product mix is constant, one unit of plastic frames is sold for every three units of glass frames. For plastic frames, the UCM is $5 ($10 – $2 – $3). For glass frames, the UCM is $7 ($15 – $3 – $5). Thus, the composite UCM is $26 ($5 + $7 + $7 + $7), and the breakeven point is 37,500 packages ($975,000 FC ÷ $26). Because each package contains four frames, the total units sold equal 150,000.
Answer (B) is incorrect because 153,947 units assumes 150,000 units of plastic frames are sold. Answer (C) is incorrect because 100,000 units equals budgeted sales of plastic frames. Answer (D) is incorrect because 300,000 units equals budgeted sales of glass frames.

**64.** The total number of units needed to break even if the budgeted direct labor costs were $2 for plastic frames instead of $3 is

A. 144,444 units.

B. 150,000 units.

C. 153,947 units.

D. 100,000 units.

The correct answer is (A). *(CMA, adapted)*
REQUIRED: The breakeven point in units if labor costs for the plastic frames are reduced.
DISCUSSION: If the labor costs for the plastic frames are reduced by $1, the composite UCM will be $27 ($26 as calculated in the preceding question + $1). Hence, the new breakeven point is 144,444 units [($975,000 FC ÷ $27) x 4 units].
Answer (B) is incorrect because 150,000 units is the BEP given no changes in variables. Answer (C) is incorrect because 153,947 units assumes 150,000 units of plastic frames are sold and no changes in the other variables. Answer (D) is incorrect because 100,000 units equals budgeted sales of plastic frames.

**65.** The total number of units needed to break even if sales were budgeted at 150,000 units of plastic frames and 300,000 units of glass frames with all other costs remaining constant is

A. 144,444 units.

B. 150,000 units.

C. 153,947 units.

D. 450,000 units.

The correct answer is (C). *(CMA, adapted)*
REQUIRED: The total number of units needed to break even if the product mix is changed.
DISCUSSION: The UCM for plastic frames and glass frames are $5 and $7, respectively. If the number of plastic frames sold is 50% of the number of glass frames sold, a composite unit will contain one plastic frame and two glass frames. Thus, the composite UCM will be $19 ($5 + $7 + $7), and the breakeven point in units will be 153,947 [($975,000 ÷ $19) x 3 units].
Answer (A) is incorrect because 144,444 units assumes direct labor cost and sales of plastic frames are $2 and 100,000, respectively. Answer (B) is incorrect because 150,000 units assumes no changes in variables. Answer (D) is incorrect because 450,000 units equals total budgeted sales.

**66.** Which of the following will result in raising the breakeven point?

    A.  A decrease in the variable cost per unit.

    B.  An increase in the semivariable cost per unit.

    C.  An increase in the contribution margin per unit.

    D.  A decrease in income tax rates.

The correct answer is (B). *(CIA, adapted)*
    **REQUIRED:** The change in a CVP factor that will raise the breakeven point.
    **DISCUSSION:** The BEP equals fixed cost divided by the UCM (selling price − unit variable cost). An increase in semivariable costs increases fixed costs and/or variable costs. An increase in either will raise the BEP. If fixed costs increase, more units must be sold, assuming the same UCM, to cover the greater fixed costs. If variable costs increase, the UCM will decrease and again more units must be sold to cover the fixed costs.
    Answer (A) is incorrect because, if other factors are constant, an increase in sales price or a decrease in unit variable cost increases the CM and lowers the BEP. Answer (C) is incorrect because an increase in the CM decreases the BEP. Answer (D) is incorrect because, if income taxes are taken into account, they are treated as variable costs. A decrease in variable costs lowers the BEP.

## 8.6 Targeted Income

**67.** In using cost-volume-profit analysis to calculate expected unit sales, which of the following should be added to fixed costs in the numerator?

    A.  Predicted operating loss.

    B.  Predicted operating income.

    C.  Unit contribution margin.

    D.  Variable costs.

The correct answer is (B). *(CPA, adapted)*
    **REQUIRED:** The addition to fixed costs when calculating expected unit sales.
    **DISCUSSION:** When a targeted operating income (T) is desired, it is treated as a fixed cost (FC). Consequently, the calculation of expected unit sales is

$$(FC + T) \div UCM = Units$$

    Answer (A) is incorrect because predicted operating loss would be subtracted from fixed costs, not added.
Answer (C) is incorrect because the UCM is the denominator.
Answer (D) is incorrect because variable costs are a component of UCM.

**68.** Last year, the contribution margin ratio of Lamesa Company was 30%. This year, fixed costs are expected to be $120,000, the same as last year, and revenues are forecasted at $550,000, a 10% increase over last year. For the company to increase operating income by $15,000 in the coming year, the contribution margin ratio must be

    A.  20%

    B.  30%

    C.  40%

    D.  70%

The correct answer is (B). *(CPA, adapted)*
    **REQUIRED:** The contribution margin ratio to increase annual operating income by a targeted amount.
    **DISCUSSION:** Determining the CMR to increase operating income by $15,000 in the coming year requires the calculation of last year's operating income. Last year's revenues must have been $500,000 ($550,000 ÷ 110%). The CMR for last year is given as 30%, resulting in a $150,000 CM ($500,000 x .3). Fixed costs equaled $120,000 last year. Thus, last year's operating income was $30,000 ($150,000 CM − $120,000 FC).
    The targeted operating income in the coming year is therefore $45,000 ($30,000 + $15,000 increase). Fixed costs remain at $120,000. Accordingly, a $165,000 CM is necessary. Next year's revenues are forecasted at $550,000. Dividing $165,000 by $550,000 gives a CMR of 30%.
    Answer (A) is incorrect because a 20% CMR would result in a loss of $10,000. Answer (C) is incorrect because a 40% CMR would result in $100,000 of income. Answer (D) is incorrect because a 70% CMR would result in $265,000 of operating income.

Questions 69 and 70 are based on the following information. An organization sells a single product for $40 per unit that it purchases for $20. The salespeople receive a salary plus a commission of 5% of sales. Last year the organization's net income (after taxes) was $100,800. The organization is subject to an income tax rate of 30%. The fixed costs of the organization are

| | |
|---|---|
| Advertising | $124,000 |
| Rent | 60,000 |
| Salaries | 180,000 |
| Other fixed costs | 32,000 |
| Total | $396,000 |

**69.** The breakeven point in unit sales for the organization is

   A.  8,800 units.

   B.  18,000 units.

   C.  19,800 units.

   D.  22,000 units.

The correct answer is (D). *(CIA, adapted)*
   **REQUIRED:** The breakeven point in unit sales.
   **DISCUSSION:** The breakeven point in unit sales equals total fixed costs divided by unit contribution margin. The UCM is $18 [$40 unit price – $20 CGS – (5% x $40) sales commission]. Hence, the breakeven point in unit sales is 22,000 units ($396,000 ÷ $18).
   Answer (A) is incorrect because 8,800 units equals total fixed costs divided by the contribution margin ratio. Answer (B) is incorrect because 18,000 units divides the total fixed costs by the unit variable cost. Answer (C) is incorrect because 19,800 units divides the total fixed costs by the unit variable cost of sales.

**70.** The organization is considering changing the compensation plan for sales personnel. If the organization increases the commission to 10% of revenues and reduces salaries by $80,000, what revenues must the organization have to earn the same net income as last year?

   A.  $1,042,000

   B.  $1,350,000

   C.  $1,150,000

   D.  $1,630,000

The correct answer is (C). *(CIA, adapted)*
   **REQUIRED:** The revenues needed to earn the same net income as the previous year.
   **DISCUSSION:** Last year's operating income before taxes was $144,000 ($100,800 ÷ 70%). The new UCM is $16 [$40 unit price – $20 CGS – (10% x $40)], and the new total fixed cost equals $316,000 ($396,000 – $80,000). If the targeted pretax operating income is treated as a fixed cost, the desired revenues equal $1,150,000 {[($144,000 + $316,000) ÷ $16] x $40}.
   Answer (A) is incorrect because $1,042,000 does not adjust net income to its pretax amount. Answer (B) is incorrect because $1,350,000 assumes fixed costs are unchanged. Answer (D) is incorrect because $1,630,000 adjusts net income to its pretax amount by dividing net income by the tax rate.

Questions 71 and 72 are based on the following information. A wholesale distributing company has budgeted its before-tax profit to be $643,500 for 1998. The company is preparing its annual budget for 1999 and has accumulated the following data:

| 1999 Data | |
| --- | --- |
| Projected annual revenues | $6,000,000 |
| Variable costs as a percent of revenues: | |
| Cost of merchandise | 30% |
| Sales commissions | 5% |
| Shipping expenses | 10% |
| Annual fixed operating costs: | |
| Selling expenses | $ 772,200 |
| Administrative expenses | $1,801,800 |

**71.** If the wholesale distributing company wants to earn the same before-tax operating income in 1999 as budgeted for 1998, the annual revenues would not be the projected $6 million but would have to be

A. $4,950,000

B. $5,362,500

C. $5,850,000

D. $7,150,000

The correct answer is (C). *(CIA, adapted)*

**REQUIRED:** The revenues needed to earn a given before-tax operating income.

**DISCUSSION:** The contribution margin ratio is 55% (100% − 30% variable cost for merchandise − 5% variable cost for sales commissions − 10% variable cost for shipping). Thus, the necessary revenues equal the sum of the fixed costs and the desired before-tax operating income, divided by the CMR, or $5,850,000 [($772,200 + $1,801,800 + $643,500) ÷ 55%].

Answer (A) is incorrect because $4,950,000 results from using a 65% contribution margin, which incorrectly excludes the 10% variable cost for shipping. Answer (B) is incorrect because $5,362,500 results from using a 60% contribution margin, which incorrectly excludes the 5% variable cost for sales commissions. Answer (D) is incorrect because $7,150,000 results from using a 45% contribution margin, which is the sum of the variable cost percentages.

**72.** Using the original $6 million projection, the wholesale distributing company's margin of safety in terms of revenues for 1999 would be

A. $82,500

B. $150,000

C. $280,000

D. $1,320,000

The correct answer is (D). *(CIA, adapted)*

**REQUIRED:** The margin of safety.

**DISCUSSION:** The margin of safety equals the difference between the projected 1999 revenues and the breakeven point. The projected revenues equal $6 million. The breakeven point equals the annual fixed operating costs of $2,574,000 ($772,200 + $1,801,800) divided by the contribution margin ratio of 55% (100% − 30% − 5% − 10%), or $4,680,000. The margin of safety is $1,320,000 ($6,000,000 − $4,680,000).

Answer (A) is incorrect because $82,500 equals the difference between the before-tax operating income for 1999 and 1998. Answer (B) is incorrect because $150,000 equals the difference between projected 1999 revenues and the revenues required to earn the same before-tax operating income in 1999 as in 1998. Answer (C) is incorrect because $280,000 equals the difference between the projected revenues for 1999 and the breakeven point based on a 45% contribution margin ratio.

**73.** Austin Manufacturing, which is subject to a 40% income tax rate, had the following operating data for the period just ended:

| | |
|---|---:|
| Selling price per unit | $ 60 |
| Variable cost per unit | 22 |
| Fixed costs | 504,000 |

Management plans to improve the quality of its sole product by (1) replacing a component that costs $3.50 with a higher-grade unit that costs $5.50 and (2) acquiring a $180,000 packing machine. Austin will depreciate the machine over a 10-year life with no estimated salvage value by the straight-line method of depreciation. If the company wants to earn after-tax income of $172,800 in the upcoming period, it must sell

A. 19,300 units.

B. 21,316 units.

C. 22,500 units.

D. 27,000 units.

The correct answer is (C). *(CMA, adapted)*
**REQUIRED:** The number of units to be sold to generate a targeted after-tax income.
**DISCUSSION:** The units to be sold equal fixed costs plus the desired pretax operating income, divided by the unit contribution margin. In the preceding year, the unit contribution margin was $38 ($60 price – $22 unit VC). That amount will decrease by $2 to $36 in the upcoming year because of use of a higher-grade component. Fixed costs will increase from $504,000 to $522,000 as a result of the $18,000 ($180,000 ÷ 10 years) increase in fixed costs attributable to depreciation on the new machine. Dividing the $172,800 of desired after-tax income by 60% (the complement of the tax rate) produces a desired before-tax operating income of $288,000. Hence, the breakeven point in units is 22,500 [($522,000 + $288,000) ÷ $36].
Answer (A) is incorrect because 19,300 units does not take income taxes into consideration. Answer (B) is incorrect because 21,316 units fails to consider the increased variable costs from the introduction of the higher-priced component. Answer (D) is incorrect because 27,000 units results from adding the entire cost of the new machine as a fixed cost.

**74.** During 1998, Thor Lab supplied hospitals with a comprehensive diagnostic kit for $120. At a volume of 80,000 kits, Thor had fixed costs of $1 million and operating income before income taxes of $200,000. Because of an adverse legal decision, Thor's 1999 liability insurance increased by $1.2 million over 1998. Assuming the volume and other costs are unchanged, what should the 1999 price be if Thor is to make the same $200,000 operating income before income taxes?

A. $120.00

B. $135.00

C. $150.00

D. $240.00

The correct answer is (B). *(CPA, adapted)*
**REQUIRED:** The price charged to earn a specified pretax operating income.
**DISCUSSION:** Assuming the volume and other costs are unchanged, Thor wishes to earn a pretax operating income of $200,000 after a $1.2 million increase in fixed costs. One approach is to treat the pretax operating income as a fixed cost and to apply the formula for the breakeven unit volume (unit volume = fixed costs ÷ unit contribution margin). Accordingly, unit variable cost is $105 [80,000 units = ($1,000,000 FC + $200,000 pretax operating income) ÷ ($120 unit price for 1998 – unit VC)], and 1999 unit price is $135 [80,000 units = ($1,000,000 FC + $1,200,000 FC + $200,000 pretax operating income) ÷ (1999 unit price – $105)].
Answer (A) is incorrect because $120.00 was the 1998 unit price. Answer (C) is incorrect because $150.00 assumes that the unit variable cost is $120. Answer (D) is incorrect because $240.00 assumes that the price must double because the sum of fixed costs and targeted operating income has doubled.

Questions 75 through 77 are based on the following information. The data below pertain to a company.

|  | Total Cost | Unit Cost |
|---|---|---|
| Revenues (40,000 units) | $1,000,000 | $25 |
| Raw materials | 160,000 | 4 |
| Direct labor | 280,000 | 7 |
| Factory overhead: |  |  |
|   Variable | 80,000 | 2 |
|   Fixed | 360,000 |  |
| Selling and general expenses: |  |  |
|   Variable | 120,000 | 3 |
|   Fixed | 225,000 |  |

**75.** In forecasting purchases of inventory for a firm, all of the following are useful except

  A. Knowledge of the behavior of business cycles.

  B. Internal allocations of costs to different segments of the firm.

  C. Information on the seasonal variations in demand.

  D. Econometric modeling.

The correct answer is (B). *(CIA, adapted)*
**REQUIRED:** The item that is not useful when forecasting inventory purchases.
**DISCUSSION:** Internal accounting allocations of costs to different segments of the firm are arbitrary assignments of already incurred costs that are irrelevant to forecasting the firm's purchases.
Answers (A), (C), and (D) are incorrect because knowing the behavior of business cycles, understanding seasonal variations in demand for the product, and using econometric models can be valuable when forecasting the required purchases of inventory.

**76.** How many units does the company need to produce and sell to make a before-tax operating income of 10% of sales?

  A. 65,000 units.

  B. 36,562 units.

  C. 90,000 units.

  D. 29,250 units.

The correct answer is (C). *(CIA, adapted)*
**REQUIRED:** The number of units to produce and sell to meet an operating income goal.
**DISCUSSION:** Revenue minus variable and fixed expenses equals operating income. If X equals unit sales, revenue equals $25X, total variable expenses equal $16X ($4 + $7 + $2 + $3), total fixed expenses equal $585,000 ($360,000 + $225,000), and operating income equals 10% of revenue. Hence, X equals 90,000 units.

$$\$25X - \$16X - \$585,000 = 10\% \times \$25X$$
$$6.5X = \$585,000$$
$$X = 90,000 \text{ } units$$

    Answer (A) is incorrect because 65,000 units is the breakeven point. Answers (B) and (D) are incorrect because 36,562 units and 29,250 units produce an operating loss.

**77.** Assuming that the company sells 80,000 units, what is the maximum that can be paid for an advertising campaign while still breaking even?

  A. $135,000

  B. $1,015,000

  C. $535,000

  D. $695,000

The correct answer is (A). *(CIA, adapted)*
**REQUIRED:** The maximum that can be paid for an advertising campaign while still breaking even.
**DISCUSSION:** The company will break even when operating income equals zero. Operating income is equal to revenue minus variable expenses and fixed expenses, including advertising. Thus, maximum advertising cost (X) is $135,000. The equation is

$$(\$25)(80,000 \text{ units}) - (\$16)(80,000 \text{ units}) - \$585,000 - X = 0$$

    Answer (B) is incorrect because $1,015,000 assumes unit variable costs of $5. Answer (C) is incorrect because $535,000 assumes unit variable costs of $11. Answer (D) is incorrect because $695,000 assumes unit variable costs of $9.

Questions 78 and 79 are based on the following information. Delphi Company has developed a new project that will be marketed for the first time during the next fiscal year. Although the Marketing Department estimates that 35,000 units could be sold at $36 per unit, Delphi's management has allocated only enough manufacturing capacity to produce a maximum of 25,000 units of the new product annually. The fixed costs associated with the new product are budgeted at $450,000 for the year, which includes $60,000 for depreciation on new manufacturing equipment.

Data associated with each unit of product are presented below. Delphi is subject to a 40% income tax rate.

|  | Variable Costs |
|---|---|
| Direct material | $ 7.00 |
| Direct labor | 3.50 |
| Manufacturing overhead | 4.00 |
| Total variable manufacturing cost | 14.50 |
| Selling expenses | 1.50 |
| Total variable cost | $16.00 |

**78.** The maximum after-tax income that can be earned by Delphi Company from sales of the new product during the next fiscal year is

A. $30,000

B. $50,000

C. $110,000

D. $66,000

The correct answer is (A). *(CMA, adapted)*

**REQUIRED:** The maximum after-tax income.

**DISCUSSION:** The maximum output (maximum sales level) is 25,000 units (given), and the unit contribution margin is $20 ($36 selling price – $16 unit VC). Thus, the breakeven point in units is 22,500 ($450,000 FC ÷ $20). At the breakeven point, all fixed costs have been recovered. Hence, pretax operating income equals the unit contribution margin times unit sales in excess of the breakeven point, or $50,000 [(25,000 unit sales – 22,500 BEP) x $20 UCM]. After-tax income is $30,000 [$50,000 x (1.0 – .4 tax rate)].

Answer (B) is incorrect because $50,000 is the pretax operating income. Answer (C) is incorrect because $110,000 fails to include depreciation as a fixed cost and ignores income taxes. Answer (D) is incorrect because $66,000 fails to include depreciation as a fixed cost.

**79.** Delphi Company's management has stipulated that it will not approve the continued manufacture of the new product after the next fiscal year unless the after-tax income is at least $75,000 the first year. The unit selling price to achieve this target income must be at least

A. $37.00

B. $36.60

C. $34.60

D. $39.00

The correct answer is (D). *(CMA, adapted)*

**REQUIRED:** The unit selling price to achieve a targeted after-tax income.

**DISCUSSION:** If X represents the necessary selling price, 25,000 equals maximum unit sales, $16 is the variable cost per unit, $450,000 is the total fixed cost, and $125,000 [$75,000 target after-tax income ÷ (1.0 – .4 tax rate)] is the desired operating income, the following formula may be solved to determine the requisite unit price:

$$25,000 \ (X - \$16) - \$450,000 = \$125,000$$
$$25,000X - \$400,000 - \$450,000 = \$125,000$$
$$25,000X = \$975,000$$
$$X = \$39$$

Answer (A) is incorrect because $37.00 does not consider income taxes. Answer (B) is incorrect because $36.60 excludes depreciation. Answer (C) is incorrect because $34.60 does not include depreciation or taxes.

Questions 80 through 82 are based on the following information. Bruell Electronics Co. is developing a new product, surge protectors for high-voltage electrical flows. The cost information in the opposite column relates to the product.

|  | Unit Costs |
|---|---|
| Direct materials | $3.25 |
| Direct labor | 4.00 |
| Distribution | .75 |

The company will also be absorbing $120,000 of additional fixed costs associated with this new product. A corporate fixed charge of $20,000 currently absorbed by other products will be allocated to this new product.

**80.** If the selling price is $14 per unit, the breakeven point in units (rounded to the nearest hundred) for surge protectors is

A. 8,600 units.

B. 10,000 units.

C. 15,000 units.

D. 20,000 units.

The correct answer is (D). *(CMA, adapted)*

**REQUIRED:** The breakeven point in units.

**DISCUSSION:** The breakeven point in units equals total additional fixed costs divided by the unit contribution margin. Unit variable costs total $8 ($3.25 + $4.00 + $.75). Thus, UCM is $6 ($14 unit selling price – $8 unit VC), and the breakeven point is 20,000 units ($120,000 FC ÷ $6).

Answer (A) is incorrect because 8,600 units (rounded) equals $120,000 divided by $14. Answer (B) is incorrect because 10,000 units equals $140,000 divided by $14. Answer (C) is incorrect because 15,000 units equals fixed costs divided by unit variable cost.

**81.** How many surge protectors (rounded to the nearest hundred) must Bruell Electronics sell at a selling price of $14 per unit to gain $30,000 additional operating income before taxes?

A. 10,700 units.

B. 20,000 units.

C. 25,000 units.

D. 28,300 units.

The correct answer is (C). *(CMA, adapted)*

**REQUIRED:** The number of units to be sold to generate a targeted pretax operating income.

**DISCUSSION:** The number of units to be sold to generate a specified pretax operating income equals the sum of total fixed costs and the targeted pretax operating income, divided by the unit contribution margin. Unit variable costs total $8 ($3.25 + $4.00 + $.75), and UCM is $6 ($14 unit selling price – $8). Thus, the desired unit sales level equals 25,000 units [($120,000 + $30,000) ÷ $6].

Answer (A) is incorrect because 10,700 units is based on a UCM equal to selling price. Answer (B) is incorrect because 20,000 units is the breakeven point. Answer (D) is incorrect because the $20,000 of allocated fixed costs is not relevant.

**82.** How many surge protectors (rounded to the nearest hundred) must Bruell Electronics sell at a selling price of $14 per unit to increase after-tax income by $30,000? Bruell Electronics' effective income tax rate is 40%.

A. 10,700 units.

B. 20,000 units.

C. 25,000 units.

D. 28,300 units.

The correct answer is (D). *(CMA, adapted)*

**REQUIRED:** The number of units to be sold to generate a specified after-tax income.

**DISCUSSION:** The number of units to be sold to generate a specified pretax operating income equals the sum of total fixed costs and the targeted pretax operating income, divided by the unit contribution margin. Given a desired after-tax income of $30,000 and a tax rate of 40%, the targeted pretax operating income must be $50,000 [$30,000 ÷ (1.0 – .4)]. Unit variable costs total $8 ($3.25 + $4.00 + $.75), and UCM is $6 ($14 unit selling price – $8). Hence, the desired unit sales level is 28,333 [($120,000 + $50,000) ÷ $6]. Rounded to the nearest hundred, the answer is 28,300.

Answer (A) is incorrect because 10,700 units is based on a UCM equal to selling price and $30,000 of pretax operating income. Answer (B) is incorrect because 20,000 units is the breakeven point. Answer (C) is incorrect because 25,000 units is based on $30,000 of pretax operating income.

**83.** Orange Company's controller developed the following variable-costing income statement for 1998:

| | | | Per Unit |
|---|---|---|---|
| Revenues (150,000 units at $30) | | $4,500,000 | $30 |
| Variable costs: | | | |
| Direct materials | $1,050,000 | | $ 7 |
| Direct labor | 1,500,000 | | 10 |
| Mfg. overhead | 300,000 | | 2 |
| Selling & mkg. | 300,000 | | 2 |
| | | (3,150,000) | $21 |
| Contribution margin | | $1,350,000 | $ 9 |
| Fixed costs: | | | |
| Mfg. overhead | $ 600,000 | | $ 4 |
| Selling & mkg. | 300,000 | | 2 |
| | | (900,000) | $ 6 |
| Operating income | | $ 450,000 | $ 3 |

Orange Company based its 1999 budget on the assumption that fixed costs, unit sales, and the sales price would remain as they were in 1998, but with operating income being reduced to $300,000. By July of 1999, the controller was able to predict that unit sales would increase over 1998 levels by 10%. Based on the 1999 budget and the new information, the predicted 1999 operating income would be

A. $300,000

B. $330,000

C. $420,000

D. $585,000

The correct answer is (C). *(CIA, adapted)*
**REQUIRED:** The projected operating income given constant FC and sales price and different estimates of unit sales.
**DISCUSSION:** Projected operating income is estimated total revenue minus estimated total costs. Given the original assumption that FC, unit sales, and sales price remain the same and that operating income will be reduced, the variable costs must increase. If the July 1999 prediction that unit sales will increase by 10% from 150,000 to 165,000 is based on the budgeted FC, sales price, and unit variable cost, predicted operating income will increase from $300,000 to $420,000.

$$TR - FC - VC = \$300,000$$
$$TR - \$900,000 - VC = \$300,000$$
$$TR - VC = \$1,200,000$$
$$CM = \$1,200,000$$

$$Budgeted\ UCM = \$1,200,000 \div 150,000\ units = \$8$$

$$Total\ CM = 165,000\ units \times \$8 = \$1,320,000$$
$$FC = (900,000)$$
$$Operating\ income\quad \$\ 420,000$$

Answer (A) is incorrect because $300,000 is the projected operating income before the increase in unit sales. Answer (B) is incorrect because $330,000 assumes a 10% increase in fixed costs. Answer (D) is incorrect because the UCM for 1999 is $8 per unit, not $9.

## 8.7 Multiproduct Breakeven

**84.** Von Stutgatt International's breakeven point is 8,000 racing bicycles and 12,000 5-speed bicycles. If the selling price and variable costs are $570 and $200 for a racer and $180 and $90 for a 5-speed, respectively, what is the weighted-average contribution margin?

A. $90

B. $202

C. $230

D. $370

The correct answer is (B). *(J.B. Romal)*
**REQUIRED:** The weighted-average contribution margin.
**DISCUSSION:** The contribution margin is selling price minus variable costs. The CM for a racer is $370 ($570 – $200), and the CM for a 5-speed is $90 ($180 – $90). The sales mix is 40% racers [8,000 ÷ (8,000 + 12,000)] and 60% 5-speeds [12,000 ÷ (8,000 + 12,000)]. Thus, the weighted-average CM is $202 [(40% x $370) + (60% x $90)].

Answer (A) is incorrect because $90 is the CM for a 5-speed. Answer (C) is incorrect because $230 is a simple average. Answer (D) is incorrect because $370 is the CM for a racer.

**85.** Bjax Corporation has a separate production line for each of two products: A and B. Product A has a contribution margin of $4 per unit, product B has a contribution margin of $5 per unit, and the corporation's nonvariable expenses of $200,000 are unchanged regardless of volume. Under these conditions, which of the following statements will always be applicable?

A. At a sales volume in excess of 25,000 units of A and 25,000 units of B, operations will be profitable.

B. The ratio of net profit to total sales for B will be larger than for A.

C. The contribution margin per unit of direct materials is lower for A than for B.

D. Income will be maximized if B only is sold.

The correct answer is (A). *(CIA, adapted)*
**REQUIRED:** The statement that is always true given contribution margins and fixed costs for two products.
**DISCUSSION:** If Bjax Corporation has a sales volume in excess of 25,000 units of A and 25,000 units of B, operations will always be profitable. Given product A's contribution margin of $4 per unit, sales of 25,000 units will yield a contribution margin of $100,000. The contribution margin per unit for product B is given as $5; therefore, sales of 25,000 units will yield a contribution margin of $125,000. The total contribution margin for the two products is $225,000 ($100,000 + $125,000). Fixed costs are $200,000. Thus, operating income is at least $25,000.
Answer (B) is incorrect because no information is given about net profit or total sales. Answer (C) is incorrect because no information is given on direct materials. Answer (D) is incorrect because, if only B is sold, the income made from A would be lost. Each product can be produced without affecting the other.

---

Questions 86 and 87 are based on the following information. The data below pertain to two types of products manufactured by Korn Corp. Fixed costs total $300,000 annually. The expected mix in units is 60% for product Y and 40% for product Z.

| | Per Unit | |
| --- | --- | --- |
| | Sales Price | Variable Costs |
| Product Y | $120 | $ 70 |
| Product Z | 500 | 200 |

**86.** How much is Korn's breakeven point in units?

A. 857

B. 1,111

C. 2,000

D. 2,459

The correct answer is (C). *(CPA, adapted)*
**REQUIRED:** The BEP in units for a two-product firm.
**DISCUSSION:** The BEP in units is equal to fixed cost divided by the difference between unit selling price and unit variable cost (UCM). The UCM for product Y equals $50 ($120 – $70), and the UCM for product Z equals $300 ($500 – $200). The weighted-average UCM is therefore $150 [(60% x $50) + (40% x $300)], and the BEP is 2,000 units ($300,000 ÷ $150).
Answer (A) is incorrect because 857 units assumes a $350 weighted-average CM. Answer (B) is incorrect because 1,111 divides fixed costs by the sum of variable costs for Y and Z. Answer (D) is incorrect because 2,459 divides fixed costs by the weighted-average variable costs.

**87.** How much is Korn's breakeven point in dollars?

A. $300,000

B. $400,000

C. $420,000

D. $544,000

The correct answer is (D). *(CPA, adapted)*
**REQUIRED:** The BEP in dollars for a two-product firm.
**DISCUSSION:** If the BEP is 2,000 units (see preceding question), the revenue (sales) mix will include 1,200 units of Y (60% x 2,000) and 800 units of Z (40% x 2,000). Hence, the BEP in dollars will be $544,000 [(1,200 x $120) + (800 x $500)].
Answer (A) is incorrect because $300,000 is the amount of fixed costs. Answer (B) is incorrect because $400,000 equals 800 units of Z times $500. Answer (C) is incorrect because $420,000 equals the sum of the UCMs of Y and Z ($50 + $300 = $350) times 1,200 units.

Questions 88 through 93 are based on the following information. The officers of Bradshaw Company are reviewing the profitability of the company's four products and the potential effects of several proposals for varying the product mix. An excerpt from the income statement and other data follow:

| | Totals | Product P | Product Q | Product R | Product S |
|---|---|---|---|---|---|
| Revenues | $62,600 | $10,000 | $18,000 | $12,600 | $22,000 |
| Cost of goods sold | 44,274 | 4,750 | 7,056 | 13,968 | 18,500 |
| Gross profit | $18,326 | $ 5,250 | $10,944 | $ (1,368) | $ 3,500 |
| Operating expenses | 12,012 | 1,990 | 2,976 | 2,826 | 4,220 |
| Income before income taxes | $ 6,314 | $ 3,260 | $ 7,968 | $ (4,194) | $ (720) |
| Units sold | | 1,000 | 1,200 | 1,800 | 2,000 |
| Sales price per unit | | $ 10.00 | $ 15.00 | $ 7.00 | $ 11.00 |
| Variable cost of goods sold per unit | | $ 2.50 | $ 3.00 | $ 6.50 | $ 6.00 |
| Variable operating expenses per unit | | $ 1.17 | $ 1.25 | $ 1.00 | $ 1.20 |

Each of the following proposals is to be considered independently of the other proposals. Consider only the product changes stated in each proposal; the activity of other products remains stable. Ignore income taxes.

**88.** If product R is discontinued, the effect on income will be

A. $4,194 increase.

B. $900 increase.

C. $1,368 increase.

D. $12,600 decrease.

The correct answer is (B). *(CPA, adapted)*
**REQUIRED:** The effect on income if one product in a mix is discontinued.
**DISCUSSION:** If product R is discontinued, the effect will be a $900 increase in income. Fixed costs are assumed to remain the same. The variable costs per unit of R are $7.50 ($6.50 + $1.00). Given that the sales price per unit is $7.00, the negative UCM is $.50 ($7.00 – $7.50). Based on sales of 1,800 units, the loss is $900. Discontinuing the R product line will therefore increase income by $900.
Answer (A) is incorrect because a $4,194 increase assumes that the fixed costs associated with product R would also be eliminated. Answer (C) is incorrect because a $1,368 increase assumes that the operating expenses are all fixed expenses. Answer (D) is incorrect because $12,600 is the revenue generated by product R.

**89.** If product R is discontinued and a consequent loss of customers causes a decrease of 200 units in sales of Q, the total effect on income will be

A. $15,600 decrease.

B. $1,250 decrease.

C. $2,044 increase.

D. $2,866 increase.

The correct answer is (B). *(CPA, adapted)*
**REQUIRED:** The effect on income if discontinuing one product also decreases sales of another product.
**DISCUSSION:** If R is discontinued, the effect on income is a $900 increase (see the previous question). Q's UCM is $10.75 ($15 SP – $3 – $1.25). Hence, a 200-unit decrease results in a reduction in income of $2,150 (200 x $10.75). The net effect is a decrease in income of $1,250 ($2,150 loss – $900 gain).
Answer (A) is incorrect because $15,600 is the decrease in sales. Answers (C) and (D) are incorrect because the total effect on income is a decrease.

**90.** If the sales price of R is increased to $8 with a decrease in the number of units sold to 1,500, the effect on income will be

A. $2,199 decrease.

B. $600 decrease.

C. $750 increase.

D. $1,650 increase.

The correct answer is (D). *(CPA, adapted)*
**REQUIRED:** The effect on income if the sales price of a product increases and sales volume declines.
**DISCUSSION:** If 1,500 units of R are sold at $8, the unit contribution margin is $.50 ($8.00 – $6.50 – $1.00 = $.50), and the total contribution margin is $750. As computed in question 88, R currently has a negative CM of $900. The net effect is an increase in income of $1,650 ($750 CM + recovery of the $900 negative CM).
Answers (A) and (B) are incorrect because the old unit price did not cover variable units. Thus, if the new unit sales price exceeds the unit variable costs, the income effect must be an increase. Answer (C) is incorrect because $750 is the CM on sales of 1,500 units of R at $8 per unit.

Refer to the information preceding question 88 on page 283.

**91.** The plant in which R is produced can be used to produce a new product, T.  Total variable costs and expenses per unit of T are $8.05, and 1,600 units can be sold at $9.50 each.  If T is introduced and R is discontinued, the total effect on income will be

A.  $3,220 increase.

B.  $2,600 increase.

C.  $2,320 increase.

D.  $1,420 increase.

The correct answer is (A).  *(CPA, adapted)*
**REQUIRED:**  The effect on income when a new product is introduced and an old one discontinued.
**DISCUSSION:**  If 1,600 units of T can be sold at $9.50 each, the unit contribution margin (UCM) is $1.45 ($9.50 – $8.05), and the total CM is $2,320 (1,600 x $1.45).  Product R currently contributes a negative CM of $900.  Hence, the net effect of discontinuing R and introducing T is a $3,220 increase in income ($2,320 + $900).
Answer (B) is incorrect because $2,600 is the increase in sales.  Answer (C) is incorrect because $2,320 is the total CM for product T.  Answer (D) is incorrect because the $900 of negative CM from R should be added to, not subtracted from, the CM generated by producing T.

**92.**  Production of P can be doubled by adding a second shift, but higher wages must be paid, increasing the variable cost of goods sold to $3.50 for each additional unit.  If the 1,000 additional units of P can be sold at $10 each, the total effect on income will be

A.  $10,000 increase.

B.  $6,500 increase.

C.  $5,330 increase.

D.  $2,260 increase.

The correct answer is (C).  *(CPA, adapted)*
**REQUIRED:**  The effect on income if additional units can be produced and variable manufacturing costs increase.
**DISCUSSION:**  The sale of the 1,000 additional units at a price of $10 and a variable cost of $3.50 results in a UCM of $5.33 ($10 – $3.50 – $1.17).  If 1,000 additional units are sold, the effect on net income will be a $5,330 increase (1,000 x $5.33).
Answer (A) is incorrect because $10,000 is the increase in revenue.  Answer (B) is incorrect because a $6,500 increase does not consider the $1.17 variable operating expense per unit.  Answer (D) is incorrect because $2,260 equals the current income before taxes of $3,260 for 1,000 units of P minus the $1,000 increase in variable costs.

**93.**  Part of the plant in which P is produced can easily be adapted to the production of S, but changes in quantities may make changes in sales prices advisable.  If production of P is reduced to 500 units (to be sold at $12 each) and production of S is increased to 2,500 units (to be sold at $10.50 each), the total effect on income will be

A.  $1,515 decrease.

B.  $2,540 decrease.

C.  $4,165 increase.

D.  $6,330 decrease.

The correct answer is (A).  *(CPA, adapted)*
**REQUIRED:**  The effect on income if the production and prices of two products change.
**DISCUSSION:**  The loss in income is $1,515 ($12,415 new total CM for P and S – $13,930 old total CM for P and S).

New CM

| | | |
|---|---|---|
| P | 500($12 – $3.67) | = $ 4,165 |
| S | 2,500($10.50 – $7.20) | = 8,250 |
| | | $12,415 |

Old CM

| | | |
|---|---|---|
| P | 1,000($10 – $3.67) | = $ 6,330 |
| S | 2,000($11 – $7.20) | = 7,600 |
| | | $13,930 |

Answer (B) is incorrect because $2,540 is the total income of P and S.  Answer (C) is incorrect because $4,165 is the new CM of P.  Answer (D) is incorrect because $6,330 is the old CM of P.

**94.** A company must decide which one of the following four products to manufacture:

| Product | Sales Price | Variable Cost | Direct Labor Hours per Unit |
|---|---|---|---|
| M | $10 | $ 7 | 1.5 |
| N | 20 | 12 | 2.0 |
| O | 5 | 2 | 0.5 |
| P | 8 | 4 | 1.0 |

Which product will result in the highest contribution margin per hour?

A. M.

B. N.

C. O.

D. P.

The correct answer is (C). *(CIA, adapted)*
**REQUIRED:** The product that will result in the highest contribution margin per hour.
**DISCUSSION:** Contribution margin equals price minus variable cost. The contribution margins of M, N, O, and P are $3 ($10 – $7), $8 ($20 – $12), $3 ($5 – $2), and $4 ($8 – $4), respectively. However, the contribution margins per hour are $2 ($3 ÷ 1.5), $4 ($8 ÷ 2.0), $6 ($3 ÷ 0.5), and $4 ($4 ÷ 1.0), respectively. Consequently, O has the highest contribution margin per hour.
Answer (A) is incorrect because product M has a CM per hour of $2.00 [($10 – $7) ÷ 1.5], whereas product O's is $6.00 [($5 – $2) ÷ 0.5]. Answer (B) is incorrect because product N has the highest contribution margin, but product O has the highest contribution margin per hour. Answer (D) is incorrect because product P has a CM per hour of $4.00 [($8 – $4) ÷ 1.0 hr.], but O's is $6.00 [($5 – $2) ÷ 0.5].

---

Questions 95 and 96 are based on the following information. A company sells two products, X and Y. The sales mix consists of a composite unit of two units of X for every five units of Y (2:5). Fixed costs are $49,500. The unit contribution margins for X and Y are $2.50 and $1.20, respectively.

---

**95.** Considering the company as a whole, the number of composite units to break even is

A. 31,500

B. 4,500

C. 8,250

D. 9,900

The correct answer is (B). *(CIA, adapted)*
**REQUIRED:** The composite breakeven point.
**DISCUSSION:** The composite breakeven point for a multiproduct firm is computed by dividing total fixed costs by a composite contribution margin. Thus, the composite CM for X and Y is $11 [2($2.50) + 5($1.20)], and the BEP is 4,500 composite units ($49,500 ÷ $11).
Answer (A) is incorrect because 31,500 equals the total units of X and Y in 4,500 composite units. Answer (C) is incorrect because 8,250 would result if the composite unit consisted only of five units of Y. Answer (D) is incorrect because 9,900 would be the breakeven point if the composite unit consisted only of two units of X.

**96.** If the company had an operating income of $22,000, the unit sales must have been

| | Product X | Product Y |
|---|---|---|
| A. | 5,000 | 12,500 |
| B. | 13,000 | 32,500 |
| C. | 23,800 | 59,500 |
| D. | 28,600 | 71,500 |

The correct answer is (B). *(CIA, adapted)*
**REQUIRED:** The computation of unit sales given profit.
**DISCUSSION:** Composite unit sales can be determined by adding profit to fixed costs and dividing by the $11 composite CM (see preceding question). To earn an operating income of $22,000, 6,500 composite units must be sold [($49,500 FC + $22,000 profit ÷ $11]. Thus, 13,000 units (2 x 6,500) of product X and 32,500 units (5 x 6,500) of product Y must have been sold.
Answer (A) is incorrect because 5,000 units of X and 12,500 units of Y will result in a $22,000 loss. Answer (C) is incorrect because 23,800 units of X and 59,500 units of Y will result in an operating income of $81,400. Answer (D) is incorrect because 28,600 units of X and 71,500 units of Y will result in an operating income of $107,800.

Questions 97 through 99 are based on the following information.  Moorehead Manufacturing Company produces two products for which the following data have been tabulated.  Fixed manufacturing cost is applied at a rate of $1.00 per machine hour.

| Per Unit | XY-7 | BD-4 |
|---|---|---|
| Selling price | $4.00 | $3.00 |
| Variable manufacturing cost | $2.00 | $1.50 |
| Fixed manufacturing cost | $ .75 | $ .20 |
| Variable selling cost | $1.00 | $1.00 |

The sales manager has had a $160,000 increase in the budget allotment for advertising and wants to apply the money to the most profitable product.  The products are not substitutes for one another in the eyes of the company's customers.

**97.** Suppose the sales manager chooses to devote the entire $160,000 to increased advertising for XY-7.  The minimum increase in sales units of XY-7 required to offset the increased advertising is

A.  640,000 units.

B.  160,000 units.

C.  128,000 units.

D.  80,000 units.

The correct answer is (B). *(CMA, adapted)*
**REQUIRED:**  The minimum increase in sales units to offset increased advertising costs.
**DISCUSSION:**  The CM for XY-7 is $1 per unit ($4 sales price – $3 variable costs).  Thus, 160,000 units of XY-7 will generate an additional $160,000 of CM, which suffices to cover the increased advertising costs.
Answer (A) is incorrect because 640,000 units results if the UCM for XY-7 is $.25.  Answer (C) is incorrect because 128,000 units implies a $1.25 UCM.  Answer (D) is incorrect because 80,000 units implies a $2.00 UCM.

**98.** Suppose the sales manager chooses to devote the entire $160,000 to increased advertising for BD-4.  The minimum increase in revenues of BD-4 required to offset the increased advertising would be

A.  $160,000

B.  $320,000

C.  $960,000

D.  $1,600,000

The correct answer is (C). *(CMA, adapted)*
**REQUIRED:**  The minimum increase in revenues to offset increased advertising costs.
**DISCUSSION:**  Revenues must increase sufficiently to cover the $160,000 increase in advertising.  The UCM for BD-4 is $.50 ($3 – $2.50 variable costs), and the CMR is 16⅔% (UCM ÷ $3 sales price).  Hence, the revenues necessary to cover the increased advertising costs equal $960,000 ($160,000 ÷ 16⅔%).
Answer (A) is incorrect because a $1 increase in revenues does not result in a $1 increase in profits.  Answer (B) is incorrect because 320,000 is the number of sales units needed to offset the increased advertising costs.  Answer (D) is incorrect because fixed manufacturing costs are not included in determining UCM.

**99.** Suppose Moorehead has only 100,000 machine hours that can be made available to produce additional units of XY-7 and BD-4.  If the potential increase in sales units for either product resulting from advertising is far in excess of this production capacity, which product should be advertised and what is the estimated increase in contribution margin earned?

A.  Product XY-7 should be produced, yielding a contribution margin of $75,000.

B.  Product XY-7 should be produced, yielding a contribution margin of $133,333.

C.  Product BD-4 should be produced, yielding a contribution margin of $187,500.

D.  Product BD-4 should be produced, yielding a contribution margin of $250,000.

The correct answer is (D). *(CMA, adapted)*
**REQUIRED:**  The more profitable product and the estimated increase in contribution margin.
**DISCUSSION:**  The machine hours must be allocated to the product(s) so as to maximize the total CM.  Given that potential additional sales of either product are in excess of production capacity, only the product with the greater UCM of scarce resource should be produced.  XY-7 requires .75 hours; BD-4 requires .2 hours of machine time (given fixed manufacturing cost applied at $1 per machine hour of $.75 for XY-7 and $.20 for BD-4).  XY-7 has a CM of $1.33 per machine hour ($1 UCM ÷ .75 hours), and BD-4 has a CM of $2.50 per machine hour ($.50 ÷ .2 hours).  Thus, only BD-4 should be produced, yielding a CM of $250,000 (100,000 x $2.50).  The key is CM per unit of scarce resource.
Answer (A) is incorrect because product XY-7 has a CM of $133,333.  Answers (B) and (C) are incorrect because product BD-4 has a CM at $250,000.

# CHAPTER NINE
# BUDGETING

A **budget (profit plan)** is an extension of CVP analysis. It is a realistic plan for the future expressed in quantitative terms. Top management can use a budget to plan for the future and communicate objectives and goals to all levels of the organization, to motivate employees, to control organizational activities, and to evaluate performance. The annual budget should be based upon an organization's goals and objectives. Thus, the annual budget is usually based on a combination of financial, quantitative, and qualitative measures.

The budget serves a vital **planning** function because organizations that prepare budgets anticipate problems before they occur. Thus, a firm with goals and objectives in the form of budgets will be able to plan and make better decisions. **Strategic budgeting** is a form of long-range planning based on identifying and specifying organizational goals and objectives. The strengths and weaknesses of the organization are evaluated and risk levels are assessed. The influences of internal and external factors are forecasted to derive the best strategy for reaching the organization's goals and objectives. External factors include general economic conditions and their expected trends, governmental regulatory measures, the labor market in the company's locale, and the activities of competitors.

The budget is also a **control** tool. For the budgetary process to serve effectively as a control function, it must be integrated with the accounting system and the organizational structure. Such integration enhances control by transmitting data and assigning variances to the proper organizational subunits. A budget helps control costs by setting cost guidelines that determine the efficiency of resource usage. A manager is less apt to incur unnecessary costs if (s)he knows that all costs will be compared with the budget and that (s)he will be accountable if controllable costs exceed budgeted amounts. Because budgets measure performance, employees should not view budgets negatively. A budget is just as likely to help as to hinder a manager's career. Furthermore, a manager can also use a budget as a personal self-evaluation tool. **Budgetary slack** (underestimation of probable performance) must be avoided, however, if a budget is to have its desired effects. The natural tendency of a manager is to negotiate for a less stringent measure of performance so as to avoid unfavorable variances from expectations. Misstating projections of costs and revenues for this purpose is behavior that is both dysfunctional and unethical.

The budget is a **motivational** tool, and employees are particularly motivated if they help prepare the budget. A manager who is asked to prepare a budget for his/her department will work hard to stay within the budget. In addition, a budget must be seen as realistic by employees before it can become a good motivational tool. Unfortunately, the budget is not always viewed in a positive manner. Some managers view a budget as a restriction. Nevertheless, employees are more apt to have a positive feeling toward a budget if some degree of flexibility is allowed.

Another purpose of a budget is **communication**. A budget can help tell employees what goals the firm is attempting to accomplish. If the firm does not have an overall budget, each department might think the firm has different goals. For example, the sales department may want to keep as much inventory as possible so that no sales will be lost, but the treasurer may want to keep the inventory as low as possible so that cash need not be spent any sooner than necessary. If the budget specifies the amount of inventory, all employees can work toward the same goals and objectives. Thus, budgets coordinate the various activities of a firm. A company's overall budget, often called the **master** or **comprehensive budget**, encompasses both the operating and financial budget processes discussed on the next page.

A **budget manual** describes how a budget is to be prepared. Items usually appearing in a budget manual include a budget planning calendar and distribution instructions for all budget schedules. Distribution instructions are important because, once a schedule is prepared, other departments in the organization use the schedule to prepare their own budgets. Without distribution instructions, someone who needs a particular schedule might be overlooked. The **budget planning calendar** is the schedule of activities for the development and adoption of the budget. It should include a list of dates indicating when specific information is to be provided to others by each information source. The preparation of a master budget usually takes several months. For instance, many firms start the budget for the next calendar year in September, anticipating its completion by the first of December. Because all of the individual departmental budgets are based on forecasts prepared by others and the budgets of other departments, a planning calendar is essential to integrate the entire process.

The **operating budget sequence** is the part of the master budget process that begins with the sales budget and culminates in the pro forma income statement. Its emphasis is on obtaining and using resources. The **sales budget** is usually the first budget prepared. Accordingly, accurate sales forecasts are crucial. Once a firm can estimate sales, the next step is to decide how much to produce or purchase. Sales are usually budgeted by product or department, and the sales budget establishes targets for sales personnel. Moreover, sales volume affects production and purchasing levels, operating expenses, and cash flow. The **production budget** (for a manufacturing firm) is based on the sales forecast, in units, plus or minus the desired inventory change. It is prepared for each department and is used to plan when items will be produced. The completed production budget and the **ending inventory budget** are the basis for three additional budgets. Direct materials usage, together with beginning inventory and targeted ending inventory data, determines the **direct materials budget**. The **direct labor budget** depends on wage rates, amounts and types of production, employees to be hired, etc. The **factory overhead budget** is a function of how factory overhead varies with particular cost drivers. The next step is preparation of the **cost of goods sold budget**, which reflects direct materials usage, direct labor, factory overhead, and the change in finished goods inventory. Other budgets prepared during the operating budget sequence are those for R&D, design, marketing, distribution, customer service, and administrative costs. These budgets, the sales budget, and the cost of goods sold budget are needed to prepare a pro forma operating income statement.

The **financial budget sequence** is the part of the master budget process that incorporates the capital budget, cash budget, and pro forma financial statements. Its emphasis is on obtaining the funds needed to purchase operating assets. The **capital budget** is not part of the operating budget because it is not part of normal operations. The capital budget may be prepared more than a year in advance to allow sufficient time to plan financing of major expenditures for long-term assets, such as equipment, buildings, and land, and to receive custom orders of specialized equipment, buildings, etc. The **cash budget** is vital because an organization must have adequate cash at all times. However, it cannot be prepared until the other budgets have been completed. Almost all organizations, regardless of size, prepare a cash budget. It is particularly important for organizations operating in seasonal industries. Even with plenty of other assets, an organization with a temporary shortage of cash can be driven into bankruptcy. Proper planning can prevent financial embarrassment. Thus, cash budgets are prepared not only annually and quarterly but also monthly and weekly. A cash budget projects cash receipts and disbursements for planning and control purposes. Hence, it helps avoid not only cash emergencies but also excessive idle cash. Moreover, cash budgeting facilitates planning for loans and other financing. A bank is more likely to lend money to a firm if the money will not be needed immediately.

The following is a summary of the operating budget sequence for a manufacturing firm that includes all elements of the value chain:

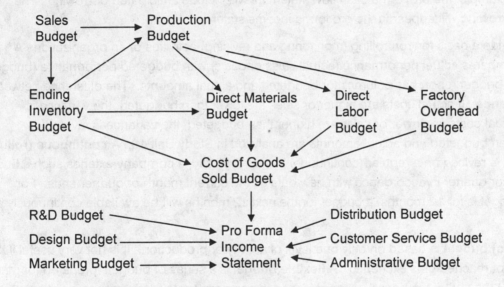

The following summarizes the financial budget sequence:

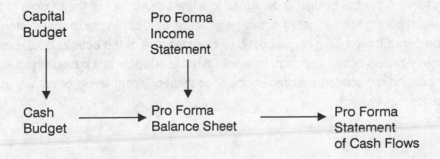

Once the individual budgets are complete, budgeted financial statements can be prepared.  They are often called **pro forma** statements because they are prepared before actual activities commence.  The **pro forma income statement** is the culmination of the operating budget sequence.  It is the pro forma operating income statement adjusted for interest and taxes.  It is used to decide whether the budgeted activities will result in an acceptable level of income.  If it shows an unacceptable level of income, the whole budgeting process must begin again.  The **pro forma balance sheet** is prepared using the cash and capital budgets and the pro forma income statement.  Thus, it and the pro forma statement of cash flows culminate the financial budget sequence.  The pro forma balance sheet is the beginning of the period balance sheet updated for projected changes in cash, receivables, payables, inventory, etc.  If the balance sheet indicates that a contractual agreement may be violated, the budgeting process must be repeated.  For example, some loan agreements require that owners' equity be maintained at some percentage of total debt or that current assets be maintained at a given multiple of current liabilities.  The **pro forma statement of cash flows** classifies cash receipts and disbursements depending on whether they are from operating, investing, or financing activities.  The direct presentation reports the major classes of gross cash operating receipts and payments and the difference between them.  The indirect presentation reconciles net income with net operating cash flow.  The reconciliation requires balance sheet data, such as the changes in accounts receivable, accounts payable, and inventory, as well as net income.  Thus, all the pro forma statements are interrelated.  For example, the pro forma cash flow statement will include anticipated borrowing.  The interest on this borrowing will appear in the pro forma income statement.

Budgets provide a basis for controlling (monitoring and revising) activities of an organization.  A **budget report** compares actual performance (actual sales or costs) with budgeted performance (budgeted sales or costs).  A budget report has columns for budgeted and actual amounts.  The difference between the two is the **variance**.  If actual costs are higher or sales are lower than budgeted, the variance is unfavorable.  If actual costs are lower or sales are higher than budgeted, the variance is favorable.  Differences between budgeted and actual amounts are analyzed in Study Unit 10.  A **continuous (rolling) budget** is one that is revised on a regular (continuous) basis.  Typically, a company extends such a budget for another month or quarter in accordance with new data as the current month or quarter ends.  For example, if the budget is for 12 months, a budget for the next 12 months will be available continuously as each month ends.

A **fixed (static) budget** is based on only one level of activity or production.  It is not very useful if the expected level is not reached or is exceeded.  A **flexible budget** is a series of budgets prepared for many levels of activity.  At the end of the period, management can compare actual performance with the appropriate budgeted level in the flexible budget.  New columns can quickly be made by interpolation or extrapolation, if necessary.  A flexible budget is designed to allow adjustment of the budget to the actual level of activity before comparing the budgeted activity with actual results.  In traditional systems, flexible budgets are usually prepared based on a single cost driver or measure of the activity level, such as direct labor hours.  In an activity-based costing system, however, flexible budgets are based on multiple cost drivers.  The result should be more accurate predictions of costs at different levels of activity than are available in traditional costing systems.

**Zero-base budgeting (ZBB)** is a budget and planning process in which each manager must justify a department's entire budget from a base of zero every year (or period). All expenditures must be justified regardless of the variance from previous years. The objective is to encourage periodic reexamination of all costs in the hope that some can be reduced or eliminated. ZBB begins with the lowest budgetary units of the entity. It requires determination of objectives, operations, and costs for each activity and the alternative means of carrying out that activity. Different levels of service (work effort) are evaluated for each activity, measures of work and performance are established, and activities are ranked according to their importance to the entity. For each budgetary unit, a decision package is prepared that describes various levels of service that may be provided, including at least one level lower than the current one. Accordingly, ZBB requires managers to justify each expenditure for each budget period and to review each cost component from a cost-benefit perspective.

A **life-cycle budget** estimates a product's revenues and expenses over its entire life cycle beginning with research and development, proceeding through the introduction and growth stages, into the maturity stage, and finally into the harvest or decline stage. Life-cycle budgeting adopts a **life-cycle cost** approach. It is intended to account for the costs at all stages of the **value chain** (R&D, design, production, marketing, distribution, and customer service). This information is important for pricing decisions because revenues must cover costs incurred in each stage of the value chain, not just production. Life-cycle budgeting emphasizes the relationships among costs incurred at different value-chain stages, for example, the effect of reduced design costs on future customer-service costs. Thus, life-cycle budgeting highlights the potential for locking in (designing in) future costs because the opportunity for cost reduction is greatest during the preproduction stages in the value chain. Indeed, it has been estimated that 90% or more of costs are committed (not incurred) before production begins. In contrast, traditional approaches focus on cost control (as opposed to cost reduction) during production and treat pre- and postproduction costs as period costs that are largely ignored in determining the profitability of specific products. Other costs that traditional methods ignore are the after-purchase costs (operating, support, repair, and disposal) incurred by customers. Accordingly, **whole-life cost** is a concept closely associated with life-cycle cost. Whole-life cost equals the life-cycle cost plus after-purchase costs. Attention to the reduction of all whole-life costs through analysis and management of all value-chain activities is a powerful competitive tool because of the potential for increasing customer satisfaction. Life-cycle and whole-life cost concepts are associated with target costing and target pricing. A firm may determine that market conditions require that a product sell at a given **target price**. Hence, a **target cost** can be determined by subtracting the desired unit profit margin from the target price. The cost reduction objectives of life-cycle and whole-life cost management can therefore be determined using target costing.

**Activity-based budgeting** applies activity-based costing principles to budgeting. It focuses on the numerous activities necessary to produce and market goods and services. This approach contrasts with the traditional emphasis on functions or spending categories. Thus, activity-based budgeting provides greater detail, especially regarding overhead, because it permits the identification of value-adding activities and their drivers. A homogeneous cost pool is established for each set of activities that have the same (or a similar) driver, and the budgeted cost for each pool is determined by multiplying the demand for the activities represented in the pool by the estimated cost of a unit of the relevant driver. Activity-based budgeting is a useful anticipatory control because it estimates the usage and costing rates of drivers before costs are locked in. After operations, it is useful for comparing actual costing rates and driver usage with the amounts budgeted.

The Japanese term **kaizen** means continuous improvement, and **kaizen budgeting** assumes the continuous improvement of products and processes, usually by way of many small innovations rather than major changes. It requires estimates of the effects of improvements and the costs of their implementation. Accordingly, kaizen budgeting is based not on the existing system but on changes yet to be made, and budget targets cannot be reached unless those improvements occur. Kaizen budget estimates may be based on learning curves, that is, expected reductions in labor time during the early stages of production as experience is gained. A kaizen budget may also relate to the product life cycle concept. The greatest improvements should occur during the early phases of the cycle, for example, during R&D and design, before costs are locked in.

**Governmental budgeting** differs from private-sector budgeting. A governmental budget is not only a financial plan and a basis for evaluating performance but also an expression of public policy and a form of control having the force of law. Thus, a governmental budget is a legal document adopted in accordance with procedures specified by applicable laws. A governmental budget must be complied with by the administrators of the governmental unit for which the budget is prepared. By law, the administrators cannot exceed the budget without a formally approved budget amendment. Moreover, because the effectiveness and efficiency of governmental efforts are difficult to measure in the absence of the profit-centered activity that characterizes business operations, the use of budgets in the appropriation process is of major importance. Accordingly, budgetary accounts may be incorporated into the formal accounting systems of governments, and a budgetary comparison statement must be issued.

## 9.1 Budget Concepts

**1.** The process of creating a formal plan and translating goals into a quantitative format is

    A. Process costing.

    B. Activity-based costing.

    C. Budgeting.

    D. Variance analysis.

The correct answer is (C). *(CMA, adapted)*

    **REQUIRED:** The term meaning the process of creating a formal plan and translating goals into a quantitative format.

    **DISCUSSION:** A budget is a realistic plan for the future expressed in quantitative terms. It is also a planning tool. Budgeting facilitates control and communication and also provides motivation to employees.

    Answer (A) is incorrect because process costing is a technique for determining the cost of manufactured products. Answer (B) is incorrect because ABC is a means of product costing that emphasizes activities as basic cost objects. Answer (D) is incorrect because variance analysis is a technique for comparing actual costs to planned costs.

**2.** Which one of the following best describes the role of top management in the budgeting process? Top management

    A. Should be involved only in the approval process.

    B. Lacks the detailed knowledge of the daily operations and should limit its involvement.

    C. Needs to be involved, including using the budget process to communicate goals.

    D. Needs to separate the budgeting process and the business planning process into two separate processes.

The correct answer is (C). *(CMA, adapted)*

    **REQUIRED:** The best description of top management's role in the budgeting process.

    **DISCUSSION:** A budget should not be dictated to lower-level employees, but top management needs to be involved. For example, the budget can be used by top management to plan for the future and communicate objectives and goals to all levels of the organization, to motivate employees, to control organizational activities, and to evaluate performance.

    Answer (A) is incorrect because top managers can use the budget for motivational and communication purposes; they should do more than merely sign off on the finished document. Answer (B) is incorrect because top managers should be involved in the budget process even though they lack detailed knowledge of daily operations; the budget can still communicate company objectives and goals. Answer (D) is incorrect because the budget process is a part of the overall planning process.

**3.** The major objectives of any budget system are to

    A. Define responsibility centers, provide a framework for performance evaluation, and promote communication and coordination among organization segments.

    B. Define responsibility centers, facilitate the fixing of blame for missed budget predictions, and ensure goal congruence between superiors and subordinates.

    C. Foster the planning of operations, provide a framework for performance evaluation, and promote communication and coordination among organization segments.

    D. Foster the planning of operations, facilitate the fixing of blame for missed budget predictions, and ensure goal congruence between superiors and subordinates.

The correct answer is (C). *(CIA, adapted)*

    **REQUIRED:** The major objectives of any budget system.

    **DISCUSSION:** A budget is a realistic plan for the future expressed in quantitative terms. The process of budgeting forces a company to establish goals, determine the resources necessary to achieve those goals, and anticipate future difficulties in their achievement. A budget is also a control tool because it establishes standards and facilitates comparison of actual and budgeted performance. Thus, it motivates good performance by highlighting the work of effective managers. Moreover, the nature of budgeting fosters communication of goals to company subunits and coordination of their efforts. Budgeting activities must be coordinated because they are interdependent.

    Answers (A), (B), and (D) are incorrect because budgets follow the creation of responsibility centers; they measure performance; and they promote, but do not ensure, goal congruence.

**4.** Which one of the following is not considered to be a benefit of participative budgeting?

    A.  Individuals at all organizational levels are recognized as being part of the team; this results in greater support of the organization.

    B.  The budget estimates are prepared by those in direct contact with various activities.

    C.  Managers are held responsible for reaching their goals, and they cannot shift their responsibility by blaming the unrealistic goals demanded by the budget.

    D.  When managers set the final targets for the budget, top management need not be concerned with the overall profitability of current operations.

The correct answer is (D). *(CMA, adapted)*
    **REQUIRED:** The item that is not considered to be a benefit of participative budgeting.
    **DISCUSSION:** Broad participation usually leads to greater support for the budget and the entity as a whole, greater understanding of what is to be accomplished, and greater accuracy of budget estimates. Managers with immediate operational responsibility for activities have a better understanding of what results can be achieved and at what costs. Also, managers cannot use unrealistic goals as an excuse for not achieving budget expectations when they have helped to establish those goals. However, top management must still participate in the budget process to insure goal congruence.
    Answer (A) is incorrect because participative budgeting promotes teamwork. Answer (B) is incorrect because a participative budget involves those most directly affected. Answer (C) is incorrect because participative budgeting improves accountability.

**5.** The budget that describes the long-term position, goals, and objectives of an entity within its environment is the

    A.  Capital budget.

    B.  Operating budget.

    C.  Cash management budget.

    D.  Strategic budget.

The correct answer is (D). *(CMA, adapted)*
    **REQUIRED:** The budget that describes the long-term position, goals, and objectives of an entity.
    **DISCUSSION:** Strategic budgeting is a form of long-range planning based on identifying and specifying organizational goals and objectives. The strengths and weaknesses of the organization are evaluated and risk levels are assessed. The influences of environmental factors are forecast to derive the best strategy for reaching the organization's objectives.
    Answer (A) is incorrect because capital budgeting involves evaluating specific long-term investment decisions. Answer (B) is incorrect because the operating budget is a short-range management tool. Answer (C) is incorrect because cash management is a short-range consideration related to liquidity.

**6.** Budgetary slack can best be described as

    A.  The elimination of certain expenses to enhance budgeted income.

    B.  The planned overestimation of budgeted expenses.

    C.  A plug number used to achieve a preset level of operating income.

    D.  The planned underestimation of budgeted expenses.

The correct answer is (B). *(CMA, adapted)*
    **REQUIRED:** The meaning of budgetary slack.
    **DISCUSSION:** A budget is a control technique that, among other things, establishes a performance standard. The natural reaction of a manager whose efforts are to be judged is to negotiate for a less stringent performance measure. Overestimation of expenses, that is, incorporation of slack into the budget, is a means of avoiding an unfavorable variance from expectations. However, this practice is both wasteful and conducive to inaccurate performance appraisal.
    Answer (A) is incorrect because building slack into a budget is the opposite of enhancing budgeting income. Answer (C) is incorrect because slack is not a plug number but an overestimation of expenses. Answer (D) is incorrect because slack is the overestimation of expenses.

**7.** The use of budgetary slack does not allow the preparer to

A. Be flexible under unexpected circumstances.

B. Increase the probability of achieving budgeted performance.

C. Use the budget to control subordinate performance.

D. Blend personal goals with organizational goals.

The correct answer is (C). *(CMA, adapted)*

**REQUIRED:** The function prevented by budgetary slack.

**DISCUSSION:** Managers often try to incorporate slack into a budget in order to provide flexibility when unexpected costs arise. In such cases, the preparer can still achieve budgeted performance even though costs are higher than actually expected. However, the existence of slack in a budget does not allow the best possible control of subordinate performance. Control entails comparison of performance with a standard. If the standard is inaccurate, the value of the comparison is diminished.

Answer (A) is incorrect because slack increases flexibility when unforeseen circumstances arise. Answer (B) is incorrect because lowering the standard of performance increases the probability of achieving budgetary goals. Answer (D) is incorrect because the existence of slack increases the likelihood that a manager will receive the personal rewards that follow from meeting the expectations of superiors.

**8.** From the perspective of corporate management, the use of budgetary slack

A. Increases the effectiveness of the corporate planning process.

B. Increases the ability to identify potential budget weaknesses.

C. Encourages the use of effective corrective actions.

D. Increases the likelihood of inefficient resource allocation.

The correct answer is (D). *(CMA, adapted)*

**REQUIRED:** The perspective of corporate management on the use of budgetary slack.

**DISCUSSION:** The existence of budgetary slack increases the probability that budgeted performance will be achieved. However, resources may not be efficiently used because the manager responsible for meeting budgetary goals will have less incentive to minimize costs.

Answer (A) is incorrect because slack decreases the effectiveness of the planning process. A budget with significant slack does not reflect the best estimate of future results. Answer (B) is incorrect because weaknesses will be overlooked if total costs are within prearranged limits, and this effect is more likely if slack is included in the budget. Answer (C) is incorrect because corrective actions (such as hiring a new manager) may not occur as quickly if slack is included in a budget.

**9.** A planning calendar in budgeting is the

A. Calendar period covered by the budget.

B. Schedule of activities for the development and adoption of the budget.

C. Sales forecast by months in the annual budget period.

D. Schedule of dates at which goals are to be met.

The correct answer is (B). *(CMA, adapted)*

**REQUIRED:** The definition of a planning calendar.

**DISCUSSION:** The budget planning calendar is the schedule of activities for the development and adoption of the budget. It should include a list of dates indicating when specific information is to be provided to others by each information source. The preparation of a master budget usually takes several months. For instance, many firms start the budget for the next calendar year some time in September in hopes of having it completed by December 1. Because all of the individual departmental budgets are based on forecasts prepared by others and the budgets of other departments, it is essential to have a planning calendar to ensure the proper integration of the entire process.

Answer (A) is incorrect because the period covered by the budget precedes the events in the planning calendar. Answer (C) is incorrect because the planning calendar is not associated with sales. Answer (D) is incorrect because a schedule of dates at which goals are to be met is a component of budget preparation, not the planning calendar.

**10.** A budget manual, which enhances the operation of a budget system, is most likely to include

    A.   A chart of accounts.

    B.   Distribution instructions for budget schedules.

    C.   Documentation of the accounting system software.

    D.   Company policies regarding the authorization of transactions.

The correct answer is (B). *(CMA, adapted)*

**REQUIRED:** The item that will most likely be included in a budget manual.

**DISCUSSION:** A budget manual describes how a budget is to be prepared. Items usually included in a budget manual are a planning calendar and distribution instructions for all budget schedules. Distribution instructions are important because, once a schedule is prepared, other departments within the organization will use the schedule to prepare their own budgets. Without distribution instructions, someone who needs a schedule may be overlooked.

Answer (A) is incorrect because the accounting manual includes a chart of accounts. Answer (C) is incorrect because software documentation is not needed in budgeting. Answer (D) is incorrect because the authorization of transactions is not necessary for budgeting.

**11.** The goals and objectives upon which an annual profit plan is most effectively based are

    A.   Financial measures such as net income, return on investment, and earnings per share.

    B.   Quantitative measures such as growth in unit sales, number of employees, and manufacturing capacity.

    C.   Qualitative measures of organizational activity such as product innovation leadership, product quality levels, and product safety.

    D.   A combination of financial, quantitative, and qualitative measures.

The correct answer is (D). *(CMA, adapted)*

**REQUIRED:** The goals and objectives upon which an annual profit plan is most effectively based.

**DISCUSSION:** Objectives vary with the organization's type and stage of development. Broad objectives should be established at the top and retranslated in more specific terms as they are communicated downward in a means-end hierarchy. Each subunit may have its own specific goals. A conflict sometimes exists in determining organizational objectives. For example, customer service may be one objective, but profitability or return on investment may be a conflicting objective. Thus, the annual profit plan is usually based on a combination of financial, quantitative, and qualitative measures.

Answer (A) is incorrect because more than financial measures are needed to prepare a profit plan. Long-term quality measures must also be considered. Answers (B) and (C) are incorrect because quantitative and qualitative measures are insufficient if financial measures are not also considered.

## 9.2 Types of Budgets

**12.** The master budget process usually begins with the

    A.   Production budget.

    B.   Operating budget.

    C.   Financial budget.

    D.   Sales budget.

The correct answer is (D). *(CMA, adapted)*

**REQUIRED:** The type of budget that usually begins the master budget process.

**DISCUSSION:** A master or comprehensive budget consolidates all budgets into an overall planning and control document for the organization. The preparation of a master budget usually takes several months. The sales budget is the first budget prepared because it is the basis for all subsequent budgets. Once a firm can estimate sales, the next step is to decide how much to produce or purchase.

Answer (A) is incorrect because the production budget normally cannot be prepared until the expected sales are known. Answer (B) is incorrect because the operating budget is another term for the budget used on a day-to-day basis for managing operations. It cannot be prepared until after the sales budget is prepared. Answer (C) is incorrect because preparation of the sales budget is the first step in the overall budgeting process.

**13.** Which of the following is normally included in the financial budget of a firm?

   A.  Direct materials budget.

   B.  Selling expense budget.

   C.  Budgeted balance sheet.

   D.  Sales budget.

The correct answer is (C). *(Publisher)*
   **REQUIRED:** The item normally included in the financial budget.
   **DISCUSSION:** The financial budget normally includes the capital budget, the cash budget, the budgeted balance sheet, and the budgeted statement of cash flows.
   Answer (A) is incorrect because direct materials budget is included in the operating budget. Answer (B) is incorrect because the selling expense budget is included in the operating budget. Answer (D) is incorrect because the sales budget is included in the operating budget.

**14.** All of the following are considered operating budgets except the

   A.  Cash budget.

   B.  Materials budget.

   C.  Production budget.

   D.  Capital budget.

The correct answer is (D). *(CMA, adapted)*
   **REQUIRED:** The item not part of the operating budget.
   **DISCUSSION:** The operating budget consists of all budgets that concern normal operating activities, including the sales, production, materials, direct labor, overhead, and cash budgets. The capital budget, which concerns new capital investment, is part of the financial budgeting process but not day-to-day operations. It is sometimes prepared more than a year in advance to allow sufficient time to secure financing for major expenditures and to receive custom orders of specialized assets.
   Answers (A), (B), and (C) are incorrect because the cash, materials, and production budgets are operating budgets.

**15.** Which one the following statements regarding selling and administrative budgets is most accurate?

   A.  Selling and administrative budgets are usually optional.

   B.  Selling and administrative budgets are fixed in nature.

   C.  Selling and administrative budgets are difficult to allocate by month and are best presented as one number for the entire year.

   D.  Selling and administrative budgets need to be detailed in order that the key assumptions can be better understood.

The correct answer is (D). *(CMA, adapted)*
   **REQUIRED:** The most accurate statement about selling and administrative budgets.
   **DISCUSSION:** Sales and administrative budgets are prepared after the sales budget. They are among the components of the operating budget process, which culminates in a budgeted (pro forma) income statement. Like the other budgets, they constitute prospective information based on the preparer's assumptions about conditions expected to exist and actions expected to be taken.
   Answer (A) is incorrect because selling and administrative budgets are no more optional than any other component of the master budget. Answer (B) is incorrect because selling and administrative budgets have both variable and fixed components. Answer (C) is incorrect because selling and administrative budgets should be prepared on the same basis as the remainder of the budget, typically on at least a monthly basis.

**16.** When sales volume is seasonal in nature, certain items in the budget must be coordinated. The three most significant items to coordinate in budgeting seasonal sales volume are

   A.  Production volume, finished goods inventory, and sales volume.

   B.  Direct labor hours, work-in-process inventory, and sales volume.

   C.  Raw material inventory, direct labor hours, and manufacturing overhead costs.

   D.  Raw material inventory, work-in-process inventory, and production volume.

The correct answer is (A). *(CMA, adapted)*
   **REQUIRED:** The three most significant items to coordinate in budgeting seasonal sales volume.
   **DISCUSSION:** The most difficult items to coordinate in any budget, particularly for a seasonal business, are production volume, finished goods inventory, and sales. Budgets usually begin with sales volume and proceed to production volume, but the reverse is sometimes used when production is more of an issue than generation of sales. Inventory levels are also important because sales cannot occur without inventory, and the maintenance of high inventory levels is costly.
   Answer (B) is incorrect because direct labor hours and work-in-process are only two components of a production budget. Answers (C) and (D) are incorrect because sales is usually the most important aspect of any budget.

**17.** Various budgets are included in the master budget cycle. One of these budgets is the production budget. Which one of the following best describes the production budget?

    A.   It includes required direct labor hours.

    B.   It includes required material purchases.

    C.   It aggregates the monetary details of the operating budget.

    D.   It is calculated from the desired ending inventory and the sales forecast.

The correct answer is (D). *(CMA, adapted)*
   **REQUIRED:** The best description of a production budget.
   **DISCUSSION:** A production budget is based on sales forecasts, in units, with adjustments for beginning and ending inventories. It is used to plan when items will be produced. After the production budget has been completed, it is used to prepare materials purchases, direct labor, and factory overhead budgets.
   Answers (A) and (B) are incorrect because the direct labor and materials purchases budgets are prepared after the production budget. Answer (C) is incorrect because the production budget is normally not prepared in monetary terms.

**18.** Which one of the following items is the last schedule to be prepared in the normal budget preparation process?

    A.   Cash budget.

    B.   Cost of goods sold budget.

    C.   Manufacturing overhead budget.

    D.   Selling expense budget.

The correct answer is (A). *(CMA, adapted)*
   **REQUIRED:** The last schedule prepared in the normal budget process.
   **DISCUSSION:** The budget preparation process normally begins with the sales budget and continues through the preparation of pro forma financial statements. The last schedule prepared before the financial statements is the cash budget. The cash budget is a schedule of estimated cash collections and payments. The various operating budgets and the capital budget are inputs to the cash budgeting process.
   Answers (B), (C), and (D) are incorrect because the cost of goods sold budget, the manufacturing overhead budget, and the selling expense budget provide information necessary to prepare the cash budget.

**19.** Which one of the following items would have to be included for a company preparing a schedule of cash receipts and disbursements for the calendar year 1998?

    A.   A purchase order issued in December 1998 for items to be delivered in February 1999.

    B.   Dividends declared in November 1998 to be paid in January 1999 to shareholders of record as of December 1998.

    C.   The amount of uncollectible customer accounts for 1998.

    D.   The borrowing of funds from a bank on a note payable taken out in June 1998 with an agreement to pay the principal and interest in June 1999.

The correct answer is (D). *(CMA, adapted)*
   **REQUIRED:** The item included in a cash budget for 1998.
   **DISCUSSION:** A schedule of cash receipts and disbursements (cash budget) should include all cash inflows and outflows during the period without regard to the accrual accounting treatment of the transactions. Hence, it should include all checks written and all sources of cash, including borrowings. A borrowing from a bank in June 1998 should appear as a cash receipt for 1998.
   Answer (A) is incorrect because the cash disbursement presumably will not occur until 1999. Answer (B) is incorrect because the cash flow will not occur until dividends are paid in 1999. Answer (C) is incorrect because bad debt expense is a noncash item.

**20.** Pro forma financial statements are part of the budgeting process. Normally, the last pro forma statement prepared is the

- A. Income statement.
- B. Statement of cost of goods sold.
- C. Statement of cash flows.
- D. Statement of manufacturing costs.

The correct answer is (C). *(CMA, adapted)*

**REQUIRED:** The last pro forma financial statement prepared.

**DISCUSSION:** The statement of cash flows is usually the last of the listed items prepared. All other elements of the budget process must be completed before it can be developed. The statement of cash flows reconciles net income with net operating cash flow, a process that requires balance sheet data (e.g., changes in receivables, payables, and inventories) as well as net income.

Answer (A) is incorrect because the income statement must be prepared before the statement of cash flows, which reconciles net income and net operating cash flows. Answer (B) is incorrect because cost of goods sold is included in the income statement, which is an input to the statement of cash flows. Answer (D) is incorrect because the statement of manufacturing costs must be prepared before either the income statement or the statement of cash flows.

## 9.3 Budgetary Control

**21.** Kallert Manufacturing currently uses the company budget as a planning tool only. Management has decided to use budgets for control purposes also. To implement this change, the management accountant must

- A. Organize a budget committee and appoint a budget director.
- B. Report daily to operating management all deviations from plan.
- C. Synchronize the budgeting and accounting system with the organizational structure.
- D. Develop forecasting procedures.

The correct answer is (C). *(CMA, adapted)*

**REQUIRED:** The action required to use a planning budget for control purposes.

**DISCUSSION:** A budget is a means of control because it sets cost guidelines with which actual performance can be compared. The feedback provided by comparison of actual and budgeted performance reveals whether a manager has used company assets efficiently. If a budget is to be used for control purposes, however, the accounting system must be designed to produce information required for the control process. Moreover, the budgeting and accounting system must be related to the organizational structure so that variances will be assigned to the proper individuals.

Answer (A) is incorrect because a budget director and committee are needed even if a budget is to be used only for planning. Answer (B) is incorrect because daily reporting is usually not necessary. Also, reporting all deviations would not be cost beneficial. Answer (D) is incorrect because the company should already be using forecasting procedures if the budget is being used as a planning tool.

**22.** Which one of the following organizational policies is most likely to result in undesirable managerial behavior?

- A. Joe Walk, the chief executive officer of Eagle Rock Brewery, wrote a memorandum to his executives stating, "Operating plans are contracts, and they should be met without fail."
- B. The budgeting process at Madsen Manufacturing starts with operating managers providing goals for their respective departments.
- C. Fullbright Lighting holds quarterly meetings of departmental managers to consider possible changes in the budgeted targets due to changing conditions.
- D. At Fargo Transportation, managers are expected to provide explanations for variances from the budget in their departments.

The correct answer is (A). *(CMA, adapted)*

**REQUIRED:** The organizational policy most likely to result in undesirable managerial behavior.

**DISCUSSION:** Control is the process of making certain that plans are achieving the desired objectives. A budget is one of the most common control devices. It is a plan for the future; it is not a contract. To interpret a budget or other plan to be as inflexible as a contract may encourage a manager to act in ways contrary to the company's best interest in a misguided effort to meet the criteria proposed.

Answer (B) is incorrect because participatory budgeting obtains the support of those involved and is likely to foster desirable behavior. Answer (C) is incorrect because changing budget targets as conditions change results in setting fairer performance goals. Answer (D) is incorrect because allowing managers to provide explanations for variances does nothing to cause undesirable behavior. If explanations are acceptable, no reason exists to manipulate statements.

**23.** A continuous (rolling) budget

A.  Presents planned activities for a period but does not present a firm commitment.

B.  Presents the plan for only one level of activity and does not adjust to changes in the level of activity.

C.  Presents the plan for a range of activity so that the plan can be adjusted for changes in activity.

D.  Drops the current month or quarter and adds a future month or quarter as the current month or quarter is completed.

The correct answer is (D). *(CMA, adapted)*
**REQUIRED:** The true statement about a continuous budget.
**DISCUSSION:** A continuous budget is one that is revised on a regular (continuous) basis. Typically, a company extends such a budget for another month or quarter in accordance with new data as the current month or quarter ends. For example, if the budget is for 12 months, a budget for the next 12 months will be available continuously as each month ends.
Answer (A) is incorrect because a continuous budget does present a firm commitment. Answer (B) is incorrect because a continuous budget can be for various levels of activity; a static budget is prepared for only one level of activity. Answer (C) is incorrect because a flexible budget presents the plan for a range of activity so that the plan can be adjusted for changes in activity.

## 9.4 Flexible Budgets

**24.** Which one of the following budgeting methodologies would be most appropriate for a firm facing a significant level of uncertainty in unit sales volumes for next year?

A.  Top-down budgeting.

B.  Life-cycle budgeting.

C.  Static budgeting.

D.  Flexible budgeting.

The correct answer is (D). *(CMA, adapted)*
**REQUIRED:** The budgeting methodology most appropriate for a firm facing significant uncertainty about unit sales volumes.
**DISCUSSION:** Flexible budgeting prepares a series of budgets for many levels of sales. At the end of the period, management can compare actual costs or performance with the appropriate budgeted level in the flexible budget. If necessary, new columns can be added to the flexible budget by means of interpolation or extrapolation. A flexible budget is designed to allow adjustment of the budget to the actual level of activity before comparing the budgeted activity with actual results.
Answer (A) is incorrect because top-down budgeting entails imposition of a budget by top management on lower-level employees. It is the antithesis of participatory budgeting. Answer (B) is incorrect because life-cycle budgeting estimates a product's revenues and costs for each link in the value chain from R&D and design to production, marketing, distribution, and customer service. The product life cycle ends when customer service is withdrawn. Answer (C) is incorrect because a static budget is for only one level of activity.

**25.** Which one of the following statements regarding the difference between a flexible budget and a static budget is true?

A.  A flexible budget primarily is prepared for planning purposes, whereas a static budget is prepared for performance evaluation.

B.  A flexible budget provides cost allowances for different levels of activity, whereas a static budget provides costs for one level of activity.

C.  A flexible budget includes only variable costs, whereas a static budget includes only fixed costs.

D.  Variances will always be larger with a flexible budget than with a static budget.

The correct answer is (B). *(CMA, adapted)*
**REQUIRED:** The difference between a flexible and a fixed budget.
**DISCUSSION:** A flexible budget provides cost allowances for different levels of activity, whereas a static budget provides costs for one level of activity. Both budgets show the same types of costs. Thus, a flexible budget is a series of budgets prepared for many different levels of activity. A flexible budget allows adjustment of the budget to the actual level of activity before comparing the budgeted activity with actual results.
Answer (A) is incorrect because both budgets are prepared for both planning and performance evaluation purposes. Answer (C) is incorrect because both budgets include both fixed and variable costs. Answer (D) is incorrect because variances tend to be smaller with a flexible budget. The figures are based on actual levels of activity, whereas the static budget may be based on an activity level far removed from actual activity.

**26.** When preparing a performance report for a cost center using flexible budgeting techniques, the planned cost column should be based on the

    A. Budgeted amount in the original budget prepared before the beginning of the year.

    B. Actual amount for the same period in the preceding year.

    C. Budget adjusted to the actual level of activity for the period being reported.

    D. Budget adjusted to the planned level of activity for the period being reported.

The correct answer is (C). *(CMA, adapted)*
    **REQUIRED:** The basis for the planned cost column in a flexible budget performance report.
    **DISCUSSION:** If a report is to be used for performance evaluation, the planned cost column should be based on the actual level of activity for the period. The ability to adjust amounts for varying activity levels is the primary advantage of flexible budgeting.
    Answer (A) is incorrect because the static budget amount is not useful for comparison purposes. The budget for the actual activity level achieved is more important. Answer (B) is incorrect because prior-year figures are not useful if activity levels are different. Answer (D) is incorrect because a budget based on planned activity level is not as meaningful as one based on actual activity level.

**27.** The difference between the actual amounts and the flexible budget amounts for the actual output achieved is the

    A. Production volume variance.

    B. Flexible budget variance.

    C. Sales volume variance.

    D. Standard cost variance.

The correct answer is (B). *(CMA, adapted)*
    **REQUIRED:** The term meaning the difference between the actual amounts and the flexible budget amounts.
    **DISCUSSION:** A flexible budget is a series of several budgets prepared for many levels of activity. A flexible budget allows adjustment of the budget to the actual level before comparing the budgeted and actual results. The difference between the flexible budget and actual figures is known as the flexible budget variance.
    Answer (A) is incorrect because production volume variance (or the idle capacity variance) is based on the difference between actual and budgeted levels of production in terms of quantities. Answer (C) is incorrect because sales volume variance is based on the difference between actual and budgeted sales volume without regard to cost. Answer (D) is incorrect because a standard cost variance is not necessarily based on a flexible budget.

**28.** The use of standard costs in the budgeting process signifies that an organization has most likely implemented a

    A. Flexible budget.

    B. Capital budget.

    C. Static budget.

    D. Strategic budget.

The correct answer is (A). *(CMA, adapted)*
    **REQUIRED:** The budget most likely implemented by a company that uses standard costs.
    **DISCUSSION:** A flexible budget is a series of budgets prepared for many levels of sales. Another view is that it is based on cost formulas, or standard costs. Thus, the cost formulas are fed into the computerized budget program along with the actual level of production or sales. The result is a budget created for the actual level of activity.
    Answer (B) is incorrect because a capital budget is a means of evaluating long-term investments and has nothing to do with standard costs. Answer (C) is incorrect because a static budget is for one level of activity. It can be based on expected actual or standard costs. Answer (D) is incorrect because a strategic budget is a long-term budget.

**29.** A difference between standard costs used for cost control and budgeted costs

    A.  Can'exist because standard costs must be determined after the budget is completed.

    B.  Can exist because standard costs represent what costs should be, whereas budgeted costs represent expected actual costs.

    C.  Can exist because budgeted costs are historical costs, whereas standard costs are based on engineering studies.

    D.  Cannot exist because they should be the same amounts.

The correct answer is (B). *(CMA, adapted)*
    **REQUIRED:** The true statement about the difference between standard costs and budgeted costs.
    **DISCUSSION:** Standard costs are predetermined, attainable unit costs. Standard cost systems isolate deviations (variances) of actual from expected costs. One advantage is that they facilitate flexible budgeting. Accordingly, standard and budgeted costs should not differ when standards are currently attainable. However, in practice, budgeted (estimated actual) costs may differ from standard costs when operating conditions are not expected to be the same as those anticipated when the standards were developed.
    Answer (A) is incorrect because standard costs are determined independently of the budget. Answer (C) is incorrect because budgeted costs are expected future costs, not historical costs. Answer (D) is incorrect because budgeted and standard costs should in principle be the same, but in practice they will differ when standard costs are not expected to be currently attainable.

**30.** A flexible budget is appropriate for

    A.  Control of direct materials and direct labor but not selling and administrative expenses.

    B.  Any level of activity.

    C.  Control of direct labor and direct materials but not fixed factory overhead.

    D.  Control of selling and administrative expenses but not factory overhead.

The correct answer is (C). *(CMA, adapted)*
    **REQUIRED:** The appropriate use of a flexible budget.
    **DISCUSSION:** A flexible budget is actually a series of several budgets prepared for many levels of operating activity. A flexible budget is designed to allow adjustment of the budget to the actual level of activity before comparing the budgeted activity with actual results. This flexibility is important if costs vary with the activity level. Thus, a flexible budget is particularly appropriate for control of direct labor and direct materials (both variable costs), but it is not necessary for control of fixed factory overhead. By definition, fixed overhead costs do not change as activity levels change.
    Answers (A) and (D) are incorrect because flexible budgets are useful for controlling variable costs, including variable factory overhead and variable selling and administrative costs. Answer (B) is incorrect because a flexible budget is prepared for a specific range of activity.

## 9.5 Other Budget Concepts

**31.** A systemized approach known as zero-base budgeting (ZBB)

    A.  Presents planned activities for a period of time but does not present a firm commitment.

    B.  Divides the activities of individual responsibility centers into a series of packages that are prioritized.

    C.  Classifies the budget by the prior year's activity and estimates the benefits arising from each activity.

    D.  Commences with the current level of spending.

The correct answer is (B). *(CMA, adapted)*
    **REQUIRED:** The true statement about zero-base budgeting (ZBB).
    **DISCUSSION:** ZBB is a planning process in which each manager must justify a department's entire budget every year. ZBB differs from the traditional concept of budgeting in which next year's budget is largely based on the expenditures of the previous year. For each budgetary unit, ZBB prepares a decision package describing various levels of service that may be provided, including at least one level lower than the current one. Each component is evaluated from a cost-benefit perspective and then prioritized.
    Answer (A) is incorrect because ZBB does represent a firm commitment. Answer (C) is incorrect because ZBB is not based on prior year's activities. Answer (D) is incorrect because ZBB starts from a base of zero.

**32.** All types of organizations can benefit from budgeting. A major difference between governmental budgeting and business budgeting is that

    A. Business budgeting is required by the SEC.

    B. Governmental budgeting is usually done on a zero base.

    C. Business budgeting can be used to measure progress in achieving company objectives, whereas governmental budgeting cannot be used to measure progress in achieving objectives.

    D. Governmental budgeting usually reflects the legal limits on proposed expenditures.

The correct answer is (D). *(CMA, adapted)*
    **REQUIRED:** The major difference between governmental and business budgeting.
    **DISCUSSION:** A governmental budget is a legal document adopted in accordance with procedures specified by applicable laws. It must be complied with by the administrators of the governmental unit for which the budget is prepared. Because the effectiveness and efficiency of governmental efforts are difficult to measure in the absence of the profit-centered activity that characterizes business operations, the use of budgets in the appropriation process is of major importance.
    Answer (A) is incorrect because business budgeting is not mandated by the SEC or any other organization. Answer (B) is incorrect because few governments (if any) actually use a zero-base budgeting system. Answer (C) is incorrect because, in some instances, governmental budgeting can be used to measure progress in achieving objectives; for example, the objective may be to expend all appropriated funds.

**33.** A manufacturing company has prepared quarterly budgets for the next 12 months. These budgets anticipate steady decreases in the unit costs of a new product. Accordingly, if unit costs for the fourth quarter are materially lower than those for the first quarter, but an unfavorable variance is reported, the company is most likely using

    A. Kaizen budgeting.

    B. Activity-based budgeting.

    C. Life-cycle budgeting.

    D. Whole-life budgeting.

The correct answer is (A). *(Publisher)*
    **REQUIRED:** The type of budgeting used by a company that anticipates continuous improvement.
    **DISCUSSION:** The Japanese term kaizen means continuous improvement, and kaizen budgeting assumes the continuous improvement of products and processes, usually by way of many small innovations rather than major changes. It requires estimates of the effects of improvements and the costs of their implementation. Kaizen budgeting is based not on the existing system but on changes yet to be made, and budget targets cannot be reached unless those improvements occur. Accordingly, an unfavorable variance may occur even if improvements occur because their magnitude is less than that budgeted.
    Answer (B) is incorrect because activity-based budgeting stresses identification of activities and driver analysis rather than functions and spending categories. Answer (C) is incorrect because the essence of life-cycle budgeting is accounting for costs at all stages in the value chain. Answer (D) is incorrect because whole-life costs include customers' after-purchase costs as well as life-cycle costs.

**34.** The budgeting tool or process in which estimates of revenues and expenses are prepared for each product beginning with the product's research and development phase and traced through to its customer support phase is a(n)

    A. Master budget.

    B. Activity-based budget.

    C. Zero-base budget.

    D. Life-cycle budget.

The correct answer is (D). *(CMA, adapted)*
    **REQUIRED:** The budget tool that involves estimating a product's revenues and expenses from R&D through customer support.
    **DISCUSSION:** A life-cycle budget estimates a product's revenues and expenses over its expected life cycle. This approach is especially useful when revenues and related costs do not occur in the same periods. It emphasizes the need to budget revenues to cover all costs, not just those for production. Hence, costs are determined for all value-chain categories: upstream (R&D, design), manufacturing, and downstream (marketing, distribution, and customer service). The result is to highlight upstream and downstream costs that often receive insufficient attention.
    Answer (A) is incorrect because a master budget summarizes all of a company's budgets and plans. Answer (B) is incorrect because an activity-based budget emphasizes the costs of activities, which are the basic cost objects in activity-based costing. Answer (C) is incorrect because a zero-base budget requires each manager to justify his/her subunit's entire budget each year.

**35.** A company's product has an expected 4-year life cycle from research, development, and design through its withdrawal from the market. Budgeted costs are

| | |
|---|---|
| Upstream costs (R&D, design) | $2,000,000 |
| Manufacturing costs | 3,000,000 |
| Downstream costs (marketing, distribution, customer service) | 1,200,000 |
| After-purchase costs | 1,000,000 |

The company plans to produce 200,000 units and price the product at 125% of the whole-life unit cost. Thus, the budgeted unit selling price is

A. $15

B. $31

C. $36

D. $45

The correct answer is (D). *(Publisher)*
    **REQUIRED:** The unit selling price.
    **DISCUSSION:** Whole-life costs include after-purchase costs (operating, support, repair, and disposal) incurred by customers as well as life-cycle costs (R&D, design, manufacturing, marketing, distribution, and research). Hence, the budgeted unit whole-life cost is $36 [($2,000,000 + $3,000,000 + $1,200,000 + $1,000,000) ÷ 200,000 units], and the budgeted unit selling price is $45 (125% × $36).
    Answer (A) is incorrect because $15 is the budgeted unit manufacturing cost. Answer (B) is incorrect because $31 is the budgeted unit life-cycle cost. Answer (C) is incorrect because $36 is the budgeted unit whole-life cost.

## 9.6 Budget Computations

**36.** Zohar Company's 1999 budget contains the following information:

Zohar Company

| | Units |
|---|---|
| Beginning finished goods inventory | 85 |
| Beginning work-in-process in equivalent units | 10 |
| Desired ending finished goods inventory | 100 |
| Desired ending work-in-process in equivalent units | 40 |
| Projected sales for 1999 | 1,800 |

How many equivalent units should Zohar plan to produce in 1999?

A. 1,800

B. 1,565

C. 1,815

D. 1,845

The correct answer is (D). *(CMA, adapted)*
    **REQUIRED:** The equivalent units to produce.
    **DISCUSSION:** The finished units needed equal 1,815:

| | |
|---|---|
| Needed for sales | 1,800 |
| Needed for ending inventory | 100 |
| Total finished units needed | 1,900 |
| Minus beginning inventory | (85) |
| Finished units needed | 1,815 |

The units to be produced equal 1,845:

| | |
|---|---|
| Finished units needed | 1,815 |
| Needed for ending inventory | 40 |
| Total units in process | 1,855 |
| Minus beginning WIP inventory | (10) |
| Units to be produced | 1,845 |

Answer (A) is incorrect because 1,800 equals projected unit sales. Answer (B) is incorrect because 1,565 equals units needed for sales minus all given inventory amounts. Answer (C) is incorrect because 1,815 equals finished units needed.

**37.** A company has the following 1999 budget data:

| | |
|---|---|
| Beginning finished goods inventory | 40,000 units |
| Sales | 70,000 units |
| Ending finished goods inventory | 30,000 units |
| Direct materials | $10 per unit |
| Direct labor | $20 per unit |
| Variable factory overhead | $5 per unit |
| Selling costs | $2 per unit |
| Fixed factory overhead | $80,000 |

What are 1999 total budgeted production costs?

A. $2,100,000

B. $2,180,000

C. $2,240,000

D. $2,320,000

The correct answer is (B). *(CIA, adapted)*
    **REQUIRED:** The total budgeted production costs.
    **DISCUSSION:** The 1999 total budgeted production costs are $2,180,000. This calculation is based on production of 60,000 units (70,000 sold + 30,000 EI – 40,000 BI).

| | | |
|---|---|---|
| Direct materials | 60,000 × $10 = | $  600,000 |
| Direct labor | 60,000 × $20 = | 1,200,000 |
| Variable overhead | 60,000 × $ 5 = | 300,000 |
| Fixed overhead | | 80,000 |
| | | $2,180,000 |

Answer (A) is incorrect because $2,100,000 ignores fixed overhead. Answer (C) is incorrect because $2,240,000 includes selling costs and excludes fixed overhead. Answer (D) is incorrect because $2,320,000 includes selling costs.

**38.** Cook Co.'s total costs of operating five sales offices last year were $500,000, of which $70,000 represented fixed costs. Cook has determined that total costs are significantly influenced by the number of sales offices operated. Last year's costs and number of sales offices can be used as the bases for predicting annual costs. What would be the budgeted cost for the coming year if Cook were to operate seven sales offices?

A. $700,000

B. $672,000

C. $602,000

D. $586,000

The correct answer is (B). *(CPA, adapted)*
**REQUIRED:** The budgeted costs.
**DISCUSSION:** Using the formula y = a + bx, y is the total budgeted cost, a is the fixed costs, b is the variable cost per unit, and x is the number of budgeted sales offices. The fixed costs are $70,000, the variable cost per unit is $86,000 [($500,000 – $70,000) ÷ 5], and the number of budgeted sales offices is 7. Thus, the budgeted cost for the coming year assuming seven sales offices is $672,000 [$70,000 + ($86,000 x 7)].

Answer (A) is incorrect because $700,000 assumes the total costs are variable. Answer (C) is incorrect because $602,000 excludes fixed costs. Answer (D) is incorrect because $586,000 is last year's total costs plus the per-unit variable cost.

**39.** Butteco has the following cost components for 100,000 units of product for 1999:

| | |
|---|---|
| Raw materials | $200,000 |
| Direct labor | 100,000 |
| Manufacturing overhead | 200,000 |
| Selling/administrative expense | 150,000 |

All costs are variable except for $100,000 of manufacturing overhead and $100,000 of selling and administrative expenses. The total costs to produce and sell 110,000 units during 1999 are

A. $650,000

B. $715,000

C. $695,000

D. $540,000

The correct answer is (C). *(CMA, adapted)*
**REQUIRED:** The flexible budget costs for producing and selling a given quantity.
**DISCUSSION:** Raw materials unit costs are strictly variable at $2 ($200,000 ÷ 100,000 units). Similarly, direct labor has a variable unit cost of $1 ($100,000 ÷ 100,000 units). The $200,000 of manufacturing overhead for 100,000 units is 50% variable, and the variable unit cost is $1 ($100,000 ÷ 100,000 units). Selling costs are $100,000 fixed and $50,000 variable for production of 100,000 units, and the variable unit selling expense is $.50 ($50,000 ÷ 100,000 units). The total unit variable cost is therefore $4.50 ($2 + $1 + $1 + $.50). Fixed costs are $200,000. At a production level of 110,000 units, variable costs are $495,000 ($4.50 x 110,000 units). Hence, total costs are $695,000 ($495,000 + $200,000).

Answer (A) is incorrect because $650,000 is the cost at a production level of 100,000 units. Answer (B) is incorrect because $715,000 assumes a variable unit cost of $6.50 with no fixed costs. Answer (D) is incorrect because total costs are $695,000 based on a unit variable cost of $4.50 each.

**40.** Based on past experience, a company has developed the following budget formula for estimating its shipping expenses. The company's shipments average 12 lbs. per shipment:

Shipping costs = $16,000 + ($0.50 × lbs. shipped)

The planned activity and actual activity regarding orders and shipments for the current month are given in the following schedule:

| | Plan | Actual |
|---|---|---|
| Sales orders | 800 | 780 |
| Shipments | 800 | 820 |
| Units shipped | 8,000 | 9,000 |
| Sales | $120,000 | $144,000 |
| Total pounds shipped | 9,600 | 12,300 |

The actual shipping costs for the month amounted to $21,000. The appropriate monthly flexible budget allowance for shipping costs for the purpose of performance evaluation would be

A. $20,680

B. $20,920

C. $20,800

D. $22,150

The correct answer is (D). *(CMA, adapted)*
**REQUIRED:** The appropriate budgeted amount for shipping costs.
**DISCUSSION:** The flexible budget formula is

Shipping costs = $16,000 + ($.50 × lbs. shipped)

Thus, to determine the flexible budget amount, multiply the actual pounds shipped (12,300) times the standard cost ($.50) to arrive at a total expected variable cost of $6,150. Adding the variable cost to $16,000 of fixed cost produces a budget total of $22,150.

Answer (A) is incorrect because $20,680 is based on the variation in the actual number of sales orders from those planned, rather than on pounds shipped. Answer (B) is incorrect because $20,920 is based on the number of shipments, not the number of pounds shipped. Answer (C) is incorrect because $20,800 is based on planned pounds shipped of 9,600, not actual pounds shipped of 12,300.

**41.** RedRock East Company uses flexible budgeting for cost control. RedRock produced 10,800 units of product during March, incurring an indirect materials cost of $13,000. Its master budget for the year reflected an indirect materials cost of $180,000 at a production volume of 144,000 units. A flexible budget for March production should reflect indirect materials costs of

A. $13,975

B. $13,500

C. $13,000

D. $11,700

The correct answer is (B). *(CMA, adapted)*
**REQUIRED:** The indirect materials costs shown on a flexible budget prepared for a given volume.
**DISCUSSION:** If ahnual costs are $180,000 for 144,000 units, the unit cost is $1.25 ($180,000 ÷ 144,000 units). Thus, at a production volume of 10,800, the total costs budgeted are $13,500 ($1.25 x 10,800 units).
Answer (A) is incorrect because indirect materials costs budgeted for March production equals $13,500 [10,800 units x ($180,000 ÷ 144,000 units)]. Answer (C) is incorrect because $13,000 is the actual indirect materials costs incurred during March. The indirect materials cost for March as determined by the flexible budget is the budgeted cost per unit of $1.25 ($180,000 ÷ 144,000) times the actual units produced of 10,800. Answer (D) is incorrect because $180,000, not $156,000 ($13,000 x 12), should be used as the annual indirect materials cost budgeted.

**42.** Barnes Corporation expected to sell 150,000 board games during the month of November, and the company's master budget contained the following data related to the sale and production of these games:

| | |
|---|---:|
| Revenue | $2,400,000 |
| Cost of goods sold | |
|    Direct materials | 675,000 |
|    Direct labor | 300,000 |
|    Variable overhead | 450,000 |
|    Contribution | $ 975,000 |
| Fixed overhead | 250,000 |
| Fixed selling/administration | 500,000 |
|    Operating income | $ 225,000 |

Actual sales during November were 180,000 games. Using a flexible budget, the company expects the operating income for the month of November to be

A. $225,000

B. $270,000

C. $420,000

D. $510,000

The correct answer is (C). *(CMA, adapted)*
**REQUIRED:** The expected operating income based on a flexible budget at a given sales level.
**DISCUSSION:** Revenue of $2,400,000 reflects a unit selling price of $16 ($2,400,000 ÷ 150,000 games). The contribution margin is $975,000, or $6.50 per game ($975,000 ÷ 150,000 games). Thus, unit variable cost is $9.50 ($16 – $6.50). Increasing sales will result in an increased contribution margin of $195,000 (30,000 x $6.50). Assuming no additional fixed costs, net operating income will increase to $420,000 ($225,000 originally reported + $195,000).
Answer (A) is incorrect because $225,000 is the net operating income before the increase in sales. Answer (B) is incorrect because net operating income was originally $1.50 per game. The $270,000 figure simply extrapolates that amount to sales of 180,000 games. Answer (D) is incorrect because $510,000 assumes that variable overhead is fixed. Variable overhead is a $3 component ($450,000 ÷ 150,000 units) of unit variable cost.

**43.** DeBerg Company has developed the following sales projections for calendar year 1999:

| | |
|---|---:|
| May | $100,000 |
| June | 120,000 |
| July | 140,000 |
| August | 160,000 |
| September | 150,000 |
| October | 130,000 |

Normal cash collection experience has been that 50% of sales is collected during the month of sale and 45% in the month following sale. The remaining 5% of sales is never collected. DeBerg's budgeted cash collections for the third calendar quarter are

A. $450,000

B. $440,000

C. $414,000

D. $360,000

The correct answer is (C). *(CMA, adapted)*
**REQUIRED:** The budgeted cash collections for the third quarter.
**DISCUSSION:** If 50% of sales is collected in the month of sale and 45% in the next month, with the balance uncollectible, collections during the third quarter will be based on sales during June, July, August, and September. As calculated below, total budgeted collections are $414,000.

| | | | |
|---|---|---|---:|
| June | $120,000 × 45% | = | $ 54,000 |
| July | 140,000 × (50% + 45%) | = | 133,000 |
| August | 160,000 × (50% + 45%) | = | 152,000 |
| September | 150,000 × 50% | = | 75,000 |
| | | | $414,000 |

Answer (A) is incorrect because $450,000 equals total projected sales for the third quarter. Answer (B) is incorrect because $440,000 equals total projected sales for August, September, and October. Answer (D) is incorrect because $360,000 does not include collections for June sales of $54,000 ($120,000 x 45%).

**44.** A company has budgeted sales for the upcoming quarter as follows:

|  | January | February | March |
|---|---|---|---|
| Units | 15,000 | 18,000 | 16,500 |

The ending finished goods inventory for each month equals 50% of the next month's budgeted sales. Additionally, 3 pounds of raw materials is required for each finished unit produced. The ending raw materials inventory for each month equals 200% of the next month's production requirements. If the raw materials cost $4.00 per pound and must be paid for in the month purchased, the budgeted raw materials purchases (in dollars) for January are

A.  $216,000

B.  $207,000

C.  $198,000

D.  $180,000

The correct answer is (A). *(CIA, adapted)*
**REQUIRED:** The budgeted raw materials purchases.
**DISCUSSION:** The budgeted amount of raw materials purchases is computed as follows:

|  | January | February |
|---|---|---|
| Sales (finished units) | 15,000 | 18,000 |
| Desired ending FG inventory | 9,000 | 8,250 |
|  | 24,000 | 26,250 |
| Est. beginning FG inventory | (7,500) | (9,000) |
| Production requirements (units) | 16,500 | 17,250 |
| Materials per finished unit | 3 | 3 |
| Materials required for production | 49,500 | 51,750 |
| Desired ending raw materials inventory (2.0 × 51,750) | 103,500 | |
| Total requirements | 153,000 | |
| Est. beginning raw materials inventory (2.0 × 49,500) | (99,000) | |
| Purchases (pounds) | 54,000 | |
| Cost per pound | $    4 | |
| Purchases (in dollars) | $216,000 | |

Answer (B) is incorrect because $207,000 equals materials required for February's production. Answer (C) is incorrect because $198,000 equals materials required for January's production. Answer (D) is incorrect because $180,000 equals materials required for January's sales.

**45.** A company is preparing its cash budget for the coming month. All sales are made on account. Given the following:

|  | Beginning Balances | Budgeted Amounts |
|---|---|---|
| Cash | $ 50,000 | |
| Accounts receivable | 180,000 | |
| Sales | | $800,000 |
| Cash disbursements | | 780,000 |
| Depreciation | | 25,000 |
| Ending accounts receivable balance | | 210,000 |

What is the expected cash balance of the company at the end of the coming month?

A.  $15,000

B.  $40,000

C.  $45,000

D.  $70,000

The correct answer is (B). *(CIA, adapted)*
**REQUIRED:** The expected cash balance of the company at the end of the coming month.
**DISCUSSION:** Collections on account equal beginning accounts receivable of $180,000, plus sales on account of $800,000, minus budgeted ending accounts receivable of $210,000, or $770,000. The beginning cash balance of $50,000, plus cash collections on account of $770,000, minus budgeted cash disbursements of $780,000 equals $40,000. Depreciation of $25,000 is excluded because it is a noncash expense.

Answer (A) is incorrect because $15,000 includes depreciation expense which should be excluded because it is a noncash expense. Answer (C) is incorrect because $770,000 ($180,000 + $800,000 – $210,000), not $800,000, was the amount of cash collected for receivables. Also, the $25,000 of depreciation should not be deducted because it is a noncash expense. Answer (D) is incorrect because $770,000 ($180,000 + $800,000 – $210,000), not $800,000, was the amount of cash collected for receivables.

**46.** National Warehousing is constructing a corporate planning model. Cash sales are 30% of the company's sales, with the remainder subject to the following collection pattern:

| | |
|---|---|
| One month after sale | 60% |
| Two months after sale | 30 |
| Three months after sale | 8 |
| Uncollectible | 2 |

If $S_n$ is defined as total sales in month n, which one of the following expressions correctly describes National's collections on account in any given month?

- A. $0.6S_{n-1} + 0.3S_{n-2} + 0.08S_{n-3}$
- B. $0.42S_{n+1} + 0.21S_{n+2} + 0.056S_{n+3}$
- C. $0.42S_{n-1} + 0.21S_{n-2} + 0.056S_{n-3}$
- D. $0.42S_{n-1} + 0.21S_{n-2} + 0.056S_{n-3} - 0.014S_n$

The correct answer is (C). *(CMA, adapted)*
**REQUIRED:** The equation that correctly describes collections on account.
**DISCUSSION:** Because the company will collect 30% of its sales at the time of sale, only 70% is on account. Of this amount, 60% is collected in the month after the sale, 30% in the second month, and 8% in the third month. Thus, the collections in any given month will be 42% (60% x 70% total sales) of the previous month's sales ($S_{n-1}$), 21% (30% x 70%) of the second preceding month's sales ($S_{n-2}$), and 5.6% (8% x 70%) of the third preceding month's sales ($S_{n-3}$).
Answer (A) is incorrect because cash sales are 30% of total sales. Answer (B) is incorrect because the previous month's sales are represented by $S_{n-1}$, the second preceding month's sales are represented by $S_{n-2}$, etc. Answer (D) is incorrect because the uncollectible sales should not be deducted from the collections on account.

**47.** A company is formulating its plans for the coming year, including the preparation of its cash budget. Historically, the company's sales are 30% cash. The remaining sales are on credit with the following collection pattern:

| Collections on Account | Percentage |
|---|---|
| In the month of sale | 40% |
| In the month following the sale | 58% |
| Uncollectible | 2% |

Sales for the first 5 months of the coming year are forecast as follows:

| | |
|---|---|
| January | $3,500,000 |
| February | 3,800,000 |
| March | 3,600,000 |
| April | 4,000,000 |
| May | 4,200,000 |

For the month of April, the total cash receipts from sales and collections on account would be .

- A. $3,729,968
- B. $3,781,600
- C. $4,025,200
- D. $4,408,000

The correct answer is (B). *(CIA, adapted)*
**REQUIRED:** The cash receipts in April.
**DISCUSSION:** The cash receipts for April equal April's cash sales (30% x $4,000,000 = $1,200,000), 40% of April's credit sales, and 58% of March's credit sales. Consequently, total cash receipts equal $3,781,600 [$1,200,000 + (40% x 70% x $4,000,000) + (58% x 70% x $3,600,000)].
Answer (A) is incorrect because $3,729,968 results from improperly calculating the collections of April and March credit sales. The 2% uncollectible amount should not be removed from the credit sales before the collection percentage is applied. Answer (C) is incorrect because $4,025,200 includes the collection of May credit sales rather than March credit sales. Answer (D) is incorrect because $4,408,000 improperly calculates the collections of March credit sales. The calculation treats the entire sales figure for March as credit sales.

Questions 48 and 49 are based on the following information. The operating results in summarized form for a retail computer store for 1998 are

| Revenue | |
|---|---|
| Hardware sales | $4,800,000 |
| Software sales | 2,000,000 |
| Maintenance contracts | 1,200,000 |
| Total revenue | $8,000,000 |
| Costs and expenses | |
| Cost of hardware sales | $3,360,000 |
| Cost of software sales | 1,200,000 |
| Marketing expenses | 600,000 |
| Customer maintenance costs | 640,000 |
| Administration expenses | 1,120,000 |
| Total costs and expenses | $6,920,000 |
| Operating income | $1,080,000 |

The computer store is in the process of formulating its operating budget for 1999 and has made the following assumptions:

- The selling prices of hardware are expected to increase 10%, but there will be no selling price increases for software or maintenance contracts.
- Hardware unit sales are expected to increase 5% with a corresponding 5% growth in the number of maintenance contracts; growth in units software sales is estimated at 8%.
- The cost of hardware and software is expected to increase 4%.
- Marketing expenses will be increased 5% in the coming year.
- Three technicians will be added to the customer maintenance operations in the coming year, increasing the customer maintenance costs by $120,000.
- Administrative costs will be held at the same level.

**48.** The retail computer store's budgeted total revenue for 1999 would be

A. $8,804,000

B. $8,460,000

C. $8,904,000

D. $8,964,000

The correct answer is (D). *(CIA, adapted)*

**REQUIRED:** The budgeted total revenue for 1999.

**DISCUSSION:** Hardware selling prices will increase by 10% and unit volume by 5%. Thus, hardware revenue will be $5,544,000 ($4,800,000 sales in 1994 x 1.10 x 1.05). Given that unit sales of software will increase by 8%, software revenue will increase to $2,160,000 ($2,000,000 sales in 1998 x 1.08). The number of maintenance contracts is expected to increase by 5%, so maintenance contracts revenue will increase to $1,260,000 ($1,200,000 sales in 1998 x 1.05). Budgeted revenue will therefore be $8,964,000 ($5,544,000 + $2,160,000 + $1,260,000).

Answer (A) is incorrect because $8,804,000 omits the growth in software sales. Answer (B) is incorrect because $8,460,000 omits the increase in the selling price of hardware. Answer (C) is incorrect because $8,904,000 omits the growth in maintenance contracts.

**49.** The retail computer store's budgeted total costs and expenses for the coming year would be

A. $7,252,400

B. $7,526,960

C. $7,558,960

D. $7,893,872

The correct answer is (B). *(CIA, adapted)*

**REQUIRED:** The budgeted total costs and expenses for 1999.

**DISCUSSION:** Hardware unit sales are expected to increase by 5%, and the cost of hardware is expected to increase by 4%. Hence, the cost of hardware sales should be $3,669,120 ($3,360,000 costs in 1998 x 1.05 x 1.04). Software unit sales are expected to increase by 8%, and the cost of software is expected to increase by 4%. Accordingly, the cost of software sales should be $1,347,840 ($1,200,000 cost in 1998 x 1.08 x 1.04). Marketing expense will increase to $630,000 ($600,000 in 1998 x 1.05) and customer maintenance costs to $760,000 ($640,000 in 1998 + $120,000). Administrative costs are expected to remain at $1,120,000. Consequently, total costs and expenses will be $7,526,960 ($3,669,120 + $1,347,840 + $630,000 + $760,000 + $1,120,000).

Answer (A) is incorrect because $7,252,400 omits the increase in hardware and software cost of sales attributable to the volume increase. Answer (C) is incorrect because $7,558,960 increased customer maintenance costs by 5% before the $120,000 for technicians was added. Answer (D) is incorrect because $7,893,872 includes an additional 10% increase for hardware cost of sales.

Questions 50 and 51 are based on the following information. A company produces a product that requires 2 pounds of a raw material. It is forecast that there will be 6,000 pounds of raw material on hand at the end of June. At the end of any given month, the company wishes to have 30% of next month's raw material requirements on hand. The company has budgeted production of the product for July, August, September, and October to be 10,000, 12,000, 13,000, and 11,000 units, respectively. As of June 1, the raw material sells for $1.00 per pound.

**50.** The cost of inventory is determined using the last-in, first-out (LIFO) method. If the price of raw material increases 10% as of June 30, what will be the effect of this increase on the cost of purchases from July to September?

A.  $600 increase.

B.  $7,060 increase.

C.  $9,200 increase.

D.  $60 increase.

The correct answer is (B). *(CIA, adapted)*

**REQUIRED:** The effect of an increase in the price of the raw material on the cost of purchases.

**DISCUSSION:** The amount of purchases can be calculated as follows:

|           | BI    | Current Requirements | Purch              | EI    |
|-----------|-------|----------------------|--------------------|-------|
| July      | 6,000 | 20,000               | 21,200             | 7,200 |
| August    | 7,200 | 24,000               | 24,600             | 7,800 |
| September | 7,800 | 26,000               | 24,800             | 6,600 |
|           |       |                      | 70,600 lbs.        |       |

The current requirement for each month is the budgeted production multiplied by the materials needed per product (2 pounds). Ending inventory is 30% of budgeted production for the next month times the materials needed per product. Purchases equals the sum of current requirements and ending inventory, minus beginning inventory. Hence, the effect of the change in price is to increase the cost of purchases by $7,060 (10% x $1 per pound x 70,600 pounds).

Answer (A) is incorrect because $600 equals 10% of the ending inventory in June. Answer (C) is incorrect because $9,200 equals $.10 times the pounds required for production from July through October. Answer (D) is incorrect because $60 results from taking the difference between June and September ending inventory and multiplying it by $.10.

**51.** In the month of September, raw material purchases and ending inventory, respectively, will be (in pounds):

A.  24,800 and 6,600.

B.  32,600 and 6,600.

C.  13,000 and 3,900.

D.  24,800 and 3,900

The correct answer is (A). *(CIA, adapted)*

**REQUIRED:** The total (in pounds) of raw material purchases and ending inventory for September.

**DISCUSSION:** The ending inventory equals 6,600 pounds [30% x (11,000 units x 2 pounds) required in October]. The requirements for September equal 26,000 pounds (13,000 units x 2 pounds), and the beginning inventory is 7,800 pounds (30% x 26,000 pounds). Thus, September purchases equal 24,800 pounds (26,000 pounds currently required + 6,600 pounds EI – 7,800 pounds BI).

Answer (B) is incorrect because 32,600 results from adding beginning inventory to purchases. Answers (C) and (D) are incorrect because 13,000 is the budgeted production in units, and 3,900 is the number of units that can be produced using the ending inventory of raw material for August.

Questions 52 and 53 are based on the following information. The Raymar Company is preparing its cash budget for the months of April and May. The firm has established a $200,000 line of credit with its bank at a 12% annual rate of interest on which borrowings for cash deficits must be made in $10,000 increments. There is no outstanding balance on the line of credit loan on April 1. Principal repayments are to be made in any month in which there is a surplus of cash. Interest is to be paid monthly. If there are no outstanding balances on the loans, Raymar will invest any cash in excess of its desired end-of-month cash balance in U.S. Treasury bills. Raymar intends to maintain a minimum balance of $100,000 at the end of each month by either borrowing for deficits below the minimum balance or investing any excess cash. Expected monthly collection and disbursement patterns are shown in the column to the right.

- *Collections.* 50% of the current month's sales budget and 50% of the previous month's sales budget.
- *Accounts Payable Disbursements.* 75% of the current month's accounts payable budget and 25% of the previous month's accounts payable budget.
- All other disbursements occur in the month in which they are budgeted.

### Budget Information

|  | March | April | May |
|---|---|---|---|
| Sales | $40,000 | $50,000 | $100,000 |
| Accounts payable | 30,000 | 40,000 | 40,000 |
| Payroll | 60,000 | 70,000 | 50,000 |
| Other disbursements | 25,000 | 30,000 | 10,000 |

**52.** In April, Raymar's budget will result in

A. $45,000 in excess cash.

B. A need to borrow $50,000 on its line of credit for the cash deficit.

C. A need to borrow $100,000 on its line of credit for the cash deficit.

D. A need to borrow $90,000 on its line of credit for the cash deficit.

The correct answer is (C). *(CMA, adapted)*
**REQUIRED:** The effect on cash at the end of April.
**DISCUSSION:** April's cash collections are $45,000 [(50% x $50,000 April sales) + (50% x $40,000 March sales)]. Disbursements for accounts payable are $37,500 [(75% x $40,000 April payables) + (25% x $30,000 March payables)]. In addition to the accounts payable disbursements, payroll and other disbursements will require an additional $100,000. Hence, total disbursements are estimated to be $137,500. The net negative cash flow (amount to be borrowed) is $92,500 ($137,500 – $45,000). Because the line of credit must be drawn upon in $10,000 increments, the loan must be for $100,000.

Answer (A) is incorrect because $45,000 equals cash receipts. Answer (B) is incorrect because the cash deficit will be $92,500 without borrowing. Answer (D) is incorrect because a loan of only $90,000 leaves the company $2,500 below its desired ending cash balance.

**53.** In May, Raymar will be required to

A. Repay $20,000 principal and pay $1,000 interest.

B. Repay $90,000 principal and pay $100 interest.

C. Pay $900 interest.

D. Borrow an additional $20,000 and pay $1,000 interest.

The correct answer is (D). *(CMA, adapted)*
**REQUIRED:** The transaction required in May.
**DISCUSSION:** The company will have to borrow $100,000 in April, which means that interest will have to be paid in May at the rate of 1% per month (12% annual rate). Consequently, interest expense is $1,000 (1% x $100,000). May receipts are $75,000 [(50% x $100,000 May sales) + (50% x $50,000 April sales)]. Disbursements in May are $40,000 [(75% x $40,000 May payables) + (25% x $40,000 April payables)]. In addition to the May accounts payable disbursements, payroll and other disbursements are $60,000, bringing total disbursements to $101,000 ($60,000 + $40,000 + $1,000). Thus, disbursements exceed receipts by $26,000 ($101,000 – $75,000). However, cash has a beginning balance of $7,500 ($100,000 April loan – $92,500 negative cash flow for April calculated in the preceding question). As a result, the company needs to borrow an additional $18,500 to eliminate its cash deficit. Given the requirement that loans be in $10,000 increments, the May loan must be for $20,000.

Answers (A) and (B) are incorrect because no funds are available to repay the loan. May receipts are less than May disbursements. Answer (C) is incorrect because the 1% interest is calculated on a $100,000 loan, not a $90,000 loan.

Questions 54 through 56 are based on the following information. Rokat Corporation is a manufacturer of tables sold to schools, restaurants, hotels, and other institutions. The table tops are manufactured by Rokat, but the table legs are purchased from an outside supplier. The Assembly Department takes a manufactured table top and attaches the four purchased table legs. It takes 20 minutes of labor to assemble a table. The company follows a policy of producing enough tables to insure that 40% of next month's sales are in the finished goods inventory. Rokat also purchases sufficient raw materials to insure that raw materials inventory is 60% of the following month's scheduled production. Rokat's sales budget in units for the next quarter is as follows:

| July | 2,300 |
| August | 2,500 |
| September | 2,100 |

Rokat's ending inventories in units for June 30, 1999 are

| Finished goods | 1,900 |
| Raw materials (legs) | 4,000 |

**54.** The number of tables to be produced during August 1999 is

   A.  1,400 tables.

   B.  2,340 tables.

   C.  1,440 tables.

   D.  1,900 tables.

The correct answer is (B). *(CMA, adapted)*
   **REQUIRED:** The number of tables to be produced during August given the budget requirements.
   **DISCUSSION:** The company will need 2,500 finished units for August sales. In addition, 840 units (40% × 2,100 September unit sales) should be in inventory at the end of August. August sales plus the desired ending inventory equals 3,340 units. Of these units, 40% of August's sales, or 1,000 units, should be available from beginning inventory. Consequently, production in August should be 2,340 units.
   Answer (A) is incorrect because 1,400 tables is the number to be produced in July. Answer (C) is incorrect because 1,440 tables is based on July's beginning inventory. Answer (D) is incorrect because 1,900 tables equals July's beginning inventory.

**55.** Disregarding your response to question 54, assume the required production for August and September is 1,600 and 1,800 units, respectively, and the July 31, 1999 raw materials inventory is 4,200 units. The number of table legs to be purchased in August is

   A.  6,520 legs.

   B.  9,400 legs.

   C.  2,200 legs.

   D.  6,400 legs.

The correct answer is (A). *(CMA, adapted)*
   **REQUIRED:** The number of table legs to be purchased in August.
   **DISCUSSION:** The August production of 1,600 units will require 6,400 table legs. September's production of 1,800 units will require 7,200 table legs. Thus, inventory at the end of August should be 4,320 legs (60% × 7,200 legs). The total of legs needed during August is 10,720 (6,400 + 4,320), of which 4,200 are available from the July 31 ending inventory. The remaining 6,520 legs must be purchased during August.
   Answer (B) is incorrect because 9,400 legs is based on an ending inventory of 100% of September's production. Answer (C) is incorrect because 2,200 legs fails to consider the legs needed for the ending inventory. Answer (D) is incorrect because 6,400 legs is the amount needed for August production.

**56.** Assume that Rokat Corporation will produce 1,800 units in the month of September 1999. How many employees will be required for the Assembly Department? (Fractional employees are acceptable since employees can be hired on a part-time basis. Assume a 40-hour week and a 4-week month.)

   A.  15 employees.

   B.  3.75 employees.

   C.  600 employees.

   D.  1.5 employees.

The correct answer is (B). *(CMA, adapted)*
   **REQUIRED:** The number of employees required for September production.
   **DISCUSSION:** Each unit requires 20 minutes of assembly time, or 1/3 of an hour. The assembly of 1,800 units will therefore require 600 hours of labor (1/3 × 1,800). At 40 hours per week for 4 weeks, each employee will work 160 hours during the month. Thus, 3.75 employees (600 ÷ 160) are needed.
   Answer (A) is incorrect because 15 employees assumes production occurs in a single 40-hour week. Answer (C) is incorrect because 600 is the number of hours needed, not the number of employees. Answer (D) is incorrect because 1.5 employees is based on only 40% of production, not total production.

Questions 57 through 59 are based on the following information. Super Drive, a computer disk storage and backup company, uses accrual accounting. The company's Statement of Financial Position for the year ended November 30, 1998 is as follows:

### Super Drive
### Statement of Financial Position
### November 30, 1998

Assets

| | |
|---|---|
| Cash | $ 52,000 |
| Accounts receivable, net | 150,000 |
| Inventory | 315,000 |
| Property, plant and equipment | 1,000,000 |
| Total assets | $1,517,000 |

Liabilities

| | |
|---|---|
| Accounts payable | $ 175,000 |
| Common stock | 900,000 |
| Retained earnings | 442,000 |
| Total liabilities and shareholders' equity | $1,517,000 |

Additional information regarding Super Drive's operations include the following:

- Sales are budgeted at $520,000 for December 1998 and $500,000 for January 1999.
- Collections are expected to be 60% in the month of sale and 40% in the month following the sale.
- 80% of the disk drive components are purchased in the month prior to the month of sale, and 20% are purchased in the month of sale. Purchased components are 40% of the cost of goods sold.
- Payment for the components is made in the month following the purchase.
- Cost of goods sold is 80% of sales.

**57.** The budgeted cash collections for the month of December 1998 are

A. $208,000

B. $520,000

C. $402,000

D. $462,000

The correct answer is (D). *(CMA, adapted)*
**REQUIRED:** The budgeted cash collections for the month of December.
**DISCUSSION:** Collections are expected to be 60% in the month of sale and 40% in the month following the sale. Thus, collections in December consist of the $150,000 of receivables at November 30, plus 60% of December sales. Total collections are therefore $462,000 [$150,000 + (60% x $520,000)].
Answer (A) is incorrect because $208,000 equals 40% of December sales. Answer (B) is incorrect because total sales are not collected in the month of sale. Answer (C) is incorrect because 100% of receivables will be collected, not 60%.

**58.** The projected balance in accounts payable on December 31, 1998 is

A. $161,280

B. $166,400

C. $416,000

D. $201,600

The correct answer is (A). *(CMA, adapted)*
**REQUIRED:** The projected balance in accounts payable on December 31, 1998.
**DISCUSSION:** Payments are made in the month following purchase. The balance in accounts payable on November 30 is $175,000; this amount will be paid in December. The account is credited for purchases of a portion of components to be used for sales in December (20% of December components) and a portion for sales in January (80% of January components). Cost of goods sold is 80% of sales, and components are 40% of cost of goods sold. Thus, December component needs are $166,400 (40% x 80% x $520,000 sales), and January component needs are $160,000 (40% x 80% x $500,000 sales). The December purchases of December component needs equal $33,280 (20% x $166,400). December purchases of January component needs are $128,000 (80% x $160,000). Hence, the total of December purchases (ending balance in accounts payable) equals $161,280 ($33,280 + $128,000).
Answer (B) is incorrect because $166,400 equals December component needs. Answer (C) is incorrect because $416,000 equals cost of sales for December. Answer (D) is incorrect because $201,600 assumes that purchased components are 40% of sales.

**59.** Refer to the information preceding question 57 on page 313. The projected gross profit for the month ending December 31, 1998 is

A. $416,000

B. $104,000

C. $536,000

D. $0

The correct answer is (B). *(CMA, adapted)*
**REQUIRED:** The projected gross profit for December.
**DISCUSSION:** Given that cost of goods sold is 80% of sales, gross profit is 20% of sales. Consequently, pro forma gross profit is $104,000 (20% x $520,000).

Answer (A) is incorrect because $416,000 is cost of goods sold (80% of sales). Answer (C) is incorrect because gross profit cannot be greater than sales. Answer (D) is incorrect because gross profit is earned when cost of goods sold is less than 100% of sales.

---

Questions 60 through 64 are based on the following information. Superflite expects April sales of its deluxe model airplane, the C-14, to be 402,000 units at $11 each. Each C-14 requires three purchased components shown below. Factory direct labor and variable overhead per unit of C-14 total $3.00. Fixed factory overhead is $1.00 per unit at a production level of 500,000 units. Superflite plans the following beginning and ending inventories for the month of April and uses standard absorption costing for valuing inventory.

|  | Purchase Cost | Number Needed for Each C-14 Unit | Part No. | Units at April 1 | Units at April 30 |
|---|---|---|---|---|---|
| A-9 | $ .50 | 1 | C-14 | 12,000 | 10,000 |
| B-6 | .25 | 2 | A-9 | 21,000 | 9,000 |
| D-28 | 1.00 | 3 | B-6 | 32,000 | 10,000 |
|  |  |  | D-28 | 14,000 | 6,000 |

---

**60.** The C-14 production budget for April should be based on the manufacture of

A. 390,000 units.

B. 400,000 units.

C. 424,000 units.

D. 500,000 units.

The correct answer is (B). *(CMA, adapted)*
**REQUIRED:** The number of units upon which the production budget should be based.
**DISCUSSION:** Sales are expected to be 402,000 units in April. The beginning inventory is 12,000 units, and the ending inventory is expected to be 10,000 units, a decline in inventory of 2,000 units. Thus, the budget should be based on production of 400,000 units because the April sales will come from the 2,000 units taken from inventory and the 400,000 units to be manufactured.

Answer (A) is incorrect because 390,000 units does not consider the need to produce for ending inventory. Answer (C) is incorrect because 424,000 units is the sum of sales and beginning and ending inventories. Answer (D) is incorrect because 500,000 is the denominator base used in allocating fixed costs.

---

Without prejudice to your response in question 60, assume for questions 61 through 64 that Superflite plans to manufacture 400,000 units in April.

---

**61.** Superflite's April budget for the purchase of A-9 should be

A. 379,000 units.

B. 388,000 units.

C. 402,000 units.

D. 412,000 units.

The correct answer is (B). *(CMA, adapted)*
**REQUIRED:** The purchases budget for component A-9.
**DISCUSSION:** Each of the 400,000 units to be produced in April will require one unit of A-9, a total requirement of 400,000 units. In addition, ending inventory is expected to be 9,000 units. Hence, 409,000 units must be supplied during the month. Of these, 21,000 are available in the beginning inventory. Subtracting the 21,000 beginning inventory from 409,000 leaves 388,000 to be purchased.

Answer (A) is incorrect because 379,000 units fails to consider the 9,000 units in the ending inventory. Answer (C) is incorrect because 402,000 units equals sales for the month. Answer (D) is incorrect because 412,000 results from adding the decline in inventory of 12,000 to production needs instead of subtracting it.

**62.** The total April budget for all purchased components should be

A. $1,580,500

B. $1,600,000

C. $1,608,000

D. $1,700,000

The correct answer is (A). *(CMA, adapted)*

**REQUIRED:** The total purchases budget.

**DISCUSSION:** Each of the 400,000 units to be produced in April will require one unit of A-9, a total requirement of 400,000 units. In addition, ending inventory will be 9,000 units. Thus, 409,000 units must be supplied. Of these, 21,000 are available in the beginning inventory. Subtracting the 21,000 beginning inventory from 409,000 leaves 388,000 to be purchased. At $.50 each, these 388,000 units will cost $194,000. The inventory of component B-6 will decline by 22,000 units. Subtracting this number from the 800,000 units (2 x 400,000 units of C-14) needed for production leaves 778,000 to be purchased at $.25 each, a total of $194,500. The inventory of component D-28 will decline by 8,000 units. Subtracting this number from the 1,200,000 units needed for production (each product requires three units of D-28) leaves 1,192,000 to be purchased at $1 each. The total cost of the components to be purchased equals $1,580,500.

Answer (B) is incorrect because $1,600,000 assumes an extra purchase for ending inventories. Answer (C) is incorrect because $1,608,000 added the beginning and ending inventories. Answer (D) is incorrect because $1,700,000 is based on a misstatement of the number of components needed.

**63.** The book value of the planned April 30 inventories is

A. $53,000

B. $83,000

C. $93,000

D. $128,500

The correct answer is (C). *(CMA, adapted)*

**REQUIRED:** The book value of planned ending inventories.

**DISCUSSION:** The 9,000 units of A-9 would be valued at $.50 each, or $4,500 in total. The 10,000 units of B-6 at $.25 each would total $2,500. The 6,000 units of D-28 cost $1 each and would total $6,000. The 10,000 units of the finished product, C-14, would be valued as follows:

| Raw materials: | A-9 (1 × $.50) | $ .50 |
|---|---|---|
| | B-6 (2 × $.25) | .50 |
| | D-28 (3 × $1) | 3.00 |
| Labor and variable overhead | | 3.00 |
| Fixed overhead | | 1.00 |
| Total standard cost | | $8.00 |

At a standard cost of $8 each, the 10,000 units of C-14 would total $80,000. Adding the four inventory items together ($4,500 + $2,500 + $6,000 + $80,000) results in total budgeted April 30 inventory of $93,000.

Answer (A) is incorrect because $53,000 fails to include the cost of the raw materials in the finished product. Answer (B) is incorrect because $83,000 omits the fixed overhead. Answer (D) is incorrect because $128,500 is the value of the beginning inventories.

**64.** Refer to the information preceding questions 60 and 61 on page 314. Superflite's budgeted gross margin for April is

A. $1,105,500

B. $1,200,000

C. $1,206,000

D. $1,608,000

The correct answer is (C). *(CMA, adapted)*

**REQUIRED:** The gross margin.

**DISCUSSION:** With sales of 402,000 units at $11 each, the total revenue would be $4,422,000. The standard cost of these units would be $8 each as calculated in the preceding question. Multiplying $8 times 402,000 units results in a cost of goods sold of $3,216,000. Subtracting cost of goods sold from revenues produces a budgeted gross margin of $1,206,000. Underabsorbed fixed overhead is normally ignored in budgeted monthly financial statements because it is based on an annual average and will be offset by year-end.

Answer (A) is incorrect because gross margin is based on a unit price of $11, a unit cost of $8, and unit sales of 402,000. Answer (B) is incorrect because $1,200,000 is based on production volume, not sales volume. Answer (D) is incorrect because $1,608,000 is the cost of sales minus the raw materials included in cost of sales.

# CHAPTER TEN
# STANDARD COSTS AND VARIANCES

**Standard costs** are budgeted unit costs used to motivate optimal productivity and efficiency. Establishing standards is necessary if management is to know when actual costs differ significantly from target or standard costs. Thus, a standard cost is a monetary measure with which actual costs are compared. It is not an average of past costs but a scientifically determined estimate of what costs should be. A standard cost system can be used in manufacturing, service, and not-for-profit entities and in both job-order and process costing systems to isolate variances. Furthermore, because of the effects of fixed costs, standard costing is most effective in a flexible budgeting system. When actual costs and standard costs differ, the difference is a variance. A favorable (unfavorable) **variance** arises when actual costs are less (greater) than standard costs. To avoid constant unfavorable variances, management will usually set standards so that they are currently attainable. If standards are set too high (or tight), they may be ignored by workers, or morale may suffer. Standard costs also must be kept current. For example, if prices have changed considerably for a particular raw material, a variance will always occur if the standard cost is not changed. Much of the usefulness of standard costs is lost if a large variance is always expected.

In manufacturing settings, standard costs are usually determined for materials, labor, and factory (manufacturing) overhead. These standards can then be used to calculate variances. The broadest type of variance is the **static budget variance**, or the difference between the static (master) budget amount and the actual results. Its components are the flexible budget variance and the sales volume variance. The **flexible budget variance** is the difference between the actual results and the budgeted amount for the actual level of activity. It may be analyzed in terms of a variety of specific variances related to sales prices, input costs, and input quantities. The **sales volume** (sales activity) **variance** is the difference between the flexible budget and static budget amounts if selling prices and costs are constant. Its components are the sales mix variance and the sales quantity variance. The latter may be decomposed into the market share variance and the market size variance.

**Direct materials variances** are usually divided into price and efficiency components. Part of a total materials variance may be attributed to using more raw materials than the standard and part to a cost that was higher than standard. The **direct materials quantity (usage) variance** (an efficiency variance) is the actual quantity minus standard quantity, times standard price: $(AQ - SQ)SP$. The **direct materials price variance** is the actual price minus the standard price, times the actual quantity: $(AP - SP)AQ$. The price variance may be isolated either at the time of purchase or at the time of transfer to WIP. The advantage of the former method is that the variance is identified earlier. Normal spoilage is considered in the calculation of standard direct materials cost per unit. The direct materials quantity (usage) variance is sometimes supplemented by the direct materials mix variance and the direct materials yield variance. These variances are calculated only when the production process involves combining several materials in varying proportions (when substitutions are allowable in combining materials). The **direct materials mix variance** equals total actual quantity times the difference between the weighted-average unit standard cost of the budgeted mix of ingredients and the weighted-average unit standard cost of the actual mix. The **direct materials yield variance** is the weighted-average unit standard cost of the budgeted mix multiplied by the difference between the actual quantity of materials used and the standard quantity. Certain relationships may exist among the various materials variances. For instance, an unfavorable price variance may be offset by a favorable mix or yield variance because materials of better quality and higher price are used. Also, a favorable mix variance may result in an unfavorable yield variance, or vice versa.

**Productivity measures** are related to the efficiency, mix, and yield variances. They can be developed for both manufacturing and service entities, although the latter may sometimes find that output is difficult to measure. Productivity is the relationship between outputs and inputs (including the mix of inputs). The higher this ratio, the greater the productivity. Improvements in productivity depend on technical efficiency and input trade-off efficiency. A process becomes more technically efficient when, for any set of inputs that will produce a given output, nonvalue-added activities are eliminated, and value-added activities use the minimum resources needed to produce the given output. Input trade-offs are efficient when the least costly set of inputs that will produce the given output is selected. A **partial productivity** measure may be stated as the ratio of output to the quantity of a single factor of production, or as a financial ratio (e.g., revenue per labor dollar). Factors of production may include direct materials, direct labor, overhead, or capital (for example, use of machinery instead of direct labor). Partial productivity measures, for example, the number of finished units per direct labor hour or per pound of direct materials, are useful when compared over time, among different factories, or with benchmarks. A partial productivity measure comparing results over time determines whether the actual relationship between inputs and outputs has improved or deteriorated. A disadvantage of a partial productivity measure is that it relates output to a single factor of production and therefore does not consider tradeoffs among input factors. Thus, **total productivity** (also known as total factor productivity) ratios may be calculated to compensate for that drawback. Total productivity is the ratio of output to the cost of all relevant inputs used. This ratio should increase from one period to the next as technological improvements permit greater output to be extracted from a given amount and mix of inputs. A less costly input mix also increases the ratio. Accordingly, the change in total costs from one period to the next is attributable to three factors: output levels, input prices, and quantities and mix of inputs. In the same way that a variance can be decomposed into components, the effect of each of the foregoing factors can be isolated by holding the others constant. For example, in the diagram on the next page, the cost of Year Two output can be calculated based on Year One (base period) input prices and input relationships (actual inputs that would have been used in Year One to produce the Year Two output). The difference between this amount and actual Year One costs is the change in costs attributable solely to output change. Similarly, the cost of Year Two output at Year Two prices based on Year One input relationships can also be calculated.  The difference between this amount and the cost of Year Two output based on Year One input prices and input relationships is the change in costs attributable to price changes.  The difference between the actual cost of Year Two output and the cost of Year Two output based on Year Two prices and Year One input relationships is the change attributable solely to the change in the quantities and mix of inputs.

Factors Causing the Cost Change

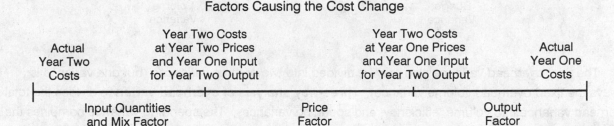

**Direct labor variances** are similar to direct materials variances.  For example, the direct labor rate and efficiency variances are calculated in much the same way as the direct materials price and quantity variances, respectively.

**Factory overhead variances** include variable and fixed components.  The total **variable factory overhead variance** is the difference between actual variable factory overhead and the amount applied based on the budgeted application rate and the standard input allowed for the actual output.  In **four-way analysis of overhead variance**, it includes the **spending variance**, or the difference between actual variable factory overhead and the product of the budgeted application rate and the actual amount of the allocation base (activity level or amount of input), and the **efficiency variance**, or the budgeted application rate times the difference between the actual input and the standard input allowed for the actual output.  Variable factory overhead applied equals the flexible-budget amount for the actual output level.  The reason is that unit variable costs are assumed to be constant within the relevant range.  The third column in the diagram below gives the flexible budget amount (also the amount applied).  If variable factory overhead is applied on the basis of output, not inputs, no efficiency variance arises.

Variable Factory Overhead Variances

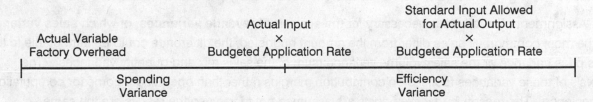

The **total fixed factory overhead variance** is the difference between actual fixed factory overhead and the amount applied based on the budgeted application rate and the standard input allowed for the actual output.  In four-way analysis of variance, it includes the **budget variance** (spending variance), or the difference between actual fixed factory overhead and the amount budgeted, and the **volume variance** (idle capacity variance, production volume variance, or output-level variance), or the difference between budgeted fixed factory overhead and the product of the budgeted application rate and the standard input allowed for the actual output.  Fixed factory overhead applied does not necessarily equal the flexible-budget amount for the actual output.  The reason is that the latter amount is assumed to be constant over the relevant range of output.  Thus, the second column in the diagram on the next page represents the flexible-budget amount, and the third column represents the amount applied.  No efficiency variance is calculated because budgeted fixed factory overhead is a constant at all relevant output levels.

## Fixed Factory Overhead Variances

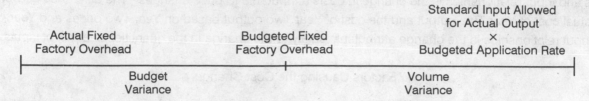

| Actual Fixed Factory Overhead | Budgeted Fixed Factory Overhead | Standard Input Allowed for Actual Output × Budgeted Application Rate |
|---|---|---|
| Budget Variance | | Volume Variance |

The total overhead variance also may be divided into two or three variances (but one variance is always the fixed overhead volume variance). **Three-way analysis of overhead variance** divides the total overhead variance into volume, efficiency, and spending variances. The spending variance combines the fixed overhead budget and variable overhead spending variances. The variable overhead efficiency and fixed overhead volume variances are the same as in four-way analysis. **Two-way analysis of overhead variance** divides the total overhead variance into two variances: volume and controllable (the latter is sometimes called the budget, total overhead spending, or flexible-budget variance). The variable overhead spending and efficiency variances and the fixed overhead budget variance are combined.

Analysis of revenues and revenue variances involves allocating or, preferably, tracing revenues to specific products, services, customers, etc. Revenue allocation is necessary when, for example, products, services, etc., are bundled (e.g., software packages). A **bundled product or service** is sold for one price but consists of distinct items that may be sold separately. The difference between allocation and tracing of revenues and revenue-related items, such as sales returns, is similar to that between allocation and tracing of costs. Moreover, the consequences of an arbitrary assignment of revenues (a broad averaging of revenue items over products, services, etc., that is, peanut-butter revenue assignments) are similar to the dysfunctional effects of inaccurate cost assignments. Like costs (see Chapter 6), revenues may be allocated using a stand-alone or an incremental method. **Stand-alone revenue allocation** may use a weighting scheme based on unit selling prices, for example, average actual prices, which is the theoretically preferable method; unit costs; or physical units in the bundle. **Incremental revenue allocation** establishes priorities among the items in a bundle. The primary product is assigned 100% of its stand-alone revenue, with the remaining revenue from the bundle assigned sequentially to the other items.

Assignment of revenues is necessary for the analysis of **revenue variances**, of which **sales variances** are the most common. If sales differ from the amount budgeted, the difference could be attributable to the sales price variance or the sales volume variance (sum of the sales mix and quantity variances). The analysis of these variances focuses on contribution margins rather than operating income for computational convenience. The reason is that fixed costs are assumed not to vary, so the results are the same. Furthermore, sales variances exclude consideration of cost variances. The sales price variance may also be called the **flexible-budget variance for revenues**. This variance and the sales volume variance are the components of the **static-budget variance for revenues**, which is the difference between the actual revenues and the amount in the static (master) budget.

For a single-product firm, the **sales price variance** is the change in the contribution margin because of the change in selling price [actual unit sales × (actual unit price – budgeted unit price)]. The **sales volume variance** is the change in contribution margin caused by the difference between the actual and budgeted volume [budgeted UCM × (actual unit sales – budgeted unit sales)]. Its components are the sales mix and sales quantity variances, but the sales mix variance is zero because the firm sells only one product. Hence, the sales volume variance for the single-product firm equals the **sales quantity** variance.

If a company produces two or more products, the sales variances reflect not only the effects of the change in total unit sales but also any difference in the mix sold. In the multiproduct case, the **sales price variance** may be calculated as described on the previous page for each product. The results are then added. An alternative is to multiply the actual total units sold times the difference between the weighted-average price based on actual units sold at actual unit prices and the weighted-average price based on actual units sold at budgeted prices. One way to calculate the multiproduct **sales volume variance** is to determine the variance for each product and to add the results. An alternative is to determine the difference between the following: (actual total unit sales times the budgeted weighted-average UCM for the actual mix) and (budgeted total unit sales times the budgeted weighted-average UCM for the planned mix). The **sales quantity variance** (the sales volume variance for a single-product company) is the difference between the budgeted contribution margin based on actual unit sales and the budgeted contribution margin based on expected sales, assuming that the budgeted sales mix is constant. One way to calculate this variance is to multiply the budgeted UCM for each product times the difference between the budgeted unit sales of the product and its budgeted percentage of actual total unit sales and then to add the results. An alternative is to multiply the difference between total actual unit sales and the total expected unit sales by the budgeted weighted-average UCM based on the expected mix. The **sales mix variance** is the difference between the budgeted contribution margin for the actual mix and actual total quantity of products sold and the budgeted contribution margin for the expected mix and actual total quantity of products sold. One way to calculate this variance is to multiply the budgeted UCM for each product times the difference between actual unit sales of the product and its budgeted percentage of actual total unit sales and then to add the results. An alternative is to multiply total actual unit sales times the difference between the budgeted weighted-average UCM for the expected mix and the budgeted weighted-average UCM for the actual mix. Multiple-country variance analysis applies the computations for sales volume, sales quantity, and sales mix variances in a multiproduct setting to sales of a single product (or service) in different countries. Results for each country are analogous to the results for a separate product because budgeted UCMs vary from country to country.

The components of the sales quantity variance are the market size and the market share variances. The **market size variance** equals the budgeted market share percentage, times the difference between the actual market size in units and the budgeted market size in units, times the budgeted weighted-average UCM. The **market share variance** equals the difference between the actual market share percentage and the budgeted market share percentage, times the actual market size in units, times the budgeted weighted-average UCM.

Variances usually do not appear on the financial statements. They are used for managerial control, and are recorded in the ledger accounts. When standard costs are recorded in inventory accounts, variances are also recorded. Thus, direct labor is recorded as a liability at actual cost, but it is charged to WIP control at its standard cost for the standard quantity used. The direct labor rate and efficiency variances are recognized at that time. Direct materials, however, should be debited to materials control at standard prices at the time of purchase. The purpose is to isolate the direct materials price variance as soon as possible. When direct materials are used, they are debited to WIP at the standard cost for the standard quantity, and the materials quantity variance is then recognized. Actual overhead costs are debited to overhead control and credited to accounts payable, wages payable, etc. Applied overhead is credited to an overhead applied account (or to overhead control) and debited to WIP control. The simplest method of recording the overhead variances is to wait until year-end. The variances can then be recognized separately when the overhead control and overhead applied accounts are closed (by a credit and a debit, respectively). The balancing debits or credits are to the variance accounts.

**Disposition of variances** is accomplished most often by closing them to cost of goods sold or income summary if they are immaterial. Variances that are material may be prorated. A simple approach to proration is to allocate the total net variance to WIP, finished goods, and cost of goods sold based on the balances in those accounts. However, more complex methods are possible.

Several alternative approaches to the timing of recognition of variances are possible. For example, direct materials and labor might be transferred to WIP at their actual quantities. In that case, the direct materials quantity and direct labor efficiency variances might be recognized when goods are transferred from WIP to finished goods. Furthermore, the direct materials price variance might be isolated at the time of transfer to WIP. These methods, however, delay the recognition of variances. Early recognition is desirable for control purposes.

Traditional variance analysis assumes that flexible budget amounts are determined using a single unit-level cost driver, such as direct labor hours. The costing formula used to develop the **flexible budget** defines certain costs as fixed in total and certain other costs as fixed per unit of the driver. In an **ABC** setting, however, the costing formula is based on multiple drivers, and activities having the same driver are grouped for computational convenience. The results should be better understanding of which activities add value, more detailed and accurate predictions of costs at different levels of activity, and more meaningful variance analysis and performance measurement. These benefits arise because, in effect, a flexible budget is developed for each group of activities having the same driver.

## 10.1 Standard Cost Concepts

**1.** A standard cost system may be used in

    A.  Job-order costing but not process costing.

    B.  Either job-order costing or process costing.

    C.  Process costing but not job-order costing.

    D.  Neither process costing nor job-order costing.

The correct answer is (B). *(CPA, adapted)*
    **REQUIRED:** The cost accumulation system(s) that may use standard costing.
    **DISCUSSION:** A standard cost system costs the product at standard (predetermined) costs and compares expected with actual cost. This comparison allows deviations (i.e., variances) from expected results to be identified and investigated. A standard cost system can be used in both job-order and process costing systems to isolate variances.
    Answers (A), (C), and (D) are incorrect because a standard cost system may be used in both process costing and job-order costing.

**2.** A difference between standard costs used for cost control and the budgeted costs of the same manufacturing effort

    A.  Can exist because standard costs represent what costs should be, whereas budgeted costs are expected actual costs.

    B.  Can exist because budgeted costs are historical costs, whereas standard costs are based on engineering studies.

    C.  Can exist because budgeted costs include some slack, whereas standard costs do not.

    D.  Cannot exist because the amounts should be the same.

The correct answer is (A). *(CMA, adapted)*
    **REQUIRED:** The difference between standard costs and budgeted costs.
    **DISCUSSION:** In the long run, these costs should be the same. In the short run, however, they may differ because standard costs represent what costs should be, whereas budgeted costs are expected actual costs. Budgeted costs may vary widely from standard costs in certain months, but, for an annual budget period, the amounts should be similar.
    Answer (B) is incorrect because standard costs are not necessarily determined by engineering studies. Answer (C) is incorrect because standard costs are usually based on currently attainable standards applicable when a process is under control. They are set without regard to variances or slack. Answer (D) is incorrect because budgeted costs include expected deviations from the standards.

**3.** When a manager is concerned with monitoring total cost, total revenue, and net profit conditioned upon the level of productivity, an accountant should normally recommend

| | Flexible Budgeting | Standard Costing |
|---|---|---|
| A. | Yes | Yes |
| B. | Yes | No |
| C. | No | Yes |
| D. | No | No |

The correct answer is (A). *(CPA, adapted)*
    **REQUIRED:** The technique(s) for monitoring cost, revenue, and profit given different levels of activity.
    **DISCUSSION:** A flexible budget is a set of static budgets prepared in anticipation of varying levels of activity. It permits evaluation of actual results when actual production and expected production differ. Setting cost standards facilitates preparation of a flexible budget. For example, a standard unit variable cost is useful in determining the total variable cost for a given output.
    Answers (B), (C), and (D) are incorrect because flexible budgeting and standard costing should be used.

**4.** Which of the following is a purpose of standard costing?

    A.  Determine breakeven production level.

    B.  Control costs.

    C.  Eliminate the need for subjective decisions by management.

    D.  Allocate cost with more accuracy.

The correct answer is (B). *(CPA, adapted)*
    **REQUIRED:** The purpose of standard costing.
    **DISCUSSION:** Standard costing is used to isolate the variances between expected costs and actual costs. It allows management to measure performance and to correct inefficiencies, thereby helping to control costs.
    Answer (A) is incorrect because a standard costing system Is not needed to perform breakeven CVP analysis. Answer (C) is incorrect because standard costs are used by management as an aid in decision making. Answer (D) is incorrect because standard costing does not allocate costs more accurately, especially when variances exist.

**5.** Which one of the following is true concerning standard costs?

    A.  Standard costs are estimates of costs attainable only under the most ideal conditions, but rarely practicable.

    B.  Standard costs are difficult to use with a process costing system.

    C.  If properly used, standards can help motivate employees.

    D.  Unfavorable variances, material in amount, should be investigated, but large favorable variances need not be investigated.

The correct answer is (C). *(CPA, adapted)*
    **REQUIRED:** The true statement about standard costs.
    **DISCUSSION:** Standards are used as a norm against which actual results may be compared. One of the benefits of a standard cost system is that it can be used to motivate employees to achieve specified goals.
    Answer (A) is incorrect because standard costs should be attainable under conditions of efficient operation. Answer (B) is incorrect because a standard cost system is ideally suited to a process costing system. Answer (D) is incorrect because all material variances should be investigated, whether favorable or unfavorable.

**6.** When standard costs are used in a process costing system, how, if at all, are equivalent units of production (EUP) involved or used in the cost report at standard?

    A.  Equivalent units are not used.

    B.  Equivalent units are computed using a special approach.

    C.  The actual equivalent units are multiplied by the standard cost per unit.

    D.  The standard equivalent units are multiplied by the actual cost per unit.

The correct answer is (C). *(CPA, adapted)*
    **REQUIRED:** The way equivalent units are used in a standard cost report.
    **DISCUSSION:** A process costing system is used to account for continuous production of homogeneous goods. EUP are calculated to determine how many complete units could have been produced, given no BWIP and no EWIP. For example, if 100 units in EWIP are 40% complete, the same amount of work could have produced 40 complete units. To determine the cost of the units produced, these EUP are multiplied by the standard cost per unit.
    Answer (A) is incorrect because equivalent units are used to calculate costs. Answer (B) is incorrect because equivalent units are computed in the regular manner. Answer (D) is incorrect because standard EUP is a nonsense term.

**7.** The difference between the actual amounts and the flexible budget amounts for the actual output achieved is the

    A.  Production volume variance.

    B.  Flexible budget variance.

    C.  Sales volume variance.

    D.  Standard cost variance.

The correct answer is (B). *(CMA, adapted)*
    **REQUIRED:** The term for the difference between the actual amounts and the flexible budget amounts.
    **DISCUSSION:** A flexible budget is a series of several budgets prepared for many levels of activity. A flexible budget allows adjustment of the budget to the actual level before comparing the budgeted and actual results. The difference between the flexible budget and actual figures is known as the flexible budget variance.
    Answer (A) is incorrect because the production volume variance equals under- or overapplied fixed factory overhead. Answer (C) is incorrect because the sales volume variance is the difference between the flexible budget amount and the static budget amount. Answer (D) is incorrect because a standard cost variance is not necessarily based on a flexible budget.

**8.** The sales volume variance equals

   A.  A flexible budget amount minus a static budget amount.

   B.  Actual operating income minus flexible budget operating income.

   C.  Actual unit price minus budgeted unit price, times the actual units produced.

   D.  Budgeted unit price times the difference between actual inputs and budgeted inputs for the actual activity level achieved.

The correct answer is (A). *(Publisher)*

**REQUIRED:** The definition of the sales volume variance.

**DISCUSSION:** The sales volume variance assumes that, unit prices and costs and total fixed costs remaining constant, the only variable is the sales activity level. Thus, the difference between a given flexible budget amount and the corresponding static budget amount is the sales volume variance.

Answer (B) is incorrect because actual operating income minus flexible budget operating income is the definition of the flexible budget variance (actual result – flexible budget amount for the actual activity) for operating income. Answer (C) is incorrect because actual unit price minus budgeted unit price, times the actual units produced, is the price variance. Answer (D) is incorrect because budgeted unit price times the difference between actual inputs and budgeted inputs for the actual activity level achieved is an efficiency variance.

**9.** An efficiency variance equals

   A.  A flexible budget amount minus a static budget amount.

   B.  Actual operating income minus flexible budget operating income.

   C.  Actual unit price minus budgeted unit price, times the actual units produced.

   D.  Budgeted unit price times the difference between actual inputs and budgeted inputs for the actual activity level achieved.

The correct answer is (D). *(Publisher)*

**REQUIRED:** The definition of an efficiency variance.

**DISCUSSION:** An efficiency variance compares the actual use of inputs with the budgeted quantity of inputs allowed for the activity level achieved. The variance equals this difference multiplied by the budgeted unit price. The result is to isolate the cost effect of using more or fewer units of input than budgeted.

Answer (A) is incorrect because a flexible budget amount minus a static budget amount is a volume variance. Answer (B) is incorrect because an efficiency variance cannot be determined using only income amounts. Answer (C) is incorrect because actual unit price minus budgeted unit price, times the actual units produced, is a price variance.

**10.** The flexible-budget variance in operating income is

   A.  Actual operating income minus flexible budget operating income.

   B.  Budgeted unit price times the difference between actual inputs and budgeted inputs for the actual activity level achieved.

   C.  A flexible budget amount minus a static budget amount.

   D.  Actual unit price minus budgeted unit price, times the actual units produced.

The correct answer is (A). *(Publisher)*

**REQUIRED:** The definition of the flexible-budget variance in operating income.

**DISCUSSION:** This analysis determines the difference in operating income between actual results and the flexible budget. The flexible budget is based on standard costs and the actual activity level. Deviations from that budget should be explained by changes in any of the items shown on the flexible budget except the activity level, for example, revenues, variable costs, contribution margin, and fixed costs.

Answer (B) is incorrect because budgeted unit price times the difference between actual inputs and budgeted inputs for the actual activity level achieved is an efficiency variance. Answer (C) is incorrect because a flexible budget amount minus a static budget amount is a volume variance. Answer (D) is incorrect because actual unit price minus budgeted unit price, times the actual units produced, is a price variance.

**11.** In analyzing company operations, the controller of the Jason Corporation found a $250,000 favorable flexible budget revenue variance. The variance was calculated by comparing the actual results with the flexible budget. This variance can be wholly explained by

A. The total flexible budget variance.

B. The total static budget variance.

C. Changes in unit selling prices.

D. Changes in the number of units sold.

The correct answer is (C). *(CMA, adapted)*
**REQUIRED:** The cause of a favorable flexible budget revenue variance.
**DISCUSSION:** A flexible budget revenue variance is the difference between actual revenue and the revenue budgeted for the actual activity level (quantity sold). Consequently, it isolates the effect of price changes because the sales quantity is held constant.
Answer (A) is incorrect because the total flexible budget variance includes items other than revenue. Answer (B) is incorrect because the total static budget variance includes many items other than revenue. Answer (D) is incorrect because, by definition, a flexible budget's volume is identical to actual volume.

**12.** The best basis upon which cost standards should be set to measure controllable production inefficiencies is

A. Engineering standards based on ideal performance.

B. Normal capacity.

C. Engineering standards based on attainable performance.

D. Practical capacity.

The correct answer is (C). *(CMA, adapted)*
**REQUIRED:** The best basis upon which cost standards should be set.
**DISCUSSION:** A standard cost system separates the expected cost from the actual cost. Thus, deviations from expected results are identified on a routine basis. The best standards are based on attainable performance so that any deviation will denote inefficiencies that deserve review and have a reasonable probability of responding to management attention. Attainable standards also motivate employees.
Answer (A) is incorrect because ideal standards assume the most efficient operations, which usually cannot be achieved or maintained. They tend to have a negative motivational effect. Answer (B) is incorrect because normal capacity is the activity level that satisfies average consumer demand over the long run and includes seasonal, cyclical, and trend factors. Answer (D) is incorrect because practical capacity is the maximum level at which the entity can possibly operate most efficiently, i.e., ideal capacity minus allowances for weekends, holidays, downtime, and external contingencies such as supply shortages.

**13.** Which one of the following statements about ideal standards is incorrect?

A. Ideal standards are also called theoretical or maximum-efficiency standards.

B. Ideal standards do not make provisions for workers with different degrees of experience and skill levels.

C. Ideal standards make no allowance for waste, spoilage, and machine breakdowns.

D. Ideal standards can be used for cash budgeting or product costing.

The correct answer is (D). *(CMA, adapted)*
**REQUIRED:** The false statement about ideal standards.
**DISCUSSION:** Ideal (perfect, theoretical, or maximum-efficiency) standards are standard costs that are set for production under optimal conditions. They are based on the work of the most skilled workers with no allowance for waste, spoilage, machine breakdowns, or other downtime. Ideal standards can have positive behavioral implications if workers are motivated to strive for excellence, for example, in a TQM environment. However, they are not in wide use because they can have negative behavioral effects if the standards are impossible to attain. Ideal standards are ordinarily replaced by currently attainable standards for cash budgeting, product costing, and budgeting departmental performance. Otherwise, accurate financial planning will be impossible.
Answer (A) is incorrect because ideal standards are perfection standards. Answer (B) is incorrect because ideal standards are based solely on the most efficient workers. Answer (C) is incorrect because ideal standards assume optimal conditions.

**14.** Which one of the following statements pertaining to practical standards is incorrect?

    A.  Practical standards can be used for product costing and cash budgeting.

    B.  A firm using practical standards has no reason to make any midyear adjustments to the production standards if an old machine is replaced by a newer, faster machine.

    C.  Under practical standards, exceptions from standards are less likely; consequently, managers will be better able to practice management by exception.

    D.  Practical standards are more likely to be attained by workers making diligent efforts.

The correct answer is (B). *(CMA, adapted)*
    **REQUIRED:** The false statement about practical standards.
    **DISCUSSION:** Practical or currently attainable standards may be defined as the performance that is reasonably expected to be achieved with an allowance for normal spoilage, waste, and downtime. An alternative interpretation is that practical standards represent possible but difficult to attain results. The use of practical standards does not, however, negate the need to adjust standards if working conditions change.
    Answer (A) is incorrect because practical standards are more appropriate than ideal standards for purposes of cash budgeting, product costing, and departmental performance budgeting. Under one interpretation of the term, practical standards are the expected results. Answer (C) is incorrect because practical standards reflect expectations or at least standards that are more likely to be attainable than ideal standards. Consequently, unfavorable variances indicate that operations have not been normally efficient and effective. Answer (D) is incorrect because practical standards reflect either reasonable expectations or at least possible results attainable with very efficient operations.

**15.** Which of the following factors should not be considered when deciding whether to investigate a variance?

    A.  Magnitude of the variance and the cost of investigation.

    B.  Trend of the variances over time.

    C.  Likelihood that an investigation will eliminate future occurrences of the variance.

    D.  Whether the variance is favorable or unfavorable.

The correct answer is (D). *(CIA, adapted)*
    **REQUIRED:** The factor not relevant in deciding whether to investigate a variance.
    **DISCUSSION:** A variance shows a deviation of actual results from the expected or budgeted results. All material variances should be investigated, whether favorable or unfavorable.
    Answer (A) is incorrect because only material variances should be investigated. Also, the benefits of each step in the entire standard cost process must be cost effective. Answer (B) is incorrect because the trend of variances over time should be considered. A negative variance that has been getting progressively smaller may not need investigating, whereas a variance that is increasing should be investigated promptly. Answer (C) is incorrect because the objective of variance investigation is pinpointing responsibility and taking corrective action.

**16.** Standard costing will produce the same income before extraordinary items as actual costing when standard cost variances are assigned to

    A.  Work-in-process and finished goods inventories.

    B.  An income or expense account.

    C.  Cost of goods sold and inventories.

    D.  Cost of goods sold.

The correct answer is (C). *(CPA, adapted)*
    **REQUIRED:** The account(s) to which the standard cost variances should be allocated.
    **DISCUSSION:** Assigning variances to cost of goods sold and inventories (proration) based on production and sales for the period will effectively convert standard costing to actual costing. This conversion is necessary for external reporting purposes when the amounts involved are material.
    Answer (A) is incorrect because a substantial portion of the variance usually needs to be allocated to CGS. Answer (B) is incorrect because standard cost variances need to be allocated to cost of goods sold and inventories. Answer (D) is incorrect because the variance also needs to be allocated to the inventory account.

**17.** If the total materials variance (actual cost of materials used compared with the standard cost of the standard amount of materials required) for a given operation is favorable, why must this variance be further evaluated as to price and usage?

A. There is no need to further evaluate the total materials variance if it is favorable.

B. Generally accepted accounting principles require that all variances be analyzed in three stages.

C. All variances must appear in the annual report to equity owners for proper disclosure.

D. Determining price and usage variances allows management to evaluate the efficiency of the purchasing and production functions.

The correct answer is (D). *(CPA, adapted)*

**REQUIRED:** The reason for evaluating a favorable variance as to price and usage.

**DISCUSSION:** A standard cost system differentiates expected cost from actual cost, which allows deviations from expected results to be identified on a timely basis. An overall variance may include both unfavorable and favorable variances. Separately analyzing the components of the overall variance results in more useful information. Thus, the price variance is used to evaluate the purchasing department, and the usage variance pinpoints any production inefficiencies.

Answer (A) is incorrect because all material variances should be investigated, regardless of the direction of the variance. Answer (B) is incorrect because GAAP do not require standard costing. Answer (C) is incorrect because variances usually are not reported to third parties and do not appear in the annual report.

**18.** When items are transferred from stores to production, an accountant debits work-in-process and credits materials accounts. During production, a materials quantity variance may occur. The materials quantity variance is debited for an unfavorable variance and credited for a favorable variance. The intent of variance entries is to provide

A. Accountability for materials lost during production.

B. A means of safeguarding assets in the custody of the system.

C. Compliance with GAAP.

D. Information for use in controlling the cost of production.

The correct answer is (D). *(CIA, adapted)*

**REQUIRED:** The intent of variance entries.

**DISCUSSION:** One step in the control process is measurement of actual results against standards. For example, the standard quantity of materials for a given output is established prior to production. If the actual materials usage exceeds the standard, the variance is unfavorable and corrective action may be needed.

Answer (A) is incorrect because accountability is adequately established by the inventory entries. Answer (B) is incorrect because variance entries cannot safeguard assets; they can only provide information for use in controlling the cost of production. Answer (C) is incorrect because internal cost accounting information need not comply with GAAP.

**19.** Which department is customarily held responsible for an unfavorable materials usage variance?

A. Quality control.

B. Purchasing.

C. Engineering.

D. Production.

The correct answer is (D). *(CPA, adapted)*

**REQUIRED:** The department usually responsible for an unfavorable materials usage variance.

**DISCUSSION:** Responsibility for variances should bear some relationship to the decision and control processes used. Materials usage should be the primary responsibility of the production management personnel.

Answer (A) is incorrect because quality control is responsible for quality standards, not material usage during production. Answer (B) is incorrect because purchasing usually is responsible for a materials price variance. Answer (C) is incorrect because engineering is responsible for design, engineering, and quality standards.

**20.** At the end of its fiscal year, Graham Co. had several substantial variances from standard variable manufacturing costs. The one that should be allocated between inventories and cost of sales is the one attributable to

  A. Additional cost of raw material acquired under a speculative purchase contract.

  B. A breakdown of equipment.

  C. Overestimates of production volume for the period resulting from failure to predict an unusual decline in the market for the company's product.

  D. Increased labor rates won by the union as a result of a strike.

The correct answer is (D). *(CPA, adapted)*

  **REQUIRED:** The standard variable manufacturing cost variance allocated to inventory and CGS.

  **DISCUSSION:** A standard cost system differentiates the expected cost from the actual cost. Thus, deviations from expected results are identified on a routine basis. Increased wages are a part of doing business and usually increase the cost of the items made and sold.

  Answer (A) is incorrect because gains and losses on speculation are not product costs. Answer (B) is incorrect because, during a breakdown, variable manufacturing costs should not be incurred. Answer (C) is incorrect because a volume variance concerns fixed rather than variable manufacturing costs.

**21.** The standard unit cost is used in the calculation of which of the following variances?

| | Materials Price Variance | Materials Usage Variance |
|---|---|---|
| A. | No | No |
| B. | No | Yes |
| C. | Yes | No |
| D. | Yes | Yes |

The correct answer is (D). *(CPA, adapted)*

  **REQUIRED:** The variance(s) using standard unit costs.

  **DISCUSSION:** The materials price variance is calculated by multiplying the difference between actual price and standard price by the actual units purchased. The materials usage variance is calculated by multiplying the difference between the actual usage and the standard usage by the standard price. Thus, the standard unit cost is used to compute both the materials price variance and the materials usage variance.

  Answers (A), (B), and (C) are incorrect because standard unit cost is used in the calculation of both materials price variances and materials usage variances.

**22.** How should a usage variance that is significant in amount be treated at the end of an accounting period?

  A. Reported as a deferred charge or credit.

  B. Allocated among work-in-process inventory, finished goods inventory, and cost of goods sold.

  C. Charged or credited to cost of goods manufactured.

  D. Allocated among cost of goods manufactured, finished goods inventory, and cost of goods sold.

The correct answer is (B). *(CPA, adapted)*

  **REQUIRED:** The treatment of a usage variance at the end of a period.

  **DISCUSSION:** Allocating a variance among work-in-process, finished goods, and cost of goods sold will properly match the variance with the items produced. This procedure adjusts the respective accounts, which are expressed in terms of standard costs, to actual costs.

  Answer (A) is incorrect because some of the variance should be allocated to cost of goods sold. Answers (C) and (D) are incorrect because the cost of goods manufactured is the cost of the goods transferred from WIP to finished goods, not a balance at year-end.

**23.** What is the normal year-end treatment of immaterial variances recognized in a cost accounting system using standard costs?

  A. Reclassified to deferred charges until all related production is sold.

  B. Allocated among cost of goods manufactured and ending work-in-process inventory.

  C. Closed to cost of goods sold in the period in which they arose.

  D. Capitalized as a cost of ending finished goods inventory.

The correct answer is (C). *(CPA, adapted)*

  **REQUIRED:** The normal year-end treatment of immaterial variances accumulated in a standard cost system.

  **DISCUSSION:** Normally, all immaterial variances are closed to CGS in the period in which they arose. This process is simpler than allocating the variance among the inventories and CGS.

  Answer (A) is incorrect because immaterial variances cannot be said to provide future benefit. Answer (B) is incorrect because, if allocated, the allocation should be to EWIP, FG inventory, and CGS in proportion to the relative flow of goods. However, for cost-benefit reasons, only material variances are usually allocated in this manner. Answer (D) is incorrect because immaterial variances should be closed to cost of goods sold, not capitalized, in the period in which they arose.

**24.** The budget for a given cost during a given period was $80,000. The actual cost for the period was $72,000. Considering these facts, the plant manager has done a better-than-expected job in controlling the cost if

- A. The cost is variable and actual production was 90% of budgeted production.
- B. The cost is variable and actual production equaled budgeted production.
- C. The cost is variable and actual production was 80% of budgeted production.
- D. The cost is a discretionary fixed cost and actual production equaled budgeted production.

The correct answer is (B). *(CPA, adapted)*
   **REQUIRED:** The circumstances in which the plant manager has done a better-than-expected job.
   **DISCUSSION:** When comparing the actual job performance with the budget, the deviations must be noted and compared with the appropriate budget that would have been in effect had perfect information been available. In this case, if the cost is variable and actual production matched the budgeted production, $80,000 is the expected actual cost. Given that the actual cost was $72,000, the plant manager has done a good job in controlling the cost.
   Answer (A) is incorrect because, if the cost is variable and actual production was 90% of budgeted production, the plant manager has merely met the standard (90% x $80,000 = $72,000). Answer (C) is incorrect because, if the cost is variable and actual production was 80% of budgeted production, the plant manager has done a less-than-adequate job in controlling the cost assuming a standard of $64,000 (80% of $80,000). Answer (D) is incorrect because the question does not state whether the discretionary fixed cost was controlled by the plant manager.

**25.** Which of the following is not an acceptable treatment of factory overhead variances at an interim reporting date?

- A. Apportion the total only among work-in-process and finished goods inventories on hand at the end of the interim reporting period.
- B. Apportion the total only between that part of the current period's production remaining in inventories at the end of the period and that part sold during the period.
- C. Carry forward the total to be offset by opposite balances in later periods.
- D. Charge or credit the total to the cost of goods sold during the period.

The correct answer is (A). *(CPA, adapted)*
   **REQUIRED:** The unacceptable treatment of factory overhead variances at an interim reporting date.
   **DISCUSSION:** Factory overhead variances may be carried to future interim periods as deferred charges or credits, charged or credited to CGS, or apportioned among inventories and CGS. To apportion the total only between WIP and FG would not allocate a proper proportion to CGS.
   Answer (B) is incorrect because allocating the variance among CGS and inventories is the usual process for material variances. Answer (C) is incorrect because APB 28, *Interim Financial Reporting*, states, "Purchase price variances or volume or capacity variances that are planned and expected to be absorbed by the end of the annual period should ordinarily be deferred at interim reporting dates." Answer (D) is incorrect because charging or crediting the variance to CGS is appropriate when the variance is immaterial.

## 10.2 Direct Materials

**26.** In a standard cost system, the materials price variance is obtained by multiplying the

- A. Actual price by the difference between actual quantity purchased and standard quantity used.
- B. Actual quantity purchased by the difference between actual price and standard price.
- C. Standard price by the difference between standard quantity purchased and standard quantity used.
- D. Standard quantity purchased by the difference between actual price and standard price.

The correct answer is (B). *(CPA, adapted)*
   **REQUIRED:** The method used to compute the materials price variance.
   **DISCUSSION:** The materials price variance measures the difference between the amount actually paid for the goods purchased and the standard amount allowed for the goods purchased. Thus, it equals the difference between actual price and standard price, multiplied by the actual quantity purchased. This question assumes that price variances are isolated at the time of purchase. If they are isolated when the materials are issued, the variance is the difference between standard and actual price, times the amount issued (not amount purchased).
   Answer (A) is incorrect because the materials price variance measures the difference between the actual price and standard price for the goods purchased. Answer (C) is incorrect because multiplying the standard price by the difference between standard quantity purchased and standard quantity used gives the standard change in inventories. Answer (D) is incorrect because the actual quantity must be used to determine the materials price variance.

**27.** An unfavorable price variance occurs because of

A. Price increases for raw materials.

B. Price decreases for raw materials.

C. Less-than-anticipated levels of waste in the manufacturing process.

D. More-than-anticipated levels of waste in the manufacturing process.

The correct answer is (A). *(CPA, adapted)*

**REQUIRED:** The reason an unfavorable price variance occurs.

**DISCUSSION:** A standard cost system differentiates the expected cost from the actual cost. Thus, deviations from expected results are identified on a routine basis. An increase in the actual price of raw materials over the standard price will result in an unfavorable price variance.

Answer (B) is incorrect because a decrease in price would result in a favorable price variance. Answer (C) is incorrect because less waste would result in a favorable materials usage variance. Answer (D) is incorrect because more waste would result in an unfavorable materials usage variance.

**28.** If a company follows a practice of isolating variances as soon as possible, the appropriate time to isolate and recognize a direct materials price variance is when

A. Materials are issued.

B. Materials are purchased.

C. Materials are used in production.

D. The purchase order originates.

The correct answer is (B). *(CPA, adapted)*

**REQUIRED:** The earliest appropriate time to isolate a direct materials price variance.

**DISCUSSION:** The time of purchase is the most appropriate moment to isolate and recognize a price variance. Analysis at that time permits the earliest possible examination of variances.

Answer (A) is incorrect because time elapses between purchase and issuance of materials; thus, the earliest time to isolate price variances is upon purchase. Answer (C) is incorrect because a materials price variance can be isolated at purchase. Answer (D) is incorrect because the transaction has not yet been consummated when the purchase order originates.

**29.** Under a standard cost system, the materials price variances are usually the responsibility of the

A. Production manager.

B. Cost accounting manager.

C. Sales manager.

D. Purchasing manager.

The correct answer is (D). *(CMA, adapted)*

**REQUIRED:** The individual responsible for the materials price variance.

**DISCUSSION:** The materials price variance is the difference between the standard price and the actual price paid for materials. This variance is usually the responsibility of the purchasing department. Thus, the purchasing manager has an incentive to obtain the best price possible.

Answers (A), (B), and (C) are incorrect because the production manager, cost accounting manager, and sales manager have no control over the price paid for materials.

**30.** Under a standard cost system, the materials efficiency variances are the responsibility of

A. Production and industrial engineering.

B. Purchasing and industrial engineering.

C. Purchasing and sales.

D. Sales and industrial engineering.

The correct answer is (A). *(CMA, adapted)*

**REQUIRED:** The functions responsible for the materials efficiency (quantity) variance.

**DISCUSSION:** The materials efficiency variance is the difference between actual and standard quantities used in production, times the standard price. An unfavorable materials efficiency variance is usually caused by waste, shrinkage, or theft. Thus, it may be the responsibility of the production department because excess usage occurs while the materials are in that department. Industrial engineering may also play a role because it is responsible for design of the production process.

Answer (B) is incorrect because purchasing is less likely to affect the materials efficiency variance. Answers (C) and (D) are incorrect because sales has no effect on the materials efficiency variance.

**31.** Price variances and efficiency variances can be key to the performance measurement within a company. In evaluating the performance within a company, a materials efficiency variance can be caused by all of the following except the

A. Performance of the workers using the material.

B. Actions of the purchasing department.

C. Design of the product.

D. Sales volume of the product.

The correct answer is (D). *(CMA, adapted)*

**REQUIRED:** The item not a cause of a materials efficiency variance.

**DISCUSSION:** An unfavorable materials quantity or usage (efficiency) variance can be caused by a number of factors, including waste, shrinkage, theft, poor performance by production workers, nonskilled workers, or the purchase of below-standard-quality materials by the purchasing department. Engineering changes in the design of the production process or of the product can also affect the quantity of materials used. Sales volume should not be a contributing factor to a materials efficiency variance.

Answers (A), (B), and (C) are incorrect because worker performance, purchasing department actions, and product design are possible causes of a materials efficiency variance.

**32.** A favorable materials price variance coupled with an unfavorable materials usage variance would most likely result from

A. Machine efficiency problems.

B. Product mix production changes.

C. Labor efficiency problems.

D. The purchase of lower-than-standard-quality materials.

The correct answer is (D). *(CMA, adapted)*

**REQUIRED:** The cause of a favorable materials price variance and an unfavorable materials usage variance.

**DISCUSSION:** A favorable materials price variance is the result of paying less than the standard price for materials. An unfavorable materials usage variance is the result of using an excessive quantity of materials. If a purchasing manager buys substandard materials to achieve a favorable price variance, an unfavorable usage variance could result from using an excessive amount of poor quality materials.

Answers (A), (B), and (C) are incorrect because machine efficiency, a change in product mix, and labor efficiency have no effect on the price of materials and would not explain the price variance.

**33.** The materials mix variance equals

A. (Inputs allowed − inputs used) x budgeted weighted-average materials unit price for the planned mix.

B. (Budgeted weighted-average labor rate for planned mix − budgeted weighted-average labor rate for actual mix) x inputs used.

C. (Inputs allowed − inputs used) x budgeted weighted-average labor rate for the planned mix.

D. (Budgeted weighted-average materials unit cost for planned mix − budgeted weighted-average materials unit cost for actual mix) x inputs used.

The correct answer is (D). *(Publisher)*

**REQUIRED:** The definition of the materials mix variance.

**DISCUSSION:** Materials yield and mix variances are the components of the materials usage variance. They are useful only if certain classes or types of materials can be substituted for each other. The materials mix variance is calculated to isolate the effects of the change in the mix of materials used. Thus, it equals the materials actually used times the difference between the budgeted weighted-average materials unit cost for the planned mix and the budgeted weighted-average unit cost for the actual mix. Because substitutability of materials may not be possible in every situation, the materials mix variance is suitable for analysis only when the manager has some control over the composition of the mix.

Answer (A) is incorrect because it states the definition of the materials yield variance. Answer (B) is incorrect because it describes the labor mix variance. Answer (C) is incorrect because it defines the labor yield variance.

**34.** The materials yield variance equals

    A.  (Inputs allowed – inputs used) x budgeted weighted-average materials unit price for the planned mix.

    B.  (Budgeted weighted-average labor rate for planned mix – budgeted weighted-average labor rate for actual mix) x inputs used.

    C.  (Inputs allowed – inputs used) x budgeted weighted-average labor rate for the planned mix.

    D.  (Budgeted weighted-average materials unit cost for planned mix – budgeted weighted-average materials unit cost for actual mix) x inputs used.

The correct answer is (A). *(Publisher)*
    **REQUIRED:** The definition of materials yield variance.
    **DISCUSSION:** The yield variance is the difference between actual input and the standard input allowed, times the budgeted weighted-average unit price. The materials yield variance is a calculation based on the assumption that the standard mix was maintained in producing a given output.
    Answer (B) is incorrect because it states the definition of the labor mix variance. Answer (C) is incorrect because it describes the labor yield variance. Answer (D) is incorrect because it defines the materials mix variance.

**35.** The efficiency variance for either labor or materials can be divided into a

    A.  Yield variance and a price variance.

    B.  Volume variance and a mix variance.

    C.  Mix variance and a price variance.

    D.  Yield variance and a mix variance.

The correct answer is (D). *(CMA, adapted)*
    **REQUIRED:** The components into which a labor or materials efficiency variance can be divided.
    **DISCUSSION:** An efficiency variance equals the difference between standard and actual resource usage times the standard price or rate per unit of the resource. The efficiency variances can be divided into yield and mix variances. A yield variance is the difference between the actual quantity and the standard quantity of the resource, assuming a constant mix. A mix variance measures the effect of a deviation from standard proportions of inputs. These variances are calculated only when the production process involves combining several materials or classes of labor in varying proportions (when substitutions are allowable in combining resources).
    Answers (A) and (C) are incorrect because an efficiency variance pertains to quantity used, not price. Answer (B) is incorrect because a volume variance is based on fixed costs, whereas an efficiency variance is based on variable costs.

Questions 36 through 38 are based on the following information. ChemKing uses a standard costing system in the manufacture of its single product. The 35,000 units of raw material in inventory were purchased for $105,000, and two units of raw material are required to produce one unit of final product. In November, the company produced 12,000 units of product. The standard allowed for material was $60,000, and there was an unfavorable quantity variance of $2,500.

**36.** ChemKing's standard price for one unit of material is

A. $2.50

B. $3.00

C. $5.00

D. $6.00

The correct answer is (A). *(CMA, adapted)*
**REQUIRED:** The standard price for one unit of raw materials.
**DISCUSSION:** Given that the company produced 12,000 units with a total standard cost for materials of $60,000, the standard cost must be $5.00 ($60,000 ÷ 12,000 units) per unit of finished product. Because each unit of finished product requires two units of raw materials, the standard unit cost for raw materials must be $2.50.
Answer (B) is incorrect because $3 is the actual cost per unit of raw materials. Answer (C) is incorrect because $5 is the total standard cost of raw materials for each unit of finished product. Answer (D) is incorrect because $6 is the actual cost of raw materials per unit of finished product.

**37.** The units of material used to produce November output totaled

A. 12,000 units.

B. 23,000 units.

C. 24,000 units.

D. 25,000 units.

The correct answer is (D). *(CMA, adapted)*
**REQUIRED:** The number of units of materials used to produce November output.
**DISCUSSION:** The company produced 12,000 units of output, each of which required two units of raw materials. Thus, the standard input allowed for raw materials was 24,000 units at a standard cost of $2.50 each (see preceding question). An unfavorable quantity variance signifies that the actual quantity used was greater than the standard input allowed. The materials quantity variance equals the difference between actual and standard quantities, times the standard price per unit. Consequently, since 1,000 ($2,500 U ÷ $2.50) additional units were used, the actual total quantity must have been 25,000 units (24,000 standard + 1,000).
Answer (A) is incorrect because 12,000 units is the number of units of finished product. Answer (B) is incorrect because 23,000 units assumes a favorable quantity variance. Answer (C) is incorrect because 24,000 units assumes no quantity variance.

**38.** The materials price variance for the units used in November was

A. $2,500 unfavorable.

B. $15,000 unfavorable.

C. $12,500 unfavorable.

D. $2,500 favorable.

The correct answer is (C). *(CMA, adapted)*
**REQUIRED:** The materials price variance for the units used in November.
**DISCUSSION:** The price variance equals actual quantity times the difference between the actual and standard prices. Actual usage and the standard price were calculated in the two preceding questions as 25,000 units and $2.50, respectively. Actual price was $3.00 ($105,000 total cost ÷ 35,000 units purchased). Consequently, the materials price variance is $12,500 unfavorable [($3.00 − $2.50) x 25,000 units].
Answer (A) is incorrect because $2,500 unfavorable is the materials quantity variance. Answer (B) is incorrect because $15,000 unfavorable is the total materials variance. Answer (D) is incorrect because the price variance is unfavorable.

Questions 39 and 40 are based on the following information. The information was presented as part of Question 5 on Part 4 of the June 1982 CMA examination.

A company produces a gasoline additive. The standard costs and input for a 500-liter batch of the additive are presented below.

| Chemical | Standard Input Quantity in Liters | Standard Cost per Liter | Total Cost |
|---|---|---|---|
| Echol | 200 | $.200 | $ 40.00 |
| Protex | 100 | .425 | 42.50 |
| Benz | 250 | .150 | 37.50 |
| CT-40 | 50 | .300 | 15.00 |
| | 600 | | $135.00 |

The quantities purchased and used during the current period are shown below. A total of 140 batches were made during the current period.

| Chemical | Quantity Purchased (Liters) | Total Purchase Price | Quantity Used (Liters) |
|---|---|---|---|
| Echol | 25,000 | $ 5,365 | 26,600 |
| Protex | 13,000 | 6,240 | 12,880 |
| Benz | 40,000 | 5,840 | 37,800 |
| CT-40 | 7,500 | 2,220 | 7,140 |
| Total | 85,500 | $19,665 | 84,420 |

**39.** What is the materials mix variance for this operation?

A. $294 favorable.

B. $388.50 favorable.

C. $94.50 unfavorable.

D. $219.50 favorable.

The correct answer is (B). *(Publisher)*

REQUIRED: The materials mix variance.

DISCUSSION: The materials mix variance equals the actual total quantity used times the difference between the budgeted weighted-average standard unit cost for the budgeted mix and the budgeted weighted-average standard unit cost for the actual mix. This variance is favorable if the standard weighted-average cost for the actual mix is less than the standard weighted-average cost for the budgeted mix. The standard mix weighted-average standard unit cost is $.225 per liter ($135 standard total cost ÷ 600 liters).

The standard cost of the actual quantity used was $18,606 (see below). Thus, the actual mix weighted-average standard unit cost was $.220398 ($18,606 ÷ 84,420 liters used), and the mix variance was $388.50 favorable [($.220398 – $.225) x 84,420 liters].

| | | | |
|---|---|---|---|
| $.200 | × | 26,600 = | $ 5,320.00 |
| .425 | × | 12,880 = | 5,474.00 |
| .150 | × | 37,800 = | 5,670.00 |
| .300 | × | 7,140 = | 2,142.00 |
| | | | $18,606.00 |

Answer (A) is incorrect because $294 favorable is the materials quantity variance. Answer (C) is incorrect because $94.50 unfavorable is the materials yield variance. Answer (D) is incorrect because $219.50 favorable is based on the actual mix of purchases.

**40.** What is the materials yield variance for this operation?

A. $294.50 favorable.

B. $388.50 favorable.

C. $94.50 unfavorable.

D. $219.50 favorable.

The correct answer is (C). *(Publisher)*

REQUIRED: The materials yield variance.

DISCUSSION: The materials yield variance equals the difference between the actual input and the standard input allowed for the actual output, times the budgeted weighted-average standard cost per input unit at the standard mix. The standard input for the actual output was 84,000 liters (140 batches x 600 liters per batch). The standard mix budgeted weighted-average standard unit cost is $.225 per liter ($135 total cost ÷ 600 liters). Thus, the yield variance is $94.50 unfavorable [(84,420 liters used – 84,000 liters allowed) x $.225].

Answer (A) is incorrect because $294.50 favorable is the materials quantity variance. Answer (B) is incorrect because $388.50 favorable is the materials mix variance. Answer (D) is incorrect because $219.50 favorable is based on the actual mix of purchases.

**41.** Productivity is defined as the ratio of outputs of a production process to the inputs that are used. Consider a process that currently produces 2,000 units of output with 500 hours of labor per day. This process can be redesigned to produce 2,520 units of output requiring 600 labor hours per day. The percentage change in productivity from redesigning the process is

A. 5%

B. 10%

C. 20%

D. 26%

The correct answer is (A). *(CIA, adapted))*

**REQUIRED:** The percentage change in productivity after a process change.

**DISCUSSION:** Before redesign, productivity equaled 4 units per hour (2,000 units ÷ 500 hours). After redesign, productivity equaled 4.2 units per hour (2,520 units ÷ 600 hours). Thus, the percentage change in productivity was 5% [(4.2 − 4.0) ÷ 4.0].

Answer (B) is incorrect because a 10% change requires output of 2,640 units. Answer (C) is incorrect because 20% is the percentage change in labor hours per day. Answer (D) is incorrect because 26% is the percentage change in units of output per day.

**42.** A manufacturing cell's partial productivity can be measured using data on

A. Inventory shrinkage.

B. Inventory turnover.

C. Direct materials usage.

D. Scrap.

The correct answer is (C). *(CIA, adapted)*

**REQUIRED:** The data used in measuring a manufacturing cell's partial productivity.

**DISCUSSION:** A partial productivity measure may be stated as the ratio of output to the quantity of a single factor of production (e.g., materials, labor, or capital). Partial productivity measures, for example, the number of finished units per direct labor hour or per pound of direct materials, are useful when compared over time among different factories or with benchmarks. A partial productivity measure comparing results over time determines whether the actual relationship between inputs and outputs has improved or deteriorated.

Answer (A) is incorrect because inventory shrinkage measures the effectiveness of internal control. Answer (B) is incorrect because inventory turnover measures the efficiency of asset usage. Answer (D) is incorrect because scrap is neither an input nor a good output.

**43.** Data regarding four different products manufactured by an organization are presented below. Direct material and direct labor are readily available from the respective resource markets. However, the manufacturer is limited to a maximum of 3,000 machine hours per month.

|  | Product A | Product B | Product C | Product D |
|---|---|---|---|---|
| Selling price/unit | $15 | $18 | $20 | $25 |
| Variable cost/unit | $ 7 | $11 | $10 | $16 |
| Units produced per machine hour | 3 | 4 | 2 | 3 |

The product that is the most profitable for the manufacturer in this situation is

A. Product A.

B. Product B.

C. Product C.

D. Product D.

The correct answer is (B). *(CIA, adapted))*

**REQUIRED:** The product that is the most profitable for the manufacturer.

**DISCUSSION:** When resources are limited, maximum profits are achieved by maximizing dollar contribution margin per limited or constraining factor. In this situation, machine hours are the constraining factor. Product B has a contribution margin per machine hour of $28 [4 x ($18 − $11)], which is greater than that of Product A [3 x ($15 − $7) = $24], Product C [2 x ($20 − $10) = $20], or Product D [3 x ($25 − $16) = $27].

Answer (A) is incorrect because Product A does have the greatest contribution margin ratio (53%), but when resources are limited, maximum profits are achieved by maximizing dollar contribution margin per limited or constraining factor, which in this case is machine hours. Answer (C) is incorrect because Product C does have the greatest dollar unit contribution margin ($10), but when resources are limited, maximum profits are achieved by maximizing dollar contribution margin per limited or constraining factor, which in this case is machine hours. Answer (D) is incorrect because Product D does have the greatest selling price per unit ($25), but when resources are limited, maximum profits are achieved by maximizing dollar contribution margin per limited or constraining factor, which in this case is machine hours.

Questions 44 and 45 are based on the following information. Fabro Inc. produced 1,500 units of Product RX-6 last week. The inputs to the production process for Product RX-6 were:

- 450 pounds of Material A at a cost of $1.50 per pound
- 300 pounds of Material Z at a cost of $2.75 per pound
- 300 labor hours at a cost of $15.00 per hour

**44.** What is the total factor productivity for Product RX-6?

- A. 2.00 units per pound.
- B. 5.00 units per hour.
- C. 0.25 units per dollar input.
- D. 0.33 units per dollar input.

The correct answer is (C). *(CMA, adapted)*

**REQUIRED:** The total factor productivity.

**DISCUSSION:** Total factor productivity equals units of output divided by the cost of all inputs. It varies with output levels, input prices, input quantities, and input mix. Hence, the total factor productivity equals 0.25 units per dollar input {1,500 units ÷ [(450 pounds of A x $1.50) + (300 pounds of Z x $2.75) + (300 hours x $15)]}.

Answers (A) and (B) are incorrect because the total factor productivity is measured in units of output per dollar of input. Answer (D) is incorrect because 0.33 units per dollar input is based only on labor costs. All input costs should be included.

**45.** What is the best productivity measure for the first-line supervisor in Fabro Inc.'s production plant?

- A. 5.00 units per labor hour.
- B. $2.00 per pound.
- C. 0.33 units per dollar input.
- D. $15.00 per labor hour.

The correct answer is (A). *(CMA, adapted)*

**REQUIRED:** The best productivity measure for the first-line supervisor in the production plant.

**DISCUSSION:** A first-line supervisor's primary job is employee supervision, so his/her productivity should be measured on the basis of output per labor hour. Thus, 5 units per labor hour expended (1,500 units ÷ 300 labor hours) measures productivity based on the factor over which the first-line supervisor has the most control.

Answers (B) and (D) are incorrect because a first-line supervisor normally does not control the price paid for either raw materials or labor. Answer (C) is incorrect because the first-line supervisor does not control the prices paid for raw materials or labor. Accordingly, output per dollar of input is not a meaningful measure.

## 10.3 Direct Labor

**46.** A debit balance in the direct labor efficiency variance account indicates that

- A. Standard hours exceed actual hours.
- B. Actual hours exceed standard hours.
- C. Standard rate and standard hours exceed actual rate and actual hours.
- D. Actual rate and actual hours exceed standard rate and standard hours.

The correct answer is (B). *(CPA, adapted)*

**REQUIRED:** The cause of a debit balance in the labor efficiency variance account.

**DISCUSSION:** A debit balance denotes an unfavorable labor efficiency variance; that is, actual hours exceed standard hours.

Answer (A) is incorrect because, if standard hours exceed actual, the result is a credit balance. Answer (C) is incorrect because, if standard rate and standard hours exceed actual rate and actual hours, the result would be a credit balance in both the labor efficiency and the labor rate variance accounts. Answer (D) is incorrect because both the labor efficiency and the labor rate variance accounts would have a debit balance.

**47.** An unfavorable direct labor efficiency variance could be caused by a(n)

   A. Unfavorable variable overhead spending variance.

   B. Favorable variable overhead spending variance.

   C. Unfavorable fixed overhead volume variance.

   D. Unfavorable materials usage variance.

The correct answer is (D). *(CMA, adapted)*
   **REQUIRED:** The cause of an unfavorable direct labor efficiency variance.
   **DISCUSSION:** An unfavorable direct labor efficiency variance results when production requires more labor hours than expected, for example, because employees take longer work breaks than anticipated when the standards were established. The variance can also be the result of production delays, such as those caused by poor quality materials or materials shortages. Thus, an unfavorable materials usage variance could indicate that excessive materials were used.
   Answers (A) and (B) are incorrect because a variable overhead spending variance may be affected by, but does not affect, the direct labor efficiency variance. Variable overhead includes indirect, not direct, labor. Answer (C) is incorrect because the volume variance is unrelated to the direct labor efficiency variance.

**48.** Which of the following unfavorable variances is directly affected by the relative position of a production process on a learning curve?

   A. Materials mix.

   B. Materials price.

   C. Labor rate.

   D. Labor efficiency.

The correct answer is (D). *(CPA, adapted)*
   **REQUIRED:** The variance affected by the learning curve.
   **DISCUSSION:** The efficiency of the employees varies with how long they have been performing the particular task. Thus, more experienced employees are expected to be more efficient, which affects the labor efficiency variance.
   Answer (A) is incorrect because the learning curve has little correlation with materials mix variances. Answer (B) is incorrect because a materials price variance is primarily the result of external factors. Answer (C) is incorrect because the labor rate variance should not be affected by the learning curve.

**49.** Under a standard cost system, labor price variances are usually not attributable to

   A. Union contracts approved before the budgeting cycle.

   B. Labor rate predictions.

   C. The assignment of different skill levels of workers than planned.

   D. The payment of hourly rates instead of prescribed piecework rates.

The correct answer is (A). *(CMA, adapted)*
   **REQUIRED:** The factor that usually does not affect the labor price variance.
   **DISCUSSION:** The labor price (rate) variance is the difference between the actual rate paid and the standard rate, times the actual hours. This difference may be attributable to a change in labor rates since the establishment of the standards, using a single average standard rate although different employees are paid different rates, assigning higher-paid workers to jobs estimated to require lower-paid workers (or vice versa), or paying hourly rates but basing standards on piecework rates (or vice versa). A union contract approved before the budgeting cycle would not cause a variance because it would have been incorporated into the standards.
   Answer (B) is incorrect because predictions may have been inaccurate. Answer (C) is incorrect because assigning higher-paid (and higher-skilled) workers to jobs not requiring such skills causes an unfavorable variance. Answer (D) is incorrect because paying hourly rates when standards were based on piecework rates causes a variance.

**50.** Excess direct labor wages resulting from overtime premium will be disclosed in which type of variance?

- A. Yield.
- B. Quantity.
- C. Labor efficiency.
- D. Labor rate.

The correct answer is (D). *(CPA, adapted)*
**REQUIRED:** The variance that will reflect overtime premiums.
**DISCUSSION:** A standard cost system differentiates the expected cost from the actual cost. Thus, deviations from expected results can be identified on a routine basis. Depending on the circumstances, the premium paid for overtime hours may be treated as overhead or as a direct labor cost. In the latter case, it increases the labor rate and is reflected in the labor rate variance.
Answers (A), (B), and (C) are incorrect because overtime wages do not affect the direct labor yield efficiency (quantity) variances. They concern the amount, not the price, of direct labor.

**51.** On the diagram below, the line OW represents the standard labor cost at any output volume expressed in direct labor hours. Point S indicates the actual output at standard cost, and Point A indicates the actual hours and actual cost required to produce S.

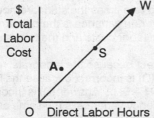

Which of the following variances are favorable or unfavorable?

|    | Rate Variance | Efficiency Variance |
|----|---------------|---------------------|
| A. | Favorable     | Unfavorable         |
| B. | Favorable     | Favorable           |
| C. | Unfavorable   | Unfavorable         |
| D. | Unfavorable   | Favorable           |

The correct answer is (D). *(CPA, adapted)*
**REQUIRED:** The nature of the direct labor variances.
**DISCUSSION:** Point S is to the right of Point A. Consequently, the standard direct labor hours allowed for the actual output exceeded the actual hours required, and the labor efficiency (quantity or usage) variance is favorable. Point A is above the line OW. Thus, the actual hourly rate must have been greater than the standard rate, and the labor rate (price) variance is unfavorable. The total labor variance, however, is favorable because Point S (total standard labor cost of the actual output) is higher than Point A (total actual labor cost).
Answer (A) is incorrect because the rate variance is unfavorable and the efficiency variance is favorable. Answer (B) is incorrect because the rate variance is unfavorable. Answer (C) is incorrect because the efficiency variance is favorable.

**52.** Which of the following is the most probable reason a company would experience an unfavorable labor rate variance and a favorable labor efficiency variance?

- A. The mix of workers assigned to the particular job was heavily weighted toward the use of higher-paid, experienced individuals.
- B. The mix of workers assigned to the particular job was heavily weighted toward the use of new, relatively low-paid unskilled workers.
- C. Because of the production schedule, workers from other production areas were assigned to assist in this particular process.
- D. Defective materials caused more labor to be used to produce a standard unit.

The correct answer is (A). *(CPA, adapted)*
**REQUIRED:** The probable reason for an unfavorable labor rate variance and a favorable labor efficiency variance.
**DISCUSSION:** More experienced people may perform more efficiently, but they usually cost more to use.
Answer (B) is incorrect because the use of unskilled workers may result in an unfavorable labor efficiency variance. Also the labor rate variance would be favorable because they are paid less. Answer (C) is incorrect because the use of untrained workers who are paid at unbudgeted amounts may result in both an unfavorable labor efficiency variance and an unfavorable labor rate variance. Answer (D) is incorrect because defective materials are not likely to cause an unfavorable labor rate variance.

**53.** How is labor rate variance computed?

    A.  The difference between standard and actual rates, times standard hours.

    B.  The difference between standard and actual hours, times actual rate.

    C.  The difference between standard and actual rates, times actual hours.

    D.  The difference between standard and actual hours, times the difference between standard and actual rates.

The correct answer is (C). *(CPA, adapted)*

**REQUIRED:** The formula for computing the labor rate variance.

**DISCUSSION:** The labor rate variance is computed by finding the difference between the standard and the actual rates and then multiplying by actual hours: AH(AR − SR).

Answer (A) is incorrect because the actual hours must be used to determine the labor rate variance. Answer (B) is incorrect because this formula gives no useful variances. Answer (D) is incorrect because the difference between standard and actual hours, times the difference between standard and actual rates, is the rate/usage variance in three-way analysis of labor variances (not widely used).

**54.** The difference between the actual labor rate multiplied by the actual hours worked and the standard labor rate multiplied by the standard labor hours is the

    A.  Total labor variance.

    B.  Labor rate variance.

    C.  Labor usage variance.

    D.  Labor efficiency variance.

The correct answer is (A). *(CPA, adapted)*

**REQUIRED:** The variance defined by the difference between total actual labor costs and total standard costs allowed.

**DISCUSSION:** The total actual labor cost is found by multiplying the actual labor rate times the actual labor hours. The total standard cost for good output is found by multiplying the standard rate times the standard hours allowed. The total labor rate variance is the difference between the total actual labor costs and the total standard labor costs.

Answer (B) is incorrect because the labor rate variance is AH(AR − SR). Answer (C) is incorrect because the labor usage variance is SR(AH − SH). Answer (D) is incorrect because the labor efficiency variance is the same as the labor usage variance, which is SR(AH − SH).

**55.** Listed below are four names for different kinds of standards associated with a standard cost system. Which one describes the labor costs that should be incurred under efficient operating conditions?

    A.  Ideal.

    B.  Basic.

    C.  Maximum-efficiency.

    D.  Currently attainable.

The correct answer is (D). *(CPA, adapted)*

**REQUIRED:** The type of cost incurred under efficient operations.

**DISCUSSION:** Currently attainable standards apply to the efficient operation of labor and resources. They are difficult but possible to achieve.

Answer (A) is incorrect because ideal standards are impossible to reach; i.e., they include no waste at all. Answer (B) is incorrect because basic standards is a nonsense concept in this context. Answer (C) is incorrect because maximum-efficiency standards are like the ideal and are not readily achievable.

**56.** The following is a standard cost variance analysis report on direct labor cost for a division of a manufacturing company:

| Job | Actual Hours at Actual Wages | Actual Hours at Standard Wages | Standard Hours at Standard Wages |
|---|---|---|---|
| 213 | $3,243 | $3,700 | $3,100 |
| 215 | $15,345 | $15,675 | $15,000 |
| 217 | $6,754 | $7,000 | $6,600 |
| 219 | $19,788 | $18,755 | $19,250 |
| 221 | $3,370 | $3,470 | $2,650 |
| Totals | $48,500 | $48,600 | $46,600 |

What is the total flexible budget direct labor variance for the division?

A. $100 favorable.

B. $1,900 unfavorable.

C. $1,900 favorable.

D. $2,000 unfavorable.

The correct answer is (B). *(CIA, adapted)*

**REQUIRED:** The total flexible budget direct labor variance.

**DISCUSSION:** The total flexible budget direct labor variance equals the difference between total actual direct labor cost and standard direct labor cost (standard rate x standard hours) allowed for the actual output. It combines the direct labor rate and efficiency variances. For this company, the variance is $1,900 U ($48,500 actual wages at actual hours – $46,600 standard wages at standard hours).

Answer (A) is incorrect because the direct labor rate variance is $100 F ($48,500 – $48,600). Answer (C) is incorrect because the total labor variance is unfavorable. Answer (D) is incorrect because the direct labor efficiency variance is $2,000 U.

**57.** The flexible budget for the month of May was for 9,000 units at a direct materials cost of $15 per unit. Direct labor was budgeted at 45 minutes per unit for a total of $81,000. Actual output for the month was 8,500 units with $127,500 in direct materials and $77,775 in direct labor expense. The direct labor standard of 45 minutes was maintained throughout the month. Variance analysis of the performance for the month of May would show a(n)

A. Favorable materials usage variance of $7,500.

B. Favorable direct labor efficiency variance of $1,275.

C. Unfavorable direct labor efficiency variance of $1,275.

D. Unfavorable direct labor price variance of $1,275.

The correct answer is (D). *(CMA, adapted)*

**REQUIRED:** The result of variance analysis based on a flexible budget for direct labor and materials.

**DISCUSSION:** Because labor for 9,000 units was budgeted at $81,000, the unit labor cost is $9. Thus, the labor budget for 8,500 units is $76,500, and the total labor variance is $1,275 ($77,775 – $76,500). Because the actual cost is greater than the budgeted amounts, the $1,275 variance is unfavorable. Given that the actual time per unit (45 minutes) was the same as that budgeted, no labor efficiency variance was incurred. Hence, the entire $1,275 unfavorable variance must be attributable to the labor rate (price) variance.

Answer (A) is incorrect because the materials usage cannot be calculated with the given data. Answers (B) and (C) are incorrect because budgeted hours equaled actual hours for 8,500 units.

**58.** Yola Co. manufactures one product with a standard direct labor cost of 4 hours at $12.00 per hour. During June, 1,000 units were produced using 4,100 hours at $12.20 per hour. The unfavorable direct labor efficiency variance was

A. $1,220

B. $1,200

C. $820

D. $400

The correct answer is (B). *(CPA, adapted)*

**REQUIRED:** The amount of an unfavorable direct labor efficiency variance.

**DISCUSSION:** The direct labor efficiency (quantity) variance equals standard rate times the difference between actual and standard amounts of labor hours. Thus, the direct labor efficiency variance is $1,200 {$12 standard rate x [4,100 actual hours – (4 standard hours x 1,000 units)]}. The variance is unfavorable because more labor hours were used than the standard.

Answer (A) is incorrect because $1,220 uses the actual labor rate. Answer (C) is incorrect because $820 is the labor rate variance. Answer (D) is incorrect because $400 is the difference between the direct labor efficiency variance and the cost difference ($.20) times the standard hours.

**59.** Information on Hanley's direct labor costs for the month of January is as follows:

Actual direct labor rate                      $7.50
Standard direct labor hours allowed          11,000
Actual direct labor hours                    10,000
Direct labor rate variance - favorable       $5,500

The standard direct labor rate in January was

    A.  $6.95

    B.  $7.00

    C.  $8.00

    D.  $8.05

The correct answer is (D). *(CPA, adapted)*
    **REQUIRED:** The standard direct labor rate for the month.
    **DISCUSSION:** The labor rate variance equals actual hours times the difference between the actual and standard rates. The variance is favorable, so the standard rate must exceed the actual rate.

$$10,000(SR - \$7.50) = \$5,500$$
$$SR = \$7.50 + (\$5,500 \div 10,000)$$
$$SR = \$8.05$$

    Answer (A) is incorrect because $6.95 treats the $.55 variance per unit as unfavorable. Answer (B) is incorrect because actual hours, not standard hours, are used to determine the SR. Furthermore, the favorable variance should be added, not subtracted, in calculating the standard rate. Answer (C) is incorrect because actual hours, not standard hours, should be used in determining the standard rate.

**60.** Tub Co. uses a standard cost system. The following information pertains to direct labor for product B for the month of October:

Standard hours allowed for
  actual production            2,000
Actual rate paid per hour        $8.40
Standard rate per hour           $8.00
Labor efficiency variance        $1,600 U

What were the actual hours worked?

    A.  1,800

    B.  1,810

    C.  2,190

    D.  2,200

The correct answer is (D). *(CPA, adapted)*
    **REQUIRED:** The actual hours worked.
    **DISCUSSION:** The standard hours allowed equaled 2,000, and the labor efficiency variance was $1,600 unfavorable; i.e., actual hours exceeded standard hours. The labor efficiency variance equals the standard rate ($8 per hour) times the excess hours. Given that the variance is $1,600, 200 excess hours ($1,600 ÷ $8) must have been worked. Thus, 2,200 actual hours (2,000 standard + 200 excess) were worked.
    Answer (A) is incorrect because the 200-hour difference between AH and SH should be added to, not subtracted from, the standard hours allowed. Answer (B) is incorrect because the difference between AH and SH must be determined using the standard rate per hour. The efficiency variance was also incorrectly treated as favorable and subtracted from the SH. Answer (C) is incorrect because the difference between AH and SH must be determined using the standard rate per hour.

**61.** Sullivan Corporation's direct labor costs for the month of March were as follows:

Standard direct labor hours               42,000
Actual direct labor hours                 40,000
Direct labor rate variance - favorable    $8,400
Standard direct labor rate per hour       $6.30

What was Sullivan's total direct labor payroll for the month of March?

    A.  $243,600

    B.  $252,000

    C.  $264,600

    D.  $260,400

The correct answer is (A). *(CPA, adapted)*
    **REQUIRED:** The direct labor payroll for March.
    **DISCUSSION:** When the actual direct labor rate is unknown, the total direct labor payroll is found by multiplying the actual hours by the standard rate, then subtracting the favorable labor variance.

$$(40,000 \times \$6.30) - \$8,400 = \$243,600$$

    Answer (B) is incorrect because $252,000 equals actual hours times the standard rate. Answer (C) is incorrect because $264,600 equals standard hours times the standard rate. Answer (D) is incorrect because the favorable rate variance should be subtracted from the payroll calculated at the standard rate for the actual hours.

**62.** The following direct labor information pertains to the manufacture of product Glu:

| | |
|---|---|
| Time required to make one unit | 2 direct labor hours |
| Number of direct workers | 50 |
| Number of productive hours per week, per worker | 40 |
| Weekly wages per worker | $500 |
| Workers' benefits treated as direct labor costs | 20% of wages |

What is the standard direct labor cost per unit of product Glu?

A. $30

B. $24

C. $15

D. $12

The correct answer is (A). *(CPA, adapted)*
**REQUIRED:** The standard direct labor cost per unit.
**DISCUSSION:** The hourly wage per worker is $12.50 ($500 ÷ 40 hrs.). The direct labor cost per hour is $15 [($12.50 x 1.0) + benefits equal to 20% of wages]. Consequently, the standard direct labor cost per unit is $30 ($15 x 2 hrs.).
Answer (B) is incorrect because the weekly wages and benefits per worker ($500 x 1.2) should be divided by 40 hours per week, not by 50 workers. Answer (C) is incorrect because $15.00 is the DL cost per hour. Two DL hours are required per unit. Answer (D) is incorrect because the weekly wages and benefits per worker ($500 x 1.2) should be divided by 40 hours per week, not by 50 workers. Furthermore, 2 DL hours are required per unit.

**63.** The labor yield variance equals

A. (Inputs allowed – inputs used) x budgeted weighted-average materials unit price for the planned mix.

B. (Budgeted weighted-average labor rate for planned mix – budgeted weighted-average labor rate for actual mix) x inputs used.

C. (Inputs allowed – inputs used) x budgeted weighted-average labor rate for the planned mix.

D. (Budgeted weighted-average materials unit cost for planned mix – budgeted weighted-average materials unit cost for actual mix) x inputs used.

The correct answer is (C). *(Publisher)*
**REQUIRED:** The definition of the labor yield variance.
**DISCUSSION:** The labor yield variance isolates the effect of using more or fewer total units of labor. The key to analyzing labor yield variances is that the labor rate and the mix of labor inputs are held constant. The labor yield variance equals the difference between the actual units of labor used and the standard units allowed for the actual output, times the standard weighted-average labor rate.
Answer (A) is incorrect because it defines the materials yield variance. Answer (B) is incorrect because this formula defines the labor mix variance. Answer (D) is incorrect because it states the materials mix variance.

**64.** The labor mix variance equals

A. (Inputs allowed – inputs used) x budgeted weighted-average materials unit price for the planned mix.

B. (Budgeted weighted-average labor rate for planned mix – budgeted weighted-average labor rate for actual mix) x inputs used.

C. (Inputs allowed – inputs used) x budgeted weighted-average labor rate for the planned mix.

D. (Budgeted weighted-average materials unit cost for planned mix – budgeted weighted-average materials unit cost for actual mix) x inputs used.

The correct answer is (B). *(Publisher)*
**REQUIRED:** The definition of the labor mix variance.
**DISCUSSION:** The labor mix variance isolates the effect of using different proportions of classes of labor. It equals the units of labor input actually used times the difference between the budgeted weighted-average labor rate for the planned mix and the budgeted weighted-average labor rate for the actual mix.
Answer (A) is incorrect because this formula defines the materials yield variance. Answer (C) is incorrect because this is the equation for the labor yield variance. Answer (D) is incorrect because this formula defines the materials mix variance.

Questions 65 through 67 are based on the following information. The information was presented as part of Question 4 on Part 4 of the June 1978 CMA exam.

A company's standard direct labor rates in effect for the fiscal year ending June 30 and standard hours allowed for the output in April are

| | Standard DL Rate per Hour | Standard DLH Allowed for Output |
|---|---|---|
| Labor class III | $8.00 | 500 |
| Labor class II | 7.00 | 500 |
| Labor class I | 5.00 | 500 |

The wage rates for each labor class increased on January 1 under the terms of a new union contract. The standard wage rates were not revised.

The actual direct labor hours (DLH) and the actual direct labor rates for April were as follows:

| | Actual Rate | Actual DLH |
|---|---|---|
| Labor class III | $8.50 | 550 |
| Labor class II | 7.50 | 650 |
| Labor class I | 5.40 | 375 |

**65.** What is the labor yield variance (rounded)?

A. $500

B. $320

C. $820

D. $515

The correct answer is (A). *(Publisher)*

**REQUIRED:** The labor yield variance for April.

**DISCUSSION:** The labor yield variance is the difference between actual and budgeted inputs, times the budgeted weighted-average rate for the planned mix. Total hours worked were 1,575 (550 + 650 + 375), standard hours allowed equaled 1,500 (500 + 500 + 500), and the budgeted weighted-average rate for the planned mix was $6.67 {[(500 x $8) + (500 x $7) + (500 x $5)] ÷ 1,500 standard DLH}. Thus, the variance is $500 unfavorable ($6.67 x 75).

Answer (B) is incorrect because $320 is the labor mix variance. Answer (C) is incorrect because $820 is the labor efficiency variance. Answer (D) is incorrect because $515 is based on the budgeted weighted-average rate for the actual mix.

**66.** What is the labor mix variance (rounded)?

A. $50.00

B. $320.00

C. $66.67

D. $500.00

The correct answer is (B). *(Publisher)*

**REQUIRED:** The labor mix variance for April.

**DISCUSSION:** The labor mix variance is the difference between the budgeted weighted-average rates for the actual and planned mixes, times the actual labor inputs. The budgeted weighted-average rate for the planned mix is $6.67 (see preceding question). The budgeted weighted-average rate for the actual mix is $6.873 [(550 x $8) + (650 x $7) + (375 x $5) ÷ 1,575 actual DLH]. Thus, the mix variance is $320 [($6.873 − 6.67) x 1,575].

Answer (A) is incorrect because $50.00 is the variance for labor class II only [($7 − $6.67) x (650 DLH − 500 DLH)]. Answer (C) is incorrect because $66.67 is the variance for labor class III only [($8 − $6.67) x (550 DLH − 500 DLH)]. Answer (D) is incorrect because $500 is the labor yield variance.

**67.** The labor mix and labor yield variances together equal the

A. Total labor variance.

B. Labor rate variance.

C. Labor efficiency variance.

D. Sum of the labor efficiency and overhead efficiency variances.

The correct answer is (C). *(Publisher)*

**REQUIRED:** The variance composed of labor mix and labor yield variances.

**DISCUSSION:** Labor mix and labor yield variances are the components of the total labor efficiency variance. For example, in the two preceding questions, the labor yield variance was $500 U and the labor mix variance was $320 U. The two variances sum to the total labor efficiency variance of $820 U.

Answer (A) is incorrect because the total labor variance equals the labor efficiency and labor rate variances. Answer (B) is incorrect because the labor rate variance is the variance of the price of the labor. Answer (D) is incorrect because the efficiency variance is not a labor variance.

## 10.4 Factory Overhead

**68.** Differences in product costs resulting from the application of actual overhead rates rather than predetermined overhead rates could be immaterial if

A. Production is not stable.

B. Fixed factory overhead is a significant cost.

C. Several products are produced simultaneously.

D. Overhead is composed only of variable costs.

The correct answer is (D). *(CPA, adapted)*

**REQUIRED:** The circumstance in which the difference between actual and predetermined overhead rates may be immaterial.

**DISCUSSION:** Actual overhead and predetermined amounts of overhead are most likely to be similar if overhead is composed primarily of variable costs. In principle, unit variable overhead should fluctuate little with the activity level.

Answers (A) and (B) are incorrect because fluctuating production levels could cause significant differences between actual and applied fixed factory overhead. Fixed factory overhead per unit changes with the activity level. Answer (C) is incorrect because a change in the product mix may cause significant differences between the predetermined and actual factory overhead rates.

**69.** The variance in an absorption costing system that measures the departure from the denominator level of activity that was used to set the fixed overhead rate is the

A. Spending variance.

B. Efficiency variance.

C. Sales volume variance.

D. Production volume variance.

The correct answer is (D). *(CMA, adapted)*

**REQUIRED:** The difference between actual production and the denominator level of production.

**DISCUSSION:** A denominator level of activity must be used to establish the standard cost (application rate) for fixed factory overhead. The production volume variance is the under- or overapplied fixed factory overhead, that is, the difference between budgeted fixed factory overhead and the amount applied (standard fixed factory overhead per unit of input times the standard units of input allowed for the actual production).

Answer (A) is incorrect because the fixed overhead spending variance is the difference between actual fixed factory overhead and the budgeted amount. Answer (B) is incorrect because the efficiency variance is a variable overhead variance. Answer (C) is incorrect because the sales volume variance is the effect on the contribution margin of the difference between actual and budgeted volume.

Questions 70 through 72 are based on the following information. Dori Castings is a job-order shop that uses a full-absorption, standard cost system to account for its production costs. The overhead costs are applied on a direct-labor-hour basis.

**70.** Dori's choice of production volume as a denominator for calculating its factory overhead rate has

A. An effect on the variable factory overhead rate for applying costs to production.

B. No effect on the fixed factory overhead budget variance.

C. No effect on the fixed factory overhead production volume variance.

D. No effect on the overall (net) fixed factory overhead variance.

The correct answer is (B). *(CMA, adapted)*
**REQUIRED:** The effect of using production volume as the denominator in calculating the factory overhead rate.
**DISCUSSION:** The use of a production volume as the denominator in calculating the factory overhead rate has no effect on the fixed factory overhead budget variance. This variance is the difference between actual fixed factory overhead and the lump sum budgeted.
Answer (A) is incorrect because, by definition, the total variable factory overhead varies with the activity level, but unit variable factory overhead does not. Answer (C) is incorrect because the fixed factory overhead production volume variance is the difference between budgeted fixed factory overhead and the amount applied based on the predetermined rate. Answer (D) is incorrect because the overall (net) fixed factory overhead variance is the difference between the actual fixed factory overhead and the amount applied based on the predetermined rate.

**71.** A production volume variance will exist for Dori in a month when

A. Production volume differs from sales volume.

B. Actual direct labor hours differ from standard allowed direct labor hours.

C. The fixed factory overhead applied on the basis of standard allowed direct labor hours differs from actual fixed factory overhead.

D. The fixed factory overhead applied on the basis of standard allowed direct labor hours differs from the budgeted fixed factory overhead.

The correct answer is (D). *(CMA, adapted)*
**REQUIRED:** The definition of a production volume variance.
**DISCUSSION:** A production volume variance is the difference between the budgeted fixed factory overhead and the amount applied based on a predetermined rate and the standard input allowed for the actual output.
Answer (A) is incorrect because sales volume is irrelevant. Answer (B) is incorrect because the difference between actual input and standard input allowed is the basis of the variable factory overhead efficiency variance. Answer (C) is incorrect because the difference between fixed factory overhead applied and the actual fixed factory overhead is the total fixed factory overhead variance.

**72.** The amount of fixed factory overhead that Dori will apply to finished production is the

A. Actual direct labor hours times the standard fixed factory overhead rate per direct labor hour.

B. Standard allowed direct labor hours for the actual units of finished output times the standard fixed factory overhead rate per direct labor hour.

C. Standard units of output for the actual direct labor hours worked times the standard fixed factory overhead rate per unit of output.

D. Actual fixed factory overhead cost per direct labor hour times the standard allowed direct labor hours.

The correct answer is (B). *(CMA, adapted)*
**REQUIRED:** The fixed factory overhead application basis.
**DISCUSSION:** Fixed factory overhead in a standard costing system is applied to the product based on the predetermined rate multiplied by the standard input allowed for the actual output. Thus, the applied fixed factory overhead is limited to the standard amount.
Answer (A) is incorrect because the standard input allowed for the actual units of finished output is used. Answer (C) is incorrect because application of fixed factory overhead is based on standard units of input. Answer (D) is incorrect because the applied fixed factory overhead is limited to the standard cost.

**73.** The fixed factory overhead application rate is a function of a predetermined activity level. If standard hours allowed for good output equal this predetermined activity level for a given period, the volume variance will be

A. Zero.

B. Favorable.

C. Unfavorable.

D. Either favorable or unfavorable, depending on the budgeted overhead.

The correct answer is (A). *(CPA, adapted)*

**REQUIRED:** The volume variance when standard hours allowed for good output equal the predetermined activity.

**DISCUSSION:** The volume variance is the difference between the budgeted fixed factory overhead and the amount applied based upon standard input allowed for good output. Thus, given no difference between the predetermined activity level and the standard input allowed for the actual output, no variance occurs.

Answer (B) is incorrect because a favorable volume variance means standard input allowed for the actual output exceeds the predetermined (budgeted) amount. Answer (C) is incorrect because an unfavorable volume variance means that standard input allowed for the actual output is less than the amount budgeted. Answer (D) is incorrect because no variance occurs.

**74.** Which of the following standard costing variances would be least controllable by a production supervisor?

A. Overhead volume.

B. Overhead efficiency.

C. Labor efficiency.

D. Materials usage.

The correct answer is (A). *(CPA, adapted)*

**REQUIRED:** The variance least controllable by a production supervisor.

**DISCUSSION:** The production volume variance measures the effect of not operating at the budgeted activity level. This variance can be caused by, for example, insufficient sales or a labor strike. These events are out of the production supervisor's control. Thus, the production volume variance is the least controllable by a production supervisor.

Answer (B) is incorrect because the variable factory overhead efficiency variance is wholly attributable to variable overhead. Answer (C) is incorrect because the efficiency of employees affects the labor efficiency variance. Answer (D) is incorrect because the materials usage variance is typically influenced most by activities within the production department.

Questions 75 and 76 are based on the following information. The diagram below depicts a factory overhead flexible budget line DB and standard overhead application line OA. Activity is expressed in machine hours, with Point V indicating the standard hours required for the actual output in September. Point S indicates the actual machine hours (inputs) and actual costs in September.

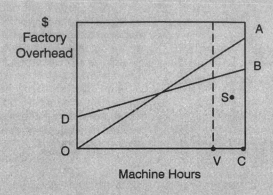

**75.** Are the following factory overhead variances favorable or unfavorable?

| | Volume (Capacity) Variance | Efficiency Variance |
|---|---|---|
| A. | Favorable | Favorable |
| B. | Favorable | Unfavorable |
| C. | Unfavorable | Favorable |
| D. | Unfavorable | Unfavorable |

The correct answer is (B). *(CPA, adapted)*
**REQUIRED:** The nature of the volume and efficiency variances.
**DISCUSSION:** The production volume variance (fixed factory overhead budgeted – fixed factory overhead applied) is favorable when actual activity exceeds the budgeted level, that is, when fixed factory overhead applied exceeds the amount budgeted. Line OA (standard overhead applied) is above line DB (the flexible budget) at Point V. Thus, total overhead applied exceeded the amount budgeted at activity level V. Because variable factory overhead applied equals the flexible-budget amount at all activity levels within the relevant range, the difference between OA and DB is solely the result of the volume variance. Fixed factory overhead costs applied equaled the flexible-budget amount at the intersection of OA and DB, which is to the left of V. Accordingly, at all points on OA to the right of the intersection, the volume variance is favorable. The efficiency variance (budgeted variable factory overhead rate x the difference between actual hours and the standard hours allowed) is unfavorable because Point S (actual hours) is to the right of Point V (standard hours allowed).
Answers (A), (C), and (D) are incorrect because the volume variance is favorable and the efficiency variance is unfavorable.

**76.** The budgeted total variable factory overhead cost for C machine hours is

A. AB.

B. BC.

C. AC minus DO.

D. BC minus DO.

The correct answer is (D). *(CPA, adapted)*
**REQUIRED:** The budgeted total variable factory overhead cost for C machine hours.
**DISCUSSION:** DB is the flexible budget line for total factory overhead. At O (zero machine hours), budgeted variable factory overhead is zero. Hence, DO must equal the fixed factory overhead cost. At C, BC represents total budgeted factory overhead, and BC minus DO must therefore equal the budgeted total variable factory overhead.
Answer (A) is incorrect because AB is the overapplied fixed factory overhead for C hours. Answer (B) is incorrect because BC is the total budgeted factory overhead for C hours. Answer (C) is incorrect because AC minus DO is the sum of the budgeted variable factory overhead for C hours and the overapplied fixed factory overhead.

**77.** A spending variance for variable factory overhead based on direct labor hours is the difference between actual variable factory overhead and the variable factory overhead that should have been incurred for the actual hours worked. This variance results from

A. Price and quantity differences for factory overhead costs.

B. Price differences for factory overhead costs.

C. Quantity differences for factory overhead costs.

D. Differences caused by variations in production volume.

The correct answer is (A). *(CPA, adapted)*
**REQUIRED:** The source of a spending variance for variable factory overhead.
**DISCUSSION:** Variable factory overhead includes numerous items, and an overall rate is required. The spending variance results not only from differences in the prices of variable factory overhead items but also from differences in the quantities used. Some of these are favorable and some unfavorable. The spending variance is the difference between actual variable factory overhead incurred and budgeted variable factory overhead based on the application of a predetermined rate to actual hours worked.
Answers (B) and (C) are incorrect because the spending variance is concerned with quantity differences and price differences. Answer (D) is incorrect because a change in production volume affects the fixed factory overhead volume variance.

**78.** Variable factory overhead is applied on the basis of standard direct labor hours. If, for a given period, the direct labor efficiency variance is unfavorable, the variable factory overhead efficiency variance will be

A. Favorable.

B. Unfavorable.

C. Zero.

D. The same amount as the labor efficiency variance.

The correct answer is (B). *(CMA, adapted)*
**REQUIRED:** The effect on the variable factory overhead efficiency variance of an unfavorable direct labor efficiency variance.
**DISCUSSION:** If the variable factory overhead efficiency variance and the direct labor efficiency variance measure the effect of the difference between actual and standard hours, both variance calculations will be based on the same activity base. Thus, if the direct labor efficiency variance is unfavorable, the variable factory overhead efficiency variance will also be unfavorable.
Answers (A), (C), and (D) are incorrect because both variances are based on the same activity base. If one is unfavorable, the other must be unfavorable.

**79.** If factory overhead is applied on the basis of units of output, the variable factory overhead efficiency variance will be

A. Zero.

B. Favorable, if output exceeds the budgeted level.

C. Unfavorable, if output is less than the budgeted level.

D. A function of the direct labor efficiency variance.

The correct answer is (A). *(CMA, adapted)*
**REQUIRED:** The effect on the variable factory overhead efficiency variance of an application rate based on output.
**DISCUSSION:** The variable factory overhead efficiency variance equals the product of a standard application rate and the difference between the standard input for the actual output and the actual input. Hence, the variance will be zero if variable factory overhead is applied on the basis of units of output. Any difference between standard and actual input cannot be recognized.
Answers (B) and (C) are incorrect because the variance will be zero. Answer (D) is incorrect because the correlation between the variable factory overhead and direct labor efficiency variances occurs only when overhead is applied on the basis of direct labor.

**80.** Under the two-variance method for analyzing factory overhead, the difference between the actual factory overhead and the factory overhead applied to production is the

A. Controllable variance.

B. Net overhead variance.

C. Efficiency variance.

D. Volume variance.

The correct answer is (B). *(CPA, adapted)*
**REQUIRED:** The difference between the actual factory overhead and factory overhead applied.
**DISCUSSION:** The net factory overhead variance is the difference between the sum of actual fixed and variable factory overhead and the sum of the fixed and variable overhead applied (total overhead rate x the standard input allowed for the actual output).
Answer (A) is incorrect because the controllable (budget) variance is the difference between actual total overhead incurred and budgeted overhead at the standard input allowed. Answer (C) is incorrect because the efficiency variance is not separately calculated in two-way analysis. Answer (D) is incorrect because the volume variance is the difference between budgeted fixed factory overhead and the amount applied.

**81.** Under the two-variance method for analyzing factory overhead, which of the following variances consists of both variable and fixed overhead elements?

| | Controllable (Budget) Variance | Volume Variance |
|---|---|---|
| A. | Yes | Yes |
| B. | Yes | No |
| C. | No | No |
| D. | No | Yes |

The correct answer is (B). *(CPA, adapted)*
**REQUIRED:** The variance(s), if any, including both fixed and variable elements.
**DISCUSSION:** In two-way analysis, the total factory overhead variance equals the volume variance (total fixed factory overhead budgeted – fixed factory overhead applied based on standard input allowed for the actual output) and the controllable (budget) variance [total actual factory overhead – (lump-sum fixed factory overhead budgeted + variable factory overhead based on the standard rate and the standard input allowed for the actual output)]. Consequently, only the controllable (budget) variance contains both fixed and variable elements.
Answers (A), (C), and (D) are incorrect because the controllable variance, not the volume variance, consists of both variable and fixed factory overhead.

**82.** Which one of the following variances is of least significance from a behavioral control perspective?

A. Unfavorable materials quantity variance amounting to 20% of the quantity allowed for the output attained.

B. Unfavorable labor efficiency variance amounting to 10% more than the budgeted hours for the output attained.

C. Favorable materials price variance obtained by purchasing raw material from a new vendor.

D. Fixed factory overhead volume variance resulting from management's decision midway through the fiscal year to reduce its budgeted output by 20%.

The correct answer is (D). *(CMA, adapted)*
**REQUIRED:** The variance of least significance from a behavioral control perspective.
**DISCUSSION:** A fixed factory overhead volume variance is often not the responsibility of anyone other than top management. It is the difference between budgeted fixed factory overhead and the amount applied. It can be caused by economic downturns, labor strife, bad weather, or a change in planned output. Thus, a variance resulting from a top management decision to reduce output has fewer behavioral implications than other variances.
Answer (A) is incorrect because an unfavorable materials quantity variance reflects on production management and possibly the purchasing function. It may indicate an inefficient use of materials or the purchase of poor quality materials. Answer (B) is incorrect because an unfavorable labor efficiency variance reflects upon production workers who have used too many hours. Answer (C) is incorrect because the purchasing function is responsible for a favorable materials price variance.

**83.** Under the two-variance method for analyzing factory overhead, which of the following is used in the computation of the controllable (budget) variance?

| | Budget Allowance Based on Actual Hours | Budget Allowance Based on Standard Hours |
|---|---|---|
| A. | Yes | Yes |
| B. | Yes | No |
| C. | No | No |
| D. | No | Yes |

The correct answer is (D). *(CPA, adapted)*
**REQUIRED:** The item(s), if any, used in the computation of the controllable (budget) variance.
**DISCUSSION:** In two-way analysis, the total factory overhead variance equals the volume variance (total fixed factory overhead cost budgeted – fixed factory overhead applied based on standard input allowed for the actual output) and the controllable (budget) variance [total actual factory overhead – (lump-sum fixed factory overhead budgeted + variable factory overhead based on the standard rate and the standard input allowed for the actual output)]. Hence, the budget allowance based on standard, not actual, hours is used in the computation of the controllable (budget) variance.

Answers (A), (B), and (C) are incorrect because only the budget allowance based on standard hours is used in the computation of the controllable variance.

**84.** Under the three-variance method for analyzing factory overhead, the difference between the actual factory overhead and the factory overhead applied to production is the

A. Net factory overhead variance.

B. Controllable variance.

C. Efficiency variance.

D. Spending variance.

The correct answer is (A). *(CPA, adapted)*
**REQUIRED:** The difference between the actual factory overhead and the factory overhead applied.
**DISCUSSION:** Three-way analysis calculates spending, efficiency, and production volume variances. However, regardless of whether two-, three-, or four-way analysis is used, the net factory overhead variance is the difference between actual total factory overhead and the total applied to the product.

Answer (B) is incorrect because the controllable (budget) variance is calculated in two-way analysis. Answer (C) is incorrect because the efficiency variance is calculated in three- or four-way analysis. Answer (D) is incorrect because, in three-way analysis, the spending variance is the difference between actual total factory overhead and the sum of budgeted fixed factory overhead and the variable factory overhead based on the actual input at the standard rate. It combines the variable factory overhead spending and the fixed factory overhead budget variances used in four-way analysis.

**85.** Under the three-variance method for analyzing factory overhead, the difference between the actual factory overhead and the budget allowance based on actual input is the

A. Efficiency variance.

B. Spending variance.

C. Volume variance.

D. Idle capacity variance.

The correct answer is (B). *(CPA, adapted)*
**REQUIRED:** The difference between the actual factory overhead and the budget allowance based on actual input.
**DISCUSSION:** In three-way analysis, the spending variance is the difference between actual total factory overhead and the sum of budgeted (lump-sum) fixed factory overhead and the variable factory overhead based on the actual input at the standard rate. It combines the variable factory overhead spending and the fixed factory overhead budget variances used in four-way analysis.

Answer (A) is incorrect because the efficiency variance equals the standard rate for variable factory overhead times the difference between actual input and the standard input. Answers (C) and (D) are incorrect because the production volume (idle capacity) variance is the difference between the budgeted (lump-sum) fixed factory overhead and the amount applied.

**86.** Under the three-variance method for analyzing factory overhead, which of the following is used in the computation of the spending variance?

|     | Actual Factory Overhead | Budget Allowance Based on Actual Input |
|-----|--------|-----------------|
| A.  | No     | Yes             |
| B.  | No     | No              |
| C.  | Yes    | No              |
| D.  | Yes    | Yes             |

The correct answer is (D). *(CPA, adapted)*
  **REQUIRED:** The components of the spending variance.
  **DISCUSSION:** In three-way analysis, the spending variance is the difference between actual total factory overhead and the sum of budgeted (lump-sum) fixed factory overhead and the variable factory overhead based on the actual input at the standard rate. It combines the variable factory overhead spending and the fixed factory overhead budget (spending) variances used in four-way analysis.
  Answers (A), (B), and (C) are incorrect because the actual total factory overhead and the budget allowance based on actual input are used in the computation of the spending variance.

**87.** During the current year, a department's three-variance factory overhead standard costing system reported unfavorable spending and volume variances. The activity level selected for allocating factory overhead to the product was based on 80% of practical capacity. If 100% of practical capacity had been selected instead, how would the reported unfavorable spending and volume variances have been affected?

|     | Spending Variance | Volume Variance |
|-----|-------------------|-----------------|
| A.  | Increased         | Unchanged       |
| B.  | Increased         | Increased       |
| C.  | Unchanged         | Increased       |
| D.  | Unchanged         | Unchanged       |

The correct answer is (C). *(CPA, adapted)*
  **REQUIRED:** The effects on unfavorable spending and volume variances of increasing the budgeted activity level.
  **DISCUSSION:** In a three-way analysis, the spending variance combines the fixed factory overhead budget variance (actual – budgeted fixed factory overhead) and the variable factory overhead spending variance (actual variable factory overhead – the amount applied based on actual input). The budget variance is not based on any allocations of overhead. The spending variance is based on the assumption that unit variable factory overhead is constant within the relevant range. Thus, a change in the denominator activity does not affect the variable factory overhead application rate and therefore the amount applied based on actual input. Because actual variable factory overhead is likewise unaffected, the spending variance is unchanged. However, the volume variance (budgeted fixed factory overhead – the amount applied) is affected by the increase in the denominator activity because the application rate for fixed factory overhead must decrease. Hence, the amount applied is lower, and the already unfavorable variance (fixed factory overhead exceeding the amount applied) must increase.
  Answers (A), (B), and (D) are incorrect because the spending variance will be unchanged and the volume variance will increase.

**88.** Union Company uses a standard cost accounting system. The following factory overhead and production data are available for August:

| | |
|---|---:|
| Standard fixed overhead rate per DLH | $1 |
| Standard variable overhead rate per DLH | $4 |
| Budgeted monthly DLH | 40,000 |
| Actual DLH worked | 39,500 |
| Standard DLH allowed for actual production | 39,000 |
| Overall overhead variance - favorable | $2,000 |

The applied factory overhead for August should be

  A. $195,000

  B. $197,000

  C. $197,500

  D. $199,500

The correct answer is (A). *(CPA, adapted)*
  **REQUIRED:** The applied factory overhead for the month.
  **DISCUSSION:** The applied factory overhead equals the standard direct hours allowed for actual production multiplied by the total standard overhead rate per hour.

$$39,000(\$4\ VOH + \$1\ FOH) = \$195,000$$

  Answer (B) is incorrect because $197,000 includes the $2,000 favorable overhead variance. This variance should not be added to the $195,000 applied factory overhead. Answer (C) is incorrect because the actual DLH worked were used to determine the applied FO when the standard DLH allowed for actual production should have been used. Answer (D) is incorrect because the actual DLH worked were used instead of the standard DLH allowed. Furthermore, the $2,000 favorable overhead variance should not be included.

**89.** Nil Co. uses a predetermined factory overhead application rate based on direct labor cost. For the year ended December 31, Nil's budgeted factory overhead was $600,000, based on a budgeted volume of 50,000 direct labor hours, at a standard direct labor rate of $6 per hour. Actual factory overhead amounted to $620,000, with actual direct labor cost of $325,000. For the year, overapplied factory overhead was

A. $20,000

B. $25,000

C. $30,000

D. $50,000

The correct answer is (C). *(CPA, adapted)*
**REQUIRED:** The overapplied factory overhead for the period.
**DISCUSSION:** Nil Co. applies factory overhead using a predetermined overhead rate, based on direct labor cost. Overhead was budgeted for $600,000 based on a budgeted labor cost of $300,000 ($6 x 50,000 hrs.). Thus, $2 of overhead was applied for each $1 of labor. Given actual labor cost of $325,000, $650,000 ($2 x $325,000) of overhead was applied during the period. Actual overhead was $620,000, so $30,000 ($650,000 – $620,000) was overapplied.
Answer (A) is incorrect because $20,000 is the difference between budgeted and actual factory overhead. Answer (B) is incorrect because $25,000 is the difference between budgeted direct labor costs and actual direct labor costs. Answer (D) is incorrect because $50,000 is the difference between the applied factory overhead and the budgeted amount.

**90.** Peters Company uses a flexible budget system and prepared the following information for the year:

| Percent of capacity | 80% | 90% |
|---|---|---|
| Direct labor hours | 24,000 | 27,000 |
| Variable factory overhead | $48,000 | $54,000 |
| Fixed factory overhead | $108,000 | $108,000 |
| Total factory overhead rate per DLH | $6.50 | $6.00 |

Peters operated at 80% of capacity during the year but applied factory overhead based on the 90% capacity level. Assuming that actual factory overhead was equal to the budgeted amount for the attained capacity, what is the amount of overhead variance for the year?

A. $6,000 overabsorbed.

B. $6,000 underabsorbed.

C. $12,000 overabsorbed.

D. $12,000 underabsorbed.

The correct answer is (D). *(CPA, adapted)*
**REQUIRED:** The factory overhead variance for the year.
**DISCUSSION:** The total overhead variance is computed by determining the difference between the actual overhead and applied overhead. Given that actual factory overhead was equal to the budgeted amount for the attained capacity, the only variance was caused by under- or overabsorption of fixed overhead. The fixed overhead rate at the 90% activity level is $4 ($108,000 fixed overhead ÷ 27,000 DLH). Given that the actual activity level achieved was 80% and that 24,000 standard hours were allowed, $96,000 (24,000 x $4.00) of fixed overhead was absorbed. Hence, underabsorbed (underapplied) fixed overhead was $12,000 ($108,000 – $96,000).
Answers (A) and (B) are incorrect because $96,000 of overhead was absorbed. Answer (C) is incorrect because the overhead variance for the year is $12,000 underabsorbed, not overabsorbed.

**91.** Simson Company's master budget shows straight-line depreciation on factory equipment of $258,000. The master budget was prepared at an annual production volume of 103,200 units of product. This production volume is expected to occur uniformly throughout the year. During September, Simson produced 8,170 units of product, and the accounts reflected actual depreciation on factory machinery of $20,500. Simson controls manufacturing costs with a flexible budget. The flexible budget amount for depreciation on factory machinery for September should be

A. $19,875

B. $20,425

C. $20,500

D. $21,500

The correct answer is (D). *(CMA, adapted)*
**REQUIRED:** The amount of depreciation expense shown on the flexible budget for the month.
**DISCUSSION:** Because straight-line depreciation is a fixed cost, it will be the same each month regardless of production. Consequently, the budget for September should report depreciation of $21,500 [($258,000 annual depreciation x 1/12)].
Answer (A) is incorrect because $19,875 equals 1/12 of $258,000 minus $20,500. Answer (B) is incorrect because $20,425 depreciation is found by allocating depreciation based on units of production [$258,000 x (8,170 ÷ 103,200)]. Answer (C) is incorrect because $20,500 is the actual depreciation on the factory machinery.

**92.** Margolos, Inc. ends the month with a volume variance of $6,360 unfavorable. If budgeted fixed factory overhead was $480,000, overhead was applied on the basis of 32,000 budgeted machine hours, and budgeted variable factory overhead was $170,000, what were the actual machine hours (AH) for the month?

A.   32,424

B.   32,000

C.   31,687

D.   31,576

The correct answer is (D). *(J.B. Romal)*
**REQUIRED:** The actual machine hours.
**DISCUSSION:** The volume variance (VV) arises from the difference between budgeted fixed factory overhead and the amount applied at the standard rate based on the standard input allowed for actual output. The overhead rate is $15 per machine hour ($480,000 ÷ 32,000).

$$VV = Budgeted - Applied$$
$$\$6,360 = \$480,000 - (\$15 \times AH)$$
$$\$15 \times AH = \$480,000 - \$6,360$$
$$AH = \$473,640 \div \$15$$
$$AH = 31,576$$

Answer (A) is incorrect because 32,424 assumes the variance is favorable. Answer (B) is incorrect because 32,000 is the amount of budgeted hours. Answer (C) is incorrect because 31,687 assumes budgeted fixed factory overhead is $650,000 ($480,000 + $170,000).

**93.** Selo Imports uses flexible budgeting for the control of costs. The company's annual master budget includes $324,000 for fixed production supervisory salaries at a volume of 180,000 units. Supervisory salaries are expected to be incurred uniformly through the year. During September, 15,750 units were produced and production supervisory salaries incurred were $28,000. A performance report for September should reflect a budget variance of

A.   $350 F.

B.   $350 U.

C.   $1,000 U.

D.   $1,000 F.

The correct answer is (C). *(CMA, adapted)*
**REQUIRED:** The budget variance given budgeted and actual fixed costs and sales.
**DISCUSSION:** The budget (spending) variance for fixed factory overhead equals actual minus budgeted amounts. The $324,000 cost of supervisory salaries is fixed and is incurred at a rate of $27,000 per month. Thus, the variance is the difference between actual costs of $28,000 and the budgeted costs of $27,000, or $1,000 unfavorable.

Answers (A) and (D) are incorrect because the variance is unfavorable. Answer (B) is incorrect because supervisor salaries are expected to be incurred uniformly through the year; thus, supervisor salaries are based on time, not units produced.

**94.** Universal Company uses a standard cost system and prepared the following budget at normal capacity for the month of January:

| | |
|---|---|
| Direct labor hours | 24,000 |
| Variable factory overhead | $48,000 |
| Fixed factory overhead | $108,000 |
| Total factory overhead per DLH | $6.50 |

Actual data for January were as follows:

| | |
|---|---|
| Direct labor hours worked | 22,000 |
| Total factory overhead | $147,000 |
| Standard DLH allowed for capacity attained | 21,000 |

Using the two-way analysis of overhead variances, what is the budget (controllable) variance for January?

A.   $3,000 favorable.

B.   $13,500 unfavorable.

C.   $9,000 favorable.

D.   $10,500 unfavorable.

The correct answer is (A). *(CPA, adapted)*
**REQUIRED:** The controllable (budget) variance.
**DISCUSSION:** In two-way analysis, the budget (controllable) variance is the total factory overhead variance not attributable to the volume variance. The total factory overhead variance equals the difference between actual total factory overhead and the factory overhead applied based on the standard input allowed for the actual output, or $10,500 unfavorable [$147,000 actual – ($6.50 x 21,000 DLH) applied]. The volume variance (budgeted fixed factory overhead – amount applied) is $13,500 unfavorable {($108,000 budgeted) – [($108,000 ÷ 24,000 DLH) x 21,000 DLH]}. Thus, the controllable variance must be $3,000 favorable ($13,500 unfavorable – $10,500 unfavorable).

Answer (B) is incorrect because the $13,500 unfavorable is the volume variance. Answer (C) is incorrect because $9,000 favorable equals the difference between total actual factory overhead and factory overhead budgeted at normal capacity. Answer (D) is incorrect because $10,500 unfavorable equals the total factory overhead variance.

**95.** The following information is available from the Tyro Company:

| | |
|---|---|
| Actual factory overhead | $15,000 |
| Fixed overhead expenses, actual | $7,200 |
| Fixed overhead expenses, budgeted | $7,000 |
| Actual hours | 3,500 |
| Standard hours | 3,800 |
| Variable overhead rate per DLH | $2.50 |

Assuming that Tyro uses a three-way analysis of overhead variances, what is the spending variance?

A. $750 favorable.

B. $750 unfavorable.

C. $950 favorable.

D. $200 unfavorable.

The correct answer is (A). *(CPA, adapted)*
**REQUIRED:** The spending variance assuming a three-way variance analysis.
**DISCUSSION:** The spending variance is the difference between the actual total factory overhead and the budgeted amount for the actual input.

| | |
|---|---|
| Budgeted $7,000 + (3,500 × $2.50) | $15,750 |
| Actual | (15,000) |
| | $ 750 F |

Answer (B) is incorrect because the spending variance is favorable. Answer (C) is incorrect because $950 favorable is based on actual fixed factory overhead. Answer (D) is incorrect because $200 unfavorable is the fixed factory overhead spending (budget) variance.

---

Questions 96 and 97 are based on the following information. Tiny Tykes Corporation had the following activity relating to its fixed and variable factory overhead for the month of July:

**Actual costs**

| | |
|---|---|
| Fixed overhead | $120,000 |
| Variable overhead | 80,000 |

**Flexible budget**
(Standard input allowed for actual output achieved × the budgeted rate)

| | |
|---|---|
| Variable overhead | 90,000 |

**Applied**
(Standard input allowed for actual output achieved × the budgeted rate)

| | |
|---|---|
| Fixed overhead | 125,000 |
| | |
| Variable overhead spending variance | 2,000 F |
| Production volume variance | 5,000 U |

**96.** If the budgeted rate for applying variable factory overhead was $20 per direct labor hour, how efficient or inefficient was Tiny Tykes Corporation in terms of using direct labor hours as an activity base?

A. 100 direct labor hours inefficient.

B. 100 direct labor hours efficient.

C. 400 direct labor hours inefficient.

D. 400 direct labor hours efficient.

The correct answer is (D). *(CMA, adapted)*
**REQUIRED:** The efficiency variance stated in terms of direct labor hours.
**DISCUSSION:** The variable factory overhead spending and efficiency variances are the components of the total variable factory overhead variance. Given that actual variable factory overhead was $80,000 and the flexible budget amount was $90,000, the total variance is $10,000 favorable. Given a variable factory overhead spending variance of $2,000 favorable, the efficiency variance must be $8,000 favorable ($10,000 total – $2,000 spending). At a rate of $20 per hour, this variance is equivalent to 400 direct labor hours ($8,000 ÷ $20).

Answers (A) and (C) are incorrect because the variances are favorable. Answer (B) is incorrect because 100 direct labor hours are equivalent to the spending variance ($20 x 100 hours = $2,000).

**97.** The fixed factory overhead efficiency variance is

A. $3,000 favorable.

B. $3,000 unfavorable.

C. $5,000 favorable.

D. Never a meaningful variance.

The correct answer is (D). *(CMA, adapted)*
**REQUIRED:** The fixed factory overhead efficiency variance.
**DISCUSSION:** Variable factory overhead variances can be divided into spending and efficiency components. However, fixed factory overhead variances do not have an efficiency component because fixed costs, by definition, are unaffected by changing levels of output within the relevant range. The total fixed factory overhead variance is typically divided into a budget (or fixed factory overhead spending) variance and a volume variance. The latter is a measure of capacity usage, not the efficiency with which inputs are employed.

Answers (A), (B), and (C) are incorrect because efficiency variances are applicable to variable costs.

Questions 98 through 102 are based on the following information. Nanjones Company manufactures a line of products distributed nationally through wholesalers. Presented below are planned manufacturing data for 1998 and actual data for November 1998. The company applies overhead based on planned machine hours using a predetermined annual rate.

| | 1998 Planning Data | | | Data for November 1998 |
|---|---|---|---|---|
| | Annual | November | | |
| Fixed factory overhead | $1,200,000 | $100,000 | Direct labor hours (actual) | 4,200 |
| Variable factory overhead | 2,400,000 | 220,000 | Direct labor hours (plan based on output) | 4,000 |
| Direct labor hours | 48,000 | 4,000 | Machine hours (actual) | 21,600 |
| Machine hours | 240,000 | 22,000 | Machine hours (plan based on output) | 21,000 |
| | | | Fixed factory overhead | $101,200 |
| | | | Variable factory overhead | $214,000 |

**98.** The predetermined factory overhead application rate for Nanjones Company for 1998 is

A. $5.00

B. $25.00

C. $50.00

D. $15.00

The correct answer is (D). *(CMA, adapted)*

**REQUIRED:** The predetermined factory overhead application rate.

**DISCUSSION:** The predetermined factory overhead application rate is $15 [($1,200,000 FOH + $2,400,000 VOH) ÷ 240,000 machine hours].

Answer (A) is incorrect because $5 is the fixed overhead application rate. Answer (B) is incorrect because $25 is the fixed overhead per labor hour. Answer (C) is incorrect because $50 is the variable overhead rate per labor hour.

**99.** The total amount of factory overhead applied to production for November 1998 was

A. $315,200

B. $315,000

C. $300,000

D. $324,000

The correct answer is (B). *(CMA, adapted)*

**REQUIRED:** The total factory overhead applied to production for the month.

**DISCUSSION:** Overhead is applied on the basis of planned machine hours. The predetermined overhead application rate is $15 [($1,200,000 FOH + $2,400,000 VOH) ÷ 240,000 machine hours]. Thus, total overhead applied was $315,000 ($15 x 21,000 planned machine hours based on output).

Answer (A) is incorrect because $315,200 is the actual overhead incurred. Answer (C) is incorrect because $300,000 is based on planned direct labor hours at $75 per hour. Answer (D) is incorrect because $324,000 is based on actual machine hours.

**100.** The amount of over- or underapplied variable factory overhead for November was

A. $6,000 overapplied.

B. $4,000 underapplied.

C. $20,000 overapplied.

D. $6,000 underapplied.

The correct answer is (B). *(CMA, adapted)*

**REQUIRED:** The amount of over- or underapplied variable factory overhead for the month.

**DISCUSSION:** Variable overhead applied in November was $210,000 [21,000 planned machine hours based on output x ($2,400,000 planned annual VOH ÷ 240,000 planned machine hours)]. Because the applied overhead was less than actual ($214,000), underapplied variable overhead equaled $4,000.

Answers (A) and (C) are incorrect because overhead was underapplied. Answer (D) is incorrect because $6,000 is based on the 22,000 hours planned for November rather than the planned hours for actual output.

**101.** The variable factory overhead spending variance for November 1998 was

    A.  $2,000 favorable.

    B.  $6,000 favorable.

    C.  $14,000 unfavorable.

    D.  $6,000 unfavorable.

The correct answer is (A). *(CMA, adapted)*
    **REQUIRED:** The variable factory overhead spending variance.
    **DISCUSSION:** The variable factory overhead spending variance equals the difference between actual variable factory overhead and the variable factory overhead based on actual activity. At a rate of $10 per machine hour ($2,400,000 ÷ 240,000 hours), the total variable factory overhead standard cost for the 21,600 actual hours was $216,000. Given actual costs of $214,000, the favorable variance is $2,000.
    Answer (B) is incorrect because $6,000 is based on planned machine hours of 22,000. Answers (C) and (D) are incorrect because the variance is favorable.

**102.** The fixed factory overhead volume variance for November 1998 was

    A.  $1,200 unfavorable.

    B.  $5,000 unfavorable.

    C.  $5,000 favorable.

    D.  $1,200 favorable.

The correct answer is (C). *(CMA, adapted)*
    **REQUIRED:** The fixed factory overhead volume variance.
    **DISCUSSION:** The fixed factory overhead volume (idle capacity) variance is the difference between budgeted fixed costs and the amount applied based on the standard input allowed for the actual output. Budgeted fixed costs for the month were $100,000. The standard fixed factory overhead applied was $105,000 [21,000 machine hours planned for actual output x ($1,200,000 planned annual FOH ÷ 240,000 planned annual machine hours) FOH application rate]. Hence, the volume variance was $5,000 favorable.
    Answers (A) and (B) are incorrect because the variance was favorable. Answer (D) is incorrect because $1,200 is the fixed factory overhead budget variance.

Questions 103 through 105 are based upon the following information. Patie Company uses a standard FIFO, process cost system to account for its only product, Mituea. Patie has found that direct machine hours (DMH) provide the best estimate of the application of overhead. Four (4) standard direct machine hours are allowed for each unit.

Using simple linear regression analysis in the form y = a + b(DMH), given that (a) equals fixed costs and (b) equals variable costs, Patie has developed the following overhead budget for a normal activity level of 100,000 direct machine hours:

| ITEM (y) | a | b |
|---|---|---|
| Supplies | | $ 0.50 |
| Indirect labor | $ 54,750 | 6.50 |
| Depreciation -- plant and equipment | 27,000 | |
| Property taxes and insurance | 32,300 | |
| Repairs and maintenance | 14,550 | 1.25 |
| Utilities | 3,400 | 4.75 |
| Total overhead | $132,000 | $13.00 |

**103.** What is the standard overhead rate?

A. $13.00 per DMH.

B. $11.68 per DMH.

C. $1.32 per DMH

D. $14.32 per DMH.

The correct answer is (D). *(L.J. McCarthy)*
**REQUIRED:** The standard overhead rate.
**DISCUSSION:** The total overhead equation is

$$y = \$132,000 + \$13(DMH)$$

This equation is derived by summing individual overhead items. The fixed portion needs to be converted to a rate by dividing it by normal capacity. Thus, the fixed overhead rate is $1.32 ($132,000 ÷ 100,000). To calculate the total overhead rate, the fixed rate is added to the variable rate. Hence, the total overhead rate per DMH is $14.32 ($1.32 + $13.00).

Answer (A) is incorrect because $13.00 is the variable overhead rate per machine hour. Answer (B) is incorrect because $11.68 equals $13 minus $1.32. Answer (C) is incorrect because $1.32 is the fixed overhead rate per machine hour.

**104.** If 23,500 equivalent units were produced during the year using 98,700 direct machine hours, how much overhead should be applied to production?

A. $1,413,384

B. $1,432,000

C. $1,346,080

D. $1,222,000

The correct answer is (C). *(L.J. McCarthy)*
**REQUIRED:** The standard overhead applied to production.
**DISCUSSION:** Overhead is applied using the standard activity allowed for actual production. The standard activity allowed is the standard activity per equivalent unit times the actual production, or 94,000 hours (4 DMH x 23,500). The overhead applied is $1,346,080 (94,000 x $14.32).

Answer (A) is incorrect because $1,413,384 is based on 98,700 actual DMF. Answer (B) is incorrect because $1,432,000 is for the original 100,000 DMH budgeted. Answer (D) is incorrect because fixed overhead costs should also be included.

**105.** Assuming actual fixed overhead incurred was $133,250 and actual variable overhead incurred was $1,225,000, what is the total overhead variance?

A. $12,170 unfavorable.

B. $12,170 favorable.

C. $55,134 unfavorable.

D. $55,134 favorable.

The correct answer is (A). *(L.J. McCarthy)*
**REQUIRED:** The total overhead variance for the year.
**DISCUSSION:** The total overhead variance is the difference between applied overhead and the actual overhead. In the previous question, the applied overhead was determined to be $1,346,080. The actual overhead is $1,358,250 ($133,250 + $1,225,000). Thus, the underapplied overhead is $12,170 U ($1,358,250 – $1,346,080).

Answers (B) and (D) are incorrect because the variance is unfavorable. Answer (C) is incorrect because $55,134 unfavorable is based on the actual DMH.

## 10.5 Sales

**106.** For a single-product company, the sales volume variance is

A. The difference between actual and master budget sales volume, times actual unit contribution margin.

B. The difference between flexible budget and actual sales volume, times master budget unit contribution margin.

C. The difference between flexible budget and master budget sales volume, times actual budget unit contribution margin.

D. The difference between flexible budget and master budget sales volume, times master budget unit contribution margin.

The correct answer is (D). *(CIA, adapted)*

**REQUIRED:** The definition of sales volume variance.

**DISCUSSION:** For a single-product company, the sales volume variance is the difference between the actual and budgeted sales quantities, times the budgeted UCM. If the company sells two or more products, the difference between the actual and budgeted product mixes must be considered. In that case, the sales volume variance equals the difference between (1) actual total unit sales times the budgeted weighted-average UCM for the actual mix and (2) budgeted total unit sales times the budgeted weighted-average UCM for the planned mix.

Answers (A) and (C) are incorrect because budgeted, not actual, UCM is used to calculate this variance. Answer (B) is incorrect because the flexible budget volume is the actual volume, resulting in a zero variance.

**107.** For a company that produces more than one product, the sales volume variance can be divided into which two of the following additional variances?

A. Sales price variance and flexible budget variance.

B. Sales mix variance and sales price variance.

C. Sales efficiency variance and sales price variance.

D. Sales quantity variance and sales mix variance.

The correct answer is (D). *(CMA, adapted)*

**REQUIRED:** The components of the sales volume variance.

**DISCUSSION:** The sales quantity variance is the change in contribution margin caused by the difference between actual and budgeted volume, assuming that budgeted sales mix, unit variable costs, and unit sales prices are constant. Thus, it equals the sales volume variance when the sales mix variance is zero. In a multiproduct case, a sales mix variance occurs when the sales mix differs from that budgeted. For example, an unfavorable sales mix variance can be caused by greater sales of a low-contribution product at the expense of lower sales of a high-contribution product.

Answers (A), (B), and (C) are incorrect because the sales price variance is a separate variance and is not a component of the sales volume variance.

**108.** The sales quantity variance equals

A. Actual units x (budgeted weighted-average UCM for planned mix – budgeted weighted-average UCM for actual mix).

B. (Actual units – master budget units) x budgeted weighted-average UCM for the planned mix.

C. Budgeted market share percentage x (actual market size in units – budgeted market size in units) x budgeted weighted-average UCM.

D. (Actual market share percentage – budgeted market share percentage) x actual market size in units x budgeted weighted-average UCM.

The correct answer is (B). *(Publisher)*

**REQUIRED:** The definition of the sales quantity variance.

**DISCUSSION:** The sales volume variance equals the difference between the flexible budget contribution margin for the actual volume and that included in the master budget. Its components are the sales quantity and sales mix variances. The sales quantity variance focuses on the firm's aggregate results. It assumes a constant product mix and an average contribution margin for the composite unit. It equals the difference between actual and budgeted total unit sales, times the budgeted weighted-average UCM for the planned mix.

Answer (A) is incorrect because this equation defines the sales mix variance. Answer (C) is incorrect because this equation defines the market size variance. Answer (D) is incorrect because this equation defines the market share variance.

**109.** The sales mix variance equals

A. Actual units x (budgeted weighted-average UCM for planned mix – budgeted weighted-average UCM for actual mix).

B. (Actual units – master budget units) x budgeted weighted-average UCM for the planned mix.

C. Budgeted market share percentage x (actual market size in units – budgeted market size in units) x budgeted weighted-average UCM.

D. (Actual market share percentage – budgeted market share percentage) x actual market size in units x budgeted weighted-average UCM.

The correct answer is (A). *(Publisher)*
**REQUIRED:** The definition of the sales mix variance.
**DISCUSSION:** The sales mix variance may be viewed as a sum of variances. For each product in the mix, the difference between actual units sold and its budgeted percentage of the actual total unit sales is multiplied by the budgeted UCM for the product. The results are added to determine the mix variance. An alternative is to multiply total actual units sold by the difference between the budgeted weighted-average UCM for the planned mix and that for the actual mix.

Answer (B) is incorrect because this equation defines the sales quantity variance. Answer (C) is incorrect because this equation defines the market size variance. Answer (D) is incorrect because this equation defines the market share variance.

**110.** The market size variance equals

A. Actual units x (budgeted weighted-average UCM for planned mix – budgeted weighted-average UCM for actual mix).

B. (Actual units – master budget units) x budgeted weighted-average UCM for the planned mix.

C. Budgeted market share percentage x (actual market size in units – budgeted market size in units) x budgeted weighted-average UCM.

D. (Actual market share percentage – budgeted market share percentage) x actual market size in units x budgeted weighted-average UCM.

The correct answer is (C). *(Publisher)*
**REQUIRED:** The definition of the market size variance.
**DISCUSSION:** The components of the sales quantity variance are the market size variance and the market share variance. The market size variance gives an indication of the change in contribution margin caused by a change in the market size. The market size and market share variances are relevant to industries in which total level of sales and market share are known, e.g., the automobile industry. The market size variance measures the effect of changes in an industry's sales on an individual company, and the market share variance analyzes the impact of a change in market share.

Answer (A) is incorrect because this equation defines the sales mix variance. Answer (B) is incorrect because this equation defines the sales quantity variance. Answer (D) is incorrect because this equation defines the market share variance.

**111.** In the budgeted profit-volume chart below, EG represents a two-product company's profit path. EH and HG represent the profit paths of products #1 and #2, respectively.

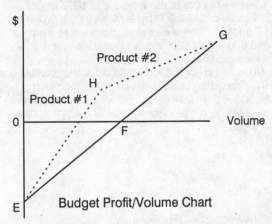

Budget Profit/Volume Chart

Sales prices and cost behavior were as budgeted, actual total sales equaled budgeted sales, and there were no inventories. Actual profit was greater than budgeted profit. Which product had actual sales in excess of budget, and what margin does OE divided by OF represent?

| Product with Excess Sales | OE ÷ OF |
|---|---|
| A. #1 | Contribution margin |
| B. #1 | Gross margin |
| C. #2 | Contribution margin |
| D. #2 | Gross margin |

**112.** The market share variance equals

A. Actual units x (budgeted weighted-average UCM for planned mix – budgeted weighted-average UCM for actual mix).

B. (Actual units – master budget units) x budgeted weighted-average UCM for the planned mix.

C. Budgeted market share percentage x (actual market size in units – budgeted market size in units) x budgeted weighted-average UCM.

D. (Actual market share percentage – budgeted market share percentage) x actual market size in units x budgeted weighted-average UCM.

The correct answer is (A). *(CPA, adapted)*
  **REQUIRED:** The product with actual sales over budget and the significance of OE divided by OF.
  **DISCUSSION:** Sales prices and total unit sales volume were as budgeted, costs expected to be fixed or variable behaved as anticipated, and no inventories existed. Thus, the excess of actual over budgeted profit must be attributable to a favorable sales mix, that is, to selling more units of the product with the higher UCM and fewer units of the product with the lower UCM. The profit path of product #1 has a steeper slope (contribution per unit of volume) than that for product #2. Consequently, product #1 had a higher UCM than product #2. Because a favorable sales mix variance arises from selling more of the product with the higher UCM, given that total unit sales equaled the budgeted amount, the sales of product #1 must have exceeded the budget.
  Given that EG is the company's profit path, OE must represent the loss at zero sales volume. No variable costs are incurred at this volume, so OE must equal total fixed costs. OF is the unit sales volume at which no profit is earned or loss incurred (the breakeven point). At the breakeven point, the total contribution margin [(unit price – unit variable cost) x unit sales] equals the fixed costs. Accordingly, OE (fixed costs) divided by OF (unit sales) must equal the UCM.
  Answer (B) is incorrect because OE divided by OF is the UCM. Answer (C) is incorrect because product #1 had actual sales in excess of the budget. Answer (D) is incorrect because OE divided by OF is the UCM, and product #1 had actual sales in excess of the budget.

The correct answer is (D). *(Publisher)*
  **REQUIRED:** The definition of the market share variance.
  **DISCUSSION:** The market share variance gives an indication of the amount of contribution margin gained (forgone) because of a change in the market share.
  Answer (A) is incorrect because this equation defines the sales mix variance. Answer (B) is incorrect because this equation defines the sales quantity variance. Answer (C) is incorrect because this equation defines the market size variance.

**113.** The gross profit of Reade Company for each of the years ended December 31, 1998 and 1997 was as follows:

|  | 1998 | 1997 |
|---|---|---|
| Sales | $792,000 | $800,000 |
| Cost of goods sold | (464,000) | (480,000) |
| Gross profit | $328,000 | $320,000 |

Assuming that 1998 selling prices were 10% lower, what was the decrease in gross profit caused by the change in selling prices?

A. $8,000

B. $72,000

C. $79,200

D. $88,000

The correct answer is (D). *(CPA, adapted)*
**REQUIRED:** The change in gross profit given a reduction in selling price.
**DISCUSSION:** With a 10% decrease in prices in 1998, that year's sales were 90% of the amount at 1997 prices. Dividing 1998 sales of $792,000 by 90% gives $880,000 of sales at 1997 prices. Thus, sales and gross profit were $88,000 ($880,000 – $792,000) lower because of the 10% decrease in selling price.
Answer (A) is incorrect because $8,000 is the decrease in sales from the preceding year. Answer (B) is incorrect because $72,000 is the 1997 sales multiplied by 90% and then by 10%. Answer (C) is incorrect because $79,200 is 10% of 1998 sales.

**114.** Teezer Co. bundles three of its software products into a package that sells for $540. The following are the stand-alone unit selling prices and manufacturing costs and the rankings for incremental allocation purposes of the three products in the package:

|  | Price | Cost | Ranking for Incremental Allocation |
|---|---|---|---|
| Item A | $360 | $60 | 1 |
| Item B | $240 | $48 | 2 |
| Item C | $120 | $24 | 3 |

What is the difference between the unit revenue allocated to Item B using the incremental method and the amount allocated using the stand-alone method based on unit selling prices?

A. $270

B. $180

C. $90

D. $0

The correct answer is (D). *(Publisher)*
**REQUIRED:** The difference between the unit revenue allocated to Item B using the incremental method and the amount allocated using the stand-alone method based on unit selling prices.
**DISCUSSION:** Given that Item B is second in the revenue-allocation sequence, it will receive $180 ($540 unit price of the package – $360 unit price of the primary product) under the incremental method. It will also receive $180 {[[$240 unit price of B ÷ ($360 + $240 + $120)] × $540} under the stand-alone method based on unit selling prices. Thus, the difference is $0 ($180 – $180).
Answer (A) is incorrect because $270 is the amount allocated to A under the stand-alone method. Answer (B) is incorrect because $180 is the amount allocated to B under either method. Answer (C) is incorrect because $90 is the amount allocated to C under the stand-alone method. It is also the difference between the amounts allocated to C under the two methods. The incremental allocation to C is $0.

**115.** Actual and budgeted information about the sales of a product are presented below for June:

|  | Actual | Budget |
|---|---|---|
| Units | 8,000 | 10,000 |
| Sales revenue | $92,000 | $105,000 |

The sales price variance for June was

A. $8,000 favorable.

B. $10,000 favorable.

C. $10,000 unfavorable.

D. $10,500 unfavorable.

The correct answer is (A). *(CIA, adapted)*
**REQUIRED:** The sales price variance for the month.
**DISCUSSION:** The sales price variance is the difference between actual price and budgeted price, times actual units. Actual price was $11.50 ($92,000 ÷ 8,000). Budgeted price was $10.50 ($105,000 ÷ 10,000). Sales price variance is therefore $8,000 [($11.50 – $10.50) x 8,000 actual units]. The variance is favorable because actual sales price was greater than budgeted sales price.
Answers (B) and (C) are incorrect because $10,000 is based on the budgeted sales. Answer (D) is incorrect because $10,500 is 10% of budgeted revenue.

**116.** The exhibit below reflects a summary of performance for a single item of a retail store's inventory for the month ended April 30, 1998.

| | Actual Results | Flexible Budget Variances | Flexible Budget | Static (Master) Budget |
|---|---|---|---|---|
| Sales (units) | 11,000 | -- | 11,000 | 12,000 |
| Revenue (sales) | $208,000 | $12,000 U | $220,000 | $240,000 |
| Variable costs | 121,000 | 11,000 U | 110,000 | 120,000 |
| Contribution margin | $ 87,000 | $23,000 U | $110,000 | $120,000 |
| Fixed costs | 72,000 | -- | 72,000 | 72,000 |
| Operating income | $ 15,000 | $23,000 U | $ 38,000 | $ 48,000 |

The sales volume variance is

A. $10,000 F.

B. $10,000 U.

C. $11,000 F.

D. $12,000 U.

The correct answer is (B). *(CIA, adapted)*
**REQUIRED:** The sales-volume variance.
**DISCUSSION:** The sales-volume variance for a single-product firm is the difference between the flexible-budget contribution margin and the static (master) budget contribution margin. The contribution margin is used rather than operating income because fixed costs are the same in both budgets. Unit sales price and variable cost are held constant so as to isolate the effect of the difference in unit sales volume. Because the flexible budget contribution margin ($110,000) is less than the master budget amount ($120,000), the variance ($10,000) is unfavorable.
Answer (A) is incorrect because the variance is unfavorable. Answer (C) is incorrect because $11,000 is the difference between actual and flexible budget variable costs. Answer (D) is incorrect because $12,000 is the difference between the flexible budget revenue ($220,000) and the actual revenue ($208,000).

Questions 117 through 121 are based on the following information. Folsom Fashions sells a line of women's dresses. Folsom's performance report for November is shown below and to the right.

The company uses a flexible budget to analyze its performance and to measure the effect on operating income of the various factors affecting the difference between budgeted and actual operating income.

| | Actual | Budget |
|---|---|---|
| Dresses sold | 5,000 | 6,000 |
| Sales | $ 235,000 | $ 300,000 |
| Variable costs | (145,000) | (180,000) |
| Contribution margin | $ 90,000 | $ 120,000 |
| Fixed costs | (84,000) | (80,000) |
| Operating income | $ 6,000 | $ 40,000 |

**117.** The effect of the sales quantity variance on the contribution margin for November is

A. $30,000 unfavorable.

B. $18,000 unfavorable.

C. $20,000 unfavorable.

D. $15,000 unfavorable.

The correct answer is (C). *(CMA, adapted)*
**REQUIRED:** The effect of the sales quantity variance on the contribution margin.
**DISCUSSION:** The sales quantity variance is the difference between the actual and budgeted units, times the budgeted UCM.

$$(5,000 - 6,000) \times \frac{\$120,000}{6,000} = \$20,000 \ U$$

Answer (A) is incorrect because $30,000 is the difference between the actual and budgeted contribution margins. Answer (B) is incorrect because $18,000 equals the difference between actual and budgeted unit sales times the actual UCM. Answer (D) is incorrect because $15,000 is the sales price variance.

Refer to the information preceding question 117 on page 363.

**118.** The sales price variance for November is

A. $30,000 unfavorable.

B. $18,000 unfavorable.

C. $20,000 unfavorable.

D. $15,000 unfavorable.

The correct answer is (D). *(CMA, adapted)*

**REQUIRED:** The amount of the sales price variance for the month.

**DISCUSSION:** The sales price variance is the actual number of units sold (5,000), times the difference between budgeted selling price ($300,000 ÷ 6,000) and actual selling price ($235,000 ÷ 5,000).

$$(\$50 - \$47) \times 5,000 = \$15,000 \ U$$

Answer (A) is incorrect because $30,000 is the difference between the actual and budgeted contribution margins. Answer (B) is incorrect because $18,000 equals the difference between actual and budgeted unit sales times the actual UCM. Answer (C) is incorrect because $20,000 is the sales quantity variance.

**119.** The variable cost flexible budget variance for November is

A. $5,000 favorable.

B. $5,000 unfavorable.

C. $4,000 favorable.

D. $4,000 unfavorable.

The correct answer is (A). *(CMA, adapted)*

**REQUIRED:** The variable cost flexible budget variance.

**DISCUSSION:** The variable cost flexible budget variance is equal to the difference between actual variable costs and the product of the actual quantity sold and the budgeted unit variable cost ($180,000 ÷ 6,000 = $30).

$$(\$30 \times 5,000) - \$145,000 = \$5,000 \ F$$

Answer (B) is incorrect because the variance is favorable. Answers (C) and (D) are incorrect because $4,000 is the amount of the fixed cost variance.

**120.** The fixed cost variance for November is

A. $5,000 favorable.

B. $5,000 unfavorable.

C. $4,000 favorable.

D. $4,000 unfavorable.

The correct answer is (D). *(CMA, adapted)*

**REQUIRED:** The fixed cost variance for the month.

**DISCUSSION:** The fixed cost variance equals the difference between actual fixed costs and budgeted fixed costs.

$$\$84,000 - \$80,000 = \$4,000 \ U$$

Answers (A) and (B) are incorrect because $5,000 is the variable cost variance. Answer (C) is incorrect because the variance is unfavorable.

**121.** What additional information is needed for Folsom to calculate the dollar impact of a change in market share on operating income for November?

A. Folsom's budgeted market share and the budgeted total market size.

B. Folsom's budgeted market share, the budgeted total market size, and average market selling price.

C. Folsom's budgeted market share and the actual total market size.

D. Folsom's actual market share and the actual total market size.

The correct answer is (C). *(CMA, adapted)*

**REQUIRED:** The additional information necessary for a market share variance calculation.

**DISCUSSION:** A change in market share reflects a change in relative competitiveness. To isolate the effect on operating income of an increase or a decrease in market share, the company must know its budgeted and actual market shares, the actual size of the market for November, and the budgeted weighted-average unit contribution margin. Such computations may help Folsom to determine whether its decline in sales resulted from a loss of competitiveness or a shrinkage of the market.

Answers (A) and (B) are incorrect because Folsom will need to know the actual total market size. Answer (D) is incorrect because Folsom will need to know the budgeted market share.

| | Actuals | Static Budget |
|---|---|---|
| Unit sales | 12,000 | 10,000 |
| Sales | $132,000 | $100,000 |
| Variable costs of sales | 70,800 | 60,000 |
| Contribution margin | 61,200 | 40,000 |
| Fixed costs | 32,000 | 30,000 |
| Operating income | $ 29,200 | $ 10,000 |

Questions 122 and 123 are based on the following information. Clear Plus, Inc. manufactures and sells boxes of pocket protectors. The static master budget and the actual results for May 1998 appear in the opposite column.

**122.** The operating income for Clear Plus, Inc. using a flexible budget for May 1998 is

A. $12,000

B. $19,200

C. $30,000

D. $18,000

The correct answer is (D). *(CMA, adapted)*

**REQUIRED:** The flexible-budget operating income.

**DISCUSSION:** A flexible budget is formulated for several different activity levels. Assuming that unit sales price ($100,000 ÷ 10,000 units = $10), variable costs of sales ($60,000 ÷ 10,000 units = $6), and total fixed costs ($30,000) do not change, a flexible budget may be prepared for the actual sales level (12,000 units). Hence, the budgeted contribution margin (sales – variable costs of sales) equals $48,000 [(12,000 units × $10) – (12,000 units × $6)]. The operating income is therefore $18,000 ($48,000 CM – $30,000 FC).

Answer (A) is incorrect because $12,000 assumes that all costs are variable. Answer (B) is incorrect because $19,200 is based on actual variable costs. Answer (C) is incorrect because $30,000 is based on actual sales revenues.

**123.** Which one of the following statements concerning Clear Plus, Inc.'s actual results for May 1998 is correct?

A. The flexible budget variance is $8,000 favorable.

B. The sales price variance is $32,000 favorable.

C. The sales volume variance is $8,000 favorable.

D. The fixed cost flexible budget variance is $4,000 favorable.

The correct answer is (C). *(CMA, adapted)*

**REQUIRED:** The true statement about the actual results.

**DISCUSSION:** The sales volume variance is the change in contribution margin caused by the difference between the actual and budgeted unit volume. It equals the budgeted unit contribution margin times the difference between actual and expected volume, or $8,000 [($10 – $6) × (12,000 – 10,000)]. The sales volume variance is favorable because actual sales exceeded budgeted sales.

Answer (A) is incorrect because the flexible budget variance for actual results is $11,200 favorable ($29,200 actual operating income – $18,000 flexible budget operating income). Answer (B) is incorrect because the sales price variance is $12,000 [$132,000 actual sales – ($10 × 12,000 units sold)]. Answer (D) is incorrect because the fixed cost budget variance is $2,000 unfavorable ($32,000 actual – $30,000 budgeted).

Questions 124 through 126 are based on the following information. The following are the relevant data for calculating sales variances for Fortuna Co., which sells its sole product in two countries:

|  | Gallia | Helvetica | Total |
|---|---|---|---|
| Budgeted selling price per unit | $6.00 | $10.00 | NA |
| Budgeted variable cost per unit | 3.00 | 7.50 | NA |
| Budgeted contribution margin per unit | $3.00 | $ 2.50 | NA |
| Budgeted unit sales | 300 | 200 | 500 |
| Budgeted mix percentage | 60% | 40% | 100% |
| Actual units sold | 260 | 260 | 520 |
| Actual selling price per unit | $6.00 | $ 9.50 | NA |

**124.** The sales volume variance for the two countries is

A. $130 U.

B. $120 U.

C. $30 F.

D. $150 F.

The correct answer is (C). *(Publisher)*

**REQUIRED:** The sales volume variance for sales in multiple countries.

**DISCUSSION:** The sales volume variance for Gallia is $120 U [$3.00 budgeted UCM x (260 actual units sold – 300 budgeted unit sales)]. The sales volume variance for Helvetica is $150 F [$2.50 budgeted UCM x (260 actual units sold – 200 budgeted unit sales)]. Thus, the multiple-country sales volume variance is $30 F ($150 F – $120 U).

Answer (A) is incorrect because $130 U is the multiple-country sales price variance. Answer (B) is incorrect because $120 U is the sales volume variance for sales in multiple countries for Gallia. Answer (D) is incorrect because $150 F is the sales volume variance for sales in multiple countries for Helvetica.

**125.** The sales quantity variance for the two countries is

A. $156 U.

B. $30 F.

C. $56 F.

D. $100 F.

The correct answer is (C). *(Publisher)*

**REQUIRED:** The sales quantity variance for sales in multiple countries.

**DISCUSSION:** The sales quantity variance for Gallia is $36 F {[(520 actual total units sold × .6 budgeted percentage) – 300 budgeted unit sales] × $3 budgeted UCM}. The sales quantity variance for Helvetica is $20 F {[(520 actual total units sold × .4 budgeted percentage) – 200 budgeted unit sales] × $2.50 budgeted UCM}. Thus, the multiple-country sales quantity variance is $56 F ($36 F + $20 F).

Answer (A) is incorrect because $156 U is the sales mix variance for Gallia. Answer (B) is incorrect because $30 F is the multiple-country sales volume variance. Answer (D) is incorrect because $100 F is the combined sales price and sales volume variance.

**126.** The sales mix variance for the two countries is

A. $156 U.

B. $26 U.

C. $56 F.

D. $150 F.

The correct answer is (B). *(Publisher)*

**REQUIRED:** The sales mix variance for sales in multiple countries.

**DISCUSSION:** The sales mix variance for Gallia is $156 U {[260 actual units sold – (520 actual total units sold × .6 budgeted percentage)] × $3 budgeted UCM}. The sales mix variance for Helvetica is $130 F {[260 actual units sold – (520 actual total units sold × .4 budgeted percentage)] × $2.50 budgeted UCM}. Thus, the multiple-country sales mix variance is $26 U ($156 U – $130 F).

Answer (A) is incorrect because $156 U is the sales mix variance for Gallia. Answer (C) is incorrect because $56 F is the multiple-country sales quantity variance. Answer (D) is incorrect because $150 F is the sales volume variance for Helvetica.

## 10.6 Variances in the Ledger Accounts

**127.** Company Z uses a standard cost system that carries materials at actual price until they are transferred to the WIP account. In project A, 500 units of X were used at a cost of $10 per unit. Standards require 450 units to complete this project. The standard price is established at $9 per unit. What is the proper journal entry?

A.
| | | |
|---|---|---|
| Work-in-process | $4,950 | |
| DM price variance | 500 | |
|   DM quantity variance | | $ 450 |
|   Inventory | | 5,000 |

B.
| | | |
|---|---|---|
| Work-in-process | $5,950 | |
| DM price variance | | $ 500 |
| DM quantity variance | | 450 |
| Inventory | | 5,000 |

C.
| | | |
|---|---|---|
| Work-in-process | $4,050 | |
| DM price variance | 500 | |
| DM quantity variance | 450 | |
|   Inventory | | $5,000 |

D.
| | | |
|---|---|---|
| Work-in-process | $5,000 | |
|   Inventory | | $5,000 |

The correct answer is (C). *(Publisher)*

**REQUIRED:** The journal entry to record direct materials issued and related variances.

**DISCUSSION:** The entry to record direct materials used is to debit WIP at standard prices and standard quantities (450 units x $9 = $4,050). In this question, all direct materials variances are recorded at the time WIP is charged. The materials price variance and the materials quantity variance must be calculated. The project used more units at a higher price than estimated, so both variances will be unfavorable (debits). The materials quantity variance is $450 U [(500 – 450) x $9]. The materials price variance is $500 U [500 units x ($10 – $9)]. Inventory is credited for the actual prices and actual quantities (500 x $10 = $5,000).

Answer (A) is incorrect because the unfavorable DM quantity variance should be a debit. Answer (B) is incorrect because the unfavorable DM price and quantity variances should be debits. Answer (D) is incorrect because this entry fails to record the variances.

**128.** If a project required 50 hours to complete at a cost of $10 per hour but should have taken only 45 hours at a cost of $12 per hour, what is the proper entry to record the costs?

A.
| | | |
|---|---|---|
| Work-in-process | $540 | |
| DL efficiency variance | 60 | |
|   DL price variance | | $100 |
|   Accrued payroll | | 500 |

B.
| | | |
|---|---|---|
| Wage expense | $440 | |
| DL efficiency variance | 60 | |
|   Accrued payroll | | $500 |

C.
| | | |
|---|---|---|
| Work-in-process | $460 | |
| DL price variance | 100 | |
|   DL efficiency variance | | $ 60 |
|   Accrued payroll | | 500 |

D.
| | | |
|---|---|---|
| Work-in-process | $500 | |
|   Accrued payroll | | $500 |

The correct answer is (A). *(Publisher)*

**REQUIRED:** The journal entry to record accrued payroll and labor cost variances.

**DISCUSSION:** The entry to record accrued payroll is to charge WIP at the standard wage rate times the standard number of hours and to credit accrued payroll for the actual payroll dollar amount. The project required more hours but a lower wage rate than estimated. Hence, the labor efficiency variance will be unfavorable (a debit); the labor price variance will be favorable (a credit).

Labor eff. var. $(50 - 45) \times \$12 = \$60\ U$
Labor price var. $(\$12 - \$10) \times 50 = \$100\ F$

Answer (B) is incorrect because this entry omits the price variance and fails to inventory the labor costs. Answer (C) is incorrect because this entry would be the proper entry if the hourly rate were greater than estimated, but hours worked were less. Answer (D) is incorrect because the labor variances must be recognized.

**129.** Assume price variances are recorded at the time of purchase. What is the journal entry to record a direct materials price variance if materials are purchased at $5 per unit for $650 and their standard price is $4 per unit?

A.
| | | |
|---|---|---|
| Inventory | $650 | |
|   Accounts payable | | $650 |

B.
| | | |
|---|---|---|
| Inventory | $520 | |
| DM price variance | 130 | |
|   Accounts payable | | $650 |

C.
| | | |
|---|---|---|
| Inventory | $520 | |
| Work-in-process | 130 | |
|   Cash | | $650 |

D.
| | | |
|---|---|---|
| Finished goods | $520 | |
| DM price variance | 130 | |
|   Cash | | $650 |

The correct answer is (B). *(Publisher)*

**REQUIRED:** The journal entry to record a direct materials price variance at the time of purchase.

**DISCUSSION:** The entry at the time of purchase is to charge inventory for $520, which is the actual quantity purchased ($650 ÷ $5 per unit = 130 units) times the standard unit price ($4). Accounts payable is credited for $650 (actual quantity x actual price). The difference between the actual and standard prices is the price variance. Because the actual price exceeded the standard, the price variance is debited for the difference. The price variance is $130 [130 units x ($5 – $4)] unfavorable.

Answer (A) is incorrect because this entry assumes the price variance is not recorded at time of purchase. Answer (C) is incorrect because the variance should be charged to a separate account, not WIP. Answer (D) is incorrect because materials should be debited to inventory.

**130.** What is the journal entry if all materials purchased in the previous question were used to complete a project that should normally require 100 units?

A.  
| Work-in-process | $650 | |
| DM price variance | | $130 |
| Inventory | | 520 |

B.  
| Work-in-process | $520 | |
| DM price variance | 130 | |
| Inventory | | $650 |

C.  
| DM quantity variance | $130 | |
| Work-in-process | 520 | |
| Inventory | | $650 |

D.  
| Work-in-process | $400 | |
| DM quantity variance | 120 | |
| Inventory | | $520 |

The correct answer is (D). *(Publisher)*

**REQUIRED:** The journal entry to record the direct materials used.

**DISCUSSION:** The entry to record direct materials used is to charge WIP for the standard quantity requisitioned times the standard unit price (100 units x $4/unit = $400). Inventory will be credited for the actual quantity requisitioned times the standard unit price, or $520 (130 x $4). When actual quantity used exceeds standard quantity allowed, an unfavorable direct materials quantity variance results. The variance account should be charged (debited) for the $120 difference (30 extra units x $4 standard unit cost).

Answer (A) is incorrect because a quantity (not price) variance should be debited (not credited). Answer (B) is incorrect because this entry records an unfavorable price, not quantity, variance. Answer (C) is incorrect because this entry confuses the amounts of the price and quantity variances.

**131.** Alpha Company paid janitors $5 per hour to clean the production area. What is the proper journal entry to account for this expense for the month of June if 530 hours were worked by the janitors?

A.  
| Salaries expense | $2,650 | |
| Payroll | | $2,650 |

B.  
| Variable overhead control | $2,650 | |
| Variable overhead applied | | $2,650 |

C.  
| Variable overhead control | $2,650 | |
| Payroll payable | | $2,650 |

D.  
| Variable overhead applied | $2,650 | |
| Payroll payable | | $2,650 |

The correct answer is (C). *(Publisher)*

**REQUIRED:** The journal entry to record the actual variable overhead incurred.

**DISCUSSION:** The entry to record actual variable overhead incurred ($5 x 530 hours = $2,650) is to charge the variable overhead control account. A corresponding credit is made to accounts payable or any other appropriate account.

Answer (A) is incorrect because actual indirect production costs are debited to overhead control. Answer (B) is incorrect because overhead application is usually based on standard rates and a given activity base, not amounts actually incurred. Overhead is applied by crediting overhead control (or a separate applied overhead account) and debiting WIP. Answer (D) is incorrect because variable overhead is debited to variable overhead control, not variable overhead applied.

**132.** Alpha Company (see question 131) initially set its standard cost of janitorial work at $4.50 per hour. What is the appropriate entry to record the application of the 530 hours worked by the janitors?

A.  
| Work-in-process | $2,385 | |
| Variable overhead applied | | $2,385 |

B.  
| Work-in-process | $2,385 | |
| Variable overhead control | | $2,385 |

C.  
| Variable overhead control | $ 265 | |
| Work-in-process | 2,385 | |
| Variable overhead applied | | $2,650 |

D.  
| Cost of goods sold | $2,385 | |
| Variable overhead applied | | $2,385 |

The correct answer is (A). *(Publisher)*

**REQUIRED:** The journal entry to record the application of variable overhead.

**DISCUSSION:** The entry to record the application of variable overhead is to charge the WIP account and enter a corresponding credit to the variable overhead applied account for the amount of overhead computed using the predetermined overhead rate (530 x $4.50 = $2,385).

Answer (B) is incorrect because overhead control is debited for overhead incurred. Answer (C) is incorrect because the overhead application is at $4.50, not $5.00, per hour. Answer (D) is incorrect because the goods to which these costs apply are in process.

**133.** Using the information in questions 131 and 132, what entry accounts for the recognition of the variance that occurred? Assume that this was the only variable overhead variance.

A.  Variable overhead applied   $2,650
     Variance summary         $ 265
     Variable overhead control     2,385

B.  Variable overhead applied   $2,385
     Variable overhead spending
      variance          265
      Variable overhead control    $2,650

C.  Variable overhead applied   $2,385
     Variable overhead efficiency
      variance          265
      Variable overhead control    $2,650

D.  Variable overhead control   $2,385
     Variable spending variance   265
      Variable overhead applied    $2,650

The correct answer is (B). *(Publisher)*
**REQUIRED:** The journal entry to record the isolation of the variance.
**DISCUSSION:** The spending variance is recognized by a debit, given that more was spent for that activity than was estimated. The entry to record the unfavorable variable overhead spending variance is to charge the variable overhead spending variance account for the appropriate amount. The variable overhead applied account is charged for its balance. The variable overhead control account is credited for its balance. These entries will result in a zero balance in both the applied and the control accounts assuming that no variable overhead efficiency variance existed.

Answer (A) is incorrect because the variance is a debit to a spending variance account, not a credit to a variance summary. Answer (C) is incorrect because the variance is a spending variance resulting from the excess of an actual cost over a standard cost, not an efficiency variance. Answer (D) is incorrect because variable overhead applied is debited and variable overhead control is credited to close out the accounts.

**134.** To adjust finished goods inventory for external reporting purposes to reflect the difference between direct costing and absorption costing, which of the following journal entries may be made?

A.  Finished goods inventory
     adjustment account     XXX
      Fixed overhead           XXX

B.  Work-in-process       XXX
      Fixed overhead           XXX

C.  Fixed overhead         XXX
      Work-in-process         XXX

D.  Finished goods         XXX
      Work-in-process         XXX

The correct answer is (A). *(Publisher)*
**REQUIRED:** The entry to adjust finished goods inventory for external reporting purposes.
**DISCUSSION:** The journal entry to record the adjustment of FG inventory for external reporting purposes is to charge the FG inventory adjustment account for the desired amount and to credit fixed overhead. To avoid alteration of the inventory accounts, the adjustment is taken to an adjustment account.

Answer (B) is incorrect because this entry is an adjustment to WIP. Answer (C) is incorrect because costs are not transferred from WIP to overhead. Answer (D) is incorrect because this entry represents the transfer of completed units to FG.

**135.** Given a favorable variable overhead efficiency variance of $1,600 and an unfavorable spending variance of $265, what is the closing entry?

A.  Income summary     $1,335
     VOH spending variance   265
      VOH efficiency variance    $1,600

B.  Variance summary     $1,865
      Cost of goods sold       $1,865

C.  VOH efficiency variance   $1,600
      VOH spending variance    $ 265
      Income summary        1,335

D.  VOH efficiency variance   $1,600
     VOH spending variance   265
      Income summary       $1,865

The correct answer is (C). *(Publisher)*
**REQUIRED:** The journal entry to close an unfavorable variable overhead spending variance and a favorable variable overhead efficiency variance.
**DISCUSSION:** The entry to record the closing of an unfavorable variable overhead spending variance and a favorable variable overhead efficiency variance is to charge the latter and credit the former. A favorable net variance of $1,335 is the result ($1,600 F – $265 U = $1,335 F). The net favorable variance is credited to income summary (or allocated among CGS and the inventories).

Answer (A) is incorrect because the net variance is favorable and should be credited to income summary. Answer (B) is incorrect because this entry does not close the variance accounts. Moreover, the net variance is $1,335. Answer (D) is incorrect because the spending variance is unfavorable and was initially debited. Closing the account therefore requires a credit.

**136.** Omega Company would have applied $31,500 of fixed factory overhead if capacity usage had equaled the master budget. Given that 2,000 standard hours were allowed for the actual output, that actual fixed factory overhead equaled the budgeted amount, and that overhead was applied at a rate of $15 per hour, what is the entry to close the fixed factory overhead accounts?

A.  Fixed overhead control          $30,000
    Production volume
        variance                          1,500
            Fixed overhead applied                    $31,500

B.  Cost of goods sold              $31,500
            Fixed overhead control                    $31,500

C.  Work-in-process                 $30,000
    overhead price variance           1,500
            Fixed overhead applied                    $31,500

D.  Fixed overhead applied          $30,000
    Production volume
        variance                          1,500
            Fixed overhead control                    $31,500

The correct answer is (D). *(Publisher)*
   **REQUIRED:** The year-end journal entry to close the fixed overhead accounts.
   **DISCUSSION:** The entry is to debit fixed overhead applied and credit fixed overhead control for their respective balances. The difference is attributable solely to the production volume variance because the budget (spending) variance is zero (actual fixed factory overhead = the budgeted amount). The volume variance is unfavorable because fixed overhead is underapplied. The underapplication (the unfavorable volume variance debited) is $1,500 [$31,500 budgeted fixed factory overhead – (2,000 hours x $15 per hour)].
   Answer (A) is incorrect because the normal balances in the overhead applied and overhead control accounts are a credit and a debit, respectively. Hence, the closing entries must be the reverse. Answer (B) is incorrect because the fixed overhead applied account must be closed with a debit entry. Answer (C) is incorrect because this entry does not close the overhead accounts.

# CHAPTER ELEVEN
# RESPONSIBILITY ACCOUNTING,
# PERFORMANCE MEASUREMENT,
# AND TRANSFER PRICING

A **responsibility accounting system** is a managerial control device that assigns revenues, costs, and invested capital to responsibility centers. It requires development of approved plans, such as budgets, and the assignment of responsibility to particular managers for the execution of particular plans. It also requires measurement of results achieved by those managers and a comparison of the results with the plans. Furthermore, it must be consistent with the **organizational structure**, in particular with the organization's degree of **centralization** or **decentralization**. Centralization concerns the concentration of authority in an organization and the degree and levels at which it occurs. Careful selection of which decisions to push down the hierarchy and which to hold at the top is required. The degree of decentralization will be greater if more decisions are made lower in the management hierarchy, some important decisions are made lower in the management hierarchy, more functions are affected by decisions made at lower levels, and fewer approvals are required before implementation of a decision. However, centralization and decentralization are relative terms. Absolute centralization or decentralization is impossible. The degree to which either is used depends upon the situation. Decisions critical to the organization cannot be decentralized to lower levels, and decisions should not be made by those who do not have necessary information, such as knowledge of job objectives or measures for evaluation of job performance. Decisions also cannot be decentralized to people who do not have training, experience, or the ability to make decisions. Furthermore, the organization cannot decentralize below the level at which coordination must be maintained. Nevertheless, providing subunit managers with significant autonomy may result in greater awareness of the needs of important constituencies (e.g., customers, suppliers, and employees), faster decisions, more rapid management development, greater management initiative, improved morale, and a narrower and therefore sharper management focus.

The costs and benefits of decentralization arise largely from **information asymmetry** (a subunit manager's greater knowledge of his/her job). If this asymmetry is exploited properly, the result is a flexibility gain to the organization. However, loss of control occurs when a subunit manager uses an informational advantage in ways at variance with achievement of organizational goals. This loss of control results in **agency costs**, that is, the reduction in the value of the organization when an agent (a subunit manager) pursues his/her interest to the detriment of the principal's (the organization's) interest. Comparing the flexibility gain with the agency costs determines the degree of **employee empowerment** (decentralization) that should be designed into the organizational structure. Employees are empowered when they are assigned more **decision rights** over organizational resources. Thus, knowledge management is crucial to organizational design. **Knowledge management** concerns how information is presented and processed, whether by computers, individuals, or companies. It is fundamental to decision making because knowledge is the input and the output of any organization's decision support systems. Accordingly, these systems should be designed to acquire knowledge that is relevant and reliable and to transfer it to those who have decision rights. Ideally, the most knowledgeable person should make the decision. However, if knowledge is easily transferred, it may be transferred to the person who makes the decision. An example is a CEO's use of financial data. If knowledge, such as how to design a computer component, is not readily transferred, the decision right must usually be transferred to the person with the knowledge. To minimize the agency costs that arise when decision rights are decentralized, systems are established to ratify or monitor decisions.

A responsibility system should encourage the efficient achievement of organizational goals. Thus, managerial control should promote **goal congruence** and **managerial effort**. All managers should be motivated to expend the necessary effort to reach common goals. The goals should be specific, objective, and verifiable. Conversely, the system should discourage effort directed toward incongruent goals. Suboptimization occurs when one segment of an organization takes action that is in its own best interests but is detrimental to the organization as a whole. One means of attaining goal congruence is to harmonize the measures used to evaluate managers with the measures used in top management's decision models. For example, the transfer price charged by a selling division to a buying division of the same organization should be set so that individual managers acting in their own best interests will further the objectives of the organization. This result will be reached when maximizing the performance measure for a manager also provides the greatest benefit for the organization.

The alignment of managerial with organizational goals requires assigning responsibility for activities, delegating the authority to perform necessary tasks, establishing accountability, and measuring and evaluating performance. The result is a structure within which individual efforts can be coordinated to attain ultimate organizational goals. **Authority** is the power to direct and exact performance from others. It includes the right to prescribe the means and methods by which work will be done. However, the authority to direct is only as good as one individual's willingness to accept direction from another. Moreover, with authority comes responsibility and accountability. **Responsibility** is the obligation to perform. In the classical view, this obligation formally comes down from a superior position and is inherent in any job (it has its origins in the rights of private property as defined by the appropriate laws). In the behavioral view, responsibility must and should be delegated; a successive dividing and passing down of obligation occurs. The appropriate amount of authority or power must be delegated with the responsibility. However, a higher position can never rid itself of ultimate responsibility. **Accountability** is the liability for failure to meet the obligation. In practice, accountability is the duty to report performance to one's superior and the physical means for reporting or being able to substantiate performance, i.e., record keeping. The principle of single accountability or unity of command means that each subordinate should report to only one superior. The principle of unity of command permits more than one person to act as a subordinate's superior only under conditions in which coordination of plans is sufficient so that conflicting or contradicting instructions are not given.

**Controllability** is another concept important to the understanding of a responsibility system. It is the extent to which a manager can influence activities. Managerial performance theoretically should be evaluated only on the basis of those factors controllable by the manager. Thus, managers may control revenues, costs, or investment in resources. For example, a controllable cost is one that is directly regulated by a specific manager at a given level of production within a given time span. However, controllability and responsibility are rarely coextensive. One reason is that more than one manager may influence an activity. If responsibility exceeds the extent to which a manager can influence an activity, the result may be reduced morale, a decline in managerial effort, and poor performance. Such a manager encounters greater risk because his/her success depends on uncontrollable factors. Consequently, a manager in these circumstances should be compensated for the incremental risk assumed. However, if a manager is accountable solely for activities over which (s)he has extensive influence, the manager may develop too narrow a focus. For example, the manager of a cost center may make decisions based only on cost efficiency and ignore the overall effectiveness goals of the organization. By extending the manager's responsibility to profits as well as costs, the organization may encourage desirable behavior congruent with overall goals, such as improved coordination with marketing personnel, even though the manager still does not control revenues. Furthermore, a manager who does not control an activity may nevertheless be the individual who is best informed about it. Thus, a purchasing agent may be in the best position to explain price variances even though (s)he cannot control them.

A well-designed responsibility accounting system establishes responsibility centers within the organization. A **responsibility center** is an organizational subunit, such as a department, plant, division, segment, or business process, the manager of which has authority over, and is responsible and accountable for, a defined group of activities. A **cost center** is responsible for costs only. A maintenance department is an example. A **revenue center** is responsible for revenues but not costs other than those attributable to marketing. A specialty clothing department of a department store is an example. A **profit center** is responsible for revenues and expenses. An appliance department in a retail store is an example. An **investment center** is responsible for revenues, expenses, and invested capital. A branch office is an example. A **service center** exists primarily and sometimes solely to provide specialized support to other organizational subunits. It is usually operated as a cost center. A maintenance department is also an example of a service center.

The **contribution approach** to **performance measurement** is emphasized in traditional responsibility accounting because it focuses on controllability. Fixed costs are much less controllable than variable costs, so the contribution margin (sales -- all variable costs) may therefore be a fairer basis for evaluation than gross margin (also called gross profit), which equals sales minus cost of sales. A contribution approach income statement for a manufacturer may include a variety of components, for example, the **manufacturing contribution margin**, or sales minus variable manufacturing costs, and the **contribution margin**, or the manufacturing contribution minus nonmanufacturing variable costs. The **short-run performance margin** is the contribution margin minus controllable (discretionary) fixed costs. Discretionary costs are characterized by uncertainty about the relationship between input (the costs) and the value of the related output. Examples are advertising and research costs. The **segment margin** is the short-run performance margin minus traceable (committed) fixed costs. Committed costs result when a going concern holds fixed assets (property, plant, and equipment). Examples are insurance, long-term lease payments, and depreciation. **Operating income** is the segment margin minus allocated common costs.

Allocation of **central administration costs** (allocated common costs) is a fundamental issue in responsibility accounting. It has often been made based on budgeted revenue or contribution margin. If allocation is based on actual sales or contribution margin, a responsibility center that surpasses expectations will be penalized (charged with increased overhead). Research has shown that central administrative costs are allocated to organizational subunits because the allocation reminds managers that such costs exist and that the managers would incur these costs if their operations were independent. The allocation also reminds managers that profit center earnings must cover some amount of support costs. Moreover, organizational subunits should be motivated to use central administrative services appropriately. Still another reason is that managers who must bear the costs of central administrative services that they do not control may be encouraged to exert pressure on those who do. Thus, they may be able to restrain such costs indirectly. If central administrative or other fixed costs are not allocated, responsibility centers might reach their revenue or contribution margin goals without covering all fixed costs, a necessity to operate in the long run. Allocation of overhead, however, is motivationally negative; central administrative or other fixed costs may appear noncontrollable and be unproductive. Furthermore, managers' morale may suffer when allocations depress operating results, dysfunctional conflict may arise among managers when costs controlled by one are allocated to others, and resentment may result if cost allocation is perceived to be arbitrary or unfair. For example, an allocation on an ability-to-bear basis, such as operating income, penalizes successful managers and rewards underachievers and may therefore have a demotivating effect. A much preferred alternative is to budget a certain amount of the contribution margin earned by each responsibility center to the central administration based on negotiation. The hoped-for result is for each subunit to see itself as contributing to the success of the overall entity rather than carrying the weight (cost) of central administration. The central administration can then make the decision whether to expand, divest, or close responsibility centers.

Alternatives to financial performance measurement based on the contribution margin approach are **return on investment (ROI)** (income ÷ total assets or another investment base), residual income, and economic value added. The advantage of these measures is that they permit comparison of the results of entities with investment bases of different sizes. Moreover, different attributes may be used to measure the elements of the investment base, for example, historical cost, replacement cost, fair value, or present value. Invested capital also may be defined in various ways, for example, as total assets available or total assets employed, which excludes assets that are idle, such as vacant land. It may also be defined as working capital plus other assets. Current liabilities are deducted from current assets to exclude the assets provided by short-term creditors. This investment base assumes that the manager controls short-term credit. Still another investment base is shareholders' equity. A portion of long-term liabilities must be allocated to the investment center to determine the manager's resource base. One problem with this definition of the resource base is that, although it has the advantage of emphasizing return to owners, it reflects decisions at different levels of the entity: short-term liabilities incurred by the responsibility center and long-term liabilities controlled at the corporate level.

The income amounts used in financial performance measurement also may be defined in various ways. Examples of income measurements are operating income (earnings before interest and taxes), net income, net income adjusted for price level changes, and cash flow. The well-known **DuPont formula** for financial planning and control decomposes ROI into total assets (investment) turnover and profit margin:

$$\frac{Income}{Total\ assets} = \frac{Revenues}{Total\ assets} \times \frac{Income}{Revenues}$$

A variant of the DuPont formula is **return on equity**, which equals total assets (investment) turnover, times the profit margin, times the equity multiplier:

$$\frac{Income}{Equity} = \frac{Revenues}{Total\ assets} \times \frac{Income}{Revenues} \times \frac{Total\ assets}{Equity}$$

**Residual income** is the excess of ROI over a targeted amount equal to imputed interest on invested capital. The rate is ordinarily the cost of capital and, in principle, should reflect the degree of risk of the reporting responsibility center. Projects with a positive residual income should be accepted, and projects with a negative residual income should be rejected. Residual income is often touted as superior to ROI. It may be more consistent with maximizing profits than ROI because it is an amount, not a rate. **Economic value added (EVA)** is a more specific version of residual income. It equals after-tax operating income [earnings before interest and taxes x (1.0 -- the tax rate)] minus the product of the after-tax weighted-average cost of capital and an investment base equal to total assets minus current liabilities. EVA represents the business unit's true **economic profit** primarily because a charge for the cost of equity capital is implicit in the cost of capital. The cost of equity is an opportunity cost, that is, the return that could have been obtained on the best alternative investment of similar risk. Hence, the EVA measures the marginal benefit obtained by using resources in a particular way. It is useful for determining whether a segment of a business is increasing **shareholder value**. EVA differs from accounting income not only because it subtracts the cost of equity but also because it makes certain other adjustments. For example, R&D costs are capitalized and amortized over 5 years for EVA purposes, and true economic depreciation rather than the amount used for accounting or tax purposes is recognized.

EVA is one of several straightforward methods for measuring managerial performance regarding creation of shareholder value. For example, the **equity spread** calculates equity value creation by multiplying beginning equity capital by the difference between the return on equity (net income ÷ equity) and the percentage cost of equity. **Total shareholder return** equals the change in the stock price plus dividends per share, divided by the initial stock price. The **market value added** is the difference between the market value of equity (shares outstanding x market price) and the equity supplied by shareholders.

Effective management control requires performance measurement and feedback. The results affect allocation of resources to organizational subunits and decisions about managers' compensation, advancement, and future assignments. Furthermore, evaluating their performance serves to motivate managers to optimize the measures in the performance evaluation model. However, that model may be inconsistent with the organization's model for managerial decision making. To achieve goal congruence, the models should be synchronized. For example, if top management wishes to maximize results over the long term, subordinates should be evaluated over the long term. Unfortunately, information systems seldom provide information on the outcomes of individual decisions, and top managers may be unaware of desirable options not chosen. Moreover, performance feedback usually applies to specific responsibility centers for specific periods. The result is that use of the same criteria for decision making and managerial evaluation may be difficult. Feedback regarding managerial performance may take the form of **financial and nonfinancial performance measures** that may be internally or externally generated. Moreover, different measures have a long-term or short-term emphasis. An example of an external financial measure is stock price. Examples of internal financial measures are cost variances, return on investment, residual income, breakeven time, return on sales, and other financial ratios.

Nonfinancial measures are important for control. They help engineering and operations managers to assess product and process quality. In a modern dynamic environment that stresses total quality management, continuous improvement, elimination of nonvalue-adding activities, attention to all activities in the value chain, and process innovation (reengineering), standards need to relate as much to processes and change (improvement) facilitation as to static financial (especially cost) benchmarks. Examples of external nonfinancial measures are market share, customer satisfaction, returned merchandise, delivery performance, and competitive rank. Examples of internal nonfinancial measures are rework, outgoing product quality, new product development time, and manufacturing cycle efficiency.

**Product development time** is an especially important performance measure because it is a crucial competitive factor. A company that is first in the market with a new product has obvious advantages. Reducing development time is also important because product life cycles are becoming shorter, and organizations need to respond quickly and flexibly to new technology, changes in consumer tastes, and other competitive challenges. One financial measure of product development is **breakeven time**, which is the time from management approval of the project to the time when the cumulative present value of its net cash inflows equals the cumulative present value of the investment cash outflows. The most popular method of determining breakeven time calculates the time required for the present value of the cumulative cash flows to equal zero. An alternative that results in a longer breakeven time is to consider the time required for the present value of the cumulative cash inflows to equal the present value of all the expected future cash outflows. **Customer-response time** (delivery cycle time) is another crucial competitive factor. It is the delay from placement of an order to delivery of the good or service. Response time is a function of time drivers, e.g., uncertainty about arrivals of customers in the queue and **bottlenecks** (points at which capacity is reached or exceeded). Response time consists of **order receipt time** (delay between the placement of an order and its readiness for setup); **manufacturing cycle time**, sometimes called manufacturing lead time or throughput time (delay from the moment the order is ready for setup to its completion); and order delivery time. **Manufacturing cycle efficiency** equals the value-added production time (excluding such activities as inspection, moving products and materials, and waiting in lines) divided by the manufacturing cycle time.

As the preceding discussion suggests, the trend in managerial performance evaluation is toward the **balanced scorecard** approach. Multiple measures permit a determination as to whether a manager is achieving certain objectives at the expense of others that may be equally or more important. For example, an improvement in operating results at the expense of new product development would be apparent using this approach. The scorecard is a goal congruence tool that informs managers about the factors that top management believes to be important. These measures may be financial or nonfinancial, internal or external, and short term or long term. A typical scorecard includes measures in four categories: profitability; customer satisfaction; innovation; and efficiency, quality, and time.

**Transfer pricing** determines the amounts charged by one segment of an organization for goods and services it provides to another segment of the same organization. Transfer prices are used by profit and investment centers. The typical problem is the determination of exactly what transfer price should be used when one segment purchases from another. In a decentralized system, each segment theoretically may be a completely separate entity. Thus, Division A should charge the same price to Division B as would be charged to an outside buyer. The reason for decentralization is to motivate managers to achieve the best results. The best interests of Division A may not be served by giving a special discount to Division B if the goods can be sold at the regular price to outside buyers. However, having A sell at a special price to B may be to the overall organization's advantage. A transfer price should permit a segment to operate as an independent entity and achieve its goals while functioning in the organization's best interests. Hence, transfer pricing should motivate managers; it should encourage goal congruence and managerial effort. **Goal congruence** is agreement regarding the goals of the organization or the segment by both supervisors and subordinates. Performance is assumed to be optimized when the parties understand that personal and segmental goals should be consistent with those of the organization. **Managerial effort** is the extent to which a manager attempts to accomplish a goal. Managerial effort may include psychological as well as physical commitment to a goal. Motivation is the desire of managers to attain a specific goal (goal congruence) and the commitment to accomplish the goal (managerial effort). **Managerial motivation** is therefore a combination of managerial effort and goal congruence.

Transfer prices can be determined in a number of ways. They may be based on a **market price**, assuming that a market exists, or on differential outlay cost to the seller plus opportunity cost to the organization. The opportunity cost is the benefit forgone by not selling to an outsider. For example, if a good costing $4 can be sold for $10, the outlay cost is $4 and the opportunity cost is $6 (assuming no idle capacity). A full absorption cost transfer price includes materials, labor, and a full allocation of overhead. Another **cost-based price** equals cost plus a lump sum or a markup percentage. Cost may be either the standard or the actual cost. The former has the advantage of isolating variances. Actual costs give the selling division little incentive to control costs. Thus, a cost-based price ignores market prices and may not promote long-term efficiencies. A **negotiated price** may result when segments are free to determine the prices at which they buy and sell internally. Hence, a transfer price may simply reflect the best bargain that the parties can strike between themselves. It need not be based directly on particular market or cost information. A negotiated price may be especially appropriate when market prices are subject to rapid fluctuation.

Transfer pricing policy is normally set by top management at the corporate level. The decision will typically include consideration of goal congruence factors because the transfer price should promote the goals of the organization. Segmental performance factors are also relevant. The segment making the transfer should be allowed to recover its incremental cost plus the opportunity cost of the transfer. For this purpose, the transfer should be at market price. The selling manager should not lose income by selling within the company. Properly allocating revenues and expenses through appropriate transfer pricing also facilitates evaluation of the performance of the various segments. Furthermore, as discussed above, negotiation factors may affect transfer prices. If the purchasing segment could purchase the product or service outside the company, it should be permitted to negotiate the transfer price. The purchasing manager should not have to incur greater costs by purchasing within the company. Capacity factors are also pertinent because, if Division A has excess capacity, it should be used for producing products for Division B. However, if Division A is operating at full capacity and selling its products at the full market price, profitable work should not be abandoned to produce for Division B. Additional considerations are cost structure factors, given that some portions of production costs are variable and fixed. If Division A has excess capacity and it can sell to Division B at a price in excess of the variable cost, the work should be performed for Division B because a contribution to recover fixed costs will result. Tax factors are still other considerations in setting transfer prices. A wide range of tax issues on the interstate and international levels may arise, e.g., income taxes, sales taxes, value-added taxes, inventory and payroll taxes, and other governmental charges. In the international context, exchange rate fluctuations and limits on transfers of profits outside the host country are further concerns.

**Dual pricing** is another internal price-setting alternative. For example, the seller could record the transfer to another segment at the usual market price that would be paid by an outsider. The buyer, however, would record a purchase at the variable cost of production. Each segment's performance would be improved by the use of a dual-pricing scheme, and the organization would benefit because variable costs would be used for decision-making purposes. In a sense, variable costs would be the relevant price for decision-making purposes, but the regular market price would be used for performance evaluation of segments. However, under a dual-pricing system, the organization's profit will be less than the sum of the profits of the individual segments. In effect, the seller is given a corporate subsidy under the dual-pricing system. The dual-pricing system is rarely used because the incentive to control costs is reduced. The seller is assured of a high price, and the buyer is assured of an artificially low price. Thus, neither manager must exert much effort to show a profit on segmental performance reports.

## 11.1 Basis of a Responsibility System

**1.** An effective managerial control system has favorable motivational effects. Which of the following are aspects of motivation?

| | Managerial Effort | Goal Congruence |
|----|-------------------|-----------------|
| A. | No | No |
| B. | No | Yes |
| C. | Yes | Yes |
| D. | Yes | No |

The correct answer is (C). *(Publisher)*
**REQUIRED:** The aspect(s), if any, of motivation.
**DISCUSSION:** A managerial control system should encourage the efficient achievement of organizational objectives. Thus, goal congruence and managerial effort are aspects of motivation. All managers should be motivated to expend the necessary effort to reach common goals.

Answers (A), (B), and (D) are incorrect because a manager should be motivated to expend the effort required to achieve organizational objectives.

**2.** Goal congruence is most likely to be promoted when

A. A company uses a cost-based transfer price.

B. A manager of a retail store is charged imputed interest on inventory.

C. Percentage return on investment rather than residual income is used to measure managerial performance.

D. An annual accrual accounting measure is used to evaluate a manager who makes capital investment decisions.

The correct answer is (B). *(Publisher)*
**REQUIRED:** The circumstances in which goal congruence is most likely to be promoted.
**DISCUSSION:** If the measure of the retail store manager's performance does not consider opportunity costs, for example, the cost of financing inventory, (s)he may be tempted to make suboptimal decisions about inventory levels. Hence, ordering excessive inventory may help to minimize the costs for which the manager is responsible while increasing the costs for which (s)he is not.

Answer (A) is incorrect because a cost-based transfer price may provide no incentive to minimize cost. Answer (C) is incorrect because the organization may be better served if a manager maximizes an absolute dollar amount rather than a rate of return. Answer (D) is incorrect because the accrual return on investment in the first years of a capital project may be very low even though it has a positive net present value.

**3.** To make goal setting effective and worthwhile, the goals should be

A. Just beyond what subordinates are likely to reach.

B. Qualitative and approximate.

C. Based on superior performers' output.

D. Specific, objective, and verifiable.

The correct answer is (D). *(CIA, adapted)*
**REQUIRED:** The nature of desirable goals.
**DISCUSSION:** Effective goal setting requires a sufficient knowledge of employees' jobs to set specific, objective, verifiable goals. Employees must also understand how goal-oriented performance will be measured.

Answer (A) is incorrect because employees will become discouraged if the goals cannot be met. Answer (B) is incorrect because goals should be quantitative and specific. They should not be too abstract. Answer (C) is incorrect because not all employees are superior. Employees are discouraged by unreachable goals. Goals should be based on an employee's skills and capacity for improvement.

**4.** The extent to which a manager can influence organizational activities is

A. Authority.

B. Responsibility.

C. Accountability.

D. Controllability.

The correct answer is (D). *(Publisher)*
**REQUIRED:** The extent to which a manager can influence organizational activities.
**DISCUSSION:** Controllability is the extent to which a manager can influence activities and related revenues, costs, or other items. In principle, controllability is proportionate to, but not coextensive with, responsibility.

Answer (A) is incorrect because authority is the power to direct and exact performance from others. It includes the right to prescribe the means and methods by which work will be done. Answer (B) is incorrect because responsibility is the obligation to perform. Answer (C) is incorrect because accountability is the liability for failure to meet the obligation.

**5.** In a well-run organization, a manager may have responsibility for activities that (s)he cannot significantly influence. This arrangement may be justified because of the

   A. Manager's knowledge about the activities and the potential for behavioral change.

   B. Manager's knowledge about the activities but not the potential for behavioral change.

   C. Improvement in managerial morale, effort, and performance.

   D. Improvement in managerial morale and the potential for behavioral change.

The correct answer is (A). *(Publisher)*
   **REQUIRED:** The reason(s) for assigning responsibility without control.
   **DISCUSSION:** A manager who does not control an activity may nevertheless be the individual who is best informed about it. Thus, a purchasing agent may be in the best position to explain price variances even though (s)he cannot control them. Moreover, if a manager is accountable solely for activities over which (s)he has extensive influence, the manager may develop too narrow a focus. For example, the manager of a cost center may make decisions based only on cost efficiency and ignore the overall effectiveness goals of the organization. By extending the manager's responsibility to profits as well as costs without changing his/her level of control, the organization may encourage desirable behavior congruent with overall goals, such as improved coordination with marketing personnel.
   Answer (B) is incorrect because the potential for favorable behavioral change may justify assigning responsibility without control. Answers (C) and (D) are incorrect because if responsibility exceeds the extent to which a manager can influence an activity, the result may be reduced morale, a decline in managerial effort, and poor performance.

**6.** A segment of an organization is referred to as a service center if it has

   A. Responsibility for developing markets and selling the output of the organization.

   B. Responsibility for combining the raw materials, direct labor, and other factors of production into a final output.

   C. Authority to make decisions affecting the major determinants of profit including the power to choose its markets and sources of supply.

   D. Authority to provide specialized support to other units within the organization.

The correct answer is (D). *(CMA, adapted)*
   **REQUIRED:** The definition of a service center.
   **DISCUSSION:** A service center exists primarily and sometimes solely to provide specialized support to other units within the organization. Service centers are usually operated as cost centers.
   Answer (A) is incorrect because a service center has no responsibility for developing markets or selling. Answer (B) is incorrect because a production center is engaged in manufacturing. Answer (C) is incorrect because a profit center can choose its markets and sources of supply.

**7.** The least complex segment or area of responsibility for which costs are allocated is a(n)

   A. Profit center.

   B. Investment center.

   C. Contribution center.

   D. Cost center.

The correct answer is (D). *(CMA, adapted)*
   **REQUIRED:** The least complex segment or area of responsibility for which costs are allocated.
   **DISCUSSION:** A cost center is a responsibility center that is accountable only for costs. The cost center is the least complex type of segment because it has no responsibility for revenues or investments.
   Answer (A) is incorrect because a profit center is a segment responsible for both revenues and costs. A profit center has the authority to make decisions concerning markets and sources of supply. Answer (B) is incorrect because an investment center is a responsibility center that is accountable for revenues (markets), costs (sources of supply), and invested capital. Answer (C) is incorrect because a contribution center is responsible for revenues and variable costs, but not invested capital.

**8.** Which of the following techniques would be best for evaluating the management performance of a department that is operated as a cost center?

    A. Return-on-assets ratio.

    B. Return-on-investment ratio.

    C. Payback method.

    D. Variance analysis.

The correct answer is (D). *(CIA, adapted)*
    **REQUIRED:** The best method for evaluating a cost center.
    **DISCUSSION:** A cost center is a responsibility center that is responsible for costs only. Of the alternatives given, variance analysis is the only one that can be used in a cost center. Variance analysis involves comparing actual costs with predicted or standard costs.
    Answers (A) and (B) are incorrect because return on assets and return on investment cannot be computed for a cost center. The manager is not responsible for revenue (return) or the assets available. Answer (C) is incorrect because the payback method is a means of evaluating alternative investment proposals.

**9.** Responsibility accounting defines an operating center that is responsible for revenue and costs as a(n)

    A. Profit center.

    B. Revenue center.

    C. Division.

    D. Operating unit.

The correct answer is (A). *(CMA, adapted)*
    **REQUIRED:** The name given to a responsibility center that is responsible for both revenue and costs.
    **DISCUSSION:** A profit center is responsible for both revenues and costs, whereas a cost center is responsible only for costs.
    Answer (B) is incorrect because a revenue center is responsible only for revenues, not costs. Answer (C) is incorrect because a division can be any type of responsibility center. Answer (D) is incorrect because an operating unit can be organized as any type of center.

**10.** The basic purpose of a responsibility accounting system is

    A. Budgeting.

    B. Motivation.

    C. Authority.

    D. Variance analysis.

The correct answer is (B). *(CMA, adapted)*
    **REQUIRED:** The basic purpose of a responsibility accounting system.
    **DISCUSSION:** The basic purpose of a responsibility accounting system is to motivate management to perform in a manner consistent with overall company objectives. The assignment of responsibility implies that some revenues and costs can be changed through effective management. The system should have certain controls that provide for feedback reports indicating deviations from expectations. Higher-level management may focus on those deviations for either reinforcement or correction.
    Answer (A) is incorrect because budgeting is an element of a responsibility accounting system, not the basic purpose. Answer (C) is incorrect because authority is an element of a responsibility accounting system, not the basic purpose. Answer (D) is incorrect because analysis of variances is an element of a responsibility accounting system, not the basic purpose.

**11.** Decentralized firms can delegate authority and yet retain control and monitor managers' performance by structuring the organization into responsibility centers. Which one of the following organizational segments is most like an independent business?

    A. Revenue center.

    B. Profit center.

    C. Cost center.

    D. Investment center.

The correct answer is (D). *(CMA, adapted)*
    **REQUIRED:** The organizational segment most like an independent business.
    **DISCUSSION:** An investment center is the organizational type most like an independent business because it is responsible for its own revenues, costs incurred, and capital invested. The other types of centers do not incorporate all three elements.
    Answer (A) is incorrect because a revenue center is responsible only for revenue generation, not for costs or capital investment. Answer (B) is incorrect because a profit center is responsible for revenues and costs but not for invested capital. Answer (C) is incorrect because a cost center is evaluated only on the basis of costs incurred. It is not responsible for revenues or invested capital.

**12.** A successful responsibility accounting reporting system is dependent upon

A. The correct allocation of controllable variable costs.

B. Identification of the management level at which all costs are controllable.

C. The proper delegation of responsibility and authority.

D. A reasonable separation of costs into their fixed and variable components since fixed costs are not controllable and must be eliminated from the responsibility report.

The correct answer is (C). *(CMA, adapted)*
**REQUIRED:** The factor upon which a successful responsibility accounting system is dependent.
**DISCUSSION:** Managerial performance should ideally be evaluated only on the basis of those factors controllable by the manager. Managers may control revenues, costs, and/or investments in resources.
Answer (A) is incorrect because fixed costs may also be controllable, and some costs not controllable may need to be assigned. Answer (B) is incorrect because knowledge about the incurrence of a cost rather than controllability may in practice be an appropriate basis for delegation of responsibility. Answer (D) is incorrect because fixed costs can be controllable.

**13.** Costs are accumulated by a responsibility center for control purposes when using

|   | Job-Order Costing | Process Costing |
|---|---|---|
| A. | Yes | Yes |
| B. | Yes | No |
| C. | No | No |
| D. | No | Yes |

The correct answer is (A). *(CPA, adapted)*
**REQUIRED:** The product costing method that uses responsibility centers to accumulate costs.
**DISCUSSION:** A responsibility center is a subunit (part or segment) of an organization whose manager is accountable for a specified set of activities. Both job-order costing and process costing may accumulate their costs by responsibility centers.
Answers (B), (C), and (D) are incorrect because both job-order costing and process costing may accumulate their costs by responsibility centers for control purposes.

**14.** Controllable revenue is included in a performance report for a

|   | Profit Center | Cost Center |
|---|---|---|
| A. | No | No |
| B. | No | Yes |
| C. | Yes | No |
| D. | Yes | Yes |

The correct answer is (C). *(CPA, adapted)*
**REQUIRED:** The responsibility center(s), if any, that include(s) controllable revenue in a performance report.
**DISCUSSION:** A profit center is a segment of a company responsible for both revenues and expenses. A profit center has the authority to make decisions concerning markets (revenues) and sources of supply (costs). A cost center is responsible for costs only.
Answers (A), (B), and (D) are incorrect because a profit center but not a cost center should include controllable revenue in its performance reports.

**15.** The following is a summarized income statement of Carr Co.'s profit center No. 43 for March:

| | | |
|---|---|---|
| Contribution margin | | $70,000 |
| Period expenses: | | |
| Manager's salary | $20,000 | |
| Facility depreciation | 8,000 | |
| Corporate expense allocation | 5,000 | (33,000) |
| Profit center income | | $37,000 |

Which of the following amounts is most likely subject to the control of the profit center's manager?

A. $70,000

B. $50,000

C. $37,000

D. $33,000

The correct answer is (A). *(CPA, adapted)*
**REQUIRED:** The amount most likely subject to the control of the profit center's manager.
**DISCUSSION:** A profit center is a segment of a company responsible for both revenues and expenses. A profit center has the authority to make decisions concerning markets (revenues) and sources of supply (costs). However, its manager does not control his/her own salary, investment and the resulting costs (e.g., depreciation), or expenses incurred at the corporate level. Thus, a profit center is most likely to control its $70,000 contribution margin (sales − variable costs) but not the other items in the summarized income statement.
Answer (B) is incorrect because the profit center's manager does not control his/her $20,000 salary.
Answers (C) and (D) are incorrect because the profit center's manager does not control the listed period expenses and therefore does not control the profit center's income.

**16.** A segment of an organization is an investment center if it has

- A. Authority to make decisions affecting the major determinants of profit, including the power to choose its markets and sources of supply.

- B. Authority to make decisions affecting the major determinants of profit, including the power to choose its markets and sources of supply and significant control over the amount of invested capital.

- C. Authority to make decisions over the most significant costs of operations, including the power to choose the sources of supply.

- D. Responsibility for developing markets for, and selling the output of, the organization.

The correct answer is (B). *(CMA, adapted)*
**REQUIRED:** The nature of an investment center.
**DISCUSSION:** In investment centers, managers are responsible for all activities, including costs, revenues, and investments. An investment center is a profit center with significant control over the amount of capital invested. This control extends to investments such as receivables and property, plant, and equipment, as well as entry into new markets.

Answer (A) is incorrect because a profit center is responsible for controlling expenses and generating revenues. Answer (C) is incorrect because a cost center has authority only over the sources of supply. Answer (D) is incorrect because a revenue center is responsible for developing markets and selling the firm's products.

## 11.2 Performance Measurement

**17.** In a responsibility accounting system, a feedback report that focuses on the difference between budgeted amounts and actual amounts is an example of

- A. Management by exception.

- B. Assessing blame.

- C. Granting rewards to successful managers.

- D. Ignoring other variables for which the budgeted goals were met.

The correct answer is (A). *(Publisher)*
**REQUIRED:** The term for feedback reports that focus on differences between budgeted and actual amounts.
**DISCUSSION:** A responsibility accounting system should have certain controls that provide for feedback reports indicating deviations from expectations. Management may then focus on those deviations (exceptions) for either reinforcement or correction.

Answer (B) is incorrect because the responsibility accounting system should not be used exclusively to assess blame. Answer (C) is incorrect because the responsibility accounting system should not be used exclusively to give rewards. Answer (D) is incorrect because feedback reports concentrate on deviations, but not to the total exclusion of other budgeted variables.

**18.** Making segment disclosures is an advantage to a company because it

- A. Facilitates evaluation of company management by providing data on particular segments.

- B. Eliminates the interdependence of segments.

- C. Masks the effect of intersegment transfers.

- D. Provides competitors with comparative information on the company's performance.

The correct answer is (A). *(CIA, adapted)*
**REQUIRED:** The reason that making segment disclosures is an advantage.
**DISCUSSION:** Segment reporting is an aspect of responsibility accounting. It facilitates evaluation of company management and of the quality of the economic investment in particular segments.

Answer (B) is incorrect because interdependence of segments is not affected by reporting methods. Answers (C) and (D) are incorrect because masking the effects of intersegment transfers and providing information to competitors are disadvantages of segment reporting.

**19.** If a manufacturing company uses responsibility accounting, which one of the following items is least likely to appear in a performance report for a manager of an assembly line?

- A. Supervisory salaries.

- B. Materials.

- C. Repairs and maintenance.

- D. Depreciation on equipment.

The correct answer is (D). *(CMA, adapted)*
**REQUIRED:** The item least likely to be found in a performance report for a manager of an assembly line.
**DISCUSSION:** Responsibility accounting stresses that managers should be held responsible for only those factors under their control. Costs are classified as controllable and noncontrollable to assign responsibility, which implies that some revenues and costs can be changed through effective management. For example, depreciation on equipment is ordinarily not controllable by the manager of an assembly line and should not appear on his/her performance report.

Answers (A), (B), and (C) are incorrect because supervisory salaries, materials, and repairs and maintenance are costs controllable by an assembly line manager.

**20.** The receipt of raw materials used in the manufacture of products and the shipping of finished goods to customers is under the control of the warehouse supervisor, whose time is spent approximately 60% on receiving and 40% on shipping activities. Separate staffs for these operations are employed. The labor-related costs for the warehousing function are as follows:

| | |
|---|---:|
| Warehouse supervisor's salary | $ 40,000 |
| Receiving clerks' wages | 75,000 |
| Shipping clerks' wages | 55,000 |
| Employee benefit costs (30% of wage and salary costs) | 51,000 |
| | $221,000 |

The company employs a responsibility accounting system for performance-reporting purposes. Costs are classified as period or product costs. What is the total of labor-related costs reported as product costs under the control of the warehouse supervisor?

    A.  $97,500

    B.  $128,700

    C.  $130,000

    D.  $221,000

The correct answer is (A). *(CIA, adapted)*
**REQUIRED:** The total labor-related costs listed as product costs under the control of the warehouse supervisor.
**DISCUSSION:** The responsibility accounting report should list only the costs over which the warehousing supervisor exercises control. The supervisor's salary should therefore be excluded because it is controlled by the warehouse supervisor's superior. Moreover, only the product costs are to be considered. These exclude the shipping clerks' wages and fringe benefits because they are period costs (shipping is a selling expense). Thus, the only product cost under the control of the warehouse supervisor is the receiving clerks' wages ($75,000) and the related fringe benefits (.3 x $75,000 = $22,500), or a total of $97,500.
Answer (B) is incorrect because 60% of the warehouse supervisor's salary is included. None of the supervisor's salary should be included because it is controlled by the supervisor's superior. Answer (C) is incorrect because the shipping clerks' wages are periodic selling costs and are therefore not included. Additionally, the receiving clerks' benefits should be included on the responsibility accounting report. Answer (D) is incorrect because neither the warehouse supervisor's salary nor any of the shipping clerks' wages and benefits should be included on the responsibility accounting report.

**21.** A company plans to implement a bonus plan based on segment performance. In addition, the company plans to convert to a responsibility accounting system for segment reporting. The following costs have been included in the segment performance reports prepared under the current system. What is the only item that could logically be reported under the planned system?

    A.  Corporate administrative costs allocated on the basis of net segment sales.

    B.  Personnel department costs assigned on the basis of the number of employees in each segment.

    C.  Fixed computer facility costs divided equally among each segment.

    D.  Variable computer operational costs charged to each segment based on actual hours used times a predetermined standard rate; any variable cost efficiency or inefficiency remains in the computer department.

The correct answer is (D). *(CIA, adapted)*
**REQUIRED:** The item included in the segment performance reports prepared on a responsibility accounting basis.
**DISCUSSION:** The variable computer cost can be included. The segments are charged for actual usage, which is under each segment's control. The predetermined standard rate is set at the beginning of the year and is known by the segment managers. Moreover, the efficiencies and inefficiencies of the computer department are not passed on to the segments. Both procedures promote a degree of control by the segments.
Answer (A) is incorrect because the segments have no control over corporate administrative costs or the allocation basis. The allocation depends upon the segment sales (controllable) and the sales of other segments (uncontrollable). Answer (B) is incorrect because the segments have no control over personnel costs or the method of assignment, which depends upon the number of employees in the segment (controllable) and the total number of employees in all segments (not controllable). Answer (C) is incorrect because the segments have no control over fixed computer facility costs, and the equal assignment is arbitrary and bears no relation to usage.

**22.** A management decision may be beneficial for a given profit center but not for the entire company. From the overall company viewpoint, this decision leads to

    A.  Suboptimization.

    B.  Centralization.

    C.  Goal congruence.

    D.  Maximization.

The correct answer is (A). *(CPA, adapted)*
**REQUIRED:** The effect when a decision benefits a profit center but not the company.
**DISCUSSION:** Suboptimization occurs when one segment of a company takes an action that benefits itself but not the firm as a whole.
Answer (B) is incorrect because centralization describes the extent to which decision-making authority is dispersed in an organization. Answer (C) is incorrect because goal congruence occurs when the goals of subordinates and the organization are shared. Answer (D) is incorrect because maximization is the quantitative or qualitative achievement of the best results by choosing an action.

Questions 23 and 24 are based on the following information. A and B are autonomous divisions of a corporation. They have no beginning or ending inventories, and the number of units produced is equal to the number of units sold. Following is financial information relating to the two divisions.

| | A | B |
|---|---|---|
| Sales | $150,000 | $400,000 |
| Other revenue | 10,000 | 15,000 |
| Direct materials | 30,000 | 65,000 |
| Direct labor | 20,000 | 40,000 |
| Variable factory overhead | 5,000 | 15,000 |
| Fixed factory overhead | 25,000 | 55,000 |
| Variable S&A expense | 15,000 | 30,000 |
| Fixed S&A expense | 35,000 | 60,000 |
| Central corporate expenses (allocated) | 12,000 | 20,000 |

**23.** What is the total contribution to corporate profits generated by Division A before allocation of central corporate expenses?

A. $18,000

B. $20,000

C. $30,000

D. $90,000

The correct answer is (C). *(CIA, adapted)*
**REQUIRED:** The total contribution to profits by A.
**DISCUSSION:** Division A's total contribution to corporate profits includes everything except the central corporate expense allocation. Thus, the total contribution is $30,000 ($150,000 sales + $10,000 other revenue – $30,000 direct materials – $20,000 direct labor – $5,000 variable overhead – $25,000 fixed overhead – $15,000 variable S&A expense – $35,000 fixed S&A expense).
Answer (A) is incorrect because $18,000 is the result of deducting the central corporate expenses. Answer (B) is incorrect because $20,000 is the result of excluding other revenue. Answer (D) is incorrect because $90,000 is the result of failing to deduct the fixed costs.

**24.** What is the contribution margin of Division B?

A. $150,000

B. $205,000

C. $235,000

D. $265,000

The correct answer is (D). *(CIA, adapted)*
**REQUIRED:** The contribution margin of B.
**DISCUSSION:** The contribution margin equals revenue minus variable costs. Thus, Division B's contribution margin is $265,000 ($400,000 sales + $15,000 other revenue – $65,000 direct materials – $40,000 direct labor – $15,000 variable overhead – $30,000 variable S&A expense).
Answer (A) is incorrect because $150,000 is the result of subtracting fixed costs. Answer (B) is incorrect because $205,000 is the result of subtracting fixed S&A costs. Answer (C) is incorrect because $235,000 is the result of subtracting fixed S and A costs but not variable S&A costs.

**25.** The segment margin of the Wire Division of Lerner Corporation should not include

A. Net sales of the Wire Division.

B. Fixed selling expenses of the Wire Division.

C. Variable selling expenses of the Wire Division.

D. The Wire Division's fair share of the salary of Lerner Corporation's president.

The correct answer is (D). *(CMA, adapted)*
**REQUIRED:** The item not included in a statement showing segment margin.
**DISCUSSION:** Segment margin is the contribution margin for a segment of a business minus fixed costs. It is a measure of long-run profitability. Thus, an allocation of the corporate officers' salaries should not be included in segment margin because they are neither variable costs nor fixed costs that can be rationally allocated to the segment. Other items that are often not allocated include corporate income taxes, interest, company-wide R&D expenses, and central administration costs.
Answer (A) is incorrect because sales of the division would appear on the statement. Answer (B) is incorrect because the division's fixed selling expenses are separable fixed costs. Answer (C) is incorrect because variable costs of the division are included.

**26.** When using a contribution margin format for internal reporting purposes, the major distinction between segment manager performance and segment performance is

- A. Unallocated fixed cost.
- B. Direct variable costs of producing the product.
- C. Direct fixed cost controllable by the segment manager.
- D. Direct fixed cost controllable by others.

The correct answer is (D). *(CMA, adapted)*

**REQUIRED:** The major distinction between segment manager performance and segment performance.

**DISCUSSION:** Control of costs accounts for the major difference between segment manager performance and segment performance. Segment performance is based on all costs directly attributable to the segment. Segment manager performance is based on all costs directly controllable by the segment manager. All variable costs ordinarily meet the criteria for both measures. The difference usually arises because a fixed cost is directly attributable to a segment but is not controllable by the manager. For example, a profit center manager may have no control over fixed costs of the segment.

Answers (A) and (C) are incorrect because unallocated fixed costs do not affect either performance measure. Answer (B) is incorrect because direct variable costs affect both performance measures and costs controllable by the manager.

**27.** Which one of the following firms is likely to experience dysfunctional motivation on the part of its managers due to its allocation methods?

- A. To allocate depreciation of forklifts used by workers at its central warehouse, Shahlimar Electronics uses predetermined amounts calculated on the basis of the long-term average use of the services provided.
- B. Manhattan Electronics uses the sales revenue of its various divisions to allocate costs connected with the upkeep of its headquarters building. It also uses ROI to evaluate the divisional performances.
- C. Rainier Industrial does not allow its service departments to pass on their cost overruns to the production departments.
- D. Tashkent Auto's MIS is operated out of headquarters and serves its various divisions. Tashkent's allocation of the MIS-related costs to its divisions is limited to costs the divisions will incur if they were to outsource their MIS needs.

The correct answer is (B). *(CMA, adapted)*

**REQUIRED:** The firm most likely to experience dysfunctional motivation on the part of its managers.

**DISCUSSION:** Managerial performance ordinarily should be evaluated only on the basis of those factors controllable by the manager. If a manager is allocated costs that (s)he cannot control, dysfunctional motivation can result. In the case of allocations, a cause-and-effect basis should be used. Allocating the costs of upkeep on a headquarters building on the basis of sales revenue is arbitrary because cost may have no relationship to divisional sales revenues. Consequently, divisional ROI is reduced by a cost over which a division manager has no control. Furthermore, the divisions with the greatest sales are penalized by receiving the greatest allocation.

Answer (A) is incorrect because allocating depreciation on the basis of long-term average use is a reasonable basis of allocation. This basis is controllable by the division managers and reflects a causal relationship. Answer (C) is incorrect because a service department's cost overruns may not be attributable to any activities of production departments. Answer (D) is incorrect because market-based allocations of costs of services are reasonable applications of the cause-and-effect principle.

**28.** Managers are most likely to accept allocations of common costs based on

- A. Cause and effect.
- B. Ability to bear.
- C. Fairness.
- D. Benefits received.

The correct answer is (A). *(Publisher)*

**REQUIRED:** The criterion most likely to result in acceptable allocations of common costs.

**DISCUSSION:** The difficulty with common costs is that they are indirect costs whose allocation may be arbitrary. A direct cause-and-effect relationship between a common cost and the actions of the cost object to which it is allocated is desirable. Such a relationship promotes acceptance of the allocation by managers who perceive the fairness of the procedure, but identification of cause and effect may not be feasible.

Answer (B) is incorrect because allocation using an ability-to-bear criterion punishes successful managers and rewards underachievers. Answer (C) is incorrect because fairness is an objective rather than a criterion. Moreover, fairness may be interpreted differently by different managers. Answer (D) is incorrect because the benefits-received criterion is preferable when a cause-effect relationship cannot be feasibly identified.

**29.** A large corporation allocates the costs of its headquarters staff to its decentralized divisions. The best reason for this allocation is to

- A. More accurately measure divisional operating results.
- B. Improve divisional managements' morale.
- C. Remind divisional managers that common costs exist.
- D. Discourage any use of central support services.

The correct answer is (C). *(Publisher)*

**REQUIRED:** The best reason for allocating headquarters costs.

**DISCUSSION:** The allocation reminds managers that support costs exist and that the managers would incur these costs if their operations were independent. The allocation also reminds managers that profit center earnings must cover some amount of support costs.

Answer (A) is incorrect because an arbitrary allocation may skew operating results. Answer (B) is incorrect because the allocation may create resentment and conflict. Answer (D) is incorrect because efficient use of central support services should be encouraged.

**30.** A firm earning a profit can increase its return on investment by

- A. Increasing sales revenue and operating expenses by the same dollar amount.
- B. Decreasing sales revenues and operating expenses by the same percentage.
- C. Increasing investment and operating expenses by the same dollar amount.
- D. Increasing sales revenues and operating expenses by the same percentage.

The correct answer is (D). *(CMA, adapted)*

**REQUIRED:** The means by which a profitable company can increase its return on investment (ROI).

**DISCUSSION:** ROI equals income divided by invested capital. If a company is already profitable, increasing sales and expenses by the same percentage will increase ROI. For example, if a company has sales of $100 and expenses of $80, its net income is $20. Given invested capital of $100, ROI is 20% ($20 ÷ $100). If sales and expenses both increase 10% to $110 and $88, respectively, net income increases to $22. ROI will then be 22% ($22 ÷ $100).

Answer (A) is incorrect because increasing sales and expenses by the same dollar amount will not change income or ROI. Answer (B) is incorrect because decreasing revenues and expenses by the same percentage will reduce income and lower ROI. Answer (C) is incorrect because increasing investment and operating expenses by the same dollar amount will lower ROI. The higher investment increases the denominator, and the increased expenses reduce the numerator.

**31.** Which one of the following statements pertaining to the return on investment (ROI) as a performance measurement is incorrect?

- A. When the average age of assets differs substantially across segments of a business, the use of ROI may not be appropriate.
- B. ROI relies on financial measures that are capable of being independently verified, while other forms of performance measures are subject to manipulation.
- C. The use of ROI may lead managers to reject capital investment projects that can be justified by using discounted cash flow models.
- D. The use of ROI can make it undesirable for a skillful manager to take on trouble-shooting assignments such as those involving turning around unprofitable divisions.

The correct answer is (B). *(CMA, adapted)*

**REQUIRED:** The false statement about ROI as a performance measurement.

**DISCUSSION:** Return on investment is the key performance measure in an investment center. ROI is a rate computed by dividing a segment's income by the invested capital. ROI is therefore subject to the numerous possible manipulations of the income and investment amounts. For example, a manager may choose not to invest in a project that will yield less than the desired rate of return, or (s)he may defer necessary expenses.

Answer (A) is incorrect because ROI can be misleading when the quality of the investment base differs among segments. Answer (C) is incorrect because managers may reject projects that are profitable (a return greater than the cost of capital) but would decrease ROI. For example, a segment with a 15% ROI may not want to invest in a new project with a 10% ROI, even though the cost of capital might be only 8%. Answer (D) is incorrect because the use of ROI does not reflect the relative difficulty of tasks undertaken by managers.

**32.** Which one of the following items would most likely not be incorporated into the calculation of a division's investment base when using the residual income approach for performance measurement and evaluation?

    A.  Fixed assets employed in division operations.

    B.  Land being held by the division as a site for a new plant.

    C.  Division inventories when division management exercises control over the inventory levels.

    D.  Division accounts payable when division management exercises control over the amount of short-term credit used.

The correct answer is (B). *(CMA, adapted)*

    **REQUIRED:** The item most likely not incorporated into the calculation of a division's investment base.

    **DISCUSSION:** An evaluation of an investment center is based upon the return on the investment base. These assets include plant and equipment, inventories, and receivables. Most likely, however, an asset, such as land, that is being held by the division as a site for a new plant would not be included in the investment base because it is not currently being used in operations. Total assets in use rather than total assets available is preferable when the investment center has been forced to carry idle assets.

    Answer (A) is incorrect because fixed operating assets are controlled by the division manager and contribute to profits. Answer (C) is incorrect because inventories are operating assets that contribute to profits and are controlled by the division manager. Answer (D) is incorrect because the level of accounts payable is an operating decision that should be considered in the evaluation of the division manager.

**33.** Most firms use return on investment (ROI) to evaluate the performance of investment center managers. If top management wishes division managers to use all assets without regard to financing, the denominator in the ROI calculation will be

    A.  Total assets available.

    B.  Total assets employed.

    C.  Working capital plus other assets.

    D.  Shareholders' equity.

The correct answer is (A). *(CMA, adapted)*

    **REQUIRED:** The ROI denominator if managers use all assets without regard to financing.

    **DISCUSSION:** ROI equals return (income) divided by invested capital. Invested capital may be defined in various ways, for example, as total assets available, total assets employed, working capital plus other assets (current liabilities are deducted from total assets to exclude the assets provided by short-term creditors), and shareholders' equity (a portion of long-term as well as short-term liabilities must be allocated to determine the manager's resource base). Total assets available assumes the manager will use all assets without regard to financing.

    Answer (B) is incorrect because total assets employed excludes idle assets. Answer (C) is incorrect because deducting current liabilities reflects the manager's control over short-term credit. Answer (D) is incorrect because shareholders' equity is determined by deducting total liabilities from total assets. Thus, this measure also considers financing.

**34.** Which denominator used in the return on investment (ROI) formula is criticized because it combines the effects of operating decisions made at one organizational level with financing decisions made at another organizational level?

    A.  Total assets employed.

    B.  Shareholders' equity.

    C.  Working capital plus other assets.

    D.  Total assets available.

The correct answer is (B). *(CMA, adapted)*

    **REQUIRED:** The ROI denominator.

    **DISCUSSION:** ROI equals income divided by invested capital. The denominator may be defined in various ways, e.g., total assets available, assets employed, working capital plus other assets, and shareholders' equity. If shareholders' equity (total assets – total liabilities) is chosen, a portion of long-term liabilities must be allocated to the investment center to determine the manager's resource base. One problem with this definition of the resource base is that, although it has the advantage of emphasizing return to owners, it reflects decisions at different levels of the entity: short-term liabilities incurred by the responsibility center (operating decisions) and long-term liabilities controlled at the corporate level (long-term financing decisions).

    Answers (A) and (D) are incorrect because they reflect an assumption that the subunit manager does not influence the resource base (denominator of the ROI calculation). Answer (C) is incorrect because working capital plus other assets reflects the assumption that the manager controls short-term credit. However, no corporate-level decision to allocate long-term liabilities to subunits is necessary.

**35.** Return on investment (ROI) is a very popular measure employed to evaluate the performance of corporate segments because it incorporates all of the major ingredients of profitability (revenue, cost, investment) into a single measure. Under which one of the following combinations of actions regarding a segment's revenues, costs, and investment would a segment's ROI always increase?

|    | Revenues | Costs | Investment |
|----|----------|-------|------------|
| A. | Increase | Decrease | Increase |
| B. | Decrease | Decrease | Decrease |
| C. | Increase | Increase | Increase |
| D. | Increase | Decrease | Decrease |

The correct answer is (D). *(CIA, adapted)*
**REQUIRED:** The circumstances in which ROI always increases.
**DISCUSSION:** An increase in revenue and a decrease in costs will increase the ROI numerator. A decrease in investment will decrease the denominator. Therefore, the ROI must increase in this situation.
Answers (A), (B), and (C) are incorrect because ROI is certain to increase only if revenue increases and costs and investment decrease.

**36.** The following information pertains to Bala Co. for the year ended December 31, 1998:

| | |
|---|---|
| Sales | $600,000 |
| Income | 100,000 |
| Capital investment | 400,000 |

Which of the following equations should be used to compute Bala's return on investment?

A. $(4/6) \times (6/1) = \text{ROI}$

B. $(6/4) \times (1/6) = \text{ROI}$

C. $(4/6) \times (1/6) = \text{ROI}$

D. $(6/4) \times (6/1) = \text{ROI}$

The correct answer is (B). *(CPA, adapted)*
**REQUIRED:** The equation used to compute ROI.
**DISCUSSION:** ROI equals capital turnover (sales ÷ investment) times the profit margin (income ÷ sales). Thus, Bala's ROI is 25% [($600,000 ÷ $400,000) x ($100,000 ÷ $600,000)].
Answer (A) is incorrect because the ROI yielded is 400%, which is the reciprocal of the true ROI of 25%. ROI equals capital turnover (sales ÷ investment) times the profit margin (income ÷ sales). Answer (C) is incorrect because capital turnover is sales divided by investment (S ÷ I), not investment divided by sales. Answer (D) is incorrect because profit margin is income divided by sales (Inc ÷ S), not sales divided by income.

**37.** The following information pertains to Quest Co.'s Gold Division for the current year:

| | |
|---|---|
| Sales | $311,000 |
| Variable cost | 250,000 |
| Traceable fixed costs | 50,000 |
| Average invested capital | 40,000 |
| Imputed interest rate | 10% |

Quest's return on investment was

A. 10.00%

B. 13.33%

C. 27.50%

D. 30.00%

The correct answer is (C). *(CPA, adapted)*
**REQUIRED:** The return on investment.
**DISCUSSION:** ROI equals income divided by average invested capital. Consequently, ROI equals 27.50% [($311,000 sales – $250,000 VC – $50,000 FC) ÷ $40,000 average invested capital].
Answer (A) is incorrect because 10.00% is the imputed interest rate. Answer (B) is incorrect because a 13.33% ROI would result from a net income of $5,332. Answer (D) is incorrect because a 30.00% ROI would result from a net income of $12,000.

**38.** Listed below is selected financial information for the Western Division of the Hinzel Company for last year.

| Account | Amount (thousands) |
| --- | --- |
| Average working capital | $ 625 |
| General and administrative expenses | 75 |
| Net sales | 4,000 |
| Average plant and equipment | 1,775 |
| Cost of goods sold | 3,525 |

If Hinzel treats the Western Division as an investment center for performance measurement purposes, what is the before-tax return on investment (ROI) for last year?

A. 34.78%

B. 22.54%

C. 19.79%

D. 16.67%

The correct answer is (D). *(CMA, adapted)*
**REQUIRED:** The before-tax ROI for an investment center.
**DISCUSSION:** An investment center is responsible for revenues, expenses, and invested capital. Given average plant and equipment of $1,775 and average working capital of $625, the net investment is $2,400. Before-tax profit is $400 ($4,000 sales – $3,525 cost of goods sold – $75 general expenses). If before-tax ROI equals before-tax profit divided by net investment, the answer is 16.67% ($400 ÷ $2,400).
Answer (A) is incorrect because 34.78% results from subtracting working capital from plant and equipment in calculating the net investment. Answer (B) is incorrect because 22.54% fails to include average working capital in the total for the net investment. Answer (C) is incorrect because 19.79% results from not subtracting general and administrative expenses in the calculation of before-tax profit.

**39.** Residual income is a performance evaluation that is used in conjunction with, or instead of, return on investment (ROI). In many cases, residual income is preferred to ROI because

A. Residual income is a measure over time, while ROI represents the results for one period.

B. Residual income concentrates on maximizing absolute dollars of income rather than a percentage return as with ROI.

C. The imputed interest rate used in calculating residual income is more easily derived than the target rate that is compared to the calculated ROI.

D. Average investment is employed with residual income while year-end investment is employed with ROI.

The correct answer is (B). *(CIA, adapted)*
**REQUIRED:** The reason for preferring residual income to ROI.
**DISCUSSION:** Residual income equals earnings in excess of a minimum desired return. Thus, it is measured in dollars. If performance is evaluated using ROI, a manager may reject a project that exceeds the minimum return if the project will decrease overall ROI. For example, given a target rate of 20%, a project with an ROI of 22% might be rejected if the current ROI is 25%.
Answer (A) is incorrect because both measures represent the results for a single period. Answer (C) is incorrect because the target rate for ROI is the same as the imputed interest rate used in the residual income calculation. Answer (D) is incorrect because the same investment base should be employed by both methods.

**40.** Residual income is a better measure for performance evaluation of an investment center manager than return on investment because

A. The problems associated with measuring the asset base are eliminated.

B. Desirable investment decisions will not be neglected by high-return divisions.

C. Only the gross book value of assets needs to be calculated.

D. The arguments about the implicit cost of interest are eliminated.

The correct answer is (B). *(CMA, adapted)*
**REQUIRED:** The reason residual income is a better measure of performance evaluation than return on investment.
**DISCUSSION:** Residual income is the excess of the amount of the ROI over a targeted amount equal to an imputed interest charge on invested capital. The advantage of using residual income rather than percentage ROI is that the former emphasizes maximizing a dollar amount instead of a percentage. Managers of divisions with a high ROI are encouraged to accept projects with returns exceeding the cost of capital even if those projects reduce the department's ROI.
Answers (A) and (C) are incorrect because the methods use the same asset base. Answer (D) is incorrect because use of the residual income method requires a knowledge of the cost of capital; thus, arguments about the implicit cost of interest may escalate with use of the residual income method.

**41.** The imputed interest rate used in the residual income approach to performance evaluation can best be described as the

A. Average lending rate for the year being evaluated.

B. Historical weighted-average cost of capital for the company.

C. Target return on investment set by the company's management.

D. Marginal after-tax cost of capital on new equity capital.

The correct answer is (C). (CMA, adapted)

**REQUIRED:** The true statement about the imputed interest rate used in the residual income approach.

**DISCUSSION:** Residual income is the excess of the return on an investment over a targeted amount equal to an imputed interest charge on invested capital. The rate used is ordinarily set as a target return by management but is often equal to the weighted-average cost of capital. Some enterprises prefer residual income to ROI because the firm will benefit from expansion as long as residual income is earned.

Answer (A) is incorrect because the cost of equity capital must also be incorporated into the imputed interest rate. Answer (B) is incorrect because the current weighted-average cost of capital must be used. Answer (D) is incorrect because both debt and equity capital must be considered.

**42.** James Webb is the general manager of the Industrial Product Division, and his performance is measured using the residual income method. Webb is reviewing the following forecasted information for his division for next year:

| Category | Amount (thousands) |
|---|---|
| Working capital | $ 1,800 |
| Revenue | 30,000 |
| Plant and equipment | 17,200 |

If the imputed interest charge is 15% and Webb wants to achieve a residual income target of $2,000,000, what will costs have to be in order to achieve the target?

A. $9,000,000

B. $10,800,000

C. $25,150,000

D. $25,690,000

The correct answer is (C). (CMA, adapted)

**REQUIRED:** The maximum costs consistent with meeting a residual income target.

**DISCUSSION:** Residual income is the excess of the amount of the ROI over a targeted amount equal to an imputed interest charge on invested capital. If a manager has $19,000,000 of invested capital ($17,200,000 of plant and equipment + $1,800,000 of working capital), a 15% imputed interest charge equals $2,850,000. Adding $2,000,000 of residual income to the imputed interest results in a target profit of $4,850,000. This profit can be achieved if costs are $25,150,000 ($30,000,000 revenue – $4,850,000 profit).

Answers (A) and (B) are incorrect because these levels of costs would result in a residual income greater than $2,000,000. Answer (D) is incorrect because $25,690,000 results from subtracting working capital from plant and equipment in determining invested capital.

**43.** REB Service Co. is a computer service center. For the month of May, REB had the following operating statistics:

| | |
|---|---|
| Sales | $450,000 |
| Operating income | 25,000 |
| Net profit after taxes | 8,000 |
| Total assets | 500,000 |
| Shareholders' equity | 200,000 |
| Cost of capital | 6% |

Based on the above information, which one of the following statements is correct? REB has a

A. Return on investment of 4%.

B. Residual income of $(5,000).

C. Return on investment of 1.6%.

D. Residual income of $(22,000).

The correct answer is (B). (CMA, adapted)

**REQUIRED:** The true statement about the company's performance.

**DISCUSSION:** Return on investment is commonly calculated by dividing pretax income by total assets available. Residual income is the excess of the return on investment over a targeted amount equal to an imputed interest charge on invested capital. The rate used is ordinarily the weighted-average cost of capital. Some companies measure managerial performance in terms of the amount of residual income rather than the percentage return on investment. Because REB has assets of $500,000 and a cost of capital of 6%, it must earn $30,000 on those assets to cover the cost of capital. Given that operating income was only $25,000, it had a negative residual income of $5,000.

Answer (A) is incorrect because, although the firm's return on equity investment was 4%, its return on all funds invested was 5% ($25,000 pretax operating income ÷ $500,000). Answer (C) is incorrect because ROI is commonly based on before-tax income. Answer (D) is incorrect because $(22,000) equals the difference between net profit after taxes and targeted income.

**44.** Economic value added (EVA) is a measure of managerial performance. EVA equals

A. Net income after interest and taxes – (the weighted-average cost of capital × total assets).

B. [Earnings before interest and taxes × (1.0 – the tax rate)] – [the weighted-average cost of capital × (total assets – current liabilities)].

C. Earnings before interest and taxes – residual income.

D. After-tax operating income – interest on debt – dividends paid.

The correct answer is (B). *(Publisher)*
**REQUIRED:** The definition of EVA.
**DISCUSSION:** Economic value added (EVA) is a more specific version of residual income. It equals after-tax operating income [earnings before interest and taxes x (1.0 – the tax rate)] minus the product of the after-tax weighted-average cost of capital and an investment base equal to total assets minus current liabilities. EVA represents the business unit's true economic profit primarily because a charge for the cost of equity capital is implicit in the cost of capital. The cost of equity is an opportunity cost, that is, the return that could have been obtained on the best alternative investment of similar risk. Hence, the EVA measures the marginal benefit obtained by using resources in a particular way. It is useful for determining whether a segment of a business is increasing shareholder value.

Answer (A) is incorrect because interest should not be subtracted twice. The WACC includes interest. Answer (C) is incorrect because EVA is a specific way of calculating residual income. Answer (D) is incorrect because the EVA calculation subtracts an opportunity cost of equity capital, not an actual cost.

**45.** Valecon Co. reported the following information for the year just ended:

|  | Segment A | Segment B | Segment C |
|---|---|---|---|
| Pre-tax operating income | $ 4,000,000 | $ 2,000,000 | $3,000,000 |
| Current assets | 4,000,000 | 3,000,000 | 4,000,000 |
| Long-term assets | 16,000,000 | 13,000,000 | 8,000,000 |
| Current liabilities | 2,000,000 | 1,000,000 | 1,500,000 |

If the applicable income tax rate and after-tax weighted-average cost of capital for each segment are 30% and 10%, respectively, the segment with the highest economic value added (EVA) is

A. Segment A.

B. Segment B.

C. Segment C.

D. Not determinable from this information.

The correct answer is (C). *(Publisher)*
**REQUIRED:** The segment with the highest economic value added.
**DISCUSSION:** EVA equals after-tax operating income minus the product of the after-tax weighted-average cost of capital and an investment base equal to total assets minus current liabilities. Thus, the EVA for Segment C is $1,050,000 {[$3,000,000 x (1.0 – .3)] – [.10 x ($4,000,000 + $8,000,000 – $1,500,000)]}.

Answer (A) is incorrect because the EVA for Segment A is $1,000,000. Answer (B) is incorrect because the EVA for Segment B is – $100,000. Answer (D) is incorrect because the EVAs are determinable.

Questions 46 through 48 are based on the following information. Semibar Co. reports net income of $630,000. The information below for the year just ended is also available:

|  | January 1 | December 31 |
|---|---|---|
| Shareholders' equity | $4,200,000 | $4,480,000 |
| Share price | $25 | $30 |
| Shares outstanding | 400,000 | 400,000 |
| Cost of equity | 10% | 10% |
| Dividends per share |  | $1.00 |

**46.** Equity value creation is

A. $630,000

B. $448,000

C. $420,000

D. $210,000

The correct answer is (D). *(Publisher)*
**REQUIRED:** The equity value creation.
**DISCUSSION:** The equity spread calculates equity value creation by multiplying beginning equity capital by the difference between the return on equity (net income ÷ equity) and the percentage cost of equity. Thus, the equity value creation is $210,000 {[($630,000 ÷ $4,200,000) – 10%] x $4,200,000}.
Answer (A) is incorrect because $630,000 is net income. Answer (B) is incorrect because $448,000 is 10% of ending shareholders' equity. Answer (C) is incorrect because $420,000 is 10% of beginning shareholders' equity.

**47.** The market value added (MVA) is

A. $2,000,000

B. $1,720,000

C. $400,000

D. $280,000

The correct answer is (B). *(Publisher)*
**REQUIRED:** The market value added.
**DISCUSSION:** MVA is the difference between the market value of equity (shares outstanding x share price) and the equity supplied by shareholders. Hence, MVA equals $1,720,000 {[($30 x 400,000 shares) – $4,480,000 SE at 12/31] – [($25 x 400,000 shares) – $4,200,000 SE at 1/1]}.
Answer (A) is incorrect because $2,000,000 equals 400,000 shares times the increase in the share price. Answer (C) is incorrect because $400,000 is the amount of dividends paid. Answer (D) is incorrect because $280,000 is the increase in equity.

**48.** The total shareholder return is

A. 24%

B. 20%

C. 16.67%

D. 4%

The correct answer is (A). *(Publisher)*
**REQUIRED:** The total shareholder return.
**DISCUSSION:** The total shareholder return is the sum of the change in the stock price and dividends per share, divided by the initial stock price. It equals 24% {[($30 – $25) + $1] ÷ $25}.
Answer (B) is incorrect because 20% is based on a denominator equal to the ending share price. Answer (C) is incorrect because 16.67% ignores dividends and is based on a denominator equal to the ending share price. Answer (D) is incorrect because 4% ignores the share price change.

**49.** Managerial performance may be measured in many ways. For example, an internal nonfinancial measure is

    A. Market share.

    B. Delivery performance.

    C. Customer satisfaction.

    D. Manufacturing cycle time.

The correct answer is (D). *(Publisher)*
    **REQUIRED:** The internal nonfinancial measure.
    **DISCUSSION:** Feedback regarding managerial performance may take the form of financial and nonfinancial measures that may be internally or externally generated. Moreover, different measures have a long-term or short-term emphasis. Examples of internal nonfinancial measures are product quality, new product development time, and manufacturing cycle time (sometimes called lead time).
    Answers (A), (B), and (C) are incorrect because market share, delivery performance, and customer satisfaction are external nonfinancial measures.

**50.** Many forms of performance feedback are based on accounting information. For example, a divisional manager may be evaluated based on return on investment (income ÷ investment). One step in the process of developing a performance measure based on accounting information is to determine the basis for stating the measure in terms of dollars. Thus, if ROI is the chosen measure, and investment is defined as total assets, comparability issues are most likely to arise when the attribute used to calculate total assets is

    A. Current cost.

    B. Current disposal price.

    C. Historical cost.

    D. Present value.

The correct answer is (C). *(Publisher)*
    **REQUIRED:** The attribute most likely to create comparability problems.
    **DISCUSSION:** Historical cost creates comparability issues because returns on significantly depreciated assets may be higher than those on newer assets that have been acquired using inflated dollars. Thus, otherwise similarly situated managers may report different operating results. Moreover, managers may be reluctant to replace aging assets.
    Answers (A), (B), and (D) are incorrect because current cost, current disposal price, and present value are attempts to remedy the theoretical deficiencies of historical cost by presenting more accurate balance sheet values.

**51.** An organization's managerial decision-making model for capital budgeting is based on the net present value of discounted cash flows. The same organization's managerial performance evaluation model is based on annual divisional return on investment. Which of the following is true?

    A. Divisional managers are likely to maximize the measures in the decision-making model.

    B. Divisional managers are likely to maximize the measures in the performance evaluation model.

    C. The manager has an incentive to accept a project with a positive net present value that initially has a negative effect on net income.

    D. The use of models with different criteria promotes goal congruence.

The correct answer is (B). *(Publisher)*
    **REQUIRED:** The true statement about use of different models for decision making and managerial evaluation.
    **DISCUSSION:** Effective management control requires performance measurement and feedback. This process affects allocation of resources to organizational subunits. It also affects decisions about managers' compensation, advancement, and future assignments. Furthermore, evaluating their performance serves to motivate managers to optimize the measures in the performance evaluation model. However, that model may be inconsistent with the organization's model for managerial decision making.
    Answer (A) is incorrect because self-interest provides an incentive to maximize the measures used in performance evaluation. Answer (C) is incorrect because a manager evaluated on the basis of annual ROI has an interest in maximizing short-term net income, not long-term NPV. Answer (D) is incorrect because the models should be synchronized so that the goals of the organization and the manager are congruent.

**52.** Which of the following criteria would be most useful to a sales department manager in evaluating the performance of the manager's customer-service group?

    A. The customer is always right.

    B. Customer complaints should be processed promptly.

    C. Employees should maintain a positive attitude when dealing with customers.

    D. All customer inquiries should be answered within 7 days of receipt.

The correct answer is (D). *(CIA, adapted)*

    **REQUIRED:** The criterion most useful for evaluating a customer-service group.

    **DISCUSSION:** A criterion that requires all customer inquiries to be answered within 7 days of receipt permits accurate measurement of performance. The quantitative and specific nature of the appraisal using this standard avoids the vagueness, subjectivity, and personal bias that may afflict other forms of personnel evaluations.

    Answer (A) is incorrect because customer orientation is difficult to quantify. Answer (B) is incorrect because the standard specified is vague. Answer (C) is incorrect because no measure of a positive attitude has been specified for the employee.

**53.** Using the balanced scorecard approach, an organization evaluates managerial performance based on

    A. A single ultimate measure of operating results, such as residual income.

    B. Multiple financial and nonfinancial measures.

    C. Multiple nonfinancial measures only.

    D. Multiple financial measures only.

The correct answer is (B). *(Publisher)*

    **REQUIRED:** The nature of the balanced scorecard approach.

    **DISCUSSION:** The trend in managerial performance evaluation is the balanced scorecard approach. Multiple measures of performance permit a determination as to whether a manager is achieving certain objectives at the expense of others that may be equally or more important. These measures may be financial or nonfinancial and usually include items in four categories: profitability; customer satisfaction; innovation; and efficiency, quality, and time.

    Answer (A) is incorrect because the balanced scorecard approach uses multiple measures. Answers (C) and (D) are incorrect because the balanced scorecard approach uses financial and nonfinancial measures.

**54.** Maplewood Industries wants its division managers to concentrate on improving profitability. The performance evaluation measures that are most likely to encourage this behavior are

    A. Dividends per share, return on equity, and times interest earned.

    B. Turnover of operating assets, gross profit margin, and return on equity.

    C. Return on operating assets, the current ratio, and the debt-to-equity ratio.

    D. Turnover of operating assets, dividends per share, and times interest earned.

The correct answer is (B). *(CMA, adapted)*

    **REQUIRED:** The performance evaluation measures most likely to motivate division managers to concentrate on improving profitability.

    **DISCUSSION:** To improve profitability, managers should concentrate on those activities over which they have control. Thus, a division manager should aim for increased turnover of operating assets, higher gross profit margin, and greater return on equity.

    Answers (A) and (D) are incorrect because a division manager does not control dividends or times interest earned. Answer (C) is incorrect because a division manager does not control the debt-to-equity ratio.

**55.** Star Manufacturing wants its treasurer to focus on improving the company's liquidity position. The performance evaluation measures that are most likely to encourage this behavior are

    A. Accounts receivable turnover, return on assets, and the current ratio.

    B. Times interest earned, return on assets, and inventory turnover.

    C. Inventory turnover in days, the current ratio, and return on equity.

    D. Accounts receivable turnover, inventory turnover in days, and the current ratio.

The correct answer is (D). *(CMA, adapted)*

    **REQUIRED:** The performance measures most likely to encourage a treasurer to focus on improving liquidity.

    **DISCUSSION:** To be effective, performance measures must be within the control of the manager and meaningful to the area in which performance is desired. Such controls must fairly reflect the events they are designed to measure. A company's liquidity can be influenced by its accounts receivable turnover, inventory turnover, and current ratio. All of these measures are within the control of the treasurer's department.

    Answers (A) and (B) are incorrect because return on assets is not a measure of liquidity. Answer (C) is incorrect because return on equity is not a liquidity measure.

**56.** A major problem in comparing profitability measures among companies is the

- A. Lack of general agreement over which profitability measure is best.
- B. Differences in the size of the companies.
- C. Differences in the accounting methods used by the companies.
- D. Differences in the dividend policies of the companies.

The correct answer is (C). *(CMA, adapted)*

**REQUIRED:** The major problem in profitability comparisons.

**DISCUSSION:** The use of different accounting methods impairs comparability. Consequently, financial statements must be adjusted to permit intercompany comparisons.

Answer (A) is incorrect because, even if a general agreement were reached, different accounting methods would still impair comparability. Answer (B) is incorrect because differences in the size of companies do not directly affect the measure of a company's profitability to the same extent as the choice of accounting principles. Answer (D) is incorrect because differences in the dividend policies of companies do not directly affect the measure of a company's profitability to the same extent as the choice of accounting principles.

**57.** An example of an internal nonfinancial benchmark is

- A. The labor rate of comparably skilled employees at a major competitor's plant.
- B. The average actual cost per pound of a specific product at the company's most efficient plant becoming the benchmark for the company's other plants.
- C. The company setting a benchmark of $50,000 for employee training programs at each of the company's plants.
- D. The percentage of customer orders delivered on time at the company's most efficient plant becoming the benchmark for the company's other plants.

The correct answer is (D). *(CIA, adapted)*

**REQUIRED:** The internal nonfinancial benchmark.

**DISCUSSION:** Benchmarking "involves continuously evaluating the principles of best-in-class organizations and adapting company processes to incorporate the best of these practices." It "analyzes and measures the key outputs of a business process or function against the best and also identifies the underlying key actions and root causes that contribute to the performance difference" (from a pronouncement issued by a committee of the IMA). The percentage of orders delivered on time at the company's most efficient plant is an example of an internal nonfinancial benchmark.

Answers (A), (B), and (C) are incorrect because the labor rate of a competitor, the cost per pound of a product at the company's most efficient plant, and the cost of a training program are financial benchmarks.

**58.** Nonfinancial performance measures are important to engineering and operations managers in assessing the quality levels of their products. Which of the following indicators can be used to measure product quality?

I. Returns and allowances
II. Number and types of customer complaints
III. Production cycle time

- A. I and II only.
- B. I and III only.
- C. II and III only.
- D. I, II, and III.

The correct answer is (A). *(CPA, adapted)*

**REQUIRED:** The indicators of product quality.

**DISCUSSION:** Nonfinancial performance measures, such as product quality, are useful for day-to-day control purposes. Examples (indicators) of nonfinancial performance measures include the following: first class calibration yield, outgoing quality level for each product line, returned merchandise, customer report card, competitive rank, and on-time delivery.

Answers (B), (C), and (D) are incorrect because the production cycle time does not measure product quality.

**59.** When evaluating projects, breakeven time is best described as

A. Annual fixed costs ÷ monthly contribution margin.

B. Project investment ÷ annual net cash inflows.

C. The point at which cumulative cash inflows on a project equal total cash outflows.

D. The point at which discounted cumulative cash inflows on a project equal discounted total cash outflows.

The correct answer is (D). *(CMA, adapted)*
**REQUIRED:** The definition of breakeven time.
**DISCUSSION:** Breakeven time evaluates the rapidity of new product development. The usual calculation determines the period beginning with project approval that is required for the discounted cumulative cash inflows to equal the discounted cumulative cash outflows. The concept is similar to the payback period, but it is more sophisticated because it incorporates the time value of money. It also differs from the payback method because the period covered begins at the outset of a project, not when the initial cash outflow occurs.
Answer (A) is incorrect because it is related to breakeven point, not breakeven time. Answer (B) is incorrect because the payback period equals investment divided by annual undiscounted net cash inflows. Answer (C) is incorrect because the payback period is the period required for total undiscounted cash inflows to equal total undiscounted cash outflows.

---

Questions 60 and 61 are based on the following information. Wolk Corporation is a highly automated manufacturing firm. The vice president of finance has decided that traditional standards are inappropriate for performance measures in an automated environment. Labor is insignificant in terms of the total cost of production and tends to be fixed, material quality is considered more important than minimizing material cost, and customer satisfaction is the number one priority. As a result, delivery performance measures have been chosen to evaluate performance.

The following information is considered typical of the time involved to complete orders.

* Wait time:
  - From order being placed to start of production          10.0 days
  - From start of production to completion          5.0 days
* Inspection time          1.5 days
* Process time          3.0 days
* Move time          2.5 days

---

**60.** What is the manufacturing cycle efficiency for this order?

A. 25.0%

B. 13.6%

C. 37.5%

D. 33.3%

The correct answer is (A). *(CMA, adapted)*
**REQUIRED:** The manufacturing cycle efficiency statistic for an order.
**DISCUSSION:** Manufacturing cycle efficiency is the quotient of the time required for value-added production divided by total manufacturing cycle time (throughput time or velocity of production), which is the time elapsed from when an order is ready for production until it becomes a finished good. For this order, the total manufacturing cycle time is 12 days (5.0 + 1.5 + 3.0 + 2.5), and the manufacturing cycle efficiency is 25% (3 days of processing ÷ 12).
Answer (B) is incorrect because 13.6% includes the 10 days prior to production in the denominator, a period not included in the calculation of manufacturing cycle efficiency. Answer (C) is incorrect because inspection time and move time should be included in the denominator. Answer (D) is incorrect because 33.3% equals inspection and move time divided by the manufacturing cycle time.

---

**61.** What is the delivery cycle time for this order?

A. 7 days.

B. 12 days.

C. 15 days.

D. 22 days.

The correct answer is (D). *(CMA, adapted)*
**REQUIRED:** The delivery cycle time for the order.
**DISCUSSION:** The delivery cycle time is defined as the entire time from receipt of the order until delivery of the order. This period equals 22 days (10.0 + 5.0 + 1.5 + 3.0 + 2.5).
Answer (A) is incorrect because 7 days excludes the wait time. Answer (B) is incorrect because 12 days ignores the 10 days of the waiting period prior to the start of production. Answer (C) is incorrect because 15 days incorporates the wait time but not the production periods.

## 11.3 Decentralization and Transfer Pricing

**62.** The primary difference between centralization and decentralization is

- A. Separate offices for all managers.
- B. Geographical separation of divisional headquarters and central headquarters.
- C. The extent of freedom of decision making by many levels of management.
- D. The relative size of the firm.

The correct answer is (C). *(Publisher)*
**REQUIRED:** The primary difference between centralization and decentralization.
**DISCUSSION:** The primary distinction is in the degree of freedom of decision making by managers at many levels. In decentralization, decision making is at as low a level as possible. The premise is that the local manager can make more informed decisions than a centralized manager. Centralization assumes decision making must be consolidated so that activities throughout the organization may be more effectively coordinated. In most organizations, a mixture of these approaches is best.
Answer (A) is incorrect because whether all managers have separate offices is a trivial issue. Answer (B) is incorrect because geographical separation is possible in a centralized environment. Answer (D) is incorrect because relative size is a secondary factor in determining whether to centralize.

**63.** Which of the following is most likely to be a disadvantage of decentralization?

- A. Lower-level employees will develop less rapidly than in a centralized organization.
- B. Lower-level employees will complain of not having enough to do.
- C. Top management will have less time available to devote to unique problems.
- D. Lower-level managers may make conflicting decisions.

The correct answer is (D). *(CIA, adapted)*
**REQUIRED:** The item most likely to be a disadvantage of decentralization.
**DISCUSSION:** The disadvantages of decentralization include a tendency to focus on short-run results to the detriment of the long-term health of the entity, an increased risk of loss of control by top management, the increased difficulty of coordinating interdependent units, and less cooperation and communication among competing decentralized unit managers.
Answer (A) is incorrect because decentralization encourages development of lower-level managers. They will have greater responsibilities and authority. Answer (B) is incorrect because more tasks will be delegated to lower-level employees. Answer (C) is incorrect because top managers will be freed from operating problems.

**64.** Which of the following is not a cost of decentralization?

- A. Dysfunctional decision making owing to disagreements of managers regarding overall goals and subgoals of the individual decision makers.
- B. A decreased understanding of the overall goals of the organization.
- C. Increased costs for developing the information system.
- D. Decreased costs of corporate-level staff services and management talent.

The correct answer is (D). *(Publisher)*
**REQUIRED:** The item not a cost of decentralization.
**DISCUSSION:** The costs of centralized staff may actually decrease under decentralization. On the other hand, the corporate staff and the various services they provide may have to be duplicated in various divisions, thereby increasing overall costs. Suboptimal decisions may result from disharmony among organizational goals, subgoals of the division, and the individual goals of managers. The overall goals of the firm may more easily be misunderstood because individual managers may not see the larger picture. Moreover, the information system necessary for adequate reporting in a decentralized mode will tend toward redundancy, which increases costs.
Answer (A) is incorrect because dysfunctional decision making is a cost of decentralization. Answer (B) is incorrect because a decreased understanding of the overall goals of an organization is a cost of decentralization. Answer (C) is incorrect because increased costs for developing the information system is a cost of decentralization.

**65.** The CEO of a rapidly growing high-technology firm has exercised centralized authority over all corporate functions. Because the company now operates in four states, the CEO is considering the advisability of decentralizing operational control over production and sales. Which of the following conditions probably will result from and be a valid reason for decentralizing?

A. Greater local control over compliance with federal regulations.

B. More efficient use of headquarters staff officials and specialists.

C. Quicker and better operating decisions.

D. Greater economies in purchasing.

The correct answer is (C). *(CIA, adapted)*

**REQUIRED:** The condition that would be a valid reason for decentralizing.

**DISCUSSION:** Decentralization results in greater speed in making operating decisions because they are made by lower-level managers instead of being referred to top management. The quality of operating decisions should also be enhanced, assuming proper training of managers, because those closest to the problems should be the most knowledgeable about them.

Answer (A) is incorrect because compliance with governmental regulations is probably more easily achieved by centralization. A disadvantage of decentralization is the difficulty of assuring uniform action by units of the entity that have substantial autonomy. Answer (B) is incorrect because decentralization may result in duplication of efforts, resulting in less efficient use of headquarters staff officials and specialists. Answer (D) is incorrect because decentralization usually results in a duplication of purchasing efforts.

**66.** Which one of the following will not occur in an organization that gives managers throughout the organization maximum freedom to make decisions?

A. Individual managers regarding the managers of other segments as they do external parties.

B. Two divisions of the organization having competing models that aim for the same market segments.

C. Delays in securing approval for the introduction of new products.

D. Greater knowledge of the marketplace and improved service to customers.

The correct answer is (C). *(CMA, adapted)*

**REQUIRED:** The event that will not occur in a decentralized organization.

**DISCUSSION:** Decentralization is beneficial because it creates greater responsiveness to the needs of local customers, suppliers, and employees. Managers at lower levels are more knowledgeable about local markets and the needs of customers, etc. A decentralized organization is also more likely to respond flexibly and quickly to changing conditions, for example, by expediting the introduction of new products. Furthermore, greater authority enhances managerial morale and development. Disadvantages of decentralization include duplication of effort and lack of goal congruence.

Answer (A) is incorrect because, when segments are autonomous, other segments are regarded as external parties, e.g., as suppliers, customers, or competitors. Answer (B) is incorrect because autonomous segments may have the authority to compete in the same markets. Answer (D) is incorrect because decentralizing decision making results in improved service. The managers closest to customers are making decisions about customer service.

**67.** The price that one division of a company charges another division for goods or services provided is called the

A. Market price.

B. Transfer price.

C. Outlay price.

D. Distress price.

The correct answer is (B). *(CIA, adapted)*

**REQUIRED:** The price that one division of a company charges another for goods or services provided.

**DISCUSSION:** A transfer price is the price charged by one segment of an organization for a product or service supplied to another segment of the same organization.

Answer (A) is incorrect because market price is an approach to determine a transfer price. Answer (C) is incorrect because outlay price is an approach to determine a transfer price. Answer (D) is incorrect because distress price is an approach to determine a transfer price.

**68.** The most fundamental responsibility center affected by the use of market-based transfer prices is a(n)

   A. Production center.

   B. Investment center.

   C. Cost center.

   D. Profit center.

The correct answer is (D). *(CMA, adapted)*

   **REQUIRED:** The most fundamental responsibility center affected by the use of market-based transfer prices.

   **DISCUSSION:** Transfer prices are often used by profit centers and investment centers. Profit centers are the more fundamental of these two centers because investment centers are responsible not only for revenues and costs but also for invested capital.

   Answer (A) is incorrect because a production center may be a cost center, a profit center, or even an investment center. Transfer prices are not used in a cost center. Transfer prices are used to compute profitability, but a cost center is responsible only for cost control. Answer (B) is incorrect because an investment center is not as fundamental as a profit center. Answer (C) is incorrect because transfer prices are not used in a cost center.

**69.** Transfer pricing should encourage goal congruence and managerial effort. In a decentralized organization, it should also encourage autonomous decision making. Managerial effort is

   A. The desire and the commitment to achieve a specific goal.

   B. The sharing of goals by supervisors and subordinates.

   C. The extent to which individuals have the authority to make decisions.

   D. The extent of the attempt to accomplish a specific goal.

The correct answer is (D). *(Publisher)*

   **REQUIRED:** The definition of managerial effort.

   **DISCUSSION:** Managerial effort is the extent to which a manager attempts to accomplish a goal. Managerial effort may include psychological as well as physical commitment to a goal.

   Answer (A) is incorrect because motivation is the desire and the commitment to achieve a specific goal. Answer (B) is incorrect because goal congruence is the sharing of goals by supervisors and subordinates. Answer (C) is incorrect because autonomy is the extent to which individuals have the authority to make decisions.

**70.** Goal congruence is

   A. The desire and the commitment to achieve a specific goal.

   B. The sharing of goals by supervisors and subordinates.

   C. The extent to which individuals have the authority to make decisions.

   D. The extent of the attempt to accomplish a specific goal.

The correct answer is (B). *(Publisher)*

   **REQUIRED:** The definition of goal congruence.

   **DISCUSSION:** Goal congruence is agreement on the goals of the organization and/or the segment by both supervisors and subordinates. Performance is assumed to be optimized when the parties understand that personal and segmental goals should be consistent with those of the organization.

   Answer (A) is incorrect because motivation is the desire and the commitment to achieve a specific goal. Answer (C) is incorrect because autonomy is the extent to which individuals have the authority to make decisions. Answer (D) is incorrect because managerial effort is the extent of the attempt to accomplish a specific goal.

**71.** Motivation is

   A. The desire and the commitment to achieve a specific goal.

   B. The sharing of goals by supervisors and subordinates.

   C. The extent to which individuals have the authority to make decisions.

   D. The extent of the attempt to accomplish a specific goal.

The correct answer is (A). *(Publisher)*

   **REQUIRED:** The definition of motivation.

   **DISCUSSION:** Motivation is the desire to attain a specific goal (goal congruence) and the commitment to accomplish the goal (managerial effort). Managerial motivation is therefore a combination of managerial effort and goal congruence.

   Answer (B) is incorrect because goal congruence is the sharing of goals by supervisors and subordinates. Answer (C) is incorrect because autonomy is the extent to which individuals have the authority to make decisions. Answer (D) is incorrect because managerial effort is the extent of the attempt to accomplish a specific goal.

**72.** A proposed transfer price may be based upon the outlay cost. Outlay cost plus opportunity cost is

A. The retail price.

B. The price representing the cash outflows of the supplying division plus the contribution to the supplying division from an outside sale.

C. The price usually set by an absorption-costing calculation.

D. The price set by charging for variable costs plus a lump sum or an additional markup, but less than full markup.

The correct answer is (B). *(Publisher)*
**REQUIRED:** The definition of outlay cost plus opportunity cost.
**DISCUSSION:** At this price, the supplying division is indifferent as to whether it sells internally or externally. Outlay cost plus opportunity cost therefore represents a minimum acceptable price for a seller. However, no transfer price formula is appropriate in all circumstances.
Answer (A) is incorrect because the retail price is the definition of the market price, assuming an arm's-length transaction. Answer (C) is incorrect because full cost is the price usually set by an absorption-costing calculation. Answer (D) is incorrect because the variable-cost-plus price is the price set by charging for variable costs plus a lump sum or an additional markup, but less than full markup.

**73.** A proposed transfer price may be a cost-plus price. Variable-cost-plus price is

A. The price on the open market.

B. The price representing the cash outflows of the supplying division plus the contribution to the supplying division from an outside sale.

C. The price usually set by an absorption-costing calculation.

D. The price set by charging for variable costs plus a lump sum or an additional markup, but less than full markup.

The correct answer is (D). *(Publisher)*
**REQUIRED:** The definition of variable-cost-plus price.
**DISCUSSION:** The variable-cost-plus price is the price set by charging for variable cost plus either a lump sum or an additional markup but less than the full markup price. This permits top management to enter the decision process and dictate that a division transfer at variable cost plus some appropriate amount.
Answer (A) is incorrect because the price on the open market is the definition of the market price. Answer (B) is incorrect because outlay cost plus opportunity cost is the price representing the cash outflows of the supplying division plus the contribution to the supplying division from an outside sale. Answer (C) is incorrect because the full-cost price is the price usually set by an absorption-costing calculation.

**74.** A proposed transfer price may be based upon the full-cost price. Full-cost price is

A. The price on the open market.

B. The price representing the cash outflows of the supplying division plus the contribution to the supplying division from an outside sale.

C. The price usually set by an absorption-costing calculation.

D. The price set by charging for variable costs plus a lump sum or an additional markup, but less than full markup.

The correct answer is (C). *(Publisher)*
**REQUIRED:** The definition of full-cost price.
**DISCUSSION:** Full-cost price is the price usually set by an absorption-costing calculation and includes materials, labor, and a full allocation of manufacturing O/H. This full-cost price may lead to dysfunctional behavior by the supplying and receiving divisions, e.g., purchasing from outside sources at a slightly lower price that is substantially above the variable costs of internal production.
Answer (A) is incorrect because the market price is the price on the open market. Answer (B) is incorrect because the outlay cost plus opportunity cost is the price representing the cash outflows of the supplying division plus the contribution to the supplying division from an outside sale. Answer (D) is incorrect because the variable-cost-plus price is the price set by charging for variable costs plus a lump sum or an additional markup, but less than full markup.

**75.** A limitation of transfer prices based on actual cost is that they

    A.  Charge inefficiencies to the department that is transferring the goods.

    B.  Can lead to suboptimal decisions for the company as a whole.

    C.  Must be adjusted by some markup.

    D.  Lack clarity and administrative convenience.

The correct answer is (B). *(CIA, adapted)*
    **REQUIRED:** The limitation of transfer prices based on actual cost.
    **DISCUSSION:** The optimal transfer price of a selling division should be set at a point that will have the most desirable economic effect on the firm as a whole while at the same time continuing to motivate the management of every division to perform efficiently. Setting the transfer price based on actual costs rather than standard costs would give the selling division little incentive to control costs.
    Answer (A) is incorrect because inefficiencies are charged to the buying department. Answer (C) is incorrect because, by definition, cost-based transfer prices are not adjusted by some markup. Answer (D) is incorrect because cost-based transfer prices provide the advantages of clarity and administrative convenience.

**76.** Brent Co. has intracompany service transfers from Division Core, a cost center, to Division Pro, a profit center. Under stable economic conditions, which of the following transfer prices is likely to be most conducive to evaluating whether both divisions have met their responsibilities?

    A.  Actual cost.

    B.  Standard variable cost.

    C.  Actual cost plus markup.

    D.  Negotiated price.

The correct answer is (B). *(CPA, adapted)*
    **REQUIRED:** The transfer price likely to be most useful for evaluating both divisions.
    **DISCUSSION:** A cost center is responsible for costs only. A profit center is responsible for costs and revenues. Hence, the transfer from the cost center must, by definition, be at a cost-based figure. The transfer should be at standard variable cost so as to isolate any variance resulting from Core's operations. Assuming fixed costs are not controllable in the short run, the relevant variance is the difference between actual cost and the standard variable cost.
    Answer (A) is incorrect because actual cost is not appropriate for a transfer price from a cost center to a profit center. Answers (C) and (D) are incorrect because, as a cost center, Core will use cost as a transfer price.

**77.** A large manufacturing company has several autonomous divisions that sell their products in perfectly competitive external markets as well as internally to the other divisions of the company. Top management expects each of its divisional managers to take actions that will maximize the organization's goals as well as their own goals. Top management also promotes a sustained level of management effort of all of its divisional managers. Under these circumstances, for products exchanged between divisions, the transfer price that will generally lead to optimal decisions for the manufacturing company would be a transfer price equal to the

    A.  Full cost of the product.

    B.  Full cost of the product plus a markup.

    C.  Variable cost of the product plus a markup.

    D.  Market price of the product.

The correct answer is (D). *(CIA, adapted)*
    **REQUIRED:** The optimal transfer price.
    **DISCUSSION:** A market-based transfer price promotes goal congruence and sustained management effort. It is also consistent with divisional autonomy. A market transfer price is most appropriate when the market is competitive, interdivisional dependency is low, and buying in the market involves no marginal costs or benefits.
    Answer (A) is incorrect because a transfer at full cost means that the selling division will not make a profit. In addition, the selling division may be forgoing profits that could be obtained by selling to outside customers. Thus, full-cost transfer prices can lead to suboptimal decisions. Answer (B) is incorrect because a transfer at full cost plus markup results in no incentive for the selling division to control its costs. Hence, a sustained level of management effort may not be maintained. Answer (C) is incorrect because a transfer at variable cost plus markup has the same weaknesses as full cost plus markup.

**78.** The Eastern division sells goods internally to the Western division of the same company. The quoted external price in industry publications from a supplier near Eastern is $200 per ton plus transportation. It costs $20 per ton to transport the goods to Western. Eastern's actual market cost per ton to buy the direct materials to make the transferred product is $100. Actual per-ton direct labor is $50. Other actual costs of storage and handling are $40. The company president selects a $220 transfer price. This is an example of

A. Market-based transfer pricing.

B. Cost-based transfer pricing.

C. Negotiated transfer pricing.

D. Cost plus 20% transfer pricing.

The correct answer is (A). *(CIA, adapted)*
**REQUIRED:** The type of transfer price.
**DISCUSSION:** A transfer price is the price charged by one segment of an organization for a product or service supplied to another segment of the same organization. The three basic criteria that the transfer pricing system in a decentralized company should satisfy are to (1) provide information allowing central management to evaluate divisions with respect to total company profit and each division's contribution to profit, (2) stimulate each manager's efficiency without losing each division's autonomy, and (3) motivate each divisional manager to achieve his/her own profit goal in a manner contributing to the company's success. Because the $220 transfer price selected is based on the quoted external price (market), it is an example of market-based transfer pricing.
Answer (B) is incorrect because the cost-based price would be $210 ($100 + $50 + $40 + $20). Answer (C) is incorrect because no negotiations took place. Answer (D) is incorrect because cost plus 20% would be $252 ($210 x 1.20).

**79.** Which of the following is the most significant disadvantage of a cost-based transfer price?

A. Requires internally developed information.

B. Imposes market effects on company operations.

C. Requires externally developed information.

D. May not promote long-term efficiencies.

The correct answer is (D). *(CIA, adapted)*
**REQUIRED:** The most significant disadvantage of a cost-based transfer price.
**DISCUSSION:** A cost-based transfer price is a price charged in an intracompany transaction that covers only the selling subunit's costs. However, by ignoring relevant alternative market prices, a company may pay more than is necessary to produce goods and services internally.
Answer (A) is incorrect because internally developed information should be developed whether or not transfer prices are used. Answer (B) is incorrect because market effects on company operations are characteristic of a market-based transfer price. Answer (C) is incorrect because externally developed information is needed for a market-based transfer price.

**80.** Which of the following is not true about international transfer prices for a multinational firm?

A. Allows firms to attempt to minimize worldwide taxes.

B. Allows the firm to evaluate each division.

C. Provides each division with a profit-making orientation.

D. Allows firms to correctly price products in each country in which it operates.

The correct answer is (D). *(CIA, adapted)*
**REQUIRED:** The false statement about international transfer prices.
**DISCUSSION:** The calculation of transfer prices should be unique to each country. A scheme for calculating transfer prices for a firm may correctly price the firm's product in Country A but not in Country B. The product may be overpriced in Country B, and sales will be lower than anticipated. Alternatively, the product may be underpriced in Country B, and the authorities may allege that the firm is dumping its product there.
Answer (A) is incorrect because properly chosen transfer prices allow firms to minimize taxes by producing various parts of the products in different countries and strategically transferring the parts at various systematically calculated prices. Answer (B) is incorrect because properly chosen transfer prices allocate revenues and expenses to divisions in various countries. These numbers are used as part of the input for the performance evaluation of each division. Answer (C) is incorrect because transfer prices motivate division managers to buy parts and products (from either internal or external suppliers) at the lowest possible prices and to sell their products (to either internal or external customers) at the highest possible prices.

**81.** A company has two divisions, A and B, each operated as a profit center. A charges B $35 per unit for each unit transferred to B. Other data follow:

| | |
|---|---:|
| A's variable cost per unit | $ 30 |
| A's fixed costs | 10,000 |
| A's annual sales to B | 5,000 units |
| A's sales to outsiders | 50,000 units |

A is planning to raise its transfer price to $50 per unit. Division B can purchase units at $40 each from outsiders, but doing so would idle A's facilities now committed to producing units for B. Division A cannot increase its sales to outsiders. From the perspective of the company as a whole, from whom should Division B acquire the units, assuming B's market is unaffected?

A. Outside vendors.

B. Division A, but only at the variable cost per unit.

C. Division A, but only until fixed costs are covered, then from outside vendors.

D. Division A, despite the increased transfer price.

The correct answer is (D). *(CIA, adapted)*
**REQUIRED:** The purchasing decision benefiting the company.
**DISCUSSION:** Opportunity costs are $0 because A's facilities would be idle if B did not purchase from A. Assuming fixed costs are not affected by the decision, the intracompany sale is preferable from the company's perspective because A's $30 variable unit cost is less than the outside vendor's price of $40.
Answer (A) is incorrect because outside purchase will increase the company's cost of sales by $10 per unit. Answer (B) is incorrect because the transfer price is irrelevant to the decision. It does not affect overall profits. Answer (C) is incorrect because the company is initially concerned with covering variable rather than fixed costs.

**82.** An appropriate transfer price between two divisions of The Stark Company can be determined from the following data:

Fabricating Division

| | |
|---|---:|
| Market price of subassembly | $50 |
| Variable cost of subassembly | $20 |
| Excess capacity (in units) | 1,000 |

Assembling Division

| | |
|---|---:|
| Number of units needed | 900 |

What is the natural bargaining range for the two divisions?

A. Between $20 and $50.

B. Between $50 and $70.

C. Any amount less than $50.

D. $50 is the only acceptable price.

The correct answer is (A). *(CMA, adapted)*
**REQUIRED:** The appropriate transfer price.
**DISCUSSION:** An ideal transfer price should permit each division to operate independently and achieve its goals while functioning in the best interest of the overall company. Transfer prices can be determined in a number of ways, including normal market price, negotiated price, variable costs, or full absorption costs. The capacity of the selling division is often a determinant of the ideal transfer price. If the Fabricating Division had no excess capacity, it would charge the Assembling Division the regular market price. However, given excess capacity of 1,000 units, negotiation is possible because any transfer price greater than the variable cost of $20 would absorb some fixed costs and result in increased divisional profits. Thus, any price between $20 and $50 is acceptable to the Fabricating Division. Any price under $50 is acceptable to the Assembling Division because that is the price that would be paid to an outside supplier.
Answer (B) is incorrect because Assembling will not pay more than $50. Answer (C) is incorrect because Fabricating will not be willing to accept less than $20. Answer (D) is incorrect because Fabricating should be willing to accept any price between $20 and $50.

**83.** Division A of a company is currently operating at 50% capacity. It produces a single product and sells all its production to outside customers for $13 per unit. Variable costs are $7 per unit, and fixed costs are $6 per unit at the current production level. Division B, which currently purchases this product from an outside supplier for $12 per unit, would like to purchase the product from Division A. Division A will operate at 80% capacity to meet outside customers' and Division B's demand. What is the minimum price that Division A should charge Division B for this product?

    A.   $7.00 per unit.

    B.   $10.40 per unit.

    C.   $12.00 per unit.

    D.   $13.00 per unit.

**84.** The Alpha Division of a company, which is operating at capacity, produces and sells 1,000 units of a certain electronic component in a perfectly competitive market. Revenue and cost data are as follows:

| | |
|---|---|
| Sales | $50,000 |
| Variable costs | 34,000 |
| Fixed costs | 12,000 |

The minimum transfer price that should be charged to the Beta Division of the same company for each component is

    A.   $12

    B.   $34

    C.   $46

    D.   $50

The correct answer is (A). *(CIA, adapted)*

**REQUIRED:** The minimum price that should be charged by one division of a company to another.

**DISCUSSION:** From the seller's perspective, the price should reflect at least its incremental cash outflow (outlay cost) plus the contribution from an outside sale (opportunity cost). Because A has idle capacity, the opportunity cost is $0. Thus, the minimum price Division A should charge Division B is $7.00.

Answer (B) is incorrect because $7.00 is the minimum that should be charged. Answer (C) is incorrect because Division A should not include any fixed costs in its transfer price because Division A has idle capacity. Answer (D) is incorrect because, since Division A has idle capacity, the minimum transfer price should recover Division A's variable (outlay) costs.

The correct answer is (D). *(CIA, adapted)*

**REQUIRED:** The minimum transfer price that should be charged to another division of the same company.

**DISCUSSION:** In a perfectly competitive market, market price is ordinarily the appropriate transfer price. Because the market price is objective, using it avoids waste and maximizes efficiency. In a perfectly competitive market, the market price equals the minimum transfer price, which is the sum of outlay cost and opportunity cost. Outlay cost is the variable cost per unit, or $34 ($34,000 ÷ 1,000). Opportunity cost is the contribution margin forgone, or $16 ($50 – $34). Thus, the minimum transfer price is $50 ($34 + $16).

Answer (A) is incorrect because, given that Alpha Division has no idle capacity, the transfer price to Beta should be the market price of $50 per unit. Answer (B) is incorrect because the opportunity cost needs to be included. Answer (C) is incorrect because the minimum transfer price equals outlay (variable) costs plus opportunity cost, not variable costs plus fixed costs.

Questions 85 through 87 are based on the following information. Parkside Inc. has several divisions that operate as decentralized profit centers. Parkside's Entertainment Division manufactures video arcade equipment using the products of two of Parkside's other divisions. The Plastics Division manufactures plastic components, one type that is made exclusively for the Entertainment Division, while other less complex components are sold to outside markets. The products of the Video Cards Division are sold in a competitive market; however, one video card model is also used by the Entertainment Division. The actual costs per unit used by the Entertainment Division are presented in the next column.

| | Plastic Components | Video Cards |
|---|---|---|
| Direct material | $1.25 | $2.40 |
| Direct labor | 2.35 | 3.00 |
| Variable overhead | 1.00 | 1.50 |
| Fixed overhead | .40 | 2.25 |
| Total cost | $5.00 | $9.15 |

The Plastics Division sells its commercial products at full cost plus a 25% markup and believes the proprietary plastic component made for the Entertainment Division would sell for $6.25 per unit on the open market. The market price of the video card used by the Entertainment Division is $10.98 per unit.

**85.** A per-unit transfer price from the Video Cards Division to the Entertainment Division at full cost, $9.15, would

A. Allow evaluation of both divisions on a competitive basis.

B. Satisfy the Video Cards Division's profit desire by allowing recovery of opportunity costs.

C. Provide no profit incentive for the Video Cards Division to control or reduce costs.

D. Encourage the Entertainment Division to purchase video cards from an outside source.

The correct answer is (C). *(CMA, adapted)*

**REQUIRED:** The effect of a full-cost transfer price.

**DISCUSSION:** A transfer price is the amount one segment of an organization charges another segment for a product. The selling division should be allowed to recover its incremental cost plus the opportunity cost of the transfer. Hence, in a competitive market, the seller should be able to charge the market price. Using full cost as a transfer price provides no incentive to the seller to control production costs.

Answer (A) is incorrect because evaluating the seller is difficult if it can pass along all costs to the buyer. Answer (B) is incorrect because transfers at full cost do not allow for a seller's profit. Answer (D) is incorrect because a full-cost transfer is favorable to the buyer. It is lower than the market price.

**86.** Assume that the Entertainment Division is able to purchase a large quantity of video cards from an outside source at $8.70 per unit. The Video Cards Division, having excess capacity, agrees to lower its transfer price to $8.70 per unit. This action would

A. Optimize the profit goals of the Entertainment Division while subverting the profit goals of Parkside Inc.

B. Allow evaluation of both divisions on the same basis.

C. Subvert the profit goals of the Video Cards Division while optimizing the profit goals of the Entertainment Division.

D. Optimize the overall profit goals of Parkside Inc.

The correct answer is (D). *(CMA, adapted)*

**REQUIRED:** The impact of lowering the transfer price to match an outside seller's price.

**DISCUSSION:** If the seller has excess capacity, it should lower its transfer price to match the outside offer. This decision optimizes the profits of the company as a whole by allowing for use of capacity that would otherwise be idle.

Answer (A) is incorrect because this action is congruent with the goals of Parkside. The use of idle capacity enhances profits. Answer (B) is incorrect because the transfer is at a loss (relative to full cost) to the seller, although the company as a whole will benefit. Answer (C) is incorrect because the buyer is indifferent as to whether to purchase internally or externally.

**87.** Assume that the Plastics Division has excess capacity and it has negotiated a transfer price of $5.60 per plastic component with the Entertainment Division. This price will

A. Cause the Plastics Division to reduce the number of commercial plastic components it manufactures.

B. Motivate both divisions as estimated profits are shared.

C. Encourage the Entertainment Division to seek an outside source for plastic components.

D. Demotivate the Plastics Division causing mediocre performance.

The correct answer is (B). *(CMA, adapted)*

**REQUIRED:** The effect of using a negotiated transfer price that is greater than full cost but less than market price.

**DISCUSSION:** Given that the Plastics Division (the seller) has excess capacity, transfers within the company entail no opportunity cost. Accordingly, the transfer at the negotiated price will improve the performance measures of the transferor. Purchasing internally at below the market price also benefits the transferee, so the motivational purpose of transfer pricing is achieved. The goal congruence purpose is also achieved because the internal transaction benefits the company.

Answer (A) is incorrect because this arrangement creates no disincentive for the seller. It will make a profit on every unit transferred. Answer (C) is incorrect because the market price charged by outside sources is higher than the negotiated price. Answer (D) is incorrect because, given idle capacity, selling at any amount in excess of variable cost should motivate the seller.

## 11.4 Comprehensive

Questions 88 through 92 are based on the following information. Oslo Co.'s industrial photo-finishing division, Rho, incurred the following costs and expenses in 1998:

|  | Variable | Fixed |
|---|---|---|
| Direct materials | $200,000 | |
| Direct labor | 150,000 | |
| Factory overhead | 70,000 | $42,000 |
| General, selling, and administrative | 30,000 | 48,000 |
| Totals | $450,000 | $90,000 |

During 1998, Rho produced 300,000 units of industrial photo-prints, which were sold for $2.00 each. Oslo's investment in Rho was $500,000 and $700,000 at January 1, 1998 and December 31, 1998, respectively. Oslo normally imputes interest on investments at 15% of average invested capital.

**88.** For the year ended December 31, 1998, Rho's return on average investment was

A. 15.0%

B. 10.0%

C. 8.6%

D. (5.0%)

The correct answer is (B). *(CPA, adapted)*
**REQUIRED:** The return on average investment.
**DISCUSSION:** Average invested capital is $600,000 [($500,000 + $700,000) ÷ 2]. The return on average investment is 10% ($60,000 net income from operations ÷ $600,000 average invested capital).

| | |
|---|---|
| Sales (300,000 units × $2) | $600,000 |
| Variable costs | (450,000) |
| Fixed costs | (90,000) |
| Net operating income | $ 60,000 |

Answer (A) is incorrect because 15% is the imputed rate. Answer (C) is incorrect because net income should not be divided by the year-end invested capital of $700,000. Answer (D) is incorrect because (5.0%) equals the residual loss ($30,000) divided by average invested capital.

**89.** Assume that net operating income was $60,000 and that average invested capital was $600,000. For the year ended December 31, 1998, Rho's residual income (loss) was

A. $150,000

B. $60,000

C. $(45,000)

D. $(30,000)

The correct answer is (D). *(CPA, adapted)*
**REQUIRED:** The residual income (loss).
**DISCUSSION:** Residual income is equal to net operating income ($60,000) minus imputed interest on invested capital ($600,000). The imputed interest rate is 15%. Thus,

| | |
|---|---|
| Net operating income | $ 60,000 |
| Imputed interest (15% × $600,000) | (90,000) |
| Residual income | $(30,000) |

Answer (A) is incorrect because the imputed interest should not be added to net operating income. Answer (B) is incorrect because the imputed interest needs to be deducted from net operating income. Answer (C) is incorrect because the imputed interest is not 15% of the year-end invested capital.

**90.** How many industrial photo-print units did Rho have to sell in 1998 to break even?

A. 180,000

B. 120,000

C. 90,000

D. 60,000

The correct answer is (A). *(CPA, adapted)*
**REQUIRED:** The breakeven point in units.
**DISCUSSION:** The breakeven point in units is total fixed costs divided by the unit contribution margin (UCM). The UCM is the selling price minus variable costs per unit. Variable costs per unit equal $1.50 ($450,000 ÷ 300,000 units). Thus, the UCM equals $.50 ($2 – $1.50). Dividing the $90,000 of fixed costs by the $.50 UCM yields a breakeven point of 180,000 units.

Answer (B) is incorrect because selling 120,000 units would result in a loss of $.25 per unit. Answer (C) is incorrect because selling 90,000 units would result in a loss of $.50 per unit. Answer (D) is incorrect because selling 60,000 units would result in a loss of $1 per unit.

**91.** For the year ended December 31, 1998, Rho's contribution margin was

    A. $250,000

    B. $180,000

    C. $150,000

    D. $60,000

The correct answer is (C). *(CPA, adapted)*
    **REQUIRED:** The contribution margin.
    **DISCUSSION:** The contribution margin is sales of $600,000 (300,000 units x $2) minus variable costs of $450,000, or $150,000.
    Answer (A) is incorrect because contribution margin is sales minus total variable costs. Answer (B) is incorrect because all variable costs, including general, selling, and administrative, need to be deducted from sales to determine contribution margin. Answer (D) is incorrect because fixed costs are not deducted to determine contribution margin.

**92.** Assume the variable cost per unit was $1.50. Based on Rho's 1998 financial data, and an estimated 1999 production of 350,000 units of industrial photo-prints, Rho's estimated 1999 total costs and expenses will be

    A. $525,000

    B. $540,000

    C. $615,000

    D. $630,000

The correct answer is (C). *(CPA, adapted)*
    **REQUIRED:** The estimated total costs and expenses given an increase in production.
    **DISCUSSION:** Over the relevant range, fixed costs will not fluctuate. The variable cost per unit was $1.50. Thus, total costs and expenses will be

| | |
|---|---:|
| Variable ($1.50 × 350,000 units) | $525,000 |
| Fixed | 90,000 |
| Total costs and expenses | $615,000 |

    Answer (A) is incorrect because fixed costs must be considered in determining total costs and expenses. Answer (B) is incorrect because $540,000 is the total costs and expenses for 1998 based on a production of 300,000 units. Answer (D) is incorrect because, within the relevant range, fixed costs will remain constant at $90,000.

Questions 93 through 99 are based on the following information. The information was presented as part of Question 6 on Part 4 of the December 1981 CMA examination.

PortCo Products is a divisionalized furniture manufacturer. The divisions are autonomous segments, with each division being responsible for its own sales, costs of operations, working capital management, and equipment acquisition. Each division serves a different market in the furniture industry. Because the markets and products of the divisions are so different, there have never been any transfers between divisions.

The Commercial Division manufactures equipment and furniture that are purchased by the restaurant industry. The division plans to introduce a new line of counter and chair units that feature a cushioned seat for the counter chairs. John Kline, the division manager, has discussed the manufacturing of the cushioned seat with Russ Fiegel of the Office Division. They both believe a cushioned seat currently made by the Office Division for use on its deluxe office stool could be modified for use on the new counter chair. Consequently, Kline has asked Russ Fiegel for a price for 100-unit lots of the cushioned seat. The following conversation took place about the price to be charged for the cushioned seats:

Fiegel: "John, we can make the necessary modifications to the cushioned seat easily. The raw materials used in your seat are slightly different and should cost about 10% more than those used in our deluxe office stool. However, the labor time should be the same because the seat fabrication operation basically is the same. I would price the seat at our regular rate -- full cost plus 30% markup."

Kline: "That's higher than I expected, Russ. I was thinking that a good price would be your variable manufacturing costs. After all, your capacity costs will be incurred regardless of this job."

Fiegel: "John, I'm at capacity. By making the cushion seats for you, I'll have to cut my production of deluxe office stools. Of course, I can increase my production of economy office stools. The labor time freed by not having to fabricate the frame or assemble the deluxe stool can be shifted to the frame fabrication and assembly of the economy office stool. Fortunately, I can switch my labor force between these two models of stools without any loss of efficiency. As you know, overtime is not a feasible alternative in our community. I'd like to sell it to you at variable cost, but I have excess demand for both products. I don't mind changing my product mix to the economy model if I get a good return on the seats I make for you. Here are my standard costs for the two stools and a schedule of my manufacturing overhead."

Kline: "I guess I see your point, Russ, but I don't want to price myself out of the market. Maybe we should talk to Corporate to see if they can give us any guidance."

| Office Division Standard Costs and Prices | | | |
|---|---|---|---|
| | | Deluxe Office Stool | Economy Office Stool |
| Raw materials | | | |
| Framing | | $ 8.15 | $ 9.76 |
| Cushioned seat | | | |
| Padding | | 2.40 | -- |
| Vinyl | | 4.00 | -- |
| Molded seat (purchased) | | -- | 6.00 |
| Direct labor | | | |
| Frame fabrication (.5 × $7.50/DLH) | 3.75 | (.5 × $7.50/DLH) | 3.75 |
| Cushion fabrication (.5 × $7.50/DLH) | 3.75 | | -- |
| Assembly* (.5 × $7.50/DLH) | 3.75 | (.3 × $7.50/DLH) | 2.25 |
| Manufacturing | | | |
| Overhead (1.5 DLH × $12.80/DLH) | 19.20 | (.8DLH × $12.80/DLH) | 10.24 |
| Total standard cost | $45.00 | | $32.00 |
| Selling price (30% markup) | $58.50 | | $41.60 |

*Attaching seats to frames and attaching rubber feet.

| Office Division Manufacturing Overhead Budget | | |
|---|---|---|
| Overhead Item | Nature | Amount |
| Supplies | Variable—at current market prices | $ 420,000 |
| Indirect labor | Variable | 375,000 |
| Supervision | Nonvariable | 250,000 |
| Power | Use varies with activity; rates are fixed | 180,000 |
| Heat and light | Nonvariable—light is fixed regardless of production while heat/air conditioning varies with fuel charges | 140,000 |
| Property taxes and insurance taxes | Nonvariable—any change in amounts/rates is independent of production | 200,000 |
| Depreciation | Fixed dollar total | 1,700,000 |
| Employee benefits | 20% of supervision, direct and indirect labor | 575,000 |
| Total overhead | | $3,840,000 |
| Capacity in DLH | | 300,000 |
| Overhead rate/DLH | | $12.80 |

**93.** What amount of employee benefit is associated with direct labor costs?

- A. $675,000
- B. $75,000
- C. $450,000
- D. $500,000

The correct answer is (C). *(Publisher)*
**REQUIRED:** The amount of employee benefits that is associated with direct labor costs.
**DISCUSSION:** To find the amount associated with direct labor, 20% of supervision and indirect labor costs are subtracted from total employee benefits {$575,000 − [20% x ($250,000 + $375,000)]}, or $450,000.

Answer (A) is incorrect because 20% of supervision and indirect labor costs need to be subtracted from total employee benefits to determine the employee benefits associated with direct labor costs. Answer (B) is incorrect because $75,000 is the result of deducting 80% of supervision and indirect labor costs from total employee benefits. Answer (D) is incorrect because 20% of supervision also needs to be deducted.

**94.** What is the variable manufacturing overhead rate?

- A. $7.80/hr.
- B. $11.25/hr.
- C. $5.17/hr.
- D. $5.00/hr.

The correct answer is (D). *(Publisher)*
**REQUIRED:** The variable manufacturing overhead rate.
**DISCUSSION:** Variable amounts are totaled ($1,500,000) and divided by the capacity in DLH (300,000). Heat/air conditioning costs are excluded. They vary with fuel charges and therefore with production levels.

| | Total | Per DLH |
|---|---|---|
| Supplies | $ 420,000 | $1.40 |
| Indirect labor | 375,000 | 1.25 |
| Power | 180,000 | .60 |
| Employee benefits: | | |
| 20% direct labor | 450,000 | 1.50 |
| 20% indirect labor | 75,000 | .25 |
| Total | $1,500,000 | $5.00 |

Answer (A) is incorrect because $7.80/hr. is the fixed manufacturing O/H rate per direct labor hour. Answer (B) is incorrect because the variable manufacturing overhead rate is determined by dividing variable expenses (supplies, indirect labor, power, and direct and indirect labor benefits) by direct labor hours. Answer (C) is incorrect because $5.17/hr. incorrectly includes supervision benefits of $50,000.

**95.** What is the transfer price per 100-unit lot based on variable manufacturing costs to produce the modified cushioned seat?

- A. $1,329
- B. $1,869
- C. $789
- D. $1,986

The correct answer is (A). *(Publisher)*
**REQUIRED:** The transfer price based on the variable manufacturing cost.
**DISCUSSION:** The variable manufacturing cost to produce a 100-unit lot is 100 times the sum of direct materials, direct labor, and variable O/H per seat.

| Cushion materials | | |
|---|---|---|
| Padding | $2.40 | |
| Vinyl | 4.00 | |
| Total cushion materials | $6.40 | |
| Cost increase 10% (given) | ×1.10 | |
| Cost of cushioned seat | | $ 7.04 |
| Cushion fabrication labor ($7.50/DLH × .5 DLH) | | 3.75 |
| Variable overhead ($5.00/DLH × .5 DLH) | | 2.50 |
| Total variable cost per cushioned seat | | $13.29 |
| Total variable cost per 100-unit lot | | $1,329 |

Answer (B) is incorrect because $1,869 is the transfer price plus the opportunity cost of $540 of the Office Division. Answer (C) is incorrect because $789 is the transfer price minus the opportunity cost of $540 of the Office Division. Answer (D) is incorrect because the transfer price based on the variable manufacturing costs is $1,329.

Refer to the information preceding question 93 on page 410.

**96.** What is the fixed manufacturing overhead rate?

A. $7.80/hr.

B. $11.25/hr.

C. $5.17/hr.

D. $5.00/hr.

The correct answer is (A). *(Publisher)*

**REQUIRED:** The fixed manufacturing O/H rate.

**DISCUSSION:** Total fixed O/H is $2,340,000 (see below). It is divided by the 300,000-hour level of activity to determine the $7.80 hourly rate.

| | |
|---|---:|
| Supervision | $ 250,000 |
| Heat and light | 140,000 |
| Property taxes and insurance | 200,000 |
| Depreciation | 1,700,000 |
| Benefits (20% of supervision) | 50,000 |
| | $2,340,000 |

Answer (B) is incorrect because the fixed manufacturing overhead rate is determined by dividing fixed expenses (supervision, heat and light, property taxes and insurance, depreciation, and supervision benefits) by direct labor hours. Answer (C) is incorrect because $5.17/hr. incorrectly includes supervision benefits of $50,000. Answer (D) is incorrect because $5.00/hr. is the variable manufacturing O/H rate per hour.

**97.** How many economy office stools can be produced with the labor hours currently used to make 100 deluxe stools?

A. 187

B. 125

C. 100

D. 150

The correct answer is (B). *(Publisher)*

**REQUIRED:** The economy stools that can be produced in the time spent to make 100 deluxe stools.

**DISCUSSION:** The labor hours used in cushion fabrication will be used to make the modified cushioned seat. Thus, the labor time freed by not making deluxe stools equals the frame fabrication and assembly time only. The number of economy stools that can be produced is 125.

| | |
|---|---:|
| Labor hours to make 100 deluxe stools (1.5 × 100) | 150  hr. |
| Minus:  Labor hours to make 100 cushioned seats (cushion fabrication .5 × 100) | (50) hr. |
| Labor hours available for economy stool | 100  hr. |
| Labor hours to make one economy stool | ÷  .8  hr. |
| Stools produced by extra labor in economy stool production (100 ÷ .8 hr.) | 125  stools |

Answer (A) is incorrect because 187 is the number of economy stools that can be made in 150 hours. Answer (C) is incorrect because 100 is the number of hours available. Answer (D) is incorrect because 150 is the number of hours required to make 100 deluxe stools before considering the hours required to make 100 cushioned seats.

**98.** When computing the opportunity cost for the deluxe office stool, what is the contribution margin per unit produced?

    A.  $25.20

    B.  $15.84

    C.  $45.00

    D.  $33.30

The correct answer is (A). *(Publisher)*

**REQUIRED:** The contribution margin per unit of the deluxe office stool.

**DISCUSSION:** The contribution margin per unit is equal to the selling price minus the variable costs. Variable costs per unit for the deluxe office stool equal $33.30, and the selling price is $58.50. Thus, the contribution margin is $25.20 per unit ($58.50 – $33.30). The total standard cost is $45.00, which includes $11.70 of fixed O/H (1.5 hr. x $7.80), and the variable costs are $33.30 ($45.00 – $11.70).

Answer (B) is incorrect because $15.84 is the contribution margin of the economy office stool. Answer (C) is incorrect because $45.00 is the total standard cost. Answer (D) is incorrect because $33.30 is the variable cost deducted from the sales price to yield the contribution margin.

**99.** What is the opportunity cost of the Office Division if 125 economy stools can be made in the time required for 100 deluxe stools?

    A.  $789

    B.  $1,869

    C.  $1,329

    D.  $540

The correct answer is (D). *(Publisher)*

**REQUIRED:** The opportunity cost of the Office Division.

**DISCUSSION:** Opportunity cost is the benefit of the next best opportunity forgone. The opportunity cost here is the contribution margin forgone by shifting production to the economy office stool ($2,520 – $1,980 = $540).

| | Deluxe | | Economy |
|---|---|---|---|
| Selling price | $58.50 | | $41.60 |
| Costs | | | |
|    Materials | $14.55 | | $15.76 |
|    Labor ($7.50 × 1.5) | 11.25 | ($7.50 × .8) | 6.00 |
|    Variable O/H ($5 × 1.5) | 7.50 | ($5 × .8) | 4.00 |
|    Fixed O/H | -- | | -- |
| Total costs | $33.30 | | $25.76 |
| Unit CM | $25.20 | | $15.84 |
| Units produced | × 100 | | × 125 |
| Total CM | $2,520 | | $1,980 |

Answer (A) is incorrect because $789 is the transfer price of $1,329 minus the opportunity cost of $540 of the Office Division. Answer (B) is incorrect because $1,869 is the transfer price of $1,329 plus the opportunity cost of $540 of the Office Division. Answer (C) is incorrect because $1,329 is the transfer price.

Questions 100 through 112 are based on the following information.

| | Segment A | Segment B | Segment C | Segment D |
|---|---|---|---|---|
| Net income | $ 5,000 | -- | -- | $ 90,000 |
| Sales | 60,000 | $750,000 | $135,000 | 1,800,000 |
| Investment | 24,000 | 500,000 | 45,000 | -- |
| Net income as % of sales | -- | -- | -- | -- |
| Turnover of investment | -- | -- | -- | -- |
| ROI | -- | -- | 20% | 7.5% |
| Minimum ROI--dollars | -- | -- | -- | $ 120,000 |
| Minimum ROI--% | 20% | 6% | -- | -- |
| Residual income | -- | -0- | $2,250 | -- |

**100.** For Segment B, net income as a percentage of sales is

A. 8%

B. 6.67%

C. 4%

D. 10%

The correct answer is (C). *(Publisher)*

**REQUIRED:** The net income as a percentage of sales.

**DISCUSSION:** Residual income was zero, indicating that net income was equal to the minimum ROI. Given a 6% minimum ROI as a percentage of investment, 6% of the $500,000 investment is $30,000. Sales were $750,000, so net income ($30,000) is 4% of sales.

Answer (A) is incorrect because net income as a percentage of sales is calculated by dividing 6% (minimum ROI) of the investment by the sales of Segment B. Answer (B) is incorrect because 6.67% is the net income as a percentage of sales for Segment C. Answer (D) is incorrect because 10% is the minimum ROI percentage for Segment D.

**101.** For Segment C, net income as a percentage of sales is

A. 5%

B. 6.67%

C. 4%

D. 20%

The correct answer is (B). *(Publisher)*

**REQUIRED:** The net income as a percentage of sales.

**DISCUSSION:** Net income as a percentage of sales is the ROI divided by turnover of investment. The turnover of the investment is sales ($135,000) divided by the investment ($45,000), or 3. Hence, net income is 6.67% (20% ÷ 3) as a percentage of sales for Segment C.

Answer (A) is incorrect because 5% is the net income as a percentage of sales for Segment D. Answer (C) is incorrect because 4% is the net income as a percentage of sales for Segment B. Answer (D) is incorrect because 20% is the ROI for Segment C.

**102.** For Segment C, the turnover of investment is

A. 3

B. 1.5

C. 2.5

D. 4

The correct answer is (A). *(Publisher)*

**REQUIRED:** The turnover of investment for Segment C.

**DISCUSSION:** The turnover of investment for Segment C is calculated by dividing sales by investment. Given sales of $135,000 and investment of $45,000, Segment C's turnover of investment is 3.

Answer (B) is incorrect because 1.5 is the turnover of investment for Segment B. Answer (C) is incorrect because 2.5 is the turnover of investment for Segment A. Answer (D) is incorrect because the turnover of investment is calculated by dividing sales by investment.

**103.** For Segment D, the turnover of investment is

A. 3

B. 1.5

C. 2.5

D. 4

The correct answer is (B). *(Publisher)*

**REQUIRED:** The turnover of investment for Segment D.

**DISCUSSION:** The turnover of investment for Segment D is determined by dividing sales by investment. For Segment D, net income ($90,000) as a percentage of sales ($1,800,000) equals 5%. ROI is given as 7.5%. Dividing net income as a percentage of sales (5%) into ROI (7.5%) gives a turnover of investment of 1.5.

Answer (A) is incorrect because 3 is the turnover of investment for Segment C. Answer (C) is incorrect because 2.5 is the turnover of investment for Segment A. Answer (D) is incorrect because the turnover of investment is calculated by dividing sales by investment.

**104.** For Segment A, ROI is

A. 6%

B. 20%

C. 20.8%

D. 7.5%

The correct answer is (C). *(Publisher)*

**REQUIRED:** The ROI for Segment A.

**DISCUSSION:** ROI is equal to net income divided by investment. Net income equals $5,000. Investment equals $24,000. Therefore, ROI equals 20.8%.

Answer (A) is incorrect because 6% is the ROI for Segment B. Answer (B) is incorrect because 20% is the ROI for Segment C. Answer (D) is incorrect because 7.5% is the ROI for Segment D.

**105.** For Segment B, ROI is

A. 6%

B. 20.8%

C. 20%

D. 7.5%

The correct answer is (A). *(Publisher)*

**REQUIRED:** The ROI for Segment B.

**DISCUSSION:** Residual income is given as zero. Thus, the actual ROI is the same as the minimum percentage ROI of 6%.

Answer (B) is incorrect because 20.8% is the ROI for Segment A. Answer (C) is incorrect because 20% is the ROI for Segment C. Answer (D) is incorrect because 7.5% is the ROI for Segment D.

**106.** For Segment A, the minimum dollar ROI is

A. $30,000

B. $6,750

C. $4,800

D. $120,000

The correct answer is (C). *(Publisher)*

**REQUIRED:** The minimum rate of return in dollars.

**DISCUSSION:** The minimum ROI in dollars is equal to the amount of the investment times the minimum rate of return percentage. The amount of the investment is $24,000. The minimum rate of return percentage is 20%. Accordingly, the minimum ROI in dollars is $4,800.

Answer (A) is incorrect because $30,000 is the minimum dollar ROI for Segment B. Answer (B) is incorrect because $6,750 is the minimum dollar ROI for Segment C. Answer (D) is incorrect because $120,000 is the minimum dollar ROI for Segment D.

**107.** For Segment B, the minimum dollar ROI is

A. $30,000

B. $6,750

C. $4,800

D. $120,000

The correct answer is (A). *(Publisher)*

**REQUIRED:** The minimum rate of return in dollars for Segment B.

**DISCUSSION:** The ROI in dollars is equal to the amount of the investment times the minimum rate of return percentage. The amount of the investment is $500,000. The minimum rate of return percentage is given as 6%. Thus, the minimum ROI in dollars equals $30,000.

Answer (B) is incorrect because $6,750 is the minimum dollar ROI for Segment C. Answer (C) is incorrect because $4,800 is the minimum dollar ROI for Segment A. Answer (D) is incorrect because $120,000 is the minimum dollar ROI for Segment D.

Refer to the information preceding question 100 on page 414.

**108.** For Segment C, the minimum dollar ROI is

A. $30,000

B. $6,750

C. $4,800

D. $120,000

The correct answer is (B). *(Publisher)*

**REQUIRED:** The minimum rate of return in dollars.

**DISCUSSION:** The minimum ROI in dollars is equal to the minimum ROI percentage times the investment. The investment was $45,000. Neither the minimum percentage nor the minimum ROI is known. However, the ROI percentage (20%) and the investment ($45,000) are known. Hence, the net income is $9,000. Given residual income of $2,250, the minimum ROI in dollars must have been $6,750 ($9,000 − $2,250).

Answer (A) is incorrect because $30,000 is the minimum dollar ROI for Segment B. Answer (C) is incorrect because $4,800 is the minimum dollar ROI for Segment A. Answer (D) is incorrect because $120,000 is the minimum dollar ROI for Segment D.

**109.** Assume that the minimum dollar ROI is $6,750 for Segment C. The minimum percentage of ROI is

A. 20%

B. 6%

C. 15%

D. 10%

The correct answer is (C). *(Publisher)*

**REQUIRED:** The minimum percentage of ROI.

**DISCUSSION:** The minimum percentage of ROI in Segment C equals the minimum dollar ROI divided by the investment. The minimum dollar ROI is $6,750. Consequently, the minimum percentage ROI is 15% ($6,750 ÷ $45,000).

Answer (A) is incorrect because 20% is the minimum ROI percentage for Segment A. Answer (B) is incorrect because 6% is the minimum ROI percentage for Segment B. Answer (D) is incorrect because 10% is the minimum ROI percentage for Segment D.

**110.** In Segment D, the minimum percentage of ROI is

A. 20%

B. 6%

C. 15%

D. 10%

The correct answer is (D). *(Publisher)*

**REQUIRED:** The minimum percentage of ROI.

**DISCUSSION:** The minimum percentage of ROI for Segment D is the minimum ROI in dollars ($120,000) divided by the investment, which must be calculated. The ROI is given as 7.5%. The net income ($90,000) as a percentage of sales ($1,800,000) equals 5%. The turnover of investment (ROI ÷ net income as a percentage of sales) is 1.5. Given turnover of 1.5 and sales of $1,800,000, investment must have been $1,200,000. The minimum percentage ROI is $120,000 divided by the $1,200,000 investment, or 10%.

Answer (A) is incorrect because 20% is the minimum ROI percentage for Segment A. Answer (B) is incorrect because 6% is the minimum ROI percentage for Segment B. Answer (C) is incorrect because 15% is the minimum ROI percentage for Segment C.

**111.** In Segment A, the residual income is

A. $200

B. $12,000

C. $(30,000)

D. $4,800

The correct answer is (A). *(Publisher)*

**REQUIRED:** The residual income for Segment A.

**DISCUSSION:** Segment A's residual income is equal to the net income ($5,000) minus the minimum ROI in dollars. Minimum ROI in dollars equals the minimum ROI percentage (20%) times the investment ($24,000), or $4,800. Residual income is therefore $200.

Answer (B) is incorrect because $12,000 is the minimum ROI percentage multiplied by sales. Answer (C) is incorrect because $(30,000) is the residual income for Segment D. Answer (D) is incorrect because $4,800 equals the minimum ROI in dollars.

**112.** In Segment D, the residual income is

A. $2,250

B. $9,000

C. $(30,000)

D. $0

The correct answer is (C). *(Publisher)*

**REQUIRED:** The residual income for Segment D.

**DISCUSSION:** The minimum ROI in dollars is given as $120,000 and net income is given as $90,000. Thus, residual income is $(30,000) ($90,000 – $120,000). Segment D did not achieve its minimum ROI and therefore has a negative residual income.

Answer (A) is incorrect because $2,250 is the residual income for Segment C. Answer (B) is incorrect because $9,000 is 7.5% of $120,000. Answer (D) is incorrect because $0 assumes that net income is $120,000.

# CHAPTER TWELVE
# NONROUTINE DECISIONS

**Nonroutine decisions** are typically made using **incremental (differential or marginal) analysis**. The quantitative analysis emphasizes the ways in which costs and benefits vary with the option chosen. Thus, the focus is on relevant or incremental, not total, costs. For example, assume that a firm produces a product for which it incurs unit costs of $2.00 for direct materials, $3.00 for direct labor, $.50 for variable overhead, and $2.50 for fixed overhead, a total unit cost of $8.00. The product normally sells for $10 per unit. Incremental cost analysis is necessary if a foreign buyer, who has never before been a customer, offers to pay $5.75 per unit for a **special order** of the firm's product. The immediate reaction might be to refuse the offer because the selling price is less than the average cost of production by a considerable amount. However, incremental cost analysis results in a different decision. In this example, the only incremental costs are for direct materials, direct labor, and variable overhead. No additional fixed overhead costs would be incurred. Because the $5.75 selling price (incremental revenue) exceeds the $5.50 of incremental costs ($2 materials + $3 labor + $.50 variable OH), accepting the special order will be profitable. In addition to special-order situations, incremental costing can be used to make decisions about insourcing vs. outsourcing (make-or-buy), pricing, choosing a product mix, adding or dropping product lines, selling or processing further, acquiring or divesting an organizational segment, or selecting a market channel. Caution must always be used in applying incremental cost analysis. Many nonquantitative factors must be considered, including whether special price concessions violate price discrimination statutes; the effect of government contract pricing regulations; whether sales to a special customer affect sales in the firm's regular market; whether regular customers will find out about a special price and demand equal terms; and, in the case of discontinuing a product line, whether sales in the other product lines will be hurt (e.g., the dropped product may have been an unintended loss leader).

Certain cost terms are commonly used in decision analysis situations. An **avoidable cost** can be saved by not adopting a particular option. An **imputed cost** requires no dollar outlay and is not recognized in the accounting records but must be considered in an investment decision to give recognition to economic reality. An opportunity cost is an example. An **opportunity cost** is the benefit forgone by not selecting the next best use of scarce resources. A **postponable cost** may be shifted to the future with little effect on the efficiency of current operations. Routine maintenance is an example. A **relevant cost** should be considered in decision making because it is a future cost that will vary with the option chosen. A **sunk cost** cannot be avoided because the expenditure has occurred or an irrevocable decision to incur the cost has been made. Sunk costs are irrelevant to management decision making because they do not vary with the option selected.

**Insourcing vs. outsourcing** (make or buy) decisions are based on the principle that available resources should be used as efficiently as possible before outsourcing. Often, an array of products can be produced efficiently if production capacity is available. If not enough capacity is available to produce them all, the products that are produced least efficiently should be outsourced (or capacity should be expanded). Services, such as computer processing, legal work, accounting, and training, may also be outsourced. Moreover, both products and services may be outsourced internationally. Thus, computer programming, information processing, customer service via telephone, etc., as well as manufacturing tasks, may be not only outsourced but outsourced offshore.

In an insourcing vs. outsourcing decision, the manager considers only the costs relevant to the investment decision. If the total relevant costs of production are less than the cost to buy the item, it should be produced in-house. The key variable is relevant costs, not total costs, because past costs are irrelevant. For example, the costs of a production plant's prior year's repairs are irrelevant to this year's decision. Book value of old equipment is also irrelevant because it is a sunk cost. Moreover, when excess capacity is available, allocated fixed factory overhead is an irrelevant cost. This cost will be incurred whether the product is made or bought. However, at full capacity, the allocation of fixed factory overhead must be considered. Furthermore, the opportunity cost of displacing other output must be treated as a cost of insourcing. Accordingly, the issue is not whether a cost is fixed or variable but whether it is relevant.

**Product mix decisions** concern the relative amounts of each type of product or service that, given demand and resource constraints, will maximize total profits. For example, if the firm can sell as much as it can produce and has a single resource constraint, the decision rule is to maximize the contribution margin per unit of the constrained resource. However, given multiple constraints, the decision is more difficult, and more sophisticated techniques, for example, linear programming (see Chapter 17), must be used.

**Disinvestment** decisions are the opposite of capital budgeting decisions because they concern whether to terminate rather than start an operation. In general, if the marginal cost of a project is greater than the marginal revenue, the firm should disinvest. Four steps should be taken in making a disinvestment decision. First, fixed expenses that would be curtailed by the disinvestment decision, e.g., depreciation and insurance on equipment used, should be identified. Second, the revenue needed to justify continuing operations (variable cost of production) should be determined. Third, the opportunity cost of funds that will be received upon disinvestment (e.g., salvage value) should be established. Fourth, if the book value of the assets is not equal to the economic value of the capital, the decision should be reevaluated using current fair value rather than the book value. When a firm disinvests, excess capacity may exist unless another project uses this capacity immediately. The cost of idle capacity should be treated as a relevant cost.

The three significant influences on **product pricing** are consumers, competitors, and costs. The consumer must be considered in pricing decisions because of the laws of supply and demand. For example, if the price of a product is increased excessively, the consumer will choose a substitute product. Pricing decisions are also influenced by the competition. When making pricing decisions, the competitors' prices must be considered as well as the quality and durability of the product. For example, a consumer may be willing to pay a higher price for a better quality product. However, pricing products below cost to destroy competitors (**predatory pricing**) is illegal. The U.S. Supreme Court has held that a price is predatory if it is below an appropriate measure of costs and the seller has a reasonable prospect of recovering its losses in the future through higher prices or greater market share. Also illegal is price discrimination among customers. The **Robinson-Patman Act** makes such pricing illegal if it has the effect of lessening competition, although price discrimination may be permissible if the competitive situation requires it and if costs of serving some customers are lower. The Robinson-Patman Act applies to manufacturers, not service entities.  Another improper form of pricing is **collusive pricing**.  Companies may not conspire to restrict output and set artificially high prices.  Such behavior violates antitrust laws.  Still another inappropriate pricing tactic is selling below cost in other countries (**dumping**), which may trigger retaliatory tariffs and other sanctions.

The seller's costs and sales volume are other important influences on pricing.  For example, under **peak-load pricing**, prices vary inversely with capacity usage.  However, a seller cannot make any profit if the product is priced below cost.  Furthermore, sales volume must be adequate to produce sufficient revenue to cover costs incurred throughout the value chain.

A **cost-plus price** equals the cost plus a markup.  Cost may be defined in many ways.  Most companies use either absorption manufacturing cost or total cost when calculating the price.  Variable costs may be used as the basis for cost, but then fixed costs must be covered by the markup.  Following are four commonly used cost-plus pricing formulas:

1. $Price = Total\ cost + (Total\ cost \times Markup\ percentage)$

2. $Price = Absorption\ manufacturing\ cost + \left( Absorption\ manufacturing\ cost \times Markup\ percentage \right)$

3. $Price = Variable\ manufacturing\ cost + \left( Variable\ manufacturing\ cost \times Markup\ percentage \right)$

4. $Price = Total\ variable\ cost + \left( Total\ variable\ cost \times Markup\ percentage \right)$

A **target price** is the expected market price for a product, given the company's knowledge of its customers and competitors.  Subtracting the unit target profit margin determines the long-term **target cost** of the product.  Because it may be lower than the full cost of the product, the target cost may not be achievable unless the company adopts comprehensive cost-reduction measures.  The Japanese concept of **Kaizen** is relevant to target costing.  A policy of seeking continuous improvement in all phases of company activities facilitates cost reduction, often through numerous minor changes.  **Value engineering** is a means of reaching targeted cost levels.  It is a systematic approach to assessing all aspects of the value chain cost buildup for a product:  R&D, design of products, design of processes, production, marketing, distribution, and customer service.  The purpose is to minimize costs without sacrificing customer satisfaction.  Value engineering requires distinguishing between cost incurrence and locked-in costs.  Cost incurrence is the actual use of resources, whereas locked-in (designed-in) costs will result in use of resources in the future as a result of past decisions.  Traditional cost accounting focuses on budget comparisons, but value engineering emphasizes controlling costs at the design stage, that is, before they are locked in.  **Life-cycle costing** is sometimes used as a basis for cost planning and product pricing.  Life-cycle costing estimates a product's revenues and expenses over its expected life cycle.  The result is to highlight upstream and downstream costs in the cost planning process that often receive insufficient attention.  Emphasis is on the need to price products to cover all costs, not just production costs.

## 12.1 Basic Concepts

**1.** Relevant or differential cost analysis

    A.  Takes all variable and fixed costs into account to analyze decision alternatives.

    B.  Considers only variable costs as they change with each decision alternative.

    C.  Considers the change in reported net income for each alternative to arrive at the optimum decision for the company.

    D.  Considers all variable and fixed costs as they change with each decision alternative.

The correct answer is (D). *(CMA, adapted)*
    **REQUIRED:** The true statement about relevant or differential cost analysis.
    **DISCUSSION:** Relevant cost analysis considers only those costs that differ among decision options. Both fixed and variable costs are considered if they vary with the option selected.
    Answer (A) is incorrect because all costs are not considered. Answer (B) is incorrect because fixed costs will also be considered if they differ among options. Answer (C) is incorrect because cost differences are evaluated.

**2.** The relevance of a particular cost to a decision is determined by the

    A.  Size of the cost.

    B.  Riskiness of the decision.

    C.  Potential effect on the decision.

    D.  Accuracy and verifiability of the cost.

The correct answer is (C). *(CMA, adapted)*
    **REQUIRED:** The factor that determines whether a cost is relevant to a particular decision.
    **DISCUSSION:** Managerial decisions should be based on the relevant revenues and costs. A particular cost or revenue is relevant if it will vary with the option chosen. Thus, a relevant cost or revenue has the ability to affect the decision made.
    Answers (A) and (B) are incorrect because the size of the cost and the riskiness of the decision are irrelevant if the cost does not affect the decision process. Answer (D) is incorrect because some estimate must be considered regardless of its accuracy and verifiability.

**3.** The term that refers to costs incurred in the past that are not relevant to a future decision is

    A.  Full absorption cost.

    B.  Underallocated indirect cost.

    C.  Sunk cost.

    D.  Incurred marginal cost.

The correct answer is (C). *(CMA, adapted)*
    **REQUIRED:** The past costs not relevant to a future decision.
    **DISCUSSION:** A sunk cost cannot be avoided because it represents an expenditure that has already been made or an irrevocable decision to incur the cost.
    Answer (A) is incorrect because full absorption cost includes not only direct costs of production but also both variable and fixed factory overhead. Answer (B) is incorrect because an underallocated indirect cost has not yet been charged to production. Answer (D) is incorrect because an incurred marginal cost is the increment in cost as a result of producing one additional unit.

**4.** Total unit costs are

    A.  Relevant for cost-volume-profit analysis.

    B.  Irrelevant in marginal analysis.

    C.  Independent of the cost system used to generate them.

    D.  Needed for determining product contribution.

The correct answer is (B). *(CMA, adapted)*
    **REQUIRED:** The true statement about total unit costs.
    **DISCUSSION:** Marginal (incremental or differential) analysis determines the differences in costs among decision choices. Total unit costs are not relevant in marginal analysis because of the inclusion of costs that may not vary among the possible choices considered. In marginal analysis, only the incremental costs are relevant.
    Answer (A) is incorrect because fixed and variable costs behave differently and therefore receive different treatment in CVP analysis. Answer (C) is incorrect because total unit costs are a product of the system used to calculate them. Answer (D) is incorrect because variable costs are the only ones needed to determine product contribution.

**5.** The term relevant cost applies to all the following decision situations except the

    A.  Acceptance of a special order.

    B.  Determination of a product price.

    C.  Replacement of equipment.

    D.  Addition or deletion of a product line.

The correct answer is (B). *(CMA, adapted)*
    **REQUIRED:** The situation to which relevant cost does not apply.
    **DISCUSSION:** Relevant costs are expected future costs that vary with the action taken. All other costs are assumed to be constant and thus have no effect on the decision. Relevant costing is not applicable to determining a product price because this decision involves an evaluation of, among other things, demand, competitors' actions, and desired profit margin.
    Answers (A), (C), and (D) are incorrect because relevant cost is an important decision tool with regard to acceptance of a special order, replacement of equipment, and addition or deletion of a product line.

**6.** Which one of the following is most relevant to a manufacturing equipment replacement decision?

    A.  Original cost of the old equipment.

    B.  Disposal price of the old equipment.

    C.  Gain or loss on the disposal of the old equipment.

    D.  A lump-sum write-off amount from the disposal of the old equipment.

The correct answer is (B). *(CMA, adapted)*
    **REQUIRED:** The item most relevant to a manufacturing equipment replacement decision.
    **DISCUSSION:** Management decision analysis is based on the concept of relevant costs. Relevant costs differ among decision choices. Thus, incremental or differential costs are always relevant. Historical costs, such as the original cost of the equipment, because they were incurred in the past, are not relevant. Similarly, any gain or loss on the old equipment is not relevant because this amount is based on the historical cost. However, the disposal price of the old equipment is relevant because it involves a future cash inflow that will not occur unless the equipment is disposed of.
    Answer (A) is incorrect because the original cost of the old equipment is a sunk cost with no relevance to future decision making. Answer (C) is incorrect because gain or loss is based on historical cost, which is a sunk cost. Answer (D) is incorrect because a lump-sum write-off of a sunk cost is not relevant to a future decision.

**7.** A decision-making concept, described as "the contribution to income that is forgone by not using a limited resource for its best alternative use," is called

    A.  Marginal cost.

    B.  Incremental cost.

    C.  Potential cost.

    D.  Opportunity cost.

The correct answer is (D). *(CMA, adapted)*
    **REQUIRED:** The contribution to income forgone by not using a limited resource for its best alternative use.
    **DISCUSSION:** Opportunity cost is defined as the profit forgone by selecting one choice instead of another. It is the benefit provided by the best alternative use of a scarce resource.
    Answer (A) is incorrect because marginal cost is the incremental cost of producing one additional unit.
    Answer (B) is incorrect because incremental cost is the increase in costs between one option and another.
    Answer (C) is incorrect because potential cost is the cost that may be incurred in the future.

Questions 8 and 9 are based on the following information. Management accountants are frequently asked to analyze various decision situations including the following:

I.  The cost of a special device that is necessary if a special order is accepted

II. The cost proposed annually for the plant service for the grounds at corporate headquarters

III. Joint production costs incurred, to be considered in a sell-at-split versus a process-further decision

IV. The costs of alternative uses of plant space, to be considered in a make-or-buy decision

V.  The cost of obsolete inventory acquired several years ago, to be considered in a keep-versus-disposal decision

**8.** The costs described in situations I and IV are

A.  Prime costs.

B.  Discretionary costs.

C.  Relevant costs.

D.  Differential costs.

The correct answer is (C). *(CMA, adapted)*

**REQUIRED:** The term for the costs involved in special-order and make-or-buy decisions.

**DISCUSSION:** The costs of alternative uses of plant space to be considered in a make-or-buy decision and the cost of a special device necessary for acceptance of a special order are relevant costs. Relevant costs are future costs that are expected to vary with the action taken. Other costs thus have no effect on the decision.

Answer (A) is incorrect because prime costs are direct materials and direct labor costs. Answer (B) is incorrect because discretionary costs are characterized by uncertainty about the input-output relationship. Advertising and research are examples. Answer (D) is incorrect because differential cost (incremental cost) is the difference in total cost between two decisions.

**9.** The costs described in situations III and V are

A.  Prime costs.

B.  Sunk costs.

C.  Discretionary costs.

D.  Relevant costs.

The correct answer is (B). *(CMA, adapted)*

**REQUIRED:** The term for previously incurred costs.

**DISCUSSION:** Sunk costs are unavoidable. They are the results of past irrevocable decisions and have no relevance to future decisions. Joint production costs are irrelevant to deciding whether to sell at split-off or to process further. Similarly, the costs of obsolete inventory are irrelevant to future decisions. Thus, these are sunk costs.

Answer (A) is incorrect because prime costs are direct materials and direct labor costs. Answer (C) is incorrect because discretionary costs are characterized by uncertainty about the input-output relationship. Answer (D) is incorrect because relevant costs are future costs that are expected to vary with the action taken.

**10.** In a manufacturing environment, the best short-term profit-maximizing approach is to

A.  Maximize unit gross profit times the number of units sold.

B.  Minimize variable costs per unit times the number of units produced.

C.  Minimize fixed overhead cost per unit by producing at full capacity.

D.  Maximize contribution per unit times the number of units sold.

The correct answer is (D). *(CMA, adapted)*

**REQUIRED:** The best short-term profit-maximizing approach in a manufacturing environment.

**DISCUSSION:** In the short run, the best approach is to maximize the unit contribution margin (price – unit variable cost) times the units sold because fixed costs can be ignored. The important consideration is the total contribution margin available to cover fixed costs and contribute to profits.

Answer (A) is incorrect because a long-term strategy is to maximize gross profit, which is calculated after deduction of fixed costs. Answer (B) is incorrect because minimizing total variable cost ignores the role of selling price in profit maximization. Answer (C) is incorrect because, in the short run, fixed overhead does not change and is therefore not relevant.

**11.** In a decision analysis situation, which one of the following costs is not likely to contain a variable cost component?

   A. Labor.

   B. Overhead.

   C. Depreciation.

   D. Selling.

The correct answer is (C). *(CMA, adapted)*
   **REQUIRED:** The cost not likely to contain a variable component.
   **DISCUSSION:** Most types of costs either are variable or contain some mix of fixed and variable components. For example, labor and materials are primarily variable. Their amounts fluctuate with the relevant cost drivers. Selling expenses and overhead costs can be either fixed or variable. Depreciation, however, is strictly a fixed cost when viewed in a decision analysis situation because it requires no cash outlay. Instead, the initial acquisition of the long-lived asset requires the cash outlay.
   Answers (A), (B), and (D) are all incorrect because labor, overhead, and selling costs are either variable or mixed.

## 12.2 Insourcing vs. Outsourcing (Make or Buy)

**12.** A company's approach to an insourcing vs. outsourcing decision

   A. Depends on whether the company is operating at or below normal volume.

   B. Involves an analysis of avoidable costs.

   C. Should use absorption (full) costing.

   D. Should use activity-based costing.

The correct answer is (B). *(CMA, adapted)*
   **REQUIRED:** The true statement about a company's approach to a make-or-buy decision.
   **DISCUSSION:** Available resources should be used as efficiently as possible before outsourcing. If the total relevant costs of production are less than the cost to buy the item, it should be produced in-house. The relevant costs are those that can be avoided.
   Answer (A) is incorrect because whether operations are at normal volume is less important than the amount of idle capacity. The company is less likely to buy if it has sufficient unused capacity. Answer (C) is incorrect because total costs (absorption costing) are not as important as relevant costs. Answer (D) is incorrect because activity-based costing is used to allocate fixed overhead. Fixed overhead is not relevant in an insourcing vs. outsourcing decision unless it is avoidable.

**13.** Costs relevant to an insourcing vs. outsourcing decision include variable manufacturing costs as well as

   A. Avoidable fixed costs.

   B. Factory depreciation.

   C. Property taxes.

   D. Factory management costs.

The correct answer is (A). *(CMA, adapted)*
   **REQUIRED:** The costs included in the analysis of insourcing vs. outsourcing decisions.
   **DISCUSSION:** Relevant costs are anticipated costs that will vary among the choices available. If two courses of action share some costs, those costs are not relevant because they will be incurred regardless of the decision made. Relevant costs include fixed costs that could be avoided if the items were purchased from an outsider.
   Answer (B) is incorrect because depreciation should not be considered unless it can be avoided. Answer (C) is incorrect because property taxes are not affected by the decision and are therefore not relevant unless the decision to buy leads to sale of the property. Answer (D) is incorrect because factory management costs are not affected by the decision and are therefore not relevant unless the decision to buy reduces the number of factory managers.

**14.** What is the opportunity cost of making a component part in a factory given no alternative use of the capacity?

   A. The variable manufacturing cost of the component.

   B. The total manufacturing cost of the component.

   C. The total variable cost of the component.

   D. Zero.

The correct answer is (D). *(CMA, adapted)*
   **REQUIRED:** The opportunity cost of making a component if there is no alternative use for the factory.
   **DISCUSSION:** Opportunity cost is the benefit forgone by not selecting the best alternative use of scarce resources. The opportunity cost is zero when no alternative use is available.
   Answers (A), (B), and (C) are incorrect because opportunity cost is not an out-of-pocket cost. It is the benefit given up by not selecting the best alternative.

**15.** In an insourcing vs. outsourcing situation, which of the following qualitative factors is usually considered?

    A.  Special technology.

    B.  Skilled labor.

    C.  Special materials requirements.

    D.  All of the answers are correct.

The correct answer is (D). *(Publisher)*

    **REQUIRED:** The qualitative factor(s) affecting an insourcing vs. outsourcing decision.

    **DISCUSSION:** Special technology may be available either within or outside the firm that relates to the particular product. The firm may possess necessary skilled labor or the supplier may. Special materials requirements may also affect the decision process because one supplier may have monopolized a key component. Another factor to be considered is that assurance of quality control is often a reason for making rather than buying.

    Answers (A), (B), and (C) are incorrect because special technology, skilled labor, and special materials requirements are all considered in an insourcing vs. outsourcing situation.

**16.** In an insourcing vs. outsourcing decision, the decision process favors the use of total costs rather than unit costs. The reason is that

    A.  Unit cost may be calculated based on different volumes.

    B.  Irrelevant costs may be included in the unit amounts.

    C.  Allocated costs may be included in the unit amounts.

    D.  All of the answers are correct.

The correct answer is (D). *(Publisher)*

    **REQUIRED:** The advantage(s) of using total costs in an insourcing vs. outsourcing analysis.

    **DISCUSSION:** Unit costs should be used with extreme care. In each situation, they may be calculated based on a different volume level from that anticipated, so comparability may be lost. Irrelevant costs included in the unit cost should be disregarded; only relevant costs should be included in the analysis. Allocated costs should also be ignored, and only the relevant costs that will change with the option chosen should be considered.

    Answers (A), (B), and (C) are incorrect because reasons favoring total costs are that unit cost may be calculated based on different volumes and that allocated costs and irrelevant costs may be included in the unit amounts.

**17.** Which of the following qualitative factors favors the buy choice in an insourcing vs. outsourcing decision?

    A.  Maintaining a long-run relationship with suppliers is desirable.

    B.  Quality control is critical.

    C.  Idle capacity is available.

    D.  All of the answers are correct.

The correct answer is (A). *(Publisher)*

    **REQUIRED:** The qualitative factor(s) favoring buying in an insourcing vs. outsourcing decision.

    **DISCUSSION:** The maintenance of long-run relationships with suppliers may become paramount in a make-or-buy decision. Abandoning long-run supplier relationships may cause difficulty in obtaining needed parts when terminated suppliers find it advantageous not to supply parts in the future.

    Answer (B) is incorrect because, if quality is important, one can ordinarily control it better in one's own plant. Answer (C) is incorrect because the availability of idle capacity more likely favors the decision to make. Answer (D) is incorrect because the importance of quality control and the availability of idle capacity are qualitative factors favoring the make choice in an insourcing vs. outsourcing.

**18.** The ABC Company manufactures components for use in producing one of its finished products. When 12,000 units are produced, the full cost per unit is $35, separated as follows:

| | |
|---|---|
| Direct materials | $ 5 |
| Direct labor | 15 |
| Variable overhead | 10 |
| Fixed overhead | 5 |

The XYZ Company has offered to sell 12,000 components to ABC for $37 each. If ABC accepts the offer, some of the facilities currently being used to manufacture the components can be rented as warehouse space for $40,000. However, $3 of the fixed overhead currently applied to each component would have to be covered by ABC's other products. What is the differential cost to the ABC Company of purchasing the components from the XYZ Company?

A. $8,000

B. $20,000

C. $24,000

D. $44,000

The correct answer is (B). *(CIA, adapted)*

**REQUIRED:** The differential cost of purchasing the components.

**DISCUSSION:** Differential (incremental) cost is the difference in total cost between two decisions. The relevant costs do not include unavoidable costs, such as the $3 of fixed overhead. It would cost ABC an additional $20,000 to purchase, rather than manufacture, the components.

| | |
|---|---|
| Cost to purchase ($37 × 12,000) | $444,000 |
| Minus rental income | (40,000) |
| | $404,000 |
| Cost to manufacture ($32 × 12,000) | $384,000 |
| Cost differential | $ 20,000 |

Answer (A) is incorrect because $8,000 assumes that $3 of fixed overhead is avoidable. Answer (C) is incorrect because $24,000 compares the full cost of manufacturing with cost to purchase. Answer (D) is incorrect because $44,000 ignores the opportunity cost.

**19.** Listed below are a company's monthly unit costs to manufacture and market a particular product.

| | |
|---|---|
| Manufacturing costs: | |
| Direct materials | $2.00 |
| Direct labor | 2.40 |
| Variable indirect | 1.60 |
| Fixed indirect | 1.00 |
| Marketing costs: | |
| Variable | 2.50 |
| Fixed | 1.50 |

The company must decide whether to continue making the product or buy it from an outside supplier. The supplier has offered to make the product at the same level of quality that the company can make it. Fixed marketing costs would be unaffected, but variable marketing costs would be reduced by 30% if the company were to accept the proposal. What is the maximum amount per unit that the company can pay the supplier without decreasing its operating income?

A. $8.50

B. $6.75

C. $7.75

D. $5.25

The correct answer is (C). *(CMA, adapted)*

**REQUIRED:** The maximum amount paid to an outside supplier without decreasing operating income.

**DISCUSSION:** The company's avoidable unit costs total $7.75 [($2.00 DM + $2.40 DL + $1.60 VOH) + (.7 x $2.50 variable marketing costs)]. Hence, it will at least break even by paying no more than $7.75.

Answer (A) is incorrect because $8.50 assumes that all variable marketing costs are avoidable. Answer (B) is incorrect because $6.75 assumes that variable marketing costs are reduced to 30%. Answer (D) is incorrect because $5.25 results from subtracting the savings in marketing costs from the manufacturing savings.

**20.** Laurel Corporation has its own cafeteria with the following annual costs:

| | |
|---|---|
| Food | $100,000 |
| Labor | 75,000 |
| Overhead | 110,000 |
| Total | $285,000 |

The overhead is 40% fixed. Of the fixed overhead, $25,000 is the salary of the cafeteria supervisor. The remainder of the fixed overhead has been allocated from total company overhead. Assuming the cafeteria supervisor will remain and that Laurel will continue to pay his/her salary, the maximum cost Laurel will be willing to pay an outside firm to service the cafeteria is

A. $285,000

B. $175,000

C. $219,000

D. $241,000

The correct answer is (D). *(CMA, adapted)*
**REQUIRED:** The maximum that could be paid.
**DISCUSSION:** Given that overhead is 40% fixed, $66,000 (60% x $110,000) is variable, and $44,000 is fixed. Of the latter amount, $25,000 is attributable to the supervisor's salary. The $19,000 remainder is allocated from total company overhead and is unavoidable. Assuming the company will continue to pay the supervisor's salary if an outside firm services the cafeteria, the total fixed overhead is not an avoidable (incremental) cost. Thus, the total avoidable cost of the cafeteria's operation is $241,000 ($100,000 food + $75,000 labor + $66,000 VOH). This amount is the savings from hiring an outside firm. Accordingly, it is also the maximum that Laurel should be willing to pay the outside firm.

Answer (A) is incorrect because $285,000 is greater than the avoidable cost of operating the cafeteria. Answer (B) is incorrect because the company can pay more than $175,000. Its overhead costs are avoidable. Answer (C) is incorrect because the company can pay more than $219,000.

---

Questions 21 and 22 are based on the following information. A business needs a computer application that can be either developed internally or purchased. Suitable software from a vendor costs $29,000. Minor modifications and testing can be conducted by the systems staff as part of their regular workload.

If the software is developed internally, a systems analyst would be assigned full time, and a contractor would assume the analyst's responsibilities. The hourly rate for the regular analyst is $25. The hourly rate for the contractor is $22. The contractor would occupy an empty office. The office has 100 square feet, and occupancy cost is $45 per square foot.

Other related data are as follows. Computer time is charged using predetermined rates. The organization has sufficient excess computer capacity for either software development or modification/testing of the purchased software.

| | Internal Development | Purchased Software |
|---|---|---|
| Systems analyst time in hours | | |
| Development | 1,000 | N/A |
| Modifications and testing | N/A | 40 |
| Computer charges | $800 | $250 |
| Additional hardware purchases | $3,200 | N/A |
| Incidental supplies | $500 | $200 |

**21.** When applying the cost-benefit approach to a decision, the primary criterion is how well management goals will be achieved in relation to costs. Costs include all expected

A. Variable costs for the courses of action but not expected fixed costs because only the expected variable costs are relevant.

B. Incremental out-of-pocket costs as well as all expected continuing costs that are common to all the alternative courses of action.

C. Future costs that differ among the alternative courses of action plus all qualitative factors that cannot be measured in numerical terms.

D. Historical and future costs relative to the courses of action including all qualitative factors that cannot be measured in numerical terms.

The correct answer is (C). *(CIA, adapted)*
**REQUIRED:** The costs included in the cost-benefit approach.
**DISCUSSION:** The analysis of an insourcing vs. outsourcing decision is based on relevant costs. If costs do not vary with the option chosen, they are irrelevant. Moreover, the decision may be based on nonquantitative factors, for example, the desire to maintain a relationship with a vendor or to assume control over development of a product.

Answer (A) is incorrect because variable and fixed costs may be relevant or irrelevant. Answer (B) is incorrect because expected incremental out-of-pocket expenses should be considered, but common costs should not. Answer (D) is incorrect because historical costs are not relevant to cost-benefit analysis because they are sunk costs.

**22.** Based solely on the cost figures presented, the cost of developing the computer application will be

A. $3,500 less than acquiring the purchased software package.

B. $500 less than acquiring the purchased software package.

C. $1,550 more than acquiring the purchased software package.

D. $3,550 more than acquiring the purchased software package.

The correct answer is (A). *(CIA, adapted)*

**REQUIRED:** The comparison of the costs of developing and purchasing software.

**DISCUSSION:** Development cost equals the cost of the outside contractor plus the costs for hardware and supplies. Computer charges are transfer prices and do not require additional expenditures, given idle capacity. The relevant cost of supplies is $300 ($500 – $200 cost if the software is purchased). The contractor's use of an otherwise idle office is not relevant. Thus, the relevant cost of development is $25,500 [($22 hourly cost of the contractor x 1,000 hours) + $3,200 hardware purchases + $300 incremental cost of supplies]. This amount is $3,500 less than the $29,000 cost of purchase. A systems analyst's work on the new software is not relevant. It is part of the regular workload.

Answer (B) is incorrect because the contractor is not paid $25 per hour. Answer (C) is incorrect because $550 in computer charges and $4,500 in occupancy charges should not be included. Answer (D) is incorrect because the contractor is not paid $25 per hour, and 40 hours of modification and testing, $550 of the computer charges, and the occupancy costs are irrelevant.

Questions 23 through 25 are based on the following information. Richardson Motors uses 10 units of Part No. T305 each month in the production of large diesel engines. The cost to manufacture one unit of T305 is presented below.

| | |
|---|---|
| Direct materials | $ 2,000 |
| Materials handling (20% of direct materials cost) | 400 |
| Direct labor | 16,000 |
| Manufacturing overhead (150% of direct labor) | 24,000 |
| Total manufacturing cost | $42,400 |

Materials handling, which is not included in manufacturing overhead, represents the direct variable costs of the receiving department that are applied to direct materials and purchased components on the basis of their cost. Richardson's annual manufacturing overhead budget is one-third variable and two-thirds fixed. Simpson Castings, one of Richardson's reliable vendors, has offered to supply T305 at a unit price of $30,000.

**23.** If Richardson Motors purchases the ten T305 units from Simpson Castings, the capacity Richardson used to manufacture these parts would be idle. Should Richardson decide to purchase the parts from Simpson, the out-of-pocket cost per unit of T305 would

A.  Decrease $6,400.

B.  Increase $3,600.

C.  Increase $9,600.

D.  Decrease $4,400.

The correct answer is (C). *(CMA, adapted)*
**REQUIRED:** The effect on out-of-pocket cost per unit if the parts are purchased from an outside supplier.
**DISCUSSION:** The out-of-pocket cost of making the part equals the total manufacturing cost minus the fixed overhead, or $26,400 {$42,400 – [(2/3) x $24,000]}. The cost of the component consists of the $30,000 purchase price plus the $6,000 (20% of cost) of variable receiving costs, or a total of $36,000. Thus, unit out-of-pocket cost would increase by $9,600 if the components were purchased.
Answer (A) is incorrect because $6,400 assumes all of the overhead is variable. Answer (B) is incorrect because $3,600 overlooks the $6,000 of receiving costs for purchased components. Answer (D) is incorrect because $4,400 assumes that only one-third of overhead is fixed.

**24.** Assume Richardson Motors is able to rent all idle capacity for $50,000 per month. If Richardson decides to purchase the 10 units from Simpson Castings, Richardson's monthly cost for T305 would

A.  Increase $46,000.

B.  Decrease $64,000.

C.  Increase $96,000.

D.  Decrease $34,000.

The correct answer is (A). *(CMA, adapted)*
**REQUIRED:** The total change in monthly cost if components are purchased and idle capacity is rented.
**DISCUSSION:** For 10 components, the total cost increase would be $96,000 [($36,000 x 10) – ($26,400 x 10)] (see preceding question), but the $50,000 rental would reduce the net increase to $46,000.
Answer (B) is incorrect because $64,000 assumes all overhead is variable and ignores rental revenue. Answer (C) is incorrect because $96,000 overlooks the rental revenue. Answer (D) is incorrect because $34,000 assumes only one-third of the overhead is fixed.

**25.** Assume the rental opportunity does not exist and Richardson Motors could use the idle capacity to manufacture another product that would contribute $104,000 per month. If Richardson chooses to manufacture the ten T305 units in order to maintain quality control, Richardson's opportunity cost is

A.  $68,000

B.  $88,000

C.  $8,000

D.  $(96,000)

The correct answer is (C). *(CMA, adapted)*
**REQUIRED:** The opportunity cost of manufacturing components.
**DISCUSSION:** For 10 units, the additional cost of purchasing is $96,000. However, the net effect of purchasing is a gain of $8,000 ($104,000 contribution from making another product – $96,000). Opportunity cost is the benefit from the next best alternative use of the resources. Hence, the company's opportunity cost of making the part is $8,000.
Answer (A) is incorrect because $68,000 overlooks the $6,000 per unit of receiving costs for purchased components. Answer (B) is incorrect because $88,000 assumes only one-third of the overhead is fixed. Answer (D) is incorrect because $(96,000) ignores the $104,000 income from alternative production.

Questions 26 and 27 are based on the following information. Regis Company manufactures plugs used in its manufacturing cycle at a cost of $36 per unit that includes $8 of fixed overhead. Regis needs 30,000 of these plugs annually, and Orlan Company has offered to sell these units to Regis at $33 per unit. If Regis decides to purchase the plugs, $60,000 of the annual fixed overhead applied will be eliminated, and the company may be able to rent the facility previously used for manufacturing the plugs.

**26.** If Regis Company purchases the plugs but does not rent the unused facility, the company would

    A. Save $3.00 per unit.

    B. Lose $6.00 per unit.

    C. Save $2.00 per unit.

    D. Lose $3.00 per unit.

The correct answer is (D). *(CMA, adapted)*

**REQUIRED:** The amount saved or lost if the company purchases the plugs but does not rent out the unused facility.

**DISCUSSION:** Exclusive of the fixed overhead, the unit cost of making the plugs is $28 ($36 total cost – $8 fixed OH). Purchasing the plugs will avoid $2 per unit of fixed overhead ($60,000 OH applied ÷ 30,000 units). Accordingly, $6 per unit of fixed overhead is unavoidable, and the relevant (avoidable) unit cost of making the plugs is $30 [$36 total cost – ($8 fixed OH – $2 avoidable cost)]. The purchase option therefore results in a $3 per unit loss ($33 purchase price – $30 relevant cost).

Answer (A) is incorrect because the result is a $3 per unit loss. Answer (B) is incorrect because the $180,000 of unavoidable overhead ($6 per unit x 30,000 units) is not a relevant cost. Answer (C) is incorrect because all relevant costs, not just fixed overhead eliminated, must be included in determining the savings or loss per unit.

**27.** If the plugs are purchased and the facility rented, Regis Company wishes to realize $100,000 in savings annually. To achieve this goal, the minimum annual rent on the facility must be

    A. $10,000

    B. $40,000

    C. $70,000

    D. $190,000

The correct answer is (D). *(CMA, adapted)*

**REQUIRED:** The minimum annual rent on the abandoned facility to achieve a targeted annual savings.

**DISCUSSION:** Without regard to rental of idle production capacity, the company will lose $3 per unit (see preceding question) by purchasing the plugs. The total annual loss will be $90,000 (30,000 units x $3). Consequently, to achieve the targeted savings, the minimum annual rental must be $190,000 ($90,000 loss from purchasing + $100,000 target).

Answer (A) is incorrect because the $90,000 loss from purchasing should be added to the $100,000 targeted savings. Answer (B) is incorrect because $40,000 equals the $100,000 target minus the $60,000 eliminated fixed overhead. Answer (C) is incorrect because the minimum annual rental is determined by adding (subtracting) the net loss (gain) from purchasing externally to (from) the targeted savings.

Questions 28 and 29 are based on the following information. Geary Manufacturing has assembled the data appearing in the next column pertaining to two products. Past experience has shown that the unavoidable fixed factory overhead included in the cost per machine hour averages $10. Geary has a policy of filling all sales orders, even if it means purchasing units from outside suppliers.

|  | Blender | Electric Mixer |
|---|---|---|
| Direct materials | $ 6 | $11 |
| Direct labor | 4 | 9 |
| Factory overhead at $16 per hour | 16 | 32 |
| Cost if purchased from an outside supplier | 20 | 38 |
| Annual demand (units) | 20,000 | 28,000 |

**28.** If 50,000 machine hours are available, and Geary Manufacturing desires to follow an optimal strategy, it should

A. Produce 25,000 electric mixers and purchase all other units as needed.

B. Produce 20,000 blenders and 15,000 electric mixers, and purchase all other units as needed.

C. Produce 20,000 blenders and purchase all other units as needed.

D. Produce 28,000 electric mixers and purchase all other units as needed.

The correct answer is (B). *(CMA, adapted)*
**REQUIRED:** The optimal strategy with respect to producing or purchasing two products.
**DISCUSSION:** Sales (20,000 blenders and 28,000 mixers) and total revenue are constant, so the strategy is to minimize total variable cost. Each blender requires 1 machine hour ($16 OH ÷ $16 per hour), and each mixer requires 2 machine hours ($32 OH ÷ $16 per hour). For blenders, the unit variable cost is $16 ($6 DM + $4 DL + $6 VOH). For each blender made, the company saves $4 ($20 – $16), or $4 ($4 ÷ 1 hr.) per unit of the constrained resource. The unit variable cost to make a mixer is $32 ($11 DM + $9 DL + $12 VOH). The savings is $6 per mixer ($38 – $32), or $3 ($6 ÷ 2 hours) per unit of the constrained resource. Thus, as many blenders as possible should be made. If 20,000 hours (20,000 units x 1 hour) are used for blenders, 30,000 hours are available for 15,000 mixers. Total variable cost will be $1,294,000 [($16 x 20,000 blenders) + ($32 x 15,000 mixers) + ($38 x 13,000 mixers)].

Answer (A) is incorrect because producing 25,000 mixers results in a total variable cost of $1,314,000. Answer (C) is incorrect because producing 20,000 blenders and no mixers increases costs by $90,000 ($6 x 15,000 units). Answer (D) is incorrect because the company can produce at most 25,000 mixers.

**29.** With all other things constant, if Geary Manufacturing is able to reduce the direct materials for an electric mixer to $6 per unit, the company should

A. Produce 25,000 electric mixers and purchase all other units as needed.

B. Produce 20,000 blenders and 15,000 electric mixers, and purchase all other units as needed.

C. Produce 20,000 blenders and purchase all other units as needed.

D. Purchase all units as needed.

The correct answer is (A). *(CMA, adapted)*
**REQUIRED:** The optimal strategy if direct materials costs for a product are reduced.
**DISCUSSION:** Reducing unit direct materials cost for mixers from $11 to $6 decreases unit variable cost to $27 ($6 DM + $9 DL + $12 VOH) and increases the cost savings of making a mixer from $6 (see preceding question) to $11, or $5.50 per hour ($11 ÷ 2 hours per unit). Given a cost savings per hour for blenders of $4 (see preceding question), the company can minimize total variable cost by making 25,000 mixers (50,000 hours capacity ÷ 2). Total variable cost will be $1,189,000 [($27 x 25,000 mixers) + ($38 x 3,000 mixers) + ($20 x 20,000 blenders)].

Answer (B) is incorrect because producing 20,000 blenders and 15,000 mixers results in a total variable cost of $1,219,000. Answer (C) is incorrect because producing 20,000 blenders results in a total variable cost of $1,384,000. Answer (D) is incorrect because the variable cost of making these items is less than the cost of purchase.

**30.** A company needs special gears. The machinery to make the gears can be rented for $100,000 for 1 year, but the company can buy the gears and avoid the rental cost. Because the demand for the gears may be high (0.6 probability) or low (0.4 probability) and contribution margins vary, the company prepared the following decision tree:

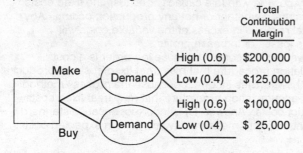

| | | | Total Contribution Margin |
|---|---|---|---|
| Make | Demand | High (0.6) | $200,000 |
| | | Low (0.4) | $125,000 |
| Buy | Demand | High (0.6) | $100,000 |
| | | Low (0.4) | $ 25,000 |

Which of the following statements is true?

  A.  The expected value of making is $20,000.

  B.  The expected value of buying is $70,000.

  C.  Making the gears is the best choice.

  D.  Buying the gears is the best choice.

The correct answer is (B). *(CIA, adapted)*
    **REQUIRED:** The true statement about a decision tree.
    **DISCUSSION:** The expected value of buying the gears is

$$.6 \times \$100,000 = \$60,000$$
$$.4 \times \$ 25,000 = \underline{\phantom{0}10,000}$$
$$\underline{\$70,000}$$

    Answer (A) is incorrect because the expected value to make the gears is $70,000 [(.6 x $200,000) + (.4 x $125,000) – $100,000 machine rental]. Answers (C) and (D) are incorrect because making the gears gives the same expected value as buying the gears, although the projected CMs for the make decision are higher than those for the buy decision.

## 12.3 Special Order

**31.** Production of a special order will increase gross profit when the additional revenue from the special order is greater than

  A.  The direct materials and labor costs in producing the order.

  B.  The fixed costs incurred in producing the order.

  C.  The indirect costs of producing the order.

  D.  The marginal cost of producing the order.

The correct answer is (D). *(CIA, adapted)*
    **REQUIRED:** The circumstances in which increased gross profit will result from a special order.
    **DISCUSSION:** Gross profit will increase if the incremental or marginal cost of producing the order is less than the marginal revenue. Marginal cost equals the relevant variable costs assuming fixed costs are not affected by the special order.
    Answer (A) is incorrect because indirect variable costs of producing a special order, such as shipping expenses, should also be considered. Answer (B) is incorrect because fixed costs should not increase as a result of producing the special order. Answer (C) is incorrect because direct labor and materials costs associated with producing a special order must be considered.

**32.** When considering a special order that will enable a company to make use of currently idle capacity, which of the following costs is irrelevant?

  A.  Materials.

  B.  Depreciation.

  C.  Direct labor.

  D.  Variable overhead.

The correct answer is (B). *(CPA, adapted)*
    **REQUIRED:** The irrelevant cost when a special order permits use of idle capacity.
    **DISCUSSION:** Because depreciation will be expensed whether or not the company accepts the special order, it is irrelevant to the decision. Only the variable costs are relevant.
    Answer (A) is incorrect because materials are relevant to a decision whether to take a special order. Answer (C) is incorrect because direct labor is relevant to a decision whether to take a special order. Answer (D) is incorrect because variable overhead is relevant to a decision whether to take a special order.

**33.** Which of the following cost allocation methods is used to determine the lowest price that can be quoted for a special order that will use idle capacity within a production area?

    A. Job order.

    B. Process.

    C. Variable.

    D. Standard.

The correct answer is (C). *(CPA, adapted)*
    **REQUIRED:** The most appropriate cost allocation method for determining the lowest price for a special order.
    **DISCUSSION:** If idle capacity exists, the lowest feasible price for a special order is one covering the variable cost. Variable costing considers fixed cost to be a period cost, not a product cost. Fixed costs are not relevant to short-term inventory costing with idle capacity because the fixed costs will be incurred whether or not any production occurs. Any additional revenue in excess of the variable costs will decrease losses or increase profits.
    Answer (A) is incorrect because job order is a cost accumulation procedure that may treat fixed costs as product costs. Answer (B) is incorrect because the process method is a cost accumulation procedure that may treat fixed costs as product costs. Answer (D) is incorrect because standard costing attempts to measure deviations from expected costs.

**34.** When only differential manufacturing costs are taken into account for special-order pricing, an essential assumption is that

    A. Manufacturing fixed and variable costs are linear.

    B. Selling and administrative fixed and variable costs are linear.

    C. Acceptance of the order will not affect regular sales.

    D. Acceptance of the order will not cause unit selling and administrative variable costs to increase.

The correct answer is (C). *(CPA, adapted)*
    **REQUIRED:** The essential assumption when only differential manufacturing costs are taken into account for special-order pricing.
    **DISCUSSION:** Granting a lower-than-normal price for a special order has potential ramifications for regular sales because other customers may demand the same price. Thus, the decision to consider differential manufacturing costs only should be based on a determination that all other costs are not relevant, that is, that these other costs do not vary with the option chosen.
    Answer (A) is incorrect because the differential analysis of a special order considers total marginal costs. Thus, unit variable costs and total fixed costs need not be constant, and any changes need not be in direct proportion to the measure of activity. Answer (B) is incorrect because the assumption is that selling and administrative costs are not relevant. Answer (D) is incorrect because the assumption is that acceptance of the order will not cause total selling and administrative costs to change.

**35.** Clay Co. has considerable excess manufacturing capacity. A special job order's cost sheet includes the following applied manufacturing overhead costs:

| | |
|---|---|
| Fixed costs | $21,000 |
| Variable costs | 33,000 |

The fixed costs include a normal $3,700 allocation for in-house design costs, although no in-house design will be done. Instead, the job will require the use of external designers costing $7,750. What is the total amount to be included in the calculation to determine the minimum acceptable price for the job?

    A. $36,700

    B. $40,750

    C. $54,000

    D. $58,050

The correct answer is (B). *(CPA, adapted)*
    **REQUIRED:** The total amount to be included in the calculation to determine the minimum acceptable price.
    **DISCUSSION:** Given excess capacity, the company presumably will not incur opportunity costs if it accepts the special order. Assuming also that fixed costs will be unaffected, the incremental cost of the order (the minimum acceptable price) will be $40,750 ($33,000 VC + $7,750 cost of external design).
    Answer (A) is incorrect because $36,700 equals variable costs plus the in-house design costs. Answer (C) is incorrect because $54,000 equals the fixed costs plus the variable costs. Answer (D) is incorrect because $58,050 equals the fixed costs, plus the variable costs, minus the in-house design costs, plus the external design costs.

Questions 36 through 38 are based on the following information. Kator Co. is a manufacturer of industrial components. One of their products that is used as a subcomponent in auto manufacturing is KB-96. This product has the following financial structure per unit:

| | |
|---|---|
| Selling price | $150 |
| | |
| Direct materials | $ 20 |
| Direct labor | 15 |
| Variable manufacturing overhead | 12 |
| Fixed manufacturing overhead | 30 |
| Shipping and handling | 3 |
| Fixed selling and administrative | 10 |
| Total costs | $ 90 |

**36.** Kator Co. has received a special, onetime, order for 1,000 KB-96 parts. Assuming Kator has excess capacity, the minimum price that is acceptable for this onetime special order is in excess of

A. $47

B. $50

C. $60

D. $77

The correct answer is (B). *(CMA, adapted)*

**REQUIRED:** The minimum acceptable price.

**DISCUSSION:** A company must cover the incremental costs of a special order when it has excess capacity. The incremental costs for product KB-96 are $50 ($20 direct materials + $15 direct labor + $12 variable overhead + $3 shipping and handling). The fixed costs will not change as a result of the special order, so they are not relevant. Thus, any price in excess of $50 per unit is acceptable.

Answer (A) is incorrect because $47 ignores the shipping and handling costs. Answer (C) is incorrect because $60 includes fixed selling and administrative costs. Answer (D) is incorrect because $77 includes fixed manufacturing overhead but omits shipping and handling costs.

**37.** During the next year, KB-96 sales are expected to be 10,000 units. All of the costs will remain the same except that fixed manufacturing overhead will increase by 20% and direct materials will increase by 10%. The selling price per unit for next year will be $160. Based on this data, the contribution margin from KB-96 for next year will be

A. $620,000

B. $750,000

C. $1,080,000

D. $1,110,000

The correct answer is (C). *(CMA, adapted)*

**REQUIRED:** The contribution margin for next year.

**DISCUSSION:** Contribution margin equals sales minus variable costs. All variable costs will remain the same except that direct materials will increase to $22 per unit (1.1 x $20). Thus, total unit variable costs will be $52 ($22 + $15 + $12 + $3), and the contribution margin will be $1,080,000 [10,000 units ($160 unit selling price – $52)].

Answer (A) is incorrect because $620,000 includes all fixed costs. Answer (B) is incorrect because $750,000 includes all manufacturing costs. Answer (D) is incorrect because $1,110,000 assumes that the fixed costs and shipping and handling are the only relevant costs.

**38.** Kator Co. has received a special, onetime, order for 1,000 KB-96 parts. Assume that Kator is operating at full capacity, and the next best alternative use of the capacity of existing equipment is to produce LB-64, resulting in a contribution of $10,000. The minimum price that is acceptable, using the original data, for this onetime special order is in excess of

A. $60

B. $70

C. $87

D. $100

The correct answer is (A). *(CMA, adapted)*

**REQUIRED:** The minimum acceptable price.

**DISCUSSION:** Given no excess capacity, the price must cover the incremental costs. The incremental costs for KB-96 equal $50 ($20 direct materials + $15 direct labor + $12 variable overhead + $3 shipping and handling). Opportunity cost is the benefit of the best alternative use of scarce resources. Because acceptance of the special order would cause the company to forgo a contribution margin of $10,000, that amount must be reflected in the price. Hence, the minimum unit price is $60 [$50 unit incremental cost + ($10,000 lost CM ÷ 1,000 units)].

Answer (B) is incorrect because $70 includes fixed selling and administrative costs. Answer (C) is incorrect because $87 includes fixed manufacturing overhead but omits shipping and handling costs. Answer (D) is incorrect because $100 is based on full absorption cost.

**39.** A company manufactures a product that is sold for $37.95. It uses an absorption cost system. Plant capacity is 750,000 units annually, but normal volume is 500,000 units. Costs at normal volume are given below.

|  | Unit Cost | Total Cost |
|---|---|---|
| Direct materials | $ 9.80 | $ 4,900,000 |
| Direct labor | 4.50 | 2,250,000 |
| Manufacturing overhead | 12.00 | 6,000,000 |
| Selling and administrative: Variable | 2.50 | 1,250,000 |
| Fixed | 4.20 | 2,100,000 |
| Total cost | $33.00 | $16,500,000 |

Fixed manufacturing overhead is budgeted at $4,500,000. A customer has offered to purchase 100,000 units at $25.00 each to be packaged in large cartons, not the normal individual containers. It will pick up the units in its own trucks. Thus, variable selling and administrative expenses will decrease by 60%. The company should compare the total revenue to be derived from this order with the total relevant costs of

A. $1,830,000

B. $1,880,000

C. $2,930,000

D. $3,150,000

The correct answer is (A). *(CIA, adapted)*
**REQUIRED:** The total relevant costs of the special order.
**DISCUSSION:** The necessary assumptions are that all fixed costs and the unit variable costs of direct materials, direct labor, and variable manufacturing overhead are not affected by the special order. Hence, the fixed costs are not relevant. The unit costs of direct materials and direct labor are given as $9.80 and $4.50, respectively. The unit variable manufacturing overhead cost is $3.00 [($6,000,000 total manufacturing overhead – $4,500,000 total fixed manufacturing overhead) ÷ 500,000 units normal volume]. The unit variable selling and administrative cost is $1.00 [$2.50 x (1.0 – .6)]. Consequently, the total relevant cost of the special order is $1,830,000 [100,000 units x ($9.80 + $4.50 + $3.00 + $1.00)].
Answer (B) is incorrect because variable manufacturing per unit is determined by using normal volume, not plant capacity, as the denominator level. Answer (C) is incorrect because the total relevant cost of the special order is $1,830,000 [100,000 units x ($9.80 + $4.50 + $3.00 + $1.00)]. Answer (D) is incorrect because fixed selling and administrative expenses of $4.20 per unit should not be included. Furthermore, variable manufacturing of $3 per unit, not total manufacturing overhead of $12 per unit, should be used in the calculation of relevant costs.

## 12.4 Other Nonroutine Decisions

**40.** Vince Inc. has developed and patented a new laser disc reading device that will be marketed internationally. Which of the following factors should Vince consider in pricing the device?

I. Quality of the new device
II. Life of the new device
III. Customers' relative preference for quality compared with price

A. I and II only.

B. I and III only.

C. II and III only.

D. I, II, and III.

The correct answer is (D). *(CPA, adapted)*
**REQUIRED:** The factors considered when pricing a new product.
**DISCUSSION:** Product pricing is a function of consumer demand, competitive factors, and the seller's cost structure and profit objectives. Thus, the seller must consider the trade-off between the price and quality effects on demand. A better-quality product, for example, one with a relatively long useful life, is more costly to produce and therefore sells for a higher price, which in turn reduces the amount demanded.
Answer (A) is incorrect because the customers' preference is also important when determining the price of a product. Answer (B) is incorrect because the life of the product should also be considered when pricing a product. Answer (C) is incorrect because the quality of a product is important when determining how much to charge for it.

**41.** When a multiproduct plant operates at full capacity, quite often decisions must be made as to which products to emphasize. These decisions are frequently made with a short-run focus. In making such decisions, managers should select products with the

A. Highest sales price per unit.

B. Highest individual unit contribution margin.

C. Highest sales volume potential.

D. Highest contribution margin per unit of the constraining resource.

The correct answer is (D). *(CMA, adapted)*
**REQUIRED:** The products to be made in the short run by a multiproduct company operating at full capacity.
**DISCUSSION:** In the short run, many costs are fixed. Hence, contribution margin (revenues – all variable costs) becomes the best measure of profitability. Certain resources are also fixed. When deciding which products to produce at full capacity, the criterion should be the contribution margin per unit of the most constrained resource. This approach maximizes total contribution margin.
Answers (A) and (C) are incorrect because the highest sales price or volume does not consider costs and constraints. Answer (B) is incorrect because the product with the highest UCM may require greater usage of the constrained resource than another product contributing a lesser amount per unit.

**42.** If a U.S. manufacturer's price in the U.S. market is below an appropriate measure of costs and the seller has a reasonable prospect of recovering the resulting loss in the future through higher prices or a greater market share, the seller has engaged in

A. Collusive pricing.

B. Dumping.

C. Predatory pricing.

D. Price discrimination.

The correct answer is (C). *(Publisher)*
**REQUIRED:** The pricing strategy characterized by charging a price that is below an appropriate measure of costs when the seller reasonably expects to recover the loss through higher prices or a greater market share.
**DISCUSSION:** Predatory pricing is intentionally pricing below cost to eliminate competition and reduce supply. Federal statutes and many state laws prohibit the practice. The U.S. Supreme Court has held that pricing is predatory when two conditions are met: (1) the seller's price is below "an appropriate measure of its costs," and (2) it has a reasonable prospect of recovering the resulting loss through higher prices or greater market share.
Answer (A) is incorrect because collusive pricing involves a conspiracy to set higher prices. Answer (B) is incorrect because dumping is defined under U.S. law as sale by a non-U.S. company in the U.S. market of a product below its market value in the country where it was produced. Such sale is illegal if it threatens material injury to a U.S. industry. Answer (D) is incorrect because price discrimination entails charging different prices to different customers for essentially the same product if the effect is to lessen competition substantially; to tend to create a monopoly; or to injure, destroy, or prevent competition.

**43.** Briar Co. signed a government construction contract providing for a formula price of actual cost plus 10%. In addition, Briar was to receive one-half of any savings resulting from the formula price's being less than the target price of $2.2 million. Briar's actual costs incurred were $1,920,000. How much should Briar receive from the contract?

A. $2,060,000

B. $2,112,000

C. $2,156,000

D. $2,200,000

The correct answer is (C). *(CPA, adapted)*
**REQUIRED:** The amount received from a cost-plus contract.
**DISCUSSION:** The formula price is 110% of actual cost, or $2,112,000 (110% x $1,920,000), a savings of $88,000 on the $2,200,000 target price. Accordingly, Briar should receive $2,156,000 {$2,112,000 + [50% x ($2,200,000 – $2,112,000)]}.
Answer (A) is incorrect because $2,060,000 equals actual costs plus 50% of the excess of the target price over actual costs. Answer (B) is incorrect because $2,112,000 is the formula price. Answer (D) is incorrect because $2,200,000 is the target price.

**44.** Power Systems, Inc. manufactures jet engines for the United States armed forces on a cost-plus basis. The cost of a particular jet engine the company manufactures is shown below.

| | |
|---|---|
| Direct materials | $200,000 |
| Direct labor | 150,000 |
| Overhead: | |
| Supervisor's salary | 20,000 |
| Fringe benefits on direct labor | 15,000 |
| Depreciation | 12,000 |
| Rent | 11,000 |
| Total cost | $408,000 |

If production of this engine were discontinued, the production capacity would be idle, and the supervisor would be laid off. When asked to bid on the next contract for this engine, the minimum unit price that Power Systems should bid is

A. $408,000

B. $365,000

C. $397,000

D. $385,000

The correct answer is (D). *(CMA, adapted)*
**REQUIRED:** The minimum unit price that should be bid.
**DISCUSSION:** The company will need to cover its variable costs and any other incremental costs. Thus, direct materials ($200,000), direct labor ($150,000), the supervisor's salary ($20,000), and fringe benefits on direct labor ($15,000) are the incremental unit costs of manufacturing the engines. The breakeven price is therefore $385,000 ($200,000 + $150,000 + $20,000 + $15,000).
Answer (A) is incorrect because depreciation and rent are allocated costs that will be incurred even if the contract is lost. Answer (B) is incorrect because the supervisor's salary will have to be covered. The $20,000 salary is an avoidable cost. Answer (C) is incorrect because depreciation is a cost that cannot be avoided.

**45.** A company has 7,000 obsolete toys carried in inventory at a manufacturing cost of $6 per unit. If the toys are reworked for $2 per unit, they could be sold for $3 per unit. If the toys are scrapped, they could be sold for $1.85 per unit. Which alternative is more desirable (rework or scrap), and what is the total dollar amount of the advantage of that alternative?

A. Scrap, $5,950.

B. Rework, $36,050.

C. Scrap, $47,950.

D. Rework, $8,050.

The correct answer is (A). *(CIA, adapted)*
**REQUIRED:** The total dollar amount of the advantage of the more desirable option.
**DISCUSSION:** The original manufacturing cost of $6 per unit is a sunk cost that is not relevant to this decision. The relevant costs are the amounts that must be expended now. Hence, selling the toys for scrap has a $5,950 advantage because rework will produce an additional $7,000 [($3 – $2) x 7,000], whereas the alternative generates an additional $12,950 ($1.85 x 7,000).
Answers (B) and (C) are incorrect because the original manufacturing cost of $6 should not be added to the sales price. Answer (D) is incorrect because $8,050 (rework) does not include the cost of the rework.

**46.** A company produces and sells three products:

| | C | J | P |
|---|---|---|---|
| Sales | $200,000 | $150,000 | $125,000 |
| Separable (product) fixed costs | 60,000 | 35,000 | 40,000 |
| Allocated fixed costs | 35,000 | 40,000 | 25,000 |
| Variable costs | 95,000 | 75,000 | 50,000 |

The company lost its lease and must move to a smaller facility. As a result, total allocated fixed costs will be reduced by 40%. However, one product must be discontinued. The expected net income after the appropriate product has been discontinued is

A. $10,000

B. $15,000

C. $20,000

D. $25,000

The correct answer is (D). *(CIA, adapted)*
**REQUIRED:** The expected net income after eliminating the appropriate product to maximize profits.
**DISCUSSION:** Product P should be eliminated because it has the smallest product margin.

| | C | J | P | TOTAL |
|---|---|---|---|---|
| Sales | $200,000 | $150,000 | $125,000 | $475,000 |
| Variable costs | 95,000 | 75,000 | 50,000 | 220,000 |
| Contribution margin | $105,000 | $ 75,000 | $ 75,000 | $255,000 |
| Separable (product) fixed costs | 60,000 | 35,000 | 40,000 | 135,000 |
| Product margin | $ 45,000 | $ 40,000 | $ 35,000 | $120,000 |
| Allocated fixed costs | | | | 100,000 |
| Net income | | | | $ 20,000 |

After discontinuing P, total product margin is $85,000 ($45,000 + $40,000), and total allocated fixed costs are $60,000 [($35,000 + $40,000 + $25,000) x (1.0 – 0.4)]. Hence, expected net income is $25,000 ($85,000 – $60,000).
Answer (A) is incorrect because $10,000 is 40% of net income after eliminating product P. Answer (B) is incorrect because $15,000 is net income if product C is eliminated. Answer (C) is incorrect because $20,000 is net income if product J is eliminated.

**47.** American Coat Company estimates that 60,000 special zippers will be used in the manufacture of men's jackets during the next year. Reese Zipper Company has quoted a price of $.60 per zipper. American would prefer to purchase 5,000 units per month, but Reese is unable to guarantee this delivery schedule. To ensure availability of these zippers, American is considering the purchase of all 60,000 units at the beginning of the year. Assuming American can invest cash at 8%, the company's opportunity cost of purchasing the 60,000 units at the beginning of the year is

A. $1,320

B. $1,440

C. $2,640

D. $2,880

The correct answer is (A). *(CMA, adapted)*

**REQUIRED:** The opportunity cost of purchasing the total annual requirement at the beginning of the year.

**DISCUSSION:** The cost of 60,000 zippers is $36,000 (60,000 x $.60). The monthly cost is $3,000 (5,000 x $.60). The company would like to purchase the items monthly, so it will invest at least $3,000 in January. Accordingly, the zippers to be used in January will be purchased at the first of the year even if no special purchase is made. Thus, the incremental advance purchase is only $33,000. Because the alternative arrangement involves a constant monthly expenditure of $3,000, the incremental investment declines by that amount each month. The result is that the average incremental investment for the year is $16,500 ($33,000 ÷ 2), and the opportunity cost of purchasing 60,000 units at the beginning of the year is $1,320 (8% x $16,500).

Answer (B) is incorrect because $1,440 is 8% of $18,000 ($36,000 ÷ 2). Answer (C) is incorrect because $2,640 equals 8% of $33,000. Answer (D) is incorrect because $2,880 equals 8% of $36,000.

**48.** Data regarding four different products manufactured by an organization are presented below. Direct materials and direct labor are readily available from the respective resource markets. However, the manufacturer is limited to a maximum of 3,000 machine hours per month.

|  | Product A | Product B | Product C | Product D |
|---|---|---|---|---|
| Selling price/unit | $15 | $18 | $20 | $25 |
| Variable cost/unit | $ 7 | $11 | $10 | $16 |
| Units produced per machine hour | 3 | 4 | 2 | 3 |

The product that is the most profitable for the manufacturer in this situation is

A. Product A.

B. Product B.

C. Product C.

D. Product D.

The correct answer is (B). *(CIA, adapted)*

**REQUIRED:** The product that is the most profitable for the manufacturer.

**DISCUSSION:** When resources are limited, maximum profits are achieved by maximizing dollar contribution margin per constraining factor, e.g., machine hours. Product B has a contribution margin per machine hour of $28 [4 x ($18 – $11)], which is greater than that of Product A [3 x ($15 – $7) = $24], Product C [2 x ($20 – $10) = $20], or Product D [3 x ($25 – $16) = $27].

Answer (A) is incorrect because Product A has the greatest contribution margin ratio (53%), but its CM per hour is $24. Answer (C) is incorrect because Product C has the greatest dollar unit contribution margin ($10), but its CM per hour is $20. Answer (D) is incorrect because Product D has the greatest selling price per unit ($25), but its CM per hour is $27.

Questions 49 and 50 are based on the following information. Whitehall Corporation produces chemicals used in the cleaning industry. During the previous month, Whitehall incurred $300,000 of joint costs in producing 60,000 units of AM-12 and 40,000 units of BM-36. Whitehall uses the units-of-production method to allocate joint costs. Currently, AM-12 is sold at split-off for $3.50 per unit. Flank Corporation has approached Whitehall to purchase all of the production of AM-12 after further processing. The further processing will cost Whitehall $90,000.

**49.** Concerning AM-12, which one of the following alternatives is most advantageous?

A.  Whitehall should process further and sell to Flank if the total selling price per unit after further processing is greater than $3.00, which covers the joint costs.

B.  Whitehall should continue to sell at split-off unless Flank offers at least $4.50 per unit after further processing, which covers Whitehall's total costs.

C.  Whitehall should process further and sell to Flank if the total selling price per unit after further processing is greater than $5.00.

D.  Whitehall should process further and sell to Flank if the total selling price per unit after further processing is greater than $5.25, which maintains the same gross profit percentage.

The correct answer is (C). (CMA, adapted)
REQUIRED: The processing and selling alternative that is most advantageous.
DISCUSSION: The unit price of the product at the split-off point is known to be $3.50, so the joint costs are irrelevant. The additional unit cost of further processing is $1.50 ($90,000 ÷ 60,000 units). Consequently, the unit price must be at least $5.00 ($3.50 opportunity cost + $1.50).

Answer (A) is incorrect because the joint costs are irrelevant. Answer (B) is incorrect because the unit price must cover the $3.50 opportunity cost plus the $1.50 of additional costs. Answer (D) is incorrect because any price greater than $5 will provide greater profits, in absolute dollars, even though the gross profit percentage declines.

**50.** Assume that Whitehall Corporation agreed to sell AM-12 to Flank Corporation for $5.50 per unit after further processing. During the first month of production, Whitehall sold 50,000 units with 10,000 units remaining in inventory at the end of the month. With respect to AM-12, which one of the following statements is correct?

A.  The operating profit last month was $50,000, and the inventory value is $15,000.

B.  The operating profit last month was $50,000, and the inventory value is $45,000.

C.  The operating profit last month was $125,000, and the inventory value is $30,000.

D.  The operating profit last month was $200,000, and the inventory value is $30,000.

The correct answer is (B). (CMA, adapted)
REQUIRED: The operating profit and inventory value after specified sales of a product.
DISCUSSION: Joint costs are allocated based on units of production. Accordingly, the unit joint cost allocated to AM-12 is $3.00 [$300,000 ÷ (60,000 units of AM-12 + 40,000 units of BM-36)]. The unit cost of AM-12 is therefore $4.50 [$3.00 joint cost + ($90,000 additional cost ÷ 60,000 units)]. Total inventory value is $45,000 (10,000 units x $4.50), and total operating profit is $50,000 [($5.50 unit price – $4.50 unit cost) x 50,000 units sold].

Answer (A) is incorrect because the $3 unit joint cost should be included in the inventory value. Answer (C) is incorrect because the $1.50 unit additional cost should be included in total unit cost. Answer (D) is incorrect because the $3 unit joint cost should be included in the cost of goods sold, and inventory should include the $1.50 unit additional cost.

Questions 51 through 53 are based on the following information. Condensed monthly operating income data for Korbin Inc. for May 31, 1998 follow:

| | Urban Store | Suburban Store | Total |
|---|---|---|---|
| Sales | $80,000 | $120,000 | $200,000 |
| Variable costs | 32,000 | 84,000 | 116,000 |
| Contribution margin | $48,000 | $ 36,000 | $ 84,000 |
| Direct fixed costs | 20,000 | 40,000 | 60,000 |
| Store segment margin | $28,000 | $ (4,000) | $ 24,000 |
| Common fixed cost | 4,000 | 6,000 | 10,000 |
| Operating income | $24,000 | $ (10,000) | $ 14,000 |

Additional information regarding Korbin's operations follows:

- One-fourth of each store's direct fixed costs will continue if either store is closed.
- Korbin allocates common fixed costs to each store on the basis of sales dollars.
- Management estimates that closing Suburban Store would result in a 10% decrease in Urban Store's sales, whereas closing Urban Store would not affect Suburban Store's sales.
- The operating results for May 1998 are representative of all months.

**51.** A decision by Korbin to close Suburban Store would result in a monthly increase (decrease) in Korbin's operating income of

A. $(10,800)

B. $(6,000)

C. $4,000

D. $10,000

The correct answer is (A). *(CMA, adapted)*
**REQUIRED:** The effect of closing Suburban Store.
**DISCUSSION:** If Suburban Store is closed, one-fourth of its direct fixed costs will continue. Thus, the segment margin that should be used to calculate the effect of its closing on Korbin's operating income is $6,000 {$36,000 contribution margin – [$40,000 direct fixed costs x (1.0 – .25)]}. In addition, the sales (and contribution margin) of Urban Store will decline by 10% if Suburban Store closes. A 10% reduction in Urban's $48,000 contribution margin will reduce income by $4,800. Accordingly, the effect of closing Suburban Store is to decrease operating income by $10,800 ($6,000 + $4,800).
Answer (B) is incorrect because $(6,000) overlooks the decline in profitability at Urban Store. Answers (C) and (D) are incorrect because profits will decline.

**52.** Korbin is considering a promotional campaign at Suburban Store that would not affect Urban Store. Increasing annual promotional expense at Suburban Store by $60,000 in order to increase this store's sales by 10% would result in a monthly increase (decrease) in Korbin's operating income during 1998 (rounded) of

A. $(5,000)

B. $(1,400)

C. $7,000

D. $12,000

The correct answer is (B). *(CMA, adapted)*
**REQUIRED:** The effect on monthly income of an advertising campaign.
**DISCUSSION:** The $60,000 advertising campaign will increase direct fixed costs by $5,000 per month ($60,000 ÷ 12). Sales and contribution margin will also increase by 10%. Hence, the contribution margin for Suburban Store will increase by $3,600 (10% x $36,000), and income will decline by $1,400 ($5,000 – $3,600).
Answer (A) is incorrect because $(5,000) is the monthly advertising cost. Answer (C) is incorrect because $7,000 omits the 10% increase in variable costs from the calculation. Answer (D) is incorrect because $12,000 is the increase in sales.

**53.** One-half of Suburban Store's dollar sales are from items sold at variable cost to attract customers to the store. Korbin is considering the deletion of these items, a move that would reduce Suburban Store's direct fixed expenses by 15% and result in a 20% loss of Suburban Store's remaining sales volume. This change would not affect Urban Store. A decision by Korbin to eliminate the items sold at cost would result in a monthly increase (decrease) in Korbin's operating income during 1998 of

A. $(5,200)

B. $(1,200)

C. $2,000

D. $6,000

The correct answer is (B). *(CMA, adapted)*
**REQUIRED:** The effect on monthly income of eliminating sales made at variable cost.
**DISCUSSION:** If 50% of Suburban Store's sales are at variable cost, its contribution margin (sales – variable costs) must derive wholly from sales of other items. However, eliminating sales at variable cost reduces other sales by 20%. Thus, the effect is to reduce the contribution margin to $28,800 ($36,000 x .8). Moreover, fixed costs will be reduced by 15% to $34,000 ($40,000 x .85). Consequently, the new segment margin is $(5,200) ($34,000 direct fixed costs – $28,800 contribution margin), a decrease of $1,200 [$(5,200) – $(4,000)].
Answer (A) is incorrect because $(5,200) is the new segment margin. Answers (C) and (D) are incorrect because operating income must decrease.

## 12.5 Comprehensive

| Questions 54 through 56 are based on the following information. Ignore taxes when answering these questions. ABC Company produces and sells a single product called Kleen. Annual production capacity is 100,000 machine hours. It takes 1 machine hour to produce a unit of Kleen. Annual demand for Kleen is expected to remain at 80,000 units. The selling price is expected to remain at $10 per unit. Cost data for producing and selling Kleen are as follows: | | |
|---|---|---|
| Variable costs (per unit) | | |
| Direct materials | | $1.50 |
| Direct labor | | 2.50 |
| Variable overhead | | 0.80 |
| Variable selling | | 2.00 |
| Fixed costs (per year) | | |
| Fixed overhead | | $100,000.00 |
| Fixed selling and administrative | | 50,000.00 |

**54.** ABC Company has 2,000 units of Kleen that were partially damaged in storage. It can sell these units through regular channels at reduced prices. These 2,000 units will be valueless unless sold this way. Sale of these units will not affect regular sales of Kleen. The relevant unit cost for determining the minimum selling price for these units is

A. $6.80

B. $6.00

C. $4.00

D. $2.00

The correct answer is (D). *(CIA, adapted)*
**REQUIRED:** The relevant unit cost for determining the minimum selling price for damaged units.
**DISCUSSION:** The unit cost relevant to determining the minimum selling price for the damaged units is the incremental cost that will be incurred. Hence, the relevant unit cost is variable selling cost, or $2.00. The other costs are considered to be sunk (irrelevant) costs because they have already been incurred.
Answer (A) is incorrect because $6.80 is the total variable cost per unit. Answer (B) is incorrect because direct materials and direct labor costs are sunk costs and should therefore not be considered. Answer (C) is incorrect because $4.00 is the prime cost per unit.

**55.** MNO Company offers to make and ship 25,000 units of Kleen directly to ABC Company's customers. If ABC Company accepts this offer, it will continue to produce and ship the remaining 55,000 units. ABC's fixed factory overhead will drop to $90,000. Its fixed selling and administrative expenses will remain unchanged. Variable selling expenses will drop to $0.80 per unit for the 25,000 units produced and shipped by MNO company. What is the maximum amount per unit that ABC Company should pay MNO Company for producing and shipping the 25,000 units?

A. $6.80

B. $6.40

C. $5.60

D. $5.20

The correct answer is (B). *(CIA, adapted)*
**REQUIRED:** The maximum unit amount that should be paid for producing and shipping the units.
**DISCUSSION:** The maximum amount per unit ABC should pay is the amount that ABC saves by not making the product.

| | |
|---|---|
| Variable manufacturing costs | |
| [25,000 × ($1.50 + $2.50 + $0.80)] | $120,000 |
| Fixed overhead ($100,000 – $90,000) | 10,000 |
| Variable selling costs [25,000 × ($2.00 – $0.80)] | 30,000 |
| Total cost savings | $160,000 |
| Units | ÷ 25,000 |
| Cost savings per unit | $   6.40 |

Answer (A) is incorrect because cost savings per unit are $6.40. Answer (C) is incorrect because $5.60 does not include the unit variable overhead cost of $.80. Answer (D) is incorrect because $5.20 does not include variable selling costs of $30,000.

**56.** ABC Company receives a one-time special order for 5,000 units of Kleen. Acceptance of this order will not affect the regular sales of 80,000 units. Variable selling costs for each of these 5,000 units will be $1.00. What is the differential cost to ABC Company of accepting this special order?

A. $39,000

B. $34,000

C. $30,250

D. $29,000

The correct answer is (D). *(CIA, adapted)*
**REQUIRED:** The differential cost of accepting a special order.
**DISCUSSION:** Differential (incremental) costs change as a result of changes in operations or objectives. The differential cost per unit includes all variable manufacturing costs and variable selling costs. Thus, the differential cost per unit is $5.80 ($1.50 + $2.50 + $.80 + $1.00). The total differential cost is $29,000 (5,000 x $5.80).
Answer (A) is incorrect because $39,000 results from including $3 of variable sales costs per unit. Answer (B) is incorrect because $34,000 includes variable selling cost per unit of $2.00. Answer (C) is incorrect because the differential cost equals the 5,000 special-order units times a unit variable cost of $5.80.

Questions 57 through 63 are based on the following information. The information was presented as part of Question 3 on Part 5 of the June 1981 CMA examination.

The Ashley Co. manufactures and sells a household product marketed through direct mail and advertisements in home improvement and gardening magazines. Although similar products are available in hardware and department stores, none is as effective as Ashley's model.

The company uses a standard cost system in its manufacturing accounting. The standards have not undergone a thorough review in the past 18 months. The general manager has seen no need for such a review because

- The materials quality and unit costs were fixed by a 3-year purchase commitment signed in July 1996.
- A 3-year labor contract had been signed in July 1996.
- There have been no significant variations from standard costs for the past three quarters.

The standard cost for the product, as established in July 1996, is presented below:

| | |
|---|---|
| Materials (.75 lb. at $1 per lb.) | $0.75 |
| Direct labor (.3 hr. at $4 per hour) | 1.20 |
| Overhead (.3 hr. at $7 per hour) | 2.10 |
| Standard manufacturing cost per unit | $4.05 |

The standard for overhead costs was developed from the following budgeted costs based upon an activity level of 1 million units (300,000 direct labor hours):

| | |
|---|---|
| Variable manufacturing overhead | $ 600,000 |
| Fixed manufacturing overhead | 1,500,000 |
| Total manufacturing overhead | $2,100,000 |

The earnings statement and the factory costs for the first quarter of 1998 are presented in the opposite column. The first quarter results indicate that Ashley probably will achieve its sales goal of 1.2 million units for the current year. A total of 320,000 units were manufactured during the first quarter to increase inventory levels needed to support the growing sales volume.

ACTION Hardware, a national chain, recently asked Ashley to manufacture and sell a slightly modified version of the product that ACTION will distribute through its stores.

ACTION has offered to buy a minimum quantity of 200,000 units each year over the next 3 years and has offered to pay $4.10 for each unit, F.O.B. shipping point.

The Ashley management is interested in the proposal because it represents a new market. The company has adequate capacity to meet the production requirements. However, in addition to the possible financial results of taking the order, Ashley must consider carefully the other consequences of this departure from its normal practices. The president

asked an assistant to the general manager to make an estimate of the financial aspects of the proposal for the first 12 months.

The assistant recommended that the order not be accepted and presented the analysis shown below to support the recommendation.

### Sales Proposal of ACTION Hardware
### First 12 Months' Results

| | |
|---|---|
| Proposed sales (200,000 at $4.10) | $820,000 |
| Estimated costs and expenses | |
| Manufacturing (200,000 at $4.05) | $810,000 |
| Sales salaries | 10,000 |
| Administrative salaries | 20,000 |
| Total estimated costs | $840,000 |
| Net loss | $ (20,000) |

Note: None of our regular selling costs are included because this is a new market. However, a 16.6% increase in sales and administrative salaries has been incorporated because sales volume will increase by that amount.

### Ashley Co.
### First Quarter Earnings
### Period Ended March 31, 1998

| | | |
|---|---|---|
| Sales (300,000 units) | | $2,700,000 |
| Cost of goods sold | | |
| Standard cost of goods | $1,215,000 | |
| Variation from standard costs | 12,000 | (1,227,000) |
| Gross profit | | $1,473,000 |
| Operating expenses | | |
| Selling | | |
| Advertising | $ 200,000 | |
| Mailing list costs | 175,000 | |
| Postage | 225,000 | |
| Salaries | 60,000 | |
| Administrative | | |
| Salaries | 120,000 | |
| Office rent | 45,000 | |
| Total operating expenses | | (825,000) |
| Income before taxes | | $ 648,000 |
| Income taxes (45%) | | (291,600) |
| Net income | | $ 356,400 |

### Ashley Co.
### Factory Costs
### For the Quarter Ended March 31, 1998

| | |
|---|---|
| Materials | $ 266,000 |
| Direct labor | 452,000 |
| Variable manufacturing overhead | 211,000 |
| Fixed manufacturing overhead | 379,000 |
| Total manufacturing costs | $1,308,000 |
| Minus: Standard cost of goods manufactured | $1,296,000 |
| Unfavorable variation from standard cost | $ 12,000 |

Questions 57 through 63 are based on the information presented on page 443.

**57.** The financial analysis prepared by the general manager's assistant is

A. Deficient in that the contribution margin is not calculated.

B. Deficient in that the sales projections are not realistic.

C. Deficient in that current changes in standard costs are recognized.

D. Adequately prepared.

The correct answer is (A). *(Publisher)*
**REQUIRED:** The deficiency in the financial analysis.
**DISCUSSION:** A primary deficiency in the financial analysis is that no contribution margin is calculated. The analysis uses a full standard cost approach to determine the profitability of a special project. Special projects should be evaluated based upon their incremental costs and benefits.
Answer (B) is incorrect because the sales projection is based on the buyer's minimum purchase quantity. Answer (C) is incorrect because a deficiency in the analysis is that current changes are not reflected. Answer (D) is incorrect because an adequate financial analysis should include CM data.

**58.** A determination should be made in regard to fixed manufacturing costs. This determination involves

A. Anticipation of a decrease because of the allocation of fixed costs to include the special order.

B. Anticipation of an increase because of the increased volume incurred as a result of the special order.

C. No consideration of fixed manufacturing costs.

D. Consideration of administrative and sales salaries.

The correct answer is (B). *(Publisher)*
**REQUIRED:** The necessary determination regarding fixed manufacturing costs.
**DISCUSSION:** The additional financial data needed for a more comprehensive analysis include an analysis of fixed manufacturing costs for any incremental increases as a result of increased volume. The special order may be such a significant proportion of the total manufacturing capacity that it will in effect increase fixed costs in a step pattern.
Answer (A) is incorrect because the special order will not decrease fixed costs. Only incremental increases in fixed costs will be allocated to the special order. Answer (C) is incorrect because a possible increase in fixed costs should be considered. Answer (D) is incorrect because administrative and sales salaries are not fixed manufacturing costs.

**59.** Revisions of standards should be made for

A. Variable overhead.

B. Labor and materials.

C. Variable overhead and labor.

D. Variable overhead, labor, and materials.

The correct answer is (D). *(Publisher)*
**REQUIRED:** The item(s) needing revision of standards.
**DISCUSSION:** Revisions of standards are appropriate for variable overhead, direct labor, and raw materials. These three components have not been reviewed in the past 18 months. They may have undergone significant change within this period, and additional change may be predicted in the immediate future.
Answer (A) is incorrect because revision of the standards should also be made for labor and materials. Answer (B) is incorrect because revision of the standards should also be made for variable overhead. Answer (C) is incorrect because revision of the standards should also be made for materials.

**60.** Assume that the factory costs incurred in the first quarter reflect the anticipated costs for the ACTION special purchase. What is the expected materials cost per unit?

A. $.75

B. $1.00

C. $.83

D. $.80

The correct answer is (C). *(Publisher)*
**REQUIRED:** The expected materials cost per unit for the special purchase.
**DISCUSSION:** The expected materials cost per unit based upon the factory costs incurred in the first quarter is equal to the materials cost in the first quarter divided by the number of units. The factory cost in the first quarter for materials was $266,000, and 320,000 units were manufactured. Thus, the unit materials cost equals $.83125.
Answer (A) is incorrect because $.75 is the standard cost of materials for the product as established in July 1996. Answer (B) is incorrect because $1.00 is the standard cost per pound of materials as established in July 1996. Answer (D) is incorrect because the unit materials cost equals the materials cost for the first quarter divided by the quantity manufactured in the first quarter.

**61.** Assume that the factory costs incurred in the first quarter reflect the anticipated costs for the ACTION special purchase. What is the total expected direct labor cost of this purchase?

   A. $240,000

   B. $452,000

   C. $282,500

   D. $200,000

The correct answer is (C). *(Publisher)*
**REQUIRED:** The total expected direct labor cost for the special purchase.
**DISCUSSION:** The total expected direct labor cost is equal to the expected direct labor cost per unit multiplied by the anticipated number of units. Based on the incurred costs in the first quarter of $452,000 and the 320,000 units manufactured, the unit direct labor cost is equal to $1.4125. The sales proposal involves 200,000 units. Hence, the expected direct labor cost equals $282,500 ($1.4125 x 200,000).

Answer (A) is incorrect because $240,000 was calculated using the standard cost of direct labor of $1.20 instead of using the unit direct labor cost of $1.4125 ($452,000 direct labor cost in the first quarter ÷ 320,000 units manufactured). Answer (B) is incorrect because $452,000 is the direct labor cost incurred in the first quarter. Answer (D) is incorrect because 200,000 is the minimum quantity of units, not dollar labor cost.

**62.** Assume that the first quarter factory costs incurred reflect the anticipated costs for the ACTION special purchase. What is the expected variable overhead cost per unit?

   A. $2.10

   B. $1.50

   C. $.60

   D. $.66

The correct answer is (D). *(Publisher)*
**REQUIRED:** The expected variable overhead cost per unit for the special purchase.
**DISCUSSION:** The expected variable overhead cost per unit based on the first quarter production is equal to the variable manufacturing overhead cost incurred divided by the number of units manufactured. Accordingly, $211,000 divided by 320,000 units equals $.659375.

Answer (A) is incorrect because $2.10 is the total standard unit manufacturing overhead. Answer (B) is incorrect because $1.50 is the standard unit fixed manufacturing overhead. Answer (C) is incorrect because $.60 is the standard unit variable manufacturing overhead.

**63.** Assume that the actual cost relationships in the quarter ended March 31, 1998 relevant to this decision about the sales proposal of ACTION Hardware are valid. What is the manufacturing contribution margin?

   A. $580,625

   B. $239,375

   C. $820,000

   D. $10,000

The correct answer is (B). *(Publisher)*
**REQUIRED:** The manufacturing contribution margin based on the cost data for the first quarter.
**DISCUSSION:** The manufacturing CM is calculated by deducting incremental manufacturing costs from the proposed sales. Assuming that the actual cost relationships for the quarter ended March 31 are valid, the per-unit costs incurred during the quarter must be used to determine the CM. Using the unit costs for materials (question 60), labor (question 61), and variable manufacturing O/H (question 62), the manufacturing CM is calculated as below.

| | | |
|---|---|---|
| Proposed sales (200,000 × $4.10) | | $820,000 |
| Incremental manufacturing costs: | | |
| Materials (200,000 × $.83125) | $166,250 | |
| Labor (200,000 × $1.4125) | 282,500 | |
| Variable O/H (200,000 × $.659375) | 131,875 | (580,625) |
| Manufacturing CM | | $239,375 |

Answer (A) is incorrect because $580,625 is the total of the incremental manufacturing costs. Answer (C) is incorrect because the proposed sales are $820,000. Answer (D) is incorrect because $10,000 is the estimated sales salaries expense for the first 12 months.

Questions 64 through 71 are based on the following information. The information was presented as part of Question 2 on Part 5 of the December 1981 CMA examination.

Jenco, Inc. manufactures a combination fertilizer and weedkiller under the name Fertikil. This is the only product Jenco produces. Fertikil is sold nationwide through normal marketing channels to retail nurseries and garden stores.

Taylor Nursery plans to sell a similar fertilizer and weedkiller compound through its regional nursery chain under its own private label. Taylor has asked Jenco to submit a bid for a 25,000-pound order of the private brand compound. Although the chemical composition of the Taylor compound differs from Fertikil, the manufacturing process is very similar.

The Taylor compound will be produced in 1,000-pound lots. Each lot will require 60 direct labor hours and the following chemicals:

| Chemicals | Quantity in Pounds |
|---|---|
| CW-3 | 400 |
| JX-6 | 300 |
| MZ-8 | 200 |
| BE-7 | 100 |

The first three chemicals (CW-3, JX-6, MZ-8) are all used in the production of Fertikil. BE-7 was used in a compound that Jenco has discontinued. This chemical was not sold or discarded because it does not deteriorate and storage facilities have been adequate. Jenco can sell BE-7 at the prevailing market price minus $.10 per pound selling and handling expenses.

Jenco also has on hand a chemical called CN-5 that was manufactured for use in another product no longer produced. CN-5, which cannot be used in Fertikil, can be substituted for CW-3 on a one-for-one basis without affecting the quality of the Taylor compound. The quantity of CN-5 in inventory has a salvage value of $500.

Inventory and cost data for the chemicals that can be used to produce the Taylor compound are

| Raw Materials | Pounds in Inventory | Actual Price per Pound When Purchased | Current Market Price per Pound |
|---|---|---|---|
| CW-3 | 22,000 | $ .80 | $ .90 |
| JX-6 | 5,000 | .55 | .60 |
| MZ-8 | 8,000 | 1.40 | 1.60 |
| BE-7 | 4,000 | .60 | .65 |
| CN-5 | 5,500 | .75 | (salvage) |

The current direct labor rate is $7 per hour. The manufacturing overhead rate is established at the beginning of the year and is applied consistently throughout the year using direct labor hours (DLH) as the base. The predetermined overhead rate for the current year, based on a two-shift capacity of 400,000 total DLH with no overtime, is as follows:

| | |
|---|---|
| Variable manufacturing overhead | $2.25 per DLH |
| Fixed manufacturing overhead | 3.75 per DLH |
| Combined rate | $6.00 per DLH |

Jenco's production manager reports that the existing equipment and facilities are adequate to manufacture the Taylor compound. However, Jenco is within 800 hours of its two-shift capacity this month before it must schedule overtime. If need be, the Taylor compound can be produced on regular time by shifting a portion of Fertikil production to overtime. Jenco's rate for overtime hours is one-and-one-half the regular pay rate, or $10.50 per hour. There is no allowance for any overtime premium in the manufacturing overhead rate.

Jenco's standard markup policy for new products is 25% of full manufacturing cost.

---

**64.** If Jenco bids this month for the special one-time order of 25,000 pounds, the total direct labor cost will be

A.  $10,500

B.  $12,950

C.  $16,250

D.  $2,450

The correct answer is (B). *(Publisher)*
**REQUIRED:** The total direct labor cost for the one-time order.

**DISCUSSION:** Given that 25 lots are produced, each requiring 60 direct labor hours, 1,500 hours will be necessary. This one-time order requires 800 hours scheduled during regular time and 700 remaining hours of overtime. Thus, overtime is a relevant cost for this order. Total direct labor cost equals $12,950 [(1,500 DLH x $7) + (700 x $3.50 hourly overtime premium)].

Answer (A) is incorrect because $10,500 does not include overtime cost of $2,450. Answer (C) is incorrect because total direct labor cost equals $12,950. Answer (D) is incorrect because $2,450 is the overtime premium cost for this order.

**65.** If Jenco bids this month for the special one-time order of 25,000 pounds, the total overhead cost used for this decision will be

A. $5,625

B. $9,000

C. $3,375

D. $5,825

The correct answer is (C). *(Publisher)*

**REQUIRED:** The total overhead cost for the one-time order.

**DISCUSSION:** The total O/H cost used for this decision will include the variable O/H only; the fixed O/H is not relevant for this one-time order. A total of 1,500 direct labor hours will be used (25 1,000-pound lots x 60 DLH per lot). The variable O/H rate is $2.25 per hour. Thus, $3,375 of total O/H is relevant to this decision (1,500 DLH x $2.25). The overtime premium is direct labor cost, not a part of overhead, because it is attributable to a particular job.

Answer (A) is incorrect because $5,625 is total fixed overhead. Answer (B) is incorrect because $9,000 includes total fixed overhead of $5,625. Answer (D) is incorrect because $5,825 equals the variable overhead plus the overtime premium.

**66.** If Jenco bids this month for the special one-time order of 25,000 pounds of the private brand, the special order's total direct materials cost will be

A. $17,050

B. $18,425

C. $14,375

D. $10,425

The correct answer is (B). *(Publisher)*

**REQUIRED:** The direct materials cost.

**DISCUSSION:** The special order will require three chemicals used in manufacturing the main product (CW-3, JX-6, MZ-8). Relevant costs are the current market prices. Chemicals not used in current production (BE-7 and CN-5) have relevant costs equal to their value to the firm. The order requires 10,000 pounds (400 lbs. per lot x 25) of CW-3. However, the 5,500 pounds of CN-5 can be substituted on a one-for-one basis at a total cost of $500 (salvage). The cost of the 4,500 pounds of CW-3 (10,000 – 5,500) is $4,050 ($.90 x 4,500). The cost of JX-6 is $4,500 (300 lbs. x 25 lots x $.60). The cost of MZ-8 is $8,000 (200 pounds x 25 lots x $1.60). The cost of BE-7 is $1,375 [100 lbs. x 25 lots x ($.65 – $.10)]. Thus, the total direct materials cost is $18,425 ($500 + $4,050 + $4,500 + $8,000 + $1,375).

Answer (A) is incorrect because $17,050 does not include the direct materials cost of $1,375 for chemical BE-7. Answer (C) is incorrect because $14,375 omits the cost of CW-3. Answer (D) is incorrect because $10,425 omits the cost of MZ-8.

**67.** The total variable cost of the special order for this month will be

A. $21,800

B. $40,375

C. $31,375

D. $34,750

The correct answer is (D). *(Publisher)*

**REQUIRED:** The total variable cost of the special order.

**DISCUSSION:** The total variable cost of the special order is the sum of direct materials, direct labor, and O/H. The cost of materials is $18,425 (question 66). Overtime is a relevant cost of this order appropriately included in the total direct labor cost (see question 64). The special order will not increase fixed O/H costs and is not a continuing product that should contribute to fixed O/H. Thus, fixed O/H is not relevant; the only relevant O/H charge is the variable O/H rate.

| | |
|---|---|
| Total direct materials cost (question 66) | $18,425 |
| Direct labor (question 64) | 12,950 |
| Variable overhead (question 65) | 3,375 |
| Total cost of special order | $34,750 |

Answer (A) is incorrect because $21,800 does not include $12,950 of direct labor cost. Answer (B) is incorrect because $40,375 includes fixed overhead. Answer (C) is incorrect because $31,375 omits variable overhead.

Questions 68 through 71 are based on the
information preceding question 64 on page 446.

**68.** What is the full cost of the one-time special order
of 25,000 pounds?

A. $18,425

B. $12,950

C. $55,906

D. $40,375

The correct answer is (D). *(Publisher)*

**REQUIRED:** The full cost of the one-time special order.

**DISCUSSION:** The full cost is the variable cost plus fixed
O/H. Fixed O/H is $3.75 per DLH, and 1,500 hours are
required.

| | |
|---|---:|
| Direct materials | $18,425 |
| Direct labor | 12,950 |
| Variable overhead | 3,375 |
| Fixed overhead ($3.75 × 1,500) | 5,625 |
| Total cost of special order | $40,375 |

Answer (A) is incorrect because $18,425 is the total direct
materials cost. Answer (B) is incorrect because $12,950 is
the direct labor cost. Answer (C) is incorrect because the
total cost of the special order is $40,375.

**69.** What will be the total direct labor cost for
recurring 25-lot orders, assuming that 60% of each
order can be completed during regular hours?

A. $12,600

B. $10,500

C. $16,500

D. $18,225

The correct answer is (A). *(Publisher)*

**REQUIRED:** The direct labor cost for recurring orders
given capacity overflow.

**DISCUSSION:** For recurring orders, the total direct labor
cost equals direct labor hours times the standard rate, with
adjustments for any overtime caused by the recurring orders.
If 60% of a batch (1,500 x .6 = 900 DLH) can be completed
during regular time, the remaining 600 DLH directly incur
overtime. The overtime premium is therefore a relevant cost
of the new product.

| | |
|---|---:|
| Regular time (1,500 DLH × $7.00 per DLH) | $10,500 |
| Overtime premium (600 DLH × $3.50 per DLH) | 2,100 |
| Total direct labor cost | $12,600 |

Answer (B) is incorrect because $10,500 does not include
$2,100 of overtime premium. Answers (C) and (D) are
incorrect because the total direct labor cost is $12,600.

**70.** What will be the total direct materials cost for recurring 25-lot orders?

A. $18,425

B. $21,500

C. $26,425

D. $23,125

The correct answer is (D). *(Publisher)*

**REQUIRED:** The total direct materials cost for the recurring orders.

**DISCUSSION:** The total direct materials cost for recurring orders will include the regular price of each product times the number of pounds. The substitution of CN-5 is no longer possible because Jenco's supply was exhausted in the first special batch.

| | |
|---|---:|
| CW-3: 10,000 lbs. × $.90/lb. | $ 9,000 |
| JX-6: 7,500 lbs. × $.60/lb. | 4,500 |
| MZ-8: 5,000 lbs. × $1.60/lb. | 8,000 |
| BE-7: 2,500 lbs. × $.65/lb. | 1,625 |
| Total direct materials cost | $23,125 |

Answer (A) is incorrect because $18,425 is the total direct materials cost for the special one-time order of 25,000 pounds of the private brand. Answer (B) is incorrect because $21,500 does not include direct materials cost of $1,625 for BE-7. Answer (C) is incorrect because the total direct materials cost for recurring 25-lot orders is $23,125.

**71.** What will be the total overhead costs for recurring 25-lot orders?

A. $5,625

B. $9,000

C. $3,375

D. $7,500

The correct answer is (B). *(Publisher)*

**REQUIRED:** The total overhead costs for recurring orders.

**DISCUSSION:** The total O/H costs for recurring orders should include both variable and fixed O/H because a continuing product should contribute to fixed O/H as well as cover all variable costs. The O/H charge will be

$$1,500 \ DLH \times \$6/DLH = \$9,000$$

Answer (A) is incorrect because $5,625 is the fixed overhead cost. Answer (C) is incorrect because $3,375 is the variable overhead cost. Answer (D) is incorrect because the total overhead costs for recurring 25-lot orders are $9,000.

Questions 72 through 77 are based on the following information. The information was presented as part of Question 2 on Part 5 of the June 1979 CMA exam.

National Industries is a diversified corporation with separate and distinct operating divisions. Each division's performance is evaluated on the basis of total dollar profits and return on divisional investment.

The WindAir Division manufactures and sells air-conditioning units. The coming year's budgeted income statement, based upon a sales volume of 15,000 units, appears below.

### WindAir Division
### Budgeted Income Statement
### For the Next Fiscal Year

| | Per Unit | Total (000 omitted) |
|---|---|---|
| Sales revenue | $400 | $6,000 |
| Manufacturing costs | | |
| Compressor | $ 70 | $1,050 |
| Other raw materials | 37 | 555 |
| Direct labor | 30 | 450 |
| Variable overhead | 45 | 675 |
| Fixed overhead | 32 | 480 |
| Total manufacturing costs | $214 | $3,210 |
| Gross margin | $186 | $2,790 |
| Operating expenses | | |
| Variable selling | $ 18 | $ 270 |
| Fixed selling | 19 | 285 |
| Fixed administrative | 38 | 570 |
| Total operating expenses | $ 75 | $1,125 |
| Net income before taxes | $111 | $1,665 |

WindAir's division manager believes sales can be increased if the unit selling price of the air conditioners is reduced. A market research study conducted by an independent firm indicates that a 5% reduction in the selling price ($20) will increase sales volume by 16% or 2,400 units. WindAir has sufficient production capacity to manage this increased volume with no increase in fixed costs. WindAir currently uses a compressor in its units that it purchases from an outside supplier at a cost of $70 per compressor. The division manager of WindAir has approached the manager of the Compressor Division regarding the sale of a compressor unit to WindAir. The Compressor Division currently manufactures and sells a unit exclusively to outside firms that is similar to the unit used by WindAir. The specifications of the WindAir compressor are slightly different, which will reduce the Compressor Division's raw materials costs by $1.50 per unit. In addition, the Compressor Division will not incur any variable selling costs for the units sold to WindAir. The manager of WindAir wants all of the compressors it uses to come from one supplier and has offered to pay $50 for each compressor unit.

The Compressor Division has the capacity to produce 75,000 units. The coming year's budgeted income statement for the Compressor Division is shown below and is based upon a sales volume of 64,000 units without considering WindAir's proposal.

### Compressor Division
### Budgeted Income Statement
### For the Next Fiscal Year

| | Per Unit | Total (000 omitted) |
|---|---|---|
| Sales revenue | $100 | $6,400 |
| Manufacturing costs | | |
| Raw materials | $ 12 | $ 768 |
| Direct labor | 8 | 512 |
| Variable overhead | 10 | 640 |
| Fixed overhead | 11 | 704 |
| Total manufacturing costs | $ 41 | $2,624 |
| Gross margin | $ 59 | $3,776 |
| Operating expenses | | |
| Variable selling | $ 6 | $ 384 |
| Fixed selling | 4 | 256 |
| Fixed administrative | 7 | 448 |
| Total operating expenses | $ 17 | $1,088 |
| Net income before taxes | $ 42 | $2,688 |

**72.** What is WindAir's current unit contribution margin on air conditioners?

A. $111

B. $125

C. $186

D. $200

The correct answer is (D). *(Publisher)*

**REQUIRED:** The unit contribution margin on air-conditioning units.

**DISCUSSION:** The current UCM is $200 because the unit selling price is $400 and the unit variable costs are $200. All the manufacturing costs are variable except $32 of fixed O/H per unit. Variable selling expenses equal $18. Thus, total variable costs are $200 ($214 – $32 + $18).

Answer (A) is incorrect because $111 is the net income before taxes. Answer (B) is incorrect because WindAir's current contribution margin on air conditioners is $200. Answer (C) is incorrect because $186 is the gross margin per unit.

**73.** How much will WindAir's net income change if it acquires the compressors from an outside source and institutes the 5% price reduction?

A.  $132,000

B.  $55,200

C.  $76,800

D.  $214,320

The correct answer is (A). *(Publisher)*

**REQUIRED:** The change in net income given a price reduction and increased sales.

**DISCUSSION:** The CM before the price decrease is $200 per unit times the 15,000 units, a total CM of $3,000,000. Given the price reduction, the unit CM decreases from $200 to $180 because the selling price declines by $20 ($400 x 5%). The units sold increase by 2,400 to 17,400. Multiplying the new $180 UCM by 17,400 units results in a new CM of $3,132,000. CM therefore increases by $132,000 ($3,132,000 − $3,000,000).

Answers (B), (C), and (D) are incorrect because the contribution margin increases by $132,000.

**74.** Another approach to analyzing the change in contribution margin covered in the preceding question is to observe that, as a result of decreasing selling price from $400 to $380, sales will increase by 2,400 units at a unit contribution margin of $180. This increase in contribution margin attributable to greater sales

A.  Must be adjusted for the $480,000 of fixed costs.

B.  Must be adjusted for the loss of the $20 unit contribution margin for 15,000 units previously budgeted.

C.  Must be adjusted for the incremental fixed manufacturing O/H (2,400 units x $32).

D.  Is the change in pretax income.

The correct answer is (B). *(Publisher)*

**REQUIRED:** The alternative approach to contribution margin analysis.

**DISCUSSION:** The increased volume of 2,400 units times the unit contribution margin results in a volume variance ($432,000 favorable). The change in volume occurs because of a lower price that creates a sales price variance ($20 per unit x 15,000 units currently budgeted = $300,000 unfavorable). Thus, the decrease in price must be considered in addition to the increase in volume.

Answers (A) and (C) are incorrect because fixed costs do not change with the increase in volume within the relevant range. Answer (D) is incorrect because the $432,000 sales volume variance must be decreased by the $300,000 sales price variance.

**75.** What will be the impact of decreasing the sales price 10% to obtain an increase in sales volume of 4,500 units?

| | Contribution Margin | Net Income Before Taxes |
|---|---|---|
| A. | $120,000 | $(480,000) |
| B. | $120,000 | $ 120,000 |
| C. | $720,000 | $ 120,000 |
| D. | $720,000 | $ 720,000 |

The correct answer is (B). *(Publisher)*

**REQUIRED:** The effect of decreasing selling price to increase unit sales.

**DISCUSSION:** The 10% price decrease ($400 x 10%) will lower the UCM from $200 to $160. The additional 4,500 units will increase the total contribution margin by $720,000 (4,500 x $160). The decrease in sales price will reduce the contribution margin by $600,000 (15,000 x $40). The net effect on both the contribution margin and net income (the fixed costs do not change) is $120,000 favorable ($720,000 F − $600,000 U).

Answer (A) is incorrect because net income before taxes is $120,000. Answer (C) is incorrect because the net effect on the contribution margin is an increase of $120,000. Answer (D) is incorrect because $720,000 is the increase in the total contribution margin from the additional unit sales volume.

Questions 76 and 77 are based on the information presented on page 450.

**76.** How much will the Compressor Division earn (lose) on the sale to WindAir of 17,400 compressors if some external sales must be forgone?

A.    Decrease net income $35,500.

B.    Decrease net income $129,800.

C.    Decrease net income $59,000.

D.    Increase net income $22,000.

The correct answer is (A). *(Publisher)*
    **REQUIRED:** The gain (loss) on the internal sale of a component given a set price and reduction of external sales.
    **DISCUSSION:** If the Compressor Division sells all 17,400 units to WindAir, its external sales will fall to 57,600 (75,000 maximum capacity – 17,400 sales to WindAir). To determine UCM, materials costs decrease by $1.50 for internal sales, and there are no variable selling expenses.

| Unit Contribution Margin | Outside Sales | WindAir Sales |
|---|---|---|
| Selling price | $100 | $50.00 |
| Variable costs | | |
|    Raw materials | $ 12 | $10.50 |
|    Direct labor | 8 | 8.00 |
|    Overhead | 10 | 10.00 |
|    Selling expenses | 6 | -0- |
| Total variable costs | $ 36 | $28.50 |
| Unit contribution margin | $ 64 | $21.50 |

The loss of the contribution from the sale of 6,400 units (64,000 – 57,600) that would otherwise be sold to outsiders is $409,600 ($64 x 6,400). The sale to WindAir will contribute only $374,100 ($21.50 x 17,400). The net result is a reduction in net income of $35,500 ($409,600 – $374,100).
    Answers (B), (C), and (D) are incorrect because there is a decrease in net income of $35,500.

**77.** If National Industries required the Compressor Division to sell 17,400 compressors to WindAir, how much will be the effect on the corporation's pretax earnings?

A.    $(409,600)

B.    $722,100

C.    $312,500

D.    $(215,400)

The correct answer is (C). *(Publisher)*
    **REQUIRED:** The net effect on corporate earnings of buying parts internally.
    **DISCUSSION:** The net effect will be the cost savings from use of an internally manufactured part minus the loss of the contribution from sales to outsiders.

| | |
|---|---|
| Outside purchase price | $  70.00 |
| Compressor Division's variable cost to produce | (28.50) |
| Savings per unit | $  41.50 |
| Number of units | × 17,400 |
| Total cost savings | $722,100 |
| Compressor Division's CM loss from sales | |
|   to outsiders ($64 × 6,400) | (409,600) |
| Increase in pretax net income | $312,500 |

Answer (A) is incorrect because $(409,600) is Compressor Division's CM loss from sales to WindAir by not selling to outside customers. Answer (B) is incorrect because $722,100 is the total cost savings of using the internally manufactured part. Answer (D) is incorrect because the increase in pretax net income is $312,500.

Questions 78 through 81 are based on the following information. The information was presented as part of Question 7 on Part 5 of the December 1978 CMA examination.

Framar, Inc. manufactures machinery to customer specifications. It operated at about 75% of practical capacity during the year. The operating results for the most recent fiscal year are presented below.

**Framar, Inc.**
**Income Statement**
**For the Year Ended September 30**
**(000 omitted)**

| | | |
|---|---:|---:|
| Sales | | $25,000 |
| Minus: Sales commissions | | (2,500) |
| Net sales | | $22,500 |
| Expenses | | |
| Direct materials | | $ 6,000 |
| Direct labor | | 7,500 |
| Manufacturing O/H-variable | | |
| Supplies | $ 625 | |
| Indirect labor | 1,500 | |
| Power | 125 | 2,250 |
| Manufacturing O/H-fixed | | |
| Supervision | $ 500 | |
| Depreciation | 1,000 | 1,500 |
| Corporate administration | | 750 |
| Total expenses | | $18,000 |
| Net income before taxes | | $ 4,500 |
| Income taxes (40%) | | (1,800) |
| Net income | | $ 2,700 |

Top management has developed the pricing formula presented below. It is based upon the operating results achieved during the most recent fiscal year. The relationships used in the formula are expected to continue during the next fiscal year. The company expects to operate at 75% of practical capacity during the next fiscal year.

APA, Inc. has asked Framar to bid on some custom-designed machinery. Framar used the formula to develop a price and submitted a bid of $165,000. The calculations are given next to the pricing formula shown below.

| Details of Formula | | APA Bid Calculations |
|---|---|---:|
| Estimated direct materials cost | $XXX | $ 29,200 |
| Estimated direct labor cost | XXX | 56,000 |
| Estimated manufacturing O/H calculated at 50% of DL | XXX | 28,000 |
| Estimated corporate O/H calculated at 10% of DL | XXX | 5,600 |
| Estimated total costs excluding sales commissions | $XXX | $118,800 |
| Add 25% for profits and taxes | XXX | 29,700 |
| Suggested price (with profits) before sales commissions | $XXX | $148,500 |
| Suggested total price equal to suggested price divided by .9 to adjust for 10% sales commissions | $XXX | $165,000 |

**78.** What will the contribution margin be if the bid is accepted?

A. $102,000

B. $63,300

C. $27,900

D. $46,500

The correct answer is (D). *(Publisher)*
**REQUIRED:** The CM if the bid is accepted.
**DISCUSSION:** The CM equals the gross revenue minus any variable costs. Variable costs include the sales commission, direct materials, direct labor, and variable manufacturing O/H. Variable manufacturing O/H for the most recent fiscal year was 30% of direct labor ($2,250 ÷ $7,500). The cost relationships are expected to continue.

| | | |
|---|---:|---:|
| Submitted bid | | $165,000 |
| Minus: Sales commission (10%) | | (16,500) |
| Net sales | | $148,500 |
| Minus variable costs: | | |
| Direct materials | $29,200 | |
| Direct labor | 56,000 | |
| Variable mfg. O/H (30% of direct labor) | 16,800 | (102,000) |
| Contribution margin | | $ 46,500 |

Answer (A) is incorrect because $102,000 is the total variable costs. Answer (B) is incorrect because $16,800 of variable manufacturing O/H should be subtracted from net sales. Answer (C) is incorrect because $27,900 is the increase in net income if the bid is accepted.

Questions 79 through 81 are based on the information preceding question 78 on page 453.

**79.** If the bid is accepted, what will be the increase in net income?

A. $27,900

B. $46,500

C. $63,300

D. $148,500

The correct answer is (A). *(Publisher)*

REQUIRED: The net increase in income if the bid is accepted.

DISCUSSION: The CM for the APA job is $46,500 (see preceding question). It will increase net income, assuming the fixed costs will be incurred even if the bid is rejected. The increase in net income equals the CM minus income taxes at a rate of 40%, or $27,900 [$46,500 x (1.0 – .4)].

Answer (B) is incorrect because $46,500 is the contribution margin if the bid is accepted. Answer (C) is incorrect because $16,800 of variable manufacturing overhead should also be subtracted from sales to arrive at the CM. Answer (D) is incorrect because $148,500 is the total net sales.

**80.** Should Framar manufacture the machinery for a counteroffer of $127,000?

A. Yes, net income will increase by $7,380.

B. Yes, net income will increase by $12,300.

C. No, net income will decrease by $12,700.

D. None of the answers are correct.

The correct answer is (A). *(Publisher)*

REQUIRED: The appropriate decision as to whether the job should be accepted at a lower price.

DISCUSSION: Acceptance of the counteroffer of $127,000 will result in a net increase in income. The incremental revenue exceeds the incremental costs.

| | |
|---|---:|
| Counteroffer | $127,000 |
| Sales commission (10%) | (12,700) |
| Net sales | $114,300 |
| Variable manufacturing costs | (102,000) |
| Contribution margin | $ 12,300 |
| Income taxes (40%) | (4,920) |
| Increase in net income | $ 7,380 |

Answer (B) is incorrect because $12,300 is the contribution margin of the counteroffer. Answer (C) is incorrect because $12,700 is the sales commission. Answer (D) is incorrect because net income will increase by $7,380.

**81.** What is the lowest price Framar can quote on this machinery without reducing its net income after taxes?

A. $114,300

B. $127,000

C. $113,333

D. $102,000

The correct answer is (C). *(Publisher)*

REQUIRED: The lowest price that can be quoted without reducing net income after taxes.

DISCUSSION: The lowest price Framar can quote is the total incremental cost associated with the job. In this case, the bid should cover the variable manufacturing costs and the sales commission. Variable manufacturing cost is $102,000, and the sales commission is 10%. Dividing $102,000 by .9 gives a minimum sales price of $113,333.

Answer (A) is incorrect because a quote of $114,300 will result in a $522 increase in net income. Answer (B) is incorrect because a quote of $127,000 will result in a $7,380 increase in net income. Answer (D) is incorrect because a quote of $102,000 will result in a $10,200 decrease in income.

# CHAPTER THIRTEEN
# CAPITAL BUDGETING

**Capital budgeting** is the process of planning expenditures for assets the returns on which are expected to continue beyond 1 year. Capital budgeting decisions are long-term. Once made, they tend to be relatively inflexible because the commitments extend well into the future. However, without proper timing, additional capacity generated by the acquisition of capital assets may not coincide with changes in demand for output, resulting in capacity excess or shortage. Thus, accurate forecasting is needed to anticipate changes in demand so that full economic benefits flow to the firm when the capital asset is available for use. Moreover, a capital budget usually involves substantial expenditures, and the sources and costs of these funds are critical. Planning is also important because of possible rapid changes in capital markets, inflation, interest rates, and the money supply. Firms constantly need to budget and plan for capital expenditures to hold a relative position in a dynamic economic environment.

Capital budgeting requires choosing among investment proposals. Thus, a ranking procedure is needed for such decisions. The first step in the ranking procedure is to determine the asset cost or net investment. The net investment is the net outlay, or gross cash requirement, minus cash recovered from the trade or sale of existing assets, plus or minus adjustments for tax effects. Cash outflows in subsequent periods must also be considered. The investment required also includes funds to provide for increases in working capital, for example, the additional receivables and inventories resulting from the acquisition of a new manufacturing plant. This investment in working capital is treated as an initial cost of the investment (a cash outflow) that will be recovered (as an inflow) at the end of the project. If the project is expected to reduce working capital during its life, the analysis should include an initial inflow and an outflow at the end of the project.

The next step is to calculate the estimated cash flows, period by period, using the acquired assets. Net cash flow is the economic benefit, period by period, resulting from the investment. Hence, reliable estimates of cost savings or revenues are necessary, and the economic life of the asset should be distinguished from its depreciable life. The **economic life** is the time period over which the benefits of the investment proposal are expected to be obtained as distinguished from the physical or technical life of the asset involved. The **depreciable life** is the period used for accounting and tax purposes over which the asset's cost is to be systematically and rationally allocated. It is based upon permissible or standard guidelines and may have no particular relevance to economic life. Finally, the disposal of the acquired assets usually increases cash inflows at the end of the project.

The third step in the ranking procedure is to relate the cash-flow benefits to their cost by using a method to evaluate the advantage of purchasing the asset. For example, the **accounting rate of return** (also called unadjusted rate of return or book value rate of return) is the increase in accounting net income divided by the required investment or the average investment. This method ignores the time value of money. Other methods are thoroughly discussed in later sections of this summary. The final step is to rank the investments and choose the best one. The rating methods can sometimes yield different solutions to an investment problem. Managers should therefore use all the methods and then use their judgment in making the final decision. These techniques consider only the economic factors in a decision, but sometimes noneconomic factors can take precedence.

Present value and future value calculations are essential to capital budgeting. They are based on the **compound interest** concept that a quantity of money sometime in the future is worth less than the same amount of money today. The difference is measured in terms of interest calculated according to the appropriate discount rate. Interest is the payment received by holders of money to forgo current consumption. Conversely, the current consumer of money pays interest for its use. Standard tables have been developed to facilitate the calculation of present and future values. Each entry in one of these tables represents the result of substituting in the pertinent present value or future value equation a payment of $1, the number of periods (n), and an interest rate (i). The **present value (PV)** of an amount is the value today of some future payment. It equals the present value of $1 (a factor found in a standard table) for the given number of periods and interest rate times the future payment. The formula is $1 \div (1 + i)^n$. The **future value (FV)** of an amount is the amount available at a specified time in the future based on a single investment (deposit) today. The FV is the amount to be computed if one knows the present value and the appropriate discount rate. It equals the future value of $1 (a factor found in a standard table) for the given number of periods and interest rate times the current payment. The formula is $(1 + i)^n$. An **annuity** is usually a series of equal payments at equal intervals of time, e.g., $1,000 at the end of every year for 10 years. An **ordinary annuity (annuity in arrears)** is a series of payments occurring at the end of the periods involved. An **annuity due (annuity in advance)** is an annuity in which the payments are made (or received) at the beginning of the periods. The difference for present value calculations is that no interest is computed on the first payment of an annuity due. For calculating the **present value of an annuity**, the same present value tables may be used for both kinds of annuities. Most tables are for ordinary annuities. The factor for an ordinary annuity of one less period (n – 1), increased by 1.0 to include the initial payment (for which no interest is computed), is the factor for an annuity due. The formula for the present value of an ordinary annuity of $1 is $\{1 - [1 \div (1 + i)^n]\} \div i$. The **future value of an annuity** is the value that a series of equal payments will have at a certain moment in the future if interest is earned at a given rate. In an ordinary annuity, the payments are made (or received) at the end of the periods, and the future value is determined at the date of the last payment. Hence, no interest is earned during the first period or on the last payment. In an annuity due, the payments occur at the beginning of the periods. The difference between an ordinary annuity and an annuity due for future value calculations is that interest is computed on the first payment of an annuity due, and the future value is determined one period after the last payment. Hence, the same future value tables may be used for both kinds of annuities. The factor for the future value of an ordinary annuity of one more period (n + 1), decreased by 1.0 to exclude the last payment (for which no interest is computed), is the factor for an annuity due. The future value of an ordinary annuity of $1 is $[(1 + i)^{n-1}] \div i$.

Risk analysis attempts to measure the likelihood of the variability of future returns from the proposed investment. Risk cannot be ignored entirely, but mathematical approaches can be difficult because of a lack of critical information. Various approaches are used to assess risk. The **informal method** calculates net present values (NPVs) at the firm's discount rate (k), and the possible projects are individually reviewed. If the NPVs are relatively close for two mutually exclusive projects, the apparently less risky project is chosen. **Risk-adjusted discount rates** are used to adjust k upward as the investment becomes riskier. By increasing the discount rate from 10% to 15%, for example, the expected flow from the investment must be relatively larger or the increased discount rate will generate a negative NPV, and the proposed acquisition/investment will be rejected. Although difficult to apply in extreme cases, this technique has much intuitive value. **Certainty equivalent adjustments** are directly drawn from the concept of utility theory. The decision maker must specify at what point the firm is indifferent to the choice between a certain sum of money and the expected value of a risky sum. The technique is not frequently used because decision makers are usually not familiar with the concept. **Sensitivity analysis** forecasts many calculated NPVs under various assumptions and compares them to determine how sensitive NPV is to changing conditions. Changing or relaxing the assumptions about a certain variable or group of variables may drastically alter the NPV, resulting in a much riskier asset than was originally forecast. **Simulation analysis** represents a refinement of standard profitability theory. A computer is used to generate many examples of results based upon various assumptions. Project simulation is frequently expensive. Unless a project is exceptionally large and expensive, full-scale simulation is ordinarily not worthwhile. **The capital asset pricing model** is derived from portfolio theory. It assumes that all assets are held in a portfolio. Each asset has variability in its returns. Some of this variability is caused by movements in the market as a whole, and some is specific to each firm. In a portfolio, the firm's specific variability is eliminated through diversification, and the only relevant risk is the market component. The more sensitive an asset's rate of return is to changes in the market's rate of return, the riskier the asset.

The principal techniques for ranking investment proposals include payback, net present value, and internal rate of return. The **payback period** is the number of years required to complete the return of the original investment, i.e., the time it takes for a new asset to pay for itself. This measure is computed by dividing the initial net investment by the periodic constant expected cash flow to be generated. If periodic cash flows are not constant, the calculation must be in cumulative form. The payback period is easy to calculate, but it ignores cash flows received after the payback period, and it does not account for the time value of money. Its strength is its simplicity. One application is to foreign investments if foreign expropriation of company assets is feared. Even in these circumstances, the payback method is most often used in addition to another, more sophisticated, method. However, it does measure risk. The longer the payback period, the more risky the investment. The **payback reciprocal** (1 ÷ payback) is sometimes used as an estimate of the internal rate of return. The **bailout payback method** incorporates the salvage value of the asset into the calculation. It measures the length of the payback period when the periodic cash inflows are combined with the salvage value. **Breakeven time** is a more sophisticated version of the payback method that is growing in popularity. Breakeven time is defined as the period required for the discounted cumulative cash inflows on a project to equal the discounted cumulative cash outflows (usually the initial cost). Thus, it is the time necessary for the present value of the discounted cash flows to equal zero. This period begins at the outset of a project, not when the initial cash outflow occurs. An alternative that results in a longer breakeven time is to consider the time required for the present value of the cumulative cash inflows to equal the present value of all the expected future cash outflows.

**Net present value (NPV)** is broadly defined as the difference between the present value of the estimated net cash inflows (positive numbers) and the present value of the net cash outflows (negative numbers). The NPV method is used when the discount rate (also known as the cost of capital, required rate of return, or hurdle rate) is specified. If n is the number of periods of future cash flows, $PCF_t$ is the periodic cash flow for period t, k is the cost of capital, and t is the time period, the formula is

$$NPV = \sum_{t=0}^{n} \frac{PCF_t}{(1 + k)^t}$$

NPV assumes the cash flows from the investment can be reinvested at the particular project's cost of capital (k), and present value tables are used to reduce the future cash flows to current dollars. If the NPV is positive, the project should be accepted. If NPV is negative, the project should be rejected.

The **internal rate of return (IRR)** is an interest rate computed such that the net present value (NPV) of the investment is zero. Hence, the present value of the expected cash outflows equals the present value of the expected cash inflows. Accordingly, the formula is

$$\sum_{t=0}^{n} \frac{PCF_t}{(1 + IRR)^t} = 0$$

The IRR can be found by trial and error using arbitrarily selected interest rates. One may go from column to column on a present value table until an NPV of zero is obtained. As long as the interest rate is greater than k (cost of capital), NPV must be greater than zero. The IRR and NPV methods may rank projects differently if the cost of one project is greater than the cost of another or the timing of cash flows differs among projects. The IRR method assumes that the cash flows will be reinvested at the IRR, not the cost of capital. If the project's funds are not reinvested at the IRR, the ranking calculations obtained may be in error. The NPV method gives a better grasp of the problem in many decision situations because the reinvestment is assumed to be the cost of capital (k). Under some circumstances, the IRR method is not totally reliable because it can give multiple answers for the same set of facts. This anomaly occurs when more than one change in the direction of net periodic cash flows occur. For example, one direction change occurs when an initial net cash outflow is followed by a series of net inflows. However, if a negative net cash flow occurs in a later period, another direction change and a second solution result. The number of solutions to the IRR formula equals the number of changes in the direction of the net cash flows. An improved version of the IRR is the modified IRR (MIRR). It assumes that reinvestment is at the cost of capital (k) rather than the IRR. The formula for the MIRR equates the present value of the investment's cash outflows discounted at k with the present value of the terminal value. The terminal value is the future value of the cash inflows assuming reinvestment at k. The MIRR is the rate at which the present value of the terminal value equals the present value of the cash outflows. If $PCOF_t$ equals the periodic cash outflow (a negative number) for time t, and $PCIF_t$ equals the periodic cash inflow for time t, the formula is

$$\sum_{t=0}^{n} \frac{PCOF_t}{(1 + k)^t} = \frac{\sum_{t=0}^{n} PCIF_t(1 + k)^{n-t}}{(1 + MRR)^n}$$

The **profitability or excess present value index** is the ratio of the present value of future net cash inflows to the present value of the initial net investment. This variation of the NPV method facilitates comparison of different-sized investments. Capital budgeting is intimately related to capital structure, that is, the permanent financing of the firm represented primarily by long-term debt, preferred stock, and common shareholders' equity (including retained earnings). **Financial leverage** is the relative amount of the fixed cost of capital, principally debt, in a firm's capital structure. Leverage, by definition, creates financial risk, which relates directly to the question of the cost of capital. The more leverage, the higher the financial risk, and the higher the cost of debt capital. Earnings per share (EPS) will ordinarily be higher if debt is used to raise capital instead of equity, provided that the firm is not over-leveraged. The reason is that the cost of debt is lower than the cost of equity because interest is tax deductible. However, greater risk results from required interest costs, creditors' liens on the firm's assets, and the possibility of a proportionately lower EPS if sales do not meet projections. The **degree of financial leverage (DFL)** is the percentage change in earnings available to common shareholders that is associated with a given percentage change in net operating income. The DFL may also be stated in terms of the second formula below, which is derived from the first (the derivation is not given).

$$\frac{\% \ \Delta \ in \ net \ income}{\% \ \Delta \ in \ net \ operating \ income} = \frac{EBIT}{EBIT - I}$$

Net income means earnings available to common shareholders, operating income equals earnings before interest and taxes (EBIT), and I equals interest expense. The greater the DFL, the riskier the firm; however, if the return on assets exceeds the cost of debt, additional leverage is favorable. If the firm has preferred stock, the second formula is modified as follows (P = preferred dividends and T = the tax rate):

$$\frac{EBIT}{EBIT - I - [P \div (1-T)]}$$

**Operating leverage** is the extent to which production costs are fixed. A firm with a high percentage of fixed costs is more risky than a firm in the same industry with a lower percentage. The **degree of operating leverage (DOL)** is the percentage change in net operating income associated with a given percentage change in sales. The DOL may also be stated in terms of the second formula below, which is derived from the first (the derivation is not given).

$$\frac{\% \ \Delta \ in \ net \ operating \ income}{\% \ \Delta \ in \ sales} = \frac{Contribution \ margin}{Contribution \ margin - Fixed \ costs}$$

The **degree of total leverage (DTL)** equals the DFL times the DOL. Thus, it also equals the percentage change in net income that is associated with a given percentage change in sales. Moreover, given that EBIT equals the contribution margin minus fixed costs, the DTL may also be stated in terms of the second formula below.

$$\frac{\% \ \Delta \ in \ net \ income}{\% \ \Delta \ in \ sales} = \frac{Contribution \ margin}{EBIT - I}$$

Firms with a high degree of operating leverage do not usually employ a high degree of financial leverage and vice versa.  One of the most important considerations in the use of financial leverage is operating leverage.  For example, assume that a firm has a highly automated production process.  Because of automation, the DOL is 2.  If the firm wants the DTL not to exceed 3, it must restrict its use of debt so that the DFL is not more than 1.5.  If the firm had committed to a production process that was less automated and had a lower DOL, more debt could be employed, and the firm could have a higher DFL.

Managers must know the cost of capital in making capital budgeting (long-term funding) decisions because investments with a return higher than the cost of capital will increase the value of the firm (shareholders' wealth).  The **cost of capital** is the weighted average of the interest cost of debt (net of tax) and the implicit cost of equity capital to be invested in long-term assets.  It represents a required minimum return of a new investment to prevent dilution of shareholders' interests.  The theory underlying the cost of capital applies to new, long-term funding because long-term funds finance long-term investments.  Short-term funds are used to meet working capital and other temporary needs.  Cost of capital is of less concern for short-term funding.  The cost of capital is a weighted average of the various debt and equity components.  The **weighted-average cost of capital** weights the percentage cost of each component by the percentage of that component in the financial structure.  The **cost of debt** equals the interest rate times one minus the marginal tax rate because interest is a tax deduction.  Hence, an increase in the tax rate decreases the cost of debt.  The **cost of retained earnings** is an opportunity cost.  It is the rate that investors can earn elsewhere on investments of comparable risk.  The cost of internally generated funds is an imputed cost.  The **cost of new external common equity** is higher than the cost of retained earnings because of stock flotation costs.  Providers of equity capital are exposed to more risk than are lenders because the firm is not obligated to pay them a return.  Also, in case of liquidation, creditors are paid before equity investors.  Thus, equity financing is more expensive than debt because equity investors require a higher return to compensate for the greater risk assumed.  The **cost of preferred stock** equals the preferred dividend divided by the net issuance price.  No tax adjustment is necessary because preferred dividends paid are not deductible.

Standard financial theory states that an **optimal capital structure** exists.  It minimizes the weighted-average cost of capital and thereby maximizes the value of the firm's stock, but it does not maximize EPS.  Greater leverage maximizes EPS but also increases risk.  Thus, the highest stock price is not reached by maximizing EPS.  The optimal capital structure usually involves some debt, but not 100% debt.  Ordinarily, firms cannot identify this optimal point precisely, but they should attempt to find an optimal range for the capital structure.  The required rate of return on equity capital (R) can be estimated in various ways, for example, by adding a percentage to the firm's long-term cost of debt.  Another method is the **Capital Asset Pricing Model (CAPM)**.  It adds the risk-free rate ($R_F$) (determined by government securities) to the product of the beta coefficient ($\beta$) (a measure of the firm's risk) and the difference between the market return ($R_M$) and the risk-free rate.  This **market risk premium** ($R_M - R_F$) is the amount above the risk-free rate required to induce average investors to enter the market.  Below is the basic equilibrium equation for the CAPM.

$$R = R_F + \beta(R_M - R_F)$$

The **beta coefficient** of an individual stock is the correlation between the volatility (price variation) of the stock market and the volatility of the price of the individual stock.  For example, if an individual stock rises 10% and the stock market 10%, the beta coefficient is 1.0.  If the stock rises 15% and the market only 10%, beta is 1.5.  Thus, assuming a beta of 1.20, a market rate of return of 17%, and an expected risk-free rate of 12%, the required rate of return on equity capital is 18% [.12 + 1.20 (.17 – .12)].

The **dividend growth model** estimates the cost of internal equity using the next expected dividend per share ($D_1$), the expected growth rate (G), and the market price ($P_0$).  Hence, to justify retention of earnings, management must expect a return at least equal to the dividend yield plus a growth rate.  The formula is

$$R = \frac{D_1}{P_0} + G$$

To determine the cost of new common stock (external equity), the model is altered to incorporate the flotation cost.  As the flotation cost rises, R increases accordingly.

$$R = \frac{D_1}{P_0 \, (1 - Percentage \ flotation \ cost)} + G$$

The dividend growth model is also used for stock price evaluation.  The stock price is affected by the dividend-payout ratio because some investors may want capital gains, but others may prefer current income.  Thus, investors will choose stocks that give the proper mix of capital gains and dividends.  The formula can be restated in terms of $P_0$ as follows:

$$P_0 = \frac{D_1}{R - G}$$

The **marginal cost of capital (MCC)** to the firm for the next dollar of new capital increases because lower-cost capital sources are used first.  Furthermore, the **marginal efficiency of investment (MEI)** declines.  The return on additional dollars of capital investment decreases because the most profitable investments are made initially.  The MEI curve is a smoothed rendering of an **investment opportunity schedule (IOS)**, which may be graphically depicted as a series of declining steps. Combining the MCC and MEI schedules (graphs) produces the equilibrium investment level (Q*) for the firm at a particular interest rate (I).

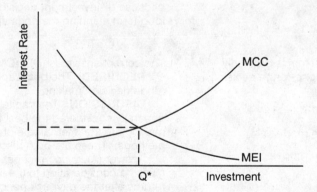

## 13.1 General Concepts

**1.** The capital budget is a(n)

    A.  Plan to insure that there are sufficient funds available for the operating needs of the company.

    B.  Exercise that sets the long-range goals of the company including the consideration of external influences.

    C.  Plan that coordinates and communicates a company's plan for the coming year to all departments and divisions.

    D.  Plan that assesses the long-term needs of the company for plant and equipment purchases.

The correct answer is (D). *(CMA, adapted)*
    **REQUIRED:** The true statement about the capital budget.
    **DISCUSSION:** Capital budgeting is the process of planning expenditures for long-lived assets. It involves choosing among investment proposals using a ranking procedure. Evaluations are based on various measures involving rate of return on investment.
    Answer (A) is incorrect because capital budgeting involves long-term investment needs, not immediate operating needs. Answer (B) is incorrect because strategic planning establishes long-term goals in the context of relevant factors in the firm's environment. Answer (C) is incorrect because an operating budget communicates a company's plan for the coming year to all departments.

**2.** Capital budgeting techniques are least likely to be used in evaluating the

    A.  Acquisition of new aircraft by a cargo company.

    B.  Design and implementation of a major advertising program.

    C.  Adoption of a new method of allocating nontraceable costs to product lines.

    D.  Sale by a conglomerate of an unprofitable division.

The correct answer is (C). *(CMA, adapted)*
    **REQUIRED:** The decision least likely to be evaluated using capital budgeting techniques.
    **DISCUSSION:** Capital budgeting is the process of planning expenditures for investments that are expected to generate returns over a period of more than one year. Thus, capital budgeting concerns the acquisition or disposal of long-term assets and the financing ramifications of such decisions. The adoption of a new method of allocating nontraceable costs to product lines has no effect on a company's cash flows, does not relate to the acquisition of long-term assets, and is not concerned with financing. Hence, capital budgeting is irrelevant to such a decision.
    Answer (A) is incorrect because new aircraft represent a long-term investment in capital goods. Answer (B) is incorrect because a major advertising program is a high-cost investment with long-term effects. Answer (D) is incorrect because disinvestment decisions should be approached with long-term planning methods applicable to investments.

**3.** The capital budgeting model that is ordinarily considered the best model for long-range decision making is the

    A.  Payback model.

    B.  Accounting rate of return model.

    C.  Unadjusted rate of return model.

    D.  Discounted cash flow model.

The correct answer is (D). *(CMA, adapted)*
    **REQUIRED:** The best capital budgeting model for long-range decision making.
    **DISCUSSION:** The capital budgeting methods that are generally considered the best for long-range decision making are the internal rate of return and net present value methods. These are both discounted cash flow methods.
    Answer (A) is incorrect because the payback method gives no consideration to the time value of money or to returns after the payback period. Answers (B) and (C) are incorrect because the accounting rate of return and the unadjusted rate of return do not consider the time value of money.

**4.** Discounted cash flow concepts concern

| | Interest Factors | Risk |
|---|---|---|
| A. | Yes | Yes |
| B. | Yes | No |
| C. | No | Yes |
| D. | No | No |

The correct answer is (A). *(Publisher)*
REQUIRED: The concept(s) underlying the time value of money.
DISCUSSION: The time value of money is concerned with two issues: (1) the investment value of money, and (2) the risk (uncertainty) inherent in any executory agreement. Thus, a dollar today is worth more than a dollar in the future, and the longer one waits for a dollar, the more uncertain the receipt is.
Answers (B), (C), and (D) are incorrect because risk and interest factors are concepts underlying the time value of money.

**5.** All of the following items are included in discounted cash flow analysis except

A. Future operating cash savings.

B. The disposal prices of the current and future assets.

C. The future asset depreciation expense.

D. The tax effects of future asset depreciation.

The correct answer is (C). *(CMA, adapted)*
REQUIRED: The item not included in discounted cash flow analysis.
DISCUSSION: Discounted cash flow analysis, using either the internal rate of return (IRR) or the net present value (NPV) method, is based on the time value of cash inflows and outflows. All future operating cash savings are considered as well as the tax effects on cash flows of future depreciation charges. The cash proceeds of future asset disposals are likewise a necessary consideration. Depreciation expense is a consideration only to the extent that it affects the cash flows for taxes. Otherwise, depreciation is excluded from the analysis because it is a noncash expense.
Answers (A), (B), and (D) are incorrect because future operating cash savings, the tax effects of future asset depreciation, and the disposal prices of the current and future assets are considerations in discounted cash flow analysis.

**6.** Which one of the following statements concerning cash flow determination for capital budgeting purposes is not correct?

A. Tax depreciation must be considered because it affects cash payments for taxes.

B. Book depreciation is relevant because it affects net income.

C. Net working capital changes should be included in cash flow forecasts.

D. Relevant opportunity costs should be included in cash flow forecasts.

The correct answer is (B). *(CMA, adapted)*
REQUIRED: The false statement about cash flow determination.
DISCUSSION: Tax depreciation is relevant to cash flow analysis because it affects the amount of income taxes that must be paid. However, book depreciation is not relevant because it does not affect the amount of cash generated by an investment.
Answers (A), (C), and (D) are incorrect because tax depreciation, net working capital changes, and relevant opportunity costs should be considered in a capital budgeting analysis.

**7.** A company considers a project that will generate cash sales of $50,000 per year. Fixed costs will be $10,000 per year, variable costs will be 40% of sales, and depreciation of the equipment in the project will be $5,000 per year. Taxes are 40%. The expected annual cash flow to the company resulting from the project is

A. $15,000

B. $9,000

C. $19,000

D. $14,000

The correct answer is (D). *(CIA, adapted)*
REQUIRED: The project's expected annual cash flow.
DISCUSSION: Depreciation expense is not a cash outflow and is not considered in the cash analysis except for its effects on taxes paid. Thus, the expected annual cash flow is $14,000 {[$50,000 cash sales − $10,000 fixed cost − (.4 × $50,000) variable costs − $5,000 depreciation] .6 after-tax income + $5,000 depreciation}.
Answer (A) is incorrect because $15,000 is the pretax income from the project. Answer (B) is incorrect because $9,000 includes depreciation as a cash outflow. Answer (C) is incorrect because $19,000 equals expected annual cash flow plus depreciation.

**8.** Future value is best described as

A. The sum of dollars-in discounted to time zero.

B. The sum of dollars-out discounted to time zero.

C. The value of a dollar-in or a dollar-out at a future time adjusted for any compounding effect.

D. None of the answers are correct.

The correct answer is (C). *(Publisher)*
**REQUIRED:** The definition of future value.
**DISCUSSION:** The future value of a dollar is its value at a time in the future given its present value. The future value of a dollar is affected both by the discount rate and the time at which the dollar is received. Hence, both dollars-in and dollars-out in the future may be adjusted for the discount rate and any compounding that may occur.

Answers (A) and (B) are incorrect because discounting to time zero is a present value calculation. Answer (D) is incorrect because future value is the value of a future cash value adjusted for the effects of compounding.

**9.** Which of the following formulas is used to determine the present value of an annuity?

A. $PV = A/(1 + i) + A/(1 + i)^2 + ... + A/(1 + i)^n$

B. $PV = A\left[\dfrac{(1 + i)^n - 1}{i}\right]$

C. $PV = A\left[\dfrac{1 - 1/(1 + i)^n}{i}\right]$

D. Both (A) and (C) are correct.

The correct answer is (D). *(Publisher)*
**REQUIRED:** The formula(s) for the present value of an annuity.
**DISCUSSION:** The present value of an annuity is the sum of the present values of several single payments. This is illustrated by the equation in answer (A), assuming that the payments are received at the end of each period, i.e., an ordinary annuity.

Answer (C) is the same formula in a different form. Equation 1 below is the same formula as in (A). Equation 2 is equation 1 multiplied by (1 + i). Equation 3 is a rearrangement of equation 2. Equation 4 is equation 3 minus equation 1. Equation 5 is equation 4 divided by i, and A is factored outside the brackets on the right side of the equation.

$$(1) \quad PV = A/(1 + i) + ... + A/(1 + i)^n$$

$$(2) \quad (1 + i)PV = A + ... + A/(1 + i)^{n-1}$$

$$(3) \quad PV + PVi = A + ... + A/(1 + i)^{n-1}$$

$$(4) \quad PVi = A - A/(1 + i)^n$$

$$(5) \quad PV = A\left[\dfrac{1 - 1/(1 + i)^n}{i}\right]$$

Answer (A) is incorrect because answer (C) is also a correct choice. Answer (B) is incorrect because it is an equation for the future value (FV), not present value (PV), of an annuity. Answer (C) is incorrect because answer (A) is also a correct choice.

**10.** Which formula is used to determine the future value that will be available if a given amount of money is invested?

A. $A(1 + i)^n$

B. $\dfrac{A}{(1 + i)^n}$

C. $A\left[\dfrac{(1 + i)^{n - 1}}{i}\right]$

D. $A\left[\dfrac{1 - 1/(1 + i)^n}{i}\right]$

The correct answer is (A). *(Publisher)*
**REQUIRED:** The algebraic formula for the future value when the present value is known.
**DISCUSSION:** The basic formula used is $PV(1 + i)^n = FV_n$; i.e., the present value times one plus the interest rate to the nth power equals the future value at the end of the nth time period. When the present amount is known (e.g., A = $100), as well as the interest rate (e.g., i = 10%) and the number of time periods (e.g., n = 2), the future value can be calculated as $100(1 + .10)^2 = $121. A is typically used in the formula, but it stands for the PV or FV (whichever is not on the other side of the equals sign).

Answer (B) is incorrect because it is the formula used to calculate the present value of an amount. Answer (C) is incorrect because it is the formula for the future value of an annuity. Answer (D) is incorrect because it is the formula for the present value of an annuity.

**11.** Essex Corporation is evaluating a lease that takes effect on March 1, 1998. The company must make eight equal payments, with the first payment due on March 1, 1998. The concept most relevant to the evaluation of the lease is

A. The present value of an annuity due.

B. The present value of an ordinary annuity.

C. The future value of an annuity due.

D. The future value of an ordinary annuity.

The correct answer is (A). *(CMA, adapted)*
**REQUIRED:** The concept most relevant to evaluating a long-term lease if the first payment is due immediately.
**DISCUSSION:** An annuity is a series of cash flows or other economic benefits occurring at fixed intervals. Present value is the value at a specified time of an amount or amounts to be paid or received later, discounted at some interest rate. In an annuity due, the payments occur at the beginning, rather than at the end, of the periods. Evaluation of an investment decision, e.g., a lease, that involves multi-period cash payments (an annuity) requires an adjustment for the time value of money. This lease should therefore be evaluated using the present value of an annuity due.
Answer (B) is incorrect because, in an ordinary annuity, each payment occurs at the end of a period. Answers (C) and (D) are incorrect because future value is the converse of present value. It is an amount accumulated in the future. Evaluation of a lease, however, necessitates calculation of a present value.

**12.** An actuary has determined that a company should have $90 million accumulated in its pension fund 20 years from now for the fund to be able to meet its obligations. An interest rate of 8% is considered appropriate for all pension fund calculations. The company wishes to know how much it should contribute to the pension fund at the end of each of the next 20 years. Which set of instructions correctly describes the procedures necessary to compute the annual contribution?

A. Divide $90,000,000 by the factor for present value of an ordinary annuity.

B. Multiply $90,000,000 by the factor for present value of an ordinary annuity.

C. Divide $90,000,000 by the factor for future value of an ordinary annuity.

D. Multiply $90,000,000 by the factor for future value of an ordinary annuity.

The correct answer is (C). *(CIA, adapted)*
**REQUIRED:** The set of instructions that correctly describes the procedures necessary to compute the annual amount the company should contribute to the fund.
**DISCUSSION:** The future value of an annuity equals the appropriate interest factor (for n periods at an interest rate of i), which is derived from standard tables, times the periodic payment. The $90 million amount is the future value of the funding payments. The amount of each funding payment can be calculated by dividing the future value of the funding payments by the interest factor for future value of an ordinary annuity for n equals 20 and i equals 8%.
Answer (A) is incorrect because the $90,000,000 is a future value figure. The interest factor to be used for the division process should be a future value factor, not a present value factor. Answer (B) is incorrect because the $90,000,000 is a future value figure. The factor to be used should be a future value factor. That factor should be used in a division, rather than a multiplication, process. Answer (D) is incorrect because the $90,000,000 should be divided by the appropriate interest factor.

**13.** The discount rate ordinarily used in present value calculations is the

A. Federal Reserve rate.

B. Treasury bill rate.

C. Minimum desired rate of return set by the firm.

D. Prime rate.

The correct answer is (C). *(Publisher)*
**REQUIRED:** The discount rate customarily used in present value calculations.
**DISCUSSION:** The discount rate most often used in present value calculations is the minimum desired rate of return as set by management. The NPV arrived at in this calculation is a first step in the decision process. It indicates how the project's return compares with the minimum desired rate of return.
Answer (A) is incorrect because the Federal Reserve rate may be considered; however, the firm will set its minimum desired rate of return in view of its needs. Answer (B) is incorrect because the Treasury bill rate may be considered; however, the firm will set its minimum desired rate of return in view of its needs. Answer (D) is incorrect because the prime rate may be considered; however, the firm will set its minimum desired rate of return in view of its needs.

Questions 14 through 16 are based on the following information. Crown Corporation has agreed to sell some used computer equipment to Bob Parsons, one of the company's employees, for $5,000. Crown and Parsons have been discussing alternative financing arrangements for the sale. The information in the opposite column is pertinent to these discussions.

| Present Value of an Ordinary Annuity of $1 | | | | |
| Payments | 5% | 6% | 7% | 8% |
| --- | --- | --- | --- | --- |
| 1 | 0.952 | 0.943 | 0.935 | 0.926 |
| 2 | 1.859 | 1.833 | 1.808 | 1.783 |
| 3 | 2.723 | 2.673 | 2.624 | 2.577 |
| 4 | 3.546 | 3.465 | 3.387 | 3.312 |
| 5 | 4.329 | 4.212 | 4.100 | 3.993 |
| 6 | 5.076 | 4.917 | 4.767 | 4.623 |
| 7 | 5.786 | 5.582 | 5.389 | 5.206 |
| 8 | 6.463 | 6.210 | 5.971 | 5.747 |

**14.** Crown Corporation has offered to accept a $1,000 down payment and set up a note receivable for Bob Parsons that calls for a $1,000 payment at the end of each of the next 4 years. If Crown uses a 6% discount rate, the present value of the note receivable would be

A. $2,940

B. $4,465

C. $4,212

D. $3,465

The correct answer is (D). *(CMA, adapted)*
**REQUIRED:** The present value of a note receivable that requires an equal payment at the end of each year.
**DISCUSSION:** The four equal payments are an ordinary annuity because they are due at the end of each period. Given a discount rate of 6%, the appropriate present value is 3.465. The present value is $3,465 ($1,000 payment x 3.465).
Answer (A) is incorrect because $2,940 assumes the note is payable in full at the end of the fourth year. Answer (B) is incorrect because $4,465 equals $1,000 times 3.465, plus $1,000. Answer (C) is incorrect because $4,212 equals $1,000 times 4.212.

**15.** Bob Parsons has agreed to the immediate down payment of $1,000 but would like the note for $4,000 to be payable in full at the end of the fourth year. Because of the increased risk associated with the terms of this note, Crown Corporation would apply an 8% discount rate. The present value of this note would be

A. $2,940

B. $3,312

C. $3,940

D. $2,557

The correct answer is (A). *(CMA, adapted)*
**REQUIRED:** The present value of a note payable in full at the end of its term.
**DISCUSSION:** A present value table for a single future amount is not given, so the first step is to derive the appropriate discount factor from the table for the present value of an ordinary annuity. The factor for four payments at 8% is 3.312. The factor for three payments is 2.577. Consequently, the difference between the factors for 3 and 4 years is .735 (3.312 – 2.577). The present value of a single $4,000 payment in 4 years is therefore $2,940 (.735 x $4,000).
Answer (B) is incorrect because $3,312 equals $1,000 times 3.312. Answer (C) is incorrect because $3,940 equals $4,000 times .735, plus $1,000. Answer (D) is incorrect because $2,557 equals $1,000 times 2.557.

**16.** If Bob Parsons borrowed the $5,000 at 8% interest for 4 years from his bank and paid Crown Corporation the full price of the equipment immediately, Crown could invest the $5,000 for 3 years at 7%. The future value of this investment (rounded) would be

A. $6,297

B. $6,127

C. $6,553

D. $6,803

The correct answer is (B). *(CMA, adapted)*
**REQUIRED:** The future value of an amount.
**DISCUSSION:** The present value of a future amount equals the amount times the appropriate interest factor. Thus, the future amount must equal the present value divided by the interest factor. The present value is given, and the interest factor for the present value of an amount can be derived from the table for the present value of an ordinary annuity. In this case, the factor is equal to the difference between the factors for three and two periods at the stipulated interest rate of 7% (2.624 – 1.808 = .816). Accordingly, the future amount of $5,000 in 3 years given an interest rate of 7% is $6,127 ($5,000 present value ÷ .816).
Answer (A) is incorrect because $6,297 equals $5,000 divided by .794 (2.577 – 1.783). Answer (C) is incorrect because $6,553 equals $5,000 divided by .763 (3.387 – 2.624). Answer (D) is incorrect because $6,803 equals $5,000 divided by .735 (3.312 – 2.577).

**17.** Janet Taylor Casual Wear has $75,000 in a bank account as of December 31, 1998. If the company plans on depositing $4,000 in the account at the end of each of the next 3 years (1999, 2000, and 2001) and all amounts in the account earn 8% per year, what will the account balance be at December 31, 2001? Ignore the effect of income taxes.

| | 8% Interest Rate Factors | |
|---|---|---|
| Period | Future Value of $1 | Future Value of an Annuity of $1 |
| 1 | 1.08 | 1.00 |
| 2 | 1.17 | 2.08 |
| 3 | 1.26 | 3.25 |
| 4 | 1.36 | 4.51 |

  A. $87,000

  B. $88,000

  C. $96,070

  D. $107,500

The correct answer is (D). *(CMA, adapted)*
  **REQUIRED:** The future value of an investment.
  **DISCUSSION:** Both future value tables will be used because the $75,000 already in the account will be multiplied times the future value factor of 1.26 to determine the amount 3 years hence, or $94,500. The three payments of $4,000 represent an ordinary annuity. Multiplying the three-period annuity factor (3.25) by the payment amount ($4,000) results in a future value of the annuity of $13,000. Adding the two elements together produces a total account balance of $107,500 ($94,500 + $13,000).
  Answer (A) is incorrect because $87,000 is the amount that would be in the account if interest were zero. Answer (B) is incorrect because the $88,000 ignores the interest that would be earned on the $75,000 initial balance. Answer (C) is incorrect because $96,070 is the amount that would be available after 2 years (December 31, 2000).

**18.** The method that divides a project's annual after-tax net income by the average investment cost to measure the estimated performance of a capital investment is the

  A.  Internal rate of return method.

  B.  Accounting rate of return method.

  C.  Payback method.

  D.  Net present value (NPV) method.

The correct answer is (B). *(CMA, adapted)*
  **REQUIRED:** The capital budgeting method that divides annual after-tax net income by the average investment cost.
  **DISCUSSION:** The accounting rate of return uses undiscounted net income (not cash flows) to determine a rate of profitability. Annual after-tax net income is divided by the average book value of the investment in assets.
  Answer (A) is incorrect because the IRR is the rate at which NPV is zero. The minimum desired rate of return is not used in the discounting. Answer (C) is incorrect because the payback period is the time required to complete the return of the original investment. Answer (D) is incorrect because the NPV method computes the discounted present value of future cash inflows to determine whether it is greater than the initial cash outflow.

**19.** The length of time required to recover the initial cash outlay of a capital project is determined by using the

  A.  Discounted cash flow method.

  B.  Payback method.

  C.  Weighted net present value method.

  D.  Net present value method.

The correct answer is (B). *(CMA, adapted)*
  **REQUIRED:** The method of determining the time required to recover the initial cash outlay of a capital project.
  **DISCUSSION:** The payback method measures the number of years required to complete the return of the original investment. This measure is computed by dividing the net investment by the constant annual cash inflow. If cash flows are not uniform, a cumulative approach is needed. The payback method gives no consideration to the time value of money or to returns after the payback period.
  Answer (A) is incorrect because the discounted cash flow method computes a rate of return. Answers (C) and (D) are incorrect because the NPV method is based on discounted cash flows; the length of time to recover an investment is not the result.

**20.** The technique that recognizes the time value of money by discounting the after-tax cash flows for a project over its life to time period zero using the company's minimum desired rate of return is the

    A.  Net present value method.

    B.  Capital rationing method.

    C.  Payback method.

    D.  Accounting rate of return method.

The correct answer is (A). *(CMA, adapted)*
    **REQUIRED:** The technique that discounts after-tax cash flows.
    **DISCUSSION:** The net present value method discounts future cash flows to the present value using some arbitrary rate of return, which is presumably the firm's cost of capital. The initial cost of the project is then deducted from the present value. If the present value of the future cash flows exceeds the cost, the investment is considered to be acceptable.
    Answer (B) is incorrect because capital rationing is not a technique but rather a condition that characterizes capital budgeting when the limited amount of capital available is insufficient to fund all profitable investments. Answers (C) and (D) are incorrect because the payback method and the accounting rate of return method do not discount cash flows.

**21.** The net present value method of capital budgeting assumes that cash flows are reinvested at

    A.  The risk-free rate.

    B.  The cost of debt.

    C.  The internal rate of return.

    D.  The discount rate used in the analysis.

The correct answer is (D). *(CMA, adapted)*
    **REQUIRED:** The assumed rate at which cash flows are reinvested under the net present value (NPV) method.
    **DISCUSSION:** The NPV method assumes that periodic cash inflows earned over the life of an investment are reinvested at the company's cost of capital (the discount rate used in the analysis). The assumptions are that the return on reinvestment is an opportunity cost and that the alternative investment has an equal degree of risk.
    Answers (A) and (B) are incorrect because the NPV method assumes that cash inflows are reinvested at the discount rate used in the NPV calculation. Answer (C) is incorrect because the IRR method assumes a reinvestment rate equal to the IRR.

**22.** The technique that reflects the time value of money and is calculated by dividing the present value of the future net after-tax cash inflows that have been discounted at the desired cost of capital by the initial cash outlay for the investment is the

    A.  Net present value method.

    B.  Capital rationing method.

    C.  Accounting rate of return method.

    D.  Profitability index method.

The correct answer is (D). *(CMA, adapted)*
    **REQUIRED:** The technique that divides the present value of future net cash inflows by the initial cash outlay.
    **DISCUSSION:** The profitability index (excess present value index) measures the ratio of the present value of future net cash inflows to the original investment. In organizations with unlimited capital funds, this index will produce no conflicts in the decision process. If capital rationing is necessary, the index will be an insufficient determinant. The capital available as well as the dollar amount of the net present value must be considered.
    Answer (A) is incorrect because the net present value method does not divide the future cash flows by the cost. Answer (B) is incorrect because capital rationing is not a technique but rather a condition that characterizes capital budgeting when insufficient capital is available to finance all profitable investment opportunities. Answer (C) is incorrect because the accounting rate of return method does not discount cash flows.

**23.** The internal rate of return (IRR) is the

A. Hurdle rate.

B. Rate of interest for which the net present value is greater than 1.0.

C. Rate of interest for which the net present value is equal to zero.

D. Accounting rate of return.

The correct answer is (C). *(CMA, adapted)*

**REQUIRED:** The true statement about the IRR.

**DISCUSSION:** The IRR is the interest rate at which the present value of the expected future cash inflows is equal to the present value of the cash outflows for a project. Thus, the IRR is the interest rate that will produce a net present value (NPV) equal to zero. The IRR method assumes that the cash flows will be reinvested at the internal rate of return.

Answer (A) is incorrect because the hurdle rate is the rate used to calculate the NPV; it is determined by management prior to the analysis. Answer (B) is incorrect because the IRR is the rate at which the NPV is zero. Answer (D) is incorrect because the accounting rate of return does not incorporate the time value of money.

**24.** Risk to a company is affected by both project variability and how project returns correlate with those of the company's prevailing business. Overall company risk will be lowest when a project's returns exhibit

A. Low variability and negative correlation.

B. Low variability and positive correlation.

C. High variability and positive correlation.

D. High variability and no correlation.

The correct answer is (A). *(CIA, adapted)*

**REQUIRED:** The circumstance in which overall company risk will be lowest.

**DISCUSSION:** A common general definition is that risk is an investment with an unknown outcome but a known probability distribution of returns (a known mean and standard deviation). An increase in the standard deviation (variability) of returns is synonymous with an increase in the riskiness of a project. Risk is also increased when the project's returns are positively (directly) correlated with other investments in the firm's portfolio; i.e., risk increases when returns on all projects rise or fall together. Consequently, the overall risk is decreased when projects have low variability and are negatively correlated (the diversification effect).

Answers (B), (C), and (D) are incorrect because overall risk is decreased when projects have low variability and are negatively correlated.

**25.** When the risks of the individual components of a project's cash flows are different, an acceptable procedure to evaluate these cash flows is to

A. Divide each cash flow by the payback period.

B. Compute the net present value of each cash flow using the firm's cost of capital.

C. Compare the internal rate of return from each cash flow to its risk.

D. Discount each cash flow using a discount rate that reflects the degree of risk.

The correct answer is (D). *(CMA, adapted)*

**REQUIRED:** The procedure for evaluating cash flows when the risks of individual components differ.

**DISCUSSION:** If risks differ among various elements of the cash flows, different discount rates can be used for different flows. The riskier the cash flows, the higher the discount rate, and the lower the present value.

Answer (A) is incorrect because the payback period ignores both the varying risk and the time value of money. Answer (B) is incorrect because using the cost of capital as the discount rate makes no adjustment for risk differentials. Answer (C) is incorrect because risk must be incorporated into the company's hurdle rate for the IRR method to be used with risk differentials.

**26.** Sensitivity analysis, if used with capital projects,

A. Is used extensively when cash flows are known with certainty.

B. Measures the change in the discounted cash flows when using the discounted payback method rather than the net present value method.

C. Is a "what-if" technique that asks how a given outcome will change if the original estimates of the capital budgeting model are changed.

D. Is a technique used to rank capital expenditure requests.

The correct answer is (C). *(CMA, adapted)*
**REQUIRED:** The true statement about sensitivity analysis.
**DISCUSSION:** After a problem has been formulated into any mathematical model, it may be subjected to sensitivity analysis, which is a trial-and-error method used to determine the sensitivity of the estimates used. For example, forecasts of many calculated NPVs under various assumptions may be compared to determine how sensitive the NPV is to changing conditions. Changing the assumptions about a certain variable or group of variables may drastically alter the NPV, suggesting that the risk of the investment may be excessive.

Answer (A) is incorrect because sensitivity analysis is useful when cash flows, or other assumptions, are uncertain. Answer (B) is incorrect because sensitivity analysis can be used with any of the capital budgeting methods. Answer (D) is incorrect because sensitivity analysis is not a ranking technique; it calculates results under varying assumptions.

**27.** When determining net present value in an inflationary environment, adjustments should be made to

A. Increase the discount rate only.

B. Increase the estimated cash inflows and increase the discount rate.

C. Decrease the estimated cash inflows and increase the discount rate.

D. Increase the estimated cash inflows and decrease the discount rate.

The correct answer is (B). *(CMA, adapted)*
**REQUIRED:** The adjustment in determining net present value in an inflationary environment.
**DISCUSSION:** In an inflationary environment, nominal future cash flows should increase to reflect the decrease in the value of the unit of measure. Also, the investor should increase the discount rate to reflect the increased inflation premium arising from the additional uncertainty. Lenders will require a higher interest rate in an inflationary environment.

Answers (A), (C), and (D) are incorrect because the estimated cash flows and the discount rate should increase.

**28.** Fast Freight, Inc. is planning to purchase equipment to make its operations more efficient. This equipment has an estimated life of 6 years. As part of this acquisition, a $75,000 investment in working capital is anticipated. In a discounted cash flow analysis, the investment in working capital

A. Should be amortized over the useful life of the equipment.

B. Should be treated as a recurring cash outflow over the life of the equipment.

C. Should be treated as an immediate cash outflow.

D. Should be treated as an immediate cash outflow recovered at the end of 6 years.

The correct answer is (D). *(CMA, adapted)*
**REQUIRED:** The true statement about an investment in working capital related to an equipment purchase.
**DISCUSSION:** The investment in a new project includes more than the initial cost of new capital equipment. In addition, funds must be provided for increases in receivables and inventories. This investment in working capital is treated as an initial cost of the investment that will be recovered in full as a cash inflow at the end of the project's life.

Answer (A) is incorrect because the investment in working capital will be needed throughout the life of the investment. Answer (B) is incorrect because the investment will occur only at the start of the project. Answer (C) is incorrect because the initial investment is an initial cash outflow that will be recovered.

**29.** Lawson Inc. is expanding its manufacturing plant, which requires an investment of $4 million in new equipment and plant modifications. Lawson's sales are expected to increase by $3 million per year as a result of the expansion. Cash investment in current assets averages 30% of sales; accounts payable and other current liabilities are 10% of sales. What is the estimated total investment for this expansion?

A. $3.4 million.

B. $4.3 million.

C. $4.6 million.

D. $5.2 million.

The correct answer is (C). *(CMA, adapted)*

**REQUIRED:** The estimated total cash investment.

**DISCUSSION:** The investment required includes increases in working capital (e.g., additional receivables and inventories resulting from the acquisition of a new manufacturing plant). The additional working capital is an initial cost of the investment, but one that will be recovered (i.e., it has a salvage value equal to its initial cost). Lawson can use current liabilities to fund assets to the extent of 10% of sales. Thus, the total initial cash outlay will be $4.6 million {$4 million + [(30% – 10%) x $3 million sales]}.

Answer (A) is incorrect because $3.4 million deducts the investment in working capital from the cost of equipment. Answer (B) is incorrect because $4.3 million equals $4 million plus 10% of $3 million. Answer (D) is incorrect because $5.2 million equals $4 million plus 30% of $4 million.

**30.** In equipment replacement decisions, which one of the following does not affect the decision-making process?

A. Current disposal price of the old equipment.

B. Operating costs of the old equipment.

C. Original fair value of the old equipment.

D. Operating costs of the new equipment.

The correct answer is (C). *(CMA, adapted)*

**REQUIRED:** The irrelevant factor when making an equipment replacement decision.

**DISCUSSION:** All relevant costs should be considered when evaluating an equipment replacement decision. These include the initial investment in the new equipment, any required investment in working capital, the disposal price of the new equipment, the disposal price of the old equipment, the operating costs of the old equipment, and the operating costs of the new equipment. The original cost or fair value of the old equipment is a sunk cost and is irrelevant to future decisions.

Answers (A), (B), and (D) are incorrect because they should be considered when evaluating an equipment replacement decision.

Questions 31 through 34 are based on the following information. In order to increase production capacity, Gunning Industries is considering replacing an existing production machine with a new technologically improved machine effective January 1, 1999. The following information is being considered by Gunning Industries:

- The new machine would be purchased for $160,000 in cash. Shipping, installation, and testing would cost an additional $30,000.

- The new machine is expected to increase annual sales by 20,000 units at a sales price of $40 per unit. Incremental operating costs include $30 per unit in variable costs and total fixed costs of $40,000 per year.

- The investment in the new machine will require an immediate increase in working capital of $35,000. This cash outflow will be recovered at the end of year 5.

- Gunning uses straight-line depreciation for financial reporting and tax reporting purposes. The new machine has an estimated useful life of 5 years and zero salvage value.

- Gunning is subject to a 40% corporate income tax rate.

Gunning uses the net present value method to analyze investments and will employ the following factors and rates:

| Period | Present Value of $1 at 10% | Present Value of an Ordinary Annuity of $1 at 10% |
|--------|---------------------------|---------------------------------------------------|
| 1 | .909 | .909 |
| 2 | .826 | 1.736 |
| 3 | .751 | 2.487 |
| 4 | .683 | 3.170 |
| 5 | .621 | 3.791 |

**31.** Gunning Industries' net cash outflow in a capital budgeting decision is

A.   $190,000

B.   $195,000

C.   $204,525

D.   $225,000

The correct answer is (D). *(CMA, adapted)*
**REQUIRED:** The net cash outflow in a capital budgeting decision.
**DISCUSSION:** The machine costs $160,000 and will require $30,000 to install and test. In addition, the company will have to invest in $35,000 of working capital to support the production of the new machine. Thus, the total investment necessary is $225,000.
Answer (A) is incorrect because $190,000 ignores the investment in working capital. Answer (B) is incorrect because $195,000 ignores the $30,000 of shipping, installation, and testing costs. Answer (C) is incorrect because $204,525 is the present value of $225,000 at 10% for 1 year.

**32.** Gunning Industries' discounted annual depreciation tax shield for the year 1999 is

A.   $13,817

B.   $16,762

C.   $20,725

D.   $22,800

The correct answer is (A). *(CMA, adapted)*
**REQUIRED:** The discounted annual depreciation tax shield.
**DISCUSSION:** Gunning uses straight-line depreciation. Thus, the annual charge is $38,000 [($160,000 + $30,000) ÷ 5 years], and the tax savings is $15,200 (40% x $38,000). That benefit will be received in 1 year, so the present value is $13,817 ($15,200 tax savings x .909 present value of $1 for 1 year at 10%).
Answer (B) is incorrect because $16,762 is greater than the undiscounted tax savings. Answer (C) is incorrect because $20,725 assumes a 60% tax rate (the complement of the actual 40% rate). Answer (D) is incorrect because $22,800 assumes a 60% tax rate and no discounting.

**33.** The acquisition of the new production machine by Gunning Industries will contribute a discounted net-of-tax contribution margin of

A.  $242,624

B.  $303,280

C.  $363,936

D.  $454,920

The correct answer is (D). *(CMA, adapted)*

**REQUIRED:** The discounted net-of-tax contribution margin from the new machine.

**DISCUSSION:** The new machine will increase sales by 20,000 units a year. The increase in the pretax total contribution margin will be $200,000 per year [20,000 units x ($40 SP – $30 VC)], and the annual increase in the after-tax contribution margin will be $120,000 [(1.0 – .4) x $200,000]. The present value of the after-tax increase in the contribution margin over the 5-year useful life of the machine is $454,920 ($120,000 x 3.791 PV of an ordinary annuity for 5 years at 10%).

Answer (A) is incorrect because $242,624 deducts fixed costs from the pretax contribution margin and applies a 60% tax rate. Answer (B) is incorrect because $303,280 deducts fixed costs from the after-tax contribution margin before discounting. Answer (C) is incorrect because $363,936 deducts fixed costs from the contribution margin before calculating taxes and the present value.

**34.** The overall discounted cash flow impact of Gunning Industries' working capital investment for the new production machine would be

A.  $(7,959)

B.  $(10,080)

C.  $(13,265)

D.  $(35,000)

The correct answer is (C). *(CMA, adapted)*

**REQUIRED:** The overall discounted cash flow impact of the working capital investment.

**DISCUSSION:** The $35,000 of working capital requires an immediate outlay for that amount, but it will be recovered in 5 years. Thus, the net discounted cash outflow is $13,265 [$35,000 initial investment – ($35,000 future inflow x .621 PV of $1 for 5 years at 10%)].

Answer (A) is incorrect because $(7,959) assumes the initial investment and its return are reduced by applying a 40% tax rate. Answer (B) is incorrect because $(10,080) assumes the initial investment was discounted for 1 year. Answer (D) is incorrect because $(35,000) fails to consider that the $35,000 will be recovered (essentially in the form of a salvage value) after the fifth year.

## 13.2 Payback

**35.** Which one of the following statements about the payback method of investment analysis is correct? The payback method

A.  Does not consider the time value of money.

B.  Considers cash flows after the payback has been reached.

C.  Uses discounted cash flow techniques.

D.  Is rarely used in practice.

The correct answer is (A). *(CMA, adapted)*

**REQUIRED:** The true statement about the payback method of investment analysis.

**DISCUSSION:** The payback method calculates the amount of time required for the undiscounted cumulative net cash inflows to equal the original investment. Although the payback method is easy to use, it has inherent problems. The time value of money and returns after the payback period are not considered.

Answer (B) is incorrect because the payback method ignores cash flows after payback. Answer (C) is incorrect because the payback method does not use discounted cash flow techniques. Answer (D) is incorrect because the payback method is often used, given its simplicity and effectiveness in risk management and cash conservation.

**36.** A characteristic of the payback method (before taxes) is that it

    A.  Neglects total project profitability.

    B.  Uses accrual accounting inflows in the numerator of the calculation.

    C.  Uses the estimated expected life of the asset in the denominator of the calculation.

    D.  Uses the hurdle rate in the calculation.

The correct answer is (A). *(CMA, adapted)*
**REQUIRED:** The characteristic of the payback method.
**DISCUSSION:** The payback method calculates the time required to complete the return of the original investment. This measure is computed by dividing the net investment by the constant expected periodic net cash inflow. If the net cash inflows are not constant, a cumulative approach is used. The payback method is easy to use but has two principal problems: it ignores the time value of money, and it gives no consideration to returns after the payback period. Thus, it ignores total project profitability.

    Answer (B) is incorrect because the net investment is the numerator. Answer (C) is incorrect because the constant expected net cash inflow is the denominator. Answer (D) is incorrect because no hurdle rate or other interest rate is used.

**37.** The bailout payback method

    A.  Incorporates the time value of money.

    B.  Equals the recovery period from normal operations.

    C.  Eliminates the disposal value from the payback calculation.

    D.  Measures the risk if a project is terminated.

The correct answer is (D). *(CMA, adapted)*
**REQUIRED:** The true statement about the bailout payback method.
**DISCUSSION:** The bailout payback period is the length of time required for the sum of the cumulative net cash inflow from an investment and its salvage value to equal the original investment. The bailout payback method measures the risk to the investor if the investment must be abandoned. The shorter the period, the lower the risk.

    Answer (A) is incorrect because the time value of money is ignored. Answers (B) and (C) are incorrect because the bailout payback includes salvage value as well as cash flow from operations.

**38.** A machine costing $1,000 produces total cash inflows of $1,400 over 4 years. Determine the payback period given the following cash flows:

| Year | After-Tax Cash Flows | Cumulative Cash Flows |
|---|---|---|
| 1 | $400 | $  400 |
| 2 | 300 | 700 |
| 3 | 500 | 1,200 |
| 4 | 200 | 1,400 |

    A.  2 years.

    B.  2.60 years.

    C.  2.86 years.

    D.  3 years.

The correct answer is (B). *(CIA, adapted)*
**REQUIRED:** The payback period given the annual cash flows.
**DISCUSSION:** Because $700 will be received in the first 2 years, only $300 will remain to be recovered in year 3. The payback period is therefore 2.6 years [2 years + ($300 ÷ $500) of year 3].

    Answer (A) is incorrect because after 2 years $300 ($1,000 – $700) remains to be recovered. Answer (C) is incorrect because the payback period is determined by adding 2 plus the percentage of year 3 cash flows necessary to recover the balance of the $1,000 original investment. Answer (D) is incorrect because, at the end of 3 years, $200 ($1,200 – $1,000) more than the original cost will have been recovered.

**39.** Jasper Company has a payback goal of 3 years on new equipment acquisitions. A new sorter is being evaluated that costs $450,000 and has a 5-year life. Straight-line depreciation will be used; no salvage is anticipated. Jasper is subject to a 40% income tax rate. To meet the company's payback goal, the sorter must generate reductions in annual cash operating costs of

A. $60,000

B. $100,000

C. $150,000

D. $190,000

The correct answer is (D). *(CMA, adapted)*

**REQUIRED:** The cash savings that must be generated to achieve a targeted payback period.

**DISCUSSION:** To achieve a payback period of 3 years, the annual increment in net cash inflow must be $150,000 ($450,000 ÷ 3 years). This amount equals the total annual reduction in cash operating costs minus related taxes. Depreciation is $90,000 per year ($450,000 ÷ 5 years). Because depreciation is a noncash deductible expense, it shields $90,000 of the cash savings from taxation. Accordingly, $60,000 ($150,000 – $90,000) of the additional net cash inflow must come from after-tax net income. At a 40% tax rate, $60,000 of after-tax income equals $100,000 ($60,000 ÷ 60%) of pretax income from cost savings, and the outflow for taxes is $40,000. Thus, the annual reduction in cash operating costs required is $190,000 ($150,000 additional net cash inflow required + $40,000 tax outflow).

Answer (A) is incorrect because $60,000 is after-tax net income from the cost savings. Answer (B) is incorrect because $100,000 is the pretax income from the cost savings. Answer (C) is incorrect because $150,000 ignores depreciation and income taxes.

**40.** Womark Company purchased a new machine on January 1 of this year for $90,000, with an estimated useful life of 5 years and a salvage value of $10,000. The machine will be depreciated using the straight-line method. The machine is expected to produce cash flow from operations, net of income taxes, of $36,000 a year in each of the next 5 years. The new machine's salvage value is $20,000 in years 1 and 2, and $15,000 in years 3 and 4. What will be the bailout period (rounded) for this new machine?

A. 1.4 years.

B. 2.2 years.

C. 1.9 years.

D. 3.4 years.

The correct answer is (C). *(CPA, adapted)*

**REQUIRED:** The bailout period for an investment in a new machine.

**DISCUSSION:** The bailout period is the time required for the sum of the cumulative net cash inflow and the salvage value to equal the original investment. During years 1 and 2, cost minus salvage value is $70,000, and the annual net cash inflow is $36,000. Hence, the incremental amount to be recovered during year 2 is $34,000 ($70,000 – $36,000). Interpolating in year 2 therefore yields a bailout period of 1.9 years [1 + ($34,000 ÷ $36,000)].

Answer (A) is incorrect because annual cash flows are $36,000, not $50,000. Answer (B) is incorrect because cost minus salvage value in year 2 is $70,000, not $80,000. Answer (D) is incorrect because the incremental amount to be recovered during year 2 is $34,000 not $14,000.

**41.** An investment project is expected to yield $10,000 in annual revenues, will incur $2,000 in fixed costs per year, and requires an initial inventory of $5,000. Given a cost of goods sold of 60% of sales and ignoring taxes, what is the payback period in years?

A. 2.50

B. 5.00

C. 2.00

D. 1.25

The correct answer is (A). *(CIA, adapted)*

**REQUIRED:** The payback period in years.

**DISCUSSION:** The payback period equals the original investment divided by the constant net cash inflow per year. Net cash inflow per year is $2,000 (see below), and the payback period is 2.5 years ($5,000 investment ÷ $2,000).

| | |
|---|---:|
| Annual revenue | $10,000 |
| CGS (60%) | (6,000) |
| Cash flow before fixed costs | $ 4,000 |
| Fixed costs | (2,000) |
| Annual net cash inflow | $ 2,000 |

Answer (B) is incorrect because 5.00 assumes a $10,000 investment. Answer (C) is incorrect because 2.00 assumes a $10,000 investment and a $5,000 constant annual net cash inflow. Answer (D) is incorrect because 1.25 equals $5,000 divided by $4,000.

**42.** Whatney Co. is considering the acquisition of a new, more efficient press. The cost of the press is $360,000, and the press has an estimated 6-year life with zero salvage value. Whatney uses straight-line depreciation for both financial reporting and income tax reporting purposes and has a 40% corporate income tax rate. In evaluating equipment acquisitions of this type, Whatney uses a goal of a 4-year payback period. To meet Whatney's desired payback period, the press must produce a minimum annual before-tax operating cash savings of

   A.  $90,000

   B.  $110,000

   C.  $114,000

   D.  $150,000

The correct answer is (B). *(CMA, adapted)*

**REQUIRED:** The minimum annual before-tax operating cash savings yielding a specified payback period.

**DISCUSSION:** Payback is the number of years required to complete the return of the original investment. Given a periodic constant cash flow, the payback period equals net investment divided by the constant expected periodic after-tax cash flow. The desired payback period is 4 years, so the constant after-tax annual cash flow must be $90,000 ($360,000 ÷ 4). Assuming that the company has sufficient other income to permit realization of the full tax savings, depreciation of the machine will shield $60,000 ($360,000 ÷ 6) of income from taxation each year, an after-tax cash savings of $24,000 (40% x $60,000). Thus, the machine must generate an additional $66,000 ($90,000 – $24,000) of after-tax cash savings from operations. This amount is equivalent to $110,000 [$66,000 ÷ (1.0 – .4)] of before-tax operating cash savings.

Answer (A) is incorrect because $90,000 is the total desired annual after-tax cash savings. Answer (C) is incorrect because $114,000 results from adding, not subtracting, the $24,000 of tax depreciation savings to determine the minimum annual after-tax operating savings. Answer (D) is incorrect because $150,000 assumes that depreciation is not tax deductible.

## 13.3 Cost of Capital

**43.** A firm's optimal capital structure

   A.  Minimizes the firm's tax liability.

   B.  Minimizes the firm's risk.

   C.  Maximizes the firm's degree of financial leverage.

   D.  Maximizes the price of the firm's stock.

The correct answer is (D). *(CIA, adapted)*

**REQUIRED:** The optimal capital structure.

**DISCUSSION:** Standard financial theory states that the optimal capital structure of a firm is the permanent, long-term financing of the firm represented by long-term debt, preferred stock, and common stock. Capital structure is distinguished from financial structure, which includes short-term debt plus the long-term accounts. The optimal capital structure minimizes the weighted-average cost of capital and thereby maximizes the value of the firm reflected in its stock price.

Answer (A) is incorrect because a high debt ratio minimizes taxes but might not maximize shareholder wealth. The risk level may be unacceptable. Answer (B) is incorrect because a low debt ratio minimizes risk but might not maximize shareholder wealth. The potential return may be unacceptable. Answer (C) is incorrect because maximum financial leverage results in excessive risk and therefore would not maximize shareholder wealth.

**44.** The firm's marginal cost of capital

   A.  Should be the same as the firm's rate of return on equity.

   B.  Is unaffected by the firm's capital structure.

   C.  Is inversely related to the firm's required rate of return used in capital budgeting.

   D.  Is a weighted average of the investors' required returns on debt and equity.

The correct answer is (D). *(CMA, adapted)*

**REQUIRED:** The true statement about the marginal cost of capital.

**DISCUSSION:** The marginal cost of capital is the cost of the next dollar of capital. The marginal cost continually increases because the lower cost sources of funds are used first. The marginal cost represents a weighted average of both debt and equity capital.

Answer (A) is incorrect because, if the cost of capital were the same as the rate of return on equity (which is usually higher than that of debt capital), there would be no incentive to invest. Answer (B) is incorrect because the marginal cost of capital is affected by the degree of debt in the firm's capital structure. Financial risk plays a role in the returns desired by investors. Answer (C) is incorrect because the rate of return used for capital budgeting should be at least as high as the marginal cost of capital.

**45.** A firm seeking to optimize its capital budget has calculated its marginal cost of capital and projected rates of return on several potential projects. The optimal capital budget is determined by

    A. Calculating the point at which marginal cost of capital meets the projected rate of return, assuming that the most profitable projects are accepted first.

    B. Calculating the point at which average marginal cost meets average projected rate of return, assuming the largest projects are accepted first.

    C. Accepting all potential projects with projected rates of return exceeding the lowest marginal cost of capital.

    D. Accepting all potential projects with projected rates of return lower than the highest marginal cost of capital.

The correct answer is (A). *(CIA, adapted)*
    **REQUIRED:** The determinant of the optimal capital budget.
    **DISCUSSION:** In economics, a basic principle is that a firm should increase output until marginal cost equals marginal revenue. Similarly, the optimal capital budget is determined by calculating the point at which marginal cost of capital (which increases as capital requirements increase) and marginal efficiency of investment (which decreases if the most profitable projects are accepted first) intersect.
    Answer (B) is incorrect because the intersection of average marginal cost with average projected rates of return when the largest (not most profitable) projects are accepted first offers no meaningful capital budgeting conclusion. Answer (C) is incorrect because the optimal capital budget may exclude profitable projects as lower-cost capital goes first to projects with higher rates of return. Answer (D) is incorrect because accepting projects with rates of return lower than the cost of capital is not rational.

**46.** In referring to the graph of a firm's cost of capital, if e is the current position, which one of the following statements best explains the saucer or U-shaped curve?

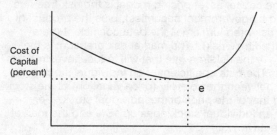

    A. The cost of capital is almost always favorably influenced by increases in financial leverage.

    B. The cost of capital is almost always negatively influenced by increases in financial leverage.

    C. The financial markets will penalize firms that borrow even in moderate amounts.

    D. Use of at least some debt financing will enhance the value of the firm.

The correct answer is (D). *(CMA, adapted)*
    **REQUIRED:** The best explanation of the U-shaped curve in a cost-of-capital graph.
    **DISCUSSION:** The U-shaped curve indicates that the cost of capital is quite high when the debt-to-equity ratio is quite low. As debt increases, the cost of capital declines as long as the cost of debt is less than that of equity. Eventually, the decline in the cost of capital levels off because the cost of debt ultimately rises as more debt is used. Additional increases in debt (relative to equity) will then increase the cost of capital. The implication is that some debt is present in the optimal capital structure because the cost of capital initially declines when debt is added. However, a point is reached at which debt becomes excessive and the cost of capital begins to rise.
    Answer (A) is incorrect because the cost of debt does not remain constant as financial leverage increases. Eventually, that cost also increases. Answer (B) is incorrect because increased leverage is initially favorable. Answer (C) is incorrect because the initial decline in the U-shaped graph indicates that the financial markets reward moderate levels of debt.

**47.** An analysis of a company's planned equity financing using the capital asset pricing model (or security market line) would incorporate only the

    A. Expected market earnings, the current U.S. Treasury bond yield, and the beta coefficient.

    B. Expected market earnings and the price-earnings ratio.

    C. Current U.S. Treasury bond yield, the price-earnings ratio, and the beta coefficient.

    D. Current U.S. Treasury bond yield and the dividend payout ratio.

The correct answer is (A). *(CMA, adapted)*
    **REQUIRED:** The components of the capital asset pricing model.
    **DISCUSSION:** The capital asset pricing model adds the risk-free rate to the product of the market risk premium and the beta coefficient. The market risk premium is the amount above the risk-free rate (approximated by the U.S. Treasury bond yield) that must be paid to induce investment in the market. The beta coefficient of an individual stock is the correlation between the price volatility of the stock market as a whole and the price volatility of the individual stock.
    Answers (B), (C), and (D) are incorrect because the price-earnings ratio and the dividend payout are not included in the model.

**48.** Which of the changes in leverage would apply to a company that substantially increases its investment in fixed assets as a proportion of total assets and replaces some of its long-term debt with equity?

|  | Financial Leverage | Operating Leverage |
|---|---|---|
| A. | Increase | Decrease |
| B. | Decrease | Increase |
| C. | Increase | Increase |
| D. | Decrease | Decrease |

The correct answer is (B). *(CIA, adapted)*
**REQUIRED:** The change applicable when fixed assets and equity increase.
**DISCUSSION:** Leverage is the amount of the fixed cost of capital, principally debt, in a firm's capital structure relative to its operating income. It is also defined as the ratio of debt to total assets or debt to capital. Leverage, by definition, creates financial risk, which relates directly to the question of the cost of capital. The more leverage, the higher the financial risk, and the higher the cost of debt capital. An increase in the equity component of the capital structure, however, decreases financial leverage. Operating leverage is based on the degree that fixed costs are used in the production process. A company with a high percentage of fixed costs is riskier than a firm in the same industry that relies more on variable costs to produce. When fixed assets increase, operating leverage also increases.

Answers (A), (C), and (D) are incorrect because financial leverage would decrease, and operating leverage would increase.

**49.** A measure that describes the risk of an investment project relative to other investments in general is the

A. Coefficient of variation.

B. Beta coefficient.

C. Standard deviation.

D. Expected return.

The correct answer is (B). *(CIA, adapted)*
**REQUIRED:** The measure of the risk of an investment relative to investments in general.
**DISCUSSION:** The required rate of return on equity capital in the capital asset pricing model is the risk-free rate (determined by government securities), plus the product of the market risk premium times the beta coefficient (beta measures the firm's risk). The market risk premium is the amount above the risk-free rate that will induce investment in the market. The beta coefficient of an individual stock is the correlation between the volatility (price variation) of the stock market and that of the price of the individual stock. For example, if an individual stock goes up 15% and the market only 10%, beta is 1.5.

Answer (A) is incorrect because the coefficient of variation compares risk with expected return (standard deviation ÷ expected return). Answer (C) is incorrect because standard deviation measures dispersion (risk) of project returns. Answer (D) is incorrect because expected return does not describe risk.

**50.** A company's beta value has decreased because of a change in its marketing strategy. Consequently, the discount rate applied to expected cash flows of potential projects will be

A. Reduced.

B. Increased.

C. Unchanged.

D. Zero.

The correct answer is (A). *(CIA, adapted)*
**REQUIRED:** The effect of a decrease in beta value on the discount rate applied to cash flows of potential projects.
**DISCUSSION:** There is a positive relationship between a firm's beta value and the discount rate applied to cash flows. Thus, a decrease in beta value will reduce the discount rate.

Answer (B) is incorrect because the discount rate will be reduced, not increased. Answer (C) is incorrect because the discount rate will be reduced. Answer (D) is incorrect because a zero discount rate incorrectly suggests that future cash flows do not need to be discounted for evaluation purposes.

**51.** A company has made the decision to finance next year's capital projects through debt rather than additional equity. The benchmark cost of capital for these projects should be

   A. The before-tax cost of new-debt financing.

   B. The after-tax cost of new-debt financing.

   C. The cost of equity financing.

   D. The weighted-average cost of capital.

The correct answer is (D). *(CIA, adapted)*
   **REQUIRED:** The benchmark cost of capital.
   **DISCUSSION:** A weighted average of the costs of all financing sources should be used, with the weights determined by the usual financing proportions. The terms of any financing raised at the time of initiating a particular project do not represent the cost of capital for the firm. When a firm achieves its optimal capital structure, the weighted-average cost of capital is minimized.
   Answers (A), (B), and (C) are incorrect because the cost of capital is a composite, or weighted average, of all financing sources in their usual proportions. The cost of capital should also be calculated on an after-tax basis.

**52.** When a company increases its degree of financial leverage (DFL),

   A. The equity beta of the company falls.

   B. The systematic risk of the company falls.

   C. The systematic risk of the company rises.

   D. The standard deviation of returns on the equity of the company rises.

The correct answer is (D). *(CIA, adapted)*
   **REQUIRED:** The effect of increasing the DFL.
   **DISCUSSION:** The DFL equals the percentage change in earnings available to common shareholders divided by the percentage change in net operating income. When the DFL rises, fixed interest charges and the riskiness of the firm rise. As a result, the variability of the returns to equity holders will increase. In other words, the standard deviation of returns on the equity of the company rises.
   Answer (A) is incorrect because an increase in the DFL increases the riskiness of the firm's stock. Thus, beta rises. Beta is a measure of the volatility of a firm's stock price relative to the average stock. Answers (B) and (C) are incorrect because systematic risk, also known as market risk, is unrelated to the DFL. Systematic risk is not specific to a company. It is the risk associated with a company's stock that cannot be diversified because it arises from factors that affect all stocks.

**53.** In its first year of operations, a firm had $50,000 of fixed operating costs. It sold 10,000 units at a $10 unit price and incurred variable costs of $4 per unit. If all prices and costs will be the same in the second year and sales are projected to rise to 25,000 units, what will the degree of operating leverage (the extent to which fixed costs are used in the firm's operations) be in the second year?

   A. 1.25

   B. 1.50

   C. 2.0

   D. 6.0

The correct answer is (B). *(CIA, adapted)*
   **REQUIRED:** The degree of operating leverage (DOL) in the second year.
   **DISCUSSION:** The DOL may be calculated as the contribution margin (sales – variable cost) divided by the excess of the contribution margin over fixed costs. The contribution margin is $150,000 [25,000 units x ($10 unit price – $4 unit variable cost)]. Hence, the DOL in the second year is 1.50 [$150,000 CM ÷ ($150,000 – $50,000 FC)].
   Answer (A) is incorrect because 1.25 ignores variable costs. Answer (C) is incorrect because 2.0 uses the first-year sales level and ignores variable costs. Answer (D) is incorrect because 6.0 uses the first-year sales level.

**54.** If a company has a higher dividend-payout ratio, then, if all else is equal, it will have

   A. A higher marginal cost of capital.

   B. A lower marginal cost of capital.

   C. A higher investment opportunity schedule.

   D. A lower investment opportunity schedule.

The correct answer is (A). *(CIA, adapted)*
   **REQUIRED:** The effect of a higher dividend-payout ratio.
   **DISCUSSION:** The higher the dividend-payout ratio, the sooner retained earnings are exhausted and the company must seek external financing. Assuming the same investments are undertaken, the result is a higher marginal cost of capital because lower-cost capital sources will be used up earlier.
   Answer (B) is incorrect because the marginal cost of capital is higher. Answers (C) and (D) are incorrect because the existence of investment opportunities is unrelated to the dividend payout.

**55.** If two companies, company X and company Y, are alike in all respects except that company X employs more debt financing and less equity financing than company Y does, which of the following statements is true?

    A.  Company X has more net earnings variability than company Y.

    B.  Company X has more operating earnings variability than company Y.

    C.  Company X has less operating earnings variability than company Y.

    D.  Company X has less financial leverage than company Y.

The correct answer is (A). *(CIA, adapted)*
    **REQUIRED:** The true statement regarding a company's debt and equity financing.
    **DISCUSSION:** Given that company X is more highly leveraged, it has greater fixed financing charges than company Y. Interest payments are fixed financing charges, but common share dividends are not. As a result, company X will be more risky and therefore will have a more volatile net income stream than company Y, if other factors are constant.
    Answers (B) and (C) are incorrect because the level of fixed financing charges does not affect operating income variability. Answer (D) is incorrect because company X has greater, not less, financial leverage than company Y. Greater use of debt financing means that a company has greater financial leverage.

**56.** A firm must select from among several methods of financing arrangements when meeting its capital requirements. To acquire additional growth capital while attempting to maximize earnings per share, a firm should normally

    A.  Attempt to increase both debt and equity in equal proportions, which preserves a stable capital structure and maintains investor confidence.

    B.  Select debt over equity initially, even though increased debt is accompanied by interest costs and a degree of risk.

    C.  Select equity over debt initially, which minimizes risk and avoids interest costs.

    D.  Discontinue dividends and use current cash flow, which avoids the cost and risk of increased debt and the dilution of EPS through increased equity.

The correct answer is (B). *(CIA, adapted)*
    **REQUIRED:** The financing arrangement that should be selected to acquire additional growth capital while attempting to maximize earnings per share.
    **DISCUSSION:** Earnings per share will ordinarily be higher if debt is used to raise capital instead of equity, provided that the firm is not over-leveraged. The reason is that the cost of debt is lower than the cost of equity because interest is tax deductible. However, the prospect of higher EPS is accompanied by greater risk to the firm resulting from required interest costs, creditors' liens on the firm's assets, and the possibility of a proportionately lower EPS if sales volume fails to meet projections.
    Answer (A) is incorrect because EPS is not a function of investor confidence and is not maximized by concurrent proportional increases in both debt and equity. EPS are usually higher if debt is used instead of equity to raise capital, at least initially. Answer (C) is incorrect because equity capital is initially more costly than debt. Answer (D) is incorrect because using only current cash flow to raise capital is usually too conservative an approach for a growth-oriented firm. Management is expected to be willing to take acceptable risks to be competitive and attain an acceptable rate of growth.

**57.** The market value of a firm's outstanding common shares will be higher, everything else equal, if

    A.  Investors have a lower required return on equity.

    B.  Investors expect lower dividend growth.

    C.  Investors have longer expected holding periods.

    D.  Investors have shorter expected holding periods.

The correct answer is (A). *(CIA, adapted)*
    **REQUIRED:** The item resulting in a higher market value for common shares.
    **DISCUSSION:** The dividend growth model is used to calculate the cost of equity. The simplified formula is

$$R = \frac{D}{P} + G$$

R is the required rate of return, D is the next dividend, P is the stock's price, and G is the growth rate in earnings per share. The equation is also used to determine the stock price.

$$P = \frac{D}{R - G}$$

Thus, when investors have a lower required return on equity, the denominator is smaller, which translates into a higher market value.
    Answer (B) is incorrect because, if investors expect lower dividend growth, the market value of common shares will decrease. Answers (C) and (D) are incorrect because the expected holding periods of investors are not related to the market value of the common shares.

**58.** Assume that nominal interest rates just increased substantially but that the expected future dividends for a company over the long run were not affected. As a result of the increase in nominal interest rates, the company's stock price should

- A. Increase.
- B. Decrease.
- C. Stay constant.
- D. Change, but in no obvious direction.

The correct answer is (B). *(CIA, adapted)*
**REQUIRED:** The effect on a company's stock price of an increase in nominal interest rates.
**DISCUSSION:** The dividend growth model is used to calculate the price of stock.

$$P_0 = \frac{D_1}{R_s - G}$$

If: $P_0$ = current price
$D_1$ = next dividend
$R_s$ = required rate of return
$G$ = EPS growth rate

Assuming that $D_1$ and $G$ remain constant, an increase in $R_s$ resulting from an increase in the nominal interest rate will cause $P_0$ to decrease.

Answers (A), (C), and (D) are incorrect because a higher interest rate raises the required return of investors, which results in a lower stock price.

**59.** A company has 10,000 outstanding shares with a market value of $25 each. It just paid a $1 per share dividend. Dividends are expected to grow at a constant rate of 10%. If flotation costs are 5% of the selling price, the cost of new equity financing is calculated by the following formula:

A. $\dfrac{\text{Dividend at time zero}}{\text{Market price}}$ + Dividend growth rate

= ($1.10 ÷ $25) + .10

= .04 + .10 = 14.00%

B. $\dfrac{\text{Dividend at time zero}}{\text{Net proceeds}}$ + Dividend growth rate

= ($1 ÷ $23.75) + .10

= .0421 + .10 = 14.21%

C. $\dfrac{\text{Expected dividend at end of period}}{\text{Market price}}$ + Dividend growth rate

= ($1.10 ÷ $25) + .10

= .044 + .10 = 14.40%

D. $\dfrac{\text{Expected dividend at end of period}}{\text{Net proceeds issuing one share}}$ + Dividend growth rate

= [$1(1.1) ÷ $23.75] + .10

= .0463 + .10 = 14.63%

The correct answer is (D). *(CIA, adapted)*
**REQUIRED:** The cost of new equity financing.
**DISCUSSION:** The cost of new equity is calculated by adding the expected dividend yield, based on the net proceeds of the new issue, to the expected dividend growth rate. The expected dividend at the end of the period equals the dividend at time zero times one plus the expected dividend growth rate. Net proceeds received by the firm when issuing one common share equals the market price of a share times one minus the flotation cost percentage. Flotation costs include items such as underwriting fees, printing, and advertising. The calculation of the cost of new equity is as follows:

$$\frac{\text{Expected dividend at end of period}}{\text{Net proceeds issuing one share}} + \text{Dividend growth rate}$$

$$= \frac{\$1(1 + .10)}{\$25(1 - .05)} + 10\%$$

$$= 14.63\%$$

Answer (A) is incorrect because the end-of-period expected dividend and the net proceeds of the issue should be included in calculating the dividend yield. Answer (B) is incorrect because the end-of-period expected dividend should be included in calculating the dividend yield. Answer (C) is incorrect because the net proceeds, not market price, should be included in calculating the dividend yield.

**60.** The marginal cost of debt for a firm is defined as the interest rate on <List A> debt minus the <List B>.

| | List A | List B |
|---|---|---|
| A. | New | Firm's marginal tax rate |
| B. | Outstanding | Firm's marginal tax rate |
| C. | New | Interest rate times the firm's marginal tax rate |
| D. | Outstanding | Interest rate times the firm's marginal tax rate |

The correct answer is (C). *(CIA, adapted)*
**REQUIRED:** The definition of the marginal cost of debt.
**DISCUSSION:** The marginal cost of debt must equal the cost of new debt minus the tax savings. Hence, marginal cost equals the cost of new debt times one minus the marginal tax rate, or $K_d(1 - T)$. This expression equals $K_d - K_dT$.

Answers (A), (B), and (D) are incorrect because the marginal cost of debt financing is the interest rate on new debt minus the firm's marginal tax rate multiplied by the interest rate. Moreover, the marginal or incremental cost of debt to the firm is based on the cost of newly issued debt, not on the cost of outstanding debt.

---

Questions 61 through 64 are based on the following information. A company has the following three investment projects available:

| Project | Cost | Internal Rate of Return |
|---|---|---|
| A | $ 50 million | 14% |
| B | $ 75 million | 12% |
| C | $125 million | 8% |

The company has a 40% debt and 60% equity capital structure. Each dollar of investment funds will be raised in these proportions (40 cents of debt and 60 cents of equity).

The marginal cost of financing increases with the amount of new funds raised, as follows:

| Interval | Amount Raised | Weighted-Average Cost of Capital |
|---|---|---|
| 1 | First $ 75 million | 6% |
| 2 | Next $100 million | 10% |
| 3 | Over $175 million | 12% |

These investment opportunities and financing costs are shown in the graph below:

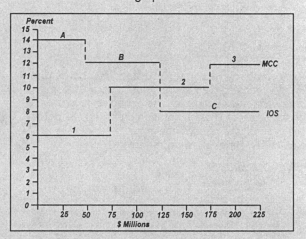

MCC - Margin cost of capital
IOS - Investment opportunity schedule

---

**61.** The investment opportunity schedule (IOS) shows, in rank order, how much money the company would invest at different rates of return. Such schedules can be drawn only for a set of projects that

A. Have the same investment cost.

B. Are mutually exclusive.

C. Have the same net present value.

D. Are independent.

The correct answer is (D). *(CIA, adapted)*
**REQUIRED:** The characteristics of projects on an IOS.
**DISCUSSION:** An IOS schedule is drawn for a set of independent projects. The decision to be made is whether to accept or reject each project without regard to other investment opportunities. Thus, the cash flows of one independent project are not influenced by those of another. Independence should be distinguished from mutual exclusivity. Projects are mutually exclusive if acceptance of one requires rejection of the other.

Answer (A) is incorrect because IOS schedules do not require that all projects have the same investment cost. The steps of the schedule can be of varying lengths. Answer (B) is incorrect because IOS schedules cannot be drawn for mutually exclusive projects. Answer (C) is incorrect because IOS schedules do not require that all projects have the same NPV. The NPV of each project depends on the investment cost and on the present value of the expected cash flows. Both costs and cash flows can vary for projects on an IOS.

**62.** The company should invest in Project(s)
<List A> and has an optimal capital budget of
<List B> million dollars.

|   | List A | List B |
|---|--------|--------|
| A. | B only | 75 |
| B. | A and B only | 125 |
| C. | A and C only | 175 |
| D. | C only | 125 |

The correct answer is (B). *(CIA, adapted)*
**REQUIRED:** The project(s) in which the company should invest and its optimal capital budget.
**DISCUSSION:** The intersection of the IOS and MCC schedules determines the cost of capital and the optimal capital budget. The company should begin with the project having the highest return and continue accepting projects as long as the IRR exceeds the MCC. The highest ranked project is A, with a $50 million cost and a 14% IRR. The MCC is only 6% over this range of financing. The next highest ranked project is B, with a $75 million cost and a 12% IRR. When $125 million has been invested, the marginal cost of the next dollar of capital is 10%, so Project B is also acceptable, bringing the optimal capital budget to $125 million. Project C is not acceptable because it has an 8% return. The MCC is 10% for the first $50 million invested in this project and 12% for the remaining $75 million.

Answer (A) is incorrect because both A and B should be undertaken. Answer (C) is incorrect because A is acceptable, but C is not. Answer (D) is incorrect because C is not acceptable. It offers an IRR less than the marginal cost of financing the project.

**63.** Without prejudice to your answer to question 36, assume that the optimal capital budget for the company is $150 million. The marginal cost of capital and the appropriate discount rate to use in evaluating investment proposals for this company would be

A. 6%

B. 8%

C. 10%

D. 12%

The correct answer is (C). *(CIA, adapted)*
**REQUIRED:** The marginal cost of capital and the appropriate discount rate.
**DISCUSSION:** The appropriate discount rate (the cost of capital used in capital budgeting) theoretically is determined at the intersection of the IOS and MCC schedules. This intersection is at an MCC of 10% and an optimal capital budget of $125 million. However, if the optimal capital budget is assumed to be $150 million, the company is still in the second interval of the MCC schedule. The marginal cost of financing in this part of the schedule is 10%.

Answer (A) is incorrect because 6% applies only to the first $75 million of new financing. Given that the optimal capital budget exceeds $75 million, 6% cannot be the discount rate. Answer (B) is incorrect because 8% is the IRR of Project C. Answer (D) is incorrect because, at an investment level of $150 million, the MCC is 10%.

**64.** The marginal cost of capital (MCC) curve for this company rises twice, first when the company has raised $75 million and again when $175 million of new funds has been raised. These increases in the MCC are caused by

A. Increases in the returns on the additional investments undertaken.

B. Decreases in the returns on the additional investments undertaken.

C. Decreases in the cost of at least one of the financing sources.

D. Increases in the cost of at least one of the financing sources.

The correct answer is (D). *(CIA, adapted)*
**REQUIRED:** The reason for the increases in the MCC.
**DISCUSSION:** The MCC is a weighted average of the costs of the different financing sources. If the cost of any source of financing increases, the MCC curve will rise. The MCC curve is upward sloping because the lowest cost financing sources are assumed to be used first. Thus, as cumulative debt increases, the cost of debt also increases.

Answers (A) and (B) are incorrect because financing costs do not depend on rates of return on investment. Answer (C) is incorrect because, as additional funds are raised, an increase in the cost of a source of financing, not a decrease, will result in an increase in the MCC.

**65.** The three elements needed to estimate the cost of equity capital for use in determining a firm's weighted-average cost of capital are

- A. Current dividends per share, expected growth rate in dividends per share, and current book value per share of common stock.

- B. Current earnings per share, expected growth rate in dividends per share, and current market price per share of common stock.

- C. Current earnings per share, expected growth rate in earnings per share, and current book value per share of common stock.

- D. Current dividends per share, expected growth rate in dividends per share, and current market price per share of common stock.

The correct answer is (D). *(CMA, adapted)*
**REQUIRED:** The three elements needed to estimate the cost of equity when determining a firm's weighted-average cost of capital.
**DISCUSSION:** The Gordon (dividend) growth model requires three elements to estimate the cost of equity capital. These are the dividends per share, the expected growth rate in dividends per share, and the market price of the stock. Basically, the cost of equity capital can be computed as the dividend yield (dividends ÷ price) plus the growth rate.
Answer (A) is incorrect because book value per share is not a consideration in computing the cost of equity capital. Answer (B) is incorrect because current dividends, not current earnings, per share are a requirement for the formula. Answer (C) is incorrect because book value per share is not a consideration in computing the cost of equity capital. Also, current dividends, not current earnings, per share are a requirement for the formula.

**66.** If k is the cost of debt and t is the marginal tax rate, the after-tax cost of debt, $k_i$, is best represented by the formula

- A. $k_i = k/t$

- B. $k_i = k/(1-t)$

- C. $k_i = k(t)$

- D. $k_i = k(1-t)$

The correct answer is (D). *(CMA, adapted)*
**REQUIRED:** The formula representing the after-tax cost of debt.
**DISCUSSION:** The after-tax cost of debt is the cost of debt times the quantity one minus the tax rate. For example, the after-tax cost of a 10% bond is 7% [10% x (1 – 30%)] if the tax rate is 30%.
Answers (A) and (B) are incorrect because the after-tax cost of debt is the cost of debt times the quantity one minus the tax rate. Answer (C) is incorrect because the cost of debt times the marginal tax rate equals the tax savings from issuing debt.

**67.** In general, it is more expensive for a company to finance with equity capital than with debt capital because

- A. Long-term bonds have a maturity date and must therefore be repaid in the future.

- B. Investors are exposed to greater risk with equity capital.

- C. Equity capital is in greater demand than debt capital.

- D. Dividends fluctuate to a greater extent than interest rates.

The correct answer is (B). *(CMA, adapted)*
**REQUIRED:** The reason equity financing is more expensive than debt financing.
**DISCUSSION:** Providers of equity capital are exposed to more risk than are lenders because the firm is not obligated to pay them a return. Also, in case of liquidation, creditors are paid before equity investors. Thus, equity financing is more expensive than debt because equity investors require a higher return to compensate for the greater risk assumed.
Answer (A) is incorrect because the obligation to repay at a specific maturity date reduces the risk to investors and thus the required return. Answer (C) is incorrect because the demand for equity capital is directly related to its greater cost to the issuer. Answer (D) is incorrect because dividends are based on managerial discretion and may rarely change; interest rates, however, fluctuate daily based on the market.

**68.** The explicit cost of debt financing is the interest expense. The implicit cost(s) of debt financing is (are) the

- A. Increase in the cost of debt as the debt-to-equity ratio increases.

- B. Increases in the cost of debt and equity as the debt-to-equity ratio increases.

- C. Increase in the cost of equity as the debt-to-equity ratio decreases.

- D. Decrease in the weighted-average cost of capital as the debt-to-equity ratio increases.

The correct answer is (B). *(CMA, adapted)*
   **REQUIRED:** The implicit cost of debt financing.
   **DISCUSSION:** Debt capital often appears to have a lower cost than equity because the implicit costs are not obvious. The implicit costs are attributable to the increased risk created by the additional debt burden. Thus, as the debt-to-equity ratio increases, the cost of both debt and equity will increase given the increased risk to both share-holders and creditors from a higher degree of leverage. An explanation based on the marginal cost of capital and the marginal efficiency of investment leads to the same conclu-sion. Lower-cost capital sources are used first. Additional projects must then be undertaken with funds from higher-cost sources. Similarly, risk is increased because the most profitable investments are made initially, leaving the less profitable investments for the future.
   Answer (A) is incorrect because both debt and equity sources increase in cost as leverage increases. Answer (C) is incorrect because equity costs decline as leverage decreases. Answer (D) is incorrect because the weighted-average cost of capital will increase with increased leverage.

**69.** All of the following are examples of imputed costs except

- A. The stated interest paid on a bank loan.

- B. The use of the firm's internal cash funds to purchase assets.

- C. Assets that are considered obsolete that maintain a net book value.

- D. Decelerated depreciation.

The correct answer is (A). *(CMA, adapted)*
   **REQUIRED:** The item not an example of imputed costs.
   **DISCUSSION:** An imputed cost is one that has to be estimated. It is a cost that exists but is not specifically stated and is the result of a process designed to recognize eco-nomic reality. An imputed cost may not require a dollar outlay formally recognized by the accounting system, but it is relevant to the decision-making process. For example, the stated interest on a bank loan is not an imputed cost because it is specifically stated and requires a dollar outlay. But the cost of using retained earnings as a source of capital is unstated and has to be imputed.
   Answer (B) is incorrect because the cost of internally generated funds is unstated. Answer (C) is incorrect because the cost of obsolete assets should be written off. Answer (D) is incorrect because understated depreciation results in unstated costs.

Questions 70 through 72 are based on the following information. Carlisle Company currently sells 400,000 bottles of perfume each year. Each bottle costs $.84 to produce and sells for $1.00. Fixed costs are $28,000 per year. The firm has annual interest expense of $6,000, preferred stock dividends of $2,000 per year, and a 40% tax rate.

**70.** The degree of operating leverage for Carlisle Company is

A. 2.4

B. 1.78

C. 2.13

D. 1.2

The correct answer is (B). *(CMA, adapted)*

**REQUIRED:** The degree of operating leverage.

**DISCUSSION:** Operating leverage is the percentage change in operating income resulting from a percentage change in sales. It measures how a change in volume affects profits. An alternative formula for operating leverage divides contribution margin by the contribution margin minus fixed costs. Companies with larger investments and greater fixed costs ordinarily have higher contribution margins and more operating leverage. The degree of operating leverage measures the extent to which fixed assets are used in the production process. A company with a high percentage of fixed costs is more risky than a firm in the same industry that relies more on variable costs to produce. Based on a contribution margin of $.16 per unit ($1 − $.84 variable cost), the degree of operating leverage is

$$(400,000 \times \$.16) \div [(400,000 \times \$.16) - \$28,000] = 1.78$$

Answer (A) is incorrect because 2.4 is obtained by overstating the contribution margin or the fixed costs. Answer (C) is incorrect because 2.13 includes a nonoperating expense (interest) as a fixed cost. Answer (D) is incorrect because 1.2 is obtained by understating the $64,000 contribution margin or understating the $28,000 of fixed costs.

**71.** The degree of financial leverage for Carlisle Company is

A. 2.4

B. 1.78

C. 1.35

D. 1.2

The correct answer is (C). *(CMA, adapted)*

**REQUIRED:** The degree of financial leverage.

**DISCUSSION:** The degree of financial leverage is the percentage change in earnings available to common shareholders that is associated with a given percentage change in net operating income. Operating income equals earnings before interest and taxes. The more financial leverage employed, the greater the degree of financial leverage and the riskier the firm. An alternative formula for financial leverage divides EBIT by EBIT minus interest and preferred dividends (before tax effect). Earnings before interest and taxes equal $36,000 [$400,000 sales − ($.84 x 400,000 units) VC − $28,000 FC]. Using the second formula, the calculation is as follows:

$$\frac{\$36,000}{\$36,000 - \$6,000 - (\$2,000 \div .6)} = \frac{\$36,000}{\$26,667} = 1.35$$

Answer (A) is incorrect because 2.4 is obtained by overstating the contribution margin or the fixed costs. Answer (B) is incorrect because 1.78 is the degree of operating leverage, not financial leverage. Answer (D) is incorrect because 1.2 is obtained by understating the $64,000 of contribution margin or understating the $28,000 of fixed costs.

**72.** If Carlisle Company did not have preferred stock, the degree of total leverage would

    A.  Decrease in proportion to a decrease in financial leverage.

    B.  Increase in proportion to an increase in financial leverage.

    C.  Remain the same.

    D.  Decrease but not be proportional to the decrease in financial leverage.

The correct answer is (A). *(CMA, adapted)*
    **REQUIRED:** The true statement about the degree of total leverage if the company did not have preferred stock.
    **DISCUSSION:** The degree of total leverage is equal to the degree of operating leverage times the degree of financial leverage. Thus, a decrease in either of these ratios results in a decrease in total leverage. If the company had no preferred stock, the DFL and the DTL would be lower because the pretax income necessary to pay the preferred dividends $[P \div (1 - t)]$ is subtracted from the denominator of the DFL.
    Answer (B) is incorrect because the DTL would decrease, not increase. Answer (C) is incorrect because the elimination of preferred stock would change the equation. Answer (D) is incorrect because the decrease would be proportional.

**73.** Colt, Inc. is planning to use retained earnings to finance anticipated capital expenditures. The beta coefficient for Colt's stock is 1.15, the risk-free rate of interest is 8.5%, and the market return is estimated at 12.4%. If a new issue of common stock were used in this model, the flotation costs would be 7%. By using the capital asset pricing model (CAPM) equation [R = RF + β(RM − RF)], the cost of using retained earnings to finance the capital expenditures is

    A.  13.21%

    B.  12.99%

    C.  12.40%

    D.  14.26%

The correct answer is (B). *(CMA, adapted)*
    **REQUIRED:** The cost of using retained earnings to finance capital expenditures under the CAPM.
    **DISCUSSION:** The CAPM determines the cost of capital by adding the risk-free rate to the product of the market risk premium and the beta coefficient (the beta coefficient is a measure of the firm's risk). The market risk premium is the amount in excess of the risk-free rate that investors must be paid to induce them to enter the market. The 7% flotation costs do not enter into the calculations because the company does not plan to issue common stock. Hence, the cost of retained earnings for Colt is 12.99% [8.5% + 1.15 (12.4% − 8.5%)].
    Answer (A) is incorrect because 13.21% results from using 7% instead of 8.5%. Answer (C) is incorrect because the estimated market return is 12.4%. Answer (D) is incorrect because 14.26% equals 1.15 times 12.4%.

**74.** Newmass, Inc. paid a cash dividend to its common shareholders over the past 12 months of $2.20 per share. The current market value of the common stock is $40 per share, and investors are anticipating the common dividend to grow at a rate of 6% annually. The cost to issue new common stock will be 5% of the market value. The cost of a new common stock issue will be

    A.  11.50%

    B.  11.79%

    C.  11.83%

    D.  12.14%

The correct answer is (D). *(CMA, adapted)*
    **REQUIRED:** The cost of financing by issuing common stock.
    **DISCUSSION:** The cost of equity using the Gordon growth model equals the quotient of the next dividend divided by the stock price, plus the growth rate in earnings per share. To account for flotation costs, the stock price is multiplied by one minus the flotation cost. Given that the next dividend is $2.332 (1.06 x $2.20), the cost of new common stock is 12.14% {[$2.332 ÷ ($40 x (1 − .05))] + .06}.
    Answer (A) is incorrect because the expected future dividend of $2.332 (1.06 x $2.20) should be divided by the adjusted stock price (current market value − the cost of issuing the new common stock). Answer (B) is incorrect because the expected future dividend of $2.332 ($2.20 x 1.06) should be used in calculating the cost of the new common stock issue. Answer (C) is incorrect because the current stock price must be adjusted for the cost of issuing the new common stock.

**75.** Datacomp Industries, which has no current debt, has a beta of .95 for its common stock. Management is considering a change in the capital structure to 30% debt and 70% equity. This change would increase the beta on the stock to 1.05, and the after-tax cost of debt will be 7.5%. The expected return on equity is 16%, and the risk-free rate is 6%. Should Datacomp's management proceed with the capital structure change?

A. No, because the cost of equity capital will increase.

B. Yes, because the cost of equity capital will decrease.

C. Yes, because the weighted-average cost of capital will decrease.

D. No, because the weighted-average cost of capital will increase.

The correct answer is (C). *(CMA, adapted)*

**REQUIRED:** The correct decision regarding a proposed capital structure change and the reason for it.

**DISCUSSION:** The important consideration is whether the overall cost of capital will be lower for a given proposal. According to the capital asset pricing model, the change will result in a lower average cost of capital. For the existing structure, the cost of equity capital is 15.5% [6% + .95 (16% – 6%)]. Because the company has no debt, the average cost of capital is also 15.5%. Under the proposal, the cost of equity capital is 16.5% [6% + 1.05 (16% – 6%)], and the weighted-average cost of capital is 13.8% [.3(.075) + .7(.165)]. Hence, the proposal of 13.8% should be accepted.

Answers (A) and (B) are incorrect because the average cost of capital needs to be considered. Answer (D) is incorrect because the weighted-average cost of capital will decrease.

**76.** Enert, Inc.'s current capital structure is shown below. This structure is optimal, and the company wishes to maintain it.

| | |
|---|---|
| Debt | 25% |
| Preferred equity | 5 |
| Common equity | 70 |

Enert's management is planning to build a $75 million facility that will be financed according to this desired capital structure. Currently, $15 million of cash is available for capital expansion. The percentage of the $75 million that will come from a new issue of common stock is

A. 52.50%

B. 50.00%

C. 56.25%

D. 56.00%

The correct answer is (D). *(CMA, adapted)*

**REQUIRED:** The percentage of the new financing needed that will come from a new issue of common stock.

**DISCUSSION:** Because $15 million is already available, the company must finance $60 million ($75 million – $15 million). Of this amount, 70%, or $42 million, should come from the issuance of common stock to maintain the current capital structure. The $42 million represents 56% of the total $75 million.

Answers (A), (B), and (C) are incorrect because the percentage of the $75 million that will come from a new issue of common stock is determined by multiplying the net cash needed for the project times the desired percentage of common equity in the capital structure and dividing this product by the total cost of the project.

**77.** Wiley's new financing will be in proportion to the market value of its present financing, shown below.

|  | Book Value ($000 Omitted) |
|---|---|
| Long-term debt | $7,000 |
| Preferred stock (100,000 shares) | 1,000 |
| Common stock (200,000 shares) | 7,000 |

The firm's bonds are currently selling at 80% of par, generating a current market yield of 9%, and the corporation has a 40% tax rate. The preferred stock is selling at its par value and pays a 6% dividend. The common stock has a current market value of $40 and is expected to pay a $1.20 per share dividend this fiscal year. Dividend growth is expected to be 10% per year. Wiley's weighted-average cost of capital is (round your calculations to tenths of a percent)

- A. 13.0%
- B. 8.3%
- C. 9.6%
- D. 9.0%

The correct answer is (C). *(CMA, adapted)*
**REQUIRED:** The weighted-average cost of capital.
**DISCUSSION:** The first step is to determine the after-tax cost of the long-term debt. Multiplying the current yield of 9% times one minus the tax rate (1 − .4 = .6) results in an after-tax cost of debt of 5.4% (9% x .6). The cost of the preferred stock is 6% (the annual dividend rate). The Gordon growth model for measuring the cost of equity capital combines the dividend yield with the growth rate. Dividing the $1.20 dividend by the $40 market price produces a dividend yield of 3%. Adding the 3% dividend yield and the 10% growth rate gives a 13% cost of common equity capital.

Once the costs of the three types of capital have been computed, the next step is to weight them according to the market values of the elements of the current capital structure. The $1,000,000 of preferred stock is selling at par. The market value of the long-term debt is 80% of book value, or $5,600,000 (80% x $7,000,000). The common stock has a current market price of $8,000,000 ($40 x 200,000 shares). Thus, the weighted-average cost of capital is 9.6% ($1,402,000 ÷ $14,600,000), as shown below.

| | | | | | |
|---|---|---|---|---|---|
| Debt | .054 × | $ 5,600,000 | = | $ 302,400 |
| Preferred | .06 × | $ 1,000,000 | = | $ 60,000 |
| Common | .13 × | $ 8,000,000 | = | $1,040,000 |
| Total | | $14,600,000 | | $1,402,400 |

Answer (A) is incorrect because 13% is the cost of equity. Answer (B) is incorrect because 8.3% is the simple average. Answer (D) is incorrect because 9% is based on book values.

## 13.4 Net Present Value

**78.** The capital budgeting technique known as net present value uses

| | Cash Flow over Life of Project | Time Value of Money |
|---|---|---|
| A. | No | Yes |
| B. | No | No |
| C. | Yes | No |
| D. | Yes | Yes |

The correct answer is (D). *(CPA, adapted)*
**REQUIRED:** The variable(s) considered in the NPV calculation.
**DISCUSSION:** The NPV is the difference between the present value of the future cash flows from the project discounted at an appropriate interest rate and the initial investment. If the NPV is zero or greater, the investment may be economically rational. The method is a technique for ranking investment proposals. Consequently, the time value of the cash flows over the life of the project is considered.

Answers (A), (B), and (C) are incorrect because the time value of the cash flows over the life of the project is considered.

**79.** If a firm identifies (or creates) an investment opportunity with a present value <List A> its cost, the value of the firm and the price of its common stock will <List B>.

| | List A | List B |
|---|---|---|
| A. | Greater than | Increase |
| B. | Greater than | Decrease |
| C. | Equal to | Increase |
| D. | Equal to | Decrease |

The correct answer is (A). *(CIA, adapted)*
**REQUIRED:** The effect on the value of the firm and its stock price of investment opportunities.
**DISCUSSION:** Investments with present values in excess of their costs (positive NPVs) that can be identified or created by the capital budgeting activities of the firm will have a positive impact on firm value and on the price of the common stock of the firm. Accordingly, the more effective capital budgeting is, the higher the stock price.

Answer (B) is incorrect because positive NPV investments will increase, not decrease, firm value and share price. Answers (C) and (D) are incorrect because investments with present values equal to their costs have a zero NPV and neither increase nor decrease firm value and share price.

**80.** A disadvantage of the net present value method of capital expenditure evaluation is that it

   A. Is calculated using sensitivity analysis.

   B. Computes the true interest rate.

   C. Does not provide the true rate of return on investment.

   D. Is difficult to adapt for risk.

The correct answer is (C). *(CMA, adapted)*
**REQUIRED:** The disadvantage of the NPV method.
**DISCUSSION:** The NPV method discounts all cash flows from a project, so a discount rate has to be stipulated by the person conducting the analysis. A disadvantage of the NPV method is that it does not provide the true rate of return for an investment; it simply indicates that the rate of return is higher or lower than the stipulated discount rate (which may be the cost of capital).
   Answer (A) is incorrect because the ability to perform sensitivity analysis is an advantage of the NPV method. Answer (B) is incorrect because the NPV method does not compute the true interest rate. Answer (D) is incorrect because the NPV method is easily adapted for risk by increasing the discount rate.

**81.** Amster Corporation has not yet decided on its hurdle rate for use in the evaluation of capital budgeting projects. This lack of information will prohibit Amster from calculating a project's

| | Accounting Rate of Return | Net Present Value | Internal Rate of Return |
|---|---|---|---|
| A. | No | No | No |
| B. | Yes | Yes | Yes |
| C. | No | Yes | Yes |
| D. | No | Yes | No |

The correct answer is (D). *(CMA, adapted)*
**REQUIRED:** The capital budgeting technique(s), if any, that require(s) determination of a hurdle rate.
**DISCUSSION:** A hurdle rate is not necessary in calculating the accounting rate of return. That return is calculated by dividing the net income from a project by the investment in the project. Similarly, a company can calculate the internal rate of return (IRR) without knowing its hurdle rate. The IRR is the discount rate at which the NPV is $0. However, the NPV cannot be calculated without knowing the company's hurdle rate. The NPV method requires that future cash flows be discounted using the hurdle rate.
   Answers (A), (B), and (C) are incorrect because the accounting rate of return and the IRR, but not the NPV, can be calculated without knowing the hurdle rate.

**82.** The proper discount rate to use in calculating certainty equivalent net present value is the

   A. Risk-adjusted discount rate.

   B. Risk-free rate.

   C. Cost of equity capital.

   D. Cost of debt.

The correct answer is (B). *(CMA, adapted)*
**REQUIRED:** The proper discount rate to use in calculating certainty equivalent net present value.
**DISCUSSION:** Rational investors choose projects that yield the best return given some level of risk. If an investor desires no risk, that is, an absolutely certain rate of return, the risk-free rate is used in calculating net present value. The risk-free rate is the return on a risk-free investment such as government bonds.
   Answer (A) is incorrect because a risk-adjusted discount rate does not represent an absolutely certain rate of return. A discount rate is adjusted upward as the investment becomes riskier. Answers (C) and (D) are incorrect because the cost of equity capital and the cost of debt capital do not equate to the certainty equivalence of a risk-free investment's return.

**83.** An advantage of the net present value method over the internal rate of return model in discounted cash flow analysis is that the net present value method

    A.  Computes a desired rate of return for capital projects.

    B.  Can be used when there is no constant rate of return required for each year of the project.

    C.  Uses a discount rate that equates the discounted cash inflows with the outflows.

    D.  Computes the maximum interest rate that can be used over the life of the project to break even.

The correct answer is (B). *(CMA, adapted)*
    **REQUIRED:** The advantage of the NPV method.
    **DISCUSSION:** The IRR method is relatively easy to use when cash inflows are the same from one year to the next. However, when cash inflows differ from year to year, the IRR can be found only through the use of trial and error. In such cases, the NPV method is usually easier to apply. Also, the NPV method can be used when the rate of return required for each year varies. For example, a company might want to achieve a higher rate of return in later years when risk might be greater. Only the NPV method can incorporate varying levels of rates of return.
    Answer (A) is incorrect because the IRR method calculates a rate of return. Answers (C) and (D) are incorrect because the IRR is the rate at which NPV is zero.

**84.** A project's net present value, ignoring income tax considerations, is normally affected by the

    A.  Proceeds from the sale of the asset to be replaced.

    B.  Carrying amount of the asset to be replaced by the project.

    C.  Amount of annual depreciation on the asset to be replaced.

    D.  Amount of annual depreciation on fixed assets used directly on the project.

The correct answer is (A). *(CPA, adapted)*
    **REQUIRED:** The matter affecting a project's net present value.
    **DISCUSSION:** To compute a project's net present value, the initial investment is subtracted from the present value of the after-tax cash flows. The proceeds from the sale of the asset to be replaced reduces the initial investment.
    Answer (B) is incorrect because the carrying amount of the asset to be replaced affects the gain or loss on the sale. Answer (C) is incorrect because the amount of annual depreciation on the asset to be replaced affects the carrying value. Answer (D) is incorrect because annual depreciation of other assets, even if used directly, does not affect the project's net present value.

**85.** The use of an accelerated method instead of the straight-line method of depreciation in computing the net present value of a project has the effect of

    A.  Raising the hurdle rate necessary to justify the project.

    B.  Lowering the net present value of the project.

    C.  Increasing the present value of the depreciation tax shield.

    D.  Increasing the cash outflows at the initial point of the project.

The correct answer is (C). *(CMA, adapted)*
    **REQUIRED:** The effect on NPV of using an accelerated depreciation method.
    **DISCUSSION:** Accelerated depreciation results in greater depreciation in the early years of an asset's life compared with the straight-line method. Thus, accelerated depreciation results in lower income tax expense in the early years of a project and higher income tax expense in the later years. By effectively deferring taxes, the accelerated method increases the present value of the depreciation tax shield.
    Answer (A) is incorrect because the hurdle rate must be stipulated by the decision maker. Answer (B) is incorrect because the greater depreciation tax shield increases the NPV. Answer (D) is incorrect because greater initial depreciation reduces the cash outflows for taxes but has no effect on the initial cash outflows.

Questions 86 and 87 are based on the following information. Federal Internal Revenue Code and Regulations in effect for the calendar year 1998 apply. The tax impact of equipment depreciation affects capital budgeting decisions. Currently, the Modified Accelerated Cost Recovery System (MACRS) is used as the depreciation method for most assets for tax purposes.

**86.** The MACRS method of depreciation for assets with 3-, 5-, 7-, and 10-year recovery periods is most similar to which one of the following depreciation methods used for financial reporting purposes?

A. Straight-line.

B. Units-of-production.

C. 150%-declining-balance.

D. 200%-declining-balance.

The correct answer is (D). *(CMA, adapted)*
   **REQUIRED:** The depreciation method most like MACRS for assets with recovery periods of fewer than 10 years.
   **DISCUSSION:** MACRS for assets with lives of 10 years or fewer is based on the 200%-declining-balance method of depreciation. Thus, an asset with a 3-year life would have a straight-line rate of 33⅓%, or a double-declining-balance rate of 66⅔%.
   Answer (A) is incorrect because the straight-line method uses the same percentage each year during an asset's life, but MACRS uses various percentages. Answer (B) is incorrect because MACRS is unrelated to the units-of-production method. Answer (C) is incorrect because the 150%-declining-balance method is the basis for MACRS for assets with lives of 15 or 20 years.

**87.** When employing the MACRS method of depreciation in a capital budgeting decision, the use of MACRS as compared with the straight-line method of depreciation will result in

A. Equal total depreciation for both methods.

B. MACRS producing less total depreciation than straight-line.

C. MACRS producing more total depreciation than straight-line.

D. MACRS producing lower annual depreciation in the early years of asset life.

The correct answer is (A). *(CMA, adapted)*
   **REQUIRED:** The effect on a capital budgeting decision of using MACRS depreciation instead of straight-line.
   **DISCUSSION:** For tax purposes, straight-line depreciation is an alternative to the MACRS method. Both methods will result in the same total depreciation over the life of the asset; however, MACRS will result in greater depreciation in the early years of the asset's life because it is an accelerated method. Given that MACRS results in larger depreciation deductions in the early years, taxes will be lower in the early years and higher in the later years. Because the incremental benefits will be discounted over a shorter period than the incremental depreciation costs, MACRS is preferable to the straight-line method.
   Answers (B) and (C) are incorrect because both methods will produce the same total depreciation over the life of the asset. Answer (D) is incorrect because MACRS produces higher annual depreciation charges during the early years of the asset's life.

**88.** Barker Inc. has no capital rationing constraint and is analyzing many independent investment alternatives. Barker should accept all investment proposals

A. If debt financing is available for them.

B. That have positive cash flows.

C. That provide returns greater than the after-tax cost of debt.

D. That have a positive net present value.

The correct answer is (D). *(CMA, adapted)*
   **REQUIRED:** The investment proposals that should be accepted by a company with no capital rationing constraints.
   **DISCUSSION:** Given unlimited capital funds, Barker should invest in all projects with a NPV greater than zero. It will be profitable to invest in any project having a rate of return greater than the cost of capital (i.e., when the NPV of the future cash flows discounted at the firm's cost of capital is positive).
   Answer (A) is incorrect because the mere availability of financing is not the only consideration; more important is the cost of the financing, which must be less than the rate of return on the proposed investment. Answer (B) is incorrect because an investment with positive cash flows may be a bad investment due to the time value of money; cash flows in later years are not as valuable as those in earlier years. Answer (C) is incorrect because returns should exceed the weighted-average cost of capital, which includes the cost of equity capital as well as the cost of debt capital.

**89.** If the net present value profiles for two mutually exclusive capital projects are shaped as in the graph below, which of the following statements is true?

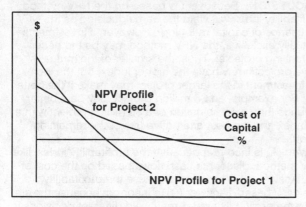

A. Project 2 has a higher internal rate of return than Project 1.

B. Project 1 has a higher internal rate of return than Project 2.

C. Project 1 has a higher net present value than Project 2.

D. Project 2 has a higher net present value than Project 1.

The correct answer is (A). *(CIA, adapted)*

**REQUIRED:** The true statement regarding the NPV profiles of two mutually exclusive capital projects.

**DISCUSSION:** The NPV is the excess of the present value of the estimated cash inflows over the net cost of the investment. Thus, Project 2 has a higher internal rate of return. The internal rate of return is the cost of capital at which the NPV is zero, that is, the cost of capital at which the NPV profile crosses the horizontal axis. The NPV profile for Project 2 intersects the horizontal axis at a higher cost of capital percentage than does that for Project 1.

Answer (B) is incorrect because Project 1 has the lower internal rate of return. Answers (C) and (D) are incorrect because the profiles of Projects 1 and 2 intersect. Neither project will have a higher NPV at all cost of capital percentages. To the left of the intersection point, Project 1 has a higher NPV. To the right of the intersection point, Project 2 has a higher NPV.

**90.** The profitability index (present value index)

A. Represents the ratio of the discounted net cash outflows to cash inflows.

B. Is the relationship between the net discounted cash inflows minus the discounted cash outflows, divided by the discounted cash outflows.

C. Is calculated by dividing the discounted profits by the cash outflows.

D. Is the ratio of the discounted net cash inflows to discounted cash outflows.

The correct answer is (D). *(CMA, adapted)*

**REQUIRED:** The true statement about the profitability index.

**DISCUSSION:** The profitability index is another term for the excess present value index. It measures the ratio of the present value of future net cash inflows to the present value of the net original investment. In organizations with unlimited capital funds, this index will produce no conflicts in the decision process. If capital rationing is necessary, the index will be an insufficient determinant. The capital available as well as the dollar amount of the present value must be considered.

Answer (A) is incorrect because the cash inflows are also discounted in the profitability index. Answer (B) is incorrect because the numerator is the discounted net cash inflows. Answer (C) is incorrect because the profitability index is based on cash flows, not profits.

**91.** If an investment project has a profitability index of 1.15, the

A. Project's internal rate of return is 15%.

B. Project's cost of capital is greater than its internal rate of return.

C. Project's internal rate of return exceeds its net present value.

D. Net present value of the project is positive.

The correct answer is (D). *(CMA, adapted)*

**REQUIRED:** The meaning of a profitability index in excess of 1.0.

**DISCUSSION:** The profitability index is the ratio of the present value of future net cash inflows to the present value of the initial net cash investment. It is a variation of the NPV method that facilitates comparison of different-sized investments. Thus, a profitability index greater than 1.0 has a positive net present value.

Answer (A) is incorrect because the IRR cannot be determined solely from the index. Answer (B) is incorrect because, if the index is 1.15 and the discount rate is the cost of capital, the NPV is positive, and the IRR must be higher than the cost of capital. Answer (C) is incorrect because the IRR is a discount rate, whereas the NPV is an amount.

**92.** The profitability index approach to investment analysis

A. Fails to consider the timing of project cash flows.

B. Considers only the project's contribution to net income and does not consider cash flow effects.

C. Always yields the same accept/reject decisions for independent projects as the net present value method.

D. Always yields the same accept/reject decisions for mutually exclusive projects as the net present value method.

The correct answer is (C). *(CMA, adapted)*
**REQUIRED:** The true statement about the profitability index.
**DISCUSSION:** Because it is based on the NPV method, the profitability index will yield the same decision as the NPV in the absence of capital rationing. However, if investments are mutually exclusive, the NPV method may be the better way of ranking projects. Thus, the smaller of the mutually exclusive projects may have the higher index, but the incremental investment in the larger project may make it the better choice. For example, an $8 million project may be a better use of funds than a combination of a $6 million project with a higher index and the best alternative use of the remaining $2 million.

Answer (A) is incorrect because the profitability index, like the NPV method, discounts cash flows based on the cost of capital. Answer (B) is incorrect because the profitability index is cash based. Answer (D) is incorrect because the NPV and the profitability index may yield different decisions if projects are mutually exclusive and differ in size.

**93.** The following data relate to two capital-budgeting projects of equal risk:

Present Value of Cash Flows

| Period | Project A | Project B |
|--------|-----------|-----------|
| 0 | $(10,000) | $(30,000) |
| 1 | 4,550 | 13,650 |
| 2 | 4,150 | 12,450 |
| 3 | 3,750 | 11,250 |

Which of the projects will be selected using the profitability-index (PI) approach and the NPV approach?

| | PI | NPV |
|---|------|-----|
| A. | B | A |
| B. | Either | B |
| C. | Either | A |
| D. | B | B |

The correct answer is (B). *(CIA, adapted)*
**REQUIRED:** The projects selected using the profitability index and the net present value approaches.
**DISCUSSION:** The profitability index (PI) is the ratio of the present value of future net cash inflows to the net cash invested. In this case, the projects have the same index.

$$\frac{\$4,550 + \$4,150 + \$3,750}{\$10,000} = 1.245$$

$$\frac{\$13,650 + \$12,450 + \$11,250}{\$30,000} = 1.245$$

The NPV of a project is the excess of the present values of future cash inflows over the net cost of the investment. Project B is preferable under the NPV approach.

$$NPV_A = \$12,450 - \$10,000 = \$2,450$$

$$NPV_B = \$37,350 - \$30,000 = \$7,350$$

Answers (A), (C), and (D) are incorrect because, using the profitability-index approach, either project will be selected because their indices are equal. Using the NPV approach, project B will be selected because it has a larger NPV.

**94.** The treasurer of a firm has an opportunity to purchase a secured 15% mortgage with 5 years remaining for $10,000. If the firm purchases the mortgage, it will receive five annual payments of $3,000 each. If the treasurer wants no less than a 12% return on long-term cash investments, the NPV of the mortgage will be

| Years: | 1 | 2 | 3 | 4 | 5 |
|--------|-----|-----|-----|-----|-----|
| Present value of $1 at 12%: | .89 | .80 | .71 | .64 | .57 |
| Present value of $1 at 15%: | .87 | .76 | .66 | .57 | .50 |

A. $80

B. $830

C. $5,000

D. Not enough information.

The correct answer is (B). *(CIA, adapted)*
**REQUIRED:** The NPV of a mortgage.
**DISCUSSION:** The NPV is equal to the sum of the discounted future cash inflows minus the required investment. Given that the firm will receive $3,000 annually over the next 5 years, the present value of the cash inflows is the sum of the products of each year's 12% discount factor and $3,000. The discount rate used is the firm's rate of return and not the mortgage's rate of return.

$$[\$3,000(.89 + .80 + .71 + .64 + .57)] = \$10,830$$
$$\$10,830 - Initial\ investment = NPV$$
$$\$10,830 - \$10,000 = \$830$$
$$NPV = \$830$$

Answer (A) is incorrect because the discount rate used should be the firm's rate of return (12%) and not the mortgage's rate of return (15%). Answer (C) is incorrect because $5,000 does not discount the annual payments. Answer (D) is incorrect because the NPV is $830.

**95.** Scott, Inc. is planning to invest $120,000 in a 10-year project. Scott estimates that the annual cash inflow, net of income taxes, from this project will be $20,000. Scott's desired rate of return on investments of this type is 10%. Information on present value factors is as follows:

|  | At 10% | At 12% |
|---|---|---|
| Present value of $1 for ten periods | 0.386 | 0.322 |
| Present value of an annuity of $1 for ten periods | 6.145 | 5.650 |

Scott's expected rate of return on this investment is

A. Less than 10%, but more than 0%.

B. 10%

C. Less than 12%, but more than 10%.

D. 12%

The correct answer is (C). *(CPA, adapted)*
**REQUIRED:** The approximate expected rate of return given the annual after-tax income, rate of return, and investment cost.
**DISCUSSION:** The initial investment of $120,000 will provide a 10-year, $20,000 annuity net of income taxes. The present value of an ordinary annuity of $1 implicit in the relationship between the investment and the net annual cash inflow from the investment is 6.00 ($120,000 ÷ $20,000). Because this figure falls between the annuity factors for 10% and 12%, the expected rate of return is greater than 10% but less than 12%.
Answers (A), (B), and (D) are incorrect because the implicit factor between the investment and the net annual cash inflow is 6.00 ($120,000 ÷ $20,000). This factor falls between the 10% and 12% annuity factors.

**96.** Each of three mutually exclusive projects costs $200. Using the table provided, rank the projects in descending NPV order.

| Year | Present Value Interest Factor (10%) | A | B | C |
|---|---|---|---|---|
| 1 | .91 | $300 | $200 | $ 0 |
| 2 | .83 | 200 | 100 | 100 |
| 3 | .75 | 100 | 0 | 100 |
| 4 | .68 | 0 | 100 | 200 |
| 5 | .62 | 0 | 200 | 300 |

A. A, B, C.

B. B, A, C.

C. C, B, A.

D. A, C, B.

The correct answer is (D). *(CIA, adapted)*
**REQUIRED:** The NPVs ranked in descending order.
**DISCUSSION:** The NPV is equal to the sum of the discounted future cash flows minus the required investment.

|  | A | B | C |
|---|---|---|---|
|  | $273 | $182 | $ 0 |
|  | 166 | 83 | 83 |
|  | 75 | 0 | 75 |
|  | 0 | 68 | 136 |
|  | 0 | 124 | 186 |
| PV | $514 | $457 | $480 |
|  | (200) | (200) | (200) |
| NPV | $314 | $257 | $280 |

Answer (A) is incorrect because C has a greater NPV than B. Answer (B) is incorrect because B has the lowest NPV. Answer (C) is incorrect because A has a greater NPV than either B or C.

**97.** On January 1, Studley Company purchased a new machine for $100,000 to be depreciated over 5 years. It will have no salvage value at the end of 5 years. For book and tax purposes, depreciation will be $20,000 per year. The machine is expected to produce annual cash flow from operations, before income taxes, of $40,000. Assume that Studley uses a discount rate of 12% and that its income tax rate will be 40% for all years. The present value of $1 at 12% for five periods is 0.57, and the present value of an ordinary annuity of $1 at 12% for five periods is 3.61. The NPV of the machine should be

A. $15,520 positive.

B. $15,520 negative.

C. $60,000 positive.

D. $25,600 negative.

The correct answer is (A). *(CPA, adapted)*
**REQUIRED:** The NPV of a machine given pretax cash flows, cost, depreciation, salvage, taxes, desired rate of return, and present value data.
**DISCUSSION:** The first step in computing the NPV is to calculate the after-tax cash flow. Depreciation is deductible for income tax purposes even though it is a noncash expense.

| | |
|---|---|
| Gross income (cash inflow) | $ 40,000 |
| Depreciation | (20,000) |
| Taxable income | $ 20,000 |
| Tax rate | × .40 |
| Tax expense (cash outflow) | $ 8,000 |

Thus, the annual cash inflow net of taxes is $32,000 ($40,000 – $8,000). The present value of the five annual cash inflows is the present value of an ordinary annuity for 5 years at 12% (3.61) times $32,000, giving a present value of $115,520. Given an initial investment of $100,000, the NPV is $15,520.
Answer (B) is incorrect because the NPV of the machine is positive. Answer (C) is incorrect because $60,000 positive does not discount the cash flows. Answer (D) is incorrect because $25,600 omits depreciation.

**98.** On January 1, a company invested in an asset with a useful life of 3 years. The company's expected rate of return is 10%. The cash flow and present and future value factors for the 3 years are as follows:

| Year | Cash Inflow from the Asset | Present Value of $1 at 10% | Future Value of $1 at 10% |
|------|------|------|------|
| 1 | $ 8,000 | .91 | 1.10 |
| 2 | 9,000 | .83 | 1.21 |
| 3 | 10,000 | .75 | 1.33 |

All cash inflows are assumed to occur at year-end. If the asset generates a positive net present value of $2,000, what was the amount of the original investment?

A. $20,250

B. $22,250

C. $30,991

D. $33,991

The correct answer is (A). *(CIA, adapted)*

**REQUIRED:** The original investment given NPV and PV and FV tables.

**DISCUSSION:** The net present value of a proposed investment is computed by subtracting the original investment from the present value of future cash flows. Accordingly, the original investment is

$$\$2,000 = (\$8,000 \times .91) + (\$9,000 \times .83)$$
$$+ (\$10,000 \times .75) - X$$
$$\$2,000 = \$7,280 + \$7,470 + \$7,500 - X$$
$$X + \$2,000 = \$22,250$$
$$X - \$20,250$$

Answer (B) is incorrect because $22,250 is the present value of future cash flows. Answers (C) and (D) are incorrect because the NPV of $2,000 needs to be deducted from the present value of future cash flows ($22,250) to yield an original investment of $20,250.

**99.** Garwood Company has purchased a machine that will be depreciated on the straight-line basis over an estimated useful life of 7 years with no salvage value. The machine is expected to generate cash flow from operations, net of income taxes, of $80,000 in each of the 7 years. Garwood's expected rate of return is 12%. Information on present value factors is as follows:

| | |
|---|---|
| Present value of $1 at 12% for seven periods | 0.452 |
| Present value of an ordinary annuity of $1 at 12% for seven periods | 4.564 |

Assuming a positive net present value of $12,720, what was the cost of the machine?

A. $240,400

B. $253,120

C. $352,400

D. $377,840

The correct answer is (C). *(CPA, adapted)*

**REQUIRED:** The cost of the machine given after-tax cash flows, present value data, and a positive NPV.

**DISCUSSION:** The net present value is defined as the excess of the present value of the future cash flows over the initial net investment. The after-tax annual cash flow is $80,000, and the present value of an ordinary annuity of $1 for 7 years at 12% is 4.564. The present value of the cash flows is thus $365,120. Given a positive NPV of $12,720, the cost of the machine must have been $352,400 ($365,120 – $12,720).

Answer (A) is incorrect because the total cash flows of $560,000 were multiplied by the present value of $1 at 12%. The present value factor of an ordinary annuity needs to be used in calculating this present value. Answer (B) is incorrect because the total cash flows of $560,000 were multiplied by the present value of $1 at 12%. The present value factor of an ordinary annuity needs to be used in calculating this present value. Furthermore, the positive NPV of $12,720 should be subtracted from the present value of the cash flows. Answer (D) is incorrect because the positive NPV of $12,720 needs to be subtracted, not added, to the present value.

## 13.5 Internal Rate of Return

**100.** The internal rate of return is

A. The discount rate at which the NPV of the cash flows is zero.

B. The breakeven borrowing rate for the project in question.

C. The yield rate/effective rate of interest quoted on long-term debt and other instruments.

D. All of the answers are correct.

The correct answer is (D). *(Publisher)*

**REQUIRED:** The true statement(s) about internal rate of return.

**DISCUSSION:** The internal rate of return (IRR) is the discount rate at which the present value of the cash flows equals the original investment. Thus, the NPV of the project is zero at the IRR. The IRR is also the maximum borrowing cost the firm could afford to pay for a specific project. The IRR is similar to the yield rate/effective rate quoted in the business media.

Answers (A), (B), and (C) are incorrect because the IRR is the discount rate at which the NPV of the cash flows is zero, the breakeven borrowing rate for projects, and the yield rate/effective rate of interest quoted on long-term debt and other instruments.

**101.** Which of the following characteristics represent an advantage of the internal rate of return technique over the accounting rate of return technique in evaluating a project?

I. Recognition of the project's salvage value
II. Emphasis on cash flows
III. Recognition of the time value of money

   A. I only.

   B. I and II.

   C. II and III.

   D. I, II, and III.

The correct answer is (C). *(CPA, adapted)*
   **REQUIRED:** The advantage(s) of the IRR technique over the accounting rate of return technique.
   **DISCUSSION:** The IRR is the interest rate that equalizes the present value of future cash flows with the initial cost of the investment. The accounting rate of return is calculated by dividing the increase in accounting net income by the required investment. However, it ignores the time value of money and does not emphasize cash flows.
   Answers (A), (B), and (D) are incorrect because both techniques recognize the project's salvage value.

**102.** Polo Co. requires higher rates of return for projects with a life span greater than 5 years. Projects extending beyond 5 years must earn a higher specified rate of return. Which of the following capital budgeting techniques can readily accommodate this requirement?

| | Internal Rate of Return | Net Present Value |
|---|---|---|
| A. | Yes | No |
| B. | No | Yes |
| C. | No | No |
| D. | Yes | Yes |

The correct answer is (D). *(CPA, adapted)*
   **REQUIRED:** The capital budgeting technique(s) that can accommodate a higher desired rate of return for longer projects.
   **DISCUSSION:** The IRR is the discount rate at which the NPV is zero. The NPV is the excess of the present value of the expected future net cash inflows over the cost of the investment. The calculation of the NPV (and therefore the IRR) can be readily adjusted for an increase in the desired return by changing the discount rate.
   Answers (A), (B), and (C) are incorrect because both methods can readily accommodate changing rates of return.

**103.** If income tax considerations are ignored, how is depreciation handled by the following capital budgeting techniques?

| | Internal Rate of Return | Accounting Rate of Return | Payback |
|---|---|---|---|
| A. | Excluded | Included | Excluded |
| B. | Included | Excluded | Included |
| C. | Excluded | Excluded | Included |
| D. | Included | Included | Included |

The correct answer is (A). *(CMA, adapted)*
   **REQUIRED:** The manner in which depreciation is handled by each capital budgeting technique.
   **DISCUSSION:** If taxes are ignored, depreciation is not a consideration in any of the methods based on cash flows because it is a noncash expense. Thus, the internal rate of return, net present value, and payback methods would not consider depreciation because these methods are based on cash flows. However, the accounting rate of return is based on net income as calculated on an income statement. Because depreciation is included in the determination of accrual accounting net income, it would affect the calculation of the accounting rate of return.
   Answers (B), (C), and (D) are incorrect because the IRR and the payback period are based on cash flows. Depreciation is not needed in their calculation. However, the accounting rate of return cannot be calculated without first deducting depreciation.

**104.** An organization is using capital budgeting techniques to compare two independent projects. It could accept one, both, or neither of the projects. Which of the following statements is true about the use of net-present-value (NPV) and internal-rate-of-return (IRR) methods for evaluating these two projects?

A. NPV and IRR criteria will always lead to the same accept or reject decision for two independent projects.

B. If the first project's IRR is higher than the organization's cost of capital, the first project will be accepted but the second project will not.

C. If the NPV criterion leads to accepting or rejecting the first project, one cannot predict whether the IRR criterion will lead to accepting or rejecting the first project.

D. If the NPV criterion leads to accepting the first project, the IRR criterion will never lead to accepting the first project.

The correct answer is (A). *(CIA, adapted)*
**REQUIRED:** The true statement about the NPV and IRR methods.
**DISCUSSION:** The NPV criterion is that the NPV is positive, and the IRR criterion is that the cost of capital is less than the IRR. When the cost of capital is less than the IRR, the NPV is positive. When it exceeds the IRR, the NPV is negative. Accordingly, when two projects are independent, the NPV and IRR criteria will always lead to the same accept or reject decision.
Answer (B) is incorrect because, if the second project's IRR is higher than the first project's, the organization would accept the second project based on the IRR criterion. Answers (C) and (D) are incorrect because, if the projects are independent, the NPV and IRR criteria indicate the same decision.

**105.** Everything else being equal, the internal rate of return (IRR) of an investment project will be lower if

A. The investment cost is lower.

B. Cash inflows are received later in the life of the project.

C. Cash inflows are larger.

D. The project has a shorter payback period.

The correct answer is (B). *(CIA, adapted)*
**REQUIRED:** The true statement about the IRR.
**DISCUSSION:** The IRR is the discount rate at which the net present value is zero. Because the present value of a dollar is higher the sooner it is received, projects with later cash flows will have lower net present values for any given discount rate than will projects with earlier cash flows, if other factors are constant. Hence, projects with later cash flows will have a lower IRR.
Answer (A) is incorrect because the present value of the cash inflows is inversely related to the discount rate; that is, if the discount rate is higher, the present value of the cash inflows is lower. If the investment cost is lower, a higher discount rate (the IRR) will be required to set the net present value equal to zero. Answer (C) is incorrect because the larger the cash inflows, the higher the IRR will be. Higher cash inflows have a higher present value at any given discount rate. A higher discount rate will be required to set the net present value equal to zero. Answer (D) is incorrect because projects with shorter payback periods have higher cash inflows early in the life of the project. Projects with earlier cash inflows have higher IRRs.

**106.** The rankings of mutually exclusive investments determined using the internal rate of return method (IRR) and the net present value method (NPV) may be different when

- A. The lives of the multiple projects are equal and the sizes of the required investments are equal.
- B. The required rate of return equals the IRR of each project.
- C. The required rate of return is higher than the IRR of each project.
- D. Multiple projects have unequal lives and the size of the investment for each project is different.

The correct answer is (D). *(CMA, adapted)*
**REQUIRED:** The circumstances in which IRR and NPV rankings of mutually exclusive projects may differ.
**DISCUSSION:** Because of the difference in the assumptions regarding the reinvestment of cash flows, the two methods will occasionally give different answers regarding the ranking of mutually exclusive projects. Moreover, the IRR method may rank several small, short-lived projects ahead of a large project with a lower rate of return but with a longer life span. However, the large project might return more dollars to the company because of the larger amount invested and the longer time span over which earnings will accrue. When faced with capital rationing, an investor will want to invest in projects that generate the most dollars in relation to the limited resources available and the size and returns from the possible investments. Thus, the NPV method should be used because it determines the aggregate present value for each feasible combination of projects.
Answer (A) is incorrect because the two methods will give the same results if the lives and required investments are the same. Answer (B) is incorrect because, if the required rate of return equals the IRR (i.e., the cost of capital is equal to the IRR), NPV would be zero, and the two methods would yield the same decision. Answer (C) is incorrect because, if the required rate of return is higher than the IRR, both methods would yield a decision not to acquire the investment.

**107.** If the net present value (NPV) of Project A is known to be higher than the NPV of Project B, it can be concluded that

- A. The internal rate of return (IRR) of Project A will definitely be higher than the IRR of Project B.
- B. The IRR of Project A will definitely be lower than the IRR of Project B.
- C. The ranking of IRRs is indeterminate based on the information provided.
- D. The payback period for Project A is definitely shorter than the payback period for Project B.

The correct answer is (C). *(CIA, adapted)*
**REQUIRED:** The significance of a higher NPV.
**DISCUSSION:** The IRR is the discount rate at which the net present value is zero. The NPV is the present value of future cash flows minus the present value of the investment. Because of a possible difference in the scale of the projects and other factors, a higher NPV does not necessarily result in a higher IRR.
Answer (A) is incorrect because the ranking of IRRs is indeterminate. Answer (B) is incorrect because the ranking of IRRs is indeterminate. Answer (D) is incorrect because the ranking for payback periods is indeterminate.

**108.** The payback reciprocal can be used to approximate a project's

- A. Net present value.
- B. Accounting rate of return if the cash flow pattern is relatively stable.
- C. Payback period.
- D. Internal rate of return if the cash flow pattern is relatively stable.

The correct answer is (D). *(CMA, adapted)*
**REQUIRED:** The item that can be approximated by a project's payback reciprocal.
**DISCUSSION:** The payback reciprocal (1 ÷ payback) has been shown to approximate the internal rate of return (IRR) when the periodic cash flows are equal and the life of the project is at least twice the payback period.
Answer (A) is incorrect because the payback reciprocal approximates the IRR, which is the rate at which the NPV is $0. Answer (B) is incorrect because the accounting rate of return is based on accrual-income-based figures, not on discounted cash flows. Answer (C) is incorrect because the payback period is a measure of time, whereas its reciprocal is a ratio.

**109.** A weakness of the internal rate of return (IRR) approach for determining the acceptability of investments is that it

    A. Does not consider the time value of money.

    B. Is not a straightforward decision criterion.

    C. Implicitly assumes that the firm is able to reinvest project cash flows at the firm's cost of capital.

    D. Implicitly assumes that the firm is able to reinvest project cash flows at the project's internal rate of return.

The correct answer is (D). *(CMA, adapted)*
  **REQUIRED:** The weakness of the internal rate of return approach.
  **DISCUSSION:** The IRR is the rate at which the discounted future cash flows equal the net investment (NPV = 0). One disadvantage of the method is that inflows from the early years are assumed to be reinvested at the IRR. This assumption may not be sound. Investments in the future may not earn as high a rate as is currently available.
  Answer (A) is incorrect because the IRR method considers the time value of money. Answer (B) is incorrect because the IRR provides a straightforward decision criterion. Any project with an IRR greater than the cost of capital is acceptable. Answer (C) is incorrect because the IRR method assumes reinvestment at the IRR; the NPV method assumes reinvestment at the cost of capital.

**110.** A company's marginal cost of new capital (MCC) is 10% up to $600,000. MCC increases .5% for the next $400,000 and another .5% thereafter. Several proposed capital projects are under consideration, with projected cost and internal rates of return (IRR) as follows:

| Project | Cost | IRR |
|---|---|---|
| A | $100,000 | 10.5% |
| B | 300,000 | 14.0 |
| C | 450,000 | 10.8 |
| D | 350,000 | 13.5 |
| E | 400,000 | 12.0 |

What should the company's capital budget be?

    A. $0

    B. $1,050,000

    C. $1,500,000

    D. $1,600,000

The correct answer is (B). *(CIA, adapted)*
  **REQUIRED:** The company's capital budget.
  **DISCUSSION:** The IRR is the discount rate at which the net present value (discounted net cash inflows – investment) of a project is zero. Hence, an investment should be profitable if the IRR exceeds the company's cost of capital. Projects B, D, and E, with a combined cost of $1,050,000, have the highest IRRs. Each is in excess of the company's maximum 11% cost of capital (10% + .5% + .5%). Because the combined cost of B, D, and E exceeds the level ($1,000,000) at which the cost of capital rises to 11%, Projects A (10.5%) and C (10.8%) must be rejected using the IRR criterion.
  Answer (A) is incorrect because any projects with an IRR of 11% or greater should be undertaken. Answer (C) is incorrect because $1,500,000 includes Project C. It should be rejected because its IRR of 10.8% is less than the 11% cost of capital. Answer (D) is incorrect because $1,600,000 includes both Projects A and C. They should be rejected because their respective IRRs are less than the 11% cost of capital.

**111.** Kern Co. is planning to invest in a 2-year project that is expected to yield cash flows from operations, net of income taxes, of $50,000 in the first year and $80,000 in the second year. Kern requires an internal rate of return of 15%. The present value of $1 for one period at 15% is 0.870 and for two periods at 15% is 0.756. The future value of $1 for one period at 15% is 1.150 and for two periods at 15% is 1.323. The maximum that Kern should invest immediately is

    A. $81,670

    B. $103,980

    C. $130,000

    D. $163,340

The correct answer is (B). *(CPA, adapted)*
  **REQUIRED:** The maximum investment given the desired IRR.
  **DISCUSSION:** The IRR is the discount rate at which the NPV is zero, that is, at which the investment equals the present value of the future net cash inflows. To determine the maximum investment that is justified given the expected cash flows and the minimum desired IRR, the cash flows must be discounted at that IRR as follows:

$$.870 \times \$50,000 = \$ 43,500$$
$$.756 \times \$80,000 = \underline{\phantom{0}60,480}$$
$$\underline{\underline{\$103,980}}$$

  Answer (A) is incorrect because the maximum that should be invested immediately is the present value of the two future cash flows. Answer (C) is incorrect because future cash flows need to be discounted using the present value factors. Answer (D) is incorrect because the cash flows need to be discounted using the present value factors, not the future value factors.

**112.** Two projects have an initial outlay of $497, and each has an income stream lasting 3 years. Project A returns $200 per year for the 3 years. Project B returns $200 for the first 2 years and $248 for the third year.

Present Value -- Amount

| n | 8% | 10% | 12% | 14% |
|---|------|------|------|------|
| 1 | .9259 | .9091 | .8929 | .8772 |
| 2 | .8573 | .8264 | .7972 | .7695 |
| 3 | .7938 | .7513 | .7118 | .6750 |

The appropriate internal rate of return valuation for Project B is

A. $200(.8772) + $200(.7695) + $248(.6750) = $496.74

B. $200(.8929) + $200(.7972) + $248(.7118) = $514.41

C. $200(.9091) + $200(.8264) + $248(.7513) = $533.42

D. $200(.9259) + $200(.8573) + $248(.7938) = $553.50

The correct answer is (A). *(CIA, adapted)*
   **REQUIRED:** The appropriate internal rate of return for Project B.
   **DISCUSSION:** The internal rate of return is the interest rate at which the present value of future cash flows is equal to the cost of the investment. Thus, the sum of the products of the discount factor for each cash inflow and the related cash inflow should equal the initial outlay ($497). In this case, the IRR is 14%.
   Answers (B), (C), and (D) are incorrect because the IRR is the interest rate at which the present value of future cash flows is equal to the cost of the initial investment.

**113.** At a company's cost of capital (hurdle rate) of 15%, a prospective investment has a positive net present value. Based on this information, it can be concluded that

A. The accounting rate of return is greater than 15%.

B. The internal rate of return is less than 15%.

C. The internal rate of return is greater than 15%.

D. The payback period is shorter than the life of the asset.

The correct answer is (C). *(CIA, adapted)*
   **REQUIRED:** The correct inference given that NPV is positive at the cost of capital.
   **DISCUSSION:** A positive NPV indicates that the PV of cash flows is greater than the initial investment. At the IRR, the PV of the cash flows equals the investment (NPV = 0). The IRR must therefore exceed the hurdle rate because the NPV is positive at the hurdle rate.
   Answer (A) is incorrect because the accounting rate of return does not use present value. Answer (B) is incorrect because the IRR is greater than 15%. Answer (D) is incorrect because the payback method does not use present value.

**114.** A project requires an initial cash investment at its inception of $10,000, and no other cash outflows are necessary. Cash inflows from the project over its 3-year life are $6,000 at the end of the first year, $5,000 at the end of the second year, and $2,000 at the end of the third year. The future value interest factors for an amount of $1 at the cost of capital of 8% are

| | Period | | |
|---|---|---|---|
| 1 | 2 | 3 | 4 |
| 1.080 | 1.166 | 1.260 | 1.360 |

The present value interest factors for an amount of $1 for three periods are as follows:

| Interest Rate | | | | |
|---|---|---|---|---|
| 8% | 9% | 10% | 12% | 14% |
| .794 | .772 | .751 | .712 | .675 |

The modified IRR (MIRR) for the project is closest to

A. 8%

B. 9%

C. 10%

D. 12%

The correct answer is (D). *(Publisher)*
   **REQUIRED:** The approximate MIRR.
   **DISCUSSION:** The MIRR is the interest rate at which the present value of the cash outflows discounted at the cost of capital equals the present value of the terminal value. The terminal value is the future value of the cash inflows assuming they are reinvested at the cost of capital. The present value of the outflows is $10,000 because no future outflows occur. The terminal value is $14,396 [(1.166 x $6,000) + (1.08 x $5,000) + (1.00 x $2,000)]. Accordingly, the present value of $1 interest factor for the rate at which the present value of the outflows equals the present value of the terminal value is .695 ($10,000 ÷ $14,396). This factor is closest to that for 12%.
   Answers (A), (B), and (C) are incorrect because the MIRR must be greater than 12%. The present value of $1 interest factor for this project that equates the present values of the costs and the terminal value is lower than the factor for 12%. The lower the present value factor, the higher the interest rate.

Questions 115 and 116 are based on the following information. A firm with an 18% cost of capital is considering the following projects (on January 1, 1998):

| | January 1, 1998<br>Cash Outflow<br>(000's Omitted) | December 31, 2002<br>Cash Inflow<br>(000's Omitted) | Project Internal<br>Rate of Return |
|---|---|---|---|
| Project A | $3,500 | $7,400 | 16% |
| Project B | 4,000 | 9,950 | ? |

Present Value of $1 Due at the End of "N" Periods

| N | 12% | 14% | 15% | 16% | 18% | 20% | 22% |
|---|---|---|---|---|---|---|---|
| 4 | .6355 | .5921 | .5718 | .5523 | .5158 | .4823 | .4230 |
| 5 | .5674 | .5194 | .4972 | .4761 | .4371 | .4019 | .3411 |
| 6 | .5066 | .4556 | .4323 | .4104 | .3704 | .3349 | .2751 |

**115.** Using the net-present-value (NPV) method, project A's net present value is

A. $316,920

B. $23,140

C. $(265,460)

D. $(316,920)

The correct answer is (C). *(CIA, adapted)*
   **REQUIRED:** The net present value of project A.
   **DISCUSSION:** The cash inflow occurs 5 years after the cash outflow, and the NPV method uses the firm's cost of capital of 18%. The present value of $1 due at the end of 5 years discounted at 18% is .4371. Thus, the NPV of project A is $(265,460) [(.4371 x $7,400,000 cash inflow) – $3,500,000 cash outflow].
   Answer (A) is incorrect because $316,920 discounts the cash inflow over a 4-year period. Answer (B) is incorrect because $23,140 assumes a 16% discount rate. Answer (D) is incorrect because $(316,920) discounts the cash inflow over a 4-year period and also subtracts the present value of the cash inflow from the cash outflow.

**116.** Project B's internal rate of return is closest to

A. 15%

B. 16%

C. 18%

D. 20%

The correct answer is (D). *(CIA, adapted)*
   **REQUIRED:** The percentage closest to project B's internal rate of return.
   **DISCUSSION:** The internal rate of return is the discount rate at which the NPV is zero. Consequently, the cash outflow equals the present value of the inflow at the internal rate of return. The present value of $1 factor for project B's internal rate of return is therefore .4020 ($4,000,000 cash outflow ÷ $9,950,000 cash inflow). This factor is closest to the present value of $1 for 5 periods at 20%.
   Answer (A) is incorrect because 15% results in a positive NPV for project B. Answer (B) is incorrect because 16% is the approximate internal rate of return for project A. Answer (C) is incorrect because 18% is the company's cost of capital.

## 13.6 Cash Flow Calculations

**117.** Regal Industries is replacing a grinder purchased 5 years ago for $15,000 with a new one costing $25,000 cash. The original grinder is being depreciated on a straight-line basis over 15 years to a zero salvage value; Regal will sell this old equipment to a third party for $6,000 cash. The new equipment will be depreciated on a straight-line basis over 10 years to a zero salvage value. Assuming a 40% marginal tax rate, Regal's net cash investment at the time of purchase if the old grinder is sold and the new one purchased is

A. $19,000

B. $15,000

C. $17,400

D. $25,000

The correct answer is (C). *(CMA, adapted)*

**REQUIRED:** The net cash investment at the time of purchase of an old asset and the sale of a new one.

**DISCUSSION:** The old machine has a book value of $10,000 [$15,000 cost – 5($15,000 cost ÷ 15 years) depreciation]. The loss on the sale is $4,000 ($10,000 – $6,000 cash received), and the tax savings from the loss is $1,600 (40% x $4,000). Thus, total inflows are $7,600. The only outflow is the $25,000 purchase price of the new machine. The net cash investment is therefore $17,400 ($25,000 – $7,600).

Answer (A) is incorrect because $19,000 overlooks the tax savings from the loss on the old machine. Answer (B) is incorrect because $15,000 is obtained by deducting the old book value from the purchase price. Answer (D) is incorrect because the net investment is less than $25,000 given sales proceeds from the old machine and the tax savings.

**118.** Garfield, Inc. is considering a 10-year capital investment project with forecasted revenues of $40,000 per year and forecasted cash operating expenses of $29,000 per year. The initial cost of the equipment for the project is $23,000, and Garfield expects to sell the equipment for $9,000 at the end of the tenth year. The equipment will be depreciated over 7 years. The project requires a working capital investment of $7,000 at its inception and another $5,000 at the end of year 5. Assuming a 40% marginal tax rate, the expected net cash flow from the project in the tenth year is

A. $32,000

B. $24,000

C. $20,000

D. $11,000

The correct answer is (B). *(CMA, adapted)*

**REQUIRED:** The expected net cash flow from the project in the tenth year.

**DISCUSSION:** The project will have an $11,000 before-tax cash inflow from operations in the tenth year ($40,000 – $29,000). Also, $9,000 will be generated from the sale of the equipment. The entire $9,000 will be taxable because the basis of the asset was reduced to zero in the seventh year. Thus, taxable income will be $20,000 ($11,000 + $9,000), leaving a net after-tax cash inflow of $12,000 [(1.0 – .4) x $20,000]. This $12,000 must be added to the $12,000 tied up in working capital ($7,000 + $5,000). The total net cash flow in the tenth year will therefore be $24,000.

Answer (A) is incorrect because $32,000 omits the $8,000 outflow for income taxes. Answer (C) is incorrect because taxes will be $8,000, not $12,000. Answer (D) is incorrect because $11,000 is the net operating cash flow.

Questions 119 through 122 are based on the following information. The following data pertain to a 4-year project being considered by Metro Industries.

- A depreciable asset that costs $1.2 million will be acquired on January 1, 1999. The asset, which is expected to have a $200,000 salvage value at the end of 4 years, qualifies as 3-year property under the Modified Accelerated Cost Recovery System (MACRS).

- The new asset will replace an existing asset that has a tax basis of $150,000 and can be sold January 1, 1999, for $180,000.

- The project is expected to provide added annual sales of 30,000 units at $20. Additional cash operating costs are variable, $12 per unit; fixed, $90,000 per year.

- A $50,000 working capital investment that is fully recoverable at the end of the fourth year is required.

Metro is subject to a 40% income tax rate and rounds all computations to the nearest dollar. Assume that any gain or loss affects the taxes paid at the end of the year in which it occurred. The company uses the net present value method to analyze investments and will employ the following factors and rates.

| Period | Present Value of $1 at 12% | Present Value of $1 Annuity at 12% | MACRS |
|---|---|---|---|
| 1 | 0.89 | 0.89 | 33% |
| 2 | 0.80 | 1.69 | 45 |
| 3 | 0.71 | 2.40 | 15 |
| 4 | 0.64 | 3.04 | 7 |

**119.** The discounted cash flow for 2002 MACRS depreciation on the new asset is

- A.   $0
- B.   $17,920
- C.   $21,504
- D.   $26,880

The correct answer is (C). (CMA, adapted)

REQUIRED: The discounted cash flow for the 2002 MACRS depreciation deduction on the new asset.

DISCUSSION: Tax law allows taxpayers to ignore salvage value when calculating depreciation under MACRS. Thus, the depreciation deduction is 7% of the initial $1.2 million cost, or $84,000. At a 40% tax rate, the deduction will save the company $33,600 in taxes in 2002. The present value of this savings is $21,504 ($33,600 x 0.64 present value of $1 at 12% for four periods).

Answer (A) is incorrect because a tax savings will result in 2002 from the MACRS deduction. Answer (B) is incorrect because $17,920 is based on a depreciation calculation in which salvage value is subtracted from the initial cost. Answer (D) is incorrect because the appropriate discount factor for the fourth period is 0.64, not 0.80.

**120.** The discounted, net-of-tax amount that relates to disposal of the existing asset is

- A.   $168,000
- B.   $169,320
- C.   $180,000
- D.   $190,680

The correct answer is (B). (CMA, adapted)

REQUIRED: The discounted, net-of-tax amount relating to the disposal of the existing asset.

DISCUSSION: The cash inflow from the existing asset is $180,000, but that amount is subject to tax on the $30,000 gain ($180,000 − $150,000 tax basis). The tax on the gain is $12,000 (40% x $30,000). Because the tax will not be paid until year-end, the discounted value is $10,680 ($12,000 x .89 PV of $1 at 12% for one period). Thus, the net-of-tax inflow is $169,320 ($180,000 − $10,680). NOTE: This asset was probably a Section 1231 asset, and any gain on sale qualifies for the special capital gain tax rates. Had the problem not stipulated a 40% tax rate, the capital gains rate would be used. An answer based on that rate is not among the options.

Answer (A) is incorrect because $168,000 fails to discount the outflow for taxes. Answer (C) is incorrect because $180,000 ignores the impact of income taxes. Answer (D) is incorrect because the discounted present value of the income taxes is an outflow and is deducted from the inflow from the sale of the asset.

**121.** The expected incremental sales will provide a discounted, net-of-tax contribution margin over 4 years of

   A. $57,600

   B. $92,160

   C. $273,600

   D. $437,760

The correct answer is (D). *(CMA, adapted)*

   **REQUIRED:** The expected net-of-tax contribution margin over 4 years.

   **DISCUSSION:** Additional annual sales are 30,000 units at $20 per unit. If variable costs are expected to be $12 per unit, the unit contribution margin is $8, and the total before-tax annual contribution margin is $240,000 ($8 × 30,000 units). The after-tax total annual contribution margin is $144,000 [(1.0 − .4) × $240,000]. This annual increase in the contribution margin should be treated as an annuity. Thus, its present value is $437,760 ($144,000 × 3.04 PV of an annuity of $1 at 12% for four periods).

   Answers (A) and (B) are incorrect because $57,600 and $92,160 are based on only 1 year's results, not 4. Answer (C) is incorrect because $273,600 improperly includes fixed costs in the calculation of the contribution margin.

**122.** The overall discounted-cash-flow impact of the working capital investment on Metro's project is

   A. $(2,800)

   B. $(18,000)

   C. $(50,000)

   D. $(59,200)

The correct answer is (B). *(CMA, adapted)*

   **REQUIRED:** The overall discounted-cash-flow impact of the working capital investment.

   **DISCUSSION:** The working capital investment is treated as a $50,000 outflow at the beginning of the project and a $50,000 inflow at the end of 4 years. Accordingly, the present value of the inflow after 4 years should be subtracted from the initial $50,000 outlay. The overall discounted-cash-flow impact of the working capital investment is $18,000 [$50,000 − ($50,000 × .64 PV of $1 at 12% for four periods)].

   Answer (A) is incorrect because the firm will have its working capital tied up for 4 years. Answer (C) is incorrect because the working capital investment is recovered at the end of the fourth year. Hence, the working capital cost of the project is the difference between $50,000 and the present value of $50,000 in 4 years. Answer (D) is incorrect because the answer cannot exceed $50,000, which is the amount of the cash outflow.

**123.** Kore Industries is analyzing a capital investment proposal for new equipment to produce a product over the next 8 years. The analyst is attempting to determine the appropriate "end-of-life" cash flows for the analysis. At the end of 8 years, the equipment must be removed from the plant and will have a net book value of zero, a tax basis of $75,000, a cost to remove of $40,000, and scrap salvage value of $10,000. Kore's effective tax rate is 40%. What is the appropriate "end-of-life" cash flow related to these items that should be used in the analysis?

   A. $45,000

   B. $27,000

   C. $12,000

   D. $(18,000)

The correct answer is (C). *(CMA, adapted)*

   **REQUIRED:** The appropriate end-of-life cash flow related to the investment.

   **DISCUSSION:** The tax basis of $75,000 and the $40,000 cost to remove can be written off. However, the $10,000 scrap value is a cash inflow. Thus, the taxable loss is $105,000 ($75,000 loss on disposal + $40,000 expense to remove − $10,000 of inflows). At a 40% tax rate, the $105,000 loss will produce a tax savings (inflow) of $42,000. The final cash flows will consist of an outflow of $40,000 (cost to remove) and inflows of $10,000 (scrap) and $42,000 (tax savings), or a net inflow of $12,000.

   Answer (A) is incorrect because $45,000 ignores income taxes and assumes that the loss on disposal involves a cash inflow. Answer (B) is incorrect because $27,000 assumes that the loss on disposal involves a cash inflow. Answer (D) is incorrect because $(18,000) ignores the tax loss on disposal.

**124.** Doro Co. is considering the purchase of a $100,000 machine that is expected to result in a decrease of $25,000 per year in cash expenses after taxes. This machine, which has no residual value, has an estimated useful life of 10 years and will be depreciated on a straight-line basis. For this machine, the accounting rate of return based on initial investment will be

A.   10%

B.   15%

C.   25%

D.   35%

The correct answer is (B). *(CPA, adapted)*
**REQUIRED:** The accounting rate of return based on initial investment.
**DISCUSSION:** The ARR is based on the accrual method and does not discount future cash flows. Accordingly, the ARR equals the decrease in annual cash expenses after taxes minus annual depreciation, divided by the initial investment. Annual straight-line depreciation is $10,000 [($100,000 cost – $0 salvage value) ÷ 10 years].

$$ARR = \frac{\$25,000 - \$10,000}{\$100,000} = 15\%$$

Answer (A) is incorrect because 10% is the depreciation rate per year. Answer (C) is incorrect because depreciation must be deducted from the $25,000 of cash expenses. Answer (D) is incorrect because depreciation must be deducted from, not added to, the $25,000 of cash expenses.

## 13.7 Comprehensive

Questions 125 through 127 are based on the following information. A company that annually reviews its investment opportunities and selects appropriate capital expenditures for the coming year is presented with two projects, called Project A and Project B. Best estimates indicate that the investment outlay for Project A is $30,000 and for Project B is $1 million. The projects are considered to be equally risky. Project A is expected to generate cash inflows of $40,000 at the end of each year for 2 years. Project B is expected to generate cash inflows of $700,000 at the end of the first year and $500,000 at the end of the second year. The company has a cost of capital of 8%.

**125.** What is the net present value (NPV) of each project when the cost of capital is zero?

|     | Project A | Project B |
|-----|-----------|-----------|
| A.  | $30,000   | $1,000,000 |
| B.  | $50,000   | $200,000  |
| C.  | $80,000   | $1,200,000 |
| D.  | $110,000  | $2,200,000 |

The correct answer is (B). *(CIA, adapted)*
**REQUIRED:** The net present value of each project.
**DISCUSSION:** The NPV is the excess of the present value of estimated cash inflows over the net cost of the investment. At a zero cost of capital, the NPV is simply the sum of a project's undiscounted cash flows. Thus, the NPV of Project A is $50,000 ($40,000 + $40,000 – $30,000), and the NPV of Project B is $200,000 ($700,000 + $500,000 – $1,000,000).

Answer (A) is incorrect because $30,000 and $1,000,000 are the initial investment outlays for A and B, respectively. Answer (C) is incorrect because $80,000 and $1,200,000 are the cash inflows for A and B, respectively. Answer (D) is incorrect because $110,000 for Project A and $2,200,000 for Project B are calculated by adding the initial outlays to the sum of the cash inflows.

**126.** The internal rate of return of Project A, to the nearest full percentage point, is

A. 10%

B. 15%

C. 25%

D. 100%

The correct answer is (D). *(CIA, adapted)*

**REQUIRED:** The internal rate of return for Project A.

**DISCUSSION:** The internal rate of return is the discount rate that sets a project's NPV equal to zero. The internal rate of return may be determined as follows if *IRR* is the internal rate of return, *t* is the time period, and *n* is the number of time periods:

$$NPV = \sum_{t=1}^{n} \frac{Annual\ net\ cash\ inflow}{(1 + IRR)^t} - Net\ investment$$

Substituting in the foregoing expression yields an internal rate of return of 100%.

$$0 = \frac{\$40,000}{(1 + IRR)} + \frac{\$40,000}{(1 + IRR)^2} - \$30,000$$

$$IRR = 100\%$$

Answer (A) is incorrect because applying a discount rate of 10% results in a NPV of $69,421. Answer (B) is incorrect because applying a discount rate of 15% results in a NPV of $65,028. Answer (C) is incorrect because applying a discount rate of 25% results in a NPV of $57,600.

**127.** Net present value (NPV) and internal rate of return (IRR) differ in that

A. NPV assumes reinvestment of project cash flows at the cost of capital, whereas IRR assumes reinvestment of project cash flows at the internal rate of return.

B. NPV and IRR make different accept or reject decisions for independent projects.

C. IRR can be used to rank mutually exclusive investment projects, but NPV cannot.

D. NPV is expressed as a percentage, while IRR is expressed as a dollar amount.

The correct answer is (A). *(CIA, adapted)*

**REQUIRED:** The difference between net present value (NPV) and internal rate of return (IRR).

**DISCUSSION:** NPV assumes that cash inflows from the investment project can be reinvested at the cost of capital, whereas IRR assumes that cash flows from each project can be reinvested at the IRR for that particular project. This underlying assumption is considered to be a weakness of the IRR technique. The cost of capital is the appropriate reinvestment rate because it represents the opportunity cost for a project at a given level of risk. The problem with the IRR method is that it assumes a higher discount rate even though a project may not have a greater level of risk.

Answer (B) is incorrect because NPV and IRR make consistent accept/reject decisions for independent projects. When NPV is positive, IRR exceeds the cost of capital and the project is acceptable. Answer (C) is incorrect because the NPV method can be used to rank mutually exclusive projects, whereas IRR cannot. The reinvestment rate assumption causes IRR to make faulty project rankings under some circumstances. Answer (D) is incorrect because IRR is expressed as a percentage and NPV in dollar terms.

Questions 128 through 131 are based on the following information. An organization has four investment proposals with the following costs and expected cash inflows:

**Expected Cash Inflows**

| Project | Cost | End of Year 1 | End of Year 2 | End of Year 3 |
|---------|------|---------------|---------------|---------------|
| A | Unknown | $10,000 | $10,000 | $10,000 |
| B | $20,000 | $ 5,000 | $10,000 | $15,000 |
| C | $25,000 | $15,000 | $10,000 | $ 5,000 |
| D | $30,000 | $20,000 | Unknown | $20,000 |

Additional information:

| Discount Rate | Number of Periods | Present Value of $1 Due at the End of n Periods (PVIF) | Present Value of an Annuity of $1 per Period for n Periods (PVIFA) |
|---------------|-------------------|------------------------|------------------------|
| 5% | 1 | 0.9524 | 0.9524 |
| 5% | 2 | 0.9070 | 1.8594 |
| 5% | 3 | 0.8638 | 2.7232 |
| 10% | 1 | 0.9091 | 0.9091 |
| 10% | 2 | 0.8264 | 1.7355 |
| 10% | 3 | 0.7513 | 2.4869 |
| 15% | 1 | 0.8696 | 0.8696 |
| 15% | 2 | 0.7561 | 1.6257 |
| 15% | 3 | 0.6575 | 2.2832 |

**128.** If Project A has an internal rate of return (IRR) of 15%, it has a cost of

A. $8,696

B. $22,832

C. $24,869

D. $27,232

The correct answer is (B). *(CIA, adapted)*
**REQUIRED:** The cost of Project A given the IRR.
**DISCUSSION:** The IRR is the discount rate that sets the net present value of the project equal to zero, so the present value of the costs equals the present value of the cash inflows. At an IRR of 15%, the present value of the inflows (and therefore the present value of the costs) for Project A equals the constant annual inflow times the present value of an ordinary annuity of $1 for three periods at 15%. Thus, the cost of Project A is $22,832 ($10,000 × 2.2832).
Answer (A) is incorrect because $8,696 uses the present value interest factor for one period at 15%. Answer (C) is incorrect because $24,869 is obtained using a 10% discount rate. Answer (D) is incorrect because $27,232 is based on a 5% discount rate.

**129.** If the discount rate is 10%, the net present value (NPV) of Project B is

A. $4,079

B. $6,789

C. $9,869

D. $39,204

The correct answer is (A). *(CIA, adapted)*
**REQUIRED:** The NPV of Project B given the discount rate.
**DISCUSSION:** The NPV is the present value of the cash inflows minus the cost of the project. The inflows for this project are not constant, so the individual cash flows may be discounted using the interest factors for the present value of $1 due at the end of a period discounted at 10%. The sum of these present values is $24,079 [($5,000 × .9091) + ($10,000 × .8264) + ($15,000 × .7513)]. Hence, the NPV is $4,079 ($24,079 − $20,000 cost).
Answer (B) is incorrect because $6,789 uses a 5% discount rate. Answer (C) is incorrect because $9,869 is the NPV of Project A at a 10% discount rate. Answer (D) is incorrect because $39,204 uses present value interest factors for annuities.

**130.** The payback period of Project C is

A. 0 years.

B. 1 year.

C. 2 years.

D. 3 years.

The correct answer is (C). *(CIA, adapted)*
**REQUIRED:** The payback period for Project C.
**DISCUSSION:** The payback period is the time necessary to recoup the investment. After 2 years, the cumulative cash inflows for Project C are exactly equal to the initial investment outlay of $25,000.
Answer (A) is incorrect because the payback period would be zero only if a project had no cost or provided immediate cash inflows at least equal to the investment outlay. Answer (B) is incorrect because after 1 year, the cumulative cash inflows for Project C are only $15,000. The initial investment outlay is $25,000. Answer (D) is incorrect because Project C pays back its initial investment outlay in only 2 years.

**131.** If the discount rate is 5% and the discounted payback period of Project D is exactly 2 years, then the year 2 cash inflow for Project D is

- A. $5,890
- B. $10,000
- C. $12,075
- D. $14,301

The correct answer is (C). *(CIA, adapted)*

**REQUIRED:** The year 2 cash inflow for Project D.

**DISCUSSION:** The discounted payback period is the time required for discounted cash flows to recover the cost of the investment. Thus, the cost of Project D must equal the present value of the end-of-year-1 cash inflow discounted at 5% plus the present value of the end-of-year-2 cash inflow. The year 2 cash inflow (X) is calculated as follows:

$$\$30,000 = (\$20,000 \times .9524) + (X \times .9070)$$
$$X = (\$30,000 - \$19,048) \div .9070$$
$$X = \$12,075$$

Answer (A) is incorrect because $5,890 uses present value interest factors for annuities. Answer (B) is incorrect because $10,000 is based on the regular payback period. Answer (D) is incorrect because $14,301 is obtained using a 10% discount rate.

Questions 132 through 134 are based on the following information. Capital Invest Inc. uses a 12% hurdle rate for all capital expenditures and has done the following analysis for four projects for the upcoming year:

|  | Project 1 | Project 2 | Project 3 | Project 4 |
|---|---|---|---|---|
| Initial capital outlay | $200,000 | $298,000 | $248,000 | $272,000 |
| Annual net cash inflows |  |  |  |  |
| Year 1 | $ 65,000 | $100,000 | $ 80,000 | $ 95,000 |
| Year 2 | 70,000 | 135,000 | 95,000 | 125,000 |
| Year 3 | 80,000 | 90,000 | 90,000 | 90,000 |
| Year 4 | 40,000 | 65,000 | 80,000 | 60,000 |
| Net present value | (3,798) | 4,276 | 14,064 | 14,662 |
| Profitability index | 98% | 101% | 106% | 105% |
| Internal rate of return | 11% | 13% | 14% | 15% |

**132.** Which project(s) should Capital Invest Inc. undertake during the upcoming year assuming it has no budget restrictions?

- A. All of the projects.
- B. Projects 1, 2, and 3.
- C. Projects 2, 3, and 4.
- D. Projects 1, 3, and 4.

The correct answer is (C). *(CMA, adapted)*

**REQUIRED:** The project(s) undertaken assuming no budget restrictions.

**DISCUSSION:** A company using the NPV method should undertake all projects with a positive NPV, unless some of those projects are mutually exclusive. Given that Projects 2, 3, and 4 have positive NPVs, they should be undertaken. Project 1 has a negative NPV.

Answers (A), (B), and (D) are incorrect because Project 1 has a negative NPV and should not be undertaken, but Projects 2, 3, and 4 have positive NPVs and therefore should be included.

**133.** Which project(s) should Capital Invest Inc. undertake during the upcoming year if it has only $600,000 of funds available?

- A. Projects 1 and 3.
- B. Projects 2, 3, and 4.
- C. Projects 2 and 3.
- D. Projects 3 and 4.

The correct answer is (D). *(CMA, adapted)*

**REQUIRED:** The project(s) undertaken given capital rationing.

**DISCUSSION:** Given that only $600,000 is available and that each project costs $200,000 or more, no more than two projects can be undertaken. Because Projects 3 and 4 have the greatest NPVs, profitability indexes, and IRRs, they are the projects in which the company should invest.

Answer (A) is incorrect because Project 1 has a negative NPV. Answer (B) is incorrect because this answer violates the $600,000 limitation. Answer (C) is incorrect because the combined NPV of Projects 2 and 3 is less than the combined NPV of Projects 3 and 4.

**134.** Refer to the information preceding question 132 on page 509. Which project(s) should Capital Invest Inc. undertake during the upcoming year if it has only $300,000 of capital funds available?

A. Project 1.

B. Projects 2, 3, and 4.

C. Projects 3 and 4.

D. Project 3.

The correct answer is (D). *(CMA, adapted)*

**REQUIRED:** The project(s) undertaken given capital rationing.

**DISCUSSION:** Given that $300,000 is available and that each project costs $200,000 or more, only one project can be undertaken. Because Project 3 has a positive NPV and the highest profitability index, it is the best investment. The high profitability index means that the company will achieve the highest NPV per dollar of investment with Project 3. The profitability index facilitates comparison of different-sized investments.

Answer (A) is incorrect because Project 1 has a negative NPV. Answers (B) and (C) are incorrect because choosing more than one project violates the $300,000 limitation.

Questions 135 through 137 are based on the following information. A company purchased a new machine to stamp the company logo on its products. The cost of the machine was $250,000, and it has an estimated useful life of 5 years with an expected salvage value at the end of its useful life of $50,000. The company uses the straight-line depreciation method.

The new machine is expected to save $125,000 annually in operating costs. The company's tax rate is 40%, and it uses a 10% discount rate to evaluate capital expenditures.

| Year | Present Value of $1 | Present Value of an Ordinary Annuity of $1 |
|------|------|------|
| 1 | .909 | .909 |
| 2 | .826 | 1.736 |
| 3 | .751 | 2.487 |
| 4 | .683 | 3.170 |
| 5 | .621 | 3.791 |

**135.** What is the traditional payback period for the new stamping machine?

A. 2.00 years.

B. 2.63 years.

C. 2.75 years.

D. 2.94 years.

The correct answer is (C). *(CIA, adapted)*

**REQUIRED:** The traditional payback period for the new stamping machine.

**DISCUSSION:** The traditional payback period is the number of years required to complete the return of the original investment. It equals the net investment divided by the average expected periodic net cash inflow. The periodic net cash inflow equals the $125,000 annual savings minus the additional taxes paid. This $125,000 increase in pretax income will be reduced by an increase in depreciation of $40,000 [($250,000 cost – $50,000 salvage) ÷ 5 years]. Hence, taxes will increase by $34,000 [$40% x ($125,000 – $40,000)], and the after-tax periodic net cash inflow will be $91,000 ($125,000 – $34,000). Accordingly, the payback period is 2.75 years ($250,000 ÷ $91,000).

Answer (A) is incorrect because 2.00 years does not consider cash flows for taxes. Answer (B) is incorrect because 2.63 years omits salvage value from the depreciation calculation. Answer (D) is incorrect because 2.94 years treats depreciation as a negative cash flow and ignores taxes.

**136.** What is the accounting rate of return based on the average investment in the new stamping machine?

   A.  20.4%

   B.  34.0%

   C.  40.8%

   D.  51.0%

The correct answer is (C). *(CIA, adapted)*

   **REQUIRED:** The accounting rate of return based on the average investment.

   **DISCUSSION:** The accounting rate of return equals annual after-tax net income divided by average investment. Annual after-tax net income equals $51,000 [($125,000 cost savings – $40,000 depreciation as calculated in the preceding question) x (1.0 – 0.4)]. Consequently, the accounting rate of return equals 40.8% [$51,000 ÷ ($250,000 investment ÷ 2)].

   Answer (A) is incorrect because 20.4% is the accounting rate of return using the original investment. Answer (B) is incorrect because 34.0% results from adding the salvage value to the original investment. Answer (D) is incorrect because 51.0% assumes an average investment of $100,000.

**137.** What is the net present value (NPV) of the new stamping machine?

   A.  $125,940

   B.  $200,000

   C.  $250,000

   D.  $375,940

The correct answer is (A). *(CIA, adapted)*

   **REQUIRED:** The net present value of the machine.

   **DISCUSSION:** The NPV of the stamping machine is the excess of the present values of the estimated cash inflows over the net cost of the investment. The annual after-tax net cash inflow from the cost savings is $91,000. In the fifth year, the cash inflows will also include the salvage value.

| Year | Cash Flow Amounts | PV Factor | PV of Cash Flow |
|---|---|---|---|
| 0 | $(250,000) | 1.000 | $(250,000) |
| 1 | $91,000 | .909 | 82,719 |
| 2 | $91,000 | .826 | 75,166 |
| 3 | $91,000 | .751 | 68,341 |
| 4 | $91,000 | .683 | 62,153 |
| 5 | $91,000 + $50,000 | .621 | 87,561 |
| | Net present value | | $125,940 |

   Answer (B) is incorrect because $200,000 is the cost of the machine minus salvage value. Answer (C) is incorrect because $250,000 is the cost of the machine. Answer (D) is incorrect because $375,940 is the NPV of the machine plus its purchase price.

Questions 138 through 144 are based on the following information. At the beginning of 1999, Garrison Corporation is considering the replacement of an old machine that is currently being used. The old machine is fully depreciated but can be used by the corporation for an additional 5 years, that is, through 2003. If Garrison decides to replace the old machine, Picco Company has offered to purchase it for $60,000 on the replacement date. The old machine would have no salvage value in 2003.

If the replacement occurs, a new machine will be acquired from Hillcrest Industries on January 2, 1999. The purchase price of $1 million for the new machine will be paid in cash at the time of replacement. Because of the increased efficiency of the new machine, estimated annual cash savings of $300,000 will be generated through 2003, the end of its expected useful life. The new machine is not expected to have any salvage value at the end of 2003.

All operating cash receipts, operating cash expenditures, and applicable tax payments and credits are assumed to occur at the end of the year. Garrison employs the calendar year for reporting purposes.

Discount tables for several different interest rates that are to be used in any discounting calculations are given below.

Present Value of $1.00 Received at End of Period

| Period | 9% | 12% | 15% | 18% | 21% |
|--------|------|------|------|------|------|
| 1 | .92 | .89 | .87 | .85 | .83 |
| 2 | .84 | .80 | .76 | .72 | .68 |
| 3 | .77 | .71 | .65 | .61 | .56 |
| 4 | .71 | .64 | .57 | .51 | .47 |
| 5 | .65 | .57 | .50 | .44 | .39 |

Present Value of an Annuity of $1.00
Received at the End of Each Period

| Period | 9% | 12% | 15% | 18% | 21% |
|--------|------|------|------|------|------|
| 1 | .92 | .89 | .87 | .85 | .83 |
| 2 | 1.76 | 1.69 | 1.63 | 1.57 | 1.51 |
| 3 | 2.53 | 2.40 | 2.28 | 2.18 | 2.07 |
| 4 | 3.24 | 3.04 | 2.85 | 2.69 | 2.54 |
| 5 | 3.89 | 3.61 | 3.35 | 3.13 | 2.93 |

For questions 139 through 141 only, assume that Garrison is not subject to income taxes.

**138.** If Garrison requires investments to earn a 12% return, the NPV for replacing the old machine with the new machine is

- A. $171,000
- B. $136,400
- C. $143,000
- D. $83,000

The correct answer is (C). *(CMA, adapted)*
**REQUIRED:** The NPV of the new machine.
**DISCUSSION:** The $300,000 of annual savings discounted at 12% has a present value of $1,083,000 ($300,000 x 3.61 PV of an ordinary annuity for five periods at 12%). The net cost of the new machine is the $1,000,000 purchase price minus the $60,000 cash inflow from the sale of the old machine, or $940,000. The resulting NPV is $143,000 ($1,083,000 present value of future savings – $940,000 cash outlay).

Answer (A) is incorrect because the $300,000 savings is an annual savings, which should be discounted at the present value of an annuity of $1 for 5 periods at 12%, or 3.61 ($300,000 x 3.61 = $1,083,000). The $300,000 annual savings should not be discounted using the present value of $1 for 5 periods at 12%, or .57 ($300,000 x .57 = $171,000). Furthermore, the properly discounted amount ($1,083,000) should be reduced by the net cash outlay ($1,000,000 – $60,000) for the new equipment. Answer (B) is incorrect because the NPV is equal to the present value of future cash savings minus net initial cash outlays. Answer (D) is incorrect because the cash inflows generated from the sale of old machinery should be added to the difference of the present value of cash inflows minus the purchase price of new machinery.

**139.** The IRR, to the nearest percent, to replace the old machine is

A. 9%

B. 15%

C. 17%

D. 18%

The correct answer is (D). *(CMA, adapted)*
 **REQUIRED:** The IRR to the nearest percent for replacing the old machine.
 **DISCUSSION:** The IRR is the discount rate at which the present value of the cash flows equals the original investment. Thus, the NPV of the project is zero at the IRR. The IRR is also the maximum borrowing cost the firm could afford to pay for a specific project. The IRR is similar to the yield rate/effective rate quoted in the business media. The formula for the IRR involving an annuity equates the annual cash flow, times an unknown annuity factor, with the initial net investment: $940,000 = $300,000 x Factor. The solution of the equation gives a factor of 3.133, which is found in the 18% column on the five-period line.
 Answers (A), (B), and (C) are incorrect because dividing the net investment by the annual savings yields a factor of 3.1333, which corresponds to an 18% IRR.

**140.** The payback period to replace the old machine with the new machine is

A. 1.14 years.

B. 2.78 years.

C. 3.13 years.

D. 3.33 years.

The correct answer is (C). *(CMA, adapted)*
 **REQUIRED:** The payback period for the new machine.
 **DISCUSSION:** The payback method determines how long it takes for the investment dollars to be recovered by the annual net cash inflows. The time is computed by dividing the net investment by the average periodic net cash inflow. The initial net cash outlay divided by the annual cash savings equals 3.13 years ($940,000 ÷ $300,000).
 Answer (A) is incorrect because the initial cash outlay divided by the annual cash savings equals 3.13, not 1.14. Answer (B) is incorrect because the initial cash outlay divided by the annual cash savings equals 3.13, not 2.78. Answer (D) is incorrect because the initial cash outlay is $940,000 ($1,000,000 outlay – $60,000 inflow).

---

Questions 141 through 144 are based on the following additional information. The assumptions are

• Garrison requires all investments to earn a 12% after-tax rate of return to be accepted.
• Garrison is subject to a marginal income tax rate of 40% on all income and gains (losses).

• The new machine will have depreciation as follows:

| Year | Depreciation |
|---|---|
| 1999 | $ 250,000 |
| 2000 | 380,000 |
| 2001 | 370,000 |
| | $1,000,000 |

---

**141.** The present value of the depreciation tax shield for 2000 is

A. $182,400

B. $121,600

C. $109,440

D. $114,304

The correct answer is (B). *(CMA, adapted)*
 **REQUIRED:** The present value of the depreciation tax shield for the second year of the machine's life.
 **DISCUSSION:** The applicable depreciation for 2000 is $380,000. At a tax rate of 40%, the savings is $152,000 ($380,000 x 40%). Its present value is $121,600 ($152,000 x .80 PV of $1 for two periods at 12%).
 Answer (A) is incorrect because the present value of the depreciation tax shield equals the present value of the product of 2000 depreciation multiplied by the tax rate of 40%. Answer (C) is incorrect because $109,440 is the present value of the tax saving discounted at 18%, not the required 12%. Answer (D) Is Incorrect because the present value of the depreciation tax shield is the PV of $1 for 2 periods at 12% times the savings of $152,000 ($380,000 x 40%).

Questions 142 through 144 are based on the information presented on pages 512 and 513.

**142.** The present value of the after-tax cash flow associated with the salvage of the old machine is

A. $38,640

B. $36,000

C. $32,040

D. $27,960

The correct answer is (A). *(CMA, adapted)*

**REQUIRED:** The present value of the after-tax cash flow associated with the salvage of the old machine.

**DISCUSSION:** The old machine will be sold for $60,000, and the entire selling price represents a taxable gain because the book value is zero. At a 40% tax rate, the tax is $24,000. However, the tax will not be paid until the end of the year. Discounting the tax payment results in a present value of $21,360 ($24,000 x .89). This amount is subtracted from the $60,000 selling price (not discounted because received immediately) to yield an after-tax NPV of $38,640.

Answer (B) is incorrect because the $24,000 tax payment to be paid at year-end should be discounted using the present value factor of .89. Answer (C) is incorrect because the $60,000 payment received for the machinery is received immediately upon sale, and therefore should not be discounted. Answer (D) is incorrect because only the discounted amount of income tax should be subtracted from the $60,000 received for the machinery.

**143.** The present value of the annual after-tax cash savings that arise from the increased efficiency of the new machine throughout its life (calculated before consideration of any depreciation tax shield) is

A. $563,400

B. $375,600

C. $433,200

D. $649,800

The correct answer is (D). *(CMA, adapted)*

**REQUIRED:** The present value of the annual after-tax cash savings that arise from the new machine without consideration of the depreciation tax shield.

**DISCUSSION:** The annual savings of $300,000 must be reduced by the 40% tax, so the net effect of purchasing the new machine is an annual cash savings of $180,000 [(1 − .4) x $300,000]. The present value of the after-tax savings is therefore $649,800 ($180,000 x 3.61 PV of an ordinary annuity for five periods at 12%).

Answer (A) is incorrect because $563,400 is the present value of the annual after-tax cash savings discounted at 18%, not the firm's required 12%. Answer (B) is incorrect because the annual savings must be reduced by the 40% tax. This is achieved by multiplying annual savings by 1 − .4, not 1 − .6. Answer (C) is incorrect because the present value is the annual after-tax savings discounted at the PV of an ordinary annuity for five periods at 12%.

**144.** If the new machine is expected to be sold for $80,000 on December 31, 2003, the present value of the additional after-tax cash flow is

A. $18,240

B. $27,360

C. $45,600

D. $48,000

The correct answer is (B). *(CMA, adapted)*

**REQUIRED:** The present value of the additional after-tax cash flow resulting from a future sale of the new machine.

**DISCUSSION:** At the time of sale, the new machine will be fully depreciated, and any sale proceeds will be fully taxable as a gain. Hence, the $80,000 taxable gain will result in $32,000 of tax ($80,000 x .40), and the after-tax cash flow will be $48,000. Its present value will be $27,360 ($48,000 x .57 PV of $1 for five periods at 12%).

Answer (A) is incorrect because the after-tax cash flow of $48,000, not the $32,000 of tax, should be discounted at the PV factor of $1 for 5 periods at 12%. Answer (C) is incorrect because the $32,000 of tax should be deducted from the sale amount before discounting the after-tax cash flow. Answer (D) is incorrect because $48,000 is the after-tax cash inflow, which needs to be discounted to its PV.

# CHAPTER FOURTEEN
# INVENTORY MANAGEMENT:
# TRADITIONAL AND MODERN APPROACHES

Traditional inventory management concerns how much of some item to have in stock, how much to order (or produce), and when to place the order (or commence production). The traditional concepts most frequently tested are the economic order quantity (EOQ) and its attendant costs, the reorder level, and safety stocks. The EOQ model can also be used to determine the optimal production run. The objective of inventory management is to maintain an adequate amount of product on hand to meet demand but at the same time to minimize the costs of keeping inventories. Too little inventory can result in both internal and external failure costs. In a production setting, an inventory shortage can result in shutting down an entire factory because sufficient components are not available. However, too much inventory can tie up funds that could be invested elsewhere or worsen such problems as obsolescence and spoilage. Thus, an organization carries inventories because of the difficulty in predicting the amount, timing, and location of both supply and demand, and the purpose of inventory management is to determine the optimal level of inventory necessary to minimize costs. However, although the traditional approach has been to minimize inventory and the related carrying costs, some organizations find inventory a good hedge against inflation. Moreover, inventory carrying costs can sometimes be transferred to either customers or suppliers. Customers can sometimes be persuaded to carry large quantities of inventory by allowing them special quantity discounts or extended credit terms. Also, if customers are willing to accept long lead times, inventory can be manufactured to order to avoid storing large quantities. Furthermore, if a manufacturer has enough control of production to know exactly when materials are needed, orders can be placed so that materials arrive no earlier than when actually needed. This just-in-time (JIT) approach relies on a supplier who is willing to take the responsibility for producing or storing the needed inventory and shipping it to arrive on time. Suppliers are more willing to provide this service when they have many competitors. JIT systems are discussed more fully below.

**Inventory costs** in addition to the costs of the purchased items have traditionally been classified as order costs, carrying costs, and stockout costs. **Order costs** include all costs associated with preparing a purchase order. **Carrying costs** include avoidable labor costs, rent, insurance, taxes, security, depreciation, and opportunity cost (i.e., the cost incurred by investing in inventory rather than making an income-earning investment). Carrying costs may also include a charge for spoilage of perishable items or for obsolescence. **Stockout costs** include the costs incurred when an item is out of stock, such as the lost contribution margin on sales, customer ill will, and production interruptions.

**Purchasing** is the inventory management function that concerns the acquisition process. It encompasses choice of vendors, contract negotiation, the decision whether to purchase centrally or locally, and value analysis. The process is initiated by purchase requisitions issued by the production control function. Purchase requisitions ultimately result from insourcing vs. outsourcing (make vs. buy) decisions made when production processes were designed. For a retailer, the purchase decision is the same as the decision about what to sell. The choice of vendors depends on price, quality, delivery performance, shipping costs, credit terms, and service. Purchasers with a competitive orientation and considerable economic power may be able to extract very favorable terms from vendors. Purchasers with a cooperative orientation adopt a longer-term approach. The purchaser and the vendor are viewed as committed to a partnership involving joint efforts to improve quality. This orientation includes the purchaser's willingness to help develop the vendor's managerial, technical, and productive capacities. Thus, it tends to result in minimizing the number of vendors.

Ordering may be a complicated task when a onetime, expensive purchase is made. It may also be as simple as a phone call or a computer message. Indeed, organizations increasingly are linked with vendors by **electronic data interchange (EDI)**. EDI permits the transmission via computer of purchase orders, invoices, and payments, thereby reducing reorder times, inventories, and document-handling costs. Moreover, an organization that has reengineered its procedures and processes to take full advantage of EDI may have eliminated even the electronic equivalents of paper documents. For example, the buyer's point-of-sale (POS) system may directly transmit information to the seller, which delivers on a JIT basis. Purchase orders, invoices, and receiving reports are eliminated and replaced with a long-term contract establishing quantities, prices, and delivery schedules; production schedules; advance ship notices; evaluated receipts settlements (periodic payment authorizations transmitted to the trading partner with no need for matching purchase orders, invoices, and receiving reports); and payments by **electronic funds transfer (EFT)**.

Tracking purchases involves following up to anticipate any deviations from delivery times, quantities, and quality. Tracking may prevent production interruptions. The receiving function verifies the time of delivery, the quality and quantity received, and the price. It also notifies purchasing, the subunit that requested the delivery, inventory control, and accounting.

Negotiation of contracts depends on the nature of the item to be purchased. For a customized item, the organization may use competitive bidding, with the contract awarded to the lowest and best bidder; it may negotiate with a **sole-source vendor** to reduce purchasing lead time; or it may order through a vendor catalog. When purchased items are standardized and in high demand, the organization may also preselect a sole-source vendor to which orders will be sent as needed. Given great enough demand, the purchaser and vendor may even agree to a long-term contract with some terms left open. A blanket contract covers numerous items, and an open-ended contract permits terms to be added or the period of the agreement to be extended. Large organizations also must decide whether to buy centrally or locally. Buying centrally increases the organization's bargaining power and allows it to exploit the expertise of corporate-level specialists. The latter consideration is important given the trend toward purchasing items abroad. Centralized buying is facilitated by developments in information technology (see the EDI discussion above). Buying locally is indicated when items are unique to decentralized subunits, when a just-in-time (JIT) system is in place, and when longer lead times are to be avoided.

Purchasing shares responsibility for **value analysis** with the production and engineering functions. Value analysis determines the purpose of an item, whether that purpose is necessary, whether a less costly standard item can be found that serves the same purpose, and whether the item can be simplified or its specifications changed to reduce the cost. Thus, value analysis is performed by teams of specialists to ascertain how the performance of an item that is either produced or purchased can be improved or its cost decreased.

**Inventory models** have been developed to assist the purchasing function. They are quantitative models designed to control inventory costs by determining the optimal time to place an order (or begin production) and the optimal order quantity (or production run). The timing of an order can be periodic (placing an order every X days) or perpetual (placing an order whenever the inventory declines to X units). **Periodic order systems** place minimal emphasis on record keeping. However, a risk of substantial overstock or understock may arise unless inventories are checked for assurance that the model is still appropriate. **Perpetual systems** detect an inventory decline to the reorder point by entering every withdrawal on a perpetual record that shows the balance. However, physical inventories should be taken to reconcile records and verify models in either a periodic or perpetual system. An alternative is to use the **two-bin method** for physical storage. In this system, the reorder level amount is stored separately from the balance of the items. When the stock clerk removes the last item from the balance bin, an order should be placed. The reorder level bin is then used until the order is received.

The basic **economic order quantity (EOQ)** model minimizes the sum of order (setup) costs and carrying costs. The following are the characteristics of this model: Demand is known and uniform throughout the period; the fixed order costs are eliminated when the total cost equation is differentiated to arrive at the EOQ; cost per order (setup) and unit carrying cost are constant, so the model is based only on variable costs; full replenishment occurs instantly when the last item is used; stockout costs are zero; and no safety stock is held. If a is the variable cost per order (setup), D is the periodic demand in units, and k is the unit periodic carrying cost, the formula for the EOQ is

$$EOQ = \sqrt{\frac{2aD}{k}}$$

The average level of inventory for this model will be one-half of the EOQ. The formula shows that the EOQ varies directly with demand and order (setup) costs, but inversely with carrying costs. Thus, the EOQ model is a push system; it is based on anticipated future demand, not the pull of actual current demand. Moreover, the EOQ is a periodic model. The number of orders (or production runs) per period is given by the periodic demand divided by the EOQ. The EOQ results from differentiating the total cost with regard to order (or production) quantity. It is the minimum point on the total cost curve. It also corresponds to the intersection of the variable carrying cost and variable order cost curves. The total cost equals the sum of variable order costs [(D ÷ EOQ) × a], variable carrying costs [(EOQ ÷2) × k], and fixed costs.

In addition to minimizing the sum of order costs and carrying costs, an organization must minimize the cost of holding safety stock and the cost of stockouts. **Safety stock** is the amount of extra inventory that is kept to guard against stockouts. It is the amount at the time of reordering minus the expected usage while the new goods are in transit. The problem may be diagrammed as follows:

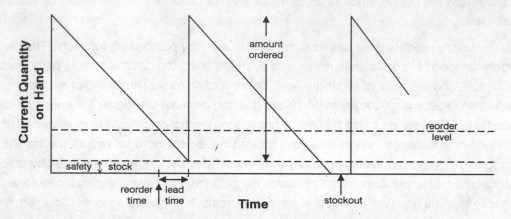

The EOQ determines order size, and the **reorder point** is the intersection of the reorder level and the downward-sloping total inventory line that allows sufficient lead time for an order to be placed and received.

Modern inventory management has departed from the EOQ approach in favor of the **just-in-time (JIT)** model. U.S. companies have traditionally built parts and components for subsequent operations on a preset schedule. Such a schedule provides a cushion of inventory so that the next operation will always have parts to work with -- a **just-in-case method**. In contrast, JIT limits output to the demand of the subsequent operation. Reductions in inventory levels result in less money invested in idle assets; reduction of storage space requirements; and lower inventory taxes, pilferage, and obsolescence risks. High inventory levels often mask production problems because defective parts can be overlooked when plenty of good parts are available. If only enough parts are made for the subsequent operation, however, any defects will immediately halt production. The focus of quality control under JIT shifts from the discovery of defective parts to the prevention of quality problems, so total preventive maintenance and zero defects are ultimate goals. Higher quality and lower inventory go together.

JIT is a reaction to the trends of global competition and rapid technological progress that have resulted in shorter product life-cycles and greater consumer demand for product diversity. Higher productivity, reduced order costs as well as carrying costs, faster and cheaper setups, shorter manufacturing cycle times, better due date performance, improved quality, and more flexible processes are goals of JIT methods. The ultimate objectives are increased competitiveness and higher profits.

JIT systems are based on a manufacturing philosophy popularized by the Japanese that combines purchasing, production, and inventory control. Minimization of inventory is a goal because many inventory-related activities are viewed as nonvalue-added. Indeed, carrying inventory is regarded as a symptom of correctable problems, such as poor quality, long cycle times, and lack of coordination with suppliers. However, JIT also encompasses changes in the production process itself. JIT is a **pull system**; items are pulled through production by current demand, not pushed through by anticipated demand. Thus, one operation produces only what is needed by the next operation, and components and raw materials arrive just in time to be used. To implement this approach and to eliminate waste of materials, labor, factory space, and machine usage, the factory is reorganized to permit what is often called **lean production**.

Plant layout in a JIT/lean production environment is not arranged by functional department or process but by **manufacturing cells**. Cells are sets of machines, often grouped in semicircles, that produce a given product or product type. Each worker in a cell must be able to operate all machines and, possibly, to perform support tasks, such as setup activities, preventive maintenance, movement of work-in-process within the cell, and quality inspection. In a pull system, workers might often be idle if they were not multi-skilled. Hence, central support departments are reduced or eliminated, space is saved, fewer and smaller factories may be required, and materials and tools are brought close to the point of use. Manufacturing cycle time and setup time are also reduced. As a result, on-time delivery performance and response to changes in markets are enhanced, and production of customized goods in small lots becomes feasible.

A cellular organization requires workers to operate as effective teams, so employee empowerment is crucial in a JIT/lean production system. Greater participation by employees is needed to achieve continuous improvement and zero defects goals, so they may, for example, have the power to stop production to correct a problem, be consulted about changes in processes, or become involved in hiring co-workers. Thus, managers in such a system usually play more of a facilitating than a support role.

The Japanese term **kanban** and JIT have often been confused. JIT is the total system of purchasing, production, and inventory control. Kanban is one of the many elements in the JIT system as it is used in Japan. The word kanban means ticket. Tickets (also described as cards or markers) control the flow of production or parts so that they are produced or obtained in the needed amounts at the needed times. A basic kanban system includes a **withdrawal kanban** that states the quantity that a later process should withdraw from its predecessor, a **production kanban** that states the output of the preceding process, and a **vendor kanban** that tells a vendor what, how much, where, and when to deliver. U.S. companies have not been comfortable with controlling production using tickets on the production floor. Computerized information systems have been used for many years, and U.S. companies have been reluctant to give up their computers in favor of the essentially manual kanban system. Instead, U.S. companies have integrated their existing systems, which are complex computerized planning systems, with the JIT system.

Another feature of the lower inventory levels in a JIT system is elimination of the need for several traditional internal controls. Frequent receipt of deliveries from suppliers often means less need for a sophisticated inventory control system and for control personnel. JIT also may eliminate central receiving areas, hard copy receiving reports, and storage areas. A central warehouse is not needed because deliveries are made by suppliers directly to the area of production. The quality of parts provided by suppliers is verified by use of statistical controls rather than inspection of incoming goods. Storage, counting, and inspecting are eliminated in an effort to perform only value-adding work. Thus, the supplier's dependability is crucial.

Organizations that adopt JIT systems therefore develop close relationships with a few carefully chosen suppliers who are extensively involved in the buyer's processes. Long-term contracts are typically negotiated to reduce order costs. Indeed, some major retailers have agreed to **continuous replenishment** arrangements whereby a supplier with superior demand forecasting ability essentially tells the buyer when and how much to reorder. Buyer-supplier relationships are further facilitated by **electronic data interchange (EDI)**, a technology that allows the supplier access to the buyer's online inventory management system. Thus, electronic messages replace paper documents (purchase orders and sales invoices), and the production schedules and deliveries of the parties can be more readily coordinated.

**Backflush costing** is often used by firms that have adopted a JIT philosophy. They regard carrying inventory as a nonvalue-added activity. Hence, components are made available just in time to be used in the production process. Backflush costing complements JIT because it simplifies costing. A traditional system tracks costs as they are incurred (sequential tracking), but backflush costing delays recording of some cost information. It treats the detailed recording of inventory data as a nonvalue-added activity. Work-in-process is usually eliminated, journal entries to inventory accounts may be delayed until the time of product completion or even the time of sale, and standard costs are used to assign costs to units when journal entries are made, that is, to flush costs backward to the points at which inventories remain.

One variation of backflush costing records materials inventory at standard cost when it is purchased. The entry is to an account such as raw and in-process inventory control. Materials arrive just in time for processing, so an entry to a separate materials inventory account is unnecessary. A materials price variance (debit or credit) may also be recorded at this time. Actual conversion costs (direct labor and overhead) are recorded when incurred in one control account. Finished goods completed during the period are debited at standard cost at the time of completion, with credits to raw and in-process inventory and conversion costs applied. After a count, raw and in-process inventory is adjusted, and a materials efficiency variance (debit or credit) is recorded for the difference between actual usage and standard usage for the amount of goods finished. The under- or overapplied conversion costs (debit conversion costs applied and credit conversion costs control) are usually closed to cost of goods sold instead of being prorated because the amounts tend to be small. The final entry is to debit cost of goods sold and credit finished goods.

A greater departure from traditional methods is to recognize completion of units only at the time of sale. Thus, instead of debiting finished goods for the number of units completed, cost of goods sold would be debited for the number of units sold. In this variation of backflush costing, only one inventory account is used (inventory control) instead of two (raw and in-process inventory and finished goods). The entry at time of sale is to debit cost of goods sold, credit inventory control, and credit conversion costs applied. A still simpler possibility is to eliminate entries to a materials inventory account altogether. Accordingly, finished goods are debited when completed and credited when sold, but no other inventory entries are made. Yet another variation of backflush costing records costs (direct materials, direct labor, and overhead) directly in cost of goods sold. At the end of the period, the standard costs of the ending work-in-process and finished goods inventories are flushed back from cost of goods sold (debit WIP and FG, credit CGS). Backflush costing may undervalue inventory and is therefore inconsistent with GAAP except when the difference is not material or an adjustment is made.

When a production process consists of interdependent operations, for example, when one part must be manufactured before another operation can continue, bottlenecks result in idle time. Thus, both items waiting in the queue to be processed by the bottleneck resource and the items waiting for the output of the bottleneck resource are idle. The **theory of constraints (TOC)** is a short-term approach to managing bottlenecks. Its basic principle is that short-term profit maximization requires maximizing the contribution margin of the constraint (the throughput contribution). However, TOC defines all costs as fixed in the short-term except direct materials costs. Accordingly, the **throughput contribution** equals sales dollars minus direct materials costs. This approach is a type of **supervariable costing** because only direct materials costs are inventoried. The objective of TOC is to maximize throughput contribution and to minimize investments (defined as materials costs of all inventories, plus R&D costs, plus fixed assets) and other operating costs (defined as all operating costs other than direct materials costs necessary to earn the throughput contribution). TOC identifies the bottleneck resource that determines the throughput contribution (the resource with large inventories waiting to be processed). The bottleneck resource establishes the processing schedule for nonbottleneck resources. Actions should then be undertaken to improve the capacity of the bottleneck so that the increase in the throughput contribution exceeds the additional costs.

Modern inventory management is often accomplished in the context of automated manufacturing, whether involving one piece of equipment, a cell, or an integrated plant. A **computer-integrated manufacturing (CIM)** system involves designing products using computer-aided design (CAD), testing the design using computer-aided engineering (CAE), manufacturing products using computer-aided manufacturing (CAM), and integrating all components with a computerized information system. Accordingly, CIM entails a holistic approach to manufacturing in which design is translated into product by centralized processing and robotics. The concept also includes materials handling. The advantages of CIM include flexibility, integration, and synergism. Flexibility is a key advantage. A traditional manufacturing system might become disrupted from an emergency change, but CIM will reschedule everything in the plant when a priority requirement is inserted into the system. The areas of flexibility include varying production volumes during a period, handling new parts added to a product, changing the proportion of parts being produced, adjusting to engineering changes of a product, adapting the sequence in which parts come to the machinery, adapting to changes in materials, rerouting parts as needed because of machine breakdowns or other production delays, and allowing for defects in materials. Benefits of CIM include improved product quality (less rework), better customer service, faster response to market changes, greater product variety, lower production costs, and shorter product development times. JIT is sometimes adopted prior to CIM because JIT simplifies production processes and provides a better understanding of actual production flow, which are essential factors for CIM success. The flexibility offered by CIM is almost a necessity for JIT suppliers. For example, a company that provides JIT deliveries to automobile plants cannot adapt to changing customer production schedules with a manual system unless a high inventory level is maintained. The emphasis is on materials control rather than the direct labor control that is dominant in most cost systems. CIM is an addition to, not a substitute for, other types of manufacturing concepts such as JIT. In other words, JIT should already be in place for CIM to work most effectively.

**Materials requirements planning (MRP)** is a computer-based information system that is more limited than CIM. It is designed to plan and control raw materials used in a production setting. MRP assumes that the demand for materials is typically dependent upon some other factor, which can be programmed into the computer. The timing of deliveries is vital to avoid production delays. For example, an auto manufacturer need only tell a computer how many autos of each type are to be manufactured. The MRP system determines how many of every component part will be needed. The computer will generate a complete list of every part and component needed. MRP, in effect, creates schedules of when items of inventory will be needed in the production departments. If parts are not in stock, the computer will automatically generate a purchase order on the proper date (considering lead times) so that deliveries will arrive on time.

**Manufacturing resource planning (MRP-II)** is a closed-loop manufacturing system that integrates all facets of a manufacturing business, including production, sales, inventories, schedules, and cash flows. The same system is used for both the financial reporting and managing operations (both use the same transactions and numbers). MRP-II uses an MPS (master production schedule), which is a statement of the anticipated manufacturing schedule for selected items for selected periods. MRP also uses the MPS. Thus, MRP is a component of an MRP-II system.

**Enterprise resource planning (ERP)** is the latest phase in the development of computerized systems for managing organizational resources. ERP is intended to integrate enterprise-wide information systems. ERP connects all organizational operations (personnel, the financial accounting system, production, marketing, distribution, etc.) and also connects the organization with its suppliers and customers.

## 14.1 Inventory Fundamentals

**1.** Economic order quantity models and two-bin systems are commonly used controls for a company's materials function. Those controls primarily relate to what part of the cycle?

   A. Materials requirements.

   B. Raw materials acceptance.

   C. Physical storage.

   D. Product distribution.

The correct answer is (A). *(CIA, adapted)*

**REQUIRED:** The part of the inventory cycle to which EOQ and two-bin systems are related.

**DISCUSSION:** Each technique is concerned with determination of need by controlling, monitoring, or analyzing the quantity of materials to purchase. The EOQ model determines the order quantity that minimizes the sum of ordering and carrying costs. Once the reorder point is established, a two-bin system may be used to signal the time to reorder when perpetual records are not kept. An inventory item is divided into two groups; when the first group is depleted, the order is placed, and the second group protects against stockout until replenishment.

Answers (B), (C), and (D) are incorrect because raw materials acceptance, physical storage, and product distribution are not part of the control cycle to which EOQ models and two-bin systems are related.

**2.** With regard to inventory management, an increase in the frequency of ordering will normally

   A. Reduce the total ordering costs.

   B. Have no impact on total ordering costs.

   C. Reduce total carrying costs.

   D. Have no impact of total carrying costs.

The correct answer is (C). *(CIA, adapted)*

**REQUIRED:** The effect of an increase in the frequency of ordering inventory.

**DISCUSSION:** Inventory carrying costs can sometimes be transferred to suppliers. If a seller has good enough control of demand schedules to know exactly when goods are needed, orders can be placed so that goods arrive no earlier than when actually needed. This practice relies on a supplier who is willing to take the responsibility for storing the needed inventory and shipping it to arrive on time. Suppliers are more willing to provide this service when they have many competitors.

Answers (A) and (B) are incorrect because total ordering costs will increase. Answer (D) is incorrect because total carrying costs are reduced.

**3.** A two-bin inventory order system is a

   A. Constant order-cycle system.

   B. Red-line system.

   C. Constant order-quantity system.

   D. Computerized control system.

The correct answer is (C). *(Publisher)*

**REQUIRED:** The nature of a two-bin inventory order system.

**DISCUSSION:** A two-bin order system divides inventory into two quantities. Inventory is reordered when the items in the first bin are used up. Essentially, the second bin provides for a safety stock plus the quantity used during the lead time before receiving the reorder. The amount of the inventory in the first bin is a constant quantity; thus, the two-bin procedure is a constant order-quantity system because the same amount is ordered each time.

Answer (A) is incorrect because the constant order-cycle describes a system in which inventory is ordered on a uniform time cycle and the quantity varies. Answer (B) is incorrect because, in a red-line system, a red line is drawn inside an inventory bin to indicate the reorder point. Answer (D) is incorrect because a two-bin system is a manual system.

**4.** Which inventory costing system results in the best inventory turnover ratio in a period of rising prices?

    A.  LIFO.

    B.  FIFO.

    C.  Weighted average.

    D.  Perpetual.

The correct answer is (A). *(Publisher)*
    **REQUIRED:** The inventory costing system resulting in the best inventory turnover ratio in a period of rising prices.
    **DISCUSSION:** The inventory turnover ratio equals cost of sales divided by average inventory. A high inventory turnover ratio is preferable because it indicates better usage of inventory. The ratio can be increased by increasing cost of sales or decreasing average inventory. In a period of rising prices, LIFO provides a lower inventory valuation because cost of sales will include the higher costs of more recently purchased goods, and inventory consists of the previously purchased, lower cost goods.
    Answer (B) is incorrect because FIFO costing results in higher inventory values when prices are rising. Answer (C) is incorrect because weighted-average costing results in higher inventory values when prices are rising. Answer (D) is incorrect because perpetual is an approach toward inventory record keeping, not an inventory costing system.

**5.** Which condition justifies accepting a low inventory turnover ratio?

    A.  High carrying costs.

    B.  High stockout costs.

    C.  Short inventory order lead times.

    D.  Low inventory order costs.

The correct answer is (B). *(Publisher)*
    **REQUIRED:** The condition that justifies acceptance of a low inventory turnover ratio.
    **DISCUSSION:** High stockout costs justify maintaining relatively large inventory levels. For example, if major customers will be lost because of stockouts, the higher costs of maintaining a large safety stock are acceptable.
    Answers (A), (C), and (D) are incorrect because high carrying costs, short lead times, and low order costs encourage more frequent orders of smaller quantities, which result in lower average inventory levels and a higher inventory turnover ratio.

**6.** Napier Company's budgeted sales and budgeted cost of sales for the coming year are $126 million and $72 million, respectively. Short-term interest rates are expected to average 10%. If Napier can increase inventory turnover from its current level of nine times per year to a level of 12 times per year, its cost savings in the coming year are expected to be

    A.  $150,000

    B.  $200,000

    C.  $350,000

    D.  $600,000

The correct answer is (B). *(CMA, adapted)*
    **REQUIRED:** The cost savings that will result from increasing inventory turnover.
    **DISCUSSION:** If budgeted cost of sales for the coming year is $72 million, and inventory turns over nine times during the year, the average investment in inventory will be $8 million ($72,000,000 ÷ 9). If the inventory turnover increases to 12 times per year, the average investment in inventory will be only $6 million ($72,000,000 ÷ 12), a decrease of $2 million. Given an interest rate of 10%, the savings are $200,000 per year.
    Answer (A) is incorrect because $150,000 is based on gross profit, not cost of sales. Answer (C) is incorrect because $350,000 is based on sales, not cost of sales. Answer (D) is incorrect because $600,000 is 10% of $6 million.

**7.** Order-filling costs, as opposed to order-getting costs, include all but which of the following items?

    A.   Credit check of new customers.

    B.   Packing and shipping of sales orders.

    C.   Collection of payments for sales orders.

    D.   Mailing catalogs to current customers.

The correct answer is (D). *(CMA, adapted)*
    **REQUIRED:** The variable not affecting order-filling costs.
    **DISCUSSION:** Order-filling costs include the costs necessary to prepare and ship the order, including the resulting payment process. Thus, clerical processing, credit checking, packing, shipping, and collecting payments are phases of the order-filling cycle. Mailing catalogs to current customers is an order-getting cost.
    Answer (A) is incorrect because credit checking of new customers, which is a clerical processing task, is an order-filling cost. Answer (B) is incorrect because the costs incurred from packing and shipping sales orders are order-filling costs. Answer (C) is incorrect because the costs incurred in billing and in collecting payments for sales orders are order-filling costs.

**8.** The control of order-filling costs

    A.   Can be accomplished through the use of flexible budget standards.

    B.   Is related to pricing decisions, sales promotion, and customer reaction.

    C.   Is not crucial because the costs are typically fixed and not subject to frequent changes.

    D.   Is not crucial because the order-filling routine is entrenched and external influences are minimal.

The correct answer is (A). *(CMA, adapted)*
    **REQUIRED:** The true statement about the control of order-filling costs.
    **DISCUSSION:** Order-filling costs can be controlled by essentially the same techniques as those used in any other cost control structure. Thus, flexible budgeting techniques could be usefully applied to controlling order-filling costs.
    Answer (B) is incorrect because the control of order-filling costs may be only indirectly related to pricing decisions, sales promotion, and customer reaction. Answer (C) is incorrect because order-filling costs may frequently change. Answer (D) is incorrect because the order-filling routine should be dynamic and flexible enough to adjust for changes in volume, etc.

**9.** Which of the following will not affect the budgeting of order-getting costs?

    A.   Market research and tests.

    B.   Location of distribution warehouses.

    C.   Policies and actions of competitors.

    D.   Sales promotion policies.

The correct answer is (B). *(CMA, adapted)*
    **REQUIRED:** The variable not affecting order-getting costs.
    **DISCUSSION:** Order-getting costs pertain to the variables necessary to obtain a particular order. Thus, budgeting and planning emphasis should be on market research, competitor analysis, promotion policies, general economic conditions, and all related policies and decisions affecting the organization up to the time of getting the order. The location of distribution warehouses is an order-filling cost consideration.
    Answer (A) is incorrect because market research and tests are necessary to obtain orders and therefore are order-getting costs. Answer (C) is incorrect because being familiar with the policies and actions of competitors is necessary to obtain orders and therefore generates order-getting costs. Answer (D) is incorrect because sales promotion policies are necessary to obtain orders and therefore are order-getting costs.

Questions 10 and 11 are based on the following information. Inventory management requires a firm to balance the quantity of inventory on hand for operations with the investment in inventory. Two cost categories of concern in inventory management are carrying costs and order costs.

**10.** The carrying costs associated with inventory management include

  A. Insurance costs, shipping costs, storage costs, and obsolescence.

  B. Storage costs, handling costs, interest on capital invested, and obsolescence.

  C. Purchasing costs, shipping costs, setup costs, and quantity discounts lost.

  D. Obsolescence, setup costs, interest on capital invested, and purchasing costs.

The correct answer is (B). *(CMA, adapted)*
  **REQUIRED:** The items included in carrying costs.
  **DISCUSSION:** Carrying costs include storage costs, handling costs, insurance costs, interest on capital invested, and obsolescence.
  Answer (A) is incorrect because shipping costs are an ordering cost, not a carrying cost. Answer (C) is incorrect because costs of purchasing, shipping, setup, and discounts lost are various ordering (or manufacturing) costs. Answer (D) is incorrect because the setup costs for a production run are equivalent to ordering costs.

**11.** The order costs associated with inventory management include

  A. Insurance costs, purchasing costs, shipping costs, and obsolescence.

  B. Obsolescence, setup costs, quantity discounts lost, and storage costs.

  C. Quantity discounts lost, storage costs, handling costs, and interest on capital invested.

  D. Purchasing costs, shipping costs, setup costs, and quantity discounts lost.

The correct answer is (D). *(CMA, adapted)*
  **REQUIRED:** The items included in order costs.
  **DISCUSSION:** Order costs include purchasing costs, shipping costs, setup costs for a production run, and quantity discounts lost.
  Answer (A) is incorrect because insurance costs are a carrying cost. Answer (B) is incorrect because obsolescence and storage costs are carrying costs. Answer (C) is incorrect because storage costs, handling costs, and interest on capital invested are all carrying costs.

## 14.2 Economic Order Quantity (EOQ)

**12.** The purpose of the economic order quantity model is to

  A. Minimize the safety stock.

  B. Minimize the sum of the order costs and the holding costs.

  C. Minimize the inventory quantities.

  D. Minimize the sum of the demand costs and the backlog costs.

The correct answer is (B). *(CIA, adapted)*
  **REQUIRED:** The purpose of the economic order quantity model.
  **DISCUSSION:** The EOQ model is a deterministic model that calculates the ideal order (or production lot) quantity given specified periodic demand, the cost per order or production run, and the periodic cost of carrying one unit in stock. The model minimizes the sum of inventory carrying costs and either ordering or production setup costs.
  Answer (A) is incorrect because the basic EOQ model does not include safety stock. Answer (C) is incorrect because, in the EOQ model, costs, not quantities, are to be minimized. Answer (D) is incorrect because quantity demanded is a variable in the model, but order costs, not demand costs, are relevant. Backlogs are customer orders that cannot be filled immediately because of stockouts. Backlog costs are not quantified in the model.

**13.** Which of the following is used in determining the economic order quantity (EOQ)?

- A. Regression analysis.
- B. Calculus.
- C. Markov process.
- D. Queuing theory.

The correct answer is (B). *(CIA, adapted)*
**REQUIRED:** The method for determining the EOQ.
**DISCUSSION:** The primary business application of differential calculus is to identify the maxima or minima of curvilinear functions. In business and economics, these are the points of revenue or profit maximization (maxima) or cost minimization (minima). The EOQ results from differentiating the total cost with regard to order quantity.

Answer (A) is incorrect because regression analysis is used to fit a linear trend line to a dependent variable based on one or more independent variables. Answer (C) is incorrect because Markov process models are used to study the evolution of certain systems over repeated trials. Answer (D) is incorrect because queuing theory is a waiting-line technique used to balance desirable service levels against the cost of providing more service.

**14.** The economic order quantity (EOQ) formula can be adapted in order for a firm to determine the optimal mix between cash and marketable securities. The EOQ model assumes all of the following except that

- A. The cost of a transaction is independent of the dollar amount of the transaction and interest rates are constant over the short run.
- B. An opportunity cost is associated with holding cash, beginning with the first dollar.
- C. The total demand for cash is known with certainty.
- D. Cash flow requirements are random.

The correct answer is (D). *(CMA, adapted)*
**REQUIRED:** The assumption not made in the EOQ model.
**DISCUSSION:** The EOQ formula is a deterministic model that requires a known demand for inventory or, in this case, the amount of cash needed. Thus, the cash flow requirements cannot be random. The model also assumes a given carrying (interest) cost and a flat transaction cost for converting marketable securities to cash, regardless of the amount withdrawn.

Answer (A) is incorrect because the EOQ model assumes that the cost of a transaction is independent of the dollar amount of the transaction and interest rates are constant over the short run. Answer (B) is incorrect because the EOQ model assumes an opportunity cost is associated with holding cash, beginning with the first dollar. Answer (C) is incorrect because the EOQ model assumes that the total demand for cash is known with certainty.

**15.** Ardmore Industries is in the process of reviewing its inventory and production policies. The company often has an excess supply of some products and shortages of other products needed for planned production runs. The method that Ardmore should use to establish its inventory policies regarding these products is

- A. Linear programming.
- B. Regression analysis.
- C. Economic production quantity analysis.
- D. Contribution margin analysis.

The correct answer is (C). *(CMA, adapted)*
**REQUIRED:** The quantitative technique that should be used for planning inventory policy.
**DISCUSSION:** The economic order quantity (EOQ) model can be used to establish inventory policy. In the case of a manufacturer, the EOQ model is called economic production quantity analysis. The objective of the model is to minimize the total of inventory holding costs and the costs of production runs (e.g., setup costs).

Answer (A) is incorrect because linear programming is used to maximize profits or minimize costs given resource constraints. Answer (B) is incorrect because regression analysis explains the behavior of a dependent variable (such as cost) in terms of one or more independent variables. Answer (D) is incorrect because a product's contribution margin is the difference between sales and variable costs.

**16.** The simple economic production lot size model will only apply to situations in which the production

    A. Rate equals the demand rate.

    B. Rate is less than the demand rate.

    C. Rate is greater than the demand rate.

    D. For the period covered equals the projected sales for the period.

The correct answer is (C). *(CMA, adapted)*

    **REQUIRED:** The situation in which the simple economic lot size model applies.

    **DISCUSSION:** This model is the same as the basic EOQ model, with the production quantity (lot) substituted for the EOQ and the cost of a production run for the order cost. In the basic model, the production rate (or time to fill an order) is deemed to be instantaneous, whereas demand is assumed to occur at a constant rate over some period of time.

    Answers (A) and (B) are incorrect because production (or resupply) is assumed to be instantaneous. Answer (D) is incorrect because the purpose of the basic model is to adjust production to match demand. This answer choice implies that production is given.

**17.** A decrease in inventory order costs will

    A. Decrease the economic order quantity.

    B. Increase the reorder point.

    C. Have no effect on the economic order quantity.

    D. Decrease the carrying cost percentage.

The correct answer is (A). *(CMA, adapted)*

    **REQUIRED:** The effect of a decrease in inventory ordering costs.

    **DISCUSSION:** A decrease in inventory order costs should decrease the economic order quantity. The effect is that more orders can be made (of smaller quantities) without increasing costs. Accordingly, in the EOQ model, ordering cost is a numerator value.

    Answer (B) is incorrect because the reorder point is based on lead time, not the EOQ model. Answer (C) is incorrect because the EOQ should decline. Answer (D) is incorrect because the carrying cost percentage will always be identical to the ordering cost percentage in accordance with the fundamental calculus underlying the EOQ model.

**18.** An increase in inventory carrying costs will

    A. Decrease the economic order quantity.

    B. Increase the safety stock required.

    C. Have no effect on the economic order quantity.

    D. Decrease the number of orders issued per year.

The correct answer is (A). *(CMA, adapted)*

    **REQUIRED:** The effect of an increase in inventory carrying costs.

    **DISCUSSION:** An increase in carrying costs will lead to a decrease in the economic order quantity. Such an increase will cause total costs to rise unless the average inventory declines. Because the average inventory will be at least half of the EOQ, the only way for the average inventory to decline (other than by changing safety stocks) is for purchases to be made more often and in smaller quantities. Thus, in the EOQ model, carrying cost is a denominator value.

    Answer (B) is incorrect because the safety stock is not a factor in the EOQ calculation. If anything, management will reduce safety stocks when inventory carrying costs increase. Answer (C) is incorrect because the EOQ will decline. Answer (D) is incorrect because the number of orders will increase. The average order size and average inventory held will be smaller.

**19.** The economic order quantity (EOQ) will rise following

  A.  A decrease in annual unit sales.

  B.  An increase in carrying costs.

  C.  An increase in the per-unit purchase price of inventory.

  D.  An increase in the variable costs of placing and receiving an order.

The correct answer is (D). *(CIA, adapted)*
  **REQUIRED:** The reason for an increase in the EOQ.
  **DISCUSSION:** The formula for the EOQ is

$$EOQ = \sqrt{\frac{2aD}{k}}$$

The variable cost per purchase order (a) and the annual unit demand (D) are in the numerator, and the annual unit carrying cost (k) is in the denominator. Consequently, an increase in a or D will increase the EOQ. A change in the fixed costs of order has no effect on the EOQ. Total inventory cost is the sum of carrying cost (a variable cost) and order cost. It is equal to variable carrying cost, plus variable order cost, plus fixed ordering cost. When this equation is differentiated, the fixed cost is eliminated. Hence, the EOQ is a function of variable costs only.

Answer (A) is incorrect because a decrease in a numerator item decreases the EOQ. Answer (B) is incorrect because an increase in a denominator item decreases the EOQ. Answer (C) is incorrect because the unit price of inventory has no effect on the EOQ if carrying cost is not affected by a change in price. But if carrying cost moves in the same direction as price changes, an increase in unit price will increase the denominator and decrease the EOQ.

**20.** One of the elements included in the economic order quantity (EOQ) formula is

  A.  Safety stock.

  B.  Yearly demand.

  C.  Selling price of item.

  D.  Lead time for delivery.

The correct answer is (B). *(CIA, adapted)*
  **REQUIRED:** The element to include in the EOQ calculation.
  **DISCUSSION:** The basic EOQ formula is used to minimize the total of inventory carrying and ordering costs. The basic EOQ equals the square root of a fraction consisting of a numerator equal to the product of twice the unit periodic demand and the variable cost per order and a denominator equal to the unit periodic carrying cost.

Answers (A), (C), and (D) are incorrect because the safety stock, the selling price of the item, and the lead time for delivery are not included in the basic EOQ formula.

**21.** Which one of the following items is not directly reflected in the basic economic order quantity (EOQ) model?

  A.  Interest on invested capital.

  B.  Public warehouse rental charges.

  C.  Setup costs of manufacturing runs.

  D.  Quantity discounts lost on inventory purchases.

The correct answer is (D). *(CMA, adapted)*
  **REQUIRED:** The item not reflected in the basic EOQ model.
  **DISCUSSION:** The basic EOQ model minimizes the sum of order (or setup) and carrying costs. Included in the formula are annual demand, ordering (or setup) costs, and carrying costs. Carrying costs include warehousing costs, property taxes, insurance, spoilage, obsolescence, and interest on invested capital. The cost of the inventory itself is not a component of the EOQ model, and neither are any quantity discounts lost on inventory purchases.

Answers (A), (B), and (C) are incorrect because interest on invested capital, public warehouse rental charges, and setup costs of manufacturing runs are all items considered in the basic EOQ model.

**22.** The calculation of an economic order quantity (EOQ) considers

    A. The purchasing manager's salary.

    B. A corporate charge for advertising expenses.

    C. The shipping costs to deliver the product to the customer.

    D. Capital costs.

The correct answer is (D). *(CMA, adapted)*
    **REQUIRED:** The true statement about the calculation of the economic order quantity.
    **DISCUSSION:** The determination of the economic order quantity balances the variable costs of ordering and carrying inventory. Factors in the equation include the cost of placing an order, unit carrying cost, and annual demand in units. Carrying costs include storage costs, handling costs, insurance, property taxes, obsolescence, and the opportunity cost of investing capital in inventory. Thus, the return on capital that is forgone when it is invested in inventory should be considered.
    Answer (A) is incorrect because the purchasing manager's salary is a fixed cost. The EOQ model includes variable costs only. Answer (B) is incorrect because advertising is not an ordering or carrying cost. Answer (C) is incorrect because the cost of shipping to customers is a selling expense.

**23.** The economic order quantity (EOQ) formula assumes that

    A. Purchase costs per unit differ because of quantity discounts.

    B. Costs of placing an order vary with quantity ordered.

    C. Periodic demand for the good is known.

    D. Erratic usage rates are cushioned by safety stocks.

The correct answer is (C). *(CPA, adapted)*
    **REQUIRED:** The assumption underlying the EOQ formula.
    **DISCUSSION:** The basic EOQ formula is a function of unit demand, the cost of placing one order, and the cost of carrying one unit for one period. A change in unit demand will cause a change in the EOQ, all other values held constant. The model assumes that demand is known and that usage is uniform.
    Answer (A) is incorrect because unit purchasing costs are constant. Answer (B) is incorrect because the costs of placing an order are deemed to be constant. Answer (D) is incorrect because the usage rate is assumed to be uniform, and no safety stock is necessary.

**24.** The following graph shows four cost curves:

• An annual inventory carrying cost curve
• An annual order cost curve
• An annual inventory total cost curve
• A fixed cost curve with respect to order quantity

The correct answer is (B). *(CIA, adapted)*
    **REQUIRED:** The annual inventory carrying cost curve.
    **DISCUSSION:** Annual inventory carrying costs (Curve 2) are a linear function of the amount of inventory carried. As the quantity ordered increases, so does the annual total carrying cost and the amount of average inventory.
    Answer (A) is incorrect because Curve 1 has a minimum point. Thus, it must be the annual total cost curve for carrying inventory. Answer (C) is incorrect because fixed costs (Curve 3) do not change with the amount of inventory held. Answer (D) is incorrect because annual order costs (Curve 4) are inversely related to the order quantity and continually decline.

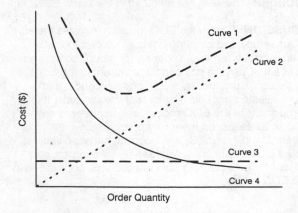

Which of the curves is the annual inventory carrying cost curve?

    A. Curve 1.

    B. Curve 2.

    C. Curve 3.

    D. Curve 4.

**25.** Given the EOQ model below, the optimal order quantity is

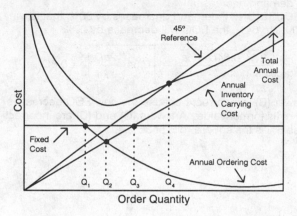

A. $Q_1$

B. $Q_2$

C. $Q_3$

D. $Q_4$

The correct answer is (B). *(CIA, adapted)*

**REQUIRED:** The optimal order quantity given the EOQ model.

**DISCUSSION:** The objective of the EOQ model is to find an optimal order quantity that balances carrying and order costs. Only variable costs should be considered. The EOQ is the intersection of the order cost and carrying cost curves. It corresponds to the minimum point on the total inventory cost curve.

Answers (A) and (C) are incorrect because fixed costs have no impact on EOQ. Answer (D) is incorrect because the intersection of the total annual cost line and the 45° reference line is meaningless.

**26.** A ski manufacturing company dates invoices seasonally so that skis delivered in September will bear an invoice due date for the following February. As a result of using this method, the manufacturer's inventory carrying costs are (lower; higher; constant) and the buyer is extended a (shorter; longer) credit period than would otherwise be true.

A. Lower, longer.

B. Higher, longer.

C. Lower, shorter.

D. Higher, shorter.

The correct answer is (A). *(CIA, adapted)*

**REQUIRED:** The effect of a manufacturer's inventory practices on inventory carrying costs and the credit period.

**DISCUSSION:** By shipping the skis in September, the manufacturer transfers warehousing costs to the purchaser. Thus, the manufacturer's carrying costs are lower than usual. By invoicing for payment in February (5 months later), the manufacturer also extends the credit period.

Answer (B) is incorrect because carrying costs will be lower because items are not held in the ski manufacturer's inventory as long. Answer (C) is incorrect because 5 months is longer than the usual credit period of, say, 20 days. Answer (D) is incorrect because carrying costs will be lower because items are not held in the ski manufacturer's inventory as long. Also, the credit period would be longer than usual.

**27.** A characteristic of the basic economic order quantity (EOQ) model is that it

A. Is relatively insensitive to error.

B. Should not be used when carrying costs are large in relation to procurement costs.

C. Is used when product demand, lead time, and order costs are uncertain.

D. Should not be used in conjunction with computerized perpetual inventory systems.

The correct answer is (A). *(CMA, adapted)*

**REQUIRED:** The characteristic of the basic EOQ model.

**DISCUSSION:** The basic EOQ model equals the square root of the quotient of (1) the product of twice the demand times the cost per order, (2) divided by the periodic carrying cost. Hence, the model is relatively insensitive to error. A given percentage error in a value results in a lower percentage change in the EOQ.

Answer (B) is incorrect because the EOQ model can be used regardless of the relationship between carrying and purchasing costs. Answer (C) is incorrect because product demand and order costs must be known with some certainty. Answer (D) is incorrect because an EOQ model can be used with any type of system.

**28.** The economic order quantity is the size of the order that minimizes total inventory costs, including ordering and carrying costs. If the annual demand decreases by 36%, the optimal order size will

- A. Decrease by 20%.
- B. Increase by 20%.
- C. Increase by 6%.
- D. Decrease by 6%.

The correct answer is (A). *(CIA, adapted)*
**REQUIRED:** The effect on the optimal order size if annual demand decreases.
**DISCUSSION:** If demand decreases by 36%, that is, from 100% to 64%, the EOQ will decrease by 20%.

$$Q_1 = \sqrt{\frac{2 \times 0.64D \times a}{k}} = \sqrt{0.64\left(\frac{2aD}{k}\right)} = 0.8Q$$

Answer (B) is incorrect because the new EOQ decreases to 80% of its former value. Answers (C) and (D) are incorrect because 6% is the square root of 36%.

---

Questions 29 and 30 are based on the following information. Based on an EOQ analysis (assuming a constant demand), the optimal order quantity is 2,500. The company desires a safety stock of 500 units. A 5-day lead time is needed for delivery. Annual inventory carrying costs equal 25% of the average inventory level. The company pays $4 per unit to buy the product, which it sells for $8. The company pays $150 to place a detailed order, and the monthly demand for the product is 4,000 units.

---

**29.** Annual inventory carrying costs equal

- A. $750
- B. $1,250
- C. $1,750
- D. $2,250

The correct answer is (C). *(CIA, adapted)*
**REQUIRED:** The annual inventory carrying costs using the EOQ technique.
**DISCUSSION:** Given that demand is constant and the EOQ is 2,500 units, the average inventory level without regard to safety stock is 1,250 units (2,500 ÷ 2). Adding safety stock results in an average level of 1,750 units (1,250 + 500). Given also that annual carrying costs are 25% of average inventory and that unit cost is $4, total annual carrying cost is $1,750 [(1,750 units x $4) x 25%].

Answer (A) is incorrect because $750 results from subtracting instead of adding the cost of carrying safety stock. Answer (B) is incorrect because $1,250 ignores safety stock. Answer (D) is incorrect because $2,250 results from double counting the cost of carrying safety stock.

**30.** Total inventory order costs per year equal

- A. $1,250
- B. $2,400
- C. $2,880
- D. $3,600

The correct answer is (C). *(CIA, adapted)*
**REQUIRED:** The total inventory order costs using the EOQ technique.
**DISCUSSION:** Total annual demand is 48,000 units (4,000 per month x 12). Hence, total annual order costs equal $2,880 [$150 cost per order x (48,000 units ÷ 2,500 EOQ)].

Answer (A) is incorrect because $1,250 equals the annual carrying cost of the average inventory, excluding safety stock. Answer (B) is incorrect because $2,400 assumes an EOQ of 3,000 units. Answer (D) is incorrect because $3,600 assumes an EOQ of 2,000 units.

Questions 31 and 32 are based on the following information. Ryerson Computer Furniture Inc. (RCF) manufactures a line of office computer chairs. The annual demand for the chairs is estimated to be 5,000 units. The annual cost to hold one unit in inventory is $10 per year, and the cost to initiate a production run is $1,000. There are no computer chairs on hand, and RCF has scheduled four equal production runs of computer chairs for the coming year, the first of which is to be run immediately. RCF has 250 business days per year, sales occur uniformly throughout the year, and production start-up is within one day. RCF is considering using the following formula for determining the economic order quantity (EOQ):

$$EOQ = \sqrt{\frac{2AD}{K}}$$

If:  A = cost to initiate a production run per purchase order
   D = annual unit demand
   K = cost of carrying one unit per year

**31.** The number of production runs per year of computer chairs that would minimize the sum of carrying and setup costs for the coming year is

A. 1

B. 2

C. 4

D. 5

**32.** If RCF does not maintain a safety stock, the estimated total carrying costs for the computer chairs for the coming year based on their current schedule is

A. $4,000

B. $5,000

C. $6,250

D. $12,500

The correct answer is (D). *(CMA, adapted)*
**REQUIRED:** The number of production runs that minimizes the sum of setup and carrying costs.
**DISCUSSION:** The EOQ minimizes the sum of carrying and setup costs. The EOQ is the amount at which carrying costs are equal to setup costs. Thus, plugging the data into the EOQ formula results in the following:

$$EOQ = \sqrt{\frac{2(\$1,000)(5,000)}{\$10}} = 1,000 \text{ units}$$

Thus, if each lot consists of 1,000 units, five production runs per year are needed to meet the 5,000-unit demand. At this level, setup costs will total $5,000 (5 x $1,000). Carrying costs will also equal $5,000 ($10 per unit carrying cost x average inventory of 500 units). Accordingly, total costs are minimized at $10,000.

Answer (A) is incorrect because a single production run indicates an EOQ of 5,000 units. The carrying costs of $25,000 [$10 x ($5,000 ÷ 2)] would exceed the $1,000 of setup costs. Answer (B) is incorrect because two production runs correspond to an EOQ of 2,500 units and an average inventory of 1,250 units. The resulting $12,500 of carrying costs would exceed the $2,000 of setup costs. Answer (C) is incorrect because four production runs correspond to an EOQ of 1,250 units and an average inventory of 625 units. The resulting $6,250 of carrying costs would exceed the $4,000 of setup costs.

The correct answer is (C). *(CMA, adapted)*
**REQUIRED:** The estimated total annual carrying costs assuming no safety stock is held.
**DISCUSSION:** Given four production runs and an annual demand of 5,000 units, each production run must generate 1,250 units. Inventory will total 1,250 units at the completion of each run but will decline to zero just prior to the next run. Thus, the average inventory is 625 units (1,250 ÷ 2), and the total carrying cost is $6,250 ($10 x 625 units).

Answer (A) is incorrect because the cost of maintaining an average inventory of 625 units is $6,250. Answer (B) is incorrect because $5,000 is based upon an EOQ of 1,000 units and an average inventory of 500 units. Answer (D) is incorrect because $12,500 is based on the maximum inventory level.

## 14.3 Other Inventory Control Techniques

**33.** Companies that adopt just-in-time purchasing systems often experience

A. A reduction in the number of suppliers.

B. Fewer deliveries from suppliers.

C. A greater need for inspection of goods as the goods arrive.

D. Less need for linkage with a vendor's computerized order entry system.

**The correct answer is (A).** *(CMA, adapted)*
**REQUIRED:** The true statement about companies that adopt just-in-time (JIT) purchasing systems.
**DISCUSSION:** The objective of JIT is to reduce carrying costs by eliminating inventories and increasing the deliveries made by suppliers. Ideally, shipments of raw materials are received just in time to be incorporated into the manufacturing process. The focus of quality control under JIT is the prevention of quality problems. Quality control is shifted to the supplier. JIT companies typically do not inspect incoming goods; the assumption is that receipts are of perfect quality. Suppliers are limited to those who guarantee perfect quality and prompt delivery.

Answer (B) is incorrect because more deliveries are needed. Each shipment is smaller. Answer (C) is incorrect because, in a JIT system, materials are delivered directly to the production line ready for insertion in the finished product. Answer (D) is incorrect because the need for communication with the vendor is greater. Orders and deliveries must be made on short notice, sometimes several times a day.

**34.** The benefits of a just-in-time system for raw materials usually include

A. Elimination of nonvalue-adding operations.

B. Increase in the number of suppliers, thereby ensuring competitive bidding.

C. Maximization of the standard delivery quantity, thereby lessening the paperwork for each delivery.

D. Decrease in the number of deliveries required to maintain production.

**The correct answer is (A).** *(CPA, adapted)*
**REQUIRED:** The benefit of a just-in-time system for raw materials.
**DISCUSSION:** Nonvalue-adding activities are those that do not add to customer value or satisfy an organizational need. Inventory activities are inherently nonvalue-adding. Thus, a system, such as JIT, that promotes lean production and reduces inventory and its attendant procedures (storage, handling, etc.) also reduces nonvalue-adding activities.

Answer (B) is incorrect because the dependability, not number of, suppliers is increased. Answer (C) is incorrect because standard delivery quality, not quantity, is increased. Answer (D) is incorrect because the number of deliveries is increased. Fewer goods are delivered at a time.

**35.** Bell Co. changed from a traditional manufacturing philosophy to a just-in-time philosophy. What are the expected effects of this change on Bell's inventory turnover and inventory as a percentage of total assets reported on Bell's balance sheet?

| | Inventory Turnover | Inventory Percentage |
|---|---|---|
| A. | Decrease | Decrease |
| B. | Decrease | Increase |
| C. | Increase | Decrease |
| D. | Increase | Increase |

**The correct answer is (C).** *(CPA, adapted)*
**REQUIRED:** The expected effects of changing to JIT.
**DISCUSSION:** A JIT system is intended to minimize inventory. Inventory should be delivered or produced just in time to be used. Thus, JIT increases inventory turnover (cost of sales ÷ average inventory) and decreases inventory as a percentage of total assets.

Answers (A), (B), and (D) are incorrect because changing to JIT increases inventory turnover and decreases inventory as a percentage of total assets.

**36.** Which changes in costs are most conducive to switching from a traditional inventory ordering system to a just-in-time ordering system?

|   | Cost per Purchase Order | Inventory Unit Carrying Costs |
|---|---|---|
| A. | Increasing | Increasing |
| B. | Decreasing | Increasing |
| C. | Decreasing | Decreasing |
| D. | Increasing | Decreasing |

The correct answer is (B). *(CPA, adapted)*
**REQUIRED:** The changes in costs most conducive to switching to a just-in-time ordering system.
**DISCUSSION:** A JIT system is intended to minimize inventory. Thus, if inventory carrying costs are increasing, a JIT system becomes more cost effective. Moreover, purchases are more frequent in a JIT system. Accordingly, a decreasing cost per purchase order is conducive to switching to a JIT system.
Answers (A), (C), and (D) are incorrect because switching to a JIT system should be considered when carrying costs increase and ordering costs decrease.

**37.** A manufacturing company is attempting to implement a just-in-time (JIT) purchase policy system by negotiating with its primary suppliers to accept long-term purchase orders which result in more frequent deliveries of smaller quantities of raw materials. If the JIT purchase policy is successful in reducing the total inventory costs of the manufacturing company, which of the following combinations of cost changes would be most likely to occur?

|   | Cost Category to Increase | Cost Category to Decrease |
|---|---|---|
| A. | Purchasing costs | Stockout costs |
| B. | Purchasing costs | Quality costs |
| C. | Quality costs | Ordering costs |
| D. | Stockout costs | Carrying costs |

The correct answer is (D). *(CIA, adapted)*
**REQUIRED:** The combination of cost changes.
**DISCUSSION:** The objective of a JIT system is to reduce carrying costs by eliminating inventories and increasing the deliveries made by suppliers. Ideally, shipments are received just in time to be incorporated into the manufacturing process. This system increases the risk of stockout costs because the inventory buffer is reduced or eliminated.
Answer (A) is incorrect because the supplier may seek a concession on the selling price that will raise purchasing costs, but the manufacturing company's stockout costs will increase. Answer (B) is incorrect because the cost of quality is not necessarily affected by a JIT system. Answer (C) is incorrect because fewer purchase orders are processed by the manufacturer, so the ordering costs are likely to decrease. However, the cost of quality is not necessarily affected by a JIT system.

**38.** In Belk Co.'s just-in-time production system, costs per setup were reduced from $28 to $2. In the process of reducing inventory levels, Belk found that there were fixed facility and administrative costs that previously had not been included in the carrying cost calculation. The result was an increase from $8 to $32 per unit per year. What were the effects of these changes on Belk's economic lot size and relevant costs?

|   | Lot Size | Relevant Costs |
|---|---|---|
| A. | Decrease | Increase |
| B. | Increase | Decrease |
| C. | Increase | Increase |
| D. | Decrease | Decrease |

The correct answer is (D). *(CPA, adapted)*
**REQUIRED:** The effect of JIT production system on economic lot size and relevant costs.
**DISCUSSION:** The economic lot size for a production system is similar to the EOQ. For example, the cost per set-up is equivalent to the cost per order (a numerator value in the EOQ model). Hence, a reduction in the setup costs reduces the economic lot size as well as the relevant costs. The fixed facility and administrative costs, however, are not relevant. The basic EOQ model includes variable costs only.
Answers (A), (B), and (C) are incorrect because the net relevant costs and the economic lot size are reduced.

**39.** In a JIT costing system, factory overhead applied should be charged to

A. Raw materials.

B. Cost of goods sold.

C. Finished goods.

D. Work-in-process.

The correct answer is (B). *(Publisher)*

**REQUIRED:** The account that factory overhead applied is charged to in JIT systems.

**DISCUSSION:** A JIT system usually has no work orders. Thus, items such as direct labor and factory overhead cannot be easily charged to specific jobs. Direct labor and factory overhead are often expensed directly to cost of goods sold. Year-end adjusting entries are required to allocate direct labor and factory overhead to the work-in-process and finished goods.

Answer (A) is incorrect because overhead is not debited to raw materials. Answer (C) is incorrect because factory overhead is not charged directly to finished goods. Instead, finished goods are adjusted to include their share of factory overhead at the end of a period. Answer (D) is incorrect because factory overhead is not charged directly to work-in-process. Instead, work-in-process is adjusted to include its share of factory overhead at the end of a period.

**40.** Backflush costing is most likely to be used when

A. Management desires sequential tracking of costs.

B. A just-in-time inventory philosophy has been adopted.

C. The company carries significant amounts of inventory.

D. Actual production costs are debited to work-in-process.

The correct answer is (B). *(Publisher)*

**REQUIRED:** The true statement about backflush costing.

**DISCUSSION:** Backflush costing is often used with a JIT system because it minimizes the effort devoted to accounting for inventories. It delays much of the accounting for production costs until the completion of production or even the sale of goods. Backflush costing is most appropriate when inventories are low or when the change in inventories is minimal, that is, when most production costs for a period flow into cost of goods sold.

Answer (A) is incorrect because traditional systems track costs as units pass through each step of production. Answer (C) is incorrect because backflush costing is inconsistent with the full-costing requirement of GAAP. The larger the inventories or the change therein, the greater the discrepancy. Moreover, larger inventories require more detailed information. Answer (D) is incorrect because backflush costing eliminates the work-in-process account.

**41.** Key Co. changed from a traditional manufacturing operation with a job-order costing system to a just-in-time operation with a backflush costing system. What is(are) the expected effect(s) of these changes on Key's inspection costs and recording detail of costs tracked to jobs in process?

| | Inspection Costs | Detail of Costs Tracked to Jobs |
|---|---|---|
| A. | Decrease | Decrease |
| B. | Decrease | Increase |
| C. | Increase | Decrease |
| D. | Increase | Increase |

The correct answer is (A). *(CPA, adapted)*

**REQUIRED:** The effects of changing to a JIT operation with backflush costing.

**DISCUSSION:** In a JIT system, materials go directly into production without being inspected. The assumption is that the vendor has already performed all necessary inspections. The minimization of inventory reduces the number of suppliers, storage costs, transaction costs, etc. Backflush costing eliminates the traditional sequential tracking of costs. Instead, entries to inventory may be delayed until as late as the end of the period. For example, all product costs may be charged initially to cost of sales, and costs may be flushed back to the inventory accounts only at the end of the period. Thus, the detail of cost accounting is decreased.

Answers (B), (C), and (D) are incorrect because both inspection costs and the detail of costs tracked to jobs decrease.

**42.** Tocon Company produces two components: A-1 and A-2. The unit contribution margins for A-1 and A-2 are $150 and $300, respectively. Each component must proceed through two processes: Operation 1 and Operation 2. The capacity of Operation 1 is 180 machine hours, with A-1 and A-2 requiring 1 hour and 3 hours, respectively. Furthermore, Tocon can sell only 45 units of A-1 and 100 units of A-2. However, Tocon is considering expanding Operation 1's capacity by 90 machine hours at a cost of $80 per hour. Assuming that Operation 2 has sufficient capacity to handle any additional output from Operation 1, Tocon should produce

|   | Units of A-1 | Units of A-2 |
|---|---|---|
| A. | 180 | 0 |
| B. | 45 | 100 |
| C. | 45 | 75 |
| D. | 0 | 60 |

The correct answer is (C). *(Publisher)*
**REQUIRED:** The optimal product mix that gives possible expansion of an internal binding constraint.
**DISCUSSION:** A-1's contribution margin per unit of the scarce resource (the internal binding constraint) is $150 ($150 UCM ÷ 1 machining hour). A-2's contribution margin per unit of the scarce resource (the internal binding constraint) is $100 ($300 UCM ÷ 3 machine hours). Consequently, Tocon should produce as much A-1 as it can sell (45 units). If Tocon adds 90 machine hours to increase the capacity of Operation 1 to 270 hours (180 + 90), it cannot produce additional units of A-1 because the external binding constraint has not been relaxed. However, it can produce additional units of A-2. Given that the UCM per machine hour of A-2 is $100 and that the cost is $80 per hour, adding capacity to Operation 1 is profitable. Thus, Tocon should use 45 machine hours to produce 45 units of A-1. The remaining 225 machine hours (270 – 45) should be used to produce 75 units (225 ÷ 3 hours) of A-2. The latter amount is within the external binding constraint.
Answer (A) is incorrect because Tocon can sell only 45 units of A-1. Answer (B) is incorrect because Tocon can produce only 75 units of A-2 if it produces 45 units of the more profitable A-1. Answer (D) is incorrect because Tocon should produce as much of A-1 as it can sell.

**43.** A major justification for investments in computer-integrated manufacturing (CIM) projects is

A. Reduction in the costs of spoilage, reworked units, and scrap.

B. Lower book value and depreciation expense for factory equipment.

C. Increased working capital.

D. Stabilization of market share.

The correct answer is (A). *(CIA, adapted)*
**REQUIRED:** The major justification for investments in CIM.
**DISCUSSION:** Automating and computerizing production processes requires a substantial investment in fixed assets and an increase in risk because of greater fixed costs. CIM also necessitates an increase in software costs and extensive worker retraining. However, the costs of spoilage, rework, and scrap are reduced along with labor costs. The qualitative advantages of CIM are increased flexibility, shorter manufacturing lead time, quicker development of new products, better product delivery and service, faster response to market changes, and improved competitiveness.
Answer (B) is incorrect because an increase in fixed assets results in higher book value and depreciation expense. Answer (C) is incorrect because working capital normally is reduced as investments shift from current to fixed assets. Answer (D) is incorrect because actual or potential market share changes may trigger investments in CIM.

**44.** The company uses a planning system that focuses first on the amount and timing of finished goods demanded and then determines the derived demand for raw materials, components, and subassemblies at each of the prior stages of production. This system is referred to as

A. Economic order quantity.

B. Materials requirements planning.

C. Linear programming.

D. Just-in-time purchasing.

The correct answer is (B). *(CIA, adapted)*

**REQUIRED:** The planning system that calculates derived demand for inventories.

**DISCUSSION:** Materials requirements planning (MRP) is a system that translates a production schedule into requirements for each component needed to meet the schedule. It is usually implemented in the form of a computer-based information system designed to plan and control raw materials used in production. It assumes that forecasted demand is reasonably accurate and that suppliers can deliver based upon this accurate schedule. MRP is a centralized push-through system; output based on forecasted demand is pushed through to the next department or to inventory.

Answer (A) is incorrect because the EOQ model focuses on the trade-off between carrying and ordering costs. Answer (C) is incorrect because linear programming is a decision model concerned with allocating scarce resources to maximize profit or minimize costs. Answer (D) is incorrect because JIT is a decentralized demand-pull system. It is driven by actual demand.

**45.** Increased competition, technological innovation, and a shift from mass production of standardized products to custom-produced products in many industries have increased the need for productivity improvement and flexibility of production systems. In response to these demands, organizations have increased their reliance on automation and the use of advanced technologies in their operations. Which of the following is an example of the use of automation and advanced technologies?

A. Flexible manufacturing system (FMS).

B. Just-in-time (JIT) system.

C. Master budgeting system (MBS).

D. Economic order quantity (EOQ).

The correct answer is (A). *(CIA, adapted)*

**REQUIRED:** The example of the use of automation and advanced technologies.

**DISCUSSION:** Flexible manufacturing is the capacity of computer-controlled machinery to perform many different programmed functions. By eliminating machine setup time, strengthening control, and automating handling processes, computer-aided manufacturing permits the efficient production of small numbers of different products by the same machines. A company can therefore more accurately match output with consumer tastes and avoid long production runs of identical goods. A flexible manufacturing system consists of two or more computer-controlled machines linked by automated handling devices such as robots and transport systems.

Answer (B) is incorrect because a JIT system involves the purchase of materials and production of components immediately preceding their use. Answer (C) is incorrect because a master budget is the detailed financial plan for the next period. Answer (D) is incorrect because the EOQ is the quantity that minimizes total costs.

**46.** Traditionally, large manufacturers have believed that economies of scale gained through large production runs of like, or similar, products are the best way to keep production costs down and remain competitive. Select the most appropriate response to whether this theory is still valid.

A. Yes, larger economies of scale continue to accrue from ever larger production runs.

B. Yes, lower-per-unit costs for standard products continue to guarantee a competitive advantage.

C. No, economies of scale can no longer be gained from long production runs.

D. No, production flexibility and diversity of products are needed to remain competitive.

The correct answer is (D). *(CIA, adapted)*

**REQUIRED:** The most appropriate evaluation of the belief that economies of scale are the best means of reducing costs.

**DISCUSSION:** Global competition and more rapidly changing consumer tastes are lessening the need for long production runs and increasing the need for diversity of products and flexibility of manufacturing. The economies of scale concept is being replaced by economies of scope, which result when flexible manufacturing methods (use of computerized machines to perform many programmed functions) permit the economical output of small numbers of many different products with the same machines.

Answers (A) and (B) are incorrect because economies of scale cannot continue to be achieved if the products are not salable. Answer (C) is incorrect because economies of scale can still be achieved from long production runs if the goods are salable.

## 14.4 Reorder Points, Safety Stock, Stockout Cost

**47.** For inventory management, ignoring safety stocks, which of the following is a valid computation of the reorder point?

A. The economic order quantity.

B. The economic order quantity times the anticipated demand during lead time.

C. The anticipated demand per day during lead time times lead time in days.

D. The square root of the anticipated demand during the lead time.

The correct answer is (C). *(CPA, adapted)*

**REQUIRED:** The valid computation of the reorder point, ignoring safety stocks.

**DISCUSSION:** The order point (the quantity of remaining inventory signaling time to order) is found by multiplying the usage per day by the lead time in days.

Answer (A) is incorrect because the EOQ is used to determine the most efficient quantity to order. Answer (B) is incorrect because the EOQ times the anticipated demand during lead time is an irrelevant number. Answer (D) is incorrect because the square root of the anticipated demand during the lead time is an irrelevant number.

**48.** What are the three factors a manager should consider in controlling stockouts?

A. Carrying costs, quality costs, and physical inventories.

B. Economic order quantity, annual demand, and quality costs.

C. Time needed for delivery, rate of inventory usage, and safety stock.

D. Economic order quantity, production bottlenecks, and safety stock.

The correct answer is (C). *(CIA, adapted)*

**REQUIRED:** The three factors a manager should consider in controlling stockouts.

**DISCUSSION:** It is desirable to minimize both the cost of carrying safety stock and the costs of running out of an item, i.e., of stockouts. Safety stock is the amount of extra stock that is kept to guard against stockouts. It is the inventory level at the time of reordering minus the expected usage while the new goods are in transit. Delivery time, usage rate, and level of safety stock are therefore considerations in controlling stockouts.

Answer (A) is incorrect because carrying costs, quality costs, and physical inventories are inventory-related concepts that do not pertain directly to stockouts. Answer (B) is incorrect because the order quantity, annual demand, and quality costs are not direct concerns. Answer (D) is incorrect because production bottlenecks result from a stockout; they are not a method of control. Also, EOQ is irrelevant to stockouts.

**49.** The elapsed time between placing an order for inventory and receiving the order is

A. Lead time.

B. Reorder time.

C. Stockout time.

D. Stocking time.

The correct answer is (A). *(CMA, adapted)*

**REQUIRED:** The period between placing an order for inventory and receiving that order.

**DISCUSSION:** The time between placing an order and receiving that order is the lead time. The basic EOQ formula assumes immediate replenishment, but in practice time will elapse between ordering inventory and its arrival. Lead time must therefore be considered in determining the order point (level of inventory at which a new order should be made).

Answer (B) is incorrect because reorder time is a nonsense answer. Answer (C) is incorrect because stockout time is a nonsense answer. The safety stock is the quantity of inventory that should be on hand when a new order arrives. Answer (D) is incorrect because stocking time is the length of time to transfer inventory to the shelves or to its place of use once it has been received by the purchaser.

**50.** A company stocks, maintains, and distributes inventory. The company decides to add to the safety stock and expedite delivery for several product lines on a trial basis. For the selected product lines, the company will experience

    A. An increase in some costs but no change in the service level.

    B. A change in the service level.

    C. An increase in ordering, carrying, and delivery costs.

    D. A decrease in ordering, carrying, and delivery costs.

The correct answer is (B). *(CIA, adapted)*
    **REQUIRED:** The effect of increasing safety stock.
    **DISCUSSION:** Safety stocks are amounts held in excess of forecasted demand to avoid the losses associated with stockouts. Safety stocks improve service to customers at the expense of increased carrying costs.
    Answer (A) is incorrect because service will improve. Answer (C) is incorrect because ordering costs will not increase. The fixed costs of the ordering department will be unaffected. Also, the department's variable costs should not change because the EOQ will be the same. However, in the first year, an additional order may be necessary to increase the safety stock. Answer (D) is incorrect because delivery costs will increase under the new delivery policy, and increasing the safety stock increases carrying costs.

**51.** When a specified level of safety stock is carried for an item in inventory, the average inventory level for that item

    A. Decreases by the amount of the safety stock.

    B. Is one-half the level of the safety stock.

    C. Increases by one-half the amount of the safety stock.

    D. Increases by the amount of the safety stock.

The correct answer is (D). *(CMA, adapted)*
    **REQUIRED:** The effect on the average inventory level of carrying safety stock.
    **DISCUSSION:** Given no safety stock, the average inventory will be 50% of the EOQ. For example, if the EOQ is 500, the average inventory will be 250. The company will have 500 units immediately after a purchase and zero immediately before the receipt of the next purchase (replenishment is assumed to be instantaneous). However, safety stock increases the average inventory by the amount of the safety stock. The modified EOQ model assumes that safety stock will never be used. Thus, given a safety stock of 100, the average inventory level will increase to 350. Inventory will be 600 units immediately upon receipt of a purchase and 100 units immediately before the receipt of the next purchase.
    Answers (A), (B), and (C) are incorrect because the average inventory increases by the amount of safety stock.

**52.** When the level of safety stock is increased,

    A. Lead time will increase.

    B. The frequency of stockouts will decrease.

    C. Carrying costs will decrease.

    D. Order costs will decrease.

The correct answer is (B). *(CMA, adapted)*
    **REQUIRED:** The effect of an increase in safety stock.
    **DISCUSSION:** The EOQ model assumes that demand and lead time are known with certainty. If these assumptions are inaccurate, stockout costs may be incurred. If safety stock is carried or the amount already carried is increased, the number of stockouts should decrease. Safety stock increases carrying costs, but these additional costs can be offset by a decrease in opportunity cost (lost sales).
    Answer (A) is incorrect because lead time will be unaffected by the level of safety stock. Lead time is the period between placing an order and its delivery. Answer (C) is incorrect because carrying costs will increase. The average level of inventory will increase. Answer (D) is incorrect because ordering costs will be constant. Safety stock does not increase the number of orders.

**53.** In inventory management, the safety stock will tend to increase if the

    A.  Carrying cost increases.

    B.  Cost of running out of stock decreases.

    C.  Variability of the lead time increases.

    D.  Fixed order cost decreases.

The correct answer is (C). *(CMA, adapted)*

    **REQUIRED:** The factor increasing safety stock.

    **DISCUSSION:** Safety stocks protect against the losses caused by stockouts. These can take the form of lost sales or lost production time. Safety stock is necessary because of the variability in lead time and usage rates. As the variability of lead time increases, that is, as the standard deviation of the probability distribution of lead times increases, the risk of a stockout increases, and a company will tend to carry larger safety stocks.

    Answer (A) is incorrect because increased carrying costs make safety stocks less economical. Thus, safety stocks would be reduced. Answer (B) is incorrect because, if the cost of stockouts declines, the incentive to carry large safety stocks is reduced. Answer (D) is incorrect because lower ordering costs encourage more frequent orders, which in turn will reduce the need for large safety stocks.

**54.** As a consequence of finding a more dependable supplier, Dee Co. reduced its safety stock of raw materials by 80%. What is the effect of this safety stock reduction on Dee's economic order quantity?

    A.  80% decrease.

    B.  64% decrease.

    C.  20% increase.

    D.  No effect.

The correct answer is (D). *(CPA, adapted)*

    **REQUIRED:** The effect of the safety stock reduction on the EOQ.

    **DISCUSSION:** The variables in the basic EOQ formula are periodic demand, cost per order, and the unit carrying cost for the period. Thus, safety stock does not affect the EOQ. Although the total of the carrying costs changes with the safety stock, the cost-minimizing order quantity is not affected.

    Answers (A), (B), and (C) are incorrect because safety stock does not affect the basic EOQ model.

**55.** A company experiences both variable usage rates and variable lead times for its inventory items. The probability distributions for both usage and lead times are known. A technique the company could use for determining the optimal safety stock levels for an inventory item is

    A.  Queuing theory.

    B.  Linear programming.

    C.  Decision tree analysis.

    D.  Monte Carlo simulation.

The correct answer is (D). *(CMA, adapted)*

    **REQUIRED:** The technique used to determine safety stock given variable usage rates and lead times.

    **DISCUSSION:** Monte Carlo simulation is often used to generate the individual values for random variables, such as lead times and usage rates. Performance under uncertainty can be investigated by randomly selecting values for each of the variables in the model (based on the probability distribution of each variable) and then calculating the value of the solution. If this process is performed a large number of times, the distribution of results can be obtained.

    Answer (A) is incorrect because queuing theory is used to minimize the costs of waiting lines. Answer (B) is incorrect because linear programming is used to minimize a cost function or maximize a profit function given constraints. Answer (C) is incorrect because decision trees are diagrams that analyze sequences of probabilistic decisions, the events that may follow each decision, and their outcomes.

Questions 56 through 58 are based on the following information. The diagram presented below represents the economic order quantity (EOQ) model.

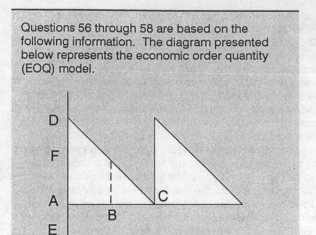

**56.** Which line segment represents the reorder lead time?

A. AB.

B. AE.

C. AF.

D. BC.

The correct answer is (D). *(CMA, adapted)*
  **REQUIRED:** The line representing the reorder lead time.
  **DISCUSSION:** The quantity of inventory on hand is represented by the y axis; time, by the x axis. The reorder lead time is represented by the line BC.
  Answer (A) is incorrect because AB is the time between receipt of the last order and the placing of the next order. Answer (B) is incorrect because AE is the safety stock. Answer (C) is incorrect because AF represents the quantity of inventory that will be used during the reorder lead time.

**57.** Which line segment identifies the quantity of safety stock maintained?

A. AB.

B. AE.

C. AC.

D. EF.

The correct answer is (B). *(CMA, adapted)*
  **REQUIRED:** The line segment representing the quantity of safety stock maintained.
  **DISCUSSION:** Quantities of inventory are shown along the y axis. Safety stock is represented by the line AE.
  Answer (A) is incorrect because AB is the time between the receipt of the last order and the placing of the next order. Answer (C) is incorrect because AC is the economic order quantity. Answer (D) is incorrect because EF represents the reorder point (the quantity available when an order is placed).

**58.** Which line segment represents the length of time to consume the total quantity of materials ordered?

A. DE.

B. BC.

C. AC.

D. AD.

The correct answer is (C). *(CMA, adapted)*
  **REQUIRED:** The line representing the time to consume all the materials ordered.
  **DISCUSSION:** Time is shown along the x axis. The line segment AC depicts the time to consume an entire order (to reduce the inventory to the safety stock).
  Answer (A) is incorrect because DE represents the total inventory on hand just after an order has been received. Answer (B) is incorrect because BC is the reorder lead time. Answer (D) is incorrect because AD is the quantity ordered.

**59.** Canseco Enterprises uses 84,000 units of Part 256 in manufacturing activities over a 300-day work year. The usual lead time for the part is 6 days; occasionally, however, the lead time has gone as high as 8 days. The company now desires to adjust its safety stock policy. The increase in safety stock size and the likely effect on stockout costs and carrying costs, respectively, would be

A. 560 units, decrease, increase.

B. 560 units, decrease, decrease.

C. 1,680 units, decrease, increase.

D. 2,240 units, increase, decrease.

The correct answer is (A). *(CMA, adapted)*
**REQUIRED:** The increase in safety stock and the likely effect on stockout costs and carrying costs.
**DISCUSSION:** Given usage of 84,000 units over 300 work days, the average usage rate is 280 units per day. Increasing the safety stock by a 2-day supply (8 days – usual 6-day lead time) increases inventory by 560 units (2 x 280). The additional inventory should decrease stockout costs and increase inventory carrying costs.
Answer (B) is incorrect because carrying costs will increase with the increased inventory size. Answer (C) is incorrect because the company is already carrying a 6-day supply of safety stock (6 days x 280 units = 1,680 units). The only additional units needed are for 2 extra days. Answer (D) is incorrect because 2,240 units equals an 8-day supply, not the increase in safety stock. Also, stockout costs will decrease and carrying costs will increase.

**60.** Each stockout of a product sold by A.W. Inn Co. costs $1,750 per occurrence. The carrying cost per unit of inventory is $5 per year, and the company orders 1,500 units of product 24 times a year at a cost of $100 per order. The probability of a stockout at various levels of safety stock is

| Units of Safety Stock | Probability of a Stockout |
|---|---|
| 0 | .50 |
| 100 | .30 |
| 200 | .14 |
| 300 | .05 |
| 400 | .01 |

The optimal safety stock level for the company is

A. 0 units.

B. 100 units.

C. 300 units.

D. 400 units.

The correct answer is (D). *(CMA, adapted)*
**REQUIRED:** The optimal level of safety stock.
**DISCUSSION:** The total expected cost of safety stock equals the sum of the expected annual stockout cost and the expected annual carrying cost. Annual expected stockout cost equals the cost per occurrence ($1,750), times the probability of a stockout per cycle, times the number of cycles (24). Annual expected carrying cost of a safety stock equals the unit carrying cost ($5) times the number of units. Hence, a safety stock of 400 units has the lowest total expected cost.

| Units Held | Carrying Cost | Expected Stockout Cost Per Cycle | Expected Stockout Cost for 24 Cycles | Total Expected Cost |
|---|---|---|---|---|
| 0 | $ 0 | $875.00 | $21,000 | $21,000 |
| 100 | 500 | 525.00 | 12,600 | 13,100 |
| 200 | 1,000 | 245.00 | 5,880 | 6,880 |
| 300 | 1,500 | 87.50 | 2,100 | 3,600 |
| 400 | 2,000 | 17.50 | 420 | 2,420 |

Answer (A) is incorrect because a safety stock of 0 units has a total expected cost of $21,000. Answer (B) is incorrect because a safety stock of 100 units has a total expected cost of $13,100. Answer (C) is incorrect because a safety stock of 30 units has a total expected cost of $3,600.

**61.** Arnold Enterprises uses the EOQ model for inventory control. The company has an annual demand of 50,000 units for part number 191 and has computed an optimal lot size of 6,250 units. Per-unit carrying costs and stockout costs are $13 and $3, respectively. The following data have been gathered in an attempt to determine an appropriate safety stock level:

| Units Short Because of Excess Demand during the Lead Time Period | Number of Times Short in the Last 40 Reorder Cycles |
|---|---|
| 200 | 6 |
| 300 | 12 |
| 400 | 6 |

The annual cost of establishing a 200-unit safety stock is expected to be

A. $2,600

B. $4,040

C. $4,260

D. $5,200

The correct answer is (B). *(CMA, adapted)*

**REQUIRED:** The annual cost of establishing a given safety stock.

**DISCUSSION:** The annual cost consists of the carrying cost of the 200 units of safety stock at $13 each, or $2,600, plus the stockout costs incurred when 200 units are insufficient. The stockout cost per unit is $3. The excess demand has been 100 units (300 – 200) greater than the proposed safety stock 30% of the time (12 ÷ 40). The cost per stockout was $300 ($3 x 100). Demand has exceeded the safety stock by 200 units (400 – 200) 15% of the time (6 ÷ 40). The cost per stockout was $600 ($3 x 200). Given 30% and 15% probabilities of $300 and $600 stockout costs, respectively, the expected stockout cost for a 200-unit safety stock for one reorder cycle is $180 [(30% x $300) + (15% x $600)]. Thus, the annual expected stockout cost for a 200-unit safety stock is $180 times the number of reorder cycles per year, or $1,440 [$180 x (50,000 ÷ 6,250 EOQ). The annual cost of a 200-unit safety stock is $4,040 ($2,600 + 1,440).

Answer (A) is incorrect because $2,600 is the carrying cost of the safety stock. Answer (C) is incorrect because $4,260 is the annual cost of establishing a 300-unit safety stock. Answer (D) is incorrect because $5,200 is the annual cost of establishing a 400-unit safety stock.

**62.** Huron Corporation purchases 60,000 headbands per year. The average purchase lead time is 20 working days, safety stock equals 7 days normal usage, and the corporation works 240 days per year. Huron should reorder headbands when the quantity in inventory reaches

A. 5,000 units.

B. 6,750 units.

C. 1,750 units.

D. 5,250 units.

The correct answer is (B). *(CMA, adapted)*

**REQUIRED:** The reorder point in units.

**DISCUSSION:** The reorder point is the quantity on hand when an order is placed. With a 20-day normal lead time, a 7-day safety stock, and usage of 250 units per day (60,000 ÷ 240), an order should be placed when 27 days of inventory is on hand, a total of 6,750 units (27 x 250).

Answer (A) is incorrect because 5,000 units does not allow for safety stock. Answer (C) is incorrect because 1,750 units covers only safety stock. Answer (D) is incorrect because 5,250 units includes only 1 day of safety stock.

**63.** If back orders can be taken (at an added cost per item back ordered),

A. EOQ will decrease.

B. EOQ will increase.

C. Lead time will decrease.

D. No change will occur. Back orders do not affect the EOQ model.

The correct answer is (B). *(CIA, adapted)*

**REQUIRED:** The effect of providing for back orders in the EOQ model.

**DISCUSSION:** A back order is a sale made when the item is not in stock. If back orders are possible, inventory can be maintained at lower levels. Hence, the EOQ model is modified for the cost (b) of back orders. The new formula is given below. The effect of the modification is to increase the EOQ because the denominator decreases.

$$\sqrt{\frac{2aD}{k\left(\frac{b}{b+k}\right)}}$$

Answer (A) is incorrect because EOQ will increase. Answer (C) is incorrect because lead time is not affected. Answer (D) is incorrect because the back-order cost must be included in the model. The back-order system replaces inventory.

# CHAPTER FIFTEEN
# PROBABILITY AND STATISTICS

**Probability** is important to management decision making because of the unpredictability of future events. Probability estimation techniques assist in making the best decisions given doubt concerning outcomes. According to a common definition adopted by many authorities, decision making under conditions of **risk** occurs when the **probability distribution** of the possible future states of nature is known, and decision making under conditions of **uncertainty** occurs when the probability distribution of possible future states of nature is not known and must be subjectively determined. Thus, probability theory provides a method for mathematically expressing doubt or assurance about the occurrence of a chance event under conditions of risk.

The field of **statistics** concerns information calculated from sample data. The field is divided into two categories: descriptive statistics and inferential statistics. Both are widely used in business. **Descriptive statistics** includes ways to summarize large amounts of raw data. **Inferential statistics** draws conclusions about a population based on a sample of the population. A **parameter** is a numerical characteristic of a population computed using every element in the population. For example, the mean and the mode are parameters of a population. A **statistic** is a numerical characteristic of a sample (taken from a population) computed using only the elements of a sample of the population. For example, the mean and the mode are statistics of the sample. **Nonparametric** or **distribution-free statistics** is applied to problems for which rank order is known, but the specific distribution is not. Thus, various metals may be ranked in order of hardness without having any measure of hardness.

A **probability distribution** specifies the values of a random variable and their respective probabilities. Certain standard distributions seem to occur frequently in nature and have proven useful in business. Distributions may be classified as discrete or continuous. If the relative frequency of occurrence of the values of a variable can be specified, the values taken together constitute a function, and the variable is known as a **random variable**. A variable is **discrete** if it can assume only certain values in an interval. For example, the number of customers served is a discrete random variable because fractional customers do not exist. A random variable is **continuous** if no gaps exist in the values it may assume. For example, the weight of an object is a continuous variable because it may be expressed as an unlimited continuum of fractional values as well as whole numbers. A hypothesis is a supposition about the true state of nature. **Hypothesis testing** uses the concepts of probability and statistics to calculate the conditional probability that both a hypothesis is true given that the sample results observed have occurred.

For decisions involving risk, the concept of **expected value** provides a rational means for selecting the best alternative. The expected value of an alternative is found by multiplying the probability of each outcome by its payoff and summing the products. It represents the long-term average payoff for repeated trials. The best alternative is the one having the highest expected value. In this probability and statistics chapter, emphasis is also placed on the expected value calculations that appear frequently on professional examinations.

## 15.1 BASIC CONCEPTS

### A. Probability

1. The sum of the probabilities of all possible events is 1.0. Accordingly, the probability of an event varies from 0 to 1.

    a. A probability of 0 means the event cannot occur, whereas a probability of 1 means the event is certain to occur.

    b. Values between 0 and 1 indicate the likelihood of the event's occurrence; e.g., the probability that a fair coin will yield heads is 0.5 on any single toss.

2. The two types of probability are objective and subjective. They differ in how they are calculated.

    a. **Objective probabilities** are calculated from either logic or actual experience. For example, in rolling dice one would logically expect each face on a single die to be equally likely to turn up at a probability of 1/6. Alternatively, the die could be rolled a great many times, and the fraction of times each face turned up could then be used as the frequency or probability of occurrence.

    b. **Subjective probabilities** are estimates, based on judgment and past experience, of the likelihood of future events. In business, subjective probability can indicate the degree of confidence a person has that a certain outcome will occur, e.g., future performance of a new employee.

3. The following are some of the basic terms related to probability theory.

    a. Two events are **mutually exclusive** if they cannot occur simultaneously (e.g., both heads and tails cannot occur on a single toss of a coin).

    b. The **joint probability** for two events is the probability that **both** will occur.

    c. The **conditional probability** of two events is the probability that one will occur given that the other has already occurred.

    d. Two events are **independent** if the occurrence of one has no effect on the probability of the other (e.g., consecutive rolls of a die).

        1) If one event has an effect on the other event, they are **dependent**.

        2) Two events are **independent** if their joint probability equals the product of their individual probabilities.

        3) Two events are **independent** if the conditional probability of each event equals its unconditional probability.

4. Probabilities can be combined using the following rules.

    a. The joint probability of two events equals the probability (Pr) of the first event multiplied by the conditional probability of the second event, given that the first has already occurred.

        1) EXAMPLE: If 60% of the students at a university are male, Pr(male) is 6/10. If 1/6 of the male students have a B average, Pr(have B average given male) is 1/6. Thus, the probability that any given student (male or female) selected at random is **both** male **and** has a B average is

$$Pr(male) \times Pr(B|male) = Pr(male \cap B)$$
$$6/10 \quad \times \quad 1/6 \quad = \quad 1/10$$

b. The probability that either one or both of two events will occur equals the sum of their separate probabilities, minus their joint probability.

    1) EXAMPLE: If two fair coins are thrown, the probability that at least one will come up heads is Pr(coin #1 is heads) plus Pr(coin #2 is heads), minus Pr(coin #1 and coin #2 are both heads), or

$$(.5) + (.5) - (.5 \times .5) = .75$$

    2) EXAMPLE: If in the earlier example 1/3 of all students, male or female, have a B average [Pr(B average) is 1/3], the probability that any given student is either male or has a B average is

$$Pr(male) + Pr(B\ avg.) - Pr(B \cap male) = Pr(male\ or\ has\ B\ avg.)$$
$$6/10\ + \quad 1/3 \quad - \quad 1/10 \quad = \quad 25/30$$

Pr(B ∩ male) must be subtracted to avoid double counting those students who belong to both groups.

c. The probabilities for all possible mutually exclusive outcomes of a single experiment must add up to one.

    1) EXAMPLE: Flipping two coins (H = heads, T = tails)

| If Coin #1 is | If Coin #2 is | Probability of This Combination |
|:---:|:---:|:---:|
| H | H | .25 |
| H | T | .25 |
| T | H | .25 |
| T | T | .25 |

Probability that one of the four possible combinations will occur     1.00 (certainty)

## B. Statistics

1. **Descriptive statistics** summarize large amounts of data. Measures of central tendency and measures of dispersion are such summaries.

    a. **Measures of central tendency** are values typical of a set of data.

        1) The **mean** is the arithmetic average of a set of numbers or, simply, the average.

            a) The mean of a sample is often represented with a bar over the letter for the variable ($\bar{x}$).

            b) The mean of a population is often represented by the Greek letter $\mu$ (mu).

        2) The **median** is the 50th percentile. If raw data are arranged in numerical order from lowest to highest, the median is the halfway value. Thus, half the values are smaller than the median and half are larger.

        3) The **mode** is the most frequently occurring value. If all values are unique, no mode exists.

4)    **Asymmetrical distributions**

a)    The following is a frequency distribution that is asymmetrical to the right (positively skewed); that is, the mean is greater than the median.

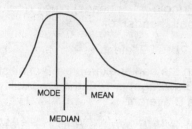

b)    Accounting distributions tend to be asymmetrical to the right.  Recorded amounts are zero or greater; many low-value items are included, but a few high-value items may also be recognized.

c)    The following is a distribution that is asymmetrical to the left; that is, the median is greater than the mean.

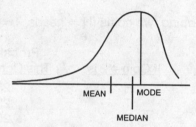

5)    For symmetrical distributions, the mean, median, and mode are the same, and the tails are identical.  Hence, there is no skew.  The normal and t-distributions (see 15.2) are symmetrical distributions.

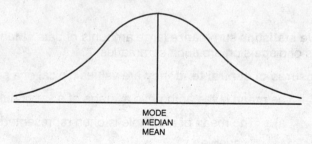

6)    EXAMPLE:  Given items of $300, $800, $1,100, $300, and $1,000, what are the mode, median, and mean?

a)    The mode (the most frequently occurring value) is $300.
b)    The median is $800 (two values lie above and two below $800).
c)    The mean is $700 [($300 + $800 + $1,100 + $300 + $1,000) ÷ 5].

b.    **Measures of dispersion** indicate the variation within a set of numbers.

1)    An important operation involved is summation, represented by the Greek letter $\Sigma$ (uppercase sigma).  The summation sign means to perform the required procedure on every member of the set (every item of the sample) and then add all the results together.

2)    The **variance** is the average of the squared deviations from the mean.  It is found by subtracting the mean from each value, squaring each difference, adding the squared differences, and then dividing the sum by the number of data items.  The variance of a population is represented by $\sigma^2$ (the lowercase Greek letter sigma squared).

    a) The formula for the variance of a set is

$$\sigma^2 \;=\; \sum_{i=1}^{N} \frac{(x_i - \mu)^2}{N}$$

        If:  N  =  the number of elements in the population. If a sample is used to estimate the population variance, use $n - 1$ instead of N, $s^2$ instead of $\sigma^2$, and $\bar{x}$ instead of $\mu$.

           $\mu$  =  the population mean

           $x_i$  =  the $i^{th}$ element of the set

3) The **standard deviation** is the square root of the variance.

    a) The formula is the square root of the variance shown above.

$$\sigma \;=\; \sqrt{\sum_{i=1}^{N} \frac{(x_i - \mu)^2}{N}}$$

    b) For a sample with the sample mean $\bar{x}$, the population standard deviation (sigma) may be estimated from the **sample standard deviation**, s.

$$s \;=\; \sqrt{\sum_{i=1}^{n} \frac{(x_i - \bar{x})^2}{n - 1}}$$

    c) The standard deviation and the sample standard deviation are always expressed in the same units as the data.

    d) The **standard error of the mean** is the population standard deviation divided by the square root of the sample size. It is the standard deviation of the distribution of sample means.

4) The **coefficient of variation** equals the standard deviation divided by the expected value of the dependent variable.

    a) For example, assume that a stock has a 10% expected rate of return with a standard deviation of 5%. The coefficient of variation is .5 (5% ÷ 10%).

    b) Converting the standard deviation to a percentage permits comparison of numbers of different sizes. In the example above, the riskiness of the stock is apparently greater than that of a second stock with an expected return of 20% and a standard deviation of 8% (8% ÷ 20% = .4).

5) The **range** is the difference between the largest and smallest values of any group.

6) **Percentiles and quartiles** are other types of location parameters (the mean and median are special cases of these parameters). A percentile is a value of X such that p% of the observations is less and (100 − p)% is greater. Quartiles are the 25th, 50th, and 75th percentiles. For example, the 50th percentile (second quartile) is the median.

c. A **frequency distribution** is used to summarize raw data by segmenting the range of possible values into equal intervals and showing the number of data points within each interval.

2.  **Inferential statistics** provides methods for drawing conclusions about populations based on sample information, including estimating the population parameters, testing hypotheses, and examining the degree of the relationship between two or more random variables.

    a.  **Sampling** is important in business because a complete census, i.e., measuring the entire population, is usually too costly, too time-consuming, impossible (as in the case of destructive testing), and error-prone. Sampling is used extensively in auditing, quality control, market research, and analytical studies of business operations.

    b.  The **central limit theorem** states that regardless of the distribution of the population from which random samples are drawn, the shape of the sampling distribution of $\bar{x}$ (the mean) approaches the normal distribution as the sample size is increased.

        1)  Given simple random samples of size n and a large sample, the mean of the sampling distribution of $\bar{x}$ will be $\mu$ (the population mean), its variance will be $\sigma^2 \div n$, and its standard deviation will be $\sigma \div \sqrt{n}$ (the standard error of the mean) .

        2)  Thus, whenever a process includes the average of independent samples of the same sample size from the same distribution, the normal distribution can be used as an approximation of that process even if the underlying population is not normally distributed. The central limit theorem explains why the normal distribution is so useful.

    c.  Population parameters may be estimated from sample statistics.

        1)  Every statistic has a sampling distribution that gives every possible value of the statistic and the probability of each of those values.

        2)  Hence, the point estimate calculated for a population parameter (such as the sample mean, $\bar{x}$) may take on a range of values.

        3)  EXAMPLE: From the following population of 10 elements, samples of three elements may be chosen in several ways. Assume that the population is normally distributed.

| Population | Sample 1 | | Sample 2 | | Sample 3 | |
|---|---|---|---|---|---|---|
| 4 | | 4 | | 7 | | 6 |
| 7 | | 5 | | 6 | | 9 |
| 9 | | 3 | | 5 | | 5 |
| 5 | $\Sigma x_i =$ | 12 | $\Sigma x_i =$ | 18 | $\Sigma x_i =$ | 20 |
| 6 | n = | 3 | n = | 3 | n = | 3 |
| 5 | | | | | | |
| 3 | $\bar{x} =$ | 12 ÷ 3 | $\bar{x} =$ | 18 ÷ 3 | $\bar{x} =$ | 20 ÷ 3 |
| 5 | = | 4 | = | 6 | = | 6 2/3 |
| 6 | | | | | | |
| 6 | | | | | | |

$\Sigma x_i = 56$
$N = 10$

$\mu = 56 \div 10 = 5.6$

$\sigma$ *(standard deviation)* $= 1.562$ *based on* $\sqrt{\Sigma(x_i - \mu)^2 \div N}$

NOTE: This sample population was chosen for computational convenience only. The population in this example is so small that inference is not required, and the samples are so small that the t-distribution (see Module 15.2) would be more appropriate than the normal distribution. A different estimate of the population mean is obtained depending upon the exact sample selected. Moreover, the central limit theorem indicates that these sample means are normally distributed around the actual population mean.

d. The quality of the estimates of population parameters depends on the sample size and the variance of the population.

e. The **precision confidence interval**, **interval estimator**, **or prediction interval** incorporates both the sample size and the population standard deviation along with a probability that the interval includes the true population parameter.

1) For the population mean, this interval is

$$\bar{x} \pm z\,(\sigma \div \sqrt{n})$$

If: $\bar{x}$ = the sample mean, which is a point estimate of the population mean

$z$ = the number of standard deviations needed to ensure a specified level of confidence

$\sigma$ = the standard deviation of the population

$n$ = the sample size

$\sigma \div \sqrt{n}$ = the standard error of the mean (square root of the variance of the sampling distribution of $\bar{x}$)

a) This representation of the confidence interval assumes that the variance ($\sigma^2$) of the population is known, the sample means are normally distributed with a mean equal to the true population mean ($\mu$), and the variance of the sampling distribution is $\sigma^2 \div n$.

b) In the more realistic case in which the population variance is not known and a sample is being evaluated, the distribution is described as a t-distribution with mean equal to $\mu$ and variance equal to $s^2 \div n$, when $s^2$ is the sample variance.

c) To compute the precision for the mean of the population given in 2.c.3), based on Sample 2, the mean ($\bar{x}$) of Sample 2 must be determined.

$$\begin{array}{c} 7 \\ 6 \\ \underline{5} \end{array} \qquad \bar{x} = 18 \div 3 = 6$$

$$\Sigma x_i = \underline{18}$$
$$n = 3$$

The sample standard deviation is

$$s = \sqrt{\frac{(7-6)^2 + (6-6)^2 + (5-6)^2}{3-1}} = 1.0$$

d) To compute the precision, the z-value is found in a table for the standard normal distribution. If a two-tailed test is desired and the confidence level is set at 95%, 2.5% of the area under the normal curve will lie in each tail. Thus, the entries in the body of the table will be .9750 and .0250. These entries correspond to z-values of 1.96 and $-1.96$, respectively. Accordingly, 95% of the area under the standard normal distribution lies within 1.96 standard deviations of the mean. Hence, the 95% confidence interval is $6 \pm 1.96\,(\sigma \div \sqrt{n})$. Because the population standard deviation is not known, the sample standard deviation ($s = 1.0$) is used. The precision then becomes

$$6 \pm 1.96\,(1.0 \div \sqrt{3}) = 6 \pm 1.13 = 4.87 \text{ to } 7.13$$

Consequently, the probability is 95% that this interval contains the population mean.

3.   **Statistical quality control** is a method of determining whether the shipment or production run of units lies within acceptable limits. It is also used to determine whether production processes are out of control.

    a.   Items are either good or bad, i.e., inside or outside of control limits.

    b.   Statistical quality control is based on the binomial distribution.

    c.   Acceptance sampling is a method of determining the probability that the defective rate in a batch is less than a certain level.

        1)   EXAMPLE: Assume that a sample is taken and the probability that the sample was from a population of 500 with a specified error rate is calculated. According to standard acceptance sampling tables, if the sample consists of 25 items and none is defective, the probability is 93% that the population error rate is less than 10%. If 60 items are examined and no defectives are found, the probability is 99% that the error rate is less than 10%. If two defectives in 60 units are observed, the probability is 96% that the error rate is less than 10%.

    d.   Statistical control charts are graphic aids for monitoring the status of any process subject to random variations. Originally developed to control the quality of production processes, they also have applications of direct interest to the management accountant, for example, unit cost of production, direct labor hours used, ratio of actual expenses to budgeted expenses, number of calls by sales personnel, and total accounts receivable.

        1)   The chart consists of three horizontal lines plotted on a horizontal time scale. The center line represents the average or mean value for the process being controlled. The other two lines are the upper control limit (UCL) and the lower control limit (LCL). The processes are measured periodically, and the values are plotted on the chart (X). If the value falls within the control limits, no action is taken. If the value falls outside the limits, the process is considered out of control, and an investigation is made for possible corrective action. Another advantage of the chart is that it makes trends visible.

            a)   **P charts** are based on an attribute (acceptable/not acceptable) rather than a measure of a variable. Specifically, it shows the percentage of defects in a sample.

            b)   **C charts** are also attribute control charts. They show defects per item.

            c)   An **R chart** shows the range of dispersion of a variable, such as size or weight.

            d)   An **X-bar chart** shows the sample mean for a variable.

        2)   EXAMPLE:   Unit Cost ($)               X  Out of control

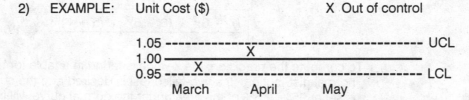

e.    Variations in the value of some process parameter may have several causes.

1)    **Random variations** occur by chance.  Present in virtually all processes, they are not correctable because they will not repeat themselves in the same manner.  Excessively narrow control limits will result in many investigations of what are simply random fluctuations.

2)    **Implementation deviations** occur because of human or mechanical failure to achieve target results.

3)    **Measurement variations** result from errors in the measurements of actual results.

4)    **Model fluctuations** can be caused by errors in the formulation of a decision model.

5)    **Prediction variances** result from errors in forecasting data used in a decision model.

f.    Establishing approximate control limits based on benchmarks is common.  A more objective method is to use the concept of expected value (see Module 15.4).  The limits are important because they are the decision criteria for determining whether a deviation will be investigated.

1)    Cost-benefit analysis using expected value provides an objective basis for setting control limits.  They should be set so that the cost of an investigation is less than or equal to the benefits derived.

a)    The expected costs include investigation cost and the cost of corrective action.

(Probability of being out of control  x  Cost of corrective action)
+  (Probability of being in control  x  Investigation cost)
Total expected cost

b)    The benefit of an investigation is the avoidance of the costs of continuing to operate an out-of-control process.  The expected value of benefits is the probability of being out of control times the cost of not being corrected.

## 15.2  PROBABILITY DISTRIBUTIONS

A.    **Discrete distributions**

1.    The **uniform distribution** is one in which all outcomes are equally likely.  The results of flipping one coin constitute a uniform distribution.

2.    In the **binomial distribution**, each trial has only two possible outcomes, e.g., accept or reject, heads or tails.  This distribution shows the likelihood of each of the possible combinations of trial results.  It is used in quality control.

a.    EXAMPLE: The social director of a cruise ship is concerned that the individuals at each dining room table be balanced evenly between men and women.  The tables have only 6, 10, or 16 seats.  If the population of the ship is exactly 50% male and 50% female [Pr(male) = .5 and Pr(female) = .5], what is the random chance for an equal balance of males and females at each table?

b.    The binomial formula is

$$\frac{n!}{r!(n - r)!} \times p^{r}(1 - p)^{n-r}$$

If:    $p$ = the probability of the given condition
      $n$ = the sample size
      $r$ = the number of occurrences of the condition within the sample
      ! = factorial, i.e., $1 \times 2 \times 3 \times ... n$, or $1 \times 2 \times 3 \times ... r$

c.    Given a .5 probability that any person in the population is male, the probability that exactly three males (and therefore three females) will be seated randomly at a table for six persons is

$$\frac{6!}{3!(6 - 3)!} \times .5^{3}(1 - .5)^{6-3} = .3125$$

d.    The probability is approximately 31% that an equally balanced group of males and females will be randomly chosen. For the tables with 10 and 16 seats, the probabilities are .2461 and .1964, respectively. The social director will have to assign seats.

3.    The **Bernoulli distribution** applies when only one trial is made. Thus, the binomial distribution reduces to the Bernoulli distribution when n is 1.

4.    The **hypergeometric distribution** is similar to the binomial distribution. It is used for sampling without replacement.

a.    For finite populations, sampling without replacement removes each item sampled from the population, thus changing the composition of the population from trial to trial.

1)    EXAMPLE: For a standard, well-shuffled deck of cards, the probability of picking the 2 of spades on the first draw is 1/52. If the card drawn is not replaced, the probability is 1/51 on the second draw, 1/50 on the third draw, etc. (unless, of course, the 2 of spades is drawn, in which case subsequent trial probabilities are 0). Sampling with replacement returns the card to the deck. The probability that any given card will be drawn is then 1/52 on every trial when sampling with replacement.

b.    For large populations and small samples, the binomial distribution approximates the hypergeometric distribution and is computationally more convenient.

5.    The **Poisson distribution** is useful when an event may happen more than once randomly during a given period of time.

a.    The Poisson distribution is defined as

$$f(k) = \frac{\lambda^{k} e^{-\lambda}}{k!} \quad \textit{mean and variance} = \lambda$$

If:    k is the number of occurrences
      e is the natural logarithm (2.71828...)

b.    When sample size is large and $\lambda$ is small (preferably less than 7), the Poisson distribution approaches the binomial distribution. In that case, $\lambda$ is assumed to equal $n \times p$.

If:    $n$ = number of items sampled and
      $p$ = probability of an event's occurrence

c.    EXAMPLE:  A trucking company has established that, on an average, two of its trucks are involved in an accident each month.  It wishes to calculate the probability of a month with no (0) crashes and the probability of a month with four crashes.  The mean of the Poisson distribution is $\lambda$, and the average monthly crash rate is 2, so $\lambda$ is 2.  The probability of 0 crashes in a given month is

$$f(0) \;=\; \frac{\lambda^0 e^{-\lambda}}{0!} \;=\; \frac{1 e^{-2}}{1} \;=\; e^{-2} \;=\; .135 \qquad (\textit{Note:}\;\; 0! = 1)$$

The probability of four crashes in a given month is

$$f(4) \;=\; \frac{\lambda^4 e^{-\lambda}}{4!} \;=\; \frac{2^4 e^{-2}}{4!} \;=\; .09$$

B.   **Continuous distributions**

1.    The **normal distribution** is the most important and useful of all probability distributions.  It describes many physical phenomena.  In sampling, it describes the distribution of the sample mean regardless of the distribution of the population.  It has a symmetrical, bell-shaped curve centered about the mean (see the diagram below).  For the normal distribution, about 68% of the area (or probability) lies within plus or minus 1 standard deviation of the mean, 95.5% lies within 2 standard deviations, and 99.9% lies within 3 standard deviations of the mean.

a.    A special type of normal distribution is called the **standard normal distribution**.  It has a mean of 0 and variance of 1.  All normal distribution problems are first converted to the standard normal distribution to permit use of standard normal distribution tables.

b.    Normal distributions have the following fixed relationships concerning the area under the curve and the distance from the mean in standard deviations.

| Distance in Standard Deviation (confidence coefficient) | Area of the Curve Within the Interval (confidence level) |
|:---:|:---:|
| 1.0 | 68.0% |
| 1.64 | 90.0% |
| 1.96 | 95.0% |
| 2.0 | 95.5% |
| 2.57 | 99.0% |

EXAMPLE:  If standard deviation ($\sigma$) = 10

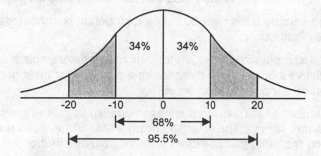

c.    The standard deviation is explained on page 549.

2.  The **exponential distribution** is related to the Poisson distribution. It is the probability of zero occurrences in a time period T.

    a.  The Poisson distribution has been defined as

    $$f(k) = \frac{\lambda^k e^{-\lambda}}{k!}$$

    The example in A.5.c.) stated that when

    $$k = 0 \text{ (no occurrences in the time period), then}$$
    $$f(0) = e^{-\lambda}$$

    b.  For the exponential distribution, M is used instead of $\lambda$

    $P = e^{-M}$
    $M = LT$ = frequency of the event's occurrence in this period
    $L$ = frequency or rate of the event's occurrence per unit of time
    $T$ = number of time units in this period
    $P$ = probability under exponential distribution

    c.  EXAMPLE: The trucking company mentioned in A.5.c. may wish to calculate the probability that a month will elapse without a single crash (the probability of a 1-month period between crashes).

    $L$ = 2 crashes per month
    $T$ = 1 month
    $M$ = 2 x 1 = 2

    The probability of a 1-month interval between crashes is then

    $$P = e^{-M} = 2.71828^{-2} = .135$$

    The probability of a 2-month period between crashes is much less likely.

    $L$ = 2
    $T$ = 2
    $M$ = 2 x 2 = 4
    $$P = e^{-M} = 2.71828^{-4} = .0183$$

3.  The **t-distribution** (also known as Student's distribution) is a special distribution used with small samples of the population, usually less than 30, with unknown population variance.

    a.  For large sample sizes (n > 30), the t-distribution is almost identical to the standard normal distribution.

    b.  For small sample sizes (n < 30) for which only the sample standard deviation is known, the t-distribution provides a reasonable estimate for tests of the population mean if the population is normally distributed.

    c.  The t-distribution is useful in business because large samples are often too expensive. For a small sample, the t-statistic (from a t-table) provides a better estimate of the variance than that from a table for the normal distribution.

    d.  See also section E. under Hypothesis Testing on page 561.

4.   The **chi-square distribution** is used in testing the goodness of fit between actual data and the theoretical distribution.  In other words, it tests whether the sample is likely to be from the population, based on a comparison of the sample variance and the population variance.

   a.   The chi-square statistic ($x^2$) is the sample variance ($s^2$), multiplied by its degree of freedom ($n - 1$), and divided by the hypothesized population variance ($\sigma^2$), if n is the number of items sampled.

   b.   A calculated value of the chi-square statistic greater than the critical value in the $x^2$ table indicates that the sample chosen comes from a population with greater variance than the hypothesized population variance.

   c.   The chi-square test is useful in business for testing hypotheses concerning populations. If the variance of a process is known, and a sample is tested to determine if it has the same variance, the chi-square statistic may be calculated.

   d.   EXAMPLE:  A canning machine fills cans with a product and has exhibited a long-term standard deviation of .4 ounces ($\sigma = .4$).  A new machine is tested, but because the tests are expensive, only 15 cans are examined.  The following is the result:

   Sample standard deviation (s) = .311

   The chi-square statistic is calculated as follows:

   $$\chi^2 = \frac{(n - 1)s^2}{\sigma^2} = \frac{(15 - 1).311^2}{.4^2} = 8.463$$

   Assume the null hypothesis ($H_o$) is that the new machine has a variance lower than or equal to the variance of the old machine, and that a probability of error ($\alpha$) of .05 is acceptable.  The $x^2$ statistic for an $\alpha$ of .05 and 14 degrees of freedom is 23.68 in the $x^2$ table.  This critical value is much greater than the sample statistic of 8.463, so the null hypothesis cannot be rejected.  Alpha ($\alpha$) error is the error of incorrectly rejecting the true hypothesis (see next module).

## 15.3 HYPOTHESIS TESTING

A.   The following are the four steps in hypothesis testing:

1.   A hypothesis is formulated to be tested for truth or falsity.

2.   Sample evidence is obtained.

3.   The probability that the hypothesis is true, given the observed evidence, is computed.

4.   If that probability is too low, the hypothesis is rejected.  Whether a probability is too low is a subjective determination dependent on the situation.  A probability of .6 that a team will win may be sufficient to place a small bet on the next game.  A probability of .95 that a parachute will open may be too low to justify skydiving.

B.   The hypothesis to be tested is known as the **null hypothesis** or $H_o$; the alternative hypothesis is denoted $H_a$.

1.   The null hypothesis, $H_o$, may state an equality (=) or that the parameter is equal to or greater (less) than ($\geq$ or $\leq$) some value.

2.   The alternative hypothesis, $H_a$, contains every other possibility.

a.   It may be stated as not equal to ($\neq$), greater than (>), or less than (<) some value, depending on the null hypothesis.

3.   The probability of error in hypothesis testing is usually labeled as

|  | Decision | |
| --- | --- | --- |
| State of Nature | Do not reject $H_o$ | Reject $H_o$ |
| $H_o$ is True | Correct | Type I Error $P(I) = \alpha$ |
| $H_o$ is False | Type II Error $P(II) = \beta$ | Correct |

a.   These are the same $\alpha$ (alpha) and $\beta$ (beta) errors familiar to auditors and accountants.

4.   EXAMPLE:  The hypothesis is that a component fails at a pressure of 80 or more lb. on the average; i.e., the average component will not fail at a pressure below 80 lb.  For a group of 36 components, the average failure pressure was found to be 77.48 lb.  Given that n is 36, $\bar{x}$ is 77.48 lb., and $\sigma$ is 13.32 lb., the following are the hypotheses:

$H_o$: The average failure pressure of the population of components is $\geq$ 80 lb.
$H_a$: The average failure pressure is < 80 lb.

a.  If a 5% chance of being wrong is acceptable, $\alpha$ (Type I error or the chance of incorrect rejection of the null hypothesis) is set equal to .05 and the confidence level at .95. In effect, 5% of the area under the curve of the standard normal distribution will constitute a rejection region. For this one-tailed test, the 5% rejection region will fall entirely in the left-hand tail of the distribution because the null hypothesis will not be rejected for any values of the test statistic that fall in the right-hand tail. According to standard tables, 5% of the area under the standard normal curve lies to the left of the z-value of –1.645. The following is the formula for the z-statistic:

$$z = \frac{\bar{x} - \mu_o}{\sigma \div \sqrt{n}}$$

If:  $\sigma$ = given population standard deviation
$\mu_o$ = hypothesized true population mean
$n$ = sample size
$z$ = number of standard deviations needed to ensure the specified level of confidence
$\bar{x}$ = the sample mean

b.  Substituting the hypothesized value of the population average failure pressure ($\mu_o$ = 80 lb.) determines the z-statistic.

$$z = \frac{77.48 - 80}{13.32 \div \sqrt{36}} = -1.135$$

c.  Because the calculated z-value corresponding to the sample mean of 77.48 is greater than the critical value of –1.645, the null hypothesis cannot be rejected.

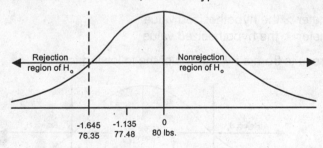

1)  The lower limit of the 95% nonrejection area under the curve is

$$80 \text{ lb.} - 1.645 \,(\sigma \div \sqrt{n}) =$$
$$80 \text{ lb.} - 1.645 \,(13.32 \div \sqrt{36}) =$$
$$76.35 \text{ lb.}$$

2)  Because a sample average of 77.48 lb. (a z of –1.135) falls within the nonrejection region (i.e., > 76.35 lb.), the null hypothesis that the average failure pressure of the population is $\geq$ 80 lb. cannot be rejected. The null hypothesis is rejected only if the sample average is equal to or less than the critical value (76.35 lb.).

C.    Hypothesis tests may be one-tailed or two-tailed.

    1.    A one-tailed test results from a hypothesis of the following form:

$H_o$: parameter $\leq$ or $\geq$ the hypothesized value
$H_a$: parameter $>$ or $<$ the hypothesized value

        a.    One-tailed test, upper tail

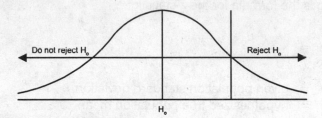

$H_o$: parameter $\leq$ the hypothesized value
$H_a$: parameter $>$ the hypothesized value

        b.    One-tailed test, lower tail

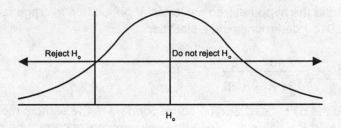

$H_o$: parameter $\geq$ the hypothesized value
$H_a$: parameter $<$ the hypothesized value

    2.    A two-tailed test results from a hypothesis of the following form:

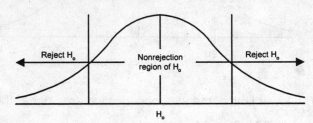

$H_o$: parameter $=$ the hypothesized value
$H_a$: parameter $\neq$ the hypothesized value

D.   A failure to prove $H_o$ is false does not prove that it is true.  This failure merely signifies that $H_o$ is not a rejectable hypothesis.  In practice, however, auditors often use acceptance as a synonym for nonrejection.

E.   Given a small sample (less than 30) and an unknown population variance, the t-statistic (t-distribution) must be used.

   1.   The t-distribution requires a number called **the degrees of freedom**, which is $(n - 1)$ when one parameter (such as the mean) is estimated.  For k parameters (any number), it is $(n - k)$.  The degrees of freedom is a correction factor that is necessary because with k parameters and n elements, only $(n - k)$ elements are free to vary.  After $(n - k)$ elements are chosen, the remaining k elements' values are already determined.

      a.   EXAMPLE:  If two numbers have an average of 5,

$$\bar{x} = \frac{x_1 + x_2}{2} = 5$$

If $x_1$ is allowed to vary but the average remains the same, $x_1$ determines $x_2$ because only 1 degree of freedom $(n - 1)$ or $(2 - 1)$ is available.

If:     $x_1 = 2, x_2 = 8$
        $x_1 = 3, x_2 = 7$

   2.   The t-distribution is used in the same way as the z or normal distribution.  Standard texts have t-distribution tables.  In the example in B.4. on page 558, if the sample size had been 25 and the sample standard deviation had been given instead of the population value, the t-statistic would have been

$$t = \frac{\bar{x} - \mu_o}{s \div \sqrt{25}} = \frac{77.48 - 80}{13.32 \div \sqrt{25}} = -.946$$

      a.   At a confidence level of 95% (rejection region of 5%) and 24 degrees of freedom (sample of $25 - 1$ parameter estimated), the t-distribution table indicates that 5% of the area under the curve is to the left of a t-value of $-1.711$.  Because the computed value is greater than $-1.711$, the null hypothesis cannot be rejected in this one-tailed test.

      b.   As the number of degrees of freedom increases, the t-distribution approximates the z-distribution.  For degrees of freedom $> 30$, the z-distribution may be used.

## 15.4 EXPECTED VALUE

A.   EXAMPLE:  An investor is considering the purchase of two different pieces of property.  The value of the property will change if a road, currently planned by the state, is built.  The following are estimates that road construction will occur:

| Future State of Nature (SN) | Probability |
|---|---|
| SN 1:  No road is ever built. | .1 |
| SN 2:  A road is built this year. | .2 |
| SN 3:  A road is built more than 1 year from now. | .7 |

1.   The following are estimates of the values of the properties under each of the three possible future states of nature.

| Property | Value if SN 1 | Value if SN 2 | Value if SN 3 |
|---|---|---|---|
| Property 1 | $10,000 | $40,000 | $35,000 |
| Property 2 | $20,000 | $50,000 | $30,000 |

2.   The expected value of each property is determined by multiplying the probability of each state of nature by the value under that state of nature and adding all of the partial results together.  Thus, Property 1 is the better investment if the two properties cost the same.

P1:  (.1 x $10,000) + (.2 x $40,000) + (.7 x $35,000) = $33,500 expected value
P2:  (.1 x $20,000) + (.2 x $50,000) + (.7 x $30,000) = $33,000 expected value

B.   Some managers are reluctant to use subjectively derived numbers, arguing that they are unmeasurable.  Certainly, the accuracy of the estimates cannot be proved.  Their use, however, makes explicit what would otherwise be decided intuitively.  Once stated, the reasonableness of subjectively derived numbers can be examined.

1.   Another criticism of expected value is that it is based on repetitive trials, whereas many business decisions involve only one trial.

a.   EXAMPLE:  A company wishes to launch a communications satellite.  The probability of launch failure is .2, and the value of the satellite if the launch fails is $0.  The probability of a successful launch is .8, and the value of the satellite would then be $25,000,000.  The expected value is therefore $20,000,000 [(.2 x $0) + (.8 x $25,000,000)].  But $20,000,000 is not a possible value for a single satellite; either it flies for $25,000,000 or it crashes for $0.

C.   **Decision trees** and **payoff tables** may be used to describe decision situations.

1.   EXAMPLE:  A dealer in luxury yachts may order 0, 1, or 2 yachts for this season's inventory, but no more or less.  The carrying cost for each excess yacht is $50,000, and the gain for each yacht sold is $200,000.  The situation may be described by the following payoff table:

| Season's Actual Demand | Pr | Order 0 | Order 1 | Order 2 |
|---|---|---|---|---|
| 0 yachts | .10 | 0 | $ (50,000) | $(100,000) |
| 1 yacht | .50 | 0 | 200,000 | 150,000 |
| 2 yachts | .40 | 0 | 200,000 | 400,000 |

a. The dealer may calculate the expected value of each course of action as follows:

| Order 0 | Order 1 | Order 2 |
|---------|---------|---------|
| .1 x 0 | .1 x $ (50,000) | .1 x $(100,000) |
| .5 x 0 | + .5 x 200,000 | + .5 x 150,000 |
| .4 x 0 | + .4 x 200,000 | + .4 x 400,000 |
| EV(0) = 0 | EV(1) = $175,000 | EV(2) = $ 225,000 |

b. The decision with the greatest expected value is to order two yachts, so, in the absence of additional information, the dealer should order two. The decision tree representation of this situation is

| Action | State of Nature | Payoff |
|--------|-----------------|--------|
| | Demand = 0 | $ 0 |
| Order 0 | Demand = 1 | 0 |
| | Demand = 2 | 0 |
| | Demand = 0 | (50,000) |
| Order 1 | Demand = 1 | 200,000 |
| | Demand = 2 | 200,000 |
| | Demand = 0 | (100,000) |
| Order 2 | Demand = 1 | 150,000 |
| | Demand = 2 | 400,000 |

**D.    Value of Perfect Information**

1.    **Perfect information** is the knowledge that a future state of nature will occur with certainty (a probability of 1.0).

    a.    The **expected value of perfect information (EVPI)** is the difference between the expected value without perfect information and the return if the best action is taken given perfect information.

    b.    EXAMPLE (from the yacht dealer problem on the previous pages):  If the yacht dealer were able to poll all potential customers and they truthfully stated whether they would purchase a yacht this year (i.e., if perfect information about this year's yacht sales could be purchased), what is the greatest amount of money the dealer should pay for this information?  What is EVPI?

        1)    If the dealer had perfect knowledge of demand, (s)he would make the best decision for each state of nature.  The cost of the other decisions is the conditional cost of making other than the best choice.  This cost may be calculated by subtracting the expected value from the expected value given perfect information.  This difference measures how much better off the decision maker would be with perfect information.  The payoff table on the page 562 gives the expected value of the best choice under each state of nature.

| Pr | State of Nature | Best Action | Best Action Payoff | Expected Value (Pr x Payoff) |
|----|-----------------|-------------|--------------------|------------------------------|
| .1 | Demand = 0 | Buy 0 | $        0 | $        0 |
| .5 | Demand = 1 | Buy 1 | 200,000 | 100,000 |
| .4 | Demand = 2 | Buy 2 | 400,000 | 160,000 |
|    |            |       |         | $260,000 |

        2)    The dealer expects to make $260,000 with perfect information about future demand, and $225,000 if the choice with the best expected value is made.  Hence, the expected value of perfect information (EVPI) is $35,000 ($260,000 – $225,000).  The dealer will not pay more than $35,000 for information about future demand because it would then be more profitable to make the expected value choice than to pay more for information.

## 15.1 Basic Concepts

**1.** To assist in an investment decision, Gift Co. selected the most likely sales volume from several possible outcomes. Which of the following attributes would that selected sales volume reflect?

    A. The midpoint of the range.

    B. The median.

    C. The greatest probability.

    D. The expected value.

The correct answer is (C). *(CPA, adapted)*
    **REQUIRED:** The attribute reflected by the selected sales volume.
    **DISCUSSION:** Probability is important to management decision making because of the unpredictability of future events. Probability theory provides a method for mathematically expressing the degree of doubt that a chance event will occur. Consequently, the most likely sales volume is the one with the greatest probability.
    Answer (A) is incorrect because the midpoint of the range is the point halfway between two points. Answer (B) is incorrect because half the values are greater and half are less than the median. Answer (D) is incorrect because the expected value is a weighted average using probabilities as weights.

**2.** Probability (risk) analysis is

    A. Used only for situations involving five or fewer possible outcomes.

    B. Used only for situations in which the summation of probability weights is less than one.

    C. An extension of sensitivity analysis.

    D. Incompatible with sensitivity analysis.

The correct answer is (C). *(CPA, adapted)*
    **REQUIRED:** The correct description of probability (risk) analysis.
    **DISCUSSION:** Probability (risk) analysis is used to estimate the likelihood of possible outcomes of a decision. Sensitivity analysis answers what-if questions about the effects of changes in the variables included in a decision model. Thus, probability (risk) analysis extends sensitivity analysis by assigning probabilities to the effects of changes in variables.
    Answer (A) is incorrect because probability analysis can be used when many outcomes are possible. Answer (B) is incorrect because the sum must equal one. Answer (D) is incorrect because probability analysis enhances sensitivity analysis.

**3.** The probability of the simultaneous occurrence of two mutually exclusive events is

    A. The probability that both events will occur.

    B. The probability that one will occur given that the other has occurred.

    C. The probability that two independent events will occur.

    D. Zero.

The correct answer is (D). *(Publisher)*
    **REQUIRED:** The definition of mutually exclusive events.
    **DISCUSSION:** Mutually exclusive events cannot occur simultaneously. The usual example is that heads and tails cannot both occur on a single toss of a coin.
    Answer (A) is incorrect because it is the definition of joint probability. Answer (B) is incorrect because it defines conditional probability. Answer (C) is incorrect because two independent events may both occur.

**4.** Joint probability is the probability that

    A. Two or more events will all occur.

    B. One event will occur given that another has occurred.

    C. One event has no effect on the probability of a second event.

    D. Mutually exclusive events will occur.

The correct answer is (A). *(Publisher)*
    **REQUIRED:** The definition of joint probability.
    **DISCUSSION:** Joint probability is the probability that two or more events will occur. The joint probability for two events equals the probability of the first event times the conditional probability of the second event.
    Answer (B) is incorrect because it defines conditional probability. Answer (C) is incorrect because it describes independent events. Answer (D) is incorrect because two mutually exclusive events cannot both occur.

**5.** Conditional probability is the probability that

    A. Two or more events will all occur.

    B. One event will occur given that the other has occurred.

    C. One event has no effect on the probability of a second event.

    D. Mutually exclusive events will occur.

The correct answer is (B). *(Publisher)*
    **REQUIRED:** The definition of conditional probability.
    **DISCUSSION:** Conditional probability is the probability that one event will occur given that another has already occurred.
    Answer (A) is incorrect because it is the definition of joint probability. Answer (C) is incorrect because it is the definition of independent events. Answer (D) is incorrect because mutually exclusive events cannot both occur.

**6.** Events are independent when

    A. Their joint probability is zero.

    B. Their joint probability is one.

    C. The conditional probability of each event is its unconditional probability.

    D. They are mutually exclusive.

The correct answer is (C). *(Publisher)*
    **REQUIRED:** The definition of independent events.
    **DISCUSSION:** Events are independent when the occurrence of one does not affect the probability of the other. For example, the tossing of two dice is usually viewed as the occurrence of two independent events.
    Answers (A) and (B) are incorrect because events are independent when their joint probability equals the product of their individual probabilities. Answer (D) is incorrect because events are mutually exclusive if their joint probability is zero.

**7.** A warehouse contains records from both the retail and the wholesale divisions of the client company. Upon inspecting the contents of one randomly selected box, the auditor discovers that they do not match the label. On average, errors of this kind have occurred in 6% of retail boxes and 2% of wholesale boxes. Unfortunately, the part of the label indicating the division of origin is illegible. The auditor does know that two-thirds of the boxes in this warehouse come from the wholesale division and one-third from the retail division. Which of the following can be concluded?

    A. The box is more likely to have come from the retail division.

    B. The box is more likely to have come from the wholesale division.

    C. The proportion of retail boxes in the warehouse is probably much larger than the auditor thought.

    D. The proportion of wholesale boxes in the warehouse is probably much larger than the auditor thought.

The correct answer is (A). *(CIA, adapted)*
    **REQUIRED:** The true probabilistic statement.
    **DISCUSSION:** Two-thirds of the boxes are from the wholesale division. Of these, 2% are mislabeled. Hence, about 1.33% (66⅔% × 2%) of all the boxes are mislabeled and originated in the wholesale division. One-third of the boxes are from the retail division. Of these, 6% are mislabeled. Hence, about 2% (33⅓% × 6%) of all the boxes are mislabeled and originated in the retail division. The probability is therefore about 60% [2% ÷ (1.33% + 2%)] that the box came from the retail division.
    Answer (B) is incorrect because the box is more likely to have come from the retail division. Answers (C) and (D) are incorrect because the contents of any one box are an insufficient basis for a conclusion about the population of boxes in the warehouse.

**8.** Which one of the following is a correct rationale for using a nonparametric statistic rather than a more conventional statistic?

    A. It is not known how the variable being tested is distributed.

    B. The event or difference to be tested is fairly small, and therefore you need a more sensitive test.

    C. The sample was not drawn randomly.

    D. The variable being tested is measured on a continuous scale.

The correct answer is (A). *(CIA, adapted)*
    **REQUIRED:** The rationale for using a nonparametric statistic.
    **DISCUSSION:** Nonparametric statistics is usually defined to include techniques that are not concerned with population parameters or are not based on rigid assumptions about the distribution of the population. For example, chi-square tests of goodness of fit are nonparametric procedures.
    Answer (B) is incorrect because nonparametric tests are usually less sensitive than conventional statistics. Answer (C) is incorrect because proper inferences from nonparametric tests also require random samples. Answer (D) is incorrect because nonparametric tests are more appropriate than parametric tests for variables measured by rankings or categories but not usually for continuous variables.

**9.** A company uses two major material inputs in its production. To prepare its manufacturing operations budget, the company has to project the cost changes of these material inputs. The cost changes are independent of one another. The purchasing department provides the following probabilities associated with projected cost changes:

| Cost Change | Material 1 | Material 2 |
|---|---|---|
| 3% increase | .3 | .5 |
| 5% increase | .5 | .4 |
| 10% increase | .2 | .1 |

The probability that there will be a 3% increase in the cost of both Material 1 and Material 2 is

A. 15%

B. 40%

C. 80%

D. 20%

The correct answer is (A). *(CIA, adapted)*
**REQUIRED:** The probability of joint increases.
**DISCUSSION:** The joint probability of occurrence of two independent events equals the product of their individual probabilities. The probability that the cost of Material 1 will increase by 3% is .3. The probability that the cost of Material 2 will increase by 3% is .5. The probability that both will occur is .15 (.3 x .5).

Answer (B) is incorrect because 40% is the average of the probabilities of a 3% increase in the costs of Material 1 and Material 2. Answer (C) is incorrect because 80% is the sum of the probabilities of a 3% increase in the costs of Material 1 and Material 2. Answer (D) is incorrect because 20% is the difference between the probabilities of an increase in the costs of Material 1 and Material 2.

**10.** Thoran Electronics Company began producing pacemakers last year. At that time, the company forecasted the need for 10,000 integrated circuits (ICs) annually. During the first year, the company placed orders for the ICs when the inventory dropped to 600 units so that it would have enough to produce pacemakers continuously during a 3-week lead time before delivery of new ICs. Unfortunately, the company ran out of this IC component on several occasions, causing costly production delays. Careful study of last year's experience resulted in the following expectations for the coming year:

| Weekly Usage | Related Probability of Usage | Lead Time | Related Probability of Lead Time |
|---|---|---|---|
| 280 units | .2 | 3 weeks | .1 |
| 180 units | .8 | 2 weeks | .9 |
| | 1.0 | | 1.0 |

The study also suggested that usage during a given week was statistically independent of usage during any other week, and usage was also statistically independent of lead time. If the company reorders integrated circuits when the inventory has dropped to a level of 700 units, the probability that it will run out of this component before the order is received is

A. .0008

B. .1040

C. .0104

D. .896

The correct answer is (C). *(CMA, adapted)*
**REQUIRED:** The probability of a stockout if an order is placed when inventory has dropped to a given level.
**DISCUSSION:** Based on the given data, weekly usage must be either 280 or 180 units, and the lead time must be either 3 or 2 weeks. Whenever the lead time is 2 weeks, no stockout will occur because usage will be, at most, 560 units (2 weeks x 280 units). Thus, one condition of a stockout is a lead time of 3 weeks. A second condition of a stockout is that usage equals 280 units for at least 2 of the 3 weeks; if usage is 280 units for only 1 week, the total usage during the lead time will be only 640 units [(2 x 180) + 280]. The probability of a 3-week lead time is given as .1. Given that weekly usage is independent of lead time and of prior weeks' usage, the probability that usage will be 280 units for at least 2 weeks is the sum of the probabilities of the following combinations of events:

| Week 1 | Week 2 | Week 3 | Probability |
|---|---|---|---|
| 280 | 280 | 280 | .2 × .2 × .2 = .008 |
| 280 | 280 | 180 | .2 × .2 × .8 = .032 |
| 280 | 180 | 280 | .2 × .8 × .2 = .032 |
| 180 | 280 | 280 | .8 × .2 × .2 = .032 |
| | | | .104 |

The probability of both a 3-week lead time and usage in excess of 700 units is therefore .0104 (.1 x .104).

Answer (A) is incorrect because .0008 is the probability that lead time will be 3 weeks and that usage will be 280 units each week. Answer (B) is incorrect because .104 is the probability of usage in excess of 700 units, given a 3-week lead time. Answer (D) is incorrect because .896 is the probability of usage less than 700 units, given a 3-week lead time.

**11.** A company with 14,344 customers determines that the mean and median accounts receivable balances for the year are $15,412 and $10,382, respectively. From this information, the auditor can conclude that the distribution of the accounts receivable balances is continuous and

A.  Negatively skewed.

B.  Positively skewed.

C.  Symmetrically skewed.

D.  Evenly distributed between the mean and median.

The correct answer is (B). *(CIA, adapted)*
   **REQUIRED:** The conclusion drawn from information about the mean and median of accounts receivable.
   **DISCUSSION:** The mean is the arithmetic average, and the median corresponds to the 50th percentile; that is, half the values are greater and half are smaller. The auditor can conclude that the distribution is positively skewed because the mean is greater than the median and the distribution is continuous.
   Answer (A) is incorrect because the mean is greater than the median and the distribution is continuous, so the distribution is positively skewed. Answer (C) is incorrect because the distribution would be symmetrically skewed if the mean, median, and mode (the most frequently occurring value) were equal. Answer (D) is incorrect because distributions spread evenly between two values are uniform distributions.

**12.** Which of the following statements is correct concerning the appropriate measure of central tendency for the frequency distribution of loss experience shown below?

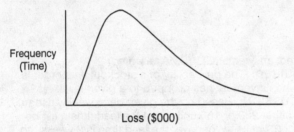

A.  The mean, median, and mode are equally appropriate because the distribution is symmetrical.

B.  The mode is the most appropriate measure because it considers the dollar amount of the extreme losses.

C.  The median is the most appropriate measure because it is not affected by the extreme losses.

D.  The mean is the best measure of central tendency because it always lies between the median and the mode.

The correct answer is (C). *(CIA, adapted)*
   **REQUIRED:** The appropriate measure of central tendency.
   **DISCUSSION:** Measures of central tendency are the mode, the median, and the mean. The mode is the most frequently occurring value, the median is the value above and below which half of the events occur, and the mean is the average or the arithmetic mean. The median is the best estimate of the central tendency for this distribution because it is not biased by extremes. The given frequency distribution of loss is skewed by the extremely high losses. The median, which consists of absolute numbers of events, is unaffected by the magnitude of the greatest losses.
   Answer (A) is incorrect because the example is an asymmetrical distribution. When the distribution is perfectly symmetrical, these three values are identical. Answer (B) is incorrect because the mode does not consider the extreme losses. It is simply the most frequently occurring value. Answer (D) is incorrect because, in this situation, the median lies between the mean and the mode. This distribution is skewed to the right because of the very high loss values. Consequently, the mean is to the right of both the mode and the median.

**13.** In sampling applications, the standard deviation represents a measure of the

A.  Expected error rate.

B.  Level of confidence desired.

C.  Degree of data variability.

D.  Extent of precision achieved.

The correct answer is (C). *(CIA, adapted)*
   **REQUIRED:** The definition of standard deviation.
   **DISCUSSION:** The standard deviation measures the variability within a population. The following is the formula for the standard deviation of a population ($\sigma$ = the standard deviation, $x_i$ = an observation, $\mu$ = the mean, and N = the number of items in the population):

$$\sigma = \sqrt{\frac{\Sigma(x_i - \mu)^2}{N}}$$

Answer (A) is incorrect because the expected error rate is associated with attribute sampling. Answer (B) is incorrect because the desired confidence level is determined by the auditor's judgment. Answer (D) is incorrect because the extent of precision achieved in variables sampling is computed using the standard deviation.

**14.** Which of the following is not a measure of dispersion of a random variable?

    A. Range.

    B. Median.

    C. Variance.

    D. Standard error of the mean.

The correct answer is (B). *(CIA, adapted)*

    **REQUIRED:** The statistical concept that is not a measure of dispersion.

    **DISCUSSION:** Measures of dispersion indicate the amount of variation within a set of numbers. Measures of central tendency, however, describe typical items in a population. The median, a measure of central tendency, is the halfway value when the raw data are arranged in numerical order from the lowest to the highest.

    Answer (A) is incorrect because it is the difference between the largest and the smallest values. Answer (C) is incorrect because the standard deviation is the square root of the variance. Answer (D) is incorrect because it is the standard deviation of sample means.

**15.** Auditors employ confidence levels in the context of audit sampling. In a given sample plan, the confidence level

    A. Is a decision variable that the auditor specifies after considering the economic consequences of drawing the wrong conclusion as a result of sampling risk.

    B. Is a characteristic of the audit population and is not under the direct control of the auditor.

    C. Is essentially a measure of the accuracy of the sample results obtained after the sample has been selected and tested.

    D. Is not normally specified before the sample size is determined. Rather, it is computed once the sample has been selected and tested.

The correct answer is (A). *(CIA, adapted)*

    **REQUIRED:** The true statement regarding confidence levels.

    **DISCUSSION:** In principle, given repeated sampling and a normally distributed population, the confidence level is the percentage of all the precision intervals that may be constructed from simple random samples of size n that will include the population value. In practice, the confidence level is regarded as the probability that a precision interval calculated from a simple random sample of size n drawn from a normally distributed population will contain the population value. The desired confidence level is specified by the auditor as a matter of judgment after determining the allowable audit risk.

    Answer (B) is incorrect because confidence is a decision variable, not a population characteristic. Answer (C) is incorrect because precision, not confidence level, is a measure of accuracy. Answer (D) is incorrect because planned confidence must be specified before sample size can be computed.

**16.** In audit sampling contexts, precision is

    A. A characteristic of the population at hand and is not under the direct control of the auditor.

    B. A measure of the accuracy with which one has generated sample estimates. Desired precision must be established before the sample is obtained and evaluated.

    C. Evaluated independently of reliability in a given sample.

    D. Important for evaluating variables samples, but not attributes samples.

The correct answer is (B). *(CIA, adapted)*

    **REQUIRED:** The definition of precision.

    **DISCUSSION:** The precision or confidence interval (allowance for sampling risk) is an interval around the sample statistic that is expected to contain the true value of the population. Precision is a variable in the sample size formula and must be estimated prior to calculating the sample size. The estimated precision interval is based upon a point estimate of the population value and the tolerable rate (for attribute sampling) or the tolerable misstatement (for variables sampling) determined by materiality considerations. The achieved (computed) precision interval is a function of population size and standard deviation, sample size, and specified confidence level.

    Answer (A) is incorrect because precision is under the auditor's control. Answer (C) is incorrect because precision and reliability are interdependent. Answer (D) is incorrect because precision applies to attribute samples as well.

**17.** An auditor wishes to determine whether the finished goods perpetual inventory records are being properly updated for completed production. To accomplish this, the auditor traces inventory quantity and cost records from production reports to perpetual inventory records, using an appropriate sample size based on a 95% confidence level, estimated error rate of 4%, and desired precision of ±2%. If the error rate in the sample is, as expected, 4%, and 2,000 production reports were posted to perpetual inventory records during the year, the auditor can be 95% sure that the number incorrectly posted was

   A.  At least 100.

   B.  At least 80.

   C.  Between 60 and 140.

   D.  Between 40 and 120.

The correct answer is (D). *(CIA, adapted)*
   **REQUIRED:** The number of errors in the inventory records.
   **DISCUSSION:** The probability is 95% that the number of errors is between 2% (4% − 2%) and 6% (4% + 2%) because the precision is ±2% and the sample error rate equals the expected rate of 4%. Consequently, the range in terms of inventory records is between 40 [(4% − 2%) x 2,000] and 120 [(4% + 2%) x 2,000].
   Answer (A) is incorrect because 100 (5% x 2,000) results from using the complement of the confidence level instead of the error rate. Answer (B) is incorrect because the actual number of errors will be more or fewer than 80 (4% x 2,000). Answer (C) is incorrect because, for the number of errors to lie between 60 and 140, the complement of the confidence level is used instead of the estimated error rate.

**18.** The principle stating that the distribution of the sample means from any underlying population is approximately normal when the sample size is large (n ≥ 30) is the

   A.  Central limit theorem.

   B.  Sample mean theorem.

   C.  Maximum likelihood theorem.

   D.  None. The given statement is not true.

The correct answer is (A). *(Publisher)*
   **REQUIRED:** The principle stating that the distribution of a sample mean is normal.
   **DISCUSSION:** Given a large enough sample size, the central limit theorem states that the probability distribution of sample means generated from any underlying probability distribution is approximately normal. The mean of this distribution is the true population mean, and the variance is $\sigma^2 \div n$.
   Answer (B) is incorrect because there is no such theorem. Answer (C) is incorrect because maximum likelihood is a form of estimation that finds the value that maximizes the joint probabilities of all random variables sampled. Answer (D) is incorrect because the statement is true.

**19.** An auditor has taken a large sample from an audit population that is skewed in the sense that it contains a large number of small dollar balances and a small number of large dollar balances. Given this, the auditor can conclude

   A.  The sampling distribution is not normal; thus, sampling based on the Poisson distribution most accurately defines the nature of the population.

   B.  The sampling distribution is normal; thus, the Z-score value can be used in evaluating the sample results.

   C.  The sampling distribution is not normal; thus, attribute sampling is the only statistical tool that can appropriately be used.

   D.  The sampling distribution is normal; thus, attribute sampling is the only statistical tool that can appropriately be used.

The correct answer is (B). *(CIA, adapted)*
   **REQUIRED:** The conclusion about a skewed population.
   **DISCUSSION:** The central limit theorem states that, regardless of the distribution of the population from which random samples are taken, the shape of the sampling distribution of the means approaches the normal distribution as the sample size increases. Hence, Z-values (the number of standard deviations needed to provide specified levels of confidence) can be used. Z-values represent areas under the curve for the standard normal distribution.
   Answer (A) is incorrect because the sampling distribution is deemed to be normal (a continuous distribution). The Poisson distribution approaches the binomial distribution (a discrete distribution) for large samples and thus is related to attribute sampling, a method applicable to binary propositions, e.g., error rates. Variables sampling is appropriate for population values. Answer (C) is incorrect because the sampling distribution can be normally distributed given a large enough sample size. Moreover, attribute sampling is not appropriate for estimating population values. Answer (D) is incorrect because variables, not attribute, sampling is appropriate in this context.

**20.** Compared with the standard deviation of the population, the standard deviation of the sampling distribution of the mean (standard error of the mean) is

- A. Larger.
- B. Smaller.
- C. The same.
- D. Indeterminate.

The correct answer is (B). *(Publisher)*
**REQUIRED:** The relationship between the standard error of the mean and the standard deviation of the population.
**DISCUSSION:** The standard deviation of the distribution of sample means (standard error of the mean) is always smaller than the standard deviation of the population ($\sigma$). It equals the standard deviation of the population divided by the square root of the sample size ($\sigma \div \sqrt{n}$). The lower number also makes intuitive sense because extreme values of a population are typically excluded because of the averaging process in calculating a sample mean.
Answers (A), (C), and (D) are incorrect because the standard error of the mean is smaller than the standard deviation of the population.

**21.** Given a normally distributed population with an unknown mean ($\mu$) but a known standard deviation ($\sigma$) of 10, the standard error of the mean for a sample size of 100 is

- A. 10
- B. 100
- C. 1
- D. .1

The correct answer is (C). *(Publisher)*
**REQUIRED:** The standard error of the mean.
**DISCUSSION:** The formula for the standard error of the mean is the standard deviation of the population divided by the square root of the sample size ($\sigma \div \sqrt{n}$). Consequently, the standard error of the mean is 1 ($10 \div \sqrt{100}$).
Answer (A) is incorrect because 10 is the population standard deviation. Answer (B) is incorrect because 100 is the sample size. Answer (D) is incorrect because .1 equals $\sigma$ divided by n.

**22.** When a decision maker is faced with a decision and the probabilities of various outcomes are known, the situation is said to be decision making

- A. Under risk.
- B. Under uncertainty.
- C. Under certainty.
- D. Through satisficing.

The correct answer is (A). *(CIA, adapted)*
**REQUIRED:** The condition in which a decision maker is faced with a decision and the probabilities of various outcomes are known.
**DISCUSSION:** Decision making under risk entails consideration of multiple possible future states of nature for each choice. The decision is under risk if a probability distribution for these states is known. Thus, the states of nature will be mutually exclusive, and the sum of their probabilities will equal 1.0. Risk increases as the variability of outcomes becomes greater. In practice, however, the terms risk and uncertainty are often treated as synonyms.
Answer (B) is incorrect because, under uncertainty, the probabilities of the possible states of nature are unknown. Answer (C) is incorrect because, under certainty, the outcome of each decision choice is known; that is, its probability is 1.0. Answer (D) is incorrect because satisficing decisions are satisfactory or sufficient but not optimal.

**23.** Decision makers are normally confronted with a choice among feasible choices. Their decisions often have to be made under conditions of risk or uncertainty, that is, with less than complete and accurate knowledge of the outcome for each alternative. Which of the following is correct?

- A. Under conditions of risk, there is only one potential outcome for each alternative.
- B. Under conditions of uncertainty, the first task is to determine the expected value of each of the multiple outcomes.
- C. Under conditions of risk, decisions are solely based on the decision maker's experience and intuition.
- D. Under conditions of uncertainty, the first task is to establish subjective probabilities of occurrence for the multiple outcomes.

The correct answer is (D). *(CIA, adapted)*
**REQUIRED:** The true statement about making decisions.
**DISCUSSION:** The two types of probability are objective and subjective. Objective probabilities are calculated from either logic or actual experience. Subjective probabilities are estimates, based on judgment and past experience, of the likelihood of future events. In business, subjective probability can indicate the degree of confidence a person has in some outcome. Under conditions of uncertainty, objective probabilities cannot be determined. A decision maker must first establish subjective probabilities; then the decision-making process proceeds as it does under conditions of risk.
Answer (A) is incorrect because, under both risk and uncertainty, there are multiple outcomes for each occurrence; certainty exists when only one outcome is possible. Answer (B) is incorrect because calculation of expected values is dependent upon probabilities.
Answer (C) is incorrect because decision makers may also rely on probabilistic information under conditions of risk.

**24.** Managers have varying attitudes regarding risk. A risk-neutral manager

    A. Avoids risk.

    B. Has a linear utility function.

    C. Tends to choose options that involve large variations of actual monetary returns about expected monetary values.

    D. Tends to choose options that have very little variation about expected monetary returns.

The correct answer is (B). *(Publisher)*
    **REQUIRED:** The characteristic of a risk-neutral manager.
    **DISCUSSION:** A risk-neutral manager neither seeks nor avoids risk. (S)he will choose investments for which the expected monetary values are equal to the manager's subjectively perceived utility values (expressed in utils, an arbitrary measure). Thus, the decision maker has a linear utility function, one in which the monetary amounts and utils have a constant or directly proportional relationship. Accordingly, (s)he is indifferent to risk.
    Answer (A) is incorrect because a risk-averse manager avoids risk. Answer (C) is incorrect because a risk-seeking manager tends to accept greater variability of returns. Answer (D) is incorrect because it describes the tendency of a risk-averse manager.

**25.** A risk-averse manager

    A. Neither seeks nor avoids risk.

    B. Has a linear utility function.

    C. Tends to choose options that involve large variations of actual monetary returns about expected monetary values.

    D. Tends to choose options that have very little variation about expected monetary returns.

The correct answer is (D). *(Publisher)*
    **REQUIRED:** The definition of a risk-averse manager.
    **DISCUSSION:** The risk-averse manager will avoid risk. (S)he prefers a certain return on investments to the risk involved in other investments with potentially large gains but also large losses. The utility function for the risk-averse manager increases at a decreasing rate.
    Answers (A) and (B) are incorrect because each is typical of a risk-neutral manager. Answer (C) is incorrect because it describes a risk-seeking manager.

**26.** A risk-seeking manager

    A. Neither seeks nor avoids risk.

    B. Has a linear utility function.

    C. Tends to choose options that involve large variations of actual monetary returns about expected monetary values.

    D. Tends to choose options that have very little variation about expected monetary returns.

The correct answer is (C). *(Publisher)*
    **REQUIRED:** The definition of a risk-seeking manager.
    **DISCUSSION:** A risk-seeking manager chooses risk. A risk seeker prefers investments that have the potential for large gains even though large losses may also be possible. The utility function for the risk seeker increases at an increasing rate; i.e., riskier investments are appealing.
    Answers (A) and (B) are incorrect because each is typical of a risk-neutral manager. Answer (D) is incorrect because it describes the risk-averse manager.

**27.** Assume a linear utility for money and a risk-neutral decision maker. From the payoff table below, one can conclude that the utility of alternative A is

| | State of Nature | | Expected |
|---|---|---|---|
| | S1 | S2 | Profit |
| Alternative A: | 100 | 200 | $160 |
| Alternative B: | 140 | 40 | $ 80 |

    A. $300

    B. High.

    C. Exactly twice that of B.

    D. Approximately twice that of B.

The correct answer is (C). *(CIA, adapted)*
    **REQUIRED:** The utility of an action given a linear utility for money, a risk-neutral decision maker, and a payoff table.
    **DISCUSSION:** The linearity assumption for the utility of money means that each additional dollar has constant utility. Risk neutrality implies that the utility of a gain (profit) equals the disutility of a loss of the same magnitude. In these circumstances, one may conclude that a profit of $160 has exactly twice the utility of a profit of $80 even though the utility function of the decision maker is not known.
    Answer (A) is incorrect because utility is measured in utils, not dollars. Answer (B) is incorrect because it requires a judgment about the utility function of the decision maker, which is unknown. Answer (D) is incorrect because the linearity assumption leads to exact statements, not approximations.

**28.** Following is a table of probabilities for two separate product lines, X and Y:

| Probability | X profit | Y profit |
|---|---|---|
| .20 | $500 | $ 50 |
| .70 | 300 | 400 |
| .10 | 600 | 800 |

The product line to obtain maximum utility for a risk-averse decision maker is

A.  X because it has the higher expected profit.

B.  Y because it has the higher expected profit.

C.  Y because it has the higher dispersion.

D.  X because it has the lower dispersion.

The correct answer is (D). *(CIA, adapted)*

**REQUIRED:** The product line that provides maximum utility for a risk-averse decision maker.

**DISCUSSION:** The expected value (mean) of X is $370 [(.2 x $500) + (.7 x $300) + (.1 x $600)]. The expected value (mean) of Y is also $370 [(.2 x $50) + (.7 x $400) + (.1 x $800)]. However, X is less risky than Y based on a mean-variance criterion (sum of the products of the squared deviations from the mean multiplied by their appropriate probabilities). Accordingly, a risk-averse decision maker, that is, one for whom the utility of a gain is less than the disutility of a loss of the same absolute amount, will prefer X because it has less variation in its possible outcomes.

### Mean-Variance of X

$$.2 \times (\$500 - \$370)^2 + .7 \times (\$300 - \$370)^2 + .1 \times (\$600 - \$370)^2 = \$8,772$$

### Mean-Variance of Y

$$.2 \times (\$50 - \$370)^2 + .7 \times (\$400 - \$370)^2 + .1 \times (\$800 - \$370)^2 = \$39,600$$

Answers (A) and (B) are incorrect because the expected values of X and Y are equal. Answer (C) is incorrect because a risk-seeking decision maker would prefer Y.

**29.** Statistical quality control often involves the use of control charts whose basic purpose is to

A.  Determine when accounting control procedures are not working.

B.  Control labor costs in production operations.

C.  Detect performance trends away from normal operations.

D.  Monitor internal control applications in computer operations.

The correct answer is (C). *(CMA, adapted)*

**REQUIRED:** The purpose of statistical quality control charts.

**DISCUSSION:** A statistical control chart is a graphic aid for monitoring the status of any process subject to random variations. The chart consists of three horizontal lines plotted on a horizontal time scale. The vertical scale represents the appropriate quantitative measure. The center line represents the average or mean value for the process being controlled. The other two lines are the upper control limit and the lower control limit. The processes are measured periodically, and the values are plotted on the chart. If the value falls within the control limits, no action is taken. If the value falls outside the limits, the process is considered out of control, and an investigation is made for possible corrective action. Another advantage of the chart is that it makes trends visible.

Answers (A), (B), and (D) are incorrect because quality control directly concerns product quality, not accounting procedures, labor costs, or computer operations.

**30.** The statistical quality control department prepares a control chart showing the percentages of defective production. Simple statistical calculations provide control limits that indicate whether assignable causes of variation are explainable on chance grounds. The chart is particularly valuable in determining whether the quality of materials received from outside vendors is consistent from month to month. What is the best term for this chart?

A.  C chart.

B.  P chart.

C.  R chart.

D.  X-bar chart.

The correct answer is (B). *(CIA, adapted)*

**REQUIRED:** The statistical quality control chart described.

**DISCUSSION:** A P chart is based on an attribute (acceptable/not acceptable) rather than a measure of a variable, specifically, the percentage of defects in a sample.

Answer (A) is incorrect because a C chart is also an attribute control chart. It shows defects per item. Answer (C) is incorrect because an R chart displays the range of dispersion of a variable, such as size or weight. Answer (D) is incorrect because an X-bar chart plots the sample mean for a variable.

## 15.2 Probability Distributions

**31.** A quantitative technique useful in projecting a firm's sales and profits is

    A.  Probability distribution theory.

    B.  Linear programming.

    C.  Gantt charting.

    D.  Learning curves.

The correct answer is (A). *(CMA, adapted)*
    **REQUIRED:** The quantitative technique useful in projecting sales and profits.
    **DISCUSSION:** Probability distribution theory is a mathematical method for making decisions about the likelihood of future events (such as sales) in the face of risk. Various estimates of sales (generated from the sales force) can be weighted with different probabilities.
    Answer (B) is incorrect because linear programming is used to minimize costs or maximize profits by determining the optimal use of resources given constraints on the production function. Answer (C) is incorrect because a Gantt chart is a bar chart used to measure progress toward a goal. Answer (D) is incorrect because a learning curve measures the benefit of experience in the early stages of a new task.

**32.** Which of the following is an attribute of a probability distribution?

    A.  The total probability associated with all possible occurrences equals zero.

    B.  It can be modeled by means of a formula or graph that provides the probability for every possible outcome.

    C.  Only one outcome is possible.

    D.  It concerns a discrete random variable only.

The correct answer is (B). *(Publisher)*
    **REQUIRED:** The attribute of a probability distribution.
    **DISCUSSION:** In a probability distribution, the probability of any random event is bounded by 0 (no chance) and 1 (certainty). The total probability of all possible random events must sum to 1. Also, a probability distribution models a random variable through the use of a formula or graph that provides the probability associated with the occurrence of certain values of the random variable.
    Answer (A) is incorrect because the total probability equals 1.0. Answer (C) is incorrect because, if only one outcome is possible, the variable is not random but constant and known with certainty. Answer (D) is incorrect because the random variable may be discrete or continuous.

**33.** What is the primary difference between a discrete and a continuous distribution?

    A.  One is not a legitimate probability distribution.

    B.  Continuous distributions are always symmetric, but discrete distributions are not.

    C.  Continuous distributions describe ranges in which any possible value has a probability of occurrence, whereas discrete distributions attribute probabilities only to a finite number of values within a range.

    D.  Continuous distributions model finite random variables only, whereas discrete distributions may model any variable.

The correct answer is (C). *(Publisher)*
    **REQUIRED:** The primary difference between a discrete and a continuous distribution.
    **DISCUSSION:** A continuous distribution describes a random variable that may take an infinite number of values. It is described by an area under a graph such that the total area bounded by its curve and the x axis equals 1.0 and the area between any two points equals the probability that the random variable is between those points. Discrete distributions model only random variables that take on a finite number of values, for example, the number of customers entering a store during a time period.
    Answer (A) is incorrect because both are legitimate probability distributions. Answer (B) is incorrect because continuous probability distributions need not be symmetric. Answer (D) is incorrect because continuous probability distributions model random variables that may take on an infinite amount of values.

**34.** Which of the following is a discrete probability distribution?

    A.  Chi-square.

    B.  Normal.

    C.  Poisson.

    D.  Exponential.

The correct answer is (C). *(Publisher)*
    **REQUIRED:** The discrete probability distribution.
    **DISCUSSION:** The Poisson distribution is a discrete distribution that measures finite events over a time interval or an area. It is similar to the binomial distribution when the sample is large and the probability of observing a desired event (p) times the sample size (n) is small, usually $np \leq 7$.
    Answers (A), (B), and (D) are incorrect because a continuous probability distribution describes a random variable that may assume an infinite number of values. For example, one may divide an interval of time into ever smaller fractional units. The normal, chi-square, and exponential distributions are continuous probability distributions.

**35.** Which of the following is a continuous distribution?

    A. Poisson.

    B. Exponential.

    C. Binomial.

    D. Hypergeometric.

The correct answer is (B). *(Publisher)*
    **REQUIRED:** The continuous distribution.
    **DISCUSSION:** The exponential distribution is related to the Poisson distribution. It is a continuous distribution used to assess the probability of observing an occurrence with a length of time greater than a specified time interval.
    Answers (A), (C), and (D) are incorrect because a discrete probability distribution is characterized by a random variable that may assume a finite number of values only. An example is the number of times a given number of coin throws may result in heads. The only possible values are whole numbers. The binomial, hypergeometric, and Poisson distributions are discrete probability distributions.

**36.** The binomial distribution is best described as one in which

    A. Each outcome has the same probability.

    B. Each event has only two possible outcomes.

    C. Sampling occurs without replacement.

    D. The curve is symmetrical and bell-shaped.

The correct answer is (B). *(Publisher)*
    **REQUIRED:** The definition of a binomial distribution.
    **DISCUSSION:** The binomial distribution, often used in quality control, gives the probability of each of the possible combinations of trial results when each trial has only two possible outcomes.
    Answer (A) is incorrect because a uniform distribution is one in which all outcomes are equally probable. Tossing one die is an example of an event with a uniform distribution. Answer (C) is incorrect because sampling without replacement occurs in a hypergeometric distribution. Answer (D) is incorrect because a normal distribution is symmetrically bell-shaped.

**37.** A hypergeometric distribution can best be described as one in which

    A. Each outcome has the same probability.

    B. Each event has only two possible outcomes.

    C. Sampling occurs without replacement.

    D. The curve is symmetrical and bell-shaped.

The correct answer is (C). *(Publisher)*
    **REQUIRED:** The best description of a hypergeometric distribution.
    **DISCUSSION:** The hypergeometric distribution is similar to the binomial distribution and is used for sampling without replacement. When the size of the population is not large relative to the sample, the probability of a certain outcome is related to what occurred on preceding trials. The number of similar outcomes or successes follows a hypergeometric probability.
    Answer (A) is incorrect because, in a uniform distribution, each outcome has the same probability. Answer (B) is incorrect because an event in a binomial distribution has but two possible outcomes. Answer (D) is incorrect because a normal distribution is symmetrical and bell-shaped.

**38.** A Poisson distribution is best described as one used

    A. To assess the probability that a certain event will occur a certain number of times in a given interval of time or space.

    B. To assess the probability of observing an occurrence at least as long (in time, e.g., life of a fuse, engine, etc.) as a specified time interval.

    C. When small samples of less than 30 are examined and the underlying population is assumed to be normal.

    D. To test the fit between the actual data and the theoretical distribution.

The correct answer is (A). *(Publisher)*
    **REQUIRED:** The best description of a Poisson distribution.
    **DISCUSSION:** A Poisson distribution models the number of times a specified event occurs over a period of time, or over a certain area or volume. It is similar to the binomial distribution when the sample is large and the probability of observing a desired event (p) times the sample size (n) is small, usually $np \leq 7$.
    Answer (B) is incorrect because an exponential distribution is used to assess the probability of observing an occurrence at least as long (in time, e.g., life of a fuse, engine, etc.) as a specified time interval. Answer (C) is incorrect because Student's t-distribution is used when small samples of less than 30 are examined and the underlying population is assumed to be normal. Answer (D) is incorrect because the Chi-square distribution tests the fit between the actual data and the theoretical distribution.

**39.** A producer of salad dressing is using queuing analysis to determine how many mechanics should be available to adjust machinery in its large filling department. Similar high-speed filling machinery is operated simultaneously on each of 13 separate production lines. Machine adjustment failures occur randomly through time such that the length of time between failures has an exponential distribution. The number of adjustment failures occurring during an 8-hour shift in the above situation is best modeled by a

A. Normal distribution.

B. Binomial distribution.

C. Poisson distribution.

D. Uniform distribution.

The correct answer is (C). *(CMA, adapted)*
**REQUIRED:** The distribution used in queuing analysis.
**DISCUSSION:** Queuing theory is a method used to examine the costs of waiting lines and of servicing them. The Poisson distribution is used in queuing theory because more than one event usually occurs in a given period of time. If λ is the value of the mean in this distribution (the average number of occurrences of an event in a given interval of time or space), k is the number of occurrences, and e is the natural logarithm (2.71828...), the Poisson distribution is defined as

$$f(k) = \frac{\lambda^k \, e^{-\lambda}}{k!}$$

Answer (A) is incorrect because normal distribution has a symmetrical, bell-shaped curve. Answer (B) is incorrect because the binomial distribution is a discrete distribution in which only two outcomes are possible. Answer (D) is incorrect because all outcomes are equally likely in the uniform distribution.

**40.** The exponential distribution is best described as one used

A. To assess the probability that a certain event will occur a certain number of times in a given interval of time or space.

B. To assess the probability of observing an occurrence at least as long (in time, e.g., life of a fuse, engine, etc.) as a specified time interval.

C. When small samples of less than 30 are examined, and the underlying population is assumed to be normal.

D. To test the fit between the actual data and the theoretical distribution.

The correct answer is (B). *(Publisher)*
**REQUIRED:** The best description of an exponential distribution.
**DISCUSSION:** The exponential distribution is related to the Poisson distribution. It is a continuous distribution used to assess the probability of observing an occurrence with a length of time greater than a specified time interval. A common use of the exponential distribution is in modeling the length of life of electronic components, engines, etc. Thus, the probability that a time unit will exceed a prespecified time unit is calculated.

Answer (A) is incorrect because a Poisson distribution is used to assess the probability that a certain event will occur a certain number of times in a given interval of time or space. Answer (C) is incorrect because Student's t-distribution is used when small samples of less than 30 are examined and the underlying population is assumed to be normal. Answer (D) is incorrect because the Chi-square distribution tests the fit between the actual data and the theoretical distribution.

**41.** Student's t-distribution is best described as one used

A. To assess the probability that a certain event will occur a certain number of times in a given interval of time or space.

B. To assess the probability of observing an occurrence at least as long (in time, e.g., life of a fuse, engine, etc.) as a specified time interval.

C. When small samples of less than 30 are examined and the underlying population is assumed to be normal.

D. To test the fit between the actual data and the theoretical distribution.

The correct answer is (C). *(Publisher)*
**REQUIRED:** The best description of Student's t-distribution.
**DISCUSSION:** Student's t-distribution is a special distribution to be used when only small samples are available and the population variance is not given. It is mound-shaped and symmetric like a normal distribution, but typically flatter with more variation. A small sample is usually deemed to be less than 30. For samples larger than 30, the t-distribution gives results similar to those provided by the standard normal distribution.

Answer (A) is incorrect because a Poisson distribution is used to assess the probability that a certain event will occur a certain number of times in a given interval of time or space. Answer (B) is incorrect because an exponential distribution is used to assess the probability of observing an occurrence at least as long (in time, e.g., life of a fuse, engine, etc.) as a specified time interval. Answer (D) is incorrect because the Chi-square distribution tests the fit between the actual data and the theoretical distribution.

**42.** A normal distribution is best described as one in which

- A. Each outcome has the same probability.
- B. Each event has only two possible outcomes.
- C. Sampling occurs without replacement.
- D. The curve is symmetrical and bell-shaped.

**43.** In a large computer manufacturer, there has been much concern about the consistency across departments in adhering to new and unpopular purchasing guidelines. An auditor has a list that rank-orders all departments according to the percentage of purchases that are consistent with the guidelines and indicates which division the department is from. The auditor performs a t-test for differences in means on the average rank of departments in Divisions A and B to see if there is any difference in compliance with the policy and finds that Division A (which has more departments) has a significantly higher (i.e., better) average rank than Division B. Which one of the following conclusions should be drawn from this analysis?

- A. Division A is complying better with the new policy.
- B. A random sample of departments should be drawn and the analysis recalculated.
- C. A t-test is not valid when the tested groups differ in size.
- D. A t-test is inappropriate for this data, and another type of analysis should be used.

**44.** Separate statistical samples of invoice payments in each of 15 branch offices of your company show a number of errors. In determining whether the quality of performance among the 15 offices is significantly different from overall quality, which of the following statistical distributions should you assume to be most applicable?

- A. Poisson distribution.
- B. Chi-square distribution.
- C. Hypergeometric distribution.
- D. Binomial distribution.

The correct answer is (D). *(Publisher)*
**REQUIRED:** The definition of a normal distribution.
**DISCUSSION:** The normal distribution is the most significant probability distribution. In sampling, it describes the distribution of the sample mean regardless of the distribution of the population, given that the sample is large (typically greater than 30). It has a symmetrical, bell-shaped curve centered around the sample mean.
Answer (A) is incorrect because, in a uniform distribution, each outcome has the same probability. Answer (B) is incorrect because, in a binomial distribution, each event has only two possible outcomes. Answer (C) is incorrect because sampling occurs without replacement in a hypergeometric distribution.

The correct answer is (D). *(CIA, adapted)*
**REQUIRED:** The true statement about application of a t-test to rank-ordered data.
**DISCUSSION:** The t-distribution is used for small samples but in the same way as the normal distribution. A t-test is not valid when used with ordinal-level data. A t-test by definition is an application of parametric statistics. Nonparametric (distribution-free) statistics is applied to problems for which rank order but not a specific distribution is known.
Answer (A) is incorrect because a t-test is not valid in this case. Answer (B) is incorrect because the auditor already has a list of the entire population and no sampling is needed. Answer (C) is incorrect because a t-test can be used with groups that differ in size.

The correct answer is (B). *(CIA, adapted)*
**REQUIRED:** The distribution used to ascertain whether the differences between samples are statistically significant.
**DISCUSSION:** The Chi-square distribution is a special distribution used in examining the fit between actual data and the theoretical distribution. It tests the probability that a particular sample was drawn from a particular population. The Chi-square statistic ($\chi^2$) equals the sample variance ($s^2$), multiplied by its degree of freedom ($n-1$), and divided by the hypothesized population variance ($\sigma^2$). Here, quality may be viewed as involving few errors and consequently a small variance. Thus, the variance of the samples of each office can be tested.
Answer (A) is incorrect because the Poisson distribution is a special case of the binomial distribution used especially in queuing analysis. Answer (C) is incorrect because the hypergeometric distribution is similar to the binomial distribution. It involves sampling without replacement. Answer (D) is incorrect because the binomial distribution applies to binary situations, e.g., a yes/no, error/no error basis.

**45.** An internal auditor is interested in determining if there is a statistically significant difference among four offices in the proportion of female versus male managers. A chi-square test is being considered. A principal advantage of this test compared with a t-test in this circumstance is that

A. Generally available software exists for the chi-square test.

B. The chi-square can both detect a relationship and measure its strength.

C. The chi-square can be applied to nominal data.

D. The chi-square is a parametric, and therefore stronger, test.

The correct answer is (C). *(CIA, adapted)*
**REQUIRED:** The principal advantage of the chi-square test over the t-test.
**DISCUSSION:** The chi-square test is used in determining the goodness of fit between actual data and the theoretical distribution. In other words, it tests whether the sample is likely to be from the population, based on a comparison of the sample variance and the population variance. The chi-square test is appropriately applied to nominal data. Nominal data simply distinguish one item from another, as male from female. The chi-square statistic equals the product of the sample variance and the degrees of freedom (number in the sample − 1), divided by the population variance. This calculated value is then compared with the critical value in the chi-square table.

Answer (A) is incorrect because software for the t-test is widely available. Answer (B) is incorrect because the chi-square test cannot measure the strength of a relationship. Answer (D) is incorrect because the chi-square test is non-parametric; thus, it is applied to problems in which a parameter is not calculated.

## 15.3 Hypothesis Testing

**46.** Hypothesis testing includes all but which of the following steps?

A. Sample data are generated, and the hypothesis is formulated.

B. The probability of the hypothesis given the sample data is computed.

C. The hypothesis is rejected or not rejected based upon the sample measure.

D. The standards are adjusted.

The correct answer is (D). *(Publisher)*
**REQUIRED:** The item not a part of hypothesis testing.
**DISCUSSION:** Adjusting standards is the final step in the control loop.

Answers (A), (B), and (C) are incorrect because hypothesis testing develops an assumption about the true state of nature. The first of the four steps is to formulate the hypothesis. Second, sample evidence is obtained. Third, the conditional probability that the hypothesis is true, given the observed evidence, and that the sample results observed have actually occurred, is computed. Fourth, the hypothesis is rejected if its probability is smaller than some subjective fixed level of probability chosen *a priori*.

**47.** An audit of accounts payable was made to determine if the error rate was within the stated policy of 0.5%. One hundred of the 10,000 accounts payable transactions were randomly selected using a 95% confidence level. No errors were found. With 95% certainty, one can conclude that the sample results

A. Indicate another sample is needed.

B. Prove there are no errors in accounts payable.

C. Indicate the null hypothesis is false.

D. Fail to prove the error rate is above 0.5%.

The correct answer is (D). *(CIA, adapted))*

**REQUIRED:** The sound conclusion if a sample contained no errors.

**DISCUSSION:** The null hypothesis is that the error rate is equal to or less than 0.5%. Given that no errors were found, no basis for disproving the null hypothesis is presented.

Answer (A) is incorrect because the sample is adequate. Answer (B) is incorrect because even an examination of all 10,000 transactions would not necessarily prove that there are no errors in accounts payable. Answer (C) is incorrect because the null hypothesis has not been disproved.

**48.** In a large computer manufacturer, there has been much concern about the consistency across departments in adhering to new and unpopular purchasing guidelines. An auditor has a list that rank-orders all departments according to the percentage of purchases that are consistent with the guidelines and indicates which division the department is from. The auditor performs a t-test for differences in means on the average rank of departments in divisions A and B to see if there is any difference in compliance with the policy and finds that division A (which has more departments) has a significantly higher (i.e., better) average rank than division B. Which one of the following conclusions should be drawn from this analysis?

A. Division A is complying better with the new policy.

B. A random sample of departments should be drawn and the analysis recalculated.

C. A t-test is not valid when the tested groups differ in size.

D. A t-test is inappropriate for this data and another type of analysis should be used.

The correct answer is (D). *(CIA, adapted))*

**REQUIRED:** The true statement about application of a t-test to rank-ordered data.

**DISCUSSION:** The t-distribution is used for small samples but in the same way as the normal distribution. A t-test is not valid when used with ordinal-level data. A t-test by definition is an application of parametric statistics. Nonparametric (distribution-free) statistics is applied to problems for which rank order, but not a specific distribution, is known.

Answer (A) is incorrect because a t-test is not valid in this case. Answer (B) is incorrect because the auditor already has a list of the entire population, and no sampling is needed. Answer (C) is incorrect because a t-test can be used with groups that differ in size.

Questions 49 through 55 are based on the following information. The ABC Company has specified that the mean number of calories in a can of its diet soda is 1 or less. A consumer testing service examined nine cans with the following amounts of calories: .9, .95, 1.0, 1.05, .85, 1.0, .95, .95, and .9. The mean of these observations is .95. The sum of the squared deviations from the mean is .03. Assume the underlying population is approximately normal.

**49.** What is the sample standard deviation?

A. .0577

B. .0612

C. .0316

D. .00375

The correct answer is (B). *(Publisher)*

**REQUIRED:** The sample standard deviation.

**DISCUSSION:** The sample mean is the sum of the observations divided by the sample size. The sample mean is typically denoted as $\bar{x}$. The following is the sample variance ($s^2$): $\sum(x_i - \bar{x})^2 \div (n - 1)$. The sample standard deviation(s) is the square root of the variance. Thus, the sample variance is .00375 [.03 ÷ (9 − 1)], and the sample standard deviation is .0612 ($\sqrt{.00375}$).

Answer (A) is incorrect because .0577 results from using n, not n-1, in the denominator. Answer (C) is incorrect because .0316 equals .03 divided by .95. Answer (D) is incorrect because .00375 is the variance.

**50.** Let $\mu$ denote the true mean calories of all diet sodas produced by ABC Company. What hypothesis should be tested to determine whether ABC's claim is valid?

A. $H_o$: $\mu = 1$
   $H_a$: $\mu \neq 1$

B. $H_o$: $\mu \leq 1$
   $H_a$: $\mu > 1$

C. $H_o$: $\mu = 1$
   $H_a$: $\mu > 1$

D. $H_o$: $\mu = 0$
   $H_a$: $\mu < 1$

The correct answer is (B). *(Publisher)*

**REQUIRED:** The hypothesis to be tested to determine whether the advertising claim is valid.

**DISCUSSION:** ABC asserts that its diet soda has, on the average, 1 calorie or less. Thus, a possible null hypothesis is $H_o$: $\mu \leq 1$. The alternative hypothesis is that the mean is greater than 1, that is, $H_a$: $\mu > 1$. Because the null hypothesis cannot be rejected if the test statistic falls in the left-hand tail of the distribution, the test is one-tailed.

Answers (A), (C), and (D) are incorrect because the null hypothesis is that the population mean is equal to or less than 1 calorie. The alternate hypothesis is that it is greater than 1.

**51.** The appropriate means for testing this hypothesis is

A. A z-statistic.

B. A t-statistic.

C. An F-statistic.

D. A Q-statistic.

The correct answer is (B). *(Publisher)*

**REQUIRED:** The appropriate statistic to test the hypothesis.

**DISCUSSION:** The t-statistic is appropriate for tests of hypotheses based on small samples. It measures how the sample mean differs from the hypothesized true mean in terms of standard deviations. The formula is

$$t = \frac{\bar{x} - \mu}{s \div \sqrt{n}}$$

If: $\bar{x}$ = sample mean
$\mu$ = hypothesized true mean
s = sample standard deviation
n = sample size

Answer (A) is incorrect because the z-statistic is appropriate when the standard deviation of the population is known or a large sample (n > 30) permits a reasonable approximation of the population standard deviation. Answer (C) is incorrect because the F-statistic tests differences in variances. Answer (D) is incorrect because Q-statistic is a nonsense term.

**52.** The value of the t-statistic is

A. −2.45

B. −.05

C. 2.45

D. 4.65

The correct answer is (A). *(Publisher)*

**REQUIRED:** The value of the t-statistic.

**DISCUSSION:** Given that $\bar{x}$ equals .95, the hypothesized value of the true mean is 1, the sample standard deviation equals .0612 (see question 47), and the sample size is 9, the value of the t-statistic is

$$t = \frac{.95 - 1}{.0612 \div \sqrt{9}} = \frac{-.05}{.0612 \div 3} = \frac{-.05}{.0204} = -2.45$$

Answer (B) is incorrect because −.05 is the difference between the sample mean and the hypothesized true mean. Answers (C) and (D) are incorrect because the value is negative.

**53.** The appropriate number of degrees of freedom for this t-statistic is

A. 8

B. 9

C. 0

D. 1

The correct answer is (A). *(Publisher)*

**REQUIRED:** The appropriate number of degrees of freedom for the t-statistic.

**DISCUSSION:** The degrees of freedom associated with the test statistic equals the sample size minus the number of parameters being tested. Measurements of calorie content were made for nine cans of diet soda; i.e., nine distinct observations were included in the sample. The only parameter tested is $\mu$, the mean calorie content of the diet sodas, so the number of degrees of freedom is 8 (9 − 1).

Answer (B) is incorrect because 9 is the sample size. Answers (C) and (D) are incorrect because one parameter is tested.

**54.** The following data are from a table of critical values of t:

| d.f. | $t_{.10}$ | $t_{.05}$ | $t_{.025}$ |
|------|-----------|-----------|------------|
| 5 | 1.476 | 2.015 | 2.571 |
| 6 | 1.440 | 1.943 | 2.447 |
| 7 | 1.415 | 1.895 | 2.365 |
| 8 | 1.397 | 1.860 | 2.306 |
| 9 | 1.383 | 1.833 | 2.262 |

The value of t defining the rejection region for testing the hypothesis that ABC's soda has 1 calorie or less per can, assuming a 95% confidence level, is

A. 2.306

B. 1.86

C. 1.833

D. 2.262

The correct answer is (B). *(Publisher)*

**REQUIRED:** The value of t defining the rejection region for testing the hypothesis at a 95% confidence level.

**DISCUSSION:** The rejection region is determined by the value of t at the appropriate degrees of freedom and the specific level of confidence. Choosing a 95% level of confidence means that the value of t will restrict the probability of a Type 1 error (rejecting the null hypothesis when the null hypothesis is true) to 5%. The rejection region is bounded by this value. Hence, the null hypothesis will be rejected if the t-statistic calculated from the formula is equal to or greater than the t-value from a table of t-values. The t-value correlates the appropriate degrees of freedom (n − 1) and the appropriate probability of making a Type 1 error (.05). In this case, with 8 degrees of freedom, the appropriate rejection region is defined by a t value of 1.86. Thus, a calculated t-statistic equal to or greater than 1.86 permits rejection of the null hypothesis $H_o$: $\mu \le 1$.

Answer (A) is incorrect because 2.306 is for a confidence level of 97.5%. Answer (C) is incorrect because 1.833 is for 9 degrees of freedom. Answer (D) is incorrect because 2.262 is for 9 degrees of freedom and a confidence level of 97.5%.

**55.** What conclusion can be drawn with 95% confidence?

A. The manufacturer's claim can be rejected.

B. The manufacturer's claim cannot be rejected.

C. No decision is possible based on current information.

D. All sodas have at most 1 calorie.

The correct answer is (B). *(Publisher)*

**REQUIRED:** The conclusion with 95% confidence.

**DISCUSSION:** The critical value of t is 1.86 (see preceding question), and the calculated t-statistic is −2.45 (see question 52). Accordingly, the 5% rejection region includes, and lies to the right of, the t-value of 1.86. Because the computed value is less than (to the left of) 1.86 in this one-tailed test, the null hypothesis cannot be rejected.

Answers (A) and (C) are incorrect because the null hypothesis cannot be rejected. Answer (D) is incorrect because some sodas have more than 1 calorie.

Questions 56 and 57 are based on the following information. J.R. Smythe, the manager for a company that manufactures custom desks, is designing a series of statistical tools to be used in the measurement and control of costs. The desks are accounted for on a job-order basis.

**56.** The production management has expressed the concern that the average per-unit cost to manufacture desks has increased. In developing a statistical test to determine whether the average cost has increased, Smythe constructs a hypothesis about the difference in means that will imply

A. A two-tailed test.

B. A single-valued test.

C. An operating characteristic test.

D. A one-tailed test.

The correct answer is (D). *(CMA, adapted)*
**REQUIRED:** The true statement about a test to determine average unit cost.
**DISCUSSION:** One possible hypothesis to be tested is whether the mean has increased, i.e., whether the mean is greater than a certain value. The alternative hypothesis is that the average per-unit cost is equal to or less than the former estimate. Consequently, a one-tailed test is appropriate because it determines whether the new average is in the upper tail of the distribution.
Answer (A) is incorrect because, if a two-tailed test is constructed, the hypothesis may be rejected if the sample value is in the upper or lower tail of the distribution. Answer (B) is incorrect because a single value is not a probability distribution. Answer (C) is incorrect because operating characteristic test is a nonsense term.

**57.** In developing the statistical test described in the previous question to determine whether manufacturing costs have increased, a null hypothesis is formulated. In this case, the null hypothesis to be tested could be: Manufacturing costs have not increased. This testing procedure can lead to the wrong decision (e.g., Type I or alpha error, Type II or beta error). What decision(s) is(are) wrong?

A. To reject the null hypothesis that the cost has not increased when the cost in fact has increased.

B. To reject the null hypothesis that the cost has not increased when the cost in fact has not increased.

C. To accept the null hypothesis that the cost has not increased when the cost in fact has increased.

D. Both (B) and (C) are wrong decisions.

The correct answer is (D). *(CMA, adapted)*
**REQUIRED:** The wrong decision(s) that may be made when testing a hypothesis.
**DISCUSSION:** Wrong decisions are of two types: Type I, or alpha error, and Type II, or beta error. To reject the hypothesis that the costs have not increased when in fact they have not increased is a Type I, or alpha error. It is also incorrect to accept the hypothesis that costs have not increased when in fact they have increased (a Type II, or beta error). Thus, both (B) and (C) are wrong decisions.
Answer (A) is incorrect because it is an appropriate decision. (The question calls for a wrong decision.) Answers (B) and (C) are incorrect because both are wrong decisions.

**58.** A company is producing a machine part whose diameter must be 1.000 inches ± .010. Historical records show that the mean diameter of all parts produced since the project began has been 0.995 inches. A sample of five observations (0.985, 1.015, 1.012, 0.988, 0.980, with a mean of 0.996) will be

A. Rejected by a quality control system that uses a mean chart ($\bar{x}$ chart) only.

B. Accepted by a quality control system that uses a mean chart ($\bar{x}$ chart) only.

C. Accepted by a quality control system that uses a range chart (R chart) only.

D. Accepted by a quality control system that uses both mean and range charts.

The correct answer is (B). *(CIA, adapted)*
**REQUIRED:** The true statement about acceptance or rejection of a machine part using a range or mean chart.
**DISCUSSION:** The sample has a mean of 0.996. Because the mean of the sample must lie between 0.990 and 1.01 (1.000 inches ± .010), the sample will be accepted if a mean ($\bar{x}$) chart is used. A mean chart displays central tendencies, whereas a range chart shows an acceptable high-low range.
Answer (A) is incorrect because the sample will be accepted if a mean ($\bar{x}$) chart is used. Answers (C) and (D) are incorrect because each observation falls outside the required range, so the sample will be rejected if a range chart is used.

**59.** A consultant is reviewing the age composition of the employees of Giant National Bank as part of a study of the bank's hiring policies. A recent industry report shows that the percentage of workers over 50 years of age in individual banks is normally distributed and has an arithmetic mean of 10%. Using a t-test and a 95% confidence level, the consultant tested the hypothesis that no difference exists between the employees' age composition of Giant and that of other banks. A random sample of 100 Giant employees included four persons over 50 years of age. The calculated t-value was 4.0. How should the consultant interpret this t-value?

A. Four percent of Giant's employees are over 50 years old.

B. Because a t-value of 4.0 is considered small, no significant difference exists between the number of people over 50 years of age employed by Giant and by other banks.

C. Because a t-value of 4.0 is considered large, the risk is less than 5% that the sample result would have occurred if the number of Giant's employees over age 50 were identical to that of other banks.

D. Because a t-value of 4.0 is considered large, there is a 95% likelihood that the number of Giant's employees over age 50 does not differ from that of other banks.

The correct answer is (C). *(CIA, adapted)*
**REQUIRED:** The interpretation of the calculated t-value.
**DISCUSSION:** Student's t-distribution should be useful whenever confidence intervals for a population are required, the sample is small (usually less than 30), and the underlying population is assumed to be approximately normal. For this two-tailed t-test, the null hypothesis that no difference exists between the age composition of Grant's employees and that of employees at other banks is accepted when the calculated t-statistic is less than the t-value found in the table at the desired level of confidence and the appropriate degrees of freedom. The null hypothesis is rejected when the t-value calculated is greater than the value found in the table. A t-value of 4.0 is usually considered large. Consequently, it most likely exceeds the critical value of t found in a standard table (see, for example, question 54), and the null hypothesis ($H_o$: $\mu$ = 10%) can be rejected.

Answer (A) is incorrect because the t-value is not a percentage. It is a variable with a probability distribution very similar to the standard normal distribution except that its shape is dependent upon the number of degrees of freedom. When the size of the sample is large (more than 30), the values associated with the standard normal and t-distributions are the same. Answer (B) is incorrect because a t-value of 4.0 is considered large, not small. Answer (D) is incorrect because a t-value of 4.0 means that the null hypothesis can be rejected.

## 15.4 Expected Value

**60.** Sweivel Company is preparing its 1999 budget and, taking into consideration the recent pace of economic recovery, has developed several sales forecasts and the estimated probability associated with each sales forecast. To determine the sales forecast to be used for 1999 budgeting purposes, which one of the following techniques should Sweivel use?

A. Expected value analysis.

B. Continuous probability simulation.

C. Monte Carlo simulation.

D. Sensitivity analysis.

The correct answer is (A). *(CMA, adapted)*
**REQUIRED:** The technique for determining a sales forecast given different forecasts and their probabilities.
**DISCUSSION:** Expected value analysis provides a rational means for selecting the best alternative in decisions involving risk. The expected value of an alternative is found by multiplying the probability of each outcome by its payoff, and summing the products. It represents the long-term average payoff for repeated trials.

Answer (B) is incorrect because simulation is not necessary. Several estimates are known. Answer (C) is incorrect because the Monte Carlo simulation method is often used to generate the individual values for a random variable; the performance of a quantitative model is investigated by randomly selecting values for each of the variables in the model (based on the probability distribution of each) and then calculating the value of the solution. Answer (D) is incorrect because sensitivity analysis determines how sensitive a solution is to changes in estimates.

**61.** The Booster Club at Blair College sells hot dogs at home basketball games. The group has a frequency distribution of the demand for hot dogs per game and plans to apply the expected value decision rule to determine the number of hot dogs to stock. The Booster Club should select the demand level that

A. Is closest to the expected demand.

B. Has the greatest probability of occurring.

C. Has the greatest expected opportunity cost.

D. Has the greatest expected monetary value.

The correct answer is (D). *(CMA, adapted)*

**REQUIRED:** The demand level that should be selected.

**DISCUSSION:** The Booster Club should select the demand level that maximizes profits, that is, the level with the greatest expected monetary value. This level may not include the event with the highest conditional profit because this profit may be accompanied by a low probability of occurrence. Alternatively, the event with the highest probability of occurrence may not be selected because it does not offer a high conditional profit.

Answer (A) is incorrect because stocking an amount equal to expected demand (the sum of the products of the possible amounts demanded and their respective probabilities) does not necessarily maximize expected profits. Answer (B) is incorrect because the number of bags to stock is not necessarily the same as the amount demanded with the highest probability. The inventory decision should be based on the relation of the probability distribution to the monetary outcomes. Answer (C) is incorrect because the greatest opportunity cost is not factored into the analysis.

**62.** The expected value of perfect information is the

A. Same as the expected profit under certainty.

B. Sum of the conditional profit (loss) for the best event of each act times the probability of each event's occurring.

C. Difference between the expected profit under certainty and the expected opportunity loss.

D. Difference between the expected profit under certainty and the expected monetary value of the best act under uncertainty.

The correct answer is (D). *(CMA, adapted)*

**REQUIRED:** The true statement about the expected value of perfect information.

**DISCUSSION:** The expected value under uncertainty is found by multiplying the probability of each outcome (event) by its payoff (conditional profit or loss) and summing the products. Perfect information is the knowledge that a future state of nature will occur with certainty. The expected value of perfect information is the difference between the expected value under certainty and the expected value of the optimal decision under uncertainty. In this question, uncertainty is synonymous with risk; that is, the specific future event is unknown, but its probability distribution is known. The expected value under certainty equals the sum of the products of the profit-maximizing payoffs of perfect forecasts and the related probabilities.

Answers (A) and (B) are incorrect because the value of perfect information is limited to the excess of the profit under certainty over the best return without perfect information. Answer (C) is incorrect because opportunity losses are not a consideration in expected value analysis.

**63.** A firm will produce product A or B. The total costs (TC) for both products can be estimated by the equations

Product A: TC = $300,000 + ($23 × Sales volume)
Product B: TC = $100,000 + ($29 × Sales volume)

The firm believes there is a 20% chance for the sales volume of each product to equal 10,000 units and an 80% chance they will both equal 20,000 units. The selling price of product A is $42, and the selling price of product B is $40. The expected profit from producing product B equals

A. $98,000

B. $120,000

C. $390,000

D. $680,000

The correct answer is (A). *(CIA, adapted)*

**REQUIRED:** The expected profit from producing product B.

**DISCUSSION:** The expected profit equals the expected value of unit demand [(20% x 10,000 units) + (80% x 20,000 units) = 18,000 units] times unit price ($40), minus fixed costs ($100,000), minus variable costs ($29 x 18,000 units), or $98,000 ($720,000 – $100,000 – $522,000).

Answer (B) is incorrect because $120,000 is the profit for product B at a volume of 20,000 units. Answer (C) is incorrect because $390,000 is the total cost of product B at a volume of 10,000 units. Answer (D) is incorrect because $680,000 is the total cost of product B at a volume of 20,000 units.

**64.** A company is evaluating the following information in an effort to determine which of two products, A or B, it should manufacture during the coming year. Disregard income tax effects.

| Product A | | Product B | |
|---|---|---|---|
| Expected Sales | Probability (Units) | Expected Sales | Probability (Units) |
| 7,000 | .60 | 9,000 | .75 |
| 8,000 | .40 | 10,000 | .25 |
| | 1.00 | | 1.00 |

| | Product A | Product B |
|---|---|---|
| Selling price | $20 | $15 |
| Variable cost per unit | $10 | $ 8 |
| Annual fixed manufacturing costs (all cash) | $50,000 | $40,000 |
| Annual company non-manufacturing expenses (all cash) | $20,000 | $20,000 |

The company is considering engaging a market research firm to better estimate its sales. Assuming that the research firm can estimate sales with 100% accuracy, what is the value of this perfect information to the company?

A. $750

B. $2,100

C. $4,750

D. $6,850

The correct answer is (B). *(CIA, adapted)*

**REQUIRED:** The value of perfect information to the company.

**DISCUSSION:** The expected values of making A and B are $4,000 and $4,750, respectively.

| | Product A | | Product B | |
|---|---|---|---|---|
| Units | 7,000 | 8,000 | 9,000 | 10,000 |
| Revenues | $140,000 | $160,000 | $135,000 | $150,000 |
| Variable costs | (70,000) | (80,000) | (72,000) | (80,000) |
| Contribution margin | $ 70,000 | $ 80,000 | $ 63,000 | $ 70,000 |
| Other costs | (70,000) | (70,000) | (60,000) | (60,000) |
| Profit | $ 0 | $ 10,000 | $ 3,000 | $ 10,000 |
| × Probability | .6 | .4 | .75 | .25 |
| = Expected value | $ 0 | $ 4,000 | $ 2,250 | $ 2,500 |

The expected value of perfect information is the expected value of the decision made with perfect information ($6,850) minus the expected value of the preferred action made with existing information ($4,750), or $2,100.

(1) Possible sales estimates and related profits:

| Case | Estimate | Product Made | Profit |
|---|---|---|---|
| 1 | A, 7,000; B, 9,000 | B | $ 3,000 |
| 2 | A, 8,000; B, 9,000 | A | 10,000 |
| 3 | A, 7,000; B, 10,000 | B | 10,000 |
| 4 | A, 8,000; B, 10,000 | A or B | 10,000 |

(2) Expected value with perfect information:

| | | | | | | | | |
|---|---|---|---|---|---|---|---|---|
| 1 | .6 | × | .75 | = | .45 | × $ 3,000 | = | $1,350 |
| 2 | .4 | × | .75 | = | .30 | × 10,000 | = | 3,000 |
| 3 | .6 | × | .25 | = | .15 | × 10,000 | = | 1,500 |
| 4 | .4 | × | .25 | = | .10 | × 10,000 | = | 1,000 |
| | | | | | | | | $6,850 |

Answer (A) is incorrect because $750 is the expected value of A minus the expected value of B. Answer (C) is incorrect because $4,750 is the expected value of B. Answer (D) is incorrect because $6,850 is the expected value with perfect information.

Questions 65 through 67 are based on the following information. A beverage stand can sell either soft drinks or coffee on any given day. If the stand sells soft drinks and the weather is hot, it will make $2,500; if the weather is cold, the profit will be $1,000. If the stand sells coffee and the weather is hot, it will make $1,900; if the weather is cold, the profit will be $2,000. The probability of cold weather on a given day at this time is 60%.

**65.** The expected payoff for selling coffee is

A. $1,360

B. $2,200

C. $3,900

D. $1,960

The correct answer is (D). *(CMA, adapted)*
**REQUIRED:** The expected payoff for selling coffee.
**DISCUSSION:** The expected payoff calculation for coffee is

$$.4(\$1,900) + .6(\$2,000) = \$1,960$$

Answer (A) is incorrect because the least the company can make by selling coffee is $1,900. Answers (B) and (C) are incorrect because the most the company can make by selling coffee is $2,000.

**66.** The expected payoff if the vendor has perfect information is

A. $3,900

B. $2,200

C. $1,960

D. $1,950

The correct answer is (B). *(CMA, adapted)*
**REQUIRED:** The expected payoff if the vendor has perfect information.
**DISCUSSION:** The vendor would like to sell coffee on cold days ($2,000) and soft drinks on hot days ($2,500). Hot days are expected 40% of the time. Hence, the probability is 40% of making $2,500 by selling soft drinks. The chance of making $2,000 by selling coffee is 60%. The payoff equation is

$$.4(\$2,500) + .6(\$2,000) = \$2,200$$

Answer (A) is incorrect because the most the vendor can make is $2,500 per day. Answers (C) and (D) are incorrect because the least the vendor could make by having perfect information is $2,000 on cold days.

**67.** Disregarding questions 65 and 66, if the probability of hot weather given a hot weather forecast is 50%, how much would the vendor be willing to pay for the forecast?

A. $600

B. $300

C. $1,000

D. $800

The correct answer is (B). *(CMA, adapted)*
**REQUIRED:** The amount the vendor should be willing to pay for a forecast.
**DISCUSSION:** If the weather is hot and coffee is served, the vendor earns $1,900. If the vendor knows the weather will be hot, (s)he sells soft drinks and makes $2,500, a $600 increase. Thus, the vendor should be willing to pay up to $600 for perfect information regarding hot weather. However, if the forecasts are only 50% accurate, the information is not perfect. Accordingly, the vendor should be willing to pay only $300 (50% x the $600 potential increase in profits) for the sometimes accurate forecasts.
Answer (A) is incorrect because the vendor would pay $600 for perfect information, but the forecasts are only 50% accurate. Answers (C) and (D) are incorrect because the most the vendor could profit from perfect information on hot days would be $600 ($2,500 – $1,900).

Questions 68 and 69 are based on the following information. Bilco Oil Company currently sells three grades of gasoline: regular, premium, and regular plus, which is a mixture of regular and premium. Regular plus is advertised as being at least 50% premium. Although any mixture containing 50% or more premium gas could be sold as regular plus, it is less costly to use exactly 50%. The percentage of premium gas in the mixture is determined by one small valve in the blending machine. If the valve is properly adjusted, the machine provides a mixture that is 50% premium and 50% regular. Assume that, if the valve is out of adjustment, the machine provides a mixture that is 60% premium and 40% regular.

Once the machine is started, it must continue until 100,000 gallons of regular plus have been mixed. Cost data available:

| | |
|---|---|
| Cost per gallon -- premium | $.32 |
| -- regular | $.30 |
| Cost of checking the valve | $80.00 |
| Cost of adjusting the valve | $40.00 |

Subjective estimates of the probabilities of the valve's condition are estimated to be

| Event | Probability |
|---|---|
| Valve in adjustment | .7 |
| Valve out of adjustment | .3 |

**68.** The conditional cost of not checking the valve when it is out of adjustment is

A. $80

B. $200

C. $92

D. $320

The correct answer is (B). *(CMA, adapted)*
**REQUIRED:** The conditional cost of not checking the valve when it is out of adjustment.
**DISCUSSION:** The conditional cost is the difference between the cost of the fuel if the valve works properly ($31,000) and the cost if it does not ($31,200), a difference of $200.

| | | |
|---|---|---|
| 100,000 × .5 × $.30 = | $15,000 | |
| 100,000 × .5 × $.32 = | 16,000 | |
| Cost when in adjustment | $31,000 | |
| | | |
| 100,000 × .4 × $.30 = | $12,000 | |
| 100,000 × .6 × $.32 = | 19,200 | |
| Cost out of adjustment | $31,200 | |

Answer (A) is incorrect because $80 is the cost of checking the valve. Answer (C) is incorrect because $92 is the expected cost of checking and adjusting the valve. Answer (D) is incorrect because $320 equals the conditional cost of not checking the valve when it is out of adjustment, plus the cost of checking the valve, plus the cost of adjusting the valve.

**69.** Using the criterion of minimum expected cost, the valve should not be checked unless the probability that the valve is out of adjustment falls in the range of

A. .13 – .2499 inclusive.

B. .25 – .3799 inclusive.

C. .38 – .4999 inclusive.

D. .50 – 1.00 inclusive.

The correct answer is (D). *(CMA, adapted)*
**REQUIRED:** The range of probability that justifies checking the valve.
**DISCUSSION:** Given that P is the probability of maladjustment, the expected cost of not checking a maladjusted valve is $200P (see preceding question). The cost of checking is $80, and the expected cost of a needed adjustment is $40P. If the expected cost of not checking is equated with the expected cost of checking and adjusting ($200P = $80 + $40P), P is found to be .5. The cost of checking the valve assuming a 50% chance of adjustment is $100 [$80 + ($40 x .5)]. The expected cost of not checking is $100 ($200 x .5). For any value of P greater than .5, the expected cost of not checking exceeds the expected cost of checking the valve, so .5 is the lowest value of P for which the valve should be tested.
Answers (A), (B), and (C) are incorrect because, for a value of P less than .5, checking the valve is more costly than not checking it.

**70.** Management of a company has asked the internal auditing department to assist in determining whether a new automated system should be implemented and whether the supporting software should be developed in-house, purchased, or leased. This will require evaluating a sequence of alternatives, each of which will result in different outcomes. The most effective tool the company can use to evaluate these choices would be

- A. Ratio analysis.
- B. Payoff tables.
- C. Queuing theory.
- D. Decision tree.

The correct answer is (D). *(CIA, adapted)*
**REQUIRED:** The most effective tool to evaluate the choice of whether to develop, lease, or purchase software.
**DISCUSSION:** A decision tree is useful when the most beneficial series of decisions is to be chosen. The possible decisions for each decision point, the events that might follow from each decision, the probabilities of these events, and the quantified outcomes of the events should be known.
Answer (A) is incorrect because ratio analysis considers only one part of the decision to be made. Ratio analysis is useful when analyzing costs and efficiencies. Answer (B) is incorrect because payoff tables are useful in assessing an individual decision. Answer (C) is incorrect because queuing theory is an approach to minimize the costs of waiting lines.

**71.** Which one of the following statements does not apply to decision tree analysis?

- A. The sum of the probabilities of the events is less than one.
- B. All of the events are mutually exclusive.
- C. All of the events are included in the decision.
- D. The branches emanate from a node from left to right.

The correct answer is (A). *(CMA, adapted)*
**REQUIRED:** The statement not applicable to decision tree analysis.
**DISCUSSION:** In a decision tree, the events following from a decision are mutually exclusive. Also, all possible events are included. Thus, the sum of the probabilities of the events is 1.0.
Answers (B), (C), and (D) are incorrect because they are true statements with respect to decision trees.

**72.** A local charitable organization orders and sells Christmas trees to raise funds. It wants to know the optimal quantity to order. Any merchandise not sold will be discarded without scrap value. This is an example of a single-period inventory model that is solved using

- A. Economic order quantity (EOQ).
- B. Payoff tables.
- C. Materials requirements planning (MRP).
- D. Game theory.

The correct answer is (B). *(CIA, adapted)*
**REQUIRED:** The quantitative technique used to solve a single-period inventory model.
**DISCUSSION:** Payoff table analysis is appropriate for single-period inventory. A payoff table performs the same function as a decision tree by relating possible decisions, events that follow those decisions, and the quantified outcomes (payoffs) of the events.
Answer (A) is incorrect because EOQ models deal with a nearly constant demand. Answer (C) is incorrect because MRP is a technique for dependent-demand inventories. Answer (D) is incorrect because game theory is a mathematical approach to decision making in which each decision maker takes into account the courses of action of competitors.

**73.** A firm must decide whether to introduce a new product A or B. There is no time to obtain experimental information; a decision has to be made now. Expected sales can be classified as weak, moderate, or strong. How many different payoffs are possible in a decision tree under these circumstances?

- A. 2
- B. 3
- C. 5
- D. 6

The correct answer is (D). *(CIA, adapted)*
**REQUIRED:** The number of different payoffs possible in a decision tree.
**DISCUSSION:** A decision tree represents the possible decisions, the events or states of nature that might follow from each decision, the probabilities of these events, and the quantified outcomes (payoffs) of the events. Given two possible decisions (A or B) and three events (low, medium, or high demand) that might follow each decision, six outcomes or payoffs are possible.
Answer (A) is incorrect because 2 equals the number of decisions. Answer (B) is incorrect because 3 equals the possible states of nature. Answer (C) is incorrect because 5 equals the sum of 2 decisions and 3 states of nature.

**74.** The legal department of a firm prepared the decision tree below for a possible patent infringement suit.

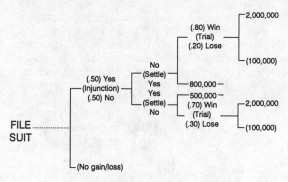

Based on the decision tree, the firm should

    A.  Not file the suit.

    B.  File suit; settle if injunction granted.

    C.  File suit; settle if injunction not granted.

    D.  Carry suit to trial.

The correct answer is (D). *(CIA, adapted)*

    **REQUIRED:** The action that should be taken based on the decision tree.

    **DISCUSSION:** To solve this problem, expected outcomes for all possibilities must be computed. If the suit is filed and an injunction granted, the following expected outcomes exist:

E(Trial) = 0.5[0.8($2,000,000) + 0.2($–100,000)]
           = $790,000

E(Settle) = 0.5($800,000) = $400,000

    If the suit is filed, but the injunction is not granted, the following expected outcomes exist:

E(Trial) = 0.5[0.7($2,000,000) + 0.3($–100,000)]
           = $685,000

E(Settle) = 0.5($500,000) = $250,000

All outcomes are positive, so the suit should be filed. In addition, because the expected outcomes are greater, the suit should be taken to trial.

    Answer (A) is incorrect because not filing results in no gain. Answers (B) and (C) are incorrect because going to trial always has a higher expected value than settlement.

# CHAPTER SIXTEEN
# REGRESSION ANALYSIS

**Correlation analysis** is used to measure the strength of the linear relationship between two or more variables. Correlation between two variables can be seen by plotting their values on a single graph to form a scatter diagram. If the points tend to form a straight line, correlation is high. If they form a random pattern, there is little correlation. Correlation measures only linear relationships.

**Regression analysis** extends correlation to find an equation for the linear relationship among variables. The behavior of the dependent variable is explained in terms of one or more independent variables. Thus, regression analysis determines functional relationships among quantitative variables. Forecasts are the basis for business plans, including budgets. In addition to intuition, many quantitative methods are useful in projecting the future from past experience. Examples of forecasts include sales projections, inventory demand, cash flow, and future capital needs. Computer models are often used in the forecasting process to simulate real-world conditions. These quantitative models may be investigated by randomly assigning values to the variables (based on the probability distribution of each variable). Solutions are then calculated. Given many iterations, a distribution of results is obtained that is useful in predicting how the system will behave. The reliability of the forecast should be determined before using it, but no objective method can determine the reliability of judgmental forecasts. When quantitative methods are used, however, measurement of reliability is usually possible.

## 16.1 CORRELATION ANALYSIS

A. If the points on a scatter diagram form a curve, several possibilities exist.

   1. A linear relationship (a straight line) may be used to approximate a portion of the curve.

   2. A linear relationship exists between some other function of the independent variable x (e.g., log x) and the dependent variable y.

   3. No relationship exists.

B. In standard notation, the coefficient of correlation is r.

   1. The coefficient of determination is $r^2$.

C. The **coefficient of correlation** measures the relative strength of the linear relationship. It has the following properties:

   1. The magnitude of r is independent of the scales of measurement of x and y.

   2. $-1.0 \leq r \leq 1.0$

      a. A value of $-1.0$ indicates a perfectly inverse linear relationship between x and y.
      b. A value of zero indicates no linear relationship between x and y.
      c. A value of $+1.0$ indicates a perfectly direct relationship between x and y.

D.   Scatter diagrams may be used to demonstrate correlations. Each observation creates a dot that pairs the x and y values. The linearity and slope of these observations are related to the coefficient of correlation by the previously stated rules.

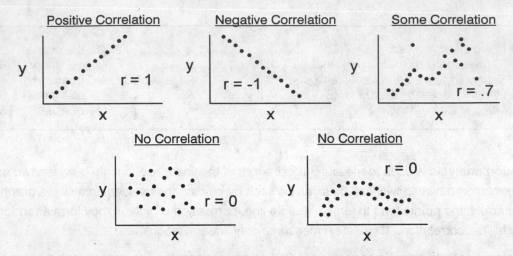

E.   The **coefficient of determination** ($r^2$), or the coefficient of correlation squared, may be interpreted as the proportion of the total variation in y that is explained or accounted for by the regression equation.

1.   It is equal to 1 minus the quotient of the unexplained variation divided by the total variation. The following is the formula:

$$r^2 = 1 - \frac{\Sigma (y_i - \hat{y})^2}{\Sigma (y_i - \overline{y}_i)^2}$$

If:  $r^2$ = the coefficient of determination
     $\Sigma$ = summation
     $y_i$ = an actual data point
     $\hat{y}$ = a point on the regression line
     $\overline{y}_i$ = the mean of the observed data points

2.   EXAMPLE: The assertion that new car sales are a function of disposable income with a coefficient of correlation of .8 is equivalent to stating that 64% ($.8^2$) of the variation of new car sales (from average new car sales) can be explained by the variation in disposable income (from average disposable income).

3.   Because $r^2$ increases as the number of independent variables increases, regardless of whether the additional variables are actually correlated with the dependent variable, $r^2$ may be adjusted (reduced) to allow for this effect. If k is the number of independent variables and n is the number of observations, the formula for adjusted $r^2$ is

$$r^2 - \frac{(k - 1)}{(n - k)} \times (1 - r^2)$$

## 16.2 REGRESSION (LEAST SQUARES) ANALYSIS

A.   **Simple regression** has only one independent variable, and **multiple regression** has more than one.

1.   EXAMPLE: A variable such as sales is dependent on advertising, consumer income, availability of substitutes, and other independent variables.

2.   **Multicollinearity** is the condition in which two or more independent variables are strongly correlated. The effect is greater uncertainty regarding the coefficient of the variables; that is, their standard errors increase. Multicollinearity is a concern in multiple regression.

3. Regression analysis is used to find trend lines in business data, such as sales or costs (time series analysis or trend analysis), and to develop models based on the association of variables (cross-sectional analysis, a method that is not time related as is trend analysis). The results are used in forecasting. Examples are the

    a. Trend in product sales
    b. Trend in overhead as a percentage of sales
    c. Relationship of direct labor hours to variable overhead
    d. Relationship of direct materials usage to accounts payable

## B. Qualifications

1. Some reasonable basis should exist for expecting the variables to be related.

    a. If they are obviously independent, any association found by regression is mere coincidence.

    b. Regression does not determine causality, however. One may conclude that x and y move together, but the apparent relationship may be caused by some other factor.

        1) EXAMPLE: A strong correlation exists between car-wash sales volume and sunny weather, but sales volume does not cause sunny weather.

    c. The statistical relationships revealed by regression and correlation analysis are valid only for the range of the data in the sample.

2. The simple regression equation is

$$y = a + bx + e$$

    If: y = the dependent variable
    a = the y-axis intercept (the fixed cost in cost functions)
    b = the slope of the regression line (the variable portion of the total cost in cost functions)
    x = the independent variable
    e = the error term (also called the residual or disturbance term)

    a. Assumptions of the model are that

        1) For each value of x, a distribution of values exists for y. The means of these distributions form a straight line. Hence, x and y are linearly related.

        2) The error term (e) is normally distributed with a mean or expected value equal to zero.

            a) The y-intercept (a) and the slope of the regression line (b) also have normal distributions.

        3) Errors in successive observations are statistically independent.

            a) Thus, the estimators are unbiased.

            b) **Autocorrelation (serial correlation)** occurs when the observations are not independent; in other words, later observations may be dependent on earlier ones.

        4) The distribution of y around the regression line is constant for different values of x.

            a) Thus, the observations are characterized by **homoscedasticity** or **constant variance**. The deviation of points from the regression line does not vary significantly with a change in the size of the independent variable.

                i) **Heteroscedasticity** is the condition in which the variance of the error term is not constant.

b)    Graphically, the model is represented by a series of normal distributions (subpopulations of y) around the regression line. As noted on the previous page, these subpopulations have the same variance.

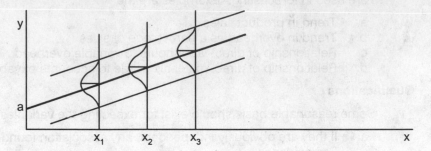

3.    From linear algebra, the equation for a straight line may be stated as follows:

$$y = a + bx$$

If:  a  =  the y-axis intercept
     b  =  the slope of the line

a.    Regression analysis uses the method of least squares, which minimizes the sum of the squares of the vertical distance between each observation point and the regression line.

b.    EXAMPLE:  Observations are collected on advertising expenditures and annual sales for a firm.

| Sales ($000,000s) | Advertising ($000s) |
|---|---|
| 28 | 71 |
| 14 | 31 |
| 19 | 50 |
| 21 | 60 |
| 16 | 35 |

1)    The regression equation that results from using least squares computations is y = 4.2 + .31(x), or

*Expected sales = 4.2 + (.31 × Advertising expenditures)*

2)    Graphically:

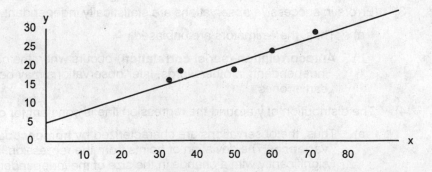

4.    Regression analysis is particularly valuable for budgeting and cost accounting purposes. For instance, it is almost a necessity for computing the fixed and variable portions of mixed costs for flexible budgeting.

C. The following equations can be used to determine the equation for the least squares regression line (the equation for the line is in the form of y = a + bx):

$$\sum y = na + b(\sum x)$$
$$\sum xy = a(\sum x) + b(\sum x^2)$$

1. EXAMPLE: The use of the two equations can be illustrated using the following sample of six observations (n = 6):

| y | x |
|---|---|
| $ 6 | 2 |
| 7 | 3 |
| 5 | 2 |
| 4 | 1 |
| 8 | 3 |
| 6 | 2 |
| Σy = $36 | Σx = 13 |

| Σxy | Σx² |
|---|---|
| 6 x 2 = 12 | 4 |
| 7 x 3 = 21 | 9 |
| 5 x 2 = 10 | 4 |
| 4 x 1 = 4 | 1 |
| 8 x 3 = 24 | 9 |
| 6 x 2 = 12 | 4 |
| 83 | 31 |

a. Substituting into the two equations gives

$$36 = 6a + 13b$$
$$83 = 13a + 31b$$

b. Solving simultaneously for the two unknowns,

$$1116 = 186a + 403b$$
$$\underline{1079 = 169a + 403b}$$
$$\underline{37 = 17a}$$

c. Thus, a = 2.176. Solving for b in the second original equation gives

$$83 = 13(2.176) + 31b$$
$$83 = 28.288 + 31b$$
$$31b = 54.712$$
$$b = 1.765$$

d. Hence, future costs can be predicted by the following formula:

$$y = \$2.176 + \$1.765x$$

e. Alternative formulas that are ordinarily simpler to use are given below.

1) The slope may be expressed as

$$b = \frac{n\sum xy - \sum x \sum y}{n\sum x^2 - (\sum x)^2}$$

2) The y-intercept may be expressed as

$$a = \bar{y} - b(\bar{x})$$

D.  The statistical significance of the slope of the regression line is important because, if its true value is zero, changes in the independent variable have no effect on the dependent variable.

1.  Because the distribution of b is normal, the t-distribution (see Chapter 15) may be used to determine whether b is significantly different from zero, that is, whether one can reject the null hypothesis that b equals zero.

a.  One approach is to divide b by the standard error of the estimate of b. (The formula is not given here. The standard error is usually provided in the computer output.) If the result exceeds the critical value of t determinable from a standard table, the conclusion is that b is not zero. For example, this critical value is 2.0 for a sample of 60, 58 degrees of freedom (60 − 2 parameters of a and b estimated), and a 95% confidence level.

b.  Another approach is to construct a precision interval (b ± t × the standard error of the estimate of b). If the interval does not contain zero, the null hypothesis may be rejected.

1)  The value of t is the critical value for the given sample size, degrees of freedom, and confidence level used in the first approach.

E.  The **high-low method** is used to generate a regression line by basing the equation on only the highest and lowest of a series of observations.

1.  EXAMPLE: A regression equation covering electricity costs could be developed by using only the high-cost month and the low-cost month. If costs were $400 in April when production was 800 machine hours and $600 in September when production was 1,300 hours, the equation would be determined as follows:

| High month | $600 | for | 1,300 hours |
|---|---|---|---|
| Low month | 400 | for | 800 hours |
| Increase | $200 | | 500 hours |

Costs increased $200 for 500 additional hours, so the variable cost is $.40 per machine hour. For the low month, the total variable portion of that monthly cost is $320 ($.40 × 800 hours). Because the total cost is $400, and $320 is variable, the remaining $80 must be a fixed cost. The regression equation is y = 80 + .4x.

2.  The major criticism of the high-low method is that the high and low points may be abnormalities not representative of normal occurrences.

## 16.3 SEPARATING FIXED AND VARIABLE COSTS

See preceding outlines.

## 16.4 OTHER FORECASTING METHODS

A.  **Time series or trend analysis** relies on past experience. Changes in the value of a variable (e.g., unit sales of a product) over time may have several possible components.

1.  In time series analysis, the dependent variable is regressed on time (the independent variable).

2.  The **secular trend** is the long-term change that occurs in a series. It is represented by a straight line or curve on a graph.

3.  **Seasonal variations** are common in many businesses. A variety of analysis methods include seasonal variations in a forecasting model, but most methods make use of a seasonal index.

4.  **Cyclical fluctuations** are variations in the level of activity in business periods. Although some of these fluctuations are beyond the control of the firm, they need to be considered in forecasting. They are usually incorporated as index numbers.

5.  **Irregular or random variation** is any variation not included in the categories above. Business can be affected by random happenings -- weather, strikes, fires, etc.

B.  **Exponential smoothing** is a technique used to level or smooth variations encountered in a forecast. This technique also adapts the forecast to changes as they occur. The simplest form of smoothing is the moving average, in which each forecast is based on a fixed number of prior observations. Exponential smoothing is similar to the moving average. The term "exponential" means that greater weight is placed on the most recent data, with the weights of all data falling off exponentially as the data age. The selection of alpha ($\alpha$), the smoothing factor, is important because a high alpha places more weight on recent data. The equation for the forecast (F) for period t+1 is

$$F_{t+1} = \alpha(x_t) + (1 - \alpha)F_t$$

If: $x_t$ = the observation for period t

$t$ = the most recent period

$\alpha$ = the smoothing factor ($0 \leq \alpha \leq 1$)

$F_t$ = the forecast for period t

## 16.5 MULTIPLE CALCULATIONS

See preceding outlines.

## 16.1 Correlation Analysis

**1.** Correlation is a term frequently used in conjunction with regression analysis and is measured by the value of the coefficient of correlation, r. The best explanation of the value r is that it

A. Interprets variances in terms of the independent variable.

B. Ranges in size from negative infinity to positive infinity.

C. Is a measure of the relative relationship between two variables.

D. Is positive only for downward-sloping regression lines.

The correct answer is (C). *(CMA, adapted)*
**REQUIRED:** The best explanation of the coefficient of correlation (r).
**DISCUSSION:** The coefficient of correlation (r) measures the strength of the linear relationship between the dependent and independent variables. The magnitude of r is independent of the scales of measurement of x and y. The coefficient lies between −1.0 and +1.0. A value of zero indicates no linear relationship between the x and y variables. A value of +1.0 indicates a perfectly direct relationship, and a value of −1.0 indicates a perfectly inverse relationship.
Answer (A) is incorrect because the coefficient relates the two variables to each other. Answer (B) is incorrect because the size of the coefficient varies between −1.0 and +1.0. Answer (D) is incorrect because a downward-sloping regression line indicates a negative correlation. A downward slope means that y decreases as x increases.

**2.** Quality control programs employ many tools for problem definition and analysis. A scatter diagram is one of these tools. The objective of a scatter diagram is to

A. Display a population of items for analysis.

B. Show frequency distribution in graphic form.

C. Divide a universe of data into homogeneous groups.

D. Show the vital trend and separate trivial items.

The correct answer is (A). *(CIA, adapted)*
**REQUIRED:** The objective of a scatter diagram.
**DISCUSSION:** The objective of a scatter diagram is to demonstrate correlations. Each observation is represented by a dot on a graph corresponding to a particular value of X (the independent variable) and Y (the dependent variable).
Answer (B) is incorrect because the objective of a histogram is to show frequency distribution in graphic form. Answer (C) is incorrect because the objective of stratification is to divide a universe of data into homogeneous groups. Answer (D) is incorrect because regression analysis is used to find trend lines.

**3.** If the coefficient of correlation between two variables is zero, how might a scatter diagram of these variables appear?

A. Random points.

B. A least squares line that slopes up to the right.

C. A least squares line that slopes down to the right.

D. Under this condition, a scatter diagram could not be plotted on a graph.

The correct answer is (A). *(CPA, adapted)*
**REQUIRED:** The scatter diagram if the coefficient of correlation is zero.
**DISCUSSION:** Each observation creates a point that represents x and y values. The collinearity of these relationships and slope of the observations are visible. If the coefficient of correlation is zero, there is no relationship between the variables, and the points will be randomly distributed.
Answer (B) is incorrect because it describes a direct (positive) relationship. Answer (C) is incorrect because it describes an inverse (negative) relationship. Answer (D) is incorrect because the points could be plotted on a scattergram, although it would have no meaning other than to confirm the lack of correlation between the variables.

**4.** In regression analysis, which of the following correlation coefficients represents the strongest relationship between the independent and dependent variables?

A. 1.03

B. −.02

C. −.89

D. .75

The correct answer is (C). *(CIA, adapted)*
**REQUIRED:** The correlation coefficient with the strongest relationship between independent and dependent variables.
**DISCUSSION:** Because the range of values is between −1.0 and 1.0, −.89 suggests a very strong inverse relationship between the independent and dependent variables. A value of −1.0 signifies a perfect inverse relationship, and a value of 1.0 signifies a perfect direct relationship.
Answer (A) is incorrect because 1.03 is an impossible value. Answer (B) is incorrect because −.02 is a very weak correlation coefficient. Answer (D) is incorrect because .75 is .25 from the maximum value, whereas −.89 is .11 from the minimum value.

**5.** The coefficient of correlation between direct materials cost and units produced is nearest

   A.  −0.75

   B.  0.50

   C.  0.0

   D.  1.00

The correct answer is (D). *(CIA, adapted)*
   **REQUIRED:** The coefficient of correlation between direct materials cost and units produced.
   **DISCUSSION:** The coefficient of correlation measures the relative strength of the linear relationship between two variables. It varies from −1.00 for a perfectly inverse relationship to 1.00 for a perfectly direct relationship. The number of units produced is strongly and directly related to direct materials cost; thus, a coefficient of 1.00 best indicates the relationship.
   Answer (A) is incorrect because a negative correlation coefficient indicates an inverse relationship between two variables. Answer (B) is incorrect because a correlation coefficient of 0.50 indicates some relationship between the two variables but not one as strong as that between direct materials and units produced. Answer (C) is incorrect because a value of zero indicates no linear relationship between the two variables.

**6.** Using regression analysis, Fairfield Co. graphed the following relationship of its cheapest product line's sales with its customers' income levels:

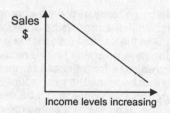

If there is a strong statistical relationship between the sales and customers' income levels, which of the following numbers best represents the correlation coefficient for this relationship?

   A.  −9.00

   B.  −0.93

   C.  +0.93

   D.  +9.00

The correct answer is (B). *(CPA, adapted)*
   **REQUIRED:** The correlation coefficient for this relationship.
   **DISCUSSION:** The coefficient of correlation measures the relative strength of the linear relationship. The range of the coefficient (r) is $-1.0 \leq r \leq +1.0$. The value of −1.0 indicates a perfectly inverse linear relationship between x and y (i.e., as x increases, y decreases). A value of zero indicates no linear relationship between x and y. A value of +1.0 indicates a perfectly direct relationship between x and y. Because Fairfield's sales decrease as income levels increase, the inverse linear relationship is very strong. This inverse relationship is best represented by −.93.
   Answers (A) and (D) are incorrect because −9.00 and +9.00 fall outside of the coefficient of correlation's range. Answer (C) is incorrect because +0.93 represents a direct relationship between x and y.

**7.** In regression analysis, the coefficient of determination is a measure of

   A.  The amount of variation in the dependent variable explained by the independent variables.

   B.  The amount of variation in the dependent variable unexplained by the independent variables.

   C.  The slope of the regression line.

   D.  The predicted value of the dependent variable.

The correct answer is (A). *(CIA, adapted)*
   **REQUIRED:** The definition of the coefficient of determination.
   **DISCUSSION:** The coefficient of correlation, which has a range from −1.00 to +1.00, is a measure of the relative strength of the linear relationship between two or more variables, that is, of how well the least squares line fits the given observations. Squaring the coefficient of correlation gives the coefficient of determination, which is a measure of the amount of variation in a dependent variable that can be explained by independent variables.
   Answer (B) is incorrect because the complement of the coefficient of determination is the unexplained variation. Answer (C) is incorrect because the slope is the change in the dependent variable in relation to the change in the independent variable. Answer (D) is incorrect because the predicted value of the dependent variable is calculated by the regression formula ($y = a + bx$ for simple regression).

**8.** The auditor of a bank has developed a multiple regression model that has been used for a number of years to estimate the amount of interest income from commercial loans. During the current year, the auditor applies the model and discovers that the $r^2$ value has decreased dramatically, but the model otherwise seems to be working well. Which conclusion is justified by the change?

   A. Changing to a cross-sectional regression analysis should cause $r^2$ to increase.

   B. Regression analysis is no longer an appropriate technique to estimate interest income.

   C. Some new factors, not included in the model, are causing interest income to change.

   D. A linear regression analysis would increase the model's reliability.

The correct answer is (C). *(CIA, adapted)*
   **REQUIRED:** The implication of the decrease in $r^2$.
   **DISCUSSION:** The coefficient of determination ($r^2$) is the variation in the dependent variable (interest income) that is explained by the independent variables. In this case, less of the change in interest income is explained by the model. Thus, some other factor must be causing interest income to change. This change merits audit investigation.
   Answer (A) is incorrect because cross-sectional regression analysis is inappropriate. The auditor is trying to estimate changes in a single account balance over time. Answer (B) is incorrect because regression analysis may still be the most appropriate method to estimate interest income, but the auditor should first understand the factors that may be causing $r^2$ to decrease. The reason may be a systematic error in the account balance. Answer (D) is incorrect because linear regression models are simpler, but the auditor should be searching for a systematic error in the account balance or applying a more complex model.

**9.** An auditor asks accounting personnel how they determine the value of the organization's real estate holdings. They say that valuations are based on a regression model that uses 17 different characteristics of the properties (square footage, proximity to downtown, age, etc.) to predict value. The coefficients of this model were estimated using a random sample of 20 company properties, for which the model produced an $r^2$ value of 0.92. Based on this information, which one of the following should the auditor conclude?

   A. The model's high $r^2$ is probably due in large part to random chance.

   B. 92% of the variables that determine value are in the model.

   C. The model is very reliable.

   D. This sample of properties is probably representative of the overall population of company holdings.

The correct answer is (A). *(CIA, adapted)*
   **REQUIRED:** The true statement about a regression model.
   **DISCUSSION:** Mathematically, $r^2$ always approaches 1.0 as the number of variables in the regression approaches the number of observations in the sample (even if the predictors are unrelated to the dependent variable). This model has a very large number of predictors for the small sample size.
   Answer (B) is incorrect because the true model is unknown. Accordingly, this inference cannot be drawn. Answer (C) is incorrect because the model has too many predictors for the small sample size. Answer (D) is incorrect because a high $r^2$ can occur in a bad sample with a bad model just as easily as in a good sample and a good model.

**10.** A firm regressed overhead on units produced over the past year and found a coefficient of determination equal to 0.85 with a U-shaped residual error pattern. It is reasonable to conclude that the relationship between overhead and units produced is

   A. Weak.

   B. Causal.

   C. Nonlinear.

   D. Linear.

The correct answer is (C). *(CIA, adapted)*
   **REQUIRED:** The relationship between overhead and units produced.
   **DISCUSSION:** A coefficient of determination measures the proportion of the total variation in y that is explained or accounted for by the regression equation. In this case, the relationship is strong because 85% of that variation is explained. However, the relationship is curvilinear because the residual error pattern is U-shaped. The residual error pattern consists of the plots of the estimates of the error term in the linear regression equation.
   Answer (A) is incorrect because the relationship is strong (coefficient of determination = .85). Answer (B) is incorrect because regression analysis measures the strength of the relationship among variables, but it does not establish causation. Answer (D) is incorrect because the U-shaped residual error pattern reflects a nonlinear relationship.

**11.** Sago Co. uses regression analysis to develop a model for predicting overhead costs. Two different cost drivers (machine hours and direct materials weight) are under consideration as the independent variable. Relevant data were run on a computer using one of the standard regression programs, with the following results:

| Machine hours | Coefficient |
|---|---|
| Y Intercept | 2,500 |
| B | 5.0 |
| $r^2$ = .70 | |

| Direct materials weight | |
|---|---|
| Y Intercept | 4,600 |
| B | 2.6 |
| $r^2$ = .50 | |

Which regression equation should be used?

   A.  $y = 2,500 + 5.0x$

   B.  $y = 2,500 + 3.5x$

   C.  $y = 4,600 + 2.6x$

   D.  $y = 4,600 + 1.3x$

The correct answer is (A). *(CPA, adapted)*
   **REQUIRED:** The regression equation.
   **DISCUSSION:** The simple regression equation is $y = a + bx$, given that y is the dependent variable, a is the y-axis intercept, b is the slope of the regression line, and x is the independent variable. To determine which cost driver to use, the coefficient of determination ($r^2$) is computed. The value of $r^2$ indicates the proportion of the total variation in y that is explained by the regression equation. Because machine hours has a higher $r^2$ than direct materials weight, the coefficients for machine hours are used to predict costs. Consequently, the regression equation is $y = 2,500 + 5.0x$.
   Answer (B) is incorrect because $y = 2,500 + 3.5x$ incorrectly multiplies the slope by $r^2$. Answer (C) is incorrect because machine hours has a higher $r^2$ than direct materials. Answer (D) is incorrect because the machine hours coefficients should be used to predict overhead costs.

**12.** If regression analysis is applied to the data shown below, the coefficients of correlation and determination will indicate the existence of a

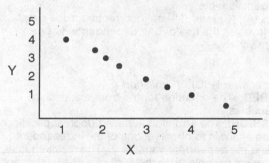

   A.  Low linear relationship, high explained variation ratio.

   B.  High inverse linear relationship, high explained variation ratio.

   C.  High direct linear relationship, high explained variation ratio.

   D.  High inverse linear relationship, low explained variation ratio.

The correct answer is (B). *(CIA, adapted)*
   **REQUIRED:** The implications of the scatter diagram regarding the coefficients of correlation and determination.
   **DISCUSSION:** The coefficient of correlation measures the degree and direction of the linear relationship between two or more variables. The relationship ranges from perfectly inverse (–1) to perfectly direct (1). If there is no relationship, the coefficient of correlation is 0. The coefficient of determination is the proportion of the variance of the dependent variable explained by the independent variable. It equals the coefficient of correlation squared ($r^2$). Given that the plotted points are almost in a straight line with a negative slope, the coefficient of correlation is almost –1, and the coefficient of determination is nearly +1.
   Answers (A), (C), and (D) are incorrect because a high inverse linear relationship exists, and a high degree of variation is explained.

## 16.2 Regression (Least Squares) Analysis

**13.** The manager of the assembly department of a company would like to estimate the fixed and variable components of the department's cost. To do so, the manager has collected information on total cost and output for the past 24 months. To estimate the fixed and variable components of total cost, the manager should use

A. Regression analysis.

B. Game theory.

C. Sensitivity analysis.

D. Queuing theory.

The correct answer is (A). *(CIA, adapted)*
**REQUIRED:** The technique used to estimate the fixed and variable components of total cost.
**DISCUSSION:** Regression analysis is a statistical technique for measuring the relationship between variables. It estimates the component of the dependent variable that varies with changes in the independent variable and the component that does not vary.
Answer (B) is incorrect because game theory is a mathematical approach to decision making in which the actions of competitors are considered. Answer (C) is incorrect because sensitivity analysis studies how changes in one or more variables affect the solution of a quantitative model. Answer (D) is incorrect because queuing theory is used to minimize the sum of the costs of waiting lines and servicing waiting lines when items arrive randomly at a service point and are serviced sequentially.

**14.** Simple regression analysis involves the use of

|    | Dependent Variables | Independent Variables |
|----|---------------------|-----------------------|
| A. | One                 | None                  |
| B. | One                 | One                   |
| C. | One                 | Two                   |
| D. | None                | Two                   |

The correct answer is (B). *(CPA, adapted)*
**REQUIRED:** The number of dependent and independent variables involved in simple regression analysis.
**DISCUSSION:** Regression analysis assumes that a change in the value of a dependent variable is related to the change in the value of an independent variable. Regression analysis attempts to find an equation for the linear relationship among variables. In simple regression analysis, one independent variable is used to predict the changes in one dependent variable. In multiple regression analysis, multiple independent variables are used to predict the changes in one dependent variable.
Answers (A), (C), and (D) are incorrect because simple regression involves the use of one dependent and one independent variable.

**15.** Simple linear regression is a method applied when the underlying relationship between two variables is believed to be linear. The least squares process estimates this hypothesized true relationship by minimizing the sum of squared errors of the observations in a sample about a fitted line. Which equation properly represents the underlying true relationship between variables?

A. $y = a + x$

B. $y = a + bx$

C. $y = a + bx + e$

D. $y = a + bx^2 + e$

The correct answer is (C). *(Publisher)*
**REQUIRED:** The equation for the true relationship between variables.
**DISCUSSION:.** The equation is based upon application of regression analysis to observations of the independent variable x and the dependent variable y. The result equates y (the dependent variable) with the sum of a (the y-intercept), bx (b is the slope and x is the independent variable), and e (an error term). The error term indicates the degree of uncertainty.
Answers (A) and (B) are incorrect because an error term should be included. Answer (D) is incorrect because a simple regression should be a linear function.

**16.** Which equation properly represents the least squares estimates of the relationship between variables? Let ^ denote a least squares estimate of a value.

A. $y = â + \hat{b} + x$

B. $\hat{y} = â + \hat{b}x + e$

C. $\hat{y} = â + \hat{b}x$

D. $y = â + \hat{b}x^2$

The correct answer is (C). *(Publisher)*
**REQUIRED:** The equation for a least squares estimate.
**DISCUSSION:** The least squares estimate is based upon the relationship that is found and described in the preceding question. The estimate has no provision for the error term, however. Rather, the error term is incorporated in the standard error of the estimate. An estimate of y is based on estimates of both a and b. Least squares estimates are deterministic, not probabilistic, estimates of the variable, so no error term should be included.
Answer (A) is incorrect because y is the actual value, and an error term should be included. Answer (B) is incorrect because the equation should include no error term.
Answer (D) is incorrect because the estimated relationship should be linear.

---

---

**17.** The dependent variable is

  A.  a.

  B.  y.

  C.  b.

  D.  x.

The correct answer is (B). *(Publisher).*

**REQUIRED:** The symbol for the dependent variable.

**DISCUSSION:** The dependent variable in the regression equation is the item to be estimated (or calculated or predicted), i.e., y. In regression analysis, the objective is to predict a value of one variable (dependent) in terms of the values of one or more other variables (independent).

Answer (A) is incorrect because a is the y-axis intercept. Answer (C) is incorrect because b is the slope of the line. Answer (D) is incorrect because x is the independent variable.

**18.** The y-axis intercept is

  A.  a.

  B.  b.

  C.  x.

  D.  e.

The correct answer is (A). *(Publisher)*

**REQUIRED:** The symbol for the y-axis intercept in the regression equation.

**DISCUSSION:** The y-axis intercept is equal to a in the equation. If the relevant range includes zero volume, a is a fixed cost in the usual cost function. It is the expected value of y when x is zero, provided that it lies within the relevant range of the sample. The relevant range of the regression analysis is the portion of the least squares line between the minimum and maximum values of the independent variable. The predictive ability of regression should be limited to this region.

Answer (B) is incorrect because b is the slope of the line. Answer (C) is incorrect because x is the independent variable. Answer (D) is incorrect because e is the error term.

**19.** The slope of the line is

  A.  y.

  B.  b.

  C.  x.

  D.  e.

The correct answer is (B). *(Publisher)*

**REQUIRED:** The symbol for the slope of the line.

**DISCUSSION:** The slope of a line is a constant equal to the proportionate change along the y axis for each change along the x axis. Thus, in a regression equation, slope represents the variable portion of the total cost in the cost function, i.e., the change in cost that occurs for each one-unit change in activity.

Answer (A) is incorrect because y is the dependent variable. Answer (C) is incorrect because x is the independent variable. Answer (D) is incorrect because e is the error term.

**20.** The independent variable is

  A.  a.

  B.  y.

  C.  b.

  D.  x.

The correct answer is (D). *(Publisher)*

**REQUIRED:** The symbol for an independent variable.

**DISCUSSION:** The independent or explanatory variable (x) is the variable that is permitted to change. These changes are used to predict values of the dependent variable (y).

Answer (A) is incorrect because a is the y-axis intercept. Answer (B) is incorrect because y is the dependent variable. Answer (C) is incorrect because b is the slope of the line.

**21.** The error term is

  A.  a.

  B.  y.

  C.  b.

  D.  e.

The correct answer is (D). *(Publisher)*

**REQUIRED:** The symbol for the error term in the regression equation.

**DISCUSSION:** The error term in the equation is e. The error term is usually assumed to have a mean of zero in linear regression, thereby permitting calculations using the formula $y = a + bx$.

Answer (A) is incorrect because a is the y-axis intercept. Answer (B) is incorrect because it is the dependent variable. Answer (C) is incorrect because it is the slope of the line.

**22.** In determining cost behavior in business, the cost function is often expressed as y = a + bx. Which one of the following cost estimation methods should not be used in estimating fixed and variable costs for the equation?

    A.   Graphic method.

    B.   Simple regression.

    C.   High- and low-point method.

    D.   Multiple regression.

The correct answer is (D). *(CMA, adapted)*
    **REQUIRED:** The cost estimation method that should not be used to generate a function expressed as y = a + bx.
    **DISCUSSION:** Regression analysis can be used to find an equation for the linear relationship among variables. However, multiple regression is not used to generate an equation of the type y = a + bx because multiple regression has more than one independent variable. In other words, a multiple regression equation would take the form: y = a + bx1 + cx2 + dx3 + . . . .
    Answer (A) is incorrect because the graphic approach can be used to estimate a linear function. Answer (B) is incorrect because simple regression, which is based on one independent variable, is the best means of expressing a linear cost function. Answer (C) is incorrect because the high-low method, although unsophisticated, can often give a good approximation of a linear cost function.

**23.** Autocorrelation or serial correlation

    A.   Defines the proportion of the variance explained by the independent variable.

    B.   Means that observations are not independent.

    C.   Means that independent variables are correlated with each other.

    D.   Is the failure of random samples to represent the population.

The correct answer is (B). *(Publisher)*
    **REQUIRED:** The true statement about autocorrelation.
    **DISCUSSION:** Autocorrelation and serial correlation are synonyms meaning that the observations are not independent. For example, certain costs may rise with an increase in volume but not decline with a decrease in volume.
    Answer (A) is incorrect because it is the definition of the coefficient of determination. Answer (C) is incorrect because it is the definition of multicollinearity. Answer (D) is incorrect because it is the definition of bias.

**24.** Multicollinearity occurs when

    A.   A proportion of the variance is explained by the independent variable.

    B.   Observations are not independent.

    C.   Independent variables are correlated with each other.

    D.   A random sample fails to represent the population.

The correct answer is (C). *(Publisher)*
    **REQUIRED:** The definition of multicollinearity.
    **DISCUSSION:** Multicollinearity is the condition in which two or more independent variables are correlated with each other. Thus, multicollinearity occurs only in multiple regression equations.
    Answer (A) is incorrect because it defines the coefficient of determination. Answer (B) is incorrect because it is the definition of autocorrelation. Answer (D) is incorrect because it is the definition of bias.

**25.** Bias occurs when

    A.   A proportion of the variance is explained by the independent variable.

    B.   Observations are not independent.

    C.   Independent variables are correlated with each other.

    D.   The parameters obtained from random sampling fail to represent the population.

The correct answer is (D). *(Publisher)*
    **REQUIRED:** The definition of bias.
    **DISCUSSION:** Bias is the condition in which the random sample has failed to represent the population and therefore does not estimate the true parameters of the underlying data. For example, if the mean of random samples does not on average represent the true population mean, the sample mean is biased.
    Answer (A) is incorrect because it is the definition of the coefficient of determination. Answer (B) is incorrect because it is the definition of auto or serial correlation. Answer (C) is incorrect because it is the definition of multicollinearity.

**26.** The confidence interval for the value of y in the simple linear regression equation represents

A.  A measure of variability of the actual observations from the least squares line.

B.  A range of values constructed from the regression equation results for a specified level of probability.

C.  A variability about the least squares line that is uniform for all values of the independent variable in the sample.

D.  The proportion of the variance explained by the independent variable.

The correct answer is (B). *(Publisher)*
**REQUIRED:** The definition of confidence interval.
**DISCUSSION:** The confidence interval is a range of values constructed from the regression results that is expected to contain the true population value. It equals the estimate of y plus or minus the number of standard errors of the estimate appropriate for the desired level of confidence (probability that the interval contains the true value). This involves taking the mean, adjusting for the standard deviation and the appropriate probability distribution, to arrive at the range.

Answer (A) is incorrect because it describes the standard error of the estimate. Answer (C) is incorrect because it describes constant variance. Answer (D) is incorrect because it describes the coefficient of determination.

**27.** In a simple linear regression model, the standard error of the estimate of y represents

A.  A measure of variability of the actual observations from the least squares line.

B.  A range of values constructed from the regression equation results for a specified level of probability.

C.  A variability about the least squares line that is uniform for all values of the independent variable in the sample.

D.  The proportion of the variance explained by the independent variable.

The correct answer is (A). *(Publisher)*
**REQUIRED:** The definition of the standard error of the estimate.
**DISCUSSION:** The standard error of the estimate represents the variance of actual observations from the regression line. It is calculated based upon the sample drawn from the population. If $y_i$ is a data point, $\hat{y}$ is the estimate of y from the regression equation, n is the sample size, and s is the standard deviation of the sample, the standard error may be stated as follows for a simple linear regression:

$$s = \sqrt{\frac{(y_i - \hat{y})^2}{n - 2}}$$

Answer (B) is incorrect because it describes a confidence interval. Answer (C) is incorrect because it describes constant variance. Answer (D) is incorrect because it describes the coefficient of determination.

**28.** All of the following are assumptions underlying the validity of linear regression output except

A.  The errors are normally distributed and their mean is zero.

B.  Certainty.

C.  The variance of the errors is constant.

D.  The independent variables are not correlated with each other.

The correct answer is (B). *(CMA, adapted)*
**REQUIRED:** The assumption that does not underlie linear regression.
**DISCUSSION:** Users of linear regression make several assumptions: that there are no changes in the environment, that errors are normally distributed with a mean of zero, that the variance of the errors is constant, and that the independent variables are not correlated with each other. However, regression is only a means of predicting the future; certainty cannot be achieved.

Answers (A), (C), and (D) are incorrect because implied assumptions of the regression model are that the errors are normally distributed and their mean is zero, that the variance of the errors is constant, and that the independent variables are not correlated with each other.

**29.** Constant variance means

A.  A measure of variability of the actual observations from the least squares line.

B.  A range of values constructed from the regression equation results for a specified level of probability.

C.  A variability about the least squares line that is uniform for all values of the independent variable in the sample.

D.  The underlying assumptions of the regression equation that are not met.

The correct answer is (C). *(Publisher)*
**REQUIRED:** The definition of constant variance.
**DISCUSSION:** Constant variance signifies a uniform deviation of points from the regression line. This uniformity is based on the assumption that the distribution of the observations and errors is not affected by the values of the independent variable(s).

Answer (A) is incorrect because it describes the standard error of the estimate. Answer (B) is incorrect because it describes a confidence interval. Answer (D) is incorrect because constant variance is one of the basic assumptions underlying regression analysis.

**30.** If the error term is normally distributed about zero, then

    A.  The parameter estimates of the y-intercept and slope also have a normal distribution.

    B.  The estimate of the slope can be tested using a t-test.

    C.  The probability that the error term is greater than zero is equal to the probability that it is less than zero for any observation.

    D.  All of the answers are correct.

The correct answer is (D). *(Publisher)*

**REQUIRED:** The true statement(s) about an error term normally distributed about zero.

**DISCUSSION:** All three statements are true. This ideal situation permits t-tests (based on the t-distribution) to be performed to evaluate the significance of the estimates. For example, a confidence interval may be constructed around the estimate of the slope (b) of the regression line using the critical value of the t-statistic (based on the specified confidence level, sample size, and degrees of freedom) and the standard error of b. In other words, the interval equals b plus or minus the t-value times the standard error of b. If this interval does not include zero, one may conclude that the true slope is not zero and that the estimate is statistically significant (not affected solely by random factors).

Answer (A) is incorrect because a and b are assumed to be normally distributed. Answer (B) is incorrect because the t-distribution may be used in hypothesis testing of the estimate of b. Answer (C) is incorrect because the mean of the error term is assumed to be zero.

**31.** Omaha Sales Company asked a CPA's assistance in planning the use of multiple regression analysis to predict district sales. An equation has been estimated based upon historical data, and a standard error has been computed. When regression analysis based upon past periods is used to predict for a future period, the standard error associated with the predicted value, in relation to the standard error for the base equation, will be

    A.  Smaller.

    B.  Larger.

    C.  The same.

    D.  Larger or smaller, depending upon the circumstances.

The correct answer is (B). *(CPA, adapted)*

**REQUIRED:** The relationship of the standard error associated with the predicted value to the standard error for the base equation.

**DISCUSSION:** The standard error associated with a predicted value is always larger because it takes into account two types of error. It contains the standard error of the estimate, which is the variability of the y values about the least squares line, and a measure of the fact that the least squares line only approximates the true relationship between x and y.

Answers (A), (C), and (D) are incorrect because the standard error associated with a predicted value is always larger because it takes into account two types of error.

**32.** When the relationship between the independent and dependent variables is not expected to remain constant, an appropriate method of analysis is

    A.  Cluster analysis.

    B.  Simple linear regression.

    C.  Curvilinear regression.

    D.  Simplex linear programming.

The correct answer is (C). *(CIA, adapted)*

**REQUIRED:** The analytical method useful when the relationship between the independent and dependent variables is not expected to remain constant.

**DISCUSSION:** Simple regression analysis involves one independent variable. Multiple regression concerns two or more. If the relationship among the variables can be described by a straight line, the regression is linear. Otherwise, the regression is curvilinear. Linear regression is appropriate when the relationship among the variables is constant for all variables, and curvilinear regression is used when it is not. For example, rainfall may increase crop yields up to a certain point, but excessive rain may have the opposite effect.

Answer (A) is incorrect because it is not meaningful in this context. Answer (B) is incorrect because a straight line indicates a constant relationship. Answer (D) is incorrect because linear programming optimizes a revenue or cost function subject to resource constraints. The simplex method is an algorithm for finding the optimal solution.

**33.** An auditor used regression analysis to evaluate the relationship between utility costs and machine hours. The following information was developed using a computer software program:

| | |
|---|---|
| Intercept | 2,050 |
| Regression coefficient | .825 |
| Correlation coefficient | .800 |
| Standard error of the estimate | 200 |
| Number of observations | 36 |

What is the expected utility cost if the company's 10 machines will be used 2,400 hours next month?

   A.  $4,050

   B.  $4,030

   C.  $3,970

   D.  $3,830

The correct answer is (B). *(CIA, adapted)*
   **REQUIRED:** The expected utility cost.
   **DISCUSSION:** The following is the basic equation for a simple regression (y = the dependent variable, or the utility cost; a = the y-intercept, or fixed cost; b = the regression coefficient; and x = the independent variable, or machine hours):

$$y = a + bx$$

The expected utility cost is $4,030 [$2,050 + (.825 x 2,400)].
   Answer (A) is incorrect because $4,050 equals the intercept plus 10 times the standard error. Answer (C) is incorrect because $3,970 results from using the correlation coefficient instead of the regression coefficient. Answer (D) is incorrect because $3,830 equals expected utility cost minus $200.

**34.** A division uses a regression in which monthly advertising expenditures are used to predict monthly product sales (both in millions of dollars). The results show a regression coefficient for the independent variable equal to 0.8. This coefficient value indicates that

   A.  The average monthly advertising expenditure in the sample is $800,000.

   B.  When monthly advertising is at its average level, product sales will be $800,000.

   C.  On average, for every additional dollar in advertising, sales increase by $.80.

   D.  Advertising is not a good predictor of sales because the coefficient is so small.

The correct answer is (C). *(CIA, adapted)*
   **REQUIRED:** The significance of the regression coefficient for the independent variable.
   **DISCUSSION:** The regression coefficient represents the change in the dependent variable corresponding to a unit change in the independent variable. Thus, it is the slope of the regression line.
   Answer (A) is incorrect because a regression coefficient is unrelated to the means of the variables. Answer (B) is incorrect because, to predict a specific value of sales, the value of the independent variable is multiplied by the coefficient. The product is then added to the y-intercept value. Answer (D) is incorrect because the absolute size of the coefficient bears no necessary relationship to the importance of the variable.

## 16.3 Separating Fixed and Variable Costs

**35.** Thompson Company is in the process of preparing its budget for the next fiscal year. The company has had problems controlling costs in prior years and has decided to adopt a flexible budgeting system this year. Many of its costs contain both fixed and variable cost components. A method that can be used to separate costs into fixed and variable components is

   A.  Trend analysis.

   B.  Monte Carlo simulation.

   C.  Dynamic programming.

   D.  Regression analysis.

The correct answer is (D). *(CMA, adapted)*
   **REQUIRED:** The method that can be used to separate costs into fixed and variable components.
   **DISCUSSION:** The basic regression formula (y = a + bx) explains the behavior of a dependent variable (y) in terms of an independent variable (x). Fixed cost (a) corresponds to the value of y when x (the measure of activity) is zero. The coefficient of x is the variable cost.
   Answer (A) is incorrect because time series or trend analysis uses regression to find trend lines in data (e.g., sales or costs) for forecasting purposes. Answer (B) is incorrect because Monte Carlo simulation involves adding random numbers to otherwise deterministic models to simulate the uncertainty inherent in real-world situations. Answer (C) is incorrect because dynamic programming is used for problems that involve probabilistic variables and time-staged decisions, that is, decisions affected by previous decisions. It involves an iterative formulation of problems. A decision tree with probabilities for each branch illustrates a time-staged decision process that could be evaluated with dynamic programming.

**36.** Given actual amounts of a semivariable cost for various levels of output, which of the following will give the least precise mathematical measure of the fixed and variable components but be easiest to compute?

    A. Bayesian statistics.

    B. High-low method.

    C. Scattergram approach.

    D. Least squares method.

The correct answer is (B). *(Publisher)*
    **REQUIRED:** The quantitative method that most easily but least precisely separates fixed and variable costs.
    **DISCUSSION:** The high-low method uses only two observations, a representative high point and a representative low point, to determine the slope of the line defining the relationship between activity and the variable cost. Thus, it is susceptible to error but is easy to compute.
    Answer (A) is incorrect because it is a technique in which future probabilities are based upon past probabilities and occurrences. Answer (C) is incorrect because a scatter diagram may be used to estimate correlations, but it is not a mathematical approach. Answer (D) is incorrect because least squares is much more precise than high-low.

**37.** Jacob Corp. wishes to determine the fixed portion of its maintenance expense (a semivariable expense), as measured against direct labor hours, for the first 3 months of the year. The inspection costs are fixed; the adjustments necessitated by errors found during inspection account for the variable portion of the maintenance costs. Information for the first quarter is as follows:

| | Direct Labor Hours | Maintenance Expense |
|---|---|---|
| January | 34,000 | $610 |
| February | 31,000 | $585 |
| March | 34,000 | $610 |

What is the fixed portion of Jacob's maintenance expense, rounded to the nearest dollar?

    A. $283

    B. $327

    C. $258

    D. $541

The correct answer is (B). *(Publisher)*
    **REQUIRED:** The fixed portion of expense as measured against direct labor hours.
    **DISCUSSION:** The high-low method can be used to determine the fixed and variable cost components of a mixed cost. The variable cost is found by dividing the change in total cost (TC) by the change in activity, e.g., DLH. The fixed cost is found by substituting the variable cost into either of the activity/cost functions. Alternatively, the fixed cost is the cost given a zero level of activity.

$$\frac{\text{Change in TC}}{\text{Change in DLH}} \quad \frac{\$25}{3,000} = \$.00833$$

$$FC = TC - VC$$
$$FC = \$585 - (31,000 \times \$.00833) = \$327$$
$$FC = \$610 - (34,000 \times \$.00833) = \$327$$

    Answer (A) is incorrect because $283 equals variable cost for January or March. Answer (C) is incorrect because $258 equals variable cost for February. Answer (D) is incorrect because $541 equals variable cost for February and March.

**38.** The management of an airline is interested in the relationship between maintenance costs and the level of operations of its aircraft. Using regression analysis on cost and activity data collected over 12 months, the relationship below was estimated.

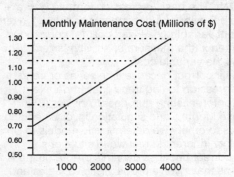

The estimated increase in the monthly maintenance cost for each additional hour of operation is

    A. $150 per hour.

    B. $300 per hour.

    C. $450 per hour.

    D. $850 per hour.

The correct answer is (A). *(CIA, adapted)*
    **REQUIRED:** The estimated increase in the monthly maintenance cost for each additional hour of operation.
    **DISCUSSION:** The change in monthly maintenance cost per hour of operation is the slope of the cost function.

$$\frac{\$1,000,000 - \$850,000}{2,000 - 1,000} = \$150 \text{ per hour}$$

    Answer (B) is incorrect because $300 per hour equals $1,150,000 minus $850,000, divided by 1,000 hours. Answer (C) is incorrect because $450 per hour equals $1,300,000 minus $850,000, divided by 1,000 hours. Answer (D) is incorrect because $850 per hour equals $850,000 divided by 1,000 hours.

Questions 39 and 40 are based on the following information. The Mulvey Company derived the following cost relationship from a regression analysis of its monthly manufacturing overhead cost.

C = $80,000 + $12M

If:  C = monthly manufacturing overhead cost
     M = machine hours

The standard error of the estimate of the regression is $6,000. The standard time required to manufacture one six-unit case of Mulvey's single product is 4 machine hours. Mulvey applies manufacturing overhead to production on the basis of machine hours, and its normal annual production is 50,000 cases.

**39.** Mulvey's estimated variable manufacturing overhead cost for a month in which scheduled production is 5,000 cases will be

A. $80,000

B. $320,000

C. $240,000

D. $360,000

The correct answer is (C). *(CMA, adapted)*
REQUIRED: The estimated variable manufacturing overhead for a month given production volume.
DISCUSSION: Each case requires 4 hours of machine time. Thus, 5,000 cases will require 20,000 hours (5,000 cases x 4). At $12 per hour, the variable costs will total $240,000 ($12 x 20,000 hrs.).
Answer (A) is incorrect because $80,000 equals the fixed cost. Answer (B) is incorrect because $320,000 equals the total cost. Answer (D) is incorrect because $360,000 assumes that the standard time is 6 hours per case.

**40.** Mulvey's predetermined fixed manufacturing overhead rate would be

A. $1.60 per machine hour.

B. $1.20 per machine hour.

C. $4.00 per machine hour.

D. $4.80 per machine hour.

The correct answer is (D). *(CMA, adapted)*
REQUIRED: The predetermined fixed overhead application rate per machine hour.
DISCUSSION: According to the regression equation, the monthly fixed costs are $80,000. On an annual basis, the total is $960,000 (12 months x 80,000). For normal production of 50,000 cases, 200,000 hours (4 hrs. x 50,000) of machine time is required. Allocating the $960,000 of fixed costs over 200,000 hours of machine time results in a cost of $4.80 per machine hour ($960,000 ÷ 200,000).
Answer (A) is incorrect because $1.60 equals $320,000 divided by 200,000 hours. Answer (B) is incorrect because $1.20 equals $240,000 divided by 200,000 hours. Answer (C) is incorrect because $4.00 equals $80,000 divided by 20,000 hours.

## 16.4 Other Forecasting Methods

**41.** To facilitate planning and budgeting, management of a travel service company wants to develop forecasts of monthly sales for the next 24 months. Based on past data, management has observed an upward trend in the level of sales. There are also seasonal variations with high sales in June, July, and August, and low sales in January, February, and March. An appropriate technique for forecasting the company's sales is

A. Time series analysis.

B. Queuing theory.

C. Linear programming.

D. Sensitivity analysis.

The correct answer is (A). *(CIA, adapted)*
REQUIRED: The appropriate forecasting technique.
DISCUSSION: In time series analysis, the dependent variable is regressed on time (the independent variable). The secular trend is the long-term change that occurs in the series. It is represented by a straight line or curve on a graph. A variety of methods include seasonal variations in this forecasting model, but most adjust data by a seasonal index.
Answer (B) is incorrect because queuing theory is used to minimize the sum of the costs of waiting in line and servicing waiting lines. Answer (C) is incorrect because linear programming optimizes a given objective function subject to constraints. Answer (D) is incorrect because sensitivity analysis studies the effects of changes in one or more variables on the results of a decision model.

**42.** What are the four components of a time series?

A.   Trend, cyclical, seasonal, and irregular.

B.   Alpha, cyclical, seasonal, and irregular.

C.   Alpha, cyclical, seasonal, and repetitive.

D.   Trend, cyclical, seasonal, and repetitive.

The correct answer is (A). *(CIA, adapted)*

**REQUIRED:** The four components of a time series.

**DISCUSSION:** Time series analysis or trend analysis relies on past experience. Changes in the value of a variable (e.g., unit sales of a product) may have several possible components. In time series analysis, the dependent variable is regressed on time (the independent variable). The secular trend is the long-term change that occurs in a series. It is represented by a straight line or curve on a graph. Seasonal variations are common in many businesses. A variety of methods include seasonal variations in a forecasting model, but most methods adjust data by a seasonal index. Cyclical fluctuations are variations in the level of activity in business periods. Whereas some of these fluctuations are beyond the control of the firm, they need to be considered in forecasting. They are usually incorporated as index numbers. Irregular or random variations are any variations not included in the three categories above. Business can be affected by random happenings, e.g., weather, strikes, or fires.

Answers (B), (C), and (D) are incorrect because alpha and repetitive are not meaningful terms in this context.

**43.** The four components of time series data are secular trend, cyclical variation, seasonality, and random variation. The seasonality in the data can be removed by

A.   Multiplying the data by a seasonality factor.

B.   Ignoring it.

C.   Taking the weighted average over four time periods.

D.   Subtracting a seasonality factor from the data.

The correct answer is (C). *(CMA, adapted)*

**REQUIRED:** The means by which seasonality can be removed from time series data.

**DISCUSSION:** Seasonal variations are common in many businesses. A variety of methods exist for including seasonal variations in a forecasting model, but most methods divide by a seasonal index. Alternatively, seasonal variations can be removed from data by using a weighted average of several time periods instead of data from individual periods.

Answer (A) is incorrect because adding or subtracting a seasonality factor to a forecast based on trend analysis is a means of adjusting for seasonality. Answer (B) is incorrect because seasonality factors cannot be ignored; they are reflected in the data and must be considered for a model to be accurate. Answer (D) is incorrect because the seasonality adjustment for a single season's data may be an increase or a decrease.

**44.** Violation of which assumption underlying regression analysis is prevalent in time series analysis?

A.   Variance of error term is constant.

B.   Error terms are independent.

C.   Distribution of error terms is normal.

D.   Expected value of error term equals zero.

The correct answer is (B). *(Publisher)*

**REQUIRED:** The assumption frequently violated in time series analysis.

**DISCUSSION:** Time series analysis is a regression model in which the independent variable is time. In time series analysis, the value of the next time period is frequently dependent on the value of the time period before that. Hence, the error terms are usually correlated or dependent on the prior period; i.e., they are characterized by autocorrelation (serial correlation).

Answers (A), (C), and (D) are incorrect because the other three major requirements of regression analysis -- constant variance of the error term, normal distribution of the error term, and an expected value of the error term equal to zero -- are usually met.

**45.** An internal auditor for a large automotive parts retailer wishes to perform a risk analysis and wants to use an appropriate statistical tool to help identify stores that are at variance with the majority of stores. The most appropriate statistical tool to use would be

A. Linear time series analysis.

B. Cross-sectional regression analysis.

C. Cross tabulations with chi square analysis of significance.

D. Time series multiple regression analysis to identify changes in individual stores over time.

The correct answer is (B). *(CIA, adapted)*

**REQUIRED:** The best statistical tool for identifying stores that deviate from the majority.

**DISCUSSION:** Time series data pertain to a given entity over a number of prior time periods. Cross-sectional data, however, pertain to different entities for a given time period or at a given time. Thus, cross-sectional regression analysis is the most appropriate statistical tool because it compares attributes of all stores' operating statistics at one moment in time.

Answer (A) is incorrect because linear time series analysis is inapplicable. It is a simple model that compares data for an individual store over time. Answer (C) is incorrect because cross tabulations have to be built on a model of expectations. Unless the model is built, the analysis is not useful. Answer (D) is incorrect because the objective is to compare stores at one moment in time. Multiple regression time series analysis compares the performance of an individual store over a period of time.

**46.** The moving-average method of forecasting

A. Is a cross-sectional forecasting method.

B. Regresses the variable of interest on a related variable to develop a forecast.

C. Derives final forecasts by adjusting the initial forecast based on the smoothing constant.

D. Includes each new observation in the average as it becomes available and discards the oldest observation.

The correct answer is (D). *(CIA, adapted)*

**REQUIRED:** The item best describing the moving-average method of forecasting.

**DISCUSSION:** The simple moving-average method is a smoothing technique that uses the experience of the past N periods (through time period t) to forecast a value for the next period. Thus, the average includes each new observation and discards the oldest observation. The forecast formula for the next period (for time period t+1) is the sum of the last N observations divided by N.

Answer (A) is incorrect because cross-sectional regression analysis examines relationships among large amounts of data (e.g., many or different production methods or locations) at a particular moment in time. Answer (B) is incorrect because regression analysis relates the forecast to changes in particular variables. Answer (C) is incorrect because, under exponential smoothing, each forecast equals the sum of the last observation times the smoothing constant, plus the last forecast times one minus the constant.

**47.** As part of a risk analysis, an auditor wishes to forecast the percentage growth in next month's sales for a particular plant using the past 30 months' sales results. Significant changes in the organization affecting sales volumes were made within the last 9 months. The most effective analysis technique to use would be

A. Unweighted moving average.

B. Exponential smoothing.

C. Queuing theory.

D. Linear regression analysis.

The correct answer is (B). *(CIA, adapted)*

**REQUIRED:** The most effective analysis technique to forecast the percentage growth in next month's sales.

**DISCUSSION:** Under exponential smoothing, each forecast equals the sum of the last observation times the smoothing constant, plus the last forecast times one minus the constant. Thus, exponential means that greater weight is placed on the most recent data, with the weights of all data falling off exponentially as the data age. This feature is important because of the organizational changes that affected sales volume.

Answer (A) is incorrect because an unweighted average will not give more importance to more recent data. Answer (C) is incorrect because queuing theory is used to minimize the cost of waiting lines. Answer (D) is incorrect because linear regression analysis determines the equation for the relationship among variables. It does not give more importance to more recent data.

## 16.5 Multiple Calculations

Questions 48 through 51 are based on the following information. Below is an examination of last year's financial statements of MacKenzie Park Co., which manufactures and sells trivets. Labor hours and production costs for the last 4 months of the year, which are representative for the year, were as follows:

| Month | Labor Hours | Total Production Costs |
|---|---|---|
| September | 2,500 | $ 20,000 |
| October | 3,500 | 25,000 |
| November | 4,500 | 30,000 |
| December | 3,500 | 25,000 |
| Total | 14,000 | $100,000 |

Based upon the information given and using the least squares method of computation with the letters listed below, select the best answer for each question.

If: a = Fixed production costs per month
    b = Variable production costs per labor hour
    n = Number of months
    x = Labor hours per month
    y = Total monthly production costs
    Σ = Summation

**48.** The equation(s) required for applying the least squares method of computation of fixed and variable production costs can be expressed as

A. $\Sigma xy = a\Sigma x + b\Sigma x^2$

B. $\Sigma y = na + b\Sigma x$

C. $y = a + bx^2$
   $\Sigma y = na + b\Sigma x$

D. $\Sigma xy = a\Sigma x + b\Sigma x^2$
   $\Sigma y = na + b\Sigma x$

The correct answer is (D). *(CPA, adapted)*
**REQUIRED:** The equation(s) expressing the relationship between fixed and variable costs.
**DISCUSSION:** The least squares method of computing fixed and variable production costs minimizes the sum of the squares of the vertical deviation from the points to a line depicted on a scatter diagram. The least squares equation minimizes the deviation from the expected linear relationship to provide the closest approximation of the relationship of fixed and variable production costs. The normal equations for least squares analysis are given in (D).
Answers (A) and (B) are incorrect because one of the equations is omitted. Answer (C) is incorrect because the first equation should be $\Sigma xy = a\Sigma x + b\Sigma x^2$.

**49.** The cost function derived by the simple least squares method

A. Is linear.

B. Must be tested for minima and maxima.

C. Is parabolic.

D. Indicates maximum costs at the function's point of inflection.

The correct answer is (A). *(CPA, adapted)*
**REQUIRED:** The characteristic of the cost function derived by the least squares method.
**DISCUSSION:** The cost function derived by the least squares method is linear, containing both fixed and variable elements. Although it is useful over the relevant range, it is probably not completely accurate.
Answer (B) is incorrect because using calculus to test for minimum and maximum points is not appropriate in a linear function. Answer (C) is incorrect because the function is not curvilinear. Answer (D) is incorrect because, if maximum costs are at the function's point of inflection, the relationship is curvilinear.

**50.** Monthly production costs can be expressed

A. $y = ax + b$

B. $y = a + bx$

C. $y = b + ax$

D. $y = \Sigma a + bx$

The correct answer is (B). *(CPA, adapted)*
**REQUIRED:** The equation expressing monthly production costs.
**DISCUSSION:** The least squares method of computation results in an equation with a dependent variable (y), a constant (a), plus a variable coefficient (b), and an independent variable (x). Thus, $y = a + bx$ expresses total monthly production cost (y) in terms of fixed cost (a) plus the variable cost (b) times the activity level (x).
Answers (A) and (C) are incorrect because b is the coefficient of x. Answer (D) is incorrect because the summation symbol should be omitted.

**51.** Using the least squares method of computation, the fixed monthly production cost of trivets is approximately

A. $100,000

B. $25,000

C. $7,500

D. $20,000

The correct answer is (C). *(CPA, adapted)*

**REQUIRED:** The fixed monthly production cost.

**DISCUSSION:** Using the least squares method, the fixed monthly production cost is the constant. It can be calculated by substituting into the equations below.

$$a = \bar{y} - b\bar{x} \qquad b = \frac{\Sigma xy - n\bar{x}\bar{y}}{\Sigma x^2 - n\bar{x}^2}$$

| x | y | xy | x² |
|---|---|---|---|
| 2,500 | $ 20,000 | $ 50,000,000 | $ 6,250,000 |
| 3,500 | 25,000 | 87,500,000 | 12,250,000 |
| 4,500 | 30,000 | 135,000,000 | 20,250,000 |
| 3,500 | 25,000 | 87,500,000 | 12,250,000 |
| 14,000 | $100,000 | $360,000,000 | $51,000,000 |

$\bar{x} = 3,500$; $\bar{y} = \$25,000$; $n = 4$

$$b = \frac{\$360,000,000 - 4(3,500)(\$25,000)}{\$51,000,000 - 4(3,500)^2} = \$5$$

$a = \$25,000 - \$5(3,500) = \$7,500$

Answer (A) is incorrect because $100,000 is $\Sigma y$.

Answer (B) is incorrect because $25,000 is $\bar{y}$. Answer (D) is incorrect because $20,000 equals total cost for September.

Questions 52 through 59 are based on the following information. Armer Company is accumulating data to be used in preparing its annual profit plan for the coming year. The cost behavior pattern of the maintenance costs must be determined. The accounting staff has suggested that linear regression be employed to derive an equation in the form of $y = a + bx$ for maintenance costs. Data regarding the maintenance hours and costs for last year and the results of the regression analysis are as follows:

| | Hours of Activity | Maintenance Costs |
|---|---|---|
| January | 480 | $ 4,200 |
| February | 320 | 3,000 |
| March | 400 | 3,600 |
| April | 300 | 2,820 |
| May | 500 | 4,350 |
| June | 310 | 2,960 |
| July | 320 | 3,030 |
| August | 520 | 4,470 |
| September | 490 | 4,260 |
| October | 470 | 4,050 |
| November | 350 | 3,300 |
| December | 340 | 3,160 |
| Sum | 4,800 | $43,200 |
| Average | 400 | 3,600 |

Average cost per hour $(43,200 \div 4,800) = \$9.00$

| | |
|---|---|
| a coefficient | 684.65 |
| b coefficient | 7.2884 |
| Standard error of the a coefficient | 49.515 |
| Standard error of the b coefficient | .12126 |
| Standard error of the estimate | 34.469 |
| $r^2$ | .99724 |
| t-value a | 13.827 |
| t-value b | 60.105 |

Single-Tailed Values of t

| Degrees of Freedom | $t_{.100}$ | $t_{.05}$ | $t_{.025}$ | $t_{.01}$ |
|---|---|---|---|---|
| 8 | $1_{.40}$ | $1_{.86}$ | $2_{.31}$ | $2_{.90}$ |
| 9 | $1_{.38}$ | $1_{.83}$ | $2_{.26}$ | $2_{.82}$ |
| 10 | $1_{.37}$ | $1_{.81}$ | $2_{.23}$ | $2_{.76}$ |
| 11 | $1_{.36}$ | $1_{.80}$ | $2_{.20}$ | $2_{.72}$ |
| 12 | $1_{.36}$ | $1_{.78}$ | $2_{.18}$ | $2_{.68}$ |
| 13 | $1_{.35}$ | $1_{.77}$ | $2_{.16}$ | $2_{.65}$ |
| 14 | $1_{.35}$ | $1_{.76}$ | $2_{.15}$ | $2_{.62}$ |

**52.** The statistic used to determine if the estimate of the slope is significantly different from zero is the

   A.  Coefficient of determination.

   B.  Standard error of the a coefficient.

   C.  Standard error of the estimate.

   D.  t-value of b.

The correct answer is (D). *(Publisher)*
   **REQUIRED:** The statistic used to determine if the slope is significantly different from zero.
   **DISCUSSION:** The t-value of b (the slope of the line of the equation) states how far removed the estimate of b is from zero in terms of standard deviations, given the assumption that the true value of b is zero. The greater the t-value of b, the greater the probability that zero is not the true value.
   Answer (A) is incorrect because it is the portion of total variance explained by the independent variable. Answer (B) is incorrect because it describes the variance of the constant term a. Answer (C) is incorrect because it measures the variability of the actual values around the least squares line.

**53.** If Armer Company uses the high-low method of analysis, the equation for the relationship between hours of activity and maintenance cost will be

   A.  $y = 400 + 9.0x$

   B.  $y = 570 + 7.5x$

   C.  $y = 3,600 + 400x$

   D.  $y = 570 + 9.0x$

The correct answer is (B). *(CMA, adapted)*
   **REQUIRED:** The equation for the relationship based on the high-low method.
   **DISCUSSION:** The high-low method compares the highest and the lowest activity levels with the highest and lowest maintenance costs. The difference establishes the coefficient of x. Thus, b is 7.5 [($4,470 − $2,820) ÷ (520 hr. − 300 hr.)], and the constant term a is $570 [$4,470 − ($7.5 x 520 hr.)].
   Answers (A), (C), and (D) are incorrect because 400 is the average activity, and 9.0 equals $3,600 average cost divided by 400.

**54.** Assume the t-value of b is 3.0 and that maintenance costs are expected to increase as hours of activity increase. If the null hypothesis is that b is zero, is the estimate of b significantly different from zero?

    A. No, with 95% confidence.

    B. No, with 99% confidence.

    C. Yes, with 95% confidence.

    D. Yes, because the estimate of b is positive.

The correct answer is (C). *(Publisher)*

    **REQUIRED:** The correct interpretation of the t-value.

    **DISCUSSION:** If the null hypothesis is that the true value of b is zero, the formula below indicates how much the observed estimate of b differs from zero in terms of standard deviations.

$$\frac{\hat{b} - 0}{\text{Standard deviation of b}}$$

The greater the difference, the lower the probability that the true value of b equals zero. A t-table may be used to find the critical t-value needed to assure the desired level of confidence. The absolute value of the statistic derived from the formula must be equal to or greater than the value from the t-table. Because the null hypothesis that b is zero implies a two-tailed test (the alternate hypothesis is that b is not zero), at a 95% confidence level, the appropriate t-value is found in the $t_{.025}$ column [$(1.0 - .95) \div 2$] and the 10 degrees of freedom row (n–2 parameters tested = 12 – 2). Because 3.0 (the given t-value) is greater than 2.23, the upper critical value for this two-sided test, one can be at least 95% confident that the estimate of b is different from zero.

    Answers (A) and (B) are incorrect because the null hypothesis can be rejected with 95% confidence. Answer (D) is incorrect because b may be negative.

**55.** Based upon the data derived from the regression analysis, 420 maintenance hours in a month would mean the maintenance costs would be budgeted at

    A. $3,780

    B. $3,461

    C. $3,797

    D. $3,746

The correct answer is (D). *(CMA, adapted)*

    **REQUIRED:** The budgeted maintenance cost at the given activity level.

    **DISCUSSION:** Substituting the given data into the regression equation results in a budgeted cost of $3,746 (rounded to the nearest dollar).

$$y = a + bx$$
$$y = 684.65 + 7.2884(420)$$
$$y = \$3,746$$

    Answers (A), (B), and (C) are incorrect because the budgeted maintenance costs are $3,746.

**56.** The coefficient of correlation for Armer's regression equation for the maintenance activities is

    A. $34.469 \div 49.515$

    B. .99724

    C. $\sqrt{.99724}$

    D. $(.99724)^2$

The correct answer is (C). *(CMA, adapted)*

    **REQUIRED:** The coefficient of correlation for the maintenance activities.

    **DISCUSSION:** The coefficient of correlation determines the relative strength of the relationship between two variables. It equals the square root of $r^2$ (the coefficient of determination). Given that $r^2$ is .99724, the coefficient of correlation is $\sqrt{.99724}$.

    Answer (A) is incorrect because 34.469 is the standard error of the estimate, and 49.515 is the standard error of a. Answer (B) is incorrect because .99724 is $r^2$. Answer (D) is incorrect because the square root of $r^2$ should be taken.

Questions 57 through 59 are based on the information presented on page 614.

**57.** The percentage of the total variance that can be explained by the regression equation is

A.  99.724%

B.  69.613%

C.  12.126%

D.  99.862%

The correct answer is (A). *(CMA, adapted)*

**REQUIRED:** The percentage of total variance that can be explained by the regression equation.

**DISCUSSION:** The percentage of the total variance that can be explained by the regression equation is $r^2$, or the coefficient of determination. It is expressed as the percentage of the total variance that is equal to one minus the proportion of the total variance not explained. Here, $r^2$ is given as .99724, or 99.724%.

Answer (B) is incorrect because 69.613% equals the standard error of the estimate divided by the standard error of a. Answer (C) is incorrect because .12126 is the standard error of b. Answer (D) is incorrect because 99.862% is the square root of $r^2$.

**58.** Armer can be 95% confident that what interval contains the true value of the marginal maintenance cost?

A.  $7.02 – $7.56

B.  $7.17 – $7.41

C.  $7.07 – $7.51

D.  $6.95 – $7.62

The correct answer is (A). *(CMA, adapted)*

**REQUIRED:** The 95% confidence interval for the marginal maintenance cost.

**DISCUSSION:** Marginal maintenance cost is the coefficient of b ($7.2884). The 95% confidence interval for a two-tailed test may be constructed using the single-tailed value of t. The interval is two-tailed because both ends of the possible range are of concern. Thus, the $t_{.025}$ column is used because 2.5% of the distribution $[(1.0 - .95) \div 2]$ is in each tail. The number of degrees of freedom equals n (the number of time periods) minus the number of parameters estimated (a and b) in the least squares equation. Hence, the appropriate t-value at 10 degrees of freedom (12 – 2) in the $t_{.025}$ column is 2.23. The standard error of the b coefficient is $.12126, and the 95% confidence interval is $7.2884 plus or minus $.2704098 ($.12126 x 2.23). The interval is therefore $7.02 ($7.2884 – $.2704098) to $7.56 ($7.2804 + $.2704098).

Answer (B) is incorrect because $7.17 – $7.41 is based on a t-value of 1.0. Answer (C) is incorrect because $7.07 – $7.51 is based on a t-value of 1.81. Answer (D) is incorrect because $6.95 – $7.62 is based on a t-value of 2.76.

**59.** At 400 hours of activity, Armer management can be approximately two-thirds confident that the maintenance costs will be in the range of

A.  $3,550.48 – $3,649.52

B.  $3,551.70 – $3,648.30

C.  $3,586.18 – $3,613.83

D.  $3,565.54 – $3,634.47

The correct answer is (D). *(CMA, adapted)*

**REQUIRED:** The 66⅔% confidence interval for actual average maintenance costs.

**DISCUSSION:** A 66⅔% confidence interval can be established by adding and subtracting approximately one standard error of the estimate to/from the predicted value of maintenance costs. When activity is 400 hours, the predicted maintenance cost is $3,600 [$684.65 + ($7.2884 x 400)]. The standard error of the estimate is given as $34.469. The 66⅔% confidence interval is therefore $3,600 ± $34.469, or $3,565.54 to $3,634.47.

Answer (A) is incorrect because $3,550.48 – $3,649.52 is based on the standard error of a. Answer (B) is incorrect because $3,551.70 – $3,648.30 adds (subtracts) the sum of the standard error of the estimate and the t-value of a. Answer (C) is incorrect because $3,586.18 – $3,613.83 adds (subtracts) the t-value of a.

# CHAPTER SEVENTEEN
# LINEAR PROGRAMMING

**Linear programming** is a technique used to optimize an **objective function**, that is, to maximize a revenue or profit function or to minimize a cost function, subject to constraints, e.g., limited (scarce) resources or minimum/maximum levels of production, performance, etc. In business, linear programming is used for planning resource allocations. Managers are often faced with problems of selecting the most profitable or least costly way to use available resources.

## 17.1 LINEAR PROGRAMMING CONCEPTS

A.  EXAMPLE: A manufacturer should minimize production costs while satisfying production requirements, maintaining required inventory levels, staying within production capacities, and using available employees. The objective function is the production cost to be minimized; the constraints are production requirements, inventory levels, production capacity, and available employees.

　　1.  Other business applications include

　　　　a.  Selecting a product mix
　　　　b.  Blending chemical products
　　　　c.  Scheduling flight crews
　　　　d.  Assigning jobs to machines
　　　　e.  Determining transportation routes

　　2.  The conditions that restrict the optimal value of the objective function are the **constraints**.

　　　　a.  A **shadow price** is the amount by which the value of the optimal solution of the objective function in a linear programming problem will change if a one-unit change is made in a binding constraint.

　　　　　　1)  A nonbinding constraint is one that has excess capacity; the optimal solution does not use all of the given resource. The shadow price for a nonbinding constraint is zero because a one-unit change will not affect the optimal solution when excess capacity exists.

　　　　　　2)  The calculation of shadow prices is a simple example of **sensitivity analysis**, which is any procedure to test the responsiveness of the solution indicated by a model to changes in variables, alternative decisions, or errors.

　　3.  The unknowns used to construct the objective function and the constraints are the decision **variables**. In the example beginning on page 623, the variables are the two products, G and J.

　　　　a.  The values of the variables are limited by the constraints.

　　4.  Values that are fixed for purposes of solving the model (but are not permanently fixed) are **cost/profit coefficients** for the objective function, **technical coefficients** for the constraints, and the **constants** on the right-hand side of the constraints.

5.    When the number of constraint equations equals the number of variables, a unique solution exists.  When the number of variables exceeds the number of constraint equations, an infinite number of possible solutions usually exists.

   a.    Values of the variables are the outputs of the linear programming process.

   b.    The constraint equations usually reflect the types of input or types of resources being allocated, e.g., available machine hours or raw materials.

   c.    The objective of linear programming is to choose the best solution from a potentially infinite number of possibilities.

6.    Management accountants should recognize situations in which linear programming may be applicable.  When an application is attempted, qualified operations research experts should assist in providing guidance in formulating and solving the problem.  Linear programming is a powerful planning tool for management, but it is complex and usually requires the use of computer software.

B.    Several methods are available to solve linear programming problems.

1.    The **graphical method**, although the easiest technique, is limited to problems with two variables.

2.    The **algebraic method** is a trial-and-error technique.  Pairs of constraints are solved algebraically to find their intersection.  The values of the decision variables are then substituted into the objective function and compared to find the best combination.

   a.    The basic rule is that the optimal solution will be at the intersection of two or more constraint equations.

   b.    Thus, all intersections can be computed and each solution evaluated in the objective function to determine which solution is optimal.  See the graphical example in Module 17.2 beginning on page 623.

3.    The **simplex method** is the technique most commonly used to solve linear programming problems.  It is an algorithm to move from one corner solution to a better corner solution.  When a better solution cannot be found, the optimal solution has been reached.

   a.    The simplex method relies on an area of mathematics called matrix algebra.  The equations that form the constraints are arranged in a matrix of coefficients and manipulated as a group with matrix algebra.

   b.    Almost all practical applications of linear programming require the use of computers.  Most computer facilities have a linear programming package that uses the simplex algorithm to find the optimal solution.

C. **Transportation Method**

1.   The transportation model applies to a special type of LP problem.  It concerns physical movement (transportation) of goods from sources of supply (such as factories) to destinations (warehouses).

  a.   EXAMPLE:  A fleet of trucks may be available for daily deliveries in a city.  Each day the transportation manager must determine the best route for each truck.  Many possible combinations of trucks and destinations satisfy the constraints of meeting all deliveries with the available trucks, but the manager would like to have the minimum cost combination.  In effect, the manager must allocate the available trucks (scarce resources) to the required destinations in a way that minimizes costs.

2.   The objective function includes the transportation cost of each item from each source to each destination.

  a.   The constraints are the output for each supply point and the demand of each destination.

  b.   EXAMPLE:  A manufacturer has four plants.  Assume that each plant could ship products to any of 20 warehouses.  Each plant has a maximum capacity, and each warehouse has a minimum demand.  Management would like to know how much should be shipped from each plant to each warehouse to minimize transportation cost.

  c.   To formulate a general linear programming model, the amount to be shipped from each plant to each warehouse would have to be stated as a separate variable.  The result would be 80 variables (4 plants x 20 warehouses).  Each plant's capacity and each warehouse's demand would be a constraint, giving 24 constraints (4 plant constraints + 20 warehouse constraints).

3.   The **assignment method** is a special case of the transportation method.  It is used to assign employees to jobs, jobs to machines, sales associates to territories, bidders to contracts, etc.

  a.   The difference from the transportation method is that each agent (employee, machine, etc.) can be assigned to only one task.

  b.   The purpose of the assignment is to optimize a given objective, such as minimizing cost, minimizing time, or maximizing profits.

  c.   The assignment model can be modified to accommodate certain variations.  They include the following:

  1)   Tasks exceed the available number of agents.
  2)   Certain assignments are unacceptable.
  3)   More than one agent may be required for some tasks.

4. **Vogel's Approximation**, or the **penalty method**, solves transportation problems easily. The name penalty method comes from the amount that must be paid if the lowest cost alternative is not selected in each row and each column.

   a. EXAMPLE: Assume that a company has two factories that produce 18 and 14 units of product, respectively, during a period of time. Three distribution warehouses demand 15, 10, and 7 units, respectively, during the same period. The table below depicts this information along with the shipping costs per unit (e.g., $4 to ship one unit from factory 1 to warehouse C). The objective is to minimize total shipping costs. The penalties (in dollars) are shown in parentheses to the right of, and below, the table.

| to \ from | A | B | C | Supply | |
|---|---|---|---|---|---|
| 1 | $8 | $5 | $4 | 18 | (1) |
| 2 | $5 | $6 | $7 | 14 | (1) |
| Demand | 15 | 10 | 7 | 32 / 32 | |
| | (3) | (1) | (3) | | |

   1) For row 1: If the lowest cost alternative is not used ($4 for C), the shipment must go to B, whose cost of shipping is $1 higher than shipping to C. The firm would suffer a $1 penalty for not selecting the lowest cost box. For column A, the penalty would be $3 ($8 -- $5) if the lowest cost box is not used.

   2) The objective under the penalty method is to avoid the highest penalties; those columns or rows where the highest penalties might occur are filled first. Because columns A and C have the highest penalties, one of these (it does not matter which) should be filled first. Choose column C. The lowest cost box in the selected column should be filled with the maximum possible number of units. The maximum that can be placed into box 1C is 7 units because warehouse C only needs 7 units; this step eliminates column C from further consideration. Draw a line through column C and recompute the penalties for the remaining columns and rows (if necessary) as shown below.

| to \ from | A | B | C | Supply | | |
|---|---|---|---|---|---|---|
| 1 | $8 | $5 | $4  7 | 18 | (1) | (3) |
| 2 | $5 | $6 | $7 | 14 | (1) | |
| Demand | 15 | 10 | 7 | 32 / 32 | | |
| | (3) | (1) | (3) | | | |

3) Because column A still shares the highest penalty, fill its lowest cost box to the maximum extent possible; i.e., assign 14 units to box 2A. The row 2 total supply is 14, thus limiting the number of units that can be assigned to box 2A. This assignment of 14 units equals the row 2 constraint, so row 2 is crossed out (it no longer needs to be considered).

4) The final units are then assigned to row 1, columns A and B, as shown in the following table:

| to \ from | A | B | C | Supply | | |
|---|---|---|---|---|---|---|
| 1 | $8   1 | $5   10 | $4   7 | 18 | (1) | (3) |
| 2 | $5   14 | $6 | $7 | 14 | (1) | |
| Demand | 15 | 10 | 7 | 32 / 32 | | |
| | (3) | (1) | (3) | | | |

5) The total shipping costs based on the assignments can be calculated by multiplying the number of units shipped times the shipping cost per unit, as follows:

$$1(\$8) + 10(\$5) + 7(\$4) + 14(\$5) = \$156$$

6) The use of the penalty method resulted in the optimal solution in this example, which is not always true. The penalty method will occasionally result in a very good solution, but not the optimum. There is a quantitative technique to test for the optimality of a solution, but it is quite complicated and beyond the scope of this discussion.

## D. Goal Programming

1. Goal programming was first introduced as a specialized type of linear programming to solve problems that had no feasible solution under regular linear programming.

2. Goal programming permits an ordinal specification (ranking) and solution to problems with multiple goals.

   a. With its ability to incorporate multiple goals, the method has the potential for solving problems with both financial and nonfinancial goals.

E.   **Integer Programming**

1.   Integer programming (IP) concerns problems in which some variables are not continuous. Linear programming, on the other hand, assumes that all variables are continuous and all functions are linear (i.e., graphed with straight lines). Variables are therefore allowed to take fractional values; 9, 9.367, and 10 are all possible values. In integer programming, fractions are not possible.

   a.   EXAMPLE: An oil company may be able to build 12 or 13 gas stations on a stretch of highway, but the meaning of an optimal solution of 12.72 gas stations is unclear.

   b.   Integer programming problems are also known as **discrete** models because the variables take on discrete, noncontinuous values.

2.   One way to solve IP problems is to solve them as LP problems and round to satisfy the integrality condition.

   a.   In the example, the decision might be to build 13 gas stations by rounding 12.72 to 13.0.
   b.   Rounding raises several problems.

      1)   The rounded solution may violate constraints.

      2)   The rounded solution may be farther from the optimal solution than some other integer combination.

3.   A certain class of IP problems concerns variables that are constrained to take on values of 1 or 0, and no other values. These are "yes or no" or "go/no-go" decisions. This class of problems may be solved only with algorithms designed to handle these constraints. Rounding is never acceptable because the error induced would be too great.

F.   **Dynamic Programming**

1.   **Dynamic programming** is an approach to solving problems, not a particular algorithm. It divides a large mathematical model into smaller, more manageable pieces in such a way that, once the smaller problems have been solved, the result is the optimal solution to the overall model. This type of model is useful for problems that involve multistage decisions, that is, decisions affected by previous decisions.

   a.   Typically, dynamic programming is applied to decisions involving fewer variables and constraints than LP.

   b.   Dynamic programming is useful for such problems as

      1)   Inventory reordering rules
      2)   Production scheduling in the face of fluctuating demand
      3)   Spare parts level determination
      4)   Capital budgeting for new ventures
      5)   Systematic search for scarce resources
      6)   Finding the shortest route through a network

2.   The key features of dynamic programming problems are

   a.   The probabilistic (stochastic) nature of the variables. However, deterministic variations exist.

   b.   The iterative formulation of the problems. The optimal solution is reached by a repetitive process.

3.   A decision tree with probabilities of occurrence for each branch is a good example of a time-staged decision process that could be evaluated with dynamic programming.

## 17.2 GRAPHS

A.   **LP** EXAMPLE:  A company produces products G and J.  Product G contributes $5,000 per unit sold and product J contributes $4,000 per unit sold.

1.   The company seeks to maximize profits, so the objective function is

Maximize 5G + 4J (the maximum profit in thousands of dollars).

2.   The objective function is subject to the following constraints:

G +   J  ≥  5        (minimal production requirement)

G        ≤  3J        (market balance requirement)

10G + 15J  ≤  150    (production capacity constraint)

G, J  ≥  0        (nonnegativity constraint)

3.   **Graphical solution**.  To plot this set of constraints,

a.   Change inequalities to equalities.
b.   Plot the equalities.
c.   Identify the correct side of the line for the original inequalities.

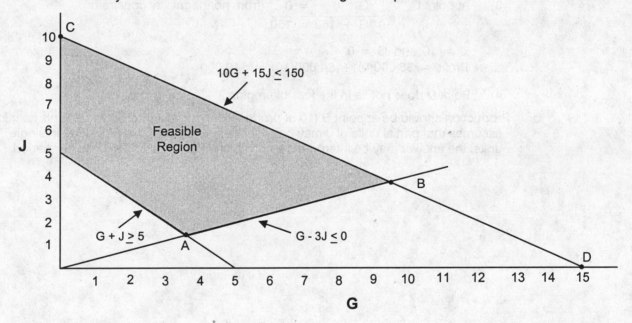

4.  **Algebraic solution**. The combination of G and J that maximizes the objective function will occur at one of the extreme points or corners of the feasible region.

    a.  Simultaneously solving the constraints intersecting at those corners and substituting into the objective function,

        1)  At point A:

            $$G + J = 5$$
            $$-G + 3J = 0$$
            $$\overline{\phantom{-G + }4J = 5}$$

            $$J = 1.25 \text{ and } G = 3.75$$
            $$\text{Profit} = \$5,000(3.75) + \$4,000(1.25) = \underline{\$23,750}$$

        2)  At point B:

            $$G - 3J = 0 \longrightarrow \qquad 5G - 15J = 0$$
            $$\underline{10G + 15J = 150} \qquad + \underline{10G + 15J = 150}$$
            $$\qquad\qquad\qquad\qquad 15G \qquad\quad = 150$$

            $$G = 10 \text{ and } J = 3.333$$
            $$\text{Profit} = \$5,000(10) + \$4,000(3.333) = \underline{\$63,333}$$

        3)  At point C:

            $$\underline{G \qquad\quad = 0} \quad \text{(from nonnegativity constraint)}$$
            $$10G + 15J = 150$$

            $$J = 10 \text{ and } G = 0$$
            $$\text{Profit} = \$5,000(0) + \$4,000(10) = \underline{\$40,000}$$

        4)  Point D does not lie in the feasible region.

    b.  Production should be at point B (10 of product G and 3.333 of product J). This solution assumes that partial units of J may be produced. If product J is produced in single units, the answer may be interpreted as production at a rate of $3\frac{1}{3}$ units per period.

## 17.3 and 17.4 FORMULATION, CALCULATIONS

A.  **The simplex method** is a systematic means of examining the corners (also called vertices or extreme points) of the feasible region while in search of the optimal solution. The algorithm always moves in the direction of improving the solution and terminates at the optimal solution.

    1.   The algorithm proceeds in several iterations.

        a.   Iteration I seeks an initial corner. If no corner is found, the problem is inconsistent and the algorithm terminates.

        b.   Iteration II generates a set of corners adjacent to the initial corner (found in Phase I). The objective function will not become less optimal and will ordinarily become more optimal at each successive corner.

        c.   The algorithm terminates after the optimal corner is reached.

B.  EXAMPLE (adapted from a CPA question): The Wineroot Company manufactures two garden benches, small and large. Each model is processed as follows:

|             | Machining | Polishing |
|-------------|-----------|-----------|
| Small (X)   | 2 hours   | 3 hours   |
| Large (Y)   | 4 hours   | 3 hours   |

The available time for processing the two models is 100 hours a week in the Machining Department and 90 hours a week in the Polishing Department. The contribution margin expected is $5 for X and $7 for Y.

    1.   The objective function is the formula for the maximum total contribution margin. Because each X produces a $5 CM, and each Y produces a $7 CM, the total CM will be 5X + 7Y. This function is to be maximized.

    2.   A constraint equation can be set up for the Machining Department, which has a total of 100 hours available each week. Each X requires 2 hours of time from that department, and each Y requires 4 hours. Accordingly, the total Machining Department time taken by production is 2X + 4Y, which must be equal to or less than the 100 hours available.

$$2X + 4Y \leq 100$$

    3.   The constraint equation for the Polishing Department is found in a similar manner. The Polishing Department has a total of 90 hours available each week. Each unit of X or Y requires 3 hours. Thus, the constraint for this department is that 3X + 3Y must be equal to or less than 90.

$$3X + 3Y \leq 90$$

4.  Both constraints are inequality expressions of the form "less than or equal to."  To transform them to an equality form, a positive variable called the **slack variable** must be added to the left-hand side of each constraint.

$$2X + 4Y \qquad \leq 100$$
$$2X + 4Y + S_1 \quad = 100$$

$$3X + 3Y \qquad \leq 90$$
$$3X + 3Y + S_2 \quad = 90$$

a.  In general, each slack variable makes zero contribution to the value of the solution.

b.  Before the tableau is constructed, the linear programming problem may be restated as follows:

$$\text{Maximize } 5X + 7Y + 0S_1 + 0S_2 \text{ subject to}$$
$$2X + 4Y + 1S_1 + 0S_2 = 100$$
$$3X + 3Y + 0S_1 + 1S_2 = 90$$

$$\text{If:} \qquad X \geq 0$$
$$Y \geq 0$$
$$S_1, S_2 \geq 0$$

5.  The initial simplex tableau (in its most common format) can be constructed from the Wineroot Company's LP problem.  Rows run horizontally and columns run vertically.

| $C_j$ | 5 | 7 | 0 | 0 | RHS |
|---|---|---|---|---|---|
| Variables | X | Y | $S_1$ | $S_2$ | |
| CB | | | | | |
| 0 | 2 | 4 | 1 | 0 | 100 |
| 0 | 3 | 3 | 0 | 1 | 90 |
| $Z_j$ | 0 | 0 | 0 | 0 | 0 |
| $C_j - Z_j$ | 5 | 7 | 0 | 0 | |

a.  After converting the constraint equations to equalities, the tableau is constructed beginning with the variables row, which consists first of the constraint variables (X and Y) and then the slack variables ($S_1$ and $S_2$).  It is essentially a row of labels.

b.  The $C_j$ row lists the payoff coefficients for a profit-maximizing problem (or the cost coefficients for a cost-minimizing problem) given by the coefficients of the objective function.

1)  The slack variables have payoff/cost coefficients of 0.

2)  Thus, in constructing this tableau, the $C_j$ row consists of the coefficients from the objective function ($5X + 7Y + 0S_1 + 0S_2$).

3)  The $C_j$ row is 5, 7, 0, 0.

c. The machining and polishing constraint rows in the simplex tableau are formed from the constraint equalities, which were

$$2X + 4Y + 1S_1 + 0S_2 = 100$$
$$3X + 3Y + 0S_1 + 1S_2 = 90$$

Using these coefficients, the constraint rows (resource coefficient rows) are

$$
\begin{array}{ccccc}
2 & 4 & 1 & 0 & 100 \\
3 & 3 & 0 & 1 & 90
\end{array}
$$

1) The resource coefficient rows in the tableau must equal the constraints.

d. There are as many basic variables as constraints.

1) Basic variables exist in the current tableau as a possible solution (not necessarily optimal).

2) In this example, the initial basic solution sets $S_1$ equal to 100 and $S_2$ equal to 90.

3) Nonbasic variables are the variables that are equal to zero in the current solution, e.g., X and Y.

e. The basic variables are those that form an identity matrix. That is, their corresponding variable columns consist of zeros and a single 1. The variable columns are those beneath the variables, i.e., beneath X, Y, $S_1$, and $S_2$.

1) Referring to the sample tableau on page 626, $S_1$ has 1, 0 in its column, and $S_2$ has 0, 1; that is, they form an identity matrix.

2) In this tableau, the basic variables are also the slack variables.

a) But they may not necessarily be next to each other in other problems.

f. The values for the basic variables are given in the right-hand side (RHS) column of the tableau.

1) Because the entry 1 for the $S_1$ variable is on the first row of the identity matrix, the value of S is given in the first row of the RHS column as 100.

2) The entry of 1 for $S_2$ is in the second row, and its value is found in the second row under RHS to be 90.

3) The values 100 and 90 come from the right-hand side of the constraint equations. Thus, the RHS values are also the amounts of available resources.

g. The CB column consists of payoff (cost) coefficients of the basic variables in profit-maximization (cost-minimization) problems.

1) Hence, the column consists of as many numbers as there are basic variables (i.e., two for this tableau).

2) The numbers entered are the same as for the basic variables found in the $C_j$ row (0 and 0).

3) $Z_j$ and $C_j - Z_j$ are not part of the CB column.

h.    The first element of the $Z_j$ row is the sum of the products of multiplying each element (payoff or cost coefficient) in the CB column by each element in the first column, $(0 \times 2) + (0 \times 3) = 0$.

1)    The subsequent elements are obtained by multiplying each element in the CB column by each element in the appropriate column and adding the products.

2)    For example, the third element in the $Z_j$ row is $(0 \times 1) + (0 \times 0) = 0$.

3)    The elements in the $Z_j$ row are opportunity costs.

i.    The index row is the last (bottom) row. It provides a measure of the direction of improvement of the objective function value for a corresponding change in the tableau.

1)    It is obtained by subtracting each element in the $Z_j$ row from each element in the $C_j$ row.

$$C_j - Z_j = 5 \ 7 \ 0 \ 0$$

2)    Positive elements in the index row for a maximization problem or negative elements for a minimization problem indicate that the solution could be improved.

j.    The current (but not the optimal) solution to this simplex problem is obtained by multiplying the CB column times the RHS column and adding the products.

1)    The result is found in the far right column (RHS) in the $Z_j$ row, which here is zero.

2)    The current solution does not always equal zero, although it does in this case because CB = 0.

k.    Professional examinations test familiarity with the simplex tableau format, but they do not customarily test further manipulation of the tableau to achieve an optimal solution.

6.    The following is the graphical solution to the foregoing problem:

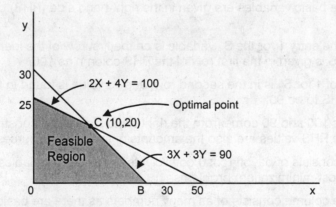

a.    Given the objective function (OF) $5X + 7Y$, the extreme points of the feasible region yield the following values:

| At point | OF |
|----------|----:|
| (0, 0) | 0 |
| (0, 25) | $(0 \times 5) + (25 \times 7) = 175$ |
| (30, 0) | $(30 \times 5) + (0 \times 7) = 150$ |
| (10, 20) | $(10 \times 5) + (20 \times 7) = 190$ |

7.    Computer software packages have been developed to manipulate linear programming problems with many more constraints. It is usually sufficient for the management accountant to recognize the basic method and its implications.

## 17.1 Linear Programming Concepts

**1.** An investment company is attempting to allocate its available funds between two investment alternatives, stocks and bonds, which differ in terms of expected return and risk. The company would like to minimize its risk while earning an expected return of at least 10% and investing no more than 70% in either of the investment alternatives. An appropriate technique for allocating its funds between stocks and bonds is

    A. Linear programming.

    B. Capital budgeting.

    C. Differential analysis.

    D. Queuing theory.

The correct answer is (A). *(CIA, adapted)*
    **REQUIRED:** The technique for allocating funds.
    **DISCUSSION:** Linear programming is a mathematical technique for planning resource allocation to optimize a given objective function that is subject to certain constraints. In this case, the maximum investment is constrained by a 70% limit on either investment choice and a minimum required return.
    Answer (B) is incorrect because capital budgeting is used to analyze and evaluate long-term capital investments. Answer (C) is incorrect because differential analysis is used for decision making when differences in costs (revenues) for two or more options are compared. Answer (D) is incorrect because queuing theory is used to minimize the sum of the costs of waiting lines and servicing waiting lines when items arrive randomly and are serviced sequentially.

**2.** Linear programming is an operations research technique that allocates resources. Mathematical expressions are used to describe the problem. The measure of effectiveness that is to be maximized or minimized is the

    A. Constraints.

    B. Set of decision variables.

    C. Objective function.

    D. Derivative of the function.

The correct answer is (C). *(CMA, adapted)*
    **REQUIRED:** The measure of effectiveness to be maximized or minimized.
    **DISCUSSION:** The objective function in a linear programming model symbolically represents the outcome to be optimized, e.g., total contribution margin, operating income, or total cost.
    Answer (A) is incorrect because constraints are the resource limitations and other conditions within which the objective function is to be optimized. Answer (B) is incorrect because variables are the unknowns used to construct the objective function and constraints. Answer (D) is incorrect because it is a calculus term that is irrelevant in this context.

**3.** The constraints in a linear programming model are

    A. Included in the objective function.

    B. Costs.

    C. Scarce resources.

    D. Dependent variables.

The correct answer is (C). *(CIA, adapted)*
    **REQUIRED:** The description of constraints.
    **DISCUSSION:** LP models are mathematical techniques in which an objective function is maximized or minimized subject to constraints. Constraints are mathematical statements expressed as equalities or inequalities. They describe conditions, usually resource limitations, to which values of the variables are subject. These constraints must be specified before a linear programming problem can be solved.
    Answer (A) is incorrect because the objective function incorporates the variables to be optimized. Answer (B) is incorrect because costs are included in the objective function. Answer (D) is incorrect because the constraints are given and are independent.

**4.** United Industries manufactures three products at its highly automated factory. The products are very popular, with demand far exceeding the company's ability to supply the marketplace. To maximize profit, management should focus on each product's

    A. Gross margin.

    B. Segment margin.

    C. Contribution margin.

    D. Contribution margin per machine hour.

The correct answer is (D). *(CMA, adapted)*
    **REQUIRED:** The measure used to determine the profit maximizing output.
    **DISCUSSION:** When demand far exceeds a company's ability to supply the marketplace, management will want to maximize its profits per unit of scarce resource. If the scarce resource is raw materials, the products that provide the greatest contribution margin per unit of raw materials should be emphasized. If machine hours are the constraint, profits are maximized by emphasizing the contribution margin per machine hour.
    Answers (A), (B), and (C) are incorrect because the company can sell as much of each product as it can produce. Thus, sales are limited by production constraints, e.g., machine hours. The company should therefore seek to maximize its return per unit of the constraint.

| Questions 5 through 7 are based on the following information. Manders Manufacturing Corporation uses the following model to determine its product mix for metal (M) and scrap metal (S). | Max Z = \$30M + \$70S<br>If:  3M + 2S ≤ 15<br>2M + 4S ≤ 18 |
| --- | --- |

**5.** These mathematical functions are an example of a(n)

   A.  Simulation model.

   B.  Linear programming model.

   C.  Economic order quantity model.

   D.  Present value model.

The correct answer is (B). *(CMA, adapted)*

**REQUIRED:** The type of model typified by the maximization and constraint functions illustrated.

**DISCUSSION:** Linear programming is a technique used to maximize a revenue or profit function, or minimize a cost function, subject to constraints such as limited resources. Linear programming is often used for planning scarce resource allocations. The optimization, or objective, function (Max Z = \$30M + \$70S) indicates that a company is attempting to maximize its contribution margin on two products. The two constraint functions suggest that either the scarcity of resources or a lack of demand limits the amount of each product that can be produced.

Answer (A) is incorrect because a simulation model is a technique for experimenting with models using a computer. It does not necessarily use maximization and constraint functions. Answer (C) is incorrect because the EOQ is based on a single equation that includes a square root. Answer (D) is incorrect because the present value model is based on a single equation that incorporates a rate of return.

**6.** The two inequality functions are

   A.  Contributions.

   B.  Shadow points.

   C.  Objectives.

   D.  Constraints.

The correct answer is (D). *(CMA, adapted)*

**REQUIRED:** The term for the two inequality functions.

**DISCUSSION:** The restrictions on the optimal value of the objective function in linear programming are known as constraints. They are depicted by means of inequalities.

Answer (A) is incorrect because contributions to revenue are included in the objective (maximization) equation. Answer (B) is incorrect because a shadow point, or shadow price, is the amount by which the value of the optimal solution of the objective function will change if a one-unit change is made in a binding constraint. Answer (C) is incorrect because objectives refer to the components of the objective (maximization) equation.

**7.** The point at which M = 2 and S = 3 would

   A.  Minimize cost.

   B.  Lie in a corner.

   C.  Be a feasible point.

   D.  Be the optimal solution point.

The correct answer is (C). *(CMA, adapted)*

**REQUIRED:** The true statement about a given point in a linear programming model.

**DISCUSSION:** The point at which M = 2 and S = 3 is a feasible point because it does not violate either of the constraint functions. A graphic depiction of the constraints will show whether the point lies in a corner, which is not the case. Because it does not lie in a corner, it cannot be the optimal solution point. In a linear programming problem, the optimal solution lies at a corner in the feasible area. Thus, all that can be said for certain about the point is that it lies within the feasible area.

Answer (A) is incorrect because nothing can be said with respect to costs. Costs are not mentioned in any of the equations. Answer (B) is incorrect because the point does not lie in a corner. Answer (D) is incorrect because the point cannot be the optimal solution point unless it is a corner point.

**8.** The procedure employed to solve linear programming problems is

A. Calculus.

B. Simulation.

C. Expected value.

D. Matrix algebra.

The correct answer is (D). *(CMA, adapted)*

**REQUIRED:** The procedure used to solve linear programming problems.

**DISCUSSION:** Matrix algebra is a method of manipulating matrices (rectangular arrays) formed from the coefficients of simultaneous linear equations. Similar rectangular arrays can be combined to form sums and products. Matrix algebra is used to solve linear programming problems (assuming that a computer is not available). This use of matrix algebra is the simplex method.

Answer (A) is incorrect because calculus is used to find maxima and minima. Answer (B) is incorrect because simulation is a technique for experimenting with mathematical models. Answer (C) is incorrect because expected value is a probabilistically weighted average of possible outcomes.

**9.** To solve a linear programming problem, slack, surplus, and artificial variables must be employed. A slack variable represents

A. Opportunity costs.

B. Unused capacity.

C. Outside variables with high cost.

D. The variable with the most negative value.

The correct answer is (B). *(CMA, adapted)*

**REQUIRED:** The definition of a slack variable.

**DISCUSSION:** A slack variable represents unused capacity using the simplex method. Because linear programming formulations are often stated as inequalities, unused capacity is possible even at the optimal production level. To convert inequalities of the ≤ type to equalities, slack variables are added to account for the unused capacity. If an inequality is of the ≥ type, a surplus variable is subtracted. In the latter case, a second variable, called an artificial variable, is added to prevent violation of the nonnegativity constraint.

Answer (A) is incorrect because opportunity costs are the benefits forgone by using a scarce resource in a given way. Answers (C) and (D) are incorrect because a slack variable has a payoff or cost coefficient of zero.

**10.** In linear programming, the shadow price refers to the

A. Measurement of the value of relaxing a constraint in a problem with dual variables.

B. Marginal change in profit associated with a change in the contribution margin of one of the variables.

C. Unused capacity available once the optimal solution is obtained.

D. Solution variable that is located outside the feasible area.

The correct answer is (A). *(CMA, adapted)*

**REQUIRED:** The definition of a shadow price.

**DISCUSSION:** A shadow price is the amount by which the value of the optimal solution of the objective function will change if a one-unit change is made in a binding constraint. The calculation of shadow prices is an example of sensitivity analysis, which is any procedure that tests the responsiveness of a solution to changes in variables.

Answer (B) is incorrect because the change is in the limited resource, not in the contribution margin of one of the variables. Answer (C) is incorrect because shadow prices are concerned with binding constraints, not nonbinding constraints; the shadow price of unused capacity, a nonbinding constraint, is zero. Answer (D) is incorrect because a shadow price is the benefit of moving the feasible area.

**11.** Shadow prices in linear programming solutions are ordinarily considered to be the same as

A. Relevant costs.

B. Differential cost.

C. Alternative costs.

D. Opportunity costs.

The correct answer is (D). *(CIA, adapted)*

**REQUIRED:** The equivalent of shadow prices.

**DISCUSSION:** A shadow price is the amount by which the value of the optimal solution of the objective function in a linear programming problem will change if a one-unit change is made in a binding constraint. The calculation of a shadow price is a simple example of sensitivity analysis. An opportunity cost is the maximum benefit forgone by using a scarce resource for a given purpose. It is the benefit from the next best use of that resource. Thus, shadow prices and opportunity costs are related concepts.

Answer (A) is incorrect because relevant costs are expected future costs that will vary with the decision taken. They are reflected in the objective function and constraints of linear programming problems. Answer (B) is incorrect because a differential cost is the net relevant cost. Answer (C) is incorrect because the term alternative costs is seldom used in either managerial/cost accounting textbooks or in the literature on decision theory.

**12.** Sensitivity analysis in linear programming is used to

A. Test the accuracy of the parameters.

B. Develop the technological matrix.

C. Determine how the optimal solution will react to changes in parameters.

D. Develop objective function coefficients.

The correct answer is (C). *(CMA, adapted)*

**REQUIRED:** The purpose for which sensitivity analysis is used in linear programming.

**DISCUSSION:** Sensitivity analysis in linear programming determines how the optimal solution will change if an objective function coefficient, the limiting value of a resource constraint, or a constraint coefficient is varied. It also considers the effect of adding a new variable or constraint.

Answer (A) is incorrect because the accuracy of the parameters cannot be tested as a part of the model. The intent is simply to measure the impact of a variance from the assumed parameters. Answer (B) is incorrect because the technological matrix is developed by production managers or engineers and is an input into the model. Answer (D) is incorrect because objective function coefficients are treated as given in the model. Sensitivity analysis can be used to determine the impact of changes in the coefficients.

**13.** Given the basic equations for the maximization of profits in a linear programming model, what quantitative technique is ordinarily employed to arrive at an optimal solution?

A. Regression analysis.

B. Markov analysis.

C. Monte Carlo analysis.

D. Simplex method analysis.

The correct answer is (D). *(CPA, adapted)*

**REQUIRED:** The usual method of solving linear programming problems.

**DISCUSSION:** The simplex method is the technique most commonly used to solve linear programming problems. It is an algorithm used to move from a possible solution to a better solution. The mathematical constraint equations are arranged in a matrix of coefficients and manipulated as a group by means of matrix algebra. Because of its complexity when numerous products and constraints are involved, the simplex method is used primarily with computers.

Answer (A) is incorrect because regression analysis measures the relationship among variables. Answer (B) is incorrect because Markov analysis is used in decision problems in which the probability of the occurrence of a future state depends only on the current state. Answer (C) is incorrect because the Monte Carlo technique is used in a simulation to generate random values for a variable.

**14.** Given below is the final solution for which type of problem?

| | | | | | | |
|---|---|---|---|---|---|---|
| $X_1$ | 8 | 0 | 1 | .5 | −.055 | 0 |
| $X_2$ | 4 | 1 | 0 | −.5 | .111 | 0 |
| $C_j$-$Z_j$: | | 0 | 0 | −20 | −6.67 | 0 |

A. Linear programming.

B. Markov absorbing chain.

C. Material requirements planning.

D. Two-line, three-server queuing system.

The correct answer is (A). *(CIA, adapted)*

**REQUIRED:** The type of problem that the given solution represents.

**DISCUSSION:** The matrix given is the final solution of a simplex tableau. The simplex method is the technique most commonly used to solve linear programming problems. It is an algorithm used to move from a possible solution to a better solution. The mathematical constraint equations are arranged in a matrix of coefficients and manipulated as a group by means of matrix algebra. The simplex method is used primarily with computers.

Answer (B) is incorrect because a sequence of events (a Markov chain) is an absorbing chain if it can reach a state that will never change. An example is the completion of a project. Answer (C) is incorrect because MRP is an inventory management technique that treats inventory as directly dependent upon short-term demand for the finished product. Answer (D) is incorrect because queuing theory is used to minimize the costs of waiting lines.

**15.** A transportation model is a special case of the

A. Markov model.

B. Linear programming model.

C. Dynamic programming model.

D. Critical path method.

The correct answer is (B). *(CMA, adapted)*

**REQUIRED:** The model of which the transportation model is a special case.

**DISCUSSION:** The transportation model is a special type of linear programming. It involves physical movement of goods from sources of supply to destinations. The objective function includes the transportation cost of each item from each source to each destination. The constraints are the output for each supply point and the demand by each destination.

Answer (A) is incorrect because a Markov model is useful in decision problems in which the probability of the occurrence of a future state depends only on the current state of nature. Answer (C) is incorrect because dynamic programming is useful for problems that involve time-staged decisions such as decisions affected by previous decisions; typically, dynamic programming is used for much smaller problems than linear programming. Answer (D) is incorrect because the critical path method is a means of managing large construction projects by focusing on the longest path in a network.

## 17.2 Graphs

**16.** The graphic method as a means for solving linear programming problems

A. Can be used given more than two restrictions (constraints).

B. Is limited to situations having two restrictions (constraints).

C. Is limited to situations with one restriction (constraint).

D. Cannot be used with any restrictions (constraints).

The correct answer is (A). *(CPA, adapted)*

**REQUIRED:** The true statement about constraints in graphic solutions of linear programming problems.

**DISCUSSION:** Linear programming (LP) problems assume linearity of relationships, and the solutions may be examined by plotting a solution (feasibility) region on a graph. The solution region is formed or bounded by the constraint lines. The objective function is also a linear relationship that may be plotted on the graph. Thus, multiple relationships and multiple constraints may be examined.

Answer (B) is incorrect because more than two restrictions (constraints) are possible. Answer (C) is incorrect because no graph is needed if only one restriction exists. The optimal solution is either all of one product, item, etc., or all of another unless the slope of the constraint line equals the slope of the objective function. Answer (D) is incorrect because all LP problems by definition have constraints.

**17.** When using the graphic method of solving a linear programming problem, which of the following is depicted on the graph?

| | Line of Best Fit | Optimal Corner Point |
|---|---|---|
| A. | No | No |
| B. | No | Yes |
| C. | Yes | No |
| D. | Yes | Yes |

The correct answer is (B). *(CPA, adapted)*
**REQUIRED:** The element(s) of a linear programming graph.
**DISCUSSION:** The graphic solution to a linear programming problem depicts the area of feasible combinations of activity given the constraints. Any point along a constraint line will have the same characteristics; thus, a point represents the line. By moving to the extreme point of the feasibility region, one finds the optimal solution.
Answers (A), (C), and (D) are incorrect because the line of best fit is found when using the least squares method, but an LP graph depicts an optimal corner point.

---

Questions 18 and 19 are based on the following information. A company produces two products, X and Y, which use material and labor as inputs. Fixed amounts of labor and material are available for production each month. In addition, the demand for Product Y each month is limited; Product X has no constraint on the number of units that can be sold.

A graphical depiction of these production and demand constraints is presented in the opposite column.

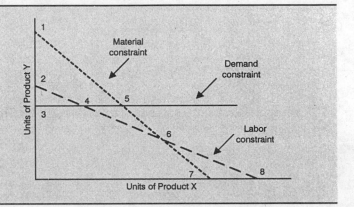

---

**18.** The feasible solution region is bounded by the lines connecting points

A. 3, 4, 6, and 7.

B. 1, 5, 6, and 8.

C. 2, 4, 5, 6, and 8.

D. 3, 5, 6, and 7.

The correct answer is (A). *(CIA, adapted)*
**REQUIRED:** The points bounding the feasible region.
**DISCUSSION:** A model consisting of a system of functions may be used to optimize an objective function. If the functions in the model are all linear, the model is a linear programming model. Linear programming is a technique used to determine optimal resource allocation. Several solution methods are available to solve linear programming problems. The graphical method, the easiest technique, is limited to simple problems. Here, the graph consists of three lines, each representing a production constraint. The lines connecting points 3, 4, 6, and 7 bound the feasible solution region. Product mixes of X and Y that lie outside this boundary cannot be produced and/or sold because the demand constraint (line 3,4), the labor constraint (line 4,6), and the material constraint (line 6,7) are binding.
Answers (B), (C), and (D) are incorrect because points 1, 2, 5, and 8 are outside the boundary.

---

**19.** If a series of profit lines for X and Y are drawn on the graph, the mix of X and Y that will result in the maximum profit can be determined from

A. The last point in the feasible solution region touched by a profit line.

B. Any point on the boundary of the feasible solution region touched by a profit line.

C. The first point on the feasible solution region boundary that intersects a profit line.

D. Any point on the demand constraint that intersects a profit line.

The correct answer is (A). *(CIA, adapted)*
**REQUIRED:** The means of determining the mix of X and Y that will result in the maximum profit.
**DISCUSSION:** A profit line has negative slope because the profit from sales of one product increases as the profit from sales of the other product declines. Moving the profit line rightward (while maintaining its slope) to the last point in the feasible region determines the solution.
Answers (B), (C), and (D) are incorrect because the last point in the feasible solution region touched by a profit line determines the solution.

Questions 20 through 27 are based on the following information. Hale Company manufactures Products A and B, each of which requires two processes, polishing and grinding. A requires 2 hours of both grinding and polishing and B requires 4 hours of grinding and 2 hours of polishing. The contribution margin is $3 for Product A and $4 for Product B. The graph to the right shows the maximum number of units of each product that may be processed in the two departments.

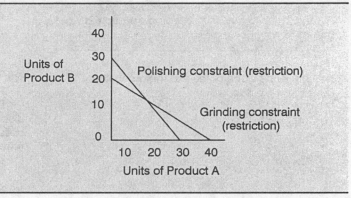

**20.** Considering the constraints (restrictions) on processing, which combination of Products A and B maximizes the total contribution margin?

A. 0 units of A and 20 units of B.

B. 20 units of A and 10 units of B.

C. 30 units of A and 0 units of B.

D. 40 units of A and 0 units of B.

The correct answer is (B). *(CPA, adapted)*
**REQUIRED:** The profit maximization point in the graph.
**DISCUSSION:** To determine the profit maximization point on an LP graph requires the examination of each of the corner points on the feasible region. For 0 units of A and 20 units of B, the contribution margin is $80 (20 units x $4 CM). At 20 units of A and 10 units of B, the CM is $100 ($60 UCM for A + $40 UCM for B). At 30 units of A and 0 units of B, the CM is $90 (30 units x $3 CM). Thus, the product mix at 20 units of A and 10 units of B maximizes the contribution margin.
Answer (A) is incorrect because the CM is $80. Answer (C) is incorrect because the CM is $90. Answer (D) is incorrect because the points representing 40 units of A and 0 units of B and 30 units of B and 0 units of A lie outside the feasible region.

**21.** What is the polishing constraint?

A. $2A + 4B \leq 80$

B. $2A + 2B \leq 60$

C. $40A + 20B \leq 20$

D. $30A + 30B \leq 30$

The correct answer is (B). *(Publisher)*
**REQUIRED:** The equation of the line representing the polishing constraint.
**DISCUSSION:** The polishing constraint on the graph consists of a line from 30B to 30A. Thus, the limitation imposed by polishing is 30A, 30B, or some combination of the two. Given that A and B both require 2 hours of polishing, 60 hours of polishing capacity must be available. Thus, $2A + 2B \leq 60$.
Answer (A) is incorrect because $2A + 4B \leq 80$ is the grinding constraint. Answers (C) and (D) are incorrect because the constraint coefficients are the amounts of resources used per unit of output, not the maximum units that can be produced.

**22.** What is the grinding constraint?

A. $30A + 30B \leq 30$

B. $2A + 4B \leq 80$

C. $40A + 20B \leq 20$

D. $2A + 2B \leq 60$

The correct answer is (B). *(Publisher)*
**REQUIRED:** The equation of the line depicting the grinding constraint.
**DISCUSSION:** The grinding constraint is a line from 20B to 40A. Thus, if B alone is produced, the output will be 20 units. If A alone is produced, the output will be 40 units. Also, A requires 2 hours of grinding and B, 4 hours. Only 80 hours of grinding capacity are available (20 units of B x 4 hours). Thus, the constraint is $2A + 4B \leq 80$.
Answers (A) and (C) are incorrect because the constraint coefficients are the amounts of resources used per unit of output, not the maximum units that can be produced. Answer (D) is incorrect because $2A + 2B \leq 60$ is the polishing constraint.

Refer to the information preceding question 20 on
page 635.

**23.** What is the slope of the polishing constraint?

A. 1/1

B. 4/3

C. 1/2

D. −1/1

The correct answer is (D). *(Publisher)*
   **REQUIRED:** The slope of the polishing constraint.
   **DISCUSSION:** The slope equals the change in vertical
distance divided by the change in horizontal distance. The
polishing constraint line decreases by 1 unit vertically as it
moves to the right (increases) horizontally by 1 unit. Thus,
the slope is −1/1.
   Answers (A), (B), and (C) are incorrect because the
slopes of the constraints are usually negative.

**24.** Constraint lines in linear programming usually
have a negative slope. Which is an example of a
constraint line that does not have a negative slope?

A. $2X + 7Y \leq 40$

B. $7X + 2Y \leq 40$

C. $X + Y \leq 40$

D. $Y \leq 40$

The correct answer is (D). *(Publisher)*
   **REQUIRED:** The constraint line that does not have a
negative slope.
   **DISCUSSION:** Each of the constraint lines given as
answer choices is downward sloping (i.e., they connect
between the Y axis and X axis) except $Y \leq 40$. When this
inequality is changed to an equality, its graphic depiction is a
horizontal line (its slope is equal to 0).
   Answers (A), (B), and (C) are incorrect because these
slopes are negative. The reason is that increasing the
amount devoted to X or Y reduces the production of the
other.

**25.** What is the slope of the grinding constraint?

A. −1/1

B. −1/2

C. −2/1

D. 1/2

The correct answer is (B). *(Publisher)*
   **REQUIRED:** The slope of the grinding constraint line.
   **DISCUSSION:** The grinding constraint line runs from
20B to 40A, decreasing 1 unit vertically for every 2 units of
horizontal increase. Accordingly, the slope is −1/2.
   Answer (A) is incorrect because −1/1 is the slope of the
polishing constraint. Answer (C) is incorrect because −2/1 is
the inverse of the slope of the grinding constraint line.
Answer (D) is incorrect because the slope is negative.

**26.** What is the slope of the objective function?

A. −1/1

B. −3/3

C. −3/4

D. 3/4

The correct answer is (C). *(Publisher)*
   **REQUIRED:** The slope of the objective function.
   **DISCUSSION:** The objective function consists of a series
of parallel lines outward from the origin having the same
profit potential. Given that each A generates $3 of CM and
each B produces a $4 UCM, the company is indifferent
between producing 4A and 3B. On this graph, such a line
will run from 30B to 40A. The change will be $3 vertically
downward for every $4 horizontal increase, for a slope of
−3/4.
   Answer (A) is incorrect because −1/1 is the slope of the
polishing constraint. Answer (B) is incorrect because −3/3 is
also the slope of the polishing constraint. Answer (D) is
incorrect because the slope is negative.

**27.** Which amounts of A and B lie on the same
objective function line?

|    | A  | B  |
|----|----|----|
| A. | 40 | 20 |
| B. | 20 | 40 |
| C. | 30 | 30 |
| D. | 40 | 30 |

The correct answer is (D). *(Publisher)*
   **REQUIRED:** The points on the objective function line.
   **DISCUSSION:** The company should be indifferent
between producing 4A and 3B. This relationship may be
depicted by a line from 30B to 40A. Each combination
represented by a point on this line provides a contribution
margin of $120.
   Answers (A), (B), and (C) are incorrect because 40A and
30B are on the same objective function line.

## 17.3 Formulation

**28.** A firm must decide the mix of production of Product X and Product Y. There are only two resources used in the two products, resources A and B. Data related to the two products are given in the following table:

|  | Products | |
|---|---|---|
|  | X | Y |
| Resource A | 3 | 7 |
| Resource B | 2 | 1 |
| Unit profit | $8 | $6 |

What is the appropriate objective function to maximize profit?

   A. 3X + 7Y

   B. 2X + Y

   C. 8X + 6Y

   D. 5X + 8Y

The correct answer is (C). *(CIA, adapted)*
   **REQUIRED:** The appropriate objective function to maximize profit.
   **DISCUSSION:** The objective function is the function to be optimized. This firm wishes to maximize profits on the sales of two products (X and Y). Based on profits per unit ($8 and $6, respectively), the objective function is 8X + 6Y.
   Answer (A) is incorrect because 3X + 7Y is a constraint. Answer (B) is incorrect because 2X + Y is a constraint. Answer (D) is incorrect because 5X + 8Y is the sum of the constraints.

---

Questions 29 through 32 are based on the following information. Merlin Company has excess capacity on two machines, 24 hours on Machine 105 and 16 hours on Machine 107. To use this excess capacity, the company has two products, known as Product D and Product F, that must use both machines in manufacturing. Both have excess product demand, and the company can sell as many units as it can manufacture. The company's objective is to maximize profits.

Product D has an incremental profit of $6 per unit, and each unit utilizes 2 hours of time on Machine 105 and then 2 hours of time on Machine 107. Product F has an incremental profit of $7 per unit, and each unit utilizes 3 hours of time on Machine 105 and then 1 hour of time on Machine 107. Let D be the number of units for Product D, F be the number of units for Product F, and P be the company's profit.

---

**29.** The objective function for Merlin Company is

   A. P = 4D + 4F ≤ 40

   B. P = 2D + 3F ≤ 24

   C. P = 2D + F ≤ 16

   D. P = $6D + $7F

The correct answer is (D). *(CMA, adapted)*
   **REQUIRED:** The objective function.
   **DISCUSSION:** The objective function is the function that the company is trying to optimize. Because the purpose is to maximize the total contribution margin, the function will equal an unknown number of units of D at a unit contribution margin of $6 plus an unknown number of units of F at a unit contribution margin of $7 (P = $6D + $7F).
   Answers (A), (B), and (C) are incorrect because the question calls for the objective function, not constraints.

---

**30.** The optimal number of units for Product D can be solved by calculating

   A. 2D + 3F ≤ 24

   B. 2D + F ≤ 16

   C. 2D + 3(16 − 2D) ≤ 24

   D. 2(16 − F) + 3F ≤ 24

The correct answer is (C). *(CMA, adapted)*
   **REQUIRED:** The equation that must be solved to determine the optimal number of D to produce.
   **DISCUSSION:** The constraint equations for machine hours are 2D + 3F ≤ 24 hours and 2D + F ≤ 16 hours. Because these equations involve two unknowns (D and F), they may be solved simultaneously. Solving for F in the second equation produces F ≤ 16 − 2D. Substituting this result into the first equation gives 2D + 3(16 − 2D) ≤ 24.
   Answers (A) and (B) are incorrect because the two equations must be solved simultaneously. Answer (D) is incorrect because D does not equal 16 − F.

Refer to the information preceding question 29 on page 637.

**31.** The equations 2D + 3F ≤ 24, D ≥ 0, and F ≥ 0 are

A. Objective functions.

B. Inequalities.

C. Deterministic functions.

D. Constraints.

The correct answer is (D). *(CMA, adapted)*
**REQUIRED:** The term for equations of the type given.
**DISCUSSION:** These are constraint equations. The objective function (P = $6D + $7F) is to be maximized subject to these constraint functions. There are four constraints: (1) the 24 hours limitation for Machine 105, (2) the 16 hours limitation for Machine 107, (3) the nonnegative production assumption for Product D, and (4) the nonnegative production assumption for Product D.

Answer (A) is incorrect because objective functions are those that management is attempting to optimize. Answer (B) is incorrect because inequalities refer to equations that do not balance. These can balance. Answer (C) is incorrect because deterministic functions are those with known (determinable) variables.

**32.** A feasible solution for Merlin Company is

A. D = 2 and F = 8.

B. D = 6 and F = 4.

C. D = 12 and F = 0.

D. D = 8 and F = 3.

The correct answer is (B). *(CMA, adapted)*
**REQUIRED:** The feasible solution.
**DISCUSSION:** This problem can be solved either graphically or by means of trial and error. The graphical approach involves drawing the constraint lines on a graph and outlining the feasible region. An easier approach is to solve the problem by trial and error. Whether the production levels violate the constraint functions below can be determined for each answer. Only answer (B) does not violate the constraints.

$$2D + 3F \leq 24$$
$$2D + F \leq 16$$

Answer (A) is incorrect because D = 2 and F = 8 violates the Machine 105 constraint. Answer (C) is incorrect because D = 12 and F = 0 violates the Machine 107 constraint. Answer (D) is incorrect because D = 8 and F = 3 violates both constraints.

Questions 33 and 34 are based on the following information. Keego Enterprises manufactures two products, boat wax and car wax, in two departments, the Mixing Department and the Packaging Department. The Mixing Department has 800 hours per month available, and the Packaging Department has 1,200 hours per month available. Production of the two products cannot exceed 36,000 pounds. Data on the two products follow:

| | Contribution Margin (per 100 pounds) | Hours per 100 Pounds | |
| --- | --- | --- | --- |
| | | Mixing (M) | Packaging (P) |
| Boat wax (B) | $200 | 5.0 | 3.6 |
| Car wax (C) | 150 | 2.4 | 6.0 |

**33.** The objective function for the linear program Keego should use to determine the optimal monthly production of each wax is

A. Z = 150B + 200C

B. 2B + 1.5C ≥ 36,000

C. 2B + 1.5C ≤ 36,000

D. Z = 200B + 150C

The correct answer is (D). *(CMA, adapted)*
**REQUIRED:** The objective function.
**DISCUSSION:** The objective function is the equation to maximize the contribution margin. Given that each 100 pounds of boat wax contributes $200 and each 100 pounds of car wax contributes $150, the company's goal is to maximize the total of these amounts. If B equals the units of boat wax, C equals the units of car wax, and Z is the total contribution margin, the objective function is Z = $200B + $150C.

Answer (A) is incorrect because the coefficients of B and C are reversed. Answers (B) and (C) are incorrect because the coefficients should be stated in dollar amounts, not as proportions, and 36,000 equals maximum production in pounds.

**34.** The mixing constraint for the Keego linear program is

   A.  $2.4M + 6P \leq 36,000$

   B.  $5B + 2.4C \geq 800$

   C.  $5B + 2.4C \leq 800$

   D.  $5B + 2.4C = 800$

The correct answer is (C). *(CMA, adapted)*
   **REQUIRED:** The mixing constraint.
   **DISCUSSION:** The Mixing Department has only 800 hours available per month, which is a limitation (constraint) on production. Thus, the total mixing time is less than or equal to 800 hours. Every 100-pound batch of boat wax (B) requires 5 hours of mixing time, and every 100-pound batch of car wax (C) requires 2.4 hours of mixing time. Accordingly, the constraint equation is $5B + 2.4C \leq 800$.
   Answer (A) is incorrect because 2.4M and 6P equal hours per unit of car wax, but 36,000 equals maximum production in pounds. Answers (B) and (D) are incorrect because total mixing time is equal to or less than 800 hours.

## 17.4 Calculations

Questions 35 and 36 are based on the following information. Patsy, Inc. manufactures two products, X and Y. Each product must be processed in each of three departments: machining, assembling, and finishing. The hours needed to produce one unit of product per department and the maximum possible hours per department are provided in the next column.

| Department | Production Hours per Unit | | Maximum Capacity in Hours |
|---|---|---|---|
| | X | Y | |
| Machining | 2 | 1 | 420 |
| Assembling | 2 | 2 | 500 |
| Finishing | 2 | 3 | 600 |

Other restrictions follow:

$$X \geq 50$$
$$Y \geq 50$$

**35.** The objective function is to maximize profits if profit equals $4X + $2Y. Given the objective function and constraints, what is the most profitable number of units of X and Y, respectively, to manufacture?

   A.  150 and 100.

   B.  165 and 90.

   C.  170 and 80.

   D.  200 and 50.

The correct answer is (C). *(CPA, adapted)*
   **REQUIRED:** The most profitable product mix.
   **DISCUSSION:** The optimal point occurs at a corner solution on a graph of the constraint equations and the objective function. The corner points define the feasibility space. Assuming the alternative answers contain the optimal solution, each alternative should be evaluated by plugging in the appropriate number of hours to eliminate the nonfeasible choices. Thus, 170 units of X and 80 units of Y should be produced [Profit = ($4 x 170) + ($2 x 80) = $840].
   Answer (A) is incorrect because profit is $800 [($4 x 150) + ($2 x 100)]. Answer (B) is incorrect because the assembling constraint is violated [(2 x 165) + (2 x 90) = 510]. Answer (D) is incorrect because the machining constraint is violated [(2 x 200) + (1 x 50) = 450].

**36.** How many constraints exist in Patsy's LP problem?

   A.  None.

   B.  Two.

   C.  Three.

   D.  Five.

The correct answer is (D). *(Publisher)*
   **REQUIRED:** The number of constraints.
   **DISCUSSION:** Each of the three departments, Machining, Assembling, and Finishing, is subject to a capacity constraint, and X and Y are subject to minimum production constraints. Accordingly, the problem has five constraint equations.
   Answer (A) is incorrect because five constraints are given. Answer (B) is incorrect because two equals the minimum production constraints. Answer (C) is incorrect because three equals the capacity constraints.

Questions 37 through 40 are based on the following information. They should be treated as completely independent.

The Marlan Company has just begun producing metal trays and storage devices. It began operations with five metal-forming machines and five metal-cutting machines rented for $300 each per month. Each machine is capable of 400 hours of production per month. No additional machines can be obtained.

#### Linear Programming Formulation

Maximize Z  =  $4T + $7S

Subject to:     T + 2S  ≤  2,000
               2T + 2S  ≤  2,000
                    T   ≤   800
                  T,S   ≥     0

If:  T  =  number of trays produced
     S  =  number of storage devices produced
     Z  =  contribution margin

#### Machine Hours per Unit

|  | Trays | Storage Devices | Total Available Machine Hrs./Mo. |
|---|---|---|---|
| Metal-cutting | 1 | 2 | 2,000 |
| Metal-forming | 2 | 2 | 2,000 |

Expected costs and revenues are as follows:

|  | Trays | Storage Devices |
|---|---|---|
| Selling price per unit | $18.00 | $27.00 |
| Variable cost per unit | 14.00 | 20.00 |

Demand for the storage devices is unlimited, but no more than 800 trays can be sold per month.

Marlan must operate within the specified constraints as it tries to maximize the contribution margin from this new operation. Marlan intends to operate at the optimal level (OP) on the graph below.

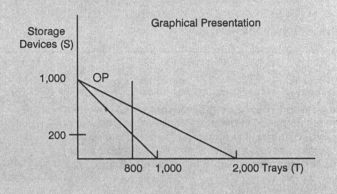

**Graphical Presentation**

**37.** If the selling price of storage devices is lowered from $27 to $23, the maximum total contribution margin Marlan can earn will

A. Decrease by $3,800.

B. Decrease by $4,000.

C. Increase by $4,000.

D. Decrease by $3,200.

The correct answer is (D). *(CMA, adapted)*

**REQUIRED:** The change in total CM given a change in selling price.

**DISCUSSION:** At the optimal point (point OP), Marlan produces 1,000 storage devices and no trays. The result is a CM of $7,000 ($7 UCM x 1,000 storage devices). Lowering the price of storage devices reduces their UCM to $3 ($23 – $20). Because trays have a UCM of $4 ($18 – $14), as many as possible should be made when the UCM of storage devices is $3. This alternative maximizes the UCM per machine hour available for metal forming (the more restrictive of the metal working constraints). Thus, the maximum number of trays (800) will be produced. Only 400 metal-forming hours will be available [2,000 – (2 x 800)], so 200 storage devices will be made. CM will be $3,800 [($4 x 800) + ($3 x 200)], and the total CM will decrease by $3,200 ($7,000 – $3,800).

Answer (A) is incorrect because $3,800 is the CM. Answers (B) and (C) are incorrect because $4,000 is the CM for 1,000 trays.

**38.** The maximum amount Marlan should be willing to spend on advertising to increase the demand for trays to 1,000 units per month is

A. $0

B. $600

C. $1,400

D. $5,400

The correct answer is (A). *(CMA, adapted)*

**REQUIRED:** The maximum amount to spend on advertising to generate targeted demand.

**DISCUSSION:** If the optimal point is 1,000 storage devices and zero trays per month, Marlan should not produce trays. Given unlimited demand for storage devices, advertising results in no marginal benefit.

Answers (B), (C), and (D) are incorrect because advertising cannot improve Marlan's CM.

**39.** If one metal-forming machine is returned to the rental agency and the rent can be avoided on it, Marlan's total profit will

- A. Be unaffected.
- B. Increase by $300.
- C. Decrease by $1,100.
- D. Decrease by $1,400.

The correct answer is (C). *(CMA, adapted)*
**REQUIRED:** The impact on total profit of returning one machine.
**DISCUSSION:** Each metal-forming machine provides 400 hours of production per month, which generates 200 storage devices. Returning one machine therefore means that CM will be reduced by $1,400 (200 units x $7). On the other hand, cost will be reduced by the $300 rent savings, so total profit will decrease by $1,100.

Answer (A) is incorrect because profit decreases. Answer (B) is incorrect because $300 is the rent saved. Answer (D) is incorrect because $1,400 is the decrease in CM.

**40.** Marlan has just realized that a material needed for the production of both products is in short supply. The company can obtain enough of this material to produce 1,200 trays. Each tray requires 2/3 as much of this material as the storage devices. Which of the following constraints will incorporate completely and correctly this additional information into the formulation of the problem?

- A. $T \leq 1,200$
- B. $2/3\ S \leq 1,200$
- C. $T + 2/3\ S \leq 1,200$
- D. $2/3\ T + 1\ S \leq 800$

The correct answer is (D). *(CMA, adapted)*
**REQUIRED:** The constraint required to express the change in available material.
**DISCUSSION:** Each question is to be treated independently. Thus, the decision to produce no trays is irrelevant here. This material constraint will limit both trays and storage devices. Either 1,200 trays or 800 (1,200 x 2/3) storage devices or some combination can be produced. Thus, the constraint is

$$2/3T + 1S \leq 800$$

Answers (A), (B), and (C) are incorrect because, assuming that one unit of the material is needed to produce one storage device, only 800 units must be available.

**41.** How is the objective function (maximization of total contribution margin) expressed?

A.  $5X + 7Y$

B.  $5X + 7Y \leq 190$

C.  $5X(3) + 7Y(7) \leq 190$

D.  $12X + 10Y$

The correct answer is (A). *(CPA, adapted)*
   **REQUIRED:** The objective function for the two models.
   **DISCUSSION:** The objective function is the formula for the maximum total contribution margin. Given that each X produces a $5 CM, and each Y produces a $7 CM, the total CM will be $5X + 7Y$.
   Answers (B) and (C) are incorrect because the objective function is not a constraint equation. Answer (D) is incorrect because the unit CMs for X and Y are $5 and $7, respectively.

**42.** How is the restriction (constraint) for the Machining Department expressed?

A.  $2(5X) + 4(7Y) \leq 100$

B.  $2X + 4Y$

C.  $2X + 4Y \leq 100$

D.  $5X + 7Y \leq 100$

The correct answer is (C). *(CPA, adapted)*
   **REQUIRED:** The constraint equation for the Machining Department.
   **DISCUSSION:** The Machining Department has a total of 100 hours available each week. Each X requires 2 hours of time from that department, and each Y requires 4 hours. Accordingly, the total Machining Department time taken by production is $2X + 4Y$, which must be equal to or less than the 100 hours available.
   Answers (A) and (D) are incorrect because 5X and 7Y are unit CMs. Answer (B) is incorrect because the hours available are omitted.

**43.** How is the restriction (constraint) for the Polishing Department expressed?

A.  $5X + 7Y$

B.  $5X + 7Y \leq 90$

C.  $2X + 4Y \leq 100$

D.  $X + 3Y \leq 90$

The correct answer is (D). *(Publisher)*
   **REQUIRED:** The constraint equation for the Polishing Department.
   **DISCUSSION:** The Polishing Department has a total of 90 hours available each week. Each X requires 1 hour of time, and each Y requires 3 hours of time. Thus, the constraint for this department is that $X + 3Y$ must be equal to or less than 90.
   Answer (A) is incorrect because $5X + 7Y$ is the objective function. Answer (B) is incorrect because 5X and 7Y are unit UCMs. Answer (C) is incorrect because $2X + 4Y \leq 100$ is the machining constraint.

**44.** How many slack variables are needed for the simplex tableau?

A.  None.

B.  One.

C.  Two.

D.  Three.

The correct answer is (C). *(Publisher)*
   **REQUIRED:** The number of slack variables necessary to construct a simplex tableau.
   **DISCUSSION:** The simplex method requires a slack variable to transform each inequality constraint into an equality. Thus, two slack variables are needed, one for each of the two inequality constraints.
   Answer (A) is incorrect because two slack variables are needed. Answer (B) is incorrect because one objective function is stated. Answer (D) is incorrect because two constraint equations and one objective function are stated.

Questions 45 through 47 are based on the following information. The final tableau for a linear programming profit maximization problem is presented below.

| | $X_1$ | $X_2$ | $X_3$ | $S_1$ | $S_2$ | |
|---|---|---|---|---|---|---|
| $X_1$ | 1 | 0 | 4 | 3 | –7 | 50 |
| $X_2$ | 0 | 1 | –2 | –6 | 2 | 60 |
| | 0 | 0 | 5 | 1 | 9 | 1,200 |

**45.** $X_1$, $X_2$, and $X_3$ represent products, slack variable $S_1$ relates to square feet (in thousands) of warehouse capacity, and slack variable $S_2$ relates to labor hours (in hundreds). The amount of $X_1$ that should be produced to maximize profit is

A. 60

B. 50

C. 1

D. 0

The correct answer is (B). *(CPA, adapted)*

**REQUIRED:** The amount of $X_1$ to produce to maximize profit.

**DISCUSSION:** $X_1$ and $X_2$ are the products in the solution. Product $X_3$ is not included because its column does not contain a 0 and 1. The rows and columns for $X_1$ and $X_2$ but not $X_3$ form an identity matrix, so $X_3$ is not a basic variable. Accordingly, using the solution values in the right-hand column, the value of the objective function is

$$50\,X_1 + 60\,X_2 = 1,200$$

Answer (A) is incorrect because 60 is the amount of $X_2$. Answers (C) and (D) are incorrect because the 1 and 0 in the $X_1$ column signify that $X_1$ is a basic variable.

**46.** The contribution to profit of an additional 100 hours of labor will be

A. 9

B. 2

C. 1

D. –7

The correct answer is (A). *(CPA, adapted)*

**REQUIRED:** The contribution to profit of an additional 100 hours of labor.

**DISCUSSION:** The number 9 in the $S_2$ column (the slack variable in the labor constraint equation) is a $Z_j$ value (the decrease in the value of the objective function from subtracting one unit of the resource). However, assuming operation within the range in which this shadow price is valid, 9 is also the amount by which the objective function will increase as the result of increasing the labor constraint by one unit (100 hours).

Answer (B) is incorrect because the 2 in the $S_2$ column means that production of $X_2$ will increase by 2. Answer (C) is incorrect because 1 is the $Z_j$ value for $S_1$ (square feet). Answer (D) is incorrect because –7 is the decrease in production of $X_1$.

**47.** An additional 1,000 square feet of warehouse space will

A. Increase $X_1$ by 3 units and decrease $X_2$ by 6 units.

B. Decrease $X_2$ by 6 units and increase $X_1$ by 2 units.

C. Decrease $X_1$ by 7 units and increase $X_2$ by 2 units.

D. Increase $X_1$ by 3 units and decrease $X_2$ by 7 units.

The correct answer is (A). *(CPA, adapted)*

**REQUIRED:** The effect of an additional 1,000 square feet of warehouse space.

**DISCUSSION:** If the square footage constraint is increased by one unit (1,000 sq. ft. of warehouse space), the effect will be to increase profit by 1, to decrease production of $X_2$ by 6, and to increase production of $X_1$ by 3.

Answer (B) is incorrect because $X_1$ increases by 3 units. Answer (C) is incorrect because increasing the labor constraint by one unit should decrease $X_1$ by 7 units and increase $X_2$ by 2 units. Answer (D) is incorrect because $X_2$ decreases by 6 units.

**48.** When using the simplex method to solve a linear programming problem for the maximization of contribution margin, the optimal solution has been reached when the values in the index row of the matrix are

    A.  All zero.

    B.  All negative or zero.

    C.  Equal to zero when added across.

    D.  Equal to a positive value when added across.

The correct answer is (B). *(CPA, adapted)*

    **REQUIRED:** The nature of the values in the index row when the optimal solution is found.

    **DISCUSSION:** Each item in the index row $(C_j - Z_j)$ gives a measure of the direction and amount of the change in the objective function value resulting from a change in the solution. If the index row has positive or zero elements (i.e., nonnegative), the solution can be improved. Each item in the $C_j$ row is the coefficient of a variable, that is, the amount by which the value of the objective function increases if the variable increases by one unit. Each item in the $Z_j$ row is the amount by which the value of the objective function decreases as a result of increasing the variable by one unit. This decrease (an opportunity cost) is caused by the shift in the use of constraint resources. In a maximization problem, the optimal solution is reached when each $C_j$ item is equal to or less than the corresponding $Z_j$ item. In a minimization problem, the foregoing is also true but with signs reversed.

    Answer (A) is incorrect because $C_j - Z_j = 0$ is true only for basic variables. The other variables, those not in the solution, have positive or negative values. Answers (C) and (D) are incorrect because each is nonsensical.

**49.** The Mix and Match Company has two products, Product X and Product Y, that it manufactures through its production facilities. The contribution margin for Product X is $15 per unit, whereas Product Y's contribution is $25. Each product uses Materials A and B. Product X uses 3 pounds of Material A, and Product Y uses 6 pounds. Product X requires 6 feet of Material B and Product Y uses 4 feet. The company can only purchase 600 pounds of Material A and 880 feet of Material B. The optimal mix of products to manufacture is

| | Product X | | Product Y |
|---|---|---|---|
| A. | 146 units | and | 0 units |
| B. | 0 units | and | 100 units |
| C. | 120 units | and | 40 units |
| D. | 40 units | and | 120 units |

The correct answer is (C). *(CMA, adapted)*

    **REQUIRED:** The optimal mix of products.

    **DISCUSSION:** The objective function ($15X + $25Y) is to be maximized subject to the two constraint functions (Material A: $3X + 6Y \leq 600$ and Material B: $6X + 4Y \leq 880$). One way to solve this problem is to graph the constraint lines and determine the feasible area. The optimal production level is at a corner of the feasible area. The corners can be determined algebraically. If X equals 0, Y equals 100 in the first constraint equation (assuming it is stated as an equality) and 220 in the second. If Y equals 0, X equals 200 in the first equation and 146 in the second. Thus, the maximum units of X and Y that can be produced are 146 and 100, respectively. Substituting into the objective function yields these results:

$$\$15(146) + \$25(0) = \$2,190$$
$$\$15(0) + \$25(100) = \$2,500$$

    A third feasible solution is to produce nothing (X = 0, Y = 0). This solution obviously yields a CM of $0. The fourth corner is the intersection of the two simultaneous constraint equations.

$$
\begin{aligned}
3X + 6Y &= 600 \\
6X + 4Y &= 880 \\
\hline
2(3X + 6Y) &= 2(600) \\
6X + 4Y &= 880 \\
\hline
8Y &= 320 \\
Y = 40 \text{ and } X &= 120
\end{aligned}
$$

    This solution results in a CM of $2,800 [($15 x 120) + ($25 x 40)].

    Answer (A) is incorrect because 146 units of X and 0 units of Y yield a CM of $2,190. Answer (B) is incorrect because 0 units of X and 100 units of Y yield a CM of $2,500. Answer (D) is incorrect because producing 120 units of Y violates the constraint for Material A.

# CHAPTER EIGHTEEN
# OTHER QUANTITATIVE APPROACHES

This chapter provides an overview of some other quantitative approaches that have received attention on the professional examinations and that are increasingly covered in cost and managerial accounting textbooks. Interpretations of the results and assumptions underlying these quantitative approaches are emphasized. **Simulation** is a technique for experimenting with logical and mathematical models using a computer. Despite the power of mathematics, many problems cannot be solved by known analytical methods because of the behavior of the variables and the complexity of their interactions, e.g., corporate planning models, financial planning models, new product marketing models, queuing system simulations, and inventory control simulations. Experimentation is neither new nor uncommon in business. Building a mockup of a new automobile, having one department try out new accounting procedures, and test-marketing a new product are all forms of experimentation. In effect, experimentation is organized trial-and-error using a model of the real world to obtain information prior to full implementation. Models can be classified as either physical or abstract. Physical models include automobile mockups, airplane models used for wind tunnel tests, and breadboard models of electronic circuits. Abstract models may be pictorial (architectural plans), verbal (a proposed procedure), or logical-mathematical. Experimentation with logical-mathematical models can involve many time-consuming calculations. Computers have alleviated much of this costly drudgery and have led to the growing interest in simulation for management. Queuing (waiting line) theory is a group of mathematical models for systems involving waiting lines. In general, a queuing system consists of a queue, or waiting line, and a service facility. Two basic costs are involved. The cost of providing service includes the facility costs and the operating costs. The waiting cost is the cost of idle resources waiting in line. It may be a direct cost, if paid employees are waiting, or an opportunity cost in the case of waiting customers. In either case, waiting has a cost. The objective of queuing theory is to minimize the total cost of the system, including both service and waiting costs, for a given rate of arrivals. Project scheduling techniques are designed to aid the planning and control of large-scale projects having many interrelated activities. Three of the more common techniques are Gantt or bar charts, PERT, and CPM. These techniques are suitable for any project having a target completion date and single start. **Gantt charts or bar charts** are simple to construct and use. To develop a Gantt chart, the project is divided into logical subprojects called activities or tasks. The start and completion times for each activity are estimated, and a bar chart is prepared showing each activity as a horizontal bar along a time scale. **Program Evaluation and Review Technique (PERT)** was developed to aid managers in controlling large-scale, complex projects. PERT diagrams are free-form networks showing each activity as a line between events. A sequence of lines shows interrelationships among activities. PERT is more complex than Gantt charts, but it has the advantages of incorporating probabilistic time estimates and identifying the critical path. **The Critical Path Method (CPM)** was developed independently of PERT and is widely used in the construction industry.  CPM may be thought of as a subset of PERT.  Like PERT, it is a network technique, but, unlike PERT, it uses deterministic time and cost estimates.  Its advantages include cost estimates plus the concept of crash efforts and costs.  **Learning curves** reflect the increased rate at which people perform tasks as they gain experience.  The time required to perform a given task becomes progressively shorter.  This technique is applicable only to the early stages of production or of any new task.  Ordinarily, the curve is expressed in a percentage of reduced time to complete a task for each doubling of cumulative production.  **Matrix algebra** is an efficient method of manipulating multiple linear equations.  The primary business application of **differential calculus** is to identify the maxima or minima of curvilinear functions.  **Integral calculus** also has a very important business application.  It permits computation of the area under a curve.  **Game (or decision) theory** is a mathematical approach to decision making when confronted with an enemy or competitor. Game theory classifies games according to how many players participate and the sum of the results.  Games are classified according to the number of players and the algebraic sum of the payoffs.

## 18.1 INTRODUCTION TO QUANTITATIVE METHODS

A.    The **simulation** procedure has five steps.

1.    **Define the objectives.**  The objectives serve as guidelines for all that follows.  The objectives may be to aid in the understanding of an existing system (e.g., an inventory system with rising costs) or to explore alternatives (e.g., the effect of investments on the firm's financial structure). A third type of objective is estimating the behavior of some new system such as a production line.

2.    **Formulate the model.**  The variables to be included, their individual behavior, and their interrelationships must be spelled out in precise logical-mathematical terms.  The objectives of the simulation serve as guidelines in deciding which factors are relevant.

3.    **Validate the model.**  Some assurance is needed that the results of the experiment will be realistic.  For example, if the model gives results equivalent to what actually happened, the model is historically valid.  Some risk remains, however, that changes could make the model invalid for the future.

4.    **Design the experiment.**  Experimentation is sampling the operation of a system.  For example, if a particular policy is simulated on an inventory model for 2 years, the results are a single sample.  With replication, the sample size can be increased and the confidence level raised. The number of runs to be made, length of each run, measurements to be made, and methods for analyzing the results are all part of the design of the experiment.

5.    **Conduct the simulation -- evaluate results.**  The simulation should be conducted with care. The results are analyzed using appropriate statistical methods.

B.    The **Monte Carlo technique** is a two-step process often employed in simulation to generate the individual values for a random variable.  A random number generator is used to produce numbers with a uniform probability distribution (equal likelihoods of occurrence).  The second step is to transform these numbers into values consistent with the desired distribution.

1.    The performance of a quantitative model may be investigated by randomly selecting values for each of the variables in the model (based on the probability distribution of each variable) and then calculating the value of the solution.  If this process is performed a large number of times, the distribution of results from the model will be obtained.

2.    EXAMPLE: A new marketing model includes a factor for a competitor's introduction of a similar product within 1 year.  Management estimates a 50% chance that this event will happen.  For each simulation, the factor must be determined, perhaps by flipping a coin, or by putting two numbers in a hat and selecting one number.  Random numbers between 0 and 1 could be generated.  Numbers under one-half would signify introduction of a similar product; numbers over one-half would indicate the nonoccurrence of this event.

C. The advantages of simulation are as follows:

    1. Time can be compressed. A corporate planning model can show the results of a policy for 5 years into the future, using only minutes of computer time.

    2. Alternative policies can be explored. With simulations, managers can ask what-if questions to explore possible policies, providing management with a powerful new planning tool.

    3. Complex systems can be analyzed. In many cases simulation is the only possible quantitative method for analyzing a complex system such as a production or inventory system, or the entire firm.

D. The limitations of simulation are as follows:

    1. Cost. Simulation models can be costly to develop. They can be justified only if the information to be obtained is worth more than the costs to develop the model and carry out the experiment.

    2. Risk of error. A simulation results in a prediction of how an actual system would behave. As in forecasting, the prediction may be in error.

E. **Sensitivity Analysis**

    1. After a problem has been formulated into any mathematical model, it may be subjected to sensitivity analysis.

       a. A trial-and-error method may be adopted in which the sensitivity of the solution to changes in any given variable or parameter is calculated.

          1) The risk of the project being simulated may also be estimated.

          2) The best project may be one that is least sensitive to changes in probabilistic inputs.

    2. In linear programming problems, sensitivity is the range within which a constraint value, such as a cost coefficient, may be changed without affecting the optimal solution. Shadow price is the synonym for sensitivity in that context.

F. **Markov Analysis**

    1. Markov processes are useful in decision problems in which the probability of the occurrence of a future state depends only on the current state.

       a. A characteristic of the Markov process is that the initial state matters less and less as time goes on because the process will eventually reach its steady state.

       b. EXAMPLE: A machine tool may be in one of two states, in adjustment or out of adjustment. The machine moves from one state to the other in 1 day with the following probabilities:

| From       To | In adjustment | Out of adjustment |
|---|---|---|
| In adjustment | .8 | .2 |
| Out of adjustment | .6 | .4 |

       c. If the machine is in adjustment on day 1, the probabilities of its being in or out of adjustment are as follows:

| | | IN | OUT | | Pr |
|---|---|---|---|---|---|
| On day 2 | $(1.0) \times (.8)$ | = .8 | $(1 - .8)$ | = | .2 |
| On day 3 | $(.8) \times (.8) + (.2) \times (.6)$ | = .76 | $(1 - .76)$ | = | .24 |
| On day 4 | $(.76) \times (.8) + (.24) \times (.6)$ | = .752 | $(1 - .752)$ | = | .248 |
| On day 5 | $(.752) \times (.8) + (.248) \times (.6)$ | = .7504 | $(1 - .7504)$ | = | .2496 |

The process approaches a probability of .75 on day n of being IN adjustment.

## 18.2 QUEUING THEORY

A.   Queuing models determine the operating characteristics of a waiting line.

   1.   The probability that no units are in the system
   2.   The average units in the line
   3.   The average units in the system
   4.   The average time a unit waits
   5.   The average time a unit is in the system
   6.   The probability that a unit must wait
   7.   The probability of a given number of units in the system

B.   Examples of queuing systems

   1.   Bank teller windows
   2.   Grocery checkout counters
   3.   Highway toll booths
   4.   Docks for ships
   5.   Airport holding patterns

C.   The structure of queuing systems depends on the number of lines and service facilities and how they are coupled.  Grocery stores usually have multiple-line, multiple-server systems.  Some banks have single-line, multiple-teller systems.  Job shops can be conceived of as multistage systems in which each machine is a server with its own queue.

D.   Mathematical solutions are available for simple systems having unscheduled random arrivals.  For other systems, simulation must be used to find a solution.

E.   The arrivals in a queuing model occur in accordance with a **Poisson process**.  The probability of occurrence of an event is constant, the occurrence of an event is independent of any other, the probability of an occurrence is proportional to the length of the interval, and, if the interval is small enough, the probability of more than one occurrence approaches zero.

   1.   The Poisson probability distribution is used to predict the probability of a specified number of occurrences of an event in a specified time interval, given the expected number of occurrences per time unit.

   2.   The related exponential distribution is used to approximate service times.  This distribution gives the probability of zero events in a given interval.  Accordingly, it gives the probability that service time will not exceed a given length of time.

F.   **Examples of Formulas for a Single Service Facility and Random Arrivals of Work Units**

   1.   If:   $B$ = average number of work units arriving in one unit of time
         $T$ = average number of work units serviced in one unit of time (if no shortage of work units), and

         Given that $\dfrac{B}{T}$ < 1 (otherwise the queue will grow to infinite length),

      a.   The average number of work units waiting in line or being serviced is

      $$N = \frac{B}{(T - B)}$$

      b.   The average number in the waiting line (Nq) is

      $$Nq = \frac{B^2}{T(T - B)}$$

c.   The average waiting time before service is

$$W = \frac{Nq}{B}$$

2.   EXAMPLE: Cars arrive at a toll booth at the average rate of 3 cars per minute.  The toll booth can serve (collect tolls from) 6 cars per minute on the average.  In the formulas,

$$B = 3$$
$$T = 6$$

a.   The average number of cars waiting in line or paying tolls at any time is

$$N = \frac{B}{(T - B)} = \frac{3}{6 - 3} = 1 \; car$$

b.   The average number in the waiting line, not being serviced, is

$$Nq = \frac{B^2}{T(T - B)} = \frac{9}{6(6 - 3)} = \tfrac{1}{2} \; car, \; or \; one \; car \; waiting \; half \; the \; time$$

c.   The average waiting time is

$$W = \frac{Nq}{B} = \frac{(\tfrac{1}{2})}{3} = 1/6 \; minute, \; or \; 10 \; seconds$$

## 18.3 NETWORK MODELS

A.   Example applications

1.   Building construction
2.   Research and development projects
3.   New product planning
4.   Feasibility studies
5.   Audit studies
6.   Book publishing

B.   The major advantage of the **Gantt chart** is its simplicity.  It forces the planner to think ahead and define logical activities.  As the project progresses, actual completion times can be compared to planned times.  Yet the technique requires no special tools or mathematics and can be used on small projects as well as large ones.

1.   The major disadvantage is that interrelationships among activities are not shown.  Several special methods have been developed to show these on a Gantt chart, but they are feasible only for simple relationships.

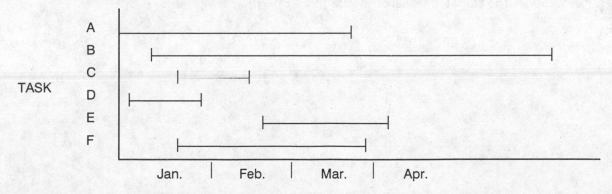

C.    In a **PERT** analysis, events are discrete moments in time representing the start or finish of an activity. They consume no resources. Activities are tasks to be accomplished. They consume resources (including time itself) and have a duration over time.

1.    The network diagram is formed by

a.    The lines (activities) connected from left to right in the necessary sequence of their accomplishment. They can be marked with time lengths.

b.    Events are shown as circles and numbered for identification.

2.    The critical path is the longest path in time through the network. It is critical in that if any activity on the critical path takes longer than expected, the entire project will be delayed. Every network has at least one critical path. Some have more than one.

a.    The mean completion time for the critical path is the sum of the means of the activity times.

b.    The standard deviation of the completion time for the critical path is the square root of the sum of the variances (squares of the standard deviations) of the activity times.

1)    EXAMPLE: If the critical path has two activities, and the standard deviations of the completion times are 3 and 4, the standard deviation for the critical path is 5, or $\sqrt{3^2 + 4^2}$.

3.    Paths that are not critical have slack time. One advantage of PERT is that it identifies this slack time, which represents unused resources that can be diverted to the critical path.

4.    Activity times can be expressed probabilistically. Computer programs are available to make the calculations and find critical paths. Several techniques have been developed to include cost information in the critical paths, often called PERT-Cost.

5.    PERT analysis includes probabilistic estimates of activity completion times. Three time estimates are made -- optimistic, most likely, and pessimistic.

a.    The time estimates for an activity are assumed to approximate a beta probability distribution. In contrast with the normal distribution, this distribution has finite endpoints (the optimistic and pessimistic estimates) and is unimodal; that is, it has only one mode (the most likely time).

b.    PERT approximates the mean of the beta distribution by dividing the sum of the optimistic time, the pessimistic time, and four times the most likely time (the mode) by six.

c.    The standard deviation is approximated by dividing the difference between the pessimistic and optimistic times by six. The basis for the latter approximation is that various probability distributions have tails that lie about plus or minus three standard deviations from the mean. For example, 99.9% of observations in the normal distribution are expected to lie within this range.

6.    EXAMPLE: If an activity can be completed in 6 days (optimistic time), 10 days (most likely time), or 20 days (pessimistic time), the expected duration is 11 days {[6 + (4 x 10) + 20] ÷ 6}.

a.    Thus, the most likely time is weighted the most heavily.
b.    The standard deviation is 2.33 [(20 − 6) ÷ 6].

7.   EXAMPLE:

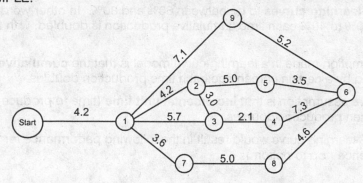

a.   For the network above, the following are the paths and path times:

| Path | Time |
|------|------|
| Start-1-9-6 | 16.5 |
| Start-1-2-5-6 | 16.9 |
| Start-1-2-3-4-6 | 20.8 |
| Start-1-3-4-6 | 19.3 |
| Start-1-7-8-6 | 17.4 |

b.   Path Start-1-2-3-4-6 is the critical path because it has the longest time.

8.   In the example above, the path of the task from 1 to 3 takes only 5.7, while the critical path events (1-2-3) take 7.2. The slack time represented by path 1 to 3 is thus 7.2 – 5.7, or 1.5. People assigned to path 1 to 3 have an extra hour and a half to help elsewhere.

D.   The **critical path method (CPM)** estimates activity times for normal effort and crash effort. Crash time is the time to complete an activity assuming that all available resources were devoted to the task (overtime, extra crew, etc.).

1.   Activity costs are also estimated for normal and crash efforts.

2.   These estimates allow the project manager to estimate the costs of completing the project if some of the activities are completed on a crash basis.

3.   The network diagram is constructed in the same manner as PERT diagrams. Once the diagram is constructed, the critical paths are found for normal and crash times. More than one critical path may exist for each diagram.

4.   Crashing the network means finding the minimum cost for completing the project in minimum time.

5.   CPM computer programs allow updating of the solution as work proceeds.

E.   Controlling **job projects** requires attention to their scope, scheduling, quality, and costs. Thus, **variance analysis** is a tool for project management.

1.   The difference between the actual cost of work performed (CWP) and the budgeted cost of work scheduled (CWS) may be analyzed in terms of two variances:

a.   The **job project-performance cost variance** is the difference between the actual CWP and the budgeted CWP. This variance may be further divided into price and efficiency variances. It measures cost overruns or underruns.

b.   The **job project-schedule cost variance** is the difference between the budgeted CWP and the budgeted CWS. It measures the extent to which the project is ahead of or behind schedule.

## 18.4 LEARNING CURVES

A.   Case studies have shown **learning curves** to be between 60% and 80%.  In other words, the time required is reduced by 20% to 40% each time cumulative production is doubled, with 20% being common.

  1.   One common assumption made in a learning curve model is that the **cumulative average time per unit** is reduced by a certain percentage each time production doubles.

   a.   The alternative assumption is that **incremental unit time** (time to produce the last unit) is reduced when production doubles.

  2.   EXAMPLE:  An 80% learning curve would result in the following performance for the lots shown, when run in sequence (top to bottom):

| Cumulative Number of Tasks | Average Time per Unit |
|---|---|
| 100 | 3.0 |
| 200 | 2.4 (3.0 × 80%) |
| 400 | 1.92 (2.4 × 80%) |
| 800 | 1.536 (1.92 × 80%) |
| 1,600 | 1.229 (1.536 × 80%) |

B.   **Graphical Presentation**

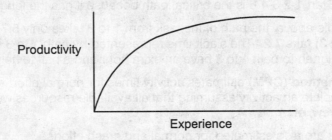

## 18.5 MATRIX ALGEBRA

A.   A **matrix** is a group of numbers ordered into rows and columns.

$$\begin{bmatrix} 6 & 4 \\ 3 & 7 \end{bmatrix}$$

6   4 is the first row.

3   7 is the second row.

6 is the first column.        4 is the second column.
3                             7

  1.   Each number in a matrix is called an **element**.  Elements are numbered by row and column.

$$\begin{bmatrix} X_{11} & X_{12} \\ X_{21} & X_{22} \end{bmatrix}$$

$X_{11}$   is in the first row and first column.
$X_{12}$   is in the first row and second column.
$X_{21}$   is in the second row and first column.
$X_{22}$   is in the second row and second column.

  2.   Matrices can be added, subtracted, and multiplied in a fashion very similar to that of variables in single equations.  Matrices must be of compatible sizes before they can be manipulated, however.

   a.   **Addition and subtraction** require matrices of the same dimensions.

1) For example, a matrix of 2 rows and 2 columns can only be added to or subtracted from another 2-row-2-column matrix.

b. Adding and subtracting matrices is accomplished by adding (subtracting) each element in the first matrix to (from) its corresponding element in the second matrix.

1) EXAMPLE:

$$\begin{bmatrix} 2 & 6 \\ 4 & 7 \end{bmatrix} + \begin{bmatrix} 3 & 9 \\ 2 & 3 \end{bmatrix} = \begin{bmatrix} 5 & 15 \\ 6 & 10 \end{bmatrix}$$

$$\begin{bmatrix} 2 & 6 \\ 4 & 7 \end{bmatrix} - \begin{bmatrix} 3 & 9 \\ 2 & 3 \end{bmatrix} = \begin{bmatrix} -1 & -3 \\ 2 & 4 \end{bmatrix}$$

c. **Multiplication** of matrices requires that the matrices conform.

1) If matrices are identified as

A (m rows × n columns) and B (n rows × p columns),

the two can be multiplied; thus, if the number of columns in the first equals the rows in the second, the matrices conform.

$$\begin{bmatrix} x & x & x \\ x & x & x \end{bmatrix} \begin{bmatrix} x & x \\ x & x \\ x & x \end{bmatrix}$$

A          B

2) Furthermore, the resulting matrix will have the number of rows of the first and columns of the second.

3) In other words, A can be multiplied by B, and AB = (m × p).

d. Matrices are actually large groups of numbers that are being manipulated.

3. **Matrix division** is accomplished by multiplying by an **inverse matrix**.

a. Multiplying an inverse matrix by its original matrix yields an identity matrix.

b. An **identity matrix** is a matrix in which all elements are zeros except the primary diagonal elements, which are ones. The primary diagonal consists of the elements that make up the line from the top left corner to the bottom right corner of the matrix. Thus, only a square matrix (rows = columns) has an inverse.

4. Matrix algebra is the basis for solving complicated linear problems.

a. These are problems with a large number of variables (which require a large number of equations).

b. A good example is the simplex tableau. See Chapter 17, Linear Programming.

B. **Boolean algebra** is the algebra of logic. It is sometimes called symbolic logic.

1. Boolean algebra is a method of expressing logic in a mathematical context.

a. It is primarily concerned with binary operations.

b. Boolean algebra is based on the commutative, associative, and distributive laws of binary operations.

2. Boolean algebra provides the theoretical concepts for computer design.

a. It is not used to solve managerial problems directly.

## 18.6 CALCULUS

A.   In business and economics, **differential calculus** is used to determine the points of revenue or profit maximization (maxima) and cost minimization (minima).

1.   Maxima or minima occur if the slope is 0. When a line becomes horizontal, it has no slope. Thus, the first step is to find the slope of the equation. Slope is the change in y over the change in x.

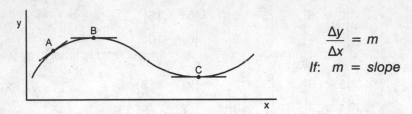

$$\frac{\Delta y}{\Delta x} = m$$

$$\textit{If: } m = \textit{slope}$$

The straight lines tangent to the curve at points B and C have a slope of 0. Point B is a maximum; point C is a minimum.

2.   The **derivative** of a function (equation) is its slope.

3.   The derivative of an equation for y that is stated in terms of a single independent variable x may be symbolized by $f'$, $\frac{dy}{dx}$, or $\frac{df(x)}{dx}$.

  a.   An equation stated in terms of x might be an expression such as
       $y = f(x) = x^2 + 12x + 7$, if x is an independent variable determining the value of y.

  b.   Thus, the derivative may be stated as $\frac{d(x^2 + 12x + 7)}{dx}$.

  c.   It may also be expressed as $f'(x^2 + 12x + 7)$.

4.   The basic formula for finding the derivative is

    $$f'(Ax^n) = nAx^{n-1}$$

    If: A  =  the constant, i.e., the number of independent variables or x's
        x  =  the variable being differentiated
        n  =  the exponent of the independent variable

  a.   EXAMPLES:    $f'(12) = 0$
                    $f'(12x) = 12$
                    $f'(12x^2) = 24x$
                    $f'(12x^3) = 36x^2$
                    $f'(12x^4) = 48x^3$
                    $f'(12x^{-2}) = -24x^{-3}$

5.   The derivative formula is applied to each term in the equation. The sum of the results is the derivative of the original equation.

  a.   EXAMPLE:    $f'(x^2 + 12x + 7) = ?$
                   $f'(x^2) = 2x, f'(12x) = 12, f'(7) = 0$
          Thus, $f'(x^2 + 12x + 7) = 2x + 12$

6.   The point(s) with zero slope on the graph of a function can be determined by

  a.   Computing the first derivative

  b.   Setting the first derivative equal to zero and solving the equation

c.   Computing the second derivative ( $f''$, $d^2y \div dx^2$, etc.) and determining whether it is positive or negative

1)   The second derivative of a function is the derivative of the first derivative.

2)   If the second derivative is positive, a point found by solving the first derivative for zero is a minimum; if it is negative, the point is a maximum.

a)   In A.5.a. on the previous page, the second derivative is positive $[f'(2x + 12) = 2]$. Consequently, the point is a minimum.

3)   If setting the first derivative equal to zero yielded two solutions, each is substituted into the second derivative.

4)   EXAMPLE:

a)   Factoring the first derivative yields:

$$f'\left( \frac{x^3}{3} - 4x^2 + 7x + 10 \right) = x^2 - 8x + 7$$

$$(x - 7)(x - 1) = 0$$
$$x = 7$$
$$x = 1$$

b)

$$f''\left( \frac{x^3}{3} - 4x^2 + 7x + 10 \right) = f'(x^2 - 8x + 7) = 2x - 8$$

$$2(7) - 8 = 6$$
$$2(1) - 8 = -6$$

c)   Accordingly, x = 7 is a minimum, and x = 1 is a maximum.

7.   EXAMPLE: The formula for the economic order quantity (EOQ) (see Chapter 14) results from differentiating the total cost with regard to the order quantity (x).

$$c = \frac{Da}{x} + \frac{xk}{2} + F \qquad \text{If:} \quad \begin{aligned} c &= \text{total cost} \\ x &= \text{EOQ} \\ a &= \text{cost per purchase order} \\ D &= \text{annual demand in units} \\ k &= \text{unit annual carrying cost} \\ F &= \text{fixed cost of ordering} \end{aligned}$$

$$f'\left( \frac{Da}{x} + \frac{xk}{2} + F \right) = \frac{-Da}{x^2} + \frac{k}{2}$$

a.   The second derivative ($2Da \div x^3$) must be positive because D, a, and x cannot be negative. Accordingly, setting the first derivative equal to zero gives the minimum total cost.

$$\frac{-Da}{x^2} + \frac{k}{2} = 0$$

$$\frac{k}{2} = \frac{Da}{x^2}$$

$$x^2 = \frac{2Da}{k}$$

$$x = \sqrt{\frac{2Da}{k}}$$

B.   **Integral calculus** is used to determine the area under a curve.  The area under a probability curve equals the probability.  Thus, integral calculus is used to evaluate the probability that events will occur.

1.   Integral calculus finds an antiderivative, i.e., the function that, if differentiated, would result in the function being integrated.

2.   The general form of the integral is $\int_a^b f(x)dx$, which is the integral of f(x) with respect to x.

3.   Some formulas for integration are

a.   $\int_a^b [kf(x)]dx = k \int_a^b f(x)dx$

1)   This formula indicates that constants (k) can be brought out of the integral.

b.   $\int x^n dx = \left[\dfrac{x^{n+1}}{n+1}\right]_a^b$

1)   The integral of $x^n$ is $x^{n+1}$ divided by n + 1.  The degenerate case is n = 1, which is the same as $x^1$, i.e., $x = x^1$.

c.   EXAMPLE:  For the function y = 4x,

$$\int_a^b ydx = \int_a^b (4x)dx = 4 \int_a^b (x)dx = 4(x^2 \div 2) = 2x^2$$

## 18.7 GAME THEORY

A.   **Game theory** classifies games according to how many players participate and the sum of the results.  In a two-person game, if the payoff is given by the loser to the winner, the algebraic sum is zero and the game is called a zero-sum game.

1.   If it is possible for both players to profit, however, it is called a positive-sum game.

B.   Mathematical models have been developed to select optimal strategies for certain simple games.

1.   Few applications of the mathematics of game theory have been made in business.  The concepts can be useful, however.

2.   For example, labor negotiations can be viewed as a two-person, nonzero-sum game.

C.   Game theorists have developed various decision rules.

1.   The **maximax criterion** is a decision rule adopted by risk-seeking, optimistic players who desire the largest possible payoff and are willing to accept high risk.  The player determines the payoff for each state of nature expected to arise after each possible decision, ascertains the maximum payoff for each decision, and then chooses the decision with the maximum payoff.

2.   A player who uses the **minimax criterion** determines the maximum loss for each decision possibility and then chooses the decision with the minimum maximum loss.  This rule produces the same result as the **maximin** technique, which determines the minimum payoff for each decision and then chooses the decision with the maximum minimum payoff.  Minimax and maximin are conservative criteria used by risk-averse players for whom the utility of a gain is less than the disutility of an equal loss.

3.   The **minimax regret criterion** is used by a player who wishes to minimize the effect of a bad decision in either direction.  It chooses the decision that has the lowest maximum opportunity cost (profit forgone).

4.    The **insufficient reason (Laplace) criterion** may be used when the decision maker cannot assign probabilities to the states of nature arising after a decision. The reasoning is that, if no probability distribution can be assigned, the probabilities must be equal, and the expected value is calculated accordingly; i.e., for each decision, the payoffs for the various states of nature are simply added, and the decision with the highest total is chosen. This criterion is risk-neutral.

5.    An **expected value criterion** might be used by a risk-neutral player, that is, one for whom the utility of a gain is the same as the disutility of an equal loss.

## 18.8 QUALITY TOOLS

A.   **Total quality management (TQM)** (see Chapter 5) emphasizes continuous improvement of processes. The following are some of the most fundamental tools for identifying and solving quality problems:

1.    **PERT** (Program Evaluation and Review Technique) and **CPM** (Critical Path Method) are similar techniques that use network diagrams to plan and control complex projects in which the proper sequencing of activities is crucial. See Module 18.3.

a.    A **Gantt chart** is a simpler project control device. It does not acknowledge the interrelationships of activities and omits calculations of activity times and costs. See Module 18.3.

2.    **Scatter diagrams** may be used to detect misstated data, relationships among variables, and unusual operating results. See Chapter 16.

3.    Also related to regression analysis are **statistical control charts**, which are graphic aids for monitoring the status of any process subject to random variations. Statistical control charts are discussed at greater length in Chapter 15.

4.    A **fishbone diagram** (also called a cause-and-effect diagram or an Ishikawa diagram) is a total quality management process improvement technique that is useful in studying causation (why the actual and desired situations differ). This format organizes the analysis of causation and helps to identify possible interactions among causes.

a.    The head of the skeleton represents the statement of the problem.

b.    The principal classifications of causes are represented by lines (bones) drawn diagonally from the heavy horizontal line (the spine).

c.    Smaller horizontal lines are added in their order of probability in each classification.

d.    Example:

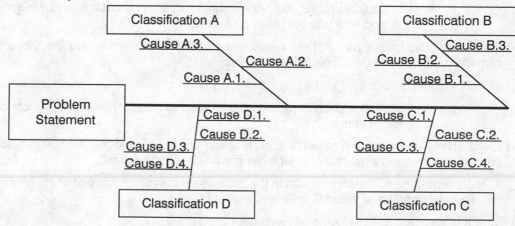

5.  **Bar charts** (bar graphs) are a two-dimensional (variables plotted on x and y axes) graphic means of quantitative comparison by using bars or rectangles with lengths proportional to the measure of the data or things being compared.

    a.  Bar charts may be vertical (column charts) or horizontal.

    b.  **Pareto analysis** is based on the concept that about 80% of results or effects are caused by about 20% of people or events. Thus, managers should concentrate on the relatively few people or events that have the most significant effects. **Pareto diagrams** are bar charts in which the frequencies of the various types of adverse conditions that may occur in a given process are depicted.

        1)  For example, an auditor might construct a Pareto diagram of the types and numbers of control deviations found in the receiving department. The tallest (or longest) bar signifies the most common type of problem.

    c.  A **histogram** is a bar chart used to depict a frequency distribution.

        1)  It is used to create a graphic representation of the results of repeated measurements of a single variable, with the class intervals on the horizontal axis and the frequency (or relative frequency) of occurrence on the vertical axis.

            a)  Whether the histogram approximates or deviates from a normal distribution is of interest for control purposes.

        2)  EXAMPLE: A histogram of the number of occurrences of various net cash flows is given below.

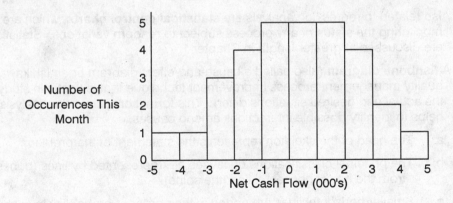

            a)  Cash flows between $0 and $1,000 occurred on 5 days; cash flows between $1,000 and $2,000 also occurred on 5 days; cash flows between –$2,000 and –$3,000 occurred on 3 days, etc.

6.  **Line charts** (also known as run, time series, or trend charts) show the frequency or amount of a variable (vertical axis) over time (horizontal axis).

    a.  For example, sales might be plotted over a period of years on a simple line chart.

        1)  A multiple-line chart compares items, such as sales of several products over a period of years.

7.  **Flowcharting** is a pictorial method of analyzing and understanding the processes and procedures involved in operations, whether manual or computerized.

    a.  Flowcharting is therefore useful in the preliminary survey and in obtaining an understanding of internal control.

    b.  It is also helpful in systems development.

    c.  Flowcharting is based on standardized symbols.

        1)  However, different systems of symbols have been devised, so care must be taken that the usage is consistent.

8.  The Taguchi quality loss function is based on the principle that quality losses occur even when items are within specified limits or tolerances. Thus, any variation from a quality target for a characteristic results in hidden quality costs.

    a.  The basic formula is

    $$L = k \, (x - T)^2$$

    If: L  = the quality costs per unit
        k  = a constant based on the entity's external failure cost experience
        x  = actual measure of the quality variable
        T  = target value of the quality variable

    1)  The estimate of the constant is

    $$k = c \div d^2$$

    If: c  = the loss at a specification limit
        d  = the difference between the target value and the specification limit

    2)  The following is the graph of a Taguchi loss function (the quality cost at the target value is $0):

    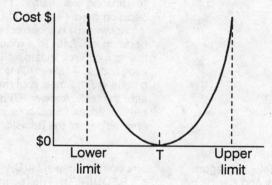

## 18.1 Introduction to Quantitative Methods

**1.** Which is the false statement about quantitative methods?

    A.   Quantitative models are usually oversimplifications.

    B.   It is impossible to include all relevant variables in each model, and the techniques may not be justifiable on a cost/benefit basis.

    C.   Every decision may be modeled mathematically and will always permit a deterministic solution.

    D.   Behavioral issues should not be taken into account in analyzing quantitative methods.

The correct answer is (D). *(Publisher)*
    **REQUIRED:** The incorrect statement about quantitative methods.
    **DISCUSSION:** It is virtually impossible to include all relevant variables in a mathematical model. Thus, the model must be reviewed in light of behavioral issues as well as other considerations.
    Answer (A) is incorrect because mathematical models are usually oversimplifications of the real world; to perform the calculations, assumptions must be made. Answer (B) is incorrect because some relevant variables may not be quantified and are therefore not included. Also, the techniques can be very complex and costly. Thus, cost-benefit analysis may not justify the use of some quantitative methods. Answer (C) is incorrect because every real-life decision situation may be modeled mathematically under certain assumptions, and a deterministic solution may be achieved.

**2.** Variables that are important to the decision-making process but are out of the control of the decision maker, e.g., economic conditions, are considered to be

    A.   Exogenous variables.

    B.   Decision variables.

    C.   Performance criteria.

    D.   Constraints.

The correct answer is (A). *(CMA, adapted)*
    **REQUIRED:** The term for variables that are outside the control of the decision maker.
    **DISCUSSION:** Exogenous or input variables are outside the control of the decision maker. Exogenous means "originating externally." These variables influence the decision model (system) but are not influenced by it.
    Answer (B) is incorrect because at least one of the decision variables in a model must be under the decision maker's control; that is, at least one variable cannot be exogenous. Answer (C) is incorrect because performance criteria are the means of measuring the results of a decision after the fact. Answer (D) is incorrect because constraints are limitations (constants, not variables) that must be considered as part of the decision process.

**3.** Through the use of decision models, managers thoroughly analyze many alternatives and decide on the best alternative for the company. Often the actual results achieved from a particular decision are not what was expected when the decision was made. In addition, an alternative that was not selected may prove to have been the best for the company. The appropriate technique to analyze the alternatives by varying expected inputs is

    A.   Expected value analysis.

    B.   Linear programming.

    C.   Program Evaluation Review Technique (PERT).

    D.   Sensitivity analysis.

The correct answer is (D). *(CMA, adapted)*
    **REQUIRED:** The technique that involves altering expected inputs during the decision process.
    **DISCUSSION:** Sensitivity modeling can be used to determine the outcome of a variety of decisions. A trial-and-error method may be adopted, usually in a computer model, to calculate the sensitivity of the solution (variability of outcomes) to changes in a variable.
    Answer (A) is incorrect because expected value analysis is used to determine an anticipated return or cost based upon probabilities of events and their related outcomes. Answer (B) is incorrect because linear programming optimizes a function given certain constraints. Answer (C) is incorrect because PERT is a network technique used to plan and control large projects.

**4.** A company is deciding whether to purchase an automated machine to manufacture one of its products. Expected net cash flows from this decision depend on several factors, interactions among those factors, and the probabilities associated with different levels of those factors. The method that the company should use to evaluate the distribution of net cash flows from this decision and changes in net cash flows resulting from changes in levels of various factors is

A. Simulation and sensitivity analysis.

B. Linear programming.

C. Correlation analysis.

D. Differential analysis.

The correct answer is (A). *(CIA, adapted)*
**REQUIRED:** The technique used to evaluate cash flows from the purchase of a machine.
**DISCUSSION:** Simulation is a technique used to describe the behavior of a real-world system over time. This technique usually employs a computer program to perform the simulation computations. Sensitivity analysis examines how outcomes change as the model parameters change.
Answer (B) is incorrect because linear programming is a mathematical technique for optimizing a given objective function subject to certain constraints. Answer (C) is incorrect because correlation analysis is a statistical procedure for studying the relation between variables. Answer (D) is incorrect because differential analysis is used for decision making that compares differences in costs (revenues) of two or more options.

**5.** Which of the following is not true about simulation models?

A. They are deterministic in nature.

B. The may involve sampling.

C. They mathematically estimate what actual performance would be.

D. They emulate stochastic systems.

The correct answer is (A). *(CIA, adapted)*
**REQUIRED:** The false statement about simulation models.
**DISCUSSION:** Simulation is a technique for experimenting with logical/mathematical models using a computer. The simulation procedure has five steps: define the objectives, formulate the model, validate the model, design the experiment, and conduct the simulation and evaluate the results. A simulation uses the laws of probability to generate values for random variables. Thus, simulation models are probabilistic, not deterministic.
Answer (B) is incorrect because simulation modeling samples the operation of a system. Answer (C) is incorrect because simulation models mathematically estimate what performance would be under various conditions. Answer (D) is incorrect because simulation models are by definition stochastic or probabilistic models.

**6.** Quick Response Plumbing (QRP), a wholesale distributor, supplies plumbing contractors and retailers throughout the Northeast on a next-day delivery basis. QRP has a centrally located warehouse to accept receipts of plumbing supplies. The warehouse has a single dock to accept and unload railroad freight cars during the night. It takes 5 hours to unload each freight car. QRP's prior records indicate that the number of freight cars that arrive in the course of a night range from zero to five or more, with no indicated pattern of arrivals. If more than two freight cars arrive on the same night, some freight must be held until the next day for unloading. QRP wants to estimate the wait time when more than two freight cars arrive in the same night. The appropriate technique to analyze the arrival of freight cars is

A. Integer programming.

B. Linear programming.

C. Sensitivity analysis.

D. Monte Carlo simulation.

The correct answer is (D). *(CMA, adapted)*
**REQUIRED:** The appropriate technique to analyze the arrival of freight cars given no indicated pattern of arrivals.
**DISCUSSION:** Monte Carlo simulation is a technique to generate the individual values for a random variable, such as the arrival of freight cars. A random number generator is used to produce numbers with a uniform probability distribution. The second step of the Monte Carlo process transforms the random numbers into values consistent with the desired distribution. The performance of the model may then be investigated by randomly selecting values for each of the variables in the model based on the probability distribution of each variable and then calculating the value of the solution. If this process is performed many times, the distribution of results from the model will be obtained.
Answer (A) is incorrect because integer programming is a variation of linear programming that concerns problems in which some variables have discrete, noncontinuous values. Answer (B) is incorrect because linear programming optimizes a function, subject to constraints. Answer (C) is incorrect because sensitivity analysis involves making several estimates of key variables and recalculating results based on the alternative estimates.

**7.** A construction firm is in the process of building a simulation model for cost estimation purposes. Management has identified all relevant variables and relationships and gathered data on past projects. The next step should be model

A.  Implementation.

B.  Design.

C.  Validation.

D.  Experimentation.

The correct answer is (C). *(CIA, adapted)*

**REQUIRED:** The next step in developing a simulation model.

**DISCUSSION:** The first step to build a simulation model is to define the objectives of the project. The next step is to formulate the model, that is, to determine the variables to be included, their behavior, and their interrelationships in precise logical and mathematical terms. The third step is to validate the model. Some assurance is needed that the results of the experiment will be realistic. For example, if the model gives results equivalent to what actually happened, the model is historically valid. Some risk remains, however, that changes could make the model invalid for the future.

Answer (A) is incorrect because implementation of the simulation follows validation. Answer (B) is incorrect because the model has already been formulated (designed). Answer (D) is incorrect because experimentation is sampling the operation of the model after validation and before full implementation.

---

Questions 8 and 9 are based on the following information. A computer store sells four computer models designated as P104, X104, A104, and S104. The store manager has made random number assignments to represent customer choices based on past sales data. The assignments are shown below.

| Model | Random Numbers |
|-------|----------------|
| P104  | 0-1            |
| X104  | 2-6            |
| A104  | 7-8            |
| S104  | 9              |

**8.** The probability that a customer will select model P104 is

A.  10%

B.  20%

C.  50%

D.  30%

The correct answer is (B). *(CMA, adapted)*

**REQUIRED:** The probability that a customer will select model P104.

**DISCUSSION:** A total of ten random numbers have been assigned. Of these, two (0 and 1) have been assigned to model P104. Assuming that each number has an equal and nonzero chance of selection, the probability is 20% that a customer will select that model.

Answer (A) is incorrect because 10% is the probability a customer will select S104. Answer (C) is incorrect because 50% is the probability associated with X104. Answer (D) is incorrect because 30% is the probability that P104 or S104 will be selected.

**9.** In running a simulation of the computer demand, the following numbers are drawn in sequence: 2, 8, and 6. The simulation indicates that the third customer will purchase

A.  Model P104.

B.  Model X104.

C.  Model A104.

D.  Model S104.

The correct answer is (B). *(CMA, adapted)*

**REQUIRED:** The model that will be purchased by the third customer when the numbers drawn are 2, 8, and 6.

**DISCUSSION:** The third customer is simulated by the third number drawn. Thus, the third customer's purchase is represented by the number six. The numbers two through six correspond to model X104. Thus, the third customer is expected to purchase model X104.

Answer (A) is incorrect because 0 and 1 are assigned to P104. Answer (C) is incorrect because 7 and 8 are assigned to Model A104. Answer (D) is incorrect because 9 is assigned to Model S104.

**10.** Probability (risk) analysis is

    A.  Used only when the sum of probabilities is less than one.

    B.  Used only for situations involving five or fewer possible outcomes.

    C.  Incompatible with sensitivity analysis.

    D.  An extension of sensitivity analysis.

The correct answer is (D). *(CPA, adapted)*

**REQUIRED:** The correct description of probability (risk) analysis.

**DISCUSSION:** Probability (risk) analysis is used to examine the array of possible outcomes given alternative parameters. Sensitivity analysis answers what-if questions when alternative parameters are changed. Thus, risk (probability) analysis is similar to sensitivity analysis: both evaluate the probabilities and effects of differing inputs or outputs.

Answer (A) is incorrect because the sum must equal one. Answer (B) is incorrect because probability analysis can be used when many outcomes are possible. Answer (C) is incorrect because probability analysis enhances sensitivity analysis.

**11.** A firm is attempting to estimate the reserves for doubtful accounts. The probabilities of these doubtful accounts follow a transition process over time. They evolve from their starting value to a changed value. As such, the most effective technique to analyze the problem is

    A.  Markov chain analysis.

    B.  Econometric theory.

    C.  Monte Carlo analysis.

    D.  Dynamic programming.

The correct answer is (A). *(CIA, adapted)*

**REQUIRED:** The most effective technique to analyze a problem involving changing probabilities.

**DISCUSSION:** A Markov chain is a series of events in which the probability of an event depends on the immediately preceding event. An example is the game of blackjack in which the probability of certain cards being dealt is dependent upon what cards have already been dealt. In the analysis of bad debts, preceding events, such as collections, credit policy changes, and writeoffs, affect the probabilities of future losses.

Answer (B) is incorrect because econometrics forecasts the impact of different economic policies and conditions. Answer (C) is incorrect because Monte Carlo analysis is a simulation technique that uses random-number procedures to create values for probabilistic components. Answer (D) is incorrect because dynamic programming is a problem-solving approach that breaks a large mathematical model into a number of smaller, manageable problems.

## 18.2 Queuing Theory

**12.** A company has several departments that conduct technical studies and prepare reports for clients. Recently, there have been long delays in having these reports copied at the company's centralized copy center because of the dramatic increase in business. Management is considering decentralizing copy services to reduce the turnaround and provide clients with timely reports. An appropriate technique for minimizing turnaround time and the cost of providing copy services is

    A.  Queuing theory.

    B.  Linear programming.

    C.  Regression analysis.

    D.  Game theory.

The correct answer is (A). *(CIA, adapted)*

**REQUIRED:** The appropriate method for minimizing turnaround time and the cost of providing copy services.

**DISCUSSION:** Queuing theory is a group of mathematical models for systems involving waiting lines. In general, a queuing system consists of a waiting line and a service facility (a copy center in this case). The objective is to minimize total costs, including both service and waiting costs (turnaround time), for a given rate of arrivals.

Answer (B) is incorrect because linear programming optimizes a given objective function subject to constraints. Answer (C) is incorrect because regression analysis estimates the relation among variables. Answer (D) is incorrect because game theory is an approach to decision making that considers the actions of competitors.

**13.** Queuing models are concerned with balancing the cost of waiting in the queue with the

- A. Cost of providing service.
- B. Number of customers in the queue.
- C. Average waiting time in the queue.
- D. Usage rate for the service being rendered.

The correct answer is (A). *(CMA, adapted)*

**REQUIRED:** The true statement about the objective of queuing models.

**DISCUSSION:** Queuing (waiting-line) models minimize, for a given rate of arrivals, the sum of (1) the cost of providing service (including facility costs and operating costs) and (2) the cost of idle resources waiting in line. The latter may be a direct cost, if paid employees are waiting, or an opportunity cost in the case of waiting customers. This minimization occurs at the point where the cost of waiting is balanced by the cost of providing service.

Answers (B), (C), and (D) are incorrect because queuing theory minimizes the sum of the costs of waiting and of providing service.

**14.** The operating condition that cannot be identified by using a queuing model is the

- A. Average percentage of time that a service facility is idle.
- B. Probability of a specified number of units in the queue.
- C. Actual amount of time each unit spends in the queue.
- D. Average number of units in the system and the mean length of the queue.

The correct answer is (C). *(CMA, adapted)*

**REQUIRED:** The operating condition that cannot be identified by using a queuing model.

**DISCUSSION:** Queuing models determine the operating characteristics of a waiting line: the probability that no units are in the system, the average units in the line, the average units in the system, the average time a unit waits, the average time a unit is in the system, the probability that a unit must wait, and the probability of a given number of units in the system. However, the actual time spent in the queue cannot be determined from the model.

Answers (A), (B), and (D) are incorrect because the queuing model calculates the average percentage of time that a service facility is idle, the probability of a specified number of units in the queue, and the average number of units in the system and the mean length of the queue.

**15.** A bank has changed from a system in which lines are formed in front of each teller to a one-line, multiple-server system. When a teller is free, the person at the head of the line goes to that teller. Implementing the new system will

- A. Decrease the bank's wage expenses because the new system uses fewer tellers.
- B. Decrease time customers spend in the line.
- C. Increase accuracy in teller reconciliations at the end of the day because fewer customers are served by each teller.
- D. Improve on-the-job training for tellers because each will perform different duties.

The correct answer is (B). *(CIA, adapted)*

**REQUIRED:** The effect of implementing the new queuing system.

**DISCUSSION:** When all customers must wait in a single queue, a decrease in waiting time is possible given multiple servers. An added effect is to increase customer satisfaction.

Answer (A) is incorrect because the number of employees is unlikely to change due to the new system. Answer (C) is incorrect because, assuming a Poisson process, the number of customers per teller will not change. Answer (D) is incorrect because tellers' duties will not change, so on-the-job training will not improve.

**16.** The drive-through service at a fast-food restaurant consists of driving up to place an order, advancing to a window to pay for the order, and then advancing to another window to receive the items ordered. This type of waiting-line system is

   A. Single channel, single phase.

   B. Single channel, multiple phase.

   C. Multiple channel, single phase.

   D. Multiple channel, multiple phase.

The correct answer is (B). *(CIA, adapted)*

   **REQUIRED:** The type of waiting-line system described.

   **DISCUSSION:** The drive-through represents a single queue (channel). Because this waiting line has three services in series, it may be said to be multiple phase. Another example is the typical factory assembly line. This terminology (channel, phase), however, is not used by all writers on queuing theory.

   Answer (A) is incorrect because service by one ticket-seller at a movie theater is an example of a single-channel, single-phase system. Answer (C) is incorrect because supermarket checkout lines are a common example of multiple single-phase servers servicing multiple lines. Answer (D) is incorrect because an example of a multiple-channel, multiple-phase system is a set of supermarket checkout lines each of which is served in sequence by a cashier and a person who packs grocery bags.

**17.** A post office serves customers in a single line at one service window. During peak periods, the rate of arrivals has a Poisson distribution with an average of 100 customers per hour and service times that are exponentially distributed with an average of 60 seconds per customer. From this, one can conclude that the

   A. Queue will expand to infinity.

   B. Server will be idle one-sixth of the time.

   C. Average rate is 100 customers per hour.

   D. Average customer waiting time is 2.5 minutes.

The correct answer is (A). *(CIA, adapted)*

   **REQUIRED:** The conclusion that can be reached about a queuing model.

   **DISCUSSION:** One hundred customers arrive in line per hour and only 60 are serviced per hour. Accordingly, the queue will expand to infinity during peak periods.

   Answers (B) and (D) are incorrect because insufficient information is given to determine overall idle time or average customer waiting time. The question gives only peak period data. Answer (C) is incorrect because peak customer service is only 60 per hour.

Questions 18 through 20 are based on the following information. A bank has two drive-in lanes to serve customers, one attached to the bank itself, the second on an island. One teller serves both stations. The bank is interested in determining the average waiting times of customers and has developed a model based on random numbers. The two key factors are the time between successive car arrivals and the time customers wait in line.

Assume that the analysis begins with cars just arriving at both service windows, both requiring 3 minutes of service time. Car 1 is at the attached window and car 2 at the island window. A car will always go to the window attached to the bank unless that window has more cars waiting than the island window. The lone teller will always serve the car that arrived first. If two cars arrive simultaneously, the one at the attached window will be served before the one at the island.

Based on a known probability distribution, the bank assigns random numbers to arrival and service times:

| Random # | Time between Arrivals | Random # | Service Time |
|----------|-----------------------|----------|--------------|
| 1        | 1 minute              | 1,2      | 1 minute     |
| 2, 3     | 2 minutes             | 3        | 2 minutes    |
| 4, 5, 6  | 3 minutes             | 4, 5, 6  | 3 minutes    |
| 7, 8     | 4 minutes             | 7, 8, 9  | 4 minutes    |

The bank then selects random numbers for the next two cars as

Random Numbers Selected:

|       | Arrival | Service |
|-------|---------|---------|
| Car 3 | #3      | #7      |
| Car 4 | #7      | #8      |

**18.** The arrival time follows which probability distribution?

   A.  Binomial.

   B.  Chi-square.

   C.  Poisson.

   D.  Exponential.

The correct answer is (C). *(CIA, adapted)*
   **REQUIRED:** The distribution of the arrival time.
   **DISCUSSION:** Queuing models assume that arrivals follow a Poisson process: the events (arrivals) are independent, any number of events must be possible in the interval of time, the probability of an event is proportional to the length of the interval, and the probability of more than one event is negligible if the interval is sufficiently small. If $\lambda$ is the average number of events in a given interval, k is the number of events, and e is the natural logarithm (2.71828...), the probability of k is

$$f(k) = \frac{\lambda^k e^{-\lambda}}{k!}$$

   Answer (A) is incorrect because the binomial distribution is a discrete distribution in which each trial has just two outcomes. Answer (B) is incorrect because the chi-square distribution is a continuous distribution used to measure the fit between actual data and the theoretical distribution. Answer (D) is incorrect because service time has an exponential distribution. This distribution gives the probability of zero events in a given interval, i.e., the probability of a specified time between arrivals.

**19.** The time that car 3 will have to wait to be serviced (not including its own service time) is

   A.  0-2 minutes.

   B.  3 minutes.

   C.  4 minutes.

   D.  5+ minutes.

The correct answer is (C). *(CIA, adapted)*
   **REQUIRED:** The time that car 3 will have to wait to be serviced (not including its own service time).
   **DISCUSSION:** Car 1 is at the attached window and will require 3 minutes to service. Car 2 must wait for car 1 to be serviced (3 minutes in the queue + 3 minutes to be serviced = 6 minutes). Car 3 arrived at the attached window 2 minutes after cars 1 and 2. It must wait 1 minute for car 1 to be serviced and 3 minutes for car 2 to be serviced, a waiting time of 4 minutes.
   Answers (A), (B), and (D) are incorrect because car 3 must wait for 4 minutes.

**20.** The time that car 4 will have to wait to be serviced (not including its own service time) is

 A.  0-2 minutes.

 B.  3 minutes.

 C.  4 minutes.

 D.  5+ minutes.

The correct answer is (C). *(CIA, adapted)*

   **REQUIRED:** The time that car 4 will have to wait to be serviced (not including its own service time).

   **DISCUSSION:** Car 4 arrives at the just-vacated island window 4 minutes after car 3. It must wait 4 minutes for car 3 to be serviced.

   Answers (A), (B), and (D) are incorrect because car 4 must wait 4 minutes.

## 18.3 Network Models

**21.** A bank is designing an on-the-job training program for its branch managers. The bank would like to design the program so that participants can complete it as quickly as possible. The training program requires that certain activities be completed before others. For example, a participant cannot make credit loan decisions without first having obtained experience in the loan department. An appropriate scheduling technique for this training program is

 A.  PERT/CPM.

 B.  Linear programming.

 C.  Queuing theory.

 D.  Sensitivity analysis.

The correct answer is (A). *(CIA, adapted)*

   **REQUIRED:** The appropriate scheduling technique.

   **DISCUSSION:** PERT/CPM is a network technique for scheduling interrelated time series activities and identifying any critical paths in the series of activities. The critical path is the longest path through the network.

   Answer (B) is incorrect because linear programming is a mathematical technique for maximizing or minimizing a given objective function subject to certain constraints. Answer (C) is incorrect because queuing theory is used to minimize the costs of waiting lines when items arrive randomly at a service point and are serviced sequentially. Answer (D) is incorrect because sensitivity analysis is a method for studying the effects of changes in one or more variables on the results of a decision model.

**22.** PERT and the critical path method (CPM) are used for

 A.  Determining the optimal product mix.

 B.  Project planning and control.

 C.  Determining product costs.

 D.  Determining the number of servers needed in a fast food restaurant.

The correct answer is (B). *(CMA, adapted)*

   **REQUIRED:** The reason for using PERT and CPM.

   **DISCUSSION:** PERT (Program Evaluation and Review Technique) and CPM are useful in the planning and control of a complex system or process. Each constructs a network of time relationships between the events or subprojects to identify those having a direct effect on the completion date of the project as a whole.

   Answer (A) is incorrect because determining product mix can be accomplished by using linear programming. Answer (C) is incorrect because product costs are determined by cost accounting. Answer (D) is incorrect because queuing theory determines the number of servers needed in a restaurant.

**23.** The primary difference between PERT and CPM is that

 A.  CPM uses probabilities on the activity times and PERT does not.

 B.  PERT considers activity costs and CPM does not.

 C.  PERT can assign probabilities to activity times and CPM does not.

 D.  CPM considers activity costs and PERT does not.

The correct answer is (D). *(CMA, adapted)*

   **REQUIRED:** The primary difference between PERT and CPM.

   **DISCUSSION:** CPM may be thought of as a subset of PERT. Like PERT, it is a network technique, but, unlike PERT, it uses deterministic time and cost estimates. Its advantages include cost estimates plus the concept of crash efforts and costs. These estimates allow the project manager to estimate the costs of completing the project if some of the activities are completed on a crash basis.

   Answers (A) and (C) are incorrect because a less significant difference between PERT and CPM is that PERT uses probabilistic estimates of completion times. CPM times are deterministic. Answer (B) is incorrect because CPM but not PERT uses activity costs and considers crash times.

**24.** PERT is widely used to plan and measure progress toward scheduled events. PERT is combined with cost data to produce a PERT-Cost analysis to

    A. Calculate the total project cost inclusive of the additional slack time.

    B. Evaluate and optimize trade-offs between time of an event's completion and its cost to complete.

    C. Implement computer-integrated manufacturing concepts.

    D. Calculate expected activity times.

The correct answer is (B). *(CMA, adapted)*
    **REQUIRED:** The true statement about PERT-Cost analysis.
    **DISCUSSION:** Combining PERT with cost data permits decisions as to whether the benefits of earlier completion of a project are justified in terms of the additional costs of completion. For this purpose, activity times and costs must be estimated for both normal and crash efforts.
    Answer (A) is incorrect because slack time is an inherent part of the noncritical paths on PERT projects. Answer (C) is incorrect because PERT-Cost can be used without computerization. Answer (D) is incorrect because costs are not needed for these calculations.

**25.** In a PERT (Program Evaluation Review Technique) or CPM (Critical Path Method) network, the critical path is the

    A. Least costly path through the network.

    B. Most costly path through the network.

    C. Shortest path through the network with the least amount of slack.

    D. Longest path through the network with the least amount of slack.

The correct answer is (D). *(CMA, adapted)*
    **REQUIRED:** The definition of the critical path.
    **DISCUSSION:** In a PERT or CPM network, the critical path is the longest path in time through the network. It is critical because, if any activity on the critical path takes longer than expected, the entire project will be delayed. Moreover, any decrease in time for an activity not on the critical path will not shorten the project. Every network has at least one critical path. Paths that are not critical have slack time.
    Answers (A) and (B) are incorrect because the critical path relates to time, not cost. Answer (C) is incorrect because the shortest path has the most slack and is therefore not critical.

**26.** A Gantt chart

    A. Shows the critical path for a project.

    B. Is used for determining an optimal product mix.

    C. Shows only the activities along the critical path of a network.

    D. Does not necessarily show the critical path through a network.

The correct answer is (D). *(CMA, adapted)*
    **REQUIRED:** The true statement about a Gantt chart.
    **DISCUSSION:** A Gantt or bar chart is sometimes used in conjunction with PERT or CPM to show the progress of a special project. Time is shown on the horizontal axis, the length of a bar equals the length of an activity, and shading indicates the degree of completion. However, the Gantt chart is not as sophisticated as PERT or CPM in that it does not reflect the relationships among the activities or define a critical path.
    Answer (A) is incorrect because the critical path is not shown on a Gantt chart. Answer (B) is incorrect because linear programming is used to determine an optimal product mix. Answer (C) is incorrect because a Gantt chart shows the activities to be completed but not their sequencing.

**27.** In the Program Evaluation Review Technique (PERT), slack is the

    A. Uncertainty associated with time estimates.

    B. Path that has the largest amount of time associated with it.

    C. Excess time available in the completion of the project after crashing the critical path.

    D. Number of days an activity can be delayed without forcing a delay for the entire project.

The correct answer is (D). *(CMA, adapted)*
    **REQUIRED:** The meaning of slack in a PERT analysis.
    **DISCUSSION:** The critical path is the longest path in time through the network. That path is critical because, if any activity on the critical path takes longer than expected, the entire project will be delayed. Paths that are not critical have slack time. Slack is the number of days an activity can be delayed without forcing a delay of the entire project.
    Answer (A) is incorrect because uncertainty is reflected in the use of probabilistic estimates of completion times. Answer (B) is incorrect because the path with the largest amount of time associated with it is the critical path. Answer (C) is incorrect because slack will exist for some activities whether or not the critical path is crashed.

**28.** When making a cost/time trade-off in PERT analysis, the first activity that should be crashed is the activity

   A. On the critical path with the lowest unit crash cost.

   B. On the critical path with the maximum possible time reduction.

   C. With the lowest unit crash cost.

   D. With the largest amount of slack.

The correct answer is (A). *(CMA, adapted)*
   **REQUIRED:** The first activity to be crashed when making a cost/time trade-off in PERT analysis.
   **DISCUSSION:** When making a cost/time trade-off, the first activity to be crashed (have its completion time accelerated) is one on the critical path. To select an activity on another path would not reduce the total time of completion. The activity chosen should have a completion time that can be accelerated at the lowest possible cost per unit of time saved.
   Answer (B) is incorrect because the time reduction should be related to its cost. Answer (C) is incorrect because the activity with the lowest unit crash cost may not be on the critical path. The activity selected must be on the critical path. Answer (D) is incorrect because the activity must be on the path with the least slack (the critical path).

**29.** Which of the following terms is not used in project management?

   A. Dummy activity.

   B. Latest finish.

   C. Optimistic time.

   D. Lumpy demand.

The correct answer is (D). *(CIA, adapted)*
   **REQUIRED:** The term not used in project management.
   **DISCUSSION:** Project management concerns managing teams assigned to special projects. Lumpy demand is periodic demand for a product or service that increases in large, lumpy increments.
   Answer (A) is incorrect because a dummy activity is one that consumes no time but establishes precedence among activities. It is used specifically in project management. Answer (B) is incorrect because the latest finish is the latest that an activity can finish without causing delay in the completion of the project. Answer (C) is incorrect because optimistic time is the time for completing a project if all goes well.

**30.** California Building Corporation uses the critical path method to monitor construction jobs. The company is currently 2 weeks behind schedule on Job #181, which is subject to a $10,500-per-week completion penalty. Path A-B-C-F-G-H-I has a normal completion time of 20 weeks, and critical path A-D-E-F-G-H-I has a normal completion time of 22 weeks. The following activities can be crashed:

| Activities | Cost to Crash 1 Week | Cost to Crash 2 Weeks |
|---|---|---|
| BC | $ 8,000 | $15,000 |
| DE | 10,000 | 19,600 |
| EF | 8,800 | 19,500 |

California Building desires to reduce the normal completion time of Job #181 and, at the same time, report the highest possible income for the year. California Building should crash

   A. Activity BC 1 week and activity EF 1 week.

   B. Activity DE 1 week and activity BC 1 week.

   C. Activity EF 2 weeks.

   D. Activity DE 1 week and activity EF 1 week.

The correct answer is (D). *(CMA, adapted)*
   **REQUIRED:** The activity that should be crashed (speeded up at additional cost) to maximize income.
   **DISCUSSION:** Activities that are to be crashed in a CPM problem should be on the critical (longest) path. Thus, activity BC should not be selected because it is not on the critical path. To finish activity BC 2 weeks early would not reduce the total time to complete the project. Thus, the only feasible choices are DE and EF on the critical path. The total cost to crash DE and EF for 1 week each is $18,800 ($10,000 + $8,800), which is less than the cost to crash either activity for 2 weeks. Thus, DE and EF should be crashed for 1 week each because the total cost is less than the $21,000 ($10,500 x 2) 2-week delay penalty.
   Answers (A) and (B) are incorrect because BC is not on the critical path. Answer (C) is incorrect because crashing activity EF 2 weeks costs $19,500, which exceeds the cost of crashing DE 1 week and EF 1 week.

**31.** When using PERT (Program Evaluation Review Technique), the expected time for an activity when given an optimistic time (a), a pessimistic time (b), and a most likely time (m), is calculated by which one of the following formulas?

A. (b – a) ÷ 2

B. (a + b) ÷ 2

C. (a + 4m + b) ÷ 6

D. (4abm) ÷ 6

The correct answer is (C). *(CMA, adapted)*
   **REQUIRED:** The formula for calculating the expected time for an activity when using PERT.
   **DISCUSSION:** PERT analysis includes probabilistic estimates of activity completion times. Three time estimates are made: optimistic, most likely, and pessimistic. These estimates are assumed to approximate a beta probability distribution. PERT approximates the mean of the beta distribution by dividing the sum of the optimistic time, the pessimistic time, and four times the most likely time by six.
   Answers (A) and (B) are incorrect because the most likely time estimate should be in the formula. Answer (D) is incorrect because all time estimates are not weighted equally.

**32.** In a PERT network, the optimistic time for a particular activity is 9 weeks, and the pessimistic time is 21 weeks. Which one of the following is the best estimate of the standard deviation for the activity?

A. 2

B. 6

C. 9

D. 12

The correct answer is (A). *(CMA, adapted)*
   **REQUIRED:** The standard deviation for the completion time of a PERT project given an optimistic time and a pessimistic time.
   **DISCUSSION:** PERT approximates the standard deviation by dividing the difference between the pessimistic and optimistic times by six. The basis for this approximation is that various probability distributions have tails that lie about plus or minus three standard deviations from the mean. Accordingly, the estimated standard deviation is 2 weeks [(21 weeks – 9 weeks) ÷ 6].
   Answer (B) is incorrect because 6 is the approximate number of standard deviations in various probability distributions. Answer (C) is incorrect because 9 is the pessimistic time. Answer (D) is incorrect because 12 is the optimistic time minus the pessimistic time.

**33.** A PERT network has only two activities on its critical path. These activities have standard deviations of 6 and 8, respectively. The standard deviation of the project completion time is

A. 7

B. 10

C. 14

D. 100

The correct answer is (B). *(CMA, adapted)*
   **REQUIRED:** The standard deviation of the project completion time.
   **DISCUSSION:** The standard deviation of the project completion time is the square root of the sum of the variances (squares of the standard deviations) of the times for activities on the critical path. The standard deviation of the project completion time (time for the critical path) is therefore the square root of $(6^2 + 8^2)$, or 10.
   Answer (A) is incorrect because 7 is the mean of the standard deviations. Answer (C) is incorrect because 14 is the sum of the standard deviations. Answer (D) is incorrect because 100 is the sum of the variances.

**34.** Using the critical path method, what is the earliest finish for activity h?

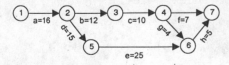

A. 61

B. 45

C. 47

D. 87

The correct answer is (A). *(CIA, adapted)*
   **REQUIRED:** The earliest finish for an activity.
   **DISCUSSION:** The earliest finish for activity h is dependent on the time required for the antecedent activities (a, b, c, d, e, and g). These activities will be completed in 56 time units (path a-d-e requires 56 time units, whereas path a-b-c-g requires 42 time units). Hence, the earliest at which activity h can be completed is 61 time units (56 + 5).
   Answer (B) is incorrect because path a-b-c-f requires 45 time units and excludes activity h. Answer (C) is incorrect because path a-b-c-g-h requires 47 time units and is shorter than path a-d-e-h. Answer (D) is incorrect because activity h can be completed in fewer than 87 time units. Some antecedent activities can be done concurrently.

Questions 35 and 36 are based on the following information. The PERT network diagram and corresponding activity cost chart for a manufacturing project at Networks, Inc. is presented below. The numbers in the diagram are the expected times (in days) to perform each activity in the project.

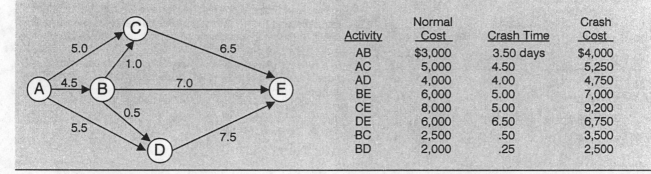

| Activity | Normal Cost | Crash Time | Crash Cost |
|----------|-------------|------------|------------|
| AB | $3,000 | 3.50 days | $4,000 |
| AC | 5,000 | 4.50 | 5,250 |
| AD | 4,000 | 4.00 | 4,750 |
| BE | 6,000 | 5.00 | 7,000 |
| CE | 8,000 | 5.00 | 9,200 |
| DE | 6,000 | 6.50 | 6,750 |
| BC | 2,500 | .50 | 3,500 |
| BD | 2,000 | .25 | 2,500 |

**35.** The expected time of the critical path is

A. 12.0 days.

B. 13.0 days.

C. 11.5 days.

D. 12.5 days.

The correct answer is (B). *(CMA, adapted)*
**REQUIRED:** The expected time of the critical path.
**DISCUSSION:** The critical path is the longest path. The longest path in the diagram is A-D-E, which requires 13 days (5.5 + 7.5) based on expected times.
Answer (A) is incorrect because 12.0 days are required for A-B-C-E. Answer (C) is incorrect because 11.5 days are required for A-B-E and for A-C-E. Answer (D) is incorrect because 12.5 days are required for A-B-D-E.

**36.** To keep costs at a minimum and decrease the completion time by 1½ days, Networks, Inc. should crash activity(ies)

A. AD and AB.

B. DE.

C. AD.

D. AB and CE.

The correct answer is (A). *(CMA, adapted)*
**REQUIRED:** The activity(ies) that can be crashed by a specified number of days at the least cost.
**DISCUSSION:** The critical path (A-D-E) requires 13 days (see preceding question). However, to decrease completion time to 11.5 days, paths A-B-C-E (4.5 + 1.0 + 6.5 = 12 days) and A-B-D-E (4.5 + .5 + 7.5 = 12.5 days) must also be shortened. Hence, A-D-E must be reduced by 1.5 days, A-B-C-E by .5 day, and A-B-D-E by 1.0 day. The only way to decrease A-D-E by 1.5 days is to crash activity AD (5.5 expected time – 4.0 crash time = 1.5 days). Crashing DE results in a 1.0-day saving (7.5 – 6.5) only. Crashing AB is the efficient way to reduce both A-B-C-E and A-B-D-E. The incremental cost of crashing AB is $1,000 ($4,000 crash cost – $3,000 normal cost). The alternatives are more costly.
Answer (B) is incorrect because crashing DE saves only 1.0 day (7.5 – 6.5) and does not reduce A-B-C-E. Answer (C) is incorrect because crashing AD does not reduce A-B-C-E or A-B-D-E. Answer (D) is incorrect because AB and CE are not on the critical path.

**37.** The Gantt chart below shows that the project is

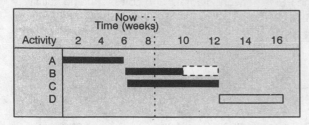

A. Complete.

B. Ahead of schedule.

C. On schedule.

D. Behind schedule.

The correct answer is (B). *(CIA, adapted)*

**REQUIRED:** The status of a project according to the Gantt chart.

**DISCUSSION:** Assuming that each of the bars represents the expected time necessary to complete an activity and that the shaded regions represent the portions completed, activity A has been completed as scheduled and activities B and C are ahead of schedule. Consequently, the project is ahead of schedule.

Answers (A), (C), and (D) are incorrect because the project is ahead of schedule, but activity D has not yet been started, much less completed.

## 18.4 Learning Curves

**38.** Seacraft Inc. received a request for a competitive bid for the sale of one of its unique boating products with a desired modification. Seacraft is now in the process of manufacturing this product but with a slightly different modification for another customer. These unique products are labor intensive and both will have long production runs. Which one of the following methods should Seacraft use to estimate the cost of the new competitive bid?

A. Expected value analysis.

B. Learning curve analysis.

C. Regression analysis.

D. Continuous probability simulation.

The correct answer is (B). *(CMA, adapted)*

**REQUIRED:** The method of estimating the cost of a product similar to a product now in process.

**DISCUSSION:** Learning curves reflect the increased rate at which people perform tasks as they gain experience. The time required to perform a given task becomes progressively shorter as the workers better learn their jobs. Ordinarily, the curve is expressed as a percentage of reduced time to complete a task for each doubling of cumulative production. This method is appropriate because the firm already has experience making the product. The result should be shorter production time and lower costs.

Answer (A) is incorrect because expected value analysis selects the best decision involving risk by multiplying the probability of each outcome by its payoff, and summing the products. Answer (C) is incorrect because regression analysis is used to find an equation for the linear relationships among variables. Answer (D) is incorrect because simulation would not be appropriate for a single project.

**39.** Which of the following may be scheduled in production planning by the use of learning curves?

A. Purchases of materials.

B. Subassembly production.

C. Delivery dates of finished products.

D. All of the answers are correct.

The correct answer is (D). *(CIA, adapted)*

**REQUIRED:** The use(s) of learning curves.

**DISCUSSION:** Learning curves describe the increase in production efficiencies resulting from experience. Labor assignments benefit from applications of learning curves to labor-hour budgets. Materials purchases result in efficiencies in the EOQ if the adjustments in production efficiency, as shown by the learning curve, are used in ordering. Subassembly production and delivery dates of finished products can each be more efficiently scheduled if learning curve efficiencies are considered during planning.

Answers (A), (B), and (C) are incorrect because learning curves may affect purchases of materials, subassembly production, and delivery dates of finished products.

**40.** If a firm is considering the use of learning curve analysis in the determination of labor cost standards for a new product, it should be advised that this technique ordinarily is most relevant to situations in which the production time per unit decreases as additional units are produced and the unit cost

   A.  Decreases.

   B.  Does not change.

   C.  Increases or decreases in an unpredictable manner.

   D.  Increases slightly.

The correct answer is (A). *(CPA, adapted)*
   **REQUIRED:** The unit cost behavior when using the learning curve approach.
   **DISCUSSION:** The learning curve is a cost function showing that the time required for production and therefore the average cost per unit decrease as production rises.
   Answers (B), and (D) are incorrect because, as production increases, efficiency also increases, resulting in lower unit costs. Answer (C) is incorrect because the unit cost decreases in a predictable manner.

**41.** A company has developed a learning (improvement) curve for one of its newer processes from its accounting and production records. Management asked internal audit to review the curve. Which of the following events tend to mitigate the effects of the learning curve?

   A.  Labor costs incurred for overtime hours were charged to an overhead account.

   B.  The number of preassembled purchased parts used exceeded the plan.

   C.  Newly developed processing equipment with improved operating characteristics was used.

   D.  All of the answers are correct.

The correct answer is (D). *(CIA, adapted)*
   **REQUIRED:** The event(s) that tend(s) to mitigate the effects of the learning curve.
   **DISCUSSION:** The learning curve is developed with a plan of all the factors of production. Any changes in the skill level of workers, processing equipment, parts used, or method of labor cost allocation will make the predesigned learning curve less useful.
   Answers (A), (B), and (C) are incorrect because each changes the results of the learning curve.

**42.** A learning curve of 80% assumes that direct labor costs are reduced by 20% for each doubling of output. What is the cost of the sixteenth unit produced as an approximate percentage of the first unit produced?

   A.  32%

   B.  40%

   C.  51%

   D.  64%

The correct answer is (B). *(CIA, adapted)*
   **REQUIRED:** The cost of the last unit produced.
   **DISCUSSION:** A learning curve may be based on the assumption that the time to produce the last unit is reduced by a constant percentage when cumulative production doubles. Under this assumption, the labor time (and labor cost) of unit 16 should be 40.96% [(80% x 100%) x (80%) x (80%) x (80%)].
   Answer (A) is incorrect because 32% is the time required for the thirty-second unit. Answer (C) is incorrect because 51% is the time required for the eighth unit. Answer (D) is incorrect because 64% is the time required for the fourth unit.

**43.** The average labor cost per unit for the first batch produced by a new process is $120. The cumulative average labor cost after the second batch is $72 per product. Using a batch size of 100 and assuming the learning curve continues, the total labor cost of four batches will be

A.   $4,320

B.   $2,592

C.   $17,280

D.   $28,800

The correct answer is (C). *(CMA, adapted)*
   **REQUIRED:** The total labor cost given a learning curve.
   **DISCUSSION:** One common assumption in a learning curve model is that the cumulative average time (and labor cost) per unit is reduced by a certain percentage each time production doubles. Given a $120 cost per unit for the first 100 units and a $72 cost per unit when cumulative production doubled to 200 units, the learning curve percentage must be 60% ($72 ÷ $120). If production is again doubled to 400 units (four batches), the average unit labor cost should be $43.20 (60% x $72). Hence, total labor cost for 400 units is estimated to be $17,280 (400 x $43.20).
   Answer (A) is incorrect because $4,320 equals the cost of the items in the fourth batch. Answer (B) is incorrect because $2,592 represents the labor cost of 100 units at the unit rate expected after another doubling of production to eight batches. Answer (D) is incorrect because $28,800 is based on an average cost of $72, the rate after two batches.

---

Questions 44 through 46 are based on the following information. LCB, Inc. is preparing a bid to produce engines. The company has experienced the following costs:

| Cumulative Units Produced | Total Cumulative Costs Materials | Labor |
|---|---|---|
| 10 | $ 60,000 | $120,000 |
| 20 | 120,000 | 192,000 |
| 40 | 240,000 | 307,200 |

At LCB, variable overhead is applied on the basis of $1.00 per direct labor dollar. Based on historical costs, LCB knows that the production of 40 engines will incur $100,000 of fixed overhead costs. The bid request is for an additional 40 units; all companies submitting bids are allowed to charge a maximum of 25% above full cost for each order.

---

**44.** LCB, Inc.'s rate of learning on the 3-year engine contract is

A.   64%

B.   100%

C.   80%

D.   62.5%

The correct answer is (C). *(CMA, adapted)*
   **REQUIRED:** The learning curve percentage.
   **DISCUSSION:** The cumulative average unit labor cost for 10 units was $12,000 ($120,000 ÷ 10). The cumulative average unit labor cost for 20 units (a doubling of production) was $9,600 ($192,000 ÷ 20). The cumulative unit average for the next doubling was $7,680 ($307,200 ÷ 40). Because $9,600 is 80% of $12,000 and $7,680 is 80% of $9,600, an 80% rate of learning occurred.
   Answer (A) is incorrect because 64% equals $307,200 divided by $480,000 (4 x $120,000). Answer (B) is incorrect because 100% implies that no learning occurred. Answer (D) is incorrect because 62.5% equals $192,000 ÷ $120,000.

---

**45.** The maximum bid price that LCB, Inc. can submit for the 40 units is

A.   $760,800

B.   $608,640

C.   $885,800

D.   $708,640

The correct answer is (C). *(CMA, adapted)*
   **REQUIRED:** The maximum bid price.
   **DISCUSSION:** Given a learning curve of 80% and a cumulative average unit labor cost for 40 units of $7,680 (see preceding question), estimated cumulative average unit labor cost for 80 units is $6,144 (80% x $7,680). Estimated total labor cost for 80 units is $491,520 (80 units x $6,144), so the incremental labor cost of the last 40 units is expected to be $184,320 ($491,520 − $307,200). Variable overhead is also $184,320. Thus, full cost is $708,640 ($184,320 DL + $184,320 VOH + $240,000 DM + $100,000 FOH). The bid price should be $885,800 (125% x $708,640 full cost).
   Answer (A) is incorrect because $760,800 is 125% of the minimum bid. Answer (B) is incorrect because $608,640 is the minimum bid. Answer (D) is incorrect because $708,640 is the full cost.

**46.** To ensure that the company will not lose money on the project, LCB, Inc.'s minimum bid for the 40 units will be

   A. $760,800

   B. $608,640

   C. $885,800

   D. $708,640

The correct answer is (B). *(CMA, adapted)*

   **REQUIRED:** The minimum bid.

   **DISCUSSION:** The full cost of the incremental production is $708,640 (see preceding question). However, that amount includes $100,000 of fixed overhead that would presumably not increase as a result of the production. Thus, if the company obtains the contract at a price of $608,640 ($708,640 – $100,000), it will break even. The minimum bid is therefore $608,640: the incremental cost of labor, variable overhead, and materials.

   Answer (A) is incorrect because $760,800 is 125% of the minimum. Answer (C) is incorrect because $885,800 is the maximum bid. Answer (D) is incorrect because $708,640 is the full cost.

---

Questions 47 and 48 are based on the following information. Moss Point Manufacturing recently completed and sold an order of 50 units that had costs as shown in the next column.

The company has now been requested to prepare a bid for 150 units of the same product.

| | |
|---|---:|
| Direct materials | $ 1,500 |
| Direct labor (1,000 hours × $8.50) | 8,500 |
| Variable overhead (1,000 hours × $4.00)* | 4,000 |
| Fixed overhead** | 1,400 |
| | $15,400 |

*Applied on the basis of direct labor hours
**Applied at the rate of 10% of variable cost

---

**47.** If an 80% learning curve is applicable, Moss Point's total cost on this order will be estimated at

   A. $26,400

   B. $35,800

   C. $38,000

   D. $41,800

The correct answer is (A). *(CMA, adapted)*

   **REQUIRED:** The total cost of a new order.

   **DISCUSSION:** Only the labor and variable overhead costs (labor-related) will be affected by the learning curve. The average cost per lot for labor and variable overhead after 100 units have been produced should be 80% of the costs of the first lot of 50 units. Thus, the average labor and variable overhead cost per lot will be $10,000 (80% x $12,500). If production doubles again, the cumulative average cost for labor and variable overhead will be $8,000 per lot (80% x $10,000), and the total cost for labor and variable overhead will be $32,000 (4 lots x $8,000). Adding $6,000 for materials ($1,500 per 50-unit lot) gives a total variable cost of $38,000. Fixed overhead is 10% of total variable cost, so total cost is $41,800. The total cost for the last 150 units is $26,400 ($41,800 – $15,400).

   Answer (B) is incorrect because $35,800 equals total cost minus materials cost. Answer (C) is incorrect because $38,000 is total variable cost. Answer (D) is incorrect because $41,800 is total cost.

---

**48.** If Moss Point had experienced a 70% learning curve, the bid for the 150 units would

   A. Show a 30% reduction in the total direct labor hours required with no learning curve.

   B. Include increased fixed overhead costs.

   C. Include 2,560 total direct labor hours at $8.50 per hour.

   D. Include 6.40 direct labor hours per unit at $8.50 per hour.

The correct answer is (D). *(CMA, adapted)*

   **REQUIRED:** The true statement about the bid for an incremental 150 units given a 70% learning curve effect.

   **DISCUSSION:** The sum of the direct labor hours for the initial lot of 50 units was 1,000. A second lot of 50 will reduce the cumulative hours per lot to 700 (70% x 1,000). A doubling to four lots will reduce the cumulative hours per lot to 490 (70% x 700). Thus, for an output of 200 units, the total hours worked will be 1,960 (4 x 490), with 960 hours (1,960 – 1,000) needed for the last 150 units. The per-unit time will be 6.4 hours (960 hours ÷ 150 units).

   Answer (A) is incorrect because, with no learning curve, estimated total hours will be 4,000 instead of 1,960, a change of more than 50%. Answer (B) is incorrect because fixed costs applied per lot will decrease given that labor hours are declining. Answer (C) is incorrect because an estimated 960 hours will be required for the last 150 units.

## 18.5 Matrix Algebra

**49.** A company has two production and two service departments. Each service department provides service to the two production departments and to the other service department. In allocating service department costs, the company would like to account for the service provided by each service department to the other. To do so, it could use

    A.  Matrix algebra.

    B.  Regression analysis.

    C.  Game theory.

    D.  Sensitivity analysis.

The correct answer is (A). *(CIA, adapted)*

**REQUIRED:** The quantitative method useful for applying the reciprocal method of service cost allocation.

**DISCUSSION:** Matrix algebra is a mathematical technique for solving a set of simultaneous equations. Matrices consisting of the coefficients of the variables of the equations may be manipulated by addition, subtraction, multiplication, and inversion. Because the two service departments simultaneously provide services to each other, recognition of these reciprocal services requires solution of a set of simultaneous equations.

Answer (B) is incorrect because regression analysis is a statistical procedure for estimation of the relation between variables. Answer (C) is incorrect because game theory is a mathematical approach to decision making that considers the actions of competitors. Answer (D) is incorrect because sensitivity analysis is a method of studying the effects of changes in one or more variables on the results of a decision model.

**50.** Consider the two equations below.

$$7x + 8y = 39$$
$$4x - 3y = 21$$

The matrix algebra representation of the two equations is

    A.  $\begin{bmatrix} 7 & 8 \\ 4 & -3 \end{bmatrix} \begin{bmatrix} x \\ y \end{bmatrix} = \begin{bmatrix} 39 \\ 21 \end{bmatrix}$

    B.  $\begin{bmatrix} 7 & 8 \\ 4 & -3 \end{bmatrix} \begin{bmatrix} x & y \end{bmatrix} = \begin{bmatrix} 39 \\ 21 \end{bmatrix}$

    C.  $\begin{bmatrix} 4 & 7 \\ -3 & 8 \end{bmatrix} \begin{bmatrix} x \\ y \end{bmatrix} = \begin{bmatrix} 39 \\ 21 \end{bmatrix}$

    D.  $\begin{bmatrix} x \\ y \end{bmatrix} \begin{bmatrix} 7 & 8 \\ 4 & -3 \end{bmatrix} = \begin{bmatrix} 39 \\ 21 \end{bmatrix}$

The correct answer is (A). *(CIA, adapted)*

**REQUIRED:** The matrix algebra representation of the two equations.

**DISCUSSION:** Matrix algebra is an efficient method of manipulating multiple linear equations. Matrices can be added and subtracted if they are of the same dimensions. They can be multiplied if they conform, that is, if the number of columns in the first equals the number of rows in the second. Using the multiplication rule, the matrices in answer (A) can be transformed back into the given equations.

Answer (B) is incorrect because the two matrices on the left-hand side do not conform. Answer (C) is incorrect because the coefficient matrix is incorrect. Answer (D) is incorrect because the columns of the first matrix do not equal the rows in the second.

**51.** For a given matrix A, a unique inverse matrix $A^{-1}$ exists. Multiplication of the matrix $A^{-1}$ by the matrix A will produce

    A.  The matrix A.

    B.  Another inverse matrix.

    C.  The correct solution to the system.

    D.  An identity matrix.

The correct answer is (D). *(CPA, adapted)*

**REQUIRED:** The product of multiplying a matrix by its inverse matrix.

**DISCUSSION:** In matrix operations, ordinary division is not possible. In lieu of division, one multiplies by an inverse matrix. By definition, a matrix times its inverse will give an identity matrix. This operation is similar to dividing one number or one variable by itself and obtaining one. An identity matrix is a matrix with zeros in all elements except the principal diagonal, which contains ones.

Answers (A), (B), and (C) are incorrect because the product is an identity matrix.

**52.** The Apex Fertilizer Company is planning a new formulation to appeal to the increasing market of herb growers. Each unit of the product will require 3 pounds of chemical A, 1 pound of chemical B, and 4 pounds of chemical C. The per-pound costs of chemical A are $7.95; chemical B, $3.28; and chemical C, $6.14. Which of the following matrix algebra formulations will lead to the cost of one unit of the new fertilizer?

A. $[7.95, \quad 3.28, \quad 6.14] \begin{bmatrix} 3 & 0 & 0 \\ 0 & 1 & 0 \\ 0 & 0 & 4 \end{bmatrix}$

B. $\begin{bmatrix} 7.95 \\ 3.28 \\ 6.14 \end{bmatrix} \quad [3, \ 1, \ 4]$

C. $\begin{bmatrix} 7.95 \\ 3.28 \\ 6.14 \end{bmatrix} \quad \begin{bmatrix} 3 \\ 1 \\ 4 \end{bmatrix}$

D. $[3 \ 1 \ 4] \begin{bmatrix} 7.95 \\ 3.28 \\ 6.14 \end{bmatrix}$

The correct answer is (D). *(CIA, adapted)*
**REQUIRED:** The matrix algebra formulation to determine unit cost of fertilizer.
**DISCUSSION:** The objective is to multiply the number of pounds of each material times the cost of each material and sum the answers. This matrix appears in answer (D).

$$(3 \times 7.95) + (1 \times 3.28) + (4 \times 6.14)$$

When multiplying two matrices together, multiply the items in each row (horizontal) of the first matrix times each item in the second matrix's column (vertical), and then add the products. Here, a 1-by-3 matrix is multiplied by a 3-by-1 matrix, resulting in a 1-by-1 matrix representing the cost. Thus, the dimensions of the matrix resulting from multiplying two matrices together are equal to the number of rows in the first and the number of columns in the second.

Answer (A) is incorrect because a 1-by-3 matrix times a 3-by-3 matrix results in a 1-by-3 matrix, i.e., three separate numbers. Answer (B) is incorrect because a 3-by-1 matrix times a 1-by-3 matrix results in a 3-by-3 matrix, i.e., nine numbers. Answer (C) is incorrect because a 3-by-1 matrix times a 3-by-1 matrix results in a 3-by-1 matrix, i.e., three numbers.

**53.** Presented below is a system of simultaneous equations.

$S_1 = \quad 98,000 + .20S_2$ or $S_1 - .20S_2 = \$ 98,000$
$S_2 = 117,600 + .10S_1$ or $S_2 - .10S_1 = \$117,600$

This system may be stated in matrix form as

A. 
$$\begin{array}{ccc} A & S & B \\ \begin{bmatrix} 1 & -.20 \\ -.10 & 1 \end{bmatrix} & \begin{bmatrix} S_1 \\ S_2 \end{bmatrix} = & \begin{bmatrix} \$ \ 98,000 \\ \$117,600 \end{bmatrix} \end{array}$$

B.
$$\begin{array}{ccc} A & S & B \\ \begin{bmatrix} 1 & \$98,000 & 1 \\ -.20 & \$117,600 & -.10 \end{bmatrix} & \begin{bmatrix} S_1 \\ S_2 \end{bmatrix} = & \begin{bmatrix} \$ \ 98,000 \\ \$117,600 \end{bmatrix} \end{array}$$

C.
$$\begin{array}{ccc} A & S & B \\ \begin{bmatrix} 1 & S_1 & 1 \\ -.20 & S_2 & -.10 \end{bmatrix} & \begin{bmatrix} S_1 \\ S_2 \end{bmatrix} = & \begin{bmatrix} \$ \ 98,000 \\ \$117,600 \end{bmatrix} \end{array}$$

D.
$$\begin{array}{ccc} A & S & B \\ \begin{bmatrix} 1 & 1 & S_1 \\ -.20 & -.10 & S_2 \end{bmatrix} & \begin{bmatrix} S_1 \\ S_2 \end{bmatrix} = & \begin{bmatrix} \$ \ 98,000 \\ \$117,600 \end{bmatrix} \end{array}$$

The correct answer is (A). *(CPA, adapted)*
**REQUIRED:** The matrix form of the simultaneous equations.
**DISCUSSION:** The requirement is to multiply matrix A times matrix S to equal matrix B. In matrix multiplication, one multiplies rows by columns. In answer (A), for example, multiplying the first row of A times the first (and only) column of S results in

$$1 \times S_1 + -.20 \times S_2$$

Multiplying the second row in A times the only column in S gives

$$-.10 \times S_1 + 1 \times S_2$$

The result is the original equations:

$$S_1 - .20S_2 = \$98,000$$
$$S_2 - .10S_1 = \$117,600$$

Answer (B) is incorrect because $98,000 and $117,600 are constants, not coefficients. Moreover, the columns of A do not equal the rows of B. Answers (C) and (D) are incorrect because $S_1$ and $S_2$ are variables, not coefficients. Moreover, the columns of A do not equal the rows of B.

## 18.6 Calculus

**54.** Financial statements of a number of companies are to be analyzed for potential growth by use of a model that considers the rates of change in assets, owners' equity, and income. The most relevant quantitative technique for developing such a model is

   A. Correlation analysis.

   B. Differential calculus.

   C. Integral calculus.

   D. Program Evaluation and Review Technique (PERT).

The correct answer is (B). *(CPA, adapted)*
   **REQUIRED:** The quantitative method for analyzing rates of change.
   **DISCUSSION:** Differential calculus is used to identify the maxima or minima of nonlinear functions, which, in business and economics, are the points of revenue (profit) maximization or cost minimization. The derivative of a function measures the slope or rate of change of that function. Maxima or minima occur where the slope is equal to zero. Thus, to measure rates of change, differential calculus is the appropriate technique.
   Answer (A) is incorrect because correlation analysis measures relationships among two or more variables. Answer (C) is incorrect because integral calculus is customarily used in business applications to identify the area under a probability curve. Answer (D) is incorrect because PERT examines complex projects for processes that are critical to the timely completion of the entire project.

**55.** What process is used when calculus is employed to determine a firm's maximum profit for a given revenue function?

   A. Integration.

   B. Differentiation.

   C. Operations research.

   D. Regression analysis.

The correct answer is (B). *(CIA, adapted)*
   **REQUIRED:** The process used when calculus is employed to determine a firm's maximum profit.
   **DISCUSSION:** Differential calculus is used to identify the maxima or minima of nonlinear functions. The derivative of a function measures the slope or rate of change of that function. Maxima or minima occur where the slope is equal to zero. A maximum exists when the second derivative of the function is negative.
   Answer (A) is incorrect because integral calculus computes the area under a curve. It finds antiderivatives; the first derivative of the integral is the function that was integrated. Answer (C) is incorrect because operations research is a broad term for the application of scientific and quantitative methods to the understanding of systems, especially human-machine systems used in business. Answer (D) is incorrect because regression analysis creates an equation to explain the variation in a dependent variable caused by changes in one or more independent variables.

**56.** An internal auditing department developed the formula, Total audit cost (TC) = $a + bX + cX^2$, with X equaling internal audit resources. The director wanted to minimize TC with respect to X. The appropriate technique to use is

   A. Linear programming.

   B. Least squares.

   C. Differential calculus.

   D. Integral calculus.

The correct answer is (C). *(CIA, adapted)*
   **REQUIRED:** The appropriate technique to solve the equation.
   **DISCUSSION:** Differential calculus identifies the maxima or minima of curvilinear functions. These points occur where the slope is zero. A minimum exists when the second derivative of the function is positive.
   Answer (A) is incorrect because the formula is nonlinear with no stated constraints. Answer (B) is incorrect because least squares is related to regression analysis. Answer (D) is incorrect because integral calculus concerns areas and volume.

**57.** Which of the following statements about marginal costs is correct?

A. Marginal cost equals the derivative of the total cost function.

B. Marginal cost increases as output quantity increases.

C. Marginal cost decreases as output quantity increases.

D. Marginal cost increases when total cost increases.

The correct answer is (A). *(CIA, adapted)*
**REQUIRED:** The true statement about marginal costs.
**DISCUSSION:** Marginal cost is the incremental cost incurred to produce one additional unit of output. The derivative of the total cost function is the change in total cost per unit change in output quantity. Accordingly, it equals marginal cost. As marginal cost increases or decreases, the derivative (slope) of the total cost function increases or decreases.

Answers (B), (C), and (D) are incorrect because marginal cost may increase or decrease as output or total cost increases.

**58.** To find a minimum-cost point given a total-cost equation, the initial steps are to find the first derivative, set it equal to zero, and solve the equation. Using the solution(s) so derived, what additional steps must be taken, and what result indicates a minimum?

A. Substitute the solution(s) in the first derivative equation; a positive solution indicates a minimum.

B. Substitute the solution(s) in the first derivative equation; a negative solution indicates a minimum.

C. Substitute the solution(s) in the second derivative equation; a positive solution indicates a minimum.

D. Substitute the solution(s) in the second derivative equation; a negative solution indicates a minimum.

The correct answer is (C). *(CPA, adapted)*
**REQUIRED:** The subsequent steps in differential calculus and interpretation of results.
**DISCUSSION:** The steps in differential calculus are to (1) calculate the first derivative, (2) set the first derivative equal to zero and solve the equation, and (3) calculate the second derivative to determine whether it is positive or negative. If the second derivative is positive, it is a minimum. If the second derivative is negative, it is a maximum. The second derivative of a function is the derivative of the first derivative of a function.

Answers (A) and (B) are incorrect because the substitution must be in the second derivative. Answer (D) is incorrect because a negative solution indicates a maximum.

**59.** The mathematical notation for the total cost function for a business is $4X^3 + 6X^2 + 2X + 10$, if X equals production volume. Which of the following is the mathematical notation for the average cost function for that business?

A. $12X^2 + 12X + 2$

B. $2X^3 + 3X^2 + X + 5$

C. $.4X^3 + .6X^2 + .2X + 1$

D. $4X^2 + 6X + 2 + 10X^{-1}$

The correct answer is (D). *(CPA, adapted)*
**REQUIRED:** The formula for average cost function.
**DISCUSSION:** The average cost function equals the total cost function divided by production volume. The total cost function is $4X^3 + 6X^2 + 2X + 10$. X is the production volume. Dividing the total cost by X gives the average cost of $4X^2 + 6X + 2 + 10X^{-1}$.

Answer (A) is incorrect because $12X^2 + 12X + 2$ is the first derivative. Answer (B) is incorrect because $2X^3 + 3X^2 + X + 5$ results from dividing by 2. Answer (C) is incorrect because $.4X^3 + .6X^2 + .2X + 1$ results from dividing by 10.

**60.** The mathematical notation for the average cost function for a business is $6X^3 + 4X^2 + 2X + 8 + 2X^{-1}$, if X equals production volume. What is the mathematical notation for the total cost function for the business?

A. $6X^4 + 4X^3 + 2X^2 + 8X + 2$

B. $6X^2 + 4X + 2 + 8X^{-1} + 2X^{-2}$

C. $12X^2 + 8X + 4 + 16X^{-1} + 4X^{-2}$

D. $18X^2 + 8X + 2 - 2X^{-2}$

The correct answer is (A). *(CPA, adapted)*
**REQUIRED:** The formula for the total cost function.
**DISCUSSION:** Total cost is average cost times production volume. The average cost function is $6X^3 + 4X^2 + 2X + 8 + 2/X$. Production volume equals X. Thus, multiplying the given average cost function by X results in the total cost function: $X(6X^3 + 4X^2 + 2X + 8 + 2X^{-1}) = 6X^4 + 4X^3 + 2X^2 + 8X + 2$.

Answer (B) is incorrect because $6X^2 + 4X + 2 + 8X^{-1} + 2X^{-2}$ results from dividing by X. Answer (C) is incorrect because $12X^2 + 8X + 4 + 16X^{-1} + 4X^{-2}$ results from dividing by .5X. Answer (D) is incorrect because $18X^2 + 8X + 2 - 2X^{-2}$ is the first derivative.

**61.** The mathematical notation for the total cost for a business is $2X^3 + 4X^2 + 3X + 5$, if X equals production volume. Which of the following is the mathematical notation for the marginal cost function for this business?

A.  $2(X^3 + 2X^2 + 1.5X + 2.5)$

B.  $6X^2 + 8X + 3$

C.  $2X^3 + 4X^2 + 3X$

D.  $12X + 8$

The correct answer is (B). *(CPA, adapted)*
    **REQUIRED:** The formula for the marginal cost function.
    **DISCUSSION:** The total cost function is $2X^3 + 4X^2 + 3X + 5$. Production volume equals X. The marginal cost function notation is determined by taking the first derivative of the total cost function notation. The derivative of a function is found using the formula $nx^{n-1}$. The coefficient of the term is multiplied by the exponent, and the exponent is reduced by one. All constants are dropped. The marginal cost function is therefore $6X^2 + 8X + 3$.
    Answer (A) is incorrect because $2(X^3 + 2X^2 + 1.5X + 2.5)$ is the total cost function. Answer (C) is incorrect because $2X^3 + 4X^2 + 3X$ simply omits the constant. Answer (D) is incorrect because $12X + 8$ is the second derivative.

**62.** A second derivative that is positive and large at a critical point (i.e., within the relevant range) indicates an

A.  Important maximum.

B.  Unimportant maximum.

C.  Important minimum.

D.  Unimportant minimum.

The correct answer is (C). *(CPA, adapted)*
    **REQUIRED:** The interpretation of a large positive second derivative at a critical point.
    **DISCUSSION:** A positive second derivative indicates that the function is at a minimum. The critical point implies an important minimum; i.e., the point is critical in the context of the problem, not in the mathematical sense.
    Answers (A) and (B) are incorrect because a negative second derivative indicates a maximum. Answer (D) is incorrect because the minimum is important.

Questions 63 through 66 are based on the following information. Redler Company manufactures and sells an industrial strength cleaning fluid. The equations presented below represent the revenue (R) and cost (C) functions for the company if x is stated in terms of thousands of gallons of fluid.

$$R(x) = -\$100 + \$26x - \$0.05x^2$$
$$C(x) = \$50 + \$8x + \$0.01x^2$$

**63.** The function that represents the marginal cost to manufacture 1 gallon of cleaning fluid is

A.  $\$8x + \$0.01x^2$

B.  $\$8 + \$0.01x$

C.  $\$8 + \$0.02x$

D.  $\$8 \div \$0.02x$

The correct answer is (C). *(CMA, adapted)*
    **REQUIRED:** The function representing the marginal cost to manufacture 1 gallon of product.
    **DISCUSSION:** The marginal cost function is the derivative of the total cost function. The basic formula for the derivative is

$$f'(Ax^n) = nAx^{n-1}$$

If: A = the constant, or number of x's
    x = the variable being differentiated
    n = the exponent of the independent variable

Thus, the derivative of the cost function is

$$f'(\$50 + \$8x + \$0.01x^2) = f'(\$50) + f'(\$8x) + f'(\$0.01x^2)$$
$$= 0 + \$8 + \$0.02x$$
$$= \$8 + \$0.02x$$

Answer (A) is incorrect because $\$8x + \$0.01x^2$ is the cost function without the constant. Answer (B) is incorrect because the first derivative of $\$0.01x^2$ is $\$0.02x$. Answer (D) is incorrect because the derivative of the entire equation is the sum of the derivatives of the individual elements.

**64.** The quantity of cleaning fluid that should be produced to maximize revenue is

A. 520,000 gallons.

B. 260,000 gallons.

C. 160,000 gallons.

D. 150,000 gallons.

The correct answer is (B). *(CMA, adapted)*

**REQUIRED:** The quantity of product to be sold to maximize revenue.

**DISCUSSION:** A maximization problem is solved by setting the first derivative of the revenue function equal to zero and solving for x. The first derivative of the revenue function is 26 – .1x. Thus,

$$.1x = 26$$
$$x = 260$$

Selling 260,000 gallons of cleaning fluid would maximize revenues.

Answer (A) is incorrect because 520,000 gallons assumes the first derivative is 26 – .05x. Answer (C) is incorrect because 260,000 gallons maximizes revenue. Answer (D) is incorrect because 150,000 gallons is the profit-maximizing amount.

**65.** The quantity of cleaning fluid that should be produced to maximize profit is

A. 520,000 gallons.

B. 260,000 gallons.

C. 160,000 gallons.

D. 150,000 gallons.

The correct answer is (D). *(CMA, adapted)*

**REQUIRED:** The production level at which profit will be maximized.

**DISCUSSION:** Profit is equal to the revenue function minus the cost function [(–$100 + $26x – $0.05x$^2$) – ($50 + 8x + $0.01x$^2$)]. It is not necessary to combine terms. The profit maximum is the first derivative of this profit function (26 – .1x) – (8 + .02x), or 18 – .12x. Set this derivative equal to zero and solve for x, or 150. Thus, producing 150,000 gallons of cleaning fluid will maximize profit.

Answer (A) is incorrect because 520,000 gallons is the quantity that maximizes revenue if the first derivative of the revenue function is 26 – .05x. Answer (B) is incorrect because 260,000 gallons is the quantity of product to be sold to maximize revenue. Answer (C) is incorrect because 150,000 gallons is the profit-maximizing production.

**66.** What would the profit (loss) be if the company manufactured and sold 300,000 gallons of cleaning fluid?

A. $3,200,000

B. $(50,000)

C. $(3,350,000)

D. $(150,000)

The correct answer is (D). *(CMA, adapted)*

**REQUIRED:** The amount of profit (loss) generated given productivity and sales.

**DISCUSSION:** This question is easily solved by substituting 300 for x in the previous two equations.

Revenue = –$100 + $26(300) – $.05(90,000)
Cost = $50 + $8(300) + $.01(90,000)

The cost equation is subtracted from the revenue equation to determine profit or loss per gallon of x.

[–$100 + $7,800 – $4,500 – ($50 + $2,400 + $900)]

Profit = $3,200 (revenue) – $3,350 (costs)
= $(150)

Because x is stated in thousands of gallons, the total loss is $150,000.

Answer (A) is incorrect because $3,200,000 equals total revenues. Answer (B) is incorrect because $(50,000) equals fixed costs. Answer (C) is incorrect because $(3,350,000) equals total costs.

## 18.7 Game Theory

**67.** The marketing department of your company is deciding on the price to charge for a key product. In setting this price, marketing needs to consider the price that a major competitor will charge for a similar product because the competitor's price will affect the demand for your company's product. Similarly, in setting its price, the competitor will consider what your company will charge. An appropriate mathematical technique for analyzing such a decision is

   A.  Game theory.

   B.  Probability theory.

   C.  Linear programming.

   D.  Sensitivity analysis.

The correct answer is (A). *(CIA, adapted)*
   **REQUIRED:** The mathematical technique for analyzing the price to charge given the existence of competition.
   **DISCUSSION:** Game theory is a mathematical approach to decision making when confronted with an enemy or competitor. Games are classified according to the number of players and the algebraic sum of the payoffs. In a two-person game, if the payoff is given by the loser to the winner, the algebraic sum is zero and the game is called a zero-sum game. If it is possible for both players to profit, however, the game is a positive-sum game. Mathematical models have been developed to select optimal strategies for certain simple games.
   Answer (B) is incorrect because probability theory is used to express quantitatively the likelihood of occurrence of an event. Answer (C) is incorrect because linear programming optimizes an objective function subject to constraints. Answer (D) is incorrect because sensitivity analysis studies the effects of changes in variables on the results of a decision model.

**68.** Only two companies manufacture Product A. The finished product is identical regardless of which company manufactures it. The cost to manufacture Product A is $1, and the selling price is $2. One company considers reducing the price to achieve 100% market share but fears the other company will respond by further reducing the price. Such a scenario would involve a

   A.  No-win strategy.

   B.  Dual-win strategy.

   C.  One win-one lose strategy.

   D.  Neutral strategy.

The correct answer is (A). *(CIA, adapted)*
   **REQUIRED:** The effect of a price war.
   **DISCUSSION:** If both firms reduce the selling price of Product A, neither will gain sales and the resultant price war will cause both firms to earn lower profits. This outcome is inevitable when reduced profit margins do not result in a significant increase in sales. The effect is a no-win strategy.
   Answers (B), (C), and (D) are incorrect because both firms will experience lower profits.

**69.** Your company (Company Y) has decided to enter the European market with one of its products and is now considering three advertising strategies. This market currently belongs to Company X. Company X is aware that your company is entering the market and is itself considering steps to protect its market. An analyst for your company has identified three strategies Company X might develop and has shown the payoffs for each in the tables below.

Net Payoff Company X
(in $000,000)

Company X

|  |  | 1 | 2 | 3 |
|---|---|---|---|---|
|  |  | Take No Action | Extensive Advertising | Extensive Advertising & Price Reduction |
| 1 | Limited Advertising | −1 | 1 | 2 |
| 2 | Extensive Advertising | −3 | 0 | 1 |
| 3 | Extensive Advertising & Price Reduction | −2 | ½ | −2 |

Net Payoff Company Y
(in $000,000)

Company X

|  |  | 1 | 2 | 3 |
|---|---|---|---|---|
|  |  | Take No Action | Extensive Advertising | Extensive Advertising & Price Reduction |
| 1 | Limited Advertising | 1 | −1 | −2 |
| 2 | Extensive Advertising | 3 | 0 | −1 |
| 3 | Extensive Advertising & Price Reduction | 2 | −½ | 2 |

The analyst has formulated this problem as a

A. Zero-sum game.

B. Cooperative game.

C. Prisoner's dilemma.

D. Game against nature.

The correct answer is (A). *(CIA, adapted)*

**REQUIRED:** The type of game illustrated.

**DISCUSSION:** Game theory is a mathematical approach to decision making when confronted with an enemy or competitor. Games are classified according to the number of players and the algebraic sum of the payoffs. In a two-player game, if the payoff is given by the loser to the winner, the algebraic sum is zero, and the game is a zero-sum game. However, if it is possible for both players to profit, the game is a positive-sum game. In this situation, the sum of the payoffs for each combination of strategies is zero. For example, if X takes no action and Y chooses limited advertising, X's payoff is −1 and Y's is 1.

Answer (B) is incorrect because, in a cooperative game, the players are permitted to negotiate and form binding agreements prior to the selection of strategies. In addition, in such games the payoffs in one or more of the cells will not sum to zero. Answer (C) is incorrect because the prisoner's dilemma is a special outcome of a partly competitive game. In these games, each player has a strategy that dominates all others, and the outcome of each player's choice of the dominant strategy is less favorable to both players than some other outcome. Answer (D) is incorrect because games against nature are formulations of problems in which only one player chooses a strategy, and the set of outcomes and payoffs is not influenced by the selection.

**70.** The procedure for choosing the smallest maximum alternative loss is

    A.  Deterministic decision making.

    B.  Maximax.

    C.  Expected value decision making.

    D.  Minimax.

The correct answer is (D). *(CMA, adapted)*
    **REQUIRED:** The procedure for choosing the smallest maximum alternative loss.
    **DISCUSSION:** In game theory, the minimax decision criterion selects the strategy that will minimize the maximum possible loss. It is a technique used by a risk-averse player. The maximin criterion, which chooses the strategy with the maximum minimum payoff, gives the same results as the minimax procedure.
    Answer (A) is incorrect because deterministic decision making is based upon fixed (nonprobabilistic) inputs into the decision process. Answer (B) is incorrect because maximax is a criterion that maximizes the maximum possible profit. Answer (C) is incorrect because expected value decision making is a risk-neutral process that selects the strategy that should maximize value in the long run.

**71.** Under conditions of risk, the rational, economic decision maker will use which one of the following decision criteria?

    A.  Maximax.

    B.  Minimum regret.

    C.  Laplace.

    D.  Expected monetary value.

The correct answer is (D). *(CMA, adapted)*
    **REQUIRED:** The decision criterion that will be used by a rational decision maker under conditions of risk.
    **DISCUSSION:** A rational economic decision maker (one completely guided by objective criteria) will use expected monetary value to maximize gains under conditions of risk because (s)he is risk-neutral (the utility of a gain equals the disutility of a loss of the same absolute amount). Expected value represents the long-term average payoff for repeated trials. The best choice is the one having the highest expected value (sum of the products of the possible outcomes and their respective probabilities).
    Answer (A) is incorrect because maximax is adopted by risk seekers. Answer (B) is incorrect because the minimum regret criterion is used by a player who wishes to minimize the effect of a bad decision in either direction. Answer (C) is incorrect because the insufficient reason (Laplace) criterion applies when the decision maker cannot assign probabilities to the states of nature arising after a decision.

**72.** The decision rule that selects the strategy with the highest utility payoff if the worst state of nature occurs is the

    A.  Minimize regret rule.

    B.  Maximize utility rule.

    C.  Maximin rule.

    D.  Maximax rule.

The correct answer is (C). *(CIA, adapted)*
    **REQUIRED:** The rule that selects the strategy with the highest utility payoff if the worst state of nature occurs.
    **DISCUSSION:** The maximin rule determines the minimum payoff for each decision and then chooses the decision with the maximum minimum payoff. It is a conservative criterion adopted by risk-averse players, that is, those for whom the disutility of a loss exceeds the utility of an equal gain.
    Answer (A) is incorrect because the minimize regret rule selects the action that minimizes the maximum opportunity cost. Answer (B) is incorrect because the maximize utility rule is not a decision rule. Answer (D) is incorrect because the maximax rule selects the choice that provides the greatest payoff if the most favorable state of nature occurs.

Questions 73 through 75 are based on the following information. A bank plans to open a branch in one of five locations (labeled L1, L2, L3, L4, L5). Demand for bank services may be high, medium, or low at each of these locations. Profits for each location-demand combination are presented in the payoff matrix.

**Payoff Matrix**

| Location | L1 | L2 | L3 | L4 | L5 |
|---|---|---|---|---|---|
| Demand: | | | | | |
| High | 15 | 21 | 17 | 26 | 29 |
| Medium | 12 | 8 | 14 | 10 | 4 |
| Low | 7 | –2 | 4 | –3 | –6 |

**73.** If the bank uses the maximax criterion for selecting the location of the branch, it will select

A. L1.

B. L2.

C. L3.

D. L5.

The correct answer is (D). *(CIA, adapted)*

**REQUIRED:** The location selected assuming a maximax criterion.

**DISCUSSION:** Under the maximax criterion, the decision maker selects the choice that maximizes the maximum profit. The maximum profits for the five locations are

| Location | L1 | L2 | L3 | L4 | L5 |
|---|---|---|---|---|---|
| Maximum Profit | 15 | 21 | 17 | 26 | 29 |

The location with the greatest potential profit is L5.

Answer (A) is incorrect because L1 is the choice based on the maximin criterion. Answer (B) is incorrect because L2 is the choice based on the minimax regret criterion. Answer (C) is incorrect because L3 is the choice based on the Laplace criterion.

**74.** If the bank uses the minimax regret criterion for selecting the location of the branch, it will select

A. L1.

B. L2.

C. L3.

D. L5.

The correct answer is (B). *(CIA, adapted)*

**REQUIRED:** The location selected using the minimax regret criterion.

**DISCUSSION:** Under the minimax regret criterion, the decision maker selects the choice that minimizes the maximum regret (opportunity cost). The maximum regret for each location is

| Location | L1 | L2 | L3 | L4 | L5 |
|---|---|---|---|---|---|
| Maximum Regret | 14 | 9 | 12 | 10 | 13 |

The location with the minimum regret is L2. If demand is low, L2 has a payoff of –2, whereas L1 has a payoff of 7.

Answer (A) is incorrect because L1 is the choice based on the maximin criterion. Answer (C) is incorrect because L3 is the choice based on the Laplace criterion. Answer (D) is incorrect because L5 is the choice based on the maximax criterion.

**75.** If, in addition to the estimated profits, management of the bank assesses the probabilities of high, medium, and low demands to be 0.3, 0.4, and 0.3, respectively, what is the expected opportunity loss from selecting location L4?

A. 5.50

B. 7.90

C. 7.50

D. 5.00

The correct answer is (A). *(CIA, adapted)*

**REQUIRED:** The expected opportunity loss from selecting location L4.

**DISCUSSION:** The opportunity loss matrix is as follows:

| Location | L1 | L2 | L3 | L4 | L5 |
|---|---|---|---|---|---|
| Demand: | | | | | |
| High | 14 | 8 | 12 | 3 | 0 |
| Medium | 2 | 6 | 0 | 4 | 10 |
| Low | 0 | 9 | 3 | 10 | 13 |

The expected opportunity loss from selecting location L4 is 5.50 [(3 x 0.3) + (4 x 0.4) + (10 x 0.3)].

Answer (B) is incorrect because 7.90 is the expected opportunity loss from selecting location L5. Answer (C) is incorrect because 7.50 is the expected opportunity loss from selecting location L2. Answer (D) is incorrect because 5.00 is the expected opportunity loss from selecting location L1.

### 18.8  Quality Tools

**76.** Quality control programs employ many tools for problem definition and analysis.  A scatter diagram is one of these tools.  The objective of a scatter diagram is to

A.  Display a population of items for analysis.

B.  Show frequency distribution in graphic form.

C.  Divide a universe of data into homogeneous groups.

D.  Show the vital trend and separate trivial items.

The correct answer is (A).  *(CIA, adapted)*
 **REQUIRED:**  The objective of a scatter diagram.
 **DISCUSSION:**  The objective of a scatter diagram is to demonstrate correlations.  Each observation is represented by a dot on a graph corresponding to a particular value of X (the independent variable) and Y (the dependent variable).
 Answer (B) is incorrect because the objective of a histogram is to show frequency distribution in graphic form.  Answer (C) is incorrect because the objective of stratification is to divide a universe of data into homogeneous groups.  Answer (D) is incorrect because regression analysis is used to find trend lines.

---

Questions 77 and 78 are based on the following information.  An organization has collected data on the complaints made by personal computer users and has categorized the complaints.

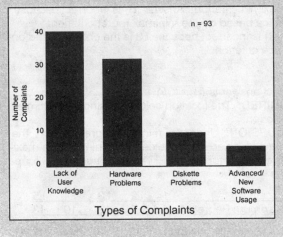

**77.** Using the information collected, the organization should focus on

A.  The total number of personal computer complaints that occurred.

B.  The number of computer complaints associated with diskette problems and new software usage.

C.  The number of computer complaints associated with the lack of user knowledge and hardware problems.

D.  The cost to alleviate all computer complaints.

The correct answer is (C).  *(CIA, adapted)*
 **REQUIRED:**  The organization's focus based on the data.
 **DISCUSSION:**  Complaints based on lack of user knowledge and hardware problems are by far the most frequent according to this chart.  Consequently, the company should devote its resources primarily to these issues.
 Answer (A) is incorrect because more detailed information is not available.  The Pareto diagram does not focus on the total quantity of computer complaints.  Answer (B) is incorrect because complaints about diskettes and software are infrequent.  Answer (D) is incorrect because cost information is not provided.

**78.** The chart displays

A.  The arithmetic mean of each computer complaint.

B.  The relative frequency of each computer complaint.

C.  The median of each computer complaint.

D.  The absolute frequency of each computer complaint.

The correct answer is (D).  *(CIA, adapted)*
 **REQUIRED:**  The information provided by the chart.
 **DISCUSSION:**  This Pareto diagram depicts the frequencies of complaints in absolute terms.  It displays the actual number of each type of complaint.
 Answers (A), (B), and (C) are incorrect because the chart does not display arithmetic means, relative frequencies, or medians of each type of complaint.

**79.** Quality Company produces a component of a machine. The target value for a key dimension of the component is 100 millimeters (mm). The quality loss per unit if the key dimension is measured at precisely the upper or lower specification limit (100 mm ± 1 mm) is estimated to be $10. The following are the measures of a sample of four units:

| Unit | Measurement |
|------|-------------|
| 1 | 99 |
| 2 | 101 |
| 3 | 99.5 |
| 4 | 100.5 |

The Quality Company produces 1,000 of the components. Based on the sample, the estimated quality loss is

A. $625

B. $6,250

C. $10,000

D. $25,000

The correct answer is (B). *(Publisher)*

**REQUIRED:** The estimated quality loss.

**DISCUSSION:** The quality loss constant (k) in the Taguchi quality loss function equation is $10 [$10 loss at the specification limit ÷ $(1 \text{ mm})^2$]. Accordingly, the quality loss for the sample may be determined as follows:

| Unit | Measurement in mm | Actual – Target $(x - T)$ | $(x - T)^2$ | $k(x - T)^2$ |
|------|-------------------|---------------------------|-------------|--------------|
| 1 | 99 | −1 | 1 | $10.00 |
| 2 | 101 | +1 | 1 | 10.00 |
| 3 | 99.5 | −.5 | .25 | 2.50 |
| 4 | 100.5 | +.5 | .25 | 2.50 |
| | | | 2.50 | $25.00 |

The average per unit quality loss for the sample is $6.25 ($25 ÷ 4). Consequently, the total estimated loss for 1,000 components is $6,250.

Answer (A) is incorrect because $625 equals $.625 times 1,000 units. Answer (C) is incorrect because $10,000 equals $10 times 1,000 units. Answer (D) is incorrect because $25,000 is based on the total loss for the sample ($25), not the unit average loss ($6.25).

# APPENDIX A

## MODULE CROSS-REFERENCES TO COST, MANAGERIAL ACCOUNTING, AND QUANTITATIVE METHODS

This appendix contains the titles and tables of contents of current textbooks with cross-references to the related modules or chapters in this study manual. The books are listed in alphabetical order by the first author. As you study a particular chapter in your textbook, you can easily determine which Gleim module(s) to study in this manual. You should review all questions and outlines in the module.

Professors, students, and accounting practitioners should all note that, even though new editions of the texts listed below may be published as you use this book, the new tables of contents usually will be very similar, if not the same. Thus, this edition of *Exam Questions and Explanations with Study Outlines* will remain current and useful.

**Cost/Managerial Accounting**

Barfield, Raiborn, and Kinney, *Cost Accounting: Traditions and Innovations*, Third Edition, South-Western College Publishing Co., 1998.

Cooper and Kaplan, *Design of Cost Management Systems*, Second Edition, Prentice Hall, 1998.

Dominiak and Louderback, *Managerial Accounting*, Eighth Edition, South-Western College Publishing Co., 1997.

Garrison and Noreen, *Managerial Accounting with Workbook-Study Guide*, Eighth Edition, McGraw-Hill, 1997.

Gordon, *Managerial Accounting: Concepts and Empirical Evidence*, Fourth Edition, McGraw-Hill Publishing Co., 1999.

Hansen and Mowen, *Cost Management: Accounting and Control*, Second Edition, South-Western College Publishing Co., 1997.

Hansen and Mowen, *Management Accounting*, Fourth Edition, South-Western College Publishing Co., 1997.

Hilton, *Managerial Accounting*, Fourth Edition, McGraw-Hill, Inc., 1998.

Horngren, Foster, and Datar, *Cost Accounting: A Managerial Emphasis*, Ninth Edition, Prentice Hall, Inc., 1996.

Kaplan and Atkinson, *Advanced Management Accounting*, Third Edition, Prentice Hall, 1998.

Maher, *Cost Accounting, Creating a Value for Management*, Fifth Edition, Richard D. Irwin, 1997.

Maher, Stickney, and Weil, *Managerial Accounting: An Introduction to Concepts, Methods, and Uses*, Sixth Edition, The Dryden Press, 1997.

Morse, Davis, and Hartgraves, *Management Accounting: A Strategic Approach*, First Edition, South-Western College Publishing Co., 1996.

Needles, Powers, Mills, and Anderson, *Managerial Accounting*, Fifth Edition, Houghton-Mifflin Co., 1999.

Raiborn, Barfield, and Kinney, *Managerial Accounting*, Third Edition, South-Western College Publishing Co., 1999.

Rayburn, *Cost Accounting: Using a Cost Management Approach*, Sixth Edition, Richard D. Irwin, 1996.

Reeve, Warren, and Fess, *Managerial Accounting*, Sixth Edition, South-Western College Publishing Co., 1999.

Vanderbeck and Nagy, *Principles of Cost Accounting*, Eleventh Edition, South-Western College Publishing Co., 1999.

Warren, Reeve, and Fess, *Financial and Managerial Accounting*, Sixth Edition, South-Western College Publishing Co., 1999.

## Quantitative Methods

Anderson, Sweeney, Williams, *Introduction to Management Science*, Eighth Edition, West Publishing Co., 1997.

Anderson, Sweeney, Williams, *Quantitative Methods for Business*, Seventh Edition, South-Western College Publishing, 1998.

Bierman, Hausman, Bonini, *Quantitative Analysis for Management*, Ninth Edition, Richard D. Irwin, 1997.

Chase, Aquilano, and Jacobs, *Production & Operations Management*, Eighth Edition, Richard D. Irwin, 1998.

Krajewski and Ritzman, *Operations Management: Strategy and Analysis*, Fourth Edition, Addison-Wesley Longman Publishing Co., Inc., 1996.

Schonberger and Knod, *Operations Management: Customer -- Focused Principles*, Sixth Edition, Richard D. Irwin, 1997.

Stevenson, *Production/Operations Management*, Sixth Edition, Richard D. Irwin, 1999.

Undoubtedly, some textbooks have been inadvertently omitted from the above lists, for which we apologize. The following 12 pages contain the tables of contents of each of these textbooks, with cross-references to modules in this study manual.

## COST/MANAGERIAL ACCOUNTING

**Barfield, Raiborn, and Kinney, *Cost Accounting: Traditions and Innovations*, Third Edition, South-Western College Publishing Co., 1998.**

Part I - Overview
    Chapter  1 -  The Contemporary Environment of Cost and Management Accounting - 1.1-1.2
    Chapter  2 -  Accounting and Organizational Strategy - N/A
    Chapter  3 -  Considering Quality in an Organization - 5.1-5.4
Part II - Selecting, Analyzing, and Tracking Costs
    Chapter  4 -  Cost Terminology and Cost Flows - 1.2-1.5
    Chapter  5 -  Allocating Indirect Costs - 6.1-6.2
    Chapter  6 -  Activity-Based Management Issues - Ch. 2
Part III - Product Costing Methods
    Chapter  7 -  Job Order Costing - 2.1-2.5
    Chapter  8 -  Process Costing - 4.1-4.8
    Chapter  9 -  Special Production Issues: Spoiled/Defective Units and Accretion - 5.2-5.3
    Chapter 10 -  Cost Allocation for Joint Products and By-Products - 6.3-6.8
    Chapter 11 -  Standard Costing - 10.1-10.4
Part IV - Cost Planning
    Chapter 12 -  Absorption/Variable Costing and Cost-Volume-Profit Analysis - Ch. 7, Ch. 8
    Chapter 13 -  Relevant Costing - Ch. 12
    Chapter 14 -  The Master Budget - Ch. 9
Part V - Cost Control
    Chapter 15 -  Designing a Cost Management System - N/A
    Chapter 16 -  Cost Control for Discretionary Costs - N/A
    Chapter 17 -  Control of Inventory and Production - Ch. 14
Part VI - Decision Making
    Chapter 18 -  Basics of Capital Budgeting - Ch. 13
    Chapter 19 -  Responsibility Accounting and Transfer Pricing in Decentralized Organizations - 11.1, 11.3-11.4
Part VII - Performance Evaluation
    Chapter 20 -  Measuring Short-Run Organizational Performance - 11.2
    Chapter 21 -  Measuring Long-Run Organizational Performance - 11.2
    Chapter 22 -  Rewarding Performance - N/A

**Cooper and Kaplan, *Design of Cost Management Systems*, Second Edition, Prentice Hall, 1998.**

Chapter　1 - Introduction to Cost Systems - 1.1-1.2
Chapter　2 - Traditional Two-Stage Cost Systems - N/A
Chapter　3 - Stage III Cost Systems to Promote Learning and Improvement - N/A
Chapter　4 - Activity-Based Costing:　Foundations - Ch. 2
Chapter　5 - Measuring and Managing Capacity Costs - 8.5
Chapter　6 - Operational and Strategic ABM:　Manufacturing Companies - Ch. 11
Chapter　7 - Using Cost Systems for Managing Customer and Supplier Relationships - Ch. 11
Chapter　8 - Using Cost Systems for Designing and Developing New Products - Ch. 11
Chapter　9 - ABC in Service Companies - Ch. 2
Chapter 10 - Developing Integrated Cost Systems - N/A
Chapter 11 - Using ABC for Budgeting and Transfer Pricing - Ch. 2

**Dominiak and Louderback, *Managerial Accounting*, Eighth Edition, South-Western College Publishing Co., 1997.**

Chapter　1 - Introduction - 1.1-1.2
Part One:　Cost-Volume-Profit Analysis and Decision Making
Chapter　2 - Profit Planning - Ch. 8
Chapter　3 - Cost Analysis - Ch. 8
Chapter　4 - Additional Aspects of Cost-Volume-Profit Analysis - Ch. 8
Chapter　5 - Short-Term Decisions and Accounting Information - Ch. 12
Part Two:　Budgeting
Chapter　6 - Operational Budgeting - Ch. 9
Chapter　7 - Financial Budgeting - Ch. 9
Chapter　8 - Capital Budgeting, Part I - Ch. 13
Chapter　9 - Capital Budgeting, Part II - Ch. 13
Part Three:　Control and Performance Evaluation
Chapter 10 - Responsibility Accounting - 11.1
Chapter 11 - Divisional Performance Measurement - 11.2
Chapter 12 - Control and Evaluation of Cost Centers - 11.2
Part Four:　Product Costing
Chapter 13 - Introduction to Product Costing - 1.1-1.2
Chapter 14 - Standard Costing and Variable Costing - 1.3-1.5, 10.1-10.4
Chapter 15 - Process Costing and the Cost Accounting Cycle - Ch. 4
Part Five:　Special Topics
Chapter 16 - Quality and Quantitative Methods in Managerial Accounting - Ch. 5, Chs. 15-18
Chapter 17 - Statement of Cash Flows - *Financial Accounting Exam Questions and Explanations* - N/A
Chapter 18 - Analyzing Financial Statements - *Financial Accounting Exam Questions and Explanations* - N/A

**Garrison and Noreen, *Managerial Accounting with Workbook-Study Guide*, Eighth Edition, McGraw-Hill, 1997.**

Part I - The Foundation:　Cost Terms, Systems Design, and Cost Behavior
Chapter　1 - Managerial Accounting and the Business Environment - 1.1-1.2
Chapter　2 - Cost Terms, Concepts, and Classifications - 1.1-1.5
Chapter　3 - Systems Design: Job-Order Costing - Ch. 3
Chapter　4 - Systems Design: Process Costing - Ch. 4
Chapter　5 - Systems Design:　Activity-Based Costing and Quality Management - Ch. 2, Ch. 5
Chapter　6 - Cost Behavior:　Analysis and Use - Ch. 15-Ch. 18
Part II - The Central Theme:　Planning and Control
Chapter　7 - Cost-Volume-Profit Relationships - Ch. 8
Chapter　8 - Variable Costing:　A Tool for Management - 1.3-1.5
Chapter　9 - Profit Planning - Ch. 8
Chapter 10 - Standard Costs and Operating Performance Measures - 10.1-10.4, 11.2
Chapter 11 - Flexible Budgets and Overhead Analysis - 9.4, 10.4
Chapter 12 - Segment Reporting, Profitability Analysis, and Decentralization - 11.1, 11.3-11.4
Part III - The Capstone:　Using Cost Data in Decision Making
Chapter 13 - Relevant Costs for Decision Making - Ch. 12
Chapter 14 - Capital Budgeting Decisions - Ch. 13
Chapter 15 - Further Aspects of Investment Decisions - Ch. 12, Ch. 13
Part IV - Selected Topics for Further Study
Chapter 16 - Service Department Costing:　An Activity Approach - 6.1-6.2
Chapter 17 - "How Well Am I Doing?" Statement of Cash Flows - *Financial Accounting Exam Questions and Explanations* - N/A
Chapter 18 - "How Well Am I Doing?" Financial Statement Analysis - *Financial Accounting Exam Questions and Explanations* - N/A

**Gordon, *Managerial Accounting: Concepts and Empirical Evidence*, Fourth Edition, McGraw-Hill Publishing Co., 1999.**

**Hansen and Mowen, *Cost Management: Accounting and Control*, Second Edition, South-Western College Publishing Co., 1997.**

**Hansen and Mowen, *Management Accounting*, Fourth Edition, South-Western College Publishing Co., 1997.**

**Hilton, *Managerial Accounting*, Fourth Edition, McGraw-Hill, Inc., 1998.**

**Horngren, Foster, and Datar, *Cost Accounting: A Managerial Emphasis*, Ninth Edition, Prentice Hall, Inc., 1996.**

Part 1 - Cost Accounting Fundamentals
    Chapter  1 - The Accountant's Role in the Organization - 1.1
    Chapter  2 - An Introduction to Cost Terms and Purposes - 1.1-1.6
    Chapter  3 - Cost-Volume-Profit Relationships - 8.1-8.7
    Chapter  4 - Costing Systems and Activity-Based Costing I:  Service and Merchandising Applications - 3.1-3.5
    Chapter  5 - Costing Systems and Activity-Based Costing Ii:  Manufacturing Applications - 2.1, 4.1-4.8
Part 2 - Tools for Planning and Control
    Chapter  6 - Master Budget and Responsibility Accounting - 9.1-9.6, 11.1-11.4
    Chapter  7 - Flexible Budgets, Variances, and Management Control I - 9.1-9.6, 10.1-10.6
    Chapter  8 - Flexible Budgets, Variances, and Management Control II - 9.1-9.6, 10.1-10.6
    Chapter  9 - Income Effects of Alternative Inventory-Costing Methods - 7.1-7.3
Part 3 - Cost Information for Decisions
    Chapter 10 - Determining How Costs Behave - 1.3, 8.3, 16.1-16.5
    Chapter 11 - Relevant Revenues, Relevant Costs, and the Decision Process - 12.1-12.5
    Chapter 12 - Pricing Decisions, Product Profitability Decisions, and Cost Management - 8.1-8.7, 11.3, 12.4
Part 4 - Cost Allocation and Revenues
    Chapter 13 - Cost Allocation:  I - 6.1-6.2
    Chapter 14 - Cost Allocation:  II - 6.1-6.2
    Chapter 15 - Cost Allocation:  Joint Products and Byproducts - 6.3-6.8
    Chapter 16 - Revenues, Revenue Variances, and Custom-Profitability Analysis - 8.1-8.7
    Chapter 17 - Process-Costing Systems - 4.1-4.8
Part 5 - Quality and JIT
    Chapter 18 - Spoilage, Reworked Units, and Scrap - 5.2-5.4
    Chapter 19 - Cost Management:  Quality, Time, and the Theory of Constraints - 5.1
    Chapter 20 - Operation Costing, Just-in-Time Systems, and Backflush Costing - 4.2
Part 6 - Capital Budgeting
    Chapter 21 - Inventory Management and Just-in-Time Systems - 14.3
    Chapter 22 - Capital Budgeting and Cost Analysis - 13.1-13.7
    Chapter 23 - Capital Budgeting:  A Closer Look - 13.1-13.7
Part 7 - Management Control Systems
    Chapter 24 - Measuring Mix, Yield, and Productivity - 10.2
    Chapter 25 - Control Systems, Decentralization, Transfer Pricing, and Multinational Considerations - 11.3
    Chapter 26 - Systems Choice:  Performance Measurement and Compensation - 11.1-11.4


**Kaplan and Atkinson, *Advanced Management Accounting*, Third Edition, Prentice Hall, 1998.**

    Introduction
    Chapter  1 - Understanding Cost Behavior - 1.1-1.2
    Chapter  2 - Short-Term Budgeting, Resource Allocations, and Capacity Cost - Ch. 9
    Chapter  3 - Assigning Resource Costs to Production Cost Centers - Ch. 11
    Chapter  4 - Activity-Based Costing - Ch. 2
    Chapter  5 - Activity-Based Management - Ch. 2
    Chapter  6 - Cost-Based Decision Making - Ch. 12, Ch. 13
    Chapter  7 - Decentralization - 11.3
    Chapter  8 - The Balanced Scorecard:  Measuring Total Business Unit Performance - 11.2
    Chapter  9 - Financial Measures of Performance - 11.2
    Chapter 10 - Financial Measures of Performance:  Return on Investment (ROI) and Economic Value Added (EVA$^{TM}$) - 11.2
    Chapter 11 - Measuring Customer, Internal Business Process, and Employee Performance Process Perspective - 11.2
    Chapter 12 - Investing to Develop Future Capabilities Technology - N/A
    Chapter 13 - Incentive and Compensation Systems - N/A
    Chapter 14 - Formal Models for Budgeting and Incentive Contracts - N/A

**Maher, *Cost Accounting, Creating a Value for Management*, Fifth Edition, Richard D. Irwin, 1997.**

**Maher, Stickney, and Weil, *Managerial Accounting:  An Introduction to Concepts, Methods, and Uses*, Sixth Edition, The Dryden Press, 1997.**

**Morse, Davis, and Hartgraves,** *Management Accounting: A Strategic Approach*, **First Edition, South-Western Publishing Co., 1996.**

**Needles, Powers, Mills, and Anderson,** *Managerial Accounting*, **Fifth Edition, Houghton Mifflin Co., 1999.**

**Raiborn, Barfield, and Kinney,** *Managerial Accounting*, **Third Edition, South-Western College Publishing Co., 1999.**

**Rayburn, *Cost Accounting: Using a Cost Management Approach*, Sixth Edition, Richard D. Irwin, 1996.**

Part I - Cost/Management Accounting Concepts
    Chapter  1 - Cost Accounting in a Contemporary Environment - N/A
    Chapter  2 - Cost Concepts and Cost Flows - 1.1, 3.2
    Chapter  3 - Cost Behavior and Cost Estimation - N/A
    Chapter  4 - Volume-Based Cost Assignments - N/A
    Chapter  5 - Activity-Based Cost Systems and Strategic Cost Analysis - 2.1
Part II - Product Cost Allocation and Accumulation Procedures
    Chapter  6 - Job Order Costing - 3.1-3.5
    Chapter  7 - Process Costing--Weighted-Average and FIFO - 4.1-4.8
    Chapter  8 - Process Costing--Addition of Materials and Lost Units - 5.1-5.4
    Chapter  9 - Joint Product and By-Product Costing - 6.3-6.8
Part III - Cost Data for Performance Evaluation
    Chapter 10 - Strategic Planning and Budgeting - 9.1-9.6
    Chapter 11 - Nonmanufacturing Budgets, Forecasted Statements, and Behavioral Issues - 9.1-9.6
    Chapter 12 - Target Costing, Kaizen Costing, and Standard Costing for Materials and Labor - 5.1, 10.1-10.3
    Chapter 13 - Standard Costs and Factory Overhead Variances - 10.1, 10.4
Part IV - Cost Planning and Control
    Chapter 14 - Cost-Volume-Profit Analysis - 8.1-8.7
    Chapter 15 - Product Quality and Inventory Management in a JIT Environment - 5.1, 14.3
    Chapter 16 - Payroll Accounting and Incentive Plans - N/A
Part V - Cost Accounting/Cost Management for Decision Making
    Chapter 17 - Decision Models and Cost Analysis under Uncertainty - 15.1-15.4
    Chapter 18 - Performance Evaluation and Segment Analysis - 11.1-11.2
    Chapter 19 - Transfer Pricing in Multidivisional Companies - 11.3
    Chapter 20 - Capital Budgeting - 13.1-13.7
    Chapter 21 - Capital Budgeting--Additional Topics - 13.1-13.7
    Chapter 22 - Activity-Based Management for Marketing and Pricing Decisions - 2.1
    Chapter 23 - Variable Costing - 7.1-7.3
    Chapter 24 - Revenue Variances, Material Mix and Yield Variances, and Labor Mix and Yield Variances - 10.2, 10.5
          10.6
    Chapter 25 - Gantt Charts, PERT, and Decision Tree Analysis - 15.4
    Chapter 26 - Linear Programming and the Cost Accountant - 17.1-17.4


**Reeve, Warren, and Fess, *Managerial Accounting*, Sixth Edition, South-Western Publishing Co., 1999.**

    Chapter  1 - Introduction to Managerial Accounting and Job Order Cost Systems - 1.1-1.2, Ch. 3
    Chapter  2 - Process Cost Systems - Ch. 4
    Chapter  3 - Cost Behavior and Cost-Volume-Profit Analysis - Ch. 8
    Chapter  4 - Profit Reporting for Management Analysis - N/A
    Chapter  5 - Budgeting - Ch. 9
    Chapter  6 - Performance Evaluation Using Variances from Standard Costs - Ch. 10
    Chapter  7 - Performance Evaluation for Decentralized Operations - 11.3
    Chapter  8 - Differential Analysis and Product Pricing - 18.6
    Chapter  9 - Capital Investment Analysis - Ch. 13
    Chapter 10 - Cost Allocation and Activity-Based Costing - Ch. 2, Ch. 6
    Chapter 11 - Cost Management for Just-in-Time Manufacturers - 14.3


**Vanderbeck and Nagy, *Principles of Cost Accounting*, Eleventh Edition, South-Western Publishing Co., 1999.**

    Chapter  1 - Introduction to Cost Accounting - 1.1-1.6
    Chapter  2 - Accounting for Materials - Chs. 1-11
    Chapter  3 - Accounting for Labor - Chs. 1-11
    Chapter  4 - Accounting for Factory Overhead - Chs. 1-11
    Chapter  5 - Cost Accounting for Service Businesses - 2.1
    Chapter  6 - Process Cost Accounting--General Procedures - 4.1-4.8
    Chapter  7 - Process Cost Accounting--Additional Procedures - 4.1-4.8
    Chapter  8 - Standard Cost Accounting--Materials and Labor - 10.1-10.3
    Chapter  9 - Standard Cost Accounting--Factory Overhead - 10.4
    Chapter 10 - Cost Analysis for Management Decision Making - Chs. 7, 8, 10, 11, 12, 16

**Warren, Reeve, and Fess, *Financial and Managerial Accounting*, Sixth Edition, South-Western College Publishing Co., 1999.**

Chapter  1 - Introduction to Accounting Concepts and Practice - N/A
Chapter  2 - Analyzing Transactions - N/A
Chapter  3 - The Matching Concept and the Adjusting Process - N/A
Chapter  4 - Completing the Accounting Cycle - N/A
Chapter  5 - Accounting for Merchandising Businesses - N/A
Chapter  6 - Accounting Systems, Internal Controls, and Cash - N/A
Chapter  7 - Receivables - N/A
Chapter  8 - Inventories - N/A
Chapter  9 - Fixed Assets and Intangible Assets - N/A
Chapter 10 - Current Liabilities - N/A
Chapter 11 - Corporations:  Organization, Capital Stock Transactions, and Dividends - N/A
Chapter 12 - Corporations:  Income and Taxes, Stockholders' Equity, and Investments in Stocks - N/A
Chapter 13 - Bonds Payable and Investments in Bonds, Statement of Cash Flows, Financial Statement Analysis - N/A
Statement of Cash Flows - *Financial Accounting Exam Questions and Explanations*
Annual Reports and Financial Statement Analysis - *Financial Accounting Exam Questions and Explanations*
Chapter 14 - Managerial Accounting and Job Order Cost Systems - 1.1-1.6, 3.1-3.5
Chapter 15 - Process Cost Systems - 4.1-4.8
Chapter 16 - Cost Behavior and Cost-Volume-Profit Analysis - 1.6, 8.1-8.7, 16.1-16.5
Chapter 17 - Profit Reporting for Management Analysis - 11.1-11.2
Chapter 18 - Budgeting - 9.1-9.6
Chapter 19 - Performance Evaluation Using Variances from Standard Costs - 10.1-10.6
Chapter 20 - Performance Evaluation for Decentralized Operations - 11.1-11.4
Chapter 21 - Differential Analysis and Product Pricing - 12.1-12.5
Chapter 22 - Capital Investment Analysis - 13.1-13.7
Chapter 23 - Cost Allocation and Activity-Based Costing - 2.1
Chapter 24 - Cost Management for Just-in-Time Manufacturers - 14.3

## QUANTITATIVE METHODS

**Anderson, Sweeney, Williams, *Introduction to Management Science*, Eighth Edition, West Publishing Co., 1997.**

Chapter  1 - Introduction - 1.1-1.2
Chapter  2 - Linear Programming:  The Graphical Method - 17.2
Chapter  3 - Linear Programming:  Formulation, Computer Solution, and Interpretation - 17.3
Chapter  4 - Linear Programming Applications - 17.1
Chapter  5 - Linear Programming:  The Simplex Method - 17.3, 17.4
Chapter  6 - Simplex-Based Sensitivity Analysis and Duality - 17.3
Chapter  7 - Transportation, Assignment, and Transshipment Problems - 17.1
Chapter  8 - Integer Linear Programming - 17.1
Chapter  9 - Network Models - 18.3
Chapter 10 - Project Scheduling:  PERT/CPM - 18.3
Chapter 11 - Inventory Models - 14.1-14.4
Chapter 12 - Waiting Line Models - 18.2
Chapter 13 - Simulation - 17.1
Chapter 14 - Decision Analysis - Ch. 15, 17.1, 17.7
Chapter 15 - Multicriteria Decision Problems - N/A
Chapter 16 - Forecasting - 16.1-16.5
Chapter 17 - Markov Process - 17.1
Chapter 18 - Dynamic Programming - 17.1

**Anderson, Sweeney, Williams, *Quantitative Methods for Business*, Seventh Edition, South-Western College Publishing, 1998.**

Chapter  1 - Introduction - 1.1-1.2
Chapter  2 - Introduction to Probability - 15.1
Chapter  3 - Probability Distributions - 15.2
Chapter  4 - Decision Analysis - Ch. 15, 17.1
Chapter  5 - Utility and Decision Making - 15.1, 15.4
Chapter  6 - Forecasting - 16.1-16.5
Chapter  7 - Linear Programming:  The Graphical Method - 17.2
Chapter  8 - Linear Programming:  Computer Solution - 17.3
Chapter  9 - Linear Programming Applications - 17.1
Chapter 10 - Transportation, Assignment, and Transshipment Problems - 17.1
Chapter 11 - Integer Linear Programming - 17.1
Chapter 12 - Project Scheduling:  PERT/CPM - 18.3
Chapter 13 - Inventory Management:  Independent Demand - 14.1-14.4
Chapter 14 - Waiting Line Models - 18.2
Chapter 15 - Computer Simulation - 17.1
Chapter 16 - Markov Processes - 18.1
Chapter 17 - Multicriteria Decision Problems - N/A

**Bierman, Hausman, Bonini, *Quantitative Analysis for Management*, Ninth Edition, Richard D. Irwin, 1997.**

Chapter  1 - Introduction to Analysis and Model Building - 18.1
Chapter  2 - Introduction to Linear Programming - 17.1
Chapter  3 - Solution of Linear Programming Problems - 17.2-17.4
Chapter  4 - Special Topics in Mathematical Programming - Ch. 17
Chapter  5 - Introduction to Probability - 15.1
Chapter  6 - Decision Making & Uncertainty - 15.1-15.4
Chapter  7 - Decision and Risk Analysis - Ch. 15
Chapter  8 - Inventory Control and Management - 14.1-14.4
Chapter  9 - Queuing Theory: Congestion in Processing Systems - 18.2
Chapter 10 - Simulation - 18.1
Chapter 11 - PERT:  Program Evaluation and Review Technique - 18.3
Chapter 12 - Forecasting - Ch. 16

**Chase, Aquilano, and Jacobs, *Production & Operations Management*, Eighth Edition, Richard D. Irwin, 1998.**

Section I - Nature and Context of Operations Management
Chapter  1 - Introduction to the Field - N/A
Chapter  2 - Operations Strategy and Competitiveness - 18.7
Chapter  3 - Project Management - N/A
Section II - Product Design and Process Selection
Chapter  4 - Product Design and Process Selection--Manufacturing - N/A
Chapter  5 - Product Design and Process Selection--Services - N/A
Chapter  6 - Quality Management - 5.1
Section III - Design of Facilities and Jobs
Chapter  7 - Strategic Capacity Management - 13.1-13.7
Chapter  8 - Just-in-Time Production Systems - 14.3
Chapter  9 - Facility Location - N/A
Chapter 10 - Facility Layout, Job Design, and Work Measurement - N/A
Chapter 11 - Learning Curves - 18.4
Section IV - Managing the Supply Chain
Chapter 12 - Supply Chain Management - 2.1
Chapter 13 - Forecasting - 16.1-16.5
Chapter 14 - Aggregate Planning - N/A
Chapter 15 - Inventory Systems for Independent Demand - Ch. 14
Chapter 16 - Inventory Systems for Dependent Demand:  MRP-Type Systems - 14.3
Chapter 17 - Operations Scheduling - 18.3
Section VI - Revising the System
Chapter 18 - Operations Consulting - N/A
Chapter 19 - Business Process Reengineering - N/A
Chapter 20 - Theory of Constraints and Synchronous Manufacturing - N/A

**Krajewski and Ritzman, *Operations Management:  Strategy and Analysis*, Fourth Edition, Addison-Wesley Logman Publishing Co., Inc., 1996.**

        Chapter  1  -  Operations As a Competitive Weapon - N/A
Part One - Strategic Choices
        Chapter  2  -  Operations Strategy - N/A
        Chapter  3  -  Process Management - N/A
        Chapter  4  -  Total Quality Management - Ch. 5
        Chapter  5  -  Statistical Process Control - Ch. 15
Part Two - Design Decisions
        Chapter  6  -  Work-Force Management - N/A
        Chapter  7  -  Capacity - N/A
        Chapter  8  -  Location - N/A
        Chapter  9  -  Layout - N/A
Part Three - Operating Decisions
        Chapter 10  -  Forecasting - Ch. 16
        Chapter 11  -  Materials Management - Ch. 14
        Chapter 12  -  Independent Demand Inventory Systems - Ch. 14
        Chapter 13  -  Aggregate Planning - N/A
        Chapter 14  -  Material Requirements Planning - 14.3
        Chapter 15  -  Just-in-Time Systems - 14.3
        Chapter 16  -  Scheduling - 18.2, 18.3
        Chapter 17  -  Managing Complex Projects - Ch. 18


**Schonberger and Knod, *Operations Management:  Customer -- Focused Principles*, Sixth Edition, Richard D. Irwin, 1997.**

Part One:  Introduction to Operations Management
        Chapter  1  -  Operations--Producing Goods and Providing Services - N/A
        Chapter  2  -  Competitive Strategies and Principles - 18.7
        Chapter  3  -  The Quality Imperative - 5.1
Part Two:  Design and Control for Customer Satisfaction
        Chapter  4  -  Designed-in Quality:  Products, Services, Processes - 5.1
        Chapter  5  -  Quality Control and Process Improvement - 5.1
Part Three:  Translating Demand Into Orders
        Chapter  6  -  Demand Management and Forecasting - 16.1-16.4
        Chapter  7  -  Master Planning for Capacity and Output - N/A
        Chapter  8  -  Flow-Control Systems Overview - N/A
        Chapter  9  -  Purchasing and Order Fulfillment - N/A
        Chapter 10  -  Timing:  JIT/Kanban, MRP, and Related Topics - 14.3
        Chapter 11  -  Quick-Change Flexibility and Lot Sizing - 14.2
Part Four:  Translating Planned Orders Into Outcomes
        Chapter 12  -  Process Selection and Layout - N/A
        Chapter 13  -  Managing Continuous and Repetitive Operations - N/A
        Chapter 14  -  Managing Job and Batch Operations - N/A
        Chapter 15  -  Managing Projects - 18.2, 18.3
Part Five:  OM Resources:  Measurement, Management, Improvement
        Chapter 16  -  Productivity and People - N/A
        Chapter 17  -  Facilities Management - N/A
        Chapter 18  -  What's Next--for YOU and for OM? - N/A

**Stevenson, *Production/Operations Management*, Sixth Edition, Richard D. Irwin, 1999.**

How to Use This Appendix:

Gleim modules are cross-referenced to the textbooks' tables of contents listed on these pages. Following each chapter title is a number or group of numbers indicating which Gleim modules you should study and review to prepare for that chapter.

**Gleim Publications, Inc.**
P.O. Box 12848
Gainesville, FL 32604

| TOLL FREE: | (800) 87-GLEIM |
| LOCAL: | (352) 375-0772 |
| FAX: | (888) 375-6940 (toll free) |
| INTERNET: | http://www.gleim.com |
| E-MAIL: | sales@gleim.com |

Customer service is available:
8:00 a.m. - 7:00 p.m., Mon. - Fri.
9:00 a.m. - 2:00 p.m., Saturday
Please have your credit card ready
or save time by ordering online!

## CPA REVIEW (98-99 Ed.)

| | Books | Audiotapes | CPA Test Prep Software | |
|---|---|---|---|---|
| Auditing . . . . . . . . . . . | ☐ @ $24.50 | ☐ @ $75.00 | ☐ @ $35.00 | $_____ |
| Business Law . . . . . . | ☐ @ $24.50 | ☐ @ $75.00 | ☐ @ $35.00 | _____ |
| TAX-MAN-GOV . . . . . | ☐ @ $24.50 | ☐ @ $75.00 | ☐ @ $35.00 | _____ |
| Financial . . . . . . . . . | ☐ @ $24.50 | ☐ @ $75.00 | ☐ @ $35.00 | _____ |

☐ A System for Success (112 pp.) (FREE with any Gleim CPA Review book)

**Save 15% on the Complete Gleim CPA System** (add $16 S&H below) . . . . . . $457.00 _____
[5 books, 4 audiocassette albums (41 tapes), 4 CPA Test Prep diskettes, and bonus canvas book bag]

## CMA/CFM REVIEW

| | Books | Audiotapes | CMA/CFMTP Software | CPE (book required) | |
|---|---|---|---|---|---|
| Part 1 . . . . . . . . . . . . . . . . | ☐ @ $22.95 | ☐ @ $60.00 | ☐ @ $35.00 | ☐ @ $25.00 | $_____ |
| Part 2CMA . . . . . . . . . . . . . | ☐ @ $22.95 | ☐ @ $60.00 | ☐ @ $35.00 | ☐ @ $25.00 | _____ |
| Part 2CFM . . . . . . . . . . . . . | ☐ @ $22.95 | ☐ @ $60.00 | ☐ @ $35.00 | ☐ @ $25.00 | _____ |
| Part 3 . . . . . . . . . . . . . . . . | ☐ @ $22.95 | ☐ @ $60.00 | ☐ @ $35.00 | ☐ @ $25.00 | _____ |
| Part 4 . . . . . . . . . . . . . . . . | ☐ @ $22.95 | ☐ @ $60.00 | ☐ @ $35.00 | ☐ @ $25.00 | _____ |

## CIA REVIEW

| | Books | CIATP Software | CPE (book required) | |
|---|---|---|---|---|
| Part I, Internal Audit Process | ☐ @ $22.95 | ☐ @ $35.00 | ☐ @ $25.00 | $_____ |
| Part II, Internal Audit Skills | ☐ @ $22.95 | ☐ @ $35.00 | ☐ @ $25.00 | _____ |
| Part III, Management Control and Information Technology | ☐ @ $22.95 | ☐ @ $35.00 | ☐ @ $25.00 | _____ |
| Part IV, The Audit Environment | ☐ @ $22.95 | ☐ @ $35.00 | ☐ @ $25.00 | _____ |

## "THE GLEIM SERIES" EXAM QUESTIONS AND EXPLANATIONS BOOKS & CPE

| | Book Only | Book & CPE | | |
|---|---|---|---|---|
| Auditing & Systems . . . . . . . . . . . . . . | ☐ $19.95 | ☐ $125.00 | (49-98 hours) | $_____ |
| Business Law/Legal Studies . . . . . . . . | ☐ $16.95 | ☐ $ 95.00 | (48-96 hours) | _____ |
| Federal Tax . . . . . . . . . . . . . . . . . . . . | ☐ $19.95 | ☐ $125.00 | (51-102 hours) | _____ |
| Financial Accounting . . . . . . . . . . . . . | ☐ $19.95 | ☐ $125.00 | (46-92 hours) | _____ |
| Cost/Managerial Accounting . . . . . . . . | ☐ $19.95 | ☐ $125.00 | (41-82 hours) | _____ |

Shipping (nonrefundable): **First item = $5; each additional item = $1** . . . . . . . . . . . . . . . _____

Add applicable sales tax for shipments within Florida. . . . . . . . . . . . . . . . . . . . . . . . . . . . . . . . _____

Fax or write for prices/instructions for shipments outside the 48 contiguous states.  **TOTAL** $_____

1. We process and ship orders daily, within one business day over 98.8% of the time. Call by noon for same-day service!

2. Please PHOTOCOPY this order form for use by others.

3. No CODs. Orders from individuals must be prepaid. Library and company orders may be purchased on account.

4. Gleim Publications, Inc. guarantees the immediate refund of all resalable texts and unopened software and audiotapes if returned within 30 days. Applies only to items purchased direct from Gleim Publications, Inc. Our shipping charge is nonrefundable.

NAME (please print) _____

ADDRESS _____ Apt. _____
(street address required for UPS)

_____

CITY _____ STATE____ ZIP_____

____ MC/VISA/DISC/AMEX ____ Check/M.O.   Daytime Telephone (____)_____

Credit Card No. _____ - _____ - _____ - _____

Exp. ____/____   Signature _____
Mo. / Yr.

Printed 12/98. Prices subject to change without notice.

# Index

Please forward your suggestions, corrections, and comments concerning typographical errors, etc., to **Irvin N. Gleim • c/o Gleim Publications, Inc. • P.O. Box 12848 • University Station • Gainesville, Florida • 32604**.  Please include your name and address so we can properly thank you for your interest.

1. _____

2. _____

3. _____

4. _____

5. _____

6. _____

7. _____

8. _____

9. _____

10. _____

11. _____

12. _____

☞  For updates and other important information, visit our home page (www.gleim.com).

13. _____

14. _____

15. _____

16. _____

17. _____

18. _____

19. _____

20. _____

| Remember for superior service: | Mail, e-mail, or fax questions about our books or software. Telephone questions about orders, prices, shipments, or payments. |
|---|---|

Name: _____

Address: _____

City/State/Zip: _____

Telephone:    Home: _____    Work: _____    FAX: _____

E-mail: _____